Scale and Scope

SCALE AND SCOPE

The Dynamics of Industrial Capitalism

ALFRED D. CHANDLER, JR.

with the assistance of
Takashi Hikino

THE BELKNAP PRESS OF
HARVARD UNIVERSITY PRESS
Cambridge, Massachusetts
London, England
1990

Library of Congress Cataloging in Publication Data

Chandler, Alfred Dupont.
　　Scale and scope : the dynamics of industrial
　capitalism / Alfred D. Chandler, Jr. with the
　assistance of Takashi Hikino.
　　　　p.　cm.
　　Includes bibliographical references.
　　ISBN 0-674-78994-6 (alk. paper)
　　1. Big business—United States—History. 2. Big
　business—Great Britain—History. 3. Big
　business—Germany—History. 4. Big business—
　Germany (West)—History. I. Hikino, Takashi. II.
　Title.
　HD2785.C474　1990
　338.6′44′09—dc20　　　　　　　　　　　89-36288
　　　　　　　　　　　　　　　　　　　　　　　　　CIP

*To the Business History Group
of the Harvard Business School
which contributed so much
to the making of this book*

Acknowledgments

Many have contributed over the past decade to the making of this book. The German Marshall Fund and the Alfred P. Sloan Foundation provided the funding needed to get the project under way. The Division of Research, Graduate School of Business Administration, Harvard University, then supported the project through its completion. I am greatly indebted to the heads of that division—Richard S. Rosenbloom, E. Raymond Corey, and Jay W. Lorsch— and to Deans Lawrence A. Fouraker and John H. McArthur for their continued enthusiastic support of the work. In addition, my research benefitted from a stay at the European Institute for Advanced Studies in Management, Brussels, where I was a visiting professor in 1979.

As in the past, my research and writing have been carried out in a traditional manner. They have been pieced together from reading and discussing business records, government reports, other original sources, and a multitude of secondary works. Thus the creative assistance of Takashi Hikino became indispensable in the writing of this book. He was extraordinarily successful in locating information. His knowledge of economics was invaluable as we defined and redefined concepts and generalizations. *Scale and Scope* is indeed the product of a several-year partnership. Without Takashi Hikino it could not have been written.

Other scholars made major contributions. Herman Daems worked closely with me in initiating and carrying out research in Europe, and later in reviewing the successive chapters he provided excellent criticism and suggestions. Others who read all or large parts of the manuscript include Robert D. Cuff, David H. Hounshell, William Lazonick, David C. Mowery, William N. Parker, Barry E. Supple, Richard S. Tedlow, Richard H. K. Vietor, and Mira Wilkins. I am particularly indebted to Barry Supple for urging me to indicate the importance of the industries analyzed in this book in regard to economic growth and transformation, to Thomas K. McCraw for his wise advice in the shaping of the last chapter, to William Lazonick for his insistence that human skills and motivations are central to any economic analysis, and to Mira Wilkins for her detailed, careful, and very valuable review of the first full draft. Leslie Hannah, William J. Reader, and Steven Tolliday all added insights and information to the chapters on Britain.

The chapters on Germany were an even more cooperative effort. Given my limited grasp of the language, Herman Daems, Franz Mathis, Clemens Verenkotte, and John Watt all played a central role in the translation of German documents and books. Colleen Dunlavy, while in Germany doing her comparative study of the beginnings of the American and Prussian railroad systems, located a number of important sources. Her own work provided essential materials for my brief review of German railway development. The chapters on Germany also benefitted greatly from the comments and criticisms of Wilfried Feldenkirchen, Gerald Feldman, Peter Hertner, Heidrun Homburg, Jürgen Kocka, and Robert Locke.

All the chapters of the book were presented in the seminar of the Business History Group at the Harvard Business School and in other seminars at Harvard and a number of other universities. The constructive responses of the commentators and the participants of these seminars were invaluable. Particularly useful were those of Richard E. Caves, Richard S. Rosenbloom, and Oliver E. Williamson.

I also want to express my appreciation to the librarians and archivists who helped carry out my research. Here the assistance of Lothar Schoen and Sigfried von Weiher at the Siemens Archives in Munich, and of Peter Göb of the Bayer Archives in Leverkusen, was all that a scholar could ask for in locating the significant files and then in photocopying and mailing the selected documents. This was also true of the help I received from A. M. Fisher and Maureen Staniforth at Unilever and from A. A. Cole, J. D. Cousin, and Sue Harvey at Imperial Chemical Industries. I am indebted to Ronald W. Ferrier, the historian at British Petroleum, who furnished valuable information from the company archives. In the United States, the librarians at the Hagley Library in Greenville, Delaware, and the Owen D. Young Library, St. Lawrence University, provided valuable documents. Most helpful of all was the Baker Library staff at the Harvard Business School who over the years provided every kind of assistance.

I am grateful to those who constructed the appendix tables of the 200 largest industrial enterprises in the United States, Great Britain, and Germany. The lists of American companies for 1930 and 1948 were compiled, and the companies classified by industry, by Regina Pisa. The list for 1917 was based on a published article by Thomas R. Navin in the *Business History Review* (Autumn 1970). All three tables of British companies were originally compiled by Margaret Ackrill, and the companies classified by industry by Peter Grant. The tables of German companies were initially compiled by Marc Vanheukelen and then were reworked and expanded by Takashi Hikino and Clemens Verenkotte. Takashi Hikino generally coordinated the efforts of compilation and determined the product lines for all the tables.

Once the manuscript was complete Max Hall's attentive reading much improved the structure of the chapters and the clarity of the prose. Jeffrey Rayport carefully checked several chapters, and almost every page benefited from Dorothy Whitney's meticulous copy editing. I am indebted to them, as I am to Elizabeth Suttell, Senior Editor, and Aida Donald, Editor-in-Chief, of the Harvard University Press for their admirable care and patience in guiding the book through all the phases of publication. I also thank Carol Leslie, Associate Editor, for her work during the production process.

Violette Gray Crowe played an indispensable part in transferring rough, original copy and dictation into finished typescript as the manuscript progressed through draft after draft. Without her careful, accurate work and her dedication to the task, this book would never have been completed on schedule. Essential too were the contributions of the Word Processing Center at the Harvard Business School, particularly those of Aimee B. Hamel and Anne M. O'Connell.

As has been the case for more than forty years, the constant encouragement and support of my wife, Fay, have been essential in carrying out and completing my historical writing.

Many have contributed to this book but the final text is mine, and for it I take full responsibility.

Alfred D. Chandler, Jr.
Cambridge, Massachusetts

Contents

PART III

Great Britain: Personal Capitalism   235

Contents

Tables

Figures

· I ·

Introduction:
Scale and Scope

In the last half of the nineteenth century a new form of capitalism appeared in the United States and Europe. Before the coming of modern transportation and communication—that is, before the railroad and the telegraph, the steamship and the cable—the processes of production, distribution, transportation, and communication in capitalistic economies had been carried on by enterprises personally managed by their owners. The number of salaried managers in these enterprises was tiny. And those few managers worked closely with the owners.

The building and operating of the rail and telegraph systems called for the creation of a new type of business enterprise. The massive investment required to construct those systems and the complexities of their operations brought the separation of ownership from management. The enlarged enterprises came to be operated by teams of salaried managers who had little or no equity in the firm. The owners, numerous and scattered, were investors with neither the experience, the information, nor the time to make the myriad decisions needed to maintain a constant flow of goods, passengers, and messages. Thousands of shareholders could not possibly operate a railroad or a telegraph system.

The new forms of transportation and communication, in turn, permitted the rise of modern mass marketing and modern mass production. The unprecedented increase in the volume of production and in the number of transactions led the entrepreneurs who established the new mass-producing and mass-distributing enterprises—like the railroad men before them—to recruit teams of salaried managers. As these enterprises expanded their activities and moved into new markets, the shareholdings of the founding entrepreneurs and their families were dispersed and operating decisions became concentrated in the hands of the managers.

Thus came into being a new economic institution, the managerial business enterprise, and a new subspecies of economic man, the salaried manager. With their coming, the world received a new type of capitalism—one in which the decisions about current operations, employment, output, and the allocation of resources for future operations were made by salaried managers who were not owners of the enterprise. Once modern transportation and communication systems were in place, the new institution and the new type of economic man provided a central dynamic for continuing economic growth and transformation.

ONE

The Modern Industrial Enterprise

In an earlier study, *The Visible Hand,* I investigated the coming of managerial capitalism by examining the evolution of several types of modern business enterprises in a single country, the United States. Here I examine the beginnings and growth of managerial capitalism globally, focusing on the history of its basic institution, the modern *industrial* enterprise, in the world's three leading industrial nations.

Of all the new forms of managerial enterprise, the modern industrial enterprise played the most fundamental role in the transformation of Western economies. They had been rural, agrarian, and commercial; they became industrial and urban. That transformation, in turn, brought the most rapid economic growth in the history of mankind. At the center of the transformation were the United States, Great Britain, and Germany, which accounted for just over two-thirds of the world's industrial output in 1870. Before the coming of the depression of the 1930s they still provided just under two-thirds (Table 1). And the speed with which the output of the United States and Germany surpassed Great Britain, the world's first industrial nation, was striking.

In each country industrial activities played the central role in transforming an agrarian commercial economy into a modern industrial economy. The significance of industrial output to economic growth has been emphasized by Simon Kuznets, who divides national economies into three basic sectors—agriculture, industry, and services. He subdivides industry, in turn, into mining, manufacturing, construction, utilities (electricity, gas, water), and transportation and communication.[1] In all three countries the largest economic growth came in the industrial sector, while agriculture drastically declined in the long run (Table 2). The industrial sector grew significantly in the United States and Germany; in Great Britain the development was slower, but sustained. Just as the industrial sector led the way in economic growth, so industrial growth was concentrated

Table 1.   Distribution of world's industrial production, 1870–1938 (in percentages).

Years	United States	Great Britain	Germany	France	Russia	Japan	Rest of world
1870	23	32	13	10	4	—	17
1881–1885	29	27	14	9	3	—	19
1896–1900	30	20	17	7	5	1	20
1906–1910	35	15	16	6	5	1	21
1913	36	14	16	6	6	1	21
1926–1929	42	9	12	7	4	3	22
1936–1938	32	9	11	5	19	4	21

Source: W. W. Rostow, *The World Economy: History and Prospect* (Austin, Tex., 1978), pp. 52–53.

in the manufacturing subdivision (Table 3). And again, growth in manufacturing was more notable in the United States and Germany than in Great Britain. By the twentieth century manufacturing accounted for the largest share of the gross domestic product in the industrial sector in all three economies.

The significance of industrial activities can further be illustrated by reference to employment. In the first half of the twentieth century in each of the three countries, industry created more employment opportunities than did either agriculture or service (Table 4). Again, whereas Great Britain experienced only a moderate change of employment structure after the 1880s, the United States, and Germany to a lesser degree, showed a dramatic transformation from an agrarian to a modern economy in which almost half of the employment centered in industry.

Finally, within the manufacturing subdivision the branches that showed the greatest growth in the United States from 1880 to 1948 were those capital-intensive industries in which large manufacturing firms predominated. Data on the growth of these branches, which were compiled by Kuznets for the United States only, are given in Chapter 6.

The manufacturing enterprises whose collective histories are presented in this study—those enterprises that were most responsible for the economic growth of the world's three largest industrial nations—have provided a fundamental dynamic or force for change in capitalist economies since the 1880s. They remain today at the core of their national economies.[2] These enterprises were not just manufacturing firms. They also entered into mining and other activities of the industrial sector, and their hierarchical organizational characteristics resembled those of the other subdivisions of that sector, with the exception of construction, which continued to include more personally managed enterprises. The manufacturers also created both national and international

Table 2. Long-term changes in shares of major sectors in total output, United States, Great Britain, and Germany (in percentages).[a]

Country	Shares in current price volumes			Shares in constant price volumes		
	Agri-culture	Industry	Service	Agri-culture	Industry	Service
United States						
National income, 1859 prices						
1839	42.6	25.8	31.6	44.6	24.2	31.2
1889–1899	17.9	44.1	38.0	17.0	52.6	30.4
GNP, 1929 prices						
1889–1899	—	—	—	25.8	37.7	36.5
1919–1929	—	—	—	11.2	41.3	47.5
1953	—	—	—	5.9	48.4	45.7
Change, 1839 to 1953	—	—	—	−47.5	+39.1	+8.4
Great Britain–United Kingdom						
Great Britain, NDP, 1865 and 1885 prices						
1801–1811	34.1	22.1	43.8	33.2	23.0	43.8
1851–1861	19.5	36.3	44.2	19.3	36.4	44.3
1907	6.4	38.9	54.7	6.7	37.0	56.3
Change, 1801–1811 to 1907	−27.7	+16.8	+10.9	−26.5	+14.0	+12.5
Great Britain, GDP						
1907	6.4	48.9	44.7	—	—	—
1924	4.2	53.2	42.6	—	—	—
United Kingdom, GDP						
1924	4.4	55.0	40.6	—	—	—
1955	4.7	56.8	38.5	—	—	—
Change, 1907 to 1955	−1.9	+6.1	−4.2	—	—	—
Germany						
Pre–World War II, NDP, 1913 prices						
1850–1859	40.9	59.1[b]		44.8	22.8	32.4
1935–1938	13.6	84.4		16.2	56.3	27.5
Change, 1850–1859 to 1935–1938	−27.3	+27.3		−28.6	+33.5	−4.9
Federal Republic, excluding Saar and West Berlin, NDP, 1936 prices						
1936	13.4	58.0	26.6	13.4	58.0	28.6
1950	12.4	59.9	27.7	11.1	57.3	31.6
Change, 1936 to 1950	−1.0	+1.9	−0.9	−2.3	−0.7	+3.0

Source: Simon Kuznets, *Economic Growth of Nations: Total Output and Production Structure* (Cambridge, Mass., 1971), pp. 144–147.

a. For a detailed explanation of the collection of the data, see Kuznets's footnotes, ibid., pp. 148–151, and for his own interpretation of the table see pp. 143–159.

b. Both industry and service.

Table 3. Long-term changes in shares of subdivisions of the industrial sector in total output, United States, Great Britain, and Germany (in percentages).

Country	Mining	Manufacturing	Construction	Electricity, gas, and water	Transportation and communication	Total
United States						
1859 prices						
1839	0.4	10.7	6.3		6.8[a]	24.2
1889–1899	2.1	24.2	4.7		21.6	52.6
Change, 1839 to 1889–1899	+1.7	+13.5	−1.6		+14.8	+28.4
1929 prices						
1889–1899	2.1	21.1	6.3		8.2	37.7
1919–1929	2.4	23.8	4.1		11.0	41.3
1953	1.6	29.6	3.7		13.5	48.4
Change, 1889–1899 to 1953	−0.5	+8.5	−2.6		+5.3	+10.7
United Kingdom						
Current prices						
1907	6.3	27.1	3.9	1.6	10.0	48.9
1963–1967	2.3	33.8	7.0	3.2	8.3	34.6
Change, 1907 to 1963–1967	−4.0	+6.7	+3.1	+1.6	−1.7	+5.7
Germany						
1913 prices						
1850–1859	1.0	18.5	2.5	0.0	0.8	22.8
1935–1938	3.1	39.9	5.0	2.3	6.0	56.3
Change, 1850–1859 to 1935–1938	+2.1	+21.4	+2.5	+2.3	+5.2	+33.5

Source: Simon Kuznets, *Economic Growth of Nations: Total Output and Production Structure* (Cambridge, Mass., 1971), table 22, pp. 160–161.
a. Both electricity, gas, and water, and transportation and communication.

Table 4. Long-term changes in the sectoral distribution of the labor force, United States, Great Britain, and Germany (in percentages).

United States, 1880–1950

	Distribution by sectors[a]			
Year	Agriculture and fishing	Industry	Trade and transportation	Other services
1880	51.9	25.9	14.3	7.9
1900	43.0	30.0	18.7	8.2
1920	30.9	38.7	23.6	6.9
1940	25.5	37.4	28.2	9.0
1950	17.5	43.0	30.0	9.5

Great Britain, 1881–1951

	Distribution by sectors[b]			
Year	Agriculture, forestry, and fishing	Industry	Trade and transportation	Other services
1881	12.6	43.5	21.3	22.7
1901	8.7	46.3	21.4	23.7
1921	7.1	47.6	20.3	25.0
1931	6.0	45.3	22.7	26.0
1951	5.0	49.1	21.8	24.1

Germany, 1882–1950[c]

	Distribution by sectors[d]		
Year	Agriculture and forestry	Industry and craft	Commerce, communications, and other services
1882	42.2	35.6	22.2
1907	33.9	39.9	26.2
1925	30.3	42.3	27.4
1939	25.0	40.8	34.2
1950	24.6	42.7	32.7

Sources: For the United States, compiled from Stanley Lebergott, *Manpower in Economic Growth: The American Record since 1800* (New York, 1967), p. 510; for Great Britain, Phyllis Dean and W. A. Cole, *British Economic Growth, 1688–1959,* 2d ed. (Cambridge, 1967), p. 142; for Germany, Gustav Stolper et al., *The German Economy: 1870 to the Present* (New York, 1967), p. 23.

a. For persons engaged (employees, self-employed, and unpaid family workers), age 10 and over.

b. For the total occupied population.

c. Adjusted for territorial changes.

d. For the total gainfully employed.

purchasing and distribution networks. Kuznets lists such activities as "trade," a subdivision of the service sector, and thus his tables somewhat underrepresent the significance of industrial enterprises; for the manufacturing firms in the industrial sector were involved in trade far more than the enterprises in the trade subdivision of the service sector were involved in manufacturing. In my view these large manufacturing companies were the prototypes of the modern industrial enterprise.

As a result of the regularity, increased volume, and greater speed of the flows of goods and materials made possible by the new transportation and communication systems, new and improved processes of production developed that for the first time in history enjoyed substantial economies of scale and scope. Large manufacturing works applying the new technologies could produce at lower unit costs than could the smaller works.

In order to benefit from the cost advantages of these new, high-volume technologies of production, entrepreneurs had to make three sets of interrelated investments. The first was an investment in production facilities large enough to exploit a technology's potential economies of scale or scope. The second was an investment in a national and international marketing and distributing network, so that the volume of sales might keep pace with the new volume of production. Finally, to benefit fully from these two kinds of investment the entrepreneurs also had to invest in management: they had to recruit and train managers not only to administer the enlarged facilities and increased personnel in both production and distribution, but also to monitor and coordinate those two basic functional activities and to plan and allocate resources for future production and distribution. It was this three-pronged investment in production, distribution, and management that brought the modern industrial enterprise into being.

The first entrepreneurs to create such enterprises acquired powerful competitive advantages. Their industries quickly became oligopolistic, that is, dominated by a small number of first movers. These firms, along with the few challengers that subsequently entered the industry, no longer competed primarily on the basis of price. Instead they competed for market share and profits through functional and strategic effectiveness. They did so *functionally* by improving their product, their processes of production, their marketing, their purchasing, and their labor relations, and *strategically* by moving into growing markets more rapidly, and out of declining ones more quickly and effectively, than did their competitors.

Such rivalry for market share and profits honed the enterprise's functional and strategic capabilities. These organizational capabilities, in turn, provided an internal dynamic for the continuing growth of the enterprise. In particular, they stimulated its owners and managers to expand into more distant markets in their own country and then to become multinational by moving abroad. They also encouraged the firm to diversify by developing products competitive in markets other than the original one and so to become a multiproduct enterprise. Industries where the new technologies provided cost advantages of scale and scope came to be operated through the system I have called managerial capitalism. Salaried managers, not owners, came to make the decisions about current operating activities and long-term growth and investment.[3] Their decisions determined the ability of their enterprises, and of the industries in which they operated, to compete and grow.

Because this study is the history of a human institution, I focus on the decisions within the institution that led to changes in production and distribution, rather than on changes in the broader economy as indicated by economic statistics—changes that resulted from such decisions. The institutional history told here is the outcome of innumerable decisions made by individual entrepreneurs, owners, and managers. For these decision-makers the choices among alternatives were limited and the outcomes uncertain, but almost always there *were* choices. Indeed, where they made decisions collectively, the decision-makers disagreed as often as they agreed.

Despite the variability of these individual decisions, taken cumulatively they produced clear patterns of institutional change. In the industries that were being transformed—or in many cases created—by new technologies and expanding markets, individual decisions within an enterprise determined whether it became a major player in the industry, was relegated to a secondary position, or was eliminated altogether. If a firm became a major player, the decisions of its senior managers shaped the ways in which it continued to respond to changing technological innovation, to market demand, to the availability of supplies, and to the more encompassing depressions and global wars. Because in each of the new industries there were only a small number of major players, the responses of their managers often determined the ways in which entire industries and even national economies responded to the changing market, technological, economic, and political environment.

Because the context, that is, the specific situations, in which such decisions were made differed greatly from industry to industry, from country to country, and from one time period to the next, the content of managerial responses differed widely. These responses varied from industry to industry for economic reasons, such as the availability of markets, supplies, capital, and labor—and also because each industry had its own production technologies and distribution requirements. They varied from country to country for cultural reasons. Educational and legal systems affected both the day-to-day operating and long-term strategic decisions: national differences in educational systems influenced the training and recruitment of managers and workers, while national legal systems defined in different ways the basic rules of the game. They varied from one time period to the next for the obvious reason that the technologies, markets, and competition confronting an enterprise and the industries and nations within which it operated differed substantially, often dramatically, in each decade from the 1880s to the 1940s. Obviously, too, the performance of an enterprise and its industry in one decade reflected investments made, personnel hired, technologies adopted, and markets obtained in the previous and earlier decades.

Because there were such major differences among industries, nations, and time periods, historical evidence can easily be found to support almost any set of hypotheses, propositions, or other generalizations concerning the growth and evolution of industries and enterprises. To be valid, historical analyses must be comparative. They must compare the histories of enterprises within the same industry, and then they must compare the collective history of the enterprises within that particular industry with that of other industries in the same nation and also with that of the same industry in other nations. Only such broad-based data can provide the comparisons that indicate common patterns of institutional growth and reveal the impact of cultural, economic, and historical differences on institutional evolution. Such comparisons, in turn, provide the underpinnings for a systematic analysis of the dynamics of modern industrial capitalism.

The first step in writing this institutional history of the modern industrial enterprise was to record the collective histories of individual companies within the same core industries in the world's three leading industrial nations from their appearance in the last quarter of the nineteenth century until the 1940s. The individual companies studied were the two hundred largest manufacturing firms in each of the three countries at three points in time—during World War I, at the end of the prosperous 1920s, and at the beginning of the post–World War II era. (The specific years chosen differ somewhat among the three countries, for reasons given in the introduction to the appendixes.) These companies are listed in the appendix tables.

The data used are those traditionally used by historians. The information on individual companies has come from a wide variety of sources—company and industry histories; monographs; journal articles and other secondary sources; investment directories such as *Moody's Manual* for the United States, the *Stock Exchange Year-Book* for Great Britain, and the *Handbuch der deutschen Aktien-Gesellschaften* for Germany; published company and governmental reports; and, for those companies whose histories were most revealing for this study, from archival records. These sources provide information on changing product lines, production processes, shifts in markets, and sources of supply. They also indicate the timing of growth by direct investment, by merger and acquisition, by expansion overseas, and by expansion into new product lines. For nearly all the companies listed they identify the senior decision-makers.

The book is divided into five sections. In Chapter 2 of this first part, I provide a more detailed but still highly generalized description and analysis of the creation and dynamic evolution of the central institution of managerial capitalism—the modern industrial enterprise. I do so by focusing on the *similarities* in the beginnings and growth of this institution in the three countries over a period of more than six decades. In that chapter are given the definitions, concepts, explanations, and generalizations necessary to make precise comparisons among industries and countries and time periods. These concepts and generalizations are then used to develop an explanatory theory concerning the beginnings and continuing evolution of the modern industrial enterprise. In the concluding section to the volume, I draw together its underlying themes—particularly those that explain the dynamics of industrial capitalism—and then relate these themes to the evolution of the modern industrial enterprise after World War II. In between, I concentrate not on the similarities but on the *differences*. I describe the differences and demonstrate how they support the generalizations and explanatory theory developed in Chapter 2.

In Parts II, III, and IV, I present, country by country, the collective histories of the two hundred largest manufacturing companies—the prototypes of the modern industrial enterprise—in the United States, Great Britain, and Germany. Each of these parts is introduced by a chapter on the historical environment of the nation in which the institution developed: its geographical size, population, domestic and foreign markets, the timing and impact of its revolutions in transportation and communication, and the resulting changes in distribution and then in production. In these introductory chapters I also review each nation's financial, educational, and legal systems, insofar as they impinge directly on the institution under study. In the subsequent chapters in each part are given the collective histories of the companies, or players, in each industry where the modern industrial enterprise developed. Within each industry in a given country at a given time these players were faced by the same general problems and challenges: changes in the technologies of production, the location of markets and supplies, and the requirements of marketing and distribution.

These histories provide the context in which critical decisions were made and actions taken—decisions and actions that did much to determine the performance of individual firms, industries, and even nations. They also include information which can be helpful in answering questions that have long concerned economists and historians—questions about changes in internal organization and management; the roles of families, financiers, and salaried executives in directing the enterprise; competition and cooperation among firms; growth through horizontal combination, vertical integration, expansion into foreign markets, and diversification into new product lines; and finally, questions on how growth and performance were affected by legal requirements, government rulings, educational systems, and cultural values.

The history of the American experience is told in Part II. In the United States the modern industrial enterprise came into being and evolved in the manner described earlier. There were many more such enterprises in the United States than in either Britain or Germany. As early as World War I the new institution dominated the core industries in the United States. The founders of the new enterprises had made extensive investments in new and improved processes of production, had assembled the essential marketing networks, recruited the salaried teams, and developed the organizational capabilities that assured them places as long-term leaders in their industries. By World War I nearly all of these enterprises were being administered by teams of full-time, experienced, largely salaried managers. And since these firms competed for market share and profits at home and abroad, it can be said that the industries had come to be operated through a system of *competitive managerial* capitalism.

The British experience, described in Part III, was different because in Britain the commitment to *personal* capitalism continued. The failure of British entrepreneurs to make the investments, recruit the managers, and develop the organizational capabilities needed in order to obtain and retain market share in many of the new industries often meant that they lost their markets not only abroad but at home. As a result of this continuing commitment to personal management, Britain became a late industrializer in many of the new industries of the Second Industrial Revolution. These British industries only became competitive with those of the United States and Germany after modern industrial firms were belatedly created. Even then they remained handicapped in national and international markets because of their late start.

The German experience, related in Part IV, was closer to the American. German entrepreneurs made the investments and created the organizational capabilities needed to form a number of major industries. But the new large enterprises in Germany concentrated on the production of industrial goods, whereas those in the United States produced and distributed consumer goods as well. The basic difference between the two countries was, however, that industrial leaders in the United States continued to compete functionally and strategically for market share, while in Germany they often preferred to negotiate with one another to maintain market share at home and in some cases abroad. In the United States managerial capitalism was more competitive; in Germany it became more cooperative. This brand of modern industrial capitalism—*cooperative managerial* capitalism—was one aspect of the arrival in Germany of what scholars have termed organized capitalism.

In preparing this study of hundreds of enterprises in many industries in three countries over a period of more than half a century, I have had to limit the amount of material extracted from the mass of historical detail I examined. I have retained only those events that created the original enterprise and those that determined the path of growth taken and the organizational capabilities developed. References are made to specific decisions only when these directly reshaped enterprises or industries. Details of decisions of less general signifi-

TWO

Scale, Scope, and Organizational Capabilities

The similarities in the beginnings and evolutionary paths of modern industrial enterprises in the United States, Great Britain, and Germany between the 1880s and the 1940s can be set out briefly by means of a dynamic framework. This analytical framework includes the definitions, concepts, and generalizations, that are needed to clarify a complex mass of historical detail, to make the comparisons between industries, countries, and time periods more precise, and to provide the ingredients for an explanatory theory concerning the creation and growth of the institution. The complexities, variations, and exceptions revealed by the detailed historical story will be described in later chapters.

The New Institution

In *The Visible Hand* I described the modern *business* enterprise (of which the modern industrial enterprise is a subspecies) as having two basic characteristics: it contains a number of distinct operating units, and it is managed by a hierarchy of full-time salaried executives. The modern *industrial* enterprise is the particular subspecies that carries out modern production processes. It has more than a production function, however. It is also a "governance structure," to use Oliver Williamson's term.[1] It governs units that carry out different production as well as commercial and research functions and so integrates these activities. In such an enterprise each unit—a factory, a sales or purchasing office, or a research laboratory—has its own administrative office, its own managers and staff, its own set of books, as well as its own resources (physical facilities and personnel) to carry out a specific *function* involved in the production or distribution of a specific *product* in a specific *geographical* area. Each unit—each factory, sales office, purchasing office, research laboratory—could theoretically act as an independent business enterprise. Indeed, many business

cance have been left to the histories of individual firms and ind
and educational systems are considered only when they had a di
the evolution of the institution being studied. An evaluation of th
broader cultural environment on the evolution of the modern in
prise and on the coming of managerial capitalism has also been
So, too, has the labor story; for although the recruitment, train
bilities of the work force and the evolving relationship between
workers in both production and distribution are, indeed, central
of the industrial enterprise, a careful analysis of these factors
demanded a second volume as extensive as this one. Finally, the
relationships between decision-makers and local and national
bodies—which differ so much from country to country—have bee
torians of business-government relationships. In a word, this study
history of the central institution in managerial capitalism, rather tha
of the broader impact of that institution on the polity or society
appeared.

enterprises still consist of just one such unit. In the modern multiunit enterprise the activities of the managers of these units (lower-level managers) are monitored and coordinated by middle-level managers. The latter, in turn, are monitored and coordinated by a full-time top-level executive, or a team of such executives, who plan and allocate resources for the operating units and the enterprise as a whole. The decisions of these top managers normally have to be ratified by a board of directors, legally defined as representatives of the owners (Figure 1).

Such boards of directors nearly always include both top managers (the inside directors) and part-time representatives of the owners (the outside directors). When the owners are an identifiable group of individuals or institutions, their representatives and the inside directors select the company's top management. When the owners are either widely scattered or have little interest in the details of the company's operations, the inside directors normally select the outside directors, and together they select the successors to top management.

Thus the institution under consideration, the modern industrial firm, can be defined as a collection of operating units, each with its own specific facilities and personnel, whose combined resources and activities are coordinated, monitored, and allocated by a hierarchy of middle and top managers. It is the existence of this hierarchy that makes the activities and operations of the whole enterprise more than the sum of its operating units.

As the definition of the institution suggests, its size, its managerial team or hierarchy, and the nature of the resources it controls are directly related to the number of its operating units; in fact, it is the number of these units, rather than total assets or the size of the work force, that determines the number of middle and top managers, the nature of their tasks, and the complexity of the institution they manage. Size in terms of assets, market value of shares, or labor force is the most readily available statistical proxy for such administrative complexity; but statistics cannot convey either the complexity or the nature and functions of the institution.

It then becomes critical to explain how and why the institution grew by adding new units—units that carried out different economic functions, operated in different geographical regions, and handled different lines of products. An initial explanation is that manufacturing enterprises became multifunctional, multiregional, and multiproduct because the addition of new units permitted them to maintain a long-term rate of return on investment by reducing overall costs of production and distribution, by providing products that satisfied existing demands, and by transferring facilities and skills to more profitable markets when returns were reduced by competition, changing technology, or altered market demand.

There were, of course, other reasons why the managers of an industrial enterprise invested in new units of production and distribution: to assure access

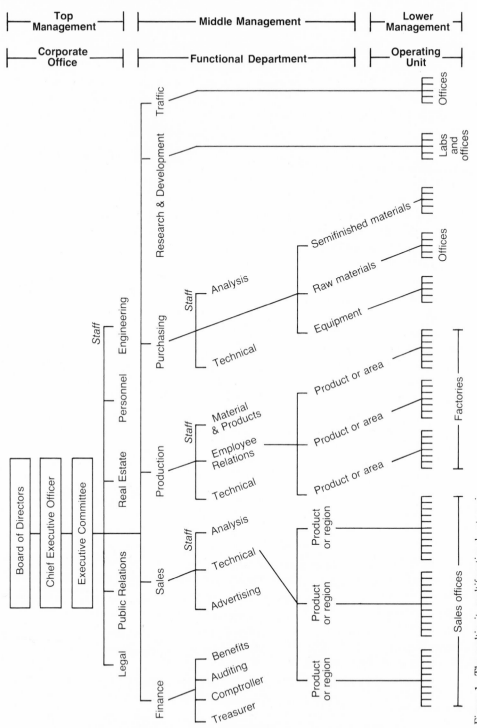

Figure 1. The multiunit, multifunctional enterprise.

to markets and supplies or to prevent competitors from obtaining such access, to obtain control over competitors, to eliminate competition in other ways, or merely to reinvest retained earnings. In more recent years financial reasons have played a role: to improve the firm's overall tax position, to alter the price of its securities, to carry out other financial manipulations, or merely to extend its portfolio of investments. Furthermore, managers have added units in order to acquire greater control over the work force, or simply to gain personal status and power.

Whatever the initial motivation for its investment in new operating units, the modern industrial enterprise has rarely continued to grow or maintain its competitive position *over an extended period of time* unless the addition of new units (and to a lesser extent the elimination of old ones) has actually permitted its managerial hierarchy to reduce costs, to improve functional efficiency in marketing and purchasing as well as production, to improve existing products and processes and to develop new ones, and to allocate resources to meet the challenges and opportunities of ever-changing technologies and markets. Such a process of growth has provided this bureaucratic institution with the internal dynamic that has made it powerful and enabled it to maintain its position of dominance as markets and technologies have changed and as world wars and depressions have come and gone.

Reductions in costs and efficient resource utilization have resulted, the explanation continues, from the exploitation of economies of scale in production and distribution, from exploiting economies of joint production or joint distribution, or from reduction in the costs of transactions involved.

Economies of scale may be defined initially as those that result when the increased size of a single operating unit producing or distributing a single product reduces the unit cost of production or distribution.

Economies of joint production or distribution are those resulting from the use of processes within a single operating unit to produce or distribute more than one product. (I use the increasingly popular term "economies of scope" to refer to these economies of joint production or distribution.)[2]

Transaction costs are those involved in the transfer of goods and services from one operating unit to another. When these transactions are carried out between firms or between individuals, they usually involve the transfer of property rights and are defined in contractual terms.[3] When they are carried out within the enterprise, they are defined by accounting procedures. The costs of such transactions are reduced by a more efficient exchange of goods and services *between* units, whereas the economies of scale and scope are closely tied to the more efficient use of facilities and skills *within* such units.

Transaction cost economies are, of course, closely related to those of scale and scope. The economies of scale and those of scope within a single unit of production or distribution permit that unit to expand the output of goods and services, which, in turn, increases proportionately the number of recurring commercial transactions and contractual relations the enterprise must carry on with other operating units. Just as changes in the processes of production and distribution within units have a powerful impact on the nature of transactions between units (as they are defined through contractual relations), so do changes in contractual relations affect the operations carried on within units.

Differences in economies of scale and scope in different industries, different countries, and different time periods result from differences in the technologies of production and distribution and differences in the sizes and locations of markets. Thus changes, particularly technological innovations in production and changes in market size, continually alter the economic environment (as differentiated from the political and social environment) in which the institution appears and grows. So do changes in per-capita income and demographic shifts, such as those from rural to urban areas and from city to suburb. External changes, by affecting the economies of scale and scope, alter contractual arrangements between units in production and those in distribution, finance, and other business activities.

It was the development of new technologies and the opening of new markets, which resulted in economies of scale and of scope and in reduced transaction costs, that made the large multiunit industrial enterprise come when it did, where it did, and in the way it did. These technological and market changes explain why the institution appeared and continued to cluster in certain industries and not in others, why it came into being by integrating units of volume production with those of volume distribution, and finally, why this multifunctional enterprise continued to grow (though not in all cases) by becoming multinational and multiproduct.

Historical Attributes

The ability of the modern industrial enterprise to exploit fully the economies of scale, scope, and transaction costs was the dynamic that produced its three most significant historical attributes. First, such enterprises clustered from the start in industries having similar characteristics. Second, they appeared quite suddenly in the last quarter of the nineteenth century. Finally, all were born and then continued to grow in much the same manner.

The industries in which the new institution first appeared, and in which it continued to cluster throughout the twentieth century, are indicated in Tables 5–8. The location, country by country and industry by industry, of all the industrial corporations in the world which in 1973 employed more than 20,000 workers is shown in Table 5. These industries are those defined by the U.S.

Table 5. Distribution of world's largest industrial enterprises with more than 20,000 employees, by industry and country, 1973.[a]

Group	Industry	United States	Outside United States	Great Britain	West Germany	Japan	France	Others	Total
20	Food	22	17	13	0	1	1	2	39
21	Tobacco	3	4	3	1	0	0	0	7
22	Textiles	7	6	3	0	2	1	0	13
23	Apparel	6	0	0	0	0	0	2	6
24	Lumber	4	2	0	0	0	0	2	6
25	Furniture	0	0	0	0	0	0	0	0
26	Paper	7	3	3	0	0	0	0	10
27	Printing and publishing	0	0	0	0	0	0	0	0
28	Chemicals	24	28	4	5	3	6	10	52
29	Petroleum	14	12	2	0	0	2	8	26
30	Rubber	5	5	1	1	1	1	1	10
31	Leather	2	0	0	0	0	0	0	2
32	Stone, clay, and glass	7	8	3	0	0	3	2	15
33	Primary metals	13	35	2	9	5	4	15	48
34	Fabricated metals	8	6	5	1	0	0	0	14
35	Machinery	22	12	2	3	2	0	5	34
36	Electrical machinery	20	25	4	5	7	2	5	45
37	Transportation equipment	22	23	3	3	7	4	7	45
38	Instruments[b]	4	1	0	0	0	0	6	5
39	Miscellaneous	2	0	0	0	0	0	0	2
—	Conglomerate	19	3	2	1	0	0	0	22
	Total	211	190	50	29	28	24	59	401

Sources: Compiled from "The Fortune Directory of the 500 Largest Industrial Corporations," *Fortune*, May 1974, pp. 230–257; "The Fortune Directory of the 300 Largest Industrial Corporations outside the U.S.," *Fortune*, August 1974, pp. 174–181.

a. The *Fortune* lists include enterprises of noncommunist countries only.

b. Medical equipment and supplies, photographic equipment and supplies, and watches and clocks.

Bureau of the Census as two-digit groups in its Standard Industrial Classification, or SIC. (The SIC divides its basic two-digit industry categories—those numbered from 20 to 39 for manufacturing—into three-digit categories. The appendixes show these three-digit classifications within the two-digit category.) In 1973, 289 (72.0%) of the 401 companies were clustered in food, chemicals, petroleum, primary metals, and the three machinery groups—nonelectrical and electrical machinery and transportation equipment.[4] Ninety-one, or just under 23%, were in three-digit subcategories of six other two-digit classifications—three-digit classifications which had the same industrial characteristics as those two-digit classifications in which the 72% clustered. These included cigarettes in tobacco; tires in rubber; newsprint in paper; plate and flat glass in stone, clay, and glass; cans and razor blades in fabricated metals; and mass-produced cameras in instruments. Only 21 companies (5.2%) were in the remaining two-digit categories—textiles, apparel, lumber, furniture, leather, printing and publishing, and miscellaneous.

A second fact illustrated by Table 5—one that is central to understanding the evolution of the modern industrial enterprise—is the predominance of American firms among the world's largest industrial corporations. Of the total of 401 companies employing more than 20,000 persons, over half (211, or 52.6%) were American. Great Britain followed with 50 (12.5%), Germany with 29 (7.2%), Japan with 28, and France with 24. Only in chemicals, primary metals, and electrical machinery did all the non-American firms outnumber the American firms by as many as four or five.

Earlier in the twentieth century the large industrial corporations in the United States had clustered in the same industrial groups as those in which they were concentrated in 1973 (Table 6). The pattern was much the same for Britain and Germany (Tables 7 and 8). The American firms, however, were bigger and more numerous than those in other countries (see appendixes). Well before World War II the United States had many more and many larger managerial hierarchies than did the other nations.

Basic differences within the broad pattern of evolution are also suggested by the tables. For example, in the United States throughout the twentieth century the great enterprises produced both consumer and industrial goods. Britain had proportionately more large firms in consumer goods than did the United States, while the biggest industrials in Germany concentrated much more on producer's goods. Even as late as 1973, close to one-third—sixteen of the fifty—firms in Great Britain employing more than 20,000 persons were engaged in the production and distribution of food and tobacco products, whereas Germany, and also France and Japan, each had only one firm in the same two categories (Table 5). On the other hand, before World War II Germany had had many more firms than Britain in chemicals and heavy machinery.

Table 6.   Distribution of the 200 largest industrial enterprises in the United States,
           by industry, 1917–1973.[a]

Group	Industry	1917	1930	1948	1973
20	Food	29	31	27	22
21	Tobacco	6	5	5	3
22	Textiles	6	4	8	3
23	Apparel	3	0	0	0
24	Lumber	3	4	2	4
25	Furniture	0	1	1	0
26	Paper	5	8	6	9
27	Printing and publishing	2	2	2	1
28	Chemicals	20	20	23	28
29	Petroleum	22	26	22	22
30	Rubber	5	5	5	5
31	Leather	4	2	2	0
32	Stone, clay, and glass	5	8	6	7
33	Primary metals	31	23	23	19
34	Fabricated metals	11	10	6	5
35	Machinery	17	19	23	16
36	Electrical machinery	5	5	7	13
37	Transportation equipment	24	23	29	19
38	Instruments	1	2	1	4
39	Miscellaneous	1	2	2	1
—	Conglomerate	0	0	0	19
	Total	200	200	200	200

Sources: Appendixes A.1–A.3 for 1917, 1930, and 1948; figures for 1973 compiled from
Fortune, May 1974, pp. 230–257.
   a. Ranked by assets.

Economies of Scale and Scope in Production

The major innovations made in the processes of production during the last
quarter of the nineteenth century created many new industries and transformed
many old industries. These processes differed from earlier ones in *their potential
for exploiting the unprecedented cost advantages of the economies of scale and
scope.*

In the older, labor-intensive industries, increases in the output of a manufacturing establishment came primarily by adding more machines and more
workers to operate them. In newer industries, expanded output came by a
drastic change in capital-labor ratios. It came by improving and rearranging
inputs; by using new or greatly improved machinery, furnaces, stills, and other

Table 7. Distribution of the 200 largest industrial enterprises in Great Britain, by
industry, 1919–1973.[a]

Group	Industry	1919	1930	1948	1973
20	Food	61	63	53	33
21	Tobacco	3	4	6	4
22	Textiles	26	21	17	10
23	Apparel	0	1	2	0
24	Lumber	0	0	0	2
25	Furniture	0	0	0	0
26	Paper	3	5	6	7
27	Printing and publishing	5	10	7	7
28	Chemicals	14	11	17	21
29	Petroleum	3	4	3	8
30	Rubber	3	3	2	6
31	Leather	1	1	1	3
32	Stone, clay, and glass	2	7	8	16
33	Primary metals	40	24	25	14
34	Fabricated metals	1	8	7	7
35	Machinery	7	6	10	26
36	Electrical machinery	6	10	11	14
37	Transportation equipment	23	17	21	16
38	Instruments	0	2	1	3
39	Miscellaneous	2	3	3	1
—	Conglomerate	0	0	0	2
	Total	200	200	200	200

Sources: Appendix B.1–B.3 for 1919, 1930, and 1948; figures for 1973 compiled from *The
Times 1000, 1974/75* (London, 1974), table 15.
a. Ranked by market value of quoted capital.

equipment; by reorienting the processes of production within the plant; by
placing the several intermediary processes employed in making a final product
within a single works; and by increasing the application of energy (particularly
that generated by fossil fuel).

The first set of industries remained labor-intensive. In industries such as
apparel, textiles made from natural fibers, lumber, furniture, printing and publishing—in which the large modern firm remained relatively rare—improvements in equipment and plant design did bring economies of scale, but they
were not extensive. A sharp reduction of unit costs did not accompany an
increase in the volume of materials processed by the plant. In these industries
the large mills, factories, or works often had observable, but not striking, cost
advantages over the smaller ones.

In the second set, the more capital-intensive industries, new processes of

Table 8. Distribution of the 200 largest industrial enterprises in Germany, by industry, 1913–1973.[a]

Group	Industry	1913	1929	1953	1973
20	Food	26	28	22	24
21	Tobacco	1	1	0	6
22	Textiles	15	24	26	4
23	Apparel	1	1	1	0
24	Lumber	1	0	0	0
25	Furniture	0	0	0	0
26	Paper	4	5	3	2
27	Printing and publishing	0	1	0	6
28	Chemicals	30	24	24	30
29	Petroleum	5	7	6	8
30	Rubber	4	2	5	3
31	Leather	2	5	2	1
32	Stone, clay, and glass	7	7	6	15
33	Primary metals	49	33	40	19
34	Fabricated metals	5	3	5	14
35	Machinery	25	19	28	29
36	Electrical machinery	7	11	8	21
37	Transportation equipment	16	24	18	14
38	Instruments	2	3	3	2
39	Miscellaneous	0	2	3	1
—	Conglomerate	0	0	0	1
	Total	200	200	200	200

Sources: Appendix C.1–C.3 for 1913, 1929, and 1953; figures for 1973 compiled from *Handbuch der deutschen Aktiengesellschaften, 1974–75.*

a. Ranked by sales for 1973 and by assets for the other three years.

production were invented or existing ones vastly improved in the late nineteenth century—processes for the refining and distilling of sugar, petroleum, animal and vegetable oil, whiskey and other liquids; for the refining and smelting of iron, steel, copper, and aluminum; for the mechanical processing and packaging of grain, tobacco, and other agricultural products; for the manufacturing of complex light, standardized machinery through the fabrication and assembly of interchangeable parts; and for the production of technologically advanced industrial machinery and chemicals by a series of interrelated mechanical and chemical processes. In these capital-intensive industries, investment in new facilities greatly increased the ratio of capital to labor involved in producing a unit of output. Production units achieved much greater economies of scale—that is, the cost per unit dropped more quickly as the volume of materials being processed increased. Therefore large plants operating at their "minimum efficient scale" (the scale of operation necessary to reach the lowest cost per unit) had an impressive cost advantage over smaller plants that did not reach that scale.[5]

The economies of joint production, or scope, also brought significant cost reduction. Here the cost advantage came from making a number of products in the same production unit from much the same raw and semifinished materials and by the same intermediate processes. The increase in the number of products made simultaneously in the same factory reduced the unit costs of each individual product.

These potential cost advantages, however, could not be fully realized unless a constant flow of materials through the plant or factory was maintained to assure effective capacity utilization. If the realized volume of flow fell below capacity, then actual costs per unit rose rapidly. They did so because fixed costs remained much higher and "sunk costs" (the original capital investment) were also much higher than in the more labor-intensive industries. Thus the two decisive figures in determining costs and profits were (and still are) rated capacity and throughput, or the amount actually processed within a specified time period. (The economies of scale theoretically incorporate the economies of speed, as I use that term in *The Visible Hand,* because the economies of scale depend on both size—rated capacity—and speed—the intensity at which the capacity is utilized.) In the capital-intensive industries the throughput needed to maintain minimum efficient scale requires careful coordination not only of the flow through the processes of production but also of the flow of inputs from suppliers and the flow of outputs to intermediaries and final users.

Such coordination did not, and indeed could not, happen automatically. It demanded the constant attention of a managerial team or hierarchy. The potential economies of scale and scope, as measured by rated capacity, are the physical characteristics of the production facilities. The actual economies of scale or of scope, as determined by throughput, are organizational. Such economies depend on knowledge, skill, experience, and teamwork—on the organized human capabilities essential to exploit the potential of technological processes.

The significance of economies of scale and those of scope in production, as measured by throughput, can be illustrated by two well-known examples: the Standard Oil Company, one of the very first modern industrial enterprises (as differentiated from transportation, communication, or distribution enterprises) in the United States; and the three oldest and largest German chemical companies.

In 1882 the Standard Oil alliance formed the Standard Oil Trust. (Its successor, Exxon, is still the world's largest oil company.) The purpose was not to obtain control over the industry's output: the alliance, a loose federation of forty companies, each with its own legal and administrative identity but tied to

John D. Rockefeller's Standard Oil Company through interchange of stock and other financial devices, already had a monopoly. At that time, in fact, the members of the alliance produced 90% of America's output of kerosene.[6] Instead, the Standard Oil Trust was formed to provide a legal instrument to rationalize the industry and exploit economies of scale more fully. The trust provided the essential legal means to create a central or corporate office that could do two things. First, it could reorganize the processes of production by shutting down some refineries, reshaping others, and building new ones. Second, it could coordinate the flow of materials, not only through the several refineries, but from the oil fields to the refineries and from the refineries to the consumers.

The resulting rationalization made it possible to concentrate close to a quarter of the world's production of kerosene in three refineries, each with an average daily charging capacity of 6,500 barrels, with two-thirds of their product going to overseas markets. (At this time, refined petroleum products were by far the nation's largest nonagricultural export.) Imagine the *diseconomies* of scale (the increase in unit costs) that would result from placing close to one-fourth of the world's production of shoes, textiles, or lumber into three factories or mills! In those instances the administrative coordination of the operation of miles and miles of machines and the huge concentration of labor needed to operate those machines would make neither economic nor social sense.

The reorganization of the trust's refining facilities brought a sharp reduction in the average cost of producing a gallon of kerosene. In 1880 the average cost at plants with a daily capacity of 1,500 to 2,000 barrels was approximately 2.5¢ per gallon. By 1885, according to the industry's most authoritative history, the average cost for plants of that size had been reduced to 1.5¢.[7] Data compiled for the trust's Manufacturing Committee showed that the average cost of processing a gallon of crude for all its works had dropped from 0.534¢ in 1884 to 0.452¢ in 1885 with a resulting increase in the profit margin from 0.530¢ in 1884 to 1.003¢ in 1885. (That profit margin was the core of four of the world's largest industrial fortunes, those of the Rockefellers, Harknesses, Paynes, and Flaglers.) As these averages indicate, the unit costs of the giant refineries were far below those of any competitor. To maintain this cost advantage, however, these large refineries had to have a continuing daily throughput of 5,000 to 6,500 barrels, or a threefold to fourfold increase over the earlier daily flow of 1,500 to 2,000 barrels, with resulting increases in transactions handled and in the complexity of coordinating the flow of materials through the processes of production and distribution.

Even as Standard Oil was investing in its large refineries to exploit the economies of scale, the German dye makers were making still larger investments to permit them to exploit fully the economies of scope. The enlarged plants produced literally hundreds of dyes, as well as many pharmaceuticals, from the same raw materials and the same set of intermediate chemical compounds. The first three enterprises to make such investments to exploit the cost advantages of scale and then those of scope—Bayer, Hoechst, and BASF—were able to reduce the price of a new synthetic dye, red alizarin, from 270 marks per kilogram in 1869 to 9 marks in 1886, and to make comparable price reductions in their other dyes.[8] A new dye or pharmaceutical added little to the production cost of these items, and the additions permitted a reduction in the unit cost of the others. On the other hand, the development of new dyes and pharmaceuticals was not only costly, but each new product increased the tasks of quality control and coordination of product flow.

Standard Oil and the German chemical companies were by no means unique. In the 1880s and 1890s new mass-production technologies—those of the Second Industrial Revolution—brought a sharp reduction in costs as plants reached minimum efficient scale. In many industries the throughput of plants of that scale was so high that a small number of them could meet the existing national and even global demand. The structure of these industries quickly became oligopolistic, and the few large enterprises in each competed world-wide. In many instances the first company to build a plant of minimum efficient scale and to recruit the essential management team remained the leader in its industry for decades.

The differentials between the potential scale-and-scope economies of different production technologies indicate not only why the large hierarchical firms appeared in some industries and not in others, but also why they appeared suddenly in the last decades of the nineteenth century. It was not until the 1870s, with the completion of the modern transportation and communication networks—the railroad, telegraph, steamship, and cable—and of the organizational and technological innovations essential to operate them as integrated systems, that materials could flow into a factory or processing plant and finished goods move out at a rate of speed and volume and with the precise timing required to achieve substantial economies of throughput. Transportation that depended on the power of animals, wind, and current was too slow, too irregular, and too uncertain to maintain a level of throughput necessary to achieve the potential economies of the new technologies. Thus the revolution in transportation and communication created opportunities that led to a revolution in both production and distribution.

The essential first step in exploiting the new technologies of production—the step that led to the creation of the modern industrial enterprise—was, therefore, the investment in production facilities large enough to exploit the full potential of the economies of scale and scope inherent in the new or improved technologies. The critical entrepreneurial act was not the invention—or even the initial commercialization—of a new or greatly improved product or process. Instead it was the construction of a plant of the optimal size required to exploit fully the economies of scale or those of scope, or both.

Several points need to be made about such an investment. First, to repeat, different production technologies have different scale-or-scope economies. Costs decrease and increase more sharply in relation to volume in some production processes than in others. In some industries, such as oil, steel, and aluminum, the cost-curve gradient (to use an economist's term) was steep, and the penalties for producing below minimum efficient scale were severe. In others, such as soap, cereal, and similar branded packaged products, the cost gradient was less steep and the penalties for operating below minimum efficient scale were less severe. So too, the potential for exploiting the economies of scope varied widely from industry to industry.

Moreover, the optimal plant size for a specific product was related as much to existing demand as to the potential output of a technology. The number of plants in an industry that could operate at minimum efficient scale at a given point in time was limited by the size of the market for that industry's product. A plant, built at minimum efficient scale for an existing technology, that could produce more than the market could absorb had higher unit costs than a smaller plant whose output was more closely calibrated to market demand. In such a situation the optimal plant size would be smaller than the size of one built to the technology's minimum efficient scale. Therefore, I use the term "optimal plant size" to mean the most efficient size of a plant at a given time and place. The term reflects not only the state of the existing production technology but also the anticipated size of markets at the time the plant was built; furthermore, it reflects the elasticity of demand. Because the products of the new technologies were often new themselves (or much improved), the lower prices made possible by scale-or-scope economies greatly increased the demand, thus further increasing optimal plant size, at least until the technological limits were reached.

Both technologies and markets were dynamic. Changes in technology could increase or decrease minimum efficient scale. Changes in market size increased or decreased optimal plant size. In addition, the capital required to build a plant of optimal size varied from industry to industry. Steel mills needed much greater capital investments than did oil refineries, which in turn were more costly than factories producing cigarettes and other branded packaged products. For these reasons the sizes and costs of production plants differed widely from industry to industry.

Optimal size, as just defined, refers only to a production unit of the type described earlier, that is, a manufacturing establishment as defined in the U.S. Census, or its physically adjoining establishments, and not to the enterprise as a whole. Most enterprises became multiplant, for in few cases were single works of optimal size able to continue to meet the demand, particularly in growing markets. Decisions concerning where and when to build new plants involved a complex equation, one that changed as technology and markets changed. Key considerations included not only the cost advantages of operating at minimum efficient scale but also estimates of anticipated share of these markets, as well as size and location of markets plus transportation costs and other costs of distribution and supply. If the plant was to be in a foreign country, the costs resulting from tariff laws and other restrictive legislation needed to be computed. The relationship between the efficient size of plant and the efficient size of a multiplant enterprise is complex. But whatever the size of an investment in production, an enterprise could realize the cost advantages of that investment only if a management team effectively coordinated the fluctuating flow of a variety of materials into the several production facilities, through them, and then to the wholesalers, retailers, and final consumers.

Manufacturers quickly appreciated the importance of the relationship between cost and volume and the penalties of operating below minimum efficient scale. By the early twentieth century, managers, particularly in the United States, were using the concept of "over and under absorbed burden" as a way to place such variations in cost on their accounting sheets. If the plant operated at less than its standard volume (based on estimates of market size as well as anticipated throughput at rated capacity), the resulting loss was listed as "under absorbed burden"; if it operated at more than that volume the resulting gain was listed as "over absorbed burden."[9] Over and under absorbed burden became critical items on the cost sheets of individual plants and on the profit-and-loss accounts of the enterprise as a whole.

Economies of Scale and Scope in Distribution

The economies of scale and those of scope as measured by throughput in the production process help explain why large firms appeared in the industries where they did and when they did, but these economies do not explain why the firms initially grew in the way they did: that is, by integrating forward into distribution and backward into purchasing. The new mass producers might well have continued to buy from and sell to commercial intermediaries—particularly wholesalers and manufacturers' agents. By doing so they would have been spared the expense of investing in personnel and costly distribution and purchasing facilities. Explaining such vertical integration requires a more precise understanding of the processes of volume distribution—particularly why the wholesalers and other commercial intermediaries lost their cost advantage vis-à-vis the volume producer.

The intermediaries' cost advantage had resulted from exploiting the economies of both scale and scope. Because they handled the products of many manufacturers, they achieved a greater volume and lower costs per unit than did any one manufacturer in the marketing and distribution of a *single* line of products (scale). Moreover, they increased this advantage by the broader scope of their operation—that is, by handling a *number* of related product lines through a single set of facilities (scope). This was true of the new volume wholesalers and the new mass retailers—the department store, the mail-order house, and the chain store. These full-line wholesalers and mass retailers came into being only after the railroad, telegraph, steamship, and cable made possible new high-volume, high-speed, regularly scheduled transportation.

Both wholesalers and retailers were organized specifically to exploit the economies of scale and scope. The organizational core of a volume distributor was its buying departments, one for each major line handled. The buyers determined the price, the quantity, and the physical specifications (size, weight, and quality) of goods ordered. They were responsible for maintaining the high-volume flow of goods through the enterprise by working closely with its traffic department in arranging specific shipments and deliveries and with its selling force in arranging displays, catalogue copy, or advertising. The critical measure of performance in coordinating this flow through the enterprise was "stock-turn," that is, the volume of goods processed in relation to inventory by a single set of facilities and personnel within a specified period of time. Stock-turn was to mass distributors what throughput was to refiners and other mass producers. The greater the stock-turn, the more intensive the use of existing personnel, facilities, and capital invested in inventory; therefore, the lower the cost per unit. The buying departments, each coordinating the flow of a single line of products, were the units that permitted the new volume distributors to take advantage of economies of *scale*. The traffic departments, the selling facilities, and the geographically distant purchasing offices and facilities used by all the buying departments permitted the enterprise to achieve economies of *scope*— that is, to use the same facilities to market and distribute different products.

Yet the wholesalers' advantages of both scope and scale had their limits. When these limits were reached, it became more advantageous for the manufacturers themselves to make the investment in purchasing, marketing, and distribution facilities. When a manufacturer's volume attained a scale that would reduce the cost of transporting, storing, and distributing products to the level of that achieved by the wholesaler through his volume economies, the intermediary lost his cost advantage. As Scott Moss points out: "Provided that such a minimum efficient scale in transactions exists, the intermediary will have a cost advantage over its customers and suppliers only as long as the volume of transactions in which he engages comes closer to that scale than do the transactions volumes of his customers or suppliers."[10] A manufacturer of a single product rarely achieved such a volume in retailing, except in highly concentrated urban markets. On the other hand, he often did so in the wholesaling of both consumer and industrial goods.

Just as the volume distributor's cost advantages of scale were lost when the manufacturer increased his output to a volume that would bring comparable advantages, so the cost advantages of joint distribution or scope were reduced when products required specialized facilities and skills in their marketing and their distribution. (I use the term "marketing" to refer to promoting and selling goods and the term "distribution" to refer to the physical flow of goods from manufacturers to customers.) The more the products required such specialized skills and such specialized storage and transportation facilities, the less were the opportunities for the intermediary to achieve economies of scope resulting from the ability to handle a number of related products for a number of manufacturers. This was also true for transactions involved. If contractual arrangements for the sale and delivery of related products were relatively straightforward and standardized, then a single intermediary might easily handle all transactions involved in the distribution of a manufacturer's output. But if the transactions were complex, if specialized knowledge was required in order to sell, install, and maintain the products and to provide the necessary credit arrangements, and if costly specialized facilities were required to distribute the goods, then the intermediary had to hire personnel with these specialized skills and invest in these specialized facilities—skills and facilities that often were applicable to only one particular product line. Moreover, if the intermediary did make the investment in facilities and personnel, he became increasingly dependent on the few manufacturers of the product in question and on the cash flow needed to stay in business. The manufacturer, in addition, usually had a more accurate understanding of the specialized facilities, skills, and services required to distribute and market his specific products than did the wholesaler, who handled a variety of lines for a number of producers. Thus the increasing product-specificity of the investment required to market a product in volume reduced the intermediary's cost advantage and otherwise discouraged him from making the necessary investment. At the same time, of course, it increased the incentive of the manufacturer to make the expenditures.

Still another incentive for the manufacturer to invest in a sales force of his own was competition. The new production technologies with their historically unprecedented output created a new type of competition. In those industries where a few large plants could meet existing demand, these few quickly began to compete for a substantial share of national and often international markets. Cost advantages of scale reflected a manufacturer's market share. Normally, loss of share to a competitor not only increased his production costs but also decreased those of his competitor.

Thus in the new capital-intensive, oligopolistic industries the few large competitors could no longer afford to depend on commercial intermediaries who made their profits by handling products of more than one manufacturer. The manufacturers needed a sales force of their own to concentrate full-time on advertising, canvassing for customers, assuring delivery on schedule, and providing installation, service and repair, customer credit, and other services for their particular line of products. A sales force became the most dependable instrument for obtaining and holding a market share large enough to assure the cost advantages of scale. In addition, it provided a steady flow of information about markets and customer needs and tastes. In these ways the manufacturer's sales force reduced potentially high transaction costs.

For these reasons, as the scale of firms' output increased and as the specialized facilities and services required for volume distribution narrowed the intermediaries' potential to exploit the economies of scope, leading enterprises in the new capital-intensive industries invested in product-specific distribution facilities and recruited and trained personnel to provide specialized marketing services.

The motives for integrating backward by building a purchasing organization to take the place of commercial intermediaries were, of course, much the same as those for integrating forward into wholesaling. The establishment of a central purchasing office provided the enterprise with skilled, product-specialized buyers who searched out sources of supplies and contracted with suppliers on price, specification, and delivery date. They worked closely with their production departments to schedule flows and with the traffic departments which were responsible for the actual shipment of goods to the plants.

Although fewer product-specific services and facilities were needed in purchasing than in distribution, they were often quite essential in coordinating flows and reducing costs. The processors of branded packaged dairy and chocolate products and of canned milk, canned vegetables, and canned meat needed refrigerated storage facilities and careful scheduling to assure continuous year-in-and-year-out flows into the processing plants. Other processors, such as cigarette makers and distillers, whose raw materials required aging and curing, made comparable investments. Furthermore, the purchasing of manufactured supplies in volume directly from the manufacturers reduced costs just as it did for mass retailers. In these ways integrating backward into purchasing, like integrating forward into distribution, replaced the existing commercial intermediaries.

Building the Integrative Hierarchy

As I have emphasized, the initial step in the creation of the modern industrial enterprise was the investment in production facilities large enough to achieve the cost advantages of scale and scope. The second step, which often occurred almost simultaneously, was the investment in product-specific marketing, distributing, and purchasing networks. The third and final step was the recruiting and organizing of the managers needed to supervise functional activities pertaining to the production and distribution of a product, to coordinate and monitor the flow of goods through the processes, and to allocate resources for future production and distribution on the basis of current performance and anticipated demand.[11]

The resulting managerial hierarchies were established along functional lines. Each function was administered by a department (see Figure 1). The largest and first to be formed were those for production and sales, with a smaller one for purchasing. At the headquarters of these functional departments middle managers coordinated and monitored the activities of the lower-level managers who administered the enterprise's operating units—its several factories, its sales and purchasing offices, and its research laboratories. They also had to provide the incentive for plant and office managers to perform effectively, just as those lower-level executives had to motivate the operating personnel in their units. Normally, the functional departments were organized along the line-and-staff principle, with line officers having executive authority and staff officers having an advisory role. In production the line officers had charge of the specific processes used in the output of goods, and staff officers had charge of personnel records, labor relations, cost accounting, and quality and inventory control. In sales the line officers usually headed regions or managed specific products, while the staff officers were specialists in accounting, advertising, and market analysis. In addition, smaller departments were established to carry out other functional activities.

Of the smaller departments, research and development became one of the most significant in those enterprises operating in technologically advanced industries. The new enterprise's laboratories were created to assist in assuring proper control of production processes and in maintaining the quality of the product. The creation of a research organization geographically and administratively separate from production came only after the production and marketing organizations had been firmly established. In their early years such research departments concentrated on improving product and process; they also located new markets for existing products. Only in later years did they begin to develop new materials or finished goods for new markets.

The amount of investment in research reflected the technical complexities of the products and the production processes. Not surprisingly, industrial research in the United States and Europe remained concentrated in a small number of industries. In the United States in 1921 (the first year for which information is available), close to half the scientific personnel in industrial research were employed in two industries—chemicals and electrical equipment. Also not surprising was the close relation that developed between research managers and those in marketing and production.[12] The sales force maintained a careful watch on product performance and customer needs. Its managers worked closely with the product designers and plant managers, as well as laboratory chiefs, in improving both product and process. In the chemical and electrical machinery industries the resulting network of information flows became a major force in continuing technological innovation.

Industrial firms invested in research and development for much the same reasons that they invested in marketing and distribution. Specialized firms existed in both areas, although there were far fewer specialized research firms than marketing firms. Like wholesalers and retailers, research and development firms made their profits by providing the same or related services to a number of manufacturers (scope). The manufacturer's primary interest, however, was in improving a specific product line. The improvement of products and processes required product-specific skills and facilities, as well as close coordination between marketing, plant, and laboratory personnel and the facilities handling that product. Moreover, in the technologically advanced industries, improved products and processes became major competitive weapons to maintain and enlarge market share. Whereas there was little incentive for a separate research firm to invest heavily in highly product-specific personnel and facilities, since its function was to serve many customers, the manufacturer with a strong proprietary interest in the development of his particular products had every incentive to do so. As a result, product-specific industrial research and development remained concentrated in the offices and laboratories of the integrated industrial enterprises. These firms, however, continued to use the specialized research companies, such as Arthur D. Little and Stone & Webster in the United States, for testing, setting standards, and other more routine, less proprietary activities. [13]

In addition to the departments for production and marketing and the smaller ones for purchasing and research and development, other smaller functional departments included traffic (to move goods over transportation networks), engineering (to construct plants and other facilities), legal, real estate, and, somewhat later, personnel and public relations. Again as in the case of research and development, the volume of activity and the product-specific nature of the tasks led to the creation of these smaller internal departments. The enterprise continued to rely on outside specialists for routine or part-time specialized assistance and advice.

The other large department was finance. Its functions were somewhat less product-specific. Its tasks were to coordinate the flow of funds through the enterprise's many units and to provide a steady flow of information to enable top management to monitor performance and allocate resources. The ability to plan and schedule cash flows was an important advantage gained from internalizing distribution units; for internalization eliminated the danger of delayed or intermittent payments from wholesalers—receipts whose steady flow was essential to pay suppliers and workers and to stabilize and reduce the costs of working capital. To provide information concerning performance and resource allocation, the financial department set up uniform accounting and auditing procedures. It also became responsible for external financial affairs, including the raising of new capital and the payment of dividends and interest on bonds.

The heads of the major functional departments, the president, and sometimes a full-time chairman of the board composed the senior decision-making unit of integrated industrial enterprises. In the United States these executives usually formed the Executive Committee of the Board; in Germany they made up the Vorstand. In Britain and Japan they became Managing or Executive Directors. Individually the full-time salaried top managers, the "inside directors" and their staffs, monitored the activities and performance of the middle managers who were responsible for the day-to-day operations of the functional departments. They supervised the flow of goods through the enterprise. Jointly they determined corporate policies, planned long-range strategy and allocated the resources—facilities and personnel—necessary to maintain the long-term health and growth of the enterprise. In making broad strategic decisions they worked closely with the "outside directors," the part-time representatives of families, banks, and other shareholders. The completed structures of these centralized, functionally departmentalized hierarchies were variations on the structure of the modern industrial enterprise (Figure 1), the central institution of managerial capitalism.

First-Mover Advantages and Oligopolistic Competition

The entrepreneurs who invested in plants big enough to exploit the economies of scale or scope in production, in product-specific facilities and skills in distribution (and also in research in technologically advanced industries), and in the managerial organization essential for coordination of those activities brought into being the modern industrial enterprise. The first to do so acquired powerful competitive advantages, or (to use the economists' term) "first-mover" advantages. This was particularly true in industries producing new or greatly improved products and using new and greatly improved processes. To compete with the first movers, rivals had to build plants of comparable size and make the necessary investment in distribution and, in some industries, in research. They also had to recruit and then train a managerial hierarchy. But to build a plant of the size needed to achieve comparable economies of scale or scope might mean that the total capacity of the industry would exceed the existing demand. Thus if latecomers were to maintain enough capacity utilization to assure competitive unit costs, they would have to take customers away from the first movers.

This was a challenging task. While the latecomer's production managers were learning the unique characteristics of what was usually a new or greatly improved technology and while its sales force was being recruited and trained, the first movers' managers had already worked out the bugs in the production processes. They had already become practiced in assuring prompt delivery. They knew how to meet customers' special needs and to provide demonstrations, consumer credit, installation, and after-sales repair and maintenance. In branded packaged products, where advertising was an important competitive weapon, the first movers were already investing some of the high profits resulting from low-cost operations in massive advertising campaigns.

The first movers had other advantages. In the more technologically complex industries the first to install research laboratories and to train technicians were the first to become fully aware of the attributes and intricacies of the new products and processes—an advantage that was often reinforced and expanded by patents. Moreover, in most of the new industries the latecomers had to make a much larger initial outlay of capital than their predecessors. They could rarely finance either the necessarily large investment in the scale of production or in the size of their marketing networks from retained earnings, as had the first movers, because to compete they had to build plants of comparable optimal size. The latecomers' investments not only had to be larger, they were also riskier, precisely because of the first movers' competitive strength.

Thus the first movers were not only the leaders in exploiting the cost advantages of scale and scope, but they had a head start in developing capabilities in all functional activities—production, distribution, purchasing, research, finance, and general management. Again to borrow a useful term from the economists, the first movers were apt to be well down the learning curve in each of the industry's functional activities before challengers went into full operation. Such advantages made it easy for first movers to nip challengers in the bud, to stop their growth before they acquired the facilities and developed the skills needed to become strong competitors. And such advantages could be and often were used ruthlessly.

This distinction between first movers and challengers is of major importance to this history. First in the development of a new set of improved products or processes came the inventors, usually the individuals who obtained the patent. Then came the pioneers, the entrepreneurs who made the investment in facilities needed to commercialize a product or process—to bring it into general use.[14] The first movers were pioneers or other entrepreneurs who made the three interrelated sets of investments in production, distribution, and management required to achieve the competitive advantages of scale, scope, or both, inherent in the new and improved products and processes. (I also use the term "first movers" for the enterprises thus created.) The challengers were the latecomers who took on the first movers by making a comparable set of investments and by developing comparable skills needed to obtain comparable competitive capabilities.

Although the barriers to entry into an industry that were raised by a first mover's investments were intimidating, challengers did appear. They came most often when rapid demographic changes had altered existing markets and when technological change had created new markets and diminished old ones. But in those industries where scale or scope provided cost advantages, the number of players remained small, and there was little turnover among the leaders. These industries quickly became and remained oligopolistic and occasionally monopolistic. A few large integrated firms competed for market share and profits in national and often world markets in what was a new, oligopolistic manner: they no longer competed primarily on price, as firms had done previously and as firms continued to do in the more fragmented labor-intensive industries. The largest firm (usually the first to make the three-pronged investment in production, distribution, and management) became the price leader, basing prices on estimates of demand in relation to its own plant capacities and those of its competitors.

Price remained a significant competitive weapon, but these firms competed more forcefully for market share and increased profits by means of functional and strategic efficiency, that is, by carrying out more capably the processes of production and distribution, by improving both product and process through systematic research and development, by locating more suitable sources of supply, by providing more effective marketing services, by product differentiation (in branded, packaged products, primarily through advertising), and finally by moving more quickly into expanding markets and out of declining ones.[15] The test of such competition was changing market share, and in most of the new oligopolistic industries market share and profits changed continually.

Competition for market share and profits tended to sharpen the skills of the middle managers responsible for the functional activities. It also tested and enlarged the skills of the top managers in their responsibilities for coordination, strategic planning, and resource allocation. The combined capabilities of top and middle management can be considered the skills of the organization itself. These skills were the most valuable of all those that made up the *organizational capabilities* of the new modern industrial enterprise.

These organizational capabilities included, in addition to the skills of middle and top management, those of lower management and the work force. They also included the facilities for production and distribution acquired to exploit fully the economies of scale and scope. Such capabilities provided the profits that in large part financed the continuing growth of the enterprise. Highly product-specific and process-specific, these organizational capabilities affected, indeed often determined, the direction and pace of the small number of first movers and challengers, and of the industries and even the national economies in which they operated.

Continuing Growth of the Modern Enterprise

Once the investment in production and distribution was large enough to exploit fully the economies of scale or scope, and once the necessary managerial hierarchy was in place, the industrial enterprise grew—it added new units—in four ways. One was by acquiring or merging with enterprises using much the same processes to make much the same product for much the same markets; that is, it grew by horizontal combination. Another was by taking on units involved in the earlier or later stages of making a product, from the mining or processing of raw materials to the final assembling or packaging; that is, it grew by vertical integration. The third way of growth was to expand geographically to distant areas. The fourth was to make new products that were related to the firm's existing technologies or markets. The initial motive for the first two strategies of growth was usually defensive, to protect the firm's existing investments. In the other two strategies, firms used their existing investments and above all their existing organizational capabilities—their facilities and skills—to move into new markets and into new businesses.

HORIZONTAL AND VERTICAL COMBINATION

In a large number of cases the incentive for acquisition or merger of enterprises producing competitive products was to gain more effective control of output, price, and markets. Such horizontal combination increased organizational capabilities and productivity *only* if a single, centralized administrative control was quickly established over the merged or acquired companies and then the facilities and personnel were rationalized to exploit more fully the economies of scale and scope. Such was the case, for example, when the Standard Oil associates legally consolidated to form the Standard Oil Trust. And such horizontal combination often permitted a number of pioneers to come together and then to make the investments in production and distribution and management necessary to achieve first-mover advantages. But if the companies acquired or those coming into the merger were not administratively centralized and rationalized but instead continued to operate autonomously much as they had before the change, the enlarged enterprise remained little more than a federation of firms. The resulting cost advantages were minimal.

The reasons for vertical integration—growth through obtaining facilities along the chain of production—were more complex. Faster throughput and with it significant cost reductions and increased productivity in terms of output per worker or unit of equipment rarely resulted from vertical integration unless the additional processes were directly connected to the firm's existing ones by its own rails, conveyors, or pipes. Such integration was particularly successful in the production of chemicals, metals, and machinery. Where the facilities to make related processes were located at a distance, increased throughput was less feasible.

The motive for such investments in growth by vertical integration was primarily defensive, but not in the same way as through horizontal combination. Sometimes the aim was to withhold supplies from competitors and so create barriers to entry in the industry. Far more often, however, the motive for such vertical integration was to assure a steady supply of materials into the enterprise's production processes, which was essential if the cost advantages of scale and scope were to be maintained. It provided insurance against great cost increases resulting from fluctuating production or even shutdown. It reduced the cost of high inventory storage and other carrying costs. It lowered the risk that suppliers would fail to carry out contractual agreements—risks from what economists and organizational theorists have termed "bounded rationality" (human fallibility) and "opportunism" (self-interest with guile). The greater the investment in capital-intensive facilities and the greater the optimal size of these facilities, the greater the incentive for insurance against such transaction costs. Thus the more concentrated the facilities of production and the more concentrated the sources of supply, the more likely was the integration of the two within a single enterprise.

Nevertheless, as long as such integration did not directly increase economies of scale or scope, as long as alternate sources of supply were available at a reasonable price, and as long as legal and personal ties and relationships helped to assure the fulfillment of contractual arrangements, manufacturers usually preferred to buy their supplies rather than invest in and manage the production of those supplies. If the investment was not made to reduce the cost of transaction risks, it might be made merely as a profitable portfolio investment. But most manufacturers preferred other routes to growth—those of adding units in areas and in products where their existing facilities and organizational capabilities gave them a distinct competitive advantage.

GEOGRAPHICAL EXPANSION AND PRODUCT DIVERSIFICATION

When managers of industrial enterprises combined horizontally or vertically for defensive or strategic reasons, they did so in response to specific historical situations that varied from time period to time period, from country to country, from industry to industry, even from firm to firm. For example, in the U.S. automobile industry during the interwar years, for specific historical reasons Ford remained fully vertically integrated, General Motors had a policy of controlling one-quarter of its suppliers, and Chrysler obtained nearly all of its supplies from independent producers (see Chapter 6).

Far more central to the continuing evolution of the modern industrial enterprise were the strategies that led to adding production units in distant places, usually abroad, and that led to manufacturing related products. Geographical expansion into distant markets provided a way for the enterprise to continue to exploit its competitive advantages, those based primarily on organizational capabilities that had been developed by exploiting economies of scale. Product diversification came from opportunities to use existing production, marketing, and research facilities and personnel by developing products for new and more profitable markets. Such expansion was based on organizational capabilities that had been developed by exploiting economies of scope. The efforts to utilize these organizationally based competitive advantages became the driving force—the underlying dynamic—in the growth of the modern industrial enterprise and industrial capitalism. The development and implementation of these two strategies of growth, carried out to employ more profitably the organizational capabilities that had been honed through functional competition, permitted the modern industrial enterprise to counter the bureaucratic inertia inherent in any hierarchical institution.

Obtaining distant production facilities obviously came after, not before, a first mover had made its initial investments in production, distribution, and management. The first expansion of production usually occurred at home with the enlargement of the original plant, particularly when such expansion brought greater economies of scale or scope. As the marketing organization was geographically extended and as the original plant reached minimum efficient scale, new plants were built to an optimal size based on the extent of the more distant domestic markets, on transportation costs, and on availability of materials and labor.

Much the same incentives led to direct investment abroad. In addition, tariff laws and other discriminatory legislation, by raising the cost of finished goods shipped across national borders, provided major reasons for constructing distant production facilities. At times factories were built to forestall competition in a new market, or to exploit potential market growth, or to produce a variation of the product line to meet local needs. In nearly every case, however, such investment was made on the assumption that the enterprise had a competitive advantage over local producers.[16]

The large integrated enterprise also expanded abroad, just as it did at home, for defensive reasons: to obtain assured sources of essential supplies, usually mineral or agricultural products, for its domestic and later its foreign processing plants. Again, it usually did so only when such supplies were not available at home and where local entrepreneurs had not developed the needed resource, as was often the case with direct investment in oil fields, mines, or rubber plantations.

The primary reason, however, for a firm's direct investment abroad was to expand its market share in distant countries and to lower the costs of making and selling its products in those markets. As I have already suggested, the decisions to establish plants abroad and to determine their size and location depended on a calculus that balanced, on the one hand, the costs of producing both primary and intermediate products in plants of optimal size with, on the other hand, the costs of transportation, distribution, tariffs, and other regulatory measures. For this reason most firms became multinational by building facilities to produce their basic lines in advanced rather than developing economies, for markets for new and improved industrial and consumer products were larger in those economies with high per-capita income. For this reason, too, such investment in distant production facilities followed, rather than preceded, that in marketing.[17]

Those first movers with the strongest competitive advantages went abroad most quickly. The first movers among American producers of mass-produced light machinery—sewing, office, and agricultural machines, automobiles (later), and a variety of comparable products, such as elevators and printing presses—were marketing and then producing abroad well before World War I. By that time the German producers of dyes and pharmaceuticals dominated world markets. By then, too, the first movers in Germany and the United States in the electrical equipment industry had taken over world markets. With the competitive advantages derived from economies of scale or scope these first movers long remained dominant firms in foreign countries, as well as in their own. By contrast, if an industry's technology of production provided little in the way of such competitive advantages, as was the case in the processing of natural fibers, the firms that went overseas rarely retained their initial market position.

Expansion by diversification into related industries—the other continuing strategy of growth—utilized the economies of scope at all three levels of the organization—the operating units, the functional departments, and the top or corporate office. And the stimuli for such diversification were both external and internal.

Changes in the environment often reduced demand for existing products and created markets for closely related ones. Basic technological innovations (electricity, electronics, and the internal combustion engine, for example), demographic shifts, and wars and depressions all affected product markets. In addition, as demand for existing products leveled off and as capacity became calibrated with or overreached existing demand, the search for new products intensified.

Internal stimulus came from the needs and opportunities to use existing facilities and capabilities more fully.[18] Indeed, the initial investment in facilities large enough to exploit the cost advantage of scale sometimes in itself encouraged new product development. Thus in the production of aluminum and synthetic ammonia the scale economies were so high that the aluminum and chemical companies had to search for new products that could take some of the output of the most efficient plants.

An impetus to diversification at the operating level was the emergence of by-products, such as fertilizer, soap, and glue in meatpacking and petrochemicals in oil refining. But unless the volume of output was high enough to warrant the creation of a new and separate marketing organization, these by-products remained by-products, and were marketed through wholesalers or other intermediaries who sold related products and so could continue to benefit from their economies of scope. Where the volume was large enough, as it was in the case of fertilizer and leather for the largest meatpackers, nationwide sales organizations were established, managers hired, and integrated subenterprises or divisions were thus formed to market such products and to coordinate the flow of goods through the enterprise.

The most common stimulus to diversification, however, was the potential for economies of scope existing in an enterprise's major functional units—production, distribution, and research. At most enterprises the first step toward such product diversification was the development of a full line that exploited the firm's facilities and capabilities in all three major activities. Thus a reaper company and a plow company began to compete directly as each moved into the other's markets by developing a full line of agricultural implements. So, too, automobile manufacturers embarked on producing and distributing a full line of cars, trucks, buses, and other commercial vehicles. Although the expansion of the line often required the building of new plants or even new sales departments, such growth relied primarily on expanding existing facilities or adding comparable ones using existing capabilities.

When diversification moved beyond producing a full line, the story was different. Where it came by exploiting the economies of scope in production to make goods sold in new and different markets, new marketing personnel and facilities had to be acquired. When American agricultural-equipment companies entered the construction-equipment business, when German dye makers moved into pharmaceuticals, or when Du Pont's rayon division developed cellophane, they all made more effective use of existing production facilities and personnel and of existing intermediate processes and materials. All also had to recruit and train new sales forces. Often, too, the resulting integration of production and distribution led to the formation of research and development units for each of the new product lines.

Where diversification resulted from the economies of scope in marketing and distribution, the establishment of new processing and purchasing units was often called for. Such economies existed because distribution and marketing networks, even though product-specific, could be used to handle more than a single product line. Thus the meatpackers began to send dairy products and fruit through their refrigerated networks. Distribution facilities created to assure daily delivery of fresh yeast to bakers and brewers were easily adapted to daily delivery of ground coffee to grocers. Nonrefrigerated facilities for moving one type of processed grain product could be used for others; and capabilities in marketing one set of branded packaged products were easily transferable to another.

In research and development, which was concentrated in the technologically advanced industries, facilities and organizational capabilities were even less product-specific and the opportunities to exploit economies of scope were even greater than in production and distribution. The knowledge required for research and development came from physics, chemistry, and other sciences, disciplines that far transcended the needs of one product line. The scientific disciplines acquired to improve processes and products in explosives were transferable to the development of new chemically produced fibers, fabrics, films, and plastics, as well as better paints, varnishes, and other finishes, since those products were all based on the same cellulose technology. The scientific training needed to improve machinery for the generation and transmission of electricity was applicable to developing electrical appliances, vacuum tubes, X-ray and electronic equipment, and other technologically complex devices.

Even more important, the chemical producers and electrical manufacturers had mastered the specialized technical and organizational skills needed to move a new or improved product into full commercial use: that is, they became even more skilled in development than in research. They understood the complexities that are inherent in market research, in building pilot plants and then in scaling up production facilities to minimum efficient size, and in recruiting and training a nationwide sales network—activities that absorb by far the greatest part of the cost of completing successfully the long haul from product innovation to volume production for world markets.

Finally, successful diversification required a team of experienced managers at corporate headquarters capable of monitoring and allocating resources for not one but several product lines. They not only had to evaluate current performance and functional competitive effectiveness in each of several product lines, but they also had to decide whether to expand or contract long-term investment in the lines. Of even more importance for the long-term performance of the enterprise, they had to determine whether or not to initiate research and development on a new product. Above all, they had to decide whether or not to make the extensive investment necessary to build production facilities of optimal size, and to recruit the management and the sales force needed to produce and sell a product that might not show a profit for many years after its development was authorized or even several years after the investment in production and other operating facilities had been made. Such evaluations and decisions called for managers experienced in the technological and marketing processes on which the competitive advantage of the new product rested. It was in carrying out a continuous strategy of growth through product diversification that the economies of scope at the enterprise level, as differentiated from the functional level, had their greatest significance.

Growth by adding units abroad or in related industries led to a modification of the enterprise's administrative structure.[19] Initially expansion abroad called for only a moderate adjustment—the formation of an international committee and then an international department to supervise distant marketing and distribution. In the few cases where overseas investment was primarily in basic materials, the supervisory body often became known as the raw materials department. Only after extensive expansion overseas did an enterprise adopt a multidivisional structure by which major geographical regions were administered through integrated area divisions.

Diversification into related industries brought far more thoroughgoing administrative restructuring. Diversifying companies adopted, some more quickly than others, a multidivisional structure (see Figure 2). This structural change came when the senior managers realized that they had neither the time nor the necessary information to coordinate and monitor day-to-day operations and at the same time devise and implement long-term plans for the several product lines. The administrative overload had simply become too great. The solution was to establish a structure consisting of divisional offices to administer each of the major product lines and a general or corporate office to administer the enterprise as a whole.

Each divisional office included a general manager, his staff, and the heads of the functional activities involved. The general manager was fully responsible for his division's performance and profits. In other words, each division became a replica of the enterprise's original centralized, functionally departmentalized organization, except that the highest ranking officer in the division had become a middle manager reporting to the top executives in the corporate office. Each division competed functionally and strategically with other firms or with the divisions of other firms within the same industry.

At the corporate office the top managers became general executives without day-to-day operating responsibilities. They concentrated on continually evaluating performance of the operating divisions and on planning and implementing long-term corporate strategy through the allocation of funds, facilities, and personnel. They were assisted by a corporate staff who provided a constant flow of information and offered specialized skills, not only to the general executives at the corporate headquarters but also to the middle managers who headed the operating divisions. The corporate staff included the enterprise's enlarged financial department with its specialists in accounting, auditing, and other numbers-oriented activities. It also included a corporate personnel office that collected information on the training and experience of both employees and managers. Its central research laboratory helped to provide technological advice and develop new products and processes not clearly related to the work of the divisional laboratories. Its development department planned corporate strategy. Often there were corporate offices for marketing and production. These corporate staff departments remained only advisory, not decision-making offices, but they enhanced the capabilities of the organization as a whole by providing a systematic and continuous internal exchange of information on new developments in facilities, processes, and products.

The multidivisional structure was the administrative response to growth based on further utilization of firms' organizational capabilities. A division was

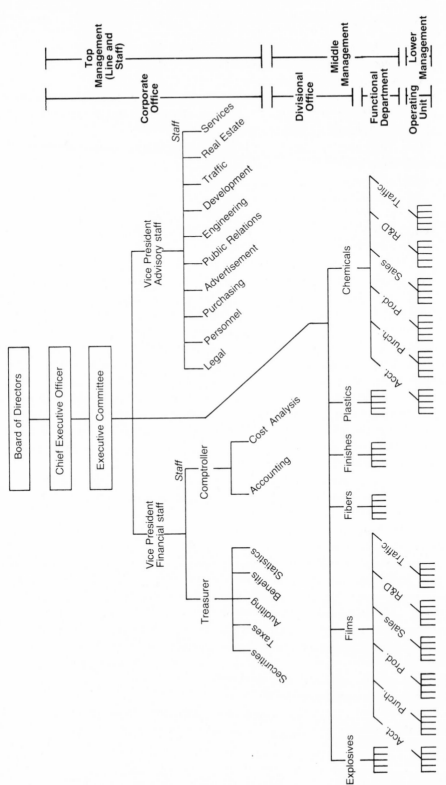

Figure 2. The multidivisional structure.

responsible for a single product line, or in some cases for a geographical area. In other words, the multidivisional structure provided the means to administer several different, though related, product lines; and it also provided the means to administer a single line which was sold worldwide by creating comparable integrated divisions for major geographical regions.[20] Thus the corporate office was able to monitor and advise and so to increase the competitive capabilities of the several divisions. In this manner diversified, multidivisional enterprises were able to intensify competition within the industry or region into which they moved and at the same time to transfer resources from older, more stable industries or markets to newer, more dynamic ones.[21]

The Modern Enterprise in Labor-Intensive Industries

It should be stressed that these broad descriptive patterns and the resulting explanations of the dynamics of the modern industrial enterprise relate to those industries where the technologies of production had the potential for extensive economies of scale and scope and where product-specific marketing organizations provided further competitive advantages. Where this was *not* the case— that is, in industries where, owing to their technology, the optimal size of plant was small, where mass distribution did not require specialized skills and facilities, and where coordination of flows was a relatively simple task—manufacturers had much less incentive to make the three-pronged investment in production, distribution, and management. In the more labor-intensive industries, such as publishing and printing, lumber, furniture, textiles, apparel, leather, seasonal and specialized food processing, and specialized instruments and machinery, the large integrated firm had few competitive advantages. In some, such as textiles and lumber, careful coordination of flows within manufacturing units did increase throughput and lower unit costs. Also costs were often lowered by producing a variety of differently designed items from the same machines and materials. But the resulting cost advantages were far fewer than those in the capital-intensive industries. They rarely created major barriers to entry. Indeed size, by making the large firm less flexible in meeting changes in demand and style, might be a competitive disadvantage. This was often the case in apparel (both cloth and leather) and in a number of industries processing food and drink. In the labor-intensive industries many small single-unit firms continued to prosper, and in them competition continued to be based on price and the ability to move quickly with changing demand.

Significantly, it was in several of these more fragmented industries—textiles, apparel, furniture, and some food processing—that the mass retailers (the department stores, mail-order houses, and chain stores) began to coordinate the flow of goods from manufacturer to consumer. In those industries where substantial economies of scale and scope did not exist in production, high-volume flows through the processes of production and distribution came to be guided—and the resulting cost reductions achieved—by the buying departments of mass retailers, retailers who handled a variety of related products through their facilities. Their efficiency, in turn, further reduced the economic need for the wholesaler as a middleman between the manufacturer and the retailer.

Where the economies of scale and scope and the creation of product-specific marketing organizations did bring competitive advantage, the history of the modern industrial enterprise followed in a general way the patterns outlined in this chapter. Here I have attempted to provide the framework—that is, the common terminology, the set of concepts, and the explanatory theory—that is needed to comprehend fully the complex, interrelated historical developments described in the following chapters.

· II ·

The United States:
Competitive Managerial Capitalism

In this comparative historical study of the beginnings and dynamic evolution of the modern industrial enterprise the American story must be told first. From the 1890s on, the United States was the world's leading industrial nation (Table 1). By 1913 it was producing 36% of the world's industrial output as compared with Germany's 16% and Britain's 14%. As a consequence there have always been a greater number of large modern industrial enterprises in the United States than in any other nation—even more than the percentage of output might indicate. Indeed, in 1973 (when the U.S. share of total world output had dropped to about a third) more than half of the 401 enterprises with more than 20,000 employees were based in the United States (Table 5). And many of those firms were larger than any abroad. A rough estimate indicates that before World War II only about a quarter of the 200 largest industrial enterprises in Britain and even less than a quarter in Germany (as listed in Appendixes A.1–A.3, B.1–B.3, and C.1–C.3) had assets greater than those of the 200th largest American firm. In addition, because many of these American firms quickly expanded abroad, they played from the start a major role in global competition, even though their managers concentrated on the home market. By the 1920s there were more American-owned subsidiaries on the list of the top 200 British firms than there were British industrials on the American list. And more of the top 200 in the United States had subsidiaries operating in Germany than the leading German firms had in the United States.

By 1917—the year for which the first list of the top 200 industrials in the United States was compiled—the great majority of these enterprises had integrated volume production with volume distribution. Nearly all of these companies had national sales organizations, and a large number had marketing subsidiaries abroad. At least a third had invested in production in foreign countries; yet only a small number had invested in research and development. Diversification was still to become a way of growth. Also by 1917 the great majority of these integrated enterprises had adopted a centrally functionalized, departmentalized structure. None of them, not even the most diversified or most geographically extended, had worked out more than an embryonic version of the multidivisional organization structure. They remained centralized, functionally departmentalized, multiunit enterprises.

In the United States, family control of these large industrial enterprises was still common during World War I. By then, however, families rarely attempted to manage all the day-to-day operations of the business themselves. The individual operating units had become too numerous and their administration and coordination too complex for such personal administration. Owners continued to participate as full-time executives in decisions establishing top-level policy and resource allocation. But in making even these decisions the family members worked closely with full-time salaried top- and middle-level managers who had little or no equity in the enterprise. Enterprises that had become large through merger and acquisition had on their boards members of banks or other financial institutions who had participated in financing this type of growth. Although such bank representatives, as part-time directors, rarely if ever participated in the day-to-day decisions regarding coordination and monitoring of flows through the stages of production and distribution, they still had a say in the formulation of general policies and the allocation of resources.

In 1917 the major stockholders in most large U.S. industrial enterprises were still represented on the board of directors, but these boards had become primarily ratifying bodies. The outside directors had the power to veto proposals made by the managers. The inside directors, however, set the agendas. They remained the primary—indeed nearly always the only—source of the information with which decisions were made and action taken. They also implemented the decisions made by the boards.

After World War I the modern industrial enterprise in the United States continued to compete and grow in the manner outlined in Chapter 2. Nearly all of these firms were substantially larger in terms of assets in 1930 than they had been in 1917, and they grew at an even greater rate between 1930 and 1948 (Appendixes A.1–A.3). During the 1920s and 1930s they grew more by moving into new geographical markets and diversifying into related products than by horizontal combination and vertical integration (as had been the case before the war). After 1920 investment in research and development increased. More companies expanded overseas. Diversification became an accepted strategy of growth.

Such growth enlarged the size of managerial hierarchies and greatly increased the complexity of decision-making at the top. As a result, by World War II a number of these enterprises had adopted and others were moving toward a multidivisional administrative structure. Such complexities further reduced the influence of part-time outside directors. Moreover, as most of the growth was financed by retained earnings, investment bankers or venture capitalists were not called on to raise funds to the same extent as before the 1920s. Such funds as were raised in the capital markets came from the sale of equity, thus increasing the company's shareholders and decreasing the influence of the founders or large investors whose families held inherited positions on boards.

Thus by World War II managerial capitalism had become firmly established in the United States in the industries where the modern industrial enterprise has clustered ever since. This was less evident elsewhere. In Germany families, large investors, and banks continued to play a more influential role, at least until the coming of the Nazi regime. In Britain, even in the 1940s, personal and family control and management were still more the rule than the exception.

THREE

The Foundations of Managerial Capitalism in American Industry

Why did the modern, integrated, multiunit enterprise appear in greater numbers and attain a greater size in a shorter period of time in the United States than it did in Europe? Why, by World War I, were managerial hierarchies becoming more extensive and the resulting separation of ownership and management becoming more clear-cut in the United States than in other economies? What crucial differences in the nature of markets and in the speed of adopting new technologies led American industrialists to make a greater investment in new units of distribution, purchasing, production, and research and development than did industrialists in other economies? How did the availability of capital and the laws regulating business activities, particularly antitrust legislation, affect this growth? In sum, what were the conditions that caused the United States to breed these large integrated enterprises in such abundance and so to become the seedbed of modern managerial capitalism?

The Domestic Market

What most strikingly differentiated the United States from Great Britain and Germany in the late nineteenth century were the geographical size and very rapid growth of its domestic market. Britain's area, including Northern Ireland, is 94,241 square miles, smaller than the combined area of three American states—New York, Pennsylvania, and Ohio. The domestic market of Britain was concentrated in an even smaller area—the London, Cardiff, Glasgow, Edinburgh quadrangle. The area of pre-World War I Germany was 208,780 square miles—smaller even than the state of Texas (though larger than California). Not only was the American population spread out over a much larger land mass, but it was more rural than that of either Britain or Germany. For example, by 1851 half the population of Britain lived in towns of 5,000 or more. That ratio was not reached in the United States until 1960, more than a century later. The vast physical space and scattered population help explain why American industrial enterprises set up more units of production and distribution in their domestic markets than did their overseas counterparts.

In addition to its size, from the 1870s until the Great Depression of the 1930s the American domestic market grew faster than that of any other nation. Until the depression the United States outdistanced other leading industrial economies in the growth of both population and per-capita income—the two basic ingredients that determined overall consumer demand. In the 1880s this population was one-and-a-half times that of Great Britain.[1] By 1900 it stood at twice Great Britain's, and by 1920 at three times. From 1870 to World War I, Gross Domestic Product (GDP) increased more than five times in the United States, while in Great Britain it slightly more than doubled and in Germany it increased 3.4 times (Table 9). During the same period the estimated growth in GDP per capita was 2.4 times for the United States, 1.5 for Great Britain, and 2.0 for Germany. As Simon Kuznets has stressed, the American accomplishment was to maintain a high rate of per-capita output and income while enjoying the largest rate of population growth of any major economy.[2] This rapid, continuing rate of growth of consumer demand, like the geographical extent of the market, provided American entrepreneurs with more opportunities—in more industries— to exploit the economies of scale and scope than existed anywhere else in the world. Because they had the world's largest and fastest-growing domestic

Table 9. Population and GDP per capita at 1970 U.S. prices, United States, Great Britain, and Germany, 1870–1979.

Country	1870	1913	1950	1979
United States				
Population (thousands)	39,305	97,227	152,271	220,584
GDP (millions)	$30,497	$176,278	$487,938	$1,335,678
GDP per capita	$764	$1,813	$3,204	$6,055
Great Britain				
Population (thousands)	31,257	45,649	50,363	55,952
GDP (millions)	$30,365	$68,082	$105,471	$222,749
GDP per capita	$972	$1,491	$2,094	$3,981
Germany[a]				
Population (thousands)	39,231	66,978	49,983	61,359
GDP (millions)	$20,998	$71,838	$68,688	$303,508
GDP per capita	$535	$1,073	$1,374	$4,946

Source: Compiled from Angus Maddison, *Phases of Capitalist Development* (New York, 1982), tables 1.4, A3, B2, B3, and B4.

a. Figures for 1950 and 1979 represent West Germany.

market, American manufacturers were much less dependent on foreign trade than were those of Britain and Germany. Hence they were less handicapped than their counterparts by the difficulties of trading in markets with different laws, customs, tastes, and, just as important, different transportation systems and distribution channels.

The Impact of the Railroads and Telegraph

The steady high volume, or throughput, needed to achieve and maintain potential economies of scale and scope could rarely be attained as long as the flow of goods depended on the energy provided by horse, man, wind, and current, and while its regularity was hampered by the vagaries of ice, drought, wind, and tides. Therefore, in the half century before the coming of the railroad and the telegraph, although the total volume of goods produced, transactions handled, and number of enterprises increased enormously, the size and scale of industrial operations remained small. They did become increasingly specialized, nearly always handling a single function, product, or service in a single geographical area. Nearly all remained partnerships, and the partners managed as well as owned the business. As a result, the number of salaried managers in 1850, except for plantation overseers, was still tiny. Owners managed and managers owned.

The railroad provided the technology, not only to move an unprecedented volume of goods at unprecedented speed, but to do so on a precise schedule, that is, a schedule stated not in terms of weeks or months but of days and even hours. And the telegraph made possible, for the first time in history, almost instantaneous communication between distant points.

Yet this new continental transportation and communication system could not be created overnight. The construction of the new nationwide networks, the development of the organizational capabilities of the enterprises that provided such transportation and communication, and the working out of the essential intercompany arrangements required more than half a century.

In the United States the geographical extent of the country (even before the West was won) as well as the distances between urban centers meant that far greater mileage had to be constructed than in other industrial countries. Thus by 1860, when Britain had completed just over 9,000 miles of road, the United States had built more than 30,000; by 1880 the figures were 15,563 for Britain and 93,292 for the United States.[3] By 1910, when the national system was virtually completed, the U.S. first-track mileage was more than ten times that of Britain, some 240,000 miles as compared with 20,000. In Germany the mileage constructed was greater than in Britain but still much less than in the United States, rising from 21,000 to 38,000 between 1880 and 1910. But because the Germans played a major role in financing, building, and supplying the railroads of eastern and southern Europe, the advent of the railroad had a greater impact on Germany than those figures suggest.

In all three countries the mileage of telegraph wires laid grew even more rapidly than railroad mileage. Expansion of the telegraph went hand in hand with the growth of the railroad; for the railroad provided the right-of-way for the telegraph, and the telegraph became a critical instrument in assuring safe, rapid, and efficient movement of trains. This was particularly true in the United States and Germany, where more single-track roads were built than in Great Britain.

The efficient operation of this transportation and communication infrastructure required a series of organizational as well as technological innovations.[4] Most critical was the creation of managerial hierarchies for the individual roads, to schedule—and to coordinate administratively with utmost precision—the flow of trains and traffic across the railroad's different operating units or "divisions," as they came to be called. Such coordination was essential for safety alone, because nearly all early American railroads were single-track lines. The coordination was also essential to assure the fast, regular, and carefully scheduled movement of a wide variety of goods shipped from hundreds of locations to as many destinations.

Thus during the 1850s American railroads became the pioneers in modern management. Because of the complexities of their operations they formed almost overnight the nation's first managerial enterprises. In the larger railroads—those over one hundred miles in length—managers with almost no equity in the enterprise made the operating decisions. And as the roads grew, these managers came to play a critical role in determining the strategy of their growth and competition.

These managers subdivided their operations into smaller operating groups and then appointed middle managers to supervise, monitor, and coordinate the different functional activities on each division: the movement of trains; the handling of traffic (that is, all activities concerned with the movement of freight and passengers); the maintenance of motive power, equipment, and roadbed; and the handling of and accounting for the thousands of daily financial transactions. To operate such an organization, railroad managers devised a line-and-staff system of administration. The managers responsible for the movement of trains were the line officers, acting on the line of authority running from the president to the general manager, to the general superintendent, to the division superintendent. The managers responsible for the other functions—the movement of freight and passengers, maintenance, and finances—were designated staff executives. Line officers ordered the movement of men and trains; the staff executives set the standards and policies for their functional departments. Railroad executives like Daniel C. McCallum (in the 1850s) and Albert Fink (in the 1860s) devised the accounting and informational systems needed to control the movement of trains and traffic, to account for the funds handled, and to determine profit and loss for the several operating units and for the enterprise as a whole. These systems provided basic techniques used by the founders of early multiunit industrial enterprises to create their internal control and accounting systems.

Because the cost of constructing and equipping railroads was so much higher than that of all previous business ventures, railroad transportation became the first modern high-fixed-cost business, and so the first in which continuous capacity utilization became a major concern. In the 1880s the costs that did not vary with traffic were estimated to be two-thirds of total cost. In order to achieve the traffic necessary to maintain profitability and even financial solvency, a road's traffic department had to set rates and to schedule flows in ways that would come close to assuring the continuous use of equipment. Because the primary flow of bulk (commodity) traffic in the United States was from the agricultural West to the industrial East, the pricing and scheduling of return traffic became particularly complex and challenging tasks.

In maintaining this traffic flow, the railroads benefited from the economies of scope. From the start they moved a wide variety of goods: as early as the 1850s the Pennsylvania Railroad listed more than two hundred types of products carried.[5] Indeed, as the investment in freight-moving equipment became more product-specific, the problems of scheduling and of maintaining capacity became more difficult. This is why the railroads preferred to have the Standard Oil Company and its associates build and schedule newly invented tank cars; why the railroads, once they had accepted the practicability of refrigerated cars, left their construction and ownership to the meatpackers; why the roads encouraged brewers, chemical manufacturers, and other producers to make their own investment in the product-specific transportation and storage facilities they needed; and why they preferred to turn over the building, owning, scheduling, and maintenance of specialized sleeping cars to companies such as that of George Pullman. The manufacturers, on the other hand, by building and maintaining rolling stock rather than relying on the railroad to provide it, could be sure that the equipment would be available when and where they needed it.

One reason the railroads were able to encourage such investments and industrialists were willing to make them was that during the 1870s the railroads perfected the intricate details of moving freight cars belonging to one enterprise across the lines of several different railroad companies. To move freight cars without interruption over several roads between hundreds of points of shipment and destination, railroad managers had to standardize track gauges and equipment, such as couplers, air brakes, and signals. They also had to perfect organizational procedures, such as the through bill of lading, intercompany billing, and the operation of the car accountant's office (which kept track of "foreign" cars on its road and its own cars on other roads). This type of technological and organizational standardization, planned and carried out by quasi-professional associations of railroad managers, such as the Society of Railroad Accounting Officers and the American Society of Railroad Superintendents, meant that loaded cars could be moved from one part of the country to another without a single transshipment. By the 1880s freight moved from Philadelphia to Chicago in two days or less, whereas in the 1840s before the spread of the railroad the trip via wagons and barges had taken at least three weeks and usually more, and the freight had had to be unloaded and reloaded as many as nine times. Once the cooperative techniques were perfected, the traffic departments of railroad companies quickly took over—that is, internalized—most of the activities previously undertaken by express companies, freight forwarders, and other specialized transportation intermediaries which had come into being precisely in order to provide delivery of goods to distant destinations on schedule. Carefully defined contractual relationships between connecting railroad companies made possible the standardization required to coordinate flows. And coordinated flows brought lower costs for railroads and shippers alike, thus providing the essential underpinnings of modern, high-volume, industrial production with its economies of scale and scope.

What such contractual arrangements did *not* achieve was the maintenance of uniform rates charged by lines competing for the same traffic. From the 1850s on, both competing and connecting roads made agreements to establish through rates, while at the same time individual railroad managers under pressure from high fixed costs secretly undercut and then openly broke these rate agreements. The pressure to cut rates in order to assure traffic flows sufficient to cover costs in this high-fixed-cost industry was too strong to resist. As long as capacity was underutilized, the temptation existed to offer lower rates than those posted (usually by means of rebates) that would still cover the variable costs of the equipment and labor needed to carry that freight. The only dependable way for competitors to regain the traffic lost by such opportunism (self-interest with guile) was to offer comparable rate cuts.

To prevent what railroad managers had come to consider ruinous competition and to assure the continuing flow of traffic needed for economic survival, the railroads formed regional federations such as the Southern Railway & Steamship Association, formed in 1875, and the Eastern Trunk Line Association, established two years later. These cartels began by allocating traffic but soon found it easier to pool profits and then divide them according to an accepted ratio.

Even though these railroad pools set up managerial teams of their own to allocate and monitor mutually satisfactory rates, they rarely succeeded in stabilizing them for any extended period of time. There was constant pressure to meet high fixed costs through rate cutting; moreover, such rate agreements, traffic allocations, and profit pools were not enforceable in courts of law. Indeed, with the passage of the Interstate Commerce Act in 1887 such agreements became explicitly illegal. In Britain and Germany such arrangements were wholly acceptable. Only in the United States did the protests of shippers, expressed in terms of antimonopoly values, result in legislation to guarantee continuous competition between companies serving the same regions.

By the early 1880s railroad managers had decided, and the investors' representatives on their boards had agreed, that the only way to ensure a continuing flow of traffic over their roads, that is, to prevent it from being captured by rival concerns, was to construct new tracks or buy existing roads in order to form giant "self-sustaining" systems. These strategic investments provided companies with their own tracks into the major commercial cities and raw-material-producing areas in the regions where they operated. In little more than a decade nearly all the systems had been completed. Thirty railroad companies, each administering lines between 1,500 and 10,000 miles long, owned and operated two-thirds of the total railroad mileage in the United States.[6] Most areas of the country were served by two or more competing systems. The corporations operating them remained for many years the world's largest business enterprises, administered by the world's largest managerial hierarchies. In order to obtain the funds needed to acquire these massive facilities, the senior managers of the systems had developed close ties with eastern investment bankers, particularly those who had access to European sources of capital. These bankers increasingly replaced local and individual investors on the boards of directors.

The purpose of such system-building was not, it should be stressed, to provide more efficient and lower-cost transportation services and facilities. Many such efficiencies had already been achieved by contractual arrangements for the handling of through traffic, just as the standardization of equipment had been worked out through the quasi-professional associations of railroad managers. The purpose was wholly defensive. These heavy investments were made as a form of insurance to guarantee the enterprises the continuing flow of traffic they needed to operate at minimum efficient scale. In this sense, the investments were made to reduce transaction costs. If interfirm agreements on rates, allocation of traffic, and pooling of profits had been legally enforceable in the courts, as they were in other countries, a powerful incentive for system-building by acquisition, merger, and new construction would have disappeared.

Besides being the first businesses to be administered through extensive hierarchies and the first to compete in a modern oligopolistic manner, the railroads were the first enterprises to be funded by modern financial institutions.[7] The unprecedented capital requirements for constructing the American railroad network led to the centralizing and institutionalizing of the nation's money market in New York City. In volume of transactions and complexity of operations the New York money market quickly became second to that of London.

From the 1850s to the late 1890s the institutions and instruments of finance on Wall Street were used almost exclusively to finance the railroads. In fact, nearly all the instruments and techniques of modern finance in the United States were perfected in order to fund the construction of railroads and to facilitate their growth through merger and acquisition. Before 1900 the great investment banks that were to play an important role in the financing of industrial mergers at the turn of the century and in the subsequent rationalization of facilities and personnel—such houses as J. P. Morgan; Kuhn, Loeb; Lee, Higginson; Kidder, Peabody; and Winslow, Lanier—concentrated on railroad finance. They acted as conduits for the flow of European capital that helped finance the American railroad (as well as telegraph and telephone) systems. Before the merger movement at the turn of the century nearly all securities traded on the New York Stock Exchange were those of railroads and closely allied enterprises, such as Western Union, the Pullman Palace Car Company, and a few coal enterprises.

Moreover, the railroads, as the first managerial enterprises with extensive managerial hierarchies, had no choice but to pioneer in the area of management-labor relations. By the 1890s collective bargaining procedures had been worked out and defined in a national railroad arbitration law. And finally, because the railroads and their networks were the first high-fixed-cost business to compete oligopolistically, railroad companies were the first, after the passage of the Interstate Commerce Act of 1887, to become federally regulated in the modern American manner.

The Revolution in Distribution

Between the 1850s and the 1880s the transportation and communication networks established the technological and organizational base for the exploitation of economies of scale and scope in the processes of production and distribution. The entrepreneurial response to the resulting opportunities came more quickly in distribution than in production, because innovations in distribution were primarily organizational rather than technological.[8] They were an almost immediate response to the recent innovations in transportation and communication.

Before the 1850s, American merchants rarely took title to goods; instead, they sold on commission. They preferred to have the manufacturers run the high risks and pay the high inventory costs of distributing the products—some of them already on a continental scale—through the slow and uncertain transportation network. Manufacturers had few alternatives if they were to sell beyond their immediate area. Among the wholesalers, only those in the large eastern cities, who bought their goods (imported from Europe) at auction, took title to them. But once the railroad, telegraph, and coastal steamship appeared, reducing risks and inventory costs and increasing the potential volume of sales, merchants moved quickly to profit from the new opportunities. They did so by taking title to the goods and making their income from markup rather than commissions.

The potentials of both scale and scope economies encouraged such middlemen to purchase goods directly from growers, processors, and manufacturers. In the 1850s commodity dealers who bought from farmers and at grain exchanges and sold to processors quickly replaced factors and other commissioned merchants in the marketing of agricultural crops. In like manner, "full-line, full-service" wholesalers bought directly from manufacturers and sold the finished goods to retailers. The new commodity dealers and full-line wholesalers relied on the telegraph to transact their increasing volume of business and on the railroad to deliver their goods on precise schedules.

Full-line, full-service wholesalers specialized in one of the broad product categories that had already appeared in retailing: dry goods, wet goods (liquor), groceries, furniture, hardware, drugs, jewelry, and so on. They usually had a central headquarters with extensive storage facilities, as well as a sizable force of salesmen who called on the specialized retail stores in towns and cities and on the many small general stores that dotted the countryside. Because the United States had a larger and geographically more scattered rural population than Europe, the ubiquitous general store was a uniquely American retailing phenomenon. As the wholesalers' hinterland grew, they invested in regional sales offices and storage facilities.

After the Civil War such wholesalers began to be replaced by the new mass retailers: the department store, the mail-order house, and the chain store. Of the new mass retailers, the department store was the oldest. Beginning with the mass retailing of apparel and textiles and then of furniture and other household goods, they appeared initially in the most concentrated urban areas along the eastern seaboard in the 1850s and 1860s; a little later in Chicago, Washington, and San Francisco; and then in the 1880s in smaller regional centers. The names of the pioneers remained household words in their respective cities for the next hundred years or more: Macy's, Lord & Taylor, Arnold Constable, and B. Altman's in New York; Jordan Marsh and R. H. White in Boston; Strawbridge & Clothier and John Wanamaker of Philadelphia; Hutzler in Baltimore; Marshall Field and Carson, Pirie, Scott in Chicago; Woodward & Lothrop in Washington; and the Emporium in San Francisco.

The two giant mail-order houses of Montgomery Ward, founded in 1872, and Sears, Roebuck, which grew large in the 1890s, came to dominate the huge rural market. They extended the scope of their lines far beyond that of the department store to include nearly everything a farm family needed, with the exception of heavy agricultural machinery. The pioneering chain stores, the Great Atlantic & Pacific Tea Company and Woolworth, began by selling groceries and novelties. Their major growth, however, came only in the early twentieth century, when they concentrated their outlets more in middle-sized towns and cities than in metropolitan centers or predominately rural areas.

The new wholesalers and mass retailers quickly recruited teams of managers. But because their investment in physical facilities was relatively small compared with that required in manufacturing, and tiny compared with that of the railroads, the founders and their families continued to retain the controlling share of stock in their enterprises. Where such owners became and remained full-time executives, they worked with their managers to make and implement top-level decisions. Where they became part-time outside directors, the salaried managers increasingly took over this critical function.

Wholesale and retail firms were organized along similar lines, although their sales staffs and facilities were quite different. At headquarters, each had a centralized buying office for each major line of goods. Every office, or "buyer," determined for its particular line the amount, quality, design, and price paid and sold; and each coordinated the flow from the purchasing office to the sales organization. Both types of firm also established purchasing offices and depots in commercial and manufacturing centers in the United States and often in Europe. Both made their profits by selling the standardized products of many manufacturers in high volumes at low prices.

As indicated in Chapter 2, these enterprises were organized to take advantage of the economies of scale and scope. Each of their several buying departments was responsible for maintaining the high-volume stock-turn (similar to the throughput in production) on which profits were based: their task was to exploit the economies of scale. In addition, these buying departments, all of which used the same set of functional personnel to do the actual purchasing and storage, to arrange for transportation, and to make the final sales, benefited from the economies of scope. By the 1870s the new mass marketers were operating on a modern scale. Marshall Field, still primarily a wholesaler, achieved a stock-turn of five times a year while Macy's, wholly a retailer, was maintaining by the 1880s a stock-turn of almost twice that much—impressive even by today's standards.[9]

From the 1880s on, the mass retailers took a larger and larger share of trade away from the big wholesalers and their small retailing clients. They did so because they achieved greater economies of both scale and scope than did the wholesalers. The department stores, which sold their goods over the counter to customers in rapidly growing urban markets—customers who could be readily reached through advertising in local newspapers—soon came to carry many more product lines than did the wholesalers. By the 1880s Macy's, for example, was handling not only a wide variety of dry goods, clothing, and shoes, but also jewelry, furniture, chinaware, silverware, books and toys.[10] The economies gained by the chain store were the same as those of the department store, but they were achieved through having not one, but many sales outlets. These outlets were usually smaller than department stores and carried fewer lines.

The two giant mail-order houses—Montgomery Ward and Sears, Roebuck— served the largest American market. Therefore, their investment in facilities, the volume of their operations, and the number of lines carried early in the twentieth century exceeded those of the largest department or chain store. The technologies (machinery and plant layout) used in achieving the economies of scale and scope are illustrated by the following description of Sears's Chicago mail-order plant published in the company's 1905 catalogue: "Miles of railroad tracks run lengthwise through, in and around this building for the receiving, moving and forwarding of merchandise; elevators, mechanical conveyors, end- less chains, moving sidewalks, gravity chutes, apparatus and conveyors, pneu- matic tubes and every known mechanical appliance for reducing labor, for the working out of economy and dispatch is to be utilized here in our great Works."[11]

The heart of the operation, however, was the scheduling system, which helped assure consistently high stock-turn. A complex, rigidly enforced time- table made it possible to fill a steady stream of orders from a large number of different departments. Each department was given fifteen minutes to send to the assembling rooms the items listed on a specific order. If any items failed to appear within that time period, the order was shipped without them. The delayed part of the order was sent by prepaid express as soon as it was ready, and the negligent department was charged both for the extra express cost and for a fine of fifty cents per item. The new system permitted the Chicago plant to fill 100,000 orders a day. Very few traditional merchants of prerailroad days handled that many transactions in a lifetime.

Because the greatest cost advantage of wholesaling and retailing on a mass scale came from exploiting the economies of both scale and scope in distribution, the new mass distributors were not pressed to integrate backwards into man- ufacturing. They did so only when they were unable to obtain a product at the price, quantity, or specification required, or when they needed a product in such large volume that they could produce it steadily at minimum efficient scale and therefore as cheaply as independent suppliers. In 1906 Sears (shortly after it perfected the operations of its Chicago plant) owned nine factories wholly or in part; by 1910 the number had reached sixteen.[12] Most of these factories made shoes, clothing, furniture, lumber, hardwood, tools, plumbing goods, stoves, and other products for which the economies of scale did not give a large plant an attractive cost advantage over a small one. Sears also had plants, such as those making sewing machines and light farm machinery, where scale advan- tages did exist. Once a reliable source was assured, however, Sears and other mass retailers often preferred to sell out their interest, even if their orders guaranteed operations at minimum efficient scale, because the management of production facilities was very different from that of mass retailing. Indeed, several mass producers of consumer durables obtained their first hold on the national market and a place in their national oligopoly by initially being suppliers for Sears or Montgomery Ward. Rarely did more than 10% or 15% of Sears's total sales come from goods made in its own factories.[13] For the new mass marketers, backward integration remained essentially a defensive strategy.

The Revolution in Production

The new forms of transportation and communication not only brought about an organizational revolution in distribution; they also created an even greater revolution in production, stimulating impressive technological as well as organizational changes. The laying down of railway and telegraph systems precipitated a wave of industrial innovation in western Europe and the United States far more wide-ranging than that which had occurred in Britain at the end of the eighteenth century. This wave has been quite properly termed by historians the Second Industrial Revolution.

The new technologies transformed the processing of tobacco, grains, whiskey, sugar, vegetable oil, and other foods. They revolutionized the refining of oil and the making of metals and materials—steel, nonferrous metals (particularly copper and aluminum), glass, abrasives, and other materials. They created brand new chemical industries that produced man-made dyes, fibers, and fertilizers. They brought into being a wide range of machinery: light machines for sewing, agricultural, and office uses; and heavier, standardized machinery, such as elevators, refrigerating units, and greatly improved printing presses, pumps, and boilers.

No innovations in the last decades of the nineteenth century had a more profound impact than those of Thomas A. Edison, Werner Siemens, and other inventors that led to the mass production and distribution of electric power. That new energy source not only transformed the mechanical processes of production within factories and created a new form of urban transportation, but it also revolutionized the making of many metals and chemicals. Indeed, nearly all the innovations in any one industry—not just electricity—had a significant impact on many other industries. Such wide-reaching, interrelated, and interdependent technological innovations brought modern industries into being and played a major role in the development of modern industrial economies. As Nathan Rosenberg has rightly emphasized: "The growing productivity of industrial economies is the complex outcome of large numbers of interlocking, mutually reinforcing technologies, the individual components of which are of a very limited economic consequence by themselves."[14]

Technological innovations, however, were not sufficient. In most cases, if their potential was to be realized and the new products and processes were to become available worldwide, entrepreneurs had to make the three-pronged investment described in Chapter 2. They had to decide to invest enough, first, to realize the cost advantages of scale and scope in production; second, to create a product-specific marketing network; and third, to recruit and train a team of salaried managers who would assure the continuing flow of goods through the processes of production and distribution. It was the investment in the new and improved processes of production—not the innovation—that initially lowered costs and increased productivity. It was the investment, not the innovation, that transformed the structure of industries and affected the performance of national economies. It was investment that created the new institution—the modern industrial enterprise—and it was investment that built the specific enterprises in the new or reshaped industries in which further, cumulative innovations in product and process would come. It was investment, not innovation, that determined entrepreneurial success or failure in the new industries of the Second Industrial Revolution.

In industries where the innovations were particularly revolutionary, the initial investment provided the first movers with such significant competitive advantages that as a general rule they remained dominant for decades. In industries where the innovations were more cumulative and interrelated, the investments that established the major players and the structure of an industry followed, in most cases, the consolidation of a number of enterprises. Such investments resembled those that were made after the formation of the Standard Oil Trust in 1881.

The major investments of the critical decades of the 1880s and 1890s transformed American industry and had a powerful impact on the legal, financial, and educational environment in which the modern industrial enterprise operated in the United States throughout the twentieth century.

BRANDED, PACKAGED PRODUCTS

Of all the industries in which the modern enterprise appeared in the 1880s and clustered from then on, those that produced new branded, packaged goods had the lowest potential for cost advantages of scale in production and the simplest requirements in terms of product-specific facilities and personnel in distribution. Yet in both areas the large enterprise had a competitive advantage over smaller firms. In the production of food and consumer chemicals (such as soap, drugs, and paints) the innovations included new packaging techniques as well as new processing techniques. The cost advantages of both were enough to transform industries and to create powerful new enterprises. Such a transformation occurred in the 1880s in two of the nation's oldest industries—tobacco and grain.

In 1884 James B. Duke took a lease on a cigarette-making machine invented by James Bonsack that produced 125,000 cigarettes a day, as compared with the 3,000 that the fastest worker could roll daily. The reduction in costs was dramatic.[15] (In Britain the Wills brothers, W. D. and H. D., who made a comparable investment, estimated that one machine reduced costs per thousand cigarettes from five shillings—sixty pence—to ten pence.) Duke himself invented a crush-proof package, as well as machinery for packaging the cigarettes. He immediately enlarged his factory in Durham, North Carolina, and built a new plant in New York City, established a national and then an international sales network, and set up corporate headquarters in New York.

Meanwhile the transformation of the grain-processing industries had begun in Minneapolis. Cadwallader Colden Washburn and his leading rival, the Pillsbury brothers, combined a series of innovations—some borrowed from Hungarian and other European millers, others invented at home—that brought into being the "automatic, all-roller, gradual-reduction mills" to mass-produce flour.[16] Henry P. Crowell did the same for oats in 1882. His company, which became the Quaker Oats Company, created a nationwide marketing network and a smaller purchasing organization and became a first mover in the new breakfast-cereal industry.

Like Duke, the grain processers began to package, and also to brand, their product as part of the production process. In so doing these manufacturers took over a basic function of the wholesaler, that of dividing bulk shipments into small units to be distributed to retailers. When packaging became part of the production process, the manufacturer rather than the wholesaler placed its brand name on the packaged product and began to advertise it. Unlike wholesalers who sold locally, manufacturers advertised nationally.

The packaging revolution got another boost in 1883 when the Norton brothers, Edwin and O. W., built the first automatic-line canning factory with machines capable of soldering cans at the rate of 50 a minute, along with other machines that added tops and bottoms at the rate of 2,500 to 4,400 units an hour. On the basis of this new technology Gail Borden quickly expanded his facilities for canning milk and his organization for marketing it. The Dorrances of Philadelphia did the same for their Campbell Soup products. So, too, did Henry John Heinz in Pittsburgh with his "57 varieties" of pickles, sauces, and other products. Libby, McNeill & Libby created a similar enterprise that produced canned meat in Chicago.

During that same decade large processing and packaging plants transformed the industries producing consumer chemicals. Procter & Gamble became a first mover in 1885 by building Ivory Dale, a model factory in Cincinnati, to produce Ivory and other branded soap products. Henry Colgate quickly followed with a comparable plant in New York City. In the same decade both Sherwin-Williams in paints and Parke, Davis in drugs expanded their production facilities and built international marketing networks.[17]

From the branch offices of the national and increasingly international sales networks, the salesmen (or "travelers") for these food and chemical companies called on retailers and often on wholesalers in order to sell their goods, renew orders, and arrange for scheduled deliveries. Soon they were advising retailers on how best to display the products. The manufacturing companies, however, continued to use wholesalers for the physical distribution of the goods (on a fixed markup or commission basis), because mass sales of these branded and packaged products demanded little in the way of specialized facilities or services. In the words of one economist, existing wholesalers became "essentially shipping agents for the manufacturers."[18] All the new enterprises reinforced their first-mover advantages by spending much of the income resulting from the cost advantages of scale on massive national advertising campaigns. In addition, these firms all developed extensive purchasing networks that often included product-specific facilities, such as those used by Duke for storing and curing tobacco and those used by Borden, Heinz, and Campbell Soup for storing seasonally grown products in quantities large enough to assure continuing throughput of canning plants year in and year out.

Producers of fresh meat and other perishable products made their initial investment in distribution.[19] In 1882 Gustavus F. Swift, a Chicago meatpacker from the East who had financed the development of the refrigerator car, began to build a nationwide distributing organization which owned, besides many such cars, a network of refrigerated warehouses that also served as branch offices for the company's wholesale marketing forces. During the next two years Swift and the largest meatpacker of the day, Armour & Company of Chicago, raced to obtain the best sites for their branch units in relation to railroad transportation and urban markets. Four other firms quickly followed. Of these, all but one were to dominate the industry for the next half century.

In the 1880s the Milwaukee and St. Louis brewers (Schlitz, Pabst, Blatz, and Anheuser Brewing) expanded into the national market by creating comparable, though smaller, networks. Their expansion was facilitated by the development at Anheuser Brewing of specialized refrigerator cars for transporting beer. A little later the Fleischmann Company developed a refrigerated network for the daily distribution of yeast to more than a thousand bakeries. And in the early 1890s Andrew Preston, whose firm became the core of the United Fruit Company, began to build a network of refrigerated cars, ships, and depots comparable to the networks of the packers and brewers.

To administer their extensive investments, all the producers of packaged products hired lower-level managers to operate the several units of production, marketing, and purchasing. They recruited middle and top managers to coordinate and monitor the activities of these operating units, as well as to allocate resources for the continuing growth of the enterprise.

MASS-PRODUCED LIGHT MACHINERY
At the same time similar developments occurred in the production of machinery and equipment made by fabricating and assembling standardized parts—a process, originally developed to produce small arms, that had become known by

the 1850s as the "American system of manufacturing." The three interrelated investments in manufacturing, marketing, and management made by these machinery producers, which were generally larger than those of the producers of branded, packaged products, brought such powerful advantages to the American first movers that they dominated world markets for decades.

In sewing machines and agricultural machinery a small number of pioneers had become predominant before the 1880s. Nevertheless, it was in the years immediately following the depression of the 1880s that the two largest—the Singer Sewing Machine Company and the McCormick Harvesting Machine Company—completed the construction of the factories that solidified their position of dominance. David Hounshell has shown that in the early 1880s these firms, both exemplifiers of the "American system," adopted the first modern mass-production methods of fabricating and assembling fully interchangeable parts.[20] Perfected techniques permitted McCormick to double throughput in its Chicago works from 30,000 machines in 1881 to 60,000 annually by the middle of the decade. In the late 1870s the Singer Sewing Machine Company built and enlarged its plant at Elizabethport, New Jersey; by 1883 full interchangeability of fabricated parts had been perfected, and by the middle of the 1880s the plant was producing more than half a million machines a year. In 1886 the company built a factory of comparable size and capacity in Scotland to produce for markets in Europe and the Eastern Hemisphere. By the late 1880s these two plants were making an estimated 75% of the world's sewing machines.

In the same years both Singer and McCormick made major investments in marketing and distribution. After Edward Clark, the business brains of the Singer enterprise, became its president in 1876, he decided to eliminate all independent sales agents at home and abroad and to replace them with salaried executives. At the same time, the existing branch offices with their teams of canvassers, repairmen, and accountants were enlarged and new ones established. During the same period Cyrus McCormick was also replacing independent intermediaries with salaried branch officers, but he chose a much less expensive retailing strategy. He recruited franchised dealers, who were supported and monitored by the company's national wholesaling network, to do the retailing. At both Singer and McCormick the branch offices assured a steadier flow of machines from the factory to the customer—and of payments from the retailer to the central office—than had independent distributors. In both companies the internal organization also provided customers with more reliable service and more uniform credit for the expensive products whose operation had to be demonstrated and whose maintenance and repair required trained mechanics.

The reliability of service and the availability of credit were particularly important in the sale of agricultural machinery. A reaper was a large capital investment for a farmer, but he only needed it during the two or three weeks of harvesttime.

If it broke down, the result could be disaster. McCormick's company, therefore, reduced production at the Chicago factory during harvesttime in order to send workers into the field to help the regular mechanics at the branch offices assure immediate maintenance and repair of the machines.[21] Existing intermediaries were rarely able to recruit experienced personnel for this seasonal work, nor did they have the experience or financial resources to provide the essential consumer credit. McCormick's leadership, based on product reliability and credit, prevailed even though its prices were higher than those of most competitors.

Innovations in office machinery came later than in sewing machines and harvesters, but they were quickly followed by the tripartite investments in production, distribution, and management.[22] The Remington Typewriter Company, an offshoot of E. Remington and Sons, makers of rifles, began in 1881 to produce the typewriter invented by Christopher L. Scholes after it had proved commercially viable. The company hired a small team to set up a national sales force, first at home and then abroad; and in 1886 when the arms company went bankrupt (various foreign buyers had failed to pay their bills), the typewriter sales team bought out the company's typewriter interests. Beginning in 1884 another firm, John Patterson's National Cash Register Company, built the plants and the national and then international marketing network that soon resulted in global domination. The same was true in the next decade for William S. Burrough's adding machines and A. B. Dick's mimeograph machines.

George Eastman invented the mass-produced camera in order to develop a market for another of his innovations, mass-produced celluloid photographic film. In 1880 he built a large plant at Rochester and quickly put together a worldwide marketing network of branch offices to supervise salesmen, service cameras, and develop and print pictures. By 1890 the Eastman Kodak Company had established production as well as service and developing facilities in Britain.

Most of the new light-machinery makers—John Deere, J. I. Case, and other makers of plows and harrows, as well as those producing less complex farm machines—followed McCormick's lead by investing in wholesaling and not in retailing. The retailing, again, was done by dealers who held an exclusive franchise for the manufacturer's product while also carrying complementary lines of other companies. A dealer with a McCormick franchise for reapers was apt to sell Deere plows, J. I. Case seeders, and the wagons and carriages of local manufacturers. On the other hand, in typewriters, cash registers, and cameras the leaders—Remington, National Cash Register, and Eastman Kodak—followed Singer's example by building a network of retail stores, owned and operated by the company, in concentrated urban areas.[23] Such stores were able to provide services on a neighborhood basis because they were in easy reach by foot or tramway. Eastman Kodak also used such outlets as places to develop film. But these firms remained the exception among American manufacturers, whose investment in marketing and distribution has been almost wholly in wholesaling, not retailing.

The makers of boilers, pumps, printing presses, and the other standardized industrial machinery that was volume-produced by fabricating and assembling standardized parts grew in much the same manner as did the makers of mass-produced light machinery. The differences were that their daily output was smaller and their finished products larger, more complex, and more tailored to the customer's need.[24] In the 1880s manufacturers of such machinery concentrated production in one or two large factories. Marketing called for specialized skills in demonstration, installation, and maintenance, as well as in providing credit. Independent commercial intermediaries had neither the incentive nor the experience to provide such services, but the manufacturer had both. In 1881 Babcock & Wilcox, makers of steam boilers, built an extensive factory at Bayonne, New Jersey (financed partly by the profits from Singer) and by the 1890s had a worldwide distribution organization in place. Worthington Pump established a comparable managerial hierarchy for production and distribution about the same time, as did Mergenthaler Linotype, maker of a new machine that helped transform the processes of printing and publishing. By the 1880s George Westinghouse, the inventor of the air brake for trains, had set up his overseas marketing organization. When electricity became available as a source of power in the same decade, Otis Elevator began its worldwide domination of that industry.

Nearly all of these producers of standardized machinery supported their foreign marketing organizations by building factories in Canada and overseas. Their plants long remained the largest producers in their industries in Britain, Germany, France, and other industrial nations.[25] The same American companies continued to be leaders of their national and global oligopolies until well after World War II.

ELECTRICAL EQUIPMENT

In the critically important electrical-equipment industries, the first movers' investments came quickly. The enterprises created in the 1880s to commercialize the inventions of Thomas Edison, Elihu Thomson, and George Westinghouse concentrated production in a few plants and immediately recruited the essential production teams and set up sales forces. In order to design, test, and manufacture in volume the recently invented equipment for generating, transmitting, and using electric power and light, larger numbers of more technically trained managers were required than for mass-producing packaged products or light machinery. Trained engineers were also needed to market, install, and service the new machines, for faulty installation could result in death by electrocution or fire. The company's engineers almost always knew more about the safe and efficient use of the new power machinery than did their customers.

In addition, because of the much higher cost of the equipment, these companies often found that they had to extend far greater amounts of credit to industrial buyers than did the producers of lighter machines.

Of the first three electrical manufacturers to build large works at optimal scale, Thomson-Houston, under the guidance of Charles Coffin, created the most effective sales organization both at home and abroad.[26] After it merged with Edison General Electric to form the General Electric Company in 1892, and General Electric and Westinghouse formed a patent pool in 1896, these two firms came to dominate the American electrical manufacturing industry. By the early 1900s General Electric and Westinghouse, working closely with two European first movers, Siemens & Halske and Allgemeine Elektricitäts Gesellschaft (AEG), had become the leaders of a global oligopoly that would remain little changed until well after World War II.

In allied fields American entrepreneurs quickly achieved an equally strong position. In the 1880s, with the spread of the newly invented telephone, Western Electric, the manufacturing subsidiary of Bell Telephone and then of its successor, American Telephone & Telegraph, expanded its sales organization overseas. By 1914 Western Electric was operating plants in Canada, Britain, Germany, France, Austria, Italy, Russia, Belgium, and Japan.[27] The Electric Storage Battery Company made its investment in production in 1893 and quickly enlarged its sales force overseas after reaching licensing agreements with the leading European producers, particularly Accumulatoren-Fabrik AG (AFA). In 1901 it acquired a leading British producer. From then on Electric Storage Battery and AFA dominated global markets. In the mass production and distribution of phonographs and records, two American companies, Victor Talking Machine and Columbia Phonograph, soon dominated their new industry. They set up sales subsidiaries abroad before 1900 and manufacturing subsidiaries shortly thereafter.[28]

INDUSTRIAL CHEMICALS

In the late 1880s and early 1890s American entrepreneurs made the investments and created the managerial teams necessary to exploit new electrolytic technologies in chemistry and also metallurgy.[29] In chemicals these included James T. Morehead, Thomas L. Willson, and Charles Brush in carbon-electrodes, H. Y. Castner in bleaching powder and caustic soda, and Herbert H. Dow in chlorine and magnesium. After building massive plants, these entrepreneurs and their associates organized national and international sales forces. Both the manufacturing and marketing of these products required engineers with skills as complex as those called for in the making of electrical machinery. They needed the knowledge of chemistry as well as physics—knowledge that was rare among managers of existing commercial intermediaries.

During these same years American entrepreneurs quickly built integrated firms to exploit the patents on chemical products invented abroad. In the 1880s and 1890s they set up enterprises to produce and distribute dynamite under Alfred Nobel's patent, synthetic alkalies made by the processes invented by the Solvay brothers, and industrial gases by Carl von Linde's liquefication process. They were, however, far behind German entrepreneurs in exploiting the new processes for producing man-made dyes, pharmaceuticals, and film on the basis of coal-tar chemistry. Nevertheless, in the 1880s large American firms did make other chemicals based on coal and coke. The Semet-Solvay and Barrett companies, for example, made roofing, creosote, asphalt, and other important chemical intermediaries such as toluene and benzene. These new chemical enterprises differed from those in branded packaged products, light machinery, and even electrical and heavy machinery in that they rarely extended their marketing and distribution organizations overseas. This was largely because German entrepreneurs had responded even more rapidly and efficiently to the new opportunities and had achieved a strong competitive advantage in the all-important European markets. By World War I, however, American chemical enterprises were beginning to make impressive investments in research and development. Much larger than those of British firms, these investments greatly enhanced American organizational capabilities after World War I.

METALS

Central to the continuing wave of innovation and investment in all these industries—and the increasing efficiency of rails, wire, and other transportation and communication equipment—were the achievements of American entrepreneurs in metals. In ferrous metals, mass production of steel by the new Bessemer and open-hearth processes only became substantial in the 1880s. In 1879 Andrew Carnegie had completed what was at that time the world's largest integrated Bessemer rail mill by installing blast furnaces at his Edgar Thomson works in Pittsburgh.[30] The impressive output of steel in the 1880s and early 1890s marked the beginnings of the modern American steel industry (Table 19). In nonferrous metals the transformation resulted from the perfecting in 1891 of a high-voltage generator that made possible electrolytic refining. In that year the construction of five giant copper refineries began a major transformation of that industry. In electrolytic copper refining the minimum efficient scale was so great that only fifteen refineries were built in the United States before World War II. In 1895 Arthur Vining Davis and Alfred E. Hunt built the giant aluminum plant at Niagara Falls to exploit Charles Hall's electrolytic process, and they began to establish a marketing organization that would assure the Aluminum Company of America's monopoly position in the Western Hemisphere. Indeed, at Niagara Falls, that most impressive source of hydroelectric power, first movers in electrochemicals (Union Carbide, Castner Electrolytic Alkali Company, Mathieson Alkali Works) and those in abrasives (Norton and Carborundum) established plants between 1889 and 1892.[31]

The carefully planned industrial development at Niagara Falls, an entrepreneurial achievement in its own right, provides a striking illustration of the revolution in production techniques that occurred in the 1880s and early 1890s. The sea change in the ways of manufacturing was as sudden as it was wide-ranging. No two earlier decades in man's history had witnessed the creation of so many new industries and the transformation of so many old ones. This was as much the case for western Europe as it was for the United States. The scale and variety of innovation and investment, its suddenness and pervasiveness, all testified to the interdependence and the cumulative impact of technological innovation. Developments in one industry very quickly led to developments in others.

Merger, Acquisition, and Rationalization

In the industries where only one or two pioneering enterprises made interrelated investments in production, distribution, and management, these enterprises quickly dominated the market. Among such first movers were the entrepreneurs who built the plants at Niagara Falls; the producers of branded packaged products, such as Borden, Heinz, Campbell Soup, Swift, Armour; and the machinery makers—Singer, Otis, Dick, Eastman, and Westinghouse. More often however, the modern industrial enterprise in the United States appeared after merger or acquisition. Leaders among the pioneers acquired or merged with competitors; and then they consolidated production facilities into plants of optimal size, established the necessary marketing networks, and recruited the managerial organization.

In such industries the pioneering entrepreneurs made investments in facilities and personnel that were large enough to augment capacity to levels of existing demand but not large enough to drive out the smaller, higher-cost firms. In such industries, pioneers were plagued by overcapacity and declining throughput. As throughput dropped, costs rose. This phenomenon occurred even in established industries, where improved technology brought more modest cost advantages than it did for those in the new industries of the Second Industrial Revolution. It occurred even in industries such as textiles, iron, simple tools, hardware, and the milling of rice and other specialized grains.[32] Increasing output and overcapacity intensified competition and drove down prices. Indeed, the resulting decline of prices in manufactured goods characterized the economies of the United States and the nations of western Europe from the mid-1870s to the end of the century.

On both continents the standard response by manufacturers to intensified competition and the resulting price decline was, first, to reach informal agreements as to price and output, and then to make more formal agreements (enforced by trade associations) to reduce output, set prices, and allocate regional markets. By the 1880s formal agreements enforced by industry-wide associations had become an accepted way of organizing markets. Agreements and associations appeared in industry after industry in Britain and Germany as well as the United States. For example, in the American hardware industry alone more than fifty trade associations managed cartels for as many specialized product lines.[33] The incentive to form such associations was particularly strong in the new capital- and energy-intensive industries where several entrepreneurs had simultaneously adopted innovative technologies of production.

Such cartels, however, remained unstable. The difficulty lay in providing mechanisms to enforce the decisions of the members of the association and thus to prevent members from secretly cutting prices by granting rebates or falsifying their books. In the United States and Britain such opportunistic behavior was particularly rampant because contractual arrangements between manufacturers (and also between associations of manufacturers and associations of wholesalers) could not be enforced in courts of law as they could be in continental Europe. Under common law, combinations in restraint of trade were illegal.

Enforcement became even more difficult in the United States after 1890, when Congress, in response to the political protest engendered by the great wave of horizontal combinations (usually trade associations) formed during the preceding decade, passed the Sherman Antitrust Act. That act not only reinforced the common law by declaring such combinations illegal; it also provided, as the common law did not, an instrument—the executive branch of the federal government—to bring action in the courts against presumed violators.

The Sherman Antitrust Act was to have a profound impact on the evolution of modern industrial enterprises in the United States. Technology and markets determined when such enterprises appeared and in what industries they were located, but it was the Sherman Act that defined the continuing interrelationships between the new enterprises within a single industry. Because the act forbade monopoly or any form of contract or combination in restraint of trade, close interfirm cooperation was defined as illegal collusion.

The legislation was more an expression of fundamental American values than the result of pressure groups at work. Unlike the Interstate Commerce Act passed three years earlier, its enactment had not been demanded by a powerful group of shippers and wholesalers. Indeed, it was passed with relatively little debate and even less opposition. The vote in the Senate was 52-1 and in the House 242-0 with 85 members not voting. Not surprisingly, the terms of the statute were imprecise and therefore ambiguous, but it made clear the strong antimonopoloy bias of the American public. This legislation, amplified by the Supreme Court's decisions in the 1890s and enforced by the executive branch in the early years of the next century, remained uniquely American; no other nation adopted a comparable law before World War II. That legislation and the values it reflected probably marked the most important noneconomic cultural difference between the United States and Germany, Britain, and indeed the rest of the world insofar as it affected the long-term evolution of the modern industrial enterprise.

Shortly before the passage of the Sherman Antitrust Act, the state of New Jersey enacted a set of general incorporation laws authorizing the formation of holding companies that might operate on a national scale. Before that time such a company could only be chartered through a special act of a state legislature. For a small fee, these New Jersey laws permitted the formation of a company that could hold the stock of existing corporations chartered in any state. After the passage of the acts, members of trade associations, as well as other corporations, were able to exchange their stock for shares in a new holding company. The creation of holding companies (the few existing trusts soon transformed themselves into such companies) thus centralized legal control of the constituent firms in a board of directors whose decisions as to prices and output of each could be legally enforced.

Of more importance for the development of the modern industrial enterprise, such legal combinations were also a prerequisite for centralizing the administration of constituent companies. The new legal form permitted rationalization of facilities and personnel (that is, the concentration of production in a small number of large plants of optimal size), the consolidation or creation of nationwide sales forces, and the recruitment of a managerial hierarchy to operate and plan for the enterprise as a whole. Such rationalization was difficult within a trade association, whose members were rarely willing to vote to shut down their own plants, to enlarge those of others, or to build factories in which they had no direct interest.

One of the very first enterprises to follow this path was, of course, John D. Rockefeller's Standard Oil Trust, which had come into being in 1882 to achieve the same ends, seven years *before* the New Jersey laws made the formation of holding companies easy. (The certificates exchanged by the trust for the shares of the constituent companies coming into the combination permitted it to acquire legal control similar to that of a holding company.) During its first five years the trust's centralized administrative board reduced the number of refining units from fifty-three to twenty-two and concentrated output in three refineries that provided the massive economies of scale described in Chapter 2. A number of the smaller refineries were converted to the production of petroleum specialties, such as lubricants, paraffin, wax, and vaseline.[34] Then the managers of the trust turned to building nationwide purchasing, marketing, and distribution networks. In 1884 the company centralized purchasing in its wholly owned Joseph Seep Agency. Between 1885 and the end of the decade it invested heavily in tank cars, storage depots, packaging facilities, and sales offices, both by acquiring existing wholesalers and by setting up wholly owned subsidiaries, such as Continental Oil and the Standard Oil Company of Iowa. This national marketing organization was administered in the 1890s through nine regionally defined marketing subsidiaries. Meanwhile, in the late 1880s the trust expanded its overseas distribution by establishing a wholly owned subsidiary in Britain, the Anglo-American Petroleum Company, and joint ventures with leading distributors in Germany, Holland, Italy, and Denmark. In addition, the trust sent out its own marketers and set up its own storage facilities, first in the Far East and Latin America and then throughout most of the rest of the world. In the same decade Standard Oil also completed its massive product-specific investment in distribution—in pipelines (which included some four thousand miles of short gathering lines at the oil fields and of long-distance lines connecting oil fields, refineries, and shipping points in the American Northeast), in a railroad tank-car fleet that operated nationally, and in a flotilla of five oceangoing tankers for the Atlantic crossing.

By 1886 the trust's headquarters at 26 Broadway in New York City housed what was then the world's largest industrial managerial hierarchy, which coordinated, monitored, and planned the activities of this integrated global enterprise. The hierarchy, by coordinating a constant flow of crude oil from the oil fields through a small number of large refineries to markets throughout the world, made Standard Oil the low-cost producer in many world markets. Its only serious competitor in Europe was the first mover on that continent, the Nobel Brothers Petroleum Company. The Nobels made very much the same investment in production, distribution, and management in Russia as did Rockefeller's Standard Oil Trust, and at precisely the same time. (The Standard Oil story is continued in Chapter 4, and the Nobel Brothers' story is told in Chapter 11.)

Growth through merger and acquisition (the response to intensified competition), whether in order to control price and output or to centralize and rationalize operations in the manner of Standard Oil, became increasingly widespread during the last two decades of the nineteenth century. Such consolidations clustered in three time periods.

The first period came in the 1880s before the passage of the New Jersey laws of 1889. Several groups of allied firms legally consolidated either by creating a trust or by obtaining a special state charter allowing one company to hold the shares or purchase the assets of the others.[35] In that decade such consolidations occurred almost wholly in the refining and distilling industries, where the new technologies had brought impressive increases in daily throughput. They came not only in petroleum but also in vegetable oil, linseed oil, sugar, whiskey, and paint. In those industries, however, only two trusts (American Cotton Oil and American Lead, which was more a producer of paints than a lead processor) followed the Standard Oil pattern of centralization, rationalization, and integration. By 1891 the American Cotton Oil Trust already owned and operated 326 tank cars, had an oceangoing tanker under construction, and had built a major storage depot in Rotterdam.

The second period of mergers began in 1890 after the passage of the New Jersey general incorporation laws for holding companies and lasted until the coming of a severe economic depression in 1893. In this short period more mergers occurred than in the previous decade. Former trusts, such as National Lead, American Sugar Refining, and Southern Cotton Oil, became holding companies. (The Standard Oil Trust did not take the legal move that made it the Standard Oil Company of New Jersey until 1899.) New consolidations included American Tobacco, United States Rubber, Pittsburgh Plate Glass, American Cereal (renamed Quaker Oats), Washburn-Crosby, General Electric, Colorado Fuel & Iron, Tennessee Coal & Iron, and National Tube Works. Soon several of these enterprises began the move toward administrative centralization and rationalization.

After 1897 began the largest and certainly the most significant merger movement in American history.[36] It came partly because of continuing antitrust legislation and activities by the states, partly because of the increasing difficulty of enforcing contractual agreements by trade associations during the depression of the mid-1890s, and partly because the return of prosperity and the buoyant stock market that accompanied it facilitated the exchange of shares and encouraged bankers and other financiers to promote mergers. The merger boom reached its climax between 1899 and 1902, after the Supreme Court had indicated by its rulings in the Trans-Missouri Freight Rate Association case (1897), the Joint Traffic Association case (1898), and the Addyson Pipe and Steel case (1899) that cartels carried on through trade associations were vulnerable under the Sherman Act. In the earlier E. C. Knight case of 1895 the Court had appeared to consider the holding company relatively immune. The merger movement died down in 1903 following a circuit court's decision in the Northern Securities case (upheld by the Supreme Court in 1904), which appeared to withdraw that immunity.

During this final and massive wave of mergers, legal consolidations occurred in almost every type of business and for almost every type of business motive. The predominant motive behind the majority of mergers was to achieve or maintain market power by transforming existing trade associations into holding companies or by uniting nonassociated competitors under a single corporate roof. Another motive was to profit from the marketing and manipulation of securities; for as the merger movement picked up speed, investment bankers and stock brokers began to participate in the process. These financial firms—some long-established enterprises, others newcomers—brought together the participants, arranged the terms of the merger (nearly all were carried out by exchanging the stock of the new holding company for that of the constituent firms), executed the legal and financial arrangements, and underwrote and marketed the new securities that had to be issued, taking in return both promotion and underwriting commissions. Often, too, these promoters, as insiders, had a chance to speculate successfully on the securities they issued. Indeed, entrepreneurs such as Charles R. Flint, James and William Moore, and John W. "Bet-a-Million" Gates became specialists in mergers.

Although market control through legally enforceable combinations and promoters' profits were the two most significant motives for mergers at the turn of the century, a number of merger-makers saw such combinations as the legal prerequisite to administrative centralization and rationalization. Like John D. Rockefeller and his associates, they realized that scale economies based on carefully scheduled high-volume flows provided a far more certain source of profit and market power than did legally enforced cartelization by means of a holding company.

This strategy was particularly well defined by the three young du Pont cousins who took over their family enterprise in 1902 and began the next year to reorganize and rationalize the American explosives industry through merger and acquisition. During the previous decade their family holdings had been part of two horizontal federations—the Gunpowder Trade Association formed in the 1880s and the Eastern Dynamite Company, a holding company formed in 1895. As the du Pont cousins—Alfred, Coleman, and Pierre—and a couple of close associates reviewed the operations of these two groups, they were increasingly astonished by the ways in which the members of the Gunpowder Trade Association and the Eastern Dynamite Company had been able to avoid, violate, and subvert the directives of the association or holding company. They then decided to achieve more certain market power by exploiting potential scale economies.[37] The goal was most precisely enunciated in a letter written by one of the young reorganizers, Albert Moxham, to Coleman du Pont, who was then in California investigating the complex activities of associated firms on the West Coast:

> I have been urging upon our people the following arguments. If we could by any measure buy out all competition and have an absolute monopoly in the field, it would not pay us. The essence of manufacture is steady and full product. The demand of the country for powder is variable. If we owned all therefore when slack times came we would have to curtail product to the extent of diminished demands. If on the other hand we control only 60% of it all and made the 60% cheaper than others, when slack times came we could still keep our capital employed to the full and our product to the maximum by taking from the other 40% what was needed for this purpose. In other words, you could count upon always running full if you make cheaply and control only 60%, whereas, if you own it all, when slack times came you could only run a curtailed product.

This advice was followed. The legal consolidation, E. I. du Pont de Nemours Powder Company, incorporated in New Jersey in 1903, did not include four of the industries' strong smaller firms.[38] Administrative centralization quickly followed the merger. Then came rationalization. Some plants were shut down or expanded and new ones built; a national sales organization was established, and a large office building was constructed in Wilmington to house the many salaried managers needed to administer the industry's dominant firm. Later, largely for defensive reasons, the company built its own glycerin plants, purchased sulphur mines, and then bought nitrate beds in Chile. This last move was not completed until 1911.

The managers of other mergers, such as those that resulted in the formation of American Cotton Oil, Southern Cotton Oil, National Lead, Virginia-Carolina Chemical, National Biscuit, American Tobacco, American Radiator, General Electric, Pittsburgh Plate Glass, and United Fruit moved almost as quickly as Standard Oil and Du Pont from a strategy of horizontal combination to one of vertical integration, from a strategy of achieving market control through contractual cooperation to one of achieving market dominance through exploiting the cost advantages of scale.[39]

At both American Sugar Refining and Corn Products Refining the change in strategy was delayed because some of the senior executives remained strongly committed to the older traditional strategy of market control. In still other companies, such as United States Rubber, International Paper, and International Harvester, the change came in a more evolutionary manner as senior executives responded to a series of day-to-day problems or opportunities.[40] Finally, such mergers as Allis-Chalmers, Worthington Pump, Distillers Securities, and the predecessors of Corn Products Refining had to endure the trauma of bankruptcy and financial reorganization before senior managers agreed that administrative centralization and rationalization were more profitable than attempting to control price and output by means of a decentralized holding company.

A very small number of these mergers, including the giant United States Steel Corporation, continued to be managed as federations. Their corporate offices remained more concerned about controlling price and output than about fully exploiting the economies of throughput (Chapter 4). Yet, even in the giant steel company the facilities of the operating subsidiaries, particularly the primary producers of fabricated products, such as American Steel & Wire, National Tube, and American Sheet & Tin Plate, were consolidated and administratively centralized in order to exploit the economies of scale to a greater extent than did comparable federations abroad. In fact, the turn-of-the-century merger movement brought a rationalization of production and distribution that did not occur in many of the same industries in Britain or on the Continent until well after World War I.

Whatever the initial motive for their formation—whether it was control through legally enforceable contractual arrangements, gains from promotion and financing, personal aggrandizement, or market power through technological and administrative efficiencies—nearly all the mergers that lasted did so only if they successfully exploited the economies of scale and (to a much lesser extent) those of scope. Few enterprises resulting from merger remained among the two hundred leaders unless they transformed themselves from a mere holding company into an operating one by creating a central administrative office to rationalize and manage the constituent companies' manufacturing personnel and facilities, by moving forward into distribution and backward into purchasing, and then by building an extensive managerial hierarchy that administered through a centralized, functionally departmentalized structure. And even merged companies that did all those things were not apt to remain among the largest two hundred industrials unless they were in industries whose production technologies gave large plants cost advantages over small ones and unless their product-specific distribution and marketing needs warranted an investment in a sales organization of their own.

This transformation of holding companies into centralized operating enterprises occurred largely in the years between the merger movement at the turn of the century and the nation's entry into World War I. In those years the successful mergers had made their shift from a holding company of previously competing firms to an operating company that integrated volume production and distribution, and so took advantage of the economies of scale. At the same time, the few combinations that continued to operate old, outmoded, poorly located plants or did not build new ones that were close to optimal size failed to grow and usually failed to make as satisfactory a return on their invested capital.[41]

Political and Legal Responses

The political and legal environment of the first decade of the new century hastened the transformation of holding companies into operating ones and the accompanying rationalization of industries. During the decade the Theodore Roosevelt and Taft administrations began to enforce the Sherman Antitrust Act vigorously. Then in 1911 antitrust action in the courts resulted for the first time in the dissolution of three major integrated industrial enterprises—Standard Oil Company of New Jersey, American Tobacco Company, and the Du Pont company. In the election of 1912, federal regulation of big business, particularly the modern industrial enterprise, became the single most important political issue. In that campaign all four candidates, not the usual two, had explicit positions on ways to regulate or control the "trusts."

One of the strongest pressure groups to fuel the political protest against big business was small business. Small businessmen included not only manufacturers whose small operations gave them a cost disadvantage, but also wholesalers, manufacturers' agents, and other middlemen who were being driven out of business as the volume-producing manufacturers moved forward and the mass retailers moved backward into wholesaling. Such displaced merchants were the leading businessmen in the smaller cities and the towns and villages across the nation. Combined they formed a much more powerful political constituency than did the much smaller number of dispossessed manufacturers.

The antitrust protest and the resulting enforcement of existing laws, along with the passage of new legislation after the 1912 election—the Federal Trade Commission Act and the Clayton Act were both passed in 1914—firmly prohibited the maintenance of market power through contractual cooperation. These executive and congressional actions, however, did not prevent increases in market share through functional and strategic effectiveness. This was because many who enforced the antitrust laws agreed that large industrials were able to increase productivity and so reduce prices. Many in the executive branch accepted Theodore Roosevelt's distinction between a good trust (one based on cost reduction) and a bad trust (one based on collusion). In breaking up Standard Oil, the Supreme Court enunciated its rule of reason. Again, efficiency appeared to be more reasonable than collusion. Ironically, then, antitrust legislation and its enforcement brought little relief to its strongest supporters, the small manufacturers and distributors in those industries where big business dominated. Indeed, the large majority of antitrust cases before World War II were brought against trade associations in the more fragmented, labor-intensive industries where the large enterprise had few competitive advantages and no firm or set of firms was able to stabilize prices.[42]

Nevertheless, the Sherman Act (reinforced by the Clayton Act of 1914) and its enforcement by the Justice Department (and after 1914 the Federal Trade Commission) did prevent agreements, both formal and informal, to set price and output—agreements that had become standard business practice in other industrializing nations. In the United States the large integrated firms in the new, concentrated industries continued to compete functionally and strategically for market share more vigorously than firms in Germany, Britain, or other European countries—or in Japan after World War II.

The Response of Financial Institutions

The merger movement was the most important single episode in the evolution of the modern industrial enterprise in the United States from the 1880s to the 1940s. Not only did it set in place the structure of the new capital-intensive industries and define their major players for much of the rest of the twentieth century, but also it permitted the rationalization of American industries in a way that did not begin in Britain and Germany until the 1920s. In addition, because successful mergers were those that were followed by administrative centralization and rationalization (which rarely happened in Britain), the governance of many large corporations was altered.

The nationwide consolidations within an industry reduced family control. The owners of the small companies coming into the merger exchanged their stock for a much smaller amount of shares of the new, consolidated firm. After facilities and personnel had been rationalized, salaried managers with little or no equity in the firm increasingly took over the management of the consolidated enterprise.

These mergers put representatives of investment banks and other financial institutions on the boards of American industrial enterprises for the first time. Financiers participating in these mergers did more than just promote and expedite consolidations. The financing of mergers involved little more than an exchange of stock, which required only a small amount of cash, but major inflows of capital were essential to finance the relocation and reshaping of old facilities and the building of new ones in order to exploit fully the cost advantages of the economies of scale.

Prior to the mergers of the 1890s, investment in American industrial enterprises had been far more personal than institutional. Unlike the railroads, which had high initial capital costs, the new industrial firms had rarely relied on investment bankers to finance their initial investment in production and distribution facilities. In most of the industries in which the large firm clustered entrepreneurs creating new enterprises had obtained funds for the initial investment in plant and facilities from local businessmen, and working capital largely from local banks. When their requirements had outrun local sources, industrialists had turned to wealthy individuals who had made fortunes in railroads or traction companies, in industry, or (to a lesser extent) in land, commerce, and banking. Such investors, who in the *Who's Who* of their day often identified themselves as capitalists, included the Rockefellers, the Harknesses, Oliver H. Payne, and Henry M. Flagler (all of Standard Oil), the Armours, the Dukes, the Clarks of Singer Sewing Machine, the McCormicks, the Vanderbilts, the Forbeses, the Boston Associates (the entrepreneurial group that made the first fortunes in textiles), and such traction magnates as P. A. B. Widener, Anthony N. Brady, Thomas F. Ryan, and William C. Whitney—men who had made their fortunes by replacing horse-drawn street railways with new electric-powered trolleys and subways.

The most successful of these venture capitalists were the Mellons of Pittsburgh, particularly Andrew W. Mellon, who in 1882 at the age of twenty-seven took charge of his family's private bank. He and his brother Richard concentrated their investments in Pittsburgh. They put funds accumulated from Pittsburgh coal and steel companies into other Pittsburgh enterprises, including Alcoa, Carborundum, Koppers, and, on a smaller scale, Pittsburgh Plate Glass. In addition, they financed a nephew, William L. Mellon, an experienced oil man, in his venture into Texas oil, the Gulf Oil Corporation. The Mellons invested their own personal funds. They did not underwrite and syndicate security issues in the manner of J. P. Morgan & Company and the other investment banking houses. Not until shortly before World War I did they convert the Union Trust Company, which they had acquired in 1903, into just such an institution to market securities of Pittsburgh-based firms.[43] The Mellons, like the other local capitalists, joined the boards of the firms in which they invested.

Such venture capitalists, however, played a relatively small role in the great merger movement. These mergers were instigated and financed by promoters, by investment bankers, or by individual manufacturers. Standard Oil and Du Pont were prime examples of manufacturers who financed their own mergers. The promoters included Charles Flint (who put together United States Rubber, American Woolen, American Chicle, and others), the Moore brothers (who were responsible for National Biscuit, American Can, American Tin-Plate, and National Steel, among others) and John Gates of American Steel & Wire and Republic Iron & Steel.[44] As the merger movement got under way, the investment bankers, many long experienced in railroad finance, turned their attention to industry. Besides such railroad financiers as J. P. Morgan & Company; Kuhn, Loeb; Kidder, Peabody; Lee, Higginson; Winslow, Lanier; and Brown Brothers, Harriman, they included James Stillman's National City Bank and George F. Baker's First National Bank. These firms and a few others like them funded the rationalization of American industries in that period.

The relationship of the promoters and even the investment bankers to the merged enterprises on whose boards they sat remained, like that of the venture capitalists, more personal than institutional. Even the largest incorporated investment banks—such as those of James Stillman and George F. Baker— were still operated like the house of Morgan, the most respected and most powerful of them all: that is, they were personally run enterprises with small staffs.[45] Their structure and functions were very different from those of the German "great banks" that played such a significant role in the financing of modern German industrial enterprises. They were more like the large British merchant banks, which, however, played only a small part in the financing of British industry. The representatives of the American banks on the boards of the newly consolidated American industrial enterprises had little personal knowledge of the businesses they had helped to finance, and they continued to rely almost wholly on the managers of each company for essential information on the company's internal affairs and its external challenges and opportunities. Therefore, as the knowledge and experience of the full-time managers on the board increased and the new enterprise succeeded in financing its current operations and long-term growth primarily from retained earnings, the influence of the financiers waned.

By the end of World War I, as David Bunting and Mark Mizruchi have pointed out, the capitalists on boards "were rarely succeeded by other finance capitalists. Indeed the control of their various companies passed, mostly by default, to subordinates [that is, salaried managers] who had been retained to manage particular companies."[46] Only in those industries having the largest capital requirements (the electrical-equipment industry is a notable example) did the leading enterprises retain ties with the bankers who had provided funds in their earlier years, so that representatives of the banks continued to sit as outside directors on their boards. And investment bankers played no significant role in those enterprises to which they had not provided capital—those that had been financed initially by individual investors and were subsequently funded by retained earnings. Industrial firms, of course, continued to use the services of banks to handle international monetary exchanges and transfers of stocks and bonds and to advise and assist in providing short-term credit and long-term underwriting of the securities that supplemented retained earnings in financing new and improved facilities. Hence their boards were apt to include representatives of the banks providing such services. But it was only when retained earnings fell off and companies underwent financial difficulties—particularly during the sharp post-World War I recession and the Great Depression of the 1930s—that investment bankers returned in any number to the boards of large American industrial enterprises. Even then their continuing influence appears to have been short-lived.

The Response of Educational Institutions

The merger movement and the resulting rationalization of production and distribution had a major impact on American educational institutions. When the expansion in the size and complexities of managerial hierarchies increased the demand for trained executives, American colleges and universities responded quickly. Graduates of land-grant colleges and other institutions that offered engineering courses began to join the managerial ranks of the new industrial enterprises even before the turn of the century. In their early years such schools concentrated on training the civil engineers so essential to the building of the railroads. In the 1880s many started to offer the courses in mechanical engineering needed to equip and operate the new factories. In that decade the Massachusetts Institute of Technology, Purdue, Wisconsin, and the Stevens Institute of Technology all established mechanical engineering departments. Case Institute expanded its offerings; and Cornell's Sibley College, after reorganizing its structure and curriculum in 1885, became the leading professional school for mechanical engineering.[47] In the 1890s the Massachusetts Institute of Technology and other schools opened departments of electrical engineering, and, in the first decade of the next century, departments of chemical engineering.

After 1900 the relationship between higher education and the industrial enterprise became closer. The Massachusetts Institute of Technology (M.I.T.) provides a good example. From M.I.T.—where Elihu Thomson (one of the founders of what later became the General Electric Company) had joined the electrical engineering faculty in 1894—General Electric recruited Willis R. Whitney and William D. Coolidge to command its new corporate research department. The company continued to rely heavily on M.I.T.'s electrical engineering department, which by World War I was reputed to be the best in the world for both technical expertise and the training of potential managers.[48] Gerard Swope, who received his electrical engineering degree from M.I.T. in 1895, became General Electric's most competent operating executive during the interwar years. The three du Pont cousins who reorganized the explosives industry in 1903 and 1904 were all graduates of M.I.T., and they continued to rely on William Walker's chemical engineering department for technical knowledge and recruitment of managers. In the same way Standard Oil (New Jersey) and other oil companies depended a few years later on Warren K. Lewis's petroleum engineering group within that department. Other graduates, Alfred P. Sloan of General Motors and Paul Litchfield of Goodyear Tire & Rubber, retained close ties with M.I.T. In Germany, too, comparable connections developed between the rising technical schools and the new industrial enterprises. They did not, however, exist to any extent in Britain.

The rationalization of production and distribution that followed the great merger movement created a demand for executives in other areas besides production. Managers in accounting, finance, marketing, and general management were needed in much greater numbers. Again, the American institutions of higher learning responded with speed.[49] Before 1900 only the University of Pennsylvania's undergraduate Wharton School of Commerce and Finance, founded in 1881, offered courses in business. In the decade after 1899 the nation's best-known colleges and universities added business education to their curriculum. The University of Chicago and the University of California set up undergraduate schools of commerce in 1899, followed by New York University in the next year. In 1900 Dartmouth's Amos Tuck School of Administration and Finance became the country's first school of business to enroll graduate students. By the time Harvard opened its Graduate School of Business Administration in 1908, professional postgraduate work in business education was already off to a good start. By 1914 the Harvard Business School was offering courses in marketing, corporate finance, and even business policy. The purpose of the last course, according to a history of the school, was "to develop an approach to business problems from the top-management point of view."[50] As in the case of engineering, German higher education also responded to the need by setting up courses in accounting, finance, and business economics; but again, this rarely occurred in Britain.

The Coming of Competitive Managerial Capitalism

By the time the United States entered World War I, the revolutionary transformation of American industry that had taken off in the 1880s had stabilized. By 1917 the underlying industrial structure of the nation had taken shape. Large, integrated industrial corporations had come to dominate the capital-intensive industries, where economies of scale and (to a lesser degree) those of scope gave size a cost advantage. In the labor-intensive industries, where the size of production units did not promote scale advantages, firms remained relatively small. Even there, however, the largest of them—those few that appeared on the list of the top two hundred—had integrated distribution with production.

In nearly all cases the new corporations, once integrated, continued to grow in the manner I described in Chapter 2. They exploited their functional expertise and their organizational capabilities by extending their sales organizations abroad, first to Europe and then to the less industrially advanced areas of the world. By 1914 nearly one-third of the top two hundred firms had supported their marketing organizations by building plants abroad when their cost calculations as to optimal size, transportation, tariffs, and the potential size and share of markets had appeared to warrant such an investment. The most numerous firms to take this step were the makers of machinery.[51]

A smaller number of the new large industrial enterprises, those that were in the most technologically advanced industries, had invested in research and development. In 1921, when the first survey of industrial laboratories in the United States was taken, personnel employed in research in American industry totaled only 6,693. Of these, 78% were working in five industries—industries in which the large firms concentrated—and more than half were in just two. Electrical-machinery firms accounted for 30.6% of the total, chemical firms 24.3%, primary metals 8.0%, rubber 7.8%, and transportation equipment 6.9%.[52]

In 1917 the large American industrial firms still concentrated mainly on producing and distributing a single product. A few, such as the largest meatpackers and metal makers, manufactured in some volume the by-products of their processes of production and distribution. A few others, particularly the makers of agricultural implements, were developing a full line of products for the same market. An even smaller number had begun to diversify by using the same production processes to make lines of products for new and different markets or by using the same distribution facilities for more than one product line. But no large American firm had yet embarked on a considered, systematic strategy of product diversification.

Nearly all of the two hundred top firms were organized as centralized, functionally departmentalized operating structures—a variation of that shown in

Figure 1. In most cases the major departments were organized internally on a line-and-staff basis, headed by a deputy director, his assistants, and an extensive staff. The departmental activities of these middle managers were coordinated and monitored by a team of top managers, usually vice presidents in charge of the major departments. Together with the president and occasionally a full-time chairman of the board, these vice presidents also planned the corporation's future and allocated resources to carry out their plans. Some of the enterprises were, of course, far more carefully structured than others. While some had completed their organizational structures early in the century, in others the structures were still evolving in 1917. In the great majority of cases, however, a hierarchy of middle and top managers coordinated and monitored the operations of many geographically scattered units of production and distribution. The organizational charts used at Armour in 1907 and at the Du Pont company after 1911 (See Figures 3 and 4), indicate more specifically than the generalized chart (Figure 1) the size and activities of the large managerial hierarchies that had been created in the United States well before the coming of World War I.

The rapid growth of these hierarchies in the two decades before 1917 was already bringing about a separation of ownership from management. The very act of entrepreneurship in commercializing the new products of the Second Industrial Revolution required the recruiting of teams of managers. The more complex the processes of production and distribution, and the more geographically extended the resulting enterprise, the larger the hierarchy. Few families could fill all the major posts with their own members or those of related kinship groups. If they were to compete successfully in the new national and global oligopolies, they had to share short-term operating decisions and then long-term resource-allocation decisions with salaried managers.

By 1917 the distinction between "inside" and "outside" directors was becoming clear in the United States. The inside directors, who were full-time managers, included senior members of the salaried hierarchy and members of the founder's family who were also full-time top managers. The outside directors, who were part-time directors with other business and social interests, represented major stockholders, including family members who were not full-time managers. As time passed, these representatives of families, banks, or large investors found it increasingly difficult at the monthly, or often only quarterly, board meetings to acquire a firm grasp of the many current issues. So the full-time inside directors managed. The part-time outside directors, even if they had a controlling share of stock and outnumbered the inside directors on the board, had neither the time, the information, nor the experience to do more than advise the full-time managers and to ratify or, in rare cases, to veto their suggestions. The outside directors enjoyed legal power over the activities of the corporation; they enjoyed the status that comes with wealth and position;

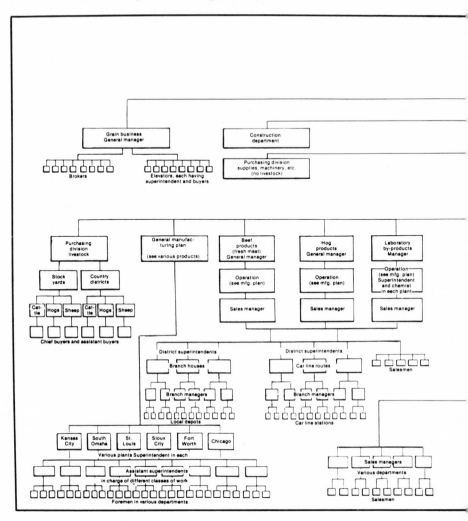

Figure 3.   Organization chart of Armour & Company, 1907. From *System* 12:220 (Sept. 1907).

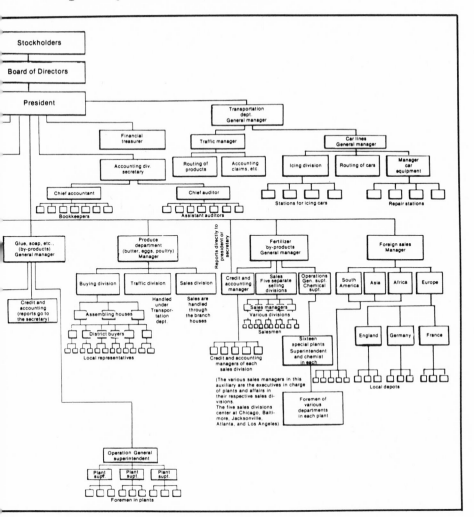

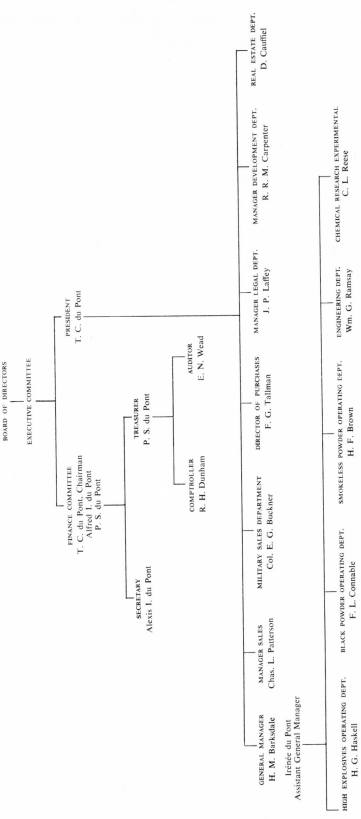

Figure 4. Du Pont Company structure after the reorganization of 1911. From Alfred D. Chandler, Jr., and Stephen Salsbury, *Pierre S. du Pont and the Making of the Modern Corporation* (New York, 1971), following p. 306.

and they may have possessed the privileges and prerogatives of power. But the inside directors increasingly controlled the *instruments* of power.[53]

By World War I managerial capitalism had taken root in those industries most essential to the continuing health and growth of the American economy. Three basic factors had encouraged the expansion of the new modern industrial enterprise: (1) the large, rapidly growing, geographically extensive, affluent domestic market; (2) the continuing development of capital-intensive technologies of production; and (3) the legal environment that prevented the enforcement of the contractual price-and-output arrangements that were attempted through horizontal federations of small firms. Given these conditions the first movers and the small number of challengers in capital-intensive industries had begun to grow by adding new units to their marketing and distribution networks and then by establishing production facilities to support them in distant markets. The founding entrepreneurs, venture capitalists, and, in case of merger, the investment bankers and promoters, but most important of all the managers of the enterprises themselves (through retained earnings) had provided the necessary funds for such expansion; and the nation's technical schools and universities were beginning to train the growing number of personnel required.

In the United States the structure of the new industries had become, with rare exceptions, oligopolistic, not monopolistic. This was partly because of the size of the market place and partly because of the antitrust legislation that reflected the commitment of Americans to competition as well as their suspicion of concentrated power. In these oligopolies the new managerial enterprises continued to compete functionally and strategically for market share and profit. By World War I the system of competitive managerial capitalism in capital-intensive industries in the United States was already different from the continuing personal or family capitalism practiced in Britain and the cooperative or organized capitalism developing in Germany.

FOUR

Creating Organizational Capabilities: Vertical Integration and Oligopolistic Competition

The industry-by-industry review of the collective histories of the leading manufacturing firms in the United States, which begins with this chapter, provides the evidence on which the generalizations and explanatory theories developed in this book are based. The review was made easier, indeed it was possible, because, first, the modern industrial enterprise continued to cluster in the same industries and, second, roughly the same set of enterprises remained the leaders in each industry.[1]

In the United States in 1917, 148 (or 74.0%) of the 200 largest industrial enterprises were located in seven of the twenty two-digit manufacturing categories of the U.S. Standard Industrial Classification or SIC (see Table 6)—that is, in food, chemicals, petroleum, primary metals, and the three machinery groups. In 1948 the number was 154 (77.0%). In six other two-digit groups—tobacco, rubber, glass, paper, fabricated metals, and instruments—the enterprises belonged to subcategories (that is, three-digit industries) with characteristics comparable to those of these seven two-digit groups. Their number was 29 in 1917 (14.5% of the top 200) and 24 in 1948 (12.0%). The remaining two-digit categories—textiles, apparel, lumber, furniture, printing and publishing, leather, and miscellaneous—included only 19 enterprises (or 9.5%) in 1917 and 17 (8.5%) in 1948.

The changing numbers within these classifications primarily reflect basic technological changes. Between 1917 and 1948 the number of food companies dropped from 29 to 27 and primary metal enterprises from 31 to 23, while the number of chemical firms rose from 20 to 23, nonelectrical machinery increased by six, and electrical machinery by two. The firms that moved onto the list of the top 200 did so largely by responding to the opportunities created by the new primary sources of power—the internal combustion engine and electricity—and by the basic innovations in chemicals and electrical and electronic products. Those that dropped off the list were makers of products that were being replaced by these basic innovations, such as natural dyes, natural fertilizers, railway equipment, and ships.

In all the industries where the nation's largest enterprises clustered, the first movers—the first to make the essential, interrelated, three-pronged investments in production, distribution, and management—remained the leaders from the 1880s to the 1940s. This was as true for Great Britain and Germany as it was for the United States. It was true even though these decades were marked by continuing technological innovation, profound changes in markets, and dramatic fluctuations in demand. During this period cities and suburbs, with their rapidly growing industries, replaced farms, rural towns, and traditional commercial centers as the major markets; and years of prosperity were followed by years of deep depression. Furthermore, the turnover that did come in the top two hundred firms in established industries resulted far more from mergers and acquisitions among existing leaders than from the entry of new companies.

Even though the leaders remained much the same within their industrial groups, in an industry-by-industry review of the collective histories of these companies the focus must be sharp. Once again, each set of industries used different technologies of production and served markets with different needs and requirements; hence each industry had different potentials in relation to the economies of scale and scope. Each called for different types of marketing organization and therefore required and developed different types of marketing capabilities. Moreover, within the individual industries the abilities of the senior decision-makers differed from company to company, and they changed as one group of company leaders was succeeded by another. Thus in the collective histories of these enterprises I focus first on the processes by which the leaders in each industry were selected—that is, on how the first movers in each became established—and then on the enterprises' dynamic evolution, their continuing relationships with one another, and their response to a small number of challengers.

Even though the evolution of industrial enterprises varied from industry to industry, growth in nearly all of them before World War I was achieved primarily by horizontal combination or vertical integration. After World War I, however, expansion resulted increasingly from moves into new geographical markets at home and abroad and into new product markets in related industries. Nevertheless, in some American industries the major players continued to compete and grow in much the same manner throughout the whole period. Their predominant strategies of growth continued to be horizontal combination and vertical integration.

In presenting the American story, I will begin with the detailed collective histories of two industries—oil and rubber—from their beginnings through World War II. In the rest of this chapter I will consider those industries in which the strategies of growth remained much the same both before and after World War I. The histories of these industries—paper, stone, clay and glass, fabricated metals, and primary metals—focus on the period before World War I. In Chapters 5 and 6, I will review the more dynamic industries—food, chemicals, and the three machinery groups—where the organizational capabilities developed through exploiting the cost advantages of scale encouraged investment abroad, and those developed through utilizing the economies of scope led to investment in related products. In those chapters I will examine only briefly the selection and early growth of the players before World War I, concentrating instead on the way they used their organizational capabilities—honed by oligopolistic competition—to expand abroad and into new product lines during the interwar years. The appendix tables list the firms in each of these industries that were among the largest two hundred in 1917, 1930, and 1948, giving their ranking, assets, and product lines. These tables provide a list of the players in the stories being told in the text about each industry.

Oil: From Monopoly to Oligopoly

From its beginning the oil industry (Group 29; see Appendixes A.1–A.3) has captured the imagination of the American public, particularly its journalists, business critics, and historians. The first mover—John D. Rockefeller's Standard Oil Company—has for the past century remained a symbol of American big business. Of more importance for this study, oil refining provides a striking example of an industry in which cost advantages of scale critically shaped the growth of firms and determined the structure of the industry.

The Standard Oil Company was one of the first enterprises in the world to exploit the economies of scale by making the three interrelated investments in production, marketing, and management. The oil industry, however, differs from the other American industries I will review in that from its beginning its major market was Europe, not the United States. As late as the 1883–1885 period, 69.0% of the kerosene refined in the United States was exported, of which 70.0% went to Europe and 21.6% to Asia.[2] Until 1900 kerosene was the industry's major product, with light and heavy lubricants, naphthas, and medicinal oils the minor ones. A strong demand for gasoline came only after 1900.

CREATING THE MONOPOLY

In oil, as in many other industries, it was the processors, not the producers of raw materials, that created the modern industrial enterprise. The potential for exploiting economies of scale was much greater in refining oil than in extracting crude oil out of the ground. And in processing, John D. Rockefeller, from the very start, built a near monopoly based on the exploitation of these potential economies of scale. When he joined forces with Samuel Andrews in 1865, six years after the discovery of oil at Titusville, Pennsylvania, the two partners operated one of the first refineries with a daily rated capacity of five hundred barrels.[3] By 1869 their operation was refining well over one thousand barrels a day. By 1870, when they and three other partners incorporated as the Standard Oil Company, their works in Cleveland were the largest in the world. They were the first to reach what the industry's historians have described as an "entirely new scale in plant and still size"—a scale that reduced unit cost by almost one-half from somewhat more than five to less than three cents a gallon.[4] The scale of these operations and their resulting cost advantage can be better understood in light of the fact that the size of Rockefeller's works by 1869 was already equal to that of the combined size of the next three largest refineries in Cleveland.

The resulting volume of output gave the partners a powerful weapon with which to reduce transportation costs. In oil, as in nearly every other American industry, competition between railroads increased the power of the large shippers; for the intense pressure exerted upon the railroads by their very high fixed costs led their operators to grant reduced rates, usually in the form of rebates, for higher-volume shipments. The larger the volume, the larger the rebate. It was Standard's unprecedented throughput that brought the reduced rates—not the reduced rates that brought the unprecedented throughput. Rockefeller did not go to the railroads. For example, in April 1868 the railroads, in the persons of Commodore Cornelius Vanderbilt of the New York Central and Amasa Stone of the Lake Shore, two of the nation's most powerful businessmen, came to the twenty-eight-year-old refiner.[5] The lower transportation rates the company received, combined with Rockefeller's much lower production costs resulting from high throughput, gave Rockefeller the economic power needed to bring together the Standard Oil alliance.

The purpose of the alliance was to control output and price. It came into being after trade associations, both those of crude oil producers and those of refiners, had failed to prevent sharp fluctuations and continuing decline of prices as more and more crude and refined oil came on the market. As would occur in many American industries, the largest firm took the lead in organizing its industry. Standard Oil Company did so by exchanging its stock for stock holdings in more than thirty other refining companies. The interlocking financial structure that resulted provided the disciplinary apparatus to maintain prices. The members of the alliance remained independent legally and administratively. Stocks of the members were held by individual directors of the Standard Oil Company. In many cases Standard's holdings gave it only partial control. Although committees were formed to coordinate marketing and distribution, no central office existed to coordinate or monitor the activities of the alliance as a whole or to allocate resources for future production and distribution.

It was a technological innovation in distribution, not refining, however, that transformed this federation into the Standard Oil Trust. The innovation was the long-distance pipeline, and the innovators were the producers of crude oil. In 1878 a group of producers, in order to break the alliance's hold on railroad rates, formed the Tide Water Oil Company to build the first long-distance pipeline—one that ran from the oil regions of northwest Pennsylvania across the mountains to the East Coast. Although the Standard Oil group fought its construction by every legal and some illegal means, Tide Water by June 1879 had completed the line, with a daily delivery capacity of six thousand barrels, to Williamsport, Pennsylvania, whence the Reading Railroad, which previously had transported no oil, carried it to tidewater. The pipeline itself was soon extended to Bayonne, New Jersey.[6]

As they vigorously fought the long-distance pipeline, the refiners in the Standard Oil alliance began to realize the potential cost advantages of this new form of transportation. Not only did it greatly reduce shipping costs, but it also provided magnificent storage areas and thus assured a much greater and steadier flow of crude oil into the refineries. The alliance quickly made an investment of more than $30 million in pipelines, at a time when the Standard Oil Company's total assets were valued at $3 million. As the new pipelines neared completion, the members of the Standard Oil alliance formed the Standard Oil Trust, which then rationalized the American petroleum-refining industry (see Chapter 2), reducing its average unit costs from 1.5 cents to 0.45 cents a gallon. Investment in a national and international sales organization quickly followed, as did the centralization of purchasing of crude oil (see Chapter 3). In the same years— the mid-1880s—an extensive managerial hierarchy began to coordinate, monitor, and plan for this global industrial empire from its multi-storied headquarters at 26 Broadway in New York City.[7]

While the original investment in the Cleveland refinery (which was accompanied by a second investment in distribution facilities in New York harbor and by the opening of contacts with European marketers) had made Standard Oil the most powerful first mover in the United States, the interrelated three-pronged investment in production, distribution, and management after the formation of the trust made it a first mover on a global scale. It permitted the company to market kerosene (refined in the United States) at a lower price in Europe than the kerosene that the European refineries made from Russian oil, and to sell the same product in China at lower prices than that made from the oil of the Dutch East Indies. At the same time, the profits were massive enough to create several of the world's largest industrial fortunes, not only for the Rockefellers but also for their close associates, including the Harknesses, Payne, Henry Flagler, and others.

In the United States the initial challenges to the Standard Oil Trust came from the crude-oil producers. The few specialty refiners of lubricants and other by-products lacked the financial resources to build a refinery of minimum efficient scale or to create the necessary marketing and distributing organizations. Tide Water, whose building of the pipeline over the mountains had forced Standard Oil to construct its own pipeline network and then to form a trust, quickly built a refinery at Bayonne with a daily capacity of six thousand barrels. Further expansion made it, by 1899, the largest refinery in the world. But Tide Water had not developed the organizational capabilities to create a substantial overseas marketing organization. Instead it turned to Standard Oil. By the late 1880s Standard Oil was marketing 50% to 75% of Tide Water's export sales at a time when Europe still was as important a market as the United States. Not surprisingly, Tide Water soon came under the financial control of Standard Oil. This same fate overtook a second challenger, the Crescent Pipe Line Company, headed by William L. Mellon of the Pittsburgh banking family. Mellon built a 270-mile pipeline over the mountains to tidewater at Marcus Hook on the Delaware River and then constructed a refinery there, which was quickly absorbed by Standard Oil in 1893.[8] More successful was the Pure Oil Company, formed in 1895 at Bradford, Pennsylvania. This producing company, after merging with United States Pipe Line (which had completed a pipeline over the mountains in 1893), also established a refinery at Marcus Hook and invested in distributing facilities at home and then abroad (including an oceangoing tanker). By 1904 it was a fully integrated enterprise.

Meanwhile, the opening of new fields in the late 1880s on the Ohio-Indiana border, together with the depletion of the Pennsylvania oil fields, created new opportunities for challengers to Standard Oil. As the output of the Pennsylvania fields declined, the crude-oil producers were able to combine for the first time to control prices. Simultaneously, entrepreneurs not only were obtaining potential drilling sites in the new fields but were beginning to build refineries and marketing organizations. At least one, the Sun Oil Company, made investments large enough to compete with Standard Oil in the Midwest.[9]

As a result of the declining output of the old fields and the opening of new ones, in 1889 Standard Oil felt forced to make its first move (a defensive one) into the production of crude oil.[10] By 1892 the company was already producing 25% of the nation's crude. Even earlier—toward the end of 1889—it had begun constructing at Whiting, Indiana, close to Chicago, a refinery even larger than the three built in the early 1880s to process crude oil from the Indiana fields. Thus, as the century came to a close the Standard Oil Company still completely dominated the market. It had become the Standard Oil Company of New Jersey when, in May 1899, the companies forming the old Standard Oil Trust came under the control of the new holding company incorporated in New Jersey.

Abroad, the threat to Standard's dominance, particularly in the lucrative European markets, came from refiners, not producers. In Europe the discovery of oil fields near Baku on the Caspian Sea in the late 1870s opened up fields comparable to those in Pennsylvania. There Ludwig Nobel, of the innovative and entrepreneurial Swedish family, became the first mover in refining, much as Rockefeller did in the United States (see Chapter 11). The Nobels, in turn, were challenged by the Rothschilds, Europe's most powerful banking family, who financed the construction of a railroad from the Caspian to the Black Sea to bypass Nobel's distributing organization and to provide crude oil to their refineries in Europe. Nevertheless, Standard Oil continued successfully to meet these challenges. Negotiations conducted in 1895 among Standard Oil, the Nobels, and the Rothschilds were based on the presumption that the American company would have 75% of the world's export trade.

CHANGING MARKETS AND SOURCES OF SUPPLY

The first decade of the twentieth century saw the sudden transformation of the American oil industry from a near monopoly to an oligopoly, which resulted from a rapid shift in the demand for refined products and an almost simultaneous opening of vast new sources of supply. This was the most dynamic decade of the first century of the industry's history. The coming of the automobile created a new demand for gasoline just as the widespread availability of electricity was threatening the market for kerosene. At the same time new sources of crude oil were discovered in Texas, California, the Far East, and eastern Europe. By 1910 the producers in these new fields had integrated forward into refining and marketing. By then there were already eight integrated oil companies among the nation's two hundred largest industrial enterprises: Standard Oil, The Texas Company (later Texaco), Gulf Oil, Associated Oil, Union Oil of California, Shell Oil, Tide Water Oil, and Sun Oil. In addition, there was Pure Oil, whose assets were not large enough to place it on the list of the top two hundred. Gulf, Texas, Sun, and a subsidiary of Standard Oil were the first enterprises to invest in refineries of optimal size using crude from the Texas fields, and so were able to take full advantage of the economies of scale. They were also the first to set up extensive marketing and distribution networks. They remained the leaders in the Southwest.[11] In California the first to make such investments were Union, Associated Oil, a subsidiary of Standard (Standard Oil of California), and a subsidiary of Royal Dutch–Shell (Shell Oil). In this way the American oil industry was transformed from a monopoly to an oligopoly *before*, not after, the Court ordered the dissolution of Standard Oil in 1911. That court decision, of course, increased the size of the oligopoly. Of the sixteen major companies spun off from Standard Oil of New Jersey, five were on the 1917 list of the nation's two hundred largest industrials. (Besides those with the Standard name, these included Vacuum Oil and Atlantic Refining.)

In Europe comparable changes in markets and the opening of new sources of supply brought similar changes. Royal Dutch, the first to build refineries of optimal size in the newly opened fields in the Dutch East Indies, quickly allied itself with Shell Transport and Trading, the largest distributor and marketer of

Far Eastern oil products. The two formally merged in 1907 under the name of Royal Dutch–Shell. At the same time, two of the great German banks were bringing together a number of smaller producing, refining, and distributing companies to form two large integrated companies—Deutsche Petroleum and Deutsche Erdöl (see Chapter 11). The breakup of Standard Oil in 1911 weakened—though not substantially—Standard's power abroad. Of the successor companies only Standard Oil of New York (Socony), which began as a marketing company, became active in the European market, while Standard Oil of California remained a major player in Asiatic markets.

VERTICAL INTEGRATION AND OLIGOPOLISTIC COMPETITION

In the United States during the second decade of the century both old and new members of the domestic oligopoly grew through vertical integration and continued to compete for market share functionally and strategically. At the time of the Standard Oil breakup in 1911 the first movers in the Texas and California fields were already fully integrated companies. Most of the new companies carved out of Standard, however, were not, since the court had divided that giant enterprise along functional lines. Of the newly formed companies only the Standard Oil Company (New Jersey), the remnant of the original Standard Oil Company of New Jersey, and Standard Oil of California remained fully integrated—from production of crude to marketing in retail outlets. [12] (Yet Jersey Standard, as the New Jersey company was usually called, had become primarily a company that did its refining in the United States and its marketing abroad.) A few of the new companies had both refining and marketing facilities. The rest were either crude-oil producers, transporters, or marketers.

But this soon changed. In the decade following the court order these new Standard companies grew rapidly through vertical integration in order to obtain and maintain a share of the swiftly growing gasoline trade, the smaller but also expanding lubricant trade, and the new fuel-oil business. The ones that were largely refining enterprises built or expanded their marketing facilities and personnel. Those that were primarily marketing companies quickly constructed their own refineries. [13] By 1917 eight of the former Standard companies had extensive refining, transportation, and distribution facilities. To assure themselves of continuing supplies, four of these had moved backward into crude-oil production. A fifth, Standard Oil of Indiana, followed in 1919. The remnant of the original company, Jersey Standard, expanded its domestic refining and marketing facilities.

Six of the seven independents on the list of the largest two hundred industrials in 1917 which have not already been mentioned—Pan American Petroleum & Transport, Midwest Refining, Cosden, General Petroleum, Magnolia Oil, and Pierce —were less integrated and would be acquired by existing integrated firms. The seventh, Sinclair Oil & Refining, which had begun as a pipeline company, moved into crude production and refining and during the 1920s built an extensive national and international organization in marketing and distribution and expanded its managerial personnel.

The investment by refiners in crude-oil production emphasizes the defensive nature of this strategy. The refiners that integrated backward into crude were far more numerous than the producers that moved forward into refining. Thus, even though crude-oil production remained the most competitive branch of the industry, the Federal Trade Commission reported in 1919 that thirty-two firms produced 59.4% of total crude output, and that, of these, integrated firms accounted for 35.4%. Extensive backward integration continued apace; by 1931, 51.9% of the nation's crude was being produced by the twenty largest integrated oil companies, which by then held 77.4% of crude-oil stocks. By 1937 these figures were 52.5% and 96.5%.[14] Such integration, however, was by no means balanced. Some medium-sized companies, such as Sinclair, concentrated on crude pipelines and refining; others focused on refining and marketing. None of the major firms attempted to balance crude, transportation, refining, and marketing. Some continued to be crude-heavy and others crude-light.

Although the pace and extent of backward integration varied with time and circumstances, forward integration into marketing did not. In the years after 1910 the leaders concentrated on building marketing and distribution networks for the sale of gasoline; these required more complex and extensive organizations than those for the sale of kerosene. They called for an investment in more and larger storage-tank stations, delivery trucks, and roadside pumps—an expensive investment that refiners had more incentive to make than did independent jobbers.[15] By 1929, therefore, only 18.9% of refinery products were still sold through independent wholesalers.[16] Many of these were captives of the processors of their supplies, for in that year 91.4% of the total number of bulk storage stations were owned by the refiners—17,972 bulk stations in all, a significant investment in product-specific distribution facilities.

Although the integrated refiners invested extensively in wholesaling, they were reluctant to do so in retailing. In 1929 only 7.6% of sales of refined petroleum products were distributed through company-owned retail outlets. Not only was the cost of this investment high, involving the purchase of real estate in hundreds of scattered locations, but also it required the establishment of an extensive administrative network. In marketing gasoline, firms increasingly preferred to "lease, lend, or sell gasoline pumps and storage to owners of retail outlets who in turn would distribute the products of the company supplying the equipment."[17] Like the makers of office and agricultural machinery in the 1880s, gasoline producers preferred to reduce potential transaction costs in retailing by organizing networks of franchised dealers. The number of company-owned retailing outlets dropped off quickly during the depression of the 1930s. By 1939 only 1.7% of the total output reached the final customer through such outlets.

As their marketing networks expanded, the major companies enlarged their output. But only those that had established their marketing positions abroad before World War I continued to have substantial sales abroad. These included four Standard Oil companies—those of New Jersey, New York, and California, as well as Vacuum Oil, a producer of lubricants.[18] They also included The Texas Company and Gulf. (Pure Oil's European marketing had come under Standard's control in 1911 just before the Supreme Court's decision.) These companies continued to do their refining in the United States. As late as 1928 Jersey Standard, which remained the largest oil company in the world, still concentrated 80.6% of its domestic output (much of which was still shipped abroad) in four U.S. works—two neighboring refineries in New Jersey, one in Louisiana, and one in Texas.[19]

In the 1920s these companies began to build refineries in Canada and Europe, partly to support the requirements of their marketing organization, partly because of rising tariffs, and partly because of the reduced costs of shipping crude oil.[20] In the making of these investments abroad the cost calculations to determine optimal plant size became increasingly complex. In competing for market share in world trade, Jersey Standard remained the leader; but it was losing its share to Socony and Texas, to a small degree, and, to a greater degree, to the two leading international challengers—Royal Dutch–Shell and Anglo-Persian Oil. (Anglo-Persian Oil—which would become British Petroleum—had replaced the prewar German oil companies to become, after Royal Dutch–Shell, the third major player in the global oligopoly.)

The extent and nature of this investment abroad is indicated by a report made in 1932 by the U.S. Bureau of Foreign and Domestic Commerce.[21] At that time eleven American companies were operating sixty-one refineries in foreign countries. Most were small and were designed to meet local demand (particularly for special products), to supplement primary flows, and to get under tariff barriers. Total employment at the sixty-one was only 1,793. In 1939 the number of refineries abroad was fifty-eight. Of these, nineteen were located close to crude-oil-producing fields and were refining largely for local markets, and thirty-nine had been built near the major consumer markets. Of the latter, twenty-five were located in Europe. Fifty of the fifty-eight refineries were owned by three companies—Jersey Standard with twenty-eight, Socony-Vacuum with fifteen, and Texas with seven.[22] (Socony had merged with Vacuum in 1931, and in 1936 Standard Oil of California and Texaco—name changed from Texas Company in 1926—formed a joint venture, Caltex, to market in the Orient.) For these three, especially Jersey Standard, the coordination of flows from the oil fields to the refineries and to the marketing outlets became an increasingly complicated task—one of the most critical functions carried out by the central corporate office.[23]

American oil companies also moved abroad through backward integration. Between the end of World War I and about 1927, shortages of domestic crude caused the American firms to explore, obtain, and extract crude oil in many parts of the world in order to assure themselves control of a minimum certain supply. But in 1926 the opening of vast new fields in East Texas and Louisiana brought a massive oversupply, which was intensified when the Great Depression stabilized and then reduced demand. The resulting surplus caused a number of leading American oil firms, including Standard of Indiana, Atlantic Refining, Associated Oil, Tide Water, and Union Oil, to withdraw from their overseas investments in production.[24]

Those who withdrew usually sold out to the most active firms marketing abroad—Jersey Standard, Socony-Vacuum, and Texaco. Meanwhile, two other American firms, Standard of California and Gulf, retained their overseas marketing networks and did not withdraw from overseas crude production. Accordingly, five American companies—Jersey Standard, Socony-Vacuum, Texaco, California Standard, and Gulf—found themselves in a strong position to exploit the massive post–World War II increase in demand for oil. And those five American companies, along with Royal Dutch–Shell and British Petroleum—the so-called Seven Sisters—continued to dominate the global oligopoly after World War II.

The rest of the major U.S. oil producers concentrated on the domestic market, which grew rapidly, at least until the Great Depression. There the leaders competed less on the basis of price and more by effective performance in each of the functional activities. Until 1911 the Standard Oil Company of New Jersey had set the industry's prices, although after 1900 the independents had challenged its leadership on the West Coast and in the Southwest. The breakup of the company, the further opening of new fields, and the automobile boom created a much more competitive situation. Between 1913 and 1915 the former Standard Oil companies became the price leaders in their own regional marketing areas. (The Court in its 1911 decision initially restricted the newly formed companies to specific areas.)[25] As the Federal Trade Commission pointed out in 1920, "In most of the marketing areas east of the Rocky Mountains, as in California, Standard . . . companies usually take the lead in announcing price changes, while other companies follow. Occasionally the Texas company and the Gulf company take the initiative. [But] prices announced by the Standard companies are generally the accepted market price."[26] Such price leadership did not call for collusion. The leaders based the prices on their costs, reflecting both capacity and demand, and the others followed. The leaders kept the prices high enough for the smaller firms to make a profit, thus assuring themselves (given their volume) an even greater profit. Only in the worst years of the depression, from 1931 to 1935, did the industry experience a severe "price war"—discounting and rebating.[27] Otherwise, the leaders had little incentive to cut prices: not only was the demand for petroleum products relatively inelastic, but the Standard companies were sensitive to the accusation of price cutting, which had been a major charge against Standard Oil in the antitrust case of 1911.

Indeed, as the Federal Trade Commission reported in 1920, "competition is more directed to developing facilities for getting business than obtaining it by underselling."[28] But this functional competition included more than marketing. In refining, transportation, and crude-oil production it meant constant effort to reduce costs and improve performance. In refining, this effort was focused on ways to increase the minimum efficient scale of production and to extract more gasoline—increasingly the most profitable product—from the crude-oil input. The companies' refining departments and their recently established research departments developed, and then invested in, the means to achieve more continuous production processes and to produce improved, higher-octane gasoline.[29] Their innovations included continuous distillation (Atlantic Refining), the Burton thermal-pressure cracking process (Standard Oil of Indiana), the Holmes-Manly process (Texaco), the tube and tank process and the fluid continuous catalytic process (Jersey Standard), and the Houdry catalytic cracking process (developed in the United States by Sun Oil). The only major innovation developed by a firm not among the leading companies was the Dubbs cracking process, financed by J. Ogden Armour from his meatpacking fortune. By the end of the twenties the large refineries on the Gulf Coast had raised minimum efficient scale to a daily throughput of thirty-two thousand barrels of crude, the greater part of which became gasoline.[30] As a result, between 1919 and 1929 refinery throughputs expanded nearly 270%, while the number of establishments increased by only about 22% and the number of employees by about 29%.

Strategic competition for market share, as contrasted with functional competition, primarily involved expansion into new geographical areas.[31] Texas and California companies expanded north and east, and the former Standard companies moved out of their original marketing regions established by the dissolution decree. Some expanded by direct investment in marketing and distribution facilities, others by acquisition.[32] Some firms moved more quickly and aggressively into new products, such as lubricants for automobiles and fuel oil for home heating.[33] In all cases, expansion required close attention to the marketing organizations—that is, to locating bulk stations, selecting franchise dealers, and advertising both locally and nationally.

As a result of such strategic competition, rival companies were able to increase their share substantially in the marketing areas that had originally been those of the former Standard companies. Between 1921 and 1926 the share controlled by the Standard group in the domestic market fell from an estimated 50–55% to 37–40%.[34] Estimates for the group are not available for the period immediately following 1926, but they do exist for individual firms. Between 1926 and 1938 the share of Jersey Standard in its domestic marketing territories dropped from 43.2% to 28.3%, that of Socony-Vacuum dropped from 46.1% to 24.3%, of Atlantic Refining from 44.5% to 21.9%, and of Standard of California from 28.7% to 17.7%. (Although the constraints of the dissolution decree had been lifted, the former Standard companies still did not sell nationally but continued to concentrate their marketing in their original regional territories.) The leading gainers were the large competitors, such as Texaco, Gulf, and Shell, not the smaller independents.

By the 1920s the oil companies were providing an almost perfect textbook case of functional and strategic competition for market share. The transformation from monopoly to modern oligopoly was complete. In the domestic markets, where all but Jersey Standard and Socony sold most of their output, the leading oil companies made no formal agreements about price and production. Abroad, it was only after the oil glut of the late 1920s that Jersey Standard, and later Socony, Texaco, Gulf, and Atlantic Refining, attempted, with varying success, to implement written agreements to stabilize price and output (see Chapter 8).

The increasing competition for market share at home and abroad encouraged the oil companies to invest in research and development. Before 1914 their research laboratories had been little more than testing and control units at the refinery. Although technicians in such units worked in an ad hoc manner to improve the quality of the product and the speed of throughput, they were few in number. In 1921—the first year data are available—the oil industry employed only 159 scientific personnel and 246 others in general research positions, well below the number employed in chemicals, electrical machinery, rubber, and transportation equipment.[35] In 1919 Walter Teagle, President of Jersey Standard, observed in a letter to A. Cotton Bedford, the chairman of the board: "The General Electric and other concerns of a like character lay great stress upon their research department. They consider this department on a parity in importance with the manufacture and sales end of their business. Our research department up to date is a joke, pure and simple; we have no such thing."[36]

During the 1920s Jersey Standard and the other large oil companies built and expanded their research facilities; they continued to do so even during the depressed 1930s. Jersey Standard had an extensive department in place by 1923. Standard Oil of California formed its research organization in 1920, Standard of Indiana in 1922, Atlantic Refining in 1924, Shell in 1928, and Gulf in 1929. By 1933 the industry employed 9.1% of the total scientific personnel working in American industry. By 1940 the percentage had risen to 10.3%, third behind chemicals and electrical machinery. These scientific personnel were concentrated in the large laboratories of the industry's leaders. By 1940, 58.5% of scientific personnel in the oil industry were employed by 19% of the industry's industrial laboratories, and these were the largest laboratories in terms of personnel and expenditures.[37]

Such investment in research brought improvements in product and process. Until World War II it led only occasionally to product diversification, because concentration on exploiting the economies of scale correspondingly reduced opportunities to exploit economies of scope. Refineries turning out a full line of petroleum products, including gasoline, kerosene, lubricants, and fuel oil, also produced petrochemicals, often as by-products; but the companies' personnel and facilities in transportation, marketing, and research were only equipped to handle petroleum, not chemicals. Williams Haynes, the historian of the American chemical industry, observed in the early 1940s:

> Production of chemicals by the petroleum industry appeared to be economically and technically sound, but most petroleum executives could not see what appeared to them to be a tiny market for a multitude of chemicals produced by a complexity of operations and sold to a long and diversified list of customers, tasks for which they had neither the technical nor the sales staffs.[38]

Of the twenty-two petroleum companies on the 1948 list of the top two hundred industrials in the United States, only four had begun to diversify into chemicals before World War II. Standard Oil of California, Shell Company of California, and Phillips Petroleum (which had become a major challenger by making the three-pronged investment in the 1920s in the newly opened Oklahoma fields) produced fertilizers and insecticides for the California market. Jersey Standard, with the industry's largest laboratories, developed and marketed antifreeze and other isopropyl products.[39] That company, however, concentrated its research effort on the development of synthetic gasoline and synthetic rubber, neither of which was commercialized before the outbreak of war. The rest of the oil companies preferred to sell their by-products as feed stock to chemical firms. For example, Union Carbide, the nation's second largest chemical company and a pioneer in the production of petrochemicals in the United States, set up one major processing plant immediately adjacent to Standard Oil of Indiana's refinery at Whiting, Indiana, and another next to South Penn Oil Company's refinery near Charlestown, West Virginia.[40] Only when World War II began and the synthetic rubber program required a large investment in petrochemicals, did the American petroleum companies acquire the skills and facilities—the organizational capabilities—necessary to compete seriously in the production and distribution of petrochemicals.

The collective history of the leading enterprises in the American oil industry from its origin through World War II provides an impressive example of the beginnings and growth of the modern industrial enterprise. The first mover solidified its position through legal consolidation, administrative centralization, and then a continuing and extensive investment in refining, marketing, and management. The first real opportunity for American companies to challenge Standard's dominance came only when demand for the specific product that was being refined changed and new sources of supply became available. The successful challengers were those that made the interrelated three-pronged investment. These challengers grew at first by vertical integration, moving backward and forward to reduce transaction costs and to protect their initial investments. When the oil glut came in the late 1920s, several sold off their crude holdings. They competed for market share and profits with one another and with the successor companies of Standard Oil through functional efficiencies much more than by price. By advertising and upgrading service stations and dealer relations they expanded market share. By improving processes of production, by more efficient coordination of flows, and by effective control over operations, they reduced costs and so increased profits—profits that were used to finance continued growth. They grew primarily by moving into new geographical markets in the United States. But because of the strength of Standard Oil and the European leaders, only the largest challengers established networks overseas. And because of their concentration on the economies of scale, even fewer attempted to diversify by utilizing the economies of scope.

Long before World War II, salaried managers with little or no equity in the companies they administered were making the decisions that determined the growth of their enterprises and of the industry as a whole. At Sun, Phillips, Sinclair, Gulf, and possibly one or two others, the founders did continue to participate as full-time managers in top-level, decision-making positions. At Gulf, for example, William Latimer Mellon (the experienced oil man who in 1902 planned and built a refinery large enough to exploit scale economies and then established a marketing network extensive enough to give Gulf first-mover advantages in the Texas fields) remained president until 1930 and continued as chairman of the board until 1948.[41] But in the former Standard companies— New Jersey, New York (Socony-Vacuum), California, Indiana, and Atlantic Refining—members of the Rockefeller family did not even participate as outside directors. By the 1930s the initial large investors were no longer influential at the older Tide Water and Pure Oil companies, nor at the newer Texaco, Union of California, and Richfield enterprises.[42] And in striking contrast to the history of the industry on the European continent (see Chapter 11), no investment banker ever played a significant, ongoing role as a decision-maker in a major American oil company. By the 1920s all firms were administered by experienced, full-time, career managers, the great majority of whom held only a tiny percentage of stock in the companies they operated.

Rubber: A Stable Oligopoly

The oil industry differed from other American industries in that during the first decades of its history its major markets were in Europe, not in the United States. It differed, too, from most other American industries because of its particularly powerful cost advantages of scale, which were equally impressive only in metals. Profound and sudden changes in both markets and sources of supply were necessary to transform the oil monopoly into an oligopoly.

In rubber (Group 30; see Appendixes A.1–A.3) improvements in the technology of production brought significant, but not comparable, cost advantages. In this industry the rapid growth in demand for automobile tires (a demand that increased a hundredfold from 1910 to 1930) created opportunities to exploit large economies of scale. The first companies to build tire plants large enough to take advantage of these economies, to create national and international marketing organizations, and to recruit the necessary managers remained the industry's leaders.

The contrasting early years of these two modern industries, oil and rubber, reflect the differences between both processes of production and the markets for their products. The overall market for finished rubber goods was much smaller than for oil, in terms of the value of output.[43] Of more importance, the processing of crude rubber permitted a much broader array of finished items to be made than did crude-oil refining. In oil the major products—kerosene, gasoline, lubricants, and fuel oil—were processed in one refinery, at times even from the same run of crude oil. In rubber each of the many items made required particular admixtures and accelerators in the chemical processes of vulcanizing, as well as different machinery for molding, extruding, and processing. The industry came to produce three basic types of goods—apparel, such as boots, gloves, and rainwear; industrial items, such as hoses, belting, flooring, and insulating materials; and, most important of all, tires.

In each of the first two subindustries the cost advantages of scale were much lower than in oil. For that reason no entrepreneur or group of entrepreneurs succeeded in achieving a monopoly comparable to that of Rockefeller's Standard Oil Company. During the last quarter of the nineteenth century, however, output rapidly increased as a result of cumulative innovations in the processes of production, as well as improved transportation. The processors responded, as they did in so many American industries, by trying to control price and production.[44] A series of attempts at combination finally culminated in the formation in 1892 of an industry-wide holding company for each of the two major product lines—the United States Rubber Company for apparel and the Mechanical Rubber Company for industrial products. (In 1899 the latter, enlarged by further acquisitions, became the Rubber Goods Manufacturing Company.) In both subindustries major companies stayed out of the combinations. Because initially neither of the combines centralized its administration, rationalized production, or invested in distribution, independent firms, such as B. F. Goodrich Company in industrial rubber, could grow large by building nationwide marketing organizations and then increasing production.[45]

In 1902, however, the new president of United States Rubber, Samuel P. Colt, began to transform the company into a centrally administered, integrated enterprise by making extensive investments in production, distribution, and management.[46] In 1905 he directed his company's takeover of the Rubber Goods Manufacturing Company and reorganized the acquisition along similar lines. In response to U.S. Rubber's move into industrial rubber, Goodrich, then the leader in that subindustry, moved into apparel. It acquired facilities and personnel for the making of boots, rainwear, and other items. And both firms began to invest in a third product line, pneumatic tires for bicycles.

The coming of the automobile, and with it a voracious demand for tires, further transformed the rubber industry, quickly creating a global oligopoly. In the United States two new companies, Firestone Tire & Rubber and Goodyear Tire & Rubber, took the lead in producing tires, soon followed by Goodrich and United States Rubber.[47] Abroad, each of the leading industrial countries quickly produced a giant of its own—Dunlop in Britain, Michelin in France, Continental in Germany, and Pirelli in Italy. All had built plants by 1906. The competitive advantages of these first movers in the American and European markets were so strong that even the two large American companies that were formed a little later to exploit the rapidly growing *replacement* tire market (that is, for tires not sold to automobile manufacturers as originals for new cars)—Fisk Rubber in 1910 and General Tire & Rubber in 1915—remained junior members of the oligopoly.[48] The sharp drop in demand during the depression eliminated (as it did for automobile makers) nearly all the small and most of the medium-sized producers. In 1935 the top four first movers in the United States accounted for 80% of the tires shipped from domestic plants.[49] As late as 1973, all four remained among the five rubber companies in the top two hundred U.S. industrials. The fifth was General Tire, which had replaced Fisk on the list when the United States Rubber Company acquired Fisk in 1939.

Although the potential for economies of scale was less in the production of footwear and other rubber apparel than in tires, it was much greater than in the making of leather boots and shoes. In 1935 the four largest makers of rubber footwear produced 80% of the output and the largest eight accounted for 100%.[50] The total number of plants producing rubber footwear in 1939 was 13. By contrast, the number of establishments making leather shoes at that time was 933. In the leather-shoe industry, where scale economies were small, the four largest companies accounted for 28% and the top eight for 33% of all domestic production.

The makers of both rubber apparel and tires continued to rely on their own sales organizations to wholesale their products. In 1935, 40.2% of rubber footwear was sold through the manufacturers' own wholesale networks, 29.7% was shipped directly from the factory to retail dealers, and 10.3% went directly to large customers. Less than 20% was sold through independent wholesalers or jobbers.

In tires the share marketed by the independent wholesalers declined even more rapidly. As the replacement market grew larger than the market for original equipment, it was eagerly sought after by mass retailers. A 1926 contract with Sears, Roebuck quickly increased Goodyear's market share. The new service stations, including those franchised or owned by the petroleum companies, also began to compete for that market by buying tires from the smaller producers. By 1929, 46.8% of the tires produced in the United States were sold through the manufacturers' wholesaling branches, primarily to franchised dealers. (Another 2.2% went to company-owned retailers.) In addition, 17.0% were sold directly to retailers and 25.6% directly to industrial users—primarily the large automobile companies—leaving only 8.2% to be sold to independent wholesalers.[51]

The rapid growth of the market and the concomitant expansion of the American tire companies' marketing organizations resulted, at least until 1930, in an increased investment in manufacturing facilities both at home and, to a lesser extent, abroad. Branch plants were built in the United States, largely to produce footwear and industrial rubber goods. The domestic production of tires, however, remained concentrated in giant works, particularly in Akron, Ohio. All the leaders built plants in Canada, to avoid the Canadian tariff and also to benefit from preference duties in the British Empire for goods manufactured in Canada. Goodrich led the American firms in European manufacturing. Before World War I it had built a tire plant in France and made an alliance with Continental, the German leader.[52] In 1917 Goodrich had seventy-five branch sales offices in the United States and twenty-one overseas. By 1921 the overseas offices totaled thirty-seven.

It was only after British automobile production started to boom in the 1920s, however, that American firms began to produce tires extensively abroad—and then, except for Goodrich, only after a British 33.3% ad valorem duty went into effect in May 1927. Goodrich built a British plant in 1924, followed by Goodyear in 1927 and Firestone in 1928. (Michelin and Pirelli did the same in 1927.) Comparable rises in tariffs led Goodyear to build plants in Australia in 1927, Argentina in 1931, and Brazil in 1937.[53] The American presence abroad, especially in Europe, prevented the single dominant company in each of the major countries from achieving a monopoly in its domestic market.

As they expanded their marketing at home and abroad, the U.S. rubber manufacturers increased their investment in research and development. The two older, more diversified firms, Goodrich and United States Rubber, made a larger investment in research and development than Firestone, Goodyear, and the other tire companies. All concentrated on the development of intermediates to provide better accelerators, to speed up processes of vulcanization, and so to improve the general performance of tires and other products. As a result of these cumulative improvements in process carried out within the major firms, production per man-hour in the tire industry increased 433% between 1914 and 1935, the greatest percentage increase of any American industry in those years.[54] Although the rubber industry was much smaller and relatively more labor-intensive than the oil industry, in 1921 more scientific personnel were employed in rubber than in oil, accounting for 5.7% of all such employees in U.S. manufacturing industries, as compared with 4.4% in oil. In total employment of scientific personnel the rubber industry was fourth, after chemicals, electrical machinery, and metals. In research intensity (the ratio of scientific and engineering personnel in research laboratories per thousand workers) rubber was second only to chemicals.[55] By World War II, however, several industries had passed rubber in numbers of personnel, but only oil and electrical equipment had passed it in research intensity.

From 1900 on, rubber manufacturers competed functionally and strategically for market share. To a greater degree than most American firms of their day, they concentrated on improving both product and process. They also competed in the purchasing of raw materials, each having a somewhat different strategy for backward integration. They differed too, in the extent and uses of their marketing organizations. And, like all mass producers of consumer products, in marketing they tried to differentiate their product from those of their competitors through extensive advertising. Nevertheless, advertising costs in 1940 were only a little over 2%, out of a total selling expense of about 15%, per dollar of net sales (see Figure 6).

There is little readily available data on price leadership in the industry, although a recent study indicates that in replacement tires "prices tended to move broadly in line and the Goodyear (earlier the B. F. Goodrich) wholesale list served as a standard." There is more information on market share. In 1915 United States Rubber was the largest producer of original tires with 21.8% of the U.S. market. Two years later when the figures for replacements became available, the company had 10.1% of that business and had dropped to 14.3% of the market for originals. During the next decade it lost market share rapidly, falling by 1924 to 4.6% of originals and 7.4% of replacements. By 1928 it had increased to 8.4% of originals and dropped to 5.6% of replacements. In 1929 members of the du Pont family acquired a sizable stock holding in United States Rubber, and they subsequently installed new management and reorganized the administrative structure. The company then embarked on a series of new marketing and production policies that made it once again an effective competitor.

In the 1930s its market share for originals averaged nearly 30%, and its share of the much larger replacement market—so essential to maintaining throughput—grew from 16.4% in 1935 to 30.9% by 1940.[56]

The leaders competed strategically as well as functionally, and their strategies for long-term growth reflected the product-specificity of their initial investments in production and distribution. Those that had begun as tire companies—Goodyear, Firestone, and the smaller General Tire and Fisk—continued to focus on exploiting the economies of scale by concentrating on their single lines. They made little attempt to transfer resources into other products. Instead they integrated backward by producing the textiles used for tire cords: Firestone and Goodyear even began growing cotton in the United States and investing in rubber plantations in Liberia and Sumatra. Those overseas investments were made partly to assure continuing high-volume inputs at precise specifications and partly to protect against price increases determined by the international crude-rubber cartel formed in 1922 by the British, Indian, Dutch, and Siamese governments.[57]

The two older leaders, United States Rubber and Goodrich, whose apparel and industrial lines antedated the automobile tire, invested much less in raw and semifinished materials and much more in research and development. By World War I their large development departments were two of the largest in American industry. Both made improvements in vulcanization and other rubber processing. In the rubber industry, as in the food and chemical industries (see Chapter 5), complex chemical processes of production encouraged the exploitation of the economies of scope because a number of products could be made from the same intermediate materials and processes. In the 1920s both companies began to use their rubber-making facilities and skills to commercialize new products for new markets. Goodrich pioneered in the development of polyvinyl chlorine resins, of plastics, and of various rubber-based chemicals. At the same time United States Rubber led the way in sprayed rubber, latex thread, and other end products based on the new methods and materials. Because these two companies employed their facilities and skilled personnel to make a number of products, not just the tire, they found it easier to develop a wider variety of commercial goods in their laboratories than did those firms that concentrated almost exclusively on tire production.[58]

Growth through diversification based on economies of scope brought administrative reorganization. Whereas the companies that continued to concentrate on tire production retained their centralized, functionally departmentalized structures until well after World War II, United States Rubber in 1929 and Goodrich in 1930 adopted a multidivisional structure to exploit the economies of scope more effectively in production, distribution, and particularly research and development.[59] But these two remained the only companies in the global oligopoly to adopt a strategy of production diversification before World War II and the only ones whose continuing growth after 1920 relied as much on the dynamics of scope as on those of scale.

The history of the leading enterprises in the rubber industry follows closely the patterns outlined earlier in this study (Chapters 2 and 3). Cumulative innovation in production brought merger. Once the merged enterprises and the leading enterprises outside the merger made the three-pronged investment in production, distribution, and management, they became the industry's leaders. The coming of a new product, the automobile tire, permitted a small number of other enterprises to enter the industry by making comparable investments in the production and distribution of tires. Although the leaders followed different strategies for backward integration, they all continued to expand their marketing organizations abroad and, primarily in order to get behind tariff walls, to build plants that supported their overseas marketing networks. All invested in research and development, but those that already had a diversified product line before the coming of the tire acquired the organizational capabilities to grow more rapidly through product diversification than did the new companies. Although the players in the oligopoly remained the same, changing market shares and profits reflected continuing functional and strategic competition.

Industrial Materials: Evolutionary and Revolutionary Technological Change

In the four material-producing industries—paper (Group 26); stone, clay, and glass (Group 32); fabricated metals (Group 34); and primary metals (Group 33)—growth by diversification was even more exceptional than it was in rubber or oil. The large firms continued to concentrate on their primary product lines and depended on economies of scale rather than scope to maintain market power and to provide for continued growth. In these two-digit industrial groups the large integrated firms appeared—and continued to thrive—primarily in those subindustries (the three- and four-digit SIC categories) whose economies of scale in production were largest and whose products went to the greatest number of customers. The material-producing industries differed from those of oil and rubber in that industrial products constituted a much greater share of their output; such products were thus marketed to businesses—manufacturers, processors, or contractors—rather than to consumers as end users. That marketing effort, however, required an extensive investment in distribution facilities and personnel. Industrial marketing was vitally important for the enterprises in these industries, and the companies' own sales forces played a major role in distributing their products (Table 10).

In the material-producing industries the coming of oligopoly reflected the rapidity of technological change in the processes of production. When this change was evolutionary, as in oil and rubber apparel (where it was based on a

Table 10. Manufacturers' domestic distribution channels and concentration ratios in materials industries, 1929–1954 (in percentages).

		Distribution channels						Concentration ratios					
		Via own channels				Via intermediaries		Four largest firms			Eight largest firms		
		Own outlets		Direct sales									
Year	Industry	Wholesale	Retail	Industrial	Consumer	Wholesalers	Retailers	1935	1947	1954	1935	1947	1954
	Group 26												
	Paper												
1929	Total	3.8	0.0	51.8	—	39.1	5.3	—	—	—	—	—	—
1939	Total	14.9	0.4	48.2	0.3	30.5	5.7	—	—	—	34	39	42
	Pulp	25.9	—	56.3	—	17.8	—	—	—	—	—	—	—
	Paper and paperboard mills	22.0	0.0	40.1	—	35.2	2.7	—	—	19	—	—	31
	Group 32												
	Stone, clay, and glass												
1929	Total	6.7	0.1	38.7	1.8	48.2	4.5	—	—	—	—	—	—
1939	Total	28.3	0.9	35.2	2.6	21.1	11.9	—	—	—	—	—	—
	Flat glass	66.4	0.0	19.5	0.0	14.1	0.0	—	—	90	—	—	99
	Glass containers	38.4	0.0	46.9	0.3	12.9	1.5	—	63	63	—	79	78
	Cement, hydraulic	39.6	0.0	20.0	0.0	17.4	23.0	29	30	31	44	45	48
	Gypsum products	67.7	0.0	5.9	0.0	21.1	5.3	—	85	90	—	94	97
	Abrasive products	37.4	0.0	37.7	0.0	24.0	0.9	67	49	50	74	56	58
	Asbestos products	56.3	0.0	22.1	—	20.1	1.5	—	—	—	—	72	73
	Group 34												
	Fabricated metals												
1929	Total	—	—	—	—	—	—	—	—	—	—	—	—
1939	Total	—	—	—	—	—	—	—	—	—	—	—	—
	Tin cans	3.0	0.0	92.1	0.2	2.9	1.8	80	78	80	85	86	88

Sources: For distribution channels, U.S. Bureau of the Census, *Distribution of Manufacturers' Sales, 1939* (Washington, D.C., 1942), table 3, appropriate industry sections; for concentration ratios, U.S. Bureau of the Census, *Concentration Ratios in Manufacturing Industry, 1958* (Washington, D.C., 1962), table 2, appropriate industry sections.

number of incremental improvements in product and process, on the availability of new sources of power, such as electricity, and on new sources of supply), the three-pronged investment usually came after merger. When changes in production process were more revolutionary, the small number of competitors grew more often by direct investment than by merger. In these cases oligopoly was only occasionally preceded by merger.

PAPER

In paper (Group 26; see Appendixes A.1–A.3), nearly all the companies on the list of the top two hundred were producers of pulp, newsprint, and paperboard, product lines where economies of scale were substantial. By 1930 more specialized firms, such as American Writing Paper and Bemis Bag, were no longer on the list. Because the production of pulp and paper demanded the availability of massive amounts of cheap power in close proximity to raw materials (transporting lumber was more expensive than shipping paper), these big companies concentrated their mills in the lumber regions of Canada.[60] They had their own sales forces to market their products. In 1939 more than 80% of the pulp and close to two-thirds of the paper and paperboard produced were sold to customers by the companies' sales forces. Their marketing organizations, however, remained small and not highly specialized.

The basic innovation that transformed papermaking from a labor-intensive to a capital-intensive industry was the development of machinery that could make the product from wood pulp rather than from rags. A growing shortage of rags, the increasing demand for paper (particularly newsprint), and the availability of timber for wood pulp led to the adoption of German processes. This innovation took hold in the United States during the 1870s. By the 1880s those pioneers that had large mills close to sources of timber and water had driven out the smaller pioneers. (The water was needed for both power and removal of waste.) By the 1890s the newsprint industry had become, in the words of Naomi Lamoreaux, "dominated by at least nine large firms that produced a homogeneous product and were equivalently equipped to compete for sales." After the 1880s technological innovation in this industry, as Avi Cohen has emphasized, "took the form of small, evolutionary changes rather than radical technological overhauls."[61]

As in many other new capital-intensive industries, increased output and intensified competition led to the formation of a nationwide holding company, in this case the International Paper Company. The merger was carried out in 1898 by the manufacturers themselves. The holding company moved rather slowly, in the manner of the United States Rubber Company, to centralize its administration, rationalize its production, and build its sales arm. Almost a decade passed before the pattern of modern oligopolistic competition emerged, with International Paper as the price leader.[62]

International Paper's delay in making the essential investments that could give it market power permitted the independents to gain a foothold in the industry. And they continued to gain market share from the leader because paper markets were extensive and growing, because the cost advantages of scale were smaller than in oil and tire production, and because marketing was relatively undifferentiated. Thus newsprint and other paper products required fewer product-specific facilities and personnel. International Paper's share of the market dropped, according to one estimate, from 65% in 1901 to 18% in 1929. Nevertheless, the share it lost was not captured by new entries into the industry but by established firms.

After the industry stabilized, the members of the oligopoly remained much the same. The changes in market share and profits are reflected in the changing position of the long-established firms on the list of the top two hundred. These firms made little attempt to market abroad. Moreover, the technology of production was not complex enough to provide an incentive for a substantial investment in research and development. By World War II the paper industry, along with fabricated metals (Group 34), had the lowest research intensity of all industries in which the large firms have always clustered. Only those labor-intensive industries where the large enterprise rarely appeared—leather, apparel, textiles, lumber, furniture, and publishing and printing—had a lower ratio of scientific personnel (in research laboratories) to employees.

STONE, CLAY, GLASS, AND CEMENT

In Group 32 (see Appendixes A.1–A.3) the large firms have clustered in glass, gypsum, abrasives, asbestos, and cement. In these industries, improved production technologies brought greater cost advantages of scale than in paper and, at the same time, required a much larger specific investment in distribution. High-volume throughput and product-specific investment in distribution brought industrial concentration (see Table 10). The glass industry remained highly concentrated because the processes of production became increasingly continuous and the distribution of fragile products required specialized facilities. The cement industry was less concentrated because the optimal size in relation to markets (markets limited by the cost of transporting the finished product) was much smaller and, as in paper, few product-specific distribution facilities were required. Not surprisingly, whereas in 1917 there were two glass and two cement firms in the top two hundred, in 1948 there were three glass companies (two were the largest in Group 32) but no cement firms. In the manufacturing of flat glass, glass containers, gypsum, abrasives, and asbestos, the pioneer firms that improved existing processes or adopted new technologies quickly dominated their respective industries. Their histories reveal significant variations in the beginning and continued growth of the modern industrial enterprise.

In glass the new large firms became concentrated in flat glass and in bottles and other containers. The category "flat glass" includes both plate glass and window glass: plate glass is heavy glass used in mirrors, store windows, and building construction; window glass is the lighter glass used mostly in residential housing. In plate glass, the high minimum efficient scale—which resulted from improving existing technology in a relatively incremental manner—quickly brought industrial concentration both in the United States and abroad. Window glass and containers continued to be produced by labor-intensive handwork until the invention of new, continuous-process machinery vastly increased throughput and revolutionized both of these subindustries.

In the production of plate glass, three developments (in addition to improved transportation and communication) greatly increased throughput and reduced unit cost during the 1880s. One was the invention, by Frederick and William Siemens of Dresden, Germany, of the continuous-process tank furnace. The second was the use of gas (instead of coal) to heat the furnace. The third was the application of electricity to power and to control the speed of glassmaking machinery. [63]

In plate glass the first mover was the Pittsburgh Plate Glass Company, formed in 1893 when John Pitcairn joined John Ford to build a large plant at Creighton, Pennsylvania, which soon incorporated these new techniques. In the depressed years of the 1890s Pitcairn merged all but three of the nation's smaller producers into the large company, which by 1900 was the acknowledged price leader in the glass industry and which has remained the largest glass company in the United States during the twentieth century. Pitcairn quickly centralized administration, concentrated and relocated production facilities to achieve greater cost advantages of scale, and then built an extensive, nation-wide network of warehouses and sales offices. This last, costly move led Pit-cairn to a break with his partner. Ford left to set up Edward Ford Plate Glass with his two brothers, thus becoming his former partner's major competitor. In 1900 Pittsburgh Plate Glass began to use its distribution facilities and per-sonnel to sell paints both to contractors and to hardware stores. To bolster this trade the company acquired a maker of paints and brushes. But that initial attempt to exploit economies of scope in distribution would not be repeated by Pittsburgh Plate Glass or any other glass company for half a century. [64]

Pitcairn's success stands in striking contrast to the two turn-of-the-century mergers of manufacturers of cut glass and tableware, which continued to use the traditional handicraft production methods. Unable to exploit the economies of scale, they failed. The United States Glass Company, formed in 1891, still operated twelve plants in 1918; but according to Warren Scoville, the leading historian of the glass industry: "It rarely had shown any profits except in its first year." The other merger led to the formation of the National Glass Company in 1899, but it had dismembered itself by 1905, turning back its factories to their original owners. This was also the course followed in 1905 by National Wall Paper, the product of a merger in another, comparably labor-intensive industry. [65]

In window glass, technological innovation may have saved the American Window Glass Company from a similar fate. This enterprise, a holding company, was formed in 1899 after earlier, unsuccessful attempts had been made by the window-glass industry to control price and production through the American Window Manufacturers' Association, established in 1880. The new company had a near monopoly on window-glass production, but it made little attempt to centralize and rationalize either production or distribution. Instead, its many plants continued to rely (in the German manner) on a selling syndicate, which had been formed in 1895 to market their products. The sales company operated until the federal government successfully brought an antitrust suit against American Window Glass in 1910. In the meantime, it had begun to invest in the newly developed production technology that was gradually replacing the existing hand processes. Although greatly increasing throughput, the new process was not a continuous one. The company was slow in adopting it, partly because of the resistance of the industry's labor union, and partly because it made no systematic attempt to build, rebuild, or relocate its plants in order to exploit the new technology fully. [66]

Therefore, when Michael Owens (who had already invented machinery to mass-produce bottles) perfected a new continuous process of pulling window glass in the form of sheets, American Window Glass was not yet effectively organized to meet the new competitor. Owens and E. L. Libbey, the senior partner and financier of the Owens Bottle Machine Company, had obtained patents for the new process in 1912 when the attempts of its inventor, Irving W. Colburn, to commercialize it had ended in bankruptcy. After spending four years perfecting the process, the two men formed the Libbey-Owens Sheet Glass Company and built a large plant at Kanawha City, West Virginia. [67] As late as 1920, executives at both American Window Glass and the largest British producer, Pilkington Brothers, still believed that glass could not be profitably produced by the Colburn process. [68] By 1921, however, throughput was already high enough to give Libbey-Owens a critical cost advantage; by 1926 it had gained 29% of the American window-glass market, and American Window Glass's share had dropped to 59%. [69]

By the 1920s Pittsburgh Plate Glass had also become a competitor by developing a third process for making window glass. In response Libbey-Owens moved into the production of plate glass by acquiring in 1920 Pittsburgh's major competitor, the smaller Ford company, and adopting the name Libbey-Owens-Ford Glass Company. Then in 1935 several smaller companies that had acquired a European (the Fourcault) process merged to form a single enterprise, Furco Glass. By then four companies were producing nearly all the window glass in the United States, with Libbey-Owens-Ford maintaining its share at 30%, Pittsburgh Plate Glass at about 25%, Furco at 25%, and American Window Glass trailing at 20%. In plate glass, Pittsburgh Plate Glass had clearly lost market share to Libbey-Owens-Ford. Thus in both plate and window glass, technological innovation proved to be a powerful factor in bringing about rapid change in market share and profits.

In the mass production of glass containers, technological change was similarly revolutionary. But because Michael Owens, who had invented the bottle-making machine in 1903, at first licensed his patent to others, production in the glass-container industry remained less concentrated than in plate and window glass. In 1910, however, after Owens and his backers had decided that large-scale production would be more profitable than licensing, the Owens Bottle Machine Company built a plant in West Virginia, set up a national sales organization, and then concentrated on expanding capacity—primarily by speeding up the production process. The company's major challenge came from the Illinois Glass Company, an early licensee that had developed a "feeder" system of production which differentiated it from the Owens vacuum process. In 1929 the two merged to become Owens-Illinois. [70]

Meanwhile, the glass industry's first movers had begun to expand overseas. Pittsburgh Plate Glass, to enhance its foreign competitive capabilities, established a plant in Belgium before World War I. In April 1921, as this plant was coming into full production after its postwar reconstruction, Libbey-Owens joined a group of Belgian investors to form the Compagnie Internationale pour la Fabrication Mechanique de Verre, which by 1929 was operating plants in France, Germany, Italy, and Spain, as well as Belgium. [71] In contrast, the Owens Bottle Machine Company pulled out of overseas manufacturing not long after its initial foray. When that firm had been licensing its patent in the United States, it was also building a works in Manchester, England; but in 1907 it sold those facilities to its British and German licensees. The purchasers, a cartel of producers using the older hand processes, shut down the Manchester plant and then used the license as a means of enforcing their price and output agreements. [72] At home, Pittsburgh Plate Glass and Libbey-Owens-Ford, while competing oligopolistically, followed the European mode of relying on contractual relations with the European first movers to maintain their market share abroad. Throughout the 1920s they remained relatively silent associates in the cartel arrangements negotiated primarily by Pilkington and the leading French firm, St. Gobain. As the depression deepened, American and European companies moved more aggressively into each other's markets. In 1934 the two American firms joined the European leaders in an agreement to divide all exports of plate glass to markets outside the United States by giving the Europeans 80% and the Americans 20%. [73]

The three largest glass firms—Pittsburgh Plate Glass, Owens-Illinois, and

Libbey-Owens-Ford—invested increasingly in research and development, as did Corning Glass, a major producer of light bulbs and other more specialized glass products. They concentrated on increasing throughput and quality. In addition, all four developed new products, such as glass fabrics, blocks, insulation, and improved optical glass. But except for Pittsburgh's very early move into paint, none of the large glass firms attempted before World War II to develop non-glass-based products.[74]

Although the two first movers in the modern abrasives industry—Norton and Carborundum—did not acquire assets large enough to be listed among the top two hundred, they were close to that group. Their most effective challenger—Minnesota Mining and Manufacturing—surpassed them to become 148th on the 1948 list. In abrasives, as in glass, technological change came in a revolutionary manner. The critical innovation was the use of electrolytic processes to produce synthetic materials at a much lower cost, and of much higher quality, than had previously been achieved with emery, garnets, crushed diamonds, and other natural abrasives. In 1891 Edward A. Acheson, the first to create a synthetic abrasive—silicon carbide—by an electrolytic process, formed the Carborundum Company. Four years later his company built a plant at Niagara Falls to assure the power needed for high-volume throughput. The Mellon family of Pittsburgh, who had assisted in the funding of this project, became the company's largest stockholders. Acheson, however, failed to build the organization essential to produce and distribute the new high-volume output. So, at the instigation of the Mellons, Frank W. Haskell took charge in 1901; he reorganized production and began building a worldwide marketing network.[75] In the same year Carborundum's major competitor, the Norton Company, which had begun operations in 1887 at Worcester, Massachusetts, obtained a comparable electrolytic synthetic (alumdum), set up its plant at Niagara Falls, and enlarged its sales force to global proportions.[76]

Both companies grew rapidly, though Carborundum moved ahead of Norton. Until the depression they produced together about two-thirds of the industry's total output.[77] Because their products—bonded abrasive paper and grinding wheels—required relatively little in the way of product-specific distribution personnel and facilities, they sold at home and abroad primarily through exclusive agents. Their own salaried sales forces worked with such agents in canvassing for sales, coordinating flow from factory to customer, and demonstrating the products; they also ran schools for grinding-machine operators. Norton's British agent was that country's leading machine maker, Alfred Herbert (see Chapter 7), and its agent in Germany and eastern Europe was Schuchard & Schutt. In 1908 Carborundum built a factory in Germany and, a little later, one in Britain to support its European sales outlets. Norton built a plant in Germany in 1909 but not in Britain—an oversight the company would long regret. Abrasives produced at Norton's Niagara Falls plant were shipped to

Worcester and to overseas plants for applications involving paper and wheels. Although both Norton and Carborundum continued to work on improving product and process, they invested relatively little in systematic research and development.[78]

In competing for market share, Carborundum was more aggressive than Norton. It not only built abroad first, and built more plants there, but it also developed a new synthetic abrasive material and moved beyond coated abrasives into the production of crystalline alumina (under the trade name Aloxite) and of super-refractories (furnace linings) used in high-temperature glazing and burnishing processes.

An even more effective challenge to Norton came from the much smaller Minnesota Mining and Manufacturing Company, or 3M. The story of 3M shows how a small, established firm could manage to overcome the first-movers' advantages and capture a place in an oligopoly through effective functional and strategic competition. Formed in 1902 to mine natural corundum, with facilities near Duluth, Minnesota, in 1918 it built a plant in St. Paul to produce natural abrasives, on a small scale, for specialized markets. It increased its market share by improving its product (by developing, for example, new methods of applying aluminum oxide to cloth) and by moving more quickly than the industry's leaders to meet the demands of the rapidly growing automobile industry. Its research laboratory, set up in 1916, was enlarged in the 1920s, and its sales force was expanded overseas. In 1928 the company built a small plant in Britain. With the coming of the depression, 3M joined Carborundum, Norton, a smaller, more specialized abrasives firm, and Armour (the meatpacker whose glue business had brought it into the abrasives industry) in forming a joint venture, Durex, in order to consolidate operations in Britain. After centralizing and rationalizing its production and distribution, Durex became the largest abrasive producer in that country.[79]

In the 1920s, 3M embarked on a strategy of growth based on exploiting the economies of scope rather than those of scale. Its initial move into a related industry was the production of a masking tape that permitted more precise painting and finishing of automobiles. In 1930 the new tape-making techniques were applied, through close cooperation with researchers from the Du Pont Company, to produce a cellophane-backed tape, now well known as Scotch tape. The development of such tapes took the company into large-scale production of a variety of adhesive products. In the 1930s 3M used its abrasive materials as a base for making granules and other roofing products. By 1937 only 37% of the value of its total sales came from its original abrasives line. Indeed, diversification had been so successful that the company's history refers to the years of the Great Depression as "a golden era." During the 1930s each of these product lines came to be administered by a separate division having "sales, production, and laboratory facilities of its own."[80] As the postwar period opened, the functions of the corporate office were reshaped to give 3M a full-fledged multidivisional structure. By 1948 Minnesota Mining and Manufacturing, with assets of $88 million, was ranked 149th among American industrials—substantially larger than either Norton or Carborundum. Besides illustrating how a smaller firm can move into an oligopoly through functional and strategic effectiveness, the 3M story shows also how a firm can grow by effectively exploiting economies of scope (the central theme of Chapters 5 and 6).

As for the new gypsum and asbestos industries, technological change during the formative years was more evolutionary than revolutionary. In these two industries, increased productivity brought industry-wide mergers in the same year, 1901: United States Gypsum in gypsum production and Johns-Manville in asbestos. In both cases, the merger-makers centralized administration, slowly rationalized production, and built extensive sales organizations. In each industry the product was sold to hundreds of thousands of builders, contractors, and suppliers. United States Gypsum was challenged by National Gypsum, a company formed in 1925 to exploit improved technology in the mass production of one special line—gypsum wallboard for ceilings and walls. By 1929, when National Gypsum was becoming a formidable competitor, United States Gypsum's market share had fallen to 64% from its high of 80% in 1901. National Gypsum, meanwhile, recruited a national network of twenty thousand sales agents, and after 1935 it acquired several smaller firms. By 1948 it had almost reached 200 on the list of the largest American companies. [81] In that year United States Gypsum was number 93. In asbestos Johns-Manville, formed in 1901 by a merger of two first movers, remained the leader in its oligopoly; it competed with several smaller companies but encountered no challenger comparable to National Gypsum in the gypsum industry. [82]

In these subindustries of Group 32, technological change affected industry structure far more than it did in pulp and newsprint. The greatest cost advantages and therefore the greatest barriers to entry came from organizational exploitation of new or improved methods of production. Technological innovations carried out within the enterprises brought shifts in market share, and they enlarged, though by only one or two, the number of players in the global oligopoly.

FABRICATED METALS

In fabricated metals (Group 34; see Appendixes A.1–A.3) the turnover at the top was comparable to that in stone, clay, and glass. Five of the six enterprises on the 1948 list had been on the 1917 list; the sixth, Gillette Razor, had assets that put it close to the top two hundred in 1917. Of the remaining five on the 1917 list, four, including American Brass, had dropped off the list by 1948 because they had merged with other companies. Of the first six, Gillette Razor had the production and distribution characteristics of other branded, packaged products, while two, American Radiator and the Crane Company (both makers of brass and iron valves and fittings for steam, gas, and water systems), had those of volume-produced machinery. Their experience was, therefore, closer to those firms discussed in the next two chapters than to those described here. The three remaining fabricated-metal firms on the 1917 and 1948 lists of the top two hundred were American Can, Continental Can, and Scovill Manufacturing (a brass-maker).

In brass the evolutionary nature of technological change brought a turn-of-the-century merger in 1902, the American Brass Company. At that time, however, American Brass failed to centralize its administration and rationalize its facilities. It did so only after being taken over in 1922 by Anaconda Copper. Indeed, before the reorganization of 1922 American Brass was one of the very few turn-of-the-century mergers that remained a federation of autonomous operating companies. Hence the Scovill Manufacturing Company, the nation's oldest and, after 1922, largest independent producer of brass, was able to expand its market share by improving production and enlarging its sales force.[83]

In 1948 the two largest enterprises in Group 34 were American Can and Continental Can. They had dominated the can industry ever since the turn of the century. The innovators in modern canning equipment had been the Norton brothers, Edwin and O. W. (no relation to the Nortons in abrasives).[84] It was their invention in 1883 that had helped bring the modern industrial enterprise to many food industries (Chapter 3). The Nortons had leased their patents not only to such food processors as Campbell Soup, H. J. Heinz, Borden's Condensed Milk, Carnation, Pet Milk, and Libby, McNeill & Libby, all of which operated their machines continuously, but also to producers of cans and canning machinery for the small processors of fruit, vegetables, and fish that only operated their machines seasonally. In 1901 nearly all the nation's producers of cans and canning machinery had merged to form American Can, with Edwin Norton as its first president. At that time the company's output accounted for 91% of the cans produced in the United States. At first American Can operated, like American Brass, as a federation of firms maintaining high prices—a strategy that encouraged the growth of the smaller independents. In 1904 most of those independents combined to form Continental Can.[85]

The two consolidations then became first movers by centralizing their administrations, rationalizing production, and investing heavily in marketing organizations that assured their customers, the seasonal processors, the facilities they needed when and where they needed them. Indeed, the effectiveness of this investment in distribution brought praise from the District Court and led to American Can's exoneration in an antitrust suit started by the federal government in 1913.[86] By then American Can's market share had dropped to 63% and Continental Can's had risen to 11.7%. By 1939 Continental, competing functionally and strategically, had further raised its share to 28.3%, while American's had fallen to 55.4%. In the 1920s both companies had moved into the European market (see Chapter 8). They both made relatively small investments in research and development, continuing instead to improve product and process in a slow and incremental manner.

This brief historical review of the leading producers of paper, glass, abrasives, gypsum, asbestos, brass, and cans (Groups 26, 32, and 34) makes it clear that the large and dominant firms in these industries appeared and continued to grow only if they made a substantial enough investment in a new or improved technology to reap the profits from scale economies, if they made the essential product-specific investment in distribution and marketing, and if they recruited management teams capable of integrating production and distribution. In most cases the threefold investment came after a merger of the leading firms. In some cases the merged companies moved slowly to make that investment, in the manner of United States Rubber rather than Standard Oil. Such delays in reducing costs and providing marketing and distribution facilities and services encouraged competition by permitting existing independents to grow by making comparable investments. In the huge American market, even when merged companies quickly centralized and rationalized their production and distribution, the barriers to entry created by their investments were still not strong enough to prevent a small number of comparably integrated challengers from continuing to compete functionally and strategically for market share and profits.

On the other hand, in those subindustries (that is, the three- and four-digit SIC classifications) of Groups 26, 32, and 34 in which technology of production did *not* bring extensive cost advantages of scale and in which product-specific investment was less essential in marketing and distribution, the modern industrial firm—and with it oligopoly—appeared much more slowly. Commercial intermediaries continued to distribute 50% or more of the product during the 1930s. These subindustries remained far less concentrated, and nationwide mergers were rarely successful. This was true in such four-digit categories of Group 26 as envelopes, writing paper, and wallpaper; in Group 32, tiles, lime, pottery, and related products, including plumbing fixtures and chinaware, cut glass, and other tableware; and in Group 34 cutlery, hardware, plumbing supplies, and oil burners.[87] There is little evidence that manufacturers in these subindustries made extensive investments either abroad or in facilities for research and development.

Primary Metals: Technology and Industrial Concentration

In primary metals (Group 33; see Appendixes A.1–A.3), basic technological innovation in the processes of production increased minimum efficient scale and brought industrial concentration comparable to that in glass and other materials.

The story of the impact of the Bessemer process in the 1870s and of the open-hearth process in the 1880s has often been told. Much less has been written about the even more dramatic impact of electrolytic smelting and refining on the production of aluminum, copper, nickel, zinc, and other nonferrous metals and of the resulting concentration of production in those fields. Whereas the basic technological innovations in the production of steel were introduced over a period of more than two decades, those in nonferrous metals made their impact almost instantaneously. The revolutionary technology not only transformed existing industries into oligopolies but also created a brand-new industry, aluminum, where the first mover swiftly achieved and long maintained a monopoly.

ALUMINUM

Early developments in the mass production of aluminum are particularly striking. In 1886 Charles Hall in the United States and Paul Heroult in Europe simultaneously invented the electrolytic method for reducing alumina (refined bauxite) into aluminum. Earlier innovations had lowered the price of that once-precious metal to twelve dollars a pound. It dropped to two dollars after two new firms moved into full production: the Pittsburgh Reduction Company, formed in 1888 to commercialize the Hall patent; and the Swiss enterprise Aluminium Industrie AG, formed in 1887 to exploit the Heroult patent and financed and managed by Germans.

The two entrepreneurs who established the Pittsburgh Reduction Company, Arthur Vining Davis and Alfred E. Hunt, realized that the successful commercialization of aluminum called for a twofold strategy. Increased throughput generated by more intensive use of electrical energy would reduce unit costs, but it had to be supplemented by strong sales efforts in order to maintain production facilities at minimum efficient scale. With financing from the nation's leading venture capitalists, the Mellons of Pittsburgh, Davis and Hunt built their giant plant at Niagara Falls in 1896. By 1898 the drastic reduction in costs allowed them to lower the price of aluminum to thirty-two cents a pound, where it remained for almost a decade with only minor fluctuations. As Davis expanded throughput, Hunt began to create what became a sophisticated sales force to build markets and an expert technical staff to develop products requiring novel techniques in both manufacture and use.[88] The new products soon included aluminum kitchen utensils, fittings, tubes, rods, castings (particularly for the new automobile market), electric wire and cable, and containers that were less costly than those made of brass or tin and just as effective. In addition, the company developed products made from aluminum alloyed with other metals. The success of these new items demanded that the sales force constantly check the new products' performance with customers and provide service when necessary. In some cases the company showed metal fabricators how to use the new metal to make finished goods. In other cases, when Pittsburgh Reduction's personnel knew more than anyone else about the properties, uses, and limitations of aluminum and some of its alloys, the company itself began to fabricate finished products.

The continuing expansion of the market led to the expansion of production facilities, in which fabricating units were often integrated with smelting operations. In 1901 a second electrolytic smelting facility, operated by a subsidiary, Alcan, was built in Shawinigan Falls, Quebec, to serve the Canadian market. Another, built in 1902 in upper New York state on the St. Lawrence, concentrated on the production of rod, wire, and cable. In 1906 a second works at Niagara Falls was completed, followed in 1913 by a plant in eastern Tennessee to serve the southern markets. In 1907 the Pittsburgh Reduction Company acknowledged this growth by changing its name to Aluminum Company of America (Alcoa).[89]

Meanwhile, the company had already begun to integrate backward to assure a steady supply of raw materials. Alcoa made its biggest investments in bauxite mines in Arkansas. In 1903 it also built a large refining plant in East St. Louis to transform the Arkansas bauxite into alumina at a rate of 30,000 pounds a day. Nevertheless it still had to rely on outside suppliers for much of its refined bauxite. Then in 1911 the adoption of a new German process increased throughput at the East St. Louis refinery to 700,000 pounds a day.[90] The new process not only ended dependence on outside suppliers but also greatly reduced unit costs of production, thus raising the already high barriers to entry.

Although Alcoa enjoyed a near monopoly of the American market, it made little effort before World War I to compete overseas. In Europe four firms produced 95% of the output. They were the Aluminium Industrie AG (known as AIAG), the first and largest European aluminum producer; two smaller French companies (one using the Heroult and the other the Hall process); and a British firm. As early as 1896 Pittsburgh Reduction and AIAG agreed to stay out of each other's major markets. In time this arrangement was extended to include the three other European producers.[91] The cartel broke down in 1909, bringing European aluminum into the American market for the first time. In 1912 the European cartel was renewed. Alcoa, then under investigation for antitrust violation, did not join. It did, however, continue to have a say in the building of a smelter by the leading French firm, L'Aluminium Français, begun in North Carolina in 1912, which was purchased by Alcoa in 1915. World War I greatly increased European capacity, primarily because the German AIAG plant was actually located just across the border in Switzerland, thus forcing the Germans to build additional giant works within their national boundaries (see Chapter 14). After the war Alcoa began purchasing European companies, largely to use them as bargaining chips in cartel negotiations, during the 1920s and 1930s, to keep the Europeans out of the American and Canadian markets.

But it never became a major player in the European market. In 1928 it divested itself of its Canadian subsidiary, Alcan, partly for internal reasons and partly in response to antitrust pressures. Alcan, however, continued to maintain close ties with its former parent.[92]

Because the cost advantages of scale in aluminum production were so high, because the product was so new, and because it therefore required such an extensive investment in marketing and development, the structure of the industry became monopolistic rather than oligopolistic. Challengers faced almost impenetrable barriers to entry. In a controversy that occurred over patents, one patent holder, the Cowles Company, won a suit against Alcoa in 1903; but without facilities, skills, and organization it had little choice but to accept the $3 million in damages. The investment required to build plants of comparable size and to recruit and train the necessary production, sales, and development forces would have been enormous. It was too late to become a serious challenger. Even the smelter that the French firm undertook to construct in North Carolina could have moved out of Alcoa's shadow only if it had developed a new way of processing alumina. Otherwise the company would have had to build a plant comparable to that of Alcoa in East St. Louis (because shipments from Europe would have been too costly) and to deploy the necessary sales and development organizations. Alcoa's monopoly was broken only after World War II when the federal government, following one of several antitrust suits against Alcoa, sold to Reynolds Metals and the Kaiser Aluminum & Chemical Corporation the smelting, refining, and fabrication capacity which Alcoa had built and operated and which the government had financed in order to meet the wartime demand.

COPPER AND OTHER NONFERROUS METALS

Whereas aluminum was one of the newest metals, copper was one of the oldest. The electrolytic revolution in copper (in which the smelting of ore preceded its refining) came in refining. Copper smelting had already benefited in the 1880s from improved transportation, evolutionary changes in furnaces, and better machinery (including converters comparable to those used in the Bessemer steel process). At that time a throughput of ten million pounds a year was required to maintain a smelter at minimum efficient scale.[93] The radical changes in refining came in 1891 with the development of a new, high-powered generator. The first five refineries in the United States to use the new electrolytic process went into operation in that year. Their scale was so high that in the next ninety years only twelve more refineries were built in this country, seven of which were in operation by 1910. Thus twelve refineries were able to supply a fivefold increase in output between 1890 and 1910, responding to the new, high levels of demand for copper wire for the production, distribution, and use of electricity, and for copper tubes and pipes for the rapidly growing American building trade and later for the automobile industry. With the exception of two works built in Montana by Anaconda Copper in 1891 and a smaller one constructed by Calumet and Hecla near Niagara Falls, all the refineries in operation before 1910 were located on the East Coast, mostly in the Long Island–Perth Amboy areas of the greater New York harbor region. There they were close to major markets and could receive smelted ("blister") copper by sea from Mexico and the southwestern United States.[94]

Because copper was an old industry with long-established channels of distribution, the giant integrated enterprises that soon dominated it were organized by copper traders rather than by the refinery operators. The important exception was Anaconda, whose Montana mine owners constructed both refineries and smelters close to their mines.

The evolution of the global copper oligopoly is a fascinating story but far too complex to relate here. The central fact is that the five largest copper producers in the United States in 1917 were also the five largest in 1930 and 1948, although their rankings had changed.[95]

They were Anaconda Copper; Phelps Dodge; American Smelting & Refining; Kennecott; and American Metal. Of the five, Anaconda was the only one not established by a copper trading family. American Smelting & Refining, formed by merger in 1899 and controlled by the Guggenheim family, centralized its administration and to some extent rationalized its production and distribution. The Guggenheims were closely allied with, and then came to control, Kennecott, a mining company that only began to produce refined copper after World War I. Both firms had their headquarters in the same office building in New York. The partners of the long-established metal-trading firm of Phelps Dodge continued to play a major role through the copper-producing company of the same name. From the start Phelps Dodge was closely allied with the Nichols Copper Company, owner and operator of a large refinery at Laurel Hill, Long Island, of which Phelps Dodge purchased full control in 1928. In 1917 American Metal was still a subsidiary of the German copper giant, Metallgesellschaft, which, founded by the Mertons, a German copper-trading family, had become the largest copper producer and distributor in Europe (see Chapters 12 and 14).

All these enterprises relied increasingly on their own sales forces of salaried personnel. Anaconda led the way in setting up a national and then an international sales organization. In the years following World War II only 10 to 15% of copper ore passed through the hands of independent agents.[96] When the postwar era opened, the four largest copper firms produced 94% of the sales of copper smelters and 90% of the sales of refined copper.[97]

The American copper companies established overseas sales offices, but they never attempted to support their marketing organizations by building refineries abroad. Because the major sources of copper were in the Western Hemisphere, transportation costs would have been prohibitive. Further, a refinery built in Europe on the American scale, by either Americans or Europeans, would have so increased worldwide capacity that it could not have operated at minimum efficient scale. This is why Metallgesellschaft made larger investments in smelting and refining in America than in Europe.

Like Alcoa in aluminum, the leading copper producers played an important role, despite American antitrust laws, in negotiating and attempting to carry out international cartel arrangements in the 1920s and 1930s. From October 1926 until the beginning of 1933, they operated Copper Exporters under the terms of the Webb-Pomerene Act, the first and probably the only Webb-Pomerene corporation to include foreign as well as American producers. As the Federal Trade Commission's 1947 report on the copper industry made clear, that cartel had little effect on prices, which sagged throughout 1927, rose sharply to peak in March 1929, and collapsed in the spring of 1930. As the Commission stated, "The operations of Copper Exporters Inc. did not appear to have benefited the members of the cartel, the copper industry, or the consumers." Despite the economic power of the American companies and the fact that it was the most formal cartel in the twentieth century in American industry, Copper Exporters had little effect in stabilizing either price or output.[98]

In the 1920s the leading copper firms made some attempt to integrate forward into fabrication. In 1922 Anaconda gained control of American Brass, the result of an industry-wide merger in 1901, which was operated through World War I as a federation of family firms in the British manner. Thereafter, the new management of American Brass quickly installed a centralized, functionally departmentalized structure and rationalized production and distribution facilities. Kennecott purchased the Chase Companies in 1929; Phelps Dodge purchased the National Electric Company in 1930; and American Smelting & Refining organized General Cable in 1924 and Revere Copper and Brass in 1928. These investments were primarily defensive, to assure outlets for the manufacturers' products. There was no attempt to reduce cost by integrating fabricating with refining within a single works. In fact, American Smelting & Refining held only between a quarter and a third of the equity of its affiliates. These downstream companies continued to enjoy full legal and financial autonomy and to be run by their own managements with relatively little oversight from the parent offices as long as they continued to perform satisfactorily.

The production of copper was closely linked with that of other nonferrous ores. Lead, silver, zinc, and nickel were apt to be located close to copper ore—often within the same mine—and all were processed by the new electrolytic methods. In fact, the Guggenheims' initial investment in metal processing, made in 1894, was for the construction of an electrolytic refinery at Perth Amboy to process lead, zinc, silver ores, and a small amount of copper (primarily from their Mexican holdings). The United States Smelting, Refining &

Mining Company, which produced little copper, acquired a refinery in the Perth Amboy area for the processing of lead and silver ores.[99] The International Nickel Company was formed in 1902 when a company operating two relatively small electrolytic plants in New Jersey (one in Camden, the other in Bayonne) combined with two copper companies, Orford Copper and Canadian Copper, which had built pioneering electrolytic works in the early 1890s in Cleveland, Ohio, and Canada. In 1929 International Nickel acquired its one North American competitor, Mond Nickel, a British company. From then on it shared a global duopoly with the Rothschild-financed La Société de Nickel.[100]

In these nonferrous metals, where the technology and markets did not change rapidly after the great transformation of the 1890s, families continued to participate as full-time executives in the companies' top management to a greater extent than in most American industries. During World War II the Guggenheims were still active in American Smelting & Refining and in Kennecott. At Kennecott, representatives of the investment houses of J. P. Morgan and Kuhn, Loeb sat on the board, for both houses had helped to finance the company's expansion first in mining and then in both smelting and refining. Major expansion in this capital-intensive industry required even more than the retained earnings that were available from the Guggenheim fortune. In like manner members of the Dodge and James families continued to participate in the management of Phelps Dodge, the Hochschilds in that of American Metal, and the Rices in that of United States Smelting, Refining & Mining. All these companies were administered by functionally defined management hierarchies. Yet, partly because of family overview and partly because operations were relatively routine, senior executives paid less attention to defining their organizational structures precisely than they did in other similarly capital-intensive American industries.[101]

The high level of concentration in nonferrous processing industries, particularly copper, was brought about by a combination of factors—the revolution in refining, the increasing capital intensity of the smelting process, the adoption after 1918 of the flotation process used to separate ore at the mine, the small amount of technical change that occurred after that innovation, and the relatively few sites that were large enough to support the high-volume extractive mining required to keep these processes running at close to minimum efficient scale. The oligopolies in copper and other nonferrous metals were even more stable than that in rubber.

STEEL

Technological innovations in iron and steel, while bringing impressive cost reductions, did not have such a dramatic impact as they had in copper and aluminum. Moreover, the steel market was much larger. During the interwar years the value of the output of steel-ingot and rolling mills was four times that of nonferrous metals. Therefore more pioneers commercialized the new technologies in steel than in nonferrous metals; and once the three-pronged investments were made, there could be more players in the oligopoly.[102]

In ferrous metals the primary technological innovations were, of course, those that made possible the mass production of steel—the basic metal required for the construction of modern transportation systems, modern cities, and modern industrial factories. In this industry, as in so many others, the first entrepreneurs to invest heavily in the new technology and to create an organization that could manage it continued to dominate. Andrew Carnegie, like John D. Rockefeller and Henry Ford, acquired industrial power and a vast personal fortune by understanding the significance of throughput. "Hard driving" was Carnegie's term for it.

The story of steel differs from that of oil, however, in that the most effective first mover sold out. Senior executives of Carnegie's successor company, the United States Steel Corporation—those who were lawyers and financiers—failed to appreciate the value of operating "steady and full." They dissipated Carnegie's first-mover advantages and thus permitted the rapid growth of challengers. Whereas, in oil, monopoly was transformed into oligopoly because of sudden massive changes in sources of supplies and markets, in steel no such changes occurred. Instead, a near monopoly was transformed into an oligopoly because of the decisions of one or two senior executives.

Andrew Carnegie was the first to exploit fully the scale economies of the new technologies in steel processing. He was not the first to install a Bessemer converter; others, beginning in 1867, had added them to their existing works. But Carnegie was the first to build from scratch a giant, integrated, Bessemer rail mill, the Edgar Thomson Works in Pittsburgh, which remained for decades the largest steel works in the world. The installation of its blast furnaces in 1879 completed the works just in time to meet the enormous demand created by the railroad boom of the 1880s.[103] When he obtained the nearby Homestead Works in 1881, Carnegie again made major investments. After improving and enlarging its rail-making facilities, he installed at Homestead a large battery of open-hearth furnaces to produce high-grade steel for beams and other structures. Of even more importance, he placed there the first "basic" open-hearth furnace (those using the Thomas-Gilchrist process) to be used in the United States to make high-quality steel for boiler tanks and ship plates.[104] In 1891 Carnegie enlarged his Pittsburgh holdings by purchasing the Duquesne Works, where the new "direct rolling" process had been developed. By 1894 the three Carnegie plants had an annual capacity of 1,710,000 tons (930,000 tons at the Edgar Thomson Works, 480,000 at Homestead, and 300,000 at Duquesne).

In the mid-1880s the entrepreneurs whose pioneering companies would combine in 1889 to form the Illinois Steel Company made a comparable investment in production. By 1894 their enterprise had a capacity of just over 2,000,000 tons (265,000 tons at the North Works, 782,000 at the South Works, 595,000 at the Union Works—all in Chicago—and 440,000 at the nearby Joliet Works). A third first mover, Jones & Laughlin Steel of Pittsburgh, a long-established enterprise, made its investment in the mid-1880s; its single works had a capacity of 850,000 tons, producing a wider variety of finished products than either Carnegie or Illinois Steel.[105] The smaller pioneers—Cambria Iron, Lackawanna Steel, Cleveland Rolling Mill, Inland Steel, Bethlehem Steel, and Pittsburgh Steel—produced mainly for regional or specialized markets (Bethlehem for ships, Inland Steel and Pittsburgh Steel for plows and other agricultural equipment).

During the 1880s and 1890s Carnegie Steel and Illinois Steel expanded their sales forces as they diversified into structures that, unlike rails, were sold to thousands of individual contractors and other customers.[106] In the same years they steadily and incrementally improved the machinery of production and the layout of their plants. This improvement vastly increased the amount of energy used, but it steadily raised daily throughput and reduced unit costs. In the words of Peter Temin:

> The speed at which steel was made was constantly rising, and new innovations were constantly being introduced to speed it further. Steam and later electric power replaced the lifting and carrying action of human muscles, mills were modified to handle steel quickly and with a minimum of strain to the machinery and people disappeared from the mills. By the turn of the century, there were not a dozen men on the floor of a mill rolling 3,000 tons a day, or as much as a Pittsburgh rolling mill of 1850 rolled in a year.[107]

As throughput increased, costs and prices fell dramatically. The price of steel rails at Pittsburgh plummeted from $67.50 a ton in 1880 to $29.25 in 1889. By the mid-1880s British steelmakers could no longer compete in the American market (see Chapter 7). In the next decade costs and prices dropped even further and profits soared. By the late 1890s Carnegie's costs had fallen to $11.25, while rail prices dropped to $18.75 a ton in 1897 and to $17.63 in 1898. Carnegie's profits rose from $7 million in 1897 to $11 million in 1898. Then in 1899, when a sharp increase in demand raised steel prices to $28.12 a ton, Carnegie's profits reached $21 million. The next year they topped $40 million.[108] As in the case of Rockefeller and oil, the low-cost, low-price production of steel generated a huge fortune.

The vast increase in throughput intensified the need for assured sources of supplies. First Carnegie acquired the Henry C. Frick Coke Company (and made Frick president of the Carnegie Steel Company). Next, at Frick's suggestion, the steel company obtained a half interest in the Oliver Mining Company in the recently opened Mesabi Iron Range of northern Minnesota. Then, after John D. Rockefeller had used some of his oil fortune to purchase the properties of the Merritt brothers (the first to open that range), Carnegie in 1895 worked out an agreement by which his company leased the ore fields, paying Rockefeller a royalty of twenty-five cents for each ton of ore extracted.[109]

Not surprisingly, Carnegie's move into the Mesabi caused Illinois Steel to embark on a similar strategy. It purchased coal and iron mines in Minnesota, Illinois, and adjoining states in the 1890s. Then in 1898, under the sponsorship of the house of Morgan, it merged with several other firms to form a large new enterprise, the Federal Steel Company. This vertical combination included, besides Illinois Steel: the Minnesota Iron Company, with 150,000 acres of ore in the Mesabi region and the adjacent railroads; and the Lorain Steel Company, with production facilities for rails and equipment for street railways and with one of the newest and largest of the nation's Bessemer works. By 1900 Federal and Carnegie together produced one-third of the country's steel, with Carnegie making 18% and Federal 15% of its steel ingots and Carnegie producing about 30% and Federal 15% of its rails and beams.[110] By then the production of primary steel—ingots, bars, rails, and structures—in the United States had become much more concentrated than it was in either Great Britain or Germany (see Chapters 7 and 12).

By contrast, the production of fabricated or, as they were termed, secondary products was much less concentrated. In these industries there were many pioneers but no first movers comparable to Carnegie Steel or Illinois Steel. Nearly all of these pioneers, like the primary producers, were integrated mills. They had their own blast furnaces and their own relatively small Bessemer and open-hearth works to supply their finishing mills. In these the potential cost advantages of scale were much smaller than in primary products. As in the production of primary steel, however, cumulative technological change increased throughput. As overall output expanded, the "fabricating" works increasingly purchased steel ingots from Carnegie Steel and Illinois Steel.

In the manufacture of tin plate (thin sheet steel coated with tin), technological change was more dramatic. This may also have been true of other secondary products. The revolutionary inventions in tin plate greatly increased output and lowered unit costs and prices. For example, the Buchanan automatic tinning machine was developed in 1892, the Record tin-plate cleaning machine in 1894, and the Duplex tin-plate duster in 1895—all of them quickly integrated so that operations became continuous. The Tinned Plate Manufacturers' Association came into being in 1896, followed by the incorporation of the American Tin-Plate Company in 1898.[111]

The tin-plate story is a short version of the history of the makers of other steel products, both secondary and primary, during these years. As increased output intensified competition, they, too, formed industry associations but had little success in controlling price and output.[112] In 1898 several of these associations also transformed themselves into industry-wide holding companies. These included American Steel & Wire, National Tube, American Steel Hoop, and American Bridge.

Although industrial promoters, such as the Moore brothers, played a major role in organizing these mergers, the manufacturers themselves clearly saw them as the means to reduce costs through centralizing administration and further rationalizing operations. In most cases the managers of the new consolidated firms began to concentrate production in more efficient, better-located plants and to systematize distribution by either combining existing sales forces or creating new national ones. As part of their rationalization program, they also started to build Bessemer and open-hearth works large enough to operate at minimum efficient scale to assure their own supply at costs almost as low as the prices they paid the primary producers. This was true at American Steel & Wire, American Steel Hoop, American Sheet Steel (formed in 1900), National Tube, and American Bridge. In addition, the promoters of the American Tin-Plate Company integrated backward by combining several small steel producers into the National Steel Company. In the words of the tin-plate industry's historian, "the two companies were managed as a single integrated concern." By the summer of 1900 all of these companies had already canceled or reduced their orders for steel ingots from the Carnegie Company.[113]

By integrating backward into steel production the new industry-wide consolidation of steel fabricators set off a chain of events that led to the formation of that giant of giants, the United States Steel Corporation.

First came Andrew Carnegie's response to the impending loss of many of his major customers. Despite the hesitancy of some of his partners, though with the strong support of his aggressive young president, Charles Schwab, Carnegie announced plans to build a great integrated works at Conneaut, Ohio, where Mesabi ore would be transformed into steel and then into wire, nails, tubes, and hoops. All agreed that, with the completion of the works at Conneaut, Carnegie could become the low-cost producer of such fabricated products as well as of steel ingots and rails.

What happened then is one of the best-known stories in American business history. J. Pierpont Morgan, the nation's preeminent investment banker, was becoming involved in financing industrial mergers. In 1898 his firm had underwritten Federal Steel, the merger that made Illinois Steel into an integrated giant, and in 1899 it had underwritten National Tube. (The Morgan firm had, however, pulled back in 1898 from underwriting American Steel & Wire.) Morgan was understandably concerned about Carnegie's well-advertised move into fabrication. Such competition threatened the dividend payments on the securities whose issues his banking house had underwritten. He therefore listened with attentive enthusiasm to a speech Charles Schwab made on December 12, 1900, urging further consolidation and rationalization of the steel industry as a way to bring even lower costs and assure industrial stability. In February 1901, Morgan agreed to buy out Carnegie at the latter's price, $480 million. Once the two leaders—Carnegie Steel and Federal Steel—were joined, negotiations began with the secondary producers. By March 1, American Steel & Wire, National Tube, American Sheet Steel, American Steel Hoop, and American Tin-Plate (and its supplier, National Steel) had been brought into the merger. Within a short time Shelby Steel and Tube, American Bridge, and the Rockefeller-owned Lake Superior Consolidated Iron Mines also joined. [114]

The resulting enterprise was unique in American industry. It was by far the world's largest industrial corporation. Only Standard Oil came close. By 1917 its assets of $2,449.5 million were more than four times those of Standard Oil (New Jersey)—which, even after the 1911 court decision, remained the nation's second largest corporation, with assets of $574.1 million—and nearly eight times that of the second largest steel company, Bethlehem Steel, with assets of $381.5 million. United States Steel was also unique in that it was a merger of many nationwide mergers in many major lines of steel products.

In addition, it had been put together in the hurried manner of speculative Wall Street promoters. In arranging the huge merger the house of Morgan did not carry out the normal, time-consuming procedures of investigating potential cost advantages of rationalization, appraising the properties of the firms coming into the merger, or negotiating the usual complex terms for the price paid through exchange of stock—procedures that the Morgan firm had followed in the formation of Federal Steel and in the 1898 initial proposal to form American Steel & Wire. [115] The procedures used in the formation of United States Steel followed more closely those of the promoters who had created such mergers as American Tin-Plate, National Steel, and Shelby Steel and Tube; that is, the Morgan firm simply accepted the valuation the incoming firms put on their own assets. As a result, the capitalization of United States Steel Corporation was $1,439.0 million, whereas the value of the securities and cash of the companies coming into the firm was only $881.2 million.

The new company remained a holding company. The existing enterprises retained both legal and administrative autonomy. Although Charles Schwab, Carnegie's protégé and the new company's first president, clearly planned to follow legal consolidation with administrative centralization and rationalization, he became too involved with other businesses and social activities to concentrate seriously on reorganization. That phase had to wait until William E. Corey became president.

Corey, another Carnegie protégé, succeeded Schwab in 1903. Corey made no attempt to create a single, centralized, functionally departmentalized structure. But he and his associates did redefine the boundaries and encourage the continuing redirection of the activities of the many subsidiaries. The Carnegie and Federal companies remained the two major steelmakers. The properties of National Steel and American Steel Hoop, both of whose facilities were concentrated in the Pittsburgh area, were folded into the Carnegie organization. All ore properties were consolidated under William J. Olcott, who was also responsible for the transportation companies that moved the ores to the mills. Marketing was reorganized so that the Carnegie company focused on the eastern market and Federal on the western. Early in 1904 came the consolidation of foreign sales into a single, worldwide marketing subsidiary, the United States Steel Products Export Company. By 1913 the export firm was operating twenty branch offices and 193 agencies in seventy countries. Then in 1905 the senior managers of Federal announced the construction in Gary, Indiana, of what would become the world's largest and most efficient steel-producing works; it went into full operation in 1911. Indeed, the Gary Works with its capacity to produce annually close to three million tons of rails, bullets, plates, slabs, axles, and merchant bars was an impressive, though belated, capstone to the post-merger rationalization at the United States Steel Corporation.[116]

Rationalization also occurred in the fabricating subsidiaries. The facilities of American Sheet Steel were combined with those of American Tin-Plate. The latter shut down more than fifteen of its thirty-nine tin-plate-producing plants, adopted new processes, and increased output in the remaining plants from five million tons in 1902 to eight million tons in 1906.[117] Rationalization, already begun before 1901, continued apace at American Steel & Wire, National Tube, and American Bridge. Though more might have been done, much was accomplished.

Because much of this rationalization had started before the formation of United States Steel, it would certainly have been carried out even if that merger of mergers had not taken place. The formation of United States Steel may have made it easier to obtain the capital necessary for rationalization, but even that view would be difficult to document. In other words, except for the construction of the Gary Works, much of the rationalization of the steel industry was not a direct result of the formation of United States Steel. Both Carnegie and Federal, acting individually, would have had the resources to build comparable works. Nor did the new enterprise achieve more than a minimum of administrative centralization.

The central headquarters of the world's largest industrial enterprise remained tiny. In striking contrast to Standard Oil in the 1890s or, later, Du Pont or General Motors, which were pioneers in creating the multidivisional form in the 1920s, staff size was too small and the senior executives too few to coordinate and monitor effectively the activities of their many autonomous operating subsidiaries. The staff included little more than legal and accounting offices. The accounting office, however, did set up a bureau of comparative statistics that became an embryonic tool of corporate control.

The general executives of the corporate office who determined policy included representatives of two groups—the investment bankers who had financed the merger and the managers who administered it. Among the representatives of the bankers were Elbert H. Gary, first chairman of the Executive Committee of the Corporation's board and after 1903 chairman of the board itself, and Robert Bacon and George W. Perkins, Morgan partners who served consecutively as chairman of the board's Finance Committee. Gary, a corporate lawyer, had no direct experience in the production and distribution of iron and steel; but as a member of the Illinois Steel board of directors he had been the driving force in the formation of Federal Steel in 1898 and had then served as chairman of its board. As chairman of United States Steel he continued to have Morgan's full confidence. The second group—the managers—included Charles Schwab, William E. Corey, and President Corey's young assistant, William B. Dickson, another aggressive Carnegie-trained manager.[118]

Once the new structure had been put into place and rationalization carried out, the senior executives at the corporate office became seriously divided over basic policies. In Gary's view the function of a corporate office was not that of coordinating, monitoring, or even systematically allocating resources to the operating units—that is, it was not to carry out what would become the normal function of a corporate headquarters. Instead, he saw the corporate office as more like that of a federation or cartel which set price and output schedules. The Carnegie-trained managers, however, wanted to continue the policy of exploiting the competitive advantages of low costs by maintaining throughput, even though this meant reducing prices. Indeed, in October 1902, when Schwab was still in command and before Gary became chairman of the board, such major fabricating subsidiaries as American Tin-Plate and American Steel & Wire followed the policy of cutting prices to keep their mills operating at minimum efficient scale.[119] But after Schwab resigned in 1903 and Gary became the Corporation's chief executive, Gary, supported by the Finance Committee, instituted a policy of price stabilization. He was willing to maintain prices even though the policy brought a sharp reduction in output and a temporary shutdown of plants. For, in Robert Hessen's words, "Gary had an aversion to any form of price competition; he considered it immoral and unprofitable."[120]

By the summer of 1904, Corey and Dickson were bitterly protesting this policy that so violated the Carnegie experience and the logic of modern high-volume production. In a letter to Corey that August, Dickson pointed out that because of Gary's pricing policies in primary products, the steel corporation was losing the respect of its competitors and the patronage of its largest customers. The policy negated one of the basic rationales for the steel merger. Dickson bemoaned:

> In economy of operations, reductions of costs, and improvement in the efficiency of our operating force, we have, I feel, accomplished even more than was expected when the Corporation was organized. All this good work is, however, to a large extent neutralized by the irregularity of operations. For some time past we have been operating at not much over 50% of our capacity, including blast furnaces. As an inevitable result costs have increased; works standing idle have deteriorated relatively more than if they were in operation; the men are disheartened and a certain amount of apathy exists. [121]

Gary's policies, so demoralizing to the managers of United States Steel, obviously delighted his competitors. By running their smaller plants "steady and full" while those of the Corporation were intentionally operating at far below capacity, other firms increased market share and profits. Charles Schwab was particularly pleased, for after leaving United States Steel he had become the largest shareholder of Bethlehem Steel and in 1904 had begun to oversee its management and to transform it from a specialized ordnance and shipbuilding company into a full-time steel producer. As Schwab's biographer points out, Gary's pricing policies permitted Bethlehem "to absorb the heavy start-up costs of the new open hearth rail mills and to put up with higher unit costs until it could match U.S. Steel's economies of scale."

Nevertheless, despite the continuing complaints of his senior operating managers and the success of his competitors, Gary persisted. When the competitors began to reduce prices to maintain share and profit, Gary instituted his famous dinners of 1907 and 1908 to urge them to support the prices that he had done so much to stabilize. On some products they did; on some they did not. United States Steel continued to lose market share. Its operating executives continued to plead for a change in policy. Finally in February 1909, Gary gave in, much to the relief of the managers. "It's better by all odds to make . . . a profit on a full output at competitive prices," Dickson wrote, "than by half output at artificial prices."[122]

With United States Steel operating at full capacity once again the independents were chastened. They held a testimonial dinner for Gary in October 1909 to urge him to return to his earlier policies. At the dinner, one that Corey refused to attend, Schwab said to Gary: "The broad principles that you brought into this business were new to all of us who had been trained in a somewhat different school. Their effect was marvelous, their success unquestioned."[123] Gary took the bait and raised prices; Corey resigned, and the independents continued to compete and take market share.

A decade of Gary's policies permitted his competitors to overcome the first-mover advantages Carnegie had achieved in the production and distribution of steel. These policies clearly did not increase U.S. Steel's earnings, for, as Carnegie had demonstrated so well and the operating managers had so strenuously maintained, larger profits came by operating steady and full and selling the larger volume at lower costs. The Gary policies, however, did permit Gary to achieve his goal of preventing the company from being broken up for violation of the Sherman Antitrust Act. In congressional hearings and in an antitrust suit against the Corporation carried on between 1911 and 1915, its competitors constantly praised Gary's policies. If Gary had followed the demands of Corey, Dickson, and other managers, charges of predatory pricing might well have led to the loss of the antitrust suit and the dismemberment of the Corporation.

Although Gary's policies meant lower productivity, higher unit costs, and lower earnings at U.S. Steel, as well as higher prices for finished steel, they did increase competition in the industry. As Gertrude Schroeder stresses, the fastest growth of the independents came in the first two decades of the twentieth century (see Figure 5). Gary's policies and then the demands of World War I made this growth possible.[124] In steel, as in rubber goods, paper, window glass, and tin cans, the failure of the new industry-wide merger to take steps to exploit fully the potential economies of scale made possible the rise of challengers and enlarged the size of the oligopoly. And these challengers were not, it must be strongly emphasized, new entrants but established firms.

By World War I the structure of the American steel industry had solidified. Gary had learned the costs of maintaining "artificial prices" at levels that were too high, while U.S. Steel's smaller competitors had come to respect the Corporation's ability to discipline price-cutting. The pattern of price leadership that emerged was comparable to that which was appearing in oil and other American industries. There were no more Gary dinners. United States Steel essentially set a price that permitted the existing companies to compete for market share but reduced the incentive to expand capacity rapidly.[125]

In steel, the major players in the oligopoly had been selected by the end of the turn-of-the-century merger movement. Of the fourteen steel producers on the 1948 list of the top two hundred industrials (they produced more than 85% of the nation's steel in that year), only three had been formed after 1900. All three—Wheeling Steel Corporation, National Steel, and Allegheny Ludlum—were mergers of long-established companies.[126] Of the eight original enterprises taking part in these mergers, only one had been established after the merger movement: this was a company that had built a plant in Detroit in the 1920s to serve the rapidly growing automobile industry. The two largest independents also expanded through merger—Bethlehem immediately after World War I and Republic between 1928 and 1930. The rest grew by direct investment in facilities and personnel rather than through acquisitions. What acquisitions they made were usually vertical (that is, to assure supplies) rather than horizontal (to absorb competitors).[127]

Though the players in the iron and steel oligopoly have remained much the same since 1903, their market shares and profits have shifted—often rapidly. In the functional and strategic competition for market share, the industry's

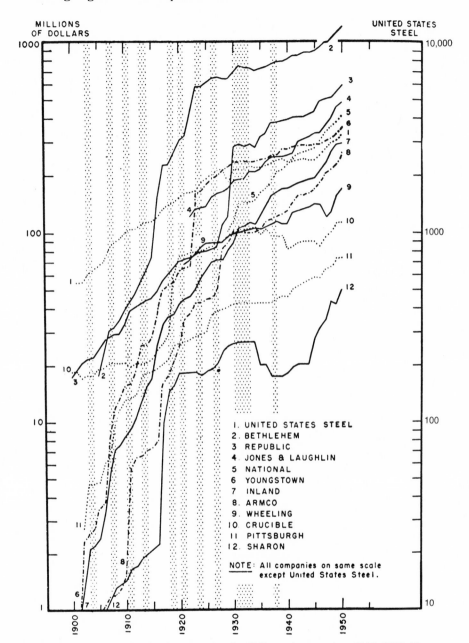

Figure 5. Change in gross fixed assets of major U.S. steel companies, 1900–1950. From Gertrude G. Schroeder, *The Growth of Major Steel Companies, 1900–1950* (Baltimore, 1953), p. 204.

Table 11. Percentage of total output produced by U.S. Steel Corporation, 1901–
           1927.

Products	1901	1911	1913	1919	1927
Iron ore	45.1	45.8	46.37	42.05	41.35
Blast-furnace products	43.2	45.4	45.47	43.97	37.70
Steel ingots and castings	65.7	53.9	53.21	49.61	41.14
Steel rails	59.8	56.1	55.51	61.96	53.26
Heavy structural shapes	62.2	47.0	54.03	43.77	38.80
Plates and sheets	64.6	45.7	49.13	44.30	36.49
Wire rods	77.6	64.7	58.44	55.42	47.42
Total finished products	50.1	45.7	47.81	44.60	37.70
Wire nails	65.8	51.4	44.55	51.86	41.99
Tin terne plates	73.0	60.7	58.64	48.44	40.46

Source: N. S. B. Gras and Henrietta M. Larson, *Casebook in American Business History* (New York, 1939), p. 612.

giant, United States Steel, continued to be the major loser (see Table 11). In many basic products its losses were dramatic—for example, it dropped from 65.7% to 41.1% in steel ingots and castings and from 64.6% to 36.5% in plates and sheets. It moved more slowly than its competitors into the new automotive, machinery, and appliance markets; it was slower to develop or adopt improved production processes, such as hot and cold continuous strip mills; and it was late in developing the new alloyed steels. The managers of its operating subsidiaries in Pittsburgh, Chicago, Duluth, and Birmingham, and of its fabricating subsidiaries, may have continued to be constrained by the Corporation's cautious finance committee.[128]

Only after Gary's death in 1927 did the executives of the Steel Corporation begin a massive structural reorganization that enlarged the activities of the corporate office and redefined the boundaries and activities of the operating subsidiaries. Not until the late 1930s did Gary's successor, Myron C. Taylor, create a version of the multidivisional firm, thus helping the Corporation to maintain market share and meet the challenge of rising demand during World War II.[129] During the interwar years its smaller competitors continued to operate through a centralized, functionally departmentalized administrative structure.

In competing for market share the members of the oligopoly increasingly relied on their own purchasing and sales forces. This was true not only of the fabricators but also of the primary producers. In 1935 only 6% of the production of steel works and rolling mills was sold through commercial intermediaries.[130] Except for United States Steel, American Rolling Mill, and Crucible Steel, steel companies in America made no aggressive efforts to sell abroad; even United

States Steel sharply reduced its investment in overseas marketing after World War I.[131] None of the American companies invested in a plant abroad if an extensive capacity already existed in that area; for as in the case of nonferrous metals, the investment required to achieve minimum efficient scale would have created massive overcapacity in the region in which the new plant was built. United States Steel sold two plants it had built in Canada to automobile companies. American Rolling Mill, however, did build a small plant in Brazil in 1912, and later it entered a joint venture with a British company to build another in Australia.

Research and development played a smaller role in the continuing competition for market share in steel than it did in any other major American industry. United States Steel did not set up a central laboratory until 1928. Republic Steel, which established its laboratory in the same year, did some useful work in developing steel alloys. But the only steel firm to exploit research effectively was American Rolling Mill, which in 1926 patented the continuous rolling process, the industry's most important innovation between the wars. It also pioneered in the production of electrical and steel alloys.[132]

With one exception, it was the industry's experienced steelmakers that made the functional and strategic decisions in competing for market share. Only in United States Steel did financiers have a significant say in policymaking. Moreover, except for the brief period between 1927 and 1930 when Cyrus Eaton attempted to carry out a strategy of growth through merger at Republic Iron & Steel, financiers played no major role in mergers or acquisitions after 1901.[133] Nor did the founders' families remain significant decision-makers for any length of time. The turn-of-the-century merger movement had eliminated family control in many sectors of the industry. Indeed, in only three independents did second-generation family members continue to participate in top-level decision-making. Where they did—at Jones & Laughlin, Inland Steel, and Pittsburgh Steel—these family participants were full-time executives who made a lifelong career of steel production and distribution.

The evolution of the structure of the American steel industry has received more detailed attention here than other industries, partly because of its fundamental place in the growth of an industrial economy and partly because the formation of the U.S. Steel Corporation differentiates steel from other industries in the United States. Yet at the same time this story of the giant merger of mergers emphasizes the importance of technology and throughput in determining the structure of an industry, as seen both in Carnegie's acquisition of and Gary's dissipation of first-mover advantages. United States Steel also provides one of the very few examples of banker control in American industry. In no other large enterprise—oil, rubber, paper, glass, or other metals or materials—did financiers and lawyers with little industrial experience make such crucial policy decisions. At United States Steel, their influence and the resulting conflict between them and the experienced operating managers provide insights into the coming of price leadership and of oligopolistic competition in American industry.

Major Trends

The most noticeable trends exemplified by the industries whose histories have just been related are, first, the close relationship between scale, vertical integration, and oligopoly, and, second, the growing separation between managers and owners.

Despite the distinctive characteristics of the steel industry, its underlying pattern was similar to that of the other industries described in this chapter— oil, rubber, paper, glass, asbestos, tin cans, aluminum, copper, and the other nonferrous metals—all of which were essential to the growth and continuing health of a rapidly industrializing and urbanizing economy. Although these industries grew in different ways, reflecting different technologies, markets, and to a lesser extent personalities, their underlying institutional history corresponds closely to the first stage of growth depicted in my simplified model (Chapter 2). The exploitation of the cost advantages of scale led to dominance by the few large enterprises. The enterprises that first made the three-pronged investment became the industry's leaders and long remained so.

In aluminum, abrasives, asbestos, automobile tires, and glass bottles the initial investments by the first movers set the structure of the industry. In other cases, however—and there were more of them—the critical investment that determined the players in and the structure of the industry came after an industry-wide merger. Where merger was *not* quickly followed by administrative centralization, rationalization, and extensive investment in production, distribution, and management, as was the case with U.S. Steel, International Paper, U.S. Rubber, American Can, and American Window Glass, competitors quickly appeared. By contrast, where such investment came quickly, challengers appeared more slowly. When they were able to establish themselves, this happened largely because of major changes in technologies, markets, and, in the case of oil, sources of supply.

The collective histories related here and the generalizations thus derived apply, of course, to capital-intensive industries where economies of scale provided powerful cost advantages. A brief look at those industries in which production technologies did not bring such advantages, and which did not require specific marketing and distribution services and facilities, helps to reinforce generalizations derived from the experience of the capital-intensive ones. Labor-intensive industries were rarely dominated by a small number of firms. Mergers in these industries were much less successful. Indeed, some combinations, such as those in cut glass and wallpaper, voluntarily disbanded into their constituent parts. In those labor-intensive, two-digit industries, such as textiles, apparel, lumber, furniture, leather, and publishing and printing, firms remained relatively small. Owners often continued to participate in their management.

Therefore, in these more traditional, labor-intensive industries, commercial intermediaries played a much larger role (Table 12). The percentage of goods sold through commercial intermediaries and the degree of concentration in the industry were roughly correlated—with a few exceptions the greater the percentage of goods sold through commercial intermediaries, the less the concentration. Moreover, a larger proportion of consumer goods produced in these labor-intensive industries went directly to retailers, of whom the mass retailers—the department stores, mail-order houses, and especially chain stores—were becoming increasingly important.

Even so, the largest firms in these industries were those that had taken over the commercial intermediaries' functions in marketing and purchasing. This was true of Simmons Company, the one furniture company, and of Weyerhaeuser Timber and Armstrong Cork, the two wood-products companies, listed among the top two hundred (Appendixes A.2–A.3). Both recruited extensive sales forces, and both sold branded products nationally.[134] This was also true of the textile companies (Group 22) that continued to grow after 1917 at a rate fast enough to stay on the list of the top two hundred. These included J. P. Stevens, Burlington Mills, United Merchants & Manufacturers, Pacific Mills, and Cannon Mills.[135] As might be expected, those companies in Group 22 that dropped off the list failed to make comparable investments. The dropouts included two subsidiaries of major foreign textile producers—American Thread, a British-controlled, turn-of-the-century combination, and Botany Mills, until 1918 a subsidiary of the largest German woolen manufacturer. Even though American Woolen, an 1899 combination of woolen producers, remained among the top two hundred, it was even less profitable than American Thread. It did little in the way of building a marketing organization, although it tried to rationalize production. Indeed, in the early 1920s, William A. Wood of American Woolen explicitly attempted to follow Henry Ford's strategy of mass production by concentrating on high-volume output of a few lines—a vision that, understandably, was never realized.[136] In textiles the creation of marketing organizations and the branding and advertising of products may have reduced costs through increased volume, but they did not provide the market power that so quickly brought concentration in the more capital-intensive industries.

Because the companies in the more labor-intensive industries did not build large distribution networks at home, they rarely tried to market directly abroad. Therefore they had little incentive to invest in distant production facilities. And because their processes and products were not technologically complex, they made almost no investment in research and development. Throughout the

Table 12. Manufacturers' domestic distribution channels and concentration ratios in labor-intensive industries, 1929–1954 (in percentages).

Year	Industry	Distribution channels						Concentration ratios					
		Via own channels				Via intermediaries		Four largest firms			Eight largest firms		
		Own outlets		Direct sales									
		Wholesale	Retail	Industrial	Consumer	Wholesalers	Retailers	1935	1947	1954	1935	1947	1954
	Group 22 Textile-mill products												
1929	Total	12.6	0.2	36.6	0.3	39.9	10.4	—	—	—	—	—	—
1939	Total	10.5	0.2	36.1	0.3	41.2	11.7	—	—	—	—	—	—
	Cotton broad-woven fabrics	9.5	0.0	25.7	0.2	54.4	10.2	—	—	18	—	—	29
	Cotton yarn	3.9	0.0	60.8	0.0	34.4	0.9	—	—	26	—	—	40
	Full-fashioned hosiery	11.6	0.2	6.2	2.2	28.1	51.7	—	—	22	—	39	31
	Synthetic broad-woven fabrics	14.5	0.2	13.9	—	68.3	3.1	—	31	30	—	39	39
	Group 23 Apparel and other fabricated textile products												
1929	Total	4.4	4.5	11.4	5.3	22.2	52.2	—	—	—	—	—	—
1939	Total	3.8	7.1	11.4	2.0	16.7	59.0	—	—	—	—	—	—
	Men's hats and caps	4.5	0.0	5.6	0.2	39.2	50.5	—	12	10	—	21	17
	Men's shirts, collars and nightwear	38.7	0.7	1.9	0.8	11.6	46.3	—	19	17	—	29	26
	Men's work shirts	13.0	0.0	1.9	0.0	38.5	46.6	—	52	54	—	68	68
	Men's suits and coats	2.7	16.1	3.4	2.7	7.0	68.1	—	9	11	—	15	18

Industry / Year													
Women's suits and coats		3.5	0.3	1.0	2.7	6.1	86.4	—	—	—	3	—	6
Millinery		3.0	1.2	0.9	0.6	21.7	72.6	—	7	—	7	10	12
Group 24													
Lumber and lumber products													
Total	1929	4.9	—	47.6	—	38.0	9.5	—	—	—	—	—	—
Total	1939	8.6	4.0	29.6	5.8	39.6	12.4	—	—	—	—	—	—
Group 25													
Furniture and fixtures													
Total	1929	4.5	2.5	28.8	2.2	19.6	42.4	—	—	—	—	—	—
Total	1939	5.5	2.0	29.6	2.5	17.0	43.4	—	7	—	8	11	—
Household furniture (wood)		2.5	2.4	9.6	1.8	17.5	66.2	—	—	—	—	—	13
Upholstered household furniture		2.0	3.0	2.5	2.8	11.0	78.7	—	14	—	15	18	18
Mattresses and bedsprings		12.0	2.4	6.0	2.7	13.6	63.3	25	36	31	34	42	40
Group 31													
Leather and leather products													
Total	1929	19.2	3.3	21.5	0.4	23.6	32.0	—	—	—	—	—	—
Total	1939	18.2	2.5	21.4	0.2	19.0	38.7	—	—	—	—	—	—
Footwear		21.7	4.3	0.9	0.2	19.3	53.6	—	28	—	30	35	36
Handbags and purses		5.2	0.0	0.5	0.0	14.1	80.2	—	7	—	8	13	14
Leather, tanned and finished		18.9	0.0	62.4	0.0	18.4	0.3	22	27	34	18	39	28

Source: For distribution channels, U.S. Bureau of the Census, *Distribution of Manufacturers' Sales, 1939* (Washington, D.C., 1942), table 3, appropriate industry sections; for concentration ratios, U.S. Bureau of the Census, *Concentration Ratios in Manufacturing Industry, 1958* (Washington, D.C., 1962), table 2. aprororiate industry sections.

period from 1921 to 1946 none of the following industries employed as much as 1% of the total scientific personnel working in American industry: apparel, leather, publishing and printing, lumber, and furniture. Textiles employed less than 1% in 1921 and 1948, and 1.36% in 1931. The only other two-digit SIC group with as little employment in research was tobacco.[137]

By contrast, in the capital-intensive industries of paper, glass, other materials, and metals, where scale economies in production and, to a lesser extent, product-specific facilities in distribution brought competitive advantages, dominant firms continued to compete functionally and strategically for market share and profits in a single industry. Although these firms were players in their larger global oligopolies and did make investments in facilities and personnel abroad, the leaders concentrated on the American market. They rarely diversified; Minnesota Mining and Manufacturing (3M) and Pittsburgh Plate Glass were the exceptions. Finally, their investment in research and development remained relatively modest.

Because these firms did not sell abroad and did not diversify, they had little need to change their organizational structure. Before World War II only International Paper and American Can created regionally decentralized multidivisional organizations, and 3M adopted a similar structure with product divisions. All the rest remained satisfied to administer their activities through a centralized, functionally departmentalized structure (depicted in Figure 1). During the 1920s those firms whose central offices had still been small and whose operations had still been informally controlled at the time of World War I formalized their organizational structures and defined more clearly the functions and activities of their middle and top managers.

The leading firms in oil and rubber made more investments abroad than did those in paper, glass materials, and metals; and more of these firms diversified into related product lines. They also made greater investments in research and development. Nevertheless, the powerful cost advantages of scale that the oil companies enjoyed in the production of kerosene and then gasoline and that the rubber companies held in tires committed them to a strategy of vertical integration and, except for the first movers, to one of concentration on domestic rather than international markets. On the contrary, the leaders in the industries whose histories will be told in the next two chapters—food, chemicals, and machinery—preferred to reinvest their profits in strategies of product diversification and expansion abroad rather than in those of vertical integration.

In many of the centralized, primarily single-industry firms the owners or their representatives still participated, at the time of World War I, in decisions that defined and implemented growth strategies; but by World War II their influence had waned. Banker domination of the type exerted in U.S. Steel was exceedingly rare in the United States. By 1920 the number of bankers on the boards of industry-wide mergers had declined sharply, as David Bunting has documented.[138] Representatives of banks never played a role in top-level decision-making comparable to that played by their counterparts in Germany and other continental European countries.

Far more influential were representatives of large individual investors, particularly when founders and their families remained or became experienced full-time managers. Thus venture capitalists such as the Mellons continued to have a say at Carborundum but far less at Alcoa and Pittsburgh Plate Glass, where the founding entrepreneurs retained control and continued as full-time top managers. The representatives of the du Ponts had a say at U.S. Rubber comparable to that of the Mellons at Carborundum, and those of the Moore family may have been in the same position at American Can. In 1917 the founders of the following firms or industries were still participating in management as full-time executives: Phillips Petroleum and Firestone Tire & Rubber; Sun Oil (the Pews); Gulf Oil (William Mellon); plate glass (the Pitcairns); flat glass (the Libbeys and Owens); abrasives (the Nortons); copper (the Guggenheims, Dodges, and Jameses); aluminum (the Hunts and Davises); and, in steel, the Laughlins and Blocks, who dominated Inland Steel, and the families who controlled Pittsburgh Steel. Unlike so many of their British counterparts, these founding families worked closely with the senior executives they had recruited, and many of the latter became members of their boards of directors.

Nevertheless, by the 1920s in nearly all the industries reviewed in this chapter, there were enterprises whose managers owned less than 1% of the stock of the company they administered. These salaried managers, unencumbered by the wishes of large stockholders (whether members of founding families, venture capitalists, or outside investors) selected their own boards of directors and nominated their own successors.

The decline of family and large-investor influence between the two world wars was even more rapid in the more dynamic set of industries (food, chemicals, and machinery) to be analyzed in the next two chapters. There the greatly enlarged number of decisions relating to increasingly complex issues—issues of production technology, of entering markets abroad, of complex research investments, and of moves into related industries—made it even more difficult for part-time outside directors to acquire the information or the understanding necessary to influence long-term investment or strategic decisions.

FIVE

Expanding Organizational Capabilities: Investment Abroad and Product Diversification in Food and Chemicals

As I have pointed out before, the continuing growth of the modern industrial enterprise came in four ways—by horizontal combination, vertical integration, expansion abroad, and diversification. Initial growth following the three-pronged investment in manufacturing, marketing, and management came largely through horizontal combination and vertical integration. These strategies were primarily defensive, aimed at protecting that sizable investment. After the players in the new oligopolies had honed their organizational capabilities and enlarged their profit streams through functional and strategic competition for market share, they continued to expand through investment abroad and the development of related product lines.

The leaders in oil and rubber, the industries that began the American story, followed this pattern in a somewhat limited way. But in the other industries described in Chapter 4, leading firms rarely diversified, and those that invested abroad rarely expanded their initial investments. During the interwar years their stories moved along in much the same way as they had before World War I. By contrast, the leaders in the food, chemical, and machinery industries expanded by making investments abroad and by diversifying into related product lines after their initial growth, and after World War I they did so extensively. Therefore, while the histories presented in the previous chapter, except for those of oil and rubber, focused on the period up to the end of World War I, this chapter (on food and chemicals) and the following chapter (on machinery) will focus on the years after World War I.

The histories related in the last chapter indicated the defensive nature of growth through horizontal and vertical combination. (After the Sherman Antitrust Act, which was enforced by Theodore Roosevelt and his successors, had restrained horizontal combination, such growth was more vertical than horizontal.) The industries reviewed in this and the next chapter continued to grow by relying on their organizational capabilities—capabilities that were sharpened through functional and strategic competition. They could do so, in part, because both their products and their processes of production and distribution provided greater potential for growth than did metals, materials, and even oil and rubber. After World War I, in fact, the leaders in these food, chemical, and machinery industries became the nation's most dynamic firms in terms of innovation (both in product and process and in organizational structure), productivity, profit, and growth. During the interwar years they accounted for just over half of the 200 largest industrial enterprises—101 in 1917 and 114 in 1948 (Table 6).

Within each of these three dynamic industries the pattern of continued growth varied. Where the dynamics for growth rested more on exploiting economies of scale, firms grew more by direct investment abroad. This was particularly the case for mass producers of nonelectrical and transportation machinery. Where the dynamics were generated more by economies of scope, the path to growth was more through diversification. This was especially true for industrial chemical firms. In food, consumer chemicals, and electrical machinery the leading companies often took both routes, becoming both multinational and multiproduct enterprises. In all cases the characteristics of their specific technologies and of their particular markets both set the course the leaders traveled and shaped the strategies they adopted. Since these characteristics varied, the histories of the three sets of industries illustrate many of the differing factors that accounted for the dynamic evolution of the modern industrial enterprise.

Branded, Packaged Products: Foods, Consumer Chemicals, Tobacco

Because the processors of foods, consumer chemicals (that is, soap, paints, drugs, and allied products), and also tobacco (Groups 20, 21, 28; see Appendixes A.1–A.4) have many characteristics in common, they are treated here as a single group. (Although the tobacco industry was far less dynamic than food and chemicals, it is included because cigarettes and other tobacco products are prime examples of branded, packaged goods.)

GENERAL CHARACTERISTICS
These industries had many characteristics in common. The most important was that their primary and most profitable lines were branded, packaged consumer goods that could be placed directly on retailers' shelves. A small number of enterprises continued to sell their products in bulk. Most, however, turned to packaging them as the final phase of the production process. Nearly all the companies were beneficiaries of packaging innovations in metals, paper, and glass. Because they did the packaging (thus taking over a basic function of a wholesaler), they branded their products and sold them nationally and interna-

tionally; and because they branded, they also advertised nationally and internationally.

A second characteristic was, then, that the food and chemical producers relied more on advertising and less on product-specific marketing services and distribution facilities than did leaders in any other industry in which the modern enterprise has clustered since the 1880s (see Figure 6). The nine groups with the highest ratios of advertising expenditures were (in order): drugs and medicines, cereal preparations, cigarettes, soaps and cooking fats, distilled liquors, malt beverages, tobacco products (other than cigarettes and cigars), cigars, and canned fruits and vegetables. The advertising expenditures in these nine industries ran from just under 5% of net sales to close to 14%, whereas for seventy-one of the ninety-one industries advertising expenditures were less than 2% of net sales. The nine industries also had the highest advertising expenses in relation to total selling expenses. Four of the nine (drugs, cereals, cigarettes, and soap) were the only industries in which advertising expenses equaled or exceeded other selling expenses. In that respect the difference between these industries and those that manufactured sewing and office machines is particularly striking, for those manufacturers, which had the largest *total* selling expenses of all (in relation to dollar sales), had relatively small advertising budgets.[1]

The leading producers of branded, packaged products, therefore, relied more than any other group of American manufacturers on that specialized intermediary, the advertising agency. That institution, which appeared in the 1870s, purchased advertising space in newspapers and other periodicals and resold it to large advertisers. At first the new mass retailers, particularly department stores, were its major clients. From the 1880s on, however, the new mass producers became even more significant users. Soon the agencies were working closely with the manufacturers' sales departments to prepare copy for the media space they sold. Such copy included texts, illustrations, and layouts that became increasingly sophisticated during the first years of the new century. A few firms, such as Royal Baking Powder and Standard Oil (before the 1911 dissolution decree), set up their own in-house advertising agencies. Nearly all of the large producers of branded, packaged products, however, continued to rely on the agencies to write copy and obtain space.[2] Such activities did not require specialized, product-specific marketing skills, such as those needed for demonstration, installation, after-sales service, and consumer credit—services that, together with the maintenance of extensive distribution facilities, accounted for the greatest part of the cost of selling American industrial products.

A third characteristic distinguishing the producers of branded, packaged products was that their essential tripartite investment in manufacturing, marketing, and management was initially smaller than that required in other industries in which the modern enterprise clustered. Not only did the marketing and distribution of these companies' goods require less in the way of product-specific personnel and facilities, but the optimal size of plants was usually much smaller. These differences meant that expansion abroad and diversification into related product lines were normally less costly and therefore less risky than comparable investments in other industries.

SELECTING THE PLAYERS, 1880 TO WORLD WAR I

For producers of branded, packaged consumer products, economies of scale came from two sources. One was inherent in the production processes themselves, that is, in the new and improved refining, distilling, and manufacturing technologies. The other derived from new packaging techniques, particularly high-speed canning. In industries where the greatest cost savings came from production processes, investments that determined the players and defined the industry's specific structure usually followed merger and acquisition. In those where cost savings came more from packaging, first movers continued to grow and develop their organizational capabilities through direct investment in their own facilities and personnel.

In the refining of sugar and vegetable oil, where the process of production was similar to that of petroleum (in fact, several of the innovations in petroleum refining were borrowed from the sugar industry), modern production methods were adopted by a number of enterprises almost simultaneously. The same thing happened in the distilling of whiskey and the processing of paint.[3] In these industries the resulting increase in output led to the establishment of the first nationwide horizontal consolidations—the small number of trusts created in the 1880s. After the passage of the New Jersey holding company law in 1889, these trusts took the legal form of holding companies, such as American Sugar Refining, American Cotton Oil, American Linseed, Distillers (formerly Distillers Securities), and National Lead (primarily a maker of paints). In the 1890s other nationwide mergers in these industries included Southern Cotton Oil and Corn Products Refining.[4]

In the production of grain, the coming of the "new process"—the automatic, all-roller, gradual-reduction mills—drastically reduced unit costs in the early 1880s; and in the production of cigarettes, the Bonsack machine did the same in the mid-1880s. Here the pioneers were leaders in the formation of industry-wide consolidations, including Henry Crowell's American Cereal Company (later Quaker Oats) in 1888 and Duke's American Tobacco in 1890. In the early 1890s the two major flour millers, Washburn-Crosby and Pillsbury, acquired competing mills. These moves, in turn, led other millers to combine into the United States Flour Milling Company (later Standard Milling).

As in other industries, the timing of post-merger administrative rationalizations and major investments in production, distribution, and management dif-

Bar chart — horizontal axis: PERCENT (0, 5, 10, 15, 20, 25, 30, 35)

Industry	Number of Companies Covered
CRUDE PETROLEUM	17
SHIPBUILDING	16
MERCHANT PIG IRON	10
COPPER SMELTING & REFINING	13
AIRCRAFT MANUFACTURE	25
IRON & STEEL FORGINGS	32
RAILROAD EQUIPMENT	14
RAYON & ALLIED PRODUCTS	30
LEAD & ZINC PRODUCTS	7
COKE OVEN PRODUCTS	27
TEXTILE DYEING & FINISHING	17
LEAD & ZINC PRIMARY SMELTING	9
TIN CANS & TINWARE	37
TANNED, CURRIED & FINISHED LEATHER	56
COTTON TEXTILES	217
GRAY & MALLEABLE IRON CASTINGS	44
WOOLEN & WORSTED MANUFACTURING	64
AUTOMOBILE PARTS & ACCESSORIES	34
ELECTRIC WIRE & CABLE	33
BOLTS, NUTS, WASHERS & RIVETS	23
MACHINE SCREW PRODUCTS	5
STEAM ENGINES & TURBINES	17
CANE SUGAR REFINING	39
STEEL CASTINGS	23
MOTOR VEHICLES	150
PAPER & PULP	77
LUMBER & TIMBER PRODUCTS	40
MACHINE TOOLS	19
POWER BOILERS, ETC.	12
FIREARMS & AMMUNITION	49
TEXTILE MACHINERY	33
INDUSTRIAL CHEMICALS	23
FERTILIZER MANUFACTURING	22
GLASS & GLASSWARE	29
MACHINE TOOL ACCESSORIES	16
PLUMBERS SUPPLIES	22
CLAY PRODUCTS (except pottery)	11
CORN PRODUCTS	13
INTERNAL COMBUSTION ENGINES	22
ELEVATORS, ESCALATORS & CONVEYORS	19
PLASTICS MANUFACTURING	23
OIL FIELD MACHINERY	9
MECHANICAL STOKERS	22
FLOUR MILLING	27
MINING MACHINERY & EQUIPMENT	

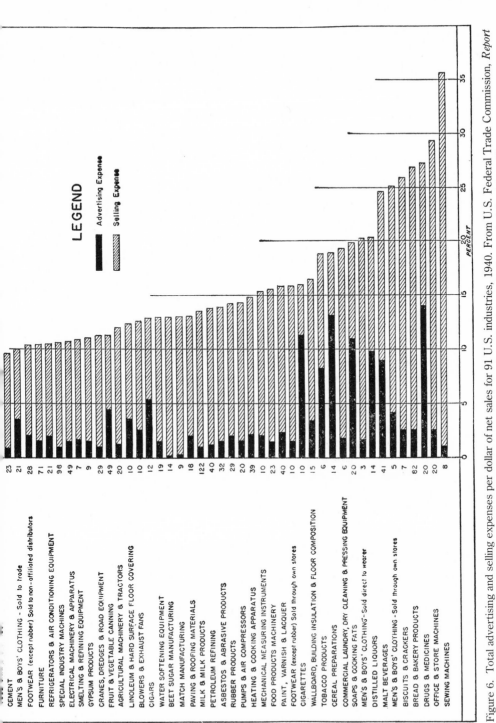

Figure 6. Total advertising and selling expenses per dollar of net sales for 91 U.S. industries, 1940. From U.S. Federal Trade Commission, *Report on Distribution Methods and Costs*, pt. V, *Advertising as a Factor in Distribution* (Washington, D.C., 1944), following p. 10.

fered, reflecting the differing perceptions and motives of the merger-makers. At Quaker Oats, American Tobacco, American Cotton Oil, National Biscuit (Nabisco), and the two leading grain millers the investments were made quickly. At American Sugar Refining, National Linseed Oil (later American Linseed), United States Flour Milling, Corn Products Refining, and Distillers Securities, they were made only after the failure of costly attempts to control price and output of bulk products through the holding company device.[5] These consolidated enterprises continued to sell in bulk lots (which were almost always branded) to food and industrial processors, mass retailers, hotels, and other institutional buyers, as well as to wholesalers. For nearly all, however, nationally advertised, branded, packaged products sold through retailers became the mainstay of their business.

After making their three-pronged investment in the 1880s, pioneers in the new high-volume packaging technologies, such as Borden in canned milk, Heinz in canned vegetables, Campbell Soup in canned soups, Libby, McNeill & Libby in canned meat, and later California Packing (Del Monte) in canned fruit, made occasional acquisitions. But the primary pattern of growth was additional investment in their own processing and marketing facilities and personnel. Moreover, because the foods they processed were perishable, they also invested in extensive purchasing and storage organizations that assured a day-to-day, year-in-year-out flow of seasonally grown products through their processing plants. (Such an investment was also essential in tobacco, where the tobacco leaves had to be cured as well as stored.) In the making of chocolate and cocoa, another industry where new packaging methods came to be combined with technologies of production that increased throughput, the leaders, Walter Baker and Hershey, also grew by direct investment in marketing and distribution rather than by merger.[6]

Like the food packagers, the producers of packaged consumer chemicals also grew primarily through direct investment. The first enterprises to exploit fully the new high-volume production and packaging technologies in soap (Procter & Gamble), paints (Sherwin-Williams), and pharmaceuticals (Parke, Davis) remained the leaders in their industries for a century. Their challengers, such as Colgate in soap and Glidden in paints, followed much the same pattern of growth. In soap, throughput economies quickly brought concentration. But in paints and in those drugs that continued to be mixed and packaged by relatively simple methods, scale provided less of a cost advantage than it did in the production of soap or the more technically complex pharmaceuticals.[7] The paint and drug industries, therefore, remained far less concentrated (see Table 13). Nevertheless, even here the first movers long remained their industry's leaders.

In these industries, as in others where new technologies brought cost advantages of scale, most of the major players had been selected by the end of the

Table 13. Manufacturers' domestic distribution channels and concentration ratios in the food, tobacco, and consumer-chemical industries, 1935–1954 (in percentages).

Industry	Distribution channels, 1939						Concentration ratios, 1935–1954					
	Via own channels				Via intermediaries		Four largest firms			Eight largest firms		
	Own outlets		Direct sales									
	Wholesale	Retail	Industrial	Consumer	Wholesalers	Retailers	1935	1947	1954	1935	1947	1954
Group 20												
Food and kindred products												
Cane sugar refining	31.4	—	15.4	—	39.6	13.6	69	70	67	88	88	86
Cottonseed oil	1.1	0.4	38.1	12.8	35.5	12.1	32	43	47	43	55	57
Cereal preparations	62.6	—	1.3	—	31.6	4.5	68	79	88	82	91	95
Flour and other grain mill products	26.3	1.4	19.3	4.1	26.0	22.9	29	29	40	37	41	52
Biscuits, crackers, and pretzels	49.5	—	1.2	0.2	15.6	33.5	—	72	71	—	78	77
Condensed and evaporated milk	33.5	7.1	12.1	2.8	34.0	10.5	—	50	55	—	63	68
Baking powder and yeast	54.4	0.7	9.8	—	33.3	1.8	57	83	80	82	94	93
Linseed oil	13.1	—	53.7	—	32.1	1.1	87	75	85	97	97	100
Group 21												
Tobacco manufactures												
Cigarettes	33.0	—	1.1	—	59.7	6.2	89	90	82	99	99	99
Group 28												
Chemicals and allied products												
Soap and glycerin	79.3	—	6.2	0.3	8.8	5.4	73	79	85	83	86	89
Paints, varnishes, and lacquers	30.9	7.4	28.7	1.4	16.4	15.2	—	27	27	—	36	37
Drugs and medicines	30.7	0.6	9.8	1.0	40.8	17.1	—	28	25	—	44	44

Sources: For distribution channels, U.S. Bureau of the Census, *Distribution of Manufacturers' Sales, 1939* (Washington, D.C., 1942), table 3, appropriate industry sections; for concentration ratios, U.S. Bureau of the Census, *Concentration Ratios in Manufacturing Industry, 1958* (Washington, D.C., 1962), table 2, appropriate industry sections.

first decade of the new century. In the succeeding years there was more turn-over at the top in these industries (but not much more) than in oil, rubber, materials, and metals. Of the twenty-seven food companies on the 1948 list, nineteen had been on the 1917 list as well. All of these nineteen had been established before the end of the turn-of-the-century merger movement.[8] Of the eight new firms, three were mergers that included companies which had been on the 1917 list. In tobacco, four of the five leaders had been part of American Tobacco before it was dissolved by a court decree in 1911. In con-sumer chemicals there was more turnover, particularly before 1930. Even so, six of the ten on the 1948 list had been there in 1930.

The food companies that dropped off the list of the top two hundred firms—such as Booth Fisheries and the two regional ice companies on the 1917 list (see Appendix A.4)—were those whose production technologies did not have scale economies comparable to those in sugar, vegetable oil, paints, or drugs. Or, in the case of sugar and vegetable oil, they were firms that failed to move, or were slow to move, from producing and selling in bulk to making branded, packaged products to be placed directly on retailers' shelves. In sugar, rapid expansion in the refining of cane sugar from Cuba and of beet sugar from the American West increased the number of competitors in the oligopoly during the 1920s; but with the coming of the depression all but two of the major sugar refiners dropped off the list. The two that remained in 1948 were American Sugar Refining, the oldest and largest of the cane processors, and Great Western Sugar, the oldest and largest of the beet-sugar processors. Of all the sugar companies only American Sugar Refining made an extended effort to concentrate on packaged products (such as its well-known Domino brand) for the retail trade.[9]

Although the largest vegetable-oil producers—American Cotton Oil and Southern Cotton Oil—did develop a variety of branded, packaged products before World War I, bulk sales to industrial users remained the major part of their business until the postwar recession of 1920–21, when both suffered severe losses through write-downs of excessive inventory. In the 1920s, there-fore, they concentrated more on their branded, nationally advertised margarine, salad dressing, washing powder, and soap. In fact, both took as their corporate names the names of their best-selling brands. American Cotton Oil became the Gold Dust Corporation, and Southern Cotton Oil became the Wesson Oil & Snowdrift Company. (In 1928 the food-making activities of American Linseed, a direct descendant of an earlier trust, became part of the Gold Dust Corpo-ration.) Nevertheless, for the producers of vegetable oil, sugar, and flour, direct sales to food and other processors and to institutional buyers remained a more important part of their business than they did for most other large food proces-sors (Table 13).[10]

CONTINUING INVESTMENT IN MARKETING AND DISTRIBUTION

As the second decade of the century came to a close, the producers of branded, packaged products began to expand by capturing markets abroad and by moving into related product lines. As might be expected, such growth was based on organizational capabilities developed in marketing and distribution more than on those developed in production and research. Nevertheless, improved skills and facilities in production and research did make important contributions. At the same time, such capabilities in marketing and distribution always reflected the nature and extent of the initial investments made in those functions. As already noted (Chapter 3), some firms, usually those with the least product-specific requirements in marketing, service, and distribution facilities, had from the start relied on the wholesaler to act as a "shipping agency" to carry out the physical distribution of goods to retailers. Others, including Sherwin-Williams, National Biscuit, Corn Products Refining, and American Cotton Oil, with their greater requirements for delivery and storage facilities, had invested in extensive distribution organizations from the start. As early as 1891 American Cotton Oil had more than three hundred tank cars, as well as an oceangoing tanker and a large depot in Rotterdam. So, too, Fleischmann by the mid-1890s had a network to distribute its perishable product daily to bakers and brewers in all parts of the nation.[11] Royal Baking Powder soon had a comparable network in place for the same market. Parke, Davis, the country's most prominent pharmaceutical firm, sold prescription drugs to pharmacies and hospitals, as well as packaged pills over the counter. It established branch offices in New York in 1881, Kansas City in 1890, Baltimore in 1897, New Orleans in 1899, and Chicago and St. Louis in 1901. It set up offices in Windsor, Canada, and London, England, in 1891; Sydney, Australia, in 1897; Montreal in 1898; and Simla, India, in 1897 (transferred to Bombay in 1907).[12]

Firms that had relied on wholesalers until World War I began after the war to replace these intermediaries with expanded organizations of their own. Not only had their output reached a scale that permitted them to distribute as cheaply as the intermediaries, but direct sales to retailers had also assured them a far better control over inventory and, therefore, of factory throughput. In 1919 Richard Deupree, the general sales manager of Procter & Gamble (later its chief executive officer), advocated direct selling to retailers. He emphasized that although consumer demand for soap and cooking oil remained steady, the orders of individual wholesalers fluctuated widely.

> If we supplied the retailer with what he needs on a week-to-week basis, the outflow from our plants would likewise be a steady week-to-week flow. If we are to avoid periodic layoffs, the solution seems to be to sell so that we will be filling retail shelves as they are empty. In that way, our outflow will be as steady as the retailer's. And we can stabilize our employment year-round to match the retailer's

year-round sales . . . The only way we can control our own production schedule
is to produce to the consumption line. [13]

His associates agreed, even though the cost was high. Overnight the sales
force had to be expanded from 150 to 600; 125 more warehouses had to be
acquired; 2,000 contracts had to be written for deliveries by trucks; and the
accounting department had to be reorganized to handle 450,000 accounts. The
investment paid off. [14] Other soapmakers followed Procter & Gamble's example.
By 1939 only 8.8% of the soap produced in the United States was distributed
through independent wholesalers (Table 13).

In the other industries making branded, packaged products, wholesalers
retained a larger share than they did in oil, rubber, metals, glass, and other
materials. Except in tobacco—where the wholesaler remained "the shipping
agency" for the manufacturers—and sugar and drugs, such intermediaries did
not handle more than a third of the goods distributed. Relatively large amounts
were sold by the companies' sales forces to retailers, increasingly chain stores
and other mass marketers (Table 13).

Functional and strategic competition in branded, packaged products brought
changes in market share. As in other industries where concentration originally
resulted from merger, the share of the dominant firm dropped. For example,
that of American Sugar, which was slow in centralizing and rationalizing, fell to
30% from 70%. But even National Biscuit, which did make the necessary
investments, fell to 42% from 70%. [15] The growth of independents in sugar
reflected not only American Sugar's delay in transforming itself from a holding
into an operating company but also the availability of new sources of supply—
the expansion of cane sugar in Cuba and the coming of beet sugar in the American West. In the case of National Biscuit, the challengers were either expanding
regional producers or other food companies diversifying their production into
biscuits and confectionery.

When one firm had acquired first-mover advantages through its initial direct
investment (rather than those made following merger), the challenges usually
came from either technological innovators or foreign firms. Canned milk is a
good example. Borden's first challenge came from abroad. In 1884 Anglo-Swiss
Condensed Milk, started by two American brothers in Switzerland in the 1880s,
opened two factories in the United States. These were sold to Borden shortly
before Anglo-Swiss merged in 1905 with another Swiss first mover, Nestlé. In
1900 Nestlé had built a plant at Fulton, New York. As part of the arrangements
of the 1905 merger, Nestlé agreed to withdraw from the condensed-milk market
in the United States, although it continued to produce baby food and milk
chocolate at Fulton. With the outbreak of World War I, however, Nestlé again
began to compete with Borden. Well before that date Borden had also been
challenged by innovators who had developed new processes for evaporating

(rather than condensing) milk—Helvetia (later Pet Milk) and Carnation. By 1918 Borden's share of the packaged milk market was 19.0%, Nestlé's 16.6%, Carnation's 12.5%, and Helvetia's 9.8%. The two leading meatpackers—Swift and Armour—together produced 9.0%. No other firm enjoyed as much as 5% of the market for packaged milk. As the Federal Trade Commission reported, the percentages had changed rapidly. Four years earlier Borden had had 23.6%, Carnation 17.8%, and Helvetia 15.1%. Nestlé had obviously proved itself an effective competitor.[16]

EXPANSION THROUGH DIRECT INVESTMENT ABROAD

The organizational capabilities developed through such oligopolistic competition encouraged American producers of branded, packaged products to invest abroad. As they enlarged their wholesaling organizations at home, they expanded them overseas, much as Parke, Davis had done in the 1880s and 1890s. Many such companies producing food and consumer chemicals waited, however, until after World War I to invest extensively in marketing abroad. Thus many more overseas manufacturing subsidiaries were set up after the war than before. Before World War I, producers of machinery led "the American invasion" of Europe (see Tables 14 and 15). Such machinery was mainly light, standardized, volume-produced equipment. Following the war, the number of new subsidiaries established by food and consumer-chemical companies nearly exceeded that set up by machinery companies. In Britain, indeed, the count of U.S. manufacturing subsidiaries established between 1918 and 1948 was fifty-five in branded, packaged products and only thirty-two in all three machinery groups: nonelectrical, electrical, and transportation. A Department of Commerce study reported that in 1932 no fewer than fifty-seven American food companies and seventy-five producers of consumer chemicals had made direct investments abroad in all parts of the world. Because the optimal size of plants was small and, therefore, required less capital, because the penalties of operating below scale were less costly than in more capital-intensive industries, and because tastes, distribution channels, and advertising media differed from country to country, the firms tended to invest in small plants for each of the different national markets. In the rich national markets of continental Europe, therefore, the value of this investment remained well below that of machinery or oil companies (but well above that of any other industry).[17]

Of the producers of branded, packaged products listed in the top two hundred, Quaker Oats, Heinz, Coca-Cola, and American Cotton Oil (all in Group 20) and Parke, Davis, United Drug, and Sherwin-Williams (in Group 28) had manufacturing plants in Europe before World War I. All expanded their production facilities during the interwar years. After the war, such firms in Group 20 as Borden, Carnation, Pet Milk, Corn Products Refining, General Foods, Royal Baking Powder, Kraft, National Biscuit, California Packing, and Wrigley

Table 14. Establishment of manufacturing operations in Great Britain by U.S. industrial enterprises, 1900–1971.

Industry	Number of cases			
	1900–1917	1918–1929	1930–1948	1949–1971
Food	2	4	24	64
Tobacco	0	0	1	6
Textiles	0	0	0	8
Apparel	0	0	0	2
Lumber	0	0	0	2
Furniture	0	0	0	3
Paper	0	0	0	8
Printing and publishing	0	0	0	2
Consumer chemicals	0	7	19	66
Industrial chemicals	1	3	12	70
Petroleum	0	5	5	22
Rubber	0	4	4	8
Leather	0	0	0	0
Stone, clay, and glass	1	1	1	31
Primary metals	0	0	2	49
Fabricated metals	1	4	3	28
Machinery	8	2	10	53
Electrical machinery	4	4	8	55
Transportation equipment	4	6	2	52
Instruments	1	1	2	12
Miscellaneous	0	1	0	3
Total	22	42	93	544

Source: Compiled by Peter Williamson from data base of Multinational Enterprise Project, Harvard Business School.

(chewing gum) invested in production facilities abroad. (Wrigley's major competitor, American Chicle, had gone overseas before 1914.) In the same years American Home Products, Sterling Drug, Procter & Gamble, Colgate, and Palmolive-Peet (all in Group 28) made comparable investments in manufacturing to support their sales organizations. All these firms also made extensive investments in Canada, which they considered an essential part of their domestic market. [18]

The specific strategies for overseas investment varied from firm to firm. Some achieved growth by acquisition (Tables 16 and 17); but more built their own plants, incorporating their wholly owned manufacturing subsidiaries. Some moved quickly; others held off. Mira Wilkins describes the strategy of both Colgate and Palmolive-Peet, which continued when they merged in 1928: "It

Table 15.   Establishment of manufacturing operations in Germany by U.S. industrial
enterprises, 1900–1971.[a]

Industry	Number of cases			
	1900–1913	1914–1930	1931–1953	1954–1971
Food	0	5	7	44
Tobacco	0	0	0	1
Textiles	0	0	0	4
Apparel	0	0	0	0
Lumber	0	0	0	1
Furniture	0	0	0	1
Paper	0	0	1	2
Printing and publishing	0	0	0	3
Consumer chemicals	0	3	1	36
Industrial chemicals	0	3	3	36
Petroleum	2	2	2	31
Rubber	0	1	2	3
Leather	0	0	0	0
Stone, clay, and glass	2	0	1	13
Primary metals	0	0	0	21
Fabricated metals	1	1	3	26
Machinery	8	6	7	30
Electrical machinery	0	2	5	43
Transportation equipment	0	3	0	24
Instruments	1	2	1	9
Miscellaneous	0	0	2	0
Total	14	28	33	330

Source: Compiled by Peter Williamson from data base of Multinational Enterprise Project,
Harvard Business School.
a. For post–World War II years, figures represent West Germany.

would export until it had obtained sufficient sales volume; then, it would contract
with an independent local soap maker to manufacture according to its formula.
It kept its own trademark and continued to do the merchandising. As volume
rose, it often purchased the foreign franchised manufacturer. Its expansion then
would proceed, primarily through invested earnings."[19]

By contrast, Colgate-Palmolive-Peet's major competitor, Procter & Gamble,
made no significant investment abroad (outside of Canada) until its major move
in the 1930s into Britain, a market long dominated by that nation's industrial
giant, Lever Brothers. It began the move by purchasing a small but long-
established firm, Thomas Hadley & Sons. After building a new, large, state-of-
the-art plant, Procter & Gamble used its skills in marketing and distribution to
cut quickly into Lever's market share.[20] Other firms, such as Quaker Oats,

Table 16. Method of U.S. firms' entry into Great Britain, 1900–1971.

	Method of entry (%)			
Categories	1900–1917	1918–1929	1930–1948	1949–1971
Newly formed subsidiaries	50.0	35.7	40.9	25.2
Reorganization of subsidiaries	4.5	4.8	5.4	2.9
Acquisition of local firms	36.5	52.4	39.7	67.1
Unclassified	9.0	7.1	14.0	4.8
Total	100.0	100.0	100.0	100.0

Source: Compiled by Peter Williamson from data base of Multinational Enterprise Project, Harvard Business School.

Table 17. Method of U.S. firms' entry into Germany, 1900–1971.[a]

	Method of entry (%)			
Categories	1900–1913	1914–1930	1931–1953	1954–1971
Newly formed subsidiaries	92.9	46.4	36.4	32.2
Reorganization of subsidiaries	0.0	3.6	0.0	1.8
Acquisition of local firms	7.1	32.1	51.5	63.0
Unclassified	0.0	17.9	12.1	3.0
Total	100.0	100.0	100.0	100.0

Source: Compiled by Peter Williamson from data base of Multinational Enterprise Project, Harvard Business School.
a. For post–World War II years, figures represent West Germany.

Heinz, and Corn Products Refining, built their own plants abroad. By the mid-1930s Corn Products Refining had its own manufacturing facilities in Britain, France, Germany, Italy, Holland, Czechoslovakia, and Yugoslavia, as well as in Asia, Latin America, Africa, and Australia.[21]

Whatever its initial strategy, a firm would usually adopt a policy of continuous investment to strengthen its competitive position abroad. It almost always made investments in production facilities to support existing sales and distribution networks in distant markets. Tariffs and other cross-border restrictions encouraged these direct investments by producers of branded, packaged products, just as they did in rubber and oil. Nevertheless, such extensive investments in Britain, where tariffs were low or nonexistent, suggests other reasons, including the reduction in transportation and inventory costs, greater flexibility in adjusting products to local taste, and further utilization of the enterprise's technical marketing and managerial skills. The overseas factories producing branded, packaged products were established to serve national markets, rather than larger regional markets, which prevailed in glass, abrasives, rubber, and machinery. This national orientation came, first, because the cost advantages of scale were relatively low, making smaller plants efficient. It came, second, because local taste helped shape the demand for branded, packaged products, and because the materials required for their processing could be obtained locally more easily than in other industries.

Once established, these integrated subsidiaries competed with local companies and the subsidiaries of other multinationals both functionally and strategically. They rarely found it necessary to take part in cartel arrangements, as did the foreign subsidiaries and their American parent companies in glass, aluminum, copper, chemicals, and electrical machinery. Because coordination of purchasing, production, and marketing was achieved most effectively at local levels, there was little need for tight home-office control over management in these subsidiaries. They operated autonomously, gently supervised by the executives of the parent company's international division.

CONTINUING GROWTH THROUGH DIVERSIFICATION

Among the leading producers of branded, packaged foods and consumer chemicals, growth through investment in new products became even more important than growth by facilities and personnel abroad. In the interwar years and even earlier, many of the largest firms—though certainly not all of them—began to grow by exploiting not only the economies of scale but also those of scope. They began to diversify into products that required either the same raw materials (which could easily be obtained by the firm's purchasing organizations), or similar (though rarely precisely the same) production processes, or, most likely of all, comparable marketing skills and distribution facilities.

Processors of foods and consumer chemicals were among the very first American enterprises to organize research units that did more than test or provide quality control. For example, Charles Wesson, a member of the class of 1883 at the Massachusetts Institute of Technology, became the chief chemist of American Cotton Oil's new "central laboratory" at Guttenberg, New Jersey, in 1893. In 1901 he moved to a comparable position with its largest competitor, Southern Cotton Oil.[22] Sherwin-Williams had hired its first chemist, another M.I.T. graduate, and had built a Chicago laboratory before the end of the century. Parke, Davis completed a new laboratory in Detroit in 1902—an establishment whose facilities and personnel received the highest praise from a leading German chemical maker, Carl Duisberg. On the other hand, Procter & Gamble, although carrying on research and developing new products, waited until 1921 to form a separate development department with its own large laboratory.[23] During the 1920s the majority of food and chemical firms that ranked among the top two hundred made equally substantial investments in laboratories and set up separate departments to administer them.

Their work and the products they developed reflected the nature of their primary products and processes, for in all cases the initial function of such research and development was to improve process and product. The less technologically complex the existing activities, the smaller the potential for new-product development. Thus the cigarette makers, which also produced packaged tobacco products, such as smoking and chewing tobacco and snuff, invested almost nothing in research and made no attempt at all to diversify. Nor did canners and packagers, such as Heinz, Campbell Soup, California Packing, Coca-Cola, and Wrigley, all of which used relatively simple processing techniques. But where the production processes were chemically or mechanically more complex, research did bring product development. By the 1930s the food companies using mechanical processes had become more diversified than those that were primarily packagers and canners, and those using more complex chemical processes with greater opportunities for exploiting scope had become more diversified than those employing mechanical ones.

The research departments of the vegetable-oil refiners—American Cotton Oil, Southern Cotton Oil, and Corn Products Refining—began well before World War I to develop new or improved branded, packaged products; these products came to play a significant role in their firms' continued profitability. These research departments originated Wesson cooking oil and Snowdrift and Gold Dust washing powder. In the 1920s they helped develop soap and paint products that used cottonseed oil as a raw material. At Corn Products Refining, in-house laboratories developed and improved such brands as Argo starch, Mazola salad and cooking oil, Karo syrup, and Kre-Mel desserts, as well as Certos, a dextrose sweetener. The research department at Corn Products also led the company into chemicals with the development of new phenol-type plastics. But rather than attempting to develop and distribute these nonfood items, Corn Products formed a joint venture (with a leading chemical enterprise, Commercial Solvents), which assumed responsibility for all production and marketing.[24]

At Borden and at the cereal companies, laboratories played a less significant role. There diversification came from exploiting the economies of scope in distribution more than those in production. The impetus for diversification came from a desire to employ more fully the expanded marketing organizations. To do so, Borden moved into the production of cereals, coffee, and other branded, packaged products. The major contribution of its laboratories in the 1920s was the development of casein and similar milk-based chemicals used in paint and other coatings. Again, as at Corn Products, Borden hesitated to make a direct investment in a relatively unknown business. Instead, it acquired in 1929 a small producer of related chemicals, the Casein Company, to process and distribute these products.[25]

The leading grain processors also diversified by taking on existing products that required similar raw materials, used similar production processes, or could be marketed through established distribution networks. Thus General Mills (the successor to Washburn-Crosby) and Pillsbury (which nearly reached the top two hundred during the interwar years) diversified into breakfast cereals, cake mixes, biscuit mixes, and then animal feeds; similarly, Ralston Purina, about the same size as Pillsbury, moved from animal feeds to cereals and other packaged foods for human consumption.[26] Each, of course, had to create a new marketing organization to sell to new kinds of customers. Quaker Oats, too, added new lines, which included wheat cereals, farina, hominy, cornmeal, macaroni, spaghetti, and, on a smaller scale, poultry feeds. Here, as at Corn Products and Borden, the research department developed a new chemical product in the early 1920s. This was furfural, made from oat hulls—a chemical that would be increasingly used by producers of resin, of agricultural and other chemicals, and, later, of synthetic rubber. In this case Quaker Oats turned over the development and marketing of the new product to an autonomous subsidiary that managed it until the 1930s.[27]

The makers of consumer chemicals concentrated primarily on developing new products, in contrast to the food companies, which mostly took on established items. At Procter & Gamble even before World War I, research chemists had developed some of the first washing powders (laundry soap flakes) sold in the United States, including Amber Flakes, White Crown, and Ivory Flakes. At the same time, their work led the company into a related line of products—cooking oils—with the development of the Crisco brand in 1911.[28] After the First World War, in collaboration with chemists at Du Pont, they introduced a wide range of new detergents, including Gardinol, Dreft, Drene, and Teel. But neither Procter & Gamble nor its competitors attempted to move beyond soap and cooking oil. Their substantial investments in high-volume, low-unit-cost systems of production and distribution for these related products deterred them from going further afield, at least until well after World War II.

The leading paint companies, Sherwin-Williams and Glidden, diversified more quickly and more extensively into new products than did Procter & Gamble and the other soapmakers. At Sherwin-Williams, work on improving pigments and lacquers during the dye shortage of World War I led the company to produce dyes and a wide range of intermediary chemicals used in the production of dyes and pigments. The new dye production was so difficult and the market so competitive, however, that after the war the company decided only to make intermediaries for other manufacturers. From this base, nevertheless, it commercialized a broad line of insecticides, fungicides, and weed killers. By the 1940s it was producing insecticides in greater volume than any other firm in the United States.

Its major competitor, Glidden, took a different route to diversification during the interwar years, concentrating its research on developing the full potential of its raw materials. From a linseed and then a soybean base came oil and margarine for the baking trade, soybean cooking oil, and then cattle and poultry feed. From the lead used in paints came a line of metal powders and from turpentine a line of naval stores.[29]

In drugs and medicines, as in paints, those firms producing complex products with sophisticated technologies grew by developing new ones. In companies where production amounted to little more than mixing and packaging, laboratories played almost no role at all. Such was the case with United Drug (along with its successors, Drug, Incorporated, and later Rexall Drug) and McKesson & Robbins. The products these companies took on, which were long-established and easily sold, were distributed through their already extensive marketing networks.[30] At Parke, Davis, however, research into complex pharmaceuticals led, mostly after World War I, to the development of such products as vitamins, hormones, and hormone-containing materials that could be packaged, branded, and mass-produced. Then came new medications for syphilis, epilepsy, leprosy, and a variety of allergies. Of the industry's leaders listed among the top two hundred, Parke, Davis, the slightly smaller American Home Products, and Sterling Drug (which grew initially through acquisition of American properties from Bayer, the giant German chemical company, in 1918) benefited most from the pharmaceutical revolution that occurred during World War II following the development of sulfa, penicillin, and other antibiotics.[31] Other beneficiaries of that revolution included Johnson & Johnson, which ranked 152d on the 1948 list, and various firms that had come close to the elite two hundred by 1948 and reached it shortly thereafter. By 1973 Abbott Laboratories, Squibb, Pfizer, and Merck had long been on the list.[32]

The pharmaceutical revolution greatly altered the industry's patterns of production, distribution, and research. Production became much more intricate as a chemical process; marketing involved reaching doctors and hospitals rather than primarily selling branded, packaged products over the counter; and research became much more science-based. The pharmaceutical revolution reshaped many American makers of branded, packaged drug products into modern, research-driven pharmaceutical companies. And I must emphasize here that the development of the new drugs and the transformation of the industry was not carried out by innovative entrepreneurial firms but by long-established enterprises.

Thus, well before World War II, American food and consumer-chemical companies had grown by making investments in facilities and personnel that permitted not only a more efficient use of existing resources but also (and this was more important) of existing technical and managerial skills within the production, purchasing, and distribution units. Increasingly these enterprises relied on their research and development departments, whose own capabilities were expanding to create new or improved products that could utilize the firm's existing resources more profitably.

DIVERSIFICATION THROUGH MERGER

In foods and consumer chemicals the merger road to growth was less common than the road of direct investment. After the turn-of-the-century merger movement, horizontal combinations in these industries were rare. Among the producers of branded, packaged products on the list of the top two hundred, only two of the firms resulting from mergers, Colgate-Palmolive-Peet (1926) and General Mills (1928), had brought together companies with competing products. The others combined large integrated firms whose complementary product lines permitted a more intensive use of their joint facilities and skills.

Some firms merged to exploit the economies of scope in distribution. Thus the main motive for the formation of Standard Brands in 1929 was to combine the distribution networks that Fleischmann and Royal Baking Powder had created in order to deliver highly perishable products to bakers and brewers on a daily basis. Another member of that merger, Chase & Sanborn Coffee, was then able to use the resulting distribution network to make daily deliveries of fresh-ground, packaged coffee throughout the nation. The 1928 merger that formed General Foods resulted in a combined distribution organization that was larger and less product-specific, but its purpose was much the same. That merger included such brand names as Calumet Baking Powder, Maxwell House Coffee, Postum Cereal, Jell-O, Walter Baker Chocolate, and Hellmann's Mayonnaise. The General Foods annual report for 1929 explained: "The demonstrated economies of selling a line of products through a single sales organization would be increased by the number of items handled by each salesman." Such mergers not only provided volume that assured the constituent companies of lower cost in their own distribution, but also permitted them to control and reduce inventory cost, as Procter & Gamble had done, and to assure a more steady throughput in production facilities.

Other consolidations benefited from the economies of scope in both production and distribution. This was true of the mergers in 1928 and 1929 of Gold Dust, American Linseed, American Cotton Oil, and Standard Milling, which in 1937 took the name of The Best Foods, Incorporated. It was also true of General Mills, which in the 1930s acquired several grocery companies using similar marketing facilities and expanded its animal-feed lines, all of which used similar production facilities. By World War II General Mills had begun to produce toasters and other appliances, which it sold through the outlets that handled its groceries.[33]

The largest merger in consumer chemicals, American Home Products (1926), included Wyeth Chemical (with its subsidiary, De Shall Laboratories) and Edward Wesley & Company. As Williams Haynes had noted, the component companies all produced "nationally advertised and distributed proprietary remedies, some having been on the market for over 30 years bearing well-known brand names." Once consolidated, this enterprise continued to grow by acquiring makers of cosmetics, dental cream, and, of greatest importance, medical and pharmaceutical products. Referring to the year 1935, Haynes states: "Under the new leadership the Corporation commenced a program of expansion and diversification in six major classifications: ethical drug preparations; food products; publicly advertised medicinal, pharmaceutical and dentifrice preparations; household products; cosmetics and toilet preparations; and chemicals, organic colors and pigments, dye stuffs and intermediates."[34] Each of these major product lines was administered by a separate integrated division, and within each division diversification continued. By the late 1930s the growth of these divisions had come more from direct investment in new and improved products developed by divisional research and development departments than from acquisitions of established lines. The Household Product Division, for example, moved first into glue and other adhesives, next into polishing and cleaning preparations, and then into sprays and disinfectants; meanwhile, the medical division had begun to develop and market chemically synthesized pharmaceuticals.

PERISHABLE PRODUCTS

Although fundamental differences existed between the producers of perishable consumer items and the makers of all other branded, packaged products, it is necessary at least to touch on the story of the perishable food industry before drawing some general conclusions.

In the production of perishable consumer products—meat, beer, dairy and bakery items—the leaders achieved their dominance by making far greater investments in distribution than in production. Gustavus F. Swift created the modern American meatpacking industry by developing the refrigerated railway car and then, in the mid-1880s, by building a national network of branch offices for his sales force (see Chapter 3). That investment, in turn, permitted much greater economies of throughput by making feasible the disassembling of cattle at Chicago and other midwestern railroad centers. By the end of the decade the few pioneer entrepreneurs who quickly followed Swift's lead—the Armours, the Cudahys, the Morrises, and the founders of Wilson & Company—by making comparable investments in distribution, production, and management had come to dominate the industry along with Swift. These firms established themselves among the nation's largest industrial enterprises and continued for decades to compete oligopolistically for market share.

So, too, did the very first national brewers—Anheuser-Busch of St. Louis and Schlitz, Pabst, and Blatz of Milwaukee. They invested in temperature-controlled tank cars and installed new equipment that permitted much greater throughput. (Adolphus Busch and other American brewers were celebrated in both Germany and the United States for having invented new forms of transportation and new brewing techniques.) In the 1880s and 1890s the American brewer established branch-office distributing networks comparable to, though smaller than, those of the meatpackers.[35] In meatpacking the greater cost advantages in production, as well as the much larger capital investment required in distribution, created barriers to entry that permitted the packers to dominate their markets more completely than the national brewers did theirs. Only in the 1920s with the coming of the truck and the rapid growth of the food retail chains—and increasingly in the 1930s with the organization of the new supermarkets—did the packers begin to lose their initial first-mover advantages to other processors.[36]

In the early years of their growth the largest makers of bread and the producers of fresh milk and dairy products were serving regional markets. From the start they delivered the largest share of product directly to retailers, often to their own retail stores. In 1929, for example, 50.8% of bread and other perishable bakery products went directly to independent retailers and another 11.1% to retailers owned by processors (by 1939 the latter figure had risen to 22.9%). In 1939 close to 60% of all commercially manufactured ice cream went directly to independent retailers, while another 25% went to company-owned outlets and 15% to wholesalers.[37]

The transformation of distribution that challenged the dominant meatpackers also created opportunities for the regional producers of bread and dairy products. Just as the truck permitted smaller packers to sell meat directly to retail butchers and, more important, to the large and growing retail food chains, such as the Great Atlantic & Pacific Tea Company (A&P), Kroger, American Stores, and First National Stores, it also permitted the large bakers, such as Ward Baking, Continental Baking, General Baking, and Purity Bakers, to become multiregional, and National Dairy (a 1923 merger of regional companies) to become national. These bakers and National Dairy standardized their geographically defined delivery systems and integrated and coordinated the activities of these systems. By World War II, National Dairy was being operated through a still embryonic multidivisional structure that included both product and regional divisions. These divisions were administered by a general office with staff units for research, quality control, market research, personnel, and management training, as well as for advertising, purchasing, and accounting.[38]

The product-specific nature of the huge distributing organizations of these producers of perishable products limited the potential for expansion into foreign markets, as well as the potential for diversification. Nevertheless, Swift and Armour, which expanded overseas and became the major suppliers of meat in Britain, were among the very oldest diversified enterprises in the United States. In the years just before World War I they entered Argentina and

Uruguay to supply the British markets, pushing aside British enterprises already in the business (Chapter 9).

And at home, in order to use their processing and distribution capabilities more fully, both Armour and Swift moved into existing related products. To market the by-products of the packing plants, they built large, separate distributing organizations for fertilizer and leather, and they formed smaller organizations to distribute glue, materials derived from animal fat (including soap, oleo oil, and stearin), and chemical and medicinal products. Indeed, by 1900 Armour and Swift had become two of the "Big Five" in the American fertilizer industry, as well as the two largest American leather producers; Armour, too, was one of the major makers of glue and abrasives.[39] And just as important, these companies used their refrigerated transportation, storage, and branch-office facilities to distribute butter, eggs, poultry, and fruit, while Armour soon became the country's largest marketer of butter. To obtain such produce the company invested in a large buying organization that had its own traffic division and its own sales force and delivery networks. The smaller members of the packing oligopoly—Wilson, Cudahy, and Morris—also diversified but on a much smaller scale. Yet by 1910 the two leaders had already realized their potential for diversification by exploiting the economies of scope; and, furthermore, the top managers of their small corporate offices, having continued to concentrate on meatpacking, had neglected to make the necessary investments in processing and marketing to challenge such first movers as Procter & Gamble and Colgate in soap, Norton and Carborundum in abrasives, and, with the coming of synthetic nitrates, Du Pont and Allied Chemical in fertilizers.

Although the meatpackers grew during the interwar years at a high enough rate to remain among the top two hundred, all but two other producers of perishable products (National Dairy and Anheuser-Busch) did not. Moreover, except for National Dairy, whose Kraft Division operated internationally, none of these others invested abroad. In short, except for National Dairy and Anheuser-Busch, all the brewers, bakers, and producers of dairy products had dropped out of the top two hundred by 1948. Clearly the producers of such perishable products had a smaller potential for growth than did those that made semiperishable branded, packaged products.

SCOPE-RELATED GROWTH

This brief review of the leading producers of branded, packaged products emphasizes that these firms grew more by expanding into new geographical and product markets than by horizontal combination or vertical integration in order to assure supplies or outlets. They grew by utilizing capabilities developed through the exploitation of the economies of scale and scope. More made direct investment abroad than did the leaders in the materials and metals industries (described in Chapter 4). The most significant difference, however, from the companies in those industries was the use of scope-related capabilities to move into related product markets.[40] Although the resources that were most easily transferable to the different product lines were connected with marketing and distribution, many firms developed products that also made use of existing capabilities in production, as well as in purchasing and research.

Such exploitation of the economies of scope came after an enterprise had created the administrative organization essential to exploit the economies of scale, and also after it had begun to compete functionally and strategically for market share with comparably integrated competitors. By then it possessed the accumulated resources that could give it a competitive advantage—and the opportunity to achieve profits—in related product lines. Yet any move made to exploit existing facilities and personnel in one functional activity required investment in another activity. The production of animal feeds, for example, although it used much the same machinery as that needed for cereals, called for the formation of a new wholesaling organization. Similarly, more intensive use of a distribution network to market an expanded line of groceries required a related investment in the processing and packaging of such products.

Many of the firms that moved into new brands and products did so in an ad hoc manner. They commercialized a new item after research had brought it into being, or they acquired an established line at an opportune time. By the 1930s a small number of the producers of branded, packaged products had explicitly developed—in the manner exemplified by American Home Products—a strategy of growth through continuing, planned diversification. Such diversification certainly increased competition within American industry. Because these big firms had the necessary resources—not only the funds for advertising but also the functional skills and facilities, particularly in marketing—they were able to invest heavily enough in both production and distribution to capture market share in another oligopoly in a way that was rarely open to the small newcomer.

Because such a strategy increased the complexities of coordination, monitoring, and resource allocation for the enterprise as a whole, it led to the adoption, again in the manner of American Home Products, of the multidivisional administrative structure. By World War II, Glidden had eight product divisions.[41] Borden had divisions for fluid milk, dairy products, and food products.[42] General Mills had two large autonomous divisions—one for flour and feed, the other for grocery products—and four smaller divisions, including one for special commodities, which at first manufactured and sold only vitamins. In 1946 General Foods, which in the 1930s had created autonomous integrated divisions for chocolate, salt, and seafood, carried out a major reorganization, creating sixteen product divisions grouped under four general executives at the corporate office. Shortly after the war Corn Products, Sherwin-Williams, and Procter & Gamble adopted their multidivisional structure and National Dairy took on its comparable structure.

In these several ways, then, the evolution of the modern industrial enterprise in branded, packaged consumer products reflected the special characteristics of this type of industry. The difference between these semiperishable consumer-goods industries and the other industries in which the modern enterprise clustered resulted from differences in their technologies of production and in their markets. Because marketing and distribution requirements were less product-specific than in the other industries, the first movers built smaller marketing organizations. Because many firms continued to rely on wholesalers for distribution, and so delayed building their own extensive marketing and distribution network, they tended to move abroad later than was the case with the leaders in machinery, rubber, and oil. Because the optimal size of their plants was smaller than in those other industries, they built more plants at home and produced for national rather than regional markets abroad. Finally, because their production processes were relatively simple and because the product could be sold in mass markets, the economies of scope through which organizational capabilities developed centered in distribution more than in production.

All this was less true for branded, packaged consumer chemicals than for branded, packaged foodstuffs, because in consumer chemicals the processes of production were more complex. In those industries the economies of scope and the resulting organizational capabilities rested on production and research as well as distribution. Thus the histories of the leading firms in consumer chemicals provide an introduction to those in industrial chemicals, where the complexities of production and distribution created the greatest potential for growth through diversification that existed in any of the industries of the Second Industrial Revolution.

Industrial Chemicals

The producers of industrial chemicals (Group 28; see Appendixes A.1–A.4), because of the characteristics of their products and processes, were the first (along with the electrical-equipment manufacturers) to embark on a strategy of growth that exploited economies of scope by developing completely new products. Further, they continued to do so more effectively than the leading enterprises in any other industry (including electrical equipment).

GENERAL CHARACTERISTICS
The producers of industrial chemicals differed most obviously from those making branded, packaged products in serving a very different set of customers. Like the processors of metals and other materials, they sold nearly all of their goods to industrial producers. Where the marketing of branded, packaged products demanded large-scale, national advertising campaigns, that of industrial chemicals required a sales force of trained chemists and chemical engineers. Precisely because chemical products and processes were more tech-

nically advanced than those of other industrial goods, the facilities and skills needed for their production and distribution provided the base for much greater diversification, particularly in the development of brand-new products.

In using and expanding their organizational capabilities to carry out strategies of growth through product diversification, the leading industrial-chemical enterprises concentrated much more on development than on research. Long-term profitability lay not in invention or innovation. It resulted from concentrating on the costly and time-consuming process of bringing new products into full-scale production. Their research and development departments built the necessary semiworks and pilot plants and made the essential studies of market demand. If the senior managers agreed that a new product was commercially viable, they authorized the investments required to build plants of optimal size, to set up an extensive marketing organization, and to recruit sufficient technical and managerial personnel (usually from the existing managerial hierarchy) to achieve first-mover advantages. To maintain these advantages they also established a specialized research and development organization to improve the products just developed and the processes of their production—an organization that itself soon became involved in the development of new or improved products and processes.

Because the continuing application of science to industrial technology was so central to their strategy of growth, it is not surprising that the companies in Group 28 (both consumer and industrial chemicals) made far greater investments in research and development than did the enterprises in any other SIC group. In 1921, 30.4% of all scientific personnel in American industries were employed in the chemical industry—and by 1946 the figure was still 30.6%, far ahead of the second-place electrical-equipment industry, with 15.2%. In those years its research intensity (defined as the ratio of scientists and engineers in laboratories per thousand employees) was also the greatest in American industry, rising from 5.2% in 1921 to 30.3% in 1946.[43]

This emphasis on research meant that more chemical firms entered the top two hundred U.S. industrials during the interwar years than did companies in any other American industry. In 1948 only about 30% of the producers of industrial chemicals on the list of the top two hundred had been on that list in 1917, whereas in oil, rubber, materials, and metals close to 60% of 1948's top two hundred had been on the earlier list (Appendixes A.1–A.3). Just as new technologies had brought several pharmaceutical firms to (or very close to) the top two hundred, burgeoning developments in electrochemicals and organic chemicals moved American Cyanamid, Dow, Monsanto, and General Aniline & Film onto the list. At the same time, former producers of dyes—United Dyewoods—and of fertilizers from natural sources—Virginia-Carolina Chemical and its major competitors (American Agricultural Chemical, International Agricultural Chemical, and Davison Chemical)—dropped off the list.

Nevertheless, despite the turnover, the first movers in industrial chemicals—

that is, those pioneers who between 1880 and 1910 saw the huge potential in new chemical technologies—remained leaders for decades. They were the firms that made sufficiently large investments to assure competitive advantage through scale economies, built the necessary product-specific marketing and distribution networks, and recruited the essential management teams of chemists and chemical engineers. They remained leaders either as independent enterprises or as complementary parts of the industry's two major mergers— Union Carbide & Carbon in 1917 and Allied Chemical in 1920. Nearly all the chemical firms listed among the top two hundred in 1948, including producers of both consumer and industrial goods, were not new but long-established companies. Nearly all had been operating since the first decade of the century.[44]

In acquiring and maintaining market power, the first movers relied initially on economies of scale. In so doing they pioneered two new production techniques. One was the use of pilot plants or semiworks to determine the most effective process and product before building a final factory scaled up to optimal size. The other was what they termed "the unit system of production." This was a method of plant layout and also of monitoring flows. Each unit represented a single physical change in the many grinding, mixing, and evaporating processes, as well as in each of the different chemical or electrolytic transformations involved.[45] In plant design the unit system of production in the chemical industries was similar to the assembly line in the machinery industries.

In addition to their extensive investments in production facilities, these first movers had to make larger investments in product-specific distribution facilities and personnel than did the producers of branded, packaged foods and consumer chemicals. Many of the industry's products were dangerous to handle. Of even more importance, the use of new or greatly improved products had to be explained to customers, and their subsequent use by these customers had to be carefully monitored.[46] In industrial chemicals the initial product-specific investment in production and distribution essential to exploit scale economies created barriers to entry even greater than those in any of the industries discussed in Chapter 4.

THE PLAYERS SELECTED
Because the new technologies were more revolutionary than evolutionary, the turn-of-the-century merger movement had less impact on industrial chemicals than it had on most other American industries. With the exception of the mergers in natural fertilizers and natural dyes, which dropped off the list of the top two hundred, there were only three mergers of significance. These resulted in the E. I. du Pont de Nemours Powder Company, formed between 1902 and 1904 when three du Pont cousins brought nearly three-quarters of the explosives industry under a single corporate roof; General Chemical, an 1899 merger of eleven producers of sulphuric and chemically related acids; and the Barrett

Company, an 1896 consolidation of several firms producing coal-tar products. In sulphuric acids and coal-tar products, technological change was significant, but its emergence was evolutionary. In explosives, the new technology was widely available because its inventor, Alfred Nobel, had licensed it to many producers.

The entrepreneurs who carried out all three of these mergers quickly followed legal consolidation with administrative centralization and so reshaped many of the industry's facilities and the activities of its personnel. Indeed, the transformation of the Du Pont Company from a holding company into a centralized, functionally departmentalized operating company provides one of the best documented examples of such industrial reorganization.[47] At General Chemical, rationalization permitted the concentration of production in high-throughput plants, which, using the unit system of processing, became even more efficient in terms of unit costs in producing sulfuric acid than the giant German firm Badische Anilin und Soda-Fabrik (BASF) at its Ludwigshafen works. Although all three of the merged enterprises concentrated their research on improving existing products and processes, they also began to diversify. By World War I, General Chemical had begun to produce and sell insecticides and fungicides as well as analin oil and salt. Barrett had moved into coal-tar intermediates such as benzene and toluene; and Du Pont had started to make artificial leather (cellulose-coated fabric) and celluloid products.[48]

Other first movers—those whose processes were based on more revolutionary technologies—grew by direct investment rather than by merger. In electrochemicals—a brand-new industry—the pioneer was a German first mover, DEGUSSA (see Chapter 12). In 1895 its subsidiary, Roessler & Hasslacher Chemical, built a plant at the new Niagara Falls industrial complex. This was the third plant to be constructed there (those of Alcoa and Carborundum were the first two); it produced metallic sodium, cyanides, and other chemicals. The German company then established another plant at Perth Amboy to make formaldehyde from methanol.[49]

The first comparable investment by an American enterprise came in 1898 when Union Carbide (predecessor of Union Carbide & Carbon) built major plants at Niagara Falls and at Sault Ste. Marie in Michigan to volume-produce calcium carbide and acetylene for lighting; these plants used the electrolytic techniques developed by James T. Morehead and Thomas L. Willson during their search for a process to produce aluminum. Morehead also helped to establish National Carbon to produce carbon electrodes for the growing arc-light systems. In 1906 Union Carbide, in order to make fuller use of its Niagara Falls plant, organized the Electro-Metallurgic Company to make silicons and ferrous-silicons used in the recovery of metals. The company quickly became a major producer of a wide variety of metal alloys, including high-carbon ferrochrome.[50]

By that time Herbert Henry Dow's enterprise in Midland, Michigan, had begun to produce chlorine electrolytically in high volume from brine and had built a bleach plant at close to optimal scale. Though still small, Dow Chemical was soon exploiting the economies of scope by making chloroform, carbon tetrachloride, insecticides, fungicides, and benzoic acid. After 1907 it moved into a new line, electrolytically producing magnesium, magnesium alloys, and compounds.[51] Another first mover, American Cyanamid, built a plant at Niagara Falls in 1909 to produce electrolytically, on the basis of a German patent, the first synthetic fertilizers made in the United States.[52]

Another revolutionary technology, the new, continuous, high-volume process that transformed the producing of caustic soda—the basic alkali used in the manufacture of glass, textiles, other chemicals, and other materials—was invented by the Solvay brothers of Belgium. Rather than attempting to manufacture abroad, the Solvays provided entrepreneurs in various countries with patents, technological know-how, and limited financing in return for a large but not controlling share of stock.[53] In the United States, Rowland Hazard in 1881 formed the Solvay Process Company on these terms. In 1895 Hazard, again acquiring patents and financing from Solvay & Cie, established the Semet-Solvay Company (which remained American-controlled) and built the by-product coke ovens essential to the production of ammonia used in the Solvay process.[54] Soon that company was also making chemicals such as benzene, toluene, and the solvent, naphtha, from crude light oils recovered from coke-oven gas; it then developed markets for them.[55]

By 1910 the structure of several branches of the American chemical industry had become clearly defined, with most of their major players well established. In explosives, synthetic alkalies, and sulfuric acid, integration of production and distribution resulted in the domination of each branch by a single large firm. In explosives, however, an antitrust decision in 1912 forced Du Pont to spin off two companies, Hercules Powder and Atlas Powder. In electrochemicals the structure was more oligopolistic; each of the leaders (including the one, powerful, German-owned firm, Roessler & Hasslacher Chemical) depended upon a somewhat different specialized technology. In the production of organic chemicals—particularly dyes and pharmaceuticals—the German first movers completely dominated American markets. Although only one German dye company, Frederick Bayer & Company, built a sizable works in the United States (at Rensselaer, New York, in 1882), the other leading German dye makers had extensive American marketing organizations.[56] By 1914 at least two major German firms chemically producing pharmaceutical products, E. Merck and von Heyden, had plants in the United States.[57] The only American challenger making organic chemicals for the American market was Monsanto Chemical, formed by John Francis Queeny in St. Louis in 1902 to produce saccharine and then caffeine, vanilla, and other fine chemicals. Even so, until World War I

Monsanto remained dependent on the German firms for intermediates and plant equipment.[58]

CONTINUING GROWTH THROUGH DIVERSIFICATION

Unlike the food companies reviewed earlier and the machinery companies to be described in the next chapter, the makers of American industrial chemicals (and also of pharmaceuticals) did not invest extensively abroad until after World War II. The product-specific investment in production and distribution made by the German first movers created almost insuperable barriers to entry into the markets of Europe and much of the rest of the world. When American chemical firms invested abroad before 1914, they did so in the Western Hemisphere. Even though the Germans lost most of their foreign plants and marketing facilities to Americans, British, French, and others during World War I, they made a quick recovery in Europe—in nearly all product lines. After 1924 they quickly regained a strong position in dyes in the United States. By the 1930s General Aniline & Film, the newly created subsidiary of the huge German chemical combination I.G. Farben, had become one of America's largest chemical enterprises (Chapter 14).

The war, however, did make a difference. In the 1920s the American chemical companies showed more interest in Europe than they had before 1914. Monsanto built a plant in Britain in 1921. Du Pont had a joint venture with Nobel Industries in 1925 to produce and distribute finishes for automobiles in Britain. Also in Britain, Union Carbide & Carbon had a small subsidiary for electrical furnace products and a larger one for producing batteries.[59] The direct investment by industrial chemical companies remained small and scattered, however. In 1931 the foreign investment in manufacturing industrial chemicals was only $21.6 million, as compared with $68.6 million made by consumer chemical companies, $149.3 million by food companies, and more than $400 million by machinery enterprises.[60]

Nevertheless, major industrial-chemical companies did not expand into related product markets as an alternative to growth by direct investment in geographical markets already preempted by German first-movers. To repeat: they embarked upon such a strategy to exploit the economies of scope and also of scale. The pioneer in developing an explicit strategy of growth through diversification was E. I. du Pont de Nemours & Company.

Although before World War I Du Pont had begun a search for new products in order to use existing plant and personnel more profitably, by 1914 only 3% of its sales came from products outside its primary line of explosives. Its huge expansion during World War I raised the unprecedented threat and challenge of underutilized resources and led its managers to seek new ways to use its physical facilities and human skills. The wartime demands, first of the Allies and then of the American military forces, vastly increased the company's investment in the production of propellants (that is, explosives to propel bullets and shells as differentiated from blasting supplies), for which there would be only a tiny market after the war. These demands also increased the company's investment in facilities that produced the intermediate chemicals required to make the propellants, including nitric and lactic acid, alcohol, and toluene, as well as the more complex chemicals—diphenylamine, ammonium picrate, and aniline. Investment, too, was made in new facilities to purify cotton linters and to make ice used in the recovery of alcohol and acid to be employed again in production processes.[61]

As early as the fall of 1915, the Executive Committee of Du Pont had established an office called the Excess Plant Utilization Division in its Development Department to find products that might be produced in its expanded facilities. But because military demand for a single product—propellants—had so vastly increased throughput, the committee agreed in February 1917 that "there are no industries which will be likely to use more than 25% to 30% of the value (costs) of these plants." Therefore, instead of searching for uses for the company's physical facilities, an investigation should be made of existing "industries which can utilize much more extensively our organization and at the same time offer good returns."[62] By "our organization" the committee explicitly meant the technical and administrative skills of its managerial personnel. The committee members fully realized that the massive wartime expansion had created capacity that was far above optimal scale for peacetime demand for explosives or any other line of products that might use those facilities. They realized too that the great increases in scale sharply limited the opportunities for scope within these facilities. They decided, therefore, to investigate the potential for scope within the enterprise as a whole rather than just that in individual operating facilities. The results were swift and impressive. In the years from 1917 to 1921 such investigations led the company into the production and distribution of paints and lacquers, pigments, dyes, films, and man-made fibers (rayon), besides into an enlargement of its earlier investment in artificial leather, celluloid products, and organic intermediates.

In the period following the sharp 1920–21 recession, the Du Pont strategy became more precise. It called for continuing diversification based primarily on the skills and experience existing within the organization; continuing vertical integration through acquisition of firms making intermediate products not yet produced by the company; and an increasing investment in research, particularly for product development. As for diversification, the company's 1924 annual report noted: "Such diversification tends to produce a more even rate of business throughout the year and tends to avoid violent fluctuation in total sales, should one industry suffer a severe depression."[63] The company's two major acquisitions—Grasselli Chemical in 1928 and Roessler & Hasslacher Chemical in 1930—fitted these goals of integration and diversification. Grasselli's primary lines, which included heavy bulk chemicals, also expanded Du Pont's line of pigments. The once German-owned Roessler & Hasslacher provided the essential bulk intermediate, metallic sodium, for Du Pont's recently developed gasoline additive, tetraethyllead. Just as important, it gave Du Pont, for the first time, a position in electrochemicals. [64]   •

Du Pont's strategy of growth rested primarily on product development, not product innovation. In the 1920s the purpose of the company's research was to develop products whose processes of production provided the cost advantages of scale and whose quality and performance promised a profitable market share. Such product development required, in addition to chemical research, the continuing pursuit of cheaper materials and intermediates, constant attention to process development, and the making of market studies.

The new strategy proved to be highly successful. It was implemented through further refinement of the multidivisional structure the company had created in 1921 to manage its new multiproduct enterprise. By 1924 its new product lines provided an income equal to that from explosives; by 1939 explosives accounted for less than 10% of the company's income. By 1947, 58% of the sales volume came from products the company had commercialized during the previous twenty years. [65] This strategy had permitted the company to turn in an impressive profit record even during the years of the Great Depression. Essential to the success of the strategy was an increasing investment in research laboratories: specialized, product-specific laboratories in the several operating divisions as well as a central research unit, administered by the corporate headquarters, which by 1928 included a laboratory—known as "Purity Hall"—explicitly devoted to fundamental research. In all but this last laboratory the Du Pont chemists and chemical engineers concentrated much more on development than on research—that is, on the commercialization phase that normally accounted for 85% to 90% of the cost of bringing a new product to market. [66]

In the 1920s and 1930s other large industrial chemical firms adopted strategies of diversification comparable to Du Pont's. Those that did not rarely stayed on the list of the top two hundred. Those that grew apace continued to expand from their initial technological bases. Like Du Pont, its two offshoots, Hercules Powder and Atlas Powder, greatly expanded production during World War I and began to diversify after the war. Hercules, which remained strong in explosives, used the nitrocellulose technology it had developed in World War I to make lacquers and protective coatings (particularly for the automobile industry), and cellulose acetate. In addition, it developed and utilized a new naval-stores technology (beginning with steam-solvent distillation of pine stumps) to produce rosin, turpentine, pine oil, and most important of all, papermaking chemicals. Atlas, also continuing in explosives, stayed closer to its original line, producing artificial leather and coated fabrics until research took it into the electrolytic production of mannitol and sorbitol, two widely used intermediates. Diversifying fairly slowly, Atlas did not grow fast enough to stay on the list of the top two hundred.[67]

American Cyanamid, the first American firm to make synthetic fertilizers from electrolytically processed calcium cyanide, initially based its growth on calcium products. After 1922 it began to move—more by acquisition than direct investment—into aluminum resins and acids, and then into consumer goods, including paint, enamel, varnishes, and water softeners. With the purchase of the Calco Chemical Company and Heller & Marz in 1929, it began to produce and sell organic chemicals. The purchase of Lederle Laboratories in the next year made it a major competitor in the pharmaceutical industry. During the Second World War, American Cyanamid moved into rubber, chemicals, and accelerators. By the 1930s each of its several product divisions was developing new lines of goods.[68]

Dow Chemical's ever-widening line of products was based on salt chemistry, which took the company into dyes and medicinal drugs and also led it to expand its lines of chlorine, phenol, ammonia, styrene, and magnesium, and, during the Second World War, synthetic rubber. In 1927 when the German chemical giant I.G. Farben threatened to move into the American market for magnesium, Dow made an agreement with Alcoa whereby Alcoa withdrew, leaving Dow the sole American producer of that metal. Monsanto Chemical, on the other hand, continued to rely on a saccharine base as it diversified into phenol and other fine chemicals and then into alcohol, rubber chemicals, and specialty chemicals.[69]

Still another diversifier was Koppers. After the outbreak of war in 1914 this small subsidiary of a German engineering company sold 80% of its holdings to an American group in which the Mellon family became the largest investors. This Pittsburgh-based group then made the major investment in production facilities and established a sales force that, with the boom created by World War I, permitted it effectively to challenge Semet-Solvay in coke and coke-based products. After the war Koppers began to produce and distribute a wide range of coke-based coal-tar products such as creosote and other wood pre-servatives, coatings for pipelines, other finishes, and roofing and road materials. It then moved into related chemicals such as styrene, ethylene, and resins and into adhesives and pharmaceuticals, and during World War II into synthetic rubber. It also volume-produced gas plants and gas holders and other metal equipment used in gas and coke works.[70]

DIVERSIFICATION THROUGH MERGER
Growth by merger remained relatively rare among makers of industrial chemicals. The industry's two major mergers after the turn-of-the-century merger movement, Allied Chemical & Dye and Union Carbide & Carbon, both came

into being, much as did those in consumer chemicals and food, to increase the economies of scope within the enlarged enterprise. They also permitted closer coordination and certainty of supplies in processing intermediates and final products. Both firms continued to grow through diversification.

The five companies that formed Allied Chemical & Dye in 1920 had long had close business relationships with one another. The five were General Chemical and the Barrett Company (two of the major turn-of-the-century mergers), Solvay Process and its offspring Semet-Solvay, and National Aniline & Chemical. In 1920 Solvay Process still concentrated on the production of synthetic alkalies, but Semet-Solvay had diversified into a wide variety of coke-oven gas products ranging from briquettes to ammonium chloride. General Chemical, while continuing to concentrate on production of sulfuric acid, had diversified into insecticides and fungicides. Barrett, which had long relied on materials provided by Semet-Solvay, had expanded its line, moving into the manufacture of coal-tar chemicals and their derivatives. In 1910 it had formed, with Semet-Solvay and General Chemical, a jointly held subsidiary, Benzol Products, which concentrated on the development of specialized coal-tar intermediates. In 1917 Benzol had merged with three small dye producers to form National Aniline & Chemical, whose goal was the high-volume production of intermediates and dyes to meet the war-engendered dye crisis.

The explicit purpose of the 1920 merger that formed Allied Chemical & Dye was to make fuller use of facilities and personnel producing these interrelated coal-based chemicals. As the committee of organization defined it:

> Among the advantages which the Committee believes are to be derived from such a consolidation are: Greater diversification of output and correspondingly greater stability of business; closer adjustment of the production of basic and intermediate materials to the requirements for manufacture and their derivatives; and greater financial strength—not to mention the various economies in operation ordinarily available only to an organization of the scope here contemplated . . . Intensive progressive research is—and will continue—an especially important feature of the chemical manufacturing business. In the opinion of the Committee, the promotion of such research, through combination of material and personnel resources of the consolidated companies, is alone a compelling reason for the proposed consolidation.

This strategy, however, was not implemented. At Allied Chemical, structure failed to follow strategy. Orlando Weber, its president throughout the interwar period, failed to create a large enough corporate headquarters—consisting of general executives and a corporate staff (including a central laboratory)—to assure coordination of flows of materials and information within the existing operating units and to plan and allocate resources for commercializing new product lines. Even though the individual divisions continued to expand their products on their relatively narrow technological bases, they did not benefit from the potential economies of scope within the enterprise. Nor did Weber reinvest earnings in research or productive facilities as did his major competitors. Until Weber's retirement after World War II, Allied Chemical remained more a holding than an operating company. As a result, the largest chemical company in the country in 1920 had dropped to third place by 1948, behind Du Pont and Union Carbide & Carbon.[71]

Union Carbide & Carbon, a comparable merger of chemical companies with complementary lines, was created in 1917. It was more successful than Allied Chemical precisely because its managers paid closer attention to creating more efficient coordinating and resource-allocating mechanisms at corporate headquarters and because they reinvested more extensively and continuously in facilities and skills. This merger included several of the first movers in the American electrochemical industry: National Carbon, producers of electrodes and Ever Ready batteries; Union Carbide, makers of calcium carbide (and its subsidiary, Electro-Metallurgical, producer of alloys); and Oxweld Acetylene, makers of acetylene and of devices using acetylene. Of the other two companies coming into the merger, one, Prest-O-Lite, was at first a maker of bicycle and automobile lamps and then of headlights and welding, heating, and cutting equipment that used acetylene; and the other was the Linde Air Products Company, which, on the basis of German patents, produced liquid oxygen essential to the production of acetylene. Following the merger the company expanded its production of metal alloys, particularly after the acquisition of Haynes Stellite in 1920. It then began to concentrate on developing other sources of gases used in acetylene and related products. These efforts resulted in the formation in 1920 of a new subsidiary, Carbide & Carbon Chemical Corporation, which became the pioneer in the United States in the development of petrochemicals and other intermediates that were soon to be used in the making of synthetic fibers, synthetic rubber, lacquers, and plastics. By the outbreak of World War II, Union Carbide & Carbon had become as diversified as Du Pont, American Cyanamid, Monsanto, and Dow.[72]

The history of the other industrial chemical companies among the top two hundred during the interwar years further documents the assertion that growth in this industry came from diversification and that the extent of diversification reflected investment in research and development. Columbia Carbon, makers of carbon black, and the two producers of commercial alcohol, Publiker Commercial Alcohol and United States Industrial Alcohol, continued to concentrate on a single product line that required neither a sophisticated sales force nor a costly research and development program to improve the product and process. All three had exited from the ranks of the top two hundred by 1948.[73] On the other hand, Air Reduction, which in 1915 had acquired a license from the French firm L'Air Liquide, built several plants during World War I to produce liquid oxygen; it also created a strong sales force, invested in research, and quickly expanded into related gases and carbides, and then into the production of specialized equipment. An effective challenger to Union Carbide & Carbon, it ranked 204th in 1930 and 144th in 1948.[74]

Nearly all the chemical companies that did diversify adopted the multidivisional administrative structure. Du Pont led the way, inventing the new form in 1920–21. Senior executives in the other firms had increasing difficulty, as had those at Du Pont, in coordinating flows, monitoring operating units, planning, and allocating resources for the future within a centralized, functionally departmentalized structure. The decision-making overload at the corporate office became too great. By the 1930s Hercules Powder, Atlas Powder, American Cyanamid, Monsanto, and Koppers were all operated through product divisions that integrated manufacturing, marketing, and development and that were administered by refashioned corporate offices at the top. At Dow, a company still dominated by its founders, product divisions had been established, but relationships between the managers in the operating divisions and those in the functional departments in the corporate office were not yet clearly defined. Of the two major mergers, United Carbide & Carbon successfully met the challenge of creating the corporate office needed to manage a multidivisional enterprise; but Allied Chemical, where Orlando Weber continued to dominate top-management decision-making, failed in this respect.[75]

The adoption of the multidivisional structure, in turn, facilitated growth through continuing diversification. Both the division laboratories and the corporate laboratories remained continuously involved in product development. In both divisional and corporate spheres, the dynamics for continuing diversification came from the organizational capabilities developed through the exploitation of economies of scope. Increasingly they came from the utilization of technical and managerial skills within the divisions and at the corporate office, rather than from those that existed within operating units responsible for day-to-day operations. In other words, they grew from exploiting the skills that the Du Pont Executive Committee had attributed to "our organization" in 1917.

THE DU PONT EXAMPLE

It is clear that the pattern of growth of the largest American producers of industrial chemicals differed from that of the enterprises in the more stable industries—oil, rubber, materials, and metals. It differed too from that of the leading producers of branded, packaged products, because the manufacturers of industrial chemicals concentrated much more on systematic product development. Because this strategy of growth was the most sophisticated one to evolve among industrial firms before World War II, because it was widely adopted in the years following the war, and because such growth was central to the intensification of competition that brought underlying changes in the strategy and structure of large American industrial firms in the 1960s, it should be examined in more detail. The Du Pont Company, the innovator in both the strategy of diversification and the multidivisional structure, offers a good example of the ways in which products were developed.

At Du Pont the decisions concerning product development were made at two levels—the corporate office and the divisional headquarters. At the corporate level the general executives on the Executive Committee who determined the strategy of the enterprise as a whole relied on two corporate staff departments: the Development Department, which became a broad planning and investigatory office that guided the direction of product development; and the Chemical Department (later called Central Research), which coordinated the company's research activities, as well as carrying out research of its own. The division managers also had their own research and development organizations with their own laboratories and auxiliary facilities. At Du Pont, product divisions were termed departments and functional offices within these departments were termed divisions. (I will use this terminology in reviewing the Du Pont experience.) Before World War II the task of the research divisions was explicitly development, not basic research. Their responsibility was to improve existing processes and products and, equally important, to commercialize new ones. This was true of the entire chemical industry in that era.

The functions of the corporate Chemical Department evolved relatively slowly.[76] At first its primary task was to undertake research work on contract from the industrial departments, but increasingly it came to coordinate and integrate the research and development work done throughout the Du Pont Company. By the end of the 1920s its director chaired the meetings of departmental research directors and took on "the responsibility of acting as a coordinating department so that overlapping of the research programs of the different manufacturing departments may be avoided as completely as possible."[77] Then in 1927 the Executive Committee, at the urging of Charles M. A. Stine, the director of the Chemical Department, authorized that department to embark on fundamental research in three closely related scientific areas—physical chemistry, colloid science, and polymerization. Thus the role of the central laboratories became research, not development; product innovation, not product commercialization. Increasingly the work concentrated on polymer chemistry. And from the research came two major product innovations—a new synthetic fiber, nylon, and a new synthetic rubber, neoprene.

Du Pont's organizational capabilities rested largely on its long experience with nitrocellulose technology used in the production of explosives and propellants. Most of the new industrial departments created in 1921 continued to build on this base. But the products and processes of two departments—Dyestuffs and Ammonia—came out of technologies first developed by German entrepreneurs and scientists. Du Pont's interest in both dyes and ammonia resulted from shortages during World War I. Even though the war removed German dye makers from American markets and made available German patents to American manufacturers, Du Pont had great difficulty in competing effectively with the Germans during the interwar years. So, too, did Allied Chemical's dye-making subsidiary, National Aniline & Chemical. Both had German patents. Du Pont had hired chemists from German firms, but it took years to develop the organizational capabilities necessary to compete.

Only in 1926 did the Du Pont dye business begin to show a satisfactory profit, and only in 1935, after eighteen years of work and an investment of $43 million, did the aggregate earnings from dyes and closely related chemicals offset the earlier losses.[78] Meanwhile, by 1929, Du Pont had obtained 26.1% of that market in the United States, which, though more than the share of Allied Chemical's National Aniline & Chemical, was still less than that of General Dyestuffs—the sales arm of those German producers who had returned to the American market in force after 1924 (Chapter 14).[79] Given this stiff competition, the director of corporate research and the research chief of the Dyestuffs Department agreed that their research unit should look for "new opportunities in organic chemistry," preferably those that permitted the exploitation of the economies of scale as well as scope.[80]

The first such opportunity came after Charles F. Kettering, who headed General Motors research, visited Wilmington in 1922 to examine dye intermediates that might be used as a gasoline additive to eliminate or suppress engine knock and increase horsepower and fuel efficiency in automobiles. Further research at both Du Pont and General Motors resulted in the development of tetraethyllead. The Dyestuffs Department then concentrated on finding ways to scale up production of this additive to assure the cost advantages of scale. In 1924 General Motors and Standard Oil (New Jersey), which had done parallel work in the initial creation of the additive, formed the Ethyl Corporation to market the product. They then contracted with Du Pont to produce it.[81]

Another profitable product developed by that department (its name was changed from Dyestuffs to Organic Chemicals in 1935) was a refrigerant for the increasingly popular household refrigerators. The product was Freon (dichlorodifluoromethane). In perfecting it, the department's chemical engineers concentrated on the development of a continuous-process, high-volume method of production, which went on line in 1931. By the end of the decade, Freon's sales were $4 million and its profits $1 million. In 1938 the fluorocarbon polymer research that stemmed from the production of Freon led in turn to the discovery of Teflon (polytetrafluoroethylene), a material that was highly resistant to acid and other corrosive substances, and one which, unlike other chemical materials, did not melt under high temperature. The successful "scaling up" of Teflon, however, had to await the end of the Second World War. Once this was achieved, it too became a profitable product.[82] The Organic Chemical Department's expertise in scaling up complex organic chemical processes led the company's executives to give the department responsibility for the development of neoprene, the new synthetic rubber, which had been discovered in the company's Central Research Department in 1930.[83]

When the Ammonia Department ventured into the production of synthetic ammonia and synthetic nitrogen from coal, water, and air, it took almost as long as the Dyestuffs Department to develop the capabilities needed for profitable operations. The technology of high-pressure synthesis, an outstanding German innovation, was far different from that used in making dyes. It had the potential for massive economies of scale, whereas the cost advantages of dye production were based almost entirely on economies of scope. During World War I, Du Pont research personnel spent time and effort searching for a successful process of nitrogen fixation. Once the war was over, the Executive Committee lost interest in this project until Allied Chemical built a small pilot plant using the German Haber-Bosch process. Du Pont then obtained the patent rights to a newer process developed by a Frenchman, Georges Claude. Both processes involved high-pressure synthesis of ammonia and its oxidation into nitric dioxide gas, which, when absorbed by water, produced nitric acid. In 1924 Du Pont and Claude formed a joint venture, Lazote. As Du Pont began to make the investment necessary to produce synthetic ammonia and nitrogen at minimum efficient scale, it acquired full control of Lazote, placing operations under the newly formed Ammonia Department. In 1926 Du Pont completed an ammonia and nitrogen plant at Belle, West Virginia, that was far larger than any in Europe using the Claude process. Its size was substantially increased in 1927, the year when Allied Chemical constructed a comparable plant at Hopewell, Virginia, which was further expanded in 1932.

Up to that time Du Pont had made little or no profit from ammonia and nitrogen; but from 1933 on, the greatly increased volume brought a threefold increase in rate of return on investment. The Ammonia Department quickly became one of the company's most profitable divisions.[84] By 1929 the Belle plant was producing 40% of the nation's synthetic ammonia and 30% of its synthetic nitrogen. By 1935 two works—Du Pont's at Belle and Allied Chemical's at Hopewell—produced 82.9% of the synthetic nitrogen made in the United States.[85]

In commercializing synthetic nitrogen and synthetic ammonia, "scaling up" paid off handsomely over time. To maintain profits the Ammonia Department did not expand its capacity further during the 1930s, preferring to run its existing plant as close to minimum efficient scale as possible. Its research division, therefore, concentrated on developing products that would help the plant to maintain such a throughput. These products included an antifreeze for automobile engines (which competed with a product developed by Jersey Standard); "longer carbon" chain alcohols used in hydraulic brake fluids; detergents for soap and other cleaners; urea for fertilizers and for synthetic resins. In developing detergents the Ammonia Department worked closely with Procter & Gamble. From urea it developed a clear, glasslike substance (methyl metracrylate) that it branded "Lucite." Its production could not be scaled up, however, until World War II greatly expanded its use in aircraft. The department later developed and then volume-produced adipic acid and hexamethylenediamine, two intermediaries from which Du Pont made nylon.

For the Rayon Department the challenge of the early 1920s was not, as it was for the Ammonia Department, to create first-mover advantages in the American market, but rather, as in the case of dyestuffs, to overcome those of others. In rayon, as in dyes and synthetic ammonia, Europeans were the first movers. American Viscose, the subsidiary of the British firm Courtaulds, dominated the American market after 1912, when it built the first plant of optimal size in the United States and set up a national distribution network. That plant produced rayon by the viscose process. Other European movers quickly followed the lead of Courtaulds. In 1918 the Belgian company Tubize built a plant in Hopewell, Virginia; then in 1925 British Celanese formed its American subsidiary to produce fibers through a different (cellulose-acetate) process. It was followed by Italians and Germans using the viscose process. (As in explosives, both processes had wood pulp as a basic ingredient.) This story is reviewed in Chapters 7, 8, and 11.

Meanwhile, Du Pont had entered the industry in April 1920 by forming a joint venture with the leading French viscose producer, Comptoir des Textiles Artificiels, in which Du Pont held 60% and its French associate 40%. Du Pont provided the money; the French provided the technology. After Du Pont had built a viscose plant of a large enough scale to compete and had organized an adequate sales force, it bought out the French minority holdings. Up to 1931 Du Pont was the only American company to overcome the first-mover advantages of the Europeans in the American market. In that year Tennessee Eastman, an Eastman Kodak subsidiary, built a cellulose acetate plant, which by 1938 had an annual capacity of 24 million pounds, in order to use more profitably the facilities and skills developed in the production of photographic film, the demand for which had dropped off during the depression. No other American firm became a major player in the new industry.[86]

To gain market share in this competitive high-volume business the Du Pont Rayon Department's research division concentrated on developing new processes, including the "cake to cone process," to reduce costs and improve the strength, texture, and appearance of rayon fiber. By 1925 Du Pont had captured 16.7% and by 1928 20% of a very profitable and still booming market. Then, after the collapse of demand following the 1929 stock market crash, the Rayon Department's research paid off. By keeping its more efficient plants at close to minimum efficient scale, it was able to maintain profits and to increase its market share during the years when greatly reduced prices eliminated five of the smaller producers. By developing products to use existing capacity, particularly rayon cord for tires and "rayon staple," a fiber that could be used on conventional textile-spinning machinery, it further strengthened its position.[87]

In the late 1920s the Rayon Department developed another product, a transparent wrapping, cellophane, whose production technology was very close to that of rayon (a cellulose-based product using much the same machinery and intermediate processes). Du Pont acquired the rights to cellophane from its French ally, Comptoir des Textiles Artificiels.[88] Again, the research group improved product and process. Then a major innovation, the discovery of a moisture-proof cellophane, gave Du Pont first-mover advantages. The building of a large plant of optimal size, coupled with the creation of an energetic marketing organization that worked closely with customers to develop specialized packaging machinery and plant layout, assured Du Pont of continuing dominance.[89] One economist estimated that a plant built by a competitor with comparable cost advantages would increase the nation's capacity by more than 40%. Only Sylvania Industrial, a subsidiary of the Belgian firm Sidac, offered any effective competition, obtaining about 17% of the overall cellophane market in 1932 and 20.7% in 1948.[90]

In paints and finishes the major Du Pont production innovation in the 1920s did not come from the Paint Department or the Chemical Department but from the laboratories of the Cellulose Products Department. In the 1921 reorganization that department was assigned to manage Du Pont's earliest ventures in diversification, those small prewar investments in the production and distribution of artificial leather and celluloid products. After the war its research division concentrated on improving product and process, so that by 1929 Du Pont's market share of pyroxylin-coated goods was 29%, rubber-coated goods 35%, celluloid articles 37%, and celluloid sheetings 45%.

The research unit's major achievement, however, was the development in 1920 of Duco, a fast-drying lacquer made from a mitrocellulose base to meet the needs of the rapidly growing automobile industry. The many days required to give an automobile several coats of paint and varnish and the week needed for drying remained a formidable barrier to increasing throughput in that industry. In developing Duco, the Du Pont chemists worked closely with Kettering's organization at General Motors. By 1924 Duco was being used in several General Motors models. By 1929 Duco's sales of $28.3 million accounted for 30% of the market for automotive finishes. Other firms, including Hercules Powder, soon developed comparable products. At the same time, the department improved lacquers for other uses, products that brought in even larger sales of $43 million, giving Du Pont 31.5% of the market for nonautomotive industrial lacquers in 1929. Here Sherwin-Williams, Glidden, and National Lead were major competitors. In 1925 the production and distribution of lacquer was placed in the Paint Department, which became the Paint, Finishes, and Chemical Department, while Cellulose Products, renamed the Plastics Department, continued to manage the artificial leather and celluloid business. After the research unit that had perfected Duco was transferred from the Plastics to the Paint Department, its chemists developed a household paint, Dulux, that helped Du Pont raise its share of the less concentrated, nonspecialized market for primary paint from 3% to 10% between 1922 and 1941, and to become the nation's third largest producer of paints—behind Sherwin-Williams (16%) and Pittsburgh Plate Glass, but ahead of Glidden and National Lead.[91]

This story of growth through diversification at four Du Pont industrial departments is incomplete and only indicates the nature of that process. It does not include the activities of the research divisions of the Plastics Department, of the older Explosives Department and the Smokeless Powder Department, or of the small Photo Products Department (which began in 1924 as the Du Pont Pathé Film Company and in time became an effective challenger to that industry's powerful first mover, Eastman Kodak). Nor does it include the Pigment Department, which had its beginnings in 1917 with the purchase of a major paint manufacturer and then expanded through the acquisition of Grasselli Chemical in 1928 and of the smaller Krebbs Pigment & Chemical Company in 1929. This department grew rapidly in the 1930s with the development of a new basic pigment—titanium dioxide—a product that made obsolete much of Du Pont's large existing investment in lithopone. Nor does my story consider the work done at Roessler & Hasslacher—which after its purchase in 1930 became the R&H Chemical Department in 1932 and the company's Electro-Chemicals Department in 1942—in developing chemicals for electroplating, bleaching, ceramics, and other industries, as well as some pesticides. Nor does it even hint at the more dramatic story of the fundamental research on polymer chemistry in the central Chemical Department, which led to the invention, development, scaling up, and further commercializing of the two totally new synthetic materials, nylon and neoprene. The story of the role of fundamental research in corporate growth is more relevant to industrial chemical companies after World War II than before, and therefore it is beyond the period of my study.[92]

The activities of these other Du Pont departments were comparable to those in Dyestuffs, Ammonia, Rayon, and Paint. And the work of all the Du Pont laboratories was paralleled during the 1920s and 1930s at Hercules, Atlas, Union Carbide, American Cyanamid, Koppers, Monsanto; and, with the corporate office playing a smaller role, at Allied Chemical and Dow. It had parallels too, albeit on a smaller scale, with new-product development at paint and drug companies and at such food companies as Borden, Corn Products, and Quaker Oats.

Diversification, Organizational Complexity, and Managerial Control

The strategies of growth developed by the first movers and a small number of challengers in the food and chemical industries had a more significant impact on the evolution of the modern industrial enterprise than did those of horizontal combination and vertical integration that characterized the leaders in the industries discussed earlier (Chapter 4). In food the utilization of organizational capabilities based on exploiting the economies of scale encouraged direct investment abroad to a greater extent than occurred in any other industry except oil and the machinery industries. In industrial chemicals the leaders invested less abroad, primarily because of the organizational strength of the great German chemical companies. Of more importance, both the food and chemical companies pioneered in the new strategy of growth that became important after World War II—that of using organizational capabilities developed through the utilization of the economies of scope to move into other established markets and to become first movers in new product lines.

In both food and chemicals, the economies of scope provided the major dynamic for continuing growth. Even though the cost advantages of scale remained the basic weapon for obtaining and maintaining market share with satisfactory profits within a single product market at home and abroad, economies of scope were more important in determining both the direction and the rate of growth of these chemical and food companies. In branded, packaged foods and consumer chemicals the leaders continued to diversify primarily by moving into the production and distribution of already existing product markets. The industrial chemical firms came more quickly to concentrate on the development of new products.

Diversification at the industrial chemical companies continued to rest on the economies of scope within the functional operating units—production, distribution, purchasing, and research and development. Increasingly, however, economies of scope within the enterprise as a whole provided an even stronger dynamic for growth. One division was able to use intermediate products produced or developed in others, to exploit research and development information and techniques perfected in other divisions, to apply knowledge acquired in other divisions that used comparable production technologies or served similar markets. Most important of all, the top and middle managers of these enterprises were able to use their experience and skill in deciding on products to be developed, in making the initial investment in production facilities of the proper size, in creating a new marketing network, and in recruiting the management teams essential to achieve and maintain first-mover advantages for their new products. And the continuing product development and commercialization further improved the facilities and honed the skills that constituted the organizational capabilities of the enterprise as a whole.

Although incentives for the initial adoption of a strategy of diversification often came from the need to employ underutilized resources, as it did at Du Pont, the incentives for a strategy of *continuing* diversification were commonly created by market opportunities. At Du Pont, for example, the moves into synthetic materials, synthetic ammonia, gasoline additives, fast-drying lacquers, refrigerants, antifreeze, titanium dioxide pigments—as well as into nylon and neoprene, developed from fundamental research—were clear responses to market opportunities. Here, Du Pont's tie with General Motors (Du Pont had invested war profits in the automobile company) was important, not only in perceiving the need but also in developing the products. The critical move in such new-product development was to "scale up" high enough and quickly enough to obtain and keep a market share that would maintain operations at minimum efficient scale. This need, in turn, led to a search for new products to maintain throughput.

Occasionally such diversification gave the first company to commercialize a product a near monopoly, such as Du Pont acquired in moisture-proof cellophane, nylon, and tetraethyllead. More often the state of technology was such that more than one firm responded to the same market opportunity or quickly followed the pioneer into the new product market. The first movers and challengers in the new product lines were not only the industrial chemical firms but also the makers of foods and consumer chemicals, as well as the few rubber and oil companies (those described in Chapter 4) that had begun to diversify before World War II. In the resulting oligopolies, the divisions of these diversified enterprises competed functionally and strategically for market share.

The new strategies of diversification, then, not only intensified competition in existing industries but helped ensure competition in new ones. The challengers that appeared in both the established and new product lines were almost never newly formed enterprises; the barriers to entry raised by first-mover advantages were too great. Instead, they were firms in related industries that had already developed their organizational capabilities and acquired competitive advantages in production, marketing, or research that permitted them to obtain and maintain a profitable share in the market into which they moved. In this way the strategy of growth through exploiting economies of scope increased competition in major American industries to a far greater extent than did any antitrust actions taken during the interwar years.

The adoption of the multidivisional structure by the diversified firms—a structure that was increasingly essential in maintaining the strategy of continuing diversification—redefined the functions of both top executives and senior middle management. The planning and carrying out of functional and strategic moves in the battle for market share became the responsibility of the division managers. Meanwhile, the responsibility of the general executives in the corporate office was threefold. First, these executives coordinated the activities of the several divisions, primarily through policies that assured continuing flows of information between divisions as to markets, supplies, production methods, and research. Second, they monitored systematically the performance of the operating divisions. Finally, on the basis of that monitoring and their evaluation of long-term supply and demand, the general executives had to decide in which industries to develop new products and markets, and then they had to allocate resources to the divisions to carry out such strategies. Such top-management decisions demanded a long-term view. Whereas the investment in new plant and facilities in a single industry—a primary concern of top managers in oil, rubber, metals, and materials—required only two or three years after the initial investment to come on stream, the time to commercialize new products in technologically complex, related industries, such as dyes, ammonia, neoprene, and nylon, often required a decade or more, as they did at Du Pont, before the very large investment began to show a profit. And that investment came from the retained earnings of the enterprise as a whole.

By the coming of World War II the new strategy supported by the new structure had proved to be so profitable that after the war diversification became a fully accepted way of growth in American industry. And by the 1960s the increased competition that resulted was beginning to transform many industrial enterprises and the industries in which they operated.

That competition was further intensified by greatly increased investments in research and development. In the years between the two world wars the basic function of those working in research departments remained that of commercializing products that had almost always been invented by others. Their primary task was to apply their knowledge of chemistry and engineering in order to acquire first-mover advantages in the production and distribution of a new product or to challenge the first-mover advantages of others. After a product division had become a successful member of a new oligopoly, the purpose of its research units was to maintain plants at close to minimum efficient scale by developing new products that used much the same processes of production. But after 1945 the leading chemical, food, oil, and rubber companies greatly increased their investment in research. With more firms making such investments and bringing new products on stream it was difficult for a single enterprise to dominate the market for one specific new product for an extended period of time. The new competition from outside the industry, in turn, stimulated firms within that industry to invest in product-development research. Such competition further prompted the leaders to invest more heavily in fundamental research. In sum, after World War II the goal of research in many firms became product innovation as much as product development.

*

The collective history of the leaders in branded, packaged products and industrial chemicals is a story of increasing complexity in decision-making at the top.

Strategic decisions on long-term investment abroad called for an understanding of distant markets characterized by ever-changing demand and an awareness of the actions and even intentions of existing and potential competitors, both foreign and domestic. The move into new product lines demanded an understanding of the technological complexities of both product and process, an evaluation of the capabilities of the firm's research units and of the enterprise as a whole, and an estimate of markets and of sources of supplies for products that might not become profitable for several years. In addition, senior managers had to evaluate the possibility that enterprises in other industries would complete the commercialization of a comparable product—and even reach the anticipated market—before they did. At the same time, besides making these long-term allocating decisions, top management had to monitor continuously the operations of their different divisions in different industries occupied by different sets of competing firms.

The increased complexities of top-level planning, resource allocation, and monitoring further separated management from ownership. Even in single-product-line companies (like many described in Chapter 4), outside directors, because they had to rely on salaried managers for information, knowledge, and experience, had difficulty in developing independent positions or in offering alternatives to the courses of action proposed by the inside directors. In the diversified firms described in this chapter, such independence was almost impossible.

Moreover, while increased complexities were strengthening the managers' control, stock ownership was becoming increasingly scattered as it passed down to the founders' children and grandchildren. Although investments abroad and in new product lines were financed primarily by retained earnings, such funding was often supplemented by equity issues that still further diluted ownership. By World War II the trend that was already apparent during World War I had been clearly defined: in a significant number of firms, no inside director held as much as 1% of the company's stock and no outside director as much as 2%.

Of the three groups of stockholders represented on the boards of directors of these diversified companies—banks, individual investors with substantial holdings, and founding families—the banks were the least significant. In the food and chemical industries, banks had not played a major role in the formation of the early trusts and turn-of-the-century mergers. Instead, the mergers in sugar, vegetable oil, and grain processing, like those that formed Du Pont, General Chemical, and Barrett, were carried out by the manufacturers themselves. So, too, were the later mergers that brought together firms producing related products, such as General Foods, General Mills, Union Carbide & Carbon, and Allied Chemical. Although banks often facilitated such mergers, it was the manufacturers that continued to make and implement significant short-term and long-term decisions. Financial institutions certainly played a more significant role when firms such as Armour and the leading vegetable-oil producers had difficulties during the post–World War I recession. But after such firms had been financially reorganized and had once again become profitable, there is little evidence to suggest that bankers affected strategic decisions.

At the board meetings of these food and chemical firms, large investors continued to have more say than the representatives of banks did. On the basis of information available on the equity held by board members in 1939 and on stockholdings in 1965, some conclusions can be drawn about the percentage of stock owned by the directors of the food and chemical companies listed among the top two hundred enterprises (Appendixes A.1–A.3).[93] The following firms had one or two outside directors holding more than 2% of the stock: National Biscuit (Moore); General Foods (Davies); General Mills (Bell); Quaker Oats (Stewart); Ralston Purina (Danforth); Colgate (Colgate); Parke, Davis (Buhl and Whitney); and Koppers (Mellon). Except for Mellon, all of these large investors were members of the founders' families. Firms with family members as inside directors (that is, full-time career managers) holding more than 2% of the stock included Swift, Cudahy, Heinz, Anheuser-Busch, Carnation, Seagram, and Wrigley in food and drink; Johnson & Johnson in consumer chemicals; and Du Pont, Dow, and Monsanto in industrial chemicals.

In the rest of the top food and chemical companies the inside directors were not troubled by influential stockholders on their boards. The firms in which no inside director held as much as 1% and no outside director as much as 2% of the stock outstanding in 1939, and which are also listed as having been management-controlled in 1965, include Armour, Borden, National Dairy, American Sugar, Great Western Sugar, California Packing, Standard Brands, and Libby, McNeil & Libby in food; Procter & Gamble, Sherwin-Williams, Glidden, Rexall Drug, Sterling Drug, McKesson & Robbins, and American Home Products in consumer chemicals; and Allied Chemical, Union Carbide & Carbon, Hercules Powder, Atlas Powder, American Cyanamid, and Air Reduction in industrial chemicals. In these companies inside directors selected the outside directors, who held even less stock than they did.

It must be stressed, however, that management control cannot be measured in terms of the amount of stock held. The managers of these companies gained control because they, not the outside directors, had the knowledge, experience, and information required to make and implement the strategies essential to keep such enterprises profitable. Only those family members who worked as full-time managers were in a position to influence such decisions. Nevertheless, during the interwar years the goal of both outside and inside directors was much the same—that of continuing to make profits over the long haul. The senior managers were well paid, and even those with shareholdings of 1% received substantial income in addition to their salaries and bonuses. Their tenure as top managers was usually relatively brief, however; and wealthy individuals or families—outside directors with substantial holdings—not only received much larger incomes from dividends than did the managers from their combined sources, but they continued to do so long after the current generation of managers had retired. They had an even greater vested interest in the long-term health and growth of the enterprise than the salaried managers had. But it was the full-time, career managers—those who controlled the instruments of power—who determined and implemented the strategies essential both to maintain current profits and to assure a profitable future.

SIX

Expanding Organizational Capabilities: Investment Abroad and Product Diversification in Machinery

This collective history of the modern industrial enterprise in the United States ends with a review of the firms that produced machinery, an industry in which America led the world. At home, machinery makers accounted for at least a quarter of the manufacturing enterprises listed among the top two hundred companies (see Appendixes A.1–A.3). In 1917 they numbered forty-six, and in 1948 they numbered fifty-nine. (In 1973 the number dropped—but only to forty-eight.) No other major industrial group—metals, chemicals, food, or oil— had half that number, except for primary metals (and then only on the 1917 list). Abroad, machinery companies headed the "American invasion" of Europe at the turn of the century that so troubled the British and so impressed the Germans.[1] During these years American firms that mass-produced machinery by fabricating and assembling interchangeable parts—a process known since the 1850s as "the American system of manufacturing"—often acquired close to a global monopoly.

General Characteristics

In machinery the trade-off between the economies of scale and those of scope was more clear-cut than in most industries. The extraordinary cost advantages of scale provided by the American system of manufacturing in the mass production of light machinery sharply reduced the opportunity for exploiting those of scope. Every part and accessory and every motion of every machine worker were designed specifically for the manufacture of a single product line. On the other hand, the construction of made-to-order machines for widely differing industries—machines that could be produced from the same materials and many of the same types of metal-working and -shaping machinery—offered the potential for exploiting the economies of scope. In this type of production German manufacturers excelled, but few American machinery companies followed the German example. Between these two extremes were the makers of volume-produced, standardized machinery for industrial uses. Although their initial cost advantages were based more on scale than scope, such American firms often did find opportunities to diversify into related products.

For such enterprises the possibility of exploiting the economies of scope through diversification usually came in one of four ways: (1) by making fuller use of a firm's existing marketing organizations, as did the food companies; (2) by exploiting the new basic innovations in energy-producing machinery—the internal combustion engine and electricity—which permitted the building of machines for many markets powered by the same energy source; (3) by building component systems that could become integral parts of larger machines (for example, braking and ignition systems for a wide variety of vehicles, and systems which generated, transmitted, or used electric power); and (4) by applying the knowledge of physics, mechanics, and other scientific fields in the developing of products and processes. This fourth factor came into play only in the electrical and electronics industries. Only there did new-product development become an instrument of growth to the extent that it did at Du Pont and the other industrial chemical companies.

Because the continuing growth of machinery firms in the United States came more from enhancing economies of scale than from economies of scope that encouraged new product development, there was less turnover among the leading corporations in machinery than in chemicals. Nevertheless, the turnover was substantial, and as in chemicals it reflected the coming of fundamental innovations. The extraordinary expansion of motor-vehicle production, the coming of volume-produced airplanes, and the development of new electronic equipment brought new firms into the top ranks. At the same time, shipbuilders and those producing locomotives and other railroad equipment dropped off. Of the fifty-nine machinery firms on the 1948 list of the top two hundred, twenty-seven had been on the 1917 list. The listings of the major firms (see Appendix A.4) do not fully reflect these changes, as most of the leaders in the automobile industry had reached the top two hundred by 1917, and those in electronics did not achieve the necessary size until after 1948.

Of the thirteen firms in transportation machinery which moved on to the list of the two hundred top industrials between 1917 and 1948, six were aircraft companies (only one of which had achieved that rank by 1930), three produced trucks, and four were makers of parts and accessories. All three of the newcomers in electrical machinery began as producers of radios.[2] Of the eleven newcomers in nonelectrical machinery, five served industries whose growth was based on the internal combustion engine: two of these (National Supply and Dresser Industries) were makers of oil machinery; one (Timken Roller Bearing) made roller bearings; another (Caterpillar) specialized in tractor and earth-moving equipment; and the fifth, International Combustion Engineering, makers of automatic stokers and power-plant equipment, was one of the few mergers carried out among the thirty-five firms. A sixth newcomer was a specialized machinery company, Food Machinery & Chemical Corporation, which had originated as a merger of several food-processing-machinery firms in the 1928–1930 period. Only the seventh, Sperry Gyroscope, was based on the commercialization of an important recent innovation. Those makers of non-electrical machinery that dropped off the list included four in shipbuilding, four in railroad equipment, and two in machine tools, all producers of older items using processes that had few opportunities for extensive exploitation of the economies of scale or scope and whose markets were declining.

Nonelectrical Machinery

The global dominance of American machinery makers using the American system of manufacturing came first in nonelectrical machinery (Group 35; see Appendixes A.1–A.4).

THE PLAYERS SELECTED

The mass producers of sewing, office, and agricultural machinery (Appendixes A.1–A.4) for a multitude of customers led the way. Those entrepreneurs who first invested in factories large enough to reap the cost advantages of scale, who set up national and international distribution networks, and who recruited the necessary managerial teams long continued to enjoy first-mover advantages throughout the world. Singer Sewing Machine, headed by Edward Clark, completed its investment in the mass-production processes at its Elizabethport, New Jersey, plant in the early 1880s and in its international sales organization soon thereafter.[3] By the end of the decade its two factories, the one at Elizabethport and another in Scotland near Glasgow, each with a capacity of ten thousand machines a week, were producing close to 75% of the world's sewing machines.

In office machinery the mass production of typewriters came first. Because the production processes and the product were relatively simple, the pioneer, Remington Typewriter Company, was quickly followed by others—by such firms as Underwood, Densmore, Smith Premier, and Yost, all of which built comparable selling organizations to market the output of their factories. In 1901 Remington engineered a merger with all but Underwood to control 75% of the industry's U.S. capacity and then rationalized that sector of the industry. In that same year John T. Underwood, who had acquired patents that greatly improved performance, began to build what became "the largest and most complete typewriter factory in existence." In typewriters, therefore, first-mover investments followed an industry-wide merger. In cash registers, adding machines, and copying machines, on the other hand, a single first mover continued to dominate more in the fashion of Singer Sewing Machine—John H. Patterson's National Cash Register, William S. Burroughs's adding-machine company, and A. B. Dick and Company in mimeograph machines. The one other office-machinery firm listed (see Appendix A.4) was a merger of three firms with complementary rather than competing products—punch cards, weighing scales, dial time recorders, and card-type time recorders. After its formation in 1911 the Computing-Tabulating-Recording Company shaped its constituent companies' marketing organizations and increased its managerial staff. A first mover in its products, it changed its name in 1924 to International Business Machines.[4]

In agricultural machinery the story followed closely that of typewriters. Several pioneers developed rather complex harvesters and reapers which, though expensive and therefore requiring consumer credit, greatly reduced farmers' costs in the long term. By dramatically extending the area that one family could cultivate, the new machines transformed the production of wheat, oats, and other grains. McCormick Harvesting Machine became the industry's leader after 1880, when Cyrus McCormick fired his conservative brother, Leander, as superintendent and replaced him with a manager who had been trained in arsenals and sewing-machine factories. Production rose rapidly to thirty thousand machines in 1881, then to sixty thousand machines annually by the middle of the decade.[5] At the same time Cyrus (who died in 1884) and his son expanded their marketing organization of franchised dealers supported by a network of branch offices. A small number of pioneers quickly followed suit, though only one—the Deering Manufacturing Company—made investments comparable to those at McCormick. The resulting intensification of competition led McCormick and Deering and three smaller firms, following several attempts to control price and production through trade associations, to combine in 1902. That merger, which formed the International Harvester Company and was financed by the house of Morgan, was actually initiated by Elbert Gary of the United States Steel Corporation. Gary acted because McCormick had proposed to follow Deering, which had integrated backward into the production of steel, thus increasing the nation's steel capacity. Gary defused the threat by bringing together the McCormicks and the Deerings.[6]

Once formed, the new combination, International Harvester, was slow to centralize administration and rationalize operations: but in 1908 it both enlarged its overseas investments and utilized more fully its personnel and facilities, particularly its marketing organization, in order to expand its product line. Thus International Harvester moved into the production of plows, spreaders, and other agricultural equipment. The existing producers of those products, including John Deere, Moline Plow, J. I. Case, Advance Rumley, and Emerson Brantingham, had built sizable plants and marketing organizations in the 1880s and 1890s. For many years these companies had attempted, always unsuccessfully, to control price and output through the Northwest Plow Manufacturers' Association. After a fruitless attempt to form an industry-wide combination in 1901, they settled down to competing functionally and strategically for market share. As International Harvester moved into their markets, they in turn added harvesters and reapers to their lines, thus using their marketing organizations more fully.[7]

In the volume production of standardized industrial machinery the story was much the same as it was in mass-produced sewing, office, and agricultural machines. Otis Elevator was the first worldwide producer of its product. Babcock & Wilcox, partially financed with the profits of Singer Sewing Machine, became an international leader in the volume production of boilers and other steam-power-plant equipment. Fairbanks, Morse pioneered in mass-produced gasoline and oil engines.[8] Link-Belt (ranked 218 among American manufacturers in 1948) had achieved its dominant position early in the century in producing conveyors and conveyor belts. About the same time, Crown Cork & Seal gained a comparable place in the production of cork and bottle caps and the machinery to make them. These first movers all followed up their initial investments in production, distribution, and management by expanding their marketing organizations at home and establishing branch offices and facilities throughout the world. To support these sales organizations, Otis Elevator, Crown Cork & Seal, and Westinghouse Air Brake had built plants abroad well before the outbreak of World War I, just as had Singer, National Cash Register, and International Harvester.

The mergers that did occur at the turn of the century in these industries were responses to the evolutionary development of their technologies; that is, they were mergers of pioneers which had simultaneously adopted and improved similar production processes. One such merger was United Shoe Machinery. Another was Worthington Pump & Machinery, a merger of seven firms of which Worthington was the largest (for some years the merged company was called International Steam Pump Company). Both had plants abroad before World War I—the first with works in four countries, the second in five. Other mergers, including Allis-Chalmers, American Radiator,[9] and Niles-Bemet-Pond, brought together only two or three major companies. Except for Niles-Bemet-Pond, these firms centralized administration, rationalized production, and created international distributing organizations. Of these, American Radiator had constructed plants in Britain, France, Germany, Austria, and Italy by 1914. And as might be expected, Niles-Bemet-Pond never became a first mover. The mergers that occurred in Group 35 industries after the turn-of-the-century merger movement were not horizontal combinations of competing firms. Instead, they were mergers comparable to those being carried out at the same time by producers of branded, packaged foods and consumer chemicals for the same reason—to exploit further the economies of scope.

Until the Great Depression these machinery makers expanded their marketing and distribution networks at home and abroad. In the United States, agricultural-machinery makers continued to use franchised dealers, supported by their wholesale organizations, to sell their products at retail, while the producers of sewing machines and typewriters continued, even after the coming of the automobile, to market through their own retail outlets. In 1935, 68.4% of agricultural machinery in the United States was distributed through company-owned wholesaler networks. Another 4.3% went directly to industrial customers, but only 1.5% was marketed through company retail outlets.[10] In sewing machines, by contrast, 72% of the dollar sales were made through company-owned intermediaries in 1935, with the lion's share transacted in retail stores. Another 10% went directly to industrial users. By then the producers of office equipment relied less on their own retail outlets.[11] In 1939, 51.2% of office equipment was distributed through wholesaler networks owned by the companies, 24.2% more through their own retail stores, and another 14.8% directly to industrial users. The sewing-machine and office-machinery industries had by far the largest total marketing expenses per dollar of net sales among manufacturing industries in the United States (see Figure 6). Of this selling expense, only a very small proportion was spent on advertising. The rest was accounted for by the enterprises' marketing services and facilities, particularly their retail networks.

The makers of standardized industrial machinery, like the makers of sewing machines, office equipment, and farm implements, relied on their own wholesaling organizations, but they sold much more of their output directly to customers. In 1935, 68.5% of heavy construction machinery went directly to industrial users and only 17.9% was handled by the companies' wholesale networks. On the other hand, firms in industries that supplied a large number of contractors and manufacturers with a wide variety of specialized products (such as pumps and compressors) sold more of their products through manufacturers' agents and other commercial intermediaries. An examination of concentration ratios in these industries, as in other American industries, indicates a rough correlation between the degree of concentration and the amount of their production that was distributed through their own marketing organizations. In 1935 the eight largest firms in the sewing-machine industry accounted for 90% of the U.S. output, and the eight largest in typewriters for 99%. The 1935 data are not available on other industries, but in 1947 the eight largest firms in tractors produced 88% of the U.S. output and in steam turbines 97%. All of these had invested heavily in marketing organizations.

CONTINUING GROWTH THROUGH EXPANSION ABROAD

These makers of nonelectrical machinery (Group 35) spearheaded the American manufacturing invasion of Europe at the turn of the century. Of the forty-one American firms that Mira Wilkins has identified as operating two or more plants abroad in 1914, almost half, or nineteen, were machinery makers. Fifteen of these were on the list of the top two hundred in 1917, and two more, Chicago Pneumatic Tool and Mergenthaler Linotype, were close to the top.[12] (In addition, Burroughs Adding Machine had one plant in England.) Of these nineteen machinery firms all but three (Ford, General Electric, and Westinghouse) belonged to Group 35. Other Group 35 companies, including Remington Typewriter, Underwood Typewriter, and Computing-Tabulating-Recording, did not build plants abroad, but relied instead on their strong marketing organizations to continue to dominate the European market.[13]

In establishing production facilities abroad the machinery firms usually invested in a smaller number of plants than did the producers of branded, packaged products, because the optimal size of plants was much greater. Some, like Singer, built single works to serve many of their markets. Others, like American Radiator and Worthington Pump (International Steam Pump), had more factories. For all, when to build overseas plants, and where, depended on a calculation that related optimal size to the existing and potential market, transportation costs, availability of supplies and of an experienced work force, and tariffs and cross-boundary regulations. Governmental regulations were important factors in establishing works in France and especially in Russia. Tariffs and other government policies encouraged both Singer and International Harvester to build, in addition to their major European works, a factory in Russia—Singer in 1904 and International Harvester in 1910.

The two largest integrated commercial enterprises in imperial Russia in 1914 were Singer Sewing Machine and International Harvester, a fact that emphasizes the global reach of American machinery firms. By then Singer was producing and distributing 679,000 machines annually in Russia with a work force of over 2,500 wage earners and 300 salaried employees in Moscow and with a sales force of 27,439 whose travels took them to outermost Siberia.[14] Harvester's 2,000 workers in Moscow produced machines that sold through a network of branch offices in eleven cities that "encompassed about 80% of the farm implement dealers in Russia."[15]

The dominance of American machinery firms in Europe testifies to the market power acquired by the first movers who exploited the competitive advantages of scale in production and built extensive product-specific sales organizations in marketing and distribution. Their power was comparable to the domination of German dye and other organic-chemical companies in the United States before World War I, resulting from their exploitation of economies of scope and the effectiveness of their marketing organizations. Few of the American machines were fully, or even partially, protected by patents. German manufacturers, for example, produced and sold sewing machines; typewriters, cash registers, adding machines, and other office machinery; harvesters, tractors, and other agricultural machinery; and elevators, pumps, heating equipment, and printing presses—all quite similar in design to those manufactured by American firms. Neither tariffs and other governmental regulations nor special relationships with bankers or members of the industrial elite can account for the American machinery companies' dominant and long-standing market share in Germany, as documented by Fritz Blaich in *Amerikanische Firmen in Deutschland, 1890– 1914* (see Chapter 11). Nor do such factors account for the comparable dominance of these firms in Great Britain, as noted by Mira Wilkins (see my Chapters 7 and 9). Surely patents, government regulations, banking ties, and personal and political relationships favored German and British companies in their own nations over the invaders from abroad.

The American machinery companies successfully "invaded" Europe because so few European enterprises were able to produce better-performing machines at comparable prices and to provide the necessary marketing services of demonstration, installation, after-sales repair and service, and consumer credit. Precisely because the market power of these American firms was based on such functional supremacy, they rarely felt the need to enter into agreements with European competitors either before or after World War I, unlike the leading American firms in oil, glass, chemicals, nonferrous metals and other materials, and electrical machinery.

The Group 35 machinery firms continued to expand their activities abroad after World War I, although they lost their properties in Russia and in a few cases in Germany and central Europe—where even the plants that were not lost were usually returned damaged or in ill repair. For most of these firms, overseas expansion continued until the depression. Those with plants enlarged them, often adding new units. Others, such as Remington Typewriter, International Business Machines, and Timken Roller Bearing, built their first manufacturing plants in Europe in these postwar years. This investment continued (see Tables 14 and 15), and in the 1920s, as might be expected, an increasing number of subsidiaries were established in Europe by companies in the more rapidly growing machinery groups—transportation equipment and electrical and electronic machinery.

GROWTH THROUGH DIVERSIFICATION

Very few companies listed in Group 35 (Appendixes A.2 and A.3) diversified as extensively as did the leading chemical firms and many large food firms. Most of them, however, came to produce closely related products for closely related markets. The leading maker of mining machinery, Ingersoll-Rand, made engines, pumps, and air-moving equipment, all essential to the operation of mines. Babcock & Wilcox produced boiler plate and air-moving equipment in addition to boilers. Fairbanks, Morse & Company manufactured electric engines along with steam and gasoline engines.

Those few that went beyond producing a full line for closely related markets followed three of the four patterns of diversification described at the beginning of this chapter: using their marketing organizations more effectively; developing new products based on recently invented gasoline and electric motors and engines; combining the mechanical parts and accessories that their factories produced into systems for a wide variety of end users. But these Group 35 companies relied much less than manufacturers of electrical equipment on the fourth route to diversification, that of exploiting the opportunities of scope in research and development.

Diversification at Remington Rand, Underwood Typewriter, International Business Machines, and the Food Machinery Corporation resulted from a desire to use more fully their respective marketing organizations. They did so primarily by merger and acquisition. Remington Rand was a 1927 merger that brought together Remington Typewriter, Rand Cardex Bureau, Dalton Adding Machine, and two smaller business-machine companies; all of these firms made products that could be sold to much the same customers through the same channels. Further diversification in the 1930s, following the development of copying machines, business accounting forms, and stationery, led to several acquisitions. In 1928 Underwood Typewriter created a combination similar to Remington Rand's by expanding its line to include cash registers and calculating machines. IBM, in contrast, did little to enlarge its line of business machines. Only in 1939 did it challenge Remington directly by entering the electric-typewriter business through the purchase of Electromatic Typewriters. The Food Machinery Corporation (FMC), a 1928 merger of producers of spray pumps, acquired producers of equipment for canning, handling citrus fruits, and other related processes in the 1930s. By 1943 the firm, already planning for the post-World War II years, purchased the producers of insecticides and fungicides already used in the company's spray pumps. After the war it grew rapidly through both acquisition and direct investment in other agricultural and industrial chemical businesses. In the utilization of marketing skills, these four companies moved into existing businesses rather than developing new ones. This was also true of International Combustion Engineering, which took on products that fitted existing resources in both production and marketing.[16]

More significant to overall industrial growth was diversification that exploited economies of scope in production through development of new product lines serving a variety of markets. Here expansion came mostly through direct investment rather than acquisition. At Allis-Chalmers and International Harvester, the oldest diversifiers among the nonelectrical machinery makers, two basic innovations—electricity and internal combustion engines—provided the impetus for getting into new products.

Allis-Chalmers was a 1901 merger of a maker of lumbering equipment and two producers of mining machinery (one of which, Fraser & Chalmers, was the nation's largest). In 1905 the Allis-Chalmers senior executives decided to use the foundries, presses, and other equipment in their much enlarged Milwaukee works to produce steam turbines. In 1913, in order to exploit economies of scope more effectively, the company closed its Chicago and Scranton works, moving personnel and some facilities to Milwaukee. (Germany's Deutsche Bank, which had helped to finance the initial merger and later expansion and rationalization may have influenced the strategy, for the German machinery firms had made good use of just such economies of scope in production—see Chapter 12.) Because the major electrical manufacturers, General Electric and Westinghouse, sold their turbines and dynamos as parts of larger systems for the generation and distribution of electric power, Allis-Chalmers, its historians note, "had no alternative but to enter electrical manufacturing." It was soon the third largest producer of electrical equipment in the United States. At the same time it developed a line of gasoline-powered engines to drive the machines it made and also to be sold separately. In the 1920s, as the company expanded its investment in flour-milling and mining machinery in addition to turbines and gasoline engines, it also began to use its know-how and facilities to build gasoline-powered tractors and then other agricultural machinery. By the mid-1930s its integrated Tractor Division, which had set up a marketing organization, was bringing in more than 50% of the company's net income. Allis-Chalmers had become the third largest producer of agricultural equipment in the United States. That enterprise used its facilities and the skills of its personnel so effectively that it was able to challenge successfully the first movers in the two established oligopolies it had entered.[17]

The International Harvester story parallels that of Allis-Chalmers. As it embarked on a full line of plows, manure spreaders, and cream separators in order to utilize its marketing organization, it also developed a gasoline-powered tractor. The reason, according to Harvester's 1907 Annual Report, was to "obtain the best results from the selling organization and to bring each manufacturing plant to its highest state of efficiency and productiveness." Actually, the company did not move into volume production of tractors until the outbreak of the war in Europe; but by 1918 it was the largest producer of tractors in the nation, with about 20% of the market. In that year, however, Henry Ford decided to invest in tractor-producing facilities that exploited the cost advantages of scale just as he had done with the Model T. By 1920 the Ford company, with its high-volume throughput, was already producing 33% of all tractors made in the United States, while Harvester's share had dropped to 14%. By 1923 Ford had captured a whopping market share of 76% to Harvester's 9%. Only five years later, however, Ford closed down its tractor production in the United States, giving Harvester an instant gain in market share. In 1928 it made 60% of the tractors produced in the nation.[18]

The primary reason for Ford's withdrawal was that, although the company was able to mass-produce, it failed to mass-distribute; or, more correctly, it failed to make the essential product-specific investment required to market tractors. Henry Ford insisted that his tractors be sold through his existing automobile-dealer network. These dealers were unable to provide either effective after-sales maintenance and repair or consumer credit. Nor did they have the intimate knowledge of the farmer's specialized needs that the Harvester sales force had acquired. Nor, again, were they able to provide information concerning customer needs to the company's design and production departments—information that Harvester used so effectively in the development of its multipurpose Farmall in the early 1920s, a machine that quickly outperformed the Ford tractor. At the end of the decade, as the worsening depression in agriculture reduced demand and led to the underutilization of the personnel and facilities producing Harvester's agricultural equipment, that company turned to manufacturing trucks and earth-moving and other construction machinery—a move that, in turn, required the creation of a new marketing organization.[19]

Then in 1944 the senior executives of Harvester reorganized the company, setting up three new autonomous divisions—Motor Truck, Industrial Power, and Steel—each with its own marketing organization. (The Steel Division operated the works inherited from the old Deering Company, which had integrated backward before the 1902 merger that established International Harvester.) Harvester's Farm Tractor, Farm Implement, and Fiber & Twine Divisions continued to sell through a single, long-established, marketing organization. By the early 1940s comparable structural reorganization—the adoption of the multidivisional form—also followed product diversification at Allis-Chalmers, Remington Rand, and the Food Machinery Corporation, as it did at Sperry and Worthington.[20] All the other firms in Group 35 (Appendix A.3) retained their centralized, functionally departmentalized structure.

Worthington Pump and the Sperry Corporation provided examples of the third way to diversify, that is, by integrating their many products into a variety of systems. Worthington, the nation's largest producer of pumps, had developed a full line of steam and gasoline-pumping equipment, and also compressors, generators, and meters. In the 1920s it began to combine these machines into systems for transferring water and heat (and later into air-conditioning equipment). It also produced extensive water-treatment and sewage-treatment systems. Sperry, whose founder invented the modern gyroscope, grew with the aircraft industry and expanded rapidly to meet the demands of World War II. During the war it made navigational equipment and aircraft instrumentation, and then it developed fire-control and other integrated mechanisms for the Navy's ships and planes, and searchlights and landing-control systems for airports. As the war came to a close, Sperry, either through acquisition or direct investment, expanded into precision instruments, motors, and generators that were integrated into peacetime systems of hydraulic transmission and electrical and magnetic control. In both companies the placing and reworking of many products into an integrated system, often for new uses, stimulated the development of new or greatly improved parts used within that system.[21]

Transportation Equipment

If the internal combustion engine transformed the agricultural-machinery industry, it revolutionized the production and distribution of transportation equipment (Group 37; see Appendixes A.1–A.4). Its coming accounts for one of the few significant sets of turnovers among the two hundred largest industrial enterprises. The assets of makers of automobiles and allied products rapidly increased, while those of producers of the older transportation equipment— ships, locomotives, and other railroad machinery—grew at a much slower rate. Almost overnight the automobile industry became the largest in the nation. By 1925 it ranked first in wages paid, in cost of materials, in value added by manufacturing, and in the value of product—and third in the number of wage earners (in 1935 it was first in wage earners too). By 1929 American manufacturers were making 85% of the automobiles produced in the world.[22] As the industry grew, the makers of specialized vehicles and automotive parts and accessories also joined the top two hundred. Shipbuilders and railroad-equipment manufacturers continued to drop off that list.

THE PLAYERS SELECTED

The central story in the growth of the American automobile industry before World War II is, of course, that of Henry Ford—his achievements as a first mover and then his failure to maintain the organizational capabilities of his enterprise. Ford was the quintessential first mover. His investment in production facilities—the Highland Park works in Detroit—became the symbol of modern mass production and the exploitation of economies of scale. Ford's completion, in the spring of 1914, of the moving assembly line quickly reduced labor time in the production of the Model T from 12.5 hours to 1.5 hours. At the same time, Ford built an international distributing and marketing network which included the industry's first branch assembly plants. He recruited able managers to operate the production facilities, to organize and administer the marketing effort, and to handle the financing of growth. As volume soared, prices dropped. In 1921 the price of a Model T ran between $440 and $455, much lower than that of its closest competitor. At the same time Ford was paying the nation's highest wages. By then he had amassed an enormous personal fortune in an even shorter time than had those earlier beneficiaries of the economies of throughput, Andrew Carnegie and John D. Rockefeller.[23]

By 1921, when the Ford Motor Company accounted for 55.7% of the passenger cars produced in the United States, the major players in the new industry had been selected. At that time Ford still concentrated wholly on the low-price market and completely dominated it. The other eight producers of automobiles listed in the top two hundred in 1917 competed in the middle and upper price ranges. Two more appeared on the 1930 list (Appendix A.4). One, the Nash Motor Company, had been formed in 1916 by Charles W. Nash, a former chief operating executive at General Motors. The other, the Hudson Motor Company, organized by Roy Chapin in 1909, moved onto the list because it first commercialized one of the industry's major innovations—the closed-body car.[24]

In 1921 General Motors, with only 12.3% of the market, was Ford's major competitor. Formed in 1908 by William C. Durant, the creator of the Buick Motor Company (which in that year was the largest producer of cars in the country), General Motors was the industry's first successful merger. Indeed, it was one of the very few carried out in the industry. For Durant, the purpose of merger was not to restrict production but rather to consolidate facilities in order to achieve greater output. His overly optimistic attitude and his failure to integrate his properties rationally, create a corporate office, and develop corporate capabilities brought General Motors into financial difficulties as soon as demand fell off, as it did first in 1910. In that year Durant sought the assistance of the venerable banking house of Lee, Higginson. He received comparable financial assistance in 1917 and again in 1920, both times from the Du Pont Company.

After the third financial fiasco the executives of the Du Pont Company appointed Pierre S. du Pont to take Durant's place as president. Du Pont and his protégé, Alfred P. Sloan, Jr., reorganized Durant's hodgepodge of operating units into a carefully coordinated multidivisional enterprise consisting of autonomous divisions that made cars, trucks, other commercial vehicles, and parts and accessories, each with its own production and distribution organization. Each of the five passenger-car divisions sold in a different price market. Keenly aware of the cost advantage of maintaining operations at minimum efficient scale, Sloan and his associates based production schedules, the hiring of workers, the purchasing of supplies—and even pricing—on annual forecasts. Production scheduling and daily throughput were more precisely calibrated to market demand by using monthly reports of new car registrations, which gave a continuous, accurate picture not only of General Motors' market share but also of that of each of its competitors. Sloan realized that automobile marketing had changed from selling customers their first car to selling them a replacement for the one they already owned—that is, he realized that trading had become an integral part of selling. General Motors concentrated on improving the style, comfort, and performance of its many different models. Sloan also cultivated good relationships with the franchised dealers who retailed the company's products.[25]

In the meantime Henry Ford was dissipating his first-mover advantages by destroying the capabilities of his managerial hierarchy. After 1919, when he bought out his partners, the Dodge brothers, he began to fire his most competent managers. Both his production chief, William Knudsen, and his sales head, Norval Hawkins, immediately took over the same posts at General Motors. In the recession of 1921 Ford demoralized his dealers by forcing cars on them after a temporary collapse in demand. From 1921 on, Ford attempted to administer his empire personally.[26]

The result was disastrous. He continued to make and produce much the same car in much the same manner. By 1925 Ford's share of the total number of passenger vehicles sold had dropped to 40%, and that of General Motors had risen to 20%. In 1927 Ford finally replaced the Model T with the Model A, a change that took a year to carry out. By 1929 Ford's share had fallen farther to 31.3%, and that of General Motors had risen to 32.3%. The Chrysler Corporation had 8.2%.

In 1928 Chrysler became the "Big Two's" most effective challenger. Walter P. Chrysler, who had acquired Dodge in order to get its plant and dealer network, introduced a new low-price car—the Plymouth—to compete with Ford and Chevrolet. In 1929 the next four largest automobile manufacturers—Hudson, Nash, Studebaker, and Packard—together accounted for a total of 12.8% of the market.

The depression years of the 1930s brought another transformation. The sharp drop in demand severely hurt the smaller, medium-price producers; for, as volume dropped, unit costs rose and profits disappeared. For example, at General Motors in 1933, 73% of the passenger-car output and 87% of the profits came from its low-price, high-volume Chevrolet division.[27] By utilizing economies of scope, particularly by using many of the same parts and accessories in all five divisions, General Motors was able to reduce the cost of its middle-priced cars. Chrysler was able to maintain its position by using the same strategy, for it had begun in 1929 to mass-produce its low-priced Plymouth and had also developed a full line, including the middle-priced Dodge, DeSoto, and Chrysler. Moreover, the Chrysler company, which had not integrated backward, was able throughout the depression to obtain parts, accessories, and bodies cheaply from outside suppliers. But the smaller automobile makers never fully recovered from the depression.[28] Soon after World War II all the independent middle-priced producers abandoned the production of automobiles, except for Willys-Overland, which had developed and mass-produced the basic military vehicle—the Jeep—the civilian version of which became the mainstay of American Motors.

Indeed, in the 1930s only two of the three producers of low-priced cars, General Motors and Chrysler, had been able to maintain a throughput large enough to remain profitable. Ford's drop in market share and profits was striking. By 1940 its share of passenger vehicles sold had fallen to 18.9%, well below Chrysler's 23.7% and far below General Motors' 47.5%. In the decade from 1927 to 1937, according to the Federal Trade Commission, Ford had a net loss of $15.9 million and a reduction in the surplus balance of another $85.6 million. In that same decade General Motors' net profits after taxes were just under $2 billion ($1,905.6 million). This difference of more than $2 billion in after-tax profits emphasizes the value of strong management and carefully thought-out administrative procedures in competing for market share and profits. For in these years Henry Ford, assisted by his son and a tiny handful of executives, continued to manage personally his huge industrial empire.

Moreover, Ford was the world's most integrated automobile company. To be sure of constant, tightly scheduled flows of materials through his huge plants—the first at Highland Park and then the River Rouge works—and thus to enhance the economies of scale, Ford made a massive investment in the production of steel and glass, parts and accessories. Therefore, as output declined, unit costs rose much more rapidly than did those of his competitors. Ford's integration was primarily within the plant. At General Motors the goal was to assure the supply of parts and accessories produced by separate and geographically distant units. Pierre du Pont and Sloan added almost no parts and accessories divisions to those acquired by Durant. Their policy, one of insurance, was to have full control over only 25% of the parts and accessories required by the automobile, truck, and other vehicle-producing divisions.[29] The Chrysler Corporation, on the other hand, did not attempt to integrate backward until after World War II, when pent-up demand and scarcity of supplies caused it to acquire an assured source of supply, Briggs Manufacturing. By using differing strategies of vertical integration both General Motors and Chrysler paid a far smaller price than Ford for operating at reduced capacity.

EXPANSION ABROAD

Direct investment abroad by American automobile manufacturers came swiftly and grew to greater value than that of any other American industry. First at home and then abroad, the establishment of sales organizations was quickly followed by the building of branch assembly plants. Ford was the first to build plants close to markets to assemble the final product in order to reduce transportation costs and at the same time assure continuing economies of throughput in large domestic fabricating plants and those producing engines, bodies, and other major components. By August 1913, when Ford began to experiment with the moving assembly line in Detroit, his company already had thirteen assembly plants operating in the United States and one in Manchester, England.[30] General Motors began to build assembly plants overseas after World War I. By 1929 six other American companies had comparable final assembly plants abroad.[31]

The management of General Motors, partly in order to increase capacity and stay in closer touch with the needs of the major foreign markets, but primarily to get under increasingly high tariffs, decided in the mid-1920s to go beyond assembly plants and to purchase existing, integrated, overseas enterprises. In 1925 the company obtained Vauxhall, a British producer of trucks and medium-sized cars, and in 1929 it purchased Adam Opel, Germany's largest producer of passenger cars. By 1937 General Motors exported 180,000 vehicles (normally assembled abroad) and manufactured 188,000 more abroad. By then it had assembly plants in Belgium, Sweden, Denmark, Spain, Egypt, Brazil, Argentina, Uruguay, Australia, New Zealand, India, Canada, South Africa, Java, China, and Japan. Ford, by contrast, relied wholly on direct investment, not acquisition, and by the 1930s had plants in several European and South American countries, as well as in Canada, Australia, India, the Union of South Africa, and Japan. Nevertheless, because of Henry Ford's dismantling of his firm's organizational capabilities, the company's performance abroad was almost as disastrous as it was at home. (The details of this story are told in Chapters 9 and 13.) As early as 1923, 54% of all cars exported to foreign markets were made in the United States, as compared with 11% made in France, 2% in Britain, and 2% in Germany. And five years later, in 1928, these figures read: 72% American, 6% French, 5% British, and 1% German. In the same year total automobile production in the United States was 4,359,000 as compared with 210,000 in France, 212,000 in Great Britain, 90,000 in Germany, and 24,000 in Japan. All but 350 of the cars in Japan were assembled by Ford and General Motors. In all five countries American firms were leaders. Given such market power, American automobile makers had no need to enter into market-sharing or price-setting agreements with competitors at home or abroad.[32]

GROWTH THROUGH DIVERSIFICATION

Precisely because the growth of the leading enterprises in the new transportation industries was based on the organizational capabilities developed in exploiting the economies of scale, these enterprises made little attempt to utilize the economies of scope. They grew far more by moving into distant geographical markets than into related product markets. Not only did the units of production concentrate wholly on mass-producing and mass-distributing motor vehicles, but, with the exception of General Motors, they made only minimal investments in research and development. This was also true of the older firms in Group 37—the builders of ships and railroad equipment. In 1931, according to David Mowery, the research intensity (scientists and engineers in laboratories per thousand employees) of the machinery makers in Group 35 was 1.68 and that of the makers of transportation equipment in Group 37 was 1.28, making them eighth and tenth in ranking—far behind chemicals, petroleum, electrical machinery, and rubber, and even below stone, glass, and clay; instruments; and metals.[33] As process and product in the auto industry became perfected and world domination followed, research investment seemed almost superfluous.

Indeed, Henry Ford was certain that the Model T and its manufacturing processes would last for a generation. Nevertheless, Ford did attempt in the 1920s to develop an all-metal, trimotor airplane, as well as a mass-produced tractor. He was as unsuccessful with airplanes as he was with tractors. He failed largely because his enterprise had been unable to acquire the organizational capabilities necessary to develop and sell these nonautomotive products.[34]

Among the Group 37 companies listed in the top two hundred (Appendixes A.1–A.3) there were only three successful diversifiers. One was General Motors. The other two were producers of parts and accessories—Borg-Warner and Bendix. Bendix Aviation enjoyed great growth, producing for the new aviation industry. Borg-Warner relied for its initial growth on replacement sales in the older motor-vehicle industry.[35] Both firms were mergers of companies with complementary lines.

Borg-Warner was a 1929 merger of single-product firms producing clutches (Borg), gears and transmissions (Warner), axles, and carburetors. After the merger it acquired makers of radiators, springs, chains, sprockets, heat-exchange elements, fuel pumps used in motor vehicles of all types, and also industrial and agricultural machinery. In 1930 Borg-Warner began to manufacture household appliances, heaters, and other consumer products that contained elements already produced by the company. By 1948 only 50% of its business was in automotive parts and equipment, and 30% was in household appliances. To assure a steady flow of specialized steels and other materials for its diversified lines during the immediate postwar years, it integrated backward, purchasing three specialty steelmakers, including United States Pressed Steel.

The Bendix Corporation started in the automotive industry. A maker of automobile ignition and braking systems, it produced the first reliable four-wheel-brake system. Then, after 1928, it took the name of Bendix Aviation and entered that industry. Through merger and acquisition it began to produce landing gears, propellers, emission systems, and navigational equipment. It also turned to making generators and carburetors for the new aviation industry. And it continued to manufacture products for automotive and then for industrial markets.

Bendix and Borg-Warner not only competed with each other but with the parts and accessory division of General Motors and with several smaller suppliers to the automobile, aircraft, and allied industries. They too soon adopted the multidivisional structure in which General Motors had pioneered.

In the 1930s General Motors began to diversify. That strategy had its seeds in the 1920s, for Pierre du Pont and Alfred Sloan, unlike the other automobile makers, believed in the value of research, particularly for product improvement.[36] They placed Charles F. Kettering, the inventor of the self-starter, in charge of a sizable research and development organization. After forming the General Technical Committee they integrated its work with that of the corporation's operating divisions. Kettering's team not only worked on short-term projects, such as improving brakes, transmissions, lubricants, and tires, but also carried out long-term investigations into metallurgy and fuels.[37]

Until the collapse of demand in the early 1930s, however, research at General Motors concentrated almost wholly on improving automotive processes and products. After 1929 Kettering's organization turned to investigating new products that might use the company's technical and managerial resources more profitably. In 1930 it began to develop a diesel-powered railroad locomotive that could be volume-produced. Production started in 1935. By 1938 manufacturing facilities of optimal size at LaGrange, Illinois, were completed. Within a decade such product development had made the steam locomotive obsolete in the United States—an impressive achievement. In 1929 the corporation enlarged its commitment to the new aviation industry by obtaining full control of the Allison Engineering Company, makers of aircraft engines, 40% of the Fokker Aircraft Corporation, and 24% of Bendix Aviation. Allison, whose design and production work used methods (as well as parts and facilities) similar to those used in the automobile company, became a division of General Motors.

On the other hand, Bendix and Fokker, a maker of airframes, remained autonomous operating subsidiaries. As Sloan later noted, "Our investments were made as a means of maintaining direct contact with developments in aviation." In 1933 Fokker became part of North American Aviation, in which General Motors held 30% of the voting shares. During World War II its activities greatly expanded. Because of the uncertain future of the airframe business and because the production and distribution of airplanes (in contrast to airplane engines) was so different from that of automobiles, the General Motors Executive Committee decided in 1943 that, at the war's end, the corporation would withdraw from the production of complete airplanes, both military and commercial. But it "should develop as complete a position in the manufacture of accessories as its capacity and circumstances make possible." After the war, overcapacity in the aircraft industry and the great, pent-up demand for automobiles caused General Motors to sell its interest in both Bendix and North American. The need to use all available technical and managerial as well as capital resources to meet the massive postwar demand for motor vehicles dampened top management's enthusiasm for moving into more distantly related products.[38]

In contrast to the three diversifiers (General Motors, Borg-Warner, and Bendix), the other Group 37 firms among the top two hundred continued to concentrate on a single line of products. White Motor, Mack Trucks, Fruehauf Trailer, and Dana produced trucks or trailers primarily for the American market. Briggs, a maker of automotive and truck bodies and parts, produced for smaller manufacturers until World War II, and for Chrysler's Plymouth Division after 1929. After the war the demise of the makers of middle-priced cars, on the one hand, and Chrysler's need for an assured supply to meet the demands of the booming automobile market, on the other, led both firms to agree (in 1953) to Chrysler's acquisition of Briggs. During the 1920s and early 1930s another specialized firm, Electric-Auto-Lite, made a variety of starting motors, spark plugs, batteries, and lamps, but they were all for the automobile market. This company's growth was quite similar to that of its counterparts in Great Britain and Germany. By 1940 the company was beginning to diversify by producing parts and systems for aircraft, tractors, and marine engines. After World War II it continued to diversify in the manner of Borg-Warner and Bendix.

The history of the leaders in Group 37 further emphasizes the difficulties of exploiting the economies of scale and scope simultaneously. Firms whose organizational capabilities rested on mass-production of cars, buses, and small trucks had few opportunities to use their skills and facilities in developing new products for new markets. Only General Motors had a research staff experienced enough and a corporate office aware and qualified enough to develop new products at a time when its divisions were operating their plants at far below minimal scale. Only those firms making parts and accessories that could be units in an integrated system had the opportunity to produce new items and new systems for a wide range of markets. Nevertheless, before World War II the nature of the technology of production and that of the products themselves deterred transportation-equipment firms from developing a systematic strategy of growth through new-product development—a strategy comparable to that adopted by Du Pont and other producers of industrial chemicals.

Electrical and Electronic Equipment

With the exception of General Electric (GE) and Westinghouse Electric and their most notable offspring, the Radio Corporation of America (RCA), the history of the volume producers of electrical products (Group 36; see Appendixes A.1–A.4) follows closely that of the other American makers of light, volume-produced, machinery in Groups 35 and 37.

THE PLAYERS SELECTED

Electric Storage Battery, Western Electric (the manufacturing arm of American Telephone & Telegraph), Victor Talking Machine, and Columbia Graphophone all produced, in a very small number of plants, a single line of products that were distributed and sold through their own international marketing organizations. By the end of the first decade of the new century they had built plants abroad. Indeed, by 1914 Western Electric was operating eight factories overseas.[39] (The reason for this large number was that nearly all telephone systems abroad were owned and operated by the state, and their managers insisted on having telephone equipment produced in plants within their own national boundaries.)

These Group 36 firms differed from American global leaders in other machinery industries in that they rarely had the field to themselves. They competed for world markets with German companies and, in the case of phonographs, with British firms during the interwar years. Because this global competition differed from competition between single-line producers in the domestic market, it will be reviewed in the histories of these British and German competitors in Chapters 9, 12, and 14.

General Electric, Westinghouse Electric, and RCA, the American first movers in modern electrical and electronic equipment, differed from the other American machinery firms in that they were able to exploit to a much greater extent the economies of scope, in addition to those of scale, and so to grow through the development of new products. The electrical-equipment manufacturers exploited all four of the routes to diversification described earlier in this chapter. They came into being by building machines for the production and use of a basic new energy source, electricity. They quickly developed a broad line of products for brand new markets. Because the generation, transmission, and uses of electric power (and also light) required the installation of systems involving a wide variety of parts and equipment, they became system builders.[40] Finally, improvement of product and process required complex technical and scientific skills and a level of investment in research and development that remained second only to that of the chemical industry.

The first movers in the electrical-equipment industry took charge as quickly as did those in motor vehicles. Just as Ford and General Motors had become the two largest producers of automobiles in less than a decade after the automobile began to be sold commercially, so ten years after the opening of the world's first central power station (Thomas Edison's Pearl Street station in New York City in 1882), the two leading American electrical manufacturers were General Electric and Westinghouse. General Electric was itself a merger in 1892 of two of the three largest manufacturers, Thomson-Houston and Edison General Electric. The two most powerful German first movers—Emil Rathenau's Allgemeine Elektricitäts Gesellschaft (AEG) and the Siemens family's Siemens & Halske—came, through merger, to dominate European markets just after the turn of the century. The two American giants and the two German firms remained the global oligopoly's Big Four until well after World War II.

Three outstanding inventors in the field of electricity accomplished what inventors rarely do. They effectively commercialized their products and then became first movers. Edison, George Westinghouse, and Elihu Thomson saw to it that large-scale investments were made in production facilities; that the necessary management teams to produce these products were recruited; and that the necessary marketing organizations were established. The three, however, worked in different ways. Edison preferred to let others—notably, Henry Villard and his young assistant, Samuel Insull—carry out the financing and build the organization. He preferred to continue to concentrate on the development of a wide variety of electrically related products at his Menlo Park laboratories. George Westinghouse, who had already created a multinational enterprise to produce and sell his air brakes for railway trains, used the funds and experience thus acquired to build an even larger personal empire in the new electrical-equipment industry. On the other hand, Elihu Thomson, whose plant in Lynn, Massachusetts, was financed by local and then by Boston venture capitalists, turned over the production and distribution of his innovations to Charles A. Coffin, who soon proved himself to be the industry's most effective enterprise builder.[41]

Coffin, the only one of these entrepreneurs without technical training, understood even more than did Villard and Westinghouse the importance of recruiting a technically trained sales force. The products were new and complex. Only men versed in the knowledge of electrical engineering were able to design, install, and maintain the new systems for electric power, light, and traction (streetcars and subways). Faulty installation and operation could have serious, often deadly, consequences. Moreover, more than in any of the other new industries of the Second Industrial Revolution, the customers, in this case new utility and traction companies, required massive credit. They normally expected to pay for their equipment, in part at least, with the stocks and bonds of their own companies. Therefore, the electrical manufacturers had to finance their customers to a uniquely great extent in order to sustain demand for their products. To do this, General Electric formed two holding companies: Edison Bond & Share to hold the securities of American utilities, and American & Foreign Power to hold those of foreign firms.

A major constraint in the commercial development of power systems and the manufacture of electric motors was the plethora of patents that were taken out during the industry's initial years of innovation. Power systems required a variety of generating, transmitting, and switching equipment, and motors contained many parts. Some patents were for viable products and technologies, others for unworkable ones. By the late 1880s inventors, at home and abroad, had patents that could block the assembling of dynamos, transformers, switch boxes, small motors, and comparable products, all of which were used in the construction of larger systems. The desire to cut through this patent maze was a major reason for the merger of Edison General Electric and Thomson-Houston in 1892 to form General Electric.

Another important reason was to bring together complementary product lines. Thomson-Houston was particularly strong in arc lighting, while Edison's forte was incandescent-lamp lighting. Thomson had pioneered alternating current systems. Edison concentrated on delivering direct current. Only in the production of electric railway and streetcar equipment did the two compete. The merger brought rationalization, with production of major product lines concentrated in single plants in order to utilize better the economies of scale and to a lesser extent those of scope. Sales forces were combined, and a centralized, functionally departmentalized structure was put into place. The 1892 merger and resulting rationalization was financed by the house of Morgan. Impressed by the capabilities of Coffin's organization, particularly in marketing and management, J. P. Morgan, supported by the representatives of Thomson-Houston's Massachusetts investors, placed Coffin and his close associates in the key managerial positions at the new General Electric Company, rather than appointing Villard and his assistants.

In 1896 General Electric and Westinghouse reduced the patent barrier still further by signing an industry-wide cross-licensing agreement. As Harold Passer's carefully researched history of the early years of the industry emphasizes, after the agreement the two first movers competed functionally and strategically for market share in the production and distribution of several product lines. Such competition strengthened the coordination of marketing, production, design, and research within each company—a linkage that was essential to the cumulative improvement of product and process in this most technologically advanced of industries.[42]

As Passer also points out, the pooling of patents obviously strengthened the two leaders' first-mover advantages. Because of the newness and complexity of the systems with their many component parts needed to generate, distribute, and use this new source of power, patents became a greater barrier to entry than in any of the other machinery industries or even in the chemical industry. Even so, in both the United States and Europe a few challengers, such as Allis-Chalmers in America and Brown, Boveri in Europe, were able to obtain a profitable market share. The first movers, in order to maintain their technological edge and their market share, invested in research and development (as did their European counterparts). Indeed, General Electric became the most prominent pioneer in industrial research in the United States.

In the competition among giants, General Electric remained the leader, partly because George Westinghouse was slow to build the necessary administrative framework and partly because he wanted to maintain financial control of his enterprise. He preferred, whenever possible, to rely on short-term debt rather than to sell equity. He did not follow General Electric and the European electrical manufacturers in setting up a finance company to assist customers to purchase his products. By 1891 his financial resources and those of local banks and bankers in Pittsburgh (the location of the Westinghouse works), had become overstretched. Westinghouse then called on the New York investment banking house of August Belmont and the Boston house of Lee, Higginson to reorganize his company's finances. Later, during the panic of 1907, cash shortages forced the company into bankruptcy. This time Kuhn, Loeb and the Chase National Bank handled the refinancing. Although the founder lost control, he stayed on as president. But financial pressures continued, and in 1911 Westinghouse left the company.[43]

In the electrical-equipment industry the combined high costs of production facilities, marketing, and product development brought investment bankers onto the boards of the two leading firms. As for the thirteen-man General Electric board, there is little evidence that the representatives of the house of Morgan or those of the Boston investors who had financed Thomson-Houston ever overruled Coffin's strategic decisions or, once Coffin had established his management team, his selection of personnel. (In 1900 the Boston representatives outnumbered the Morgan men by six to three.)[44] At Westinghouse, on the other hand, the company's financial difficulties forced the investment bankers on the board to play a more active role in both the financing of facilities and the recruitment of management.

EXPANSION ABROAD

The founders' predilections and their business abilities were reflected in the way their enterprises expanded overseas. Thomas Edison, who paid little attention to organization and sales, relied on licensing his patents to foreigners rather than investing directly in distant production and marketing. The licensee in Germany, Emil Rathenau's Deutsche Edison Gesellschaft, later called Allgemeine Elektricitäts Gesellschaft (AEG), created one of the most successful and profitable first movers in Europe. The licensees in Britain and France did little.[45] At Thomson-Houston, on the other hand, Coffin quickly built an international sales organization and then established major manufacturing subsidiaries in Britain and France. Therefore, General Electric's overseas growth in the early twentieth century rested largely on those two Thomson-Houston subsidiaries and on a continuing close relationship with Rathenau's AEG.

George Westinghouse also preferred direct investment to licensing. He, too, supported his sales organization by establishing plants abroad. Because of his entrepreneurial optimism and empire-building tendencies, however, the plants he had built were far too large for existing markets. The works constructed in 1899 at Trafford Park in Manchester, England, were much bigger than the British plant built earlier by Thomson-Houston. Indeed, it became one of Britain's most impressive industrial establishments. But this subsidiary only occasionally showed a profit, for it rarely operated at even close to minimum efficient scale. This was also true of works that Westinghouse built before World War I in France, Italy, Germany, and Russia.

High unit costs, the resulting unprofitability, continuing financial difficulties at home, and the coming of World War I caused top management at Westinghouse to withdraw from Europe. During the war the company sold its plants in Britain, France, and Italy, and after 1918 it made no attempt to regain investments lost in Germany and Russia. Nevertheless, in the interwar years Westinghouse maintained a stream of income from abroad by relying on process and patent agreements based upon the effectiveness of its own continuing research and development in Pittsburgh, and by maintaining close relationships with leading British and Continental firms (as reviewed in Chapters 9 and 13). [46]

As Westinghouse withdrew, General Electric advanced. After the war it became the world's most powerful electrical manufacturer, dominating the global oligopoly. Under Gerard Swope, who headed its international activities before becoming president in 1922, and Owen D. Young, who succeeded Coffin as chairman of the board in the same year, the company attempted to reorganize and rationalize Britain's electrical-equipment industry, to refinance that of Germany, and to continue to play the leading role in France, Mexico, South Africa, Australia, and Japan. In Japan as early as 1905 it acquired a controlling interest in Tokyo Electric, and five years later it purchased a minority interest in Shibaura Electric.

Because General Electric and Westinghouse, unlike the leading American firms making automobiles and nonelectrical machinery, had to compete for market share in international markets with powerful European first movers—primarily Rathenau's AEG, the Siemens family's combined enterprises, and the smaller Swiss firm of Brown, Boveri—they relied much more than did the leaders in the other two machinery groups on negotiations and contractual arrangements to determine market share. Success in such negotiations with competitors, however, depended on financial strength and, above all, on maintaining and expanding the state of the art by a continuing commitment to investment in research and development. Producers of more specialized electrical and electronic products also negotiated as well as competed for market share. In batteries, such firms included Electric Storage Battery and Accumulatoren-Fabrik AG. In telephone equipment they included Western Electric and then International Telephone & Telegraph (after Western Electric's parent, American Telephone & Telegraph, sold its overseas holdings to ITT), the Swedish firm of L. M. Ericsson, and Siemens & Halske. Because the changing relationship among the members of this global oligopoly had a major impact on the development of the leading electrical manufacturers in both Great Britain and Germany, the international activities of the dominant American firms are described in more detail in Chapters 9, 12, and 14.

GROWTH THROUGH DIVERSIFICATION

For the two American electrical giants, growth came as much from investment in related product lines as it did from investment abroad. Not only was this industry more science-based than any other except chemicals, but the many uses for electrical energy and the equipment and machinery powered by it stimulated further product improvement and diversification. The number of scientific and engineering personnel working in Group 36 throughout the interwar years remained second to, though still far behind, chemicals.[47] And much of that personnel was concentrated in the laboratories of General Electric and Westinghouse.

The complexity of the technology, the resulting heavy investment in research, and the variety of products used in the generation, transmission, and application of electric power led both Westinghouse and General Electric to embrace enthusiastically the development and commercialization of new products whose production and distribution made at least partial use of the companies' existing facilities and even more use of their technical and managerial skills. Here General Electric, whose early investment in research was larger than that of Westinghouse, remained more innovative. At GE, research to improve electric wire and cable resulted in the development and commercialization of new alloys, bringing the company into competition with metal-making companies such as Alcoa and chemical firms such as Dow. Investigations to improve insulation of wire led to the development of new varnishes, adhesives, and lacquers, products that brought General Electric into direct competition with Du Pont and also leading paint companies. Research on the molding of carbon for light bulbs brought product innovations in plastics that led to competition with other divisions of major chemical companies. From the research on the vacuum tube came X-ray machinery, which, in turn, brought the development of other new types of medicinal equipment.[48] Equally revolutionary was General Electric's development of the high-vacuum radio tube and the radio-frequency alternator, making the company, along with Westinghouse, Western Electric, and the American subsidiary of British Marconi, a pioneer in radio receivers and broadcasting equipment.[49]

Diversification at General Electric and Westinghouse was also stimulated by the desire to develop new products that not only used company-produced parts and machines but also increased the demand for their electrical generating and transmitting equipment. This motivation led to the volume production of household appliances, including electric refrigerators, hot-water heaters, stoves, washing machines, vacuum cleaners, and space heaters.[50] Such new appliances called for an increase in the production of small electric motors and enlarged the demand for electricity generated by the companies' primary products. In fact, the extensive investment made by these two companies in household appliances may have discouraged the rise of large single-line firms in these businesses, or at least may have kept them from becoming large enough to join the list of the top two hundred. For example, the British subsidiary of Hoover, an American maker of vacuum cleaners, quickly joined the top two hundred in that country, but its larger parent did not have enough assets to come close to a comparable ranking in the United States. To market these consumer durables, both GE and Westinghouse invested in new national and then worldwide sales networks. But because these products needed less effort for demonstration, installation, or service and repair than did the more complex industrial durables, a large share came to be distributed through independent jobbers, with the companies' own wholesaling organizations concentrating on advertising, canvassing retailers for orders, and assuring deliveries on schedule.

Such diversification into new products for new markets forced organizational change at both GE and Westinghouse. Until the 1930s both responded in an ad hoc manner. In the 1920s each created a "merchandise department" to market its consumer appliances. At GE the production and distribution of alloys and X-ray machines were carried on through separate, autonomous subsidiaries that built and managed their own plants and supervised sales forces in their specialized markets. The chemical activities were combined into an administratively comparable autonomous and integrated chemical division. The initial organizational response at Westinghouse was similar.

The organization that was developed to commercialize the newly invented radio was more complicated. In 1919 the technological pioneers in radio and broadcasting—General Electric, Westinghouse, Western Electric (AT&T's manufacturing subsidiary), and American Marconi—formed the Radio Corporation of America to pool patents. RCA absorbed American Marconi and then became the marketing outlet for radios produced for consumer markets by both General Electric and Westinghouse.[51]

David Sarnoff, RCA's energetic top executive, was determined to produce as well as distribute. His first success came in 1929 when he arranged for the purchase of Victor Talking Machine, the largest American producer of phonographs and records. Victor's senior managers had become convinced that they must move into the production of radios, particularly radio-phonograph combinations, if they were to retain market share. Sarnoff convinced them to sell out instead. That acquisition gave him his manufacturing base. He then persuaded Gerard Swope and Owen D. Young, the president and chairman of the board, respectively, at General Electric, and Andrew W. Robertson, Westinghouse's president, to let RCA take over the radio-manufacturing facilities of both companies. Three weeks after this agreement was signed in April 1930, the Department of Justice filed an antitrust suit against RCA and its owners. As a result GE, Westinghouse, and AT&T agreed to a consent decree which made RCA an independent corporation. They disposed of their stock interest and any participation in the radio company's management and direction. Sarnoff quickly consolidated the company's manufacturing and design facilities and expanded its marketing organization. He also invested heavily in research and development, and this investment helped RCA to maintain its powerful patent position and its leading edge in the new and rapidly changing electronics technology.

The demands of World War II, not just for existing products but for radar, sonar, and other electronic innovations, first permitted smaller companies like Philco and Sylvania to use the RCA patents in carrying out government contracts. The government financed their plants and provided the markets that permitted the newcomers to operate for several years at close to minimum efficient scale and thus to develop organizational capabilities so essential in overcoming RCA's first-mover advantages. After the war, Philco and Sylvania successfully brought antitrust suits against RCA, weakening the first mover's control over patents. These challengers rapidly expanded their marketing organizations and increased their investment in research and development. At the same time they began to diversify into other radio and electronic equipment and into systems using electronic parts, as well as into consumer appliances and the new television market, so that radio was soon only one of many product lines. [52]

It was only after 1948, however, that the coming of the transistor and the modern computer, in addition to advances in sophisticated instrumentation for navigation and weaponry, created an electronics revolution that would bring new entrants into the top two hundred. These new products transformed the electronics industry in much the same way as antibiotics and other "miracle" drugs were transforming the pharmaceutical industry in the same years and as chemical synthesis and the internal combustion engine had earlier transformed the chemical industry and the transportation-equipment industry.

At GE, Westinghouse, and RCA, continuing diversification brought, to each at a different pace, a multidivisional administrative structure. In 1931 Westinghouse embarked on a thoroughgoing reorganization that ended in 1934 with the final definition of the functions of the general office in Pittsburgh and the boundaries of seven divisions—steam turbines and other generating and also transmitting equipment; motors and other products for industry; lamps; X-ray equipment; appliances; elevators; and miscellaneous products. At GE the structural change came much more slowly. Until the retirement of its two highly competent senior executives, Swope and Young, that company's structure remained something of an administrative hodgepodge of functional departments, specialized sales departments, and autonomous, integrated divisions and subsidiaries. Shortly after World War II, Ralph Cordiner began a massive overhaul of the company's structure that was not completed until the mid-1950s. At RCA the changes came before they did at GE. In fact, in the early 1950s the largest division, RCA Victor, was divided into a number of product divisions. [53]

Although GE and Westinghouse as well as RCA expanded into related products by exploiting the economies of scope, those of scale continued to provide a significant cost advantage at home and abroad. As early as 1895, when GE was producing six product lines, it had more than 10,000 industrial and governmental customers and processed 104,000 separate orders. But, as time passed, what differentiated these two companies from the other machinery makers was the constant addition of new product lines. Because of the variety of products needed for a single power-generating and transmitting network (generators, transformers, motors, and switches), because of the many uses to which electricity was increasingly put (electrolytic processes in chemicals and metals, the different motors and other power sources produced for other industries, and the increasing demand for household appliances and other consumer durables), and because of the potential for improving product and process through the application of physics and electrical engineering, the number of GE's product lines (lines in which operating results were accounted for separately) rose from 10 in 1900 to 30 in 1910, to 85 in 1920, to 193 in 1930, and to 281 in 1940. By World War I, GE had developed one of the most diversified product lines of any industrial enterprise in the world. Nearly all these products were related to its electrical-equipment base; and the expansion into related product lines was carried out much more by direct investment than by acquisition—investment that was funded largely from retained earnings.[54]

Organizational Complexities and Managerial Control

In the machinery industries the exploitation of the economies of both scale and scope made top-management decisions more complex than in any other American industry except chemicals. The cost advantages of scale carried American machinery firms into global markets sooner and on a grander scale than occurred in other industries, including chemicals. To retain their first-mover advantages the machinery makers, both those making consumer durables, such as sewing machines and typewriters, and those making industrial products, such as elevators and pumping equipment, had to pay closer attention than most other American industrial companies to the details of operating in, and allocating resources for, foreign markets. They had to adjust to the different levels and types of demand, different distribution systems, different sources of supply, and different tariffs and other barriers to international trade in the many different national and the several regional markets in which they operated. The leading producers of sewing, office, and agricultural machinery; of elevators, pumps, boilers, and other volume-produced industrial equipment; of automobiles and commercial vehicles; of telephone and other electrical items—all these firms had to make strategic decisions concerning the precise location and optimal size of their overseas plants, as well as whether to build assembly plants (whose profitable operation required careful coordination with the operations of the fabricating works at home) or to buy integrated enterprises abroad. Such functional and strategic decisions had to be made in a constantly changing environment—one where a world war was followed by brief recovery, sharp recession, prosperity, depression, and another world war. After 1929 the managerial task was further complicated by an increase in economic nationalism that restricted both the flow of goods and the flow of funds.

For those firms where the potential for economies of scope encouraged growth through product diversification, top-management decisions were even more complex than those connected with geographical expansion. The decisions at International Harvester and Allis-Chalmers to utilize the internal combustion engine, those at General Motors (during the Great Depression) to move into diesel locomotives and airplane engines, those at Bendix and Borg-Warner to develop new parts and systems, and those at GE, Westinghouse, and RCA to develop a wide variety of related electrical and electronic processes for both industry and household—all these decisions required the balancing of many technological marketing, production, and financial variables. As in the chemical firms, profits on many new products were realized only years after the initial investment in development had been made.

In the machinery industries, as in the chemical and chemically oriented food industries, the complex and technical nature of decisions critical to current and future health of their enterprises meant that they were made by trained and experienced, full-time salaried managers. Here, as in chemicals, the information, knowledge, and experience of the inside directors gave them the authority to plan and implement long-term strategy, as well as to make short-term operating decisions. No part-time outside director could hope to acquire comparable data and skills.

Representatives of banks who sat on the boards of these machinery companies rarely influenced top-level decisions except during and after mergers or unless the company had financial problems. Such difficulties arose when, for example, Westinghouse was unable to meet its short-term obligations in 1907, when General Motors under William Durant was unable to do so in 1910, and when a small number of machinery companies experienced the same problem in the 1920–21 recession and others did so in the dark days of the early 1930s. Only at Westinghouse did banker influence continue for more than a short period: there the banking representatives on the board concerned themselves primarily with recruiting an effective top management. Nor did banker influence last long after mergers. At GE by 1900, Charles Coffin, not the representatives of Morgan or those of the Boston investors, was fully responsible for company affairs. By 1910 members of the McCormick family, not the Morgan representatives, were in charge at International Harvester. The investment house of Dillon, Read assisted Walter Chrysler in financing the purchase of Dodge in 1928, but Chrysler and his top managers, not the representatives of Dillon, Read, formulated and implemented Chrysler's subsequent and most successful strategies.

Far more influential was Pierre du Pont at General Motors when he became its president in 1923 after Durant's financial difficulties. Once du Pont had reorganized the enterprise and recruited a new top-management team, he turned the reins over to Alfred Sloan. From 1923 on, the representatives of the Du Pont Company on the General Motors board carefully reviewed management proposals, particularly those relating to finance, and paid close attention to management recruitment. But very rarely did they influence operating decisions or propose alternative courses of action.[55] In addition to representatives of the Du Pont Company at General Motors and those of General Motors at Bendix, wealthy investors serving as outside directors in machinery firms included the Phipps and Grace families at Ingersoll-Rand, the Ingersoll and Johnson families at Borg-Warner, and the founding Clark family at Singer.[56] None of these investors appears to have participated in board meetings more conscientiously than did the Du Pont representatives at General Motors.

By 1939 a handful of founding families were still represented on the boards as full-time *inside* directors. They included the McCormicks at International Harvester, the Deeres at John Deere, the Falks at Allis-Chalmers, the Timkens at Timken Roller Bearing, the Douglases at Douglas Aircraft, the Rands at Remington Rand, and, of course, the Fords at Ford. All of these firms except the Ford Motor Company had long been operated through an extensive managerial hierarchy whose senior executives served on their boards of directors. By World War II, Ford was one of the last personally operated enterprises among the two hundred largest American manufacturing firms. Its dramatic loss of market share and profit during the previous decade and its inability to diversify into tractors and airplanes underline the difficulty of attempting to compete in the modern American economy without a sizable team of experienced managers.

By 1939 the list of machinery companies administered by full-time executives who held only a tiny percentage of total equity was impressive. They included companies headed by the nation's best-known businessmen—IBM, where Thomas Watson held 0.85% of the stock outstanding; Chrysler, where Walter P. Chrysler had 1.5%; and RCA, where David Sarnoff held 0.4%—percentages that made the individuals wealthy but brought no assurance of control. In addition to these three, machinery companies listed among the top two hundred in which no inside director held as much as 1%, and no outside director as much as 2%, included United Shoe Machinery, National Cash Register, Burroughs Adding Machine, Otis Elevator, Caterpillar Tractor, Babcock & Wilcox, Worthington Pump, Electric Storage Battery, General Electric, Westinghouse, Studebaker, Mack Truck, White Motor, Curtiss-Wright, United Aircraft, and Underwood Typewriter.

In the machinery industries, as in the other industries described in this study, salaried managers operated, monitored, and coordinated the product flows of their companies. They devised and carried out the investment strategies that determined the direction and pace of growth of the companies and of the industries in which they operated. Well before World War II the machinery industries, like others in which large firms appeared and continued to cluster, were administered through a system of managerial capitalism.

The Dynamics of Modern Industrial Enterprise: The American Experience

The collective histories of the modern industrial enterprise in the United States recounted here are based on a neutral sample—the two hundred largest manufacturing enterprises in the United States in 1917, 1929, and 1948. These firms clustered in the most capital-intensive and the most technically advanced industries of their day.[57] They were the fastest growing industries in the fastest growing subdivisions (manufacturing) of the most dynamic sector (the industrial sector) of the American economy.

Simon Kuznets's statistics in his *Economic Growth of Nations* indicate a rough correlation between those industries in which the modern industrial enterprise clustered and those that drove economic growth. Kuznets divides thirty-eight U.S. manufacturing branches into four groups (see Table 18). Group A includes the fastest growing branches and those (with the exception of two—fertilizers and locomotives) that continued to grow throughout the entire period from 1880 to 1948. Kuznets points out:

> Most of the branches in Group A represent loci of quite recent or impending technological changes. This is certainly true of rubber products (increasingly dominated by automobile tires), petroleum (increasingly dominated by the demand for automobile fuel), and motor vehicles—which have been combined into an automobile subgroup. But it is also true of most of the other branches in A: canned foods, silk and rayon (because of recent emergence of rayon), chemical fertilizers, chemicals proper, metal building materials, electrical machinery, metal office equipment, and locomotives.[58]

In Group A twelve of the thirteen branches are industries in which the modern industrial enterprise dominated—those whose collective histories have been reviewed here. The only exception is knit goods. Group B includes industries where technological innovation appeared somewhat earlier than in those in Group A, and where the greatest growth came before 1914. Of these branches, only one—publishing and printing—was not capital-intensive or dominated by the large, integrated, industrial enterprise. Group C consists of long-established industries whose total share rose slightly until 1914 and then declined. Of the nine branches in that group, the modern industrial enterprise played a role in four—sugar refining, tobacco, agricultural machinery, and chemicals such as paints and varnishes. Group D includes the "lagging" industries whose shares sharply declined throughout the period. These are industries in

Table 18.   Changes in shares of branches of manufacturing in output of total manufacturing grouped by rapidity of growth in initial period, United States, 1880–1948.

Group	Shares in value of output (in percentages)[a]		
	1880	1914	1948
Group A. Share in 1880 of 0.6% or less; growth factor, 1880–1914, of 6 or more[b]			
Canned foods	0.4	1.0	1.6
Silk and rayon goods	0.3	0.8	1.6
Knit goods	0.3	1.0	1.3
Rubber products	0.2	0.5	2.3
Fertilizers	0.2	0.5	0.4
Chemicals proper, acids, compounds, etc.	0.4	0.8	2.2
Petroleum refining	0.3	1.2	10.4
Metal building materials and supplies	0.3	2.1	2.1
Electrical machinery and equipment, radios, etc.	0.1	1.8	4.9
Office equipment (metal)	0.1	0.4	0.5
Motor vehicles	0	1.5	6.8
Locomotives	0.6	1.4	0.7
Airplanes, etc.	0	0	0.8
Total, Group A	3.2	13.0	35.6
Automobile subgroup[c]	0.5	3.2	19.4
Other	2.7	9.8	16.2
Group B. Share in 1880 of more than 0.6%; growth factor, 1880–1914, of 6 or more			
Bakery and confectionery products	2.1	3.5	2.6
Other food products	1.6	4.4	4.6
Paper products	1.1	2.3	2.7
Printing, publishing, etc.	2.7	5.3	3.1
Stone, clay, and glass	2.2	3.5	2.4
Iron and steel	4.1	7.5	8.3
Other nonferrous metal products	1.5	4.3	2.6
Total, Group B	15.3	30.8	26.3
Group C. Growth factor, 1880–1914, of less than 6 but more than 3			
Sugar refining	1.1	1.2	0.6
Tobacco products	2.4	2.2	2.2
Cotton goods	5.2	4.2	1.2
Clothing	5.8	6.7	4.9
Allied chemical products, paints, varnishes, etc.	2.8	3.7	4.9
Hardware	1.1	1.1	0.9
Precious metal products, jewelry, etc.	0.5	0.6	0.6
Agricultural machinery, etc. (metal)	0.6	0.5	1.6
Miscellaneous machinery: factory, household, etc.	5.3	5.7	6.0
Total, Group C	24.8	25.9	22.9

Table 18   *(continued)*.

| | Shares in value of output (in percentages)[a] | | |
Group	1880	1914	1948
Group D. Lagging industries (all other); growth factor, 1880–1914, of less than 3[b]			
Mill products (food)	6.0	3.4	2.0
Packing-house products	12.4	8.4	5.0
Woolen and worsted goods	3.5	2.0	0.6
Carpets, floor coverings, tapestries, etc.	0.9	0.6	0.4
Textiles, n.e.c.	2.5	1.6	2.1
Boots and shoes	4.2	2.8	0.9
Other leather products	7.9	2.9	0.7
Sawmill and planing-mill products	11.3	5.7	1.3
Other wood products	8.0	2.9	2.2
Total, Group D	56.7	30.3	15.2
Growth factors	1880–1914	1914–1948	1880–1948
Total output	4.33	3.51	15.17
Group A	17.59	9.61	168.77
Automobile subgroup[c]	27.71	21.28	588.60
Other	15.72	5.80	91.02
Group B	8.72	3.00	26.08
Group C	4.52	3.10	14.01
Group D	2.29	1.76	4.07

Source: Simon Kuznets, *Economic Growth of Nations: Total Output and Production Structure* (Cambridge, Mass., 1971), table 47, pp. 316–318.

a. For specific year, 100% represents total value of output of all manufacturing industries in 1929 prices.

b. The growth factor for specific industries is identified as the ratio of 1914 value of output to 1880 value of output in 1929 prices. For the original data which Kuznets used, see Daniel Creamer et al., *Capital in Manufacturing and Mining: Its Formation and Financing* (Princeton, 1960), table A-10, pp. 252–258.

c. Rubber products, petroleum refining, and motor vehicles.

which, with one exception, the large industrial firm never played a significant role. In that one exception, packing-plant products, such enterprises appeared only in the distribution of fresh meat to distant markets—a product that demanded heavy investment in refrigerated facilities.

Kuznets's data support the assertion that the industries spearheading American economic growth were those dominated by a small number of large managerial enterprises. But these oligopolistic industries also included other types of business enterprises. Precisely because the leaders grew by exploiting the cost advantages of scale and scope, their standardized products often failed to meet the needs of specialized or regional markets. In addition to the smaller firms that filled such market niches, the industry contained suppliers, distributors, dealers, and others who developed a variety of relationships with the leaders. As an industry and its dominant firms grew, so did the number of niche companies and of small-scale suppliers and distributing intermediaries. Nevertheless, in the industries at the core of the rapidly growing and industrializing American economy, the critical decisions concerning current operations and the allocation of future resources were made by salaried managers of the modern industrial enterprise.

The rise and continuing growth of this enterprise and its contribution to American economic expansion cannot be fully explained by orthodox economics. For economists of the conventional school a statement that economic growth was paced by a few hierarchical enterprises competing in an oligopolistic manner is a contradiction in terms. For them and for most scholars, bureaucracy means inefficiency and oligopoly means misallocation of resources by a few firms that collect monopoly rents based on their market power.

Market power did indeed bring oligopoly; yet such power rested far more on the development of organizational capabilities than on creating "artificial" barriers to the allocative effectiveness of market mechanisms such as patents, advertising, and interfirm agreements.[59] It could, of course, be misused in predatory or antisocial ways. But such power required a sound economic base. It depended, first, on the powerful competitive advantages that resulted from the interrelated investments in manufacturing, marketing, and management required to exploit the full potential of the economies of scale and scope; and, second, on the organizational capabilities—the facilities and skills—sharpened by the enterprises' drive to obtain and maintain share and profit in distant geographical markets and in related product markets.

Patents, advertising, and interfirm agreements often reinforced first-mover advantages. But by themselves they almost never accounted for the rise of dominant firms in modern oligopolistic industries. By themselves they cannot account for the ability of first movers to drive off small competitors and to move more successfully into new markets.

The entrepreneurs who made the essential investments were rarely inventors who had patented the new products or processes. Although such famous inventors as Thomas Edison, George Westinghouse, Cyrus McCormick, and George Eastman did obtain from local capitalists and bankers the necessary financial support to commercialize their innovations, they were exceptional. Normally the entrepreneurs who became first movers were those who acquired patents. Patents without the investments required to exploit them remained of little value. Their cost, like the cost of original research, was only a small part of the investment needed to bring new or improved products and processes on stream. Entrepreneurs making the investments often had choices between comparable and competing patents. Indeed some, such as Henry Ford and other automobile makers, simply ignored existing patents.[60] Moreover, as the historian of the electric-storage-battery industry has pointed out: "Patents control a technology but they are not the technology itself." Thus, "the Brush patents described an unworkable technology, yet they were very effective in controlling storage battery technology."[61] For this reason the makers of electrical equipment and other machinery involving many components had to pool patents before full use of the new technologies was possible. In other industries, including paper, paint, soap, oil, and some food processing, patents played virtually no role in the creation of each industry in its modern form.

On the other hand, the first movers in technologically advanced industries used patents to reinforce their dominant position. Soon after the entrepreneurs creating the enterprise had recruited their management organization, patent specialists were hired to file patents to cover new processes and products developed by the enterprise and to bring suits to protect existing ones.

Nevertheless, a far greater barrier to entry into the industry than patents was the investment the first movers made in their own highly product-specific research and development activities. George Eastman, when giving the reasons for establishing an Experimental Department at Eastman Kodak in 1896, wrote: "If we can get out our improved goods every year, then nobody will be able to follow us and compete with us. The only way to compete with us will be to get out original goods the same as we do."[62] Unpatented proprietary knowledge, "trade secrets," and broad, product-specific knowledge and experience created far more powerful barriers to entry than did patents. And patents without the product-specific capabilities to develop them were of little value, as Du Pont and other American chemical firms learned painfully after they had acquired German patents for dyes, pharmaceuticals, and other organic chemicals in 1917. They needed almost a decade to develop the facilities and skills required to commercialize these patents profitably.

As the collective histories of the leaders in foods, chemicals, and the electrical-equipment industries emphasize, it was not the innovation (that is, not the research), but the development (the large investment essential to "scale up" a product so as to obtain the cost advantages of scale and scope) that was the first step in creating the modern industrial enterprise in a new industry. Development was also the critical step by which established firms became leaders in new industries and obtained profitable market share in related established industries. Individual inventors, universities and research institutes, or smaller companies provided innovations; but in most cases only large, established firms had the capabilities needed to volume-produce a new product for national and international markets.

By itself, advertising did not create first-mover advantages. The first American manufacturers to advertise nationally were the makers of patent medicines. Yet because their processing technology was so simple—primarily the blending and bottling of grain alcohol with herbs and other flavoring—the process offered little in the way of cost advantages of scale. Entry remained easy. On the contrary, in those industries with significant economies of scale in production, such as cigarettes, soap, and breakfast cereals, advertising campaigns financed by the high income generated by the cost advantages of scale became powerful deterrents to entry. Nevertheless, advertising reinforced first-mover advantages in only a few industries. In only eight of ninety-one industries studied in 1940 did companies spend as much as 5% of their net sales on advertising (Figure 6). All eight were producers of branded, packaged products. In other consumer products, such as sewing machines and typewriters, and in industrial products, the leading firms spent much more on providing marketing facilities and services than they did on advertising. A far greater deterrent to entry than advertising was the product-specific networks the first movers created to market and distribute their products on a national and international scale.

Even in branded consumer products, advertising rarely increased market share unless the enterprise enjoyed the cost advantages of scale. Thus Duke, a first mover in the making and selling of cigarettes, was able to use the same methods to dominate the snuff, pipe, and chewing tobacco trades, but he failed in cigars, which were still made largely by semiskilled hand labor. Despite the acquisition of a retail chain, repeated nationwide advertising campaigns, and destructive price wars, the struggle for the cigar industry, in the words of Richard Tennant (the most careful student of the tobacco industry), "was the one case in which the Trust's methods met complete defeat."[63] American Tobacco never acquired as much as 15% of that market.

By itself, merger did not assure market dominance. As so many American industrialists learned during the turn-of-the-century merger movement, combinations that were formed merely to replace cartels as means of controlling price and production often just encouraged new competition, attracted by the resulting higher prices. Only those consolidations that rationalized the facilities and skills of the constituent companies by making concentrated investments in manufacturing, marketing, and management became first movers in their restructured industries—and then only those in which the technological characteristics of the production process permitted such investments to reduce costs of production and in which distribution and marketing required specialized facilities and skills.[64] Where such post-merger, consolidated combinations were successfully challenged, it was by enterprises that made the comparable three-pronged investment.

Once established, the first movers and a small number of challengers continued to compete for market share and profits. In all the industries reviewed in the last three chapters the market share of individual firms changed. Such changes reflected both the success of some firms and the failure of others to enhance their organizational capabilities.

These capabilities were those of the enterprise as a unified whole. They included both its physical facilities and its human skills. Physical facilities had to be maintained and improved and the skills of the employees working in them sustained and updated if market share was to be held. Moreover, these facilities and skills had to be integrated and coordinated into a unified operating entity if the enterprise was to compete effectively on a national and international scale. The success of the enterprise in the marketplace depended heavily, therefore, on the product-specific and function-specific knowledge and skills of the middle managers in the functional departments of production, distribution, purchasing, and research, and, just as important, on their ability to coordinate, evaluate, and motivate. The long-term profitability of the enterprise depended even more on the top managers who recruited and motivated the middle managers, monitored and coordinated their activities, and determined the continuing strategies for market share and the growth of the enterprise. Combining such managerial skills was the critical element in determining the strength or weakness of the organizational capabilities of an enterprise.

Functional and strategic competition for market share between the major players of the new oligopolies was a major force in sharpening these organizational capabilities. Such competition provided a spur to counter inevitable bureaucratic inertia, and the enhanced capabilities provided profits to finance continued growth.

Of the four major strategies for growth—horizontal combination, vertical integration, expansion into new geographical markets, and expansion into new product markets—only the last two rested on a firm's organizational capabilities. Because of the enforcement of the Sherman Act, horizontal combination was never so widely used in the United States as it had been before and during the turn-of-the-century merger movement. Among the smaller number of consolidations that occurred in the 1920s, there appeared only occasionally an industry-wide horizontal combination comparable to those of the first merger movement. Usually the combining was carried out by firms whose activities were complementary rather than competing, and because it was done to exploit the economies of scope, it furthered growth through diversification.

Until the coming of the Great Depression, growth through vertical integration remained common. Such vertical growth—defined in this study as moving into processes of production, including the extraction and transportation of raw materials, that differed from a firm's original activities—came mainly through acquisition. The acquired firm tended to maintain its existing marketing organization unless the purchaser absorbed nearly all its output. These acquisitions were almost always responses to specific ad hoc situations involving reduction of transaction costs and defending existing investments. These varied from industry to industry, from time period to time period, and from one company to another. Thus, in oil, the moves of refiners back into the production and transportation of crude oil and the much smaller number of moves by crude-oil producers into refining and distribution companies varied with the availability of crude—with its scarcity in the early 1920s and its glut after 1927. After the opening of new fields brought overabundance, major refiners sold off their crude-oil holdings, while producers of crude (such as Sinclair Oil) expanded their refining and marketing investments to assure themselves of outlets. In rubber, three of the "Big Four" integrated backward into rubber plantations, but they did so at different times. The fourth—Goodrich—and the two largest second-rank firms did not do so. In metals the primary producers integrated backward into ore mining and transportation, with steel companies moving into coal mining. After the turn-of-the-century merger movement, however, the metal companies rarely integrated forward into the making of complex fabricated products and machinery, and very few machinery makers invested in their own steel, glass, and other basic supplies. Henry Ford's River Rouge works was very much the exception. In Germany many more combinations of metal and machinery makers and in Britain many more combinations of shipbuilding and metal producers were formed than in the United States.

But neither horizontal combination nor vertical integration (strategies to protect the initial investment), nor patents nor advertising (factors that reinforced the firm's existing market power) provided the dynamic for the continuing, long-term growth of the modern industrial enterprise or of the industries and economies in which they operated. That dynamic came from the organizational capabilities developed after the three-pronged investment and enhanced by continuing functional and strategic competition with other first movers and with challengers who made comparable investments. It was these organizational capabilities that provided the enterprise with the competitive edge needed to obtain and maintain market share and profits in distant lands and in related product lines. These last two strategies—expansion into foreign markets and into related markets—became, much more than horizontal combination or vertical integration, accepted paths to growth for the modern industrial enterprises in the United States whose technologies and markets permitted them to develop and expand such capabilities.

Moreover, this dynamic was often self-sustaining. Capturing new markets further expanded the capabilities of growing enterprises. Such entries into established markets were entrepreneurial achievements that individuals and newly formed small firms rarely had the financial resources, physical facilities, or technical and managerial skills to accomplish. For this reason the challengers to first movers in capital-intensive industries were almost always well-established enterprises from abroad, from related industries, or from niches within their own industry. For this reason, too, established enterprises played an impressive role from the 1920s on in creating new products and even new industries, especially in the technologically advanced chemical, pharmaceutical, electrical, and electronic fields.

The increasing number and complexity of managerial decisions resulting from expansion into new geographical or product markets led to the adoption of the multidivisional structure. The general managers of the operating divisions—still middle managers—came to monitor and coordinate the activities of production, distribution, and often research for a single line of products or a major geographical area. Top managers coordinated the activities of several operating divisions, planned and allocated resources for future production and distribution in these divisions, and determined the long-term direction of continuing growth.

The functional and general administrative capabilities developed by the middle and top managers of these enterprises through the years of competition and growth had two major consequences. First, they further intensified the separation between ownership and management. Second, they helped to make the U.S. industries in which they operated as productive and competitive as those of any country in the world.

The increase in the number of critical decisions made by managers was far more responsible for the further separation of ownership and management than was the dispersion of stock holdings. Part-time, outside directors had almost no way to obtain the detailed information or gain the broad understanding needed to make the long-term investment decisions on which the continuing health and growth of the enterprise depended. This was difficult enough for the full-time, inside directors, who had spent a lifetime in that (or a related) industry. As a result, major sectors of the American economy came to be administered through a system of managerial capitalism, where managers with little or no equity in their enterprises made operational and strategic decisions—decisions that determined each firm's competitiveness, the prosperity of the industry in which it operated, and, in part, the industrial performance of the national economy.

Until the Great Depression sharply reduced demand and so created a vast amount of overcapacity, the output and productivity per worker in many of the capital-intensive industries appears to have been greater in the United States than was the case in the same industries in other nations. In most such industries American firms were competitive abroad. In some they dominated global markets. Only in a few industrial-chemical industries (including dyes, pharmaceuticals, and rayon), most heavy-machinery industries, and a small number of light-machinery industries did European firms, primarily German, outperform their American counterparts in international trade.

To put the performance of these American managers and the industries they shaped into perspective, their work must be compared with that of managers in the same industries during the same decades in Great Britain and Germany. Because in each country the modern industrial enterprise began and evolved in a unique environment, such comparisons are needed to understand the dynamics and growth, not only of the modern industrial enterprise, and particularly of the organizational capabilities developed by its managers, but also of the specific industries in which they operated, and particularly their competitiveness in international markets.

· III ·

Great Britain:
Personal Capitalism

The history of the modern industrial enterprise in Great Britain provides a counterpart to the story just told about its beginnings and evolution in the United States. In Britain fewer such firms appeared, and they grew in a slower and more evolutionary manner. British entrepreneurs failed to make the essential three-pronged investment in manufacturing, marketing, and management in a number of the capital-intensive industries of the Second Industrial Revolution. If they did do so, their investments in production were usually large enough to benefit from the economies of scale and scope but often not large enough to utilize their full potential. Moreover, the investments in distribution were smaller and were made more slowly than was the case in the United States. Most important of all, the pioneers recruited smaller managerial teams, and the founders and their families continued to dominate the management of the enterprises.

As late as World War II, far fewer enterprises in Britain were administered through extensive managerial hierarchies than in the United States, and substantially fewer than in Germany. Those that did build such managerial organizations dominated their domestic markets even more than their American counterparts did theirs; and they represented Britain in their global oligopolies. The rest, however, included two types of companies that had become rarities among the largest American and German industrial enterprises. Either these were firms managed by individuals or by a small number of associates, often members, of founders' families, assisted by only a few salaried managers, or they were federations of such firms. These federations were holding companies. Each legally controlled its small, personally managed operating subsidiaries but did not have a large, central, corporate office for coordinating, monitoring, or resource allocation.

It was this continuing commitment to personal management and therefore to personal capitalism that fundamentally differentiates the collective histories of the large industrial enterprises in Britain from those in the United States. For this reason the British story provides a counterpoint—an antithesis—to the American experience. The continuing commitment of British enterprise to personal capitalism can provide as valuable insights concerning the rise of managerial capitalism as do the collective histories of the evolution of the managerial enterprise in the United States and Germany.

If the explanatory theory presented in Chapter 2—a theory based on a pattern drawn from the collective history of the largest United States manufacturing firms—has validity, then the collective histories of the two hundred largest British manufacturing companies should differ from those of the American companies in four essential ways.

First, the leaders that failed to make the three-pronged investment, or that did so in a slow and evolutionary manner, should have had different organizational structures from those of the leaders in American industries. And the structures of the industries in which they operated should also have been different. Second, since the investments were smaller and the barriers to entry lower, such personally managed leaders should have relied more than the Americans on what have traditionally been defined as the sources of market power— patents, advertising, and, above all, inter-enterprise cooperation in maintaining output and prices.

Third and of more importance, in those industries where British entrepreneurs failed to make the essential, interrelated investments, foreign first movers should have been able to drive British pioneers not only from international markets but from their own home markets. When British challengers did appear in these markets, they should have been the firms that had made comparable investments in production, marketing, and above all management. Only then could they have developed the organizational capabilities needed to compete effectively with foreign firms at home and abroad. Such capabilities should have been most needed to compete in the more technologically advanced growth industries, such as chemicals, electrical equipment, and other machinery where complex facilities and highly specialized technical and managerial skills were essential in obtaining and maintaining market share. On the other hand, in industries with uncomplicated technologies of production and with less need for product-specific distribution networks, as in the case of many branded, packaged products, personally managed British firms should have been less handicapped in competing with foreign first movers in international markets and in their own domestic markets.

Finally, because the continuing commitment to personal management reduced the opportunities to develop the organizational capabilities necessary to move into new geographical and product markets, British firms should have grown more slowly than American industrial enterprises. Not only would fewer resources in terms of facilities and skills have been available, but also the owner-managers might have been more hesitant to deprive themselves of short-term income in order to invest in long-term growth. As a result, British firms should have moved more slowly to expand overseas and into related products than their counterparts in the United States.

The historical record based on the collective histories of the top two hundred manufacturing enterprises in Britain in 1919, 1930, and 1948 reveals that the continuing commitment to personal capitalism actually did result in these four different patterns. To understand why the large industrial firms in the United States and Great Britain followed such different patterns of historical evolution, it is necessary to begin the British story (as I began the American one) by examining the broader environment in which the modern industrial enterprise operated.

SEVEN

The Continuing Commitment to Personal Capitalism in British Industry

Because the collective histories of the large industrial enterprises in Great Britain provide a counterpoint to those of the leading industrial enterprises in the United States—a counterpoint that is needed to understand the evolution of the modern industrial enterprise—it is important to begin the British story by pointing out the underlying differences between such enterprises in the United States and Britain. And because German enterprises, like American, became managerial, references are also made to differences between German and British companies.

Underlying Differences

In Britain the large industrial firms clustered in a small number of significant industries, as they did in the United States and Germany. Indeed, they clustered in even fewer industries. In 1919, 177 (88.5%) of the top 200 operated in seven industrial groups—food, textiles, chemicals, metals, and the three machinery groups. (For consistency the British and also the German firms have been classified by the categories of the United States Standard Industrial Classification.) Statistical data compiled by Leslie Hannah on Britain's 100 largest firms show that these leaders already produced a substantial share of total manufacturing output. The 100 largest accounted for 21% in 1924, 26% in 1930, and 23% in 1935, slightly less than the leading 100 in the United States, where the figures were 24% for 1929 and 25% for 1935.[1] The additional 100 firms listed in the appendixes probably increased the share by at least 5% in each country.

Even though the large industrial firms in Britain clustered in much the same broad categories as did those in the United States, within the categories they were concentrated in quite different subdivisions. A much larger proportion of the British enterprises produced consumer, not industrial, goods. Many more were in long-established industries, such as brewing, textiles, publishing and printing, shipbuilding, and the older branches of the chemical and machinery industries. Far fewer were in the new, technologically advanced, growth industries. Indeed, until after World War I the largest enterprises in Britain in oil, electrical equipment, and light machinery were subsidiaries of American or German enterprises.

Moreover, British industrial firms were smaller than their American counterparts. Although accurate and comparative figures are difficult to come by, it seems safe to estimate that only about fifty of the British firms on the 1930 and 1948 lists had assets that would rank them in the top two hundred in the United States.[2] Nevertheless, these were large enterprises. Except for regional breweries, nearly all sold their products throughout the British Isles, and a substantial number did so throughout the world. Also, in 1948 Britain had more firms than Germany (or Japan) with assets larger than those of the 200th firm on the American list. Since by 1948 the output of the American economy was close to five times that of Britain, the large industrial firm can be considered to have played an even more influential role in the British economy than it did in the American.

Yet many of these enterprises remained personally managed. In this review of British enterprise I use the term "personally managed" in two ways. One refers to the governance of the enterprise; the other to the ways of its management, that is, to its management "style" or, to use a more popular word, its management "culture."

Because the personal management of British enterprise differed from the management of American and also of German enterprise, I need to define more explicitly the three types of governance used by the enterprises described in this study. The first type includes those administered without benefit of an extensive managerial hierarchy. The term "extensive managerial hierarchy" refers to a hierarchy at least as large as that of one American subsidiary, British Westinghouse, in 1917, whose tables of organization are the earliest I found of a manufacturing enterprise operating in Britain (see Figure 7). I term this type a personal enterprise. The second type is that which I have called the entrepreneurial or family-controlled enterprise (entrepreneurial in the first generation and family in later generations), where the founders and their heirs recruited managerial hierarchies but continued to be influential stockholders and senior executives in their companies. Finally, there is the managerial enterprise, in which the executives in the administrative hierarchy have no connection with the founders or their families and have little or no equity in the company. What differentiated British entrepreneurial, later family-controlled, enterprises from those in the United States and Germany was that the entrepreneurs assembled smaller management teams, and until well after World War II they and their heirs continued to play a larger role in the making of middle- and top-management decisions.[3]

THE BRITISH WESTINGHOUSE ELECTRIC AND MANUFACTURING
COMPANY LIMITED

JUNE 1917

BOARD OF DIRECTORS

J. ANNAN BRYCE, M.P.—*Chairman*

W. W. Blunt   Lt. Col. Montagu Cradock, C.B., C.M.G.   Norman B. Dickson, C.B.E.

Sir Edward A. Goulding, Bt., M.P.   Alex. Spencer

Managing director: PHILIP A. LANG   *Secretary and treasurer:* A. E. Scanes

SENIOR OFFICIALS

Works

Chief electrical engineer	J. S. PECK
Chief mechanical engineer	K. BAUMANN
General works manager	H. MENSFORTH
Assistant to general works manager	M. A. McLean

Superintendents:

detail	A. M. Randolph
electrical machine	G. H. Nelson
engine	G. E. Bailey
foundries	J. E. H. Allbutt
transformer	A. P. M. Fleming
erection	——
employment	A. Walmsley
Welfare superintendent of women workers	Miss E. E. Wilson
Works engineer	H. W. Brighten
Supervisor, trade apprentice school	A. P. M. Fleming
Purchasing agent and storekeeper	J. Billington
Traffic agent	J. E. Davenport

Commercial

General sales manager	W. W. BLUNT
Assistant general sales manager	P. N. Rand

Managers:

home sales	A. G. Livesay
price and publicity	A. G. Seaman

Sales managers:

detail	P. N. Rand
meter and instrument	E. H. Miller
switchgear	E. S. M. Pritchard
transformer	A. J. Cridge

Sales managers (cont.):

gas and oil engine	J. G. Walthew
mechanical	J. N. Bailey
plant and motor	J. C. Whitmoyer
supply	J. Gibson
Manager, traction	P. S. Turner

Branch office managers:

Birmingham	G. J. Bish
Cardiff	W. J. H. Porter
Glasgow	W. J. Poole
London	O. H. Baldwin
Manchester	T. M. Kirby
Newcastle on Tyne	G. H. Tweddell
Sheffield	W. F. Mylan
Sales manager, export and continental	W. E. Bouette
Assistant manager, export	E. J. Summerhill

Branch office managers:

London	F. M. Rogers
Barcelona	P. J. Brewer
Calcutta	{G. Laird {S. A. Joyce
Bombay	H. N. Dutton
Johannesburg	A. E. du Pasquier
Melbourne	A. McKinstry
Petrograd	C. S. Richards *acting*

Westinghouse Norsk Elektrisk Aktieselskap, Christiania

Manager	G. Franklin *acting*
Assistant secretary and treasurer	J. H. Tearle
Accountant	F. J. Cobbett
Managers, patents	{A. S. Cachemaille {F. W. Le Tall

The Westinghouse Traction Bureau

Manager	P. S. Turner

Société Anonyme Westinghouse, Paris

General manager	A. Delas

Societa Italiana Westinghouse, Rome

General manager	A. Zani

Figure 7. Management of British Westinghouse in 1917. A. P. M. Fleming, supervisor, trade apprentice school, became manager of the new research department in October 1917. From John Dummelow, *1899–1949* (Manchester, Eng., 1949), p. 68.

There were far fewer hierarchical enterprises in the capital-intensive industries in Britain than there were in the United States. But there were also fewer in these industries than there were in Germany. In some industries, such as oil, rubber, rayon, explosives, and synthetic alkalies, there were one or two such firms in both Britain and Germany and several in the United States. On the other hand, in many of the industries most central to continued economic growth and industrial competitiveness there were far fewer such firms in Britain than in either Germany or the United States. This was particularly true in metals (both ferrous and nonferrous), in a wide range of light and heavy machinery, and in organic, inorganic, and agricultural chemicals. In fact, in 1919, only in branded, packaged products and glass were there more hierarchical enterprises in Britain than in Germany, and in both those industries there were many more such enterprises in the United States.

The small number of enterprises with administrative hierarchies and the smaller size of such hierarchies helped to perpetuate a commitment to personal ways of management. In most British enterprises senior executives worked closely in the same office building, located in or near the largest plant, having almost daily personal contact with, and thus directly supervising, middle and often lower-level managers. Such enterprises had no need for the detailed organization charts and manuals that had come into common use in large American and German firms before 1914. In these British companies, selection to senior positions and to the board depended as much on personal ties as on managerial competence. The founders and their heirs continued to have a significant influence on top-level decision-making even after their holdings in the enterprise were diminished. Not only were fewer senior managers placed on boards as inside directors than was the case in the United States and Germany, but outside directors were selected as much for family connections and social position as for industrial experience. In these respects, then, the personal ways or culture of British management differed from the managerial ways or culture of American and German firms.

Prototypes of British Industrial Enterprise: Cadbury Brothers and Imperial Tobacco

These differences in governance can be most clearly understood by examining the history of the two basic types of personally managed industrial enterprises. Cadbury Brothers, Ltd., (which in 1919 joined its major competitor, J. S. Fry & Sons, to form British Cocoa & Chocolate) is an example of the family firm. Imperial Tobacco exemplifies the second type, a federation of a number of such firms legally consolidated into a holding company.

Cadbury Brothers, Ltd., Britain's leading maker of cocoa and chocolate, has long been considered one of the nation's best-managed companies. Its senior executives wrote at length about their operations and governance structure. By 1930 the merger, British Cocoa & Chocolate, was already the twenty-eighth largest industrial in Britain in terms of market value of its shares, and by 1935 it was the twenty-third largest employer. By then the combined firm was comparable in size to those at the lower end of the list of the top two hundred in America.

The history of the modern Cadbury firm begins in 1861, when George and Richard Cadbury took over the small tea and coffee company their father had established in 1831. At that time it employed eleven workers. They quickly transformed it into an enterprise producing high-grade chocolate. In 1879 the brothers built a large factory with advanced processing equipment. This plant, by further reducing unit costs, solidified the firm's position as the industry's leader. Its carefully laid-out houses and recreational areas for the workers won the reputation of being a "factory in a garden." Cadbury reinforced its position by recruiting a sales force of travelers and by advertising extensively throughout the nation. In the years following 1879 production grew rapidly. The work force was 1,193 in 1889, 2,689 in 1899, 4,923 in 1909, 7,100 in 1919, and 8,381 in 1931. Small subsidiary plants to process milk for the operation appeared in the dairy areas of southwest England, the first in 1911. By 1939 there were four. In addition, in 1921 the firm integrated backward by building a large works near Worcester, England, to produce boxes, cases, tins, paper, and other packaging materials.[4]

Cadbury Brothers' initial investment in marketing and distribution was smaller, and remained much smaller, than its investment in production. Like American producers of branded, packaged products, it used existing wholesalers and large retailers to distribute its products in its domestic market. From the start, however, the firm relied on its own sales force to maintain its market share by seeking out orders from retailers as well as wholesalers and by running advertising campaigns continually. Its sales department also was responsible for making deliveries on schedule and for collections. The firm invested in domestic distribution facilities more slowly than did makers of branded, packaged products in the United States. With increasing output and the advent of truck transportation, it set up in 1921 a system of "depot distribution," with large warehouses in major cities and a growing fleet of trucks, for the specific purpose of assuring a regular and steady flow from the factory to the customers. By 1931 the company had fifteen such depots in Britain. At that time, to facilitate the flow, it formed a traffic section headed by a younger Cadbury. By then 70% of the company's products were moving through the depots. Much of the rest went directly to chain stores (or multiple shops, as they were termed in Britain) and other large retailers.

Cadbury moved overseas cautiously. In 1903 the firm had its own sales office in Sydney with branches in Melbourne, Adelaide, and Brisbane. It soon had similar sales offices in New Zealand, South Africa, and then India. Except for a branch in Spain, no effort was made to set up such offices outside the empire. To reach the rest of the world, the export office continued to rely on local agencies to distribute its products. Investment in production facilities abroad came only after World War I when, with its collaborator in British Cocoa & Chocolate, J. S. Fry & Sons, Cadbury built plants in Australia in 1920, New Zealand in 1930, Ireland in 1933, and South Africa in 1937.[5]

Until the early twentieth century Cadbury's buying organization remained small. Purchases were made through produce exchanges in London and from importers of the cocoa bean. As production expanded and as a new cocoa-growing region on the west coast of Africa came into being, Cadbury began to build a permanent buying organization. In so doing it worked closely with its two major competitors, the family firms of Fry and Rowntree. In 1910, when the first crop was planted, Cadbury set up a permanent buying office in Accra on the Gold Coast. It opened another in Nigeria in 1917 and operated it jointly with Fry, and still another in the same colony in 1919, which it operated jointly with both Fry and Rowntree.

Because the Cadbury family was prolific, the sons, daughters, and grand-children continued to manage the firm's functional activities—production, marketing, and sales—as well as the enterprise as a whole. By World War II the enterprise was still administered by a management team that was somewhat similar to that of British Westinghouse in 1917. The management, in the words of a company report published in 1944, "retained many of the essential features of a family concern . . . Since its inception, the control of the Company has been vested in a Board of Managing Directors, one of whom since 1919 has been a woman." The directors, this report continued, "meet formally as a Board once a week—more often if necessary." Each director, it said, "is personally responsible for a particular section of the business and is in constant touch with his or her colleagues," and thus "a close degree of coordination is achieved between the policies and programs of the different departments." Committees further coordinated the several functional activities (see Figure 8). "The formulation of policies, both general and departmental," the analysis continued, "is in the hands of a number of committees, each meeting under the chairmanship of a Director, through whom it reports to the Board. As each Director is at the same time responsible for the daily activities of a group of departments, the Board becomes an efficient coordinator of policies framed by the committee and of actual departmental conduct of business."[6] And during most of the interwar years, all but one of the directors were Cadburys. In 1930 Barrow Cadbury was chairman; of the other seven Managing Directors five were Cadburys (including Miss Dorothy A. Cadbury) and a sixth, Walter Barrow, was a cousin. (In Britain the term "Managing Director" is equivalent to that of inside director in the United States.) At Cadbury's even as late as the 1940s the owners managed and the managers owned.

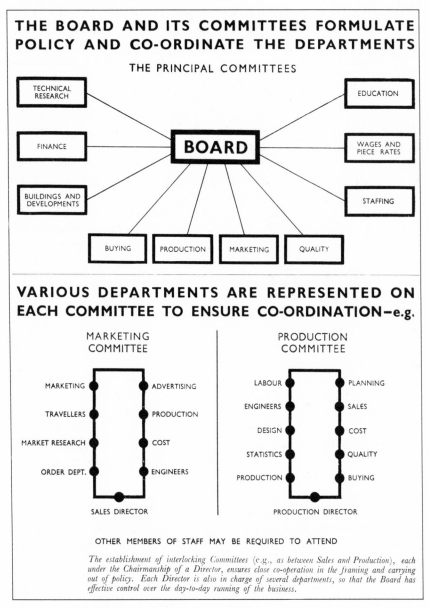

THE BOARD AND ITS COMMITTEES FORMULATE POLICY AND CO-ORDINATE THE DEPARTMENTS

THE PRINCIPAL COMMITTEES

TECHNICAL RESEARCH

EDUCATION

FINANCE

BOARD

WAGES AND PIECE RATES

BUILDINGS AND DEVELOPMENTS

STAFFING

BUYING · PRODUCTION · MARKETING · QUALITY

VARIOUS DEPARTMENTS ARE REPRESENTED ON EACH COMMITTEE TO ENSURE CO-ORDINATION–e.g.

MARKETING COMMITTEE

MARKETING — ADVERTISING
TRAVELLERS — PRODUCTION
MARKET RESEARCH — COST
ORDER DEPT. — ENGINEERS

SALES DIRECTOR

PRODUCTION COMMITTEE

LABOUR — PLANNING
ENGINEERS — SALES
DESIGN — COST
STATISTICS — QUALITY
PRODUCTION — BUYING

PRODUCTION DIRECTOR

OTHER MEMBERS OF STAFF MAY BE REQUIRED TO ATTEND

The establishment of interlocking Committees (e.g., as between Sales and Production), each under the Chairmanship of a Director, ensures close co-operation in the framing and carrying out of policy. Each Director is also in charge of several departments, so that the Board has effective control over the day-to-day running of the business.

Figure 8. Management of Cadbury's in the 1930s. From *Industrial Record, 1919–1939: A Review of the Inter-War Years,* published by Cadbury Brothers, Ltd., Bournville (London, n.d.), p. 9. The directors of Cadbury Brothers, Ltd. in 1930 were Barrow Cadbury (chairman), W. A. Cadbury, E. Cadbury, G. Cadbury, W. Barrow, L. J. Cadbury, Miss D. A. Cadbury, P. S. Cadbury, C. W. Gillett. The directors of British Cocoa & Chocolate Co., Ltd. in 1930 were Barrow Cadbury (chairman), W. A. Cadbury, Edward Cadbury, G. Cadbury, R. J. Fry, C. P. Fry, R. A. Fry, C. B. Fry, W. Barrow, A. E. Cater, L. J. Cadbury, C. R. Fry, P. S. Cadbury, Miss D. A. Cadbury, Egbert Cadbury, G. H. Boucher, C. W. Gillett.

As emphasized in the eighty-page 1944 report on the operation and administration of the enterprise during the interwar years, the function of the governance structure was almost wholly to coordinate and monitor the production and selling facilities. The study says almost nothing about budgets (operating or capital), appropriation procedures, or other capital-allocation techniques. The senior Cadburys were completely absorbed in day-to-day operational activities. They concentrated on carrying out the functions of middle, not top, management. A comparison of the size, diversity, and management structure of the family firm of Cadbury at the outbreak of World War II with those of the large, multidivisional, managerial American food firms, such as Borden and General Foods, is striking. Even more revealing is the comparison with those of one of Cadbury Brothers' major competitors in Britain, the family firm of Gebrüder Stollwerck, the leading chocolate maker in Germany (see Chapter 10).

Although the Cadburys always thought and spoke of their company as a completely independent family firm, they joined in 1919 with J. S. Fry & Sons, Britain's third largest chocolate producer, to form the British Cocoa & Chocolate Company. That company, which held the "ordinary" shares (that is, the voting shares) of the two companies, provides an example of a device widely used in Britain to permit close cooperation between the leaders of an industry. A Fry sat on the Cadbury board and three Cadburys joined the Fry board, while the board of British Cocoa & Chocolate was made up of assorted Cadburys and a smaller number of Frys.[7] The activities of the two operating companies remained separate. The preferred shares and debentures of each continued to be traded on the London Stock Exchange. Not until 1935 were these securities consolidated and retired. Even then the two companies retained their legal and administrative autonomy.

Until the 1930s the two firms, Cadbury and Fry, remained little more than allies using the holding-company board to supervise their overseas marketing and their jointly owned and operated overseas factories, and to continue to purchase supplies for both firms. In 1931 the British Cocoa & Chocolate Company operated, besides the three major depots in Nigeria and the Gold Coast, fourteen buying stations in West Africa and twenty-four smaller "bush" stores. But during the 1930s these activities came to be increasingly managed by the Cadburys. During these years, too, Fry began to use the growing Cadbury network for distribution depots in Britain. Both firms continued, however, to produce, advertise, and ship their own brands; to develop new ones; and to allocate resources for future growth. The Cadbury-Fry arrangement was typical of mergers carried out in Britain during the interwar years between two or three of an industry's largest firms.

More significant for the British economy was an earlier type of merger that brought together a large number of small family-controlled firms into an industry-wide holding company. Imperial Tobacco, which was in 1919 the fifth largest, in 1930 the second largest, and in 1948 the largest industrial enterprise in Britain in terms of the market value of its shares, is a good example of this second distinctive form of British industrial enterprise.

As was so often the case in the United States, the first mover in the industry instigated the merger. That first mover was W. D. & H. O. Wills, which, like James B. Duke's American Tobacco Company in the United States, was the first firm to deploy the mass-processing Bonsack machine in Britain. Wills also began to expand its sales force overseas, although in the international market it was outpaced by Duke. Duke's success led him to challenge Wills in Britain by acquiring a smaller British cigarette maker in 1901. In response Wills almost immediately brought together the sixteen smaller firms and united them with itself through an exchange of stock to form a new company, Imperial Tobacco.

Shortly after its formation, Imperial came to terms with Duke. The Wills family and Duke agreed that Imperial would market in Britain and Ireland, American Tobacco would market in the United States, and a jointly owned company, British-American Tobacco (BAT), would sell and distribute the output of both firms' factories in the rest of the world. Two-thirds of BAT's shares were held by American Tobacco and one-third by Imperial. BAT quickly became the overseas arm of American Tobacco and soon owned and operated factories in Germany, China, and elsewhere to support its marketing organization. Imperial continued to concentrate on the British home market. But after the U.S. Supreme Court ruling against American Tobacco in the antitrust case in 1911, that company began to sell its shares in BAT. By the 1920s BAT was controlled primarily by the British, and, as control shifted, it became increasingly the overseas arm of Imperial.[8]

From the start, Imperial was organized as a federation. A senior executive later recalled that its structure was "not unlike that of the Thirteen States of America, who, when the Federal Constitution was first adopted, gave the central government as little authority as possible and retained as much as they could in their own hands."[9] Imperial's central government was vested in the Executive Committee, consisting of members of the families operating the largest constituent companies, or "branches," as they came to be called: two Willses from Wills, a Lambert and a Butler from Lambert & Butler, and a Player from John Player & Sons. The Executive Committee's tiny staff included its secretary, an engineer who pooled technical information, a chief accountant who introduced uniform accounting into the operating companies, and a purchasing agent whose services the operating units could use (but were not required to). The staff was housed in a small office in the largest of the Wills factories. The Executive Committee's responsibility was to set prices, to determine how much each of the subsidiaries could spend on advertising—the basic competitive weapon—and to approve annual operating budgets. Thus the subsidiaries continued to produce and distribute their products independently, much as they had done before the merger. These personally managed enterprises planned and carried out their own advertising campaigns, developed new brands, and hired, fired, and set the salaries of their small teams of managers in charge of production, sales, advertising, and purchasing.

During the interwar years, Imperial Tobacco continued to be administered in much the same manner. The Executive Committee included successive generations of Willses, Players, Mitchells, and Lamberts, their sons-in-law, and the members of other families that operated their branches. It continued to set prices, approve advertising expenditures, and occasionally set company-wide policies on issues such as pension plans. "Control over branch budget" continued to amount "to little more than sanctioning proportionate increases in expenditures to match growth."[10] Within this framework, the branches competed for market share decorously through the years, with Player increasing its share at the expense of Wills. No major change in this structure occurred until the 1960s.

The contrast between Imperial and its counterpart, American Tobacco, is striking. Even before American Tobacco's founder, James Buchanan Duke, had launched his invasion of Britain in 1901, its impressive managerial hierarchy was headquartered in a multi-storied building at 111 Fifth Avenue. The New York office housed the top echelons of management, including line and staff executives of the Production Department, who supervised all manufacturing activities, and of the Leaf Department, who were responsible for purchasing, storing, and curing tobacco, monitoring the company's extensive investment in drying and packing warehouses in the bright-leaf district of North Carolina and Virginia, in the Burley district of Ohio and Kentucky, and in Turkey after Turkish tobacco became popular. Corporate headquarters also housed the Sales Department, which handled advertising and distribution on a global scale and maintained control and delivery systems that were needed to maintain steady, high throughput. A central auditing and accounting department produced a steady flow of detailed cost data, particularly on production costs. The large hierarchy of middle and top management at the corporate office had developed procedures to coordinate the flow of materials that produced and distributed four to five billion cigarettes a year, plus substantial amounts of other tobacco products. There, too, Duke and his associates planned and carried out their grand strategy.[11] While in Britain the price umbrella established by the federation permitted smaller cigarette firms to compete vigorously and to move into the top two hundred, in the United States only a Supreme Court ruling breaking up American Tobacco's cigarette business into four companies brought competition. Even after the breakup, only one firm, Philip Morris, was able to challenge the successor companies.

Thus, whereas during the interwar years the branches of Imperial Tobacco—the original, constituent family firms—remained personally managed by their owners, whose representatives met at stated intervals to assure the maintenance of gentlemanly competition, the American Tobacco Company had become a managerial enterprise well before the 1920s. With the breakup of Duke's empire in 1911, Duke sold off his holdings, after which the new American Tobacco Company—that which remained after spin-offs decreed by the court had been completed—was administered by one of America's rare managerial dynasties. In 1912 Duke hired Percival Hill, the sales manager for Bull Durham, the company's chewing-tobacco subsidiary, as president. Percival's son, George Washington Hill, became sales manager, and after successfully launching the Camel and Lucky Strike brands, took over the presidency. In time he turned the reins over to his own son, George Washington Hill, Jr.[12] In 1937 the two Georges owned 0.08% of the voting stock and Mrs. Percival Hill another 0.85%.[13] In that same year, members of the Elkins and Widener families, whose forebears had helped finance the company's expansion through acquisition and merger in the 1890s, still controlled as much as 12% of the stock. They and their representatives had little or no impact on the company's affairs, however.

These two tobacco companies underline the different natures of industrial capitalism in Britain and the United States during the first half of the twentieth century. In the United States, salaried managers with little or no equity in the enterprise, who administered it through extensive managerial hierarchies, were making the critical coordinating and allocating decisions. In Britain those decisions were still being made by the major stockholders, who had inherited their positions and continued personally to manage their enterprises.

What accounts for these fundamental differences in size, ownership, and management between the large enterprises in these two leading industrial nations? What effects did these differences have on the performance of British firms, British industries, and the British economy as a whole? How did they influence the types of industries in which large British industrial enterprises concentrated? To answer these questions it is first necessary to understand the environment in which such enterprises evolved in Great Britain.

Domestic and Foreign Markets

Great Britain is, of course, very different from the United States both geographically and demographically. Its territory of 94,214 square miles is smaller than that of the three contiguous states of New York, Pennsylvania, and Ohio.[14] Nevertheless, Britain's small area was and is far more densely populated than those three states.

In the decades before World War I, Britain's income grew more slowly than that of the United States. National income per capita increased, at 1913 prices, from £26.8 in 1870 ($131.30, with the pound at $4.90) to £48.2 in 1913

($236.10)—that is, less than twofold. In the United States gross national product per capita rose from $223, the average for 1869–1873, to $608 for 1907–1911—a little less than threefold. Angus Maddison estimates the rise of net output per capita between 1870 and 1913 as 1.3% per annum for Britain and 2.2% for the United States.[15] Moreover, not only were output and income per capita growing much faster in the United States than in Britain, but so was the population. By the 1880s the population of the United States had become one and one-half times that of Britain. By 1900 it stood at twice Britain's population, and in 1920 at three times. British entrepreneurs, therefore, had less incentive than their American counterparts to build giant plants. Given the existing size and potential growth of the domestic market, the optimal size of a plant using the same technology as its American counterpart remained smaller. Plants the size of American works would have been unable to maintain throughput close to minimum efficient scale (unless much of their output was exported). As the domestic market was geographically so much smaller, distribution networks were, of course, less extensive and less costly. And because distances were so foreshortened, there was less need to build branch plants in Britain some distance away from the original establishment. In other words, given the size and rate of growth of the domestic British market, investments in production and distribution comparable to those made by American firms in the same industries would have led to underutilization and higher costs. By the same token, the hierarchies needed to administer smaller production and distribution facilities were, of course, also smaller.

The smaller and slower-growing domestic market also meant that overseas customers were always more important to British than to American industrialists. In the broadest terms, the ratio of British foreign trade to national income ranged from 26.9% to 29.9% between 1860 and 1913, while for the same years the ratio for the United States hovered around 5%.[16] Just as important, British exports continued to be the products of older industries, those of the First Industrial Revolution. For the years 1870–1879, 55% of exports consisted of textiles (including apparel), 16% of iron and steel, 4% of machines, and 4% of coal. The 1900–1909 figures were respectively 38%, 14%, 7%, and 10%, with an additional 3% for transportation equipment (primarily ships). By contrast, the manufactured goods exported from the United States were those of the Second Industrial Revolution—refined oil, processed foodstuffs, mass-produced light machinery, and electrical equipment.[17] (Those of Germany were also those of the Second Industrial Revolution—namely, chemicals and heavy machinery, including electrical equipment, steel, and electrolytically produced nonferrous metals.) Moreover, American exports of manufactured products were dwarfed in those years by its exports of raw cotton, wheat, corn, tobacco, meat, and other agricultural products—the products that were Britain's leading imports.

Equally significant, Britain's commercial export channels to markets both at home and abroad, as well as its import channels for food and other raw materials, had been developed (more fully than those of any other industrializing nation) before the coming of the transportation and communications revolution—that is, before the advent of the railroad, the telegraph, the steamship, and the cable. These trade and distribution channels had been put into place when the speed and regularity of transportation and communication still depended on age-old methods subject to the vicissitudes of animal and wind power. Moreover, textiles made by machines, iron processed by coal, and ships constructed of iron—the core industries of the First Industrial Revolution—lacked the potential for economies of scale comparable to that of the industries of the Second Industrial Revolution. Indeed, in accounting for the differences between the development of the large-scale enterprise in Britain and its development in Britain's two major industrial challengers, one must consider not only that Britain was the first urban, industrial nation, but also that it was the only nation to industrialize and urbanize before the coming of the transportation revolution. For the United States and Germany the new transportation and communication networks and the technological opportunities they created were at the very center of the industrializing process.

Britain also differed from other industrializing nations in that by the 1870s it had almost completed its transformation from an agrarian commercial economy to an urban industrial one, a change which had begun at the end of the previous century. In 1871, 43.1% of its work force was in mining and manufacturing, 19.6% in trade and transport, 15.3% in domestic and personal services, and 6.8% in professional and public employment, while only 15.1% was engaged in agriculture, forestry, and fishing. The occupational pattern in the United States did not reach roughly similar proportions until World War II. As early as 1851, half the population of Britain lived in towns of more than five thousand. London, which ten years later had a population of 3.2 million, was already the largest metropolis in the Western world. Again, a comparable ratio of rural to urban population would not be reached in Germany until after 1900 and in the United States not until after World War II.[18]

In Britain, then, the rapid internal migration from country to city and from agriculture to industry resulted in the largest concentrated consumer market yet created. By 1850 more than 10 million persons living within the geographically small quadrangle bounded by London, Cardiff, Glasgow, and Edinburgh depended on money wages to obtain their entire supply of food, drink, clothing, and housing. Precisely because England was the first urban industrial nation, it became the world's first consumer society. That golden quadrangle remained the world's richest consumer market for more than a century. The small geographical size of the domestic market, its concentrated richness, and the excellent transportation system had as much impact as did legal, educational, and cultural factors on the continuing of personal management and personal capitalism in British industry.

Rapid industrialization and the superior pre-railroad transportation system also meant that business enterprises in both commerce and industry had become more specialized in Britain than in the United States in the pre-railroad years. As in the United States, the standard legal and administrative form of business enterprise had long been the partnership. But, again as in the United States, the partnership was a much less stable form than the incorporated stock company. Partnerships were easily formed, altered, or dissolved. New partners came; old ones left. One businessman was often a partner in two or more enterprises. The owners, that is, the partners, managed all the operations of the enterprise, assisted only by a clerk or two in the office and by foremen in the new factories. As the new factories increased the nation's industrial output early in the nineteenth century and as other continents began to supply raw materials and to provide markets for that output, the expanding volume of transactions brought increasing specialization in both production and distribution. But the internal management of the enterprise remained almost unchanged. Thus, pre-railroad Britain provided an even more believable example than pre-railroad United States of an economy operating through small, single-function, single-product, personally managed enterprises, and of the activities coordinated by the invisible hand of market forces and mechanisms.

The Impact of the Railroads

Because Britain began to industrialize well before the coming of the railroad, the telegraph, the steamship, and then the cable, these innovations in transportation and communication had much less impact on industrial institutions there than in the United States, or in Germany. Not only had Britain become an industrial urban economy before the building of the railroad network, but its much smaller geographical area had required a smaller, tighter network than did.the United States. Thus the construction, financing, and management of railroads created fewer challenges in Britain than they did in the United States. Moreover, because Britain's pre-railroad transportation system was much more efficient than that of the United States, the impact of the railroads on the processes of production and distribution was much less significant than in the United States. Not only were distances between industrial and commercial centers much shorter, but water transportation was much more available in this island economy, where few towns were more than seventy miles from the coast and where rivers and canals rarely froze for extended periods in winter. In addition, hard-surfaced roads were more numerous and their condition was far superior to those in contemporary America.

In regard to both the overall size of the railroad network of the two countries and the size of individual railroads, the differences were dramatic. By 1860 Britain had 9,069 miles of railroads and the United States 30,626; by 1880 the figures were 17,933 and 93,292. In the next year (1881) alone, just under 10,000 miles of track were laid in the United States; in 1882 the figure was just over 10,000 miles. Thus in those two years more mileage was built in the United States than had been constructed in Britain since 1830. By World War I, the American mileage of just over 240,000 was more than ten times that in Britain. Further, the major British roads operated from 600 to 1,000 miles of track, whereas American railroad companies in the 1880s and 1890s were operating from 6,000 to more than 10,000 miles. In the 1890s one American railroad company, the Santa Fe Railway, operated mileage that equaled more than half of Britain's total. [19]

Nevertheless, the British railroad companies were by far the largest business enterprise in Britain during the nineteenth century. Their operations resulted in the creation in Britain of the first managerial hierarchies with lower, middle, and top levels of management. [20] Even though the geographical distances were much smaller and the terrain and freight characteristics less varied than in the United States, the intensity of traffic—the volume carried per mile—was much greater. Because traffic and mileage were concentrated in so small a geographical area, British railroad managers became expert in moving freight and passengers on their intensively used urban rail systems. No regional markets in the United States were better served than was the golden quadrangle in Britain.

At the same time, British railroad managers were less challenged to pioneer new methods of organization and of internal control than were Albert Fink, J. Edgar Thomson, and others in the United States—methods so necessary in administering systems, several of which served geographical areas larger than all of Great Britain. British railroads, therefore, did not provide models for industrial management as did the U.S. railways. Indeed, by the end of the century British railroad managers were traveling to the United States to learn American management methods. [21]

Nor did the coming of the railroads have so great an impact on the capital markets in Britain as they did in the United States. In industrial Britain, railroad promoters were able to rely more on local capital than could their American counterparts in the rural areas of the recently settled South and West. When railwaymen did go to London, the world's largest and most sophisticated money market, they had little difficulty in raising the funds needed. [22] True, the new demand for railroad capital did lead to the development of new financial instruments—preferred stock and debentures. Industrialists would later use the same type of nonvoting securities to meet their capital needs without losing control of their enterprises. British stockbrokers, such as the partners in Foster & Braithwaite, Haseltine Powell, and Henry Cazenove, took their places on the railroad boards. In no sense, however, did they acquire the influence, both formal and informal, that the New York investment bankers enjoyed in the affairs of American railroads at the turn of the century. Moreover, because capital was raised locally, local capitalists served on railroad boards more often than they did in America, and they appear to have participated more effectively on boards and committees of boards than did their counterparts in the United States. In America the far greater capital requirements of the railroad network resulted in centralizing and institutionalizing the American capital market in New York, thus creating the second largest money market in the world. In Britain the smaller requirements of a much smaller network only enlarged and refined somewhat the activities of what had long been the world's largest financial center.

Finally, competition between railroads did not bring governmental regulation in Britain in the same way as it did in the United States. Not only was the standardization of procedures and equipment easier to work out in the smaller, more compact British network, but also as early as 1842 a Clearing House Association had been formed to settle intercompany accounts and then to maintain rates through the pooling of profits and other devices. Because pooling and other means of cooperation were encouraged and because shorter distances in the much more industrialized economy made the capture of through-traffic less critical to profits, there was less incentive to discriminate, either openly or secretly, in rate-making, and, therefore, there were fewer grievances of the kind that led to rate regulation in the United States. Even so, freight rates, because they so directly affected costs for both producers and shippers, did become a major issue late in the 1880s. Nevertheless, government regulation of British railroads resulted as much from the demands of passengers for safety, and of railroad employees for better pay and improved working conditions, as it did from the complaints of shippers and communities about discriminatory rates.[23]

The railroads in Britain, therefore, were not pioneers in modern management, in finance, or in government regulation to the extent that they were in the United States. Nor did they have the same impact on the organization and process of production and distribution. This was partly because industrialization preceded the building of the railroad network and partly because pre-railroad water and land transportation carried goods, passengers, and messages more efficiently than was the case in the United States. As T. R. Gourvish, a leading British railroad historian, has pointed out, "It is generally agreed that, with the basic industries already well established in 1830, the railway could do little more than cement the existing patterns of settlement and industrial location."[24] Although the railroads and also the telegraph did bring an expansion of markets and did encourage the introduction of large-batch and continuous processes, particularly in the mass production of branded, packaged products, the technological response to the opportunities created by new transportation and communication was much less dynamic in Britain than it was in either the United States or Germany. On the other hand, as Gourvish notes, "retailing was transformed, and essentially new traffic was encouraged in perishable goods—meat, fish, fresh milk and vegetables."[25]

The Revolution in Distribution

British entrepreneurs responded with alacrity to the opportunities for mass distribution as the new transportation and communications networks were put in place. In his classic study on the retailing trade in Britain, James B. Jefferys describes the transformation in these words:

> In contrast to this relative stability or near-stability in distributive organization and method up to the middle of the nineteenth century, the following half-century or so, particularly the period 1875–1914, witnessed a transformation of the distributive trades comparable in many ways to the revolutionary changes that had taken place in the industrial structure of the country in the previous century. In these years new techniques of selling, new methods of wholesale and retail organization, new trades, new types of consumer goods and new forms of retailing units began to emerge, at first alongside the older-established traditional methods and then in place of them. The branding of goods, their advertisement by the producers, and the determination of the retail selling prices under systems of retail price maintenance were introduced widely in some trades. Flamboyant window displays and advertisements by retailers and the use of clearly marked prices were replacing the older customs of reticence and higgling. Finally these years saw the triumph of the fixed shop as the dominant form of retail trading and the emergence on a significant scale of large-scale distributive organizations—the department store, the Co-operative Society and the multiple shop firm. These units employed hundreds and thousands of workers, in a sector of the economy hitherto the untouched preserve of the small-scale independent master employing at the most a handful.[26]

The three new types of mass retailers, then, were the department stores, the multiple shops (chain stores), and the consumer cooperatives. The cooperatives were served by two giant organizations of the Co-operative Wholesale Society (C.W.S.), one in England and the other in Scotland. In order to exploit the economies of scale and scope, the new mass retailers organized themselves in much the same manner as did their counterparts in the United States. They had buyers for each major product line—buyers who set price, output, and specifications, and who scheduled the high-volume flow from the factories to the retail shelves. In Britain, as in the United States, such administrative coordination quickly lowered unit costs, bringing both lower prices (to the consumer) and higher profits (to the merchandiser) than those resulting from market coordination among a large number of smaller, independent, wholesalers and retailers.

Yet, differences between the mass markets in the two countries led to noteworthy differences between the institutions created to serve them. Whereas the new mass marketers in the United States catered to a recently settled continental territory that was still oriented toward commerce and agriculture, those in Britain served the world's first industrial nation. In Britain there were no giant mail-order houses, such as Sears or Montgomery Ward, distributing to farmers and small merchants on a continental scale. The established institutions continued to serve the middle-class clientele—increasingly professionals and white-collar workers—who shopped on the High Street of British towns and cities. So the new mass marketers concentrated on serving the still rapidly growing working-class neighborhoods that were not adequately supplied by the older, pre-railroad, wholesale and retail enterprises. [27]

Of the three new types of mass marketers in Britain—the department stores, the multiple shops, and the cooperatives—only the department stores, particularly those in London, were oriented toward the middle-class shopper. British department stores developed much as did the American ones. Concentrated in urban areas, they normally were dry goods shops grown large. As Macy's had done in New York, Whiteley's and other British pioneers expanded the scope of their operations by adding to their original lines of dry goods and apparel such items as carpets, draperies, cabinets, beds, and a variety of other household furnishings. Although the department stores in the metropolis attracted middle-class customers, W. Hamish Fraser notes that "outside of London the new department stores at first looked to working class customers." By the early twentieth century, however, they were "concentrating on the upper end of the market." [28]

On the other hand, both the multiple shops (chain stores) and the cooperatives continued to cater almost wholly to working-class customers until the mid-twentieth century. The multiples, as they were often called, were an even more direct response to the growing, urban, working-class market than were the department stores. They came earlier than their counterparts in the United States and concentrated on a much smaller line of products. Nearly all these pioneers carried one of two lines of goods—either perishable foods or apparel (primarily shoes). Because of their narrow line they exploited economies of scale (stockturn) more than those of scope. Of the 101 multiple-shop enterprises with more than ten branch stores in operation in 1890, 51 were in food and 44 were in footwear. Of the 374 in 1928, 188 were in food (including groceries, meat, bread, milk, and confectionery) and 70 were in footwear. The rest were in other apparel, with a small number retailing household furnishings and chemist's products (branded, packaged items and generic medicines and drugs). [29] Unlike the American chains, particularly those in food, the British multiples continued to concentrate on single lines of goods. Whereas in the United States the Great Atlantic & Pacific Tea Company, Grand Union, American Stores, and Kroger expanded their lines to carry a variety of groceries, meats, condiments, canned goods, bottled goods, and local fresh produce, Lipton, Maypole, and Home & Colonial Stores in Britain sold little more than tea, sugar, bacon, ham, margarine, butter, cheese, and eggs. Eastman, Nelson, and Fletcher carried only chilled or frozen meat. Because the multiples carried so few lines, the shops were physically smaller than their American counterparts. Because their market was so much more concentrated, and because their volume of sales was very high, these enterprises integrated backward much more than American food chains did. They owned or controlled suppliers in Ireland, Holland, Denmark, and even the United States and Argentina in order to assure themselves of the supplies needed to maintain consistently high stockturn.[30]

An even more striking difference between the two countries was the rapid growth of consumer cooperatives in Britain, a movement that never became extensive in the United States. Unlike publicly held corporations, the members of cooperatives did not receive dividends on the shares they held, but on the purchases they made. James Jefferys has pointed out that "in the thirty-five years between 1881 and 1914 the membership, drawn almost exclusively from the working class, had increased nearly six times and the retail turnover at constant prices just over five times." By 1913 the cooperatives had 2.72 million members and by 1937 more than 6.50 million. The number of separate societies in existence grew as rapidly, from 400 in 1862 to 1,043 in 1882, and to a peak of 1,455 in 1903. Moreover, many of these cooperatives had a number of branches. In 1888 each of the largest 14 had more than 5,000 members, and in 1900 a quarter of the total membership was in societies with 11,000 or more.[31]

The rapidly growing need of these retail cooperatives for an assured and continuing flow of supplies led to the formation of the Co-operative Wholesale Society (C.W.S.) in England in 1862, and of a second Society in Scotland in 1866. These two wholesale cooperatives quickly became the world's largest distribution organizations. Their size, the rapidly growing number of individual members, and the resulting market encouraged both of the wholesale societies and some of their retail-store members to exploit economies of scope much more than the multiples did, though still much less than the American mass retailers. Initially, the cooperatives concentrated on food, carrying about the same lines as the multiples did. First came groceries, then meat, and then soap and other packaged products.[32] In the 1870s the cooperatives also began to market apparel, drapery, and other household furnishings. Because they had the volume and the assured sales, the two mass-wholesaler societies from which the retail cooperatives obtained their food, apparel, and other products integrated backward extensively, making a larger investment in production facilities than did the American mass retailers. By the 1890s the English C.W.S. carried on its wholesale business from large offices in Manchester, Newcastle, and London (each with extensive warehouse facilities), and from smaller ones at Bristol and Northampton. It operated supply depots on the Continent, in New York and Montreal, and in Liverpool and Longton. It soon had its own factories producing bread, biscuits, confectionery, soap, ready-made clothing, shoes, draperies, flour, tobacco, and cabinets. Ideological as well as economic reasons encouraged the investment in factories: the salaried managers of the C.W.S. and the members of its retail cooperatives firmly believed that the cooperative movement should be encouraged in all sectors, including not only manufacturing but also banking and insurance. They viewed it as an effective alternative to exploitative capitalism.

By the end of World War I the new mass retailers had captured an impressive share of three trades: perishable foods, apparel, and household furnishings. As early as 1915, department stores, multiples, and cooperatives together accounted for between 17% and 21% of total retail sales (a decided increase from their 2% or 3% share in 1875). In the same year (1915) they accounted for 31% of the groceries and provision trade, 44% of footwear, 23% of women's wear, and 20% of household furnishings.[33] In these trades they concentrated on a limited number of products. They relied on high-volume throughput (stock-turn) to reduce prices to a level low enough for the working-class customer to be willing to pay cash rather than to rely on credit as supplied by existing retail shops. (A critical function of the small, independent retail shops—and, indeed, often the reason for their continued viability in food and clothing—was that even though they and their wholesale suppliers sold at higher prices, they did provide extensive credit to their customers.)[34]

The volume handled by the new mass retailers was impressive. Thomas Lipton, who opened his first shop in Glasgow in 1874, was by 1878 selling *daily* in his Glasgow multiples "1½ tons of butter, 50 cases of rolled butter, one ton of bacon, 1½ tons of ham, ½ ton of cheese and 16,000 eggs." The requirement to maintain such throughput caused Lipton to invest even more extensively than the C.W.S. in refrigerated collection facilities in Ireland, Holland, Denmark, and the United States, as well as in Britain.[35] For the same reason the multiple-shop distributors of meat, besides investing in similar refrigerated warehouses in Australia, New Zealand, and Latin America, obtained packing plants in Argentina and Uruguay.

As the importation of perishable foods into Britain grew to unprecedented proportions, however, entrepreneurs found it profitable to construct extensive and specialized refrigerated storage facilities at major ports—London's Smith-field complex being the largest and best known of such plants. The volume of trade was large enough to encourage intermediaries like Union Cold Storage Company and one or two of the railroads to build smaller refrigerated storage units (but apparently not refrigerated cars) to serve the inland markets. Once such organizations were in place, the multiples and the two cooperative whole-sale societies did not need to make nearly so extensive an investment in product-specific refrigerated distribution facilities as did the American meat-packers in the 1880s.

In apparel, footwear, furniture, and other nonperishable consumer goods, the integration of retailing and manufacturing occurred for much the same reasons as it did in the United States. The small optimal size of plants in these labor-intensive industries meant that a relatively small number of outlets could absorb the output of a single factory. Generally, therefore, a number of multiple-shop distributors would invest in their own production facilities, which would provide an assured supply at the lowest possible unit cost (that is, by operating at minimum efficient scale). Indeed, in the United States, according to Victor S. Clark, such integration occurred in footwear and apparel at roughly the same time (the 1880s and 1890s). Most such American firms remained regional, although a small number had nationwide sales. Two of these, International Shoe and Endicott Johnson, were large enough to be on the list of the top two hundred American companies in 1917, 1930, and 1948. In Britain the integration came earlier and resulted from retailers' decision to integrate backward to control their own supplies. Only one shoe manufacturer, the Trueform Boot Company, appeared (in Group 31) on the list of the two hundred largest British companies in 1930 and 1948.[36]

In these ways Britain's smaller geographical size and greater concentration of markets brought opportunities for exploiting scale economies, and thus encouraged mass retailers of food and apparel to integrate backward more than did those in the United States. Once that investment was made, they continued to concentrate on handling a limited line of provisions, or meat, or shoes, or men's clothing, or women's wear, or one or two lines of household furnishings. These limited lines meant that fewer buyers and other middle managers were necessary than was the case with their American counterparts. Only a few of the leading London department stores, along with the two giant wholesaling societies which supplied the consumer cooperatives, had the opportunity to achieve economies of scope in addition to those of scale as measured by stock-turn. At the Co-operative Wholesale Society the addition of new lines, which allowed each to make fuller use of existing distribution facilities, provided an incentive to invest in manufacturing plants of optimal size whose output could be absorbed easily by the cooperatives' distribution organization.

A comparison of the two largest distribution enterprises in the two countries—Sears, Roebuck and the English C.W.S.—emphasizes the way in which different markets help to differentiate the marketing institutions of different nations. Just before World War I, Sears was smaller than the C.W.S., employing a total of 9,500 persons, of whom only a small number were in manufacturing.

In 1913 the C.W.S. employed 7,000 persons in distribution and 14,000 more in production. Sears had sales of $90.4 million and the C.W.S. £31.2 million (equivalent to about $150 million), which included sales from its manufacturing as well as distribution activities. (In 1913 the sales of the C.W.S. to its societies were £25.2 million, or about $123.5 million.)

At Sears a much larger managerial hierarchy, placing greater reliance on systems of control, exploited as fully as possible the economies of both scale and scope. Its broad product range included hundreds of items in addition to apparel and household furnishings; it sold a multitude of "hard lines"—cutlery, tools, hardware, firearms, washing machines, stoves, books, buggies, pumps, windmills, bathtubs, and pianos and other musical instruments. C.W.S.'s much smaller number of lines included food as well as apparel and furnishings, but no "hard lines." Because Sears handled so many different lines, it only moved into manufacturing when it could not obtain the desired article at the desired price, quantity, and quality. The operations of Sears's highly centralized administrative hierarchy of functional-line and advisory-staff managers made possible by 1905 the filling of as many as one hundred thousand orders a day from its Chicago plant. By World War I it had added only two smaller branch distributing plants, one in Dallas and one in Seattle. With this management in depth and the resulting organizational capabilities, Sears was able to attain an average return of 9.6% on sales between 1905 and 1916.[37]

The C.W.S. was, of course, a mass wholesaler, not a retailer. Its function was to serve its hundreds of retail shops. Because it handled a much smaller number of lines, and because the optimal size of the plants used in the production of those products was small, it invested in production facilities to a much greater degree than Sears. And because it had far fewer lines than Sears, and these lines required less coordinating of throughput to assure cost advantages, the English C.W.S. continued to be managed in a more personal manner. It did not need the hierarchy, the operating technology, or the control systems required by Sears to process orders at a high minimum efficient scale. It operated in a much more decentralized manner with autonomous units or "district" offices serving their respective areas—three major ones at Manchester, Newcastle, and London, and two smaller ones at Bristol and Northampton. The geographical areas served by these district offices were far smaller than the administrative districts or zones of American retail chains. The buyers for the different lines in each of these "district" offices operated quite independently of those in other district offices. In each of the five district offices, the several product departments—the buyers—were grouped into two "divisions," one for groceries and one for "draperies" (products other than food).

Even after World War I the C.W.S. had only a skeleton of a corporate office. Before the war it had had little more than the secretaries of two enterprise-wide committees, one committee for groceries and the other for draperies, that met at intervals at the C.W.S. Manchester headquarters to coordinate the buying and investment policies of the enterprise as a whole. These two committees also supervised most but not all of the factories established by the C.W.S. After the war the society recruited a small staff composed of accounting and auditing offices, an analytical laboratory, and a publicity department. These were housed next to the offices of the secretaries of the drapery, grocery, finance, and factories committees, and to those of the two senior executives, the secretary and the executive officer. At the C.W.S. the management remained nonhierarchical and the profit low. The reported profit as a percentage of sales between 1903 and 1913 ran between 1.5% and 2.5%. (Because C.W.S.'s accounting procedures are not clear, this figure may not be accurate.)[38] Moreover, maximum stockturn was not a primary objective. Profits, which were returned to the member societies, were not a major concern. A far greater concern was to keep the price and quality of goods competitive.

This comparison between the English C.W.S. and Sears demonstrates the basic differences between the mass distribution enterprises in the two countries. The British consumer cooperatives, multiples, and even department stores looked to the urban working class as their market. For this reason they handled a smaller number of product lines, nearly all of which were basic necessities. Because the number of lines was smaller, they relied more on economies of scale than of scope to reduce costs. Because they relied on scale, because the products they handled—food and clothing—had a low minimum efficient scale in production (that is, the optimal size of plants was small), they integrated backward by investing in manufacturing plants more than did their American counterparts. Because they concentrated on marketing a relatively few lines of standardized products, they required much less in the way of a managerial hierarchy. Therefore management remained much more personal (nonhierarchical) than it did among the mass distributors in the United States.

The Revolution in Production

Although British entrepreneurs responded with alacrity to the opportunities in distribution that appeared when the new railroad, telegraph, steamship, and cable systems were being completed, they reacted much more hesitantly to those offered by the revolution in production techniques that was engendered by the new transportation and communications networks. In those industries where British entrepreneurs did make the three interrelated investments that created the modern industrial enterprise, these enterprises and industries were able to compete successfully in international markets. But—and this calls for repetition and emphasis—in the new industries of the Second Industrial Revolution, British entrepreneurs too often failed to make an investment in production large enough to utilize fully the economies of scale and scope, to build a product-specific marketing and distribution network, and to recruit a team of salaried managers. And when they did, they made smaller investments and made them in a more evolutionary manner. So they continued to rely on older forms of industrial enterprise—firms that were personally managed, usually family-managed. In many of these new industries substantial tripartite investments were, indeed, made in Britain; but foreign, not British, enterprises made the investments. Foreign firms reaped the profits and developed the product-specific organizational capabilities. The failure of British entrepreneurs and enterprises to build such capabilities—in terms of both facilities and skills—continued to handicap these British industries and the British economy for decades.

ENTREPRENEURIAL SUCCESS: BRANDED, PACKAGED PRODUCTS
British entrepreneurs were most successful in the production of branded, packaged products. In these lines, where manufacturing processes were not technically complex and where extensive, product-specific, distribution facilities or specialized marketing services were not required, British entrepreneurs created profitable integrated enterprises. They adopted new production technologies for refining, distilling, milling, and processing food, drink, tobacco, and consumer chemicals. They devised new ways of packaging and branding products that could be sold directly to the consumer from retailers' shelves.

Nevertheless, these entrepreneurs failed to take up the most cost-reducing of the new packaging technologies—high-speed canning. Because British entrepreneurs failed to invest in the new canning processes that revolutionized packaging in the United States beginning in the 1880s, not a single food company in Britain before World War II was comparable in size and complexity of operation to Borden, Heinz, Campbell Soup, Del Monte, or Libby, McNeill & Libby. Nor did a large producer of metal containers and canning machinery similar to American Can and Continental Can appear before the 1930s. Until then the British companies relied primarily for their packaging on paper boxes and wrappings, glass bottles, and tin boxes.

Even so, by the turn of the century many producers of branded consumer goods were among the nation's largest and most successful industrial enterprises. These were producers of cigarettes and other tobacco products; of sugar, flour, chocolates, biscuits, and other confectionery; of jams and sauces, condiments, meat extracts, and certain other foodstuffs; of beer, whisky, and soft drinks; and of consumer chemicals such as soaps, starch, cosmetics, paints, and pills. Nearly all began, like Cadbury Brothers, as small family partnerships producing for local markets, and then expanded in the 1880s (and in a few cases earlier) by exploiting the cost advantages of scale.[39]

In the 1850s and 1860s, as railroads and steamships speeded flows of materials and expanded markets (Britain's basic rail network was near completion at least two decades earlier than that of the United States), these owner-operators adopted new high-volume processes of production and then took over the marketing functions that, until then, had been handled by intermediaries. They branded their products and advertised nationally. Most important of all, like Cadbury they sent out ever-increasing numbers of salesmen or "travelers"—sometimes salaried, sometimes on commission, and sometimes paid both ways. These travelers obtained orders from wholesalers and large urban retailers and were responsible for delivery of orders on schedule. Because their market was so geographically concentrated and so well served by a long-established network of intermediaries—in striking contrast to the United States—British producers of branded, packaged products invested much less in distribution facilities and relied more on independent distributors than their American counterparts. Even so, those with the largest output, such as Lever Brothers in soap, Peek Frean in biscuits, Schweppes in soft drinks, and Reckitt & Sons in starch and blueing, had set up branch offices and warehouses before 1900. After World War I, as the scale of such operations increased and as the automobile and truck offered more versatile forms of transportation and local delivery, more of these firms began, like Cadbury, to invest extensively in trucks and depots.[40]

As in the United States, by reducing costs the new high-volume processes of production greatly increased the funds available for nationwide advertising. Such advertising, in turn, created formidable barriers to entry by competitors in more than just local markets. Also, as in the United States, these producers relied on advertising agencies to buy space in national periodicals and in hundreds of local newspapers. In fact, such specialized intermediaries were probably established in Britain before they appeared in the United States. By the 1890s British advertising agencies, like their American counterparts, had begun to assume responsibility for preparing advertising copy for their clients.[41]

The names of these first movers in branded, packaged products are familiar today. Cadbury is a leading example. According to J. Othick, the British chocolate and cocoa industry was becoming concentrated in the late 1860s, and "by the early twentieth century the industry was very much dominated by three firms—Cadbury, Fry, and Rowntree."[42] Already leaders in the 1870s, they remained so in 1919. The largest firms in the biscuit industry were Carr of Carlisle, Huntley & Palmers, and Peek Frean. Carr was founded in 1841 and the other two in 1857. In the biscuit trade, as in chocolate making, as one historian has noted, "technology boosted production." Machinery for making biscuits in volume had been invented in the 1840s, but the leading firms' real expansion came with investments in technology for volume production during the 1870s and 1880s. By the 1880s, another historian reports, Huntley & Palmers and Peek Frean had begun to collaborate informally on determining prices, output, and other matters.[43] Although there is less information on the jam makers, it seems clear that the big three in that industry before 1900 were Crosse & Blackwell, J. Keiller, and E. Lazenby.[44] The soap trade began to become oligopolistic when in the 1880s William Lever started to mass-produce, package, brand, market, and distribute soap in a manner similar to that of Procter & Gamble in the United States. (Before that time soap had been sold in both countries in bulk, with the retailer selling slices to the consumer in the way that he sold cheese and butter.) By 1914 Lever and those leading competitors that were soon to come under Lever's control produced 61% of Britain's soap. By 1919, after they had come under Lever's full control, this figure had risen to approximately 70%.[45]

In the 1870s Scottish whisky makers came to blend "pot-still" whisky with "patent-still" grain spirits. The patent still, in the words of the industry's historian, "produced whisky more quickly, more cheaply, in much greater quantity and in a continuous process." Much of the increased income from the resulting reduced unit cost went into advertising. By the 1890s the Scotch whisky industry was dominated by six firms—Distillers Company (a merger of six patent-still operators), Haig, Dewars, Walker, Mackie (White Horse brand), and Buchanan (Black and White). In 1915 Buchanan and Dewars merged to form Scotch Whisky brands. By 1927 further mergers and acquisitions brought all of these leaders into the Distillers' Company, which like Imperial Tobacco was a federation within which each of the constituent companies produced and distributed its own well-advertised brands.[46]

In mass-produced cigarettes, as has already been told, W. D. & H. O. Wills quickly overshadowed its smaller competitors, who joined with Wills to form Imperial Tobacco when Duke's American Tobacco Company threatened to invade Britain. That federation dominated the British market for decades, although the price umbrella it provided permitted the growth of strong competitors, including Gallaher, Carreras, and Phillips.[47]

The firms that came so quickly to dominate their industries at home were soon marketing directly overseas. Indeed, many of these producers of branded, packaged products had branch offices staffed by salaried managers abroad before they had them at home. Like Cadbury—but often more aggressively—they began to sell overseas, first in what were to become the Commonwealth nations of Australia, New Zealand, Canada, and South Africa. Only a few looked toward the Indian subcontinent. Early in the twentieth century some ventured into the United States and continental Europe. Although they invested quite extensively in marketing abroad, they were slower about building plants there. By the First World War those with overseas manufacturing facilities included Liebig's Extract of Meat (beef bouillon), Reckitt (blueing), Keiller (marmalade), Bryant & May (matches), and Burroughs Wellcome (drugs and pharmaceuticals).[48]

The largest of all the makers of branded, packaged goods, Lever Brothers, the soap company that consciously followed the American example, invested the most abroad. By World War I it had plants not only in Australia, Canada, and the United States but also in Switzerland, Germany, France, Holland, Belgium, Sweden, Norway, and Japan. In all but one case the company built these plants, according to Peter Buckley and Brian Roberts, because sales volume justified local production, rather than because it wanted to avoid tariffs. The plants served national rather than larger regional markets. This was partly because of differences in currencies, laws, and tastes. But such direct investments rarely came until the sales organizations in each country had developed a volume of "trade sufficient to warrant the construction of a factory." Because minimum efficient scale in soap production was so much lower than it was, say, in machinery or chemicals, Lever Brothers found it more economical to build several small plants for national markets rather than one or two for the whole European market. Because the firm moved abroad earlier than American soapmakers such as Colgate and Procter & Gamble, and before firms in Europe or elsewhere had developed the new methods of producing and marketing packaged soap, Lever built its own plants rather than acquiring existing ones. And because few economies resulted from closely coordinating the local activities of distant plants, these integrated foreign subsidiaries operated quite autonomously, having relatively little contact with one another. They probably had less constant supervision from the home office than did the subsidiaries of their American competitors.[49]

Growing demand at home and abroad brought gradual enlargement of the main factories of these branded, packaged producers, and with it an expansion of their purchasing organizations. Until after World War I, however, the companies producing foods and consumer chemicals rarely operated more than one major factory within Britain. Even though the increase in size brought only relatively small cost advantages, the British market was so geographically concentrated and homogeneous that there was little to gain in terms of transportation costs and differentiated demand by building new capacity at a distance. On the other hand, a number of firms, including Cadbury, Lever Brothers, Rowntree, Fry, Liebig's Extract of Meat, and Bovril, had by then invested much more than their American counterparts in plantations, agencies, and trading companies in foreign lands in order to have assured sources of supply. Possibly because their supplies came from distant areas overseas, they felt a stronger need to reduce transaction costs in this way than did American companies that could rely on domestic sources.

The histories of the individual firms making branded, packaged products varied, of course. Some moved overseas earlier than others; some entered American and Continental markets with more energy and enthusiasm than their competitors. In nearly all cases, however, the growth of the enterprise took place more slowly than did that of comparable enterprises in the United States.

In industries like these, where mass production did not require the services of technically trained managers and where distribution called for little in the way of specialized services and facilities, such evolutionary growth permitted the founding families to continue to manage the enlarged enterprises. This evolutionary growth also meant that many continued to own as well as manage. Expansion of plants and facilities was financed from retailed earnings or, where earnings were paid out in dividends, by issuing debentures or other nonvoting securities. Because increasing demand was normally met by expanding the size of the original plant and because buyers and travelers continued to work out of the home office, next to the enlarged works, the enterprise could easily be managed in person by a few executives. Overseas marketing functions were left almost entirely to the local managers. Before the advent of the airplane and the overseas telephone, foreign factories, sales offices, purchasing units, and plantations simply could not be supervised as closely as an American firm could supervise its more extensive network of branch plants and sales and purchasing offices within the United States. After all, Chicago was only an overnight trip from New York, and San Francisco was only two days from Chicago, whereas a supervisory round trip from London to South Africa required at least six weeks, and one to Australia took twelve.

Thus a founding family continued to manage its growing enterprise in much the same manner as did the Cadburys, even as late as World War II. Such firms operated through functionally departmentalized organizations, with department heads who were apt to be members of the family. Working closely together at an office in or near the plant and living nearby, they had little need for charts and tables to define and explain their organization to themselves or others. Before World War I such personal management by owners assisted by a small team of managers was practiced even among the largest producers of branded, packaged products ranked in the top two hundred, including Reckitt, J. J. Colman, Beechams, Rowntree, Mackintosh, Crosse & Blackwell, Peek Frean, Huntley & Palmers, Bovril, Gilbey, Schweppes, Yardley, the sugar refiners Abram Lyle and Henry Tate, the grain millers J. Rank and Spillers, and the producers of cigarettes. Only in the case of Britain's largest, Lever Brothers, is there clear evidence that the owners were assisted by an extensive hierarchy before World War I. It was smaller in size than the hierarchies of leading American and German firms and also differed from them in structure (see Chapter 9). By 1917 Lever's corporate office included thirteen salaried managers, several of whom oversaw operations of the allied companies that Lever controlled, as well as supervising functional specialties.[50]

The brewing enterprises that appear in such profusion on the lists of the two hundred largest British industrial enterprises continued to be administered in an even more personal manner. Unlike the producers of branded, packaged foods and consumer chemicals, these firms invested heavily in retail outlets.

The capital-intensive nature of brewing technology (with its high potential for scale economies), combined with the fact that its major markets were public houses that were limited in number by law, encouraged brewers to buy or lease public houses that would sell their brand exclusively. (This large investment in "pubs" is a significant reason why there are so many brewers listed in the top two hundred, for the market value of shares on which the listings are based reflects these assets in real estate.)[51]

Although most breweries were incorporated, they continued to be run as partnerships. Kristof Glamann has noted: "As to the management structure of private partnerships, the active partners tend to take responsibility for their own particular specialist departments (brewing, public house management, accounting, distribution)."[52] Generally, each department was managed by one or more partners, usually from the founding family or families, together with a salaried specialist in the departmental function, such as Head Brewer, Head Clerk, or Head of Malt and Maltings.

There were exceptions to personal management without the assistance of hierarchy, but very few. The brewers at Burton-on-Trent, particularly Bass and Worthington, which owned relatively few pubs and concentrated increasingly on distribution to the national market, had recruited salaried sales managers and a chemist or two; they were thus beginning to build a hierarchy. This was true, too, of Watney, Combe, Reid, the largest London brewer.

The most significant exception, however, was the Irish brewer, Guinness. Guinness owned no pubs. By exploiting scale economies and investing in a marketing and distribution network throughout Great Britain, it was rapidly becoming in the 1880s—and would remain for the next century—the largest brewer in the British Isles. In 1919 it was the largest of the food and beverage enterprises among the top two hundred in Britain and the seventh largest in all categories. At first, Guinness sold almost wholly to wholesalers who were bottlers, many of them wine and spirits merchants. Thus, although Guinness quickly recruited a much larger sales force of travelers and invested more in transportation and storage facilities than any other British brewer, its marketing and distribution organization appears to have been at first smaller than those of Pabst, Schlitz, Anheuser Busch, and other national brewers in the United States; the same would have been true in comparison with Schultheiss, and possibly others, in Germany. After the turn of the century, Guinness began to do its own bottling, to advertise even more energetically, and to invest more heavily in temperature-controlled distribution and transportation facilities. To manage their profitable enterprise the Guinness family soon had a staff of full-time salaried managers who carried out day-to-day operations; thus its organizational form was becoming similar to that of American and German family firms.[53]

To summarize, it was in branded, packaged products—food and drink, tobacco, and consumer chemicals—that the British industrialists of the Victorian era made their mark. Far more of the two hundred largest enterprises in Britain clustered in these consumer industries than in any other set of related industries in Britain. Lever Brothers, Imperial Tobacco, Distillers' Company, and Guinness were among the very largest firms in Britain before and after World War I. British industrial fortunes came from these industries and not from oil, industrial chemicals, machinery, and metals, as they did in the United States and Germany. A survey of British millionaires that relied on British Census classifications for the period from 1880 to World War I revealed many more millionaires associated with Group III (food, drink, and tobacco) than with any other standard manufacturing classification.[54] This success not only reflects these industries' proximity to the world's richest and most concentrated consumer market but also points to the critical aspect of all these industries—that their production and distribution required less costly facilities and less complex managerial and technical skills than other capital-intensive industries.

ENTREPRENEURIAL SUCCESS: RUBBER, GLASS, EXPLOSIVES, ALKALIES, AND FIBERS

In branded, packaged products British entrepreneurs created national and international organizations that could still be personally managed by an extended family with a very few close associates. Such family management was much more difficult to maintain in the more technologically complex new industries. British entrepreneurs did build the managerial teams necessary to compete effectively in a number of new, high-volume, capital-intensive industries, including rubber, glass, explosives, synthetic alkalies, and man-made fibers. But they failed to do so in other industries that were even more important to the nation's health and growth, including machinery, organic chemicals and electrochemicals, and steel, copper, and other metals.

In the new capital-intensive industries where British entrepreneurs performed well, the first to make the three-pronged investment continued to dominate. Because the domestic market for the products of these first movers was smaller than its equivalent in the United States, it could absorb only the output of a very few plants operating at optimal scale. Thus in the home market the structures of these new industries became more monopolistic than oligopolistic. In global markets, on the other hand, these industries remained oligopolistic because of competition from firms of other nations.

Rubber. The Dunlop Rubber Company became Great Britain's representative in the global rubber oligopoly. Because no producer in Britain had integrated production and distribution of rubber footwear and clothing on the scale achieved by the United States Rubber Company and Goodrich, those two American companies easily established an extensive sales organization in Britain before World War I and enjoyed profitable shares of the British market.[55] In

1908, however, the Dunlop Rubber Company built the first automobile tire plant in Britain large enough to exploit the cost advantages of scale. From then on, Dunlop remained one of the world's largest manufacturers of rubber goods.

An Irish-born entrepreneur, Harvey DuCros, had formed this company in Britain in 1889 to acquire the Dunlop patent for pneumatic bicycle tires. But the company's rapid growth came with the automobile. In 1896 DuCros obtained an interest in two French bicycle makers, Alexander Darracq and Adolphe Clement, both of whom then turned to manufacturing automobiles. By 1901, the year in which Darracq produced close to a thousand cars and became one of the largest auto manufacturers in Europe, DuCros built an automobile-tire factory. Two years later he bought out Darracq, then making between two and three thousand vehicles a year, and continued to expand tire output. He quickly established an international marketing and distributing organization and within a short time was competing with the French, German, and a little later the Italian representatives in the global oligopoly, which included Michelin, Continental, Pirelli, and the four leading American tire makers.[56]

In a somewhat unsystematic and unplanned manner DuCros recruited the managerial hierarchy necessary to maintain the firm's marketing position in the global oligopoly. The firm continued to market aggressively abroad, setting up the first large tire plant in Japan in 1909. By World War I it had a research and development organization. Dunlop, like United States Rubber, invested defensively in plantations—in this case in Malaya and Ceylon. The post-World War I recession brought a thorough administrative and financial reorganization (as it did to many American enterprises). In the course of the reorganization the DuCros family lost control. By the early 1920s Dunlop had become one of the very first managerial enterprises in Britain (see Chapter 8).

Glass. In plate glass, first movers quickly took command of their industry. The technology of production and the requirements of distribution meant that the two largest producers, Pilkington Brothers and the somewhat smaller Chance Brothers, came to dominate production of plate glass in much the same way and at approximately the same time as John Pitcairn's Pittsburgh Plate Glass Company did in the United States (see Chapter 4). (On the other hand, flat glass continued to be produced in Britain by labor-intensive methods until Pilkington acquired the necessary licenses and machinery in the early 1930s from Pittsburgh Plate Glass.) The two English firms were based in the industrial town of St. Helens. They improved production processes—primarily through introduction of the Siemens continuous-tank furnace and the application of electricity to glassmaking machinery. Indeed, it was Pilkington's quick adoption of the Siemens furnace and its further investment in such new facilities, especially in 1879 and 1884, that moved the firm ahead of Chance and made it the industry's leader. Pilkington's weekly throughput increased from 350,000 feet of glass before the introduction of the new processes to 500,000 in 1877, to

900,000 in 1887, to 1,100,000 in the early 1890s, and to more than 1,600,000 by the end of the century. Such throughput assured Pilkington's position in the international oligopoly as well as its leadership in the domestic market.

Pilkington expanded its sales organization, adding new warehouses in Britain for finishing and storing plate glass and, according to company policy, to act "as much as possible as a Town Store." In these same years the firm expanded its sales forces overseas, building warehouses in eastern Canada in 1892 and 1893, then others in western Canada and still others in Australia and New Zealand. At the same time came investment on the European Continent with a sales company based in Hamburg and with depots in Paris and Naples, and the purchase of shares in 1890 in a new glass works in France. These moves were followed by the acquisition of a manufacturing plant in Canada in 1909 and full control of the one in France in 1907.[57]

Chance Brothers, overshadowed by its neighbor and rival, followed the same pattern of growth, but on a smaller scale at home and with little direct investment abroad. At home the two firms both competed and collaborated. Together they effectively negotiated price and production schedules for European markets with the small number of Continental competitors, headed by France's St. Gobain. In the American market, however, the tariff and the efficiency of the industry's leaders, Pittsburgh Plate Glass and then Libbey-Owens, discouraged Pilkington and the Europeans from making an even modest investment in distribution and production. Pilkington, however, continued to expand its sales in Canada and other Commonwealth countries, and Chance did the same on a much more modest scale.

Pilkington, for all its rapid and successful growth, remained a family firm managed much like Cadbury, except that it had a larger managerial staff. In 1894, when the firm became a limited-liability company, the four Pilkingtons of the second generation who had carried out the expansion of the previous two decades distributed shares to four more Pilkingtons of the third generation. Before World War I the only non-Pilkington on its board was Edward Herbert Couzens-Hardy, whose sister had married a Pilkington and who, with no training in the business, was put on the board in 1907 when his brother-in-law died. The number of middle managers increased in the years before the war; but the corporate office, housed at the Pilkington plate-glass works, remained small by American and German standards. The failure to expand the enterprise's managerial capabilities was to handicap the firm in the years following World War I (Chapter 8).

Three chemicals: dynamite, synthetic alkalies, and synthetic fibers. In the production of both dynamite and synthetic alkalies a single first mover quickly dominated at home and became Britain's representative in the new global oligopoly. In 1887 Alfred Nobel, dynamite's inventor, and a group of Scottish entrepreneurs headed by Charles Tennant (whose family firm was Europe's largest producer of bleaching powder) formed British Dynamite, later renamed Nobel Explosives. The new company, headquartered in Glasgow, produced explosives more efficiently and at lower cost than existing makers of black powder, just as did the users of the Nobel patents in the United States—California Powder, Giant Powder, and the Du Pont Company's Eastern Dynamite. Nobel Explosives trained a sales force and invested in distribution facilities, but on a smaller scale than the American companies. Not only was the British market smaller but, from 1886 on, overseas markets were limited by contractual agreements with competitors from other nations.

In 1886 the company joined four German firms to form the Nobel-Dynamite Trust Company, Ltd., a unique, British-chartered, multinational holding company. That enterprise, in turn, joined with other Continental and American explosive makers to allocate territories and carry out arrangements which gave the British firm the markets of the British Empire, Latin America, and Southeast Asia. In Latin America the British company worked through joint ventures with the Americans, and in Southeast Asia it cooperated with its German associates. Because its founders, Alfred Nobel and Charles Tennant and his colleagues, were deeply involved in other business activities, they recruited a small but effective team of salaried managers. For this reason, and also because of its multinational structure, Nobel Explosives was from the start a rare example of a large British-based industrial enterprise administered by salaried managers.[58]

The new technology for synthetically producing alkalies provides an impressive example of the competitive advantages of continuous-process technology. In the 1870s and early 1880s two Belgian brothers, Ernest and Alfred Solvay, perfected a new, continuous, capital-intensive process that reduced costs well below those of the small-batch, labor-intensive Leblanc process. As in the United States and also in Germany, the Solvays provided licenses and financial support to local entrepreneurs in return for a share—but not a controlling share—of the new company's stock. In Britain their affiliate, Brunner, Mond, moved into full production in 1882. By 1890 it was producing 130,000 tons of soda a year, nearly all of it in the original plant in Winnington. By then the total claimed output of the nearly fifty works in Britain producing through the older Leblanc process was 140,000, or only 10,000 tons more.[59] And while Brunner, Mond from its single plant was making a handsome profit, the Leblanc producers were suffering heavy losses. The cost differential caused the Leblanc manufacturers to form a holding company, the United Alkali Company, in 1891. Even though this holding company made a much greater effort to centralize administration than did other British mergers, it had little hope of competing with Brunner, Mond's Solvay technology in the production of soda.[60]

At Brunner, Mond, the two senior partners paid close attention to perfecting the Solvay process. They recruited a small, but soon well-trained, team of salaried managers, and, in a move that was rare in Britain, brought senior salaried executives onto the board of directors. The company's investments in sales and distribution remained relatively small, not only because its product was an undifferentiated commodity but also because it was sold to a relatively small number of large customers. Where it did not sell directly, the company relied on exclusive agents. As in the case of Nobel Explosives, its markets were restricted by agreements with other patent-holding processing companies. Of these the most important was Rowland Hazard's Solvay Process Company in the United States and Deutsche Solvay Werke headed by Karl Wessel in Germany (Chapter 5 and Chapter 11). By these agreements Brunner, Mond had for its market the British Empire, Latin America, and Southern and Southeast Asia. Its total domestic and foreign market was smaller than the domestic market enjoyed by Americans and the combined domestic and foreign market accessible to the Germans. For these reasons the managerial hierarchies of the British firm remained smaller than those of the Solvay companies in the United States and Germany.[61]

Chemically made fibers provide an even more dramatic example than synthetic alkalies of the cost advantages of exploiting scale economies. Courtaulds, the first British company to adopt and organize a new technology that would permit huge economies based on high-volume throughput, became the first mover in Britain and later in the United States. Courtaulds was a long-established crepe-making family firm. In 1904 Henry G. Tetley, a salaried manager outside the family, supported by Thomas P. Latham, another manager, persuaded the family to acquire patents for the viscose process of making artificial silk, later known as rayon. By 1907 they had put a new plant at Coventry into full production and had recruited a sales force to market the product at home and abroad. By 1912 the total value of Coventry sales was £686,176, as compared with the company's total crepe-silk and -fabric sales of £49,606. Its rayon profit margin that year was 44.4%. In the five years from 1907 to 1912 its rayon output had increased from 157,000 to 2,547,000 pounds. Within the same period, output per spindle in this one works doubled from 6.8 pounds per week to 12.3 pounds, and the pounds of yarn per worker more than doubled from 9.7 to 22.0, with the biggest jump coming in the first year. Meanwhile, in order to go under the tariff and forestall competition, in 1910 Courtaulds built a plant at Marcus Hook, Pennsylvania, comparable in size to the one in Coventry. The performance of the American plant was as impressive as that of the English one.[62] Not surprisingly, Courtaulds completely dominated rayon production in both countries before World War I. By 1919 it was already the eleventh largest industrial enterprise in Britain in terms of the market value of its securities.

After 1919 Courtaulds maintained its lead in Britain in competition with British Celanese, which pioneered the cellulose production process, and in the United States in competition with Du Pont and other European first movers.

With these it also competed effectively in Europe and other parts of the world, though in Europe Courtaulds preferred cooperation to competition. In the years immediately before World War I it joined the industry's first movers in Germany, France, Switzerland, Italy, and Spain in an unsuccessful attempt, headed by the largest of them all, the German producer, to form an international consortium to control price and output. That unsuccessful effort began in 1911 and ended with the outbreak of war in 1914 (see Chapter 11).

As at Dunlop, Pilkington, and Brunner, Mond, growth at Courtaulds, impressive as it was, was easily financed from retained earnings; so the founding families and the two managers who had moved the company into rayon continued to control the enterprise. After a financial reorganization in 1912 the Courtaulds held 32.9% of the shares outstanding; the other founding families of the original crepe-making enterprise held 26.6%; and Tetley and Latham, the innovating managers, held 18.5%. Close to 10% more were held by senior production and sales managers and other executives whom Tetley and Latham had recruited. Of these recruited executives, however, only the manager of the Coventry works came onto the board before the 1920s. (He did so in 1914.) In this way two managers outside the family turned a third-generation family firm into a powerful entrepreneurial enterprise by adopting a new technology and creating the organization essential to exploit it.[63]

Thus in rubber, glass, explosives, synthetic alkalies, and synthetic fibers the first enterprises to achieve the scale economies that were permitted by a new technology dominated the British domestic market more completely than the American first movers dominated theirs. In these industries the pattern of interfirm relations developed differently from the way it did in the United States, conforming more closely to the pattern of the other industrial nations of western Europe. In these smaller domestic markets, which could accommodate fewer plants operating at optimal scale, one or two firms came to dominate. In international markets, these national representatives in their global oligopolies normally preferred to negotiate rather than to fight functionally and strategically for market share. International agreements, however, were difficult to define and difficult to maintain. They were reached in glass, explosives, and synthetic alkalies, but they were not consummated in rayon before World War I, and they did not occur at all in rubber tires.

To summarize, in the industries in Britain where owners made the investments in production and distribution that were needed to exploit new technologies, and where they recruited even relatively small managerial hierarchies, their enterprises competed effectively in global oligopolies. Because the domestic market was smaller and because global markets were limited by cartel agreements, these managerial hierarchies remained less extensive than those of American firms, making it easier to retain family control at the top. But if British entrepreneurs failed to move quickly into a new technology, to recruit the necessary management teams, and to make a substantial investment in distribution, marketing, and purchasing organizations, they were unable to compete abroad or to have significant influence in global cartels, or even to retain their home markets.

ENTREPRENEURIAL FAILURE: MACHINERY, ELECTRICAL EQUIPMENT,
ORGANIC CHEMICALS, ELECTROCHEMICALS, AND METALS

Indeed, the British entrepreneurial response in rubber, glass, explosives, synthetic alkalies, and synthetic fibers represented the exception rather than the rule. True, these exceptions were of great importance. The organizational capabilities developed at Nobel and Brunner, Mond became the basis for the modern British chemical industry, especially after the two joined in 1925 to form Imperial Chemical Industries, just as those at Dunlop, Pilkington, and Courtaulds continued to provide Britain with its competitive strength in their respective industries. Nevertheless, in the new, dynamic industries of the Second Industrial Revolution—those at the center of industrial and economic growth—there were more failures than successes in Great Britain. In some industries such entrepreneurial failures are understandable; in others they are more difficult to explain.

In oil (both mineral and vegetable) and in meat processing a lack of supplies and natural resources limited opportunities for British entrepreneurs. Oil refining was usually carried on close to sources of supply or at major shipping points. Britain had no domestic sources of petroleum and, as the world's first urban industrial society, it had few sources of vegetable or animal oil. Not surprisingly, before World War I the British market for kerosene and then gasoline was supplied by a subsidiary of Standard Oil of New Jersey and also, after the turn of the century, by Royal Dutch–Shell and the German-financed and German-managed European Petroleum Union.[64] The largest consumers of vegetable and animal oil, that is, such soapmakers as Lever and Gossage, purchased palm plantations in Africa and Oceania to assure themselves supplies in the volume they needed, and set up their own refineries in Britain. The smaller British refiners of vegetable or animal oil bought their supplies from branch offices of American companies such as American Cotton Oil, Southern Cotton Oil, American Linseed, and from meatpackers such as Swift, Armour, and Cudahy.[65] These small refiners merged in 1899 to form the British Cake & Oil Company, a holding company which in typical British fashion made no attempt to rationalize production and distribution but remained a decentralized federation of family firms.

Britain had no great herds of cattle to provide the basis for giant meatpacking plants comparable to those in Chicago and other American cities on the edge of the cattle frontier. On the other hand, the rich British market attracted an ever-increasing flow of beef, veal, mutton, lamb, bacon, and ham from overseas. This demand led to the formation of specialized transportation and storage intermediaries, such as Union Cold Storage and the Smithfield Docks. Moreover, the demand was met not by meat processors, as in the United States, but by the new mass retailers, particularly the multiple shops. These retailers made the investment in supplementary facilities to assure high-volume flow of perishable products from the meat-growing regions of Ireland, the Continent, South America, Australia, New Zealand, and the United States. Mass retailers, rather than processors, also made the investment in distribution facilities for locally produced perishables such as fresh milk, cheese and other dairy products, and bread and other bakery products.

Although there were few entrepreneurial opportunities within Britain in the oil- and meat-processing industries, there were many in mass-produced standardized light machinery, electrical equipment, chemicals, and metals. In these industries British entrepreneurs failed to grasp the opportunities the new technologies had opened up, precisely because they failed to make the necessary, interrelated, three-pronged investment in production, marketing, and management. Those opportunities within Britain were seized instead by Germans and Americans.

Light machinery and electrical equipment. The failure in light machinery is understandable. American first movers established themselves so quickly in Britain that local firms hardly had a chance to get started. The invaders' experience with the American system of manufacturing, reinforced by their impressive scale economies in production and their proved efficiencies in marketing, made them all but invincible. Their continuing dominance is emphasized by the fact that on the 1919 list of the two hundred largest British industrials (Appendix B.1) there were no British-owned or British-managed producers of sewing machines, typewriters, cash registers, adding machines, mimeograph machines, harvesters, reapers, phonographs, storage batteries, or electrical appliances. The largest producers in Britain of such standardized equipment as elevators, pumping systems, Linotype machines, and shoemaking machinery were subsidiaries of American enterprises. Because minimum efficient scale in the production of office, agricultural, and canning machinery was so high, most American companies continued to supply their British sales branches from the United States or from newly established regional factories on the Continent. In sewing machines, however, Singer, with its factory near Glasgow employing seven thousand workers, was Britain's thirty-first-largest industrial employer in 1907.[66] Burroughs Adding Machine had a comparable plant in Britain before 1914. In 1911 the Ford Motor Company, already the largest seller of automobiles in Great Britain, completed an assembly plant in Manchester.

The American makers of volume-produced, standardized, industrial machinery invested even earlier in British factories. This was because the plants of optimal size produced a smaller number of units than did those making sewing, office, and agricultural machinery. Moreover, their products often had to be adjusted to customers' needs. Well before 1914, American Radiator, Worthington Pump, Otis Elevator, Mergenthaler Linotype, Babcock & Wilcox, Westinghouse Air Brake, United Shoe Machinery, Chicago Pneumatic Tool, Electric Storage Battery, Western Electric (the manufacturing arm of American Telephone & Telegraph), and Carborundum (makers of grinding machinery and abrasives) were operating large plants in Britain.[67] None of these factories, it should be noted, was established to get under tariff barriers, as Britain then had almost no tariff legislation. The construction of several was at least partially financed by funds raised in Britain.

In the electrical-machinery industries foreign firms did not have a head start comparable to that of the Americans in light machinery. In electrical equipment British entrepreneurs did have the opportunity to capture the home market before foreign first movers established themselves. British inventors such as Joseph Swan and Sebastian Z. Ferranti were as technologically able as Edison, Westinghouse, and Thomson in the United States and Werner Siemens and his associates in Germany. Moreover, Mather & Platt, one of Britain's most successful machinery makers, had acquired the Edison patents. Sir William Mather, its head, hired Dr. Edward Hopkinson, one of Britain's ablest electrical engineers (he had been chief assistant to Sir William Siemens at the German company's British plant producing telegraph and cable equipment), to take charge of the firm's new electrical department.[68]

Surely there was no economic reason why Sir William Mather, who was one of Britain's leading industrialists, and who had acquired the Edison patents at the same time as Emil Rathenau, was unable to build an industrial empire comparable to the one Rathenau created in Germany. The market was there; the workers were as skilled as those in Germany and the United States; and London investors were eager to profit from the new technology. But Mather and other less well established pioneers apparently did not believe that extensive investment in manufacturing, marketing, or management was necessary. In any case, they failed to make such investments before the Americans and the Germans established their marketing organizations and then built their production facilities in Britain. So the British firms remained of little significance in the development of the British electrical-machinery industry.

By World War I, two-thirds of the output of electrical equipment manufactured by British factories was made by the subsidiaries of three foreign firms—General Electric, Westinghouse, and Siemens. During the period 1911–1912 the three subsidiaries produced £3.7 million of a total value of £5.6 million. The remaining third was divided among five small British firms. The largest of these, Dick Kerr, makers of streetcars, had an estimated £0.4 million in sales, accounting for 7.3% of the total market, and General Electric Company (which had no connection with the American firm of the same name) had only 3.6% of the market. Mather & Platt had become a minor producer of specialized electrical equipment for factories. By 1912 the sales of Rathenau's company, AEG, the fourth member of the global oligopoly, were far greater in Britain than Mather & Platt's electrical sales. Not surprisingly, much of the London subway system was equipped by the General Electric Company of the United States.[69]

The British failure to create the organization necessary to exploit the new electrical technology had a lasting impact. In the years after World War I and particularly in the 1930s, British industrialists were able to win back much of the British market and to play a more significant role in the industry's global oligopoly, but it was still a far less decisive role than that played by their American and German competitors. Even after the British companies made the necessary investment in production and distribution, they continued to rely on General Electric, Westinghouse, Siemens, and AEG for new products and processes. In the 1920s and 1930s the major advances in new electrical technologies were accomplished in industrial laboratories in Schenectady, Pittsburgh, and Berlin, not in Britain.

For these reasons the relatively few machinery companies on the 1919 list of the two hundred largest British industrials (Appendix B.1) were established firms that produced equipment primarily for the industries of the First Industrial Revolution. The British-owned and British-managed companies on the list were makers of textile and mining machinery, railway equipment, and ships.[70] Or else they were specialized builders of military and naval ordnance for Britain and much of the rest of the world. Britain's largest maker of agricultural machinery, Ruston & Hornsby, was driven out of the harvester and plow trade by Americans well before the end of the nineteenth century; it came to concentrate instead on portable steam engines for farm and other uses.[71]

On the other hand, the most successful makers of textile machinery—Mather & Platt, Platt Brothers of Oldham, and Howard & Bullough—did adopt improved production methods and had begun to use sales agencies and offices at home and abroad.[72] Early in the twentieth century Alfred Herbert, who began as an agent for American manufacturing firms, built his own plant to produce machine tools for the metal-working industries, which was "described as the finest in Europe, 'with methods that were essentially American.'"[73] By 1914 these few—Alfred Herbert, Mather & Platt, Platt of Oldham, and Howard & Bullough—appear to have recruited a respectable staff of salaried managers to assist their owners and founders, who continued to maintain full control over the enterprise.[74]

With these few exceptions, however, British machinery firms remained small. Their investment in marketing and distribution was far less than that of the machinery firms on the lists of the two hundred largest American and German enterprises. In marketing overseas they relied on a combination of branches, traveling engineers, and independent agents.[75] Their trade, unlike that of the Americans, was rarely large enough to warrant the establishment of overseas plants. Except for Howard & Bullough's small textile-machinery factory built in Providence, Rhode Island, in 1894, there is little evidence of construction of any branch plants by these or other British machinery makers.[76]

Organic chemicals and electrochemicals. In industrial chemicals the opportunities were even greater for British entrepreneurs than in electrical machinery. Consider the story of organic chemicals, the pioneering and most dynamic branch of that science-based industry. In economic terms Britain enjoyed potentially striking competitive advantages in this field in 1870. In 1856 a Britisher, Sir William H. Perkin, had invented the first process for making dyes by chemical synthesis. Britain was far better endowed than Germany with the basic raw material, coal. In fact, Germany imported crude coal tar and certain processed intermediates from Britain. The British textile industry, the world's largest, remained by far the biggest single market for dyes until World War II. The one advantage German producers had was better training in chemistry. But in 1870 leading German chemists were already working in British companies. By almost any criterion the pioneering British dye makers should have quickly dominated international markets.[77]

By the mid-1880s the glowing potential had already disappeared. For it was the German, not British, entrepreneurs who made investments in giant plants, recruited managerial teams to coordinate the complex technological processes, and built the essential worldwide marketing organizations (see Chapter 12). It was the German first movers who, by exploiting the economies first of scale and then of scope, drove down the production cost of alizarin from 270 marks per kilogram in 1869 to 9 marks in 1886. They, not British marketers, instructed most of the world's textile manufacturers in the application of the new dyes. And, in recruiting managerial and technical staffs, they were the ones who offered salaries that brought German chemists back from Britain to head their companies' laboratories—laboratories which from then on led the world in exploiting the potential of the new organic-chemical industries. Well before the turn of the century Britain had become almost totally dependent on imported dyes, pharmaceuticals, and other allied products. In 1913, of the 160,000 tons of dyes produced, 140,000 were made by German companies and 10,000 by the neighboring Swiss. In that year 4,100 tons were produced in Britain (and only 3,000 in the United States).[78] Moreover, a substantial portion of the dyes produced in Britain (and in the United States) were made by subsidiaries of German firms.

British entrepreneurs also failed to exploit other products made out of coke and coal, the raw materials with which their nation was so richly endowed. They did not build enterprises comparable to Semet-Solvay, Barrett, and Koppers in the United States or to Rütgerswerke and Holzverkohlungs-Industrie in Germany in order to produce intermediates such as benzene and toluene and finished products such as creosote, roofing, and paving materials. And except for Burroughs Wellcome, no enterprises were established in Britain to process and distribute pharmaceuticals or fine chemicals, comparable to Monsanto and Mallinckrodt in the United States or to Heyden, Riedel, Schering, and Merck in Germany. In fact, Burroughs Wellcome itself was founded by two Americans.

In electrochemicals the opportunities were less obvious than in coal-based chemicals. British entrepreneurs were handicapped by the lack of major sources of electric power such as Niagara Falls or the streams of the Alps. Yet even here available opportunities were not taken. Brunner, Mond did obtain, albeit belatedly, electrolytic techniques for making bleaches through its Solvay connection. The Castner-Electrolytic Alkali Company, formed to exploit patents owned by an American, H. Y. Castner, built a small plant in Cheshire and a larger one at Niagara Falls. Albright & Wilson adopted a comparable process for the production of phosphorus and financed a works at Niagara Falls. The Castner firm, however, was soon controlled and operated by Americans, and the Albright & Wilson works at Niagara was managed by the firm's American agents, J. J. and D. S. Ricker, who joined in the financing of the enterprise.[79] It is even more significant that no enterprises appeared in Britain that were comparable in size and diversity of product lines to Dow Chemical, American Cyanamid, Union Carbide, and National Carbon in the United States, or to the even larger Griesheim-Elektron and DEGUSSA in Germany. These American and German companies all had giant plants for which electrical power was generated by lignite and coal, an energy source readily available in Britain. British entrepreneurs failed almost as badly in electrochemicals as in organic, coal-based chemicals.

Only in dynamite and synthetic soda ash (both made commercially viable by foreign innovators) did British chemical industrialists make the investment necessary to become significant players in their global oligopolies. Not surprisingly, it was a combination of those two players—Nobel and Brunner, Mond—that became the only British chemical company of international stature during the interwar years—Imperial Chemical Industries (ICI).

Nonferrous metals. In metals British entrepreneurs again failed to capitalize on opportunities created by the new technologies. In aluminum, copper, and other nonferrous-metal production they did adopt the revolutionary electrolytic techniques but failed to utilize them effectively enough to play a significant role in international markets. In steel (which will be discussed in the next section), where they pioneered in both Bessemer and open-hearth processes, they also quickly fell behind.

In the case of aluminum the British were again handicapped by lack of a water-based power source. In 1896 British industrialists formed the British Aluminium Company to utilize the Heroult patents. They obtained bauxite properties in Ireland and France. But, without the water power essential for high-volume output, they were unable to attain the great scale economies enjoyed by their international competitors. To continue to compete, the British firm built a plant in Norway but defaulted on its debentures in 1908. It went through a second financial reorganization in 1910. Until World War I it remained a weak member of the international oligopoly, which was dominated in Europe by the German-controlled and German-operated Swiss firm Aluminiumindustrie, Neuhausen, and in America by Alcoa. Only the demand created by World War I and a subsidy from the British government permitted British Aluminium to remain an active participant in the postwar oligopoly and the cartel agreements that its members spawned.[80]

In copper and other nonferrous metals, British entrepreneurs' opportunities for building international enterprises based on the new technologies were even greater than those of the Germans and almost as promising as those of the Americans. There was no economic reason why a smelting and refining complex comparable to, though somewhat smaller than, the one that arose in New York harbor area could not have been built in South Wales along the Bristol Channel or near Liverpool at the mouth of the Mersey. In the 1880s between 20% and 25% of the world's copper came from the Iberian Peninsula (the voyage from Spain to Britain was much shorter than that from Mexico or the southwest United States to New York), and one-half of the ores there were mined by the British-owned and British-managed Rio Tinto Company.[81] Although the three leading copper processors in Britain—Thomas Bolton & Sons of Widnes on the Mersey, J. H. Vivian & Sons Company, and Elliott's Metal Company, both of the latter near Swansea on the Bristol Channel—were slow in adopting the Bessemer-like converter in smelting, they did take up the new electrolytic refining.

In 1891, the year when the new high-powered dynamo was introduced (see Chapter 4), the Bolton company, which had already begun to experiment with electrolytic refining, built a completely new plant with eight dynamos and was soon producing seven hundred tons of electrolytic copper a month. At that very same time, however, Alfred Bolton, one of the founder's sons, decided that such expansion was sufficient. He made a "gentleman's agreement" with Callender's Cable, which was the second largest producer of cable in Britain (the largest was British Insulated Cable). Callender's agreed to buy all its copper requirements from the Bolton company, which, in turn, agreed not to enter the cable business. On Alfred Bolton's death in 1905, Thomas Callender, son of the founder of Callender's Cable, came on the Bolton board. From then on he remained the Bolton company's policymaker, while Thomas Bolton's sons managed the day-to-day business.[82] It should be noted here that the two cable companies (British Insulated and Callender's) invested substantially in manufacturing facilities, marketed their products throughout the world, and became not only the two leading cable companies in Britain but also major players in their industry's global oligopoly (see Chapter 9).

If Thomas Bolton & Sons lost the opportunity to capitalize fully on the new technology by becoming a captive of a leading cable company, thus limiting its output to one of several markets, the other major producers did little better. J. H. Vivian & Sons, which ran a refinery that was half the size of those of its two leading competitors, lost market share and income during the 1890s and so turned increasingly to the small-scale fabrication of copper tubes, boilers, and other finished products. Elliott's Metal Company (about which I have been able to obtain little information) remained a small refining enterprise and became a subsidiary of ICI in 1928. It may have entered into an alliance with British Insulated Cable similar to the one signed in 1891 between Bolton and Callender.[83] In any event, the largest British copper mining company, the Rio Tinto, likewise failed to invest in refining in a manner comparable to that of American copper producers or the German giant, Metallgesellschaft. In 1884 Rio Tinto did acquire a copper smelter near Swansea. "Between this time and the turn of the century, however," the company's historian emphasizes, "there are few signs that the company was interested in the revolutionary changes taking place in associated industries throughout the world."[84] By 1900 the opportunity for a British firm to become a major player in the global copper oligopoly was gone, never to return.

The processors of lead and zinc were no more successful in international markets. In the years before World War I, Metallgesellschaft controlled the international cartels in both these industries. In neither one did firms comparable in size to either National Lead or St. Joseph Lead in the United States appear.[85] In nickel, Ludwig Mond (the entrepreneur born and trained in Germany who created Brunner, Mond) did invent and commercialize an electrolytic process for refining nickel. His company, Mond-Nickel, formed in 1900, built (on the site of a major nickel mine that it had purchased in Canada) a refinery large enough to exploit scale economies. It also set up a full-scale processing works in South Wales. Mond-Nickel remained a competitor in the global nickel oligopoly until it was sold in 1929 to International Nickel.[86]

Steel. For steel, production figures for Great Britain, the United States, and Germany between 1875 and 1914 tell the story (see Table 19). Until the depression of the 1870s the British had led the way in mass production of steel through two basic technological innovations—the Bessemer process, invented in 1859, and the open-hearth process, perfected in the late 1860s. British entrepreneurs pioneered in the adoption of both. Because Bessemer steel was more brittle than that of the open hearth, the Bessemer converter was used primarily for making rails, tubes, and some sheet steel, whereas higher-grade, open-hearth steel was used increasingly for beams, other structures, and ship plate. In most cases these pioneers added Bessemer converters and open-hearth furnaces to their existing iron works, which were producing iron bars or finished iron products. The initial demand for steel was primarily for rails, but in 1860 Britain's demand for rails was still relatively small. Since much of the British rail network

Table 19. Production of steel ingots and castings, by process, Great Britain, United States, and Germany, 1875–1914 (in thousand metric tons).

Year	Bessemer process			Open-hearth process			Other processes	Total
	Acid	Basic	Total	Acid	Basic	Total		
Great Britain, 1875–1914								
1875	—	—	630	—	—	89	—	719
1880	—	—	1,061	—	—	255	—	1,316
1885	—	—	1,324	—	—	594	—	1,918
1890	—	—	2,048	—	—	1,590	—	3,638
1895	—	—	1,560	—	—	1,753	—	3,313
1900	1,275	499	1,774	2,910	298	3,208	—	4,981
1905	1,419	587	2,006	3,093	808	3,901	—	5,907
1910	1,157	651	1,808	3,066	1,604	4,670	—	6,478
1914	810	490	1,300	3,741	2,922	6,663	—	7,963
United States, 1875–1914								
1875	304	—	304	—	—	7	42	353
1880	975	—	975	—	—	92	65	1,132
1885	1,378	—	1,378	—	—	121	54	1,553
1890	3,348	—	3,348	—	—	466	67	3,881
1900	6,066	—	6,066	774	2,309	3,038	96	9,245
1905	9,928	—	9,928	1,049	7,093	8,142	101	18,171
1910	8,541	—	8,541	1,100	13,876	14,976	162	23,679
1914	5,645	—	5,645	820	14,765	15,585	107	21,337
Germany, 1880–1914								
1880	679	18	697	—	—	36	—	733
1885	379	548	927	—	—	276	—	1,203
1890	351	1,493	1,844	—	—	388	—	2,232
1895	316	2,520	3,836	—	—	1,189	—	4,025
1900	223	4,142	4,365	148	1,997	2,145	136	6,646
1905	424	6,204	6,628	166	3,087	3,253	186	10,067
1910	171	8,031	8,202	140	4,974	5,114	383	13,699
1914	100	8,144	8,244	275	5,946	6,221	481	14,946

Sources: For the United States, compiled from American Iron and Steel Institute, *Annual Statistical Report, 1914,* pp. 28–29; for Great Britain and Germany, compiled from [British] National Federation of Iron and Steel Manufacturers, *Statistics of the Iron and Steel Industries, 1922,* pp. 14 and 57.

had already been laid down and the great expansion of the American and Continental systems was still to come, British producers had little incentive to invest in integrated rail mills as large as those constructed by first movers in the United States and Germany in the late 1870s and the 1880s.

In 1880 Britain was still the world's largest producer of steel, but only barely so. As the world emerged from the severe depression of the late 1870s, American and German entrepreneurs began to make investments that fully utilized the cost advantages of the new technologies. In 1879 Andrew Carnegie placed blast furnaces to produce pig iron next to the steel-producing Bessemer converters in his new Edgar Thompson rail works, making him the world's most efficient steel-rail producer (Chapter 4). In the early 1880s, as Carnegie was converting the Homestead works from rails to structures by installing open-hearth furnaces, Illinois Steel and Jones & Laughlin were building comparably giant works. At the same time the German firms—Rheinische Stahlwerke, Hoerder Verein, Dortmunder Union Bergbau, Krupp, and GHH—began to expand their Bessemer and open-hearth facilities rapidly. In Germany much more than in the United States, the invention of the "basic" Thomas-Gilchrist process in 1879 permitted steelmakers to use readily available low-grade phosphorus ores, thus assuring them a supply of inexpensive ore large enough to utilize fully the cost advantages of scale (Chapter 12). (The term "basic" was applied to the Thomas-Gilchrist process, and the steel made without benefit of that process was termed "acid.")

In both the United States and Germany the new integrated steel works, much larger than any in Britain, were able to meet the rising demand in the 1880s for tubes, pipes, wires, cables, bridges, plate, and, above all, rails and structures as the United States and Europe rapidly urbanized and industrialized. As throughput soared (see Table 19), prices fell even more in the United States than in Germany: prices of rails at works in Pennsylvania plummeted from $67.50 per ton in 1880 to $29.25 in 1889. British producers could no longer compete on either continent. Imports of British rails into the United States from 1880 to 1883 were substantial, although not quite so large as they had been in the years before 1874 (when the depression struck). After 1883 they all but disappeared. [87] Tariffs cannot account for the British loss of the American market. The only change in tariffs on iron and steel in the decade of the 1880s was a reduction in 1883. In the same years the British lost markets in Continental countries, and then in Latin America and Asia, to the Germans—markets where the Germans had to pay the same tariff as the British. [88]

By World War I, American and German steelmakers had taken the lead in all major markets except the British Empire and Britain itself. [89] As British producers lost their overseas markets, they concentrated on domestic demand, particularly on serving the British shipbuilding industry, still the world's largest. To meet this market required a shift in the late 1880s and 1890s from Bessemer to open hearth. During the decade of the 1890s roughly half of the open-hearth steel produced in Britain (more than a quarter of the total output) went to shipbuilding. [90] But nearly all of this shift came before the adoption by British steelmakers of the technological innovations in the 1890s, including mechanical charging, hot-metal practice, and the tilting furnace, which increased minimum efficient scale in open-hearth steel production. Therefore, only the larger steel mills integrated blast furnaces, open-hearth furnaces, and finishing mills. According to one estimate, in this fragmented industry twenty-one of seventy-two mills were integrated.[91]

In the late 1890s the British makers of iron and steel lost another American market, that for tin plate, to integrated producers. Again they did so, not because of tariffs, but because of the sharp drop in prices as American manufacturers developed and integrated new tin-plate processes at greatly increased throughput. (This technology is described in Chapter 4.) The McKinley tariff enacted in 1890 can hardly account for the price reduction from $5.73 a ton in 1893, before the innovators came on stream, to $2.99 in 1898. In those same years U.S. output soared—from 113,700 tons in 1895 to 360,900 tons in 1899. By 1914 American tin-plate producers were competing vigorously with the British in international markets.[92]

By World War I the United States was producing 40% and Great Britain 10% of the world's output of pig iron and steel, and Germany had become the world's largest exporter. By then Britain was importing 29% of her home consumption of iron and steel (most ingots); more than half of the imports came from Germany and the rest from the United States and Belgium.[93] As early as 1890 the German and American first movers had already acquired powerful competitive advantages in their national markets, and this, in turn, provided a base for marketing abroad. Only a courageous and somewhat irrational set of British steelmakers and financiers would have made the investment required to build and integrate works in Britain large enough to compete in price with those of Pittsburgh and the Ruhr in order to regain these most distant markets. By not doing so, however, the British lost these markets forever. After the war the loss of markets abroad and also at home continued in an even more disastrous manner. The problem was not one of quality or of delivering on schedule. In Peter Payne's words, "The essence of the problem was costs."[94]

ACCOUNTING FOR ENTREPRENEURIAL FAILURE

Why, then, did British entrepreneurs, the heirs of the First Industrial Revolution, exploit to such a limited extent the opportunities of the new technologies of the Second Revolution? The answer to this historical question is enormously complex. I have already mentioned the incentives, and the disincentives, that made opportunities in the new industries appear less attractive and more risky to British than to American and German entrepreneurs. The nation's small geographical size, its lack of raw materials, its still profitable industries—those created before the advent of the railroad and telegraph—and its extraordinarily rich consumer markets provided incentives to invest resources (facilities and personnel) in consumer industries, particularly branded, packaged products and mass retailing, and in the older producer-goods industries of the First Industrial Revolution. With these continuing opportunities for profit, investments large enough to exploit the full potential of economies of scale and scope in the new industries—steel, electrolytically produced copper and aluminum, light machinery, electrical and other heavy machinery, and chemicals—may have appeared less attractive.

In some cases the failure of British entrepreneurs to make the investments and create the organization essential to compete at home and in the new industries was quite understandable. In steel, British entrepreneurs may have been paying the price of having been pioneers before the opportunities to fully exploit the new technology appeared. Their relatively small initial investment in new production technologies, their reliance on commercial intermediaries, and their personal management—all these reflected the presence of a market still too small to exploit fully the economies of scale. When American and European markets for rails, structures, tubes, and other steel products took off in the 1880s, American and German producers had a far greater incentive to make investments that would fully utilize the cost advantages of the new technologies. They were closer geographically and also culturally to these markets. Once they had made such investments and acquired first-mover advantages, their British competitors had little choice but to turn their production to meeting the still sizable demand of the domestic British market, and particularly of its rapidly growing shipbuilding industry.

Understandable, too, was the British failure in machinery. In the mass production of light machinery American first movers had developed, before the turn of the century, such effective competitive capabilities in both production and distribution that they remained unchallenged until well after World War II. So, too, German manufacturers who had initially exploited economies of scope to build heavy machinery for the many new and growth industries easily maintained their competitive advantages. That story will be told in more detail in the German chapters.

On the other hand, in chemicals, electrical equipment, and copper, British (and French) entrepreneurs had almost the same opportunities as the Americans and Germans. In dyes and pharmaceuticals British entrepreneurs had even greater opportunities and incentives than German industrialists to create new enterprises. In electrical equipment, British inventors were as innovative and British markets as potentially lucrative as any in the world. In copper, the owners and operators of the Rio Tinto Company and the three leading processors had an even better opportunity to dominate European markets than the Mertons who established Metallgesellschaft.

In those three industries the availability of capital in Britain was hardly a constraint; London was the largest and most sophisticated capital market in the world. The more successful British companies had no difficulty in raising funds there. German and American first movers financed their subsidiaries in London.[95] Nor, of course, was the availability of trained labor a constraint. The workers in the factories of these foreign subsidiaries were British.

Whatever the exact reasons for such entrepreneurial failure were, two points are clear. First, entrepreneurial failure in the new industries can be precisely defined. It was the failure to make the three-pronged investment in production, distribution, and management essential to exploit economies of scale and scope. Second, the time period in which that investment could have been made was short. Once first movers from other nations had entered the British market, often supplementing their marketing organizations by direct investment in production, the window of opportunity was closed.

And once closed, that window was difficult to reopen. One reason was that continuing, cumulative innovation within an industry usually occurred within established enterprises. Thus when British steelmakers attempted to modernize their industry in the interwar years, they had to rely wholly on American techniques and methods. Likewise, in chemicals—organic, electrical, agricultural—research and development had remained concentrated in Germany and the United States, at least until after World War I. In electrical equipment the innovation and commercialization of products and processes continued in Berlin, Schenectady, and Pittsburgh. Moreover, what was true of innovations in production was also true of those in distribution and marketing. Here British challengers had to compete both at home and abroad against established firms with national and international sales organizations whose experienced managers understood the many and changing needs of their customers.

Even in those industries where British entrepreneurs made the necessary three-pronged investment, they recruited fewer salaried managers and placed a smaller number of them on the governing boards of their enterprises than American and German industrialists did. In those industries British industrialists appear in general to have had a distrust or dislike of losing personal control over enterprises they had either created or inherited. Throughout the late nineteenth century British entrepreneurs continued to view their businesses in personal rather than organizational terms, as family estates to be nurtured and passed on to heirs.

Growth through Merger and Acquisition, British Style

This British bias for small-scale operation and personal management is particularly striking when one examines national differences in the patterns of industrial growth through merger and acquisition. In both the United States and Britain, approximately as many large-scale industrial enterprises were created by merger as by direct investment in marketing and distribution. In the United States, however, mergers were often planned as preliminary legal moves necessary for achieving economies of throughput by integrating high-volume production with large-scale distribution. There mergers preceded the investments in production and distribution that determined key players in the new oligopoly. In Britain this pattern rarely occurred until the 1930s. In the United States, mergers led to recruitment of centralized, corporate, managerial hierarchies and then to the development of new organizational capabilities. In Britain, mergers remained collections of small, personally run (usually family-managed) firms. Thus, whereas in the United States mergers often represented first steps in augmenting market power through functional and strategic efficiencies, in Britain they remained no more than a device to maintain market power through contractual cooperation.

In both countries, major merger movements came at almost precisely the same time: during a short period in the late 1880s—in Britain a little earlier than in the United States—and then during a longer period at the turn of the century, between 1897 and 1902. The number of mergers in Britain was smaller, however, and on average they involved fewer firms. "In 1899 alone," Leslie Hannah reports, "there were 979 firm disappearances by merger in the United States valued at $2,062 million (over £400 million), compared with 255 firm disappearances valued at only £22 million in Great Britain."[96] Moreover, while British mergers clustered in a relatively narrow range of established industries, primarily in brewing and textiles, in the United States they came in the new capital-intensive industries.

In Britain the initial drive to seek market control on a national scale through cooperative association resulted—as it did in the United States and Germany—from the expanding use of improved production technologies, which intensified competition by driving output ahead of existing demand. Prices declined about the same time in all three countries. As in the United States and Germany, British manufacturers quickly turned to informal agreements concerning price, output, and quality. "Almost every trade," Peter Mathias reports, "possessed its groupings in the 1880s."[97]

Again as in the United States, the basic problem was one of enforcement. Like their American counterparts, British industrialists soon turned to more formal agreements—cartels which supplemented price-fixing agreements with production quotas, market allocation, and even pooling of profits. Normally they formed trade associations to enforce these cartel arrangements. Still, however, enforcement remained a problem, for the precedents of British common law made such combinations in restraint of trade illegal in both countries. The significance of such common-law precedents was not that they were being used to bring action by consumers or by competitors who resented the market power acquired by these associations. Very few such cases were brought in British courts against trade associations or other combinations for anticompetitive practices. Indeed, the most important cases in the 1890s were decided in favor of maintaining such agreements.[98] The significance of common-law precedents was that such contractual agreements could not be enforced in British (or American) courts of law as they could be in Germany and the other European nations. A parliamentary report published in 1927 put it this way: "As regards terminal agreements and associations, the neutral attitude of the [British] State is qualified by the application of the doctrine of English common law that agreements 'in restraint of trade' are legally unenforceable."[99] For this reason cartels in Britain remained weak and often ineffective.

Therefore British manufacturers, like their American counterparts, turned to legal consolidation. The methods used were much the same in both countries. Occasionally a firm would acquire fellow members of an association or cartel, either by cash purchase or, more often, by using newly issued shares of the new company to pay for assets acquired. The normal way, however, was to form a holding company which exchanged its stock for that of each of the constituent enterprises. The resulting control thus assured that price, production schedules, and other arrangements could be legally maintained.

As I have already pointed out, these British holding companies were of two types. One, illustrated by Imperial Tobacco, was a combination of a large number of relatively small, single-function, family enterprises. Such horizontal combinations often included as many as sixty or eighty constituent firms. The second type, illustrated by the Cadbury-Fry alliance, was a combination of two or three leading family firms in an industry. The first type—the one with more members—occurred largely in textiles, with a small number in cement and two or three in other industries such as tobacco; the second was more common in metal making, metal fabrication (including shipbuilding), brewing, and food processing. In metals and shipbuilding, but rarely in other industries, combinations were often vertical as well as horizontal.[100]

In neither of these two types of British holding companies did legal consolidation bring administrative centralization, new investment in production and distribution facilities, or the recruitment of salaried top and middle managers. Governing boards often made arrangements for joint purchasing and occasionally even for joint research. More often, uniform financial and operating accounting was established in order to determine prices and profits in relation to output more accurately. In most cases the directors of the constituent companies remained responsible, as they had been before the merger, for the day-to-day production and distribution of their products. The parent company's central office was usually little more than a meeting place for a board of directors who, as representatives of owners of constituent firms, determined through negotiation both output and prices. Occasionally they allocated funds for a joint plant or sales activities, usually overseas.

Peter Payne has noted: "In iron and steel, as in brewing, the perpetuation of family control remained a major desideratum."[101] In the mergers involving two or three leaders in an industry, the constituent companies often continued to be listed separately in the *Stock Exchange Year Book,* as was true of Cadbury & Fry. In the mergers involving numerous firms, their boards, which included representatives from many constituent companies, were large and unwieldy. As a result, the Calico Printers' Association (controlling 85% of the industry) had a board of eighty-four members; Fine Cotton Spinners' & Doublers' Association had thirty-one; and Associated Portland Cement, in addition to its managing directors, had forty "ordinary" board members.[102] The situation was similar in the Bleachers' Association, made up of fifty-three firms; in the British Cotton & Wool Dyers' Association, consisting of forty-six firms; in Salt Union, a merger of sixty-three firms that represented close to 90% of the industry's output; and in United Alkali, a combination of forty-eight companies. Nearly all of these, as well as other similar mergers, remained loose federations. Indeed, the preamble of incorporation of both Calico Printers and English Sewing Cotton said, in words that closely followed those of the Bradford Dyers' Association: "It is intended as far as possible that control of each firm shall remain in the hands of those who have been responsible for its conduct in the past."[103]

There were, however, exceptions. A few combinations did begin to establish a small central corporate office. One was J. & P. Coats, a merger in 1896 of four family thread-making companies which had been previously allied through a joint sales agency. Though it did not centralize production management, Coats did build an extensive national and international sales organization under the guidance of a German-born and German-trained manager. It also marketed the products of English Sewing Cotton, a comparable combination. In addition, the Coats company enlarged plants that its constituent companies had already built abroad, and it constructed new ones in both the United States and Europe. Sir Arthur Coats stated in 1899 that half of his company's profits came from abroad. In 1898 J. & P. Coats and its ally, English Sewing Cotton, promoted and financed the American Thread Company, a merger of fourteen U.S. thread producers. Together the subsidiaries of Coats and English Sewing Cotton were said to control two-thirds of all cotton-thread output in the United States.[104] By 1917 American Thread was the third largest U.S. textile company, and it ranked 160th among U.S. industrial enterprises in terms of assets. Nevertheless, because its production technology could not provide major scale economies (in striking contrast to rayon), and because distribution had few product-specific requirements, American Thread lost market share, failed to grow, and made only modest profits.

The other British textile merger that began to recruit managers was the Fine Cotton Spinners' & Doublers' Association. The former owners of its constituent companies continued to manufacture and sell their specific product lines, but their activities were coordinated by the hard-driving Managing Director, Herbert Dixon. Under Dixon's guidance the company invested in cotton plantations in the United States and in a firm that exported Egyptian cotton. It set up a central purchasing office and even established a research laboratory in 1900, but the constituent companies continued to have full control over their own buying and selling. In both British textile mergers the central offices remained much smaller than those of the successful American mergers.[105]

In chemicals, two mergers—in alkalies and explosives—built embryonic hierarchies. The United Alkali Company established its central office in response to adversity. It was formed in February 1891 by producers using the Leblanc process in order to meet the competition from Brunner, Mond, which was using the much more efficient Solvay process, and it went beyond mere legal consolidation. The new company placed its works under district managers, appointed a technical director, began to centralize sales and purchasing, and set up financial controls; it then established a research laboratory. But it continued to rely more on committees than on departments to coordinate its functional activities; and according to its historian, "there was no manufacturing department in the central office."[106] Nor is it clear how much rationalization of plant and equipment actually took place. In any case, the company failed to invest in the new electrolytic process for making alkalies that would have made its production costs comparable to those of Solvay. This was due partly to a negative recommendation by its research chemist and partly to its weak financial position, which deterred it from building the costly facilities it needed to obtain cost advantages of scale from the new technology. It continued in business because of the willingness of Brunner, Mond to let its weak rival stay alive, and also because it moved away from competing directly with Brunner, Mond and concentrated on making other products, particularly pyrites and sulphuric acid, that used existing capabilities in the purchasing and processing of raw and intermediate materials.[107]

The central office of the Nobel Dynamite Trust Company, whose technology was much more suited to achieving economies of throughput, remained even smaller than that of United Alkali Company. The 1886 merger between the Nobel Explosives Company of Glasgow and the German Union—four smaller German dynamite firms whose total sales were less than those of the British company—was essentially a legal and financial arrangement. The constituent companies continued to manage their own production and distribution. The parent institution, the Nobel Dynamite Trust Company, Ltd., had no central buying office or even a research laboratory. In fact, the British subsidiary did not have research facilities until 1909, and these served primarily to improve quality control. The subsidiaries could borrow from the trust. They could also go to outside sources if they so desired. As the board of directors explained, the trust's purpose was "to check competition and to prevent the lowering of prices, and to achieve savings by lowering advertising and other marketing expenses and by reducing inventories."[108] In explosives, as in other British industries, the purpose of mergers was to assure market power through contractual cooperation.

The British merger that most closely followed the American pattern was the Metropolitan Amalgamated Railway Carriage & Wagon Company, a consolidation in 1902 of five producers of rolling stock and a maker of specialized tires and axles. Although representatives of the former family owners of the constituent companies remained on the new board and although reorganization was not achieved until six years after the merger, the company's organizer, Dudley Docker, an able Birmingham industrialist, did rationalize production and recruit a small managerial team. He centralized purchasing, instituted uniform accounting, purchased a steel plant in Belgium, closed down two factories, and improved facilities in others. These moves permitted the company to maintain its position in the domestic market, the British Empire, and Latin America; but Docker's moves came too late to regain lost markets in Europe and North America. [109]

In one sense it is surprising that hardly any British industrialists followed Docker's example. The organizational structures of Standard Oil, Du Pont, American Tobacco, General Electric, and the many other American consolidations were well known in Britain. Indeed, Henry W. Macrosty, in the introduction to his widely read *Trust Movement in British Industry,* which was published in London in 1907, emphasized "the advantages which the amalgamation possesses over the association or cartel." He said that those advantages

> arise out of its permanency and the more complete control over production. Superfluous or badly equipped plants can be closed, mills can be specialized, concentration of establishments will enable greater economies of large-scale production to be made, and, above all, the best brains of the trade in any department are put at the disposal of all branches of the combination. [110]

Such rationalization, Macrosty warned, required administrative centralization:

> When amalgamation is formed virtually on the federal principle, these interests inevitably clash and dire confusion results as in several of the textile trusts. In the most highly organized form of amalgamation all functions are carefully defined and graded so that proper subordination is observed, and the whole edifice culminates in a small board of directors who form, so to speak, the cabinet of the industry. [111]

In another sense, however, the failure to follow Docker's example or to heed Macrosty's advice is quite understandable. In industries where mergers were concentrated—in textiles, food, beverages, cement—the potential economies of scale were small and the potential for such rationalization limited. Moreover, the British mergers worked. The incorporated federations that resulted did what was expected of them, as long as they did not have to compete with companies from abroad or from related industries. They were able to control price and output, at least for the constituent firms within their enterprises.

Continuing Dominance of Personal Management

The British industrialists' success in maintaining power through contractual cooperation was one reason that the ways of personal management lasted much longer in large industrial enterprises in Great Britain than in the United States. Another reason was the geographical compactness and slow growth of the domestic market. And still another factor was the uncertainties connected with direct supervision and distant overseas activities. These legal and marketing conditions reduced pressure on British manufacturers to rationalize production and to invest extensively in distribution. By lessening the need for trained managers, they encouraged the continuance of the family firm. In Britain, sons and other relatives of the founders usually took over control of the enterprise. In some cases they selected board members from their managerial ranks, but even as late as World War II this remained the exception rather than the rule. In the United States nepotism had a pejorative connotation. In Britain it was an accepted way of life.

As Donald Coleman has suggested, the management of British companies included "gentlemen"—the sons of the founding fathers—and "players"—the salaried managers, the practical men whose ability brought them into partnership with the gentlemen. As Coleman further suggests, the primary ambition of a player was to become a gentleman. [112] In such personally managed firms, growth was not a primary objective. In Britain the more efficient family firms were less aggressive than American managerial firms, preferring cooperation to price competition. As William Reader, describing Brunner, Mond's relation to United Alkali, has put it, "the whole principle of the system was 'live and let live,' because price competition was so destructive of profit; and it depended on deliberate self-restraint by the stronger firms."[113] In addition, the profits made by the enterprise went to the owners. Many preferred current income to large-scale, long-term reinvestment in their enterprise. This view made it easy to accept live-and-let-live attitudes and to hold back on expanding investment in production, distribution, research, and development, and on the recruitment, training, and promoting of salaried managers—all of which were fundamental to the continuing, successful exploitation of the new technologies.

These values were reflected in the British institutions of higher learning. Their response to the needs of the new industrial enterprises was slow, both in regard to generating scientific information and in graduating trained managers. These were needs to which the American and German colleges, universities, and institutes responded very quickly. In Britain the gentlemen and the players received different kinds of education. The players were trained on the job, serving as apprentices in production or as articled clerks in accounting and finance. Such players—production managers or engineers, as they were termed, and accountants—established professional societies well before the turn of the century. Even after World War I the members of these societies of engineers and accountants continued to agree that practical work on the job was far more useful than spending the same amount of time at a university. For the gentlemen, education meant Oxford or Cambridge. Even those who attended the new "red brick" civic universities tended to agree with their colleagues at the ancient Oxbridge institutions about the goal of university education.[114] The aim of universities was less to search for knowledge and more, in a phrase cited by Eric Ashby, to be "a nursery for gentlemen, statesmen and administrators." Ashby adds: "Where science was beginning to be pursued, as it was at Cambridge in particular, clear distinction was made between science and vocation."[115] Training in science was a proper function of the university; vocational training was not. As a result of this belief, the critical linkage between higher education and industry, so essential to the development of long-term industrial capabilities in Germany and the United States, remained tenuous in Britain before 1914 and continued to be so during the interwar years.

Robert Locke, writing in the 1980s, noted that in Britain "the university and the business and industrial community always treat each other with indifference, if not distrust and hostility."[116] Oxford, Cambridge, and the red brick universities did establish chairs in engineering, but the professors who occupied them had few students. In 1913 the number of engineering students graduating from the universities of England and Wales was 1,129. In the same year three or four of the leading American engineering schools graduated that number, and the engineers graduating from German universities and institutes were ten times that number. Moreover, far less interest was shown in business and commercial education than in engineering. In the years when business schools in the United States and the Handelshochschulen in Germany were growing rapidly, Oxford and Cambridge taught no business subjects. They did not do so until long after World War II. Civic universities did offer undergraduate business courses, but few students attended. Until 1932, when the London School of Economics started a graduate program in commercial education, there was no graduate work in Britain in commerce or business.

Thus the limited supply of academically trained managers reflected the limited demand. In all but a handful of even the largest companies the owners preferred to recruit lower and middle managers from personnel with long on-the-job training within the company and to select top management from their own families or from those of their close associates. As a result, the educational infrastructure so essential to sustaining modern industry appeared much later in Britain than in the United States and Germany.

The continuance of management by a small number of gentlemen and players had the least impact on the performance of large enterprises in industries where the exploitation of scale economies did not call for technologically sophisticated processes of production or for specialized marketing and distribution skills or organizations. In branded, packaged foods and consumer chemicals, marketing required little more than placing advertising through specialized agencies, calling on distributors and retailers, and coordinating flows to see that deliveries arrived on time. Younger generations of gentlemen might easily learn to administer the marketers, as well as the engineers and accountants, under their command.

But where high-volume production and distribution required extensive investment in complex, product-specific production and distribution facilities and the creation of product-specific technical and managerial skills, personal management constrained the growth of enterprises and the industries in which they operated. Even where British entrepreneurs in the new industries did make the investments in manufacturing, marketing, and management that were needed to compete effectively at home and abroad, their preference for personal management slowed the development of the functional and administrative skills necessary to maintain market share and to grow by exploiting competitive capabilities. Their enterprises moved overseas more hesitantly and less successfully than those of many of their foreign competitors. They also moved more slowly and less systematically than did German and American companies into industries where economies of scope provided them a competitive advantage.

The economic costs of the commitment to personal management were high. In the new industries the period before the window of opportunity closed was brief. In many cases the time between the initial commercializing of a new product or process and the coming of the three-pronged investment that determined the players in an industry was little more than a decade. Because British entrepreneurs hesitated, Americans and Germans made the investments that permitted them to dominate British as well as international markets. They did so in copper and other nonferrous metals; in abrasives and tin containers; in organic chemicals and electrochemicals; in light mass-produced office, sewing, and agricultural machinery and automobiles; in light industrial machines from elevators to printing presses; in electrical equipment that powered the new factories and provided light and transportation to the world's growing cities; and in the heavy machinery used to produce the unprecedented volume of goods in both old and new industries.

By World War I the industrial output of the United States and of Germany was outpacing that of Great Britain. For Britishers the surge of German industrial power posed more of a threat than the American. The Americans still concentrated on their own vast and rapidly expanding domestic market. Their role in world affairs complemented rather than challenged British hegemony. The Germans, on the other hand, competed much more directly with the British in international, particularly European, markets. Moreover, German industrial strength was permitting that nation to challenge Britain's international political dominance—the first serious challenge since 1815, that is, since Napoleon's defeat at Waterloo. When, partly as a result of the growing Anglo-German rivalry, the first global war to occur for a century erupted in the summer of 1914, British industrialists and statesmen saw an opportunity to regain their nation's industrial power.

EIGHT

Creating Organizational Capabilities: Success and Failure in the Stable Industries

By World War I the British had become "late industrializers" (to use Alexander Gerschenkron's widely applied term) in the new industries that were the dynamos driving the growth of industrial capitalism after the 1880s.[1] Thus, if they were to compete at home and abroad, British manufacturers in many of these industries had to become challengers and surmount the first-mover advantages of their international rivals by investing in essential facilities and developing the necessary organizational capabilities.

The Impact of World War I

World War I provided British enterprises in the new industries with an unexpected opportunity to meet these challenges. It did so in three ways. First, the war made British industrialists more aware of the advantages of closely coordinating production and distribution. They observed improved coordination of flows and more systematic allocations of resources by government-industry committees; by government directions concerning price controls, rationing, and export licensing; by government purchasing; and even by government ownership. Second, the war forced British industry to provide chemicals and machinery for which British users had hitherto depended on German and American producers. Third, the war, by depriving German industrial enterprises of their international markets for almost half a decade, eroded their first-mover advantages. Industrialists in the Allied nations built new capacity in these industries.[2] At the same time the governments of Britain, France, the United States, Japan, and other Allied countries expropriated German factories and marketing subsidiaries and then turned them over to leading domestic manufacturers. Producers in neutral nations—the Swiss in chemicals and machinery, and the Swedes and Dutch in machinery—moved into markets vacated by the Germans.

From the war's outset British manufacturers were keenly aware of these war-created opportunities. Many agreed with the Birmingham industrialist Dudley Docker that they provided "a 'mighty solvent' for the future, a last chance to stop the German and American rivals from spoiling British industrial hegemony."[3]

The response to these opportunities came quickly. In oil the voracious demand for fuel oil and to a lesser extent gasoline and lubricants, along with the dismemberment of the two large, integrated German enterprises, permitted Anglo-Persian Oil to emerge as the third most powerful member of the global oligopoly, next to Standard Oil (New Jersey) and Royal Dutch–Shell. In rubber an increased call for tires and other products strengthened Dunlop's position at home and in the global oligopoly. In chemicals the formation of British Dyes, a government corporation, and the greatly increased production of benzol, toluol, and other intermediates helped to give Britain her second chance in the organic-chemical industry. In electrical equipment the expropriation of Siemens's British subsidiary and the acquisition of British Westinghouse Electric gave British manufacturers their first strong position in that critical industry. Although Americans continued to dominate in mass-produced light machinery, including automobiles, the demand for trucks and motorized military equipment, as well as the development of the tractor for use in Britain's agriculture, laid a base for that nation's motor vehicle industry.[4] In metals, particularly steel, an expanded capacity and greater vertical integration within works increased output and lowered unit costs.[5]

Nevertheless, although World War I led to the investment in production facilities that was necessary to achieve and maintain the cost advantages of scale, it did not bring the building of comparable marketing networks, for nearly all these products went to meet military demands. Nor did war requirements lead to the building of corporate offices of middle and top management. Instead, industrial coordination and monitoring was accomplished by the government and inter-industry bureaus and committees.

In the immediate postwar years the institutional arrangements that had brought such a great increase in output came to an end. Sidney Pollard has written that "'back to 1914' became a common cry and by the middle of 1922 the whole machinery of government control was dismantled." Industry structure soon reverted to what it had been before 1914. In industries where large firms had created organizational capability these firms continued to dominate. Where they had not, the industry operated through small, personally managed firms, though these were often tied together by trade associations or by holding companies. Wartime cooperation did strengthen trade associations and encouraged a rash of postwar mergers. Indeed, in 1919 the Parliamentary Committee on Trusts reported that it was "satisfied that Trade Associations and Combines are rapidly increasing in this country, and may, within no distant period, exercise permanent control over all important branches of British industry."[6] Yet with only a few, but significant, exceptions these mergers were not consummated in the American manner. They remained federations of small, personally managed firms that failed to rationalize facilities or to develop overall organizational capabilities thus increasing the productivity and competitiveness of the combined enterprises or the industry as a whole.

In this chapter and the next I will track the success or failure of British enterprises to exploit the opportunities created by World War I. My method will be the same as that followed for American industry: to examine industry by industry the collective history of the firms on the basis of a representative sample—the nation's largest two hundred manufacturing enterprises. In this chapter I begin (as I did in Chapter 4) with oil and rubber and then proceed to glass, paper, and other materials, followed by fabricated and primary metals. Because of the importance of textiles to the British economy I pay more attention to the man-made and natural-fiber industries than I gave the American textile industry. In the next chapter I take up the collective history of the leaders in machinery, chemicals, and branded consumer products—industries where organizational capabilities based on the exploitation of both the economies of scale and those of scope provided the greatest opportunities for enterprises to grow by expanding abroad and into related industries.

The Modern Industrial Enterprise during the Interwar Years

In Britain the two hundred largest industrial firms were even more concentrated in a few industrial groups than they were in the United States (see Table 7). In 1919, 88.5% of the top two hundred were clustered in textiles, food, chemicals, metals, and machinery. In 1948 the figure was 77.0%. The one striking difference between this concentration and that in the United States was the large number of firms in textiles—a labor-intensive industry that did not lend itself to extensive economies of scale. During the interwar years the number of firms in the older textile, food, and metal industries declined, and the number in the newer chemical, machinery, and metals industries increased slightly. Nevertheless, the continuing concentration of the large firms in the long-established industries is impressive.

The lists of the top two hundred companies show more turnover of individual firms in Britain during the interwar years than in the United States. There are several reasons for this. One is the differing criteria used for selecting firms for the lists. Although the capital assets of individual firms are readily available in the United States and Germany, they are not in Britain, for British firms were not called on to produce consolidated balance sheets until after 1948. Therefore the only available criterion by which to rank British companies is the market value of the enterprise's shares. Because these values reflect the security market's more volatile appraisal of the worth of an enterprise's shares, British companies move up and down and on and off the list more rapidly than American companies. Much more significantly, however, the smaller size, and often the lack, of managerial hierarchies meant that British firms were more susceptible to changes in product markets and sources of supplies, as well as to weaknesses in entrepreneurial and managerial skills. Not surprisingly, the British firms that did create sizable managerial hierarchies remained among the largest in the kingdom throughout the entire period. There was much less turnover among the top fifty than there was among the rest. Also, because British firms remained smaller and more personally managed, they often failed to develop the facilities and skills necessary to grow by expanding into new markets abroad or into related industries. Moreover, the owner-managers of these enterprises often preferred to pay out profits in current dividends rather than reinvesting them in the firm for long-term growth. Therefore, British industrial firms grew more by merger and acquisition than by direct investment—more through horizontal combination and vertical integration than by direct investments in new markets. During the interwar years more firms dropped off the list because they were absorbed by merger than happened among the top two hundred in the United States.

Oil: The Creation of Organizational Capabilities

In oil (Group 29; see Appendixes B.1–B.3), the Anglo-Persian Oil Company, which became the Anglo-Iranian Oil Company in 1935 and British Petroleum in 1955, is the centerpiece of Britain's story. Its history demonstrates how carefully planned, extensive investment in production, distribution, and management and the resulting creation of organizational capabilities permitted a British company to overcome the first-mover advantages of existing rivals and to become a major player in its global oligopoly.

At the turn of the century British consumers of kerosene, gasoline, lubricants, fuel oil, and other petroleum products were supplied almost completely by a Standard Oil subsidiary, Anglo-American Oil. Although Anglo-American was spun off legally from Standard Oil by the U.S. Supreme Court decision in the 1911 antitrust case, its internal organization and its relationship with its formal parent were little changed. In the first decade of the new century two more foreign enterprises began to compete vigorously for a share of the lucrative British market. One was Royal Dutch–Shell, the 1907 merger of the Royal Dutch Company and the British-owned and British-managed Shell Transport and Trading, in which the Dutch held 60% and the British 40% of the voting stock. The other was a German firm, Europäische Petroleum Union (EPU), formed in 1906 (described in Chapter 11), which quickly set up a marketing subsidiary in Britain called British Petroleum.[7]

The one large British company, Burmah Oil, which began refining in Burma after 1896, sold its product in the Eastern Hemisphere, primarily in India, where it competed with Standard Oil and worked closely with Shell. In 1909 Burmah Oil formed a subsidiary, the Anglo-Persian Oil Company, to exploit the huge field its geologists had discovered two years earlier near the Persian Gulf. This was the Anglo-Persian Oil Company which within a few crowded years became the third most influential member of the global petroleum oligopoly.[8]

Although Anglo-Persian operations were in full swing when World War I broke out in 1914, the war gave that enterprise its critical opportunity by permitting it to make the investments necessary to challenge the first movers; at the same time the war removed the two German firms that had begun to challenge Standard Oil and Royal Dutch–Shell in the decade before 1914. The company's pipeline from its Persian oil field to its refinery on the coast at Abadan was completed in 1911, and the refinery went into operation in 1912. Because its crude was heavy and therefore less suitable than most for gasoline and kerosene, its primary product was fuel oil.

In 1914 the British government paid £2.0 million for a controlling 51% interest in Anglo-Persian. The deal was made after lengthy negotiations between Winston Churchill, the First Lord of the Admiralty, who wanted an assured supply of fuel oil for the British Navy, and Anglo-Persian, which desperately needed an assured market for its high output. Burmah Oil continued to hold a sizable block of the remaining shares.[9] The transaction provided the funds for further investment in refining and an initial investment in transportation and marketing. It also meant that the Anglo-Persian Oil Company would not remain a personally owned and operated enterprise, like its parent, Burmah, and the great majority of British industrial enterprises.

Charles Greenway, an entrepreneurially minded salaried executive, taking office in 1910 as Anglo-Persian's managing director, defined its strategy of growth. This strategy reflected Greenway's experience in working for Shaw, Wallace & Company, Ltd., the managing agency that carried on Burmah Oil's refining operations. Shaw, Wallace was typical of a special type of British enterprise—the managing agency. Such firms managed the operations of several British-owned and -based companies within a single region of the Near and the Far East. While at Shaw, Wallace, Greenway had contracted to have Royal Dutch and Shell Transport and Trading market Burmah Oil's products in the Indian markets. He soon realized how dependent Burmah had become on its major competitors. Thus when he became managing director at Anglo-Persian, Greenway did his best to make his enterprise independent of the region's dominant oil firms. But in the spring of 1912 increasing difficulties in operating the recently completed refinery and lack of the funds essential to build an independent organization led Greenway to hire a Persian Gulf managing agency—Strick, Scott and Company—to operate the refinery and pipeline and to market the output in the Gulf and nearby Mesopotamia. At the same time Greenway signed a ten-year marketing agreement with Royal Dutch–Shell's Asiatic Petroleum Company to distribute Anglo-Persian's products in Asia and Africa. With its own capabilities not yet developed, Anglo-Persian had to rely on the facilities and skills of others.[10]

It was the government's purchase of 51% of the company's shares and the outbreak of war in Europe that gave Greenway the opportunity to carry out his goal of creating an integrated enterprise. He wanted, in his own words, "to build up an absolutely self-contained organization." The company's historian, Ronald W. Ferrier, writes of Greenway: "He aimed at a company producing, transporting and distributing products directly to customers 'wherever there may be a profitable outlet for them without intervention of any third parties.'"[11]

Greenway's first step was to expand what was already one of the world's largest refineries at Abadan, increasing its annual throughput from 124,000 tons (approximately 893,000 barrels) in 1913–1914 to 225,000 (1,620,000) in the next fiscal year, to 476,000 in 1916–1917, and then to 923,000 (6,645,600) in the next year. Although the company did not formally dissolve its agreement with the managing agency (Strick, Scott) until after the war, the refinery manager soon came under the direct control of the company's London headquarters.[12]

In 1915 Greenway, who had become chairman of the board as well as managing director, began the move into distribution and marketing by forming a wholly owned subsidiary, the British Tanker Company. That company was to buy, build, and operate a fleet of tankers and to achieve Greenway's goal of having 90% of the company's shipping requirements carried by its own facilities. By 1920 that fleet numbered more than thirty ships. In the meantime, in May 1917 Greenway had acquired (for £2.65 million) British Petroleum, the marketing subsidiary of the German oil company, EPU, a subsidiary which had been expropriated by the British government as enemy property. In negotiating for its purchase with the Board of Trade and the Public Trustee responsible for enemy property, Greenway argued successfully that his company would thus obtain a marketing organization in Britain "which it would take any new company many years to build up" and at the same time prevent "a foreign firm," Royal Dutch–Shell, from becoming a major influence in the British market.[13]

Further expansion came in refining. In 1917 Greenway had decided to build a refinery at Swansea in Wales with an improved refining technology that could produce gasoline and other lighter products from Persian crude for British and European markets. Finally, a small research laboratory, first set up in 1917 in the basement of a country house in Sunbury, was enlarged into "a proper laboratory" in 1921.[14]

All these investments in physical facilities were accompanied by recruitment of the necessary operating and managerial personnel. In this way Greenway's entrepreneurial vision, the government's investment in the company, and the coming of World War I, which greatly increased Britain's demand for oil and eliminated German competition, permitted Anglo-Persian Oil to challenge Standard Oil (New Jersey) and Shell in both British and international markets and so to become the third ranking player in the global oligopoly.

Aggressive expansion in all functional activities during the 1920s reinforced the company's position. Immediately after the coming of peace it established marketing subsidiaries in Norway, Denmark, Belgium, and France. In Austria, Switzerland, and Germany it purchased a controlling interest in Deutsche Erdöl's marketing subsidiaries (see Chapter 11). Then after the expiration of the ten-year contracts with Royal Dutch–Shell in Asia and Africa in 1922, the company set up its own marketing and distributing organizations in those regions. In Britain and on the Continent it followed the lead of Anglo-American and Standard's Continental subsidiaries by investing initially in a network of bulk storage plants for gasoline and then in pumps for garages and service stations. At first the company gave the pumps to retailers without charge; soon, however, it began selling them, normally at a £25 loss per installation. By 1925 Anglo-Persian's British Petroleum had 6,058 pumps in Great Britain as compared with 6,168 for Anglo-American and 4,296 for Shell's subsidiary. In these same years the company's shipping was greatly expanded, so that by 1928 the fleet included eighty seagoing tankers, five coastal vessels, and thirteen more seagoing ships on charter. Refining capacity was enlarged with the establishment of new refineries in Scotland and France. The laboratory at Sunbury expanded its activities and began to concentrate on improving gasoline and kerosene. By far the largest share of the funding for this expansion in the several functional activities came from retained earnings.[15] Such financial independence helped Greenway achieve still another of his goals by 1922—that of having the British government and the government's representatives on the board of directors "accept market forces and a special relationship of amicable indifference, perhaps diffidence, to the Company."[16] Such diffidence from Anglo-Persian's most influential outside directors continued until well after World War II.

Just as Greenway provided an outstanding example of a highly successful builder of business empires (one of the few that Britain produced), John Cadman, his successor, was one of the few effective British organization-builders. Whereas Greenway had made the essential initial investments in facilities and personnel, Cadman built up the enterprise's organizational capabilities that assured its position in the international oligopoly.

A professor of mining at the University of Birmingham, Cadman had headed the British government's wartime Petroleum Executive, an office which in 1917 took charge of allocating and distributing short-term oil supplies and planned, long-term oil flows.[17] On becoming managing director of Anglo-Persian in September 1925, Cadman immediately drafted a plan of administrative reorganization which set up a carefully defined "system of line management derived from military models and American administrative experience." In this centralized, functionally departmentalized structure, Cadman defined "four main directorates: (1) technical operations of discovery and production and refining; (2) distribution and the marketing of refined oil products; (3) finance in all its aspects; and (4) general services." Within each directorate there were several functional departments. The managing directors of these departments, as in American oil companies, sat on the board as inside directors with Cadman, who became chairman in 1927. Together the inside directors planned strategy and allocated resources to implement the plans. To assist the top managers in coordinating and monitoring activities and in allocating resources, Cadman strengthened the role of the advisory staff and adopted budgetary and capital-allocation procedures that were as advanced as any yet developed in Britain.[18] The resulting centralized, functionally departmentalized administrative organization was quite similar to that instituted by Pierre S. du Pont at his company twenty years earlier. One difference was that the outside directors at Du Pont, particularly Pierre's relatives, were less diffident than those at Anglo-Persian.

By 1927 Anglo-Persian had become a business enterprise with trained, salaried, full-time managers that, though smaller, had the competitive capabilities of Shell or Standard Oil (New Jersey). Not surprisingly then, in 1928 after the opening of the great new Texas fields and a new Anglo-Persian field in Persia had created the world's first great oil glut, it was those three companies that addressed the problem. John Cadman met with Walter Teagle of Jersey Standard and Sir Henri Deterding of Royal Dutch–Shell at Achnacarray, Scotland, in August 1928.

There they worked out the well-known "As is" agreement, by which the three global giants agreed in principle to maintain market share as it then existed, to stabilize prices, and to cooperate where possible in the use of existing resources. This arrangement was reinforced by the Memorandum for European Markets, approved in January 1930, by which the three companies agreed that their local representatives would consult on prices and selling conditions with the aim of stabilizing competition. As the glut continued and the worldwide depression became worse, the other American oil companies which still had extensive overseas holdings—Texaco, Gulf, Standard Oil of California, and Socony-Vacuum (which later became Mobil)—joined with the Big Three in an agreement in December 1932 which, with further stipulations, was signed in June 1934. Fifty years later those seven—known as the Seven Sisters—remained the leaders of the world's most renowned global oligopoly.

Committees had been set up in New York and London to monitor the agreements, but in the early 1930s these became little more than forums for the exchange of information and ideas. Because of American antitrust laws and the

inevitable disagreements among the participants—as well as the lack of enforcement procedures—the "As is" agreement remained a set of broad principles
rather than the foundation of a tight cartel. In the words of Ronald Ferrier,
"Achnacarry became a symbol of stabilization. It was never the machinery for
global implementation . . . It acted as a keel to the industry, never its rudder."[19]

Instead, the more specific arrangements continued to be handled by more
enforceable regional or local agreements. In Britain, for example, Shell's British
subsidiary (Shell-Mex) and Anglo-Persian's subsidiary (British Petroleum)
merged in 1932 in the normal British fashion to form a new distribution company, unimaginatively named Shell-Mex & BP, Ltd., with Shell having a 60%
interest and Anglo-Persian 40%. As in the case of most British holding companies the arrangement was only a legal device to set output and price. Otherwise, the two marketing subsidiaries continued to operate autonomously and
to receive their refined products from the two parent companies, Anglo-Persian
and Shell. Shell-Mex & BP and Anglo-American, the affiliate of Standard Oil
(New Jersey), continued to compete with smaller firms, including Texaco's
subsidiary, Russian Oil Products Ltd. (a distributor of Soviet oil products), and
Trinidad Leaseholds. Market share changed, with Shell-Mex & BP increasing
its share of kerosene sales in Britain from 36.3% to 42.4% between 1932 and
1938 and dropping its share of gasoline from 46.4% to 42.3% between 1934
and 1938. The kerosene share of Standard's affiliate sank from 41.9% to 38.5%
between 1931 and 1938, and its gasoline share from 30.8% to 28.9%.[20] Thus
in Britain, though the "As is" agreement did not prevent changes in market
share, these changes were less extensive than those among the leading American companies in their domestic market.

The history of the oil industry in Britain and indeed in all of Europe was
different from that in the United States. In Europe the opening of the new
sources of supply and the coming of new product markets led before World War
II to the rise of only two major industrial enterprises—Anglo-Persian and Shell.
I have chosen to review the history of Anglo-Persian because, first, it was
wholly British, whereas Shell was only 40% British. Second, its records were
more readily available than Shell's. Finally, the Shell story is more complex than
that of Anglo-Persian and could hardly be condensed into a few pages. Its
founder, Henri Deterding, made the essential three-pronged investment in manufacturing, marketing, and management, and he did so well before Greenway
did. Although Deterding's Shell had a head start, Greenway and his successor,
John Cadman, created one of Britain's first managerial enterprises; it and Shell
were the two non-American members of the Seven Sisters. Anglo-Persian Oil,
which became Anglo-Iranian Oil in 1935, retained its position even after its
massive base in Iran was nationalized in 1954 and it took the name of its
marketing subsidiary, British Petroleum. Since 1954 it has become an even
larger enterprise, carrying out its petroleum activities in many more parts of

the world and diversifying into petrochemicals and other related products by using the organizational capabilities it developed during the interwar years.

Rubber: The Enhancement of Organizational Capabilities

Dunlop Rubber Company, the British representative in its global oligopoly (Group 30; see Appendixes B.1–B.3), differed from Anglo-Persian Oil in that it was already a well-established, family-operated enterprise before the coming of World War I. By building a tire factory large enough to obtain the cost advantages of scale, by creating a global marketing network, and by recruiting a team of salaried managers, the Du Cros family had made their company the first mover in Britain and also the British global representative. But only with the end of family control shortly after the war did the company put in place an administrative structure and develop the organizational capabilities needed to maintain a strong position in global markets.

The financial crisis that ended family control in 1922 was brought on by the sharp postwar recession coupled with the financial manipulations of James White, a speculator who had become closely allied to Arthur Du Cros, son of the founder. Sir Eric Geddes, one of Britain's most talented business administrators, carried out the needed financial and administrative reorganization. In 1916 Geddes, deputy general manager of the North Eastern Railway, had become the head of military transportation in France and then in all the theaters of war. He had been appointed First Lord of the Admiralty in 1917 and had served in the cabinet as Minister of Transportation from 1919 to 1921. As Dunlop Rubber's managing director, Geddes, like Cadman at Anglo-Persian, expanded and reshaped both the functional departments and the corporate office of this multinational enterprise. Its management became increasingly professional, especially after F. R. M. de Paula, a professor of accounting at the London School of Economics and a British pioneer in cost accounting and budgeting, became the company's comptroller in 1929.[21]

As Dunlop Rubber, under Geddes's guidance, enlarged its organizational capabilities, it grew in much the same manner as the large American enterprises. It continued to expand its investments abroad and began to diversify into new product lines. It diversified more than the leading American tire companies—Goodyear and Firestone—but somewhat less than the American rubber firms established before the coming of the automobile tire, United States Rubber and Goodrich. Dunlop acquired producers of rubber footwear, outerwear, and rubber industrial goods. Of those firms, Charles Macintosh was the most important. From Dunlop's laboratories, at least one of which had been set up before the change of command in 1922, came successful commercialization of a latex foam, patented in 1933 and given the brand name of Dunlopillo. At the same time the enterprise integrated backwards, buying cotton mills and rubber plantations. Dunlop's historian has noted that integration and product diversification "prompted Geddes to reform management structure." In the early 1930s product sections or divisions were formed. Nevertheless, a full-fledged multidivisional structure was not articulated; the heads of functional departments—sales, manufacturing, and finance—continued to control their activities, and foreign subsidiaries operated quite autonomously.[22]

During these same years Geddes expanded Dunlop's overseas activities. In 1922 the company built a plant in Buffalo, New York. This venture, however, was not a success. Dunlop was never able to compete in the United States and Canada with the American first movers, whose competitive capabilities were too strong. It tried to convince the major American automobile companies to equip their exports with Dunlop tires so that the company might have a reasonable chance of selling replacements in those markets. But it was even unable to extract this favor from General Motors, whose president, Pierre du Pont, sat on the board of Dunlop's American subsidiary. Frustrated, Dunlop's managers tried to increase its share of the American replacement market by investing in a large chain of retail outlets. Again it met with little success. The competition and the onslaught of the Great Depression prevented any growth in sales. Dunlop was increasingly unable to operate its American plant even close to minimum efficient scale, and thus its unit costs remained well above those of its competitors.

On the Continent, Dunlop was more successful. In both Germany and France, small Dunlop plants that had been started as bicycle-tire factories moved into the production of automobile tires as automobile production boomed after the war. In both countries this foreign firm quickly became the second largest producer.[23] Its strategic move into France was a typical oligopolistic response: a report to the Dunlop board in 1924 noted that, without serious competition, Michelin "would be enabled to increase his prices in the French market and make corresponding decreases in the English market," and that this would have a "most serious effect" on Dunlop's business. In India the company built a plant in the 1930s, partly to forestall a move by Goodyear but also because of local government requirements. Such requirements also led to construction of factories in Australia and Ireland.[24]

The leading rubber manufacturers, as Dunlop's experience indicates, competed far more vigorously in international markets and relied far less on arrangements to control price and output and to allocate these markets than did the leaders in oil, rayon, glass, and other industries. Such agreements came almost wholly in the production of crude rubber, beginning with the so-called Stevenson plan of 1921, which followed the 1920–21 recession, and then with a second plan in 1934 during the Great Depression. Both were negotiated and enforced by governments rather than by business enterprises.[25] The nearest approach to cartel-like arrangements was an agreement made in 1934 between Dunlop and Goodyear for reciprocal manufacturing abroad, by which Goodyear manufactured Dunlop tires in Argentina and Dunlop manufactured Goodyear tires in South Africa.

Industrial Materials: Organizational Capabilities Constrained by the Ways of Personal Management

Thus in the oil and rubber industries in Britain a single large integrated enterprise, created to exploit the cost advantages of scale, came to compete successfully at home and abroad with comparably organized foreign companies. This was also the case with British producers of industrial materials (goods purchased by other producers for further processing or fabrication) whose production methods brought similar cost advantages. In these industries, however, the dominating firms differed from those in oil and rubber in that nearly all continued to be managed by their owners. They differed from Dunlop in another way too—they relied more on negotiated agreements than on functional and strategic competition to maintain market shares and profits. They also collaborated more closely with smaller specialized firms operating in the domestic market.

RAYON

Rayon (part of Group 22; see Appendixes B.1–B.3) was one of the few industries in which European first movers entered the American market as quickly as American first movers in mass-produced light machinery had entered European markets. The story of rayon thus illustrates the differences between the way of competing in Britain (and all of Europe) and in the United States. The histories of the rayon producers also emphasize that the initial exploitation of scale was little affected by national differences among the first movers. These differences become more apparent after the industries had been established and the players had been selected and had begun to compete.

The rayon story also provides a dramatic example of how differences in the technology of production affect the structure and growth of enterprises and industries. Rayon was sold in much the same markets as the yarn and cloth processed from natural materials—cotton, wool, silk, and hemp. Whereas the high minimum efficient scale associated with the technology of rayon production resulted in the development of the modern industrial enterprise and a global oligopoly, the low minimum efficient scale of the technology of processing natural materials kept those industries fragmented, with hundreds of small enterprises competing primarily on price. During the interwar years—when the rayon producers were making large profits and when, even after the coming of the depression, rayon was considered a growth industry—the industries processing natural fibers remained "sick industries" in Britain, the United States, and Germany.

The rayon industry's first mover in Britain, Courtaulds, brought its plant in Coventry into full production in 1907 (see Chapter 7). By building a works in 1912 at Marcus Hook, Pennsylvania, which like Coventry used the viscose process, it became the industry's first mover in the United States. Courtaulds' major rival in Britain was British Celanese, the pioneer in developing the cellulose acetate process, which made its major investments in manufacturing, marketing, and management shortly after World War I.

By 1930 Courtaulds was the nation's largest textile producer and British Celanese was the fifth largest. The two ranked sixth and fifth among the top two hundred (Appendix B.2). In 1928 Courtaulds accounted for 76% of the viscose rayon and 9% of the acetate produced in Great Britain, while for British Celanese the proportions were roughly reversed. The only other significant rayon producers in Britain were the subsidiaries of the Dutch firm Nederlandsche Kunstzijdefabriek (Enka) and the German firm Bemberg. The first built its plant in Britain in 1925 and the second in the following year. [26]

The war delayed the foreign invasion of the United States, as *Fortune* later viewed it, that Courtaulds had initiated. [27] In 1918 Tubize, a Belgian pioneer that had developed the Chardonnet process—one that Courtaulds had bypassed—built a works at Hopewell, Virginia, relying on financing in the United States. In 1920 the leading Italian company, Sina Viscosa, established a subsidiary with works in Cleveland, Ohio. (In 1925 it became Industrial Rayon.) In 1925 British Celanese constructed the first large acetate plant in the United States. [28] Then in 1927 Germany's first mover, Vereinigte Glanzstoff Fabriken (VGF) and its smaller ally, J. P. Bemberg, which VGF controlled, set up one factory in Johnson City, Tennessee (using the cuprammonium process which Bemberg had originally developed) and another at the same site in 1928 to produce viscose yarn. After the merger of VGF and Enka (the Dutch firm) in 1929, the resulting enterprise, Algemene Kunstzijde Unie, built a third works, also using the viscose process, at Asheville, North Carolina. Although each of the three plants had a different corporate identity, they were all administered by a single German management. [29] In the 1920s Courtaulds constructed three more plants in the United States and one in Canada, and then two more in Canada in the 1930s.

The success of this invasion can hardly be accounted for by either tariffs or patents. Tariffs did provide an impetus to build plants in the United States, however; for the tariff on rayon imports was increased in 1922 from 35% ad valorem to 45%. Its chief proponents were, of course, the foreign first movers, not the American enterprises. The leading lobbyist was Samuel Salvadge, Courtaulds' American manager. First-mover advantages were not based on patents either, for each of the different European companies had its own strong patent position. In fact, one of the first and strongest patents was that filed in 1895 by Arthur D. Little, the American chemist (the founder of one of the nation's best-known consulting firms in chemical engineering), who failed to make the investments necessary to exploit it.[30]

Instead, first-mover advantages came from the minimum efficient scale of the production process, which in the early 1920s was between 10 and 12 million pounds but through cumulative technological innovation rose to between 25 and 30 million pounds in the 1930s.[31] Even so, until the 1930s the demand was rising fast enough for the leaders to build new plants in the United States as well as in Europe.

Given this barrier to entry, only two American challengers were successful in competing with the foreign first movers. One was Du Pont, which entered the industry in 1920 through a joint venture with the leading French rayon producer and then purchased full control of that venture after it had learned and "scaled up" the process of production (see Chapter 5). The other was Tennessee Eastman, Eastman Kodak's producer of its safety-base photographic film. It turned to developing a cellulose acetate process of its own in order to use existing capacity—both facilities and skills—after the Great Depression sharply reduced the demand for film. In 1932 its 24-million-pound plant came into production.[32]

During the 1930s five foreign enterprises, together with DuPont and Tennessee Eastman, produced about 90% of the rayon made annually in the United States. Increased competition reduced Courtaulds' lead. In 1927 the American Viscose Company (AVC) accounted for 56% of the output of rayon in the United States and Du Pont for 21%. By 1938 American Viscose had 49% of the installed capacity (not output) and Du Pont 15%. Although figures on market share are not available, Donald Coleman's review of AVC's performance during the depression indicates that as the result of functional and strategic competition it lost market share and profits to Du Pont, to the Italian-sponsored Industrial Rayon, and probably to the German enterprises. Such changes reflected improved functional competition, particularly through improved technology of production. It also reflected strategic competition through expanding into tire cord and rayon staple. (Rayon staple was a new product—fibers that could be spun on machinery that was made to use natural fibers.)[33]

If the Europeans competed in this fashion for market share in the United States, in Europe (where neither of the two United States companies attempted to market) Courtaulds and British Celanese and their Continental competitors preferred to negotiate rather than to compete directly for share. Demand there boomed during the 1920s, as it did in the United States; but only two challengers, both established firms, entered the industry. They were the German companies of Köln-Rottweiller and AGFA (see Chapter 13). The first was an explosives firm; the second a dye and film producer. Both became part of I. G. Farben, the giant German chemical combine. Both of them concentrated wholly on the production and distribution of the new product, rayon staple, which had been developed during the First World War to meet German shortages in natural fibers. The other producers only moved into rayon staple in the 1930s, after the depression had stimulated the search for new lines. [34]

The movement for European cooperation in the 1920s was led by Courtaulds and the German first mover, VGF. The two negotiated with other Continental firms to control price and output. As before the war, however, agreements were difficult to reach. Once reached, they were still harder to enforce, and therefore the leaders came to rely more on bilateral alliances. Thus in 1925 Courtaulds and VGF formed a joint venture—Glanzstoff Courtaulds—to construct a large viscose factory in Cologne. In 1927 the two jointly purchased a controlling share in the Italian Sina Viscosa. Only in France, where the major competitor was less cooperative, did Courtaulds (in 1925) build a factory of its own in Calais. In the words of Samuel Courtauld, the company's chairman, the avowed purpose of these joint ventures was to assist "in the protection of the British and American markets and the profitable canalization of exports from continental producers to other markets"—that is, as a threat to discipline the Continental producers' output and flows of products. [35]

By making the alliance with VGF, Courtaulds had hoped to get the European competition out of Britain. As the Bemberg plant using the cuprammonian process for specialty products was not a direct competitor, this meant Enka. But when VGF merged with that Dutch firm in 1929 (Chapter 13), the holding company that resulted, Algemene Kunstzijde Unie, failed to shut down the Dutch factory in Britain. It continued to operate despite strong and continuing protests from John C. Hanbury-Williams, the Courtaulds director in charge of foreign affairs, who was a member of the board of the new German-Dutch holding company. In a long-drawn-out series of negotiations the two firms were unable even to effect the obvious solution—one by which Courtaulds would sell its shares in the Cologne plant and the Continental company would close its works in Britain. In rayon, more than other British industries, even formal legal ties were unable to assure control over the competitive moves of partners and subordinate firms. [36]

Although both British leaders—Courtaulds and British Celanese—did continue to expand their facilities and enhance their functional and administrative skills during the interwar years, family control constrained the full development of their organizational capabilities. Both were administered through centralized, functionally departmentalized structures. At Courtaulds, the company's home office administered production and sales in continental Europe. On the other hand, both Courtaulds' American venture and, apparently, that of British Celanese had their own fully autonomous, centralized, functionally departmentalized organizations. Neither Courtaulds nor British Celanese had an international department.

The greatest weaknesses of both firms lay in the corporate office. Their owners' continuing commitment to the ways of personal management retarded the development of managerial and technical skills that were so essential to top management's monitoring and resource allocation. By 1933 these weaknesses had become painfully apparent at Courtaulds. An internal memo on internal management made at the request of the chairman, Samuel Courtauld, noted in 1933: "Through fear of over-centralization, no adequate central organization has been set up, and now either matters of fundamental importance are decided by persons who naturally are unable to appreciate the full consequences of such decisions to the firm as a whole, or such questions are referred to London to receive the personal attention of a director." A minor reorganization in 1936 set up a committee structure of the board comparable to that at Cadbury's—with committees for finance, yarn, and textiles (but not for research or external affairs, as had been suggested in the original proposal); but the change did little to reduce the overload and expand the perspective of the top decision-makers. In 1938 leading members of the board had to agree that "the directors generally as well as the Board were much too concerned with detailed administration," and that the company thus suffered from "a lack of managers to whom the execution of policy should be devolved."[37]

The failure to build up the central office not only inhibited strategic planning, particularly abroad, but also held back investment in research and development. A small number of overworked executives, Donald Coleman notes, "wholly failed to see the implications of chemistry and to set up a serious research effort." Du Pont's Rayon Department, on the other hand, not only continued to improve the processes of producing rayon as well as the product itself but also quickly commercialized cellophane, making it one of the company's most profitable products. At the same time its central research department was developing a new and superior man-made fiber—nylon. Courtaulds only began to move into cellophane in 1930–1931 and did not build its first successful cellophane plant until 1938 after entering a joint venture with the French firm Comptoir des Textiles Artificiels, which provided the necessary technical and marketing capabilities.[38] In the years when the Du Pont company was investing heavily in the development of its own new or improved products and processes, the Courtaulds board preferred to keep large reserves aside for buying out improvements in processes and products developed by others. Only in 1938 did the chairman, Samuel Courtauld, commit the company to a significant investment in development. As he wrote: "Our Company which was a pioneer in the early days has, with its associates, rested too much on its laurels in recent years and the competitors have got ahead of us in the race."[39]

Thus during the boom years of the 1920s Courtaulds failed to reinvest profits in long-term improvements of process and product or in new product development as did Du Pont and other American firms. Instead, earnings were paid out in dividends. In addition to dividends on ordinary shares, averaging 30% in

1925, 1926, and 1927, Courtaulds in February 1928 declared a share bonus of 100%, thereby providing "the Stock Exchange with the sensation of the year," in the words of the *Economist*.[40] What was true at Courtaulds was also true at British Celanese and its American subsidiary, the Celanese Corporation of America. There the strong entrepreneurial hand of the founders, Henry and Camille Dreyfus, kept the central office small and the investment in research low.[41] Thus, although the managerial hierarchies were larger in these two companies than in any other British textile enterprise except possibly J. & P. Coats, neither developed the competitive capabilities of the sort that permitted their German and American competitors to expand market share abroad at the British companies' expense and to move more quickly into such related products as cellophane and rayon staple.

STONE, CLAY, AND GLASS

During the interwar years the firms in Group 32 (see Appendixes B.1–B.3)— stone, clay, and glass—that were on the 1919, 1930, and 1948 lists of the top two hundred industrial companies in Britain clustered in glass, cement, abrasives, and asbestos, much the same three-digit industries as in the United States. But whereas in the United States these firms were largely centrally managed, managerial firms, in Britain they were representatives of the two British types and also of a third type, the managerially operated foreign subsidiary. In abrasives an American-owned subsidiary dominated the British industry. In asbestos, cement, glass bottles, and plaster board the largest firms were federations of relatively small firms united through a holding company; while the plate-glass industry continued to be dominated by Pilkington, a family firm that had made the necessary initial investment in production, distribution, and management in the 1880s and 1890s, and whose later evolution parallels that of Courtaulds.

After World War I Americans continued to rule the British abrasives industry. In 1928 Minnesota Mining & Manufacturing, the challenger to the industry's first movers, Norton and Carborundum, built its plant in Britain. In the next year these three companies joined with several smaller specialized producers in the industry to form two Webb-Pomerene companies, one a sales company, the other the Durex Corporation to manufacture in Britain and Canada. These two companies were soon controlled by the three largest American firms and American Glue, a subsidiary of the meatpacking company, Armour. Durex's manager, Donald Kelso, concentrated British production in a single new large plant and consolidated and expanded the sales forces of the predecessor companies in Britain and on the Continent. Then in 1935 Durex set up specialized processing plants in France and Germany, making it the largest abrasives producer in Europe.[42]

In asbestos and cement, after World War I the dominant federations in Britain began to move slowly toward centralizing and rationalizing their activities. The Associated Portland Cement Manufacturers, the 1900 amalgamation, after a further merger in 1912 with the British Portland Cement Company came to include fifty constituent firms. After 1920 the central office of Associated Portland Cement began slowly to build a single sales force to market the different brands produced. Production and the scheduling of flows to consumers appear to have remained in the hands of the operating companies. Because the cost of transportation and the relatively small economies of scale in cement production meant that plants served local markets, the incentive for further centralization was reduced. The corporate office appears to have remained small. In any case, Associated Portland Cement made more of an effort to centralize control than did the second largest producer, Allied Cement, another federation. [43]

In asbestos the largest firm, Turner & Newall, made more of an effort to create an overall management structure. Formed in 1920 as a merger of four companies, it continued to expand by acquisition. By 1929 it had brought together twenty-nine companies, including producers of asbestos, asbestos cement, asbestos textiles, and asbestos brake linings, as well as a mining company in Rhodesia that was obtained to assure supplies. Constituent companies operated almost completely autonomously until 1929, when reorganization began. Then the administration of production and distribution facilities was reshaped along major product lines. By 1931 the subsidiaries were grouped into four units or divisions—mining, textile manufacturing, asbestos cement, and insulation. Rationalization continued within single or combined units—"control companies," as they were called. Subsidiaries were established abroad. But the offices of the control companies remained small, and the central office appears to have been not much more than a meeting place for the heads of the control companies and other directors, with little or no corporate staff. Members of the Turner and Newall families continued to dominate the board; its chairman in the early 1930s was a Turner and its vice-chairman a Newall. Two other Newalls and Turners sat as directors. This managerial hierarchy remained much smaller than that of the leading American asbestos producer, Johns-Manville. The reorganization and expansion strengthened the company's near-monopoly position in Great Britain and assured its place as an effective participant in the international cartel; but the reorganization did not develop organizational capabilities that would lead to direct investment abroad or to investment in research and development and in related products. [44]

In plate glass there was no need for holding companies such as Turner & Newall and Associated Portland Cement. There the two prewar first movers, Pilkington Brothers, Ltd., and its smaller neighbor, Chance Brothers, Ltd., continued to dominate between the wars and to cooperate with each other. Both firms continued to be managed by members of the founding families, even after Pilkington acquired a substantial block of Chance stock in the late 1930s.

At Pilkington the board of family directors made all the major decisions, operational and strategic, much in the manner of the board at Cadbury Brothers, Ltd. At the end of the 1920s the increasing number and increasing complexities of these decisions were beginning to overwhelm those responsible for them. By 1930 profits had fallen, so that the dividend was reduced to 2% for the first half of 1930–31 and was passed entirely in the second half. By contrast, Chance Brothers declared dividends of 5% in 1930 and 3% in 1931. The historian of the Pilkington firm writes of its chairman, Austin Pilkington, that "the efforts of running the business without sufficient delegation had at last proved too great for him . . . his health was breaking down under the strain." As was precisely the case at Courtaulds, the board's concentration on day-to-day operations prevented its members from planning strategically, both for expansion overseas and for the development of new product lines. Even more serious was the increasingly obvious inability of the senior Pilkingtons to coordinate functional activities effectively within the firm, particularly those of the works and sales departments.

In May 1931, Edward Herbert Couzens-Hardy, whose sister had married Austin Pilkington, and who had become a board member in 1908, proposed a reorganization that would make a distinction between inside and outside directors. After his proposal was put into effect, the board consisted of full-time managers who made up the executive committee and part-time "non-executive" members—including Pilkingtons. For the first time, two nonfamily managers came onto the board, one to handle legal affairs and the other sales. A third, the manager of the main works, became a member in 1939 as director of production. Younger Pilkingtons were now required to take the same intensive training course that was offered to qualified graduates of Oxford and Cambridge. Though the top jobs at Pilkington Brothers were finally opened to talent, family members still had a much greater opportunity to reach them than outsiders did. [45]

A new executive committee introduced systems of auditing and financial control based on those that F. R. M. de Paula had set up at Dunlop. It established four committees—finance, sales, technical matters, and personnel and welfare. These committees, made up of inside directors and line and staff middle managers, met regularly to coordinate these functional activities. In 1936 the technical committee finally pushed the company into setting up a separate central-research department. In 1938 the company built its first research facilities, a quarter of a century after its American counterparts had made a comparable investment. [46]

In the years following the reorganization, Pilkington's performance improved substantially. Profits rose and a dividend of 5.2% was paid in 1933, 10.7% in 1935, and 14.6% in 1937. The company's acquisition of substantial holdings in Chance Brothers, its longtime friendly rival, began in 1936, although it did not acquire full control until 1945. Investment in research encouraged the company to begin to diversify by developing and then producing glass fiber and glass bricks.

In these same years Pilkington strengthened its position abroad. In 1934 the company played a major role in negotiations that led to an agreement between the American and European producers by which the Americans were to have 20% and the Europeans 80% of the export market, that is, markets other than each producer's own domestic market. In these same negotiations Pilkington was able to bring St. Gobain, the French giant, to purchase the Pilkington works at Mauberge in France, and then to shut it down. Pilkington also got Pittsburgh Plate Glass to set up a Webb-Pomerene company (the Plate Glass Export Company) so that its Belgian subsidiary might work more closely with the European glass cartel. Beginning in 1935 Pilkington expanded its overseas production. It built safety-glass plants in Australia in 1935 and 1937 (then sold 49% of the shares to an Australian glass producer). With a local firm in South Africa it formed a joint venture in which the British company held two-thirds of the stock; the South African plant went into production in 1936. Next came a joint venture in Argentina with other European firms and a local company; the Argentine factory was completed in 1937.[47]

Thus reorganization of top management appears to have permitted Pilkington to develop, more quickly and effectively than Courtaulds, the facilities and managerial skills needed to grow through product innovation and investment overseas—organizational capabilities that provided Pilkington with the competitive edge for an impressive growth after World War II.

PAPER

The papermaking firms (Group 26; see Appendixes B.1–B.3) on the list of the two hundred largest British enterprises were, as in the United States, producers of pulp, newsprint, kraft, and cardboard. But because British companies were on the average smaller than those in the United States, the list also includes makers of specialty products and wallpaper. Except in wallpaper, these paper firms remained independent, personally managed enterprises—usually family firms.

The industry's only significant merger was Wall Paper Manufacturers, formed in 1899. Throughout the interwar years this federation continued to control close to 90% of the industry's output and to operate as a legal cartel.[48] Its longevity in this industry, where the economies of scale were so slight, stands in sharp contrast to that of a comparable American combination, National Wallpaper. The directors of the American company, which was formed by twenty-eight manufacturers in 1892, agreed by 1900 "that the Company be dissolved and the factories returned to their original owners, or sold to the highest bidder." The reason was that "the manufacturer of wallpaper is so dependent on such peculiar circumstances that independent plants can be operated to better advantage than many plants under one control."[49] In the United States legal combinations in industries where little was to be gained by administrative centralization and nationalization disbanded. In Britain they continued to enforce agreements as to price and output.

As might be expected, the British pulp and newsprint industry was even more concentrated than that in the United States. According to the British 1936 census of production, the three largest firms accounted for 70% of the output.[50] Unlike those in the United States, all three had been tied to newspaper chains. The largest of these, E. W. Bowater, had been controlled by the Rothermere and Beaverbrook interests before Eric Bowater (a son of the founder) gained independence from them in 1932. In 1936 Bowater increased his firm's size and influence by purchasing one of the other three, Edward Lloyd, from Allied Newspapers.[51] The third, Inveresk Paper, had integrated forward in the 1920s by obtaining the *Illustrated London News,* the *Lancashire Daily Press,* and United Newspapers, Ltd.

Both Bowater and Inveresk integrated backward during the 1930s by purchasing forest lands and building mills in Canada, Newfoundland, and Scandinavia, for the differential costs between transporting paper and wood meant that in order to operate at minimum efficient scale such mills had to be near extensive timber sources. By the end of the thirties Bowater had made its first investment in research and development and had begun to enlarge its lines of paper products. By 1948 these moves had helped to make it much larger than Inveresk—26th on the list of the top two hundred, while Inveresk was only 124th.

Nevertheless, Bowater continued to be managed in a personal manner. The central office remained tiny. "In spite of the size of Bowater's business," noted the historian of the company, William Reader, "the organization in the late forties remained rudimentary."[52] In the years immediately after World War II the managerial hierarchy at Bowater was somewhat enlarged; the product lines were expanded in a limited fashion; and a distribution network was established and then plants were built in the United States. Decisions at the top, however, continued to be in the hands of Sir Eric Bowater until his death in 1962.

Sir Eric's failure to develop organizational capabilities at top- and middle-management level handicapped his company's post-World War II growth—in both its expansion overseas, particularly in the United States, and its moves into related packaging materials. These managerial weaknesses were at least partially responsible for the company's financial crisis in the early 1960s, its takeover by the promoter Walker Lewis in the early 1970s, and its continuing difficulties in the following years.[53]

The makers of more specialized paper products, where the processes of production offered few economies of scale, remained small. Those listed in the top two hundred (Appendixes B.1–B.3) were John Dickinson, a producer of specialty wrapping and packaging materials; E. S. & A. Robinson, stationers; and Wiggins, Teape, producers of specialty papers including photographic paper. All three were family-operated. There were almost as many Robinsons on the Robinson board as there were Cadburys on the chocolate maker's board. In 1922 Wiggins, Teape merged with its major competitor, Alex Pirie (Merchants) Ltd., in an alliance comparable to the Cadbury-Fry merger. Dickinson and Robinson, which had long been cooperative allies, merged in the same manner in 1960.[54] These specialized producers had little impact on international markets and did little to develop related product lines. The major newsprint makers had more of an impact abroad, with Bowater becoming a major but not too successful challenger in the American market after World War II.

From this review of the British producers of industrial materials between the world wars the following points emerge. In cement, asbestos, and wallpaper the turn-of-the-century federations, though beginning to tighten central control and to rationalize production and distribution, remained federations of firms that, with the possible exception of Turner & Newall, were personally managed (nonhierarchical) enterprises. In rayon, glass, and paper, where the first movers created modern industrial enterprises, family control retarded the development of organizational capability and so held back profitable expansion abroad and successful diversification into related lines. Pilkington, by making a more thorough reorganization of top management, regained its competitive strength more quickly than Courtaulds; but in paper the failure of the founding entrepreneur to develop managerial capabilities plagued the enterprise in its effort to expand overseas and to develop a full line of products. By World War II the British leaders in these three sets of industries—rayon, glass, and paper—had not reached the size or the financial strength of the leading enterprises in the same industries in the United States.[55] In glass and paper, however, they outstripped their counterparts in Germany.

METAL FABRICATING

During the interwar years British metal fabricators (Group 34; see Appendixes B.1–B.3) were, with one notable exception, even less successful than the leading materials producers in catching up, or even holding their own, in domestic and international markets. In semifinished and fabricated brass there were no large British producers comparable to American Brass or Scovill. Moreover, in Britain the subsidiary of American Radiator continued to be the leading producer of radiators and other heating equipment, and Gillette's subsidiary continued as the leader in safety razors.

Except for Metal Box (which transformed itself into a modern industrial enterprise), the size, strategy, and structure of the British metal fabricating firms among the top two hundred changed little between the two wars. Small specialized firms such as Crittall Manufacturing, producers of metal windows and doors, and J. G. Graves, makers of cutlery and electroplate equipment, remained family-owned and family-managed firms with a minimum number of salaried executives.

The largest company among the metal fabricators, Guest, Keen & Nettlefolds (GKN), a 1902 horizontal and vertical combination of makers of screws, nuts, rods, wires, and other fabricated products—and also producers of steel—remained through the interwar period a standard example of a loose confederation. In the words of Leslie Hannah, it had "virtually no central control," for each subsidiary or branch had "its own board with direct access to the chairman of the group." During these years the GKN board included a Keen (as "Deputy Chairman and Managing Director"), a Guest, and a variety of Berrys, Beales, Llewellyns, and other descendants of the founding families.[56]

During the interwar years GKN took advantage of the growth of the automobile industry by acquiring these three firms: John Garrington, a major producer of steel forgings; John Lysaght, which throughout most of the period produced 90% of the sheet steel for British automobiles; and John Sankey, a producer of automobile wheels and chassis components. These firms operated as autonomously as the producers of GKN's original lines of screws, nuts, and bolts—items whose production offered few economies of scale and whose distribution required little in the way of marketing services. The operating units, encouraged by the GKN board, sought agreement as to price and production with their competitors. Much the same pattern was followed by Radiation, Ltd., "the gas stove combine" formed in 1919, which dominated another industry where scale economies, though greater than in nuts and bolts, were still relatively low.[57]

On the other hand, there were substantial scale economies in the fabrication of metal cans and containers, as the history of the American can industry demonstrates, and their distribution in volume called for product-specific facilities and personnel. Until 1930, however, no British entrepreneur made the investment in production and distribution needed to exploit the advantages of scale. Metal Box & Printing Industries, formed in 1922, remained until 1930 a standard British combination, which included three of the five leading producers of tins, and in which each member continued to operate on its own.

Only the threat of an American invasion in 1929 brought change. When the Metal Box directors learned that the American Can Company was planning to move into Britain, they had little difficulty in getting another major producer, Edward C. Barlow & Sons, and two small metal-box makers to join the combination. In the spring of 1930 the fifth of the leading producers, G. N. Williamson & Sons, also joined. Immediately young Robert Barlow, who had just taken over Edward C. Barlow & Sons after his father's death, began to transform the federation into a modern industrial enterprise and so gave the structure of the British canning industry its modern form.[58]

William Reader, in his history of Metal Box, emphasizes that the American canning industry of the 1920s

> had practically nothing in common with the contemporary British tin box making industry except in its main raw material: tin-plate. The tin-box makers represented a small service industry, tiny in relation to their important customers, but the can-makers worked at a much larger order of magnitude, numbering their output in the hundreds of millions of units, whereas the tin-box makers ran only to the thousands, and [the can-makers were] organized on a scale which made them much larger than most of their customers and put them on more or less even terms with all but the very biggest.

Not only did the Americans have a huge volume of output, but they provided "at the can-makers' expense a complete service of upkeep and repair."[59] The only firms in Britain in the 1920s to use continuous-process canning machinery, developed in the United States in the 1880s, were the subsidiaries of large foreign manufacturers of food, one or two of the largest British food companies, and the Co-operative Wholesale Society. Moreover, a sizable portion of the tin boxes produced in Britain by older, more labor-intensive methods were fabricated by the large users themselves, including Cadbury and Fry, J. & J. Colman, Reckitt and Sons, Crosse & Blackwell, British American Tobacco, and Imperial Tobacco.[60]

American Can's opening move into the British market was to purchase a small producer, Ernest Taylor Ltd., of Liverpool. Then, after approaching the senior Barlow without success, it began negotiations to acquire Metal Box. These broke down in November 1928, apparently because American Can wanted full control. Robert Barlow, who had taken over the family firm on his father's death, and whose firm had then joined Metal Box in July, immediately opened negotiations with American Can's rival, Continental Can. Continental Can had already responded to its competitor's move into Britain by offering to equip the G. N. Williamson plant with American machinery. (This happened before that firm had joined Metal Box.) In April 1930 Barlow signed an agreement with Continental Can to have exclusive rights to buy automatic canning machinery from Continental Can for fifteen years and, "more important" (in Reader's words), to have "exclusive rights to service and technical information, as well as patent licenses." Continental Can and Metal Box exchanged stock— a transaction that brought Continental Can's directors onto Metal Box's board but did not give Continental Can control of the company.[61]

Next, assisted by George E. Williamson (son of G. N. Williamson), Barlow began to transform the loose federation into a modern corporation, despite strong opposition from several of his fellow directors. First he set up a central purchasing department and a finance department. Then he created a national and international network for marketing and distribution, which, besides handling cans, leased and serviced equipment to canners. By August 1931 he was strong enough to buy from American Can its recently purchased British company.

In December 1933 Barlow outlined a program for rationalizing and centralizing Metal Box's operations. His memorandum began by listing three major moves:

A. The absorption of businesses acquired.
B. The creation of a central organization dealing with the main divisions of activity.
   1. Finance.
   2. Accountancy.
   3. Sales.
   4. Supplies.
   5. Production.
C. The redistribution of manufacturing, aiming at specialization for technical and geographical reasons. [62]

As these moves were carried out, Barlow, always working closely with Continental Can, enlarged both the production of cans and canning equipment and the marketing services to meet the needs of small seasonal canners. He also expanded activities overseas, using joint ventures with local firms on the Continent and direct marketing investments in the Empire. Next came the building of highly profitable production facilities in India and South Africa. [63] In 1934 the company purchased a tin-plate works and then a factory to produce the specialized machinery. [64] Finally in 1937 came the construction of the company's central research laboratory. By the outbreak of World War II, Metal Box had a practical monopoly of can production in Britain and, still working closely with Continental Can, had made the global duopoly into a "triopoly." By then its managerial hierarchy was a smaller version of the hierarchies of its two American counterparts, including salaried managers making top level decisions. The difference was that one man, the man who had transformed Metal Box into a modern industrial enterprise and who remained a substantial stockholder, continued to rule his extensive managerial staff until well after World War II.

Thus Metal Box, thanks in good part to Robert Barlow's entrepreneurial imagination and skills, made the investment in production and built the marketing organization that transformed a federation into a strong multinational enterprise. Metal Box made the transformation much more effectively than Turner & Newall, which did so more successfully than Guest, Keen & Nettlefolds. By the coming of World War II, Metal Box's position in its domestic and global markets was comparable to that of Courtaulds, Pilkington, Dunlop, and Anglo-Iranian in theirs.

METAL MAKING

In metal fabrication Metal Box was the exception that illustrates the rule. In metal making (Group 33; see Appendixes B.1–B.3) the story was even more dire. There the small, personally managed firms operating in unconcentrated industries had become too solidly entrenched to change. In almost every case the entrepreneurial failures of the 1880s and 1890s could not be reversed. Again there was only one significant exception, Stewarts & Lloyds.

The British were unable to create major enterprises in nonferrous metals such as lead, zinc, or copper during the interwar years. In 1929 Mond Nickel, a strong independent, became a subsidiary of the American giant, International Nickel. In aluminum the British continued to play a secondary role in international competition.

In lead the most important manufacturers formed Associated Lead Manufacturers, Ltd., a typical British holding company, in 1919. It accomplished only a modicum of modernization and rationalization of facilities and established only a small central office. The operating companies continued to handle their own production and distribution, even after an overseas sales company had been set up. Associated Lead and the small, personally managed (nonhierarchical) independent firms continued to rely on their trade association, the British Lead Manufacturers Association, to control competition at home and to negotiate with their international competitors abroad, negotiations that resulted in the establishment of formal agreements or "conventions" for Great Britain and then for international markets.[65]

Copper refineries remained relatively small and continued to be closely allied to the electric-cable producers. The Rio Tinto company, having lost out in copper, continued to play a significant role in the mining and distribution of pyrites. In 1926 a newly recruited managing director began to expand and reshape the company's managerial staff. That year the company formed a joint venture, the European Pyrites Corporation, with the German giant, Metallgesellschaft. It replaced the existing international cartel by beginning to market, in conjunction with the American-sponsored Copper Exporters, Inc., the output of all the major European producers. In the next year Rio Tinto expanded its activities in the United States and Europe. It bought into Davison Chemical, its major American customer, and then into Davison's chemical subsidiary, Silica Gel, helping Davison to construct processing plants in Belgium and Great Britain. It also participated with Metallgesellschaft in the formation of two holding companies, Amalgamated Metal and British Mining Corporation. But all this activity produced only feeble results. By the early 1930s the companies in which Rio Tinto had invested in both the United States and Europe had become bankrupt. Only new investment in recently opened Rhodesian mines kept Rio Tinto solvent.[66]

The story of British Aluminium during the interwar years is less depressing. Revived by wartime demand and by subsidies from the British government during and after the war, it built the largest hydroelectric complex yet to be constructed in Great Britain. It increased its bauxite mining in Ireland, expanded its aluminum-processing plants in Ireland and Great Britain, and, most important of all, enlarged its works in Norway, where cheap water power was available. In the words of one authority, the company was "an important, though secondary, factor in the world aluminum industry." Little information is available on the organization of British Aluminium, but it appears to have set up a marketing organization and recruited the managerial staff necessary to maintain its secondary position in the industry's global oligopoly.[67] It failed, however, to become a serious challenger to the German industry, even though the Germans, who had lost their aluminum works in Switzerland during World War I, had to create a wholly new enterprise to produce and distribute aluminum (see Chapter 14).

In steel the lasting effects of the entrepreneurial failure of the late nineteenth century were even more striking than in nonferrous metals. Despite the expansion of steel output during the war and the postwar boom that lasted until 1920, the British industry remained fragmented. After the war only one British steel-maker listed among the top two hundred industrial enterprises was able to achieve a strong position at home and abroad by effectively exploiting economies of scale. Nearly all the steel-producing enterprises remained personally managed. As late as 1939 only the very largest of the British steel companies had recruited managerial staffs as big as that depicted in Figure 7.

As a result, after the collapse of the postwar boom the British steel producers faced far more difficult times than they had before the war. They were unable to win back their overseas market, even though (1) they had increased their capacity during and immediately after the war; (2) the American steel producers had turned their backs on Europe in order to exploit the U.S. boom in automobiles, highways, housing, and factories; and (3) the German industry remained in disarray until the autumn of 1924, when agreements among the victorious Allies helped to stabilize the German economy. Indeed, the British continued to lose overseas markets rapidly. By the 1936–1938 period, exports had fallen to 12% of total steel production. At the same time pressures from imports increased. In addition, the British shipbuilding industry, the major domestic market, had all but collapsed in the early 1920s. The 1920s were long remembered as the steel industry's "black decade."[68]

During that decade nearly everyone concerned about the industry's plight agreed on a cure—investment in facilities modern and large enough to increase output per worker and decrease the cost per unit produced. There were opportunities within existing enterprises for such rationalization. But because the firms were relatively small, with many old and scattered facilities, nearly everyone involved—owners, managers, banks, and the British government—agreed that in most cases such rationalization must be preceded by merger and acquisition followed by administrative centralization. Yet for all this agreement, little was done. For British steel the possibility of regeneration was long gone. The personal and institutional barriers resulting from the initial failure to invest were too great, and the organizational capabilities of the industry's enterprises were too limited.

Boards of directors argued endlessly over the terms of mergers. Longtime competitors distrusted one another. Even within firms, agreement was difficult. The different branches of the founding families often disagreed, as did managers and owners. And both managers and owners had different goals from those of their creditors. Hard times had led to borrowing and to the raising of funds through the selling of shares. Banks had reluctantly become involved in the industry. They and the holders of the new securities viewed the plans for merger and rationalization from a perspective different from that of the families and managers. Moreover, many steel companies were owned by enterprises in other industries. Shipbuilding firms had obtained control of metal-making companies in order to assure themselves of supplies, and coal companies had moved forward into making iron and steel so as to be assured of outlets for their product. These firms viewed the needed investment differently from the families who owned the steel enterprises and the banks that provided them with funds. Still another perspective existed within the government. As the industry's crisis continued into the late 1920s, the central bank, the Bank of England, along with the Bankers' Industrial Development Company (BIDC), which it sponsored, embarked on its own plans for the modernization and rationalization of the industry. An underlying difficulty was finance. Funds were required not only to construct new best-practice plants but also to purchase outmoded capacity that needed to be shut down. Unless these facilities were purchased, their owners usually preferred to continue operations even when faced with bankruptcy proceedings.[69]

The history of Stewarts & Lloyds, the leading British maker of steel tubes, provides the one important exception to the generalizations just made. It was the only company in the iron and steel industry that evolved in the manner of the other successful British industrial enterprises described in this chapter. Formed in 1903 as a merger of the two leading producers of tubes, by World War I it accounted for half of the entire British output of steel tubes, and half of that half was exported. Until the end of the war the company remained a typical British merger of the two industry leaders. It continued to be operated separately by the Stewarts in Scotland and by the Lloyds and Howards in Birmingham.

Wartime expansion and plans to compete vigorously in the postwar market brought the beginnings of centralization. In 1918 the five-man General Purpose Committee, a "centralized coordinating authority," began to unify what Jonathan Boswell has termed this "long-established dual monarchy." The managerial staff was expanded, and, as was still so rare in Britain, younger, nonfamily managers came on the board. By 1921 half of the inside directors came from outside the family circle of Stewarts, Lloyds, and Howards. Nevertheless, facilities remained scattered. Although some of the works were new, others were old and technologically outmoded. The demand for weldless tubing by the oil industry was growing rapidly and the need for Bessemer steel to produce such tubes was growing even faster.[70]

Allan MacDiarmid, the first nonfamily chairman of Stewarts & Lloyds (de facto in 1925, de jure in July 1926), made a penetrating report, written when he took full command, on the need for major capital expenditures "to bring ourselves up to tone again." This was essential if the company was to maintain its position in foreign markets, particularly "when one considers the enormous wealth of America at the present moment, and the amount of money she is spending on Weldless plant and on research into methods of tube-making, and when one sees how French Tube Makers are developing and how German Tube Makers are systematically combining to cheapen production and eliminate old-fashioned plant."[71] MacDiarmid began to buy small tube-making firms. In 1927 the company turned to developing plans for a new modern facility to produce Bessemer steel for their tube-making facilities. After much discussion, the firm in October 1929 hired H. A. Brassert & Company, a Chicago-based consulting firm which was making comparable studies for other British steel companies, to advise on the construction of new facilities on company property at Corby in Scotland to provide both the open-hearth and Bessemer capacity it needed.

Brassert proposed a best-practice mill that, when operating at the estimated minimum efficient scale of 625,000 tons, would return 21.5% on capital invested. Such a throughput, however, would produce 195,000 more tons of low-priced open-hearth steel than Stewarts & Lloyds needed for its own tube making.[72] When the other steel producers learned of this proposal, their outcry was immediate and sharp. The most vocal were Dorman Long and United Steel Companies, Ltd., the nation's two largest steelmakers. In addition, the proposal jarred the regional-rationalization plans of Montague Norman, the Governor of the Bank of England and of its Bankers' Industrial Development Company (BIDC).

This opposition blocked the raising of the necessary capital. MacDiarmid had to report to his board on September 4, 1930, that "it is impossible to obtain a 'fair field' for our Corby plans, including the necessary finance, unless we agree to restrict the admitted competitive strength of Corby in such a way as to safeguard the steel industry—and the bankers' loans involved—from its attacks." Brassert returned to the drawing board to plan a mill to produce 430,000 tons of ingots annually but *only for tubes*. The mill could meet 75% of the British demand for tubes and, even if operating at 66%, might still obtain 20% return on capital invested. This move still did not satisfy the other producers. Finally, in order to get financing the Stewarts & Lloyds board agreed to build a mill of only 200,000 tons, making only Bessemer steel and *only for their own company*.[73] They further agreed to sell only tubes and no other steel products.[74] The Corby steel mill, completed in 1934 and later enlarged, remained the lowest-cost Bessemer producer in Britain, even though, because of the pressure from competitors and banks, it was forced to be built at well below optimal size. After its completion and the expansion of its tube-making facilities, the company produced 80% of the tubes made for the British market and nearly all of those exported from the country.

Stewarts & Lloyds quickly became not only the largest British tube producer but also the largest British steel producer in terms of market value of its securities, as well as one of the most profitable steel companies. At home, the company made an agreement in 1930 with Tube Investments, a typical British holding company of small producers of precision-made, specialized tubing, for the following purposes: to cooperate in research and development, to determine the products to be made by each company, to fix prices where products overlapped, and, if necessary, to exchange shares.[75] Five years later the two companies purchased British Mannesmann, the British affiliate of their leading German competitor, thereby acquiring control of more than 90% of the nation's output of tubes. At the same time Stewarts & Lloyds expanded sales overseas. It became a major force in maintaining the International Tube Cartel, which it helped to found in 1929. When that cartel fell apart in 1935, the company had the economic power to bring the German producers back into the fold by 1937. By making an extensive investment in production, which had been reduced as the result of pressure from the other steel companies, and by expanding its organizational capabilities, Stewarts & Lloyds reached a position in its global oligopoly comparable to that of Anglo-Iranian, Dunlop, Courtaulds, Pilkington, and Metal Box in their industries.

In tin plate, Richard Thomas & Company attempted to do what Stewarts & Lloyds had done in tubes, but with much less success. By the early 1920s Richard Thomas was the largest producer in the British tin-plate industry—an industry which remained primarily in Wales and which had not yet adopted the innovations in production developed in the United States in the late 1890s (see Chapter 4). Nevertheless, by 1914 the British tin-plate industry, although losing share to the American manufacturers, still accounted for 45% of the world's output. By 1930, however, it produced only 23%. The firms in the industry remained small and nonintegrated. Cartels created in times of prosperity fell apart when demand dropped off.[76]

Richard Thomas had grown large by acquisition and also by expanding its capacity during World War I. After the war its owner-manager, Frank Thomas, made little effort to rationalize its facilities, which ran the gamut from ancient mills built in the 1870s to a major, integrated, steel-producing works that the firm had constructed at Redbourn in Lincolnshire during the war. Thomas, a ruthless, arrogant autocrat, had pushed other members of the founding families out of the management of the firm but had failed to replace them with experienced steel and tin makers. Struck down by an incapacitating illness, he turned the command of his company over to William Firth in 1924. A tin merchant who had obtained his own processing works, Firth after 1918 was Thomas's most aggressive competitor until the two firms merged. Firth, who continued the Thomas style of highly personal, autocratic rule, failed to develop a managerial team comparable to that at Stewarts & Lloyds.[77]

Nevertheless, Firth was more impressed than Thomas by the advantages of technological efficiency. In May 1929 he turned to H. A. Brassert & Company for advice on the restructuring of his enterprise. (This happened a few months before Stewarts & Lloyds hired the same consultant firm.) With the Thomas company, as with Stewarts & Lloyds, Brassert urged the construction of a new integrated works that could sharply reduce the cost of producing pig iron, steel ingots, and steel bars. The American consultants were at that time advising still another British producer, the United Steel Companies, and they came to believe that the best solution was to merge Richard Thomas with United Steel. That combination could then support the construction of an integrated tin-plate plant built to optimal size. When United Steel failed to show interest (it was going through receivership at the time), Brassert proposed that the Richard Thomas firm build the plant, using the new continuous-strip process developed by American Rolling Mill in the United States. Although the proposed works would substantially increase the nation's tin-plate output, Brassert pointed out that the recently reorganized Metal Box Company was enlarging the market by rapidly expanding its demand for tin plate. (By 1933 Metal Box was already taking 18% of the home consumption of tin plate, and its consumption was to triple over the next four years.) In addition, the mill could produce sheet steel for the growing British automobile industry. Firth was impressed by the proposed cost reductions and the resulting "enormous potential advantages for the firm that would be first in the field, particularly if, as he expected, tin plate demand grew more and more rapidly."

Again, the difficulty was finance. The most efficient program, Brassert reported, would be to build a 160,000-box plant and to close down all the company's existing works. But all agreed that such a plan was much too ambitious. Yet even the smallest mill that could efficiently use the new technology— one producing 80,000 boxes—would, if Thomas did not shut down its other plants, produce close to the nation's current aggregate demand for the product.

One alternative was to build the plant and close down 75% of Thomas's existing capacity or acquire competing plants and shut them down.[78]

The threat of a new, small, but best-practice mill producing a substantial share of the nation's sheet steel brought a quick, angry response from the sheetmakers, including John Summers (the leading producer), Baldwins, and John Lysaght. The Lysaght company, by then a completely autonomous subsidiary of Guest, Keen & Nettlefolds, accounted for 90% of the sheet used in British automobile bodies. These companies and their bankers so effectively prevented Firth from raising the necessary capital that he turned to the government for political backing. That support, however, was forthcoming only if Firth agreed to build the plant, not at the Lincolnshire site which he and Brassert considered most satisfactory, but at Ebbw Vale in South Wales where unemployment was high.

As a result the plant designed to exploit the new technology was built at what Steven Tolliday calls a "hopeless location," with initially high construction costs and continuing high transportation costs. Then the coming of the recession in 1938 and a drop in the company's earnings forced Firth to go again to the City for necessary financing. To obtain it he needed the support of the British Iron & Steel Federation (formed in 1934), which, in turn, required him to place representatives of the rival companies on the Richard Thomas board. The resulting intensive boardroom warfare led in time to the replacement of those representatives by leading steel men from noncompetitive firms, including MacDiarmid of Stewarts & Lloyds and Sir James Lithgow of the foremost Scottish firm, Colville. But soon Firth himself was forced off the board because he refused to run the new works in line with the board's wishes. As the new continuous-strip mill went into full operation in 1939, it was performing in a poor location under a new management of recently recruited executives.

Although the best-practice plants of Richard Thomas and Stewarts & Lloyds were not of the size (and in Thomas's case not in the location) to assure maximum cost advantages, they were constructed without the need for a merger, because both firms were already the largest producers in their industries. For the other steel producers, mergers (usually with firms in the same region) appeared to be the essential first step to rationalization. But these mergers were so difficult to negotiate and so long in coming that they rarely resulted in the building of modern mills and equipment.[79]

In Scotland, where plates, particularly for shipbuilding, were the primary product, the critical merger took a long time to consummate—so long that rationalization, when it came, was carried out only in a piecemeal, ad hoc fashion rather than through the building of new best-practice plants. At the center of this merger was the leader, David Colville & Sons, which, like nearly all Scottish steel producers, was owned by a shipbuilder.

Although the final merger did not take place until 1936, the story begins in

1920 when the Colville family sold 90% of the ordinary shares to Harland & Wolff, shipbuilders, which, in turn, was partly owned by the Royal Mail Group, a shipping enterprise in which the Lithgow family had a major interest. After the sale, however, the Colville board "operated as a virtually autonomous enclave within the larger concern." Even before the sale, the role of the family was diminishing. At the death of David Colville four years earlier, the family had turned over its management to John Craig, an ironworker's son who had handled the company's sales for many years. Craig remained managing director for forty years, retiring in 1956 at the age of eighty-one. Family members stayed on the board, but their primary connection with the company was to provide short-term and long-term credit. This credit was supplemented by banks, of which the National Bank of Scotland became the leading supplier.[80] Thus, in Steven Tolliday's words, "the structure of authority and control at Colville was a multilayered cake of owners, managers, family and creditors."[81]

During the 1920s Craig and other industrialists and bankers discussed ways to rationalize and modernize the steel industry in Scotland. Little was done, however, until in February 1929 Craig and Sir James Lithgow, at the urging of Lord Weir, a Glasgow industrialist, asked Brassert & Company to make a comprehensive report on Scottish steel.[82] Brassert's report made it clear, in Peter Payne's words, "that *only* a fully integrated iron and steel making plant with the most modern ore dock facilities would permit the rehabilitation of the Scottish iron and steel industry."[83]

All agreed that merger must precede such a major investment. In 1931 Craig completed a merger with James Dunlop & Company, a small firm controlled by the Lithgow family (and not associated with the tire maker). The parties involved in the arrangement included Craig, the Colvilles, the Lithgows, Harland & Wolff, the Bankers' Industrial Development Company, the British Iron and Steel Federation, and the Midland Bank. Five more years passed before the parties achieved their larger objective, namely, an agreement on the merger of Colvilles with the Steel Company of Scotland and the Lanarkshire Steel Company. That 1936 merger gave Colvilles 80% of the Scottish steel capacity. By that time, however, the rapid rise in costs had made the carrying out of the Brassert scheme far more expensive than originally planned. Andrew McCance, Colvilles' brilliant technical engineer, was able to modernize the existing works in an impressive but piecemeal and improvised manner. Successful as McCance was—and that success in good part came from the rapid increase in demand— Tolliday emphasizes that the opportunity for the building of a modern, efficient works had been missed. "In the long-run the congested sites, the complex material flows, the use of already existing plant in remodeled forms severely restrained the prospects for future evolution."[84]

Colvilles with its small but highly experienced team of managers was able to consolidate the neighboring Scottish enterprises and to bring somewhat significant increases in productivity and reductions in costs. On the northeast coast of England, however, where there was the same agreement on the need to merge, rationalize, and modernize, not even this first step was achieved. That region had four major players. Dorman Long was a family firm that had grown by acquisition but had made no attempt to integrate or reorganize the acquired firms. South Durham/Cargo Fleet, an early merger of two plate makers, did consolidate operations and was controlled by the Furness family, leaders in shipping and shipbuilding. Consett Iron Company was also a plate maker with excellent local coal supplies. The fourth was Bolckow Vaughan, another family firm, which, like Dorman Long, produced rails and structural steel as well as plate. All but South Durham had expanded their capacity during World War I and the boom that immediately followed. As in other regions, expansion had come in a piecemeal fashion. Inefficient plant, excess capacity, and low profits had increased these firms' debts and brought creditors onto their boards.

The key to any major merger in the Northeast was Dorman Long. The firm in the 1920s was still headed by its founder, Arthur Dorman, who died in 1931 at the age of eighty-one. The chairmanship then went to Sir Hugh Bell, age eighty-seven, the founder of the firm that had merged with Dorman Long in 1903. Over the years the two families rarely agreed as to how the firm should be run. Indeed, the company was known locally not as Dorman Long but as "Dorman versus Bell." In the 1920s that firm attempted to expand its overseas activities with little success. Nor was the region's second largest firm, South Durham, able to move out of plate into other steel products with any more success. Neither they nor their two neighbors had the resources or organizational capabilities to modernize, much less to expand into new markets or closely related products.[85]

The first regional merger, between Dorman Long and the almost bankrupt Bolckow Vaughan, took less time than some. Negotiations began in April 1927 and were completed in July 1929. The merger was expensive for Dorman Long, and the octogenarians in charge made no attempt to reorganize facilities. Next, in 1930, negotiations began with South Durham/Cargo Fleet. "The next three years," writes Tolliday, "saw a series of bewildering complex negotiations, involving some five different schemes, several in many versions, ranging from regional operating companies to outright purchase. All ran rapidly into a complex interlocking web of sectional interests, and all proved abortive." South Durham's managing director, Benjamin Talbot, and its owners, the Furness family, could not agree among themselves on terms. Nor could the Dormans and the Bells at "Dorman versus Bell." Even after the death of the senior Dorman and the senior Bell, and the removal of Talbot by the Furness family, agreement was held off by the different demands of the debenture and preference shareholders and by the creditors, particularly Barclays Bank and the Bank of England. Each of these banking institutions wanted the other to take the financial risks of promoting the merger.[86]

After the final breakdown of negotiations in 1933, Ellis Hunter, a partner in the acccounting firm of Peat Marwick, who represented the debenture holders at Dorman Long, unofficially took charge. At first, while still at Peat Marwick (where he worked through Lawrence Ennis, the company's most effective manager), and then after 1938 as the steel company's managing director, Hunter reorganized the management, restructured the marketing organization, and began to modernize the plant, although less effectively than McCance was doing at Colvilles. These improvised improvements, Tolliday reminds us, were "not part of any centralized program to achieve full economies of integrated processes."[87]

United Steel Companies, Ltd., the largest iron and steel producer in the Midlands, was more successful than Dorman Long in reshaping its facilities, but not in achieving regional rationalization through merger. The company, a 1919 merger of three firms, made no attempt to centralize administration or to integrate and coordinate the activities of the merged firms until 1928.[88] Then Walter Benton Jones, son of the founder of one of the constituent companies, became chairman and Robert Hilton became managing director. Hilton was a former managing director of Metropolitan-Vickers. Trained at British Westinghouse, he was one of the few experienced industrial administrators in Britain. Jones and Hilton set up a corporate office at Sheffield and installed themselves and their senior functional executives there. They expanded the sales staff; and, in the words of one historian, "centralized purchasing and costing systems were established, a Central Research Department was set up, and also an Efficiency Department to concentrate on organization and methods, time studies and other similar pursuits." Nevertheless, the corporate office remained small by American and German standards. (As late as 1950 the total staff at the Sheffield head office numbered only 120 and its sales force in Britain some 130 out of a total of 28,800 employees.) Limited rationalization followed the centralization of 1928. Some coal mines were shut down, redundant plants scrapped, and manufacturing of rails and other products concentrated. At the same time an attempted takeover by a well-known financier, Clarence Hatry, benefited the company's financial position by forcing it into bankruptcy and so permitting the writing down of sizable obligations.[89]

In the early 1930s the Bank of England looked on the United Steel Companies as a potential core for regional rationalization. Again the scenario was much the same as in other regions. Brassert made a study. Lengthy merger negotiations were carried out between the Bank and two of its clients. One was Lancashire Steel, a five-company merger that had been sponsored by the Bank. The other was John Summers & Sons, a family firm which had come under control of the Bank because of a costly effort to build a continuous-strip steel mill. (The Summers story in many ways paralleled that of Richard Thomas.) Nothing came of the negotiations. So no overall rationalization occurred in the Midlands.[90]

This review of the experience of the largest British iron and steel companies is all too brief. The companies described here are in no way unique; other British steel firms listed in Appendixes B.1–B.3 had strikingly similar experiences. Even this brief review makes it clear why the British steelmakers were unable to carry out the plans that all agreed were needed to modernize their industry and make it competitive in international markets. Essentially they were paying the price for the earlier failure to make an investment large enough and to recruit a management organization large and effective enough to exploit fully the new technologies of mass-producing steel. By the 1920s too many interests were involved in trying to reach and implement the decisions necessary to modernize the industry. Except at Stewarts & Lloyds the managers were unable to define a strategy which their boards would approve. Instead, owners, family, creditors, the financial community, and the government were all involved with (or against) the managers in attempting to reach accord on courses of action. Even at Stewarts & Lloyds the managers had to give way to the wishes of competitors and banks.

In the steel industry, management itself remained small and personal. The top and middle management rarely included more than the managing director and the executives in charge of the production works, of the small sales and purchasing offices, and, less often, of the technical (engineering) office. Many of these managers continued to handle their activities until they reached their seventies or eighties. Hence there was little opportunity to build a managerial organization or develop organizational capabilities in the manner of the large American or German steel producers. As Tolliday has emphasized:

> Technical and production engineering management developed less fully. Figures like Andrew McCance (Colvilles), John E. James (South Durham, Lancashire Steel, and Richard Thomas), and Lawrence Ennis (Dorman Long), who rose to the top as technical managers, were rare. In the late 1930s James was almost the sole figure of this sort that the Bank of England could find to put in to rationalize the technical side of ailing firms, and most banks and firms turned to the American consultants H. A. Brassert & Co. for the most modern technical expertise. With the sole exception of the relationship between Sheffield University and United Steel in the 1930s, technical education did not feed directly into higher management in steel.[91]

Not surprisingly, the innovations and technical development in steel production in the interwar years came from the United States and Germany.

As a result, with the sole and important exception of Stewarts & Lloyds, no steel producer was able to exploit the economies of scale and hence to achieve dominance at home and become a major player in markets abroad as the single dominant British firm in oil, rubber, rayon, glass, and containers, and to a lesser extent paper and asbestos, was able to do. Instead the British steel producers remained small, regionally oriented, and relatively specialized. After 1931 they cooperated through the British Iron & Steel Federation to control competition at home and to work with international European cartels to control competition abroad. In the international negotiations, the British Federation was less effective than Stewarts & Lloyds in obtaining market share for British enterprises.[92] Indeed, the failure to create a strong management structure through merger—which would have made possible the rationalization and modernization of facilities—forced the steelmakers to become increasingly dependent on the trade association, the banks, and the government. That dependence in turn further inhibited the possibility of merger, administrative centralization, and rationalization of personnel and facilities.

The contrast between Britain and the United States with respect to the evolution of the large enterprise and the resulting structure of the steel industry is historically significant. More striking is the contrast between the British and German steel industries (see Chapter 14). Very few of the leading steel producers in Britain were as large as the American firms that challenged United States Steel. In 1935 there were at least forty-four American steel works with a capacity exceeding 400,000 tons, twice as large as the original integrated works of Stewarts & Lloyds at Corby. Of these, eighteen had a capacity of a million tons or more, including those of U.S. Steel, Bethlehem, Jones & Laughlin, Republic, Inland, National, and Youngstown.[93] In Britain the primary issue facing decision-makers was how best to *acquire* the cost advantages of current technology. In the United States the issue for the industry's leaders was how best to *exploit* them. In Britain the government and its central bank supported efforts to consolidate, rationalize, and modernize the industry. In the United States the chairman of United States Steel, supported by the bankers on the board, held back from fully utilizing scale economies in order to prevent the government from dismembering his enterprise.

Even more instructive is the contrast between the British steel industry and other British industries where technologies of production brought substantial economies of scale. In oil, rubber, glass, abrasives, metal containers, and steel tubes, the first movers continued to maintain market share in Britain and to compete successfully with foreign enterprises abroad. Once the necessary investments had been made in production, distribution, and management, bankers had almost no say in major decisions; nor did the government play a role comparable to its role in steel. In the detailed, documented histories of British Petroleum, Courtaulds, Pilkington, and Metal Box, there is almost no mention of bankers. Even in oil, where the government held 51% of the voting shares, the role of the directors representing the government had by 1922 become one of "amicable indifference." In Britain, as elsewhere, the organizational capabilities that permitted a firm to compete profitably at home and abroad normally assured that enterprise of earnings that kept banks and governments at a distance.

Textiles

Although my main focus in this study is on the growth of the modern enterprise in industries where new technologies brought cost advantages of scale and scope, the traditional textile industry must be reviewed for Britain in a little more detail than it was for the United States (see Chapter 4). The major difference between the profiles of the top two hundred manufacturing enterprises in Britain and those in the United States is that there are many more textile companies on the British lists. In part this difference merely reflects the fact that there were a smaller number of large British firms in oil and in the new machinery, materials, and chemistry industries, so that more companies in the long-established industries remained on the lists. But it also reflects the importance of the natural-fiber textile industry in the British economy; between the 1880s and 1940s that industry was Britain's largest in terms of total output, assets, and employment.

The largest British textile firms (Group 22; see Appendixes B.1–B.3) were, as might be expected, either industry-wide federations, most of which had been established at the turn of the century, or, like the few textile companies among the top two hundred U.S. manufacturing firms, they were enterprises that marketed as well as produced.

The federations of small, single-unit, personally managed (nonhierarchical) enterprises carried out specialized processes or made specialized products. The "process federations" included Bleachers' Association, Calico Printers' Association, and the Bradford Dyers.[94] The "product federations," such as J. & P. Coats and Linen Thread, continued to produce thread, while the Fine Cotton Spinners' and Doublers' Association concentrated on high quality yarn. In the interwar years those three product federations did enlarge their small corporate offices and even their facilities for research, but they failed to develop a structure comparable to that of Metal Box after its reorganization by Robert Barlow. The constituent companies continued to be responsible for purchasing their own materials, for processing, and for sales. The function of these holding companies remained primarily to control price and output. In addition, during the depressed years of the 1930s they did reduce excess capacity by closing down the older and less efficient mills.

The large textile firms which established their own marketing network and also integrated spinning and weaving within their mills—such firms as Horrockses, Crewdson, Joshua Hoyle, and Whitworth & Mitchell—remained very much the exceptions in the British textile industry. Well before World War I, cotton and wool processors had disintegrated vertically in response to the rapid expansion of overseas markets during the second half of the nineteenth century. By 1914 the vast majority were producing a single product or carrying out a single function—spinning, weaving, dyeing, or bleaching.[95] William Lazonick points out: "In 1930 only 26 of more than 2,000 cotton yarn and cloth producers in Britain had their own marketing facilities and only 19 combined spinning and weaving as well. These 26 firms controlled about 7 percent of the spindles and 10 per cent of the looms in the industry."[96]

Those few undoubtedly did benefit from economies of scale. But in these labor-intensive textile industries such cost differentials were far smaller than those in steel, oil, chemicals, machinery, and the other capital-intensive industries in which the modern industrial enterprise clustered. Moreover, investment in a marketing organization did not provide the advantages and create the barriers to entry that similar investment did in capital-intensive industries. So the largest textile firms in no way dominated their industries.

The hundeds of firms producing textiles in Britain had enormous difficulty in responding to the loss of export markets during the 1920s. The rapid increase in production before World War I—the increase that so encouraged vertical disintegration in the industry—came from an expanding overseas demand. During the war, producers in Japan and India captured the Asian markets for low-quality products; and during the 1920s those in western Europe and the United States increased their market share for high-quality goods. In 1922 the volume of piece goods exported was only 61% of the 1913 level; by 1929 it was only 53%.[97]

The difficulty was that many of the British mills were still relying on a technology more than a century old. Whereas in 1913 in the United States 87% of all spindles were "ring," 81% of British spindles were still "mules" (a machine first developed in the 1770s). Whereas 40% of American cotton-weaving looms in 1914 were automatic, only 1 or 2 percent of the British looms were.[98]

As in the steel industry there was general agreement on what needed to be done. Equipment should be modernized, capacity reduced, and, although there was less agreement on this point, throughput should be increased by integrating spinning and weaving within a single works. (In the United States by 1899, 84% of the spindles and 90% of the looms were in such integrated mills.)[99] But within these fragmented British industries there existed no institution capable of carrying out the transformation.

As John Maynard Keynes defined the problem in 1928: "There [is] probably no hall in Manchester large enough to hold all the directors of cotton companies, they [run] into thousands. One of the first things should be to dismiss the vast majority of these people, but the persons to whom this proposal would have to be made would be precisely those directors."[100] The Bank of England, the most powerful financial institution in Britain, attempted to use its power by merging a number of companies as the first step toward rationalization. Through its subsidiary, Bankers' Industrial Development Company, the Bank set up the Lancashire Cotton Corporation, which acquired seventy firms in 1929 and twenty-six more the next year. Yet the new corporation had little success in even achieving the first step of administrative centralization. Sir Eric Geddes, who was brought in by the Bank to review the situation in late 1931, wrote: "I think the founders of the Lancashire Cotton Corporation underestimated the enormous difficulty of creating a great amalgamation of this kind without any real strong existing organization to take over control."[101] A smaller combination of fifteen spinning mills using Egyptian cotton, which was also formed in 1929, did little better. (Lancashire Cotton used American-grown cotton.) Although these amalgamations failed to bring modernization, to increase productivity, and to decrease costs, they did eventually result in some reduction in capacity.

In the textile industries—those processing natural fibers, where firms remained small and nonintegrated and competed primarily on price—attempts to reorganize and rationalize production processes by creating large managerial enterprises seemed doomed to failure. Neither the needed organizations nor the essential organizational capabilities existed in these labor-intensive industries. In the United States the large integrated textile firms appear to have stayed relatively profitable, but the American industry as a whole remained "sick." In Germany attempts to rationalize through merger and acquisition were almost as unsuccessful as in Britain (see Chapter 13).

Costs of the Failure to Develop Organizational Capabilities

Administrative centralization and rationalization were certainly viable alternatives to continuing personal management in capital-intensive industries. In metals (and, as described in the next chapter, in machinery and chemicals) American and German industries showed the way. In copper, British firms had the opportunity, particularly during the years immediately following World War I, to become competitive; but they failed to act. In steel nearly everyone agreed on the need to merge, centralize administratively, and rationalize. No one disputed the validity of Brassert's proposal to build profitable, competitive plants. Nevertheless, even with an immense amount of effort the personally managed British firms were unable to adopt modern, best-practice technology, much less to develop it. Managements were not strong enough and competent enough during the interwar years to make the necessary investment and to create the necessary organization to compete in international markets or, often, to maintain their place in the domestic one. Only one firm, Stewarts & Lloyds, developed the necessary organizational capability.

In the late 1930s, rapid growth in the production of automobiles, together with rearmament, sharply increased the demand for steel in Britain and brought existing capacity into fuller use. Therefore the steel output per worker increased and costs declined more than in the United States, where the Great Depression cut automobile output in half and where rearmament came later. Even so, in Britain costs remained higher and productivity lower than in the United States. The author of a recent study of British steel concludes his analysis thus: "Despite the achievements, the most distinctive legacy of the inter-war years in steel was in problems unsolved and possible solutions compromised."[102] As a result the industry continued its decline. The inability to respond to change brought high economic and social costs in terms of unemployment and higher prices for the most essential of industrial materials.

On the other hand, in oil, rubber, synthetic fibers, plate glass, asbestos, paper, and metal containers, a leading enterprise in each industry took the steps required to obtain and maintain market share and profit at home and abroad. It integrated the processes of production within its works, invested in best-practice technology, built national and international marketing organizations, and recruited a small hierarchy of managers. In these industries the bankers played a much less influential role than in textiles and steel, and the leading enterprises made fewer calls on the government for assistance. In these industries the processes of production and distribution did adapt to change. Here the economic and social costs of changing markets and technology were much lower than in natural fibers and steel.

Even though these leaders did create the organizations necessary to exploit the cost advantages of scale, their managerial capabilities differed from those of their American counterparts. These differences in capabilities reflected differences in the structure of the domestic industries in which the firms operated. In the United States the coming of the new technologies with their scale economies led to the dominance of two or more large firms that competed functionally and strategically for market share. In Britain, because of the smaller size of the domestic market, only one or occasionally two such firms appeared. Most of these companies negotiated for market share with the smaller satellites in their industry and with foreign competitors in international markets.

The development of British organizational capabilities was held back not only by less vigorous competition between firms but also by the desires of the founders and their families to retain control. These desires kept the firms from making what their owners viewed as relatively risky investments in distant lands or in new and untested products and processes. If the financing of such ventures required new capital, the resulting increase in shares outstanding or long-term debt posed a threat to continuing family control. In addition, the smaller number of top executives in British firms usually meant that they had to concentrate on day-to-day operations to the detriment of long-term planning and growth. As Geoffrey Jones has noted in an introduction to a series of essays on British multinationals: "Until the 1930s many British companies paid only spasmodic attention to their foreign subsidiaries, and coherent overseas business strategies were rare."[103] The executives of leading British enterprises were slow, too, in turning their attention to the potentials of research and development and to the formulation of a considered strategy of product diversification.

So much for differences between Britain and the United States in the more stable industries—oil, rubber, synthetic fibers, natural fibers, glass, newsprint, asbestos, abrasives, metals, and textiles. The German experience further highlights these differences (see Part IV). In these industries the dynamics of growth were based largely on the cost advantages of scale. The differences between the modern industrial enterprises and their evolution in each of the nations studied were even more noticeable in the more dynamic industries— machinery, industrial chemicals, and branded, packaged products—where opportunities created by economies of scope supplemented those of scale.

NINE

Creating Organizational Capabilities:
Success and Failure in the Dynamic Industries

In the more dynamic industrial groups—food, chemicals, and machinery—the modern industrial enterprise had greater potential for growth by moving into foreign markets and related product markets than did the materials and metals industries. The organizational capabilities developed to exploit the economies of scale gave enterprises a competitive advantage in foreign markets, and those developed to exploit the economies of scope gave a similar advantage in related product markets. But precisely because so few British firms in food, chemicals, and machinery developed effective organizational capabilities—physical facilities and human skills—before 1914, they grew more slowly and more hesitantly during the interwar years through expansion overseas and into related industries than did their counterparts in the same industries in the United States. In the decades of the 1920s and 1930s British firms were still catching up with American and also German competitors, not only in international markets but even within Britain itself.

In each of these major industrial groups the processes of catching up and of continuing growth varied. In nonelectrical machinery British enterprises had little success in competing with American firms in the new light, mass-produced equipment. American first movers continued to dominate British markets until well after World War II. Although British enterprises were more successful in catching up with American first movers in electrical equipment and motor vehicles, American enterprises nevertheless remained leaders in both of these groups of British industries throughout the interwar years.

In industrial chemicals the two British firms that had developed effective organizational capabilities before World War I merged to form an enterprise, Imperial Chemical Industries (ICI), that was able to challenge German and American competitors effectively in international markets and to diversify into related lines. But ICI was the exception. Of the other listed producers of industrial chemicals (see Appendixes B.1–B.3), only one, British Oxygen, had begun to build a managerial hierarchy by World War II. These firms specialized in narrow lines of products and made limited direct investments abroad or in related industries.

In branded, packaged products—food and consumer chemicals—family firms (a few with hierarchies, but more without) continued to dominate. There the technology of production remained relatively simple, and marketing and distribution required relatively small investment in product-specific facilities and services. But when these enterprises were directly challenged by foreign competitors, they had to expand their investments in production and distribution and to recruit managers if they were to retain their market share at home and abroad. Moreover, unless they made these moves, they rarely diversified into related industries in the manner of the American producers of branded, packaged products.

Machinery

The collective histories of the three basic machinery groups—nonelectrical machinery, electrical machinery, and transportation equipment—further pinpoint differences between Britain and the United States in the evolution of the modern industrial enterprise.

In nonelectrical machinery the established firms in the older trades continued to dominate their industries. These firms, producers of textile machinery or makers of metal-working and mining equipment, had begun to develop organizational capabilities before World War I. But in the newer industries—those that made light, volume-produced machinery—all but two of the firms listed among the top two hundred enterprises were or had been subsidiaries of American first movers. In electrical manufacturing, on the other hand, the story was one of catching up with foreign first movers by enlarging small prewar facilities and by taking over existing foreign-owned and foreign-managed enterprises. In electrical, as in nonelectrical machinery, therefore, there was little turnover at the top. Many of the same firms continued to be listed among the top two hundred British enterprises, even though their size and management changed.

In transportation equipment, however, rapid adoption of the internal combustion engine caused a much greater turnover, as it did in the United States. As makers of automobiles, automobile parts, and airplanes came on the list, shipbuilders and makers of railroad equipment dropped off. In shipbuilding (including armaments) and railroad equipment the threat of financial disaster brought intervention and reorganization by the banks and the government. In automobiles, as in electrical equipment, the story was much more one of catching up.

NONELECTRICAL MACHINERY: CONTINUING FOREIGN DOMINANCE

During the interwar years British entrepreneurs and enterprises did little more than they had before 1914 to challenge American first movers in the new, volume-produced, light-machinery industries (Group 35; see Appendixes B.1–B.4). The subsidiaries of those first movers, which were partially financed in Britain and were listed in the *Stock Exchange Year-Book* (and therefore in Appendixes B.1–B.4), include British United Shoe, Linotype & Machinery, and Babcock & Wilcox. The last, the largest of the British nonelectrical machinery companies in terms of market value of shares, was formed in 1900 to take over the American parent's activities in Britain and other countries abroad. Throughout the interwar years the British enterprise remained closely tied to its American founder through technical and marketing agreements.[1]

Other first movers in Britain in nonelectrical machinery were subsidiaries of American firms whose shares were not publicly traded and thus were not listed in the *Stock Exchange Year-Book* (and therefore not in the appendixes). They too continued to dominate the British industries in which they operated. Those that had built plants in Britain before World War I included Singer Sewing Machine, Otis Elevator, Westinghouse Air Brake, Chicago Pneumatic Tool, Burroughs Adding Machine, American Radiator, Eastman Kodak, and Worthington Pump.[2] Those that obtained production facilities during the interwar years included International Business Machines, Timken Roller Bearing, and Remington Typewriter. Of all these only Worthington Pump had significant competition, but its geographical spread and its diversified product line were far more extensive than those of Britain's largest producer of pumps, G. & J. Weir.[3] Nor did British firms successfully challenge American companies such as National Cash Register, International Harvester, and Underwood Typewriter, which supplied their extensive marketing organizations from either their American or European factories.

All these subsidiaries of larger international organizations were run by salaried middle managers who coordinated and monitored British and allied businesses and reported to managers in their corporate offices in the United States, usually to those in charge of the international relations department. In all of the subsidiaries, including Babcock & Wilcox, research and development to improve product and process continued to be carried out in the United States and not in Britain.

During the interwar years the British-owned and British-managed firms in Group 35 (see Appendixes B.1–B.4) modestly developed their organizational capabilities by expanding and strengthening their marketing forces overseas. There is little evidence, however, that they established plants abroad. Alfred Herbert in metal-working machine tools and Mather & Platt in textile machinery had worldwide networks of branch offices or franchised agencies. As Mather & Platt announced in the 1930 *Federation of British Industries Register,* its offices abroad as well as in Britain were "at all times ready to offer expert advice on site, to give estimates and to render after-sale services."[4] In the 1920s Mather & Platt further expanded their line of electric meters and fire equipment, which were mainly used in the textile mills equipped by the company. By the 1930s it was beginning to invest in research and development.

The other two leading textile-machinery makers were slower than Mather & Platt to develop their organizational capabilities. In 1931 these two, Platt Brothers (not connected with Mather & Platt) and Howard & Bullough, merged with three smaller textile-machinery firms and then began hesitantly to reorganize. The sales forces were slowly consolidated. By World War II a central research and development unit had been established. A major financial reorganization, begun in 1947, gave the consolidated enterprise a new name: Platt Brothers & Company (Holdings), Ltd. Only then did the company centralize its administration and rationalize its facilities in the manner of Metal Box, setting up a functionally departmentalized structure. Although the founding families, the Platts and the Taylors, remained on the board, after 1946 Platt Brothers (Holdings), Ltd., appears to have become a managerial enterprise.[5] This may have also been true of Mather & Platt.

Yet even in the late 1940s these firms were the exceptions. Of the other machinery companies, R. A. Lister, makers of dairy and sheep-shearing machinery, continued to be managed in a personal manner—all five directors were Listers. At G. & J. Weir, makers of pumps, William, Lord Weir, was very much in charge for six decades. He became managing director in 1902, chairman in 1912, and was still chairman in the 1960s when his grandson, W. K. J. Weir, came on the board. At Herbert Morris, makers of lifting and conveying equipment, F. M. Morris was vice-chairman and managing director in 1948. At Alfred Herbert, Ltd., long Britain's premier maker of machine tools, Sir Alfred Herbert remained "Chairman and sole Governing Director" until just before World War II.[6] Before the 1950s none of the British producers of nonelectrical machinery had recruited the managerial hierarchies or developed the organizational capabilities of their American counterparts.

TRANSPORTATION EQUIPMENT

Although the players in Group 35 remained much the same and continued to operate along the lines established before the outbreak of World War I, those producing transportation equipment (Group 37; see Appendixes B.1–B.4) enjoyed far less stability. Some Group 37 firms were in older industries that suffered from declining markets and increasing international competition. Other Group 37 firms were in newer industries where they were able, as those in Group 35 were not, to challenge the American first movers successfully. The history of the leading firms in the older industries emphasizes the difficulties facing enterprises which had failed to create substantial enough organizational capabilities to adjust to a changing environment. The story of those in the new industries indicates that, although the British companies did catch up by the time of World War II, they had only just developed the capabilities needed to become strong competitors abroad and, where technology permitted, to move into new product lines.

Continued failure in the older industries. In the older industries, particularly shipbuilding, the problems were much the same as in textiles and iron and steel. During World War I the shipyards of other nations, especially the Netherlands and Japan, expanded rapidly. Then after the brief postwar boom collapsed, British shipbuilding went into a decline from which it never recovered. As in textiles and steel, the leading firms were unable to respond to the challenges of reduced demand. "Many of the problems of British shipbuilding were outside of the power of the industry to solve," wrote William Reader. "It can scarcely be doubted, however, that they were made worse by the reluctance of management and men to face drastic rationalization of productive capacity and shipbuilding methods." Compared with the explosives and chemical industries, Reader notes, rationalization in shipbuilding "started later, did not go nearly so far, and demonstrated only its negative aspect: the shutting down of uneconomic yards."[7]

The postwar situation was made more difficult by the close ties between shipbuilding, marine engineering, steel production, and armaments. This was particularly true of naval shipbuilding, for before World War I not only was Britain the world's most formidable naval power, but her yards were the world's foremost suppliers of vessels for the navies of many nations. Not only were the leading armament makers, such as Vickers, Armstrong Whitworth, and William Beardmore, major shipbuilders, but also the leading shipbuilders, such as John Brown and Cammell Laird, built naval vessels. After the war all of these firms fell on hard times.

Before 1914 Vickers and to a lesser extent Armstrong Whitworth and Beardmore (Beardmore had come under the financial control of Vickers) developed a policy of manufacturing everything that went into a warship, including engines and other power equipment, steel, naval ordnance, and gunnery-control equipment (that is, equipment to control the firing of heavy guns). In addition, Vickers produced machine guns, rifles, and small arms. In 1901 it even set up an automobile factory. "Such self-propelled machines," noted the minutes of the Vickers board, "must be of great use in future military operations." These firms invested in operations abroad—Vickers in Japan, Spain, and Turkey. To improve the effectiveness of its military and naval products, Vickers, in the opinion of historian Clive Trebilcock, evolved the most advanced research and development of any business enterprise in Great Britain before World War I.[8]

At these companies, however, the number of managers remained small. Armstrong Whitworth continued to be administered by Armstrongs and Whitworths. Throughout its history it suffered from dynastic controversies and clashes. At Beardmore the owner-entrepreneur, Sir William Beardmore, made all the major decisions, constrained only occasionally by the Vickers management. By contrast, the two Vickerses, Alfred and Douglas (brother and son, respectively, of the founder, Thomas Vickers), did bring in experienced executives. By 1900 the enterprise was managed by a seven-man "cabinet"—the two Vickerses who had the controlling shares, two technical men, two others who were responsible for sales, and a financial specialist. Yet the company had almost no central staff, nor were there middle managers between the cabinet and the plant managers. The sales force consisted of a tiny number of very effective salesmen who contacted naval and military officers at home and abroad.[9] This small managerial team successfully administered wartime expansion, but it failed dramatically to maintain profit and growth in the postwar years.

The postwar strategy of all three of the leading armaments firms, like that of Du Pont, was one of diversification into peacetime products. The difference between Du Pont and the British firms was that the latter, including even Vickers, had few of the managerial or technical skills essential to compete effectively in new product markets. The cabinet at Vickers saw diversification only in terms of using existing plants and their work forces, much as the Du Pont company had seen it before February 1917. Unlike the Du Pont Executive Committee after that date, Vickers never appreciated that successful diversification must be based on organizational capabilities, that is, product-specific facilities and skills. (For Du Pont's experience see Chapter 5.) Another historian of Vickers, J. D. Scott, describes the transformation of the company's production facilities plant by plant:

> This then was the position during 1919—Sheffield turning over to railway material, forgings and stampings; Barrow to merchant shipbuilding and the production of locomotives, boilers, turbines, reciprocating steam engines, diesel and gas engines; Erith to matchmaking machinery, machine tools, cardboard box-making machinery and gas meters; Crayford to sporting guns, sewing machines and motor car parts; Dartford to furniture, wooden toys, washing machines and so forth. Wolseley was planning the production of mass-produced cars, high-class mass-produced cars costing £800, such that no American car could compete with. It seemed that a good beginning, at any rate, had been made upon peace products.[10]

In addition to changing the product lines in these six works, Vickers used its wartime profits to move into the electrical-equipment industry. In 1917 it acquired a train-lighting company, a producer of electrical refrigerators, and an electric-cable company. Then in 1919 it purchased, for what many thought an excessively high price, Dudley Docker's Metropolitan Carriage & Wagon and also Docker's holdings in British Westinghouse. In 1917 Westinghouse senior executives in Pittsburgh, troubled by financial difficulties both at home and in

Britain, had asked Docker, the Birmingham industrialist, to sell their subsidiary to British nationals. Docker worked out an arrangement by which Vickers obtained both British Westinghouse and Metropolitan Carriage, merging them into a new company, Metropolitan-Vickers. The parent firm, however, made no attempt to unify the operations of these two very different enterprises.

Armstrong Whitworth followed a similar pattern of diversification, making an even more unrelated major investment in a new enterprise, the Newfoundland Paper Mills, which was to develop hydroelectric power and also mass-produce pulp and paper in Canada. Beardmore, with little guidance from Vickers (still its major owner), moved into the manufacturing of automobiles, airplanes, locomotives, and diesel engines at a cost of £4 million. Hadfields, which was the largest of the renowned specialty steelmakers of Sheffield, and which had produced armor-piercing projectiles and armor plate, turned to making automobiles. Cammell Laird and other shipbuilders made similar moves.

Because these companies, unlike Du Pont, had so little in the way of technical and managerial skills to transfer to their new product lines, diversification proved disastrous. They were unable to achieve a high enough level of throughput to compete in what had become high-volume industries. Douglas Vickers's plaintive lament of April 1925 tells the story: "When the manufacturer's costs are high, he cannot quote low prices; when he cannot quote low prices, he cannot fill his works; and when he cannot fill his works, his costs are higher; and so it goes from bad to worse."[11] Vickers and the others did not have the necessary sales and purchasing organizations for the new lines, nor did they invest in research and development for their new products. By 1925 Vickers was passing through the most serious financial crisis in its history, and Armstrong Whitworth, which owed the Bank of England £2.6 million, was on the verge of bankruptcy. The situations at Beardmore and Hadfields were only a little better.

The failure of the armaments firms' attempts to diversify brought massive corporate reorganization in the late 1920s, marking the beginning of the restructuring of the British shipbuilding and railroad-equipment industries. This, in turn, stimulated major efforts by the Bank of England to rationalize the steel industry. At Vickers an "advisory committee" of outsiders, headed by Dudley Docker and including Reginald McKenna of the Midland Bank and Sir William Plender, one of Britain's leading accountants, made an investigation and carried out the subsequent reorganization. At Armstrong Whitworth, Montagu Norman, head of the Bank of England, attempted a similar reorganization, and he did so by relying on Frater Taylor, a consultant who became, in the words of J. D. Scott, "in effect the comptroller of the company." At both companies new managers were recruited. Douglas Vickers was put aside at the age of sixty-five, having served thirty-eight years on the Vickers board, including eight years as chairman. In October 1927 the two were merged into Vickers-

Armstrong, Ltd., with Vickers controlling and Armstrong Whitworth becoming merely a holding company.

The new, consolidated firm, Vickers-Armstrong, concentrated on the business it knew best—armaments. Even before the merger Vickers had sold Wolseley, its automobile subsidiary, to Morris Motors, which by then was the leading automobile manufacturer in Britain. Vickers had also closed down its ventures in train lighting and refrigeration. In 1928 it sold the electrical-equipment part of Metropolitan-Vickers to the American giant, General Electric, which merged it with its existing British subsidiary, British Thomson-Houston, to form Associated Electrical Industries (AEI). Next the railway-equipment division of Metropolitan-Vickers was combined with comparable works of Cammell Laird, and both of those companies became joint owners of the new Metro-Cammell Carriage Railway & Wagon Company. The same two companies (Metropolitan-Vickers and Cammell Laird) next merged their steelmaking activities into English Steel Corporation, Ltd. In 1928, immediately after the merger, Armstrong Whitworth's Canadian venture, Newfoundland Paper Mills, was sold to the foremost American paper manufacturer, International Paper; and its steel works became part of the Lancashire Steel Corporation, sponsored by the Bank of England. Finally, in 1929, Vickers turned its cable company over to Callender's Cable. By that year Vickers, administered by a small team of salaried managers, was again little more than an essential arm of Britain's professional military establishment. [12]

At the same time Beardmore, whose controlling shares Vickers had disposed of in 1926, was rescued from bankruptcy by the Bank of England and reorganized in the fashion of Vickers and Armstrong Whitworth, with the Bank placing its own agents in charge of the company. In 1931 Hadfields liquidated its automobile venture and began to concentrate once again on specialty steels and armaments. [13]

In this ad hoc way the leading firms producing arms, naval vessels, and railroad rolling stock—and the industries in which they operated—had been reorganized before the 1930s. These reorganizations, in turn, brought the Bank of England into even broader schemes for rationalizing the British shipbuilding and steel industries. [14] Yet in shipbuilding, as in steel, the conflicting interests and the inability of the Bank to find effective managers frustrated Montagu Norman's efforts. Some consolidation occurred, some outmoded capacity was scrapped, but little modernization or increased productivity resulted. To be sure, the new nonfamily management teams became experienced enough by the late 1930s to respond effectively to increased demand as the rearmament of Britain moved into full swing. But the tradition of personal management and the resulting failure to develop broad organizational capabilities contributed to the disastrous performance of the leaders in these industries during most of the interwar period.

After the First World War one smaller, more specialized armament firm, Birmingham Small Arms (BSA), made the reconversion to peacetime markets far more effectively than Vickers and the other giants. It did so because long before the war it had moved into the high-volume production of civilian products. That firm, one of the first British companies to adopt the American system of manufacturing by fabricating and assembling interchangeable parts, had its beginnings in the 1860s, mass-producing rifles and other small arms. In the 1880s it had turned its facilities and skills to making bicycles and then in the late 1890s to producing motorcycles. In the years just prior to World War I only a quarter to a third of its total output came from military orders. After a massive wartime expansion in the output of small arms, BSA turned its facilities back to its earlier lines, primarily motorcycles, and added the production of machine tools.[15] Thus it had the facilities and skills—the organizational capabilities—to remain the dominant producer of motorcycles at home and Britain's major representative in that line abroad, in much the same way as Anglo-Persian had done in oil, Dunlop in rubber, and Stewarts & Lloyds in steel tubes.[16]

Challenging the American presence in the newer industries. In automobiles and the allied industries the story was dramatically different from that of shipbuilding and railway equipment, and it was also different from that of nonelectrical machinery. Whereas in the Group 35 industries no strong challengers to the American first movers appeared, in the automobile industry British entrepreneurs were able to compete, at least in the British market. They did so partly because of Henry Ford's errors, which undermined his company's first-mover advantages, and partly because of the ability of William Morris and Herbert Austin to design an attractive small car tailored to the needs of British motor-vehicle users, to adopt mass-production methods, and to create the necessary marketing and distributing organizations.

Under the guidance of the able Percival Perry, the Ford Motor Company became the industry's first mover in Britain. In 1905 Perry, a Londoner, began to build Ford's marketing organization in the British Isles. In 1911, at Manchester, he established Ford's first overseas assembly plant. At the end of World War I the Ford Motor Company dominated the British automobile market just as it controlled the low-priced automobile market in the United States.[17] Then Henry Ford dissipated his first-mover advantages in Britain, much as he was then doing in the United States, by destroying the organization developed by his senior managers. In 1919, when he also fired his experienced and effective executives in Detroit, including William S. Knudsen and Norval A. Hawkins, he removed Perry and Perry's subordinates in Britain. The new managerial team abruptly reshaped the sales force by abolishing the wholesale distributors and insisting on exclusive retail dealerships, and then, most serious of all, allocated these dealers increasingly larger quotas of cars that were increasingly difficult to sell. The demoralized dealers turned to Morris and Austin, who at that moment were rapidly expanding their sales organizations.[18] (At home Ford dealers were flocking to General Motors at the same time for much the same reason.) By 1924 Ford had slipped into second place behind Morris. By 1929 Morris and Austin and the somewhat smaller Singer & Co. had taken 75% of the British market. By then Ford's share had dropped to a calamitous level of 5.7%.[19]

In the following decade, however, the Americans regained ground in the British market. Britain recovered much more quickly from the Great Depression than the United States, and the 1930s witnessed a boom in automobile output, which rose from 238,805 vehicles in 1929 to 507,000 in 1937—results that helped make the British economy relatively buoyant in the mid-1930s. A recent history of the industry notes that "the principal beneficiaries of this remarkable expansion were the American subsidiaries."[20]

In 1928 Ford rehired Perry, a most uncharacteristic move. Perry rebuilt the company's managerial capabilities and had Ford's designers in Detroit create a model—the Model Y or Baby Ford—to meet the specific needs of British and Empire markets.[21] By 1937 Ford's market share had risen to 22%, and the company was neck and neck with Austin for second place.[22] Even so, profits were reduced because Henry Ford, despite Perry's protests, had pushed the construction of a new plant at Dagenham on the Thames near London. This plant was poorly located, and it was much too large for the depressed market of 1931 and even for the increased demand of the mid-1930s. Until World War II it never operated at levels close to minimum efficient scale.

General Motors, concentrating on reorganization and rationalization at home, moved relatively slowly into the British market. In 1924 it built an assembly plant in London. Then in 1925, in order to get under high import duties and be closer to the market, the General Motors Executive Committee, after an unsuccessful attempt to buy Austin, purchased Vauxhall, a small producer of relatively high-priced cars with a tiny volume of 1,500 a year.[23] Until the depression, General Motors, intent on surpassing Ford in the domestic market, paid relatively little attention to its overseas activities. But in the early 1930s its management authorized a major increase in the scale of the British plant and had its engineers design a new "Light Six" specifically for the middle-priced market in Britain. These moves gave Vauxhall a substantial share of that market.

By 1938, just before World War II, six companies accounted for 93% of British automobile production. The Big Three (Austin, Morris, and Ford) produced 62% (down from 64% in 1929), and the next three (Vauxhall, Standard, and Rootes) produced 31%.[24] Exports of private and commercial automobiles had risen from 42,000 in 1929 to 98,500 in 1937, making Britain the world's second largest exporter of automobiles.

In the production of trucks, buses, and other commercial vehicles and automotive parts and accessories the story was much the same. Subsidiaries of

American firms remained strong, with British firms growing as demand expanded. Ford and Morris led in light trucks, with Bedford (General Motors' British truck subsidiary) providing vigorous competition, while British firms— Leyland, Dennis, Associated Commercial Vehicles, and one or two others— dominated the more specialized, heavy truck and bus production.[25] In the output of bodies and large parts, Pressed Steel, a joint venture of Morris and the Budd Company of Philadelphia, competed successfully with the British subsidiary of Detroit's Briggs Manufacturing Company. In smaller parts and accessories Joseph Lucas, maker of batteries, magnetos, and other electrical parts, and S. Smith & Sons, former watchmakers, grew by acquiring smaller firms and competed successfully with Champion Spark Plug (a General Motors division) and other subsidiaries of American firms. Lucas and Smith also succeeded in moving into new product lines. Indeed, by 1948 the two had become smaller versions of such American counterparts as Bendix and Borg-Warner.[26]

Britain's three aircraft companies—Hawker Siddeley, Bristol, and De Haviland (the last was number 203 on the list of the largest industrials in 1948), producers of airframes and engines—were even more closely tied to the military than were similar firms in the United States. But just before the war the largest, Hawker Siddeley, had begun to diversify in the manner of Joseph Lucas and S. Smith. By 1948 all three of these diversifying firms—Hawker Siddeley, Lucas, and Smith—were building braking, lighting, and ignition systems that were used in tractors, marine engines, construction equipment, and other power-driven equipment, as well as in automobiles, trucks, buses, and airplanes. They had also expanded overseas. Before World War II, Lucas and Hawker Siddeley had had research laboratories although the British automobile companies had not yet made such investments. Like their American counterparts, Joseph Lucas and Hawker Siddeley enjoyed tremendous growth during World War II, and by 1948 they were continuing to deploy their resources into new product lines.[27]

Thus the British makers of automobiles, parts, and accessories succeeded between the wars in creating enterprises that permitted them to regain a major share of their domestic market and to make modest gains overseas. Nevertheless, the revival of Ford and General Motors in Britain suggests that the organizational capabilities of the British companies were still limited. So does the strength of the American parts and accessories firms in Britain. The British automobile makers were, after all, smaller than the large *divisions* of the American automobile companies—for example, the Chevrolet and Plymouth divisions of their respective companies. Indeed, in 1937 General Motors alone produced three times as many passenger cars (1.6 million) as the total output of all motor vehicles in Britain (0.5 million). British cars exported in 1937 were still only 14.4% of the world export market, whereas American exports accounted for 57.9%.[28] And in that year 84.6% of British automobiles exported went to protected Empire markets. Moreover, the British subsidiaries of Ford and General Motors, the third and fourth largest producers in Britain, contributed substantially to the total number of cars exported. It is evident, too, that no British automobile company attempted to diversify its product lines in the manner of General Motors.

Finally, the first-generation firms continued to be personally managed by their founders. William Morris remained the top-level decision-maker in his company until well after World War II. So, too, the Spurrier family at Leyland, the Rootes brothers and sons at their firm, and the Lucases and the Smiths at theirs all dominated the management of their enterprises during the interwar years.[29] Wayne Lewchuk has shown that these firms, like Courtaulds, preferred to pay out earnings in dividends rather than reinvesting them, relying instead on capital markets for expansion and even for the maintenance of facilities. By contrast, the American companies financed most of their capacity expansion from earnings. Lewchuk has also shown that lower-level managers in British automobile companies turned the coordination of the flow of material over to the foreman on the shop floor. The firms continued to pay on a piece-work basis and permitted the work force to control flows, rather than paying hourly wages and making the managers responsible for coordinating flows in the American manner.[30]

The organizational capabilities developed in the interwar years did permit the British automobile makers to respond effectively to demand after World War II and to maintain—though rarely to expand—their market share and their profit at home and abroad during the 1950s. Nevertheless, what Lewchuk terms "the underdevelopment of the managerial function" appears to have been a significant factor in the collapse of the British automobile industry that began in the 1960s.[31]

ELECTRICAL EQUIPMENT: CATCHING UP

In automobiles the idiosyncratic management decisions of Henry Ford, the American first mover, permitted competitors at home and abroad to overcome his company's competitive advantages. In the production of heavy electrical equipment (Group 36; see Appendixes B.1–B.4) the American and German leaders were more careful to sustain their first-mover advantages. Nevertheless, the much smaller British firms benefited from the mistakes of George Westinghouse in creating—as Ford did later—plants that were too large for existing markets. They also benefited from the failure of Owen D. Young and Gerard Swope of General Electric to follow through on their plan to rationalize the British industry in the late 1920s. The greatest benefit of all, however, was the removal of the German first movers, Siemens and AEG, from British and international markets after the outbreak of World War I. Even though the American presence remained a powerful one in this industry, the British companies did recruit managerial hierarchies and did develop organizational capabilities during the interwar years that permitted them to challenge the American and German first movers, at least in Britain and the British Empire.

In the production of more specialized electrical machinery (still Group 36), however, the pattern was more similar to that in nonelectrical machinery (Group 35). While in the older industries the British remained strong, in the newer industries the subsidiaries of American firms that had established themselves in Britain at the turn of the century continued to dominate the nation's markets between the wars. The American subsidiaries among the largest manufacturing firms in Britain during the interwar years included: Chloride Electrical Storage (subsidiary of Electric Storage Battery); its competitor, British Ever Ready (subsidiary of Union Carbide & Carbon); Hoover (subsidiary of the American vacuum-cleaner producer of the same name); Standard Telephone & Cables, the subsidiary of Western Electric, and its successor overseas, International Telephone & Telegraph; and the Gramophone Company, which was controlled until 1931 by Victor Talking Machine. The one exception was Columbia Graphophone, which in the early 1920s became British-owned and then led the way to building a British-managed and British-owned record and radio industry.

In the older telegraph-equipment and cable-making industries the established British firms maintained their strong global position. It was to their advantage that in the prewar years British companies had operated two-thirds of the world's cable mileage and a large part of its telegraph system. W. T. Henley's Telegraph Works remained the major producer of telegraph equipment and wires, while Callender's Cable and Construction and British Insulated Wire (which became British Insulated Cables in 1926) continued to be the two leading producers of undersea cables to transmit messages and, later, of underground cable to transmit electric power. In the interwar years they maintained their strong overseas sales organizations and enlarged their management teams. In Britain their major competitor continued to be Siemens, which in the 1920s was able to regain control of its British cable-making plant.[32]

The management of these makers of telegraph equipment and electric cable and the structure of their industry remained unchanged until well after World War II. The firms continued to be family-managed. For example, Sir Thomas Callender, who had been active in his family firm (Callender's Cable) in the 1880s, was still "Deputy Vice-Chairman and Managing Director" in 1930 (and still, apparently, the de facto head of Vivian and Sons, the copper refiners). At British Insulated Wire, Dane Sinclair, who had invented a telephone switchboard in 1883, had become chairman and general manager in 1902 and was still running the enterprise in the 1930s.[33] These two competitors worked closely together, each sitting on the board of the smaller Enfield Cable Works. Then in 1945 the two joined forces; they set up a holding company, but in the typical British manner this did not interfere with either firm's operational autonomy.

It was in the central sector of the electrical-equipment industry—the production of machinery for the generation, distribution, and use of electric power—that the greatest change occurred. World War I brought an expansion of output and moved the smaller British companies into the production and distribution of new lines. Increased wartime profits permitted Hugo Hirst's General Electric Company (GEC) to buy out the German half-ownership in Osram Lamp Works, the major British makers of light bulbs, and also to buy some smaller producers of electrical equipment. Wartime profits allowed Dick, Kerr to obtain the following firms: United Electric Car Company (a small manufacturer of streetcars and railway wagons); Coventry Ordnance (armaments producer); the British sales subsidiary of the German giant, AEG; the equipment-manufacturing plant of Siemens's British subsidiary; and other, smaller, electrical-equipment makers. In 1919 the Dick, Kerr companies were legally unified under a holding company, English Electric; according to the historians of the industry, "right from the beginning it had been decided that the parent company would interfere as little as possible with the internal organizations of the firms concerned."[34] As important as the growth of the smaller British firms was the departure of one of the two American first movers, Westinghouse, and the acquisition of its personnel and facilities by Metropolitan-Vickers.[35]

Of these British firms only Hirst's GEC made a concerted effort in the early 1920s to expand its resources. It planned to move into new product lines, including telephone and radio, and it also planned to meet an optimistically stated goal of producing "everything electric."[36] It reorganized its plant facilities and reshaped and expanded the sales network, forming thirty-one branch and sub-branch offices in Great Britain and fifteen overseas. The company established, in the words of its official historian, "complete self-acting sales centers, with warehouses and showrooms under the charge of expert salesmen and technical men." In 1922 the company opened its central research laboratory, the first in the British electric-equipment industry.[37] Then came the construction of Magnet House in Kingsway, London, to house the corporate offices.

Nevertheless, GEC remained much smaller than its foreign rivals and had not yet developed the organizational capabilities it needed to capture market share effectively. Meanwhile, at English Electric no rationalization occurred. And little was changed at the former Westinghouse subsidiary (owned by Metropolitan-Vickers) and at smaller, specialized firms, such as Reyolle, makers of switch gears, and Crompton Parkinson, producers of transformers. The British industry was still having great difficulty in challenging the American and German first movers. Its leaders became increasingly concerned about their ability to catch up. Their trade association, British Electrical & Allied Manufacturers, warned in 1927:

> The British electrical industry has two possible moves left—either to form closer associations with German and American manufacturing concerns, and so become absorbed in the international combine which may be formed ultimately, or to tighten up its own organization, to form a compact group of manufacturers with a common policy both in manufacturing (prices and orders) and in finance, and at the same time strengthen the central association. It cannot continue in the present system . . . and remain in existence . . . The industry has no more than two years in which to effect the necessary changes.[38]

The senior executives at the American General Electric Company (GE) obviously agreed. In 1927 Owen D. Young, its chairman, wrote to Montagu Norman, who, as governor of the Bank of England, was then assisting in the Armstrong Whitworth and Vickers reorganization. Young urged "an amalgamation of the electrical industries in Great Britain." He suggested that Hirst be made the chairman of the merger's executive committee and that Lord Weir be chairman of the board. "If you agree that unification is desirable and that the general set up of personnel is right, I am sure that it can be left to you with safety to find the donkey and to administer the whack."[39]

By March 1928 Young and Gerard Swope, GE's president, decided that, since Norman appeared to be too involved in other matters, they should begin the process themselves. First they purchased Metropolitan-Vickers's electrical division (the former British Westinghouse); then they proposed its amalgamation with their subsidiary, British Thomson-Houston (BTH). Young wrote to Weir in August 1928 to explain the advantages of American methods: "The combination of the volume of that company [Metropolitan-Vickers] and B.T.H. would lay the foundation for the production methods of standardized units, such as motors, lamps, meters, etc., and thereby a great saving in cost. It should also permit, in a few years, a diminution in the sales costs and a large reduction of overhead per unit."[40] By September the two firms had been unified as Associated Electrical Industries (AEI), controlled by International General Electric Company, GE's subsidiary responsible for its operations abroad.

By now Young and Swope saw the unification of the British industry and its rationalization as an effective way to stabilize the larger global oligopoly. The next step would be to bring GEC into AEI. Negotiations with GEC's founders—Hirst, Max Railing, and Hirst's son-in-law, Leslie Gamage—at first went well. In the end, however, the founders refused to give up operational control.[41]

Undaunted, Young continued to plan for a truly global organization. On November 29, 1929, he wrote to Sir Felix Pole, an experienced railroad executive whom GE had recruited to head AEI:

> The great units for the production of electrical goods are located in the United States and Germany. They have highly developed research laboratories, great production units, far-flung sales organizations, and in the case of the American companies are generously financed. If stability is assured in Germany, the great German electrical companies will be among the first to get an ample capital supply. England has no manufacturing units comparable in size to the German and American units.[42]

Young estimated that "the entire production of electrical manufactured goods, certainly in the heavy field, in England is less than one half the output of the General Electric Company in New York alone and that business is divided between five companies." Why, Young asked, did not Britain have a unit of production comparable to the American and German companies? "She has the prospective market, the technical skill, and the financial resources to do so. The only thing needed is proper mobilization and management." In France, under the guidance of GE's 60%-owned subsidiary, the industry was moving toward greater concentration. In the other Continental countries—Belgium, Switzerland, Italy, and Sweden—smaller units would not be able to grow large enough to benefit from similar economies of scale.[43]

Young concluded his letter to Pole by proposing the creation of a worldwide organization. The leaders in the different nations should "create an investment trust which should hold something less than a half the common stock or equity of all the companies," with "voting power of such an investment trust restricted to 10% of the voting rights in any particular company." That would free each national industry from the onus of international control. It would unify the interests of the companies economically, but not politically. Such an arrangement would "naturally dissuade all companies from foolish and ruinous competition, which in the end weakens and hurts the industry; but it would not have the power to control such competition." Moreover, the investment trust "could pool all research and so assure continuing development in all parts of the world," as well as strengthen the international enforcement of patents.[44]

During the summer of 1929 GE had already begun to implement this imperial scheme by financing the two German leaders. It bought $15 million worth of stock in AEG, bringing its total holdings in that German giant to $25 million. At the same time it pledged not to attempt to obtain a majority of the stock.[45] It also purchased $11 million of Siemens's debentures. (Further details of this transaction are given in Chapter 14.) Swope followed these successful negotiations with a lightning trip through Europe and Asia to reinforce financial and technical agreements with other large firms in other countries.[46]

This plan for a global investment trust was never carried out. It floundered because of the onslaught of the depression, the collapse in demand for heavy electrical equipment and the resulting financial difficulties at GE, and also because of the growing specter of antitrust action. After 1929 GE made little further investment in foreign companies. In 1931 Young and Swope settled for more modest international goals. GE joined with Westinghouse to form a Webb-Pomerene association, the Electrical Apparatus Export Association. (The Webb-Pomerene Act was the one that permitted American firms to cooperate in international trade.) In 1933, through this association, the two firms signed with the leading European firms an "International Notification and Compensation Agreement" to assist in maintaining prices.[47] GE made no further effort to rationalize the British industry. It did not even consolidate the operations of AEI's two subsidiaries, Metropolitan-Vickers and BTH. Each firm retained its own name and continued to make much the same competing lines and to sell them with two different sales forces. By World War II GE had reduced its holdings in AEI from 56% to 40%, and, largely because of U.S. antitrust action, by 1946 its share had fallen to 34%. It sold out completely in 1953.[48]

As GE's influence declined during the 1930s, the strength of its competitors increased. Hugo Hirst expanded the facilities of his own company, GEC. Slowly, its organizational capabilities improved. Crompton Parkinson enlarged its line to include electric motors and transformers. Of even more importance was the revival of English Electric, the federation formed by Dick, Kerr in 1919, which had made no attempt to centralize control and rationalize facilities.

Here Westinghouse once again entered the game. In 1929 an American financial group headed by Harley Clarke, the president of the Chicago-based Utilities Power & Light Corporation, which was a customer of Westinghouse and a promoter of utilities in Britain, formed a financial group to acquire control of English Electric. In addition to Clarke, the group included Westinghouse, the Chase National Bank of New York, and the investment banking house of Lazards, which was Clarke's British financial agent. The group appointed an experienced engineer and manager, George Nelson, who had trained at British Westinghouse, to revive English Electric. Nelson rationalized the company's facilities, created a new management organization, and moved the company's headquarters from the works at Strafford to London, where the production, sales, and accounting departments were housed under one roof. English Electric then signed a technical agreement with Westinghouse by which the American firm provided free access to its research, patents, designs, and processes.[49] After 1934, as the economy improved, English Electric and Hirst's GEC became effective enough competitors in Britain to challenge the two operating companies of GE's Associated Electrical Industries—BTH and Metropolitan-Vickers.

By the coming of World War II the leading British electrical manufacturers had recruited sizable teams of lower- and middle-salaried managers. Top-level decisions, however, continued to be made by Hirst and his brother-in-law at GEC, by George Nelson (who would be succeeded by his son) at English Electric, and by Arthur Parkinson at Crompton Parkinson.[50] Top management in electrical-equipment manufacturing was similar to that in the automobile industry, but the electrical firms appear to have had a stronger management at the lower levels.

Though market share did change, these firms preferred to cooperate on determining prices, tendering contracts, and allocating marketing territories abroad, rather than competing functionally and strategically.[51] In marketing abroad the British firms stayed within the Empire. Since only GEC had established research facilities, the industry's research and development continued to be carried out largely in the United States; so the British firms were far less successful in diversifying than were the industry leaders in the United States or Germany.

Nevertheless, the British industry was catching up. The technologies of product and process, even though many were still imported, were of the modern, best-practice type. The necessary investment had been made in distribution as well as production. Managers in the new hierarchies had been recruited and trained. Thus after World War II, when GE completed its withdrawal from Britain and Westinghouse reduced its role in English Electric, the leading firms in Britain's heavy-electrical-equipment industry developed the organizational capabilities to compete and expand in international markets over the long run more effectively than did Britain's leading automobile companies.

In the smaller phonographic-recording and radio industry the transformation came sooner. From the industry's beginning in the 1890s, it had been dominated globally by two American companies—Victor Talking Machine and Columbia Phonograph Company. Both American enterprises staked out worldwide marketing organizations and built recording and assembling (but not fabricating) plants abroad, with Victor expanding internationally more quickly than Columbia.

Victor's affiliate in Britain was the Gramophone Company. It had been financed in Britain but remained American-managed and was responsible for assembling the machines, recording the discs, and for selling both in Europe and the Eastern Hemisphere. One of the Gramophone Company's most successful subsidiaries, Deutsche Grammophon AG, was expropriated during the war and then taken over by German nationals. Research for Gramophone, as well as the fabrication of the parts and machines, continued to be done in the United States. In 1920 the American company took full financial control of the British enterprise.[52] Until 1931 Gramophone remained, in the words of Geoffrey Jones, "little more than a sophisticated marketing organization."[53]

Victor's American rival, Columbia Phonograph, suffered financial difficulties during the postwar recession of the early 1920s. As a result it sold its British subsidiary, Columbia Graphophone, to a British syndicate headed by Louis Sterling, who had grown up on New York's Lower East Side and since 1909 had headed Columbia Phonograph's British business. Then in 1925 Sterling, with the help of a loan from J. P. Morgan & Company, obtained a controlling interest in his company's former parent, Columbia Phonograph, for $2.5 million. Sterling remained in London and the British company became the parent, making the former American parent its subsidiary. In the same year Sterling also purchased Carl Lundstrom, an aggressive German enterprise that was competing successfully with Deutsche Grammophon. In 1928 Sterling obtained the leading French record producer, Pathé Frères.

The final reorganization of the consumer electronic firms and their global industry began in January 1929. In that month the Radio Corporation of America (RCA), the radio industry's first mover in the United States (jointly owned by GE, Westinghouse, and AT&T), purchased Victor Talking Machine after arranging to have RCA radios placed in Victor's Victrola cabinets. RCA's energetic young president, David Sarnoff, then went on the board of Victor's subsidiary, the Gramophone Company, in Britain. In 1930 RCA was spun off from its three parents—a transaction that engrossed much of the time and energy of GE's Young and Swope during that year (see Chapter 6). Thereupon Sarnoff, assisted by Thomas Cochran, a Morgan partner, traveled to London to negotiate for the merger of Victor's Gramophone Company with Louis Sterling's Columbia Graphophone.[54]

The result was the formation in April 1931 of Electrical & Musical Industries (EMI). The new company became British-owned and British-managed. Its chairman was Arthur Clark, the American who had headed the management of the Gramophone Company for more than two decades, and its managing director was Louis Sterling. These two British managers, who had been born and bred in the United States, consummated the merger in the American manner. They consolidated their sales forces, selectively shut down or combined manufacturing facilities, centralized administration, expanded activities at home and abroad, made extensive investment in research and development, and entered radio and audio-system manufacturing, electrical appliances, and broadcasting. EMI became a leader in the global oligopoly along with RCA. After World War II the oligopoly came to include also the German firm, Deutsche Grammophon, and two smaller, more specialized recording companies—Columbia Records, the name given to a new American enterprise formed by Columbia Broadcasting System in 1938, and Decca Records, a dynamic young British recording company that had been established in 1929.

EMI, however, was an exception among British machinery makers. In the new field of consumer electrical and electronic products it had created the organizational capabilities needed to exploit the economies of scale and scope and so to compete effectively at home and abroad. At the same time it had freed the industry from its long dependence on American management and finance. In the other machinery industries the American presence was still powerful. In the vital electrical-equipment sector, GE controlled and Westinghouse played a major role in three of Britain's four largest operating enterprises. The Americans had installed and helped to train British managers in these companies, but Americans retained control of finances and of technological developments. In automobiles the subsidiaries of General Motors and Ford remained major players in a British oligopoly of six. In the smaller electrical industries such as batteries and appliances, and in the production of automobile parts and accessories, the Americans were still the leaders. In most of the newer nonelectrical industries—those of the Second Industrial Revolution— the British had not even attempted to compete before World War II. In sum, throughout the interwar years American technology, management, and finance played a critical role in permitting the British to catch up in the production of modern machinery.

Industrial Chemicals

In industrial chemicals (Group 28; see Appendixes B.1–B.4) the catching-up process was much more homegrown than in machinery. The two chemical firms that had created managerial hierarchies and developed their organizational capabilities before World War I—Brunner, Mond and Nobel Explosives—merged in 1926. The new enterprise, Imperial Chemical Industries (ICI), centralized administration (employing American techniques in doing so), and it extensively rationalized facilities and shifted personnel. By 1930 it had developed the organizational capabilities necessary to compete with the American and German giants abroad as well as at home, and to expand through the development of new products and processes in a manner similar to its foreign counterparts. The other British producers of industrial chemicals large enough to be listed among the top two hundred during the interwar years changed much more slowly. These personally managed family firms did recruit outside managers, but only a few. The federations of such firms did begin to build corporate offices, but only small ones.

THE PERSONALLY MANAGED FIRMS

The most successful of the family firms, Albright & Wilson, producers of phosphorus for matches, had made a major investment in a new electrolytic production process before the turn of the century. In 1897 it built a plant at Niagara Falls to produce for the American and Canadian markets. In Britain it had a smaller plant, whose output was sold by its small marketing organization. At the British plant the company established a laboratory headed by a noted chemist, Sir Richard Threlfall. As a result it was able to bargain effectively in this highly specialized industry's global cartel, which included (besides Albright & Wilson) a strong German company (Griesheim Elektron) and a weaker

French firm (Coignet).[55] Abroad it left the management of its integrated American enterprise wholly to American managers, who helped to finance the subsidiary; but at home the company continued to be personally managed by its owners. The home company's cost-accounting procedures, still used during World War I some years after Du Pont had adopted the most advanced costing methods, exemplify the workings of its personal management. In the words of Kenneth H. Wilson, later the company's chairman: "The [annual] inventory was completed by *6th January* and our work, which often kept us up till 9:00 or 10:00 p.m., was finished about the 16th, when the directors met in solemn conclave around the Board Room Table and worked out the costs by long hand:—R.T.'s Fuller slide-rule, when introduced at a later date, was rather frowned upon by J.J.W." (J. J. Wilson was the senior Wilson on the board, and the company's managing director, R. T., was Richard Threlfall.) Still, the owners did add a manager or two, and in the 1930s the firm did diversify into phosphorus products for bakers. In 1935 it even set up a technical sales office for such customers. During these years the senior managers remained the Wilsons, Albrights, and Threlfalls, whose families still held 40% of the voting shares of the company in 1951.[56]

The industrial chemical federations—Fisons, Salt Union, Borax, and British Briquettes—continued to be managed in a personal manner. Fisons, a family firm that mixed fertilizers, began to acquire a number of small firms in 1929 when ICI, the major British producer of synthetic nitrates, threatened to move forward into the mixing of fertilizers. Fisons, however, made no attempt to administer or coordinate its acquisitions. Instead, in order to blunt the ICI threat, it relied on contractual agreements enforced by the Fertilizer Manufacturers' Association. Another federation, Salt Union, only began to be reorganized after ICI gained full control in 1937, while, until it became part of ICI, United Alkali retained much the same structure as it had had before World War I (see Chapter 7).

Even British Oxygen, with more technologically complex production processes and more product-specific distribution requirements, was slow in building a corporate office. As a later chairman of the board noted: "As factory units grew" and as "satellite factories in neighboring towns" were opened, each of the heads of "districts or areas" became the "one real boss of everything, with only the loosest coordination at the Board in London." In the 1930s British Oxygen did begin to reorganize and enlarge its production facilities. It also acquired new production technologies, continued to expand overseas, and moved into the manufacturing and distribution of welding equipment. In 1937 it purchased a carbide-producing plant in Norway. By 1948 it had created a functional organizational structure that resembled the organization of its American counterpart, Linde Air Products, well before that firm became part of Union Carbide & Carbon in 1917.[57]

IMPERIAL CHEMICAL INDUSTRIES: ORGANIZATIONAL ACHIEVEMENT

At the center of the British industrial-chemical industry during the interwar years was the one exception to the rule of personal and family management: ICI, the 1926 merger of Brunner, Mond, Nobel Industries, and two smaller firms. The history of the British chemical industry during the interwar years was strikingly different from that of steel, of nonferrous metals, and of all three categories of machinery—and ICI was at the heart of the difference. It was the first merger in Britain to consolidate major sectors of a basic industry in the American manner. Indeed, it provides one of the very few examples of systematically planned, large-scale, organization building in British industry before World War II comparable to that carried out in the United States and Germany in the early twentieth century. Such organization building permitted a sizable part of the British industrial chemical industry to compete effectively at home and abroad. For all these reasons ICI deserves special attention.

The First World War deeply affected Brunner, Mond and, even more profoundly, Nobel Explosives, because the coming of the war brought an end to the joint Anglo-German Nobel's Dynamite Trust. During the war the British part of that enterprise, Nobel Explosives, merged with the four more specialized British makers of explosives: Kynoch, Ltd., of Birmingham; Curtis & Harvey (a federation of family firms); Bickford Smith, Ltd., makers of safety fuses; and Eley Brothers, cartridge producers. The result was the formation, at the end of 1918, of Explosives Trades, Ltd. (which changed its name to Nobel Industries in November 1920).[58]

In 1919 Harry McGowan, the firm's managing director, and his senior associates, particularly Josiah Stamp, agreed to centralize administrative control and to rationalize production and distribution so as to exploit the economies of both scale and scope. They looked to other British firms for models but could find none. During the early months of that year they investigated what they considered the best organized among the large British industrials—J. & P. Coats, Calico Printers' Association, Bradford Dyers, United Steel, Metropolitan-Vickers, and Dunlop Rubber. Some had created a central purchasing organization, their report noted; others had gone somewhat further by creating a corporate office; but each one remained little more than an "aggregation of a number of companies."

So the reorganizers of what became in the following year Nobel Industries turned to their long-term American ally, E. I. du Pont de Nemours & Company. They traveled to Wilmington, Delaware, and reviewed with Du Pont executives the reorganization that the American company was undergoing—a reorganization which further centralized Du Pont's long-established structure (but on which the Du Pont executives would change their minds in 1921).[59] A minority of the organizing committee, however, remained skeptical about the resulting unprecedented proposal. Arthur Chamberlain of Kynoch, a member of Birmingham's best-known industrial family, urged his colleagues to "go slowly in altering the inherited and accepted notions of British Industrial Management and instead of jumping to complete control at once, only adopt it when distinctive Trades control has shown a weakness."[60]

The acceptance of the committee's report resulted in as massive an industrial reorganization as had yet occurred in Britain. First came administrative centralization and then rationalization. Functional activities of Nobel Industries were centralized in new departments for sales, finance, purchasing, and development. The full-time senior functional executives formed a general management board, later called the Central Executive Department. The enlarged hierarchy of middle and top managers was then housed in a hotel, renamed Nobel House, near Buckingham Gate.[61] Production was concentrated in larger, more efficient, best-practice works. The goal was, in the words of the company's historian, "to bring most of the group's explosives manufacturing to Ardeer, safety fuse manufacture to Bickford Smith's factory at Tuckingmill in Cornwall, all ammunition to Kynochs' at Birmingham. What McGowan called 'the metal end' of the business was also concentrated around Birmingham." By 1924 forty factories had been closed. Of these, twenty-three had been "completely realized," that is, all equipment that could be used had been moved and the rest sold along with the land and buildings.[62] As part of this process, long-established family firms such as Chilworth and Eley Brothers disappeared. Older industry leaders, including Arthur Chamberlain, distressed by these unprecedented moves, left Nobel Industries.

At the other major British producer of industrial chemicals, Brunner, Mond, the immediate postwar years were less dramatic. During and just after the war it acquired a small, competitive alkali producer that was located nearby; a small producer of caustic soda and chloride that used the Castner electrolytic method; and two sets of suppliers—one in coke and coal and the other in lime quarries.[63] The company, however, made no attempt to consolidate these acquisitions within a centralized administrative structure.

In addition, at the urging of the British government, Brunner, Mond reluctantly committed itself in April 1920 to making an extensive, direct investment in producing synthetic nitrates on the basis of the German Haber-Bosch process. "Much the largest project in the British chemical industry of the day," this nitrate facility had required by 1925 an investment of at least £3.0 million without any financial return.[64] As Du Pont and Allied Chemical had already learned, the costs of developing and scaling up comparable technological processes were very high indeed. At the same time the challenge meant that a British firm was able to develop significant capabilities in the new high-pressure technology.

It was not, however, the growth or the fortunes of these two successful firms that set off the train of events which led to the formation of Imperial

Chemical Industries. It was rather the continuing, disastrous impact of the earlier entrepreneurial failure to develop modern synthetic dyes. When the war had cut off Britain's supplies of dyes, the government sponsored and financed the formation of British Dyes, Ltd. Similarly, the war had also revived the fortunes of Levinstein, Ltd., the one remaining British dye manufacturer of any size. In order to meet postwar competition these two firms had been merged under government pressure into the British Dyestuffs Corporation, Ltd. Faced with challenges comparable to those at Du Pont, the two constituent companies still refused to cooperate even after they became part of the same enterprise.

Finally, in December 1920, the government appointed Sir William Alexander as managing director with a fiat to force centralization and rationalization. Alexander, appalled at both the existing facilities and the management capabilities, decided that reorganization would not be enough. If British Dyestuffs was to compete in world markets, it had to acquire technical know-how from the great German dye firms. He began negotiations with the Interessengemeinschaft— the I.G., or community of interest, of the eight German leaders and the forerunner of I.G. Farben—which came into being at the end of 1925 (Chapter 14). The Germans agreed, but only on terms that would give them almost complete control over the industry in Britain. By this agreement British Dyestuffs would become little more than their British selling agent. Neither Conservative nor Labor party members of Parliament were able to accept these terms.[65]

As a result, in June 1926 Reginald McKenna, chairman of the Board of Trade's committee responsible for British Dyestuffs, approached Harry McGowan, by then chairman of Nobel Industries, to ask that firm to take over the government-owned dye maker. McGowan suggested that the weak United Alkali and the strong Brunner, Mond be added to the merger. Such a "British I.G." could effectively compete with the recently formed German giant, I.G. Farben, in the global markets. Alfred Mond was less than enthusiastic about the proposal. Son of one of the founders of Brunner, Mond, Alfred had recently returned to the family firm as chairman after spending the years between 1906 and 1923 in Parliament. He did so after Roscoe Brunner, a son of the other founder, had lost, with disastrous consequences, a lawsuit to Lever Brothers, resigned as chairman, and then committed suicide. Alfred Mond himself was hoping to build a comparable enterprise that would unite his company with Solvay & Cie, I.G. Farben, and the American firm, Allied Chemical. (Allied had absorbed the American Solvay Company.) Only after that venture fell through, largely because Allied refused to go along, did Mond agree to the 1926 merger with Nobel Industries, British Dyestuffs, and United Alkali. Thus ICI was born, with Mond as its chairman and McGowan as its president, and with six full-time directors, three from Nobel Industries and three from Brunner, Mond.[66]

Again, as at the earlier reorganization of Nobel Industries, administrative centralization quickly followed legal consolidation. This time the new centralized administrative structure was defined and put into place, not by a committee or a team of executives as at Du Pont, General Motors, and other American firms, or even earlier at Nobel Industries. It was carried out almost wholly by one man—not Harry McGowan, the experienced industrialist, but Alfred Mond, who had spent little time in industry but who was chairman of the board and the largest stockholder among the senior managers.[67] He had given organizational requirements some thought, for just prior to the merger he had begun to plan a comparable centralized structure for his own enterprise.

But the structure at Nobel Industries was Mond's model. At ICI, Mond initially set up the Technical Department and the Commercial Department, each with two managers who sat on the ICI board; the Financial Department headed by another board member; and the "Centralized Administration Department" with two more board members at its head.[68] These men made up, with Mond and McGowan, the inside members of the board. During the company's first years the outside members included a Brunner, a representative of Solvay et Cie (which, with 6% of the ordinary stock, was the largest shareholder in ICI), and such eminent public figures as Lord Reading and Sir John Anderson. Mond then installed the most advanced internal accounting and other control systems.[69]

Once the consolidation of the sales, research, and accounting departments of the merged companies was completed, Mond turned to transforming the new structure into a more decentralized, multidivisional one. He correctly believed that centralization and consolidation followed by rationalization must precede decentralization and divisionalization. But by 1929 the middle and top managers at ICI's corporate headquarters in London were already overwhelmed by the multitude of tasks involved in making and implementing the myriads of operating decisions connected with the production and distribution of the numerous product lines. During 1929 Mond worked on a second reorganization in which the product groups became the primary administrative units. The reorganization went into effect shortly after Mond's death in December 1930, following several months of illness (see Figure 9). The product or manufacturing groups included Alkali, Billingham (synthetic nitrates and fertilizers), Dyes, Explosives, General Chemicals, Leathercloth, Lime, Metals, and Associated Companies. Each group had not only its own production and marketing managers but also its own research laboratories. Each was managed by an executive board made up of local and central-office representatives, assisted by a management committee of senior functional executives in that group.[70]

Although in many ways the new structure resembled that of Du Pont and other American divisionalized firms, it differed in that the integrated product groups were managed by boards of several executives rather than by a single individual. Moreover, these boards did not have full responsibility for the profits of their groups. Throughout the interwar period the ICI corporate office con-

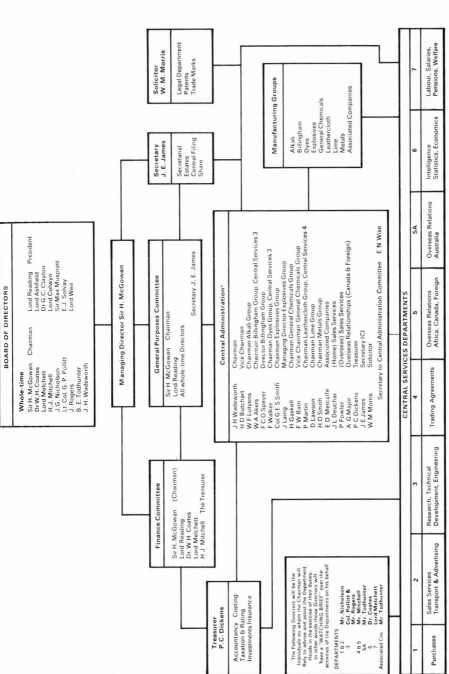

Figure 9. ICI organization chart, March 1931. From W. J. Reader, *Imperial Chemical Industries: A History,* vol. II, *The First Quarter-Century, 1926–1952* (London, 1975), p. 139.

tinued to have the final say as to price, output, and market allocation. And from the time the decentralized structure went into operation, senior executives repeatedly expressed their concern about the dangers and difficulties of having product lines managed by senior executives who lacked full responsibility and authority.

The reasons for centralizing such decision-making are easily identifiable. One was the British tradition of personal leadership at the top. Mond and McGowan, and then McGowan alone after Mond's death, continued personally to make major top-level decisions as to broad strategy and the allocation of resources. They had staff executives make reports. Other senior managers were often consulted, but often they were not. In any case, the chairman, not they, determined major policy.[71]

The other reason for continuing the tight control of the corporate office was the depression. The resulting slump in demand and the increased competition forced tighter control over operations. Equally important, hard times and excess capacity increased the pressure for contractual cooperation in international markets, particularly with powerful German competitors. Cartels, by setting prices and output through interfirm agreements, obviously kept product-group managers from making critical decisions that would affect the profits of their group.

The years 1931 and 1932 were years of cartel-making. In 1929, even before the depression, ICI had strengthened its relations with its American ally, Du Pont, by signing a patents-and-process agreement with that firm, comparable (with some modifications) to those which Du Pont and Nobel Industries (and its predecessors) had enjoyed since 1907. These agreements called for a full exchange of technical information. The resulting and improved new processes or products were then licensed in order to permit the two firms to allocate major markets between them.[72] ICI had more difficulty in coming to terms with the powerfully competent Germans. But its growing organizational capabilities gave it the bargaining power to obtain a secure foothold in international markets in three major product lines.

First, in negotiations completed in April 1931, ICI achieved its goals in a patent-process and output agreement with I.G. Farben, Standard Oil (New Jersey), and Royal Dutch–Shell in a new industry, the production of synthetic fuel from coal.[73]

Second, in April 1932 the managers of ICI signed an agreement with the German and Norwegian makers of synthetic nitrates and fertilizers. The resulting group, known as DEN, then negotiated with the larger group of international producers that formed the Convention de L'Industrie de L'Azote (CIA). ICI, the newcomer in the business, received a quota of 18.5% in the DEN group and exclusive marketing rights to the British Empire, the Dutch East

Indies, and Spain and Portugal, with shared markets in China, Japan, and Egypt.[74]

In the third industry, dyes, where the British had no position at all in the early 1920s, they received an 8.43% quota in the International Dye Cartel agreement of 1932. "From ICI's point of view," Reader notes, "the four party agreement [I. G. Farben, the Swiss I. G., Kuhlmann in France, and Imperial Chemical Industries] was a victory, for on arriving at the figure of 8.43 percent . . . the Continental Group had agreed to forego business of £195,000." Moreover, ICI considered it unnecessary to join the other three in a much tighter structure, which would have included exchange of technical information. The ICI executives felt that by then they had developed the capabilities necessary to compete. As one senior manager wrote, "The only way BDC [ICI's dyestuffs group] could get into the dye stuffs business on anything approaching a substantial scale . . . was to invent its way in. The IG never took much notice of BDC until they found out that BDC could invent."[75]

Even so, centralization of decisions as to price, output, and frequently even product development did put a damper on the potential for growth through diversification. After returning from a visit to the Du Pont company in 1937 one ICI senior executive noted: "The most striking difference between Du Pont's business and ours arises from the existence of free competition in America." Reader adds: "By that he meant that research was not impeded by agreements not to compete with other businesses, or indeed by any agreement among the du Pont divisions not to compete among themselves."[76]

Nevertheless, ICI's continuing investment in research and personnel, its increasingly closer ties with scientists at Oxford, Cambridge, London, and other universities, and its growing ability to commercialize new products (that is, capability in development as well as research) made for impressive exploitation of the economies of scope that were available within the operating units of the different product groups and within the organization as a whole. In December 1935 the Alkali Group's research laboratory invented polyethylene, which, once commercialized, became one of ICI's most profitable products.[77] In the three years from 1933 through 1935 the laboratory of the Dyestuffs Group came up with eighty-seven new products, including rubber goods, chemicals, synthetic resins and lacquers, detergents, pesticides, and pharmaceuticals, as well as new dyestuff intermediaries and new dyes. One Du Pont executive considered ICI's development of "Monastral" dyes the most important development in dye chemistry in twenty-five years.[78] The high-pressure laboratories of the Billingham (fertilizer) Group at Winnington were soon among the best in the world.

By the 1930s ICI's research capabilities were beginning to rival Du Pont's. In the 1929 accord each company had agreed to pay the other for technical information, patents, and other assistance received. During the 1930s these payments remained almost equal, with Du Pont receiving on average about $100,000 a year after the accounts were balanced. "It was astonishing," wrote Fin Sparre, the manager responsible for Du Pont's central research division, "to find that the work of the two companies had paralleled each other to such a remarkable extent."[79]

The continuing success in product development became a goad for further administrative reorganization. In 1937, however, came what Reader termed "the barons' revolt" against McGowan's "dictatorship."[80] McGowan did agree to accept a set of procedures to assure more collective and systematic strategic decision-making. But because he stayed on as chairman, at least one of the barons remained skeptical about the effectiveness of the change:

> The scheme . . . does not give the full-time Directors any more authority than they have had in the past and therefore does not meet one of our very real and recurring problems, that of the present GPC [General Purposes Committee] being faced with decisions which may not have had any "collective" consideration. It still (on paper) leaves the staff with a right—not infrequently exercised—of by-passing the whole administrative machinery . . . and seeking for decisions of the Chair by direct approach.[81]

Nevertheless, under the new procedures the top managers did become executives with real authority, and they did become involved in monitoring and planning for the enterprise as a whole. At the same time, the need to manage diversification more effectively led to the strengthening of the product groups and a more precise definition of their boundaries; the reestablishment of the Development Department to watch over new-product development (this department had been moribund during McGowan's rule); and in 1938, after a visit to Du Pont, an authorization to build a central research laboratory.[82]

The outbreak of World War II postponed the building of that central laboratory and also held off a final decision on the shape of the new organizational structure. Most executives agreed on the necessity of maintaining "a fundamental and integrating unison between production, research and selling efforts." Many were also aware of the importance of "fully developing all various units into a related balanced whole." The war, by dispersing central-office activities outside London, increased the need for overall coordination.[83] A further reorganization in 1944 attempted to achieve this balance.[84] And in the postwar years growing markets, both at home and abroad; the breakdown of the cartel networks; and the increasing competition, based on functional and strategic effectiveness rather than contractual arrangements, led to further adjustment of ICI's divisional structure. But it was not until the major reorganization of 1962, in which the American consulting firm of McKinsey & Company played an advisory role, that each division began to be administered by a single executive who was responsible for its profit and loss.[85] Nevertheless, ICI, the most diversified

British industrial enterprise, was one of only two major British firms to adopt the full-fledged multidivisional form before World War II. The story of the other, Unilever, will be told shortly.

By World War II, thanks to ICI, much of the British chemical industry had recovered from the entrepreneurial failures of the late nineteenth century. The organizational capabilities needed to produce and distribute a variety of industrial chemicals efficiently had been created. The investment made by ICI (and its predecessors) in best-practice industrial operations, in personnel and facilities for marketing, and above all in research and development permitted the British industry to compete effectively in international markets and to continue to grow by developing new products and processes. ICI had recruited as large and as experienced a managerial hierarchy as any enterprise in Britain. Very few British companies could have had "a revolt of the barons," because hardly any of them had enough barons to revolt. Moreover, the company had forged strong ties with leading universities, which provided a significant link not only in the development of new products and processes but also in the recruiting of trained chemists, chemical engineers, and managers. Yet, whereas in the United States and Germany there were many industrial chemical producers with comparable organizational capabilities, in Britain there was only ICI. The model it established helped Fisons, Albright & Wilson, British Oxygen, and other smaller, personally managed British chemical companies to develop such capabilities in the years after World War II. These companies built the organizations that made it possible to compete at home and abroad in areas of the chemical industry in which ICI did not operate. Nevertheless, the British continued to be relatively weak in other branches of the industry—in electrochemicals, fine chemicals, and certain other chemicals that were developed and produced by such German and American first movers as DEGUSSA, Griesheim, Riedel, Dow, Monsanto, and those that became parts of Union Carbide.

Branded, Packaged Products

For the leading British producers of food and consumer chemicals the challenges in the interwar years differed from those in industrial chemicals and machinery. In the case of food and consumer chemicals, unlike most machinery and industrial chemicals, British firms were first movers. They made the investments in production and distribution needed to capture home markets. The British leaders in these nondurable-goods industries (Groups 20, 21, and 28; see Appendixes B.1–B.4) continued to produce in bulk form, but the mainstays of their business increasingly became branded, packaged products to be placed directly on retailers' shelves. During the interwar years these firms remained among the largest and most profitable industrial enterprises in Britain. Seven of

Britain's ten largest enterprises in terms of the market value of their stocks produced branded, consumer products. Moreover, during these same interwar years there was little turnover at the top (see Table 20 and Appendix B.4). The changes that did occur were largely the result of acquisition and merger.

In these industries challengers came more from abroad, particularly the United States, than from within Britain. Precisely because branded, packaged products offered smaller economies of scale in production, and required less in the way of product-specific facilities and specialized skills in distribution, than was the case in other capital-intensive industries, the firms that manufactured them could be administered profitably by a smaller number of managers. During the interwar years this group remained the stronghold of the family firm. For the same reasons, however, these firms found themselves vulnerable when American first movers entered the British market after World War I. When directly challenged by American competitors, they had to update their facilities and develop their technical and managerial skills. In other words, they had to enhance their organizational capabilities if they were to maintain market share and profit.

THE BASTION OF THE FAMILY FIRM

At most food and beverage companies, the same families continued during the interwar years to manage their enterprises in a personal manner from the same offices their forebears had established next to the original factories or processing plants. Most did continue to expand their production facilities and to enlarge their marketing operations at home and then abroad in the manner of the Cadbury family. Many added warehouses and fleets of trucks to their purchasing organizations. More than their American counterparts, they invested

Table 20.   The largest industrial enterprises in Great Britain in 1919, 1930, and 1948.

1919	1930	1948
1. Burmah Oil	1. Unilever	1. Imperial Tobacco
2. J. & P. Coats	2. Imperial Tobacco	2. Anglo-Iranian Oil
3. Anglo-Persian Oil	3. Shell	3. ICI
4. Lever Brothers	4. ICI	4. Unilever
5. Imperial Tobacco	5. Anglo-Persian Oil	5. Shell
6. Vickers	6. Courtaulds	6. Distillers'
7. Guinness	7. J. & P. Coats	7. Guinness
8. Brunner, Mond	8. Distillers'	8. Courtaulds
9. Shell	9. Guinness	9. Burmah Oil
10. Nobel Explosives	10. Burmah Oil	10. Dunlop Rubber
11. Courtaulds	11. Dunlop Rubber	11. J. & P. Coats

Source: Appendixes B.1–B.3.

in overseas plantations, cattle ranches, and other sources of supply. This was the case for Liebigs, makers of beef bouillon, which continued to be owned and managed by the Carlisle and Gunther families; of its competitor, Bovril, headed by the Walker and Johnson families; of Brooke Bond, blenders and packers of tea, which the Brooke family continued to manage; of Barretts, confectionery makers, where Barretts and Sennetts worked under the board's chairman, J. Barrett-Sennett; and of Mackintosh, where the Mackintosh family continued to run their long-established toffee-making enterprise. [86]

In consumer chemicals the pattern was much the same, although there the companies did build more extensive managerial hierarchies. In soap the two largest firms, Lever Brothers and Crosfield, had sizable managerial staffs by the early 1920s. John Knight and Yardley and Company continued to be personally managed. In paint Lewis Berger & Sons, which had been purchased in 1910 by an American first mover, Sherwin-Williams, became personally managed again in 1919. In that year W. H. Cottingham, retired as Sherwin-Williams's president, purchased control of Lewis Berger, moved to Britain, and ran the smaller firm as a personal fiefdom, one that he turned over to his son in 1930. [87] In drugs and medicines, Sangers remained the domain of the Sanger and Smith families. So too, the Beechams ran Beecham's Pills until Sir Thomas Beecham decided to devote all of his energies to directing symphony orchestras and sponsoring concerts at Covent Garden, which he had also inherited from his father. [88]

A third drug firm, Boots Pure Drug, was a retail chain which, like the British meat and grocery chains, integrated backward into the production of items to be sold in their stores. It was managed by its founder, Jesse Boot, until 1920. Then he sold it to an American giant, United Drug, whose new managers installed an American-style "territorial" managerial organization, subdivided into regions and supervised by a reorganized corporate office in Nottingham. In 1933 the financial difficulties of United Drug in the United States permitted John Boot, Jesse's son, to regain control of the family firm, Boots Pure Drug, which had come to be administered through an extensive managerial hierarchy. [89]

Less is known about the most progressive of the British drug companies, Burroughs Wellcome. This company, referred to as the "Yankee Chemist" because it was founded by two Americans, continued to be run by Harry Wellcome from his partner's death in 1895 until the mid-1920s, when he turned the management of the company over to a deputy. The founders made a larger investment in production, marketing, and research than happened with the other British drug companies. The firm moved abroad more quickly and systematically than others, establishing "branch houses" in South Africa, Canada, the United States, Italy, Argentina, China, and India between 1902 and 1912. Burroughs Wellcome developed a broader product line than its competitors and was one of the very few British drug firms that produced more than packaged, over-the-counter pills and powders and whose salesmen called on doctors and hospitals.[90]

In the years immediately following World War I a number of mergers occurred among leading producers of branded, packaged food and chemical products which had worked closely with one another in their industries. After the formation of such holding companies the partners continued, however, to operate quite autonomously, in the manner of Cadbury and Fry following the establishment of British Cocoa & Chocolate in 1919. In 1921 Huntley & Palmers and Peek Frean formed Associated Biscuit Manufacturers, of which the senior Palmer became chairman and the senior Carr (of Peek Frean) became vice-chairman and secretary. Again the two families continued to run their separate firms much as they had before 1921. This was also true of a similar merger made that same year by the two leading sugar refiners, Henry Tate & Sons and Abram Lyle & Sons, which formed Tate & Lyle.[91] In 1919, when Crosse & Blackwell, producers of jams and preserves, joined James Keiller, the Dundee marmalade maker, and E. Lazenby, a maker of preserves and sauces, to form a holding company carrying the Crosse & Blackwell name, the formal agreement read, "each company will retain its complete independence."[92] H. P. Sauce was a similar merger of Lea & Perrin and other sauce makers, while Cerebos was a comparable union of producers of condiments.[93] In 1920 Cooper McDowell and Robertson was formed as a similar federation of producers of veterinary supplies. The two leading producers of starch and blueing for the laundering of cloth, Reckitt and Sons and its friendly rival, J. J. Colman, were neighbors in Hull on the northeast coast. They worked closely with each other for decades, but waited until 1938 to join in a formal merger. Thereupon a grandson of the Reckitt founder became chairman of Reckitt and Colman, Ltd., and a grandson of the Colman founder became vice-chairman.[94]

A few producers of branded, packaged products went beyond just allying with a major competitor or two; instead they grew more rapidly and expansively through acquisition. Such firms included J. Rank and Spillers, the two leading grain producers in Britain; Distillers' Company, Ltd., the Scotch whiskey makers; Beecham's Pills after it was acquired by Philip Hill in 1928; Goodlass Wall in paints; and Lever Brothers, Britain's first mover in soap. All of these firms had the opportunity, after acquisition, to rationalize and modernize through investment in new or improved facilities and to build a managerial organization. But, except for Lever Brothers, none of them took up this challenge effectively before World War II.

At the paint companies almost nothing was done. Goodlass Wall remained a federation and in 1931 merged with another federation, Amalgamated Lead Industries, to form Goodlass Wall & Lead Industries, Ltd. Few changes resulted, even though the stated purpose of the 1931 merger was to achieve the advantages of rationalization and vertical integration in the paint industry. Less is known about Pinchin Johnson, which acquired thirteen firms in the mid-1920s; the size of its board of directors indicates that it remained a typical British holding company.[95]

In grain processing more was accomplished. J. Rank, the largest, did shut down some of the more obsolete mills it acquired. Nevertheless, its other acquisitions continued to operate much as they always had. The company's official history explains: "As each mill consolidated its position and strengthened its hold upon its particular trade so it tended to become self-contained, each branch naturally striving to do the best for itself. This made for healthy competition not only within the organization but within the trade at large."[96] Spillers accomplished more, primarily because this 1919 merger of a handful of family firms, which produced not only flour but also biscuits and pet food, encountered financial losses after making several acquisitions, including mills in Canada. After passing a dividend in 1926 the ruling families called on their accounting firm, Price, Waterhouse, to advise them on reorganizing the company's administration. As a result the enterprise divided its British grain-milling operations into four geographical areas, each headed by an executive committee; set up a department of overseas sales; and placed ship biscuits and animal food in a single division, called Spillers Victoria Food. It also recruited a new managerial team which worked closely with the representatives of the Nichols, Barker, Allan, and Vernon families on the board. A modicum of rationalization followed. In 1928 Spillers joined with Rank to purchase a number of smaller mills, whose activities were then rationalized. The changes at Spillers may have helped to raise the market value of its securities from well below that of Rank in 1919 to almost its equal in 1930.[97]

At Beecham's, by 1938 Philip Hill had acquired ten companies producing medicines, proprietary drugs, toothpaste, and other toilet articles; each retained full autonomy.[98] By that date the firm's executives had fully realized that "'management' was already emerging as the primary Beecham problem." They understood that without reorganization and rationalization—including investment in production and distribution and the recruitment of a managerial team—Beecham's could not compete effectively within Britain with what one executive, H. G. Lazell, termed "the great American international businesses."[99] He referred explicitly to Colgate-Palmolive-Peet, Procter & Gamble, American Home Products, Sterling Drug, Bristol-Myers, and Chesebrough (makers of Vaseline).[100]

In the 1920s Distillers' Company, Ltd., obtained a near monopoly of the Scotch whiskey industry. Even before World War I this holding company had accounted for the largest share of that trade. Its major rival was Scotch Whisky Brands. That company was a 1916 merger of Dewars and Buchanan (Black and White), which soon acquired James Watson, Peter Dawson, Mackie, and Haig & Haig. In 1925 Distillers' acquired Scotch Whisky Brands and John Walker (in which both Distillers' and Scotch Whisky Brands had holdings). By 1927, when it took over White Horse Distillers, it had its near monopoly. In addition, it began to diversify through acquisitions, purchasing two leading gin makers as early as 1924. Because gin, unlike Scotch, was not dependent on local water and peat for its taste, Distillers' Company was able to set up gin distilleries overseas—in the United States, Canada, and Australia. In the same years it expanded its production of yeast, a central ingredient in the distilling process, and began to sell it to the large bakery market. Its yeast-making subsidiary built a specialized distributing network for this perishable product comparable to the one Fleischmann had established years earlier in the United States. Then, to make further use of this network, Distillers' purchased a company producing margarine and edible fats.[101] During World War I it had expanded its production of industrial alcohol, and after the war it used its facilities and experience to diversify into alcohol-based and yeast-based chemicals, such as solvents, acetone, and carbon dioxide, and also into plaster board and pharmaceuticals.[102]

Nevertheless, despite its growth both abroad and into related industries, the Distillers' Company remained essentially a federation of whiskey makers. The production of malt was centralized in one of the constituent firms, Scottish Malt Distilleries; but each firm produced and distributed its own brand of blended whiskey. The Distillers' board continued to be dominated by members of the whiskey-making families—the Dewars, Walkers, Buchanans, and Rosses. William Ross, who became its secretary in 1889 and managing director in 1900, and who did not retire as chairman until 1935, was for half a century the federation's major policymaker.[103] Only upon Ross's retirement did the board establish a full-time management committee to handle the supervisory and planning functions between board meetings. Top-level decisions as to strategy and the allocation of resources continued to be made from the personal perspective of a small number of whiskey producers. Because of these decision-makers and their perspectives Distillers' Company was never able to exploit effectively its moves into the production of foods and of industrial alcohol and related chemicals.

Of the leading producers of branded, packaged products that grew through acquisition, Lever Brothers (which became Unilever in 1929) was unique—it was not only the most aggressive in Britain, but it went abroad more quickly and more effectively than its competitors. Its story, which reveals much about the transformation from entrepreneurial to managerial enterprise and from personal to collective ways of management in Great Britain, will be told at the end of this chapter.

EXPANSION OVERSEAS AND PRODUCT DIVERSIFICATION

Because so many of the leading British producers of branded, packaged products remained personally managed, because so few mergers were consummated in the American manner, and because, therefore, these firms had smaller financial resources and less-developed organizational skills than their American counterparts, the pattern of their expansion provides a counterpoint to the collective histories of the leaders in the same industries in the United States. The British producers of branded, packaged products did grow in much the same manner as the American companies. But they expanded into foreign markets and diversified into related industries in a less aggressive and systematic way.

Although the British producers of branded products had set up marketing branches overseas, before World War I only a very few—such as Keiller, Reckitt, and Lever—had supported these units by establishing plants abroad. Most waited until after the war to make direct investments in overseas production facilities. Then they made such investments primarily because of the increasing tariff barriers and other import restrictions imposed by the British Commonwealth countries as well as by the Americans and Europeans. Only a very few—Tate & Lyle, H. P. Sauce, and J. Rank—did not venture overseas at all. While only a few besides Spillers followed the prewar example of such producers as Bovril, Liebig, the chocolate companies, and Lever Brothers by investing abroad in order to assure themselves supplies, the rest did make direct investments in processing plants abroad. The chocolate manufacturers did so in Canada, Australia, New Zealand, Ireland, and South Africa—largely through joint ventures. The only moves they made outside the Commonwealth came in 1928 when Cadbury and Rowntree each invested in factories in Germany (but not enough to assure control). Neither venture was successful. [104] The biscuit makers also concentrated on white Commonwealth markets, while Schweppes and Distillers' looked to American as well as Commonwealth markets. [105]

On the other hand, the makers of jams, mustard, and condiments moved, as Lever had done so effectively before the war, into both Europe and the United States. By 1930 the three firms that made up Crosse & Blackwell were operating factories in Hamburg (their only prewar plant), Paris, Buenos Aires, Brussels, Toronto, and Baltimore. [106]

Reckitt & Sons, one of the largest producers of British branded products (it ranks eighteenth, twenty-first, and fourteenth in Appendixes B.1, B.2, and B.3, respectively) was also one of the most active in going overseas. A producer which from its earliest years had made mustard as well as starch and blueing, it joined forces with its friendly neighbor and competitor, J. & J. Colman, in 1913 to form Atlantis, Ltd., for joint marketing overseas. By then Reckitt was already operating manufacturing facilities in Australia; in Hamburg, Germany; and in New Brunswick, New Jersey. In 1926 Colman purchased a major American mustard producer, R. T. French of Rochester, New York. The two allies (they would not formally merge until 1938) then formed Atlantis Sales Company to take over the marketing of the three companies in the United States, while

Atlantis, Ltd., expanded the number of its marketing branches in other parts of the world. In 1926, too, Reckitt obtained a leading Belgian manufacturer of blueing and soon was operating factories in Spain and France as well. But as Basil Reckitt reports: "The establishment of overseas factories was not the wish of the Board. It was forced on the company by the imposition of prohibitive import tariffs in country after country. Without local manufacture, trade would have been impossible because local competition would have had such an over-whelming price advantage."[107]

In consumer chemicals—soap, paints, and drugs—only Lever Brothers, the first mover in soap, had invested abroad extensively before World War I. After the war, paint companies—Pinchin Johnson and Lewis Berger—made overseas investments that were concentrated in Commonwealth countries; Pinchin Johnson acquired subsidiaries not only in India, Australia, and New Zealand but also in Italy; and Lewis Berger acquired them not only in South Africa, Australia, and New Zealand but also in France.[108] Leading drug companies, including Beecham, Sanger, and Boots, did not invest abroad. Only Burroughs Wellcome, the pioneer pharmaceutical producer in Britain, and Glaxo, a small specialized producer of powdered milk for babies and of vitamins, had plants abroad. Bur-roughs Wellcome continued to have a large and successful American subsidiary, while Glaxo, during the interwar years, established packaging plants in India, Greece, and Italy, and primary processing plants in Australia and Argentina. Tariffs and other import restrictions were the reasons for Glaxo's invest-ment.[109]

During the interwar period the British producers of branded, packaged prod-ucts, therefore, did seek new markets abroad. But they did so more as an ad hoc response to increased tariffs and other governmental restrictions than as part of a broad strategy of market penetration, as was the case during the interwar years for such American firms as Borden, Quaker Oats, Coca-Cola, Corn Products, General Foods, and Royal Baking Powder. The decision to invest overseas was usually made personally by one or two senior managers. These executives often failed to realize the significant differences between their scattered markets, even differences between the less populated Common-wealth markets and the highly concentrated one in Britain. They rarely worked out careful cost calculations as to size and location of plants. The Cadbury and Fry venture into Australia, for example, led to the building of a plant much too large for their expected share of that market. In its first years it operated at 50% capacity. Moreover, it was located on the island of Tasmania, far from the major Australian markets.[110]

Because the family managers of these firms did not want to dilute control enough to finance even these relatively small plants, and because the managerial pool was limited, the firms often preferred to carry out their expansion by joint ventures, usually with leading competitors and allies but also with local firms. Once the investment was made, the overseas subsidiary operated with little oversight. Its autonomy was encouraged by distance, by the divided control inherent in a joint venture, and by the fact that the senior executives in the home office were concentrating on day-to-day domestic operations. Supervision required little more than reviewing short reports and an occasional visit by a senior executive. By the 1930s, however, Cadbury, after it took over the management of Fry's overseas subsidiaries in addition to its own, set up an Overseas Factory Committee. Reckitt and Colman, well before their formal merger, established a Joint Overseas Committee to supervise their overseas activities.[111] Nevertheless, the directors of these firms continued to pay little attention to their foreign subsidiaries.[112] In these enterprises where the personal ways of management lingered on, expansion overseas remained limited by the lack of organizational resources—financial as well as managerial—while limited growth, in turn, held back the development of managerial capabilities.

Organizational limitations created far more powerful barriers to expansion through product diversification than they did to investment overseas. Personally managed family firms were unable to exploit the economies of scope in the manner of their American counterparts. Precisely because they invested much less in marketing and research facilities and personnel, few opportunities for exploiting organizational scope existed. Product development in most of these British firms, even the ones using relatively complex production technologies, was similar to that of the American firms that used the simplest production processes—Heinz, Campbell Soup, California Packing, Wrigley, and the cigarette companies. New brands were usually minor variations of the primary product. In some cases, as in soap, by-products were sold on a small scale. During the interwar years not one British producer of branded, packaged products developed a variety of product lines comparable to that of Corn Products, with its starch, salad and cooking oils, syrups, sweeteners, desserts, and plastics. In grain processing neither Spillers nor Rank offered an array of products comparable to those of Pillsbury, Ralston Purina, or Quaker Oats. Nor did any British paint company move into chemicals as did Sherwin-Williams, Glidden, and National Lead. Only in soap and cleaners were new products developed—by Lever and Reckitt—and even here the range was limited. Lever did so by acquisition only. It entered the margarine business only because of a wartime emergency, and then through a joint venture with a leading margarine producer. Reckitts, with its well-established research laboratory and its relatively strong marketing organization, did diversify into bath cakes and window and lavatory cleaners.[113] In drugs the contrast with American leaders is even more striking. Of the British firms, only Burroughs Wellcome developed marketing and research capabilities comparable to those of Parke-Davis, Sterling, Abbott, Merck, American Home Products, and the other drug producers among the American top two hundred. Even Glaxo Laboratories, a British pioneer in pharmaceuticals, relied on American processes to move into vitamins and other products more complex than dried milk.[114] Not surprisingly, when Beechams, Crosfields, Boots, and other British drug companies began to hire research personnel, they often recruited them from Burroughs Wellcome.[115] After World War II, when those firms and Glaxo began to produce and sell antibiotics and other miracle drugs, Burroughs Wellcome may have been their model.

In the United States the leading food and consumer-chemical companies used their research facilities during the interwar years to expand into industrial chemicals, where they became competitors of Du Pont, Union Carbide, Monsanto, and others. Such inter-industry competition rarely appeared in Britain. There only Distillers' Company, Ltd., began to exploit systematically the economies of scope available in its yeast and industrial-alcohol business and thereby to diversify into chemicals. To strengthen its rising position in the chemical industry it set up a central research laboratory in 1930. Under the guidance of H. M. Stanley the laboratory began to bring forth marketable products, particularly through its industrial-alcohol technology. Nevertheless, since that federation was still dominated by whiskey makers, the enterprise never developed the organizational capabilities needed to develop and then to commercialize these products effectively. Its chemical business remained unprofitable. Finally in 1965 it sold nearly all of its chemical interests to British Petroleum (the successor to Anglo-Iranian Oil), a firm which, like the American oil companies, began to use the capabilities it had developed in petrochemicals during World War II to move into a variety of oil-based and other chemicals.[116]

Finally, during the interwar years there were no mergers in Britain comparable to those carried out in the United States by large, integrated firms whose product lines complemented one another so as to permit more intensive use of combined marketing, distribution, and, to a lesser extent, production and research personnel and facilities. There were no combinations similar to Standard Brands, General Foods, General Mills, Best Foods, and American Home Products. In those American mergers a number of founding families, including the Fleischmanns, Pillsburys, Washburns, and Wyeths, gave up operating control. The reluctance to lose family influence may have been a deterrent to comparable consolidations in Britain.

PERISHABLE PRODUCTS

As in the United States, the meat processors were the only British producers of perishable products (chilled and frozen meat, dairy and bakery products, and beer) to make significant overseas investments. They made these investments, however, in order to assure sources of supply rather than to expand markets, and they did not diversify in the manner of their American counterparts.

Of the producers of dairy and bakery products (see Appendix B.1–B.4) all but Cow & Gate were mass retailers. Like the meat-selling chain stores and

Boots Pure Drug they had integrated backward into the production of some of the goods sold in their stores; and they did so to assure a continuing high-volume stock turn. United Dairies, a 1915 merger, was a federation of three autonomous parts: a retail organization with 470 outlets in 1920 and 700 in 1930; several milk-condensing establishments and creameries; and a producer of dairy equipment.[117] J. Lyons and Aerated Bread owned and operated tea-blending establishments and producers of ice cream and other dairy products in order to supply their chains of tea shops, restaurants, and in the case of Lyons, hotels.[118] Allied Bakeries, a chain founded only in 1935, was by World War II operating 28 bakeries for its 217 retail outlets concentrated in the London and Glasgow metropolitan regions. Cow & Gate, the only dairy enterprise without its own retailers, produced cream, ice cream, cheese, and other dairy products, as well as baby foods.[119] All five companies appear to have been managed in a personal way. There is little indication of the creation of hierarchies of the size of National Dairy and other comparable American firms.[120]

The structure of the brewing industry changed little between the wars. Except for the industry's largest firms, markets remained regional. Mergers accounted for most of the turnovers; and mergers, as in the case of other branded products, remained essentially alliances among nearby competitors. Except for Guinness, the leading firms did not build sizable managerial hierarchies. Guinness continued to expand, building a major brewery in London. It began operations there in 1938 and soon supplied 50% of the stout consumed in Great Britain. Neither the brewers nor the bakeries and dairy companies invested extensively in research. Nor did they, except for Guinness, move into markets overseas.[121]

The story of the British meatpackers has broader significance. They differed from the American meatpackers in that from the beginning they were mass retailers. During the 1880s, the innovators—Eastman's, Ltd., and Nelson—had acquired their own refrigerated ships, storage facilities at seaports and at depots in the interior, and packing plants in Argentina.[122] So too did the British-owned, British-managed, and Argentine-incorporated River Plate Fresh Meat Company, which, after its formation in 1883, built a network of retail stores in Britain with the necessary distribution facilities. W. & R. Fletcher was a comparable retailer that processed and shipped Australian meat, primarily lamb.[123] As the meat trade grew rapidly, two specialists in the transportation and storage of perishable foods, Union Cold Storage and International Cold Storage, which were established to serve Britain's rich domestic market for perishable foods, rapidly expanded their facilities and activities. By utilizing the economies of scope they provided services as cheaply and efficiently as the retailers could on their own. In so doing, they encouraged Eastman's and Nelson to sell off their own transport and storage facilities.[124]

These British meat processors and distributors continued to be personally managed (nonhierarchical) enterprises until they were challenged by the first movers in the American meat trade just before World War I. The American firms, no longer able to supply both American and trans-Atlantic markets with meat processed in the United States, decided to enter South America in order to supply their overseas demand. Swift led the way, purchasing a plant in central Argentina and then one in Uruguay and a third in Patagonia. In 1909 it joined with Armour to operate another plant. Schwartzchild & Sulzberger (Wilson & Company after 1917) and Morris soon followed. Then in 1914 Armour built the largest and most modern processing plant in South America.[125]

Quickly these American firms dominated the Anglo-Argentine meat trade. By 1910 they were already exporting 42% of the beef shipped from Argentina and Uruguay to Britain. By 1914 the figure was 63.3% (and that was before the completion of the Armour plant).[126] Swift became the leading producer in South America, shipping more than 1.0 million "quarters" in 1917, as compared with the combined output of 960,000 for the two largest British companies.[127] As output increased and prices declined (even under wartime conditions), the London *Times* reported that American firms remained profitable, while British and Argentine companies were incurring "heavy losses."[128]

After attempts to set up a profit pool failed (the Americans demanded too much), the British firms turned to merger and rationalization as an answer. In March 1914, Nelson and the River Plate Fresh Meat Company joined to form the British & Argentina Meat Company.[129] In this case, merger became more than just an alliance. Administrative centralization and rationalization did follow legal consolidation. After the two firms consolidated their production facilities and sales forces and revamped their retail stores (1,000 such stores came from Nelson and 440 from the River Plate Company), profits soon replaced losses, despite continuing investment by American firms in facilities in South America. The merged enterprise's share of exports from that continent rose from 15.0% in 1915 to 27.4% in 1917.[130]

Further merger came at the end of the war. When it came, it brought into being a single, integrated giant. The managers of that merger were the Vestey brothers, William and Edmund, the founders of the Union Cold Storage Company. In 1911 they had formed the Blue Star Line, acquiring a fleet of five refrigerated ships. In 1910 they had obtained W. & R. Fletcher, the integrated Australian and New Zealand meatpackers with retailing outlets in Britain. Then in 1916 the Vesteys had established a packing house in Argentina. In August 1920 they took control of Eastman's and then of two smaller firms (Argentina Meat and J. H. Dewhurst). Finally in 1923 they acquired the British & Argentine Meat Company. Again centralization and rationalization followed. That merger made Union Cold Storage the largest meat retailer in the world. Controlling one-third of the refrigerated storage capacity in Britain and two-thirds of the multiple-shop outlets selling fresh or frozen meat, it accounted for 20% of all meat imported into Britain. As the world's third largest meatpacking company, behind only Swift and Armour, it became as powerful a representative in its global meatpacking oligopoly as the British representatives in oil, rubber, rayon, metal containers, steel tubes, motorcycles, cables, phonographs (and records), and chemicals were in their oligopolies.[131]

Union Cold Storage, however, continued to differ from its American counterparts. In the first place, it was more centralized, more integrated, and less diversified. It owned ranches and continued to operate—though not to expand—the retail outlets that had come with the acquired companies. It made far less effort than Armour and Swift to exploit by-products such as fertilizers, glue, leather, and dairy products. It remained much more family-managed than any of the American companies, including Swift. As late as the 1970s two Vesteys, a grandson of one of the founders and a great-grandson of another, managed their worldwide business from the same "nondescript office in London's Smithfield Market" near the Thames that their forebears had occupied. In that office, *Business Week* reported, they "divide the responsibilities of empire and have half a dozen special managers reporting to them."[132]

UNILEVER: FROM PERSONAL TO COLLECTIVE MANAGEMENT

In the 1930s Unilever was a British giant, the largest industrial enterprise in the nation in terms of its work force and of the market value of its shares.[133] Its history, including that of its predecessor, Lever Brothers, concludes not only this section on branded, packaged products but also the British experience as a whole. The story of the company's growth through acquisition and merger, of its governance through federation, and of its transformation from a personally to a collectively administered enterprise reveals more about the evolution of the modern industrial enterprise in Britain than do the histories of any of the other large British firms (Table 20). Imperial Chemical Industries and Anglo-Persian Oil looked to American models in building their administrative organizations, while both Imperial Tobacco and Distillers' Company remained federations until well after World War II.

Until 1921 William Hesketh Lever individually made the critical decisions at Lever Brothers, the soapmaking enterprise that he had founded with his brother James in the 1880s. His success in mass-producing, packaging, branding, and advertising soap, and in recruiting a sizable managerial staff, made him the British industry's foremost first mover. The largest soapmaker at home, he moved abroad with much greater alacrity than his competitors, becoming a major producer first in Europe (where his competitors were Schicht and a little later Henkel) and then in the United States (where they were Procter & Gamble and later Colgate-Palmolive-Peet).[134] To assure supplies to his growing industrial empire, Lever began to look overseas for sources of copra, palm oil, and palm kernels. In 1905 he purchased coconut plantations in the

Solomon Islands in the southwest Pacific, and in 1911 he obtained large concessions in the Belgian Congo. In 1910, to assure a more certain supply from Nigeria and nearby areas, the company purchased William B. MacIver and Company, a leading West African trading company, and later obtained other trading companies in that region.[135]

At home Lever took the lead in unifying the industry under the roof of a single holding company. In 1906 he proposed a federation within which each firm would "conduct its own affairs as at present" but would be controlled by a central body "consisting of representatives of the constituent companies" according "to the *pro rata* interest each bears to the whole."[136] He made this proposal because the industry's Soap Makers' Association had been unable to control price and output as competition intensified. Consummation of the merger was thwarted, however, by a massive outcry against the proposed "soap trust" by the press, headed by the *Daily Mail*.

Nevertheless, Lever accomplished his goal in a piecemeal manner. Between 1910 and 1920, largely through exchange of stock, he acquired nearly all of his major rivals. Of these the most important were the Lancashire firms of Joseph Crosfield and William Gossage & Sons, both obtained in 1919, and John Knight of London, acquired in 1920.[137] Crosfield had been Lever Brothers' most effective competitor because it had developed the materials end of the business, producing caustic soda and other chemicals, and because it was able to acquire from Henkel, the German pioneer, processes for producing soap powders chemically.[138] The "Associated Companies," as the constituent companies were termed, retained their legal and administrative autonomy. In addition to the acquisition of competitors, William Lever, in a fit of optimistic enthusiasm during the brief period of postwar prosperity in 1919 and early 1920, obtained control of the Niger Company, the largest commercial enterprise in Nigeria; invested in the Philippine Refining Corporation; invested also in the Sanitas Disinfectant Company, a soapmaking concern in India; and founded a soapmaking company in Nigeria and another in the Congo. At the same time Lever personally purchased a fleet of Scottish trawlers and a chain of fish shops which he later sold to Lever Brothers.[139]

Although Lever, like other British entrepreneurs, continued to administer the enterprise personally, he enlarged his managerial staff from the 1890s on, thus developing what I have called an entrepreneurial enterprise. His board of directors increased from four to eight in 1897, and by 1917 it included fifteen full-time salaried managers, in addition to Lever and his son, W. Hulme Lever, who was Acting Chairman and head of the Finance Committee, and a nephew, J. Littleton.[140] A memorandum, compiled in 1917 in response to a call from the chairman for each of the board members to define his duties, indicates the ad hoc growth of the organization. Some members carried out specific functional duties. These included the directors in charge of finance, of purchasing, real estate, traffic, and legal matters. Another director handled domestic sales, another exports, and still another overseas operations. Others, however, had a wide variety of responsibilities, including oversight of one or more of the Associated Companies. Moreover, the directors rarely met as a board, except to transact "purely formal and legal business." But they did meet informally as the Policy Committee, where other executives who were not directors were brought in for discussion and advice. In addition, Hulme Lever's Finance Committee, formed in 1915, reviewed and allocated capital expenditures.

Nevertheless, it was William Lever (Lord Leverhume after 1917) who set policy and single-handedly made the top-level decisions. He corresponded directly with local managing directors or chairmen. On capital expenditures, D. K. Fieldhouse notes, "he almost certainly took all the final decisions," often deliberately allowing a committee to be "in ignorance of what he was doing."[141]

It was Lever's uninhibited and misdirected postwar expansion and the company's resulting financial crisis during the collapse of the postwar boom in the summer of 1920 that led, in Fieldhouse's words, to a shift "from personal to collective management."[142] First came the formation in January 1921 of the Special Committee, consisting of four members—the two Levers and the other two most experienced and trusted directors. The four were soon joined by Francis D'Arcy Cooper, a member of the accounting firm of Cooper Brothers, which had long served Lever Brothers. His appointment had been insisted upon by the holders of debenture (nonvoting) stock. The committee's initial purpose was, as Fieldhouse notes, "to insure that Lever acted only on proper advice and after mature consideration; and he seems to have accepted the new situation generously and fully."[143] From then on, all decisions were made collectively. This shift in management was further emphasized, indeed symbolized, by the transfer of the company's headquarters from Port Sunlight, its original and still its largest factory, to London.

After the Special Committee took command, it made further organizational changes. In 1923, in order to institute a modicum of control over the federation's many operating units, the committee placed each under a Group Board (later known as a Control Group), defined by product lines. There were boards for soap, margarine, oil cake, and apparently for the by-products. In the next year the group boards' export and overseas activities were removed from their jurisdiction and were consolidated under an export director and an export control group, thus leaving the existing control groups to oversee exclusively the production and distribution of their products within Great Britain.

William Lever's death in 1925 completed the transformation. His son Hulme, preferring not to take on the responsibilities involved, declined the chairmanship and took the title of governor. D'Arcy Cooper became the chairman. The Special Committee continued to be the top decision-making body (comparable to the executive committee in an American company). The board itself, after each weekly formal meeting, transformed itself into the Managing Directors' Conference, later the Directors' Conference, to advise the Special Committee in much the same way as the Policy Committee had done earlier. Two major new committees were established in May 1925—the Capital Expenditure Committee to handle the work carried out earlier by the Finance Committee, and the Sales Executive Committee, formed in an attempt to rationalize marketing operations. In 1926 the need for better coordination and control abroad led to the formation of the Overseas Committee. It included three directors who had been individually responsible for three different overseas areas. They met daily in the Overseas Committee, making their decisions collectively. That committee took over the functions of the Export Control Board. In this way all foreign operations were brought under a single controlling office. At the same time the Special Committee strengthened the Control Groups responsible for major product lines in the domestic market.[144] In this ad hoc, evolutionary manner Lever Brothers had by 1926 acquired an administrative structure that was a variance on the multidivisional form. It had its corporate office, its small top committee of general executives, its corporate staff, and its domestic-product and international-area divisions.

Nevertheless, the coming of a systematically defined corporate office did not in itself bring the much-needed rationalization of personnel and facilities. Lever's purchasing department cooperated and assisted the purchasing departments of the Associated Companies. A new transport department began to provide services for operating units desiring them. Other staff offices did much the same.[145] But the Control Group boards did little to rationalize facilities or to reshape the staffing of the many members of the Associated Companies in the Lever family. Costs remained high; market share declined. The continuing loss of market share emphasized the need for further reorganization. In 1921 the Lever group enjoyed 70% to 75% of the domestic soap market. But the Co-operative Wholesale Societies (English and Scottish) were rapidly increasing their market shares. British Oil & Cake Mills, a combination of processors of vegetable oil, had begun to produce its New Pin brand of soap. And by 1926 the American company, Colgate-Palmolive-Peet, was producing the largest-selling toilet soap in Britain. Therefore, by 1930 Lever's share had dropped to 60%, and it probably would have dropped further if Lever had not acquired British Oil & Cake Mills in 1925. Lever's margarine business, into which the company had moved in late 1914 largely at the request of the government when the war threatened to reduce imports from Europe, was barely making expenses. In 1925 and 1926 the dividends on ordinary (common) shares were not paid.[146]

The difficulty, all agreed, was the long-established, federated system of operations. The corporate office had developed effective techniques to monitor, plan, and allocate resources for the federation as a whole, but the Associated

Companies had their own legal and administrative autonomy and indeed controlled autonomous subsidiaries of their own. In fact, Lever Brothers in Great Britain alone had forty-nine different manufacturing companies maintaining forty-eight separate sales organizations.[147] Few disputed Chairman Cooper's claim that rationalization of overlapping marketing and distribution facilities and personnel could save two pounds sterling per ton in soap-distribution costs alone. Yet Cooper and his colleagues hesitated to alter radically the established, federated organization. As Charles Wilson puts it: "The late Chairman's ghost still walked."[148]

William Lever had long had a powerful commitment to what Arthur Chamberlain at the time of the Nobel reorganization called "the inherited and accepted notions of British industrial management." Lever explicitly distrusted and opposed rationalization, particularly when it required shutting down plants. His goal was "healthy," not "frenzied," competition between the Associated Companies of the Lever "family." "In the family the only competition is novelty and quality," he wrote in 1923. And he added, "I want us all to compete strenuously on everything but price," the "competition of efficiency being our aim and desire." The problem was how to coordinate such "friendly rivalry," particularly between the largest members of the "family"—Lever, Crosfields, and Gossage—which continued to compete vigorously at home and abroad.

It was primarily to control such intergroup competition that the Group Boards were set up in 1923 and the Export Control Board in 1924. In a further attempt to provide central control the Special Committee formed the Sales Executive Committee in 1925. It was "to be responsible to the Board for sales policy of the soap companies in the Family," so that the companies could "concentrate as little as possible on fighting each other and as much as possible on fighting outsiders." In August 1928 the company formed United Exporters, Ltd., to further carry out the same policies abroad. But, for all their exhortations, these boards and committees accomplished little.[149]

It required the merger of Lever Brothers and the Dutch firm Margarine Unie in 1929—the largest international merger carried out before World War II—to clear the way for rationalization within Lever Brothers. Margarine Unie was the dominant producer of margarine in Britain. It was itself a 1927 merger of the leading Dutch margarine makers and the British companies they had come to control, and it had been joined by the Schicht and Centra groups, the leading soap and margarine makers of eastern Europe. Long before this, the two Continental first movers—the Dutch firms of Van den Bergh and Jurgens—had entered the British margarine market, the world's largest, where they purchased control of the leading British retail grocery chains, which sold tea, bacon, butter, and margarine (see Chapter 13). In 1912 Van den Bergh consolidated its purchases into Meadows Dairy, which in 1916 took over the management of Van den Bergh's other large holding, Pearks Dairies. Before the war Jurgens obtained comparable chains, of which Shepherd's Dairy was the largest. Then in 1919 Jurgens acquired full control of one of Britain's most successful grocery chains, Home & Colonial Stores. In 1924 that firm, in turn, took over Maypole Dairy, a large and aggressive chain that had become a major margarine producer and had purchased land and other properties in West Africa. Finally, in 1926 Van den Bergh obtained control of the renowned grocery and tea company, Thomas Lipton, Ltd.[150] By then the two Dutch companies controlled six of the eight largest grocery chains in Britain.[151] Once the two Dutch giants had consolidated into Margarine Unie in September 1927 and been joined by Schicht and Centra a year later, the new margarine colossus began a massive rationalization throughout Europe.

As part of this restructuring Margarine Unie approached Lever Brothers late in 1928 to find, in Charles Wilson's words, "a device for enabling Lever Brothers and the Unie to keep out of each other's way." The goal of the negotiations was to have Lever turn over its margarine enterprises to Margarine Unie and the latter to turn over its soapmaking companies to Lever. The allocation of these properties, however, became too complex to sort out, particularly when it concerned those whose role in the production of soap or margarine was less direct, such as the cake and oil-milling processors. Moreover, D'Arcy Cooper was convinced that the edible fats had a more profitable long-term future than soap. In the end, merger seemed the best solution, even though, because of its international scope, it presented complex legal as well as administrative challenges. The new giant that came into being in 1929 took the name Unilever.[152]

The legal problems were solved through a complicated arrangement of joint governing boards and intricate dividend allocations, described in Charles Wilson's history of Unilever.[153] The administrative challenge was met, first, by selling off retail activities and, secondly, by folding Margarine Unie's operations into Lever's existing administrative structure. By the first action, Unilever became a manufacturing enterprise only, as Lever Brothers had been. The holdings in Maypole, Lipton, and Meadows/Pearks (acquired earlier by the Dutch first movers) were taken over by Home & Colonial Stores. Then the shares that Unilever held in Home & Colonial began to be sold off. These enterprises continued to be operated autonomously under the Home & Colonial Stores umbrella, and a new firm, Allied Suppliers, was created to provide many of their basic supplies. Allied Suppliers remained primarily a purchasing organization, but it soon had its own plants for grinding coffee, blending tea and butter, and packaging flour, cereal, and jam.[154] In this way the merger permitted a division by administrative fiat between mass production and mass retailing in the British food industry, similar to that which had occurred without fiat in the United States. In both cases the manufacturing enterprises took over the wholesaling (but not retailing) of volume-produced products, and the retailers took over the wholesaling (and in only a few cases the manufacturing) of goods whose production offered few cost advantages of scale.

With retailing removed, administrative centralization became less difficult. D'Arcy Cooper, clearly a talented, tactful, and thoughtful manager, was able to convince the new European directors to bring their administrative organization into that of Lever. The Special Committee at first included two British and two Continental members. The numbers were soon increased to four and four. London became the headquarters. A new and impressive Unilever House was built at the site of Lever Brothers' existing corporate offices in Blackfriars. The board meetings, which at first were held alternately in London and Rotterdam, were by 1931 held regularly in London. The meetings were followed by the informal Directors' Conference, which acted "as a center for dissemination of information and the exchange of opinions." It also acquired a more formal function, that of allocating capital expenditures, which had been carried out earlier by the Finance Committee. In the corporate office the service and advisory staffs were enlarged, as was the number of advisory committees. For Great Britain, operations were grouped by product—soap, margarine, oil mills, and foods—each headed now by the Group Executive (the new name for the older Control Group). Three comparable executive bodies supervised business abroad—the Continental Committee for Europe (with its headquarters in Rotterdam), the Overseas Committee, and the United Africa Company for activities on that continent. Below this superstructure were the managements of the many local companies.

The most important adjustment of this structure came in July 1933 after the Directors' Conference decided that the members of the Special Committee who also served on the Continental and Overseas Committees should "withdraw from the daily management of these committees" and, with the other members of the Special Committee, should concentrate on overall monitoring, planning, and resource allocation. The board members who remained on the Overseas Committee, and a little later those who remained on the Continental Committee, were no longer to make their decisions collectively.[155] Instead, each of these directors would become responsible for monitoring and coordinating the operating companies in a specified territorial region. By World War II such directors, whose number had been increased to eight, were known as Contact Directors. And with the end of World War II the office of Western European Management, with headquarters in Rotterdam, was established to take the place of the Continental Committee.

Except for the alterations having to do with Contact Directors and the formation of the Western European Management, the structure of Unilever remained relatively unchanged after 1932. In 1946 an organization chart, together with a page of explanatory notes, was distributed to the company's executives (see Figure 10). This chart shows clearly that Unilever, one of

Britain's most successful multinational giants, had come to be managed through a multidivisional structure, with a corporate office of general and staff executives, with product divisions for its domestic (British) markets, and with geographical divisions for its markets overseas.

The administrative reorganization finally brought much-needed rationalization. At all levels of the Lever organization the merger helped to break down resistance to reshaping the long-established patterns of small-scale management at the operating level. The new European members of the Special Committee (including Georg Schicht and Sidney Van den Bergh) had been deeply involved in rationalizing the European margarine trade after the formation of Margarine Unie in 1927. The way in which they shut down obsolete plants, concentrated production in reconstructed, modernized, and often new plants, and consolidated sales forces, purchasing organizations, and transport and storage networks is described in Charles Wilson's history of Unilever. The 1929 merger of Lever and Margarine Unie was followed by a comparable rationalization of a large part of the European soap industry by reshaping and combining the Lever, Schicht, and Centra soapmaking and distributing enterprises. On the Continent the pressure to rationalize had already increased because the German rival, Henkel, was making a rapid recovery in the European market.

These actions, with the continuing loss of market share in the British soap market, set the stage for reorganizing Lever's federation of soapmakers in Britain. The competition from Colgate-Palmolive-Peet and the Co-operative Wholesale Society broadened in 1930 when Procter & Gamble, intent on exploiting Unilever's weaknesses in that market, purchased a small independent soapmaker, Thomas Hedley & Sons of Newcastle. Unilever's soap rationalization began after what amounted to an ultimatum by the senior director of the Soap Executive Committee at a managers' conference in 1931. Many of the individual firms, including Gossage, were liquidated. Facilities and personnel in production and distribution were consolidated or otherwise reshaped, and their numbers were reduced. Again Wilson gives the details.[156] This process took even more time than did the changes on the Continent. By 1935, however, the goals of 1931 were on their way to being met. Even so, the changes were not so extensive as those that usually followed American mergers. For example, such long-established enterprises as Crosfield and Hudson & Knight retained much of their autonomy. Only in 1945 were agreements made between Crosfield and other Lever companies for more reciprocal production and distribution of each other's products. It was not until 1964 that Crosfield was finally incorporated into Unilever's legal and administrative structure.[157]

The reorganization of Unilever's British soap business came just in time. Procter & Gamble, which had completed a new state-of-the-art factory in Britain in 1933, used its competitive capabilities in production and marketing to increase its market share from 1.5% in 1930 to 15% in 1935. Unilever's orga-

ORGANISATIONAL STRUCTURE 1946

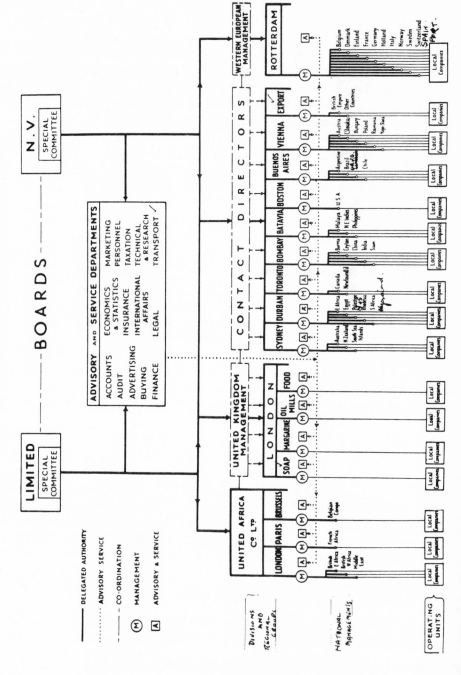

NOTES ON ORGANISATIONAL STRUCTURE — YEAR 1946

The chart printed above shows, in a necessarily simplified form, the framework of the Organisational Structure of the two Unilever Companies in 1946. This structure is not static; it will undergo change as circumstances may require.

The structure has been planned to meet certain requirements which are of extreme importance in an undertaking of this size. These are :—

(a) The principle of delegation of responsibility should be followed to the utmost extent, consistent with efficiency and co-ordination of policy.

(b) Those responsible for broad policy should be adequately and continuously informed as to events and progress throughout the whole organisation, but at the same time kept free of all matters which can be properly decided by executives. They should be enabled to form a sound judgment of the abilities and experience of all members of the staff likely to be able to play a senior part in later years.

(c) Executive responsibility at home and abroad should be placed in the hands of picked personnel supported by all necessary technical and advisory services.

(d) All the knowledge and information likely to be of interest to the organisation should be collected from both internal and external sources, collated and passed on for practical application to all concerned.

(e) Apart from the normal interchange of correspondence and documents, there should be frequent personal contact between Directors of the two Parent Companies, the Technical and Advisory Services and the Executives of operating groups or units by visits to and from the centre.

(f) It should be established practice to move suitable personnel from one activity to another within the organisation, and thus develop individual experience, give opportunities for promotion, and build up a reserve of experienced personnel from which the higher posts may be filled.

To attain these ends the structure provides :—

(1) Identical membership of the Boards of the two Parent Companies.

(2) A Special Committee consisting of a few members of the Boards, to which the two Boards have delegated power to deal with broad policy, to co-ordinate the work of other Directors, to supervise the operations of the Advisory and Service Departments, and to undertake outside contacts at the highest level. Their recommenda-

tions are submitted to the appropriate Board. Members of this Committee are free from all routine executive duties.

(3) A series of specialist Advisory and Service Departments working with the Group and National Managements. These Departments acquire and maintain competent and up-to-date knowledge within their respective spheres, and ensure that it is available throughout the whole organisation.

(4) The United Africa Company Ltd., operating as a self-contained organisation under its own Directorate, responsible for the control and management of the mercantile and industrial activities in British, Belgian and French West Africa, North Africa, East Africa and the Middle East.

(5) A U.K. Management responsible for production and distribution within the United Kingdom, arranged in the Main Divisions of Soap, Margarine, Oil Mills and Food.

(6) A panel of Contact Directors, common to the two Parent Companies, constantly visiting the Regional Groups and National Managements outside Western Europe. They act as advisers to responsible executives throughout these territories; assist in the correlation of policy and practice between territories; acquaint themselves with the personnel concerned; observe and assist the operations of the Advisory and Service Departments; and make recommendations on policy and development through the Special Committee to the Parent Boards.

(7) A Western European Management responsible for the supervision of all Unilever activities throughout Western Europe.

(8) Regional Groups, each covering several countries, in charge of Directors or senior executives to whom responsibility is delegated, subject to guidance on high policy from the Parent Boards, and which in turn delegate responsibility to National Managements.

(9) National Managements in each country comprised in a Regional Group, supervising the operating Units within their national frontiers.

(10) Two Export Divisions, one in London and the other in Rotterdam, promoting export from the most convenient production point.

It will be seen that the structure provides for the central determination of broad policy, and at the same time for freedom of action within Divisions, Groups and National Managements. In this way, rapidity of decision and action is effectively ensured.

Figure 10. Organization chart of Unilever Corporation, 1946. From Unilever Archives, London.

nizational changes permitted it to halt the inroads from the Co-operative Wholesale Society and apparently from Colgate-Palmolive-Peet. Although it still continued to lose share to Procter & Gamble, output and profit margins increased in a most satisfactory manner.[158] At the same time the company warded off Henkel's continuing challenge on the Continent. Its American soapmaking subsidiary, under the able leadership of Francis A. Countway, continued to compete vigorously with the two American leaders in the United States market. Outside of the United States and Europe, Unilever remained for several decades the dominant producer of soap, only being pressed here and there by Procter & Gamble and Colgate-Palmolive-Peet.[159]

This history of Lever Brothers and then Unilever during the interwar years tells much about British industrial management and industrial organization. First, organizational change in large British industries was not a carefully planned process, but rather the result of ad hoc responses to immediate needs. Even when the Lever enterprise was becoming managerial and its leadership collective, few if any studies or reports on organizational matters were made, comparable to those made by Du Pont, General Motors, or even ICI and its predecessor Nobel Industries. Until the merger with Margarine Unie, organizational changes were reactive. They were responses to immediate needs for financial and administrative control. The 1929 merger that presented the opportunity for major structural change was itself a response to overproduction in margarine, especially abroad. Its consummation, in turn, encouraged and indeed may have made possible the reorganization of the enterprise's soapmaking and distributing activities, which was necessary to meet the competitive threats from three other global soapmakers, two American and one German. In all these changes Lever management reacted in much the same ad hoc way as did Standard Oil (New Jersey) in its reorganization during the same years (I have described this in *Strategy and Structure*). In neither case was there detailed or serious discussion about organization qua organization.[160] And what was true of Lever was true of nearly all the other British industrial enterprises. The review of organizational needs and options that was made in 1919 by Explosives Trades (the early name of Nobel Industries) was very much the exception.

This lack of attention to corporate structure reflects a second characteristic of British enterprise. The Lever story emphasizes once again that the British preference for personal management led to a reliance on federations of relatively small enterprises rather than to the rationalizing of facilities and personnel of constituent companies in a single, centralized operating organization. By 1948 such federations, originally created as devices to control price and output (a legal cartel), which had all but disappeared in the United States after the turn-of-the-century merger movement, were a standard means of organizing even the largest of British industrial enterprises. Neither Imperial Tobacco nor Distillers' Company made any significant move to centralize and rationalize its operations until the 1960s, nor did the comparable alliances between industry leaders, such as Cadbury and Fry, Huntley and Palmer, and Tate and Lyle. The continuing hesitancy of the Lever management to undertake a drastic reshaping of its federation attests to that commitment.

Third, Unilever's story demonstrates that the reshaping and modernizing of an industry did require, as Sir Eric Geddes said of the textile industry, a "strong organization to take over control." The success of enterprises in soap, chemicals, and metal containers, and the failure of the cooperative efforts of individual companies, banks, and the government in steel and shipbuilding, suggest that the only type of organization capable of carrying out such a reorganization was the modern industrial enterprise. In Britain its formation was held back by the federations, entrenched in many industries, that were based on a continuing commitment to the ways of personal management.

Implications of the British Experience

As the story of Lever Brothers reflects the broader history of branded, packaged products, so the collective history of those industries—industries in which British enterprises continued to be the most successful—reflect the larger British experience from the 1880s until World War II. The ability to continue to compete in soap and meatpacking required the creation of an organizational structure and the development of organizational capabilities comparable to those of foreign competitors. Where the challenges in the British market were less direct—as was the case in whiskey, beer, cigarettes, chocolate, biscuits, preserves, sugar, confectionery, and other branded food products—enterprises managed in a personal manner were able to remain profitable at home and even to develop businesses abroad. They could do so, however, only in markets where they were not directly challenged by modern industrial enterprises of other countries. Nor did they expand overseas on the scale of the managerial American food and consumer-chemical companies, or even on the scale of the pre-1914 Lever Brothers, the enterprise which had the largest managerial staff in these industries.

These British producers of branded, packaged products did not expand by aggressively moving into related product lines. They did not use their distribution capabilities to take on new products in the manner of their American counterparts. British firms rarely merged in the manner of General Mills and General Foods to make use of complementary facilities and skills. Moreover, these British firms did not invest in research that might have developed products using the same raw materials and production processes. Whereas Procter & Gamble developed Crisco and other cooking oils before World War I, Lever Brothers moved into margarine only under pressure from the government during the war. In the interwar years it remained far behind Procter & Gamble and Henkel in the development of detergents and other nonsoap cleansers. Lever's diversification into trawlers and fish shops resulted from the unplanned, personal decisions of William Lever. Nor did the British food, soap, and paint companies diversify into chemicals and other nonfood products in the manner of American firms. On the other hand, the few firms that did make important investments in research, such as ICI, Burroughs Wellcome, and Dunlop, did begin to develop a broader line of products. They remained the exceptions, however. Therefore the American pattern of large firms competing in several different industries through different sets of companies began to be seen in Britain only after World War II.

The continuing failure to make such investments and to recruit and train the necessary managerial staffs may reflect differences between the basic goals of British and American enterprises, or, more properly, between enterprises managed personally or by families and those administered by salaried managers. In American managerial firms the basic goals appear to have been long-term profit and growth. Growth ensured increased assets for large investors, including founding families. Growth also ensured long-term income and long-term tenure for managers and, in many cases, for workers. In Britain the goal for family firms appears to have been to provide a steady flow of cash to owners—owners who were also managers. On the other hand, the published histories of ICI, Unilever, and British Petroleum indicate that for the relatively few British managerial firms the goal became, as it was for such American companies, long-term growth of assets financed through retained earnings.

Much more research needs to be done on this subject, but there is a good deal of evidence to support the view that in Britain a large and stable income for the family was more of an incentive than the long-term growth of the firm. For one thing, in the years before World War I the pay-out in dividends appears to have been much greater in British than in American firms, with the ratio of dividends to earnings running as high as 80% or even 90%.[161] After the war, if such companies in the automobile and other industries wished to expand facilities, they chose to raise new funds by issuing nonvoting preferred stock or debentures, rather than to use retained earnings. Courtaulds and to a lesser extent Pilkington chose to pay dividends rather than to reinvest in research and development. These and other family firms were reluctant to recruit nonfamily managers and even slower to bring such salaried executives into top management. At the same time, they were much more willing than American firms to let skilled workers take over the functions of lower-level managers.

All of these characteristics help to account for the failure of many British firms to maintain up-to-date facilities and to reinvest in product and process development. They also help to account for the failure of those companies to sharpen product-specific managerial and technical skills in the functional departments, as well as the capabilities of monitoring, planning, and resource allocation in the top corporate office. The failure to develop such organizational abilities, in turn, explains at least partially the inability of enterprises and the industries in which they operated to compete for market share abroad and even at home, or to move into more profitable related industries. Attempts by firms to maintain market power solely through the use of patents, advertising, cartel arrangements, and mergers were doomed to failure once they were challenged by enterprises that had made investments and developed capabilities. British entrepreneurs had the patents. They had access to advertising agencies. They had created enforceable cartels in the form of holding companies. They had much closer ties with and access to British financial institutions, government bureaus, and Parliament than did American and German competitors producing and selling in British markets. In a number of basic industries they enjoyed every source of market power against these competitors, except the capability to compete. Thus British entrepreneurs lost out in many of the most dynamic new industries of the Second Industrial Revolution.

On the other hand, those few entrepreneurs who did make the investment in new production machinery and product-specific marketing personnel and facilities and who also recruited managerial teams—as they did in glass, explosives, rayon, rubber, and soap—became effective competitors at home and took their place in the rising global oligopolies. Of even more significance, British enterprises that became successful later challengers to first movers in existing oligopolies did so by making comparable investments, as they did in petroleum, metal containers, steel tubes, motorcycles, cables, radios, in selected industrial chemicals (particularly after the formation of ICI), and in meatpacking. They also did so, but to a lesser extent, in automobiles and electrical equipment; there they remained less effective challengers because the founding entrepreneurs recruited fewer middle managers, because they continued to manage personally from the top, and because they invested less in research. In both industries the development of new products and processes continued to be carried on primarily in the United States and Germany.

The industries in which entrepreneurs did make the three-pronged investment and did develop organizational capabilities had relatively little need to seek the assistance of financial institutions and government bureaus. In these industries banks rarely played any significant role. Except for oil, the initial investment came from the founding families and local sources. In oil the government gave financial support to Anglo-Persian in response to an immediate military need for its product. Nevertheless, the government's part in making both short-term operating decisions and long-term strategic decisions at Anglo-Persian remained minimal. In the more fragmented industries, such as textiles and steel, the role of government officials and bankers was far more significant. There, however, the privileged access to outside support provided little help in maintaining the profits and performance of the enterprises or their industries, precisely because the industrial enterprises had failed to create competitive capabilities. Indeed, in steel this access was a positive deterrent to overall productivity and growth because some firms used such connections to prevent others from making the investment and developing the skills needed to become competitive.

The general failure to develop organizational capabilities weakened British industry and with it the British economy. In the first place, the failure to consolidate industry-wide federations into modern industrial enterprises, as Robert Barlow did in metal containers and McGowan and Mond did in chemicals, meant the lack of effective enterprises to rationalize industries by investing in state-of-the-art facilities and developing the skills essential to exploit the economies of scale and scope. Second, when British entrepreneurs did succeed in creating such enterprises in their industries, the success of those industries in international competition depended on the extent to which only one or two such firms had developed their facilities and skills. In oil, rubber, and metal containers the dominant enterprises did continue to improve products and processes and to compete effectively both functionally and strategically in the international marketplace. But in other industries, where the desire for family control and income delayed the development of such capabilities—as was the case in rayon and in glass until the mid-1930s—the British industry fell behind. Even in electrical equipment and automobiles, British enterprises remained very dependent on the United States for the development of new processes of production and, to a lesser extent, of new products. Finally, the failure to develop competitive capabilities resulted in high economic and social costs in terms of rate of return on investment and of employment. On the whole, British industries benefited far less from technological innovation than those of the United States and Germany in the years before World War II and those of Japan after that war.

In sum, the collective histories of British enterprises demonstrate the essential need to create and maintain competitive capabilities in order to assure continuing profitability and productivity in an industry. The German experience reinforces these lessons. There the three-pronged investment in production, distribution, and management permitted German industrial enterprises to become the most successful and their industries the most powerful in Europe during the years before World War I. These same organizational capabilities allowed those enterprises and their industries to recover after the 1914–1924 decade of war and crisis, and quickly to regain world markets with little direct assistance from the German government or from German financial institutions.

· IV ·

Germany:
Cooperative Managerial Capitalism

The collective histories of the largest manufacturing companies in Germany provide a third perspective—a final point of triangulation—in mapping the evolution of the modern industrial enterprise from its beginnings in the 1880s to the 1940s. This third set of collective histories is based on a neutral sample similar to those used for the United States and Britain—the two hundred largest manufacturing enterprises in roughly the same years; that is, at the time of World War I, at the end of the 1920s, and at the beginning of the post–World War II era. These histories are presented in much the same way as they were for the United States and Britain. They are told industry by industry, first for the period before World War I and then for the interwar years.

The German experience revealed by the collective industry-by-industry histories is closer to that of the United States than to that of Britain. In Germany as in the United States, but much more than in Britain, entrepreneurs did make the investment in production facilities and personnel large enough to exploit the economies of scale and scope, did build the product-specific international marketing and distribution facilities, and did recruit the essential managerial hierarchies. In Germany, again as in the United States, but much more than in Britain, the founding entrepreneurs soon shared top management with the senior managers they recruited. Therefore in Germany, as in the United States, salaried managers with little or no equity in the enterprises for which they worked participated in making decisions concerning current production and distribution, as well as in planning and allocating resources for future production and distribution. And because German entrepreneurs were so often the first in Europe to make the three-pronged investment in manufacturing, marketing, and management essential to exploit fully the economies of scale and scope, they became first movers in many of the new capital-intensive industries, not only in their homeland but in all of Europe. Moreover, because they soon developed effective organizational capabilities—in relation to both physical facilities and human skills—they continued to grow in much the same manner as American first movers. They expanded abroad; and, where their processes of production and distribution permitted, they moved into related industries. As in the United States, these capabilities provided a basic dynamic of industrial capitalism.

A central theme of the following chapters on the German experience is that the organizational capabilities of German firms gave them powerful advantages in international competition. The creation of these capabilities was certainly one reason why Germany so swiftly surpassed Britain to become Europe's leading industrial nation. Equally important, their existence helps to explain why German enterprises in these industries recovered so quickly after the 1914–1924 decade of war and postwar crises. The inability of British, and also of French, enterprises to take advantage of the opportunities created by German competitive disadvantages during that decade, as well as the swift recovery of the German firms in international markets after 1924, emphasize the critical importance of organizational capabilities to the long-term performance of industrial enterprises and of national industries and the national economy in which they operated.

Although in both Germany and the United States the technologically advanced, capital-intensive industries of the Second Industrial Revolution came to be managed through a system of managerial capitalism and so were driven by the same dynamics of growth, their collective experiences differed in significant ways.

While in the United States modern industrial enterprises appeared in about equal numbers in producer-goods and consumer-goods industries (and in Britain were more numerous in consumer goods), in Germany such enterprises were concentrated in the production and distribution of producer's goods. Nearly two-thirds of the 200 largest industrial companies in Germany were clustered in metals, chemicals, and the three machinery groups (see Table 8). In 1913 these five industrial groups accounted for 127 or 63.5% of the 200 companies; in 1929 for 111 or 55.5%; and in 1953 for 118 or 59.0%. Many of the firms in other industries such as food (particularly sugar and vegetable oil), textiles, paper, and stone, glass, and clay (listed in Appendixes C.1, C.2, and C.3) also produced goods for further processing or for industrial use. Only a small number made consumer goods for individuals and households, and of these nearly half were regional breweries.

German investment in production also differed from that in the United States and Britain in that the cost advantages of size rested as often on the exploitation of economies of scope as on the utilization of those of scale. This was particularly true of the chemical and heavy-machinery industries.

Another difference was that although German entrepreneurial and family firms recruited, trained, and promoted salaried managers in much the same manner as their American counterparts, in some German industries family control lasted longer than it did in the United States.

The greatest difference, however, came in interfirm and intrafirm relationships.

Whereas in the United States the new, large, integrated managerial firms competed aggressively for market share and profits, in Germany many of them preferred to cooperate. Whereas in the United States the passage of the Sherman Antitrust Act in 1890 and its enforcement by the federal courts reflected a shared belief in the value of competition, in Germany the strong support given to cartels and other interfirm agreements by the nation's courts reflected a shared belief in the benefits of industrial cooperation. These beliefs were also evident in the larger role played by trade associations in Germany than in the United States. So too, German manufacturers, while remaining unsympathetic to labor unions (like American managers), paid much closer attention to the needs and welfare of their working force than did most of their American counterparts. Thus the cooperation that developed between and within industrial firms can be considered as part of a larger system, which Jürgen Kocka and other historians of the German economy have termed "organized capitalism."

Part IV on the German experience rounds out my global overview of the industries in which the modern industrial enterprise has clustered since its beginnings in the 1880s. The term "global overview" seems justified because until the 1930s Germany with the United States and Britain accounted for two-thirds of the world's industrial output. Moreover, many of the leading enterprises in the other industrial nations appear in this study as competitors to American, British, and German players in the global oligopolies.

TEN

The Foundations of Managerial Capitalism
in German Industry

Although in Germany the basic story of the beginnings and dynamic evolution of the modern industrial enterprise is similar to that in the United States and Britain, there were, of course, variations in its evolution; and these variations reflected significant differences between the environment in which German enterprises operated and those in which American and British enterprises evolved.

Similarities and Differences

In Germany the modern industrial enterprise appeared quickly, as it did in the United States, following the completion of the new transportation and communication networks—networks that made possible a flow of goods and information large enough to exploit the economies of scale and scope. The new manufacturing enterprises continued to cluster in industries in which the technology of production provided the cost advantages of scale and scope, and in these industries they coordinated the flow of goods through the processes of production and distribution. But in other industries, where the technologies of production failed to bring impressive cost advantages of scale and scope, it was the new distributors—the full-line, full-service wholesalers and the new mass retailers, including department stores, mail-order houses, and chains—that began, as they did in the United States and Britain, to coordinate the flow of materials through the processes of production and distribution.

Operating in a different environment, German industrial enterprises acquired distinctive features that differentiated them from comparable enterprises in the United States and Britain. Economic differences—those of markets, sources of supply, and methods of finance—played a part in the differentiating process. So did cultural differences, as reflected in "rules of the game" (legal or otherwise) and in educational systems. The most striking legal difference—the ability to enforce cartels and other agreements between competitors in courts of law—meant that German industrials had much less incentive to merge into industry-wide holding companies. Instead, agreements as to price, output, and marketing territories were enforced through looser and more temporary federations—conventions, syndicates, and communities of interest—legal devices that were rarely used in Britain or the United States. And by the turn of the century German universities and institutes, among the best in the world, were ahead of their American counterparts in providing industrial enterprises with technical and scientific knowledge and with skilled technicians and managers—knowledge and skills central to the exploitation of the new technologies of the Second Industrial Revolution.

In the economic realm the most important difference came in the financing of enterprise. Differences in markets were important, too (differences in sources of supply were less important in the long run), but the German financial arrangements were especially distinctive. Self-financing remained the major source of growth; in Germany, however, unlike Britain and the United States, large multipurpose banks played a major role in providing funds for the initial investment in the new, capital-intensive industries—investment that was essential to achieve the economies of scale and scope. Such a role meant that the representatives of banks sat on the boards of many enterprises and so participated in top-level decisions more than was the case in either Britain or the United States. In the United States, investment bankers first appeared on boards of industrial firms during the turn-of-the-century merger movement. In Britain, bankers rarely played a role until a firm or an industry became financially distressed. Even in Germany, once the enterprise had made the tripartite investment in production, distribution, and management and had developed its organizational capabilities, bankers on boards became less influential. Nevertheless, the German industries in which banks played a significant part in an enterprise's initial creation and growth provide the best and almost the only examples of financial capitalism. Only in Germany did representatives of financial institutions help to shape top-level policy, particularly on resource allocation, over any extended period of time.

Two German Industrial Enterprises: Gebrüder Stollwerck and Accumulatoren-Fabrik AG

More complex and subtle distinctions between German and other industrial enterprises (particularly Britain's) can be best suggested by examining two enterprises in which neither bankers nor legalized cartels played a major role. One of these is Gebrüder Stollwerck, the chocolate maker, chosen because it provides an excellent counterpart to Cadbury, that successful British family firm (see the beginning of Chapter 6). The other is Accumulatoren-Fabrik AG (AFA), maker of electric batteries. It made the necessary investments in production, distribution, and management in an industry where British entrepreneurs failed to do so, and before World War I it created a managerial hierarchy that was far larger and much more systematically organized than that of any industrial enterprise in Britain. In a very short time this firm and its American counterpart squeezed their British competitors out of the world market and even out of markets within Britain. The stories of Stollwerck and AFA effectively illustrate the differences between the personal ways of British management and the more impersonal, systematic, and professional ways of German management.

Gebrüder Stollwerck and Cadbury Brothers had similar beginnings. The German firm was founded in Cologne in 1839; the British was established near Birmingham in 1831.[1] The Cadbury sons who took over their father's firm built their large factory—one that brought scale economies—in 1879. The Stollwercks did the same in Cologne a year or two earlier. Both had comparable working forces: the Birmingham factory employed 1,193 in 1889 and the Cologne works 1,500 in 1890.[2] Both families were prolific. Franz Stollwerck's five sons took over the management of the firm and its continuing expansion just as the next generation of Cadburys did.

Here the similarities end. The Stollwercks made a greater investment than the Cadburys in distribution facilities and personnel. They recruited a larger managerial team. As a result the German family firm developed organizational capabilities that allowed it to expand abroad and to diversify into new markets far more quickly and effectively than the Cadburys' family-managed enterprise.

During the 1870s and 1880s the Stollwercks paid very close attention to marketing. The company's official historian emphasizes their appreciation of the importance of marketing for the continued growth of the firm. They concentrated on packaging, particularly as a means to preserve the quality of their perishable products, and on branding, with special attention to the design of the package. They soon had a separate advertising department. Of even more importance, they quickly created a network of branch sales offices in Europe and the United States. These offices not only housed the sales forces that did the marketing, but they also supervised some packaging and administered a small number of retail stores that the company operated. As the history of the company points out, the branches, besides increasing sales, provided the management at home and abroad with information on local tastes and demands. Marketing expansion became "a pace-setter in the manufacturing and the engineering."[3] It led not only to the building of new plants at home and abroad and the development of new products, but also to the establishment of the research laboratory in 1884. All but one of that laboratory's four directors between 1884 and World War II had doctoral degrees in chemistry.[4]

Well before the turn of the century the international chocolate business began to profit from a rapid expansion of demand. Whereas Cadbury's growth continued to come from enlarging its original factory, Stollwerck's came from building new works to support its international marketing organization. In 1886 the company built a plant at Pressburg in Hungary. Then, in 1889, a second German factory was constructed to serve the fast-growing metropolitan area of Berlin. The firm established a factory in New York in 1900 and replaced it in 1906 with a much larger one at Stamford, Connecticut. By that time Gebrüder Stollwerck, according to the company's historian, was the second largest producer of chocolate in the United States. (Walter Baker was the first.) In America Stollwerck concentrated on the production of chocolate coating and powder to be sold to other confectionery manufacturers, rather than on branded, packaged products. Soon it had branch sales offices in New York, Boston, Chicago, and San Francisco. The initial success of the American venture encouraged the company to challenge the British "Big Three"—Cadbury, Fry, and Rowntree—on their own ground by setting up a plant in London in 1903. Then in 1910 it built one in Vienna, the long-acclaimed chocolate capital of the world.[5]

Because of Stollwerck's strong marketing orientation, its research technicians pioneered in the development of vending machines as an inexpensive way to sell its products. The venture was so successful that in 1894 the family formed a separate company, Deutsche Automatengesellschaft Stollwerck & Co., a limited partnership capitalized at M 1.1 million, to develop, produce, and market an increasingly wide variety of vending machines. Even before that date the enterprise, as a first mover in producing such machines, had set up vending-machine subsidiaries in Austria, Hungary, Britain, Belgium, and the United States.[6] As the firm developed a full line of vending machines, Ludwig Stollwerck formed alliances with Jasmatzi, the Dresden cigarette producer, with the German subsidiary of the American match producer, Diamond Match, and with the German subsidiary of the British soapmaker, Lever Brothers, to produce specialized vending machines for each of these products. In each of the three enterprises Ludwig became chairman of the Supervisory Board.[7] Stollwerck also built a chain of automated restaurants in Europe and another in the United States. In the United States, where representatives of the firm had worked with Thomas A. Edison in developing their vending machines, the company set up a production plant in New York City and repair facilities in Chicago, thereby producing machines to dispense chewing gum as well as the other products listed. In 1911 it formed the Auto Sales Gum & Chocolate Company in New York, which by 1916 had a capitalization of $10.4 million.[8]

The overseas expansion of Stollwerck's chocolate-making activities and its moves into vending machines were carried out by a growing managerial hierarchy. In the 1870s and 1880s a relatively small number of nonfamily senior managers in finance, production, and sales received the title of *Prokurist,* that is, a manager legally empowered to act as a company owner. By the 1880s the Stollwercks were being forced to decide whether to grow by expanding the hierarchy or whether to stay the same size, relying on the family for executives. The two older brothers were quite reluctant to give up the concept of family-centered—or, in their own terms, "patriarchalisch-familienegoistischen"—management.[9] But the third son, Ludwig, insisted that family capabilities were not enough. He had his way. He not only expanded the managerial staff abroad, but quickly built up an extensive central staff, whose size grew from 65 employees in 1886 to 154 in 1896.[10] Simultaneously he reorganized the firm's bookkeeping and cost accounting and reshaped its functional operating departments. In later years he considered these the most important actions of his business career.

Although Ludwig built up an extensive hierarchy to manage an increasingly multinational business, the Stollwerck family retained full control at the top. Family members made up both the Vorstand, or the Management Board, and the Aufsichtsrat, the Supervisory Board. (Here I will use the English term "Supervisory Board" for the Aufsichtsrat, but the German term "Vorstand" for that uniquely German governing body.) With the outbreak of World War I and the resulting management challenges, nonfamily executives joined the Vorstand. By 1920 the Supervisory Board included representatives of banks as well as the family.

Until the 1920s, however, the family dominated top-level decision-making. The Stollwerck family had relied on retained earnings, supplemented by funds provided by private banks in Bremen and Berlin and the Cologne bank of A. Schaaffhausen (which was already one of the giant German credit banks, one of the Grossbanken), to finance the initial expansion in both chocolate and vending machines. In 1902, in order to raise new capital for further plant expansion at home and abroad, the firm was incorporated as a joint-stock company, becoming Gebrüder Stollwerck AG. It was capitalized at M 14 million, of which M 9 million in stock was held by the family and the remaining M 5 million was provided primarily by the Darmstädter Bank für Handel und Industrie (another of the Grossbanken).[11] Nevertheless, the family remained in complete control until after World War I. The Darmstädter representative on the Supervisory Board of Gebrüder Stollwerck was not an executive from the bank, but Heinrich Stollwerck.

The comparison between the two family firms, Stollwerck and Cadbury—both in the same business—underlines the significance of Ludwig Stollwerck's break from personal management to the recruiting of a team of salaried managers. Those managers helped the German firm not only to become the industry's leader at home, but also to develop facilities and skills that brought much more dynamic growth in foreign markets and in related industries. Nevertheless, Stollwerck, which provides a striking contrast to its British counterpart, was not a typical German industrial firm, for it was one of the very few enterprises on the lists of the two hundred largest in Germany to mass-produce and distribute branded, packaged products. Even so, much of its turnover and profits came from selling chocolate in bulk for further processing and from the volume production and distribution of vending machines.

More representative of the typical, large, German manufacturing enterprise is Accumulatoren-Fabrik AG (AFA), the battery maker, which manufactured technologically advanced industrial products. As the technological leader of its industry in Europe, it soon began to share world markets with its American counterpart, the Electric Storage Battery Company, leaving British, French, and other producers far behind. Its history illustrates once again how the creation of organizational capabilities resulted in market power.

The storage battery was brand-new. It was an essential, though specialized, ingredient of the new technology developed in the 1880s to generate, transmit, and use electric power. The initial and, for many years, the most important use of the storage battery was to even out the fluctuating demand for electric current for power and light. Power stored in the batteries at utility plants generating electricity for power and light met peak-load demands. The batteries were then recharged during times of low demand. These batteries were of particular value in providing power for electric streetcars and subways, which required much more power than street and interior lighting. Storage-battery manufacturers also produced in volume smaller specialized units to provide power for telegraph and telephone systems; for police and fire alarms; for lighting in subways and trains; for power in electric automobiles and submarines; and after 1911 for self-starting and lighting systems in mass-produced, gasoline-driven automobiles and other vehicles. [12]

During most of the decade of the 1880s in the United States and Europe the production of nearly all electrical equipment was marked by innovation and small enterprises. The production of storage batteries was no exception. Patents, products, and small shops abounded. Only in the late 1880s and early 1890s were plants built large enough to capture economies of scale. In this industry, as in many others, the first companies to build such plants, to create a management organization to administer them, and to invest extensively in sales and service organizations continued to dominate for decades. But in Germany, as in the United States and Britain, numerous patents had to be acquired before large-scale investment could be made in large, efficient production facilities. It is in this connection that Richard H. Schallenberg states in his history of storage-battery technology: "Patents control the application of technology, but they are not the technology itself." Thus "the Brush patents described an unworkable technology; yet, they were very effective in controlling other storage battery technology." [13]

The first German entrepreneur to acquire the necessary patents and to obtain funds to build a plant of optimal size was Adolph Müller of Hagen in the Ruhr Valley. Late in 1889 Müller and a partner, operating as Müller & Einbeck, worked out an arrangement with the two European first movers in the manufacturing of electrical equipment, Allgemeine Elektricitäts Gesellschaft (AEG) and Siemens & Halske (S&H). Those two firms agreed, with the support of leading banks, to provide the funds needed to purchase patents and to finance the construction of a plant large enough to supply batteries in volume at the lowest possible cost. In return AEG and S&H agreed to purchase batteries exclusively from the new enterprise. On these terms Accumulatoren-Fabrik AG (AFA) was formed, with AEG, S&H, and the firm of Müller & Einbeck taking shares. As they completed the plant Müller and his associates established a worldwide network of branch offices to market, install, and service their batteries.[14]

AFA's story was repeated elsewhere. As Schallenberg points out, "In each country one firm rose to dominance." In the United States, Electric Storage Battery, founded in 1888 by W. W. Gibbs, who headed the largest gas-lighting utility in Philadelphia, remained small until 1893, when Adolph Müller visited Gibbs to discuss production technologies and markets.[15] Gibbs then quickly worked out an arrangement with leading Philadelphia capitalists to raise $4.0 million. The two most prominent capitalists, P. A. B. Widener and W. L. Elkins, were making their fortunes by building the new urban traction systems for which the storage battery was a basic component. With these funds Gibbs purchased several smaller companies and bought out patents belonging to Brush Electric, Edison Electric, Thomson-Houston, and other leading American electrical manufacturers. The American first movers in the electrical-equipment industry—General Electric and Westinghouse—did not, like their German counterparts, finance the new storage-battery company. They too preferred to leave this specialized component in the larger electrical systems to reliable outside manufacturers, but at that time they needed all the funds they could obtain to expand their facilities for making heavy equipment to generate and transmit electricity.

Once Gibbs had acquired the necessary financing, he brought in Herbert Lloyd, a trained engineer, from one of his other enterprises to manage Electric Storage Battery. Lloyd then supervised the construction of what was by far the largest storage-battery plant in the United States. Next Lloyd established a network of branch sales offices covering the United States and Canada. These branch offices housed a corps of electrical engineers who installed and serviced batteries under "a maintenance contract" modeled directly on one that had been devised by AFA in Germany.[16]

In 1894, the year Electric Storage Battery made its initial large-scale investment in production facilities, Lloyd signed an agreement with Müller's AFA, the leading French firm, and one of the largest British companies, Chloride

Electrical Storage Battery Syndicate, to exchange technical information—an arrangement that made possible "the unrestricted transfer of technology."[17] The details of the agreement are not known, but if it was similar to comparable international compacts in the electrical-equipment, chemical, and other technologically dynamic industries, it probably allocated markets and possibly set prices.

Whatever these arrangements were, the American firm and the German firm quickly dominated world markets. They did so because neither the British firm nor the French firm made the essential tripartite investment in production, marketing, and management. The British enterprise, Chloride Electrical, had every potential for success. Its founder (in 1891), William Mather, was the owner-manager of Mather & Platt, one of the largest textile-machinery firms in Britain, and he was also a pioneer in the new electrical technology. He had financial resources of his own and enjoyed the confidence of British investors. Indeed, his firm, Mather & Platt, had acquired the English rights to the Edison dynamo in 1883 and had become a leading pioneer of electric traction equipment by 1890. Yet Mather made little attempt to develop volume production and to bring together a trained sales and service force, either in his electric-equipment or his battery firm. In 1901 Mather sold Chloride Electrical to Electric Storage Battery.[18] At that time, Chloride Electrical "was not the dominant giant of the British storage battery industry that it subsequently became. It was simply one of several manufacturers." The American firm sent engineers and managers to Britain and "began turning it into a British version of itself."[19] Its major competitor within Britain and the British Empire was AFA. Because the American purchase of English Chloride clearly altered any existing agreements as to markets, AFA built a plant in Manchester in 1905 and set up its own sales offices in four British industrial cities and in Sydney and Calcutta. Here, then, is a revealing example of American and German entrepreneurs creating within Britain the managerial hierarchy needed to produce and distribute technologically complex products.

AFA's direct investment in Britain was part of a broader strategy to build factories in foreign lands in order to meet the demand created by its sales and service network. Until World War I three works—AFA's plant at Hagen, one that AFA built in Berlin in 1904, and Electric Storage Battery's plant in Camden, New Jersey—continued to produce most of the world's storage batteries. AFA manufactured its more specialized "movable" batteries—those for train lighting, automobiles, and lamps—in its two giant German works. But when local demand for its primary line—batteries permanently placed in power plants—was large enough, when transportation costs of this solid lead product were high enough, when local requirements were idiosyncratic enough, and when local tariffs and other regulations were costly enough, AFA built, purchased, expanded, or consolidated existing plants in various countries to operate at a scale that met regional demands. In 1899, for example, the company enlarged a plant it had purchased at Hirschwang near Vienna and consolidated there the production facilities of two smaller plants, one in Vienna and the other in Raab in Hungary, to meet more efficiently the increasing demand in southeastern Europe.[20] Other plants were built or consolidated to serve regional demands in Zaizoata, Spain, in 1897; in St. Petersburg in 1903; Budapest in 1904; Lemberg in Galicia in 1906; Jungburzlau in Bohemia in 1909; Bucharest in 1911; and Nol, Sweden, in 1914.[21] This expansion resulted from a considered plan to use the firm's competitive capabilities to acquire markets abroad systematically. It was not, as in the case of most British companies, an ad hoc reaction to tariffs and other government regulations.

As the company's organization chart for 1913 indicates (Figure 11), these branch plants became the core of national subsidiaries that had their own sales and service organizations and their own headquarters, which, except for Italy, were in the capital city—London, Madrid, Bucharest, St. Petersburg, Vienna. In Italy they were in Milan.[22] The oldest and largest of these, at Vienna, had a special status as a secondary corporate office. The areas abroad where the demand was not great enough to warrant building a local factory were served by the Export Division. That division had its own sales and service branch offices in Buenos Aires, Tokyo, Constantinople, and Cairo, and in addition it supervised and supported a network of exclusive agents throughout the world, except for the United States, Canada, and the rest of North America. By "friendly agreement" those markets were left to the Electric Storage Battery Company.

At the corporate office in Berlin an extensive hierarchy of middle and top managers administered this global enterprise. The 1913 organization chart indicates that, with the exception of production, the management of the company's functional activities was centralized in Berlin. The staff offices of the Zentral-Büro included, besides housekeeping units, the legal and financial departments. The legal department had an office for patents and one for general legal matters. The financial department included offices for cost accounting, bookkeeping, and current accounts. There was also an office for publicity and another for technical information.

Major operating activities (except for production) were administered in Berlin through "divisions" (Abteilungen). There was a division for inspection and quality control *(Prüffeld)*, one for research, and one for the development of the new process of rail welding *(Schienenschweissen)*—a related activity using the firm's welding capabilities in one of its major markets, subways. As might be expected, the sales organization was much more extensive. Division I, Division II, and the Export Division handled sales and services not carried on by the foreign subsidiaries. Division I was responsible for marketing and servicing the primary product—power-plant batteries—within Germany. Division II assisted

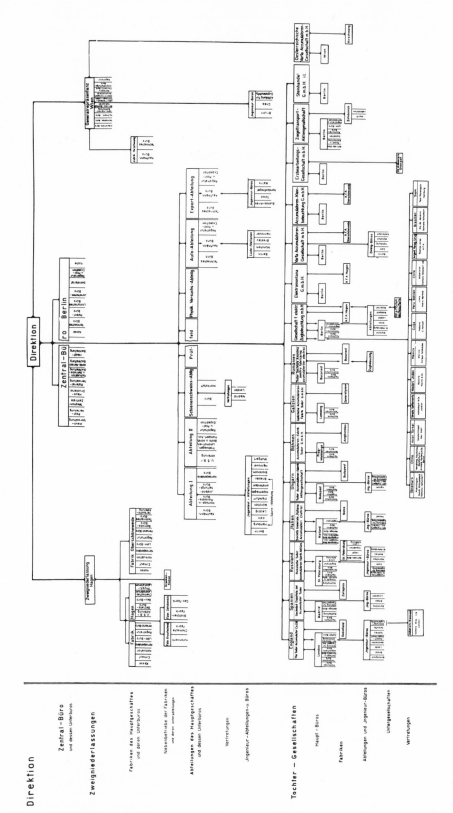

Figure 11. Organization chart of Accumulatoren-Fabrik (AFA), 1913. From Albert Müller, *25 Jahre der Accumulatoren-Fabrik Aktiengesellschaft, 1888–1913* (n.p., 1913).

the seven sales subsidiaries (legally organized as limited-liability companies) to market and distribute "movable" batteries to seven major product markets. The largest of these which sold batteries to subway systems, had its own agents in many parts of the world. In addition, there was at headquarters a recently created division, not yet incorporated, to sell batteries to the infant automobile industry.

The administration of production remained centralized at the company's oldest and largest plant (Fabrik) at Hagen. That plant and a somewhat smaller one in Berlin produced the company's primary products—storage batteries for electric power systems—which were not made by the national subsidiaries for their local markets. The senior executives at Hagen were also responsible for the production of all specialized "movable" products, except for the production of vehicle batteries for the Austro-Hungarian market made in a factory near Vienna. In addition, the Hagen headquarters supervised the smaller factories making metal cases, chemicals, wooden separators, bricks, gas, and other items used in the production of batteries.

The heads of production at Hagen; the heads of sales, research, and the smaller functional staff units at the Zentral-Büro in Berlin; and the heads of the foreign subsidiaries (Tochter-Gesellschaften) all reported to the Vorstand, which was responsible in turn to the Supervisory Board. The precise functions of the full-time managers on the Vorstand are not spelled out in the available secondary literature.[23] As in other German firms, the Supervisory Board included representatives of a small number of large investors: before World War I, representatives from Siemens, AEG, and not only the banks allied to those firms, particularly the Deutsche Bank, but also the Berliner Handels-Gesellschaft and the Nationalbank für Deutschland.[24] As at Stollwerck and the other large German industrials, the Supervisory Board also included one or two distinguished lawyers.

By the second decade of the new century, AFA had created an organizational structure that defined the activities and relationships of its plants, its sales and service offices, its purchasing units, and its laboratories far more precisely than did even the largest British multinationals. In 1913, well before any British firm had felt the need to draw up even an informal sketch of its organization, AFA had published for internal use its detailed organization chart (Figure 11), which was accompanied by one hundred pages of text describing the functions of each of the many offices and the relationships between them. It was this close attention to supervision of functional activities, to the coordination of product flows, and to the planning and allocation of resources that developed the organizational capabilities which, in turn, gave AFA and its American counterpart a powerful competitive advantage in international markets—markets where French, British, and other firms originally enjoyed the same patents and the same technological information. In both these firms the top executives, including the chief executive officers, were trained, experienced engineers. In neither firm did a member of the Müller or the Lloyd family follow his father into a command position.

Although AFA and Electric Storage Battery were similar in several respects, their structures also show important differences. First, the German firm had many more integrated regional subsidiaries, thus reflecting major differences in markets. For the Americans, the major market remained the huge domestic one. For the Germans, international trade was what counted. Second, the German firm's financial offices were fewer and smaller.[25] AFA had no treasurer's office comparable to those in American companies. Its Zentral-Büro only included offices for cost accounting and current accounts. There was no large comptroller's office with an internal auditing department, nor were there offices for stock transfers and stockholder relations. Perhaps one or more of the banks whose representatives sat on the AFA Supervisory Board acted as the company's de facto treasurer and auditor.

This brief review of the histories of Gebrüder Stollwerck and AFA before World War I, besides indicating differences between the leading German, British, and American enterprises, suggests the cooperative nature of managerial capitalism in Germany. The German Grossbanken played a much larger role in financing the Stollwerck enterprise than British banks did for Cadbury and American banks for the leading American chocolate companies. In addition, Ludwig Stollwerck served as chairman of the Supervisory Board of three enterprises that used his vending machines. As for AFA, it came into being as a cooperative venture. It was financed by its two major customers, who in turn were financed by Grossbanken.[26]

Why, then, did large German enterprises rely more on banks for financing than did their British and American counterparts? Why were there more financiers and senior executives from allied industries on the top boards of German industrial enterprises? Why were German entrepreneurs so much more successful than their British rivals in recruiting large managerial hierarchies and in creating carefully organized, multinational, industrial empires? And finally, why did the German modern industrial enterprises concentrate on the production of industrial goods, such as electrical and other heavy machinery, metals, and chemicals; and why did so few of them manufacture branded, packaged products, or mass-produced consumer durables, or other light, standardized machinery?

These questions cannot be answered without first comparing the German economic and cultural environment with that of Britain and that of the United States. The same environmental conditions will be considered here as have been examined before: the size of domestic and foreign markets; the impact of the railroads and the new institutions that financed them; changes in distribution and marketing; the laws and customs that affected competition and the growth of firms; and the educational institutions that provided the essential training and knowledge.

Domestic and Foreign Markets

The crowning of King William I of Prussia as German Emperor in the Hall of Mirrors at Versailles in 1871 symbolized the completion of both the economic and the political unification of the German states. The new emperor ruled over a nation that was more than twice the size of Great Britain, including all of Ireland—267,339 square miles to Britain's slightly more than 120,000 square miles—but still much smaller than that of the United States, with just over 3 million square miles. In 1871 Germany's population of 41.06 million was substantially larger than that of Britain (including Ireland), with 31.5 million, and almost exactly that of the United States—40.9 million.

The domestic market of the new empire differed from that of the United States in that its population was expanding at a slower rate, and it differed from Britain's in that less of it was urban in nature. By 1910 the German population had reached 64.9 million, while that of the United States had jumped to 92.4 million and that of Britain (again including Ireland) had risen to 46.2 million. In 1871 Germany was much more rural than Britain, with 63.9% of the population living in rural areas and 36.1% in urban areas, that is, in communities of more than 2,000. By 1910 that ratio had shifted dramatically. By then 60.1% lived in urban areas and more workers were employed in industry than in agriculture. This shift in favor of the urban sector came almost fifty years after it occurred in Britain but about forty years before it did in the United States.[27]

Nevertheless, Germany's urban population remained much less concentrated in large cities than that of Britain or even that of the United States. Whereas in 1871 Britain had six cities of more than 240,000, including London with a population of 3,890,000, the new German Empire had only a half dozen or so cities of more than 100,000. Berlin had 826,000, and the next largest, Hamburg, had 240,000. The total population of all German cities of over 50,000 did not add up to that of London. In 1871 the United States had fourteen cities of more than 100,000, and seven of these exceeded 250,000. Moreover, Germany's cities were not only fewer and smaller but were more geographically separated than those in Britain's golden consumer quadrangle. Even as late as World War I, only the lower Rhine-Ruhr Valley and the Berlin metropolitan area had a population density close to that of the British golden quadrangle or even of the Washington-Boston urban corridor in the northeastern United States. Indeed, regional differences between Germany's industrial West and agrarian East long remained a striking feature of its economy.

Finally and most important, Germany's gross domestic product per head (and therefore its per-capita income), while rising rapidly before World War I, remained substantially lower than that of Britain or the United States. According to the estimates of Angus Maddison, Germany's 1870 figure of $535 (in 1970 U.S. dollars) was far below Great Britain's $972 and also below the United States' $769. By 1913 Germany's rapid industrialization had almost doubled its gross domestic product per head to $1,073 (again in 1970 dollars); but by then that figure for Britain, which had increased by a half, was $1,481 and for the United States $1,813.[28] Before World War I, Germany's consumer markets, concentrated largely in its western regions, still were smaller in terms of buying power than those in Britain or the United States. At the same time, its industrial markets were growing faster than Britain's, though not so fast as those in America.

German industrialists, like their British competitors, relied much more heavily on foreign markets than did American manufacturers. In 1880 German exports were valued at £147 million (M 2,923 million), while those of Great Britain stood at £286 million. By 1913 the figures were £505 million (M 10,097 million) and £635 million. Until the turn of the century Germany's leading exports had been textiles and consumer goods (apparel, toys, pianos) for the urban markets to the west—Great Britain, the Low Countries, and the United States. But in the first years of the new century the balance of German exports shifted dramatically to industrial products—metals (particularly steel and electrolytically refined nonferrous metals), machinery, and chemicals—and total value of industrial exports soared from M 43 million in 1890 to M 780 million in 1899, to M 1,744 million in 1907, and to M 2,944 million in 1913. (For the same years exports of consumer goods in millions were M 1,132, M 1,217, M 1,758, and M 1,899.)[29]

By 1913 Germany was the world's largest exporter of chemicals and of electrical equipment and other industrial machinery. In chemicals, where one-third of the industry's output was exported, Germany accounted for 28.5% of exports sold in the world markets, with Britain's share reaching 15.6% and that of the United States 9.7%. In electrical equipment Germany's exports were even more important, accounting for 34.9% of its total domestic electrical-equipment production, whereas the United States' exports accounted for 28.9% of domestic output and Britain's for 16.0%. At the same time Germany's exports accounted for 46.4% of the world's export trade in electrical equipment, as compared with 22% for Britain (of which two-thirds was produced by subsidiaries of the United States' General Electric and Westinghouse and of Germany's Siemens), and as compared with 15.7% for the United States. In other industrial machinery, including textile and metal-working machinery, Germany had surpassed Britain by 1913. By then it accounted for 29.1% of total world production and Britain for 28.4%, while the United States claimed 26.8%. These figures emphasize that although Britain was holding its own in traditional industrial goods and materials—textiles, iron shapes, iron ships, and steam engines—Germany had decisively outpaced Britain in producing and exporting the products of the Second Industrial Revolution.[30]

The nations to the south and east offered a promising market for industrial goods produced in Germany. Although the nations of eastern and southeastern Europe, with their large rural population and smaller per-capita income, were even smaller consumer markets than Germany itself, they were beginning to industrialize. In the three decades before World War I railroad and telegraph systems were built, electrical utilities installed, and machinery and other capital equipment imported for their growing textile, metal, and other manufacturing industries. As was true for both Stollwerck and AFA, other German industrial enterprises set up their first foreign sales offices and often their first foreign plants in the Austro-Hungarian Empire. Nevertheless, Britain and the United States, which remained two of the most industrialized nations, soon became as important a market for German industrial goods as they had been earlier for German consumer goods—as important as the nations of southern and eastern Europe. Both abroad and at home these new industrial markets provided German entrepreneurs with incentives for innovation, investment, and the creation of modern industrial enterprises.

The Impact of the Railroads

The coming of the railroad (and its handmaiden, the telegraph) had a much greater impact on Germany than it did on Britain. In Germany distances were greater, the terrain was much more rugged, and the area available to coastal, canal, and other water traffic was smaller. The transportation revolution heavily influenced Germany's economic growth and the accompanying institutional changes. As in the United States, but not in Britain, the rapid growth of the railroad network was an integral part of the initial industrialization as well as the continuing industrial growth of the nation. J. H. Clapham makes this point effectively by citing an earlier eminent historian: "The railways, as [Heinrich von] Treitschke said, first dragged the nation from its economic stagnation— and with astonishing abruptness."[31] This earlier judgment has been fully supported by Rainer Fremdling in a more recent econometric study of the railroads as a leading sector in German economic growth. Fremdling concludes that without the innovation of the railroad "the Industrial Revolution cannot be explained."[32]

Even though the mileage built in Germany was much less than that in the United States, the two countries offer important parallels in the timing of railroad construction and in the consequences of railroad operations. For both countries the initial burst of growth came in the late 1840s and 1850s, the period which Treitschke and Fremdling describe. But in both countries the integration of the network had only begun by the end of the fifties. In the 1860s the major rivers were bridged and significant branch lines and connecting lines were built. In both countries a second boom came in the late 1860s and early 1870s. In both countries the mileage doubled in the decade between 1865 and 1875—from 35,080 miles to 74,100 miles in the United States, and from 8,640 miles (13,900 kilometers) to 17,380 miles (27,970 kilometers) in Germany. And most of that growth took place after 1870. At the same time the railroad mileage in eastern Europe—much of which was financed and equipped by German companies—grew rapidly. In Austria-Hungary, for example, the mileage went from 2,296 in 1865 to 6,416 in 1875, again with the larger share coming after 1870. When the onslaught of the worldwide depression of the 1870s slowed construction, the basic contours of the new transportation and communication network had been completed on both continents. One difference was that, after prosperity returned at the end of the decade, railroad construction in Germany did not take off again as it did in the United States. Instead it continued to grow moderately until it leveled off in the first decade of the twentieth century.[33]

In the 1870s the salaried managers in Germany perfected, even earlier than did their counterparts in the United States, the operating and organizational procedures needed to assure a steady, fast, regularly scheduled flow of goods over the new national, and increasingly international, network. The tasks of the German engineers were easier in one way than those of the American railway men, for they had fewer roads whose activities had to be coordinated; but the tasks were more complicated in that different German states had their own systems—some built and operated by the state, others by private companies, and still others by both public and private enterprises.

The organization that brought an essential uniformity and standardization of equipment and operating procedures was what can be called in English the Association of German Railway Administrations. It was established in 1846 when ten of the leading Prussian railways met to lobby for changes in the existing railroad law and to establish uniform financial reporting. The Association immediately enlarged its membership to include the railways of other German states. Then it began to draw up regulations for the joint handling of freight and passenger traffic. These included procedures for the mutual use of cars and the transshipment of traffic, similar to the through bill of lading and the car accountant office that were perfected a decade or so later in the United States.[34] The work of the Association was supplemented by an association of German railway civil engineers. This organization, formed in 1850, immediately began to bring uniformity in physical equipment and facilities—track gauge, permanent way, rolling stock, signaling. In 1864 the older and larger Association opened its membership to associations of roads in Austria-Hungary and other neighboring nations.[35] In this way German railroad engineers and managers embarked on creating a unified transportation system for much of continental Europe.

As in the United States, it was easier to agree on setting standards for equipment and operating procedures than on setting uniform freight rates and classifications. During the 1850s rates came to be set by regional associations. The first was the North German Traffic Association, which was followed by comparable organizations for South Germany, then for Central Germany, and then for even smaller regions. Because these regions overlapped and because their members competed for traffic, no uniform transportation rates or classifications were adopted before 1871, when a German Railway Traffic Association was created. But the German railroad companies were more successful—much more successful than American companies—in preventing competition in construction. In the late 1860s the Association of German Railway Administrations worked out a set of "fundamental regulations" for the laying down and construction of branch lines.[36]

German political unification in 1871 hastened the integration, both physically and operationally, of the railway network within Germany and with those of nations to the east and south. The new Chancellor, Otto von Bismarck, planned to consolidate the German railroads into a single system. He created the Imperial Railway Department to assure uniformity of operations and sent to the Imperial Bundesrat an Imperial Railway Act to empower the carrying out of this consolidation. The smaller states, particularly Bavaria, resisted, however, and the Railway Act was defeated three times.

As a result, Bismarck decided to achieve his goals by two other means. His first method was to rely more heavily on the Association of German Railway Administrations, which was reshaped as the German Railway Administration, and which continued to include representatives from Austria-Hungary and other neighboring states. In 1877 the reconstituted body adopted uniform rate and classification structures for all its members. Bismarck's second method was to embark on the nationalizing of the Prussian railroad lines, which in 1871 accounted for two-thirds of the mileage in the new German Empire. By 1878, 30% of the Prussian mileage was state-owned and another 20% was state-operated. By 1885 only 1,025 miles (1,650 kilometers) remained in private hands, and 13,429 miles (21,624 kilometers) were state-owned. Other German states followed suit. By 1909, of the 38,000 miles of German standard-gauge track, only 2,236 were still privately held. Until after World War I the German railways were operated through eight state systems of which the Prussian was by far the largest. The telegraph and postal systems were administered along the same lines. (From the start the telegraph system had been operated by the post office.)[37]

From the 1880s on, the Prussian Ministry of Public Works, working closely with the new German Railway Administration and the new Imperial Railway Department, provided the basic framework within which the eight systems operated, although the Bavarian system continued to enjoy showing its independence. As the roads became nationalized, the state systems began to set rates through the Railway Traffic Association, which became the central rate-making board within the empire. Then Prussia, and soon other states, passed laws setting up regional railway councils made up of representatives of trade, industry, and agriculture to work closely with the traffic association in setting rates.[38] An international agreement signed in 1890 extended the traffic association's rate structure and rate-making, as well as its billing, routing, and scheduling procedures, to all neighboring countries.[39]

By the 1880s German industrialists, like those in the United States, enjoyed the benefits of a new transportation system that permitted the movement of materials and goods and messages with unprecedented regularity and speed over a continental area—the essential precondition for achieving the cost advantages of the economies of scale and scope inherent in capital-intensive, high-volume technologies of production. The Continental railroad network that was operationally integrated by the Railway Traffic Association gave German entrepreneurs a readier access to the industrial markets of Europe than British or even French manufacturers had. The Continental network thus hastened the transformation of Germany's export trade from consumer to industrial products.

Nevertheless, because of the obvious historical differences (especially nationalization), the new German transportation and communication systems had less impact on other economic institutions than they did in the United States, though more than they did in Great Britain. Nationalization, of course, eliminated the need for public regulatory commissions. Because shippers and other users of the roads had an opportunity to participate in the rate-making decisions through the district railway councils, there was less political protest arising from rate discrimination than in the United States or even Britain. As Detlev Vagts has written, "The German rate setting mechanism was basically more parliamentary than judicial and adversary."[40] With nationalization, railroad management became increasingly that of a civil service in a land with a long civil-service tradition.

In Prussia the railway office of the Ministry of Public Works was responsible for the day-to-day operation of the railway system, as were comparable officers in each of the other seven state systems. The office's function was similar to that of the transportation and traffic departments of American railroads, except that in rate-making it worked closely with the German Railway Traffic Association and the district railway councils. The Prussian Ministry of Public Works and comparable ministries in other states also carried on the internal financial activities—that is, accounting for and auditing the multitude of financial transactions—while the ministries of finance were responsible for the external finance, that is, raising the funds that the public works ministries deemed necessary to operate, maintain, and expand their systems.[41] Thus railroad administration never provided the managerial model for industrial enterprise that it did in the United States. If there was any such model, it was that of the civil service—the Prussian bureaucracy.

Workers as well as managers were, of course, government employees. There were no unions. Strikes were not permitted. In Werner Sombart's words, the postal services and the railways were "only the civil sections of the army." In Prussia the senior managers, Sombart noted, were often generals; and in these two services were placed "three-quarters of a million men who stood at stiff attention when their superior spoke to them."[42] In Germany, in total contrast to the United States and Britain, the railroad was a representative organ of a bureaucratic state. Ministries of public works no more developed models for labor relations than they did for managerial organization in the modern industrial enterprise.

The Railroads and the New Financial Institutions

Although the coming of the railroads had far less impact on patterns of industrial management, labor relations, and government-industry relations in Germany than in the United States, its impact on industrial finance was another story. In that area the German railroads had as profound an effect as the U.S. railroads did on American corporate finance, though in quite a different way.

Until Bismarck embarked on his policy of nationalization, the majority of German roads, particularly those in Prussia, were built and operated by private corporations, not public bureaus. In Germany, capital for the first railroads was raised locally much as it had been in both the United States and Britain. It came from merchants, manufacturers, bankers, and, to a lesser extent, landowners living at the termini or along the rail lines. In Germany, as in the United States, promoters often made direct contact with foreign investors. The rapid rail growth of the late 1840s and 1850s created in both countries an unprecedented peacetime demand for capital. In the United States this demand led to the centralizing and institutionalizing of the nation's money market in New York and with it the development of nearly all the instruments and institutions of modern American corporate finance. In Germany, too, it encouraged the creation of a wholly new financial intermediary, one that became central to the later financing of large-scale industrial enterprise. This new type was the Kreditbank (plural, Kreditbanken)—a bank that provided capital on a national, indeed an international, scale. A number of such banks appeared in Germany after 1850. A handful of the largest Kreditbanken, termed Grossbanken (great banks), have dominated German finance ever since.

As Richard Tilly emphasizes, until the 1850s banking and finance were "personal and interfamilial." Then: "The railroads, and a good deal of heavy industrial enterprise which followed or accompanied their construction, involved external finance to a much larger extent than earlier types of business enterprise in Germany did. "[43] According to Jacob Riesser's classic study of the Grossbanken, the total capital invested in joint stock companies between 1851 and 1870 amounted to M 2,251.0 million. More than three-fourths of it went into railroads (M 1,722.4 million to railroad companies, as against M 273.4 million to industry and mining enterprises and M 253.2 million to banks and insurance companies). Moreover, this estimate of railroad investment did not include the funds raised by the sale of government securities for state-financed railroads. A major share of this approximately M 2 billion was raised by Kreditbanken. [44]

The earliest of the Grossbanken was a long-established, private, commercial bank, Abraham Schaaffhausen of Cologne, which was reorganized in 1849 to finance railroads and industrials in the lower Rhine. According to Riesser, however, it was the famous Credit Mobilier, which opened its doors in Paris in 1852, that became the model for the Kreditbanken. It was an all-purpose institution that came to combine the activities of a commercial bank, an investment bank, a development bank, and an investment trust within a single corporate enterprise. [45] In 1853 a Grossbank of that sort, the Bank für Handel und Industrie, was formed in Darmstadt. In 1856 the Disconto-Gesellschaft, which had been established in Berlin in 1851, was reorganized along Credit Mobilier lines. In 1856, too, came the formation of still another Grossbank, the Berliner Handels-Gesellschaft.

The central role played by railroad financing in the rise of this new and basic financial institution of German capitalism is suggested by Riesser's list of the "most important" railway transactions in which the Darmstädter Bank and the Disconto-Gesellschaft participated (see Table 21). The Berliner Handels-Gesellschaft had an important part in financing Russian, Rumanian, and Italian railroads. Cologne's Schaaffhausen concentrated more on financing the new transportation in rapidly industrializing western Germany.

The second railroad boom helped to bring into being three more of these Grossbanken—the Deutsche Bank of Berlin and the Commerz-und-Disconto-Bank of Hamburg in 1870 and the Dresdner Bank in 1872. Like the new financial institutions in the United States (the commercial firms that turned to investment banking), the all-purpose Kreditbanken, particularly the largest, the Grossbanken, were the instruments that made possible the rapid accumulation of capital on a scale vast enough to finance the building of the new Continental transportation and communication infrastructure. In Britain, where such investment was somewhat smaller, and where more local capital was available and the world's largest and most sophisticated money market existed, the provision of funds for railway building had less impact on existing financial institutions, just as British rail construction had less impact on the processes of industrial production.

In the 1880s, as the railroad network was being completed and as railroads

Table 21. The most important railway transactions of the Darmstädter Bank and the Disconto-Gesellschaft.

Darmstädter Bank

1854. Austrian State Railway (taking over of shares).
1855. Extension of the Rhine Railway from Nymwegen to Bingen.
    Theiss Railway (taking over of shares).
1856. Financing the Bingen-Aschaffenburg Railway (via Mainz) and promoting the
    Elizabeth Railway (taking over of shares).
1859. Four and one-half percent bonds of the Rhine-Nahe Railway (guaranteed by
    State), 4,500,000 thalers, jointly with the Disconto-Gesellschaft.
1861. Preference shares of the Cologne-Minden Railway.
    Private sale of shares and bonds of the Hessian Ludwig Railway.
1862. Placing of bonds of the Livorno Railway.
    Conversion of the 4¼ percent Thuringian Railway preference shares.
    Issue of 1,200,000 florin preference shares of the Hessian Ludwig Railway.
1863. Preference silver shares of the Galician Carl-Ludwig Railway, exempt from
    taxation (Rothschild syndicate), of 6,000,000 florins.
    Five percent preference shares of the Moscow-Riazán Railway of 5,000,000
    rubles, guaranteed by State.
    Four percent preference shares of the Hessian Ludwig Railway of about
    3,000,000 florins.
    Silver preference shares of the Galician Carl-Ludwig Railway of 5,000,000
    florins (Rothschild syndicate).
1866. Shares of the Hessian Ludwig Railway.
    Shares of the Magdeburg-Leipzig Railway Lit. B.
    Shares of the Altona-Kiel Railway.
    Preference shares of the Upper Silesian and South-North German Junction
    Railway (Reichenberg-Pardubitz).
1867. Common and preference shares of the Fünfkirchen-Bares Railway and
    construction of the line, as well as of the Siebenbürgen and Franz Joseph
    Railway (Rothschild syndicate).
    First preference shares of the Magdeburg-Halberstadt Railway.
    Bonds of the Russian Kozlov-Woronezh and Poti-Tiflis Railway.

were being taken over by the state, the Grossbanken began to concentrate on financing industrial enterprises, particularly in the new industries. As they had with railroad companies, these Grossbanken acted as intermediaries for the sale of securities, often taking a block of stock on their own account and usually obtaining proxy powers for the shares they sold to other investors. Even more than they had done with railroad companies, these banks provided initial capital for new industrial ventures and helped guide them through their early years of growth.

The representatives of the German Grossbanken participated to a greater

Table 21. (continued)

1868. Shares of the Hessian Ludwig Railway (1,000,000 thalers).
Five percent bonds of the Hessian Ludwig Railway (guaranteed by State, 4,000,000 thalers).
Five percent preference shares of the Hessian Ludwig Railway.
Organization of the Alföld Railway (Rothschild syndicate).
Construction of the Arad-Temesvar line (Rothschild syndicate).
Shares and bonds of the Austrian North-West Railway.
Shares of the Rhine Railway Lit. B. (5,000,000 thalers).

1869. Five percent preference shares of the Berlin-Potsdam-Magdeburg Railway of 7,000,000 thalers.
Five percent preference shares of the Upper Silesian Railway of 13,305,000 thalers.
Four and one-half percent guaranteed shares of the Thuringian Railway Lit. C of 4,000,000 thalers.
Shares of the Cologne-Minden Railway of 9,068,200 thalers.

1869–70. Purchase of the entire Brunswick railway system from the Brunswick government on behalf of a syndicate for 11,000,000 thalers, and an annual payment of 875,000 thalers for sixty-four years, and transfer of its management and of the further extension of lines to a special company.

Disconto-Gesellschaft

1853. Five percent bonds, guaranteed by the State, of the Moscow-Riazán Railway of 5,375,000 thalers; jointly with the Darmstädter Bank, the banking firm of Sal. Oppenheim jr., & Co., and a St. Petersburg house.

1856. Three and one-half percent bonds of the Upper Silesian Railway Company.

1857. Four and one-half percent bonds of the Cosel-Oderberg Railway (1,500,000 thalers).

1859. Four and one-half percent State guaranteed bonds of the Rhine Nahe Railway of 4,500,000 thalers (jointly with the Darmstädter Bank).

1866–1868. Shares and bonds of the Bergisch-Märkische Railway.

1867. First preference shares of the Nordhausen-Erfurt Railway.

1868. Shares of the Alsenz Railway.
Five percent bonds of the Charkoff-Krementshúg Railway of £1,716,000 (jointly with J. H. Schröder & Co., London).

Source: Jacob Riesser, *The German Great Banks and Their Concentration in Connection with the Economic Development of Germany* (Washington, D.C., 1911), pp. 64–65.

extent in the top-level decision-making of new industrial companies than did representatives of financial institutions in the United States and Britain. There were two reasons for this. First, the Grossbanken were larger than American investment banks in terms of assets and personnel, precisely because they were all-purpose banks. The American and British investment-banking firms consisted of little more than a few partners with a tiny secretarial staff, but the

German Grossbanken had extensive staffs. As the banks moved into industrial finance, these staffs came to include specialists with extensive knowledge of specific industries.[46] In fact, by the turn of the century members of the Vorstand of the Deutsche Bank were industry specialists responsible for the bank's relationships with firms in major industries.

Second, because the German banks had played a larger role in financing the new industrial enterprises, they had more opportunities for participation in top-level decision-making. As major shareholders and representatives of other shareholders, they sat on the Supervisory Boards of the new or greatly enlarged companies. Even when such representation was shared with the founder or his family, the banks often had a significant say (particularly in the early years of a company's history) in investment decisions, in the selection of top and even middle managers, in establishing administrative procedures, and in reviewing the internal financial management of the enterprises that they had helped to finance. Because the banks controlled many shares on their own account and also voted the proxies of many of the investors who had purchased these securities, they had stronger legal and administrative ways to supervise internal auditing, accounting procedures, and external financing than did the representatives of financial institutions on the boards of American companies.[47]

The Grossbanken were the most important institutional innovation that the railroads bequeathed to German industry. They supplied much of what today would be called venture capital. They provided the funds for the large investments necessary to exploit the cost advantages of scale and scope and thereby to acquire first-mover advantages. Because the large German enterprises clustered in industries that required greater initial capital and brought less immediate cash flow than did the production of branded, packaged products or light machinery, and because the capital markets in Berlin, Frankfurt, and Cologne were smaller and less sophisticated mobilizers of funds than those in London and even New York, these "great banks" became a primary source of initial financing of industrial enterprises in Germany in a way that banks rarely, if ever, did in the United States and Britain. Nevertheless, in several industries first movers were financed locally and did not require the services of Grossbanken. Moreover, as bank-financed enterprises began to rely on retained earnings to fund their growth, the influence of bankers on their boards declined and in some cases disappeared.

Changes in Distribution

In the United States the building of the modern transportation and communication infrastructure precipitated a revolution first in distribution and then in production. In Britain the railroad, telegraph, and even steamship had more impact on the organization of distribution than on that of production. In Germany it was the other way around; that is, the new transportation and communication networks revolutionized the processes and institutions of production but brought less innovation in those of distribution. In Germany the changes in distribution were more derivative than innovative. The revolution in production provides the themes of the next two chapters. What follows here is a brief review of the changes in distribution.

As the movement of goods and messages became faster, more regular, and greater in volume, the new institutions of distribution appeared. They came more slowly than those that had sprung up in the United States and Britain. They were smaller in size, but they evolved in much the same way. Wholesalers transformed themselves from commission merchants to jobbers who took title to their goods and made their profit on markup rather than on fixed commission. They specialized in much the same areas as in the United States and Great Britain—in dry goods, hardware, drugs, jewelry, and oil and paint. In Germany, however, there may have been more levels of wholesalers, that is, more sales from large wholesalers to smaller wholesalers. One report on the marketing of kerosene in Germany in the 1880s referred to "the usual trade organization— a hierarchy of wholesalers."[48]

The evolution of the mass retailer in Germany was not strikingly different from that in Britain. Although more mail-order stores were established than in Britain, none operated on the scale of the American giants, Montgomery Ward and Sears, Roebuck. As in Britain, the cooperative became a major retail institution. In Germany the department stores served the growing cities, as in other countries, but in Germany they did not appear in numbers until the 1890s. By the end of the century, however, leading stores such as Wertheim in Berlin had as large a stock-turn and carried as broad a line as the major department stores in New York or London. In addition, German entrepreneurs appear to have pioneered in establishing chains of small department stores. The firm of Tietz (later Kaufhof) began to build its network in the 1890s and by 1906 was operating stores in twenty-seven cities. The Karstadt chain of smaller variety stores had thirty-two outlets five years after its formation in 1920, had acquired a financial interest in another chain with thirteen outlets, and had entered into special pooled-purchasing agreements with forty-seven stores throughout the nation.[49] Among the other types of chains were a small number of specialized food and apparel enterprises. As in the United States and Britain their success encouraged retailers to form voluntary chains with their own centralized buying organization. One of those, EDEKA, established in 1907, has remained the biggest of the German chains. In 1958, the first year when a list of the one hundred largest German nonfinancial enterprises was compiled, EDEKA ranked just behind Karstadt, Kaufhof, and GEG, the wholesaler for the biggest group of consumer cooperatives.[50] These four were the largest German distributing organizations on that list.

The history of consumer cooperatives in Germany parallels that in Britain, but these cooperatives operated on a smaller scale. Ideological conflicts between socialists and their opponents over the role of cooperatives as well as more restricted consumer markets delayed their growth. The first wholesaler for a group of cooperatives was not established until 1894. That enterprise, GEG, or the Grosseinkaufs-Gesellschaft Deutscher Konsumvereine, quickly became the largest commercial enterprise in the German Empire in terms of volume of goods handled, even larger than any of the retail chains.[51] In 1903 the retail cooperative societies it served formed the Central Union of Germany Cooperative Societies, consisting of 666 affiliated societies with a total of 573,000 members and 1,597 shops, concentrated in the industrial Rhine and Ruhr regions. At that date the GEG had a capital of more than M 500,000 and annual sales of M 2.64 million.[52] Like its British counterpart it moved into the production of soap, tobacco, flour, bread, and processed meat. By 1929 it was operating fifty manufacturing works, nearly all of them small, and its total turnover was M 501.4 million, of which M 123.9 million was earned in manufacturing. In 1912 a small group of cooperatives with a Catholic orientation set up the Reich Union of German Consumers' Societies and formed a similar though much smaller wholesale organization, which began to manufacture much the same types of products. Nevertheless, the larger GEG remained much smaller than the Co-operative Wholesale Society (C.W.S.) in England. In 1914, as World War I began, GEG had a sales turnover equivalent to £7.8 million and sales of £0.50 from its production units, as compared with the C.W.S. sales in 1911 of £25.2 million to its member societies and total sales (including those from its production units) in 1913 of £31.2 million.[53] Very little information is available on the internal organization of the GEG, but what there is suggests that its management was more centralized than that of England's C.W.S.

Although mass retailers were fewer in number and handled a smaller volume than those in the United States and Great Britain, their effectiveness in reducing prices brought an even greater political protest from their competitors—the small retailers and the hierarchy of wholesalers that served them. The protesters were often successful in obtaining regional legislation that placed restrictions on the mass retailers, including taxes on turnover, store space used, and number of outlets.[54]

Even so, the mass retailers' share of the market expanded as the German economy became industrialized and urbanized. Very rough estimates for 1900 indicate that department stores accounted for only 0.33% of retail sales while consumer cooperatives claimed about 1.0%. But by 1926, when the first German census of distribution provided more accurate figures, the mass retailers were getting closer to the share held by their counterparts in Great Britain. In that year the large German department stores accounted for an estimated 3.8% of total retail sales as compared with 3.0% to 4.0% in Britain (in 1925); German multiple shops (including chains of variety shops and small department stores and manufacturers' outlets) accounted for 8.2% as compared with 9.5% to 11.5% in Great Britain. The great difference came in consumer cooperatives, which held only 2.6% of the market in Germany as compared with 7.5% to 9.0% in Great Britain. The somewhat backward nature of retailing in Germany is suggested by the fact that "peddlers and street vendors," with 6.5% of the market, sold more than department stores and cooperatives combined.[55]

The German mass retailers carried much the same lines of goods as those in Britain and the United States—dry goods, textiles, clothing (including shoes), furniture, and food—whose production offered little in the way of scale economies and whose distribution needed little in the way of product-specific investment. In these industries their market share must have been, as it was in Britain (and as the strength of the political protest they engendered suggests), well above their share of total retail sales.

These mass retailers were organized to achieve the cost advantages of scope and scale in much the same manner as in the other two countries. Profits were based on low prices and high volume. The buyers in the central purchasing organization were responsible for coordinating the flow and were evaluated on the stock-turn—the measure of throughput in distribution—in their departments. The rest of the organization provided the scope needed to sell a variety of related goods. In all three countries the mass retailers rarely integrated backward by obtaining their own suppliers unless the plants so obtained could be operated at minimum efficient scale, or unless existing suppliers could not provide products to the specification, price, and volume desired. The one exception may have been the cooperatives, which for ideological reasons encouraged the establishment of cooperative production units. Thus the growth of the mass retailers in all three countries was based much more on the cost advantages of scale and scope within a distribution unit than on the reduction of transaction costs between retailers and wholesalers or between retailers and manufacturers.

In Germany the response of commercial intermediaries to the new forms of transportation and communication was similar to that in the United States and Britain. But because in Germany final consumers were fewer and their income less, the response came somewhat later and on a smaller scale. In production the responses were much more innovative, for German industry met the needs of the rapidly industrializing and urbanizing Continent. In the great industries— metals, machinery, and chemicals—entrepreneurs made, in the 1880s and 1890s, the investment necessary to become first movers at home and abroad. In rubber, rayon, and synthetic alkalies the response was similar to that in Britain. One firm became dominant at home and represented the nation in its global oligopoly. On the other hand, in consumer-oriented industries, including kerosene and consumer durables such as sewing machines, German entrepreneurs were generally less successful, giving way to American and British producers. The transformation of production in industry was strongly influenced by Germany's legal and educational systems.

The Legal and Educational Environment

In Germany there was no common law to prohibit combinations in restraint of trade, as the common law continued to do in Britain. And, of course, there was no specific legislation to prohibit monopoly or monopolistic practices, as the Sherman Antitrust Act did in the United States. In 1897, at almost the same moment when the United States Supreme Court upheld the constitutionality of the Sherman Act and so made such interfirm agreements illegal, the German high court, the Reichsgericht, held that contractual agreements as to price, output, and allocated markets were enforceable in courts of law. Such agreements, the court added, were not only in the interest of those who signed them but were also in the public interest.[56]

In Germany the initial efforts at such contractual cooperation between competing firms came at the same time and for the same reasons as they did in the United States and Britain. As the new factories went into operation, output soared, prices declined, and competition intensified. As in the United States, the use of agreements between manufacturers as to price, output, and marketing areas began in earnest with the economic depression that struck the international economy in 1873 and set off a twenty-year decline in prices of industrial goods. Jürgen Kocka estimates that "there were four cartels in 1875; 106 in 1890; 205 in 1896; 385 in 1905," and "most were regional, unstable, and short-lived."[57] From the start these cartel agreements were fully supported by the German courts.

Even with legal sanction, however, contractual arrangements remained difficult to negotiate and even more difficult to enforce. At times competitors refused to join, enjoying price stability without restricting output. Often, those who joined devised ingenious ways to cheat on the agreement. As a result, arrangements became increasingly formal and complex. Simple agreements as to price, marketing quotas, and marketing territories were replaced by more precisely defined "conventions," consortiums, and formal associations. To assure more effective compliance, groups of firms often set up a sales syndicate to market and distribute the output of all participants in a convention or an association. In some cases, the syndicate appointed an existing wholesaler as its central agency. In others the sales organization of one of the leading companies became the agency. In still others a new organization was created. And sometimes firms used syndicates to sell undifferentiated, commodity-like products but relied on their own sales forces to market a more technologically complex line of goods. In the last case, agreements on price and markets continued to be difficult to enforce.[58]

As these sales agreements broke down, some firms decided to cooperate even more closely by pooling profits. This meant that if a sales force overran its quota, the profits of the offending company would not be increased; it would continue to receive the agreed-upon percentage. Such profit pooling was achieved through the formation of an Interessengemeinschaft (an I.G., or "community of interest"), which, besides pooling profits, often attempted to coordinate its members' policies on technical matters, sales purchases, and patents. Occasionally, firms turned to an even more centralized formal organization for determining output and price, with an even larger administrative staff to enforce its decisions. The Nobel Dynamite Trust (see Chapter 6) is an example of such a complex cartel structure.

Yet all of these arrangements were difficult to maintain. Contractual agreements, "conventions," and consortiums were, as Kocka emphasizes, usually short-lived; and while they lasted there were constant squabbles over the allocation of quotas and constant maneuvering to improve one's position in time for the next renegotiation and reallocation. The syndicates were longer-lived but remained scenes of continuing conflict and controversy. This was less true of the I.G.'s and the other more formal associations. But even here, in order to assure compliance, firms purchased shares of other enterprises in their group. Usually the larger firm obtained stock in smaller ones; occasionally large companies held each other's shares.

The legality of cartelization thus led to a much richer variety of interfirm contractual relationships in Germany than in the United States or even Great Britain. It had other significant effects, changing not only the ways of competition but also those of growth. Because cooperation was legal, there was less pressure for industry-wide mergers. Because industry-wide mergers were the prerequisite to industry-wide reorganization and rationalization, far fewer such rationalizations occurred before World War I in Germany than in the United States.

One other significant difference between Germany and the United States was the German two-board system of corporate governance. In 1884 a law was passed that required a joint-stock company, an Aktiengesellschaft (AG) to have both a management board, the Vorstand, which was responsible, to quote Norbert Horn, for "the routine running of the business," and a supervisory board, the Aufsichtsrat, which was responsible for "control and guidance with respect to long-term policy-making." As Horn points out, this division of labor was difficult to carry out in practice. Occasionally a supervisory board took over both functions. "In most cases," however, the supervisory board came to be made up of part-time representatives that included not only those representing "majority shareholders (including parent companies) but other external interest groups (banks, communities of interest)." In such cases the supervisory board became relatively "inactive, retaining . . . some reduced controlling functions (including 'crisis management' and often its legal function of selecting the management board members)."[59] Therefore the Vorstand, consisting of full-time company executives, made long-term policy as well as short-term operating decisions. Nevertheless, representatives of the banks on which companies still relied for funding and of the parent companies continued to influence policy-making; and a supervisory board, by including bankers and officers from other companies, could provide an instrument for assisting interfirm cooperation.

The two-board system applied legally to the joint-stock company only and not to a second type of incorporated company, the privately held, limited-liability company or Gesellschaft mit beschränkter Haftung (GmbH). Nevertheless, this incorporated company, whose shares were rarely traded, often used the two-board system.

By comparison with the legal framework, Germany's institutions of higher education affected the beginning and continued growth of the large German industrial enterprise in ways that were less obvious but no less significant. By the late nineteenth century these institutions were providing the best technical and scientific training in the world. The German universities had become centers for serious research and scholarship in science and technology long before their British and American counterparts. They pioneered in institutionalizing the acquisition and transfer of knowledge. They led the way in the development of the disciplines of physics and chemistry and their application to medicine and industrial technology.[60] Moreover, the Technische Hochschulen (technical universities) were specifically created to train men for industrial appointments. By 1900 such schools were established in major locations—Charlottenburg (in Berlin), Munich, Darmstadt, Hannover, Karlsruhe, Dresden, Stuttgart, Aachen, and Brunswick.[61] After 1900 others were set up at Danzig and Breslau. Between 1890 and 1900 the enrollment at these technical schools increased from 5,361 to 14,738—an increase of 170% as compared with the 10% growth of the German population in that decade. By 1910 the enrollment was 16,568.[62] By contrast, in 1913 there were only 1,129 students of engineering in all the universities of England and Wales (see Chapter 7). Moreover, the German universities, unlike the British, had established graduate programs in engineering. At the turn of the century Emperor William II had issued several decrees permitting these universities to award the degree of *Doktor Ingenieur*.

In these years the German government also sponsored research institutes where distinguished scholars spent full time working on scientific research. The best known was (in English translation) the National Physical Technical Institute—(later the Royal Institute of Physics)—which was established in 1888 in Charlottenburg near the electrical equipment works of Werner von Siemens, who had been the driving force in its founding.[63] Among the others that followed, the Kaiser-Wilhelm-Gesellschaft for chemistry, established in Berlin in 1911, was of particular importance. These institutes, with their increasing number of Nobel prize winners, soon had ties with universities, the technical schools, and the large industrial enterprises.

In the years just before and after 1900, about the same time that schools of business appeared in the United States, the first German schools to provide business education, the Handelshochschulen, were established. The first appeared at Cologne in 1898, followed by those at Aachen in 1903, Berlin in 1906, Mannheim in 1907, and Munich in 1910.[64] The curriculum, as compared with that of the American business schools, was concentrated more on accounting, finance, and generalized business economics and law than on marketing and general management. By 1920, according to Robert Locke, "it was possible to acquire a full range of undergraduate and graduate degrees in business economics, and the possession of research degrees became increasingly important for appointment to professorships in business schools."[65]

This rapid growth of an infrastructure for scientific, technical, and business education provided more than just a source of technically trained managers. As in the United States, the engineering schools and to a lesser extent the business schools became a vital source of scientific, technical, and commercial knowledge. Robert Locke has described and documented the close relationships between the new educational institutions and the new industrial enterprises, mainly those in the chemical and electrical-equipment industries but also those in metals, nonelectrical machinery, and optics. Thus in Germany the modern industrial enterprise with its production managers, design engineers, and marketers quickly provided the crucial link between the sources of technical knowledge and the needs of customers, particularly industrial customers. This linkage was much closer in Germany than in Britain, where it rarely existed at all, and even than in the United States, where at the turn of the century the process was just beginning. And only a little later a comparable set of relationships developed in finance and commerce between the large industrial enterprise and the new Handelshochschulen.

The Coming of Cooperative Managerial Capitalism

These characteristics that differentiated Germany's economic and cultural environment from that of Britain and of the United States tended to encourage cooperation between its new modern industrial enterprises. From the start the foreign market was more important to German industrialists than to the Americans or even to the British. Continental Europe provided the major market for Germans, just as the continental United States did for Americans and as the British Empire did for the British. But whereas for the Americans the continental market was largely a home market, for the Germans it consisted of many states, languages, and cultures. When German enterprises marketed and distributed in European countries, they were foreigners competing with local citizens. Outside Europe, in Latin America, Asia, and Africa, the British and to a lesser extent the Americans had already established a strong commercial presence before German enterprises moved into these areas. The challenge of meeting such competition abroad often promoted cooperation at home.

Such cooperation was further encouraged by the Grossbanken when they provided initial capital for the new industrial enterprises. Because the banks invested in a number of firms, they normally preferred cooperation to competition, particularly when competition threatened profits. As competition intensified as a result of the rapidly increasing output of the new technologies, the laws themselves further promoted cooperation. Even the educational system facilitated cooperation by providing managers for the new enterprises who came from much the same social class and received much the same technical and commercial training. By the turn of the century, after the new enterprises had been created through the three-pronged investments in manufacturing, marketing, and management, and after the players in the new oligopoly had been selected and were beginning their powerful and effective drive into foreign markets, these industrial leaders began to devise more formal and sophisticated legal forms of cooperation. The coming of World War I, the defeat of Germany, and the successive postwar crises intensified the pressure for cooperation. German industrialists believed that such cooperation was necessary if they were to maintain their position at home and win back the markets they had lost abroad. Thus the events of the decade between 1914 and 1924 helped to solidify the system of cooperative managerial capitalism that was developing before World War I within the major German industries.

ELEVEN

Creating Organizational Capabilities: The Lesser Industries

During the years between 1870 and World War I, Germany, like the United States, quickly surpassed Britain in industrial output and captured an increasing share of Britain's international and even domestic markets. At the core, this success rested on the ability of German entrepreneurs to adopt new technologies and to build the organizations necessary to exploit them. Nevertheless, the technological processes of production in the new capital-intensive industries and the markets for their output differed from one industry to another. These industries differed in the timing of technological innovation, the availability of markets and supplies, and the need for capital. Therefore they differed in their financial requirements and in the role the banks played in financing them. They differed, too, in the ways in which the legally enforceable cartels affected the growth of companies and the competition between them, and the ways in which the educational infrastructure affected the development of product and process and the recruitment of managers.

The Second Industrial Revolution

The industries in which German entrepreneurs excelled were those that lay at the heart of the Second Industrial Revolution—those that produced the materials and the machinery so essential to the rapid industrializing and urbanizing of the economies, not only of continental Europe but also of Britain and the United States. By World War I Germany's industrial strength lay in what contemporaries referred to as "the great industries." These included metals—iron and steel, copper and other nonferrous metals; heavy industrial machinery, particularly the new machines that generated, transmitted, and used electrical power; and the new chemical industries that produced man-made dyes, fibers, fertilizer, and materials used in a wide variety of industrial processes. In these industries German entrepreneurs were the first movers in Europe: they succeeded where British entrepreneurs failed. Not surprisingly, these were the industries that attracted the most attention in their day and have continued to interest historians and economists ever since.

The other industries in which the modern industrial enterprise has always clustered played a less central role in the development of the modern German economy. For this reason, probably, much less has been written about them. Nevertheless, the histories of the leading enterprises in Germany's "lesser industries" provide a somewhat different perspective from which to view the evolution of the large enterprise and the coming of managerial capitalism. In rubber, rayon, synthetic alkalies, explosives, and a small number of light-machinery industries, German entrepreneurs were first movers, competing with the British and Americans in European and global markets. In oil, German firms, financed by powerful Grossbanken, became strong challengers. But in some of the other lesser industries—most foods, glass, abrasives, and other materials, and most standardized, light machines—the German entrepreneurs' response to the new opportunities was much more limited, and their enterprises were far less effective in international trade. In these lesser industries the leading firms faced more vigorous competition from foreign enterprises both at home and abroad than did those in the great industries. Such competition resulted in somewhat different patterns of interfirm relationships and of financing than occurred in metals, machinery, and most of the chemicals.

Because World War I obviously affected the German economy much more drastically than it did that of the United States and even that of Britain, the history of its industries will be told in two parts—first, up to the outbreak of World War I, and then (in later chapters) from 1914 until the mid-1930s, when Hitler's rise to power once more transformed Germany into a command economy. The industry-by-industry review will include the same industries as those already considered for the United States and Britain. But because of the different impact of these industries on the German economy and because of the different entrepreneurial responses to the opportunities created by the coming of transportation and communication revolution, the industries will be reviewed in a somewhat different order. In this chapter on the lesser industries I begin with the branded, packaged products (food, tobacco, and consumer chemicals), in which German entrepreneurs made only limited investments. Next I discuss oil, rubber, and industrial materials (including explosives) in the same order as that used for Britain (Chapter 8). Then I turn to the few light-machinery industries in which a small number of German entrepreneurs (unlike their British counterparts) responded effectively to new opportunities. Finally, I briefly consider textiles, where again the entrepreneurial response differed from that in Britain.

Branded, Packaged Products: Limited Entrepreneurial Response

In contrast to the United States and Britain, the two hundred largest industrial enterprises in Germany included few producers of foods, tobacco, and (except for sophisticated pharmaceuticals) consumer chemicals (Groups 20, 21, and 28; see Appendixes C.1–C.4). The brewers were the major exception to this general situation. In foods, tobacco, and consumer chemicals large industrial enterprises did appear in Germany during the 1880s in the same three-digit industries as they did in the United States and Britain—vegetable oil, sugar, cocoa and chocolate, beer, soap, and drugs: that is, they appeared in all three countries in those industries where the technology of production gave large works cost advantages over smaller plants. But German entrepreneurs failed to create large enterprises in branded, packaged cereal and other grain products comparable to those in the United States and Britain.

Moreover, the German vegetable-oil and sugar companies that are listed failed to do what their counterparts in the United States and Britain did. Instead of moving into packaged and branded products that could be placed directly on retailers' shelves, they remained primarily producers of bulk or commodity products. All the sugar companies were regional beet-sugar producers which benefited from scale economies as the industry's output rose from an annual average of 2.5 million tons in the period 1866 to 1870 to 3.4 million tons between 1906 and 1910. As output expanded, the number of factories declined and, in J. H. Clapham's words, "the average factory greatly increased in size." These firms, which usually grew the beets as well as processing them, sold in bulk to confectioneries and other producers. In addition, they sold in bulk to wholesalers who packaged and branded the product for retail sale. The final consumer market for sugar was apparently too small to encourage packaging and branding by the manufacturers, as was done by American Sugar and Tate & Lyle.[1]

As vegetable oil replaced animal oils in the production of margarine, cooking oils, and other foods for human and animal consumption (and also for soap), and as palm and copra (dried coconut flesh) began to replace cottonseed oil as primary sources of vegetable oils, large firms began to concentrate their processing plants in the nation's two major ports, Hamburg and Bremen. By 1914 the four largest enterprises—Verein deutscher Oelfabriken, F. Thörl, Bremen-Besigheimer Oelfabriken, and Noblee & Thörl—along with two smaller firms, accounted for 80% to 90% of the coconut oil and more than 90% of the palm oil processed in Europe. They sold the products in bulk, primarily to producers of cattle fodder or makers of margarine.[2]

By the turn of the century German margarine production, which also enjoyed high economies of scale, was dominated by two Dutch producers—Van den Bergh and Jurgens. They had captured the German and Continental markets by being the first to build large plants in Germany (this was done in 1887 after the imposition of a tariff), and then they had rapidly expanded their networks of branch offices. In 1908 the two Dutch firms signed an agreement to take most of the output of the four largest German vegetable-oil refiners. All but one of these four were taken over shortly after World War I by the two Dutch margarine makers, which were the Continental forbears of Unilever.

German entrepreneurs were most successful in developing branded, packaged products in the cocoa and chocolate trade. The first mover, Stollwerck, remained the leader until after World War I. Its only German rival was Sarotti, which was formed in 1865 and built a large plant in Berlin in the early 1890s. By 1900 employment there had risen from less than one hundred to close to one thousand. Sarotti made no attempt to expand outside Germany or to diversify into vending machines or other nonchocolate products. Like the vegetable-oil producers it was taken over after World War I by a foreign first mover, in this case Deutsche Nestlé, a major subsidiary of the giant Swiss firm, which since the turn of the century had been the largest producer of canned milk, baby food, and other packaged dairy products in Germany.[3]

German entrepreneurs were more successful in consumer chemicals than they were in foods. They became first movers in pharmaceuticals and challenged Lever Brothers in soap. In these cases, however, success rested on capabilities in chemical processing and not in mixing, packaging, and branding soap, drugs, and paints by mechanical means in the American and British fashion. Because German pharmaceuticals grew out of the production of dyes, their history is told in the next chapter along with those of the leading producers of organic chemicals.

The story of the German challenger in soap shows how one enterprise moved into a global oligopoly by using an innovative technology of production based on existing organizational capabilities. In 1907 Fritz Henkel, a maker of bleaches used in laundries, working closely with Deutsche Gold- und Silber-Scheide-Anstalt AG (DEGUSSA), a first mover in electrochemicals, developed a new chemical-based soap powder. At that time two foreign firms dominated the German soap market, Lever Brothers and the Austro-Hungarian firm of Schicht. The Schicht firm had built a works in Aussig, Austria, in 1887 that was large enough, in the words of Lever's historian, to permit it "to reduce costs far below its competitors." It then established a Continental sales force.[4] In 1898 Lever Brothers, in order to maintain its position in the German market, built a works in Mannheim.

Henkel was able to challenge these first movers because in 1889 he had constructed a large bleach plant near Düsseldorf and had formed an extensive sales force. After developing the soap powder, Henkel and DEGUSSA signed an agreement by which DEGUSSA was to provide the basic material, sodium silicate, and Henkel was to process, package, market, and distribute the new product, given the brand name of Persil. On the basis of his new technology and existing sales force Henkel quickly became the major soap-powder producer on the Continent. Lever quickly responded by purchasing a half interest in another pioneer—Dr. Thompson's Seifenpulver—and improved that firm's product, producing a soap powder for finer fabrics. This became Lever's internationally sold Rinso brand. Possibly because of this strong response, Henkel decided not to challenge Lever directly in Britain. Instead, in 1909 he licensed his process to Crosfield's, one of Lever's friendly competitors, to make soap powder for sale in Great Britain and in the empire, with the exception of Canada, Australia, and New Zealand. The new product was clearly a superior one, for as Crosfield's historian writes: "The deal with Henkel's was ultimately to prove the most profitable stroke of business Crosfield's ever made." Henkel then made comparable arrangements for a French company to produce and sell Persil in that nation. In the rest of Europe, Henkel's Persil sales grew rapidly. In 1913 the company constructed its first foreign plant, in Switzerland. After the war it built works in other European countries.[5]

Finally, in tobacco, Georg A. Jasmatzi became the dominant enterprise after it was purchased in 1901 by the American industry's first mover, American Tobacco Company. It was then taken over by British-American Tobacco (BAT), American Tobacco's successor in international trade. BAT quickly enlarged Jasmatzi's facilities and personnel, making it the dominant tobacco-processing enterprise in Germany.

Of the two other producers of branded, packaged products listed among the top two hundred German industrials (see Appendixes C.1–C.4), one was Knorr, a producer of packaged powdered soup and baby food, and the other was "Nordsee" Deutsche Dampffischereigesellschaft. Knorr's development was similar to that of Nestlé and Borden, though on a smaller scale. The "Nordsee" story is unusual. By World War I it was operating processing plants, a fleet of ships, and nine branches that marketed both fresh and processed fish in Germany. Little information is available on this only representative of the fishing industry among the top twentieth-century enterprises in all three countries.[6]

That German companies—Nordsee, Henkel, Stollwerck—and foreign firms—Lever, Nestlé, BAT, and the Dutch margarine producers—created long-lasting, integrated, high-volume producing and distributing enterprises in Germany emphasizes that, even though consumer income was lower there than in the United States or Britain, entrepreneurial opportunities existed in the production and distribution of branded, packaged products. The success in the German market of subsidiaries of American firms such as Quaker Oats and Corn Products Refining again makes the point. These two subsidiaries quickly became the largest producers of their cereal products in Germany.[7]

The German entrepreneurial response was limited in these industries partly because foreign rather than German entrepreneurs were the first to make the necessary investment in new processing and packaging technologies and to build the necessary marketing networks and managerial organizations to exploit them effectively. Only in soap, and then only after a technological breakthrough, was a German company able to challenge foreign first movers. For Nestlé and the Dutch margarine producers, which built works large enough to obtain the cost advantages of scale, and which had only tiny domestic markets of their own, Germany was second only to Britain as an outlet for their new mass-produced goods. The creation of their Continental marketing organizations was essential to their initial success. For the British and American processors, whose initial growth had rested on their large domestic markets, the building of a comparable sales network in Germany was part of the global expansion of their marketing activities. In order to supply the growing demand they acquired production facilities within Germany, though they did so less quickly than the Dutch and Swiss companies.

In the processing of those perishable products whose volume production depended on a heavy investment in refrigerated facilities—meat, dairy products, and beer—German entrepreneurs only created large firms in beer. Because the German Empire was neither a massive importer nor a massive exporter of perishable meat and dairy products, there was less incentive to build either large, mass-producing meatpacking enterprises like those in the United States, or specialized commercial intermediaries like Britain's Union Cold Storage and International Cold Storage, or retail chains such as Britain's Eastman, Nelson, and Lipton. Nor was the urban market concentrated enough to encourage the growth of firms to equal the size of Maypole Dairy and United Dairies in Great Britain.

The brewing industry in Germany, as in Britain, was a special case. It was by far the largest consumer-goods industry in the country. At the time of the first industrial census in 1926 its capital assets were close to those of the giant electrical-machinery industry.[8] As in Great Britain, the brewers concentrated more on regional than on national markets. Unlike the British, the German brewers did not invest heavily in "pubs" or other retail outlets, however. On the other hand, they made a greater effort than the British to exploit the fundamental innovations that created the modern brewing industry in the late 1870s and early 1880s. These included the studies of Louis Pasteur, published in 1876, which "laid the foundation of modern techniques of sterilization and preservation"; Carl von Linde's invention of a cooling compressor; improved steam boiling; and new bottling techniques.[9]

The Germans quickly built breweries large enough to obtain the cost advantages of scale. As might be expected, the first companies to make the investment in the new high-volume technologies continued to dominate their regions. By 1911 fewer than 10% of the German breweries already accounted for 37% of the total beer produced.[10] As the railroad network filled in, the leading regional firms—those of Dortmund in the west, Munich in the south, Leipzig and Berlin in the center, and Breslau in the east—began to compete more with each other and to participate more in the export trade. Thus, although the German firms owned fewer retail outlets than the British, they did make a greater investment in product-specific refrigerated storage and transportation facilities. In addition, they spent more on research, and they established vocational schools and professional journals before their British counterparts did. The managerial organizations of the regional firms, however, remained relatively small and the enterprises family-controlled.

Before World War I, at least one brewing enterprise moved beyond its regional boundaries and in so doing created an extensive hierarchy of managers. This firm, Schultheiss, was the nation's biggest from the 1880s until World War II. Earlier, as one of the largest breweries in Berlin, it had begun to build an extensive network of branch offices in northern Germany, in the manner of Pabst and other American brewing firms. These branch offices, with refrigerated warehouses, numbered forty-five by 1901 and sixty-eight by 1910. This network was served by a transportation office that scheduled flows in the company's refrigerated cars. To meet the enlarged demand, in 1891 Schultheiss acquired a brewing company in Berlin, in 1896 one in Dessau to the south, and in 1898 another in Niederschöneweide to the southeast of Berlin. Earlier it had obtained its own factory to build casks and cases, as well as its own malt works. In 1898 it constructed a large central administrative office building in Berlin. Unlike comparable British enterprises, Schultheiss did not operate as a federation of breweries. Instead, it was centrally managed from the Berlin headquarters through six territorial divisions, each with its own marketing and distributing organization whose activities were planned, coordinated, and monitored from Berlin.[11]

Except in brewing, however, the modern industrial enterprise played a much smaller role in foods and consumer chemicals in Germany than it did in Great Britain, where such firms were among the very largest industrial enterprises, and in the United States, where they were among the most dynamic. Even in brewing the companies remained relatively small and family-managed. The lower per-capita income in Germany, the larger rural population, the lack of concentrated urban markets, and the entrance of foreign first movers into the German market all reduced the incentives for German entrepreneurs to make an investment in facilities and personnel large enough to exploit the cost advantages of scale available in these industries. Entrepreneurs like Ludwig Stollwerck and Fritz Henkel were very much the exception.

Other Lesser Industries: Effective Entrepreneurial Response

In the other lesser, capital-intensive, German industries where increased size of plant brought greater cost advantages than it did in branded, packaged products, German entrepreneurs responded almost as successfully as their American and British counterparts. In oil the response was late, but in European markets by World War I two German companies were challenging the first mover, Standard Oil, and its strongest rival, Royal Dutch (after 1907, Royal Dutch–Shell). In rubber, Germany, like other European countries, had one company—the first to build a tire plant large enough to obtain the cost advantages of scale—which dominated the home market and competed effectively internationally. In rayon, synthetic alkalies, explosives, and a small number of light-machinery industries German entrepreneurs made the investments and created the managerial organizations needed to participate in global markets, much as did their British counterparts in all but light machinery. By contrast, in other capital-intensive processing industries, including glass, abrasives, and asbestos, and also in most of the light-machinery industries, German entrepreneurs failed to make the investments in time to prevent foreign first movers from dominating the German market.

OIL: LATE CHALLENGERS

Because Germany had so few sources of petroleum within its boundaries, its entrepreneurs entered the oil industry late (Group 29; see Appendix C.2). They were still ahead of the British, however, and they acted primarily on the initiative of the German Grossbanken. When German entrepreneurs began to enter the European oil industry in the 1890s, it was dominated by the American first mover, Standard Oil; the European first mover, the Nobel Brothers; and two challengers—the Rothschilds, Europe's premier banking family, and Henri Deterding's Royal Dutch Company. Thus the story of the German oil industry tells of the rise of challengers in a capital-intensive industry and of the role played by the Grossbanken in establishing industrial enterprises.

As in the United States, the oil industry in Europe was dominated by its first mover until the late 1880s. Ludwig Nobel and his brothers, members of the entrepreneurial Swedish family, became the "Russian Rockefellers." Among all the refiners of crude oil from the recently opened fields at Baku on the Caspian Sea, Ludwig was the first to install a pipeline connecting a well with a refinery. He did so in 1877. This pipeline, eight miles long, gave his refinery the largest throughput of any in the Baku area. Nobel was also the first of the Baku refiners to invest in a distribution network. He built the world's first oil tanker in 1878 and used it to carry his products to rivers and to railheads on the Caspian, serving the Russian market. And in 1879, with his brothers Alfred and Robert, he formed the Nobel Brothers Petroleum Production Company. That firm put together a distribution system of flat cars (to carry barrels) and then tank cars, storage depots, and terminals throughout Russia. (Forty such terminals had been built by 1885.) In 1881 the company expanded its facilities by erecting a continuous-process refinery with the most advanced technology, having an annual throughput of 8 million puds (approximately 1.2 million barrels) of kerosene and 3 million puds (approximately 0.3 million barrels) of lubricating oil.[12] Even before he built this new refinery, Nobel was one of the three largest competitors in the Baku area, and three years later he was the leading refiner of Russian oil, "refining more than four times as much as the second largest, and more than the next five producers combined." Again the parallel to Rockefeller is striking.

Finally, the Nobels recruited a managerial organization to coordinate the flow from the oil fields through the refining facilities and the distribution network to the retailers, quickly developing sophisticated accounting and operational controls to carry out this task.[13] The managerial hierarchy remained smaller than that of Standard Oil, however. In 1883 the Nobels failed in an attempt to consolidate the industry within Russia as Rockefeller had succeeded in doing in the United States. After this failure their enterprise made no further extensive effort to expand its marketing organization beyond Russia and Scandinavia. During the 1880s, when Standard Oil was establishing its own distribution organization in western Europe, the Nobels continued to rely primarily on independent wholesalers to sell and distribute in the same market.

The dominance of the Nobels in Russia was challenged, as was Rockefeller's in the United States, when other producers and refiners found an alternate route to a market. In this case it was a railroad from Baku to Batum on the Black Sea, completed in 1885. One of Europe's most powerful banking houses played a major role in organizing and financing the new competition. The Paris Rothschilds entered the Russian oil business in 1886 by purchasing tank cars on the recently opened Baku-Batum line, by advancing loans to small refiners to purchase their own cars, and by building a factory to produce packing cases at Batum. The motive here was to provide crude oil to the refineries which a Rothschild enterprise—the Société Anonyme Commerciale et Industrielle de Naphthe Caspienne et de la Mer Noire—was financing in France, Austria, and Spain in order to serve a European distribution network which it was establishing. In addition, the new railroad route permitted Baku refiners to compete with Nobel in the Russian markets.[14]

Despite the achievements of the Nobels and their challengers, Standard Oil continued to dominate the European markets for kerosene. This was not only because the American firm had rationalized and centralized its production processes and had integrated forward into marketing and distribution abroad as well as at home. It was also, as John McKay has pointed out, because the Europeans had not been able to create a comparable, integrated organization.[15] With the failure of the Nobels' attempt in 1883 to consolidate the industry in Russia and with the opening of the new routes to the European and Russian markets, more small firms were competing than was the case in the United States, even though the Nobel and Rothschild groups continued to be the most effective challengers to Standard Oil. Standard's relative strength is indicated by a proposed agreement drawn up in March 1895, which would have assigned 75% of the world's export trade to Standard Oil and the other 25% to the Nobels and other European producers.[16]

In the first decade of the new century the European oligopoly was enlarged in much the same way as the oligopoly dominated by Standard Oil in the United States. On the one hand, new sources of supply were beginning to open up. On the other, the coming of the internal combustion engine was creating a new major market, for even before 1900 stationary gasoline engines were being produced in volume. In this restructuring of the European oil industry the Germans came to play the major role.

In the 1890s oil fields were discovered in Rumania, in Galicia in Austria, and also in Borneo and Burma. Although Standard Oil's American rival, Pure Oil, was making inroads on the European market, the major new challenger in Europe was Henri Deterding's Royal Dutch Company, the industry's first mover in Asia. That enterprise was closely allied with Marcus Samuel's Shell Transport & Trading Company, the British carrier of the newly discovered oil of southeast Asia to Europe. In 1901 Samuel arranged to purchase from the predecessors of Gulf Oil one thousand tons of crude per year from the newly opened Spindletop fields in Texas, at a fixed price, for twenty-one years. In 1902 Samuel and Deterding, with the Paris Rothschild Bank as a third partner, formed the Asiatic Petroleum Company to market oil in the Eastern Hemisphere. In the meantime, Deterding had quickly moved into the recently opened fields in Rumania and also into new fields in Russia.[17]

The smaller indigenous enterprises in the new fields, however, were able to hold their own, largely because of the German banks. The Deutsche Bank (by then the most powerful of the Grossbanken), supported by several smaller banks, financed ventures in Rumania, including the largest producer, Steaua Romana, which quickly built a substantial refinery and a local sales organization. Then in 1903 the managers of the Deutsche Bank realized, as Rockefeller and Nobel had done earlier and Charles Greenway at the Anglo-Persian Oil Company did a little later, the necessity of having an international sales organization and of consolidating refining and producing activities within a single enterprise. In January 1904, therefore, the bank formed Deutsche Petroleum AG (DPAG). At the same time, it purchased the German gasoline and naphtha sales subsidiary of Shell Transport & Trading. That subsidiary, which became Deutsche Petroleum-Verkaufs-Gesellschaft (DPVG), soon had marketing organizations in other European countries.

Then in June 1906 Arthur von Gwinner, the chairman of the Deutsche Bank's Supervisory Board, joined forces with the Nobels and Rothschilds to form the Europäische Petroleum Union (EPU), which became the western European selling arm of the three major groups producing oil in Europe—the Nobels, the

Rothschilds, and the Deutsche Bank. EPU, in turn, set up a British sales subsidiary, the British Petroleum Company, which established its own tanker company, the Petroleum Steamship Company of London. In this way, EPU became a consolidated marketing enterprise for the western European markets.[18] It was organized, however, more like a German sales syndicate than like a marketing organization of an integrated American company: that is, EPU's policy board, the Comité des Participants de la Centrale, determined the amount of refined oil to be distributed, the amount that each of the participating companies would provide, and how much should be purchased from outside suppliers, such as Gulf. "Their day-to-day management," according to Frederick C. Gerretson, "was in the hands of a Conseil d'Administration which was composed of the directors of the various amalgamated companies."[19]

It was in 1907, soon after the birth of EPU, that Deterding's Royal Dutch Company joined forces with Shell Transport & Trading Company in an arrangement which gave the Dutch company 60% and the British 40% of the new enterprise, Royal Dutch–Shell.

In the meantime Austrian producers, supported by the second most powerful of the German Grossbanken, the Disconto-Gesellschaft, and its ally, Bankhaus S. Bleichröder, were bringing together a smaller but more integrated oil enterprise. The Disconto had entered the Rumanian fields by refinancing two small producing companies. In 1905 these two joined with another to form Allgemeine Petroleum Industrie (APIAG). The Disconto also helped to finance the consolidation of several small Austrian (Galician) producers and refiners in 1899. In 1904 it supported the consolidation of a number of wholesalers into an enterprise that became known as OLEX, a trade name and the telegraph address of its coordinating headquarters. In 1905 OLEX began to move aggressively into Germany and nearby countries, creating regional marketing organizations and investing in tank cars and wagons and storage depots. In 1910 OLEX centralized its control over the regional subsidiaries by setting up headquarters in Berlin.[20]

The senior managers at the Disconto then realized that they had to decide to be either a bank or an oil company. In the first place, the oil investment was absorbing an increasing share of the bank's resources. Second, in their own words, "from the banking point of view the technical direction of undertakings which are so ramified and difficult to manage would not be practicable in the long run, because it made such demands on the co-operation of the banking management that various members would be permanently submerged in oil to the exclusion of all other activities."[21] Disconto's board, therefore, decided to concentrate its oil industry interests in the hands of Rudolf Noellenburg, an able young executive in Deutsche Tiefbohr AG, a potash and coal-mining firm that in 1906 had moved into oil production in Alsace and near Hannover. That firm had built refineries adjacent to its production operations and created a small sales organization. With Disconto's backing Deutsche Tiefbohr changed its name to Deutsche Erdöl (DEA) and took over Disconto's Rumanian holdings (APIAG); the marketing subsidiaries of OLEX in Germany, Switzerland, Belgium, and Scandinavia; and also the allied banks' producing and refining interests in Galicia. In addition, DEA obtained control of Deutsche Mineralöl-Industrie and other North German refineries. The Disconto bank, although turning over the administration of its holdings to Noellenburg's Deutsche Erdöl, remained DEA's major stockholder and continued to administer directly the finances of this new integrated oil enterprise.

Standard Oil responded quickly to the growing strength of Royal Dutch and the two German bank-sponsored enterprises. Its marketing subsidiary, Deutsch-Amerikanische Petroleum-Gesellschaft (DAPG, of which Standard had come to hold 90% of the equity), built refineries using Rumanian and Pennsylvania oil to produce kerosene, gasoline, and a variety of naphtha products. Standard's DAPG also intensified its sales and distribution efforts and sharply cut prices. In 1904, in direct response to the formation of OLEX, another of Standard's subsidiaries, Vacuum Oil, producer and worldwide distributor of lubricants, built two refineries to process Galician oil. In the same year Standard Oil formed Româno-Americana to produce, refine, and distribute Rumanian crude oil. These investments in all three activities quickly made Standard a major player in eastern Europe. It was only turned away from making a similar set of investments in Russia by the 1905 revolution and the massive destruction at the Baku and other Russian fields.[22]

Standard Oil's response was effective. After a short spell of vigorous competition, DAPG reached a series of agreements in 1907 with subsidiaries of Deutsche Petroleum and of its marketing arm, the new EPU. And these agreements once again confirmed the American company's paramount position in the markets of western Europe, including Britain. As a result of these agreements, historians of Standard Oil estimate, Standard enjoyed 75% and EPU 20% of the overall market for illuminating oil—kerosene—with OLEX and Pure Oil as competitors in particular areas. Significantly, Standard's share of gasoline was less. In 1910 Standard made a comparable marketing agreement with OLEX, the selling arm of Deutsche Erdöl.[23]

In this way, through a complex series of interactions that are hardly hinted at in this brief summary, by World War I the global petroleum industry's first mover, Standard Oil, was being challenged in all parts of the world by Royal Dutch–Shell and in European markets by two German-financed and -administered firms—Deutsche Petroleum and the smaller Deutsche Erdöl. In addition, the new integrated American firms, Texaco and Gulf, were beginning to seek foreign and particularly European markets. On the other hand, the growing global oligopoly lost an important member when Standard Oil made arrangements in 1911 with Pure Oil to handle its overseas marketing.[24] The dismemberment of Standard Oil by the Supreme Court's 1911 antitrust ruling did not substantially affect international competition during the brief period before the outbreak of World War I.

The challenge by the two German companies was more potential than real. In 1914 Noellenburg was just beginning to rationalize his producing, refining, and distributing facilities and to build the management structure essential to administer the properties which the Disconto bank had legally consolidated into Deutsche Erdöl. And Deutsche Petroleum remained little more than a loosely knit holding company. At EPU, its marketing and distribution company, Emil Georg von Stauss, the bank's specialist in oil, was building an effective transportation, distribution, and marketing organization for Europe. He also "compelled its suppliers to supply lamp oil of a certain quality which was equal in every way to Standard's White Water."[25]

As early as 1910 the Deutsche Bank's directors were becoming as concerned (and for the same reasons) as had the directors of the Disconto bank about their ability to manage a large oil enterprise. Indeed, in that year Arthur von Gwinner of the Deutsche Bank offered to sell EPU to Standard Oil and to Royal Dutch–Shell. As Standard Oil's historians have paraphrased his explanation, "the managers of the firm were bankers and they did not have the necessary time to devote to the demands of this commercial enterprise."[26] Both Standard and Shell turned down the bank's offer. The price was too high. Then von Gwinner began a campaign in the Reichstag to strike at Standard's power in Germany by nationalizing the wholesaling of kerosene. (The aim was not, it should be stressed, to nationalize the oil industry, but only the wholesaling of kerosene, the market that Standard dominated.)[27] It was only in 1913, after Standard had effectively thwarted the threat, that von Gwinner turned over the bank's holdings to von Stauss's management. Only then did von Stauss begin to concentrate on consolidating and rationalizing Deutsche Petroleum's facilities and recruiting the necessary management organization.

One reason Royal Dutch–Shell turned down von Gwinner's offer was that Deterding had his eye on the Rothschilds' holdings in Russia. He began serious negotiations in 1911. The transactions, completed early in 1912, included the purchase of crude-oil facilities with an annual output of 436,000 tons of crude and 338,000 tons of refined, as well as tankers, barges, and 800,000 tons of storage capacity.[28] In 1914 Deterding, who was still involved in building his giant integrated empire, had as yet given relatively little thought to managing it. Nevertheless, by 1914 Royal Dutch–Shell and its two German rivals were beginning to reduce Standard's share in the European market. If the war had not totally disrupted the production, refining, and distribution of oil, Deutsche Petroleum and Deutsche Erdöl would in all likelihood have remained major players in the global oligopoly.

The evolution of the oil industry in Europe was significantly different from that in the United States, even though the Nobels acquired first-mover advantages comparable to those of Rockefeller's Standard Oil, and even though the challenges to the first mover came at much the same time for much the same reasons. The main difference was that the Nobels failed to create an integrated organization comparable to that of Standard Oil. The Nobels and their major European rivals relied much more on contractual arrangements than did Standard and its American competitors. They made contracts with suppliers, marketers (both wholesale and retail), and transportation companies, as well as among themselves and their smaller competitors. Both the Nobels and Rothschilds often made investments in the same independent enterprises. These agreements rarely lasted, because the opening of new fields and the development of new products continually altered the strategy of the leaders. By 1911 when the Rothschilds sold off their major holdings, the Nobels' integrated oil enterprise operated only in Russia and Scandinavia.

Another difference between Europe and America was the entrepreneurial role of banks. Although the Rothschilds' banking activities may have been more personal (that is, family-oriented) than institutional, the German Grossbanken with their extensive managerial hierarchies were responsible for creating two major challengers to Standard Oil in Europe before the outbreak of World War I. In no American or British industry did banks play a comparable role.

FIRST MOVERS, EUROPEAN STYLE: RUBBER, RAYON, ALKALIES, AND EXPLOSIVES

In several other industries where high-volume chemical processes of production assured the cost advantages of scale economies—that is, in rubber, synthetic fibers, synthetic alkalies, and dynamite—the evolution of the large German industrial enterprise paralleled more closely the British experience. Whereas in oil, as in branded, packaged products, the Germans were latecomers, in these other industries the German entrepreneurs were first movers. They were among the first to invest in the new technologies, recruit the necessary managers, and build an international sales network. They quickly dominated the domestic market and competed with first movers of other nations in international markets. Moreover, they relied far less on banks than did the oil producers and refiners, partly because of the rapidity with which they generated profits.

Rubber. In rubber (Group 30; see Appendixes C.1 and C.2), the first German enterprise to mass-produce the automobile tire was still the nation's dominant rubber company in the 1980s. Continental-Caoutchouc-und Gutta-Percha-Compagnie differed from Britain's Dunlop and resembled Goodrich and United States Rubber in that it began by producing rubber products, albeit on a smaller scale, before the coming of the pneumatic tire.[29] At its Hannover works it made boots, apparel, and surgical rubber (but apparently not industrial items such as belting). Continental's first important growth came in meeting the demands for bicycle tires, and its dominance was assured when it built its automobile-tire plant. The number of employees jumped from 600 in 1893 to 2,200 in 1903 and to 12,000 in 1913. By 1907 tires made up 91.6% of its sales. Once the new plant was in full operation, Continental immediately became larger than the Phoenix Gummiwerke AG, at that time Germany's leading producer of rubber shoes, fabrics, and a variety of industrial rubber products, and the smaller Vereinigte Gummiwaren-Fabriken Hamburg-Wien. Neither of those two firms moved quickly into the production of tires.[30] Continental's throughput in automobile tires quickly gave it a powerful competitive advantage. Although it had made a market-sharing agreement with a nearby competitor, Hanno-versche Gummi-Kamm, to divide the domestic bicycle-tire market, with 65% going to Continental and 35% to its competitor, it refused to make a comparable agreement for the sale of automobile tires, either at home or abroad. Indeed, it was unwilling to agree on allocating foreign markets for any rubber products, even bicycle tires.

Like the first movers in other nations, Continental invested quickly in a global marketing network for its automobile tires. By 1913 it had 130 branch offices— 20 in Germany, 48 in the rest of Europe, and 62 in other parts of the world. But it had none in the United States. In 1905 Continental liquidated its American sales subsidiary, which had been set up before the coming of the automobile tire, but it did maintain close ties with one American firm, Goodrich. That company, in return for German technical advice and possibly German patents, produced and sold a tire with the Continental brand name and became a partner with Continental in joint marketing ventures in Belgium and Austria.[31]

There is little evidence of extensive interfirm cooperation in the global tire industry. (For the only other example—that between Dunlop and Goodyear— see Chapter 8.) The dominance of each European firm in its own domestic market, as well as the economic strength of the four American leaders, meant that Continental and its major European rivals competed functionally and stra-tegically rather than negotiating for market share, as so often occurred in European industries. Moreover, Continental did not have to tie itself to any of the Grossbanken. The cost advantages of high-volume throughput permitted the use of retained earnings to pay for the continuing growth of the enterprise. From 1902 to 1913 annual dividends never fell below 40%, and for several years they were higher. Generalizations concerning banker influence and cartelization made on the basis of Europe's oil industry obviously have little relevance to the history of its rubber industry.

Rayon. The history of rayon (in Group 22; see Appendix C.1) in Germany parallels that of rubber to a certain extent. One firm quickly came to dominate, and it grew by investing retained earnings rather than by bank financing. But in rayon—an industry in which Europeans pioneered—the German leader and its European competitors quickly attempted to maintain market shares and profits through contractual agreements.

The German first mover was Vereinigte Glanzstoff-Fabriken (VGF). Its story is only less dramatic than that of Courtaulds in that the first entrepreneurs to build a large rayon plant in Germany, Max Fremery and Johann Urban, used the cuprammonium process, in which scale gave less impressive cost advantages. That process also resulted in a product of more limited use than that made by the viscose process. Nevertheless, once the plant was built, the sales force organized, and the management recruited, profits came quickly, rising from M 65,000 ($15,480) in the first year, 1900, to M 1.7 million ($422,000) in 1904 and moving on up in the following years. The increasing profits financed VGF's continuing growth. After setting up two smaller plants in Alsace, it established manufacturing units at Givet in France (1903), St. Pölten in Austria (1906), and Flint in Wales (1908).

In 1911 VGF made the most significant strategic move in its history. It purchased the pioneer German producer of rayon by the viscous process (the process developed in Britain by Courtaulds), a firm headed by Count Guido Henckel von Donnersmarck that had failed to make the investments necessary to become a first mover. VGF immediately scaled up its viscous output.[32] At the same time it began to obtain a financial interest in the other large German rayon-producing firm, J. P. Bemberg, a prominent cloth dyer and finisher which had experimented not too successfully with a variation of the cuprammonium process. After 1911 VGF became almost wholly a producer of viscous rayon. As it increased its holdings in Bemberg, it influenced that firm to concentrate on the production of yarns better suited to the older cuprammonium process. (By the 1920s VGF had full control of Bemberg.)[33]

In 1911, as it was taking full command of the rayon industry in Germany, VGF began to work out an agreement with Courtaulds and the rayon producers in other nations to control price, output, and use of patents. In April of that year, VGF, Courtaulds, the Comptoir des Textiles Artificiels in France, and the Belgian firm Tubize, together with the Italian, Swiss, and Spanish viscous companies, agreed in principle to form a consortium consisting of three groups— German, Anglo-Saxon, and Latin—with each group responsible for sales in its area. The members would share patents and technical innovations and would establish a central committee which was to fix prices, set production schedules, and pool and allocate profits.[34] But to delineate these principles in a written contract acceptable to all parties proved to be an exceedingly difficult task. As Donald Coleman reports, representatives of VGF "spent the next three years vainly trying to secure such a contract."[35] Patent and process agreements were made and statistical data were collected, but disagreements on specifics continued until World War I cut off negotiations. The experience demonstrated both the desire of European competitors to negotiate rather than to compete for market share and the difficulties involved in agreeing on the specific terms of such contractual relationships.

By the outbreak of war, VGF had become second to Courtaulds among the

European producers of the first man-made fiber. After the war the German firm, maintaining a tenuous alliance with Courtaulds, remained the most influential rayon maker on the Continent. Moreover, after the European invasion of the American rayon market, VGF became responsible for the third largest output in the United States, led only by Courtaulds and Du Pont, and it was soon taking market share from the British firm (see Chapter 8).

Alkalies and explosives. In synthetic alkalies and dynamite (in Group 28; see Appendixes C.1 and C.4) the German pattern was similar to that of Britain. In both countries local entrepreneurs exploited the innovations of two foreign inventors, Ernest Solvay and Alfred Nobel.

To make alkalies by the new Solvay method, Deutsche Solvay-Werke was established in 1885 in much the same way as Brunner, Mond was in Great Britain and Solvay Process was in the United States, with Solvay & Cie of Brussels taking stock in exchange for patents and financing. The German company's head, Karl Wessel, quickly built up a comparable integrated organization. Within a year of its founding, the firm had captured a third of the German market. It differed from its British counterpart in that it obtained control of the manufacturers using the older Leblanc process; and it differed from both its British and American associates by being technologically more innovative and by quickly becoming more diversified. In Britain, Brunner, Mond negotiated with the United Alkali Company, the combination of Leblanc producers that was created to try to ward off the impact of the new technology. In Germany, Wessel of Deutsche Solvay did more than negotiate; in 1891 he took over the Syndikat Deutsche Sodafabriken formed five years earlier by the existing producers to fight Solvay. Reorganized, that syndicate was renamed Deutsche Sodafabriken Karl Wessel and became the German industry's marketing organization, which Deutsche Solvay dominated.[36] Working closely with Ernest Solvay, Wessel improved the production process by applying electrolytic techniques, particularly those for making chlorine bleach. He did this before either the British or the American firm even became interested in the new cost-reducing process.[37] As was true of the other members of the international alliance of Solvay-process firms, Deutsche Solvay's markets outside of Germany were allocated in Brussels by the representatives of all those firms, including the British, American, Russian, and Austro-Hungarian, in consultation with the Solvays.

In the explosives industry, market allocation was more complex, for Alfred Nobel was far less systematic than Ernest Solvay in licensing the patents for his new products, or in attempting to oversee the activities of the licensed firms. In Germany (and in the United States) Nobel licensed more firms than he did in Great Britain.[38] In Germany the first and largest producer of dynamite, Dynamit AG, quickly dominated the trade. In 1884 it joined with three other firms (including the second largest, Rheinisch-Westfälische Sprengstoff AG) to set price and output. The next year they formed a tighter federation, the

German Union, which determined prices, allocated profits, and had a permanent policy board and a board of managers to coordinate activities. Then in 1886 the German Union joined Britain's Nobel Explosives, the oldest dynamite enterprise in Britain and by then the largest in Europe, to form the Nobel-Dynamite Trust Company (see Chapter 7). This unusual international consolidation pooled profits and coordinated activities within the home markets and negotiated for world markets with the leading American companies and with an association of French, Italian, and Spanish explosives makers on the Continent known as the Latin Group.[39]

The Trust Company also maintained formal and informal contacts with another group of four German firms that produced propellants used in weapons, as differentiated from explosives used in construction and mining. In the mid-1880s the largest and most powerful member of that group, Vereinigte Köln-Rottweiler Pulverfabriken, had acquired a controlling share of a major British producer, Chillworth Gunpowder Company, Ltd., and was developing close relations with Vickers, the integrated British arms maker, and with the leading German maker of firearms, Ludwig Loewe's Deutsche Waffen-und Munitions-Fabriken.[40]

In the German explosives industry, market share at home and abroad was determined more by negotiations than by functional and strategic competition. Such negotiations, which never came in rubber, succeeded far more quickly in explosives than in rayon. As in rubber, rayon, and synthetic alkalies the Gross-banken played no significant role in financing the first movers in this new industry.

Other materials. In glass and abrasives (in Group 32; see Appendixes C.1 and C.2) the Germans were less successful in exploiting the new technologies for volume production than they were in rubber, rayon, synthetic alkalies, and explosives. In both industries foreign first movers—American in abrasives and American, British, and French in glass—quickly established their marketing organizations in Germany. The failure of German entrepreneurs to create strong enterprises in glass and abrasives again emphasizes the powerful competitive advantages that accrued to distant first movers even when local entrepreneurs were fully aware of best-practice technological and organizational procedures. The leading glass company on the Continent was the ancient and impressively large French enterprise, St. Gobain. At the turn of the century it owned four of the seven factories in France and operated the only two plate-glass factories of importance in Germany. St. Gobain shared its economic power in international markets with Pilkington, which operated a plant in France from the 1890s on; with Pittsburgh Plate Glass, which had one in Courcelles in Belgium; and with Libbey-Owens, which came to operate several plants in Europe after World War I (see Chapters 4 and 7).[41] From 1904 until World War II the two European leaders, St. Gobain and Pilkington, dominated the meetings that set price and production schedules and allocated markets, while the American companies played a passive role.[42]

In abrasives, which were synthetically produced by electrochemical techniques, the German subsidiaries of the two American first movers—Norton and Carborundum—remained among the largest producers in Germany until World War II. Both sold through exclusive agents. In Norton's case the agent was Schuchardt & Schütte, machine-tool makers with branches throughout Germany, eastern Europe, and Scandinavia. Both Norton and Carborundum built factories in Germany before World War I.[43]

In other processing industries small German firms produced for the domestic market, but they rarely penetrated other European markets. Not one asbestos firm listed in the *Handbuch der deutschen Aktiengesellschaften* came close to the size of Johns Manville in the United States or Turner & Newall in Britain. Nor was there a gypsum producer similar in size to United States Gypsum. In Germany, as in Britain, there were fewer paper companies listed in Group 26 than in the United States. Information on which the appendixes are based indicates that as late as 1929 the two largest employed about the same number of workers as the fifth and sixth largest American paper firms. Like the cement and porcelain companies listed in Group 32 (Appendixes C.1 and C.2), they appear to have produced primarily for local markets.

FIRST MOVERS, AMERICAN STYLE: LIGHT, MASS-PRODUCED MACHINERY

In light, volume-produced machinery (Group 35; Appendixes C.1, C.2, and C.4), the few German first movers expanded and competed differently from the first movers in rubber, rayon, synthetic alkalies, and explosives. In these last industries, first movers appeared almost simultaneously in other European countries, usually one to a country. In the light-machinery industries those that made the investment in manufacturing, marketing, and management expanded globally, much as did American firms that used similar processes of production. As they dominated world markets (except in the United States) for their particular products, they, like their American counterparts, rarely relied on cartel agreements. In those light-machinery lines where the Americans were the global first movers, local German challengers were more successful in local markets than were their British counterparts in their domestic market. And when they were unable to compete in Germany with American first movers, they responded, as the British firms did not, by turning to lines of business in which the barriers to entry were less formidable.

Thus Ludwig Loewe, one of Germany's most successful machinery makers, began his career by building sewing machines. Indeed, Loewe was the pioneer in adopting the "American system of manufacturing" in Germany. He visited the United States in 1869 to learn about the new technology at first hand and then recruited American engineers to assist in building plants, overseeing operations, and establishing testing laboratories. Unable to challenge Singer's dominance in Germany effectively, Loewe soon turned to producing small arms by the same methods of fabricating and assembling interchangeable parts. Thus the sequence in Germany was the reverse of that in the United States, where mass-production methods began with rifles and pistols and were then adapted to sewing machines. Ludwig Loewe & Co. AG, Berlin, soon became one of Europe's leading military contractors. After its small-arms factory became the core of a separate enterprise of its own, called Deutsche Waffen-und Munitions-Fabriken, the other parts of Loewe & Co. concentrated on producing machine tools and, after the mid-1880s, on light electrical machinery and motors.[44] In 1894 the firm organized a separate venture to produce and distribute a typesetting machine which was based on American patents and made by American processes and which competed with Mergenthaler Linotype in European markets.[45]

Other German firms that attempted to challenge Singer in the German market also returned to producing other products. As in the United States the move from sewing machines was usually into bicycles and then automobiles. Adam Opel, which became Germany's largest automobile maker, is a well-known example. Others moved from sewing machines into industrial machinery and machine tools, a move that rarely occurred in the United States. But two pioneers, Pfaff and Dürkoppwerke, stayed with sewing machines. By adopting production techniques comparable to Singer's, by improving the product, by concentrating on a somewhat more specialized product (that is, on a market niche), and by setting up a less extensive and less costly marketing network than Singer's (one that relied on franchised dealers rather than company-owned retail outlets), they were able to achieve a market share that provided a volume large enough to bring its costs closer to those of Singer.[46]

In office machinery no opponent challenged the American first movers as effectively as Pfaff and Dürkoppwerke did in sewing machines. National Cash Register completely dominated its industry in Germany after forming a sales subsidiary there in 1896. It set up a marketing organization that had eight district offices by 1906, and in 1903 it built an assembly plant in Berlin. The company quickly acquired the reputation of using its economic power more ruthlessly than any other American firm in Germany. It took to Europe its notorious "knock-out method," one of patent suits and price cutting. Although the German courts consistently upheld local plaintiffs in patent suits and in cases of unfair trade practice, no German firm was able, even after a victory in the courts, to challenge National Cash Register in the marketplace on the basis of price, service, and reliability. National Cash Register continued to dominate the German market. Thus its major rival, Schubert & Salzer, a maker of bicycles that had moved into cash registers and calculators, soon began to concentrate on machine tools and textile machinery.[47] In adding machines and calculating machines the American leaders—Burroughs Adding Machine, the Computing-Tabulating-Recording Company, and the Hollerith Tabulating Machine Company (the last two joined with a third enterprise in 1911 to form International Business Machines) continued to overpower German competitors even though they did not build factories in Germany to supply their marketing organizations. This was also the case with the two typewriter companies, Remington and Underwood. They were able to fend off challenges from Wanderer-Werke, Adlerwerke, and other German makers of typewriters by relying on their own German sales and service networks. Wanderer-Werke continued to produce typewriters but concentrated more on its other products—machine tools, bicycles, and automobiles. Adlerwerke dropped its typewriter line altogether, concentrating production on bicycles and then almost wholly on automobiles.[48]

In agricultural equipment the German response was closer to that in sewing machines. In 1900, as the demand in Germany for such machinery began to become substantial for the first time, McCormick Harvesting Machine established its own sales organization within the empire, with branches in Breslau, Hamburg, Königsberg, Mannheim, Munich, and Neuss. This organization became the base for the European business of International Harvester after that company was formed by merger in 1902. By 1910 the growing demand encouraged International Harvester to build a works in Germany with an annual capacity of 250,000 machines.

As in sewing machines, the most successful farm-equipment challenger, Heinrich Lanz AG, obtained and maintained market share by effective functional competition. The founder of that enterprise, Heinrich Lanz, visited the United States in 1902 to study production processes and distribution methods. He concentrated first on stationary, steam-powered, threshing machines and next on "movable" threshers; then, with the introduction of gasoline engines, Lanz became the pioneer tractor builder in Europe, developing the well-received Bulldog model. By World War I the firm had sales branches throughout Germany and in Russia, France, Britain, and southern and eastern Europe.[49] By contrast, the Hannoversche Maschinenbau, which produced agricultural machinery but also made a variety of industrial machinery, never became, in the German or the larger European market, a significant competitor to International Harvester or Lanz, or, for that matter, to smaller companies such as the American firm Walter A. Wood and the Canadian firm Massey Harris.

In volume-produced, standardized, *industrial* machinery, the first-mover advantages were most obvious for those firms that concentrated on a single line of products requiring highly specialized marketing services. Thus Otis Elevator remained unchallenged in Europe except for the Swiss firm of Schindler. United Shoe Machinery's almost complete dominance in Europe resulted from its high-quality machines and its guaranteed servicing of those machines. By licensing on a time basis rather than selling machines, it lowered the pay-out required of its customers. In licensing it was careful not to give discounts; large shoemakers were charged the same rates as small ones. Westinghouse Air Brake shared the German market with a German company, Knorr-Bremse, but largely because that firm convinced the Association of German Railway Administrations to use a domestic supplier. With this assured market Knorr-Bremse expanded it sales of air brakes throughout Europe. Chicago Pneumatic Tool came to share its market with a small German firm, Frankfurter Maschinenbau AG, and with Deutsche Niles-Werkzeugmaschinen-Fabrik AG, a joint venture between the Niles Tool Company of Hamilton, Ohio, and several German partners (more will be said about them shortly).

Two other American makers of standardized industrial machinery, American Radiator and International Steam Pump (which became Worthington Pump), were not so dominant in German and European markets as other American makers of volume-produced machinery. They were, however, powerful players in these markets. Well before 1914 each was operating large plants not only in Germany but in Britain, France, and Austria. American Radiator was the only one of all these producers of standardized light machinery to negotiate agreements with its competitors, and those agreements were only for the German market. It is, at least, the only company for which there is clear evidence of such agreements. For the rest of the American leaders, their competitive advantage was such that they had little need to negotiate for market shares with German or other European firms in European markets.[50]

Although the Americans ruled most of the standardized light-machinery industries, German entrepreneurs did become first movers in a small number of others. Like the Americans who built plants large enough to exploit fully the economies of scale, who created extensive sales and distributing networks and recruited the necessary management, they quickly became global in their operations. The storage-battery maker Accumulatoren-Fabrik (AFA) is a good example of such a first mover (see Chapter 10). So are the enterprises started by Nicolaus August Otto, Robert Bosch, and Carl von Linde. The first two of these innovators, Otto and Bosch, pioneered in the development of the internal combustion engine.

In 1868 Otto, with Eugen Langen, founded Gasmotorenfabrik Deutz to produce in volume, in their Cologne factory, a small, stationary, gasoline engine. In 1876 Otto perfected the prototype of today's internal combustion engine and then expanded his works to produce it. Even before that date the two partners had begun to build a global sales force. Production facilities quickly followed the sales force abroad. Assembly plants were constructed in Vienna in 1872, Philadelphia in 1875, Paris in 1878, and Milan in 1888. By 1913 the company had sixteen sales offices in fourteen countries, and 51% of its income resulted from overseas sales.[51]

In 1902 Robert Bosch perfected a magneto that almost immediately became the standard ignition system essential for internal combustion engines that were to furnish the power for moving vehicles—motorcycles, automobiles, tractors, boats. His firm, Robert Bosch AG, established in 1889, grew with the automobile industry, employing 45 workers in 1901, more than 500 in 1905, and more than 4,000 in 1914. He opened sales offices throughout Europe and then in the United States. This investment in marketing was followed by the building of an assembly works in Britain, a fabricating and assembly works in France, an assembly plant in New York in 1906, and then a larger fabricating and assembly works in Springfield, Massachusetts, in 1909. In the United States the company had branch sales offices in Chicago, San Francisco, and Detroit, and agencies and supply depots in more than a hundred other American cities.[52]

The enterprise created by Carl von Linde, a pioneer in the development of modern, mechanical, refrigerating machinery in the 1880s and liquid oxygen in the mid-1890s, grew in a somewhat different fashion from those of Otto and Bosch. Linde's Eismaschinen AG, established in 1887 to produce an innovative cooling compressor for German brewers, was soon manufacturing cooling equipment for other industries and in other countries. In Germany and in southern and eastern Europe the firm sold refrigeration machinery through exclusive agents. The company precisely defined the territories within which the selling agents operated, and it remained responsible for the delivery, installation, and starting up of the equipment.[53] On the other hand, in France, Britain, and the United States, Linde licensed his patents, but in neither France nor Britain did the licensee effectively develop the product. In Britain, therefore, the Linde company came to rely on a joint venture formed in 1885 with a British firm, the venture that became the British Refrigeration Company. In France, it bought back the patent and turned the French market over to its sales organization. Only in the United States did the licensee, Frederick Wolf of Chicago, develop an enterprise to produce and distribute this new product effectively.[54]

When Linde's inventive mind perfected a new process for the volume production of liquid oxygen in 1895, his company carried out a somewhat different policy of expansion. Partly because of the failure of his early licensing ventures and partly because an oxygen process developed by George Claude had brought a strong competitor into the field, Linde decided to set up foreign subsidiaries in much the same way as Ernest Solvay had done earlier. Instead of selling licenses, his firm received substantial blocks of stock in new enterprises in return for a license and often the provision of financial assistance. Through this control Linde defined specific market areas for the subsidiaries. Such "daughter companies" were quickly set up in Austria, Hungary, Norway, Sweden, Denmark, Switzerland, Great Britain, and the United States. The American company, Linde Air Products, later became part of Union Carbide. The British company, British Oxygen, remained for many decades that country's leading producer of liquid oxygen. Like Solvay, the Linde company made no attempt to administer its foreign affiliates. It did its best, however, to make sure that they stayed out of each other's national markets.[55]

The experience of the volume producers and distributors of light machinery in Germany further documents the cost advantages of economies of scale in these industries. The first mover in each industry, whether German or American, continued to be the leader abroad as well as at home. One difference was that American first movers were more dominant in European markets than German first movers were in the United States. The experience of the German light-machinery makers also emphasizes that the best way to become a challenger was to find a niche and then to make the investment and build the organizational capabilities needed to compete functionally and strategically, as Pfaff, Dürkoppwerke, and Lanz did.

Finally, the experience of German producers demonstrates the difficulty of attempting to exploit, in these mass-production industries, the economies of both scale and scope at the same time. If they continued to produce several lines in expectation of exploiting the economies of scope, they were unable to achieve production economies to match those of competitors that concentrated on a single product. At the same time, they were unable to afford the building of separate sales forces to provide specialized marketing services—demonstration of the product, after-sales maintenance, and consumer credit—for quite different products. Instead, they had to continue to rely on intermediaries to market their goods. Thus by World War I nearly all the German machinery makers that first exploited the economies of scope, except for Wanderer-Werke, had come to concentrate on a single product line, as Schubert & Salzer had in textile machinery and Adlerwerke and Adam Opel had in automobiles.[56] (For the development of the German automobile industry after World War I, see Chapter 13.)

The reverse was also true. Enterprises that were experienced in exploiting scale economies were unable to capture market share in industries where the cost advantages of production lay in scope. The experience of Deutsche Niles-Werkzeugmaschinen-Fabrik AG documents this point. The purpose of that venture, set up in 1898 by Ludwig Loewe, the electrical giant AEG, and four banks, including three Grossbanken, was to create a competitor to the leading German producer of light machine tools, Ernst Schiess Werkzeugmaschinenfabrik AG, by introducing American production equipment and methods. In this joint venture the Niles Tool Company of Ohio contributed no funds; instead it received M 500,000 worth of stock for providing machine designs and know-how. But Schiess, a well-established producer of engines, pumps, and regulators, as well as of machine tools for grinding, polishing, and stamping, had developed powerful organizational capabilities in production, marketing, and product design. So the Deutsche Niles challenge was almost a total failure. Only after the new venture completely shifted its strategy and began to concentrate on the volume production of a single product—air compressors—did it begin to show a profit.[57]

In the German light-machinery industries neither banks nor cartels played a significant role. The banks hesitated to support the challengers against powerful American competitors, and the American competitors saw little need to negotiate for market share with their rivals. And those German entrepreneurs that did become first movers did not need to go beyond personal and local sources of capital before retained earnings gave them funds for continuing growth. The first-mover advantages they achieved globally meant that they had few rivals with whom to negotiate, except in the United States where such negotiations were illegal.

The German Entrepreneurial Response in the Lesser Industries

In several of what I have termed the "lesser" of the new, capital-intensive German industries, the modern industrial enterprise developed in much the same way as it did in Britain. One first mover quickly came to dominate the domestic industry and to represent the nation in the global oligopoly. In rubber, Continental, like Dunlop in Britain, was the first firm to make an investment large enough to exploit the economies of scale and also the first to build an international marketing network and recruit the essential management hierarchy. In rayon, VGF was the counterpart to Courtaulds; and it would come to have control over its smaller competitor, J. P. Bemberg, as Courtaulds never had over British Celanese. So, too, Karl Wessel's Deutsche Solvay acquired more direct control over the alkali producers using the older Leblanc process than did Brunner, Mond. Bosch was a more successful international competitor in ignition systems than its British counterpart, J. Lucas, Ltd. In certain other volume-produced machinery—notably gasoline engines, refrigerating equipment, and electric storage batteries—the Germans never had serious British competition, just as Pilkington and St. Gobain, first movers in their industry, had little competition from German glassmakers. And German entrepreneurs in paper, abrasives, and asbestos made no real attempt to challenge foreign first movers in international markets, although a few of them were able to compete profitably in local markets.

In other industries, however, German entrepreneurs did challenge foreign first movers. In sewing and agricultural machinery, the newcomers Pfaff and Lanz acquired niches and continued to grow by improving product, process, and marketing, which permitted them to increase market share at home and to begin to move abroad. In soap, Henkel, by developing a new product based on a new process, was successful in challenging Lever and Schicht; but before World War I the company concentrated its marketing in Germany and southern and eastern Europe. In oil the challenge to Standard Oil and Royal Dutch–Shell came primarily through the entrepreneurial activities of the two leading German Grossbanken, which made the necessary investment in production and marketing and which, at the outbreak of World War I, were recruiting the essential managerial organizations in the integrated oil companies they sponsored.

Before World War I the two distinctive characteristics of German industrial development, the involvement of the Grossbanken and the legalized cooperation between competing enterprises, had relatively little impact on the evolution of the leading firms in these lesser industries. Only in oil did banks play a critical entrepreneurial role. In rubber, rayon, synthetic alkalies, soap, and volume-produced machinery the initial financing came from local sources, and growth was financed in large part through retained earnings. Again, except for oil, interfirm agreements as to price, production, and marketing territories were relatively rare. The dominant firm had little to gain at home from such agreements and found them difficult to set up and maintain abroad. In oil the challengers, after failing to increase their market share substantially, made agreements that permitted Standard Oil to keep the lion's share of European markets. On the other hand, in Germany's great industries the Grossbanken and the cartels and other forms of interfirm cooperation played a far more significant role than they did in the industries described in this chapter.

Textiles: A Labor-Intensive Industry

The textile industry (Group 22; Appendixes C.1 and C.2) was the only labor-intensive industry in which more than two or three firms appeared among the top two hundred industrial enterprises in Germany during the twentieth century. As in the case of Britain and the United States, the textile story is a counterpoise to the histories of the more capital-intensive industries that are the focus of this study. In Germany, as in Britain, the textile industry was the largest manufacturing industry in terms of employment, although its share of Germany's total employment fell from 18% in 1875 to 10.3% in the period 1911–1913.[58] In the years before World War I the industry was structured more like Britain's than like that of the United States. Compared with America, it remained more fragmented, and there was much less integration of spinning and weaving within the same mill. The nonintegrated mills did get larger, however, and their total number dropped: in the case of wool spinning, from 5,181 in 1882 to 1,193 in 1907; and in wool weaving, from 26,026 to 17,566 during the same years.[59] While the German textile industry had less integration of spinning and weaving within a single mill than was the case in the United States, it had much more organizational cooperation and coordination than was the case in Britain. For example, there were many more horizontal local and regional cartels in spinning and weaving in Germany than in Britain, where industry-wide horizontal combinations came primarily in the finishing industries—in bleaching, dyeing, and printing. In 1905 there were almost as many interfirm agreements in textiles (thirty-one) as in chemicals (thirty-two).[60] Although these contractual arrangements tended to be short-lived, they appear to have encouraged vertical integration, much as similar arrangements did in the steel industry (see Chapter 12). To avoid the cartel restrictions on price and output in one stage of production, producers took control of other firms in other stages. For example, in 1907 more than half of the wool-spinning mills (618 out of a total of 1,193) were "affiliated with clothing or other wool weaving mills."[61] Such cooperative vertical association remained rare in Britain, where most enterprises carried out a single process, as well as in the United States, where all processes were usually combined in a single mill.

In Germany a small number of the largest textile manufacturers did integrate forward into marketing. By investing in best-practice production, these integrated firms developed competitive advantages that permitted them to expand abroad successfully. Thus the large, integrated, worsted producer Stöhr & Company of Leipzig, like the British firms J. & P. Coats and English Sewing Cotton, was highly successful in the American market. After establishing a selling agency in New York in 1886, Stöhr formed the Botany Worsted Mills, which built a mill in Passaic, New Jersey, in 1890 to produce worsted yarn. The next year it completed a weaving, dyeing, and finishing plant. Further expansion came in 1903. Botany soon had sales offices in Philadelphia, Chicago, Cleveland, Boston, Detroit, St. Louis, Minneapolis, and Los Angeles. By 1917, when it was acquired by American nationals, Botany was the third largest textile company in the United States in terms of assets (English Sewing Cotton's subsidiary was the second). Botany's success attracted similar investments by four other German woolen producers—investments that helped to make Passaic the American center for the production of fine worsted yarn and high-quality woolens for men's and women's clothing.[62] Because the cost advantages of scale were relatively small and because marketing organizations provided only a small competitive advantage, these processors of natural fibers never dominated their industries at home or abroad as the makers of man-made fibers or light machinery did. Neither Botany nor English Sewing Cotton's subsidiary (American Thread) was on the list of the two hundred largest American firms in 1930 or 1948.

The natural-fibers industry in Germany never became concentrated, any more than it did in Britain and the United States. Companies such as Stöhr, J. & P. Coats, and J. P. Stevens did not have as powerful cost or marketing advantages as the firms in other industries where the modern industrial enterprise clustered. Because cartelization was legal in Germany, however, there was more vertical integration there than in Britain, and there was more horizontal combination than in the United States. The Grossbanken appear to have played a limited role in this industry, where capital requirements for individual establishments were relatively low and therefore relatively easy to satisfy locally.[63] Although the story of textiles has parallels in other less technologically complex, labor-intensive industries, including apparel, leather, lumber, and furniture, both the evolution of the individual firms and the structure of the labor-intensive industries as a whole differed from the experience of the lesser industries reviewed in this chapter, as well as from that of the great industries to be discussed in the next chapter.

TWELVE

Creating Organizational Capabilities: The Great Industries

From the beginning the modern industrial enterprise has clustered in Germany's three major sets of industries—heavy industrial machinery (including electrical and transportation equipment), chemicals, and metals. During the first half of the twentieth century, between 55% and 65% of the two hundred largest companies manufactured these lines.[1] These industries, in which Germans were the European first movers, accounted more than any others for the great burst of German exports in the decade and a half before World War I. They were also the industries in which the Germans recovered most quickly after the war, regaining a significant share of their prewar market position. In metal processing the dynamic for growth came from exploiting the cost advantages of scale, as it did in these same industries in other countries and in the lesser industries in Germany. By contrast, in industrial machinery and chemicals the dynamic came much more from the cost advantages of scope. In fact, in any country these two industries provide the most impressive early examples of economies of scope.

Nonelectrical Machinery: Exploiting Economies of Scope

In the production of nonelectrical heavy machinery, the machinery that processed, shaped, and finished the new products of the Second Industrial Revolution (Groups 35 and 37; see Appendixes C.1–C.4), gained a unique position. Their large plants, using the same materials and the same forges and foundries, turned out processing equipment for all sorts of manufacturing industries. These included textiles, food, lumber, leather, printing and publishing, steel, copper, fabricated metals, glass, paper, and chemicals. They also produced mining machinery, locomotives, rolling stock, and other equipment for railroads, including their terminals and stations, as well as machinery for shipbuilding and for use in harbors and docks. The international sales forces of these German heavy-machinery makers provided even more extensive marketing services than did those of the American and German light-machinery producers. They spent more time with industrial customers in designing products to meet their specific needs. They worked out arrangements to extend extensive credit and to provide elaborate repair and service guarantees. The German machinery makers recruited extensive managerial hierarchies to supervise and integrate their processes of production and distribution, hierarchies that were probably even larger than those of the American machinery companies. Indeed, almost no American or British producer of heavy machinery could match these German enterprises in size, systematic layout of works, and number of lines produced. One reason may have been that in both the United States and Britain industrial enterprises often preferred just to design their processing equipment and then to have it produced in relatively small, specialized, job shops.

The German heavy-machinery enterprises grew in a more evolutionary manner than did many of the American producers of light machinery. Nearly all that are listed in Group 35 (Appendixes C.1–C.3) began as small machine shops and expanded to satisfy the demands of railroads, mining companies, shipbuilders, and iron producers. Then in the 1880s and 1890s they expanded further to meet the needs for machinery and equipment in the thriving steel, chemical, and other new industries. Most of those that did not expand in this way failed to grow. They remained personally managed enterprises producing one or two specialized lines. By the 1920s they were no longer among Germany's top two hundred firms (see Appendixes C.1 and C.2). Therefore, I review here only the stories of those that continued to grow by exploiting the economies of scope. (The histories of the much smaller number that grew by exploiting those of scale have been told in Chapter 11.)

The experience of Maschinenbau-Anstalt Humboldt, established in the 1850s in Cologne to provide equipment to a leading mining firm, is representative. As Humboldt broadened its line of mining and quarrying equipment, it began to build other materials-handling machinery. Next, Humboldt met the demand for air-moving and cooling machinery in the mines—machinery which it was soon selling also to brewers and slaughterhouses.[2] In 1895, to make use of underutilized production facilities, it began to construct locomotives and railroad cars and other transportation equipment. By World War I its Cologne works had grown to a great size and included eight divisions—four concentrating on intermediate parts and carrying out intermediate processes and the other four concentrating on finished goods. The facilities used in the intermediate processes—foundries and forges, sheet-making and other fabricating equipment, dies, presses, milling and perforating equipment, and coating processes—were located in Divisions II, III, and VI, and XI of the works (see Figure 12). Division I turned out locomotives, Division VII passenger and freight cars and other

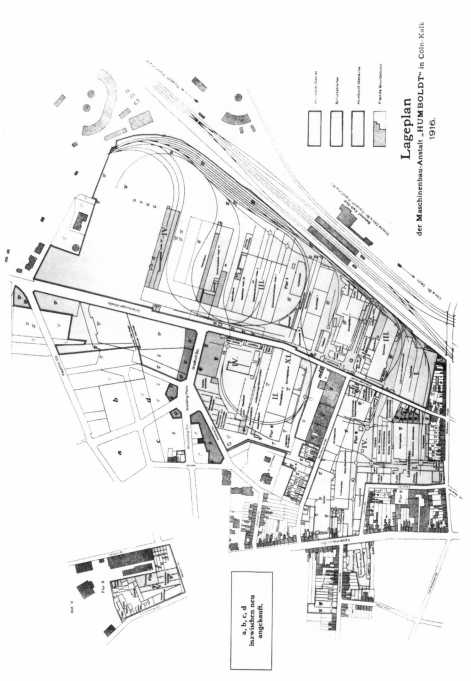

Figure 12. The Cologne factory of Maschinenbau-Anstalt Humboldt, 1916. From *Führer durch die Maschinenbau-Anstalt Humboldt: 60 Jahre technischer Entwicklung, 1856–1916* (n.p., 1919).

transportation equipment, and Divisions IV and V a variety of large and small industrial machines, including brewing and refrigeration machinery, mining and materials-handling equipment, and after 1914 military supplies.[3] Humboldt, like the storage-battery firm AFA, had an impressive sales organization, manned by trained engineers, with branches in Vienna, Budapest, Paris, and London, and a network of exclusive agents covering the rest of the world. Well before the turn of the century it had its technical division to design machinery and its testing laboratories. But because of the wide variety of products made to meet specific customer needs, it had a much smaller investment in research and development than did the leading producers of electrical equipment, whose products were both more standardized and more complex technologically.[4] As emphasized in Humboldt's own history, published in 1919, the company's continuing strategy of diversification not only reduced the costs of individual products but also spread the risk over many markets.[5]

The methods of production, distribution, and growth in the other leading German industrial-machinery firms were variations on those of Humboldt. A number began by building locomotives for railroads in the several still independent states that were soon to be unified as the German Empire. By contrast, in Britain major railroads built their own locomotives; and in the United States locomotives were made by a small number of large companies for the much greater national market. In 1869 Borsig, a pioneer locomotive producer, delivered one of the first two Siemens-Martin open-hearth works constructed in Germany. In the next two decades the firm began to make stationary steam engines, boilers, and other equipment used in steel mills; pumps and pipelines for the growing oil industry; equipment for the expanding chemical factories; and turbines, compressors, and cooling machinery for other industries. Even so, locomotives remained Borsig's primary product.[6] By contrast, Hannoversche Maschinenbau AG (Hanomag), which also began as a locomotive maker and was soon producing steam engines, pumping and heating equipment, and (less successfully) plows and other agricultural machinery, had only 19% of its business in locomotives by 1900.[7] Berliner Maschinenbau AG, vorm. L. Schwartzkopff (BEMAG) also started as a locomotive maker. It then began to specialize in the production of mines and torpedoes for naval warfare (constructing a branch plant in Venice), but it also continued to build locomotives, compressors, and other machinery. In its search for new products BEMAG developed close ties with large American companies. In 1897 it became the manufacturer of the Mergenthaler Linotype Company's typesetting machines for the European continent. Its output was sold through a joint venture with the American company, called Mergenthaler Setzmaschinen-Fabrik GmbH. BEMAG made much the same arrangement in 1908 with the Owens Bottle Machine Company, and later with an American vacuum-cleaner producer. Still another locomotive maker, Gebrüder Körting AG, produced marine engines, pumps, and brakes and became Germany's leading maker of central-heating equipment.[8]

Other heavy-machinery firms diversified in somewhat the same manner. One example is Maschinenfabrik-Augsburg-Nürnberg (MAN), a merger in 1898 of two Bavarian companies, one having a single works and the other having two. Although it never became a major locomotive maker, MAN produced railway cars, other transportation equipment, and engines powered by steam, gasoline, and then diesel oil. By World War I it had exploited the economies of scope in its three works by manufacturing an extraordinary variety of machines for the mining, metal, metal-processing, metal-fabricating, chemical, food, textile, lumber, and printing-press industries, and also for utilities. Nearly all of the machines produced by MAN in the late 1920s—one exception being the diesel engine—had been developed before World War I (see Table 22).[9] An even larger enterprise was Gutehoffnungshütte (GHH), which had been founded in the mid-eighteenth century by the Haniel family. Before 1900 it was producing iron and steel at Oberhausen; steam engines (including marine engines), boilers, bridges, and other structures near Sterkrade; and boats for the inland waterways at Walsum. By World War I the steel output produced in its own works to supply its machinery-making units made it the eighth largest producer of primary steel in Germany.[10]

Still other leading machinery makers were only a little less diversified. Deutsche Maschinenfabrik (DEMAG), a 1910 merger of three works in the Duisburg area, concentrated on machinery for blast furnaces and steel works, foundries, rolling mills, shipyards, harbors, and docks.[11] Stettiner Chamotte-fabrik AG produced furnaces and ovens for the iron and steel industry and then for the ceramic, glass, and chemical trades, as well as a wide variety of furnaces for specialized tasks.[12] Berlin-Anhaltische Maschinenbau (BAMAG), a consol-idation of two Berlin works in 1872, increasingly specialized in the production of pumps and compressors used in gas, water, and sewerage works. In 1909 BAMAG acquired a Cologne firm that made machinery for processing steel, oil, and sugar.[13] Still another firm, Maschinenfabrik Buckau R. Wolf, a merger of two neighboring works in Magdeburg, made steam and diesel engines for the mining, chemical, and construction industries, as well as setting up complete (turnkey) factories that produced briquettes, limestone, and sugar.[14] Säch-sische Maschinen-Fabrik vorm. Rich. Hartmann, while developing a broad line that included locomotives, steam engines, and pumps, continued to concentrate on textile machinery, which had been its initial product when it was established in the late 1830s.[15]

The German producers of railway equipment and ships were more diversified than their American or British counterparts. Only a very few—such as the Breslau firm of Linke-Hofmann, and Henschel, and possibly one or two other firms—continued to concentrate on their original lines.[16] Orenstein & Koppel,

Table 22.   Product line of the Maschinenfabrik Augsburg-Nürnberg (MAN) in the late
1920s.

Industries served
  Coal and metal mining industries
  Metal smelting and refining industries
  Metal fabricating industries
  Machinery-building industries
  Shipbuilding industry
  Ground, water, and air transportation industries
  Electric, gas, and water power-generating stations
  Public utilities and services
  Chemical industry
  Agriculture and food industries
  Textile and apparel industries
  Stone, clay, and glass industries
  Lumber industry
  Printing industry

Major products
  Power-generating equipment
    Diesel motors, large gas machinery, steam turbines, steam machinery, steam
    boilers, steam storage equipment, steam-pressure control equipment, steam
    transformers, waste heat exhaust equipment
  Transportation equipment
    Cranes, tip-trucks, turntables, moving stages, railroad cars, trucks, buses
  Steel structures
    Bridges, steel superstructures, gas tanks, other storage facilities, chalybeate
    water facilities
  Pressing machinery
    Mechanical presses, rotary presses, auxiliary machines
  Other equipment
    Testing equipment, hydraulic presses, vacuum equipment, heating and drying
    equipment, brewery facilities

Source: Compiled from *Werden und Wirken der MAN* (n.p., 1931), pp. 14–64.

the world's largest producer of light locomotives and narrow-gauge railways
and equipment, had created in the 1880s and 1890s an impressive multinational
enterprise which by World War I operated twelve factories—six in Germany
and six abroad (in Vienna, Prague, Budapest, St. Petersburg, one near Brussels, and a large one in Pittsburgh, established in 1893)—and ninety-five branch
offices covering Europe and most of the rest of the world.[17] Its growth pattern
was closer to that of the American light-machinery makers and of Deutz and
Bosch. For the German shipbuilders, growth came more from the incentives
provided by scope than from those provided by scale. The major German

firms—Vulcan at Stettin and Bremen, Blohm & Voss at Hamburg, Weser at Bremen, and Howaldt at Kiel—were as much producers of fabricated metal shapes, engines, boilers, and even locomotives, as of ships. The Vulcan works at Stettin, for example, built two thousand locomotives between 1859 and 1902.[18]

These heavy-machinery firms grew primarily through internal investment, although there were several mergers of two or, occasionally, three works. Those mergers rarely increased market share for a single product line and rarely resulted in further economies of scale. Their purpose, rather, was to add related product lines in order to exploit the economies of scope. These enterprises, however, were organized by function rather than by product. Their production departments helped to integrate the activities of the two or three large works. Their sales departments supervised a global marketing network. They usually had their own branches in Europe and relied on exclusive agents elsewhere. Their technical and design departments had subdivisions for the different major product lines.

These machinery makers were large. By World War I, MAN employed more than 15,000 men, as did Orenstein & Koppel. In 1912 the Vulcan works at Stettin had over 13,000 workers. Most of these enterprises, however, employed 3,500 to 5,000—large works for that day. Buckau Wolf in its single large works had 3,340 workers and 537 *Beamte* (the term used for managers and white-collar staff) in 1911. In 1912 Sächsische Maschinen-Fabrik vorm. Rich. Hartmann employed 5,000 workers (blue-collar) and 500 Beamte, and DEMAG had 4,000 workers.[19]

A few heavy-machinery firms of that size existed in the United States and Britain, but almost none had the same diversity of product line. In Britain the great armament firms (Vickers and Armstrong-Whitworth), and the largest shipbuilding and railroad-equipment firms, employed more workers than the German heavy-machinery firms; but in the production of industrial machines (products which placed these firms in Groups 35 and 36) only three British firms employed as many as 4,000 workers in 1907. These were Guest, Keen & Nettlefolds (a federation of smaller firms), with 12,500, and the two leading makers of textile machinery—Platt Brothers with 10,800, and Mather & Platt with 4,000. Little information is available on the size of the work force of such firms in the United States for the period before World War I, but even as late as 1930 only three of the nonelectrical-machinery, shipbuilding, and railroad-equipment firms (most of which continued to concentrate on a single line of products) had more than 8,500 employees. Most ran between 4,500 and 5,000. Only Allis-Chalmers, which had ties to Germany, was as diversified as its German counterparts. The rationalization following the merger that created Allis-Chalmers, which was financed by the Deutsche Bank, concentrated nearly all of the company's activities in a single large works in Milwaukee in order to exploit the economies of scope (see Chapter 6).

In German heavy machinery, agreements as to price, output, and specification were difficult to draw and to enforce because the products were rarely standardized but instead were usually designed to meet customer needs (locomotives and textile machinery were the most standardized). Therefore, although there were a few cartels (the cartel for railroad locomotives in 1909 is a well-known example), there was far less interfirm contractual cooperation in heavy, nonelectrical machinery than in the German chemical and metal industries.

Because expansion was by internal investment, which rarely called for sums like those required in the electrical-equipment, chemical, and metal-making industries, founders' families often continued to dominate their Supervisory Boards. Thus Borsig remained a family partnership until 1930. But if a company ran into financial difficulties, as Humboldt did in the 1880s, bankers quickly appeared on the Supervisory Board. By World War I, Humboldt's board included representatives of four of the six leading Grossbanken and had as its chairman the steel magnate Peter Klöckner. After the war the firm became part of the Klöckner group of companies.[20]

Electrical Machinery: Exploiting Economies of Scale and Scope

In the electrical-equipment industry (Group 36; see Appendixes C.1–C.4), the two giants—Siemens and Allgemeine Elektricitäts-Gesellschaft (AEG)—resembled in many ways the producers of heavy industrial machinery in Group 35. They concentrated production in massive works and had large global sales organizations, containing highly skilled engineers, to sell and service their products. Indeed, their sales organizations were even larger than those of the nonelectrical firms. Also, because of the technical complexity and newness of their products and processes, they made a much greater investment in industrial research. Their histories, particularly that of Siemens, provide striking examples of the exploitation of the economies of both scale and scope.

The smaller German electrical firms that successfully exploited the economies of scale remained among the top two hundred. Nearly all were single-line, volume producers, like Accumulatoren-Fabrik AG or AFA (see Chapter 10), although Felten & Guilleaume (listed in Group 33, primary metals) concentrated on cables used for both telecommunications and electric power and light. Voigt & Haeffner manufactured electrical switches in volume at its expanding plant in Frankfurt. Mix & Genest were makers of specialized telephone equipment for use in private homes, offices, factories, mines, banks, hospitals, and hotels. Polyphon Musikwerke, which before World War I had difficulty in competing with Deutsche Grammophon, the subsidiary of the British-financed and American-managed Gramophone Company (see Chapter 9), concentrated on phonographs and records. Only S. Bergmann-Elektricitäts-Werke, established by a close associate of Thomas A. Edison who had returned to Germany to produce insulating and wiring conduits, expanded its activities into the production and sale of other electrical equipment. None were able to develop the capabilities to expand widely abroad in the manner of AFA.[21]

SIEMENS AND AEG: CREATING INDUSTRIAL GIANTS

The histories of the two first movers, particularly that of Siemens, are told here in more detail than those of the other machinery companies. This is partly because Siemens and AEG, along with General Electric and Westinghouse of the United States, continued for decades to dominate one of the world's most significant industries during the whole period from the 1880s to the 1940s. It is also because their experience illustrates both the important similarities and the striking differences between Germany and the United States in the evolution of the modern industrial enterprise.

Siemens was the oldest of the global industry's "Big Four." Werner Siemens pioneered in the development of telegraph and cable equipment (a task carried out in the United States by Western Electric, the manufacturing arm, first of Western Union and then of AT&T). In the 1850s and 1860s his company, Siemens & Halske (S&H), established a multinational enterprise with its manufacturing works concentrated in the Markgrafenstrasse area of Berlin. Werner's brothers built works at St. Petersburg in Russia and at Woolwich in Britain and then managed the British branch as an autonomous enterprise, Siemens Brothers, and the Russian branch as an affiliate of S&H. In 1879 Werner's company, S&H, opened a factory in Vienna. During the 1880s the firm's innovative work in the development of equipment for the generation, transmission, and use of electric power and light was comparable to that done by Edison, Westinghouse, Joseph Swan, and other American and British inventors. S&H quickly made extensive investments in plants and facilities to manufacture these products.[22] To market the new machines and equipment as well as the larger, integrated electrical systems, the company initially recruited a network of exclusive agents, each covering a carefully specified area and working according to precisely defined contractual relations.[23]

AEG had its beginning in March 1883 when Emil Rathenau formed the Deutsche Edison-Gesellschaft to use Edison's patents and know-how to build central power and lighting stations in Berlin like those of Edison in New York City. Rathenau immediately signed an agreement with S&H by which Siemens provided all the equipment that was needed for these installations except light bulbs—a product fully covered by an Edison patent.[24]

Because of the difficulties of enforcing the Edison patents, four years later Rathenau was able to abrogate his earlier arrangements with Edison and to modify those with Siemens. With a massive infusion of capital raised by the Deutsche Bank and several smaller banks, Rathenau quickly transformed Deutsche Edison into Allgemeine Elektricitäts-Gesellschaft, an enterprise that manufactured as well as installed and operated electric power systems. By the early 1890s AEG had made, as had Siemens, the investment necessary to assure the powerful cost advantages of large-scale production of "heavy current" (high-voltage) products, but not, as Siemens had, those of the production of "light current" (low-voltage) communication equipment. In the following years AEG built and operated far more local power and traction systems in Germany, and then throughout the world, than did Siemens.

Rathenau quickly set up an international sales and service network which by 1900 included forty-two "bureaux" (offices) in Germany, thirty-seven in other European countries, and thirty-eight overseas.[25] Siemens, which was becoming painfully aware of the inadequacy of using commercial intermediaries to handle complicated transactions and to install and maintain complex machinery, followed suit. By 1903 Siemens had twenty-two technical offices in Germany and eight abroad. Each had "a commercial head alongside the technical managers" and a large staff of trained electrical engineers to design, install, and service customers' electrical equipment.[26] As at the American companies, the sales offices of AEG and Siemens provided their production, design, and research departments with a steady flow of information about customers' needs. This information propelled the rapid development of the new technology. Again like General Electric with its Electric Bond and Share Company, these German firms created financial institutions that provided customers with funds necessary to finance their purchases—equipment that was often paid for with shares of utility or traction companies. For this purpose AEG established its Bank für elektrische Unternehmungen in Switzerland in 1895, and Siemens set up the Schweizerische Gesellschaft für elektrische Industrie in the same country in 1896. Later, AEG took control of a comparable, Belgian-based, holding company—SOFINA.[27]

In the early years of the industry two other enterprises made investments in production, marketing, and management extensive enough to compete seriously with Siemens and AEG. The larger and more aggressive of the two was Schuckert & Co., which, after expanding its works in Nuremberg, set up a marketing organization even larger than that of Siemens, with thirty-six sales and technical offices in Germany and almost as many abroad as AEG had. In 1896 it purchased a factory in Vienna. The next year it organized a joint production venture with a local company in France. Then it established joint ventures in Sweden and Norway. By 1900 its sales of high-voltage products— M 77 million—within Germany were close in value to those of Siemens, although Siemens's foreign business was substantially larger, as was its extensive low-voltage business.[28] The other competitor, somewhat smaller, was Union Elektrizitäts-Gesellschaft. It was essentially the German subsidiary of the American company Thomson-Houston (which in 1892 merged with Edison General Electric to become General Electric). Ludwig Loewe & Co. and the engineering subsidiary of the Thyssen steel concern helped to finance this enterprise. Union Electrizitäts soon had works in both Germany and Austria, as well as a sales force in eastern Europe.

The following pioneering firms were still smaller: S. Bergmann, makers of insulating and wiring conduits; Lahmayer & Co., a producer of dynamos, cables, and other equipment; Helios, which had its start by providing electrical power and light equipment to the city of Cologne; O. S. Kummer & Co., which started by providing the same in Dresden; and the Swiss firm of Brown, Boveri & Cie, the one major non-American-controlled European competitor, which provided such equipment for Frankfurt.[29] During the 1890s all these pioneers grew rapidly by meeting an almost insatiable demand for electric power and light; but once demand leveled off, only three—Siemens, AEG, and Brown, Boveri— would stay the course as independent enterprises.

At the same time Siemens and AEG, in an unparalleled burst of entrepreneurial energy, diversified into related product lines. Siemens, as Europe's primary producer of telegraphic equipment, used its highly specialized facilities and skills to move into telephone equipment and to compete in Europe, at first not very successfully, with Western Electric, by then the manufacturing subsidiary of AT&T.[30] And both Siemens and AEG pioneered in the electrochemical field far more than did General Electric or Westinghouse.

Siemens developed and established subsidiaries to manufacture equipment to produce electrochemicals, particularly chlorides and other bleaches. It also established a works in Berlin that made carbon carbide through a method similar to that developed by Thomas L. Willson and Union Carbide in the United States. From the start that unit was operated through a separate company, Gebrüder Siemens & Co. Siemens also invested in a project to produce fertilizer electrolytically through the cyanamid process, and this project led to the establishment of the successful firm of Bayerische Stickstoffwerke.[31] In 1893, AEG set up its Elektrochemische Werke and leased the two new plants in 1897 to Griesheim-Elektron, which then became the largest manufacturer of electrolytic alkali in Germany.[32] Schuckert, too, established an electrolytic department, where it produced calcium carbide and other electrochemicals.

In addition, in 1898 Siemens and AEG financed the establishment of AFA (see Chapter 10), soon to become Europe's largest producer of storage batteries. AEG also financed Aluminium Industrie Neuhausen, which became Europe's largest first mover in aluminum, and for which AEG made the essential electrical equipment. In 1903 AEG and Siemens formed a fifty-fifty joint venture to develop wireless telegraphy. This was Telefunken, an enterprise that became the Continent's pioneer in radio. The year before, the two had collaborated on a project to develop electric locomotives for long-distance runs on railroads.[33]

MERGER AND RATIONALIZATION

In 1901 a downturn in the business cycle set off what the electrical industry and its historians have always referred to as "The Crisis." Demand fell, credit tightened, and liquidity was threatened. O. S. Kummer went into bankruptcy, followed by Helios in 1903. Schuckert, to solve its financial difficulties, began to negotiate for a merger with AEG. When no agreement could be reached, S&H stepped in and signed a pact in March 1903 with Schuckert, which gave Siemens full control of the merged enterprise. The next year AEG completed its "fusion" with Union Elektrizitäts-Gesellschaft, with which it had already formed a community of interest (an I.G.) in 1901. Before long the remaining pioneers—Bergmann and Lahmeyer—came under the control of the "Big Two."[34]

These two mergers, the only nationwide mergers in major German industries before the mid-1920s, brought increased international cooperation. Because General Electric had operating control of Union Elektrizitäts-Gesellschaft, AEG signed, as part of the merger transaction, a patent and exchange-of-information agreement with GE. As in comparable agreements (such as the one made three years later between Du Pont and Nobel Explosives), this one allocated markets as well as assuring technological interchange. It gave the United States and Canada to GE, and much of Europe to AEG. The two set up a joint venture in Italy. They had their subsidiaries in France and Britain draw up the arrangements for sales in those two countries. In the next year, 1905, a member of AEG's Vorstand became its "permanent representative to G.E." This alliance in time encouraged Siemens and Westinghouse to work together in a looser, less formal manner.[35] These four giants, two German and two American, continued to dominate global markets for decades. They maintained friendly relations with other European companies, of which the Swiss firm of Brown, Boveri was the largest.

These mergers, carried out by the industry's largest enterprises, brought, as such mergers often did in the United States, a further investment in manufacturing, marketing, and management that reinforced first-mover advantages. Legal consolidation was followed by administrative centralization and rationalization, the only such industry-wide rationalization to be carried out in major industries in Germany before World War I.

At Siemens in 1903 legal consolidation and administrative centralization were achieved by forming a new company, Siemens-Schuckert Werke GmbH (SSW). The controlling share of its stock was held by S&H. S&H provided four (possibly five) of the members of SSW's seven-man Vorstand and a majority of the Supervisory Board, including two sons of Werner Siemens—Arnold and Carl Friedrich. (Werner, the founder, had died in 1892.)[36] The two brothers also represented the Siemens family on the S&H Supervisory Board. By the terms of the merger, S&H took over the production and distribution of Schuckert's electrochemicals, light bulbs, and measuring instruments. Schuckert's sales and service branches were incorporated into Siemens's Technical Offices. SSW became responsible for the operations of the high-voltage facilities of both S&H and Schuckert. By this allocation of activities SSW took over the production and distribution of equipment for power, light, and traction and railway systems; small parts and accessories (such as switches, fuses, plugs, sockets); and the high-voltage electric cables used in such systems. S&H continued to make low-voltage telegraph and telephone equipment, railway signals, and cables, in addition to electrochemicals, light bulbs, and measuring instruments. Both companies were managed from the same central administration building, which housed the financial and legal offices that served both. Each, however, continued to have its own boards.[37]

After administrative centralization came a massive rationalization of the production facilities. The goal was to permit the consolidated companies to exploit further the economies of both scale and scope. At the time of the Siemens-Schuckert merger in 1903, the Siemens manufacturing facilities were already concentrated in Berlin. Almost from the beginning its low-voltage products—telegraph, underwater cable, and then telephone equipment and a variety of measuring instruments—had been produced in factories in the Markgrafen-strasse area of the Prussian capital. In the 1880s new works for the manufacture of power, light, and traction equipment had been established in the Charlotten-burg area, and in 1899 the company had built enlarged cable works farther to the west in Nonnendamm. After the 1903 merger, the Siemens brothers and senior executives decided to concentrate the production facilities of both S&H and SSW in Nonnendamm. They commissioned the municipal architect of Berlin to lay out plans for a vast industrial complex of many related works.[38]

The first of the new facilities completed at Nonnendamm was the Werner Werke, where more than 8,000 workers in one huge factory produced S&H's telecommunication equipment and instruments, including fire alarms. In its design the economies of both scale and scope were taken into account. In the words of the company's historian, Georg Siemens: "A more distinct separation was made between the manufacture of components and their assembly, and advantages taken of every means of extending rational mass production."[39] At the same time the presses and the machines for grinding, milling, polishing, drilling—indeed, for fabricating a multitude of parts used in the wide variety of final products—were placed so that they could be operated almost continuously. In 1906 SSW's new Grossmaschinenbau (large machinery works) was completed. The opening of the new Kleinmaschinenbau (small machinery works) soon followed and then that of the metal foundry. In 1910 SSW's new dynamo works was completed adjacent to the Grossmaschinenbau works, and S&H's new electrochemical works was placed next to the Werner Werke. In 1912

SSW's cable works was moved once again farther west, and the small-motor works was moved from Charlottenburg to that site. That move left only light appliances and switching equipment in Charlottenburg. The same year saw the completion of a new central office building at Nonnendamm. Reported to be larger than any government building in Berlin, it provided office space for more than 2,000 employees. By then the municipality where more than 21,000 Siemens employees worked was known as Siemensstadt and was officially designated as such in 1920.

By 1913 Berlin's Siemensstadt had become the world's most intricate and extensive industrial complex under a single management. There was nothing approaching it in either the United States or Britain. Indeed, the locational contrast between Siemens and GE is striking. A similar complex would have appeared in the United States only if the GE plants at Schenectady, New York; Lynn and Pittsfield, Massachusetts; Harrison, New Jersey; and Erie, Pennsylvania had been placed along with Western Electric's large Chicago plant, which produced nearly all of the nation's telephone equipment, at one site in the neighborhood of 125th Street in New York City, or at one near Rock Creek Park in Washington, D.C.

The two Siemens enterprises (SSW and S&H), which were administered from the same corporate office, first in Charlottenburg and then in Nonnendamm, had somewhat different structures. Once the consolidation following the merger of 1903 was completed, SSW was administered through two giant functional departments. The Fabrizierenden-Abteilungen (the production departments) were under the director of the Charlottenburg works, who was responsible for production, designing, and research activities, not only for the SSW activities at Charlottenburg and then at Nonnendamm but also for the Schuckert works at Nuremberg and the works controlled by the Siemens group in Russia, Austria, and Britain. The managers of the Vertriebs-Abteilungen (the sales departments) at the Berlin headquarters and in the worldwide network of Technical Offices were responsible for marketing, servicing, and customer relations, as well as for distribution and storage of the goods made by the production department.

After the move to Nonnendamm was completed in 1913, SSW's administrative structure was given a form that remained relatively unchanged until World War II (see Figure 14, which depicts this structure as it existed in the 1920s). By a plan that went into effect on August 1, 1913, the organization of the Production Department—renamed the Zentral-Werksverwaltung (ZW)—remained much as it had been before, though its specialized staff offices increased in number and in size. The Sales Department, now called the Zentral-Verkehrsverwaltung (ZV), supervised six major divisions, each responsible for a major line of products. In 1913 these included: central power stations; electrical machinery for industry; military and naval equipment (which also included electrical equipment for merchant marine); electric trams and railways; and a small machinery and accessories department which sold to contractors and dealers the many lighter, mass-produced items, including incandescent lamps and meters. The sixth division, formed earlier in 1908, handled export and overseas sales. Smaller staff divisions included those for personnel, purchasing, assembling and shipping, insurance, and comparable activities, and the legal, patent, graphic, and archives offices. "Over everything," wrote Georg Siemens, "and forming, as it were, the roof of the structure was the 'Central Sales Administration,' whose function it was to supervise and control the combined result."[40] In determining profit and loss the senior executives relied on the sales divisions and the auditing, accounting, statistical, credit, and collection offices. At SSW only the Cable Works remained responsible for its own sales.[41]

The structure of S&H appears to have been more decentralized, even though production of railway signals and light bulbs was controlled by the S&H hierarchy that administered the Werner Werke. S&H had its own sales force, though because much of its selling was to state-owned telegraph and telephone systems, this force was somewhat smaller than that at SSW. The sales personnel of both companies were housed in the same branch Technical Offices scattered throughout Europe and much of the rest of the world. There appears to have been closer coordination between the production and distribution offices of the several product lines at S&H than there was at SSW. It is not clear whether, in the case of those products manufactured in the Werner Werke, a single executive had full responsibility for both production and distribution for each separate product line and for the resulting profit or loss. But this was certainly the case for the managers of SSW's Cable Works and of S&H's light-bulb and railway-signal works, and also for those of a small unit of four hundred fifty employees developing an electrical automobile. Production and marketing of carbon carbide and also arc lamps continued to be carried out by Gebrüder Siemens & Co., which was legally and administratively a separate enterprise.

Thus by 1913 the Siemens facilities, increasingly concentrated at Siemensstadt, were operated through a variety of forms—centralized for some major lines and less centralized for others. These enterprises of the Siemens group were controlled at the top by the boards of S&H and SSW and by the single Finanz-Abteilung or Finance Division (see Figure 14). Four men sat on both boards. Three of these—Arnold, Wilhelm, and Carl Friedrich von Siemens—were sons of Werner (who had been ennobled in 1888), and the fourth was Friedrich A. Spiecker, the head of the joint Finanz-Abteilung. Another office for the group as a whole, besides the Finanz-Abteilung, was a small secretariat that had been established in 1907 to assist the Supervisory Board of S&H.[42] The senior line officers of the operating companies all worked in the same central office at Siemensstadt. Unlike their American counterparts, they could physically see and inspect from their offices a major part of their company's production facilities. By the outbreak of World War I the Siemens enterprises were operating through a single administrative structure which, with a corporate office of senior executives and with several autonomous product divisions, was the forerunner of the multidivisional structure which Du Pont and General Motors began to fashion in the United States shortly after the war.

Because much less has been published about AEG than about Siemens and because internal documentary evidence is less available, less can be said about the administrative centralization and rationalization that followed its merger with Union Elektrizitäts-Gesellschaft in 1904. A rationalization of major proportions did occur, but it appears to have been less extensive and less systematic than was the case at Siemens. The two sales forces of the merged firms were consolidated, more slowly abroad than at home. The production of pumps and turbines was consolidated in the Union's Berlin works and that of railway motors and controls in the AEG works. Because, in the words of the company's own history, "factories in almost all departments were now too small . . . AEG had to carry out extensive regroupings in many, varied production branches and new factory construction." Emil Rathenau was keenly aware of the advantages of integrating production facilities. (One reason he decided against a merger with Schuckert was that it would disperse production facilities between Berlin and Nuremberg.) Photographs of AEG's new factories and office buildings, constructed at the same time as Siemensstadt, indicate that Rathenau carried out plans comparable to those at Siemens to reshape the company's production facilities. He built a similar but somewhat smaller complex at Hennigsdorf, northeast of Siemensstadt, to exploit economies of scale and scope. Organizationally AEG appears to have been operated in a more decentralized fashion than Siemens, with a larger number of autonomous operating units, a smaller central office, and more personal management by Rathenau and his son Walther. A precise description of its organizational structure must await a study of the documentary record.[43]

Like their two American counterparts, Siemens and AEG continued to use their competitive capabilities to expand abroad and to move into related product lines. Of the global oligopoly's "Big Four," GE was the largest in terms of assets.[44] In 1913 both of the German firms had more assets than Westinghouse, and they were the leaders in world markets. In that year, according to the estimates of Peter Czada, Germany's share of the electrical-equipment export market was 46.4% and that of the United States 15.7%.[45] The amount produced by the American companies was actually larger, because the 15.7% figure does not take into account the exports of the European subsidiaries of GE and Westinghouse. But the German figure, 46.4%, is also understated, because the German firms, too, had extensive direct investments abroad, and their foreign plants did some exporting. The merger with Schuckert gave Siemens a third factory in Russia, a second one in Austria, a second in Hungary, and one in France. AEG by its 1904 merger acquired works in Russia and Austria-Hungary. It also operated the joint venture with GE in Italy and joined Siemens to form a cable company in Russia, where the market was too small for each to have a works of optimal size. After the mergers, and after the rationalization of facilities in Berlin, neither company added substantially to its capacity abroad. In order to exploit fully the cost advantages of scope they preferred to concentrate on production in Berlin. In 1913, therefore, 87% of all electrical equipment imported into Russia originated in Germany, as did 70% of such equipment imported into Italy.

The two German leaders continued to produce a more extensive line of equipment than the Americans. Siemens remained the largest European maker of telegraph and telephone equipment, competing internationally with AT&T's Western Electric. AEG was more active than the American firms in building and operating central power and traction systems. By 1911 AEG owned at least some part of 114 power plants which supplied 31% of German-connected electric power; and much of Berlin's power and light was provided by one of its subsidiaries, the Berliner Elektricitäts-Werke. On the other hand, SSW had part ownership in only 80 plants, which supplied 6.3% of Germany's total load.[46] Given AEG's history, its predominance here is not surprising. It is also not surprising that AEG lagged behind in the light-voltage business until after World War I, and that it had a smaller investment in research and development than the Siemens enterprises.

The nature of competition between the two giants of the German electrical-equipment industry varied from product line to product line. In some—equipment for power, light, streetcars and railways—the two competed functionally and strategically for market share, much as their two counterparts did in the United States. Each also competed in Europe with the subsidiaries of the other's American ally. In other lines, such as incandescent lamps, cables, and some types of turbines, they participated in "conventions" or in joint sales syndicates. In still others, as in wireless telegraphy and in the development of high-speed electric locomotives, the two formed joint ventures. Their joint ventures occasionally included a third partner: for example, the cable maker Felten & Guilleaume joined them in their Russian cable business. The choice between competition and cooperation reflected more the nature of the product and the existing market than the predilection of either company for one type or another of interfirm relationship. The more standardized the product and the less susceptible it was to rapid technological innovation, the greater the likelihood of cartelization.[47]

The strategic decisions as to cooperation or competition, as to product development, and as to long-term investment in production, distribution, and research were made by the Siemenses and the Rathenaus (Walther Rathenau succeeded his father, Emil, as head of AEG in 1915) and by their senior executives. Several of the Grossbanken played a major, indeed, a critical, role in financing AEG. They were less important for Siemens, for the family could rely on retained earnings from their earlier telegraphic-equipment enterprises. Nevertheless, the Deutsche Bank, whose chairman was Georg Siemens, a nephew of Werner, did facilitate the Siemens move into electric power and light equipment. This bank also facilitated AEG's rapid expansion. Indeed, Georg Siemens became chairman of AEG's Supervisory Board. Yet in the 1880s he was unable to prevent Emil Rathenau from carrying out his most important strategic decisions—the abrogation of the agreement with Siemens and Edison General Electric and the move into manufacturing. When in 1904 Rathenau brought together a consortium of the leading banks to finance the merger with Union and the rationalization that followed, the Deutsche Bank was conspicuously absent. Although Werner's nephew Georg helped in 1897 to transform the S&H partnership into a joint stock company, an AG, with a capitalization of M 35 million, he was unable to prevent Werner Siemens from including in the articles of incorporation a clause that assured his branch of the family full control of the enterprise.[48] The bank was able to have an outsider appointed chairman of the Vorstand; but, although that appointee helped to systematize the company's sales organization, he was pushed aside in 1903 ("overthrown" is the word used by a historian of the company, a later Georg Siemens) by a senior career executive, Emil Berliner, who was the "driving force in the negotiations with Schuckert" and the resulting merger. In 1906 when Berliner, this time working closely with the Deutsche Bank, attempted to centralize control in an executive committee headed by himself, Werner's son Wilhelm was again able to prevent a change that might affect family control.

Both Siemens and AEG continued to have bankers on their senior boards. Siemens continued to look to the Deutsche Bank, while AEG relied on a consortium of banks to assist in the handling of financial matters. The banks placed capital issues for both firms and acted as mediators in the industry. The Deutsche Bank helped Siemens to capture financial control of S. Bergmann in 1912. It also assisted AEG in financing the purchase of the Lahmeyer dynamo works in Frankfurt in 1910.[49] Nevertheless, as Hugh Neuburger has emphasized, the Deutsche Bank's principal task in the electrical-equipment industry was "to provide credit and advice, not to dictate policies to the firm that the bank served."[50] From the 1890s on, full-time managers (including members of the founding families), not bankers, determined the direction and pace of growth of these two giants and therefore of one of Germany's most basic and dynamic industries. Nevertheless, as Neuburger has noted, the Deutsche Bank, like the other Grossbanken, facilitated cooperation between the two leaders by supporting cartels that the two dominated and the joint ventures they embarked on.

Chemicals: Exploiting Economies of Scope

In chemicals (Group 28; see Appendixes C.1–C.4), the German entrepreneurial achievement was even more impressive than in the electrical field. In electrical machinery German entrepreneurs made the investment in production facilities, created the worldwide marketing networks, and recruited the managerial organization necessary to acquire the powerful first-mover advantages that permitted them to dominate and share world markets with the two American first movers. Like the Americans, they grew by utilizing the economies of scale; but they exploited the economies of scope in production, distribution, and research even more than did the Americans.

In chemicals the technology of production permitted the first movers to use scope economies to become even more powerful competitors than Siemens or AEG in world markets. In the production of synthetic dyes and pharmaceuticals made from organic chemicals rather than from natural substances the Germans remained unsurpassed. Indeed, before World War I they were as strong in organic chemicals in the United States as the Americans were in mass-produced light machinery in Europe. In electrochemicals they dominated the European markets and challenged the Americans in the United States. The Germans also were the first to develop synthetic fertilizers by the cyanamid process. And they led the way in the production of ammonia and nitrates from the air.

THE DYE MAKERS: CREATING CAPABILITIES

The first of the modern chemical producers were the makers of synthetic dyes. There were three giants—Badische Anilin- & Soda-Fabrik AG (BASF), Bayer, and Hoechst—and four smaller enterprises—AG für Anilin-Fabrikation (AGFA), Leopold Cassella & Co., Kalle & Co., and Weiler–ter Meer. Initially these firms had acquired their first-mover advantages by building plants large enough to exploit fully the economies of scale in the production of alizarin dye. The first was BASF, whose chief chemist, Heinrich Caro, was one of the inventors of an inexpensive production process in 1869. By 1873 the firm was producing 100 tons of alizarin annually, and by 1877 the output had reached 750 tons. Cassella and Kalle followed suit, while AGFA turned to mass-producing another line of products, aniline dyes; and Weiler–ter Meer began to concentrate on intermediates. The greatly increased output drove the price of alizarin down from M 120 per kilo in 1873 to M 23 in 1878 and M 17.5 in 1881. At the same time the companies rapidly improved their processes of production so that their colors remained fast, not fading or changing with application or use.[51]

In the late 1870s and early 1880s the three largest companies became the giants by developing or acquiring facilities to produce many lines of dyes and then pharmaceuticals and photographic film—facilities that used the same intermediate products and processes. Their efficiency brought the price of alizarin down to M 9 per kilo in 1886. They not only developed a wide variety of colors but created different types of dye to make the *same* color, depending on what sorts of materials were to be dyed—cotton, wool, silk, linen, leather—as well as what sorts of paints and pigments needed coloring. By 1900 each of the Big Three was producing several hundred different dyes. By 1913 Bayer was making more than two thousand. By contrast, their competitors in Britain produced either a very narrow line or products of low quality. The smaller German firms—AGFA, Cassella, and Kalle—continued to concentrate on a few high-quality specialty dyes, but, like the Big Three, these three also moved into pharmaceuticals and photographic film.[52]

From the late 1870s on the leaders invested heavily in marketing and distribution facilities and then in research facilities and personnel to improve product and process. Because the application of the new synthetic dyes required methods and skills that differed from those used in applying the older natural dyes, careful instruction and often the installation of new dyeing equipment were required. The new marketing organizations with their worldwide network of branches and agents were among the largest in the world. For example, the number of customers that purchased Bayer's dyes (and also its pharmaceuticals) rose from 10,000 to 25,000 between 1890 and 1902. Branch offices included experienced chemists and dyers who, like the trained sales forces of the electrical-equipment manufacturers, worked closely with their customers. These offices sent in a steady flow of information about the strengths and weaknesses of the products and suggestions for improvement—information that commercial intermediaries were rarely competent to supply. The staff people in the central sales office in Germany who received these reports worked closely with processing departments and research laboratories, both to improve and to innovate. In addition, customers were invited to spend weeks or even longer at the company's completely equipped dye house in order to better understand the products and their application. The rapid expansion of the sales network, in turn, brought a continuing investment in research and development, an investment that quickly became even larger than that of the electrical-equipment manufacturers. The new and enlarged laboratories remained for more than half a century the world's leaders in organic chemicals.[53]

The growth of sales also brought a concomitant increase in investment in production facilities. Because the profits depended so much on exploiting the economies of scope within a single works, far more capital was invested in enlarging primary plants than in building branch plants. So the dye makers concentrated their production, even more than did Siemens and AEG, in huge works. All but one of these were on the Rhine or the Main. These rivers and the railroads that paralleled them provided the transportation essential to bringing in massive amounts of fuel and raw materials. The rivers also provided the vast amounts of water needed in the production processes. Even more than at Siemens, the physical location of the many processing plants within the works determined the overall administrative structure of the enterprise.

This was certainly the case at Bayer. In 1891, because of the inadequacies of the original location at Elberfeld in the Ruhr, the company began to transfer many basic facilities to Leverkusen on the Rhine near Cologne. But by 1894 Carl Duisberg, the company's most influential manager, had become concerned by the somewhat ad hoc approach to the transfer of old facilities and the construction of new ones. Duisberg was only thirty-four years old at that time. He had joined the company ten years before and had pioneered in developing impressive research projects. In 1895, in a "Memorandum on the Construction and Organization of the Dye Works [Farben Fabriken], at Leverkusen," Duisberg outlined a works plan that he believed would meet the company's requirements for the next fifty years.[54] It was, indeed, as farseeing and as systematic a construction program as the one which the Siemens family would embark upon in Berlin a few years later.

In his memorandum Duisberg emphasized that it was "urgently necessary to depart from our practice hitherto used of manufacturing our intermediate products in the dye works and to unite them into an intermediate products works for the sake of quality control, simplification of preparation, and cost reduction." He paid the closest attention to the most efficient ways to coordinate the flow of materials from their arrival at the works through the processes of production to the storage and shipment of the final products. The plan called for five product departments, a sixth department consisting of the many workshops and offices required to service the processing plants, and Department VII, Central Administration. Department I, which included raw-materials storage and the pump house and concentrated on the production of inorganic chemicals, was situated along the Rhine wharf. Separated from it by a street 120 feet wide (such streets separated all the departments) was Department II, which produced the organic intermediates. Then came Department III, making alizarin and azo dyestuffs. Department IV produced aniline dyes. Department V made pharmaceuticals. The last row back from the river consisted of the grinding and mixing plants, the refrigeration facilities, the power station, and the packaging and other works that made up Department VI. Along the wide streets ran the canals supplying the water needed in processing, the gas and electric lines, and forty miles of railway tracks.[55]

By this plan each of the five production departments was to have its own laboratories and engineering staff, for Duisberg thought it essential "to place all chemists working in the same area in a common laboratory, so as to make possible a common working of various people, and encourage each individual by mutual stimulation." The offices of the production engineers were to be close to the chemical laboratories so "that works chemists can at any time get into direct communication with the works engineers." Throughout his memorandum Duisberg stressed the importance of having managers in direct verbal communication with each other and in close personal contact with all parts of their domains.[56]

Duisberg's plan was not fully completed until 1907. By 1914, with a few additions, the works covered 760 acres and employed 7,900 workers. Long before 1914 Leverkusen had become the model for other German chemical companies as they expanded or rebuilt their massive works.

The heart of the Bayer works was Central Administration (Department VII), the building which housed top management and the offices of the sales, purchasing, accounting, patent, and statistical departments, and also the library. Close to that building were the central "scientific" laboratory, the central "physiological" laboratory, and the dye house that provided quality control of existing production and testing of newly developed dyes.

In the largest of the offices of Bayer's Central Administration worked the members of the "Directorium," the five senior managers responsible for the health and continuing growth of the company. This equivalent of a Vorstand included Duisberg and Friedrich Bayer, the son of the founder and an able chemist. Although all five had a variety of functional activities, Duisberg and Bayer became primarily responsible for production, engineering, and research. The other three concentrated more on purchasing and, much more important, on sales. They supervised a worldwide marketing organization that was divided into six regional groups—Teutonic (that is, Germany, Austria, Holland, and Scandinavia); Latin (France, Italy, Spain, Belgium, and Switzerland); Eastern Europe; Britain; North America; and one for South America, Australia, and the Far East. A lengthy memorandum, written by Duisberg in June 1899, made precise and formal the individual and collective duties of the Directorium. In it he listed those decisions that required a majority vote of its members. Duisberg remained a strong advocate of collective management—by the Directorium at the top and by committees of the middle managers at the next level.[57]

The administrative structure thus defined in 1899 remained little changed until the Bayer Company merged with other leading chemical companies to form I.G. Farben in 1926. As the 1899 memorandum indicated, new departments had already been added and existing ones enlarged and further subdivided. The memorandum mentioned a new production department—Drying and Milling. By then new pharmaceutical and bacteriological laboratories had been established. The Engineering Department had the responsibility for the workshops and for factory maintenance and power and light. Another new central-office unit, the Welfare Department, dealt with housing and pensions for the

Beamte, and with housing, canteens, and accident and old-age insurance for the workers. Interestingly, though accounting and control offices were expanded, no comparable department was formed for external finance.

In 1912 when Friedrich Bayer retired, the Directorium was enlarged and given the traditional name, the Vorstand. By then it consisted of five Vorstand members, six deputy Vorstand members, and four deputy directors, so that all departments of the business were represented in the new directorate. By then a small photographic film department had been added to the list of production departments. The Sales Department, which since the 1880s had included a worldwide organization of the marketing of dyes and then a smaller one, made up of entirely different personnel, for pharmaceuticals, had added a third organization for the marketing of photographic film and a fourth and even smaller one for the sale of intermediate products. By then, according to the eighty-page *Handbuch für die Abteilungsvorstände,* the directors' duties had increased substantially in number but remained much the same in function.[58] Thus the same basic functional structure was simply spread over the large and more diversified industrial empire.

Because Bayer and the other major dye firms had grown large by exploiting the economies of scope, they had become by 1900 as diversified as any other industrial enterprise in the world. When Bayer made the move to Leverkusen, it was already producing pharmaceuticals developed in its laboratories. The earliest was Phenacetin, developed in 1888. Then came the first of Bayer's sedatives, Sulfonal, which was superseded by Trional and then replaced in 1904 by the barbiturate Vernal. In 1898 Bayer put on the market its best-known drug, Aspirin. Then in 1902 began the small venture into photographic film, fixers, and developers. Hoechst, even more innovative in pharmaceuticals, brought to the market in 1892 one of the first serums for diphtheria. Then it developed Novocain and other pain-killers, fever-depressing drugs, and vaccines to control cholera and tetanus. At Hoechst, Paul Ehrlich invented, and the company commercialized, the earliest chemotherapeutical drug, Salvarsan, the first effective remedy for syphilis. BASF did less in pharmaceuticals; but from the start it made even more intermediates than it needed for its own use, selling them to other producers of organic chemicals, including the more specialized Swiss and German pharmaceutical companies. BASF also became the pioneer in the development of mass-produced, synthetic ammonia and nitrates from the air. Of the smaller firms, AGFA was the most diversified. While making pharmaceuticals and specialty dyes, it led the way in photochemicals, which by 1914 reportedly provided 30% of its income. At the outbreak of World War I, all of these firms were searching vigorously for products that would use their resources more profitably.[59] Their laboratories, according to the dye industry's historian, John Beer, were "engaged in research projects that were aimed at opening up tremendous new markets"—synthetic rubber, plastics, varnishes, resins, insecticides, aromatics, and pigments.[60]

The economies of scope, which provided the dynamic for the growth of these firms through product diversification, also restrained them from making extensive direct investment abroad, except for marketing facilities and personnel. Economies in production and administration could be obtained abroad only if very large plants were built. Because of high tariffs and transportation costs, Bayer did obtain a financial interest in a plant at Rensselaer, New York, to produce a limited line of aniline dyes (primarily blues and blacks) for leather processors. In 1905 that plant was enlarged to make pharmaceuticals. Hoechst did construct a relatively small works in Cheshire in Britain in 1910, to avoid the possible loss of major trade secrets under the British Patent Law of 1907. By 1914 BASF still had three plants abroad. After building their giant works at home, where economies of scope so lowered costs, the German dye firms reduced output and shut down the plants they had set up earlier in other nations. The more distant establishments were used primarily for packaging (and branding) pharmaceuticals and photographic supplies and for repacking bulk dye shipments. Even in Russia, where tariffs were especially high, branch works processed only the final stages of production, making up about 20% of value added.[61]

THE DYE MAKERS: INTERFIRM COOPERATION

Until the turn of the century the dye makers competed for market share—functionally by improving product and process, marketing, and purchasing, and strategically by moving into new products and new markets—but they competed more from necessity than by intent. Cartels were attempted, but the dynamic technology of production and the number and variety of products made them difficult to establish and to enforce. Thus the same downturn of the business cycle after 1901 which brought the industry-wide mergers in the electrical-equipment industries led the producers of organic chemicals to search for other ways to maintain profits. Some argued for profit pools in the form of an Interessengemeinschaft (an I.G., or community of interest).[62]

Others, led by Carl Duisberg, saw greater opportunities in merger. Duisberg had made a trip to the United States in the spring of 1903, inspecting plants and talking to senior executives. Among the American consolidated enterprises that he visited were Standard Oil, United States Steel, Corn Products Refining, American Smelting & Refining, and the best-known machinery makers, including Singer and Westinghouse.[63] He may also have been influenced by the rationalization that at the end of 1903 was just beginning to result from the Siemens-Schuckert merger.

In January 1904 in a memorandum to Gustav von Brüning, the senior manager at Hoechst, Duisberg proposed an industry-wide merger along American lines. He described the cost savings and other advantages of rationalization that would follow such a merger. Sales departments could be consolidated, thereby reducing sales personnel, storage facilities, and offices. The small finishing and packaging plants, especially those abroad, could also be consolidated. Purchasing could be more systematized. Less efficient plants could be closed and production transferred to a few large, efficient facilities, as Duisberg had already done at Bayer. As the volume of output increased, the production of a larger number of specialized intermediates could be produced within the merged enterprise. The ending of corporate secrecy would accelerate research and development, and individual laboratories could specialize in different lines of products. To achieve these goals Duisberg wanted the merger to include the leading producers of pharmaceuticals as well as the makers of dyestuffs.

Duisberg's plan met resistance. Hoechst, which had just perfected a new synthetic indigo process, refused to join. So did the more specialized pharmaceutical companies. Only Heinrich von Brunck, the chairman of BASF, was enthusiastic. Even so, negotiations between von Brunck and Duisberg moved slowly until the two learned that Hoechst had made an alliance with Cassella, one of the smaller dye companies, by which Hoechst bought 25% of Cassella's shares and Cassella bought 20% of Hoechst's. BASF and Bayer then brought one of the other smaller firms, AGFA, into their negotiations. Finally in October 1904 the three formed an I.G. The agreement creating this "Dreibund" called for the pooling of profits (BASF and Bayer each to get 43% and AGFA 14%) and for the coordination of policies on technical activities, sales purchases, and patents. Such policies, Duisberg hoped, would give the I.G. the benefits of merger.[64]

The substitution of an I.G. for the proposed merger, however, prevented an extensive rationalization of facilities similar to that which was being carried out in many American industries and in the German electrical-equipment industry, and which was to occur in the chemical industry after the formation of I.G. Farben in 1925. AGFA did agree not to expand its dye line but instead to concentrate increasingly on photochemicals. Yet the Dreibund carried out no systematic plans for relocating or consolidating production or distribution activities. Even the cooperation on functional matters was less than anticipated. Though collaboration by the technicians of the three companies did occur in production and accounting, it was "nonexistent among the commercial staff."[65] By 1910 Duisberg was writing that the Dreibund had failed to increase productivity and to lower costs, becoming "little more than an organization for mutually safeguarding profits."[66]

The Hoechst-Cassella combination, based as it was on interlocking stock participations, was more tightly controlled than the I.G. uniting Bayer, BASF, and AGFA. In 1908 Hoechst and Cassella acquired 88% of the stock of Kalle & Co., the third of the four smaller dye producers. These three, located close to one another in the Frankfurt area, were able to cooperate successfully on functional matters. Nevertheless, there was no rationalization or consolidation of facilities and personnel.

Moreover, the I.G. and the Hoechst-led combination continued both to compete and to cooperate in domestic and global markets. By 1913 these German first movers overwhelmingly dominated the world's industry. They accounted for 140,000 tons of the 160,000 tons of dyes produced in the world (Swiss neighbors added another 10,000 tons). By that time, the British were producing only 4,100 tons and the Americans hardly any at all. The Big Three in Germany—BASF, Bayer, and Hoechst—were responsible for sales valued at £10.5 million out of a German total of £13.5 billion. The remainder was accounted for by the Little Four—AGFA, Kalle, Cassella, and Weiler–ter Meer, along with Griesheim Elektron, a leading electrochemical firm that had developed a new electrolytic method of making dyes.[67] The history of the dye makers differed, therefore, from that of the electrical-equipment manufacturers in that the use of I.G.'s and the availability of stock participations held off merger and further rationalization.

The dye makers' experience differed also in that, once established, they relied far less on banks. As in oil and electrical equipment, banks did play an important role in assisting the dye founders to establish their companies. They also helped to finance the rapid growth in the 1880s and 1890s, which called for heavy investment in new facilities and in research and development. Unlike the electrical manufacturers, however, the dye makers did not need to provide customers with extensive credit. Once established, they relied almost wholly on retained earnings to finance further expansion. Indeed, profits were so great that from 1890 on Hoechst and probably others were able to continue their impressive growth and still pay an average annual dividend of over 20%. With such profits, banker influence disappeared. Financiers were not involved in the negotiations in 1904 and 1905 that led to the formation of the two major groups.[68] After 1900, too, founders and their families were not a significant force in top-level decision-making, as they continued to be in electrical equipment. At Bayer, for example, Carl Duisberg, not the founder's son Friedrich Bayer, guided that company's development. The founding families were even less influential in the other leading firms. By World War I the German dye companies had become the world's first truly managerial industrial enterprises.

OTHER WORLD LEADERS IN PHARMACEUTICALS, AGRICULTURAL CHEMICALS, AND ELECTROCHEMICALS

The histories of the leading companies in other branches of the German chemical industries are not so dramatic as those of the dye makers. Nor do they provide such striking examples of the German ability to commercialize the new science-based technologies and particularly to utilize the economies of scope. Nevertheless, in pharmaceuticals, in less complex coal- and wood-based chemicals, in electrochemicals, and in synthetic fertilizers, German enterprises quickly became and remained the leaders in world markets. Only a small number of companies, nearly all American, were effective competitors.

In pharmaceuticals the leaders, including Schering AG, E. Merck & Co., and

Chemische Fabrik von Heyden, quickly built global enterprises. J. D. Riedel developed its overseas network a little later, opening its American branch in New York City in 1908. Unlike most British and American drug firms, which continued to concentrate on grinding and mixing branded, packaged products to be sold over the counter, the Germans produced new drugs by chemical synthesis. Spurred by increasing competition as the dye makers moved into pharmaceuticals, they invested heavily in research and set up worldwide marketing organizations.[69] Of their Anglo-Saxon rivals, only Parke, Davis in the United States and Burroughs Wellcome (founded by Americans) in Britain made comparable investments in research and in marketing abroad.[70]

The cost advantages of scope were less for the German pharmaceutical firms than for the dye makers. Not only did they carry fewer lines, but the need for greater purity and more careful quality control meant that they could not risk using the same intermediates—and particularly the same pieces of equipment—to produce related products. Therefore, the pharmaceutical companies were less reluctant than the dye firms to build plants abroad to support their extensive sales organizations. Merck in 1899 and Heyden in 1900 began producing pharmaceuticals and fine chemicals in the United States. Merck was particularly strong in alkaloids and organotherapeutical compounds, and Heyden excelled in saccharine. In 1907 Schering built a plant in Britain and the next year one in Russia. After 1900 these firms began to diversify. For example, Schering moved into photographic chemicals and films and into the production of synthetic camphor.[71]

After refusing to join Duisberg's proposed merger of organic chemical producers, five of the leading pharmaceutical firms, including Merck and Riedel, formed an interest group of their own, Pharma I.G., in 1905. This I.G. was more successful than the two groups of dye makers in achieving the benefits of cooperation. Besides pooling profits, its members were able to avoid duplication of production, maintain prices, exchange technical information, and work together in purchasing and export sales.[72] The I.G., however, brought no extensive rationalization of production or distribution. Moreover, such powerful first movers as Schering and even Heyden did not join the I.G. These firms and the pharmaceutical departments of the dye makers continued to compete functionally and strategically with the members of the I.G. Banks did help to finance the initial growth of these leading pharmaceutical companies, and representatives of banks sat on their boards. The readily available evidence does not indicate that they influenced the making of critical decisions to expand production or to form the I.G., but they most likely encouraged cooperation through "conventions" and other interfirm agreements.

Larger in terms of assets than the pharmaceutical producers, but still smaller than the leading dye companies, were those firms that produced the less complex products distilled from wood and coal tar. The most important of these were Rütgerswerke and Holzverkohlungs-Industrie AG (HIAG).

By the late 1870s Rütgerswerke, Europe's leading producer of waterproof (creosoted) wooden sleepers for railroad tracks and telephone poles, had integrated backward into the growing and shipping of wood, and was operating plants in Austria, Russia, Denmark, and Holland. As the basic transportation and communication networks were completed, the company turned its resources to producing wood-distilled products, particularly intermediates for the rapidly growing dye industry. In 1909 the company purchased the Baekeland patents and began to produce phenol-formaldehyde (Bakelite) and other synthetic resins used for molding, extrusion, laminating, and insulation. Then in 1912 it took over a company, initially sponsored by AEG, that produced graphite from anthracite and then made carbon electrodes. (In 1927 Rütgerswerke merged this company with Siemens's carbon and arc-light subsidiary, Gebrüder Siemens & Co., to form Siemens-Planiawerke AG.) Although less able than the dye and pharmaceutical firms to utilize the economies of scope in its operating facilities, Rütgerswerke did utilize these economies on the management side, and thus it provides an excellent example of a management employing its organizational capabilities to move successfully from one industry to another as old markets declined and new ones appeared. [73]

HIAG, a large wood-distilling firm that produced turpentine, chemical briquettes, and most important of all, intermediates for dyes, was never so aggressive as Rütgerswerke in moving into new and technologically advanced products. As a result the firm, ranked 77th on the 1913 list of Germany's top two hundred companies, disappeared from the 1929 list. A third firm, Oberschlesische Kokswerke & Chemische Fabriken, which operated tar-distillation and roofing factories, moved to exploit coke and coke gases much as Koppers did in the United States, although on a smaller scale. It also entered more slowly than the American firm into other related product lines (see Chapter 14). [74]

The leading German electrochemical firms, Griesheim and DEGUSSA, were as innovative and as dynamic as the electrochemical companies that appeared simultaneously in the United States. In the 1880s Chemische Fabrik Griesheim, a producer of alkalies by the Leblanc process, pioneered in ways to produce caustic soda, liquid chlorine, and bleaches by electrolyzing brine. In 1898, when it merged with AEG's Chemische Fabrik Elektron to become Griesheim-Elektron, it operated two large electrochemical plants leased from AEG (one coal-powered and the other water-powered) and so became the largest manufacturer of electrolytically produced bleaching powders in Europe. Griesheim-Elektron then began to use its production and research capabilities more effectively by diversifying into sodium metal and magnesium, in much the same ways as its counterpart, Dow, did in the United States. It also moved into carbide furnaces and then into acetates and liquid gases. (In 1907 it acquired the Claude liquidation patents, dividing the German market for industrial gases with Linde's Eismaschinen.) After 1900 this technologically innovative firm even pioneered in the use of electrolytic processes for the making of dyes, and thereby became the first significant challenger to the first movers in that industry.[75]

In the 1880s Deutsche Gold-und Silberscheide-Anstalt (DEGUSSA), became Germany's largest producer of cyanides by the electrolytic process. A partnership formed in 1868 by two families of assayers and traders in precious metals, the Roesslers and Cohens, the firm had already begun to produce ceramics and chemicals. In 1895 it joined with a British firm, Aluminium, Ltd., of Oldbury, to set up a plant at Niagara Falls to produce metallic sodium as well as sodium cyanide. In 1898 DEGUSSA established another works at Rheinfelden near the plants that AEG had leased to Griesheim-Elektron. Like Griesheim, DEGUSSA set up an international marketing organization. In the first decade of the new century it increased production both at home and abroad.[76] Its American subsidiary, Roessler & Hasslacher Chemical Company, which was operating the Niagara Falls plant (of which it had obtained full control), was soon operating two more works at Perth Amboy, one concentrating on the production of formaldehyde, the other producing a broader line of cyanides, bleaching agents, and salts. A fourth plant at St. Albans, West Virginia, produced sodium and crude chloroform. Roessler & Hasslacher also had sales offices in ten American cities.[77] (Roessler & Hasslacher was purchased by Du Pont in the 1920s, becoming that company's Electrochemical Department— see Chapter 5.)

Two major challengers to these first movers in electrochemicals (Griesheim and DEGUSSA) were Kunheim, the largest chemical firm in Berlin, which produced inorganic chemicals and ammonia, and the potash producer, Consolidirte Alkaliwerke Westeregeln AG, which became even more successful than Kunheim.[78] Nearly all of the remaining chemical firms listed among the top two hundred industrials in Germany at the beginning of World War I were producers of potash and phosphates, with which they made fertilizers and other agricultural chemicals. As in the United States and Britain these processors were primarily mixers. Because their mixing technology was simple and their products undifferentiated from company to company, they developed little in the way of extensive production or distribution facilities. All the companies participated in a government-sponsored sales syndicate established in 1910. That syndicate was one of the very few government-sponsored cartels in Germany, and the only one before World War I.[79] With one or two exceptions—Consolidirte Alkaliwerke Westeregeln was a notable one—these firms invested little in research and so failed to develop capabilities for diversification into related product lines.

Again as in the United States, these producers of fertilizers from natural sources quickly gave way to the makers of synthetic products. The first major producer of cyanides for fertilizers using the Frank-Caro electrolytic calcium process was Bayerische Stickstoffwerke, which was established in 1908 by Siemens and Kunheim and was financed by the Deutsche Bank. That enterprise pioneered in Germany in the way that American Cyanamid did in the United States. Its first rival was Aktiengesellschaft für Stickstoffdünger, which began full-scale operations in 1910 and soon came under the control of Hoechst. In 1912 Chemische Werke Albert joined with two other producers of superphosphates and AG für Stickstoffdünger in a joint venture to produce cyanamides on a large scale, but this did not get under way before the war. Finally, in 1913 BASF began the commercial production of ammonia through the Haber-Bosch ammonia synthesis process, the most successful technology for manufacturing man-made fertilizers. That process had a very high minimum efficient scale, resulting in huge scale economies. In 1917 and 1918 ammonia made at BASF's Oppau plant and its new Leuna works already accounted for 45% and 50%, respectively, of the ammonia-based nitrogen compounds produced in Germany. As in the United States, however, the full impact of the revolution in the production of man-made fertilizers based on the Haber-Bosch and other, similar processes was not felt until after World War I.[80]

To summarize, in chemicals the Germans led the way. More quickly than the Americans and much more quickly than the British, they made the necessary investment in the new physical facilities of production; recruited the managerial production teams necessary to exploit the economies of scale and, particularly in organic chemicals and electrochemicals, those of scope; built extensive marketing organizations, usually worldwide; made large investments in innovative research and development; and recruited the integrating managerial hierarchies. The resulting first-mover advantages gave the Germans domination of European and global markets in five major branches of the industry—dyes, pharmaceuticals, wood and coal-tar distillates, electrochemicals, and fertilizers. Americans were able to compete successfully in their home markets in all but dyes; but only a very few firms—Parke, Davis was one—attempted to challenge the Germans on their own continent. The British remained out of the game almost entirely. They had no enterprises with plants and marketing forces that approached the German dye, film, or coal-chemical companies, or the electrochemical firms, or those that produced synthetic fertilizers or, except possibly for Burroughs Wellcome, pharmaceuticals. The British had access to the technology, access to markets, and access to raw materials, but they failed to make the investments and to create the organizations essential to develop the new products commercially.

After the sharp 1901–1903 recession the German chemical firms turned from price and output agreements, which were difficult to establish and enforce, to two other forms of interfirm cooperation—to I.G.'s, as did the dye and pharmaceutical firms, and to sales syndicates, as did the producers of agricultural chemicals.[81] The I.G.'s, by pooling and allocating profits, removed the incentive to undercut price and output agreements, for lower prices and increased market share made no difference to the accepted allocation of profits. The I.G.'s also permitted exchange of information and other types of interfirm cooperation. But in carrying out such cooperation, producers in the organic and the electro-chemical branches of the industry, at least, no longer looked to the banks for financial assistance. Their highly profitable operations had made them indepen-dent of financial institutions.

Metals: Exploiting Economies of Scale

In metals (Group 33; see Appendixes C.1–C.3) German entrepreneurs were as successful as they were in chemicals and heavy machinery in making the investments and creating the organizations needed to profit from the introduc-tion of the new technologies. In metals, however, the cost advantages lay in scale, not in scope. In nonferrous metals Germans adopted, as quickly as did the Americans, the new electrolytic techniques of refining that so increased output and decreased costs. In ferrous metals large-scale investment in Bes-semer and open-hearth mills came only after the Thomas-Gilchrist process, developed in 1879, had made possible the use of cheaper, more available ore with high phosphorus content in the production of high-grade steel.

FIRST MOVERS IN NONFERROUS METALS

In aluminum Europe's first mover was an enterprise created by Emil Rathenau's AEG. In October 1888, shortly after Rathenau's decision to go into the pro-duction of electrical equipment, AEG joined with the Kunheim firm and the Frankfurt banking house Gebrüder Sulzbach to take over a Swiss enterprise formed a year earlier to exploit the Heroult patent. (Both the American Charles Hall and the Frenchman P. T. Heroult had patented their different electrolytic processes in 1886.) The new firm was named Aluminium Industrie Neuhausen AG (AIAG). Swiss interests continued to hold only 20% of the capital. In this German-controlled and German-managed company, Germans, not Swiss, made the essential investment in processing, distribution, and management. AEG provided the electrical equipment for the new giant aluminum works just in-side the Swiss border. At first it also took the responsibility of finding a mar-ket for the new product, but AIAG soon had its own marketing network. It remained the largest producer and distributor in Europe. Although operating in Switzerland, AIAG continued to be Germany's powerful representative in the global oligopoly until the outbreak of World War I.[82]

In tin, a small firm named Th. Goldschmidt AG grew to become the industry's leader after 1890, when it developed an electrolytic technique that greatly reduced the cost of both detinning scrap and processing ore. It soon developed an improved detinning process using liquefied chlorine which was made electrolytically. In 1909 it reportedly processed 50,000 tons of the 75,000 tons of scrap detinned in Germany. By then it had processing plants in Austria, Britain, and France and also in the United States, where its works were at Wyandotte, Michigan; Carteret, New Jersey; and East Chicago, Indiana. These American plants not only detinned scrap but also produced tin tetrachloride and other chemicals. [83]

In copper, lead, zinc, and nickel the impact of the new electrolytic processes was even more dramatic than in the production of aluminum and tin. In Germany, as in the United States, the organizations necessary to exploit the new technology were built by established metal traders.

Because much less copper ore was available in Europe than in North America and transatlantic shipping was very costly, the two electrolytic copper refineries built on the Continent before 1912 were too small to exploit fully the cost advantages of the new technologies. But German traders, unlike the British processors, created a giant international enterprise to utilize North America's more abundant sources of ore. Here the first mover was Wilhelm Merton, a third-generation member of the metal trading firm of Merton and Cohen. In 1860 that partnership had established a branch in Britain that came to be managed by Henry Merton, Wilhelm's brother. In 1881 Wilhelm organized Metallgesellschaft AG, which included Henry's British branch and whose stock was held by Wilhelm, Henry, and a brother-in-law. Wilhelm quickly recognized the significance of the new electrolytic refining processes and the importance of the United States as a source of copper ore and a market for refined copper. In 1887 he formed the American Metal Company with headquarters in New York, which soon came to be managed by Berthold Hochschild, the younger brother of the chairman of Metallgesellschaft's Vorstand. Shortly after this move the Mertons, using knowledge developed at DEGUSSA (in which the Cohen family were partners) and some British financing, took control of the Norddeutsche Affinerie of Hamburg. There they installed the first modern electrolytic copper refinery in Europe (a small experimental electrolytic refinery had been tested in 1875), and at the same time enlarged its managerial staff.

In 1891, the year in which the development of the new dynamo led to the building of five electrolytic refineries in the United States, the company's American subsidiary (the American Metal Company) moved immediately to exploit the new opportunity. It helped to establish, at Balbach, New Jersey, one of these five refineries. This refinery had an annual capacity of 48 million pounds of copper and other nonferrous metals. American Metal also invested in the much larger Nichols Refinery on Long Island, which by 1905 had been enlarged to a capacity of 500 million pounds a year. Meanwhile, American Metal had established subsidiaries to process and sell copper, lead, and zinc, as well as to mine these metals in Mexico. By World War I it owned and operated smelters in Mexico, Colorado, Oklahoma, Kansas, Ohio, and Pennsylvania, and was producing annually in the United States between 100 and 125 million pounds (that is, between 50,000 and about 62,000 tons) of electrolytic copper, 75,000 to 100,000 tons of zinc, and 72,000 to 90,000 tons of lead. In Europe, Metallgesellschaft obtained control of smaller mining and processing properties. In 1912 at Hoboken, Belgium, it built the largest refinery yet constructed in Europe to process the ore from the newly opened mines at Katanga in the Belgian Congo.[84]

In the meantime the Merton enterprises, which had been financed by retained earnings, reshaped their administrative and financial structures. In 1897 they formed Metallurgische Gesellschaft AG (always known as Lurgi), to administer the many processing and mining activities from its large corporate office in Frankfurt, leaving Metallgesellschaft, the senior company, to handle the commercial activities. Then in 1906 the Mertons formed a third firm, Berg-und Metallbank, a financial company, to hold the securities of their major British and American subsidiaries. This new enterprise also served as the financial department for the group as a whole, handling internal accounting and other control systems as well as external financing. Finally in 1910 the holding company and the industrial companies were merged in order to centralize the finances, as well as the administration, of the domestic enterprises. At the same time Wilhelm Merton established a holding company in Switzerland to hold the controlling shares of the consolidated enterprises and the British branch.[85]

In this way, by World War I Metallgesellschaft had become the one major European contender in the global copper oligopoly. In addition, it was a leader in the production and distribution of zinc and lead in the United States, it also dominated those industries in Europe. In 1908, working with two other leading metal-trading firms and the other zinc producers in Germany, it formed and managed a marketing syndicate for the distribution of zinc (the Zinkhüttenverband). Then in 1911 it brought together other German and European producers into an International Zinc Syndicate. In 1909 Metallgesellschaft had also become the exclusive agent for the "International Lead Convention."[86] As a result of earlier agreements with International Nickel and that American company's predecessors, it was already the leading distributor of nickel in Germany and much of Europe.[87] Metallgesellschaft thus came to be as dominant in nonferrous metals as Continental was in rubber, VGF in rayon, AFA in storage batteries—all industries where a small number of plants of optimal size could meet national and world demand. And as in the others, Metallgesellschaft's retained earnings financed growth.

STEEL: EUROPE'S LEADERS

The markets for iron and particularly for the new mass-produced steel were more varied and much larger than those for nonferrous metals; therefore, as in the United States and Britain, many more companies competed for market share. Chronologically, the growth of the German steel industry closely paralleled that of the United States. One difference was that there was no first mover comparable to Andrew Carnegie. Instead, as the depression of the 1870s receded, a number of entrepreneurs made large enough investments in the new processes of production to exploit their cost advantages effectively— investments that defined the structure of the industry and determined its leading players.

In both countries a major expansion of iron production came in the 1850s, partly in response to the growth of demand as the railroad network spread rapidly, and partly in response to the increased throughput made possible by technological innovation—the use of coal instead of charcoal as fuel and of coal-fired puddling and rolling mills instead of water-powered forges. In that decade older firms, such as those of the Krupp, Haniel, and Stumm families, expanded their capacity; and new firms, including Phoenix, Hoerder Verein, Bochumer Verein, Kattowitzer, and Vereinigte Königs-und Laurahütte, were founded. The railroad boom of the late 1860s and early 1870s encouraged a second expansion. The new demand was met by the rapidly increasing capacity of existing companies and the formation of three major, large enterprises— Thyssen & Co., Rheinische Stahlwerke (Rheinstahl), and Dortmunder Union für Bergbau, Eisen- und Stahlindustrie, the last being a merger of three companies.

At that moment, again as in the United States, the new technology for the mass production of steel was just being introduced. The first Bessemer plants in Germany were built between 1868 and 1872, and the construction of the first Siemens-Martin open-hearth furnace in Germany came in 1869. The new plants were just getting under way when the sharp economic depression began in 1873. Again as in the United States, the depression years after 1873—those plagued by excess capacity and losses—were followed in the 1880s by a period of strong though fluctuating demand. The German steelmakers, however, did not enjoy a railroad construction boom comparable to that which in the United States permitted Carnegie and his rivals to exploit so effectively the economies of scale inherent in the Bessemer process. Nevertheless, it was in the decade of the 1880s that the German iron and steel industry took on its modern structure.

In both countries the growing demand permitted a throughput large enough to realize the economies of the new technologies. In Germany, however, another technological innovation was required to assure the steady supply of ore needed if works were to be operated at minimum efficient scale. Unlike the American steelmakers, the Germans were handicapped by a lack of inexpensive, high-grade ores. Most local ores, as well as those of nearby Sweden and those of Lorraine (the *minette* ores), had too high a phosphorous content to be used either in the Bessemer or the Siemens-Martin process. In 1879 two British cousins, Sidney Gilchrist Thomas and Sidney Gilchrist, devised a way to dephosphorize ores by adding limestone. They did so by placing a new lining in both the Bessemer converter and the open-hearth furnace that permitted the use of limestone in the transformation process. Immediately three of the industry's leaders, including Hoerder and Phoenix, installed new Thomas-Gilchrist "basic" Bessemer converters. Others quickly relined their existing converters and furnaces.[88]

In 1890, 1.84 million tons of Bessemer steel were produced in Germany—all but 0.35 million tons by the Thomas-Gilchrist process—and only 0.39 million by the open-hearth method (see Table 19). The relatively low-grade, more brittle Bessemer steel made from phosphoric ores supplied the continuing demand for rails, wire, and tubes. The next decade saw a rapid expansion of markets for and output of higher-grade, basic, open-hearth steel, that is, steel made largely from wrought iron and scrap and used for beams and other structures, ship plates, and machinery. By the mid-1890s the basic investment in facilities using these two processes had been completed. By then the players in the German steel industry had been selected. From then on, entrepreneurs and enterprises did not enter the industry by building new facilities but by acquiring existing ones.[89]

In iron and steel the banks played a larger role than they did in the other great industries in financing the new enterprises and assisting them to survive the depression of the 1870s. In the 1850s and again in the 1870s Cologne's Schaaffhausen'scher Bankverein was the financial godfather to the leading iron and steel firms in the Ruhr. The Berlin banks, particularly the Disconto-Gesellschaft and the Berliner Handels-Gesellschaft, were active in the Ruhr and also provided capital for steelmakers in Silesia, Lorraine, and other parts of Germany. Such banking support continued to be important in sustaining the companies during the depression. After 1879 the banks also helped finance the installation of the new Thomas-Gilchrist basic Bessemer furnace and the open-hearth furnace. In those years each company's financial support usually came from a single bank, whose representatives then took seats on the company's Supervisory Board.

After the first movers came into full production in the 1880s the influence of the banks declined. The banks themselves, reacting to the close financial calls of the late 1870s, preferred to avoid direct capital participation in these industrial enterprises. At the same time, increased output made possible by the new technology permitted steelmakers to meet demand with their existing capacity for over a decade. In the late 1890s increased demand did call for a broad expansion of facilities. By then, however, the companies were able to finance much of this expansion from retained earnings, supplemented by the sale of securities, primarily bonds. They relied on the banks to market these issues and also to provide short-term working capital.[90]

The managerial teams recruited in the 1880s and 1890s to exploit the economies of throughput were as large as those of the American steelmakers. These salaried managers increasingly participated in top-level decisions. As Gerald Feldman has noted: "The importance of the great general director who stood at the summit of this growing bureaucracy of 'leading employees' (Leitende Angestellte) in the great concerns was already in evidence before the turn of the century," in such persons as Emil Kirdorf of Gelsenkirchener Bergwerks AG (GBAG) and William Bankenberg of Phoenix AG. During the first decade of the new century such salaried general directors as Dr. Feodor Goecke and then Johann Hasslacher of Rheinstahlwerke, Albert Vögler of Deutsch-Luxemburgische Bergwerks-Hütten AG, the Springorums (father and son) at Eisen- und Stahlwerk Hoesch, and Paul Reusch at Gutehoffnungshütte (GHH) were as powerful in their enterprises as American managers ever were in theirs.[91] Moreover, the owners who still controlled—the Thyssens, the Krupps, the Klöckners, and Hugo Stinnes—were experienced steel industrialists who ruled their hierarchies in a most knowledgeable manner. In Germany, unlike Britain, the operation of steel enterprises was firmly centralized in the hands of tested managers who knew their business intimately.

By the end of the century the German steelmakers, again like the Americans but unlike the British, were beginning to build extensive marketing organizations. Before the outbreak of World War I the Thyssen iron and steel enterprises had distributing offices and facilities in Berlin, Stettin, Duisburg, Ludwigshafen, Königsberg, and Buenos Aires; while Gelsenkirchener Bergwerks-AG, a giant, integrated mining and steel-producing enterprise, had offices and subsidiaries in a dozen German cities and exclusive agents in as many more, as well as branch offices and agents in nearly all the major European cities and also in China, Egypt, Morocco, Ceylon, South Africa, Brazil, Uruguay, and Chile.[92] Like the Americans, the German steelmakers rarely built works abroad to support their marketing organizations, for the capacity required to compete with existing plants in those markets was too costly and would have increased output too much to be worth the investment.

The Germans and their American counterparts, by investing more in the new technology and by creating the essential (and quite similar) organizations to administer the new processes of production and distribution, quickly outproduced and undersold their British rivals. In the 1880s the Germans captured the European markets for rails and preempted that for structures and wire almost as quickly as Carnegie, Illinois Steel, and Jones & Laughlin did in America (see Chapter 7). In the late 1890s the British started to lose their Latin American and Asian markets. In the first decade of the new century the Germans were beginning to move into *British* markets. In 1913 Britain imported 15% of the world's exports of steel, 58.4% coming from Germany and the rest from the United States and Belgium.

Although the German and American steel industries quickly became the world's leaders, there were significant differences between the two. First, the German industry remained less concentrated than the American. Second, the German steel companies were from the start more vertically integrated than the American (and also more than the British); that is, more of the leading firms became involved in all the stages of production from raw materials to finished machinery. Third, in addition to relying more on banks for their initial financing than did the Americans, the Germans relied on interfirm cooperation to determine market share in a way that was not open to Americans. Both the move to vertical integration and the ability to form cartels are helpful in explaining why the German industry remained less concentrated than the American.

In the United States, Carnegie, who so confidently and relentlessly exploited the economies of scale, and other first movers—Illinois Steel and Jones & Laughlin Steel—concentrated on the production of primary steel (that is, on making ingots, bars, billets, and rails and structures). In Germany, where overall demand, especially that for rails, was smaller (and hence the number of works that could operate at minimum efficient scale was also smaller), the steelworks made a greater variety of products. The largest firms, like second-rank American companies, produced not only primary products but also secondary ones such as wire, plates, rods, pipes, tubes, and cast and forged pieces. A number of them manufactured final products, as American steel companies rarely did. Friedrich Krupp AG, for example, was making armaments before the 1880s, and machinery makers like GHH and Oberschlesische Eisenbahn-Bedarfs-AG added Bessemer converters and open-hearth furnaces to supply their own needs. After the adoption of the Thomas-Gilchrist process, the new leaders, such as Phoenix and Rheinstahl, did not integrate forward into machinery; but nearly all of the major German steel firms produced secondary as well as primary products.[93]

Thus, whereas in 1900 Carnegie Steel and Federal Steel (the successor to Illinois Steel) together accounted for 35% of the steel ingots produced in the United States and 45% of its rails, no major steelmaker in the Ruhr produced as much as 10% of Germany's primary steel products. In 1904, with the establishment of a cartel administered by the Steel Works Association, the largest German steelmaker, Krupp, was given 9.3% of the primary steel output. By 1912 the two largest, which by then were Krupp and Deutsch-Luxemburg, together had a total primary-steel allocation of 18.5%. The thirteen largest producers ranged from 4% to about 9% of total output. Cartels helped to maintain this relatively low level of concentration.[94]

The Steel Works Association (Stahlwerkband), formed in 1904, included twenty-nine companies controlling 74.5% of the industry's output. Its formation was the steelmakers' response to the same business downturn that had brought about the Dreibund and the Hoechst alliance in chemicals and the Siemens and

AEG mergers in the electrical-equipment industry. Although the new association managed the steel industry's first nationwide cartel in a full line of products, nearly all of its members had already had experience with cartels. For most, the experience had been less than reassuring because most cartels had been short-lived, temporary solutions. Even the most inclusive and best known of them—the International Rail Syndicate—had only lasted from 1883 to 1886.

Several steelmakers had participated in one of the first successful cartels in Germany, the Rhenish-Westphalian Coal Syndicate. In 1893 the leading coal-mining operators of that leading coal-mining region (these included iron and steel companies that had integrated backward into coal mining), had established a syndicate in the form of a limited private company—a GmbH—to market their products. By controlling distribution, this selling syndicate was able to maintain prices and enforce the production allocations. Three years later several steel producers participated in the formation of the Rhenish-Westphalian Pig Iron Syndicate, the first of such regional selling agencies for pig iron. That syndicate, however, had "a troubled history and suffered dissolution, along with all the other regional associations except for the Upper Silesia Pig Syndicate, in 1908."[95]

These regional coal and pig-iron cartels provided the model for the steelmakers. But even at that time some of their number were calling for merger. Early in 1905 August Thyssen insisted that "the time of syndicates is passed, and we must move on to the time of trusts." Only through merger, Thyssen (and later, Hugo Stinnes) argued, could the industry be rationalized in the American manner so that further scale economies in production might be utilized and marketing services and distribution facilities be systematically integrated. The majority, however, preferred the less radical response. The members of the Steel Works Association agreed that a sales syndicate to distribute output according to allocated percentages was workable for primary products—semifinished steel, rails, and structures—which they termed Class A products. But they also agreed that such a plan would be much more difficult to institute for the distribution of secondary or Class B products. Instead, Class B products continued to be sold through the individual companies' sales forces, with the association setting prices and prescribing quotas on output.[96]

The Steel Works Association was less than successful in achieving its goals. It did maintain prices for a few years, particularly in primary products, and was effective in somewhat increasing the German share of foreign markets. A recent study shows that by stabilizing prices and output the association did permit a fuller and steadier, and therefore a more profitable, utilization of capacity. Yet, as was true of all such negotiated arrangements, the participants constantly bickered as to prices and the allocation of output. By 1907 the association had finally dropped tentative plans to create a marketing syndicate for Class B products. By 1912 it no longer attempted even to set price and output schedules for the B products. Indeed, by then "less than one-third of the industry's production was encompassed by the Steel Works Association in any form because of the decartelization of the B products. The famed Association had become a 'torso.'"[97]

Although it was only a limited success, the cartel did have a powerful impact on the growth and structure of the industry. Of most significance, it prevented nationwide mergers and therefore the industry-wide rationalization of facilities and services that Thyssen and others desired. Horizontal mergers did occur on a limited regional scale. Phoenix acquired Westfälische Union in 1898 and Hoerder Verein in 1906. Hugo Stinnes made his initial major investment in steel in 1901 by creating Deutsch-Luxemburg to take over a financially troubled, integrated firm with operations in Luxemburg. In 1907 that company acquired control of two more firms, Schalker Gruben- und Hüttenverein, and Aachener Hüttenaktienverein Rote Erde, and in 1910 it also took over Dortmunder Union.[98] Nevertheless, these acquisitions by Phoenix and Deutsch-Luxemburg brought little rationalization in production facilities. The works were operated much as they had been before acquisition, although increased cooperation did occur in sales.

Thus in Germany before World War I there was no shutting down of certain facilities, expanding of others, and building of new ones, comparable to that which occurred as a result of the turn-of-the-century mergers in the United States: for example, after the formation of National Tube, American Tin Plate, American Steel & Wire, and even the United States Steel Corporation. Nor was there a steel rationalization comparable to that carried out by Siemens and AEG after their 1904–05 mergers with other firms. This essential revamping and continuing modernization of the industry had to wait until the German economy was finally stabilized in 1925 after the series of crises that followed World War I.

Although cartelization restrained horizontal mergers and with them rationalization, it did encourage growth of firms through vertical mergers; for cartelization in one branch of the industry created an incentive for one company to avoid cartel rulings by obtaining other companies in other branches. By integrating backward through the acquisition of coal-mining companies, the primary steel producers did not have to pay the coal cartel's price for its product because transactions within an enterprise did not come under cartel rulings. Such moves, in turn, encouraged coal-mining and ore firms to provide assured outlets by moving into steel production. Thus one of the largest German coal producers, GBAG, became one of the nation's biggest steelmakers in the first decade of the new century. So, too, Mannesmannröhren-Werke, the developer of an innovative process for making seamless steel tubes, quickly obtained its own steelmaking facilities in order to avoid paying cartel prices. At the same time, steel producers like August Thyssen and Hugo Stinnes moved still further forward by the acquisition of machinery-making firms.[99]

The objective of this strategy of vertical integration through acquisition was essentially defensive. It rarely led to decreased costs through increased throughput or to improved quality by the reshaping of production facilities. Such economies could only be achieved if the works of the acquired company were geographically adjacent to one of the purchasing enterprises. Such vertical acquisitions were instead a form of insurance to guarantee a steady flow of supplies at a reasonable price or to have protected markets for at least a portion of output. Vertical integration in the steel industry in prewar Germany provides an excellent example of growth through acquisition to reduce transaction costs (but only indirectly production costs).

In the years following the recession of 1901–1903 the influence of the banks on the steel industry may have increased, for they were years of strong demand that brought extensive investment in new capacity. In these years bankers appeared to have a stronger say in companies administered by salaried managers than in those where the family remained the major shareholder. At Phoenix the representatives of the Schaaffhausen'scher Bankverein encouraged the board to make the acquisitions that it did. Furthermore, as an advocate of cooperation, the bank all but forced the firm to join the Steel Works Association in 1904. The Disconto-Gesellschaft helped to carry out GBAG's strategy of growth through vertical integration. The Deutsche Bank, in classic German manner, financed the initial three-pronged investment at Mannesmann that permitted that firm to become the dominant producer of seamless steel tubes. This investment made it possible for Mannesmann to declare its first dividend in 1906, to expand its two plants in Germany and one in Bohemia, and to acquire works in Austria and Silesia, Italy and Britain. On the other hand, such family-controlled firms as Krupp, Haniel, and Stumm made less use of the banks. Moreover, after 1903 most of the established firms used a consortium of banks rather than a single institution to finance their continuing growth. Wilfried Feldenkirchen's study of banks and steel in the Ruhr concludes that, even with the increased call for funds resulting from acquisitions and expanded capacity, "after 1895 the enterprises were increasingly able to free themselves from the influence of the banks." In these years the banks' role appears to have been primarily one of facilitating interfirm cooperation, but new ventures like Mannesmann did continue to rely on banks for their initial financing.[100]

If the bankers on Supervisory Boards became less influential in well-established enterprises as time passed, those founders and their families who continued to participate as full-time executives in their firms continued to have a powerful say in top-level decision-making. The Krupps, the Thyssens, the Stumms, Peter Klöckner, and a little later Hugo Stinnes determined and carried out strategies of growth, competition, and cooperation. Even the Haniel family, who relied heavily on an able general director, Paul Reusch, kept a careful watch on their investments. In so doing, all built more integrated and diversified groups or Konzerne than did any American maker of iron or steel. The steel

Konzerne, it should be noted here, differed from the Siemens electrical group and the Merton copper group in that they were personally, rather than collectively, managed at the top. Although German families continued to play a larger role in top-level decisions than American families, particularly after the formation of United States Steel had eliminated family control from such large segments of the industry, they, unlike the British families, operated through large hierarchies of salaried executives.[101]

To summarize, in steel as in nonferrous metals the Germans exploited the new technologies as effectively as the Americans and far more effectively than the British. They quickly made the necessary investments in physical facilities and established the organizations necessary to exploit them fully. The German experience differed from that of both Americans and British in that the Grossbanken played a large role in the initial financing, just as they did in other major German industries. But as in electrical equipment, chemicals, and other industries, the influence of bankers on the boards of individual firms declined as the steel industry moved into full-scale utilization of the new technology and as the enterprises were able to finance continuing growth out of retained earnings. In Germany, as in Britain, the founders and their families continued to play a more significant role in the industry than they did in the United States. The difference between the German and British entrepreneurs, of course, was that the Germans recruited large managerial hierarchies to assist them in administering their enterprises. Finally, the German steelmakers, having different legal traditions and somewhat different attitudes toward competition, used formal cartels more than either the Americans or the British. Though such contractual arrangements proved difficult to negotiate and difficult to enforce, they did help to stabilize prices and output and so permitted a fuller and steadier utilization of capacity. They helped, too, to keep the industry less concentrated than in the United States. As in chemicals, they held back the formation of industry-wide mergers, which, after 1905, a number of German steelmakers believed were the essential precondition for the further rationalization and continuing modernization and increased productivity of their industry.

Organizational Capabilities and Industrial Power

The great industries spearheaded Germany's rapid rise as an industrial power. And in these industries it was the entrepreneurs and the enterprises that they created—those described in this chapter—that were primarily responsible for making Germany the most powerful industrial nation in Europe in 1914. In the lesser industries—oil, rubber, rayon, explosives, synthetic alkalies, and a small number of light-machinery industries—entrepreneurs built enterprises comparable to those in Britain and the other European nations. In these lesser industries one or two first movers dominated domestic markets and represented the nation's industry in international trade. In the great industries, how-ever—in heavy machinery (including electrical equipment), industrial chemicals (except for explosives and synthetic alkalies), and aluminum, copper, and steel—the Germans by 1914 had few competitors in Europe. And these were precisely the industries in which Britain, the world's first industrial nation, had had powerful economic advantages when the new technologies of the Second Industrial Revolution had begun to come on stream. In the 1870s Britain was the largest producer of steel and the major source of rails for both continental Europe and the United States. In copper British refineries were as productive as any in Europe, and in Europe a British-owned and -managed mining enter-prise mined a quarter of the world's output of copper ore. In industrial chemicals and nonelectrical industrial machinery, British enterprises were, as they were in steel, the leaders. In the new electrical-machinery industry, British inventors were as ingenious as those in the United States and Germany; and in the mid-1880s one of Britain's foremost industrial enterprises, Mather & Platt, acquired the Edison patents, which should have further assured Britain a strong position in that industry.

By 1914, however, British enterprises had given way to German organiza-tional capabilities in all of these great industries. British comparative advantages had been destroyed by German competitive advantages. The loss reflected the failure of British entrepreneurs and the success of German entrepreneurs to make large enough investments in the new production technologies to exploit fully the economies of scale and scope, to build the marketing networks needed to distribute goods on an international scale, and to recruit and train the essen-tial managerial teams.

At the core of Germany's industrial strength lay the organizational capabilities (the physical facilities and human skills) of the leading enterprises in the great industries. That strength was centered in the vast electrical-equipment-producing complex at Siemensstadt and a somewhat smaller complex at nearby Hennigsdorf in Berlin, in the huge chemical works of Leverkusen, Ludwigs-hafen, and Frankfurt, and in the massive machinery works and steel mills in the Ruhr and along the Rhine. Comparable works did not exist in Britain.

Even more important, that industrial power rested on the skills of the workers in the factories, laboratories, and offices. And most important of all, it depended on the very product-specific skills of lower, top, and middle manage-ment. It depended on the lower-level managers who trained and motivated the work force and coordinated the activities in the plants, the laboratories, and far-flung sales offices; on the middle managers (the heads of the departments of production, research, sales, purchasing) who coordinated and monitored the functional activities of the enterprise; and on the skills of the top managers who monitored, recruited, promoted, and motivated the lower and middle managers, who coordinated the overall flow of goods through the processes of production and distribution, and who planned and allocated resources for future production and distribution.

In these same industries during the same decades between the 1870s and World War I, British enterprises failed to invest in comparable production facilities essential to exploit the economies of scale and scope. They only rarely created comparable facilities to improve existing processes and products and to develop new ones, or comparable international sales networks to market and distribute finished products. Nor did the British firms have comparable hierarchies of lower, top, and middle managers. Even in the more efficient British enterprises a smaller number of middle managers were responsible for coordinating and supervising the lower-level plant managers whose output was so essential to the long-term success of the enterprise, the heads of laboratories and research offices who concentrated on improving product and process, and the managers of the sales offices who worked closely with their industrial customers—the users of the new metals, materials, and machinery. Nor did the British firms have the skilled top managers who monitored, recruited, promoted, and motivated the lower-level and middle managers and who coordinated the overall flow of goods through the processes of production and distribution and planned and allocated resources for future production and distribution.

In creating the organizational capabilities that undergirded the power of the great German industries in international markets in the years before World War I, government played a role, but only a minor one. It did not provide direct subsidies to the producers of metals, machinery, and chemicals. Its tariffs were no higher than those of the leading Continental nations and the United States. Of more importance, tariffs enacted by the German government soon became, to use the word that Steven B. Webb applies to the duties on steel, "redundant." Webb notes that "even with free trade, Germans would have regularly imported only tin-plate and special types of pig and bar iron."[102] In organic chemicals and electrochemicals and in electrical and other heavy machinery, the Germans exported more and imported less than they did in steel. Even with no tariffs at all, foreign competitors in these industries could have competed in only a few specialty products. In markets of other nations where the Germans drove out British competitors, each had to pay the same tariff.

Nor were domestic patents an essential spur. The first all-German patent law was not enacted until 1877. It followed closely those already established in Britain, France, and other nations. As in these other countries, the patent law encouraged investment in research and development. The new German law made it easier to extend initial patents. But because German researchers in their great industries were far more inventive than those of other European countries, they benefited more from the patent laws of other nations than from their own. Indeed, the Swiss were careful not to have patent laws. As Haber points out in connection with chemicals, a "prerequisite to the establishment of the manufacture of such dyestuffs was the absence of patent protection. For had the Germans patented their processes in Switzerland, the local industry would have been unable to expand and so withered away."[103]

Financial and educational institutions played a more important role than the government in the development of organizational capabilities. The German Grossbanken, however, were neither the creatures of government nor of industry. They had come into being, as had the American investment banking houses, primarily to finance the railroads. Like the American investment houses, they had assisted their own and foreign governments in marketing government bonds and other securities. But before World War I that government business was only indirectly related to the financing of industrial enterprises. And once the new industrial firms were firmly established, the banks left the decisions as to the development of physical assets and human skills within an enterprise almost wholly to its senior, full-time managers. As the top executives of the two leading German banks that financed the German oil enterprises emphasized, the functions of their banks were financial and not industrial. They had neither the resources nor the facilities to manage both activities.

So, too, German educational systems helped to foster the organizational capabilities of the enterprises in the great industries. Yet before the establishment of the new enterprises—before German entrepreneurs had made the tripartite investment in these industries—technically trained German graduates were finding employment outside of the country, particularly in Britain. It was the demand of the new industrial enterprises for engineers, chemists, and managers—a demand that was never strong in Britain—that encouraged the rapid growth of the Technische Hochschulen and then the Handelshochschulen. Nevertheless, Germany's organizational capabilities can hardly be attributed entirely to the symbiosis that developed in Germany—but not in Britain— between the country's industrial enterprises and its financial and educational institutions.

Another reason for the continuing success of the German enterprises may have been simply location. Germany was closer both geographically and culturally to the Continental markets for the new materials and machines needed by the rapidly industrializing and urbanizing European nations. This proximity undoubtedly gave the steel and copper producers an advantage. But it was hardly important in chemicals, especially in dyes, where the world's largest market was the British textile industry. Nor did proximity make much difference in the electrical and other heavy-machinery industries, for the British were unable to compete effectively in these products, even in their own domestic market.

Far more important to the building of organizational capabilities and the resulting market power of the German enterprises than geographical proximity was the willingness of German entrepreneurs to rely on teams of salaried managers, in contrast to the continuing preference of British entrepreneurs for personal ways of management. German entrepreneurs were more ready than the British and, in most cases, than the French to give up, in Ludwig Stollwerck's words, "patriarchalisch-familienegoistische Auffassungen," and instead to recruit teams of managers, to give those managers wide responsibility, and to share top-level decision-making with them.

The concept of managerial hierarchy may have been less foreign to German than to British entrepreneurs and managers, for Germany had a long tradition of bureaucratic management. In a country where the civil service was highly respected, the new salaried managers, even on the lowest supervisory level, carried the title of *Privatbeamte,* that is, private civil servant.[104] In Britain, even the most senior salaried executives continued to be referred to as "company servants." Before the 1920s only a few were admitted to boards of directors. In Germany by 1900, salaried managers, especially those with university or Doktor Ingenieur degrees, moved into and often dominated the Vorstände and appeared on the Supervisory Boards of German industrial enterprises. Because of industry's close ties with universities (as was the case also in the United States)—universities that served both as training grounds for managers and as sources of technological information and innovation—the partnership of science and technology so essential to the continued growth of the new industries and of the economy as a whole continued to flourish. In Britain, where before World War I the family managers rarely looked to the universities for "company servants," this partnership did not develop.

The growth of German industrial power and the weakening of British industrial power resulted not so much from the differences of location or of government policy toward industry, or even from differing types of financial and educational institutions. Rather, it resulted from the ability of German entrepreneurs and the failure of British entrepreneurs to make the investments in physical facilities and human skills that were necessary to exploit fully the competitive advantages of scale and scope, and then to continue to reinvest in facilities and to develop technical and managerial skills. German industrial growth and the concomitant British industrial decline emphasize the importance of organizational capabilities in providing the underlying dynamic for modern industrial capitalism.

The differences between the United States and Germany in both the growth of the modern industrial enterprise and the industries in which such enterprises operated was less pronounced than the differences between Britain and Germany. In both the United States and Germany the enterprise became managerial and quickly developed effective organizational capabilities. The German firms differed from the American in that the family often continued to have a powerful, even a decisive, say in management. Commitment to family control also held back mergers. A German industrialist was more reluctant than an American to relinquish his independence and lose the identity of the firm his family had founded. In the words of one German industrialist, "Germany is not the U.S.A." Fritz Blaich points out that "the personal element and the historical background, family possession and tradition"—all these militated against the fusing of several firms into a single, legally consolidated, centrally administered enterprise.[105]

The most critical difference, however, concerned the relations between the firm and its competitors and other enterprises. Once the German enterprises were fully established, they began to compete functionally and strategically for market share. But as soon as competition intensified, as it did during the downturn of demand from 1901 to 1903, German firms in the great industries began to work out sophisticated ways to cooperate in maintaining market share and profits. That is why, whereas the American story illustrated the emergence of competitive managerial capitalism, the German story exemplifies the coming of cooperative managerial capitalism.

Legally permitted interfirm cooperation in Germany was not, it should again be emphasized, the result of legislation; rather, it reflected a fundamental legal difference between continental and Anglo-Saxon law. That agreements between firms as to price, production, and markets were legally enforceable in courts of law affected the growth of the industrial enterprise in two ways. First, it meant that German firms had less incentive than those in the United States to attempt to control markets through mergers and acquisitions. Second, it led to a more complex set of formal ties between companies than those that developed in either Britain or the United States. In Germany, therefore, in the years before the war, large industrial firms grew more by direct investment and less by merger and acquisition than did those in the other two countries. A study by Richard Tilly shows that, between 1880 and 1914, mergers and acquisitions accounted for only one-fifth of the total growth of assets of nearly forty leading industrial enterprises.[106] Moreover, more of these mergers were the result of strategies of vertical integration and diversification than of horizontal combination (as usually occurred in the United States and Britain).

The responses of the first movers in the great industries also indicate the variety of alternatives available by which to structure interfirm relationships. After the first sharp downturn in prices to follow the adoption of the new technologies—the downturn that began in 1901—the first movers in steel opted for an industry-wide cartel enforced by a trade association. Those in chemicals and pharmaceuticals turned to I.G.'s, while the electrical-equipment manufacturers merged into giant, consolidated enterprises. In electrical equipment, however, there was far more cooperation between the two leaders, in the form of conventions, cartels, and joint ventures, than there ever was in the American electrical duopoly.

*

On the eve of World War I the modern industrial enterprise in Germany and the industries in which it operated had taken on their modern form. The enterprises that acquired first-mover advantages by making the necessary investments in production and distribution and by creating the managerial organization essential to exploit fully the economies of scale and scope had become the major players in their industries at home and abroad. By 1914 these enterprises had driven the British out of international markets in a wide variety of chemicals and machinery and in nonferrous metals, and had driven them out of many of the Continental markets for steel. In electrical equipment they shared world markets with the Americans. In rubber, rayon, explosives, and synthetic alkalies they had become the German representatives in the global oligopolies. Only in light, volume-produced machinery and in branded, packaged products were German home markets dominated by foreign first movers. Even in light machinery a few German first movers had created worldwide organizations comparable to those of the Americans.

Then, abruptly, the competitive position of these German industries in international markets was shattered. In August 1914 the sudden outbreak of war between Germany and Austria-Hungary, on one side, and Britain, France, and Russia—joined by Italy, Japan, and several small European powers, and then by the United States—on the other, followed by the British blockade, removed German first movers from major markets. Foreign competitors in the Allied nations acquired German properties, which their governments had expropriated. Challengers in the neutral nations had an opportunity to expand production, create marketing organizations, and build the organizational capabilities necessary to compete before the Germans once again returned to the international markets. The loss of markets tested the organizational capabilities of German industrial enterprises when they returned to international trade after the German defeat in 1918. That loss also increased the pressure for interfirm cooperation in Germany.

THIRTEEN

War and Crises:
Recovery in the Lesser Industries

The Great War of 1914–1918 had a more powerful impact on the evolution of the industrial enterprise in Germany than it had in Britain, precisely because the war offered British industrialists a potential opportunity to regain lost markets, while their German competitors had to face the realities of lost markets and lost investments in foreign lands. The continuing series of postwar crises further dissipated the competitive advantages of the German first movers. The sudden armistice was followed by political revolution, and a new and weak government. Moreover, the Treaty of Versailles imposed heavy reparations and the loss of certain industrial areas. Then in March 1921 began the occupation of the Rhineland and the Ruhr, the heartland of industrial Germany, by French and Belgian troops. Soon afterward inflation became hyper-inflation. For almost a decade after 1914 German industrialists simply could not plan ahead. Instead, until the autumn of 1924, when the Allied and German governments completed the arrangements, known as the Dawes Plan, that stabilized the German economy, they had to concentrate on adjusting to constantly changing economic and political conditions.

After 1924 the swift recovery of German industrial enterprises in international markets was most impressive. The story of German industry in the very brief period between stabilization at the end of 1924 and the coming of the Great Depression in 1930 demonstrates the resilience of the organizational capabilities developed before World War I by the leading industrial enterprises. Within two or three years German industrialists regained markets abroad which the British, and also the French, had had every opportunity to acquire during the years of Germany's disarray.

War and Postwar Crises

More than in Britain and France, and much more than in the United States, the central government of Germany took over the allocation of resources to—and the coordination of flows through—industrial facilities. Because the German government and its military command expected the war to be short, full-scale mobilization of the economy came slowly. The first step was the creation, in late 1914, of the Raw Materials Section of the Prussian War Ministry, headed by Walther Rathenau of AEG. By the end of 1915 a War Industry Administration had been established. But it was only after the long, bitterly fought battles of Verdun and the Somme had dispelled hopes of an early peace that the Reichstag passed (in 1916) the Hindenburg Plan that completely militarized the German economy.[1] During this mobilization—with the resulting increase in government control over imports, exports, prices, priorities, and profits—leading industrialists, including Carl Friedrich von Siemens, Ernst Borsig, and Hugo Stinnes, served as members of the German War Industries Administration.[2] The war greatly disrupted the processes of production. The scarcity of supplies and the drafting of workers into the military caused overall productivity and output to fall well below 1913 levels. Indeed, coal, iron, and steel did not return to prewar levels of output until the late 1920s.[3]

More critical to the future of German industry than the transformation to war production was the loss of foreign markets. Even more disastrous was the takeover of direct investments made by German enterprises in foreign lands. Nearly all the production and marketing subsidiaries of the major German producers of chemicals, pharmaceuticals, machinery, and metals located in the United States, Britain, France, and Italy were acquired by their leading competitors in those nations. After 1917 German subsidiaries in Russia became the property of the new Soviet state. At the same time, competitors in neutral countries were able to take over markets as the Allied blockade and other restrictions removed the German presence. In Switzerland these competitors included Ciba, Geigy, and Sandoz in chemicals and Brown, Boveri in electrical equipment; in Sweden there was L. M. Ericsson in telephone equipment; and in Holland there was Philips in electrical equipment. All were able to expand their markets and enlarge their organizational capabilities, thus assuring themselves a strong position in their global oligopolies after the war.

The harsh but hardly unexpected terms of the armistice of November 11, 1918, were a prelude to the peace treaty signed at Versailles in June 1919. By that treaty France acquired the coal and ore lands of Lorraine and the potash beds and textile industry of Alsace. The ownership of the rich industrial areas of upper Silesia and the Saar was to be decided by future plebiscites. The treaty also required Germany to consent to the sale of properties expropriated by Allied countries. Tariffs were to be on a most-favored-nation basis until 1925, thereby preventing the development of systematic and uniform tariff policies. Finally, Germany was to pay an unspecified amount of reparations to the victors for damage done by the German armies to Allied property. These reparations, which were later extended to include pensions to Allied soldiers and sailors and their beneficiaries, were finally set in 1921 at $35 billion. In addition, the Germans were to deliver 70 million tons of coal to France, 80 million to Belgium, and 34.5 million to Italy over a period of ten years, as well as large quantities of benzol, coal tar, ammonium sulfate, and other chemicals and dyes.

As James Angell wrote in 1929:

> The Germany of 1920 was thus very different from the Germany of 1913. She had lost or ceded 13% of her 1913 population, 13% of her European territory, all her colonies, about 15% of her total productive capacity. The whole structure of her industry and commerce had been forced into new channels by the War, and then had been completely disorganized by the cessions under the Treaty. She had been through a political revolution, and had of necessity signed the Reparations blank check. She was far weaker economically and politically than she had been in 1913, but she was being compelled to take on burdens which in 1913 would have seemed impossible.

The series of crises, resulting primarily from the terms of the treaty and lasting until 1924, had more serious consequences for German industry than the war itself. In Angell's terms, "even after all allowances for the direct effects of the Treaty cessions, industrial Germany was far weaker at the close of 1923 than she had been at the beginning of 1919."[4] Reparations, along with the required exports of coal and chemicals, hastened monetary inflation, which became hyper-inflation by July 1922. In March 1921 disputes over reparation payments had brought military occupation of Düsseldorf, Duisburg, and Ruhrort on the rim of the Ruhr Basin, followed by an influx of French and Belgian troops into the Ruhr in January 1923. Germans resisted the occupation of the Ruhr with sabotage and a continuing campaign of passive resistance, which, in turn, brought more coercion by the French, including the removal of German officials and imprisonment of industrial and labor leaders. At the same time, inflation took off at an unprecedented speed. In 1923 the exchange rate with the dollar was 40,000 to 1, and it continued to accelerate until November. That autumn Germany's future was indeed uncertain. The French were encouraging separatist revolt in the Rhineland; the Socialist government of Saxony was defying Berlin; and Adolf Hitler attempted a right-wing coup in Bavaria.

Although efforts at stabilization were begun at the end of 1923, they were not completed until the close of the following year. First the Reichsbank brought inflation under control by issuing a new currency, the Rentenmark, which replaced the old mark at a ratio of a trillion to one. The Reichsbank also stopped accepting government debt and took other measures. Not until June 1924, however, was the stabilization of the mark complete and all controls on foreign exchange lifted. In July and August, at a conference in London, representatives of the Allied nations and Germany agreed to the so-called Dawes Plan, that is, to the recommendations of an expert committee (of the larger Allied Reparations Committee) headed by General Charles G. Dawes, which provided a schedule of payments fitted to Germany's ability to pay. The representatives also agreed on the withdrawal of troops from the Ruhr (but not the Rhineland) and on other matters essential to the stabilization of the German economy.

Stabilization brought a relatively severe but brief economic recession beginning in the early fall of 1925 and going into the spring of 1926, which resulted in business failures and increased unemployment. Nevertheless, as 1925 began, German industrialists were no longer overwhelmed by swiftly moving political and economic events. For the first time since August 1914 they were able to consider details of the financial and industrial reorganization needed to compete in the postwar world and were able to plan long-term investments based on credible assessments of demand, cost of equipment and supplies, and availability of capital. Capital was still limited at home, but stabilization made it possible to obtain funds from abroad, particularly from the United States— funds that were needed to finance the restructuring and equipping of German industries, particularly those that had been the source of prewar Germany's industrial strength.

Impact on Interfirm Relationships

War and the postwar crises not only restrained and distorted the evolution of the industrial enterprise in Germany. They also altered relationships among firms and those between industrial enterprises and financial institutions. The place of cartels and the role of banks in German industry were very different in 1925 from what they had been in 1914. During the war and inflation, cartels had proved to be of little value to industrialists. So, too, war and inflation had lessened the ability of the credit banks, particularly the Grossbanken, to provide capital for constructing new facilities and reshaping existing plants, or for carrying out acquisitions or mergers. Therefore, it is essential to consider the impact of these changing interfirm relationships and the role of banks before 1924 in all of Germany's industries before beginning the industry-by-industry review of the recovery of its industrial enterprises—first those in the lesser industries and then (in the next chapter) those in the great industries.

THE GROWTH OF I.G.'S AND KONZERNE

The reasons that cartels were of little value throughout the war and upheaval are obvious enough. During the war, government agencies set prices and directed output. After the war the continuing crises, particularly inflation, made pricing and marketing agreements very difficult to establish and to maintain. Instead of such agreements the large German firms relied increasingly on more formal alliances by joining together either in I.G.'s (Interessengemeinschaften or "communities of interests") or in Konzerne through the interchange of stocks. (The German word "Konzern"—plural, "Konzerne"—refers to a group of firms financially controlled by a few individuals, usually a family.) In both of these legal forms the member firms kept their legal and administrative identities. They cooperated in marketing, research, purchasing, and other functional activities; and in the case of the I.G.'s they pooled profits. Before 1925, however, few attempts were made to go beyond such federations and to merge or "fuse" the constituent companies into a single enterprise that was legally and administratively centralized. Political and economic uncertainties were too great to permit working out the details of such permanent arrangements.

I.G.'s and Konzerne had existed, of course, before 1914. I.G.'s had been formed in the dye and pharmaceutical industries and Konzerne in iron and steel (Chapter 12). Prewar Konzerne included the group of firms in steel brought together by Hugo Stinnes and the groups in steel and machinery brought under the control of Peter Klöckner, August Thyssen, and the Krupp and Haniel families. (They differed from the Siemens group of electrical-equipment companies and the Merton group in copper in that those groups were administered through large, central corporate offices.) From 1918 until the autumn of 1924, the number of such Konzerne increased rapidly, as did the number of I.G.'s. This expansion resulted from the need felt by industrialists to cooperate during the years of turmoil and uncertainty. They used these two legal devices, and variations of them, to handle all three of the basic interfirm relationships— horizontal (that is, between competitors), vertical (between firms in different stages of the processes of production and distribution), and related (between firms producing related products). Although I.G.'s and Konzerne appeared in many industries, they were most prominent in the great industries—chemicals, metals, and machinery.

During the war the chemical industry led the way in these innovations in interfirm relations. In a memorandum written in July 1915, Carl Duisberg, who in 1903 had sought an industry-wide merger of dye makers, proposed to combine the two existing chemical groups (those which had been created following his earlier plan) and two other leading chemical companies into a single I.G. The General Council (Gemeinschaftsrat) of the proposed I.G. would have more power than those of the two existing cooperative arrangements. Duisberg argued that further cooperation was called for by current war needs, by the challenge of regaining foreign markets after the war, and by the requirements of financing the existing, costly, war-engendered ventures. These ventures included a new, high-pressure nitrate works at BASF, the development of acetic acid for acetylene at Hoechst (which called for the purchase of Knapsack's

Carbide Works), and Griesheim's construction, in conjunction with Metallgesellschaft, of new aluminum works, as well as the enlargement of Griesheim's magnesium works. No action was taken on Duisberg's proposal, however, until the logic of his arguments was reinforced by the stalemate on the western front.

Then, on August 18, 1916, the dye firms signed the agreement that brought into being the new I.G., the Interessengemeinschaft der deutschen Teerfarbenfabriken. They were Bayer, BASF, and AGFA of the Dreibund; Hoechst, Cassella, and Kalle of the other earlier group (which had been cemented by an exchange of stock); Griesheim-Elektron, a first mover in electrochemicals; and Weiler–ter Meer, the independent producer of intermediates. The corporate identities and internal administrative organizations of the eight companies remained untouched. The General Council appointed by the member companies met periodically to approve new projects, to arrange for raising the necessary funds, to consider acquisitions of licenses and also acquisitions of other companies, to exchange technical and operational information, and to review and renew cartel, convention, and syndicate arrangements. All decisions required a 70% vote of the Council's members. Those affecting the closing of works, restrictions on production, and reorganization of marketing activities called for a unanimous vote. The agreement also listed the percentage of profits to be allocated to each of the member companies.

The I.G. agreement of 1916, however, was not all-inclusive. Excluded were BASF's pioneering activities in nitrogen fixation, as were those of Hoechst in acetylene and of Griesheim in aluminum and magnesium. Even so, the I.G. appears to have played a major role in the financing of these projects. Nevertheless, although it provided a pool of capital, of technical information, and of economies in purchasing, it failed to reorganize and rationalize personnel and facilities in production, distribution, and research in ways that Duisberg and the other managers had expected. The required votes in the General Council could not be obtained. Evidently federation was not enough. As the economy began to stabilize late in 1924, the members of the I.G. turned to merger (Chapter 14).[5]

When the war was coming to an end, the makers of iron and steel proposed the formation of a similar I.G. In October 1918 Hugo Stinnes of Deutsch-Luxemburg asked his general director, Albert Vögler, to draw up a memorandum advocating a "triple alliance," including Emil Kirdorf's Gelsenkirchener Bergwerks AG (GBAG) and the Phoenix company. In the following July, Vögler updated his memorandum, calling for an I.G. which would embrace these three and also the other leading producers in the Rhenish-Westphalian region. Explicitly based on Duisberg's chemical I.G., it was to last for fifty years. Although its constituent companies were to maintain their corporate and administrative identity, it promised rationalization in production, marketing, and administration. August Thyssen, who had urged an industry-wide merger in 1905, enthusiastically supported Vögler's proposal, as did Paul Reusch, the general director of Gutehoffnungshütte (GHH), though with somewhat less ardor. But Hugo Stinnes, Vögler's own chief, and Johann Hasslacher, the senior manager of Rheinische Stahlwerke (Rheinstahl) were no longer receptive. They had become "obsessed by present problems and opportunities," which they preferred to work out in their own ways.

Continuing inflation and the unsettled market were encouraging entrepreneurs to speculate in materials and then in industrial enterprises, as well as in industrial securities. To exploit these opportunities Stinnes not only enlarged his coal, iron, and steel interests but began, through financial shrewdness and manipulation, to build up a huge industrial Konzern that also included paper, pulp, and oil, along with newspapers, shipping, and other commercial companies. Hasslacher was less aggressive. He, like most steelmakers, preferred to place his earnings as quickly as possible into fixed assets, usually in plant and equipment.[6] But because these renewed or re-equipped facilities were often poorly designed and badly located, they merely intensified the need for reorganization and rationalization of the industry when stabilization came.[7]

The continuing uncertainty brought more Konzerne and I.G.'s in steel, although not on an industry-wide scale as Vögler and Thyssen had envisaged. In July 1920, Stinnes and Vögler began negotiations to create a vertically integrated I.G. combining their Deutsch-Luxemburg with the coal-rich GBAG and two of Germany's largest machinery makers, Siemens-Schuckert Werke and Maschinenfabrik Augsburg-Nürnberg (MAN). For the manufacturing firms the incentive to join was one of insurance—to assure an essential supply of steel and also of funds. Stinnes's Deutsch-Luxemburg was at that moment financially well placed because it had cash from the sale of its properties in Lorraine to French steelmakers—cash that encouraged Stinnes to build his industrial conglomerate. At the same time, Siemens-Schuckert Werke and MAN offered assured outlets for the two steel and coal companies. Although, in Feldman's words, "the quest for security constituted the fundamental reason" for the proposed I.G., its stated goal was much broader. This goal was rationalization on a grand, indeed, a grandiose, scale.[8] As a Siemens-Schuckert Werke director, Heinrich Jastrow, wrote:

> The first thing to do is to set up an economic program for the new economic body (*Wirtschaftskörper*) to regulate imports and exports and the exchange question: to reduce the costs of new acquisitions; to consolidate foreign enterprises and representatives; to appropriately deal with business cycles, preparing ahead for future better periods in times of slack, limiting sharp recessions through production for stockpiling (*Lagerfabrikation*) of appropriate items. We need to take advantage of technical improvements . . . . and to create an economic body which ought not to go unnoted and unasked for [by] any project that comes up in this world.

The first step was the combination of Deutsch-Luxemburg and GBAG into an entity called Rheinelbe-Union. This came quickly, on August 18, 1920. The Siemens managers remained enthusiastic about the project. During the fall, however, MAN began to be wooed by another suitor, the Haniel family's GHH. That large, integrated, machinery and steel Konzern had ample supplies of ore and steel and was financially strong. GHH's highly competent chief executive officer, Reusch, soon persuaded MAN to join his Konzern by forming "'a kind of community of interest' that 'requires no contracts or arrangements,'" namely, 'participation by taking over a large portion of stock.'" The MAN Supervisory Board agreed that such arrangements would leave MAN with a "certain dependence" through the stock participation. Nevertheless, believing there would be generous treatment with "far-reaching freedom of action and an arrangement that would involve no diminution of MAN's external status," its Supervisory Board signed an agreement on November 9, 1920. Even though Reusch acquired majority control in the following year, MAN maintained throughout the interwar years broad legal and operational autonomy within the GHH Konzern.[9]

With MAN out of the picture, Siemens and Stinnes joined forces. By the end of that same November (1920), the agreements had been signed and the new I.G., the Siemens-Rheinelbe-Schuckert Union (SRSU), came into being. Besides Siemens, Deutsch-Luxemburg, and GBAG, it soon included Bochumer Verein (over which Deutsch-Luxemburg had obtained control in October), and it was further enlarged in the following spring by the acquisition of a controlling interest in an Austrian steel and iron works.[10]

The SRSU, however, never brought close collaboration between its members. Its grand goals were chimerical. Once Siemens was fully back into production, its managers realized that it could take only about 10% of the output of the SRSU steelmaking enterprises, and much of this was in the form of special orders. It easily found other suppliers of both steel and coal that produced better-quality products and delivered more promptly. Nor were the commercial organizations of Stinnes and Siemens able to make use of each other's marketing facilities. The Siemens personnel had neither the training nor the facilities for selling steel or coal, and certainly the other members of the I.G. had no capabilities in selling technologically complex electrical equipment. Nor was there, particularly during the inflation, any realistic way to pool profits between such disparate enterprises.[11] Therefore, after Stinnes's death in the spring of 1924 and the coming of economic stability later in the year, the SRSU disintegrated. This disintegration, however, set the stage for the formation of the first nationwide merger of German iron and steel companies in 1925.

While the Stinnes-Siemens I.G. failed, the GHH-MAN combination was successful. It succeeded because the acquisition of MAN was part of a larger strategy on the part of GHH to use its organizational and financial strengths to meet the uncertainties of the times by creating a self-contained industrial empire. Its story provides an excellent example of Konzern building during the postwar crisis years.[12] It differed from similar Konzern building by the Krupp, Thyssen, Klöckner, and Stumm families only in that it was directed at the top by a full-time salaried manager, Paul Reusch, who had the full support of the Haniel family, which still held 70% of GHH's shares as late as 1945.[13]

The companies whose control Reusch obtained between 1918 and 1923 included an allied enterprise, Haniel & Lueg, which was an integrated Düsseldorf producer of machinery, presses, and other metal-shaping equipment; Maschinenfabrik Esslingen, which made not only locomotives and cars but also lifting gear, loading bridges, and refrigeration machinery; L. A. Riedinger, producers of refrigeration machinery in Augsburg; Fritz Neumeyer and another, smaller machinery maker; a shipyard (Deutsche Werft) in Hamburg; a locomotive works near Düsseldorf (Waggon-Fabrik AG in Uerdingen); two wire and cable works (Osnabrücker Kupfer-und Drahtwerk, and Hackethal-Draht-und Kabel-Werke); an iron works in Nuremberg; and the Swabian Smelting works at Stuttgart. In these same years Reusch also expanded the group's selling capabilities by acquiring two Dutch marketing firms with strong international connections. All these acquisitions were financed from within. The Haniel family's own wealth—banks had had little involvement in their enterprises—and their firm's continuing retained earnings permitted Reusch to say (as paraphrased by Feldman) that "the GHH acted as a 'credit bank' for the concern members as part of a deliberate policy to prevent the firm from building up bank debts."[14] At GHH financial, technical, and managerial cooperation strengthened the members of the Konzern and helped them to weather the economic storms of the early 1920s.

SRSU and GHH were among the most prominent of the many postwar I.G.'s and Konzerne in the metal and machinery industries. Steelmakers, while using I.G.'s, preferred to add to their own Konzerne or to join other Konzerne. The Krupp Konzern maintained "consortorial connections" (meaning stock participations) in Rheinmetall and Mannesmann; it also entered into I.G.'s with a small agricultural-equipment firm (Fahr), a Dresden photographic-equipment enterprise, and a small automobile company. In addition, as part of this Konzern's strategy of diversifying out of war industries, it further increased its holdings in Deutsche Schiff-und Maschinenbau AG, a merger of Vulcan Werke Hamburg and Aktiengesellschaft Weser. August Thyssen obtained control of the shipbuilding firm Bremen Vulcan Werke in 1919 and of assorted machinery firms after the war. He joined Peter Klöckner to acquire large works in Siegerland, including the Geisweider Eisenwerke. Klöckner, who had formed I.G.'s with two other steelmakers, Hasper and Georgs-Marien, joined with Thyssen and Otto Wolff, a leading iron and steel distributor, in refinancing the firm of Van der Zypen. Of even more importance for the future growth of the Klöckner Konzern was the purchase of blocks of stock in two major machinery-making firms, Deutz and Humboldt. The Stumm family's Konzern, which, like Klöckner's had properties in the "lost territories" (some of which were paid for), made similar investments in other firms, both small and large. Hoesch formed an I.G. with a leading coal company. Rheinmetall made a comparable arrangement with another mining group.[15]

Several, though not all, of the major shipbuilding firms had become part of steelmaking Konzerne, but the railroad-equipment producers relied more on I.G.'s. Thus Henschel, the specialized locomotive builder, formed an I.G. with the much more diversified Hannoversche Maschinenbau (Hanomag) and with a small number of coal, iron, and steel producers known as the Lothringen group. At the same time, Linke-Hofmann, Henschel's major competitor and a producer of railway cars as well as locomotives, formed an I.G. with the steelmaker Lauchhammer and the great electrical company AEG. Then these firms joined in an I.G. with Oberschlesische Eisenindustrie. (This I.G. was the creation of Friedrich Flick, a successful financier, who had begun to build a coal, iron, and steel complex in Upper Silesia.) Borsig made less formal ties with Rheinmetall and AEG.[16]

In these ways, during the postwar years of inflation, speculation, and political uncertainty, I.G.'s and stock participations took the place of cartels, and also of full-scale acquisition and merger, as ways to achieve combinations, either horizontal, vertical, or complementary. These methods were less costly, less permanent, and more flexible than merger. After economic stabilization, merger and acquisition became the preferred route. With the centralization of control and the rationalization of facilities that followed merger came also the return of cartels, conventions, and syndicates to control price and output. Their establishment and enforcement was easier than it had been in the past because of the increased concentration within industry and the resulting economic power of the merged enterprises.

THE CHANGING ROLE OF BANKS

The same uncertainties that encouraged the much greater use of communities of interest and spurred the growth of Konzerne through stock participations also reduced the influence of the banks in industrial decision-making. Their ability to provide industrialists with short-term working capital, and particularly with long-term investment capital, was quickly undermined as rapidly escalating inflation made lending increasingly, if not impossibly, risky. Indeed, by 1923 interest rates had reached 20% a day (7,300% a year) and were changing almost daily.[17] Firms, instead of paying dividends, invested profits in real assets and facilities. They built or obtained plants, not according to any long-term plan of growth, but rather as a hedge against inflation or to take advantage of a financial opportunity. There is little evidence that the Grossbanken played an influential role in building and shaping postwar I.G.'s or Konzerne. Indeed, as has been suggested, an important incentive to form I.G.'s was to provide a pool of capital resources, that is, to act, in Reusch's terms, as a "credit bank" for members of an allied group. As early as May 1920 a director of the Hannoversche Bank emphasized to a member of the Supervisory Board of the Deutsche Bank that "the great industrial corporations generally dominate the banks and not the reverse."[18]

The German banks remained powerful financial institutions. Their directors continued to sit on the Supervisory Boards of major industrial enterprises. After stabilization they continued to carry out effectively their basic functions of providing short-term and long-term capital. They underwrote sales of securities and assisted firms in financial difficulties. Nevertheless, after stabilization they were unable to regain their entrepreneurial role of providing funds for new ventures to the same extent as they had done in the early years of the modern chemical, steel, and electrical-equipment industries and, later, in the oil industry. Nor were they able to play a major role in financing post-stabilization expansion through the construction of new facilities or the rationalization of existing ones. After the years of instability and inflation they simply did not have access to the necessary financial resources. To a great extent the capital to finance, reorganize, and expand German industry after 1924 had to come from abroad, particularly from the United States. Nevertheless, the banks did continue to play a significant role in guiding the flow of funds from abroad and in assisting the less strongly established enterprises, particularly those in what I have termed the lesser industries.

Recovery in the Lesser Industries after Stabilization

The rapid recovery of German industry after 1924 was selective. It came in those industries where entrepreneurs, well before the outbreak of the war, had made the investment in production large enough to exploit the cost advantages of scale and scope, had built their international marketing networks, had recruited the necessary management teams, and had perfected their organizational capabilities. In most cases they regained their earlier position with impressive swiftness. But industries in which German entrepreneurs had failed to develop their organizational capabilities before 1914 were unable to compete internationally. In the great industries—heavy machinery, metals, and chemicals—German firms once again became world leaders. And in those lesser industries where German enterprises had strong organizational capabilities—in rubber, rayon, and a small number of mass-produced light-machinery industries—recovery was as effective as it was in the great industries. But in those lesser industries where German firms either had failed to create these capabilities—as was the case in most branded, packaged products, glass, and other materials, and in many light-machinery industries—or had just begun to develop such capabilities—as was the case in oil—the international and even the German domestic markets continued to be dominated by foreign industrial enterprises.

Since organizational capabilities created before 1914 determined the ability of an enterprise and an industry to recover, it is not surprising that few new names appeared on the list of the top two hundred manufacturing enterprises during the interwar years, and that most of these were of long-established firms. Moreover, much of the change between the 1929 and 1953 lists (Appendixes C.2 and C.3) came after 1945, including that imposed by the victors of World War II, who broke up earlier mergers.

Far less has been written about the lesser industries after World War I than about the great industries. Yet their stories continue to provide an important perspective on the evolution of the industrial enterprise in Germany, for the failure of leaders in branded, packaged products, textiles, and oil to maintain even their limited prewar position is as revealing as is the successful recovery of the dominant firms in rubber, rayon, explosives, alkalies, and light machinery.

BRANDED, PACKAGED PRODUCTS AND TEXTILES: WEAK RECOVERY

The turnover among the top two hundred was as small during the interwar years among the producers of branded, packaged products (Groups 20, 22, and 28; see Appendixes C.1–C.4) as it was in any German industry. That which did occur came both from merger and from acquisition by foreign firms. The large enterprises remained concentrated in those industries which, as in the United States and Great Britain, enjoyed the cost advantages of scale—in sugar, vegetable oil, chocolate, beer, cigarettes, and soap. In brewing there was little turnover. One reason for such stability was the legislation which ruled that regional specialists could only brew in their specific region. Mergers were rare, therefore. Only the largest brewer, Schultheiss, made major acquisitions during the interwar years, acquiring Patzenhofer in 1920 and Ostwerke, the nation's second largest, in 1930. Both of these acquisitions were Berlin brewers, like Schultheiss.[19]

By contrast, the postwar histories of firms in sugar and vegetable oil are marked by mergers and acquisitions. The major sugar companies turned from cartels to I.G.'s during the early 1920s, and then to mergers to control price and output and to standardize the process of production. In 1926 five firms, led by the largest, Zuckerfabrik Frankenthal, merged to form Süddeutsche Zucker AG. Rationalization followed, but the combination apparently made little attempt to brand and package products in the manner of American Sugar and Tate & Lyle. It cooperated closely with the other sugar refiners in the German market, but neither it nor its cooperative competitors sold extensively abroad. In the 1920s worldwide overproduction led to agreements among leading international producers, supported by their national governments, to allocate marketing territories, but German firms had relatively little influence in negotiating and shaping these agreements.[20]

While the German sugar producers managed to maintain their independence, the major producers of vegetable oil were quickly taken over by foreign firms. During the war the German leaders had built new hardening and extraction plants, and at least one had moved forward into the production of margarine. Early in 1919 six of the largest firms formed the Interessengemeinschaft Deutscher Ölmühlen (IGO), to pool profits as well as to bring cooperation in purchasing raw materials, selling the product, setting prices, and exchanging technical information. The I.G.'s primary task, however, was to provide a united front against the major buyers of their products—the two Dutch margarine makers, Jurgens and Van den Bergh.

In the resulting conflict the Dutch buyers won easily because the German producers did not have the resources to maintain their independence. In 1920 Anton Jurgens obtained a majority holding of Bremen Besigheimer Oelfabriken and of a small producer, Gross-Gerau. By 1921 Van den Bergh had gained control of Verein Deutscher Ölfabriken, and later it acquired F. Thörl's Vereinigte Harburger Ölfabriken. From then on, the industry's largest firms and their I.G. remained under the control of the two Dutch firms. These two merged in 1927 with two other Continental producers to form Margarine Unie, and in 1929 that merger combined with Lever Brothers to form Unilever (Chapter 9).[21]

In chocolate making the smaller of the two industry's leaders, Sarotti, weakened by a serious fire in its Berlin factory in 1922, sold out to Nestlé in 1928. That Swiss company's German subsidiary had long been the country's leading producer of condensed milk for babies and other packaged milk products, and it had recently moved into the chocolate business.[22]

The largest German chocolate maker, the highly successful Gebrüder Stollwerck, never fully recovered from the wartime expropriation of its profitable American properties and its factory and marketing facilities in Britain. It further weakened its financial position in 1921 by distributing as dividends the funds it had received from the American expropriation (which came far below the true value of the properties), instead of putting them back in the business. After 1921 its financing came from Grossbanken, primarily from the Deutsche Bank and A. Schaaffhausen. During the interwar years Stollwerck remained a major producer of chocolates and vending machines in eastern Europe, building a small plant in Rumania shortly after the war and one in Budapest in 1924, and re-equipping its existing plants in Vienna and Pressburg. The eastern European market, however, in no way compensated for those lost in the United States and Britain. Hard hit by the depression, the company passed its dividends in 1930 and 1931. In 1930, at the urging of two of the Grossbanken it underwent a financial and administrative reorganization that included the adoption of new internal accounting and control systems and the replacement of all but one of the family directors on the Supervisory Board with representatives of the two banks.[23]

Two other producers of branded, packaged products that were listed among the two hundred largest German companies in 1929—"Nordsee" Deutsche Hochseefischerei (the name had been changed from Dampffischerei in 1928) and Knorr—also had difficulty in recovering from the years of war and crisis. Nordsee had to turn to the banks for financial support even earlier than Stollwerck did, so that by 1929 eight members of its Supervisory Board represented banks, both local banks and such Grossbanken as Darmstädter, Disconto, and the Deutsche Bank. Knorr not only turned to banks during its financial difficulties, but also to an American food processor, Corn Products Refining. As a result of such financing the president of Corn Products' German subsidiary, Deutsche Maizena Gesellschaft GmbH, became vice-chairman of Knorr's Supervisory Board in 1925 and then its chairman. By 1931 only one member of the Knorr family remained on the Vorstand.[24]

In pharmaceuticals and soap the firms that developed their organizational capabilities before 1914 recovered much more quickly and effectively than did Stollwerck in chocolate making. (For pharmaceuticals, which were part of the great German chemical industry, see Chapter 14.) The effect of the war on Henkel, the leading soap producer, was exactly the opposite of its effect on Stollwerck. Henkel had no investments overseas that could be appropriated. Even more important, its British rival, Lever Brothers, withdrew from Germany at the war's outbreak, selling to German nationals its soapmaking plant in Mannheim and its half interest in Dr. Thompson's Seifenpulver (soap powder). After the war Lever was able to buy into its former soap subsidiary, Sunlicht Gesellschaft. "The German connection," Charles Wilson has noted, "was reestablished—after a struggle—but native interest had come into the business and Lever's could hardly claim to be masters in their own house."[25]

The loss of Lever's first-mover advantages in Germany permitted Henkel to become the British firm's "most formidable rival" in Europe. Wilson comments that Henkel's operations "were as ubiquitous in Europe as Unilever themselves." Soon Henkel built plants to support its growing sales force. One was established in Denmark in 1923. Major expansion, however, had to wait until after stabilization. Then plants were built in Switzerland and Austria in 1927, Belgium in 1929, Norway in 1930, Holland in 1932, and Italy in 1933. Tariffs appear to have played a role in such direct investments, but evidence of this is certain only for the Norway factory. Thus, because of the small optimal size of soapmaking plants, Henkel, like Lever and Colgate, built plants to produce for national rather than Continental or other transnational markets. In the same years it integrated backward into the production of packaging materials—wood and paper—and also obtained shares in Noblee & Thörl, the only vegetable-oil producer not yet under the control of the Dutch margarine makers. In 1930 Henkel also obtained control of the rival soap-powder producer, Dr. Thompson's Seifenpulver.[26]

Henkel thus expanded its organizational capabilities in much the same manner as the leading British and American soapmakers. It relied less than other German firms on cartels to negotiate market share. It expanded its sales force and built plants abroad to support its marketing organization. Because it had only begun to operate multinationally before the coming of rearmament and Hitler's command economy, it did not have the opportunity to diversify into cooking and salad oils, toothpaste, and cosmetics, as did Procter & Gamble and Colgate. But after World War II it grew both by expanding abroad and by diversifying into these product lines.

The war that helped Henkel to challenge Lever also permitted Germany's largest cigarette producer, Georg Jasmatzi, to free itself from British American Tobacco. In 1916 a consortium of German bankers purchased the controlling shares of that company from British American Tobacco. During the years of war and continuing crisis Jasmatzi worked closely with a smaller competitor, Reemtsma. In the autumn of 1925, after having signed an I.G. in August, the two tobacco processors merged, using a Dutch holding company, N.V. Handelsmaatschappij Caland, as a financial instrument to carry out the merger. Further reorganization consolidated the two companies in 1929 into Reemtsma Cigarttenfabriken GmbH. By then the merged enterprise controlled more than 50% of the production of cigarettes in Germany; but it made little attempt to market outside of the country.[27]

Thus, with the exception of Henkel, German leaders in the production and distribution of branded, packaged products did not become strong international competitors. Some came under the wing of foreign firms—of Nestlé in powdered milk and chocolates, of Corn Products Refining in powdered soup and baby food, and of Unilever in margarine (though not in soap). In grain processing, American producers such as Corn Products Refining and Quaker Oats, both of which were established on the Continent before the war, remained more aggressive in building their German and Continental business, thereby becoming the largest producers of processed grain products in Germany. Henkel's success resulted in good part from Lever's pullout in 1914, which weakened that first mover's competitive advantages. And certainly the war was responsible for Jasmatzi's independence.

For textiles (Group 22; see Appendixes C.2 and C.3) recovery after years of war and crisis was even more difficult than for the producers of branded, packaged products. The experience in Germany of that one labor-intensive industry in which the large industrial enterprise appeared in all three countries differed from that in the United States and Britain in ways that could be expected. By 1914 the industry in Germany was less fragmented than it was in Britain, but it continued to be more fragmented than in the United States. Instead of integration, the processors of natural fibers in Germany relied on interfirm cooperation in the form of I.G.'s, Konzerne, and loose mergers. Through such organizations they were able to be somewhat more successful than the British processors in reducing excess capacity and modernizing facilities. Nevertheless, precisely because scale economies were small and product-specific marketing needs were limited, few firms in this labor-intensive industry had developed the capabilities required to rationalize and modernize. As Robert Brady pointed out in his *Rationalization Movement in German Industry*, little occurred in textiles. Rationalization had to be preceded by horizontal and vertical mergers. Brady reported in 1933: "The road leading to a combination of either type . . . has been strewn by corpses of repeated failure, but here and there with occasional success."[28]

The experiences of five of the largest German producers of textiles from natural (as differentiated from man-made) fibers that appear on the 1929 list (Appendix C.2) support Brady's statement. Kammgarnspinnerei Stöhr, like Stollwerck, was never able to recover from its losses abroad, particularly the loss of its profitable American subsidiary, Botany Worsted Mills of Passaic, New Jersey. In 1928, when it was close to bankruptcy, it went through a financial reorganization, with the assistance of several banks, that permitted it to continue as a viable enterprise. During the years of war and crisis the largest German textile company in 1929, Norddeutsche Wollkämmerei & Kammgarn-spinnerei (Nordwolle), had obtained stock interests in more than twenty companies. In 1927 it merged these and other holdings into a single enterprise for the explicit purpose of integrating more efficiently the processes of spinning, weaving, and finishing, and of improving (through integration) the purchasing of raw materials, the marketing of finished goods, and the development of processes and products. But by 1931 the merged enterprise had been forced into bankruptcy. Two of the other large firms, Christian Dierig and Hammersen, family Konzerne that had acquired sizable holdings during the inflation, formed an I.G. early in 1924. Because Dierig concentrated on cotton spinning and Hammersen on cotton weaving, they saw their salvation in joint research, investment in best-practice facilities, and improved coordination of flows through the processes of production and distribution. By the late 1920s, however, the I.G. had disintegrated, and the Dierig enterprise had brought legal action against Hammersen.

Another leader, Vereinigte Jute Spinnereien-und Webereien was somewhat more successful, probably because its industry was smaller, in terms of numbers of workers and firms, than the cotton and wool trades. After the war two brothers, Joseph and Alfred Blumstein, brought together a Konzern that included nearly all the processes of making jute bagging. Then in the late 1920s the Blumsteins, working closely with the Bank für Textilindustrie and four other banks, merged the companies into a single legal enterprise. It remained a family Konzern however, with each operating company administering its own production and distribution. Except for some plant shutdowns, little rationalization appears to have occurred.[29]

In Germany the tradition of interfirm cooperation was of value in the rationalization and restoration of the capital-intensive industries. But it was unable to assist the labor-intensive, fragmented, textile industry to restructure itself; although that restructuring attempt was somewhat more successful than in the case of the personally managed, single-unit firms in Britain. The turnover of textile firms between 1929 and 1952–53 (Appendixes C.1–C.3) indicates this instability. Again, the impact of the differences in technology on industrial structure was striking. While the producers of natural fibers in Germany, Britain, and the United States had great difficulty in coping with changing markets during the 1920s and 1930s, the very few enterprises in the capital-intensive processing of man-made fibers were able to expand their output rapidly and to maintain their profits even during the Great Depression.

OIL: DISMEMBERMENT

The oil and rubber industries differed from branded, packaged products and textiles in that their production enjoyed substantial economies of scale. Yet the postwar experiences of the two industries differed dramatically. These differences, in turn, reflected the state of the organizational capabilities each had developed by 1914. In rubber the first mover, which had effectively developed such capabilities, quickly became even more dominant abroad and more powerful at home than it had been in 1914. But in oil (Group 29; see Appendixes C.1–C.3), where organization building had just begun, the two German leaders disintegrated. In 1913 those two, already the third and fourth in the global oligopoly (behind Jersey Standard and Royal Dutch–Shell), were the pride of their parents, the two most powerful German Grossbanken. Yet by the late 1920s they had become minor appendages of the Anglo-Persian Oil Company.

After 1918 Deutsche Petroleum and Deutsche Erdöl and their financial sponsors, the Deutsche Bank and the Disconto-Gesellschaft, respectively, tried valiantly to retain their prewar position in European markets despite the loss of their properties in Britain, Poland, and Rumania. Early in 1920 Emil Georg von Stauss, the Deutsche Bank's expert on the oil industry and a senior executive at Deutsche Petroleum, proposed to merge the assets of the two oil groups into a single enterprise in which Deutsche Petroleum and Deutsche Erdöl would each have a 50% interest. Both groups, however, were so financially and organizationally weak that nothing came of this proposal. Instead, in January 1923 Deutsche Petroleum formed an I.G. with Rütgerswerke AG, the chemical firm which before the war had begun to integrate backward to assure itself of supplies of coal, lignite, and shale oil.[30]

Then, with economic stabilization, the German oil industry took on its interwar structure. In December 1924 the Deutsche Bank approached Heinrich Riedemann, still a senior manager of Jersey Standard's German subsidiary, Deutsch-Amerikanische Petroleum-Gesellschaft AG (DAPG), with an offer to merge Deutsche Petroleum with DAPG.[31] Although he was tempted, Riedemann turned it down. The two banks, Deutsche Bank and Disconto-Gesellschaft, then agreed that they could not compete with Standard and Shell, which together were selling half of the oil products consumed in Germany. So the two banks early in 1925 engineered a complicated deal which resulted in the consolidation of the German firms and the formation of close links with Britain's Anglo-Persian Oil Company.

The main features of the rearrangement were as follows. The two banks turned over their shares in Deutsche Petroleum and Deutsche Erdöl to Deutsche Erdöl and the chemical firm Rütgerswerke. Those two processing companies, in turn, consolidated their oil activities under Deutsche Petroleum. The shares of Deutsche Petroleum were held 54% by Deutsche Erdöl and 46% by Rütgerswerke. Then Deutsche Petroleum consolidated its refining facilities. At the same time, it merged its marketing activities into a single subsidiary, OLEX Deutsche Petroleum-Verkaufs-Gesellschaft (OLEX DPVG), with von Stauss as chairman of its Supervisory Board. Other members of the two banks remained on the boards of Deutsche Petroleum and OLEX DPVG, although the banks no longer held any equity in them.

Deutsche Petroleum then opted to work with the newest and smallest member of the global "Big Three," the Anglo-Persian Oil Company; it did so by selling the British firm a 40% interest in its sales subsidiary, OLEX DPVG. In return Anglo-Persian agreed to provide the crude oil needed by Deutsche Petroleum's refineries. Four years later, in 1929, the British firm acquired 75% of OLEX DPVG and in 1931 obtained full control. In this way Deutsche Petroleum became a small refiner, buying much of its crude from Anglo-Persian and selling Anglo-Persian its products. Deutsche Erdöl, besides holding the controlling shares in Deutsche Petroleum, became a producer of coal and lignite and the products made from them, including coke, gas, bituminous coal tar, paraffin, and briquettes.

After 1925 the German market for gasoline, kerosene, fuel oil, and other petroleum products continued to be dominated by the three major international oil companies. In 1938 Jersey Standard's DAPG accounted for 26.1% of all the oil products delivered in Germany and Shell's Rhenania-Ossag Mineralölwerke accounted for 22% (with a joint venture of the two, which produced specialties, adding another 1.6%), while OLEX DPVG, owned by Anglo-Iranian Oil (successor to Anglo-Persian Oil) had 9.6%.[32] For Standard, Germany remained the largest market (except for Britain) outside the United States.[33] The biggest independent oil company in Germany, Benzol-Verband, a distributor of Russian oil, delivered 16.3% of these oil products; and the distributor of new synthetic gasoline, Deutsche Gasolin, accounted for 3.9%.[34] Of the several companies distributing the remaining 20.5%, probably the most important was a subsidiary of the American company Socony-Vacuum; however, in Germany that subsidiary remained primarily a producer of crude oil.

In this way, the war and the crises that followed destroyed the possibility of Germany's fielding players in the global oligopoly. If the war had not occurred, the new British player, Anglo-Persian Oil, would have had great difficulty in moving into European markets. If, again, the two German firms had had time to build their organizations and develop their competitive capabilities before the war, they might well have been able after the war to regain their ties with Rumanian crude-oil producers; to control German crude, whose production rose from 51,000 to 230,000 tons between 1923 and 1932; and even more important, to become outlets, after the extended oil glut that began in 1927, for other American producers besides Jersey Standard.[35] As it was, during the interwar years Deutsche Petroleum continued to operate under the wing of Anglo-Persian. Until the Nazi drive for self-sufficiency, the "Big Three" continued to set the pace. In the early 1930s they began to implement the principles of the "As is" agreement by making local arrangements, of which the Benzol (gasoline) Convention of August 1932 was probably the most important.

RUBBER, RAYON, ALKALIES, EXPLOSIVES, AND LIGHT MACHINERY: STRONG RECOVERY

Whereas the oil story was marked by failure, rubber (Group 30; see Appendixes C.1–C.3) was one of several lesser industries that made a strong recovery after 1925. In rubber the German first mover, Continental-Cautchouc-Compagnie AG, regained its prewar position with surprising speed.[36] It did so in part through the assistance of its American ally, B. F. Goodrich Company. In April 1920 the two companies reached an agreement under which, in addition to their earlier arrangements for exchange of technical information, Goodrich was to obtain the supplies of crude rubber needed by Continental and to provide the funds to modernize Continental's plant. This was done by making a loan to Continental and purchasing a "share packet," which amounted to 25% of Continental's shares.[37] As a result, Continental had the financial strength to return to international markets with an improved product—the cord tire—developed jointly by the two firms. Thus Continental was able to adopt best-practice technology and update its facilities by using recently developed American machinery, particularly the automatic winder (*Wickelmaschine*), which substantially increased throughput.

As Continental regained markets abroad, it increased its dominance at home. As early as November 1922 the senior managers of Continental and of its neighbor in Hannover, Hannoversche Gummiwerke "Excelsior" AG (the second largest rubber producer in Germany), began plans for a merger. As in other German industries, such plans had to await stabilization. In 1926 both Continental's general director and the head of its legal staff joined Excelsior's Supervisory Board. Then in 1928 the two companies merged. Early the next year three of the four other rubber producers joined the consolidation. Only Phoenix Gummiwerke, which still did not produce tires, stayed out. As part of the reorganization the new consolidated company, Continental Gummi-Werke AG, was able to buy back the shares held by Goodrich. This refinancing was made easier because one of Continental's major customers, Adam Opel, the automobile maker, had just been purchased by General Motors. The Opel family decided to invest the monies received from the American company in Continental, with Dr. Fritz Opel becoming the chairman of Continental's Supervisory Board.

Administrative centralization and rationalization of facilities and personnel followed quickly, much in the American manner. Production, except for a few specialties, was concentrated in the two large Hannover works, with one producing intermediate products and carrying out the initial processing and the other doing the finishing of tires, clothing, and industrial rubber. The sales forces of the different firms were consolidated, with the marketing subsidiaries abroad operating under an umbrella company that was soon marketing in thirty-six countries. By 1935, Continental Gummi-Werke AG had built its first plant abroad, in Spain (the first major tire factory to be built there). Within Germany, in this industry where there had been no cartels, the first price agreement with Phoenix (and probably with the small specialty producers on the 1952–53 list—see Appendix C.3) appeared shortly after the 1928 merger in response to the reduction of demand caused by the depression. The corporate history of Continental does not say whether the agreement included foreign firms. If it did, this would have been a first for the industry.[38]

Despite its technical skills and its close ties to Goodrich, Continental did not diversify as much as either Goodrich or United States Rubber in America or as Dunlop in Britain. This may have been because the depression followed so closely on the heels of the 1928 merger and the rationalization. Moreover, when German rearmament got under way in the mid-1930s, Continental's research units began to concentrate almost wholly on developing synthetic rubber and synthetic (rayon) tire cord as part of Hitler's drive for self-sufficiency.

For rayon (Group 22, Appendix C.2) and synthetic alkalies and explosives (Group 28, Appendix C.2), where scale economies brought cost advantages and where organizational capabilities had been honed before the war, the interwar history of the leading enterprises was quite similar to that of Continental in rubber. The German first mover in rayon, Vereinigte Glanzstoff-Fabriken (VGF), and the first mover in synthetic alkalies, Deutsche Solvay-

Werke, quickly regained their prewar positions. The leading explosives firms, however, were less successful in regaining strong positions in internal markets. Before the war they had been part of the Nobel Dynamite Trust and so had had fewer opportunities to develop skills in process and product improvement and in marketing, particularly abroad.

Because VGF, the rayon leader, had not built extensive marketing networks abroad before the war, it did not suffer serious losses through expropriation, comparable to those of the German oil companies and even of Continental. After stabilization it expanded production at home, enlarged its research facilities, speedily recovered its position in Europe, and moved aggressively into the American market. In these moves it worked closely with the two smaller rayon producers, J. P. Bemberg (which had subsidiaries in Britain, France, and Italy, and in which VGF had long had a financial interest) and Fr. Küttner, a firm whose growth had been sparked by wartime demand. It increased its holdings in Bemberg, and in 1921 it obtained shares of Küttner. In Europe it worked closely with Courtaulds, the industry's leader (Chapter 8), joining with the British firm in 1925 in a fifty-fifty venture to build a large, best-practice plant near Cologne. Later the two companies took over control of the largest Italian producer, Sina Viscosa. Then in 1929 VGF (and Bemberg, which VGF had fully controlled since 1925), with the blessing of Courtaulds, joined the Dutch producer Nederlandsche Kunstzijdefabriek (Enka) to form Algemene Kunstzijde Unie (AKU). In this Dutch-based holding company VGF, Bemberg, and Enka maintained their legal identities, but VGF dominated the management. Though the Supervisory Board included only three representatives of the German firm, along with three of the Dutch and one from Courtaulds, five of the seven members of the management committee—the "working" committee—were from VGF.[39]

These were the same years, the 1920s, when VGF used its organizational capabilities to move into the American market. In 1925 its junior partner, Bemberg, built a plant in Tennessee using the cuprammonium process. Then came the formation of the American Glanzstoff Corporation with headquarters in New York, which in 1928 constructed a viscose plant, also in Tennessee. That same year Enka built another viscose plant. In 1929 the three plants, operated by a single management team, all became legally a part of the VGF-controlled Dutch holding company, AKU. By 1929 this venture had become the third largest producer of rayon in the United States, after Courtaulds and Du Pont.[40] Successful abroad, VGF had little difficulty at home in warding off the threat of competition from the new, huge chemical combine, I.G. Farbenindustrie (Chapter 14).

As in rayon and rubber, the postwar evolution of the leading producers of synthetic alkalies and explosives reflected their prewar history. Deutsche Solvay-Werke, undoubtedly aided by other members of the Solvay group, recovered quickly. After the formation of I.G. Farben in the fall of 1925, it was the fifth largest chemical processor in Germany. Moreover, because the British and American Solvay companies had been taken over by larger national enterprises (ICI and Allied Chemical), the German company had become the most important member of the Solvay group.[41]

The explosives companies, on the other hand, came back more slowly. The largest one that made high explosives, Dynamit AG, which before the war had been part of the Nobel Dynamite Trust Company, Ltd., was able to gain a place in the global oligopoly by moving quickly into South America. The situation was different for Köln-Rottweiler Pulverfabriken, the leading producer of smokeless powder. In Germany, unlike the United States and Britain, high explosives and propellants were made by different companies. Köln-Rottweiler was deprived of its propellant market by the Versailles Treaty, which forbade the German production of military materials. The company, like Du Pont, turned to using its cellulose-based intermediate materials to produce paint, lacquers, and rayon; but it simply did not have the resources, particularly during the postwar crises, to commercialize these new products. Dynamit AG, however, was able to compete effectively enough to bring the largest American and British producers, Du Pont and Nobel Industries (before 1914 Nobel's predecessor had been the largest firm in the Nobel Dynamite Trust) to the negotiating table. The result was the formation in the spring of 1925 of a marketing company for South America, in which the German company held 25% of the shares and Nobel and Du Pont equally divided the remaining 75%.[42] After that settlement, Nobel and Du Pont agreed in the following November to provide Köln-Rottweiler, as well as Dynamit AG, with financial assistance by taking M 7.5 million or 10% of the increased capital (but not the voting rights) of each of the two German companies.[43]

At that moment, however, the formation of I.G. Farben was transforming the German chemical industry. In June 1926 I.G. Farben acquired full control of Köln-Rottweiler. With the necessary resources now available, Köln-Rottweiler's plant became the major producer of rayon in the new I.G. Farben complex. Nevertheless, until Germany moved to a program of self-sufficiency in the 1930s, the company had difficulty competing with VGF. Meanwhile, I.G. Farben also formed an I.G. with Dynamit AG. Then in 1931 Dynamit took over its major competitor, Rheinisch-Westfälische Sprengstoff, and integrated it into its operating structure.[44] Thus, whereas VGF and Deutsche Solvay and the two industries they dominated remained independent of I.G. Farben, by the 1930s the German explosives industry had been consolidated and brought securely under I.G. Farben's wing.

In volume-produced light machinery (Groups 35 and 37; see Appendix C.2) the pattern was much the same as in these materials-producing industries. The greater the organizational capacity based on the economies of scale acquired before the war, the swifter was an enterprise's recovery. Except for the automobile industry, new challenges to American prewar dominance in light machinery were rare. Even in the automobile industry the American presence remained strong. On the other hand, in those industries where, before 1914, German challengers to American first movers had made the investments and recruited the managers on the scale required to compete in international markets, these challengers continued to maintain and often expand their markets.

In sewing machinery, G. M. Pfaff AG and Dürkoppwerke, and in agricultural machinery Heinrich Lanz AG, continued to compete with the dominant producers—Singer Sewing Machine and International Harvester, respectively. Lanz, the agricultural machinery firm, did so more effectively than Pfaff and Dürkoppwerke. During the war Lanz had lost its sales branches in Allied nations. Nevertheless, even before 1924 it improved its Bulldog tractor line and its other farm machines and redesigned and rebuilt its plant. By rationalizing internal flows it sharply increased throughput. Then it built an even more extensive marketing network than it had had in 1914.[45] Another farm-machinery firm, Maschinenfabrik Fahr, with which Krupp the steelmaker had formed an I.G. shortly after the war as part of its diversification program, became large and competitive enough to be listed among the top two hundred in 1953.[46]

In office machinery, on the other hand, German producers continued to be unable to compete successfully with National Cash Register, Burroughs Adding Machine, International Business Machines, and the American typewriter companies. Not surprisingly, after the war the German firms that produced office machinery chose to exploit the economies of scale more than those of scope by concentrating on a single product line. Schubert & Salzer Maschinenfabrik dropped its other lines to become a major producer of textile machinery. By 1933 the company claimed to have "the largest, most diversified [*vielseitigste*] and most competitive textile machinery factory in the world."[47] After 1925 Adlerwerke, which had already turned to automobile production before the war, became a leading producer in that industry. Only Wanderer-Werke remained in office machinery. In 1932 it merged its automobile-producing facilities into Auto Union and from then on concentrated wholly on the production of office machinery, setting up its first sales and service organization for office equipment.[48]

Those few German first movers in light machinery—Gasmotorenfabrik-Deutz, Robert Bosch, Linde's Eismaschinen, and Müller's Accumulatoren-Fabrik—recovered even more quickly than Lanz, Pfaff, and Dürkoppwerke, even though they suffered more from the loss of their overseas facilities. Like Lanz, they rebuilt their foreign sales and service forces and also introduced assembly lines and other American-style production techniques to increase throughput. They concentrated, too, on improving product as well as process. Even more important, they pioneered in developing closely related, technologically advanced products. Thus Gasmotorenfabrik-Deutz, while continuing to concentrate on the volume production of gasoline motors, moved swiftly into improving and producing the relatively new diesel engine. After 1924, in an impressively short time, Deutz recovered the markets it had lost during the war. By the fiscal year 1929–30, more than 53% of its production was sold abroad. (In 1913 the figure had been 51%.)[49] The steel magnate Peter Klöckner had obtained control of the Deutz firm during the crisis years, and it quickly became the showpiece of his growing steel and machinery Konzern.

Bosch's response was as effective as Deutz's. It rebuilt its worldwide sales organization, adopted new, assembly-line production methods, formed a joint venture with Joseph Lucas in Britain (CAV-Bosch), and established a new subsidiary in the United States. After several lawsuits, in 1930 its American subsidiary regained control of Bosch's prewar American subsidiary, which had been sold to American nationals by the Alien Property Custodian after 1917. At home after 1924 Bosch diversified more quickly than Lucas in Great Britain and comparable firms in the United States, using its organizational capabilities to move into batteries, injection pumps for diesels, electric hand tools (by 1938 it was the largest producer of such tools in Europe), household appliances, radios, and film projectors, as well as its traditional electrical systems for a wide variety of vehicles. By 1936 the firm was employing more than twenty thousand workers.[50]

Carl Linde, it will be recalled, had created two enterprises, one to produce refrigeration machinery and the other to make liquid oxygen. The differing postwar evolution of these two firms reflected their differing prewar development.

Of particular significance was Linde's move into the rapidly growing market for household refrigerators. The final rationalization of facilities awaited an agreement in 1927 with Gutehoffnungshütte, or GHH (see Chapter 14). The result of this agreement was that Linde's production of large refrigerating machinery was concentrated in one plant, while the smaller household refrigerators, for which demand was rapidly growing, were placed in two other plants with new-style assembly lines. (The production of still another line of large refrigerating machinery was concentrated in one of GHH's major plants.) At the same time, separate design, sales, and service organizations were established for the two kinds of refrigeration products, which went to quite different markets. After this rationalization Linde was once again Europe's largest producer of refrigerating machinery.

By contrast, Linde's second enterprise, the producer of liquid oxygen, which had licensed and financed "daughter companies" in the manner of Solvay and which had not created a central organizational capability, never really recovered. Ties with the American, British, and Italian firms, which had been completely severed during the war, could not be restored, and those with other associated companies remained weak. At the same time, competition had increased and demand for oxygen (except for that used in the production of synthetic nitrates) had leveled off.[51]

Still another German first mover, Accumulatoren-Fabrik (AFA), may have been helped in its recovery by its American ally, the Electric Storage Battery Company. During the winter of 1920–21, at least, the president of the American firm visited AFA's headquarters to renew prewar agreements. (The record does not show whether the American company provided funds, as Goodrich had in assisting the revival of Continental in the rubber industry.) Once the period of crisis was passed, AFA improved its older products and quickly began to expand its newer products, such as batteries for automobiles and radios, while at the same time cutting back on the production of large stationary batteries. Its sales force, reorganized in 1926, expanded at home and throughout Europe, also going into India, Egypt, and South Africa. In 1928 AFA returned to Britain, setting up Brittannia Batteries, Ltd., with a plant at Redditch, and placing its Calcutta branch under the control of this new subsidiary. In 1936, possibly because of events in Germany, AFA turned over the control of Brittannia Batteries to the British subsidiary of Electric Storage Battery and reaffirmed its earlier arrangements with the American company.[52]

The rapid recovery of German enterprises in light machinery provides a revealing contrast to the performance of British firms. It was the Germans, not the British, that challenged the American dominance in Europe during the interwar years, in spite of having been out of the game for almost a decade. No British enterprise developed the diesel engine or volume-produced refrigeration equipment as Deutz or Linde did. Bosch appears to have competed abroad and diversified more successfully than Lucas, and it seems to have benefited at least as much as Lucas from the relatively rapid growth of the British automobile industry in the 1920s and 1930s. AFA soon regained its place in the British market for storage batteries and related products, sharing that market with its American ally, Electric Storage Battery. Britain had no counterparts to Lanz in agricultural machinery and to Pfaff in sewing machines. Thus the organizational capabilities the Germans had developed before the war in light, volume-produced machinery permitted them to compete functionally and strategically with the Americans in ways that eluded the British, despite a decade of opportunity.

TRANSPORTATION EQUIPMENT: A NEW START

In the production of transportation equipment (Group 37; see Appendixes C.1–C.4) during the interwar years, the older, long-established shipbuilding and railroad-equipment firms, quite understandably, moved down and often off the list of the top two hundred, and the makers of automobile and automotive equipment began to take their places. This shift occurred to a lesser extent than it did in the United States and Britain, partly because the German firms, particularly the shipbuilders, continued to be more diversified than those in Britain or America and so were less dependent on a single market. Most railway-equipment enterprises, especially those locomotive makers that produced to specifications and designs submitted by their customers, suffered after 1925 from overproduction, excess capacity, and low profits. The producers of more standardized equipment, Knorr-Bremse in air brakes and Orenstein & Koppel in light, narrow-gauge railway equipment, were more successful. The first remained the major European competitor to Westinghouse Air Brake; while Orenstein & Koppel, unable to regain their extensive properties in the United States and other Allied nations, needed the support of several banks to reassert its dominance in European and Eastern Hemisphere markets.[53]

The evolution of the producers of automobiles and automotive equipment differed in Germany and in Britain, mainly because in Germany the American presence only made itself felt after the war, and then not until after stabilization. At the outbreak of the war the German automobile industry was still in its infancy. In 1913 the two largest German producers, Daimler and Benz, builders of high-priced luxury automobiles and craft-built trucks, were sixteenth and nineteenth in output of vehicles among the world's producers, behind fourteen American and two French companies (Peugeot and Renault, ranking thirteenth and fifteenth). In Germany the ratio of automobiles to inhabitants was still far below that in the United States and well below that in Canada and Britain. Production expanded rapidly during the war, with Adam Opel taking the lead in number of vehicles produced. In 1919 and 1920 German industrialists and bankers discussed the possibility of creating a German automobile industry, but little could be accomplished along these lines until the end of 1924.[54]

With the coming of economic stabilization the German automobile industry took off. Annual production rose from 40,000 vehicles in 1923 to 140,000 in 1929. By 1932 the investments made in production, distribution, and management had established the industry's players—with one exception, the Hitler-sponsored "people's car," the Volkswagen, which only began to be produced in 1940, several months after the outbreak of World War II. Late in 1924 Adam Opel started to install American fabricating and assembling facilities, and these came into full production in 1928. By that date Opel's more than seven hundred sales outlets gave it the most effective dealer organization in Germany.[55] Also late in 1924 the long-established firms of Daimler (which for years had produced the famous Mercedes) and Benz formed an I.G. and then in 1926 completed a full merger. During the resulting rationalization, moving assembly lines were introduced into the plants of Daimler-Benz. In 1926, too, Adlerwerke, by then concentrating wholly on motor vehicles, modernized its production facilities.

After stabilization, foreign producers immediately moved into the German market. The Ford Motor Company AG was incorporated on January 5, 1925.

By June 1926, when Ford's German assembly plant in Berlin came on stream, the Berlin plants of both General Motors and Chrysler were nearing completion. By 1928, in addition to the American cars assembled in Berlin, 40% of the cars sold in Germany were imports. The resulting cry of domestic producers for protection caused the tariff on foreign cars to be sharply raised in 1927.[56] This protection, in turn, caused the Bayerische Motorenwerke (BMW), producers of airplane engines, and the Zschopauer Motorenwerke (known as DKW), manufacturers of motorcycles, to begin making automobiles. Then in 1932, partly because of the Great Depression, DKW merged with three other nearby firms in the State of Saxony to form Auto Union. These three were Audi, Horch, and the automotive works of Wanderer-Werke.[57]

The financing of the automobile industry suggests the modified role carried out by the Grossbanken during the interwar years in providing venture capital for new industries. The Deutsche Bank did play a major part in the financing of Daimler-Benz and BMW. As the bank moved out of oil in 1925, it turned to automobiles and airplane engines. Indeed, Emil Georg von Stauss, the chairman of the dismembered Deutsche Petroleum, became a member of the Supervisory Board at Daimler in 1925 (later becoming chairman of the merged Daimler-Benz). In 1926 he also became chairman at BMW, two years before that producer of airplane engines turned to automobile production.

The rest of the industry relied much less on banks to provide funds for its initial investments in large-scale production and distribution facilities. Adam Opel, like Ford in the United States, financed itself largely from retained earnings. Adlerwerke used funds earned in its other product lines to finance the move into automobiles. In 1932 that company did turn to the Darmstädter Bank to raise funds to help it through a depression-caused crisis. The resulting Supervisory Board, however, was dominated more by industrialists than by bankers. The board's chairman was a senior manager at DEGUSSA, and other members were managers at Siemens. Still another member was the steel magnate Friedrich Flick. Auto Union, the 1932 merger, obtained financing from the State of Saxony, the region where the participants in the merger operated.[58]

After the raising of the tariff, Ford and General Motors were the only foreign producers that attempted to maintain large-scale production in Germany. Each responded quite differently to the situation. Ford's response reflected Henry Ford's idiosyncratic personal decision-making; General Motors' was the result of more carefully planned, collective decisions. Early in 1929 Alfred Sloan and the staff of the company's international office (the General Motors Export Companies) purchased for $33.4 million an 80% interest in Adam Opel, Germany's leading producer. (Sloan had taken an option to buy the company in the previous April.) The combined organizational skills of General Motors and Adam Opel quickly assured Opel's place as Europe's largest automobile producer. Its share of the German market rose from 26% in 1928 to 37.7% in March 1933 and then leveled off at about 40%. In 1938 it made 114,000 passenger cars, more than the next three German producers combined. (In 1938 Morris, the largest British automaker, produced just over 80,000 cars.) In these years Adam Opel continued to concentrate on the low-priced market, Daimler-Benz on the high-priced luxury models, and Adlerwerke and BMW on cars in the middle price range.[59]

Ford's performance in Germany was even worse than it was in Britain. Until 1929 the company did well. In 1930, indeed, Ford with an output of 11,150 vehicles had the second largest output in Germany, though it lagged far behind Adam Opel, which produced 24,000 in that year. In the same year Henry Ford decided, in view of a proposed substantial increase in the tariff, that his company should not only assemble but also fabricate parts in Germany. To do this he expanded an assembly plant then under construction in Cologne so that it could produce engines and some parts. The enlarged plant, relatively small by American standards, was still larger than the optimal size for the German or even the European market at a time when the Continent, and particularly Germany, was feeling the brunt of the depression. After its completion in the spring of 1931, the plant operated at only 13% capacity, and the resulting high unit cost forced the company to price itself out of the market. By 1932 its German market share had dropped to 1.9%, while its ranking in output had dropped from second to ninth in two years. The Cologne plant provides an even more dramatic example than the Ford works at Dagenham (near London) of the penalty paid for building a plant too large for existing demand.[60]

Recovery did come. In March 1933 Ford held 5.5% of the German market and was in sixth place in the output of automobiles. Then with the development of new models and the lower costs permitted by increasing demand and therefore increasing output, Ford was able by 1938 to edge ahead of Adlerwerke into fourth place and to press Daimler-Benz for third. Ford did even better in the production of trucks, reaching second place, behind Opel but ahead of Daimler-Benz.[61]

Thus in automobiles the Americans moved quickly into the German market once the opportunity appeared. Indeed, if Henry Ford had learned to relate capacity to existing demand, his company probably would have remained the second largest producer in Germany after General Motors' Adam Opel. But, scorning General Motors' type of careful market analysis, Ford completely misjudged demand. At the laying of the cornerstone for the new Cologne factory in October 1930, he was asked if he thought that hard times would diminish the buying power of the Germans. According to a history of Ford's foreign operations, he retorted stubbornly: "I don't see any hard times. The people look well fed and busy. Everywhere I've been I've seen people working, even little children."[62] By contrast, General Motors was able to use its technical and financial capabilities to expand and then maintain Adam Opel's strong market

share. General Motors engineers improved Opel's interchangeable-parts manufacturing, greatly increasing throughput, and its Product Study Group
designed new models for the German subsidiary.[63] Only in the years after World
War II did the German automobile manufacturers seriously challenge the Americans at home and abroad.

The history of the German automobile companies differs from that of the
makers of other volume-produced machinery in that the automobile industry
was a latecomer. The basic large-scale investment in production and personnel
that was needed to assure the cost advantage of scale did not occur until after
World War I. The machinery makers that had made such an investment before
the war—Lanz, Pfaff, Deutz, Bosch, Linde, Knorr-Bremse, Orenstein &
Koppel, and AFA—swiftly regained their European and, in most cases, their
overseas markets. But most of the German manufacturers of light, volume-
produced machinery had not developed organizational capabilities based on the
utilization of scale before the war, and therefore after the war they failed to
become a significant force, either at home or abroad.

Recovery as a Function of Organizational Capabilities

The experience of the leaders in what I have called Germany's lesser industries
between 1924, when the acceptance of the Dawes Plan assured the stabilization
of the German economy, and the mid-1930s, when Hitler began to place the
country on a war footing, does more than just underline the central importance
of organizational capabilities to postwar recovery. It also records changes in
those distinctively German patterns of competition and cooperation between
firms and in the relations between industrial enterprises and the banks.

To repeat, where such capabilities had been established before 1914,
recovery and a return to international competition came quickly in nearly all
cases despite major losses of foreign assets. Where, as in the case of oil and
branded, packaged products, such capabilities had not been fully developed,
German enterprises became parts of large foreign firms that had such capabilities—Anglo-Iranian in oil, Nestlé in chocolate, Corn Products in packaged
soup, and Jurgens and Van den Bergh in margarine.

So too, in industries where German challengers to foreign first movers in
European and international markets had not appeared before the Great War,
they rarely did so after 1924. For example, of the three glass companies in
Group 32 (see Appendixes C.2 and C.3), one was a subsidiary of Libbey-
Owens-Ford incorporated in 1925 and another, AG für Glasindustrie vorm.
Friedrich Siemens, had financial ties with Owens-Illinois. The foreign firms
Norton and Carborundum remained leaders in Germany in abrasives. The
majority of firms in the same group on the German lists (Appendixes C.2 and
C.3) were cement makers. They produced for local markets, and this was also

true of the pulp and paper producers listed in Group 26. In Group 34—fabricated metal products—there were no German firms comparable to Metal Box and the two American leaders in the production of metal containers, nor to Gillette in safety razors. The interwar years offered entrepreneurs in these industries few incentives to make the extensive investment in facilities and personnel necessary to compete in more than local markets.

After the stabilization of the German economy, mergers (usually nationwide) came in sugar, textiles, rubber, rayon, and explosives. In light machinery, growth came more from direct investment, with some acquisitions. Though cartels and conventions continued, they appear to have been less widespread than in the great industries. In the lesser industries the leaders relied more on functional and strategic effectiveness to compete for market share and profits, for in all cases they competed with foreign first movers in international markets, where cartels were rarely effective. This is particularly true of the light-machinery producers—Lanz, Pfaff, Linde, Deutz, Bosch, and the automobile companies. But it is also true of Continental, VGF, Deutsche Solvay, and Dynamit AG, which remained the German players in their global oligopolies. For both Deutsche Solvay and Dynamit AG, international agreements were far less effective after 1924 than they had been before 1914; and in rayon such agreements, as Donald Coleman's history of Courtaulds emphasizes, continued to be hard to establish and difficult to maintain.

Possibly because of such continuing competition the German enterprises in these lesser industries continued to grow, after a hiatus of a decade, in much the same manner as American firms. One difference was that, given the very brief period of recovery before the Nazis turned Germany to rearmament and self-sufficiency, the enterprises had far less opportunity than their American counterparts to expand through diversification. But diversification did become a major path to growth in the 1950s and 1960s after the German economy had once again recovered, this time from an even more devastating war.

The German banks, weakened as they were after 1924, played an even less significant role in the affairs of the leaders of the lesser industries than they had before 1914. Only when firms like Stollwerck and "Nordsee" Deutsche Hoch-seefischerei encountered financial difficulties, did they increase their influence. The banks, of course, continued to provide the usual services. Their representatives continued to sit on the boards of many companies, but they were often joined by industrialists whose firms had provided the necessary funds. Nor were the banks able to carry out energetically their earlier entrepreneurial role of financing industrial start-ups. Their support in financing the new automobile industry after the war was much less aggressive and less imaginative than their participation in the oil industry had been before 1914. After 1924 even German oil enterprises relied much more on industrial organizations—Rütgerswerke and Anglo-Persian Oil—than on banks for financing. In rubber, rayon, synthetic alkalies, explosives, and several of the light-machinery industries, the banks played an even smaller role than they had before 1914. In the interwar years financing came from American sources, including Goodrich in rubber, Du Pont and ICI in explosives, and probably Electric Storage Battery in electrical equipment.

These changes in interfirm relationships and the role of banks that occurred in the lesser industries during the interwar years were even more evident in the history of the great German industries—heavy machinery, chemicals, and metals—where the evolution of the German enterprises was less tempered by functional and strategic competition with foreign firms. And in those great industries the impact of existing organizational capabilities on German industrial recovery was even more substantial.

FOURTEEN

Recovery in the Great Industries

The great industries—heavy industrial machinery, metals, and chemicals—continued to overshadow other German industries in the years after 1924 as they had before 1914. This was true even though more firms in the lesser industries had moved into the list of the top two hundred. Before the war, 63.5% of the two hundred were clustered in the great industries; by 1929 the percentage was 55.5%. As in the lesser industries, only those firms that had developed their organizational strengths before the war were able to come back after the decade of war and crises.

In the great industries, with the exception of nonelectrical industrial machinery, cartels had played a larger role before the war than they had in the lesser industries. During the decade of war and crises, I.G.'s and Konzerne were generally preferred (see Chapter 12), and they were more prevalent than in the lesser industries. After 1924 mergers and acquisitions and the resulting rationalizations were on a grander scale than in other industries. On the other hand, in the years after the war the banks, which had played a significant role in the great industries before 1914, had even less influence than they did in the lesser industries.

Within the great industries rationalization and recovery after the stabilization of the economy in late 1924 differed, of course, from industry to industry. In industrial machinery—both electrical and nonelectrical—rationalization and recovery were carried out more by direct investment than by acquisition and merger. Here the most successful enterprises were those that were able to use their organizational capabilities to develop new products and processes or substantially improve existing ones. This was also the case in nonferrous metals and pharmaceuticals. In steel and in industrial chemicals, however, activity centered more on the rationalization of existing facilities, a rationalization made possible by the final realization of plans for legal consolidation and administrative centralization that had been under discussion during the preceding two decades.

Nonelectrical Industrial Machinery: Revival and Rationalization

After 1924 the makers of heavy industrial machinery (Group 35; see Appendixes C.1–C.4)—those uniquely German enterprises that had become successful before 1914 by exploiting the economies of scope—quickly became again the leading producers of machines for European factories, mines, ports, railway terminals, utilities, and commercial centers. Indeed, the leaders expanded the number of lines they produced. This was evident, for example, in the wide variety of markets served by Maschinenfabrik Augsburg-Nürnberg (MAN) in the late 1920s (see Table 22). In this kind of manufacturing, where product performance and service were far more important competitive weapons than price, the leading firms made as little use of cartels after stabilization as they had before the war. Once the economy had settled down, they rarely sought to enter existing I.G.'s or Konzerne or to form new ones of their own. Existing I.G.'s were often disbanded, and the Konzerne rarely acquired additional enterprises. Therefore it was largely within those Konzerne that had expanded between 1918 and 1924 that most of the interfirm rationalization in heavy machinery occurred.

Those enterprises that remained independent continued to produce much the same products as they had before the war—such firms as Berlin-Anhaltische Maschinenbau (BAMAG), Deutsche Maschinenfabrik (DEMAG), Hannoversche Maschinenbau (Hanomag), Berliner Maschinenbau Schwartzkopff, Maschinenfabrik Buckau Wolf, Sächsische Maschinen-Fabrik vorm. Rich. Hartmann, Ernst Schiess, Ludwig Loewe & Co., Stettiner Chamottefabrik, and the shipbuilders Blohm & Voss and Howaldtswerke. (See Chapter 12 for a description of the products of these companies.)

Of these enterprises only BAMAG and DEMAG made major acquisitions. In 1924, before stabilization, BAMAG acquired Meguin, a producer of coal, iron, sheet steel, structures, and bridges, which had been forced to move out of the Saar. The purchase, like that of other enterprises, was a defensive move to assure supplies for BAMAG and outlets for Meguin.[1] DEMAG's growth came after stabilization. In 1926, as part of nationwide merger in steel, it took over the machinery units of Fritz Thyssen's Konzern.

The machinery firms that were relatively diversified—both the independents and those that had become members of larger Konzerne—continued to prosper. Because they exploited scope rather than scale in production, they had built few plants abroad, and therefore they lost less by expropriation during the war than did other German manufacturers. They appear to have regained their original markets with little difficulty.

On the other hand, those that remained less diversified—and stayed too close to declining industries, such as railroad equipment and textile machinery—fared less well. By 1929 many of the specialized machinery firms that had been among the two hundred largest companies before the war were no longer in that group (see Appendixes C.1 and C.2). Some had been acquired by large enterprises, including Konzerne. Several may even have gone out of business. Even the stronger of the less diversified machinery firms suffered severe financial losses in the early 1930s. Thus Borsig, for decades a leader among producers of locomotives and railway equipment, sold its locomotive works to AEG, shut down its main Tegeler Works at the end of 1931, and then went into receivership early in 1932. After the Borsig family had been forced to withdraw, financial reorganization was initiated by the steel producer Rheinmetall (rather than by a bank) in a transaction that led to the formation of Rheinmetall Borsig AG.[2] So, too, Sächsische Maschinen-Fabrik vorm. Rich. Hartmann went into receivership in 1930. Financial reorganization was followed by a merger with three other neighboring textile-machinery companies in the city of Chemnitz. After rationalization the consolidated enterprise once again became profitable.[3]

Major rationalizations in the industrial-machinery industry—those that involved more than one firm—came primarily within the new and enlarged Konzerne, those of Krupp, Klöckner, Thyssen, and GHH, rather than in the independents. Although such industrial reorganizations were extensive, little has been written about them. I will use two examples to illustrate the process.

One is the rationalization of the German manufacture of refrigerating machinery instigated by Paul Reusch, general director of Gutehoffnungshütte (GHH). In building its Konzern after the war GHH had acquired three works producing such machinery—the MAN works at Augsburg, the works of L. A. Riedinger Maschinen- und Bronzewaren-Fabrik (also in Augsburg), and those of Maschinenfabrik Esslingen (to the west, near Stuttgart). The last had the largest output of these specialized machines. In 1927 Reusch and the senior managers of MAN opened negotiations with the managers of Carl Linde's Eismaschinen, the industry's leader. They quickly agreed (as described in Chapter 13) that GHH would concentrate more on large industrial refrigeration machinery and Linde would manufacture the small, more standardized, increasingly mass-produced refrigerators. All of GHH's production was then placed in the Esslingen works, where an experienced work force also produced the large compressors and boilers that were used in such industrial refrigerating machinery. The other two works, those of MAN and Riedinger, stopped making refrigerating machinery. Their facilities were redesigned and integrated in order to exploit the economies of scope in the production of diesel engines and of offset and other types of printing presses, new products which MAN was then bringing on stream; while Linde devoted the facilities of two factories to small refrigerator equipment, including household units, for which the demand was growing rapidly. (One line of more specialized small refrigerators which did not compete directly with those at the Linde works continued to be produced at the Esslingen factory.) Moreover, Linde's Eismaschinen took over the designing, selling, and servicing of all machines, small and large, because it had far greater capabilities and facilities in marketing and product development than the Esslingen enterprise had. Linde then reorganized its sales force into two separate divisions to deal with its two very different sets of customers.[4]

The other example of rationalization concerned the two firms Deutz and Humboldt, both members of the Klöckner Konzern. Peter Klöckner, the iron and steel producer, had been chairman of the Supervisory Board of each firm since 1920 when he had become a major shareholder in each. In 1924 he united the two in an I.G. whose primary purpose was to provide Deutz with the facilities to expand production of its new lines of diesel engines and diesel-driven vehicles. Humboldt had enlarged its production of railroad equipment, particularly locomotives, during the war, and by 1924 was suffering from over-capacity like the rest of the industry. In 1925, therefore, Klöckner turned over part of the Humboldt works to Deutz for the production of diesel-powered tractors, and later he turned over its facilities to diesel locomotives. Humboldt's equipment for making steam locomotives was then sold off, as were the facilities for producing cranes, boilers, and excavators. The remaining departments concentrated on Humboldt's original product lines of machinery for mining and processing coal and ore. In addition, a new Humboldt department was formed to produce pulverizing and cement-making equipment. In 1930 Humboldt and Deutz were formally merged into an AG. Six years later the consolidated company, Humboldt-Deutz, acquired Magirus, a leading producer of diesel fire engines. (The diesel fire engine with its obvious advantages over gasoline power had captured that market.) Then in 1938 Klöckner legally consolidated his diversified machinery maker into the family's iron, steel, and mining enterprises. In this way, in the years immediately following stabilization, the Klöckner Konzern effectively transferred its facilities and skills from the old, declining, steam-driven and gasoline-driven equipment into new diesel equipment, thus permitting Deutz to compete successfully with another diesel pioneer, MAN, and preventing Humboldt from suffering the same fate as Borsig.[5]

These two examples of rationalization and development in two major mechanical technologies—refrigeration and motive power—indicate how interfirm cooperation within Konzerne and also with outside firms helped to modernize German industry after 1924 and to enhance its competitive capabilities. Such cooperative arrangements rarely occurred in the United States, where they would have been considered violations of the antitrust laws. There, such rationalization and product development took place within large diversified firms such as General Electric and General Motors. In refrigerators the two American companies concentrated on small, mass-produced consumer products. In diesels they both moved much more slowly than MAN and Humboldt-Deutz. In Britain little was done to develop either of these product lines. There such interfirm rationalizations rarely occurred, because so few firms had the managerial resources and incentives to carry them out. Finally, these examples emphasize that after 1924 in Germany such product development and rationalization was financed, as well as planned and carried out, by industrial companies, with the banks playing only a minor role.

Electrical Machinery

In electrical equipment (Group 36; see Appendixes C.1–C.4) the structure of the industry and the number and characteristics of the leaders were less changed by the events of 1914–1924 than was the case in nonelectrical machinery. This was true, in part at least, because of the mergers and rationalizations in the electrical field that had occurred in 1904. The two groups differed in that in nonelectrical machinery one firm did not overshadow the others, while the electrical-machinery group continued to be dominated by its two giants.

Although Siemens and AEG became even more diversified than before 1914, the smaller producers continued to concentrate on narrow lines of products. Of these the biggest was Bergmann-Elektricitäts-Werke, in which both Siemens and AEG came to have substantial investments (although in 1928 the two controlled less than 50%); Bergmann was able to increase its output of specialized lines of equipment with the approval of its two major shareholders. Much more independent was Voigt & Haeffner, maker of electrical switchboards, which added starters, radiators and fuses for automobiles to its line, thus challenging Robert Bosch. The other firms listed among the top two hundred (see Appendixes C.1–C.3) remained more narrowly specialized. Julius Pintsch, a maker of specialized machinery, had produced gas lamps for ships and trains. During World War I Pintsch pioneered in the development of tungsten filament for electric lamps, and then it shifted to producing closely related electric-lighting equipment. Felten & Guilleaume continued to produce cables for both light-voltage and heavy-voltage equipment, while Mix & Genest and C. Lorenz AG remained producers of specialized communication equipment. One new firm listed among the top two hundred in 1929, Polyphonwerke, was one of the few German companies to gain from the wartime expropriation. In 1917 it obtained Deutsche Grammophon, the German subsidiary of the British-financed, American-managed Gramophone Company in England. Despite a barrage of lawsuits in the 1920s, Polyphonwerke continued to fend off the former owner's attempts to regain control of Deutsche Grammophon.[6] During the interwar years these smaller firms, all administered through centralized, functionally departmentalized structures, remained very much under the shadow of the industry's two giants, the Siemens group (including Siemens & Halske, or S&H, and Siemens-Schuckert Werke, or SSW) and Allgemeine Elektricitäts-Gesellschaft (AEG).

Thus while the companies in the nonelectrical machinery group developed along characteristically German lines, the structure of the electrical-machinery industry and of the firms in it, as well as the dynamics of their growth, paralleled in many ways those of their American counterparts, but with two basic differences. Besides the fact that interfirm cooperation and agreements remained entirely legal, the two German firms had suffered severe losses during the decade of war and crises.

RAPID RECOVERY AND CONTINUED MODERNIZATION

Siemens and AEG lost more by wartime expropriation than the leaders in Germany's other great industries—nonelectrical machinery, metals, and even chemicals—for they had greater investments abroad. Siemens lost its plants and technical bureaus in Britain, France, and Russia. In Russia the government took over the three Siemens works, one of AEG's works, and their jointly owned cable-making company. Equally disastrous was the loss of foreign markets, during the decade of war and crises, to producers in neutral countries, particularly Brown, Boveri of Switzerland (whose German subsidiary also remained an effective small competitor in the German market), L. M. Ericsson of Sweden, N. V. Philips of the Netherlands, and, most significant of all, the two American first movers—General Electric and Westinghouse. Of the two German leaders, AEG, with its emphasis on heavy equipment and its concentration on foreign sales, probably lost the most.[7] As a result, the German share of the world's export market for electrical equipment dropped from 46.4% in 1913 to 25.8% in 1925, while that of the United States rose from 15.7% to 24.9%, that of Britain from 22.0% to 25.1%, that of France from 4.2% to 5.6%, and that of the Netherlands, Sweden, and Switzerland (together) from 7.2% to 10.0%.[8] Serious, too, was Siemens's loss of control over its Swiss holding company, and AEG's loss of its Swiss holding company and also its Belgian company (SOFINA)—holding companies that were used to finance customers in international markets.[9]

In the period of instability from 1918 to 1924 both enterprises relied on stock participations to cement interfirm relationships. Siemens, in addition to the I. G. with Stinnes's iron and steel enterprises (SRSU), joined with AEG to invest in the electric-cable makers Felten & Guilleaume, and both increased their investment in Bergmann. AEG also took a large block of shares of Mix & Genest in order to obtain a window on the telephone business. In 1920 the two leaders sponsored the formation of Osram GmbH to produce their light bulbs. Soon the bulb-making facilities of Bergmann, Pintsch, and a specialized bulb producer,

Auer, were brought into Osram. In 1924 Osram signed the Phoebus agreement with leading foreign producers, which effectively controlled the international markets for electric bulbs. [10]

These last agreements were related to broader accords made by both of the leaders with the Americans. In 1923 AEG and General Electric renewed their prewar arrangements for exchange of technical information and for defining markets. By the resulting allocations General Electric agreed to stay out of Europe except for France, Spain, and Portugal, and AEG agreed to stay out of the United States and Canada. In the following year Siemens and Westinghouse signed a comparable pact. [11] Thus when stabilization came, the German leaders in the electrical-equipment industry had already returned to international trade as major players.

After 1924 they moved in earnest to regain foreign markets. First, however, came a proposal and negotiations for merger, one that would have been similar to those that were being carried out in the same year (1925) in steel and chemicals. But when AEG initiated negotiations, the Siemens managers hesitated. [12] They had already put aside their I.G. with the Stinnes group because they had long since ceased to look at that steel enterprise as a source of supplies or funds. [13] The more carefully they reviewed the merger proposal, the less attractive it became.

The incentives to merge were limited. The two firms had already carried out extended rationalization and modernization following the mergers of 1904. Moreover, during and after the war Siemens had gone further than AEG in maintaining and improving its facilities and also in investing in research and development. Karl Dihlmann, director of the Zentral-Werksverwaltung (Production Department) of SSW from 1914 to 1920, and his successor, Carl Köttgen, had drawn up and carried out detailed plans to increase throughput and decrease unit costs—plans which included the application of American continuous-belt and conveyor techniques. In the same period, Siemens had adopted and further perfected the most advanced inventory and accounting controls, including some of American origin. For these reasons Siemens emerged from the decade of war and crises financially, technologically, and organizationally stronger than its primary competitor—particularly in heavy equipment, where AEG had earlier had an edge. Therefore the Siemens managers decided in 1925 to continue the prewar pattern of both competing and negotiating with AEG for market share rather than merging. In 1930 and 1931, when the onslaught of the depression brought a second set of proposals and negotiations for a merger, Siemens again said no. [14]

After 1924 both firms quickly rebuilt their marketing networks of technical bureaus, sales offices, and agents which had been disrupted by the war and continued to expand the existing ones at home and in neutral countries. By the 1930s Siemens's international organization included close to two hundred subsidiaries, and AEG had more than three hundred marketing and distribution offices throughout the world.[15] Siemens continued to do well in Scandinavia and particularly in eastern Europe. To support its eastern European sales organization it operated three works in Vienna, one in Budapest, and another in Czechoslovakia. In Czechoslovakia and also in Italy and France it was forced to set up factories to produce telephone equipment, because all three nations required such equipment to be manufactured by national producers.[16] In addition, Siemens regained its place in Britain through an agreement with its former subsidiary, Siemens Brothers, by which the two firms exchanged stock and shared research results and technical information. It also expanded its investment in Japan by forming a joint venture with Furukawa, a long-established zaibatsu (family-controlled business group) that focused on the mining and processing of copper. The joint enterprise was called Fuji Denki Seizo (Fuji Electric Manufacturing).

Siemens recovered from the devastating losses of facilities and markets more quickly and successfully than AEG, but their joint performance was very impressive. From 1925 to 1931 the German share of the export market in their industry rose from 25.8% to 32.7%, while that of the United States declined slightly from 24.9% to 23.2% and that of Britain fell much more sharply from 25.1% to 13.8%. By 1933, however, the German share had dropped back to 26.5% and the British had risen to 18.9%, reflecting in part the fact that the depression did not hit the British economy so hard as it hit the Continent (and the United States), and possibly also reflecting the increased capabilities of British industry.[17]

In the years immediately following stabilization the greatest challenge facing the two German leaders was finance. Funds were needed to maintain the quality of product and process at home. They were also essential for competing abroad, particularly for large utility projects in which the customers expected to be at least partly financed by the manufacturer. In Latin America, for example, where AEG and Siemens worked closely together, they lost out to General Electric in sales to utilities. And in telephone equipment Siemens had difficulty in competing with Western Electric in Europe as well as in Latin America and Asia, and then after 1925 with International Telephone & Telegraph (ITT), to which Western Electric had sold its overseas holdings. The German banks, even the Grossbanken, lacked the necessary funds. So did the holding companies in Switzerland and Belgium, which Siemens and AEG had revived after stabilization.

As in other industries the money had to come from America. In January 1925, therefore, Max Haller, the Siemens financial chief, completed negotiations with Dillon, Read, an aggressive New York investment banker, for a $10 million loan, which was soon increased to $25 million. Other loans followed under the auspices of the Bank of America as well as Dillon, Read. At the same time AEG took out loans from the National City Bank. At Siemens the American financing, which reached a total of RM 130 million ($32 million), was used to renovate old facilities and to build new ones, including a new, high-rise, switch-gear factory in Siemensstadt and additions to the Werner Works; to start a subsidiary in Ireland; to expand foreign offices; and to help finance customers.[18]

It was the continuing financial needs of the German giants that encouraged Owen D. Young and Gerard Swope of General Electric to organize the industry on a global basis (see Chapter 9). Young wrote to one of his senior British executives late in 1929 that whereas British industry needed "proper mobilization and management," the Germans required "an ample capital supply." To provide this capital and the influence that came with the transaction, GE in July 1929 acquired 16.66% of Osram, the light-bulb company that had been formed in 1920 under the sponsorship of Siemens and AEG. The price was RM 37 million, or $8.8 million. Then, in October, GE acquired $5 million worth of AEG shares, which, by increasing GE's holdings to 25% of the stock outstanding, made it the German company's largest shareholder.[19] Siemens refused to sell GE a minority holding of a comparable size. But at a meeting on January 26 and 27, 1930, in New York between Swope and Carl Köttgen of Siemens, Swope agreed that GE would take $11 million of the $14 million gold debentures to be repaid in 999 years—an issue that Dillon, Read had underwritten. Both Swope and Carl Friedrich von Siemens agreed that the arrangement would provide a basis for "exchange of patents, technical experience, and information" between GE, AEG, and Siemens.[20]

Although the severity of the depression forced Swope and Young to put aside their ambitious plans to unify the world's electrical-equipment producers, Siemens and AEG maintained close contact with their American ally. Both kept GE informed of their abortive negotiation for merger in 1930 and 1931, of an agreement between the two of them on export prices, and of an agreement made between Siemens and Brown, Boveri on patents and processes. In 1933, as was pointed out in Chapter 9, the major players in the global oligopoly agreed to the International Notification and Compensation Agreement, which was administered after 1936 through the International Electric Apparatus Export Association in Zurich. By this agreement, marketing territories for electrical apparatus were allocated. For specified territories, procedures were established by which each company was required to notify the Association's international secretary of its bid on a major project. After the bids were reviewed, the successful company had to "compensate" the other bidders. A similar arrangement was created for the sale of telephone and telegraph equipment, and still another was made for cables.[21] Thus, by the mid-1930s, changes in market share in the global electric-equipment industry had come to be negotiated rather than competed for. Nevertheless, Siemens continued to rely on its technical excellence to strengthen its negotiating position and so to maintain and, indeed, increase its market share.

Within Germany the two leaders and the smaller producers continued to be tied together through a complex network of interfirm arrangements. After stabilization the electrical-equipment manufacturers continued to rely on joint ventures and stock participations to influence price and output, more than on formal cartel agreements. Thus AEG and Siemens formed a joint venture (Klangfilm) to produce equipment for talking movies and one for radio broadcasting (Transradio, a broadcasting subsidiary of the prewar Telefunken). They remained shareholders in Bergmann and Osram, and they took holdings in Deutsche Grammophon and in a combination of smaller producers of electric calculators and cash registers, and even in a maker of glass products. They also remained shareholders in Vereinigte Eisenbahn-Signal Werke, a 1927 merger of an S&H subsidiary, Siemens & Halske Blockwerke, the Railway Signal Department of AEG, and a small competitor—a merger that was followed by rationalization of the consolidated facilities. The two continued close technical and marketing cooperation with Accumulatoren-Fabrik AG and Felten & Guilleaume. In 1929 the American firm ITT formed a joint venture for the production of telephone equipment with AEG and Felten & Guilleaume, a venture in which the American company soon acquired a controlling interest. That ITT-dominated joint venture, in turn, obtained control of Mix & Genest and C. Lorenz, the two smaller telephone-equipment makers on the 1929 list (see Appendix C.4), and also of two other small specialized firms.[22]

Thus in the electrical-equipment industry, during the interwar years, cooperation became far more common than competition, even though there was no merger comparable to those that occurred in steel and chemicals.

THE EVOLVING STRUCTURE OF THE LEADERS

The organizational framework in which the two leaders made and implemented day-to-day operating and long-term strategic decisions was central to the performance of the German electrical-equipment industry. Both companies, it will be recalled, had created their internal administrative structures after rationalizing production and distribution following the turn-of-the-century mergers. The structure of Siemens and that of AEG (about which much less is known) evolved slowly during the years after 1914. There were no major reorganizations similar to those which occurred at Westinghouse in the mid-1930s and at GE in the early 1950s.

In 1921 the Siemens group included, as it had before 1914, S&H as the parent company—producers of telegraph, telephone, cable, and other light-current equipment—SSW, which was controlled by S&H, and a number of foreign and domestic subsidiaries. S&H and SSW were administered from the headquarters building in Siemensstadt, and they shared the same corporate financial staff in the Finanz-Abteilung, or Finance Division.

In 1921 the Siemens group readjusted its basic organizational structure to incorporate wartime developments. New product lines, particularly in instruments, medical equipment, and telecommunications, had been added, and after 1918 the production of military equipment was dropped. Sales forces were reshaped to adjust to wartime losses. Of more importance was the growth of the overall corporate office during the war. By 1921 the Finance Division, headed by Max Haller and serving both S&H and SSW, included the central or corporate offices for internal accounting, purchasing, legal affairs, taxes, statistics, tariffs, and archives, and new departments such as a central research department with chemical and physical laboratories, an enlarged patents department, and departments to perform several housekeeping duties. One office for "economic policy" (comparable to a development department in a large American firm) and another for "social policy," primarily labor relations, were established in 1919. Another department in the Finance Division was created to coordinate the activities of the technical bureaus at home and abroad that were used by the Siemens enterprises in marketing goods. At the top, the administrative hinge between S&H and SSW became stronger than it had been before 1914, because Carl Friedrich von Siemens had become chairman of the Supervisory Board of each company. He and the two boards were served by a new office for supervision of personnel, as well as by the older general secretariat.[23] By 1921, then, the Siemens group had a corporate office of staff and general managers whose operations resembled (even more than they had in 1914) the corporate offices that Du Pont and General Motors were just beginning to create in 1921.

The overall structure at Siemens remained much the same throughout the interwar period (see Figures 13 and 14).[24] The Finance Division and the staff of each Supervisory Board not only served both S&H and SSW but also the firms in which S&H had major stock participations. During the 1920s the internal organization of each of these major operating enterprises—S&H and SSW—remained much as it had been before the war. At S&H (Figure 13) production and distribution were administered along more decentralized, divisional lines than was the case at SSW. Werner Works F made and sold telecommunications equipment; Werner Works M made and marketed measuring and medical equipment. In 1932 Werner Works M was legally separated to become Siemens-Reinigerwerke. A third division, Werner Works Central Administration, supervised such divisional staff departments as research, construction, personnel, labor relations, patents, and technical literature. It also supervised an electro-chemical subsidiary until 1933 (which in that year became a separate legal and administrative subsidiary), a subsidiary for leasing equipment, another for production and distribution of low-voltage cables, and a fourth for aircraft engines and equipment. Finally, it was responsible for the Wiener (Vienna) Works, which supervised production and distribution of selected lines in eastern Europe. These autonomous subsidiaries reported through the head of the Finance Division to the S&H Vorstand.

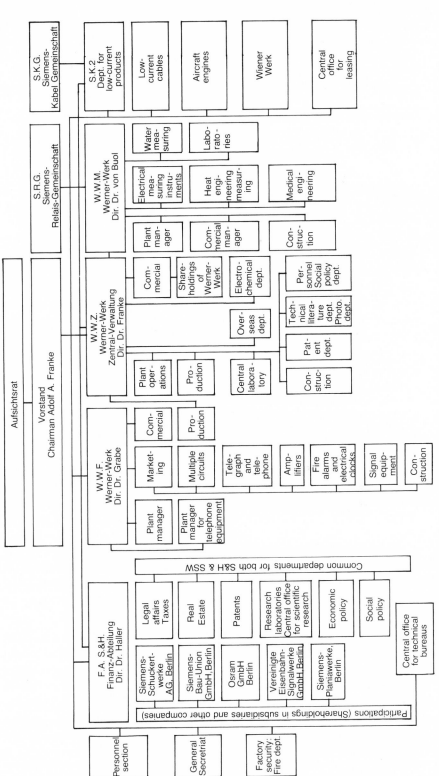

Figure 13. Organization of Siemens & Halske, August 1930. Adapted from Siemens Archives, SAA 68/vi 187, Personnel Department, Werner-Werk, Munich.

While S&H became further decentralized along product lines, SSW continued to be operated through a centralized, functionally departmentalized organization (Figure 14). The Zentral-Werksverwaltung continued to administer the company's giant plants, each manufacturing a major product line.[25] The departments of the Zentral-Verkehrsverwaltung supervised sales, marketing, and distribution to each of the major product markets—power stations, industrial customers, wholesalers, and railways. The overseas department, established before the war, continued to watch over marketing abroad, while another office oversaw the SSW technical bureaus in Germany and Europe.

The Finanz-Abteilung and the Supervisory Board of S&H were also responsible (see Figure 13) for the other wholly or partly owned enterprises, and they kept an eye on the joint holdings of S&H and AEG. Besides Osram and Vereinigte Eisenbahn-Signal Werke, these other enterprises included Siemens-Plania-Werke and Bau-Union. Of the last two, the first was a 1927 merger of Gebrüder Siemens & Co. (the electrochemical company Siemens had established in the 1880s) and the plants of Rütgerswerke, producing carbon electrodes and other amorphous carbons. Siemens held 51% and the Rütgerswerke 49% of the shares of the new firm. The second, Bau-Union, was an engineering subsidiary which had been formed in 1921 primarily to build power plants and hydroelectric projects.[26]

As for AEG, much less information is available on the evolution of its internal structure during the interwar years. It had almost as wide a range of products as Siemens, having moved into telecommunications after the war, and it distributed and marketed its goods in all parts of the world. Observers agreed that it was more decentralized than Siemens. "Each plant constitutes a separate organizational unit," wrote Robert Brady in 1933, "which is self-sufficient" in "the conduct of all internal operations." In the 1920s AEG followed Siemens in introducing American-style "automatic machinery and continuous flow methods."[27] But AEG does not seem to have developed a corporate office as powerful as that of Siemens. For example, it did not establish a central research laboratory until 1928.

At both companies, coordination of closely related activities carried on by the many operating units remained a continuing problem. Harm Schröter's study of Siemens's activities in central, southern, and southeastern Europe during the interwar years describes the complex organizational lines of command that ran between the corporate headquarters in Siemensstadt, the works in Vienna, the other production and distribution facilities, and the sales offices of the different integrated divisions and subsidiaries in eastern Europe. Coordination of production also raised problems. Thus an internal I.G. had to be formed to facilitate a joint operation and resolve conflicts between SSW and S&H in the production of cables and relays.[28]

The structure of the two leading firms and the industry as a whole changed

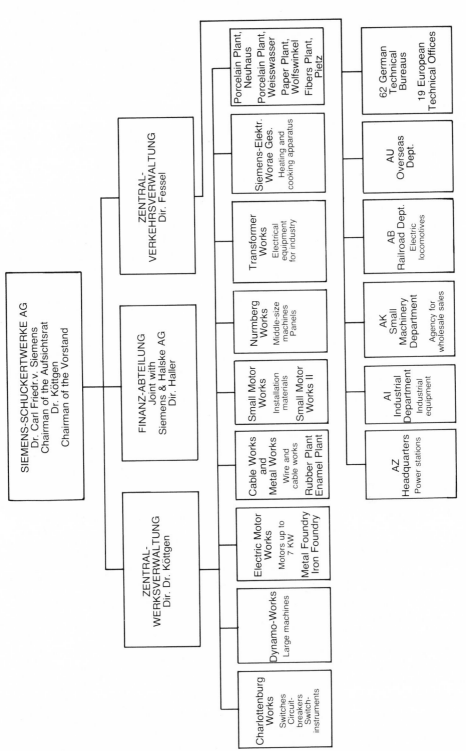

Figure 14. Organization of Siemens-Schuckertwerke, August 1927. From Siemens Archives, Elmo 7152.

little in the 1930s. At Siemens in 1932, when the medical-equipment division was spun off from the Werner Works to become legally and administratively independent, the rest of the S&H operations were arranged in four autonomous divisions—telecommunications, light electrical equipment, electrochemicals, and small-lot sales (wholesaling). In the following year, at the request of the Defense Ministry, the top management formed Siemens Apparate und Maschinen GmbH to handle all government orders. Increased wartime demands may also have helped to bring to a successful conclusion, in October 1941, the negotiations that had been going on for three years between Siemens and AEG over the control of their several joint ventures and participations. By this agreement Siemens turned over its shares of Telefunken to AEG and in turn received AEG shares in Bergmann, Vereinigte Eisenbahn-Signalwerke, Deutsche Grammophon, and Klangfilm. This move gave each of the parent companies stronger and firmer administrative control over the long-established operating enterprises whose shares they had received.[29]

Of all the great German industries the electrical-equipment industry was most similar, in its evolution, to its American counterpart. In both Germany and the United States the two first movers quickly became colossal enterprises, and this quartet continued to dominate global markets during the half-century covered in this study. More than other leading German enterprises the two electrical companies grew through merger and acquisition. The rationalization that followed the industry-wide mergers at the beginning of the century permitted an intensive exploitation of the economies of both scale and scope, probably more than occurred in the American firms. In this most critically placed industry of the Second Industrial Revolution the German firms invested heavily in research and development and grew by adding related product lines, as well as by making direct investments abroad. By 1929 Siemens and AEG had become two of the world's largest industrial enterprises. In that year, S&H and SSW together employed 116,000 workers and reported assets of RM 690.2 million ($180 million). For AEG the figures were 70,000 and RM 548.4 million ($154 million). The only firms in Germany that were larger were the recent mergers in steel and chemicals. In 1929 these two industries were still establishing their consolidated structures and rationalizing facilities and personnel. The German electrical-machinery companies in 1929 employed substantially larger work forces than their American counterparts, but the value of their assets was less. In 1930 GE had assets of $493.9 million and a work force of 78,380, and Westinghouse had assets of $246.1 million and a work force of 36,974. If the work force of Western Electric (the manufacturing arm of American Telephone & Telegraph) had been added to those of GE and Westinghouse, the total number of employees would have been about the same, although the assets of the American firms were much higher.[30] Except for telephone and telegraph equipment, the product lines of the German and American companies were much the same.

Both Germans and Americans continued to pioneer in the development of new electrical and electronic products, including radios, talking movies, stoves, vacuum cleaners, other household appliances, and X-rays and other medical equipment. GE appears to have commercialized more of the alloys and chemicals (plastics and varnishes) developed to improve the equipment that produced and distributed electricity than did the German companies, and the Germans continued to play a larger role in the production and distribution of electrochemicals.

Although the Siemens organization changed in an evolutionary manner, it appears to have been more carefully and systematically defined than the structure of GE before its post–World War II reorganizations and than that of Westinghouse before its major restructuring that began in 1933—and even, apparently, more clearly defined than the structure of AEG. Nevertheless, by the 1930s each of these four companies did have a central corporate office with staff and general executives who supervised, monitored, coordinated, and allocated resources for a number of autonomous, self-contained operating units.

The most obvious difference between the Germans and the Americans was the complex and varied arrangements that the German firms had with each other and with the smaller competitors and producers of related projects within Germany and Europe, including joint ventures, stock participations, cartels, conventions, and agreements involving patents, processes, and marketing— nearly all of which were illegal in the United States. Did the antitrust laws, then, make a significant difference? Did they make American industry more effective and German industry less so? The initial success of the two German leaders, their industry's quick recovery after the war, and the relatively parallel development in the growth and the structures of the first movers in each of the two countries suggest that they did not.

In both of the German companies, as in the American, salaried managers ran the business. After Walther Rathenau was assassinated in 1922, family influence came to an end at AEG. But at Siemens, Carl Friedrich and his two nephews, all experienced managers, continued to work through an impressive hierarchy of able managers that the Siemens family had recruited to administer the enterprise from the 1880s onward. In neither company did banks and bankers direct the policy-making. The Siemens group had always kept its favored bank, the Deutsche Bank, at arms length. At Siemens it was Max Haller, its financial chief, and not the bankers on the board, who negotiated the American loans. Bankers probably had a larger say at AEG, but their primary task appears to have been to assist in the flow of American funds to the company. In 1930 the AEG Supervisory Board included Swope, Young, and three other GE executives—five men who probably had as much influence on that board as did all the others, the half-dozen bankers, representing different Grossbanken, and the larger number of industrial leaders, mostly from the steel and chemical industries. In any case, it was the full-time senior executives in these giant capital-using enterprises who conceived, determined, and carried out the strategies and the tactics that permitted them to regain lost international markets and to expand existing markets and create new ones through improved processes and products, and to do this despite the growing organizational capabilities of the British electrical-equipment companies and the smaller European competitors—N. V. Philips; Brown, Boveri; and L. M. Ericsson.

Metals

The histories of the leading metal makers (Group 33; see Appendixes C.1–C.4) during the interwar years follow more distinctly German lines than do those of the electrical-equipment producers. After stabilization, Krupp rationalized the personnel and facilities of the many firms in its Konzern in much the same manner as did GHH and Klöckner. Large centralized enterprises such as Hoesch, Mannesmann, and Metallgesellschaft rebuilt and expanded their activities along prewar lines, much as did many of the makers of machinery, both light and heavy. What was new—what differentiated iron and steel from both electrical and nonelectrical machinery—was the industry-wide merger in 1926 that formed Vereinigte Stahlwerke (VSt), an enterprise even larger than Siemens or AEG. This merger reflected the steel industry's past weaknesses and its current needs, weaknesses and needs that had been recognized before the war and had intensified during the decade between 1914 and 1924. The resulting administrative reorganization, which created an enterprise comparable to the United States Steel Corporation, permitted a rapid rationalization and modernization of the industry, something that the British steel industry was unable to achieve during the interwar years. The differing responses dramatically emphasize how differing commitments to management—the British commitment to the ways of personal, nonhierarchical enterprise and the German adoption of managerial enterprise—affected industrial structure and performance.

STEEL: MERGER, RATIONALIZATION, AND RESTRUCTURING

For the makers of steel, the war, the peace terms, and the postwar crises were more devastating than they were to any of the other German industries. During the war the German producers lost their overseas markets to other nations, particularly the United States. In addition, the Versailles Treaty deprived Germany of 72% of her iron-ore reserves, 43.4% of her pig-iron output, 36.3% of her crude steel, 53.9% of her steel-bloom output, and 30% of her rolling capacity. Though 60% of pig-iron production had come from domestic ores in 1913, only 18% did so in 1925 and 11.85% in 1927. Especially serious was the breakup of the closely coordinated, integrated industrial complexes by the permanent loss of Alsace-Lorraine and the temporary occupation of the Ruhr and Rhineland.[31]

In 1925 the iron and steel industry was probably in greater need of reorganization and rationalization than any other German industry. During the war and postwar years Europe had greatly expanded its output of steel.[32] Before 1925 most of the increased German capacity was built in a relatively unplanned, ad hoc manner, either to meet specific military needs during the war or to place capital in real assets during the period of inflation. Moreover, unlike the makers of light machinery and pharmaceuticals, the steelmakers were not able to go under tariffs by building abroad, for a plant constructed at optimal size in a particular market would increase capacity far beyond that market's existing demand. Nor were steelmaking facilities and skills easily transferable to related products for existing or for new and growing markets.

Finally, the industry's leaders had not rationalized and modernized equipment before World War I in the manner of their American counterparts or their contemporaries in the German electrical-equipment industry. There had been no nationwide mergers. The call of August Thyssen for merger and reorganization in 1905 and that of Albert Vögler in 1919 had gone unheeded. Even though the prewar German steel industry was larger and more productive than Britain's, its situation in the mid-1920s was similar to Britain's. In both countries the proposed answer was much the same—reorganization and modernization. The German steelmakers succeeded; and their success, especially when it is contrasted with the failure of their British counterparts, is striking and instructive.

As soon as the economy moved toward stabilization, the leading steelmakers turned their attention once again to consolidation. The brief "stabilization crisis" in the spring of 1925 emphasized the industry's plight by driving down prices and creating a financial stringency that brought some of the weaker steel companies close to bankruptcy. Early that summer the strong proponents of merger, Thyssen and Vögler, began negotiations with the senior managers of Rheinstahl. (Vögler, after Hugo Stinnes's death in April 1924, had taken command of the coal, iron, and steel properties of the Stinnes Konzern—that is, of Deutsch-Luxemburg, Bochumer Verein, and GBAG.) Other leading firms were soon invited to join the discussions. Three major producers, those which concentrated on end products more than on primary steel—GHH, the Klöckner Konzern, and the tube maker Mannesmann—showed little interest in participating. The managers of the Stumm Konzern, which was suffering severe financial losses, also stayed away.[33]

The negotiations lasted for months, unlike those that led to the formation of the United States Steel Corporation. At first the participants held back from complete fusion, favoring an I.G. Fritz Springorum, the general director at Hoesch, then withdrew from the negotiating table. He was willing to sell out to a merger but did not want to play second fiddler in an I.G. Nor did he want to take part in negotiations involving confidential information if he was not serious about accepting the final outcome.[34] Krupp also withdrew. Not only did the Krupp family want to keep its independence, but the negotiators had difficulty integrating that Konzern's machinery, shipbuilding, and other finished products into the proposed combination. Most important of all, Krupp was able to obtain a promise from the Prussian government of a substantial loan to provide the essential financing the steelmaker needed.[35]

Finance was, indeed, a major issue in the continuing merger negotiations. Representatives of the German banks, which now saw themselves as little more than intermediaries with foreign financial interests, felt that fusion was a more likely course than any other to bring rationalization and lower costs, and thereby to increase the possibility of obtaining funds abroad, particularly in the United States.[36] Taxes, too, raised difficulties, as recent legislation had placed high taxes on mergers. In addition, the negotiators continued to argue over what plants were to be shut down or expanded and over other requirements for rationalization. In time the negotiators appointed a committee to work out these complex financial and industrial problems and to develop a plan that would reshape the industry on a national scale. On March 26, 1926, the participants finally accepted that committee's findings.

The combination was a fusion, not an I.G. The companies coming into the merger turned most of their assets over to Vereinigte Stahlwerke AG (VSt), and were paid RM 800 million in the shares of the new enterprise (see Figure 15, center panel, for names of the founding companies). Not all the properties of the founders went into VSt. The coal mines of Rheinstahl were turned over to the recently formed I.G. Farben, which held 35% of the stock in Rheinstahl. Excluded too was a major coal mine belonging to GBAG. Thyssen's machinery companies were merged into the long-established DEMAG, giving Thyssen a majority shareholding of that machinery company. Thus the existing companies receiving VSt stock were the Thyssen group (including Phoenix and Vereinigte Stahlwerke van der Zypen und Wissener Eisenhütten), Rheinstahl (Rheinische Stahlwerke), and the Rheinelbe-Union companies of the former Siemens-Stinnes I.G., the SRSU, which was transformed into a company to hold the shares of Siemens and others in VSt.

VSt, shortly after its formation, acquired the properties of AG Charlotten-hütte, those of the financially strapped firm of Rombach, and those of AG Friedrichshütte. The new company also leased the properties of the Stumm Konzern. By the end of 1926 it had obtained control of the Mitteldeutsche Stahlwerke, a new merger of several small works in central Germany. Later, as part of the rationalization process, VSt formed Deutsche Edelstahlwerke, which produced high-grade specialty steels, and then in 1930 it established Ruhrstahl, a merger that integrated operations of four small firms in the Ruhr.

Administrative centralization quickly followed legal consolidation. The initial function of the central administration of VSt was to supervise rationalization of

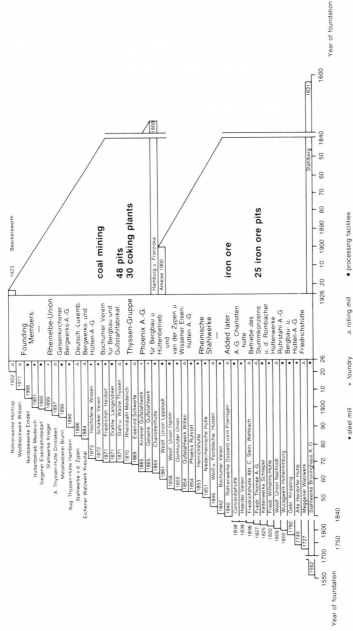

Figure 15. The historical background of Vereinigte Stahlwerke Aktiengesellschaft, 1926. From Wilfried Feldenkirchen, "Big Business in Interwar Germany: Organizational Innovation at Vereinigte Stahlwerke, I. G. Farben, and Siemens," *Business History Review* 61:423 (Autumn 1987).

production facilities and to provide a core of central services. Individually, the different producing units continued to be administered as they had been before the fusion. Although they were placed together in groups that paralleled the old corporations, no attempt was made to create administrative offices for these groups. Each of the major operating units became the responsibility of a member of the very large Vorstand, which numbered forty-one in 1926 but was reduced as rationalization was carried out.[37]

Though the metal-processing activities remained decentralized, the mining, purchasing of raw materials, research, finance and accounting, and other, less basic, functional activities were more centralized. The coal-mining operations were put into four regional groups with central headquarters in Essen. The supervision of the mining and processing and of the marketing and purchasing of ore and other raw materials—scrap, limestone, dolomite, clay, and quartz—was centralized in the Raw Materials Group with headquarters at Dortmund. Sales units for primary products were reorganized under a Central Group for Sales, which had its offices in the company's new headquarters at Düsseldorf. Exports were handled by Stahlunion-Export GmbH, which essentially took over the operations of the Otto Wolff firm, with Wolff becoming a large shareholder in VSt and a member of its Supervisory Board. Another sales company handled the marketing of by-products.

In addition, the Düsseldorf headquarters housed the central legal, patent, tax, and real estate departments and also a social and an economic department comparable to those at Siemens. A central costing office was assigned to develop data systematically, and a central auditing office to review accounts. A central research division supervised and coordinated the work of the control and testing laboratories within works. It, Robert Brady reported, "established in Dortmund a special research institute whose function is to devote its labor solely to further development of steel types and methods of iron and steel production, unencumbered by the labor of testing for control purposes."[38] The laboratories in the institute included those for ferro-chemistry, physical chemistry, metallurgy, coal chemistry, and silicate chemistry, as well as a physics laboratory and one that concentrated on the reworking of iron. These research facilities were much more extensive than anything yet established at the United States Steel Corporation or any other steel company in the world, with the possible exception of American Rolling Mill. Nothing like them existed in Britain.

As the new structure was being put into place, the rationalization of production facilities began (Table 23). This massive reorganization was financed by loans of more than $100 million raised in the United States, almost all underwritten by the New York investment-banking house of Dillon, Read. Rationalization proceeded along two lines. One was the reorganization and relocation of works so that they could be more efficiently located in relation to sources of

Table 23. Rationalization in the production of Vereinigte Stahlwerke (VSt), 1933.

Production facilities	Before VSt		In 1933	
	Number of plants	In companies	Number of plants	In groups
Blast-furnace plants	23	8	9	5
Siemens-Martin steel mills	20	8	8	6
Bar-and-profile iron mills	17	8	10	6
Strip-iron mills	7	5	3	3
Wire mills	7	4	2	2
Tube mills	13	6	6	4
Sheet mills	7	4	2	1
Hammer mills	8	6	4	3
Iron foundries	11	6	6	1
Steel foundries	10	6	4	4
Wire-rod mills	9	5	4	1
Tin-plate mills	3	3	3	1
Wheel-set mills	6	5	1	1
Fittings plants	3	3	3	1

Source: Thyssen Archive, VSt 1588, quoted in Wilfried Feldenkirchen, "Big Business in Interwar Germany: Organizational Innovation at Vereinigte Stahlwerke, IG Farben, and Siemens," *Business History Review* 61:425 (Autumn 1987).

raw materials, transportation, and markets. The other was the concentration of production and the physical integration of processes within a single works, or a few works in close proximity, to permit steady, high-level throughput at minimum efficient scale.

Thus the works on the Rhine, with its cheap water transportation, concentrated on the production of exports and also of crude steel; and those in the interior, where transportation costs were higher, produced higher-grade steel and machinery and other finished products. The production of secondary products was concentrated in large integrated works with their own blast furnaces and steel mills. Production of rails, which had been carried on in nine plants, was placed in a single, modern, best-practice, integrated plant. The number of wire-rod works was reduced from nine to four, with a central mill at Hamm producing a major portion of the output. The plants making other types of wire dropped from seven to two. Seven sheet mills were reduced to two, while those producing tubes fell from thirteen to six. Of the six tube mills at least four manufactured specialized tubing.[39] In addition, existing integrated works were modernized. For example, the new facilities at the giant Thyssen works at Hamborn increased output by 75% with no increase in its labor force. Fully integrated works, wrote Brady in 1933, became the rule rather than the exception. Pure rolling mills, for example, are practically non-existent. Steel plants are nearly always attached directly to iron smelting works, and these in turn to coal mines, coking ovens, and, where possible (Siegerland), to iron ore extraction. And steel and rolling mills are usually combined with pipe, wire, bar iron, special alloy, heavy machinery, and other special works.

As a result of reorganization and modernization, Brady further noted, VSt had by 1930 "in large part carried through plans for closing down completely seven smelting works, equipped with 19 blast furnaces, and 8 steel plants equipped with 39 open-hearth furnaces." In addition, Wilfried Feldenkirchen records, sixteen mining pits, eleven rolling mills, and one coke furnace had also been shut down.[40] After 1930 the depression brought further closings—closings that were carried out according to plans already instituted.

In 1933, as the German as well as the international economy began to recover, the senior executives at VSt completed the administrative reorganizations they had begun in 1926. The architect of the final plan, Heinrich Dinkelbach, made de jure that which had already been achieved de facto by way of improving the coordination of the flow of materials through the processes of production and distribution and at the same time permitting top management to monitor current operations more effectively and to allocate resources for future activities more systematically. The major operating divisions were regrouped along regional and product lines and were legally transformed into either joint stock companies (AGs) or privately held limited-liability companies (GmbHs) (see Figure 16). The coal-mining groups headquartered at Essen became an AG. The Raw Materials Group at Dortmund became a GmbH. A third subsidiary (Deutsche Eisenwerke) concentrated on the production of pig iron and foundry products. Four more were the company's basic steel producers in each of the major producing regions—one each for the Rhine and Siegerland and two for the Ruhr. Three other subsidiaries produced secondary products—tubes, wire rods, and wire hoops, respectively. Another manufactured rails and railway equipment. There were a bridge-building subsidiary and also a ship-building subsidiary. Two others produced different varieties of wires, screws, and hardware. Another produced fine specialized steel. Still other subsidiaries—GmbHs—were new sales companies, which were structured, as might be expected, along product lines. Those for primary products continued to have their offices at the Düsseldorf headquarters. Those for secondary materials such as wire, rods, and specialized steel were housed at the units manufacturing their products and became the marketing arms of their production counterparts.

These twenty-six operating subsidiaries (twelve AGs, and fourteen GmbHs) were administered by a corporate office which included general and staff executives. The staff offices, though somewhat enlarged, remained much the same as they had been before the final reorganization. The ten general executives who by then made up the VSt Vorstand concentrated on overall monitoring

A) OPERATING COMPANIES AND OFFICES

MINING

Gelsenkirchener Bergwerks-AG, Essen
 Dortmund Group
 Bochum Group
 Gelsenkirchen Group
 Hamborn Group

IRON AND STEEL WORKS WITH ROLLING MILLS

August Thyssen-Hütte AG, Hamborn
 Thyssenhütte, Hamborn
 Blast Furnace Works Operation
 Lower Rhine Works
 Ruhort-Meiderich Works
 Vulkan Works

Deutsche Röhrenwerke AG, Düsseldorf
 Phoenix Works, Düsseldorf
 Thyssen Works, Mülheim
 Thyssen Works, Dinslaken

Westfälische Union AG für Eisen- und
 Drahtindustrie, Hamm
 Westfälische Union, Hamm
 Lippstadt Works
 Langendreer Wire Works
 Knipping Wire Works
 Iburg Rope Industry

Bandeisenwalzwerke AG, Dinslaken

FABRICATING COMPANIES

"Wurag" Eisen- und Stahlwerke AG,
 Hohenlimburg
 Hohenlimburg Works
 Wickede Works

Dortmunder Union Brückenbau AG,
 Dortmund
Eisenwerk Rothe Erde GmbH, Dortmund
Kettenwerke Schlieper GmbH, Grüne

OFFICES

Raw Materials Distribution of
 Vereinigte Stahlwerke GmbH, Dortmund
Roheisenkontor GmbH, Gelsenkirchen

Walzeisenkontor GmbH, Düsseldorf

Westdeutsches Bandeisenkontor GmbH,
 Mülheim

RAW MATERIALS GROUP

Raw Materials Group of Vereinigte
 Stahlwerke GmbH, Dortmund
 Limestone and Dolomite Department
 Westenwald Mining Administration
 Bayern Mining Administration
 Siegerland Mining Administration

Dortmund-Hoerder Hüttenverein AG,
 Dortmund
 Dortmund Works
 Hörde Works
Bochumer Verein für Gu stahl-
 fabrikation AG, Bochum
Deutsche Eisenwerke AG, Mülheim
 Schalker Federation
 Friedrich Wilhelms Works
 Foundry Works Operation
 Hilden Foundry

Hüttenwerke Siegerland AG, Siegen
 Wissen Works
 Charlotte Works
 Eichen Rolling Mill, Kreuztal
 Attendorn Works
 Weidenau Rolling Mill
 Nachrodt Works
 Meggener Rolling Mill
 Hüsten Works

Kleineisen- und Schraubenfabrik
 Steel GmbH, Essen-Steele

Eisenwerk Wanheim GmbH, Duisburg-
 Wanheim

Concordiahütte GmbH, Engers
Siegener Eisenbahnbedarf AG, Siegen
Gebr. Knipping Nieten- und Schrauben-
 fabrik GmbH, Altena
Nordseewerke Emden GmbH, Emden

Grob- und Mittelblechkontor GmbH,
 Düsseldorf
Westdeutsches Feinblechkontor GmbH,
 Siegen
"Union" Rheinisch-Westfälisches
 Drahtkontor GmbH, Hamm
Thomasmehlkontor GmbH, Dortmund

B) MAJOR ASSOCIATED COMPANIES AND PARTICIPATIONS

MINING

Hürtherberg Trade Association,
 Hermülheim near Cologne
Essener Steinkohlenbergwerke AG,
 Essen
Concordia Bergbau AG, Oberhausen

IRON AND STEEL WORKS WITH ROLLING MILLS

Stahlwerke Brüninghaus AG, Werdohl
 Vorhalle Department
 Westhofen Department

Eisenindustrie zu Menden und Schwerte
 AG, Schwerte

Ruhrstahl AG, Witten
 Witten Steel Casting Works
 Henrich Works, Hattingen
 Gelsenkirchen Steel Casting Works
 Krieger Steel Works
 Annen Steel Casting Works
 Brackwede Forging Works

FABRICATING COMPANIES

Wagner & Co. Werkzeugmaschinenfabrik,
 Dortmund
Vereinigter Rohrleitungsbau GmbH,
 Berlin-Mariendorf

SALES COMPANIES

Thyssen Eisen- und Stahl-AG, Berlin

Heinr. Aug. Schulte Eisen AG, Dortmund

Thyssen-Rheinstahl AG, Frankfurt

Raab Karcher GmbH, Karlsruhe

OTHER COMPANIES

Westdeutsche Wohnhauser AG, Essen

Rheinische Wohnstätten AG, Duisburg

Rheinisch-Westfälische Haushalt-
 versorgung AG, Bochum

RAW MATERIALS GROUP

Louise Trade Association,
 Weickartshain
Rheinische Kalksteinwerke GmbH,
 Wülfrath
Rheinisch-Westfälische Kalkwerke,
 Dornap
Westdeutsche Kalk- und Portland-
 zementwerke AG, Cologne
Silika- und Schamottefabriken
 Martin & Pagenstecher AG, Cologne

Friedrich Thomée AG, Werdohl

Bergbau- und Hütten-AG, Friedrichs-
 hutte, Herdorf
Deutsche Edelstahlwerke AG, Krefeld
 Krefeld Steel Works Department
 Bergisch Steel Works Department
 Dortmund Magnet Plant Department
 Brüninghaus Forging Works

Bergische Stahl-Industrie KG,
 Remscheid

Geisweider Eisenwerke AG, Geisweid

Vereinigte Economischerwerke GmbH,
 Hilden
Christine Trade Association,
 Essen-Kupferdreh

Vereinigte Stahlwerke Schrotthandel
 GmbH, Dortmund

Vereinigte Haozgesellschaften GmbH,
 Essen

Stahlunion Export GmbH, Düsseldorf

Westfälische Wohnstätten AG,
 Dortmund

"Wehag" Westdeutsche Haushalt-
 versorgung AG, Gelsenkirchen

Figure 16. Structure of Vereinigte Stahlwerke Aktiengesellschaft, 1934. From Wilhelm Treue and Helmut Uebbing, *Die Feuer verlöschen nie: August Thyssen-Hütte, 1926–1966* (Düsseldorf, 1969), pp. 66–67.

and resource allocation. In addition, the Vorstand remained responsible for, but did not directly administer, the enterprises in which VSt held controlling shares. The most important of these were Ruhrstahl, Deutsche Edelstahlwerke, and Stahlunion-Export.[41]

The completed structure was, in fact, quite similar to the one being put in place about the same time at United States Steel following the death of its long-tenured chief executive officer, Elbert Gary, though the circumstances and timing of the reorganizations had little in common.[42] Although the two giants had somewhat different product lines, their integrated subsidiaries manufactured comparable products and were administered in comparable ways. But the VSt corporate staff was larger than that at U.S. Steel, and sales for primary products appear to have been more centralized.

One difference between the two was that there was less apparent banker influence in the German company than in the American one. At U.S. Steel, representatives of the investment-banking house of J. P. Morgan still dominated the Finance Committee, whereas at VSt the overall Supervisory Board included six bankers out of twenty-four members, and each of these represented a different Grossbank.[43] These bankers were far outnumbered by industrialists. And although no American was on the VSt board, Dillon, Read, which between 1926 and 1928 had underwritten about $100 million worth of loans for rationalization, must have had more influence than any single German financial institution. Another difference was that the rationalization carried out at VSt was more sweeping and entailed more reshaping and rebuilding of physical facilities than that which had occurred early in the century at U.S. Steel, and even than that which was carried out there in the 1930s after Gary's death. The earlier rationalization at U.S. Steel reflected only twenty or twenty-five years of competitive growth, whereas the German company had to reshape the industry after a half-century of such expansion.

After 1925 the leading steel companies that did not become part of VSt made somewhat less sweeping reorganizations and rationalizations. Krupp, in the manner of GHH and Klöckner, readjusted pieces of its Konzern to assure a better fit in production and distribution. GHH and Krupp borrowed $10 million apiece in the United States for the initial financing of these changes. Hoesch concentrated on remaining an efficient producer of primary and secondary steel products, for it had never been an important maker of machinery and other finished items.[44] Mannesmann, which lost less than the other steelmakers because of the war, quickly regained its prewar market position. It concentrated on reshaping its organization to assure its dominance in central and southeast Europe. Its major non-German rival remained the British firm of Stewarts & Lloyds, to which it sold its British subsidiary in 1935.[45]

VSt and those five enterprises—Krupp, Hoesch, Mannesmann, GHH, and Klöckner—along with a smaller Konzern created by Friedrich Flick after 1925, completely dominated the German steel industry. Other makers of iron and steel were relatively small satellites in which the larger firms often had stock participations or agreements as to price, output, and markets. The most independent of the smaller steel firms were Ilseder Hütte and Buderus'sche Eisenwerke, both strong, integrated regional companies.[46]

In these ways the German steel industry acquired a structure that was strikingly different from that of Britain but somewhat closer to that of the United States. As in the United States there were one giant and several strong independents, although the independents in the United States were more numerous and less vertically integrated than those in Germany. There were two other major differences between the German and American steel industries. The first concerned the nature of interfirm relationships, and the second had to do with the internal organization of the independents.

First, as soon as stabilization occurred and rationalization began, the German steelmakers returned to using cartels to control price and output at home, and they became the major participants in the International Steel Cartel formed in 1926. Nevertheless, as Robert Brady pointed out in 1933, the cartels and sales syndicates covered "only certain specified types of materials and are usually made for comparatively short periods."[47] Although price competition was temporarily stabilized, the VSt and the independents jockeyed functionally and strategically for market share at home and abroad, at least until Germany's economy moved to a war footing in the mid-1930s.[48]

Indeed, the industry remained loosely enough structured to permit the rise of a new Konzern. Friedrich Flick, through a series of financial transactions—both acquisitions and divestments—built an integrated multicorporate enterprise in eastern Germany whose major holdings included Eisenwerk Maximilianshütte (acquired from VSt), AG Charlottenhütte, and Mitteldeutsche Stahlwerke (VSt retained 25% of the shares of this firm). These enterprises remained closely tied to the machinery companies in Upper Silesia that Flick had acquired during the inflation period.[49]

Second, the German independent steelmakers were organized differently from those in the United States. Although Hoesch and Mannesmann remained producers of primary and secondary steel products and in this way were quite similar to the American independent steelmakers, the organization and activities of Krupp, GHH, Klöckner, and Flick were uniquely German. The rapid growth of personal or family-controlled, multicorporate, vertically integrated Konzerne reflected the unsettled years of crisis following Germany's defeat. As a defensive strategy their owners and managers acquired machinery companies, shipbuilders, and other metal-using manufacturers. In Britain such integration occurred primarily in shipbuilding, and there it was usually the shipbuilders that acquired the steelworks. In the United States only United States Steel, temporarily during World War I, and Bethlehem, because of the particular circumstances of its birth in 1903, operated shipbuilding firms. Neither these nor any other American steel company developed a strategy of acquiring machinery makers. Furthermore, after the turn-of-the-century merger movement American machinery makers, with the exception of Henry Ford and possibly one or two others, did not feel the need to have their own large steelworks.

The German steel Konzerne were family-controlled financial holding companies whose operating enterprises were legally and administratively independent of one another. These Konzerne had only the tiniest central or corporate offices, nothing like those of Siemens, Metallgesellschaft, or VSt. At the Haniel family's GHH, its manager Paul Reusch instituted quarterly meetings of the heads of the production units in 1921, primarily so that they could get to know one another. But GHH had little in the way of other committees or other coordinating devices. Reusch expected the corporations under his controlling supervision to operate independently but to work together when the need arose. "To march apart but to hit united" was his principle.[50] But GHH and the other vertically integrated holding companies did develop a self-sufficiency that permitted them to maintain successful arms-length negotiations with VSt and other Konzerne. Their bargaining power permitted continuing competition for market share through functional and strategic effectiveness.

It was this industry structure and its interfirm relationships that permitted the German steel and machinery makers to rationalize and modernize their industries during the interwar years in a way that proved impossible in Britain. The interfirm cooperation that existed before the war became even stronger during the postwar crises. The building of Konzerne, the formation of I.G.'s, and then the industry-wide merger centralized strategic decision-making in a way that was essential to large-scale rationalization. In Britain, by contrast, where family members, other shareholders, and creditors continued to have a say in the management of personally administered enterprises, such centralization rarely occurred. Those personally run, nonhierarchical firms developed little organizational capability or organizational structure. Owners, managers, and creditors were unable to reach the agreements within and between enterprises that were essential to obtain the funds and carry out the plans for modernization.

In Germany the steel companies had been managed since the 1880s through hierarchies of salaried administrators. Experienced managers built the Konzerne and carried out the industry-wide merger. VSt was formed by salaried managers and administered almost wholly by them. At Hoesch, as at GHH and Mannesmann, salaried managers ran the show. At the Krupp and Klöckner Konzerne, experienced family members had long administered their many enterprises through hierarchical organizations. In these firms the managers were able to devise, agree upon, and implement the complex plans so essential in bringing their enterprises—and therefore the industry as a whole—up to its technological potential. Only at Mannesmann did the representatives of a Grossbank (in this case the Deutsche Bank) continue to have a strong influence on the Supervisory Board. These representatives, like the bankers on the boards of the other leading steelmakers, worked closely with the managers to arrange for the extensive funds required for reconstruction. Because the managers' plans made sense to foreign investors in terms of increasing productivity per worker and per unit of capital, and because they had been drawn up and were to be carried out by experienced steelmakers, the Germans had little difficulty in finding funds, primarily in the United States, to pay for these changes. Thus where VSt was able to raise more than $100 million, the United Steel Companies and other British steel firms had problems in raising $5 million to rationalize and update facilities.

In 1930 the American funds dried up, but by that time the German industry had been modernized. At that time, too, aggregate demand dropped off sharply (far more sharply than it did in Britain), and the German works were saddled with the cost of operating at far below minimum efficient scale. Nevertheless, when demand increased, the German steel firms embodied much more efficient organizational capabilities (physical facilities and human skills) than did the British. Even with all the damage done in World War II, by the time the high demand of the immediate postwar years had leveled off, the German industry was much more healthy and more competitive than the British steel industry.

NONFERROUS METALS: THE RETURN OF METALLGESELLSCHAFT

In nonferrous metals, where the coming of electrolytic processes had brought technological change that was more revolutionary than that in iron and steel, where overall demand was smaller, where customers were less varied, and hence where far fewer enterprises existed, the story of German recovery was essentially that of a single firm, Metallgesellschaft. That enterprise not only regained Germany's global place in copper and other nonferrous metals in which it had previously excelled. It also was partly responsible for immediately making the nation a major aluminum producer, even though before 1914 no aluminum had been manufactured on its soil. Again the comparison with the British experience is striking.

The war created a challenge in aluminum. It did so because the initial German-financed and German-managed aluminum enterprise had been built across the border in Switzerland. After war broke out, Metallgesellschaft and Griesheim-Elektron, the two German firms experienced in the electrolytic processing of metals, established three small, essentially experimental aluminum-producing works.[51] In 1916, when it was realized that the war would not be short, plans were made to build a modern, state-of-the-art works at Lautawerk in the Lausitz region, using brown coal as the energy source. The works were to be made large enough to compete in postwar world markets. To finance construction

Metallgesellschaft and Griesheim provided half the capital of a new company, the Vereinigte Aluminium-Werke, and the German government provided the other half. That new company immediately acquired the three small works that had already been completed. As the Lautawerk plant came on stream in the summer of 1918, construction was beginning on a second large works in Bavaria, one that relied on the water power of the River Inn and was financed largely by increasing the government's participation in the company.

In 1919 the Reichstag, then dominated by the Socialist and Catholic Center parties, insisted that the German government take over the two large plants that had been heavily financed by government funds. Vereinigte Aluminium-Werke, the joint venture of Metallgesellschaft and Griesheim, was able to keep and operate one of the small works, the one located at Bitterfeld. The other two were shut down. Of much more importance, the state-owned aluminum enterprise commissioned Metallgesellschaft to market all its output, thus assuring the private company complete dominance in the German aluminum industry. After stabilization, the Griesheim-Metallgesellschaft joint venture enlarged the Bitterfeld works. (Griesheim continued to participate, although it had just become part of I.G. Farben.) In 1927 Metallgesellschaft joined with Th. Goldschmidt AG, still the leading tin processor in Germany, and three smaller firms to form Vereinigte Leichtmetallwerke to produce a variety of fabricated aluminum products.[52]

In copper Metallgesellschaft remained the largest German producer, continuing to control Norddeutsche Affinerie and then obtaining a participation with AEG (a major copper user) and Otto Wolff (closely allied to VSt) in the second largest producer, Mansfeld AG. For a time these three, in fact, controlled Mansfeld.[53]

In the meantime, Metallgesellschaft also regained its position as the one powerful European member of the global copper oligopoly. It did so despite the wartime loss of its recently built refinery at Hoboken in Belgium and its major holdings in Britain, the United States, Latin America, and Australia. Its former British subsidiary, which had been taken over by the British Metal Corporation headed by Sir Cecil Budd, remained the leading copper-trading company in Britain.[54] Although Metallgesellschaft's former American subsidiary, the American Metal Company, was expropriated by the U.S. Alien Property Custodian, it was purchased by a consortium that included its former managers. It remained a major player in world markets, maintaining close personal, though not legal and administrative, ties with its former parent. Indeed, the four men who consecutively held the offices of president and board chairman of American Metal for forty years, from 1917 until 1957, were Berthold Hochschild, the brother of the chairman of Metallgesellschaft's Vorstand in the 1880s who had established the American company; L. Vogelstein, the German copper trader who with Hochschild obtained the controlling share of American Metal's stock after the war; and Hochschild's two sons.[55]

After stabilization Metallgesellschaft began a series of moves that permitted it to regain its holdings from the British Metal Corporation by 1926 and to participate in the founding of Copper Exporters, the American consortium formed under Webb-Pomerene legislation (see Chapter 4).[56] Metallgesellschaft quickly became the leading non-U.S. associate in Copper Exporters. At the same time the German company entered into a joint venture with British Metal; and in 1929, through the formation of Amalgamated Metal, a holding company, it further strengthened its influence over the British nonferrous metals industries. Meanwhile, in Germany, Metallgesellschaft soon dominated the zinc, nickel, lead, and silver trades, either by holding shares in, or acting as sales agent for, the smaller producers.

In 1928 Metallgesellschaft further centralized its legal and administrative structure. Since 1910 it had operated through two legal units—Metallgesellschaft, which was responsible for commercial activities, and Metallbank und Metallurgische Gesellschaft, which was responsible for the industrial and financial activities. In 1928 the commercial activities were integrated into the industrial organization, with the new consolidated company keeping the original name, Metallgesellschaft.[57]

To summarize, this German first mover in the modern European copper industry was able to use its organizational capabilities to become very quickly a world leader in aluminum, while also recapturing its leadership in copper and other nonferrous metals. Again the capabilities established before World War I, together with the inability of the British, French, and other European enterprises to develop such capabilities, permitted the Germans to regain their dominant position in Europe. At the same time, as the dominant firm in Germany, Metallgesellschaft strengthened its control over smaller firms in all the nonferrous metals, much as Siemens and AEG did over their satellite firms in the electrical-equipment industry and as Continental and VGF did in rubber and rayon, respectively.

Chemicals

In chemicals (Group 28; see Appendixes C.1–C.4) the massive post-stabilization merger was even more all-encompassing than its counterpart in steel. The creation of I.G. Farbenindustrie AG (I.G. Farben for short) not only consolidated the makers of dyes and other coal-tar-based products; it also developed close ties in the form of stock participations, joint ventures, selling companies, I.G.'s, and cartels with the leaders of allied products—other organic chemicals (including pharmaceuticals), fertilizers, rayon, and explosives. As in nearly all the other German industries, the basic changes came in 1925 and 1926.

THE FORMATION OF I.G. FARBEN

The creation of I.G. Farben, like that of VSt, was the culmination of proposals initiated more than two decades earlier. Carl Duisberg of Bayer had proposed a nationwide merger of the producers of organic chemicals in 1904, shortly before Thyssen's call for a national steel trust. Duisberg's call, however, had a more immediate effect than Thyssen's. It resulted in 1904 in the two alliances which in 1916 were combined into that single industry-wide I.G. whose formal name was the Interessengemeinschaft der deutschen Teerfarbenfabriken (Community of Interest of the German Dye Works). This I.G. comprised not only the seven leading dye makers (which were also producers of pharmaceuticals and films), including the Big Three—Bayer, Hoechst, and BASF—but also Griesheim-Elektron, the first mover in electrochemicals which had pioneered in applying electrochemical techniques to the production of intermediates and then dyes (see Chapter 12).

The formation and operation of I.G. Farben deserves to be described in some detail. I.G. Farben became Germany's most powerful industrial enterprise at home and abroad. The merger and rationalization involved many more products and indeed more industries than the merger in steel (VSt included only producers of primary and secondary steel products, for the machinery-making activities of the constituent companies were spun off), or than any other German or European merger. Most important of all, the merger represented the culmination of an extended process of industrial consolidation in a nation where interfirm cooperation was legal and valued.

The I.G. Farben story provides a fitting conclusion to this study of the evolving industrial enterprise in Germany, much as the Unilever history did for Britain. Because I.G. Farben was more central to the development of the German chemical industry than Unilever was to the British branded-packaged trades, its story is even more closely related than Unilever's to those of the other leaders in its industry. The following pages focus, therefore, on both the giant firm and the chemical industry as a whole.

By the time stabilization finally came in 1924, the senior executives of the member firms in the existing I.G. agreed that a more centralized effort was needed if their enterprises were to strengthen their organizational capabilities at home and so regain their prewar dominance abroad. Their losses from the war and the peace treaty were extensive, though smaller than those of the steel and electrical-machinery makers. Finishing works in Russia and France had been lost, as had Bayer's American properties and Hoechst's smaller investments in Britain. But because these firms exploited the economies of scope extensively, they had made relatively few major investments abroad in plant and other facilities. Nor did they have holdings and raw materials in the lost territories comparable to those of the iron and steel companies. Nevertheless, the Treaty of Versailles forced the chemical manufacturers to turn over half of their existing stocks of dyes, pharmaceuticals, and intermediaries to the Allied Reparations Commission, to sell a quarter of their current output to that commission at prices set by the commission, and to deliver annually 30,000 tons of sulfate of ammonia to France.[58] During the years of crisis they continued to lose markets, so that whereas in 1913 Germany accounted for 28.5% of total chemical products exported, by 1925 the figure had dropped to 23.0%. In the same period U.S. exports rose from 9.7% to 16.0% of the total, and those of France from 9.7% to 13.2%. Britain's share, even in these years of opportunity, dropped from 15.6% to 13.6%.[59]

As might have been expected, the initial push for reorganization as the economy stabilized came from Carl Duisberg, still the senior executive at Bayer. In the summer of 1924 he prepared a proposal and circulated it for consideration at the October meeting of the General Council of the existing I.G. In the discussions that had led to the 1916 I.G., Duisberg had pointed out that one inherent weakness of such an I.G. was its inability to consolidate sales forces, to rationalize production, and to change the production mix of the various giant works. This was not only because the firms within the I.G. remained independent legal and administrative entities, but also because they could withdraw from the I.G. at will.[60] Nevertheless, in 1924 the managers of most of these long-established, highly successful German enterprises still held back from losing their historical identities through merger. Therefore Duisberg, supported by the representatives of Hoechst, proposed the formation of a management company to act for the eight companies in the existing I.G. in the reorganization and management of their personnel and facilities.[61]

Carl Bosch, the senior director at BASF, argued strongly against the Bayer-Hoechst proposal, calling instead for a complete fusion. Bosch, who with Fritz Haber had invented and perfected the first high-pressure ammonia-synthesis process, had in 1919 made an extended visit to the United States. This view of American industry had convinced him that nothing short of merger could create the organization required to carry through the necessary rationalization and restructuring of the German chemical industry. Duisberg quickly agreed, and others were soon won over. At its November 1924 meeting the I.G.'s General Council decided to transform the existing I.G. into an AG and then, after legal consolidation, to centralize its administration and rationalize its personnel and facilities.

At that November meeting Duisberg outlined a plan to carry out the fusion and to create the more centralized structure. To avoid taxes on merger, the shareholders of the constituent companies would exchange their shares for those of BASF. That firm would greatly increase its capitalization, turn over the new shares to the eight companies, and finally change its corporate name to I.G. Farbenindustrie AG. The existing companies could keep their names in correspondence and trademarks and in carrying on internal activities. The headquarters of the new fused enterprise would be in Frankfurt. All members of the existing Supervisory Boards and Vorstände of the eight constituent firms would become members of the Supervisory Board and the Vorstand of I.G. Farben. Each of these two boards would then select a small, full-time committee of members to act for it in governing the new enterprise.[62]

Because the legal arrangements were complex and required the final approval of the stockholders of the eight constituent companies, the Council realized that it could be a year before I.G. Farben became a legal entity. To cover this transition period Duisberg proposed the formation of an "overpass delegation," or transition committee, selected from the existing I.G.'s General Council, to have responsibility for the affairs of the existing I.G. and to begin setting up the administrative structure for the consolidated enterprise. This committee would differ from the current I.G.'s General Council in that it would be an executive body (not a legislative body), making decisions acting directly rather than through its members.

Duisberg then went on to propose an organizational structure for the merged enterprise. The management of the production facilities of the eight constituent firms was to be placed in four regional Operating (or Plant) Communities, "no matter to which firm they belonged." Each community was to have its own board of directors, "with extensive self-government under the supervision of one headquarters."[63] The administration of marketing and distribution activities was to be placed in five Sales Communities classified by products. The existing I.G.'s Commercial Committee and its many product subcommittees would continue to coordinate the sales for the several communities. So, too, the long-established Technical Committee and its subcommittees would continue to coordinate production, purchasing, and research and development. Duisberg urged that the new Operating and Sales Communities be set up as quickly as possible. This organization plan, outlined by Carl Duisberg of Bayer in his memorandum of November 8, 1924, did become the basic organizational structure of I.G. Farben for the more than twenty years of its existence, but only after months of debate and negotiations.

At that November meeting, BASF's Bosch, who was thirteen years younger than Duisberg, challenged Duisberg on several points. He stressed, even more than Duisberg had in his memorandum, the need to move slowly so as not to undermine proven arrangements and capabilities. He considered the proposal to create Operating and Sales Communities too radical. He was also disturbed by Duisberg's attempt to spell out an organizational plan in detail before the merger was completed. What counted, Bosch insisted, was the selection of the most qualified managers. Appoint the right people and the necessary organi-

zation would follow. For Bosch, "our most valuable resources" are "the relatively few persons who lead and develop in our plants." He continued, "In other
words: organization is the best possible allocation of the current management
force."[64] (Interestingly, a similar debate on the relationship of men and organization had occurred a short time before at Du Pont, with Pierre du Pont
arguing that the selection of men should come before the redesigning of the
organization, and Harry Haskell, the senior vice-president, arguing for first
laying out the new structure and then selecting the executives to fill it.)

According to the General Council's rules, its chairmanship rotated. After the
November 1924 meeting it was BASF's turn to be in the chair. Therefore
Bosch, the new chairman, took over the implementation of what the previous
chairman, Duisberg, had proposed. By then Bosch appears to have accepted
Duisberg's plans for the Operating and Sales Communities. But now he wanted
to concentrate executive power. He agreed with Duisberg on his proposal to
form two small committees—the "Governing Board" of the large Supervisory
Board and a "Working Committee" of the Vorstand—to govern the coming
merger. He also agreed that, under the supervision of the two new senior
committees, the existing committees of the old I.G., of which the Technical
and the Commercial were the most important, would continue to carry out their
coordinating functions.

In a memorandum of February 24, 1925, however, Bosch argued that the
Governing Board should have minimal power—only that required by law. He
insisted that it should *not* be expected to work closely with the small Working
Committee of the Vorstand. Its members should not even be permitted to
attend the Working Committee's meetings as nonvoting participants. The
Working Committee must provide "the real management" of the enterprise,
"as far as no laws hinder it."[65] In addition, it should be as small as possible.
Without such concentrated executive control Bosch feared that the weakness
of the existing I.G.'s form of governance would not be overcome. Only a powerful executive board at the center could control and direct long-established
operating units. He then listed the broad executive powers that the proposed
Working Committee should be given. In this same memorandum Bosch urged
that the name of the consolidated enterprise be changed from I.G. Farbenindustrie to Verein deutscher Teerfarbenfabriken (Union of German Dye Works),
or something comparable. The enterprise, after all, was an Aktiengesellschaft,
or AG, not an I.G. Moreover, such a name might be useful in recapturing
markets where the names of the individual firms remained well known, whereas
the term "I.G." smacked of cartelization and aggressive marketing.

While Duisberg was less concerned about the name, he argued strongly for
giving the Governing Board a significant role. He appears to have been supported by several senior managers of the constituent companies. Even though
Bosch had urged that the senior executives be given full authority to meet their

responsibilities, they themselves must have feared that such centralization would jeopardize their control over activities they had long managed. In the continuing discussion during the winter and spring of 1925, both Bosch and Duisberg argued that their goal was "decentralized centralism," and each said that the other's plan had elements of the "autocratic."

Agreement was not reached until October 2, 1925, when all the members of the Supervisory Boards and Vorstände of the eight companies finally signed the merger agreement. That final agreement was closer to the position of Duisberg than of Bosch. The name was to be I.G. Farbenindustrie AG. The agreement established, as Duisberg had originally proposed, four regional Operating Communities or Departments (the terms Betriebsabteilungen and Betriebsgemeinschaften were used interchangeably), and five Sales Communities. By the terms of the agreement each Operating Community "shall *manage its own work* as far as possible under supervision of a central office, shall *control* its own and compete with other Operating Communities in ideal competition (*idealem Wettbewerb*)."[66] This was Duisberg's concept of decentralization, which fitted closely with his often expressed views of the value of such internal competition as a means of promoting efficiency in a near monopoly. Duisberg also achieved his goal of giving the Governing Board, which he was to chair, significant power. Besides overall supervision and control, it had the final say on the selection of senior personnel and the authorization of all capital expenditures of more than RM 100,000. Its members could participate, but not vote, in the meetings of the Working Committee and the meetings of other major committees.

The Working Committee, which Bosch was to chair, was to make and implement the critical decisions. Although Bosch did not get all he wanted, its broad but specifically enumerated powers followed closely in order and in substance the Bosch memorandum of February 24. They comprised the determination of capital expenditures "including participation in other enterprises," plant closings and reshapings, other reorganization matters, "conventions, cartels and syndicates," all labor concerns, recruiting and promotion of all managers with salaries of RM 10,000 and over, and all financial matters including dividend payments (which required final authorization by the Governing Board).[67] The long-established Technical, Commercial, and Financial Committees and the smaller functional committees of the existing I.G. would continue to coordinate the flow of goods through the Operating and Sales Communities. They would also continue to monitor these units, and on the basis of such coordinating and monitoring would provide the Working Committee with advice and suggestions on long-term strategies and the allocation of resources to carry them out. Of these committees the Finance Committee of only four members was expected to play a major role.

By the end of 1925 the huge corporation I.G. Farbenindustrie was a reality. The shareholders of the constituent companies had given their approval of the merger. The members of the two senior boards had been decided upon. So too had the members of the Technical and Commercial Committees and of the more specialized, functional, coordinating committees—including those for purchasing (EK), social and labor relations (Seko), legal and patents (Juko), traffic (Veko), and production (Fako). Since each of these committees had been part of the old I.G., each had its own full-time *Büro* or staff, housed in either Frankfurt, Ludwigshafen, Leverkusen, or Berlin.[68] In December 1925 the Central Accounting Department was established in Frankfurt, and Central Finance was set up a little later in Berlin.

By then the Operating (Plant) Communities had been formed. They were Upper Rhine, Middle Rhine, Lower Rhine, and Middle Germany. So too had the five Sales Communities: (1) nitrogen, (2) dyes and other dye by-products, (3) inorganic chemicals and inorganic intermediates, (4) pharmaceuticals and veterinary products, and (5) photographic products.

The new structure was essentially a compromise in which all agreed that the goal of the merger should be to bind together more effectively the existing administrative offices and committees. Almost no new offices were created. The senior executives on the two top boards, particularly the Working Committee, and also the members of the more specialized, functional committees, continued to carry out the administrative tasks they had had in the pre-merger I.G. Some continued to manage the same giant works as they had before 1925, works which became centers of the new Operating Communities. Other members of the senior committee, continuing as the sales chiefs of the leading companies, became the senior executives of the new Sales Communities. Certain members of the Working Committee carried on as chairmen or members of the long-established Technical and Commercial Committees (Figure 17).

RATIONALIZATION AT I.G. FARBEN

The rationalization that came on the heels of the restructuring, while impressive, was no more radical than the restructuring. It was far less drastic than the one that was to get under way in 1926 at the steel firm VSt or, for that matter, than those that had been carried out by Siemens and AEG early in the century. One reason, of course, was that in the German chemical industry there was less need to replace outmoded equipment and outmoded skills. The companies coming into the merger had been able to maintain their facilities and the skills of their personnel at close to the state-of-the-art level. The Germans still led the way in most industrial chemicals. Rationalization, therefore, was marked less by the massive closing down of old works, the reshaping of other works, and the building of new ones than occurred in iron and steel. More often it took the form of changing the product mix and concentrating products in plants best suited for their manufacture.

Dyestuff production ceased at Elberfeld (the smaller of Bayer's two factories), at the Weiler–ter Meer works at Uerdingen, at the Kalle works at Biebrich, and at the Griesheim works. Vat dyes were concentrated at Hoechst.

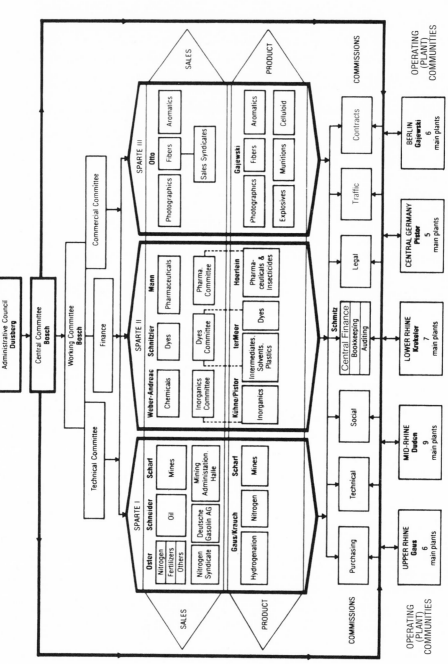

Figure 17. Organization of I.G. Farben, 1930. From Peter Hayes, *Industry and Ideology: I.G. Farben in the Nazi Era* (Cambridge, Eng., 1987), p. 388.

The Leverkusen works of Bayer (the center of the Lower Rhine Operating Community) increased its dye output by more than 25%. BASF gained a little in dye output and Hoechst lost a little. Because Duisberg, like William Lever, was strongly committed to internal competition as an essential spur to efficiency, dye production was not further concentrated. In this rationalization the number of dyes produced was sharply cut. From 1927–28 to 1932 the number decreased from 33,000 (marketed under 55,000 brand names) to 6,000. Uerdingen became a supplier of bulk intermediate chemicals, while the Kalle works began to make a new product, cellophane. Hoechst (the headquarters of the Middle Rhine Operating Community) remained the leading producer of pharmaceuticals, with Leverkusen handling the rest. Besides producing vat dyes, Hoechst took over the production of all chemicals made from acetylene, including a new product, polyvinyl acetate. BASF (center of the Upper Rhine Operating Community) continued to produce intermediates, dyes, and closely related organic chemicals at its Ludwigshafen works. But its primary activity soon became the manufacture of synthetic ammonia and of nitrogenous fertilizers at the adjoining Oppau works and at the Leuna works to the east of Leipzig. Between 1926 and 1928 those works expanded their annual output of nitrogen from 350,000 to 650,000 tons. The Griesheim works at Bitterfeld (headquarters of the Middle Germany Operating Community) concentrated on light metals, particularly magnesium, and also, as its joint venture with Metallgesellschaft, on aluminum. AGFA, the headquarters of what became the Berlin Operating Community (making five in all), carried out the production of photographic film and took over the management of the production and distribution of photographic products, including paper produced at Leverkusen and cameras made in Munich. Another member of that community, Köln-Rottweil, purchased in 1926 (see Chapter 13), produced all three types of rayon, though not in large volume until the mid-1930s.[69]

Rationalization of the same sort took place in research. Again the aim was not to make radical changes in existing arrangements. The Operating Communities had their own Central Laboratories and some specialized laboratories as well. At Leverkusen, the Central Laboratory for the Lower Rhine Community naturally concentrated on dyes. Also located at Leverkusen were the specialized Color Laboratory, the Moth Laboratory (for developing mothproof clothing as well as insecticides), and the Rubber Laboratory, where much work was done in the 1930s on synthetic rubber. At Hoechst, research concentrated on pharmaceuticals, but the Central Laboratory for the Middle Rhine Community continued to focus also on vat dyes. Another laboratory did research on acetylene. At Ludwigshafen, location of the major producer of intermediates in the earlier I.G., the Central Laboratory for the Upper Rhine Community devoted its attention to the development of synthetic intermediates, such as resins, styrene, and ethylene, while the laboratory at nearby Oppau focused on high-pressure synthesis.[70]

In this way the major laboratories in the major works continued to concentrate on much the same product areas as they had before the merger, and indeed, since their beginnings in the late nineteenth century. As E. K. Bolton, the senior Du Pont research executive, was told on a visit to Germany in 1936: "In order to preserve the traditions of each laboratory in the different fields of work there appears to be some overlapping, but Dr. ter Meer feels that it is relatively unimportant and that above all he wishes to preserve, as far as feasible, the traditions of each research laboratory."[71] Bolton also reported that there appeared to be relatively little fundamental research carried out at I.G. Farben. It had no central corporate laboratory where such research was concentrated, as it was at Du Pont.

In sales, rationalization moved more slowly but along the same lines as in research and production. The sales forces of the constituent companies were quickly consolidated, permitting a reduction of major sales agencies from ninety-one to forty-five. Fertilizers and other nitrogen products continued to be sold through the government-sponsored, nonprofit Nitrogen Syndicate, formed in 1919. After gasoline began to be produced synthetically in 1927, the new product was marketed through Deutsche Gasolin, in which I.G. Farben held a 45% interest, while Standard Oil's DAPG held 25% and Royal Dutch–Shell was the other major participant. The marketing of coal continued to be carried out by the Mining Department, which processed as well as mined. (I.G. Farben had acquired the coal mines of Rheinstahl at the formation of VSt.) All photographic business (film, paper, and cameras) came under AGFA, which also sold rayon and aromatic products made in nearby factories in the Berlin area. Dyes, organic intermediates, and pharmaceuticals—I.G. Farben's primary products— continued to be marketed from much the same offices as they had been before the fusion—those in Leverkusen, Frankfurt, and Ludwigshafen. They were sold through regional agencies in Germany and through country bureaus abroad. The difference was that the Commercial Committee and its superior, the Working Committee, had the administrative power to implement policy and operating decisions quickly. In the consolidation of sales, as of production and research, the senior managers of this huge merger were careful to build on the highly developed organizational capabilities of the constituent enterprises.[72]

Recovery abroad followed reorganization at home. The regaining of markets in the United States provides a good example. In July 1925, even before the arrangements for the merger were completed, the "transition committee" of the existing I.G. incorporated the General Dyestuffs Corporation to market all of its products (dyes and all its other goods) in the United States. By 1928 I.G. Farben had acquired from Grasselli Dyestuffs Company not only the dye-making section of the former Bayer works in Rensselaer, New York, which Grasselli had purchased from the U.S. Alien Property Custodian, but also Grasselli's new dye works at Linden, New Jersey. These two dye plants were reincorporated as the General Aniline & Film Company (GAF). In addition, I.G. Farben acquired in 1926 a 50% interest in Winthrop Chemical, a subsidiary of Sterling Drug. (Sterling Drug was the company that had purchased the pharmaceutical-producing section of Bayer's Rensselaer works at auction from the U.S. Alien Property Custodian.) Winthrop then sold pharmaceuticals made by both Sterling and I.G. Farben to physicians and hospitals directly. By 1929 the General Dyestuffs Corporation, selling the products of General Aniline and the dyes produced by I.G. Farben in Germany, was already the leading marketer of dyes in the United States. As late as 1939 General Dyestuffs still outsold its competitors—having 26.3% of the market, based on the value of sales, compared with Du Pont's 25.5%, Allied Chemical's subsidiary National Aniline's 15.9%, and the Swiss I.G.'s subsidiary's 14.9%.[73]

In 1928 I.G. Farben purchased Ansco, a small enterprise that was attempting to challenge the American first mover in photographic equipment, Eastman Kodak, on the basis of a successful patent suit. As a historian of the American photographic industry has noted, this acquisition "brought to Ansco engineering and production talent, capital and access to its [I.G. Farben's] all-important scientific and technical research facilities in Germany."[74] Thus, by acquiring Ansco, renamed Agfa-Ansco, I.G. Farben provided a small American patent holder with the organizational capabilities necessary to become Eastman Kodak's first successful challenger in the American market.

In 1929 the American I.G. Chemical Corporation was formed to hold securities of the three new companies, namely, General Aniline, General Dyestuffs, and Agfa-Ansco.[75] The American I.G. was, in turn, controlled by the International Corporation for Chemical Engineering (ICCE) in Basel, Switzerland. Formed in 1928, that Swiss company also controlled I.G. Farben's holdings in Latin America and Europe. Of these, the 25% share of Norsk Hydro which I.G. Farben had received in 1927 in return for the use of the Haber-Bosch process and the necessary know-how to use it, was probably the most important.

By 1929 the new sales organization at I.G. Farben had made advances in Europe and Asia that matched its achievements in North and South America, although it was more successful in dyes and films than in pharmaceuticals. William Reader had documented this recovery in the British Empire. Verena Schröter has done the same for I.G. Farben's success in eastern Europe. Reader has noted that although in 1929 American, French, and British manufacturers were holding their own in their domestic markets, the Swiss I.G., consisting of Sandoz, Ciba, and Geigy, was "the only effective competitor, in world markets, of I.G. Farbenindustrie."[76]

I.G. FARBEN'S CHANGING STRUCTURE: FAILURE TO ACHIEVE OVERALL CONTROL

The completion of the rationalization of production and the drive to regain world markets brought an increasing demand for closer coordination between production and distribution and a greater centralization of control at the top. As early as February 1927, Dr. Hans Kühne, a young and rising member of the Working Committee (he would head the Leverkusen operations by the end of the 1930s), urged Bosch to centralize marketing and distribution of the major lines of products—dyes, pharmaceuticals, organic and inorganic chemicals—in Frankfurt. Kühne further proposed that for each major product line "a chemist," that is, a product manager, should work closely with a commercial executive in adjoining offices in Frankfurt. The commercial executive would set sales policies and distribution arrangements for the several products in the major product line; and the product manager would coordinate the development of these products and their distribution to the marketing organization. Neither would be directly involved in day-to-day operations. Production would remain the responsibility of the Operating Communities, and distribution that of the Sales Communities. Besides coordinating product flow, the two managers should "review at least twice weekly their whole world-wide business."

In addition Kühne urged, as Bosch had done earlier, that the overall management of I.G. Farben be placed in the hands of a small central board (Zentraldirektorium) made up of representatives of the Operating and Sales Communities with "dictatorial authority and responsibility over the operating units." He further proposed that all the heads of Operating and Sales Communities should also have their offices at the Frankfurt headquarters. Working there with the other senior executives, they would "create new ideas and transfer them to the operating departments."[77]

Action came slowly on Kühne's proposals to integrate and coordinate distribution more effectively with production and to create an overall corporate office in Frankfurt. In 1929 the Working Committee did centralize sales of dyes and of inorganic and organic chemicals at Leverkusen and sales of pharmaceuticals at Frankfurt. Each of these offices was given its own accounting, statistical, and legal bureaus. Then came the formation of three Hauptgruppen (Chief Groups—the Sparte in Figure 17), which included a new set of product managers. Despite Kühne's proposal no comparable set of commercial managers was appointed. Instead, in the new Hauptgruppen the heads of the Sales Communities (their number was increased from five to seven) continued to be the senior commercial executives. The most important of these, Hauptgruppe II, handled the enterprise's central product lines, including chemicals, dyes, and pharmaceuticals. It also had the overall supervision and coordination of newer products that were not yet bringing in significant income, such as pesticides, detergents, finishes, cellophane, and compressed gases. Hauptgruppe I concentrated on high-pressure chemistry, which produced nitrogen and synthetic gasoline. It was also responsible for I.G. Farben's coal mines. Hauptgruppe III, with headquarters in Berlin, included photographic supplies, rayon, explosives, and aromatics.[78]

Finally in spring of 1930, Bosch's arguments of 1925 and Kühne's of 1927 for strengthening overall control were heeded. Possibly the severe impact of the depression on industrial markets permitted Bosch to get his way at last. At that time the Working Committee agreed to drop Duisberg's policy of having some of the same products made in different plants to encourage internal competition. It apparently had become too expensive.[79] In September 1931 a directive issued from the Working Committee's staff office defined the seven-member Central Committee (Zentral-Ausschuss) of the existing Working Committee with Bosch as chairman (Figure 18). The directive was short and to the point. The new committee's powers were general, not specific. It was to be "the highest organ of real management [*eigentlichen Geschäftsführung*]. The orders of the Central Committee are binding on all Divisions [*Sparten*, as Hauptgruppen were renamed], Operations [*Betriebe*] and Committees [*Kommissionen*]."[80] The new Central Committee had an extensive staff working in its offices in Frankfurt.

The duties of the existing major committees were redefined to carry out the intent of the directive. Those of the Governing Board, consisting of about eleven members of the Supervisory Board (which itself was reduced to twenty-eight members) became only those absolutely required by law, exactly as Bosch had proposed in 1925. Those of the existing top committees—the Working Committee (whose name was changed shortly to the Executive Committee), the Technical Committee, the Commercial Committee, and the Finance Committee, were only advisory: "to review and resolve issues" for I.G. Farben as a whole and to recommend action to the Central Committee.[81] The new Central Committee received directly the detailed accounting and financial reports compiled by the central finance office. These had previously gone to the Finance Committee for action, but that committee was now to receive them for information only.[82] Although this reorganization explicitly centralized authority and responsibility, it still was not followed by the establishment of a corporate headquarters at Frankfurt. The senior executives of the major plants (who also headed the Operating Communities), the leading marketers (who headed the Sales Communities), the product managers (most of whom were on the new Central Committee or other senior committees), and the heads of many staff departments continued to live and have their offices in Leverkusen, Frankfurt, Ludwigshafen, Bitterfeld, or Berlin.

Nor were many changes made at the operating level (Figure 17). Although the Hauptgruppen were renamed Sparten, their functions remained unchanged. Bosch and others did consider further centralization in the marketing of chemicals—along product rather than regional lines. But they agreed that the money saved in reduction of personnel would in no way counterbalance the loss of organizational experience, particularly in the handling of the vast numbers of conventions and other price, production, fabricating, and patent agreements. So within Sparte II, marketing policies continued to be determined by the heads of the Sales Communities and the product managers, while the day-to-day

Prof. Dr. Carl Bosch: (Ludwigshafen)
— Central Committee (chairman)
— Working Committee of the Vorstand (chairman)
— Finance Committee
— Technical Committee (chairman)
— Commercial Committee

Dr. Hermann Schmitz: (Ludwigshafen)
— Central Committee (vice-chairman)
— Working Committee of the Vorstand
— Technical Committee
— Finance Committee
— Commercial Committee (chairman)
— Director of Central Financial Management and Central Bookkeeping

Prof. Dr. Paul Duden: (Frankfurt am Main)
— Central Committee
— Working Committee of the Vorstand
— Technical Committee
— Director of the Joint Operations — Middle Rhine
— Senior Manager — Hoechst

Director Dr. Wilhelm Gaus: (Ludwigshafen)
— Central Committee
— Working Committee of the Vorstand
— Technical Committee
— Director of the Joint Operations — Upper Rhine
— Senior Manager — Ludwigshafen works

Director Dr. Karl Krekeler: (Leverkusen)
— Central Committee
— Working Committee of the Vorstand
— Director of the Joint Operations — Lower Rhine
— Deputy Manager — Leverkusen (C. Duisberg, Senior Manager)

Director Dr. Georg von Schnitzler: (Frankfurt am Main)
— Central Committee
— Working Committee of the Vorstand
— Technical Committee
— Commercial Committee
— Dyes Sales Committee (director)

Prof. Erwin Selck: (Frankfurt am Main)
— Central Committee
— Working Committee of the Vorstand
— Technical Committee
— Commercial Committee

Figure 18. Operating responsibilities of the members of the Central Committee of I.G. Farben after 1930. Compiled from sources at Bayer Archives, Leverkusen.

coordination of flows of individual products was carried out by product committees, the major ones having been in existence since 1916.[83]

The only important change at the operating level was one that shortly followed the 1930 reorganization. That was the abolishing of committees for the coordinating of minor functional activities. Instead, their staffs or Büros (renamed *Zentralstellen*) became responsible for such coordination throughout the enterprise. In Berlin were housed the Zentralstellen for purchasing, legal affairs and patents, economic policy and statistical, foreign and governmental relations, personnel, housekeeping arrangements, and finance.[84] In Frankfurt were located those for engineering, social and labor relations, central accounting, insurance and taxes. Ludwigshafen housed those for traffic and contracts. Of all these, Central Finance in Berlin was probably the most important. It handled payments of wages and of suppliers, as well as providing short-term working capital and long-term investment capital. From the start it worked closely with the Deutsche Länderbank, which I.G. Farben soon owned and operated as its in-house bank.

The minor organizational adjustments that occurred after 1931 reflected changes in top personnel and in German military mobilization. In 1935, on Duisberg's death, Bosch took his place as chairman of the Governing Board, and Hermann Schmitz, who had long managed I.G. Farben's complex financial affairs, became chairman of the Vorstand. Bosch, however, continued to attend meetings of the Central Committee and, after 1937, of the Vorstand. In that year the Vorstand was reduced to twenty-one members, the Executive Committee was abolished, and the Central Committee of the new Vorstand handled only special finance and personnel matters.[85]

In 1937, too, despite opposition within the enterprise, the Nazification of I.G. Farben's senior management began. Jewish members began to be expelled and other senior members joined the Nazi party.[86] Even before that date small organizational changes had been made to meet the demands of the expanding German war machine.[87]

In the early 1930s, before German industry was called on to build a self-sufficient military state, I.G. Farben was moving toward a multidivisional structure. The Sparten (originally the Hauptgruppen) were embryonic product divisions, and the Central Committee was an embryonic central or corporate decision-making body. As yet, however, the functions of both the operating and the top management of this huge enterprise continued to be carried out by the same executives, who managed through committee. And I.G. Farben was huge. In terms of its assets of RM 2,090 million ($520 million) in 1929, it was the largest industrial enterprise in Germany; and with 114,185 workers it was second only to VSt in employment. Its assets were somewhat below the $617.6 million of the largest American chemical company, Du Pont, but only because Du Pont's assets included its large investment in General Motors (over a quarter of the shares outstanding), and it employed four times Du Pont's work force. Committees remained responsible for coordination of product flow, the monitoring of current operations, the planning of strategy, and the allocating of resources for future production and distribution.

At I.G. Farben, top management remained intimately involved in day-to-day operations. Some members of the Working Committee—and then, after 1930, of the smaller, all-powerful Central Committee—also served as chairmen or members of the Technical, Commercial, and Finance Committees and of the major production, research, and marketing committees for the different product lines. Still others headed the Operating and Sales Communities and were the product managers in the Sparten. The operating responsibilities of the members of the small, all-powerful Central Committee in the early 1930s were unusually varied and time-consuming (Figure 18). In addition, the members of the Central Committee participated in negotiating major international agreements far more than did the senior executives at Du Pont or ICI.[88] Moreover, these senior executives worked and lived in different cities. The staffs of the senior committees, the offices of the heads of the Operating and Sales Communities, and those of the product managers were also in different locations. The scheduling of meetings must have been a complex task, to say the least.

The staffs of the committees and the functional staff officers were large, specialized, and well trained. The information the senior managers received at their many meetings was probably as accurate and detailed as the information produced at that time by staff offices in any industrial enterprise in the world. Yet, given the number of meetings that the senior executives had to attend in different places, they had little time to absorb and evaluate the massive data they received for long-term strategic planning. Instead, they continued to use the data more for short-term decisions concerning the day-to-day production and distribution activities in which they were so intimately involved. Unlike Du Pont, they had no corporate or general office where general executives, largely free from operating duties, concentrated on monitoring performance; on allocating resources on the basis of that monitoring and of their own understanding of economic, technological, market, and political considerations; and then on defining and implementing long-term strategies.

These differences clearly reflected I.G. Farben's own particular history. Its organization had evolved in a very different way from those of large American and British industrial combinations, proceeding as it had from two alliances in 1904 and to a single I.G. in 1916 and then to a merger in 1925. In no other merger at home or abroad had the constituent firms worked so closely together for so many years before the final consolidation. This is why Duisberg and Bosch agreed on the need to avoid radical changes, and why in the pre-merger discussion so little was said about organization qua organization.[89] Instead, discussion focused on practical ways to create overall supervision and control in order to make more effective use of existing facilities and skills. The Duisberg-Bosch debate was over the methods to be used to assure quicker responses to changing technologies and markets without constraining existing capabilities in production and distribution. Because the constituent firms already had long-established organizational means to coordinate activities, there was less need to create a corporate office to coordinate, monitor, and allocate resources for the enterprise as a whole—a need acutely felt by the American mergers, which, as was the case with Allied Chemical and Union Carbide, brought together long-established companies producing different but complementary lines. Finally, because the senior managers at I.G. Farben had so effectively exploited the economies of scope, and so for years had been more diversified than American chemical and machinery companies, they were not faced with the challenges that forced Du Pont, Hercules Powder, Monsanto Chemical, Westinghouse, International Harvester, and others to restructure their organizations when production moved from a single line to several lines of products for several different markets.

Despite all their efforts, two of Germany's most forceful industrial managers, Carl Duisberg and Carl Bosch, were unable to transform a merger based on two decades of uniquely German interfirm cooperation into a coherent whole. They were unable to achieve what D'Arcy Cooper was finally able to bring about at Unilever—a uniquely British federation of personally managed companies. They were unable either to create a set of divisions based on product markets, or to build a single corporate office where senior managers could devote their whole attention to essential top-management functions. Once Bosch left the Vorstand in 1935 to chair the Supervisory Board, and Hermann Schmitz had firmly established himself as the Vorstand's chairman, top-level control began to disintegrate. Soon Schmitz's Vorstand no longer governed effectively. As Peter Hayes noted in his study of I.G. Farben during the Nazi era:

> Whether in committee or as a whole, they [the senior executives] assembled less to deliberate on common policy than to inform one another, to the degree that each saw fit, about their highly specialized fields and to answer questions. Still less did they familiarize their colleagues with the operations and finances of the subsidiaries to whose boards they were assigned. The members lacked the time or inclination to meddle in one another's bailiwicks; where their concerns overlapped, they reached agreement privately or in some lower-level committee. Consequently *Vorstand* meetings seldom lasted longer than four hours, formal votes were almost never taken, and the participants nearly always ratified the course of action that had worked its way on to the agenda. After 1938, each member saw only that portion of the minutes and I.G.'s balance sheets related to his sphere of operations.

For these executives the information provided by their staffs was used to make decisions about their own particular operations and not about the enterprise as a whole. The information they received at a particular meeting was only relevant to the operational issue at hand. The corporate appraisals of operating performance and the long-term financial and strategic planning that Bosch had hoped for no longer existed. In the words of its managers it became increasingly governed on "the Habsburg Model," which Peter Hayes defines as a "composite of pyramided dynastic unions, proud local magnates, and heterogeneous dominions."[90]

Did these differences in structure that resulted from very different historical circumstances make a difference in overall performance? With its committee structure, I.G. Farben quickly regained and then maintained market position and profits for its established products. In addition, it successfully developed new products that involved investment in production on a massive scale, such as synthetic gasoline and synthetic rubber, which were essentially commodities. In developing a wide variety of more specialized products, particularly those that were sold to consumer-oriented industries, it was less successful than Du Pont, Union Carbide, Siemens, ICI, and the other large enterprises that had adopted the multidivisional form of organization. The Du Pont output and profits in the interwar years came largely from new products. By World War II more than half of Du Pont's sales volume came from lines that the company had not been producing commercially twenty years earlier—some of which had not even been invented twenty years earlier—such materials as rayon, detergents, refrigerants, paints, varnishes, finishes (including Duco), moisture-proof cellophane, brake fluids, antifreezes, Lucite, and Teflon. For several of these Du Pont had been a first mover. By contrast, I.G. Farben's sales in the late 1930s came primarily from product lines developed well before World War I—chemicals, dyes, and film—and from such massive projects as the production of nitrogen from the air just before that war, aluminum and magnesium during the war, synthetic gasoline after 1925, and synthetic rubber in the 1930s (see Figure 19). It had far less success in developing new lines such as rayon, cellophane, detergents, finishes, and pesticides.[91] In 1929 the failure to produce rayon competitively caused the Working Committee to shut down a plant at Hölken and to break off its joint venture with VGF for the production of acetate rayon.[92] Only after Hitler demanded national self-sufficiency did rayon become profitable for I.G. Farben, and then it was largely rayon staple. For example, in 1937 the company planned to produce 50,000 tons of staple and only 10,000 tons of filament.[93]

This significant difference in performance between Du Pont and I.G. Farben reflects other basic differences besides organizational structure. At I.G. Farben new-product development in the interwar years appears to have paid much less attention to marketing—to commercial surveys, tests with customers, and constant adjustment to customers' concerns—than was the case at Du Pont. For I.G. Farben the commercialization of a product remained essentially technological. There were no central corporate-development or research staffs to

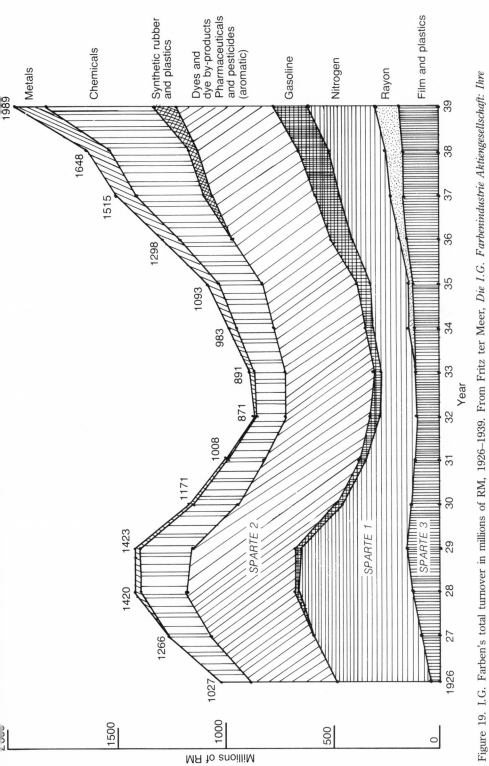

Figure 19. I.G. Farben's total turnover in millions of RM, 1926–1939. From Fritz ter Meer, *Die I.G. Farbenindustrie Aktiengesellschaft: Ihre Entstehung, Entwicklung, und Bedeutung* (Düsseldorf, 1953), following p. 116.

bring new products and new market opportunities to the attention of both middle managers in the operating units and the enterprise's senior managers, or to begin work on such projects when they were not taken up by the divisional laboratories. For example, I.G. Farben does not appear to have adopted a strategy similar to that of Du Pont or Union Carbide by which new products systematically replaced old ones—nylon replacing rayon and Orlon and Dacron taking over parts of the nylon market. Nevertheless, the difference in methods of product development was not just a matter of history and the resulting organizational structure; it was also a matter of opportunity. I.G. Farben had far less opportunity to exploit such consumer-oriented materials than its overseas competitors did. The demands of recovery after World War I, followed by depression and then military rearmament, and also the smaller consumer markets in Germany and Europe than in the United States and Britain, militated against the development of new consumer-oriented materials.

If I.G. Farben differed from its foreign counterparts and the dominating enterprises in the other German great industries in its internal structure, it also differed from Du Pont and other American firms—but was quite similar to Siemens, VSt, Metallgesellschaft, and other German industrial leaders—in its relationship to other firms within its basic industry. Through interfirm and contractual relations it dominated its industry even more thoroughly than Siemens, AEG, and VSt did theirs. To American and even British managers the number of arrangements it had with competing firms would be considered extraordinary. Reviewing the company's organization for the marketing of chemicals in August 1931, Eduard Weber-Andreae, the head of the Chemical Sales Community, wrote that the selling of 2,000 chemical products (300 with an annual turnover of more than RM 20,000 apiece) to more than 60 industrial product markets involved 95 broad "conventions" and 53 marketing, 15 fabrication, 15 closing, 12 production-control, and 7 price-fixing agreements. The complex and intricate specialized knowledge required to make, monitor, and maintain these agreements was in Weber-Andreae's opinion a basic reason for not making significant changes in administering the marketing of chemicals.[94]

In addition to its many formal contractual agreements (and often as a means of enforcing them), I.G. Farben had stock participations in, and joint ventures with, other leaders in the chemical and closely related industries. Through its holdings in Dynamit AG it dominated the explosives industry. Through Vereinigte Aluminium-Werke, the joint venture of one of its founding companies, Griesheim, with Metallgesellschaft, it continued to have a tie with the production of aluminum as well as magnesium. Through Griesheim it had comparable financial ties with DEGUSSA, Griesheim's only major rival in the German electrochemical industry. DEGUSSA had been weakened by the loss of its highly successful American subsidiary, Roessler & Hasslacher, to American nationals during the war. When Griesheim was absorbed by I.G. Farben in the 1925 merger, the existing I.G. arrangement that Griesheim had had with DEGUSSA during the crisis period was replaced with an arrangement by which three companies—I.G. Farben, Henkel (the soap maker), and Metallgesellschaft— each took one-third of DEGUSSA's preference shares. Then I.G. Farben made a long-term contract with DEGUSSA to market its metallic sodium (and Henkel did the same for sodium perobate). In 1930 these interlockings were further extended when DEGUSSA acquired full control of Holzverkohlungs-Industrie, a leading producer of intermediate chemicals by wood distillation, which had been allied with DEGUSSA since the turn of the century.[95] I.G. Farben also acquired a say in the potash industry when it made agreements with Kali-Chemie, a 1928 merger of two leading producers, Kaliwerke Friedrichshall and Rhenania-Kunheim, to market a wide range of Kali-Chemie's products.[96] Farben's 1926 joint venture with VGF, the dominant rayon maker, to produce rayon by the acetate process in Berlin and Hölken strengthened, at least temporarily, its position in that industry. Important too were the shares it held in Norsk Hydro-Elektrisk A/S, the producer of nitrogenous fertilizers that was one of Norway's largest industrial enterprises.[97]

Although most of these interlocking stockholdings were with German firms and the contractual agreements were with German and Continental companies, I.G. Farben was also, of course, a major player in broader international agreements, particularly those that came into being after the depression intensified global overcapacity in several of its industries. It was the dominant firm in the nitrogen cartel established in 1930 and the dyestuffs cartel instituted in 1932. The latter allocated 65.5% of world export sales to I.G. Farben. Because of its strong patent position, it was a moving spirit in the cross-licensing agreements for producing synthetic gasoline from coal that were signed in April 1931 by I.G. Farben, ICI, Royal Dutch–Shell, and Standard Oil (New Jersey).[98]

In any case, the German chemical industry's quick return to international markets was based largely on organizational capabilities—on the production, marketing, and research facilities and technical and managerial skills of the companies that had formed I.G. Farben in 1925. The new administrative structure created by the merger facilitated rationalization at home and recovery abroad. Yet the old ways of cooperative, autonomous management were hard to change, just as those of personal management were hard to change in Britain. Moreover, the enterprise was so large and its activities so complex and diversified that it might have been unmanageable no matter what organizational structure it had. In the years following World War II, after the Allied Control Council had broken up I.G. Farben into three companies, no suggestions were made to merge them once again into a larger enterprise. These three companies—Bayer, BASF, and Hoechst—had the same names, much the same facilities, and the same locations as they had had before the merger in 1925. Cassella, which the council placed under the control of Hoechst, expanded its product line by purchasing Riedel–de Haën in 1955. AGFA remained under the control of Bayer, and Griesheim and Kalle under that of Hoechst. In the postwar years all of I.G. Farben's successors adopted variations of the multidivisional form. A century after their founding their entrepreneurs had made the initial three-pronged investment in manufacturing, marketing, and management. The industry's first Big Three were still the three largest chemical companies in Germany.[99]

THE INDEPENDENTS

Despite I.G. Farben's dominating position in so much of the chemical industry, a few strong German competitors enjoyed a larger market share in specific product lines—and often a stronger bargaining position in negotiations relating to those products. Such competitors included the first movers in rayon and synthetic alkalies. When I.G. Farben closed down its Höklen rayon plant in 1929, VGF happily pulled out of its joint venture with the chemical giant, realizing it had little to fear from the chemical company's competition at home and abroad.[100] After 1925 Deutsche Solvay-Werke increased its control over the alkali trade and at the same time helped to build a direct competitor to I.G Farben in the 1930s by investing in Kali-Chemie, the 1928 merger of potash producers. After that merger Kali-Chemie centralized its administrative structure and rationalized its facilities. Next it took back the marketing of products it had turned over to I.G. Farben at the time of the merger. Then, by using the funds received from Solvay (in exchange for shares which gave Solvay control), Kali-Chemie began to challenge I.G. Farben directly by moving into pharmaceuticals and specialty dyes. It also diversified into X-rays. After World War II it administered these product lines through a multidivisional structure.[101]

Other potash producers besides Kali-Chemie remained relatively independent of I.G. Farben. Of these only Consolidirte Alkaliwerke Westeregeln, which before the war had become a producer of electrochemicals as well as of potash, was as dynamic as Kali-Chemie.[102] The other producers (the largest was Kali-Industrie, a 1927 merger) remained as much mining as processing firms; they relied on the potash cartel which had been reinstituted by the government in 1919 to control price and production. During the interwar years, still another successful independent, Bayerische Stickstoffwerke, remained the largest producer of cyanamide, with its output well ahead of that of I.G. Farben, the second largest producer.[103]

Even more independent was Rütgerswerke. During the crises that followed the war it had expanded its activities by investing in shale and petroleum companies (see Chapter 13). After 1925 it continued to enlarge its three main lines: building materials, basic chemicals, and plastics and synthetics. In 1927 it spun off its carbide-production enterprise into a joint venture with Siemens to form Siemens-Planiawerke. As at Kali-Chemie, its three product groups were administered as autonomous divisions (Sparten) after World War II.[104] Little information is available on two other chemical companies listed among the top two-hundred in 1929, namely, AG für chemische Produkte vorm. Scheidemandel, which dominated the German glue industry, and Saccharin-Fabrik, a leading producer of saccharine. Neither appears to have had financial ties with I.G. Farben.

The leading producers of pharmaceuticals also operated quite independently of I.G. Farben, as they had of the chemical I.G.'s that preceded it. The information available on the pharmaceutical companies is less voluminous than that for the other German chemical companies, but what does exist indicates that the prewar leaders—von Heyden, Merck, Riedel, and Schering—quickly regained their marketing position abroad as well as at home. In the United States both Merck and von Heyden made arrangements with the Alien Property Custodian that put them in a position similar to that of Metallgesellschaft in relation to American Metals. Their prewar American subsidiaries became independent but retained personal ties with the former German parent, permitting an extensive exchange of personnel and technical information. In this way newly independent American branches could continue to benefit from the organizational capabilities of their parents.[105] After 1924 J. D. Riedel rebuilt its marketing organization abroad with branch offices in New York, London, and Milan and expanded its product line at home. Riedel also acquired E. D Haën AG, specialists in fine chemicals.[106] Merck, von Heyden, and Schering supported their rejuvenated marketing organizations in Europe and elsewhere by building small finishing factories, primarily to get under tariffs.[107] Because these enterprises exploited the economies of scope to a lesser extent than the makers of industrial chemicals, most preferred not to diversify beyond drugs and pharmaceuticals. Until after World War II they continued to be administered through centralized, functionally departmentalized organizational structures.

One exception was Schering, the largest of the German pharmaceutical firms during the interwar years. It grew more by acquisition than by direct investment. Its history provides a rather curious example of Konzern building during the postwar crisis years. In 1922 and 1923 Oberschlesische Kokswerke & Chemische Fabriken, a firm which (along with Rütgerswerke and Holzverkohlungs-Industrie) had pioneered in coal and wood distillates, obtained control of Schering and three other companies—Kahlbaum, a producer of fine chemicals; Voigtländer & Sohn AG, Germany's oldest camera maker; and a firm producing dyeing, washing, and cleaning chemicals. After the stabilization of the German economy Schering and Kahlbaum were legally merged and administratively centralized. The rationalization of Schering-Kahlbaum followed, primarily in sales. Five regionally defined sales departments were established for the worldwide marketing of pharmaceuticals, chemicals, and pesticides, and three more for the products of the other subsidiaries of Oberschlesische Kokswerke. At the same time, Oberschlesische Kokswerke set up a central office and central laboratory in Berlin. Then came further diversification through the acquisition of a soap and cosmetics firm and an Austrian chemical company and through the creation of a joint venture with Du Pont (Duco AG) to sell the American company's finishes in Germany. Finally in 1937 Schering-Kahlbaum and its parent, Oberschlesische Kokswerke, were formally merged, with the new company taking the Schering-Kahlbaum name. Its operations were then consolidated into two large departments—mining and chemicals. The first included five divisions—coke and coal products, fertilizer, sulfuric acid, mining machinery, and bricks—all of which had been produced by the former parent company. The chemical department had five divisions (including one for film and cameras), which produced and distributed products hitherto handled by Schering-Kahlbaum and the other two subsidiaries. With the creation of these product divisions and the enlargement of the Berlin corporate office, Schering-Kahlbaum had acquired a multidivisional structure much like that of American chemical firms.[108]

*

This review of the performance of the German chemical industry—the nation's most impressive industrial achievement—provides what can be considered a classic example of cooperative capitalism. At the center of the industry was the giant, I.G. Farben, still evolving from an alliance of first movers. These had cooperated at first through cartels and other contractual agreements, then had formed a "community of interests," and finally had fashioned a complete fusion. In 1937 the resulting consolidated enterprise accounted, according to a postwar estimate, for 98% of the dyestuffs produced in Germany, 50% of the pharmaceuticals, 60-70% of the photographic film, 70% of the nitrogen, and 100% of the magnesium.[109] As late as 1939 it continued to operate largely through intrafirm committees that had begun as interfirm committees years earlier. Around this core clustered a number of allied enterprises—joint ventures and firms in which I.G. Farben had large stock participations.

Beyond that sphere were the firms which had developed organizational capabilities that permitted them to maintain and often increase market share at the expense of the central giant. Their functional and strategic effectiveness gave them a strong hand in negotiating output, price, and other agreements. These smaller enterprises, which (except for the pharmaceuticals) grew by exploiting the economies of scale more than those of scope, remained organized along centralized, functionally departmentalized lines. When they diversified, as did Schering-Kahlbaum, Rütgerswerke, and Kali-Chemie, they moved toward a multidivisional type of structure, although their general offices were smaller than those of their American counterparts.

The satellites and the independent German chemical firms were somewhat smaller than the American leaders; but, like the American companies, they had larger managerial hierarchies than any British chemical firm except ICI and, probably, Burroughs Wellcome. Except for these two firms and Albright & Wilson (a specialized producer comparable to Scheidemandel and Saccharin-Fabrik in Germany), by the 1930s no British chemical company had developed the organizational capabilities needed to compete effectively in their global oligopolies. They failed even though they had been given a decade (from 1914 to 1924) to accomplish this task.

This was also true of the industry in France. There, only two large enterprises, Kuhlmann and Rhône-Poulenc, concentrated on the production of chemicals between the world wars. Two other important chemical producers, St. Gobain and Pechiney, remained the major producers of glass and aluminum, respectively. Rhône-Poulenc, a 1928 merger of organic chemical producers, made little attempt to rationalize production, distribution, or research in order to meet German competition. Kuhlmann, which had started by producing dyes during World War I, was even less resilient than ICI in challenging I. G. Farben's terms for international competition. Indeed, after 1925 the most effective competition the German companies had in international trade came from the Swiss in dyes and pharmaceuticals and from the Americans (to some extent) in pharmaceuticals and (to a much greater extent) in newer products such as finishes, fibers, fabrics, and cellophane.[110]

The German Experience: The Evolution of Cooperative Managerial Capitalism

The collective histories of modern industrial enterprises in Germany from their beginnings in the 1880s to the coming of the Nazi regime provide a third perspective on the evolution of the institution at the core of managerial capitalism.

In the United States the three-pronged investment that created these enterprises came quickly, and the first movers began to compete oligopolistically at home and very soon abroad. As time passed, they continued to exploit their organizational capabilities by moving into new geographical markets and by diversifying, primarily through direct investment, into related industries.

In Britain fewer entrepreneurs made the essential investments. Even when they did, they were slow to develop the organizational capabilities essential to compete at home and abroad. By relying on the more accepted methods of market control—patents, advertising, cartels, and mergers without rationalization—many further sapped their competitive strength. They moved abroad more slowly than their foreign competitors and diversified less extensively into related industries through direct investment.

In Germany more entrepreneurs made the necessary investments and developed the functional and strategic skills. Where they became first movers, as they did in chemicals, machinery, and metals, they quickly became major players in the new global oligopolies. Soon they too, moved into related industries when economies of scope gave them the opportunity. On the other hand, in industries where entrepreneurs only occasionally made the essential initial investments in manufacturing, marketing, and management, as was the case in branded, packaged products and oil, and also in sewing, office, and agricultural equipment and other light machinery, either the American or the other European first movers became dominant in Germany. Where German entrepreneurs did develop organizational capabilities, they reinforced their position by continuing close interfirm cooperation. But where they failed to develop these capabilities, such cooperation was in itself of little value in acquiring and maintaining market power in international markets.

The organizational capabilities developed by the German first movers in the industries of the Second Industrial Revolution—the industries so central to the growth of a modern economy—were more responsible for the rise of Germany's industrial power than those developed by American firms were for the industrial growth of the United States. American entrepreneurs who created the new industrial enterprises benefited from a much larger domestic market in terms of growth of population and the income of that population and also from having a much greater abundance of natural resources—oil, coal, iron, copper, and other nonferrous metals—and a larger output of agricultural products. On the one hand, the greater dependency of German industrial enterprises on foreign raw materials, and, even more important, foreign markets encouraged interfirm cooperation. On the other hand, the great importance of the international market provided a constant goad for German firms to maintain their facilities and to sharpen their functional, technical, and strategic skills that might otherwise have been diluted through cartels and other interfirm agreements. Even where prices and markets were negotiated, those that maintained such facilities and skills were in a far better negotiating position than those that did not.

Moreover, Germany's industrial strength lay in its producer-goods industries—in industrial chemicals, machinery, and metals. The initial investment in such industries was larger than that in any other. At the same time, Germany's capital markets were smaller and less developed than those of the United States and Britain. Therefore financial institutions, particularly the new, all-purpose Grossbanken, played a greater role in financing the first movers' initial investment in production and distribution, and hence a greater role in their subsequent governance, than was the case in the other two countries. And because they served several clients and were committed from the start to maintaining the long-term viability, and therefore profits, of their investments, they remained a strong force for interfirm and inter-industry cooperation.

The organizational capabilities so central to Germany's industrial growth before 1914 were also responsible for the successful return of German industry after a decade of war and crises. The loss of international markets during these years and the declared intention of the industrialists of the victorious nations, particularly those of Britain and France, to take over markets that had been held by Germans intensified the pressure for cooperation. Because the Gross-banken had been weakened during the period of war and inflation, cooperation between the enterprises themselves became increasingly desirable.

The extent of this distinctively German industrial and financial cooperation varied not only from industry to industry but also from period to period. These variations, in turn, reflected differences in the changing characteristics of production, of markets, and of competition from foreign enterprises. In nonstandardized heavy machinery (those companies in Group 35), banks played a less significant role and cartels were much less used than was the case in electrical equipment, metals, and chemicals, where the initial investment was large and paybacks on that investment in many cases came more slowly. So, too, in industries where scale provided rapid payback of initial investments and where a single first mover came to dominate its specific product markets, as was true in rubber (Continental), rayon (VGF), nonferrous metals (Metallgesellschaft), light machinery (Bosch, Linde, and Deutz), and soap (Henkel), banks never played an essential role. In these industries the first movers moved quickly into foreign markets, and as cartels in international markets were difficult to negotiate and implement (at least until the Great Depression), these firms, like American firms, continued to compete functionally and strategically for market share. Though the firms did begin to diversify into related products, they did so less aggressively than American firms, partly because the opportunity for such expansion during the interwar decades was available to the German enterprises only between 1925 and the coming of the depression five years later.

In steel, electrical equipment, and chemicals, where there was more than one first mover, banks participated to a greater extent in initial financing and in encouraging interfirm cooperation. As the first movers became established, as the organizational capabilities were developed, and as the structure of these industries became clearly defined, the role of banks diminished and that of formal cooperation increased.

Effective industry-wide cartels came only after an industry's structure had been stabilized. Even then, agreements as to price, output, and marketing territories remained difficult to reach and to enforce. Because quotas were regularly renegotiated, leading firms continued to maintain their functional strength to gain market share, in order to be in a position to claim these gains in the next set of negotiations.

The instability of the cartels encouraged the formation of two new forms of industrial organization—the I.G. and the Konzern. The I.G. as a profit pool reduced the incentives to cheat on price and output agreements, and by cooperation in functional activities the member firms enhanced their industry's position in foreign markets. The Konzerne were more vertically integrated, for they were often established for the defensive purpose of assuring the central enterprise of sources of supply and outlets for its products. Although I.G.'s and Konzerne appeared before 1914, they became much more widely used in the crisis years following the German defeat in World War I. Then, by providing pools of capital as well as sources of supplies and outlets, they helped many firms to survive. They appeared not only in the great industries but also in lesser ones like margarine, sugar, oil, rubber, and automobiles.

The weakness of the I.G. and even of the Konzern, as German industrial leaders such as Duisberg and Thyssen had argued from the turn of the century on, was that they did not permit the industry-wide rationalization of facilities and personnel needed to exploit fully the cost advantages of scale and scope or to replace obsolescent equipment with modern, state-of-the-art facilities. Only in the electrical-equipment industry had such mergers occurred before World War I. Then, once the German economy was stabilized after 1924, mergers took place in both the steel and chemical industries, permitting rationalization. They also occurred in sugar, rubber, and automobiles. The resulting organizational structures developed in the steel and chemical mergers were, by the time of the Nazi military mobilization, moving toward variations of the multidivisional form. In chemicals the size and complexity of the operations and the long tradition of cooperation among powerful, long-established constituent companies forestalled the creation of an effective corporate office comparable to that of Siemens in Germany, ICI in Britain, and the leading chemical and food firms in the United States.

The post-stabilization rationalization of German industry was carried out not only in mergers but also in existing Konzerne and in the large, functionally departmentalized enterprises. In all these types of enterprises it was executed by experienced managers who could no longer look to the Grossbanken for financing. Those institutions simply did not have the necessary financial resources required by the major firms for modernization and rationalization. The banks did continue to assist smaller firms in the great industries, as well as such companies as Stollwerck and "Nordsee" Deutsche Hochseefischerei in the lesser industries. But during the interwar years similar individual enterprises also received financing from strong industrial companies such as Rheinmetall, Henkel, Rütgerswerke, Deutsche Solvay, and such giants as VSt and I.G. Farben. Even American companies—including Corn Products Refining, Goodrich, Du Pont, and probably Electric Storage Battery—became significant sources of funding. For these reasons, by 1930 industrialists had usually come to outnumber bankers on the Supervisory Boards of leading German industrial enterprises.

In the great industries, the leading companies looked even less to the banks for major financial assistance. Those in electrical equipment and steel turned to foreign capital, using American investment-banking houses to underwrite their loans. AEG, Siemens, VSt, GHH, and Krupp looked to Dillon, Read, National City Bank, and other such houses, and not to the Deutsche Bank or the Disconto Gesellschaft. Indeed, these two industries accounted for two-thirds ($254.2 million) of the total of $384.0 million borrowed in the United States by German industrial enterprises up to 1927.[111] The third great industry, chemicals, was much more self-financed. It borrowed only a total of $22.5 million. I.G. Farben even took over its own banking functions by acquiring the Länderbank.

By the 1930s, too, families were playing a less influential role than they had earlier in tactical and strategic decision-making. In chemicals and steel the giant mergers had eliminated much of what remained of family influence within these enterprises. So had the building of Konzerne during the postwar crises. Thus by 1930 there were fewer entrepreneur- or family-controlled enterprises in Germany than there had been in 1914. Individuals and families controlling Konzerne—such as the Krupps, Klöckners, Haniels, and Flicks—managed a larger number of companies with a greater variety of activities than did leading American industrial families such as the du Ponts or Mellons. Whether a German family-dominated enterprise was administered through a small corporate office of a Konzern or a much larger central office of a consolidated group, as in the case of the Siemens and Merton families, the decisions concerning day-to-day coordination of its activities and those involving long-term allocation of resources were made and implemented by teams of salaried managers who had no blood relationship to the founders or their families and who held few (or no) shares in the enterprise.

It was the number and size of such managerial hierarchies that differentiated industrial capitalism in Germany and the United States from that in Britain. In Britain, as the post-World War II era opened, more of the large industrial companies were still run by founding families or their descendants. Fewer nonfamily members were recruited into top management from smaller pools of middle managers. In Britain in the late 1940s the commitment to the ways of personal management was still strong.

The following extract from the minutes of the board of Pilkington Brothers, one of Britain's most successful industrial enterprises, dated November 29, 1945, makes this point. It refers to the recruitment of Alastair Pilkington, whose development of the float-glass processes in the 1950s was to give that company its most effective competitive edge during the postwar years. At issue here was Alastair's name, for he was not a member of the glass-making family. How then should he be brought into the firm?

The Directors considered a report furnished by Col. Phelps of an interview which he and Mr. W. H. Pilkington had had with Col. Lionel G. Pilkington on the subject of the possibility of his second son, Alastair, joining the P.B. Organization after completing his studies at University. The matter had arisen from an almost casual introduction by Mr. Richard Pilkington. The Directors felt that it should be pointed out to Mr. Richard Pilkington that the method of introduction was very irregular. Mr. L. G. Pilkington's branch of the Family broke away at least 15 generations ago [i.e., as far back as Richard Pilkington's researches had been able to take him]. It was agreed, however, that a member of the Pilkington Family, however remote, could be accepted only as a potential Family Director. After considerable discussion, the Board agreed that, in principle, they were prepared to open the door wider to really promising candidates . . .

With regard to the particular case under discussion, it was considered that before any action in respect of Alastair Pilkington was taken, we should take steps to learn more about Col. L. G. Pilkington—in particular his business and Family background. He is the Managing Director of Pulsometer Engineering Co., Reading, which Lord Cozens-Hardy pointed out was a small but old and well established company, he believed, of Quaker origin.[112]

Such a discussion concerning the recruitment of a lower-level manager would be hard to find in the minutes of a large American or German enterprise in the capital-intensive industries of the twentieth century.

This commitment to personal rather than professional management characterized British industrial capitalism. It was also this commitment that made industrial capitalism less dynamic in Britain than in the United States and Germany, in terms of the development of new products and processes and of the growth and competitiveness of enterprises and industries.

In both the United States and Germany by the 1930s managerial capitalism had replaced personal capitalism in major sectors of the economy, in ways that were only beginning to be evident in Britain. The difference between the two brands of managerial capitalism was that one was oriented toward competition and the other toward cooperation. Industry leaders in the United States competed functionally and strategically for markets and profits, whereas in Germany they often preferred to negotiate rather than to compete. Nevertheless, in order to negotiate from strength at home, as well as to compete with foreigners at home and in international markets, the managers of these enterprises were well aware of the value of maintaining their organizational capabilities—their physical facilities and human skills. After the Allied victory in 1945 brought a strong commitment to competition in Europe, German managers accepted the American ways of competition but continued to cooperate more than their American counterparts. So, too, in the years after World War II, British enterprises became increasingly managerial even though their preference for the ways of personal management continued.

The Dynamics of Industrial Capitalism

The German story completes the examination of the collective histories of the two hundred largest industrial enterprises in the three nations that produced two-thirds of the world's industrial output from the 1880s until the depression of the 1930s. The sample that provides the data on which this history is based is both representative and comprehensive. Some firms, particularly privately held firms not listed in stock-exchange manuals or year books, have undoubtedly been missed, but there are only a few of them. Not all the companies that were listed and have been included in the appendixes of this study have been mentioned, but their experience parallels those of other leaders in their respective industries.

For the historian relying on this broad sample the collective histories of these enterprises provide a story of economic growth and transformation. Economists, particularly those of the more traditional mainstream school, have not developed a theory of the evolution of the firm as a dynamic organization. For many of them the modern industrial enterprise is little more than an extractor of monopolistic or oligopolistic rents. Nor have sociologists and other social scientists developed such a theory. Indeed, for many scholars the large industrial enterprise represents a prime example of an inefficient, bureaucratically managed organization. But in the history just told the modern industrial enterprise played a central role in creating the most technologically advanced, fastest-growing industries of their day. These industries, in turn, were the pace setters of the industrial sector of their economies—the sector so critical to the growth and transformation of national economies into their modern, urban industrial form. Therefore the enterprises whose collective histories have been reviewed here provided an underlying dynamic in the development of modern industrial capitalism.

Organizational Capabilities as the Core Dynamic

At the core of this dynamic were the organizational capabilities of the enterprise as a unified whole. These organizational capabilities were the collective physical facilities and human skills as they were organized within the enterprise. They included the physical facilities in each of the many operating units—the factories, offices, laboratories—and the skills of the employees working in such units.

But only if these facilities and skills were carefully coordinated and integrated could the enterprise achieve the economies of scale and scope that were needed to compete in national and international markets and to continue to grow. Thus even more important to the maintenance of market share than the capabilities of the lower-level managers in charge of the operating units were those of the middle managers responsible for the performance of the lower-level executives. These middle managers not only had to develop and apply functional-specific and product-specific managerial skills, but they also had to train and motivate lower-level managers and to coordinate, integrate, and evaluate their work. And most critical to the long-term health and growth of the industrial enterprise were the abilities of the senior executives—the top operating managers and those in the corporate office—who recruited and motivated the middle managers, defined and allocated their responsibilities, and monitored and coordinated their activities, and who, in addition, planned and allocated the resources for the enterprise as a whole.

Such organizational capabilities, of course, had to be created, and once established, they had to be maintained. Their maintenance was as great a challenge as their creation, for facilities depreciate and skills atrophy. Moreover, changing technologies and markets constantly make both existing facilities and skills obsolete. One of the most critical tasks of top management has always been to maintain these capabilities and to integrate these facilities and skills into a unified organization—so that the whole becomes more than the sum of its parts.

Such organizational capabilities, in turn, have provided the source—the dynamic—for the continuing growth of the enterprise. They have made possible the earnings that supplied much of the funding for such growth. Even more important, they provided the specialized facilities and skills that gave the enterprise an advantage in foreign markets or in related industries. Because of these capabilities the basic goal of the modern industrial enterprise became long-term profits based on long-term growth—growth that increased the productivity, and so the competitive power, that drove the expansion of industrial capitalism.

Profits are, of course, essential to the survival and growth of all capitalist enterprises. If income is less than costs over an extended period of time, the enterprise cannot remain commercially viable. In personally managed, personally owned enterprises (and here British companies provide the best examples), assured income rather than appreciation of assets was usually the goal. The individuals and families who managed the enterprises that they controlled did invest earnings to maintain existing facilities. But they often preferred to pay out earnings in dividends rather than using them to make the extensive investments required to move into foreign markets or to develop new products in related industries. Because their firms grew slowly and because they hired only a small number of managers, the founders and their families remained influential in the affairs of the enterprise and so affected dividend policy. And in many cases that policy continued to favor current dividends over long-term growth.

On the other hand, where the investment in production and distribution necessary to exploit fully the economies of scale and scope required more funds than an individual or family had available, and where the management of the enterprise required more managers than the family could provide, long-term profits based on long-term growth were a goal on which managers and major investors could agree. Here American and German enterprises provide examples. Such a goal not only helped to assure tenure for the senior executives, but it also enhanced the opportunity for advancement for the more junior managers. (In the personally owned and managed firms in Britain, the key managerial positions were usually reserved for the owning family.) In firms with long-term goals the major investors, who were wealthy individuals almost by definition, were promised long-term appreciation of their assets.

Until well after World War II, both the managers with little equity in the enterprise (the inside directors) and the representatives of the major stockholders (the outside directors) agreed that retained earnings should be reinvested in facilities and personnel in industries where the enterprise had developed competitive advantages based on its organizational capabilities. They agreed that such investment carried lower risk and higher probability of a satisfactory rate of return than making comparable investments in industries where the firm did not have such advantages. Wealthy investors continued to prefer to keep their capital in enterprises whose organizational capabilities they understood, and whose inside directors they might influence—rather than to invest through the capital markets in enterprises whose capabilities and managers they did not know. Even small investors who had no direct contact with managers made the distinction between investing for current income and for long-term growth. From the beginning of the modern securities markets such investors looked for income to bonds with fixed returns, and looked for growth to stocks with no stated returns.

The development and maintenance of organizational capabilities not only helped to assure the continuing growth of the enterprise but also affected the growth of the industries and of the nations in which the new modern industrial enterprise appeared. Such organizational capabilities provided a dynamic for growth that helped to make the economies of the United States and Germany, in the three decades before World War I, the most productive and most competitive in the world. These capabilities made possible global domination by Americans in light machinery, by Germans in dyes and other organic chemicals and in heavy machinery, and by both American and German makers of electrical equipment and metals. On the other hand, the continuing commitment of British manufacturers to more personal, nonhierarchical management, and therefore their failure to develop such capabilities in these basic industries of the Second Industrial Revolution, held back or prevented British enterprises and the industries in which they operated from becoming competitive and so played a significant part in weakening Britain's industrial strength in relation to her two major rivals.

The development and maintenance of these capabilities affected the performance of enterprises, industries, and economies in the years between World War I and World War II as profoundly as they had before World War I. The maintenance and renewal of such capabilities were essential for the rapid recovery of German competitive strength in world markets after the decade of war and crisis following 1914. The lack of such capabilities prevented British, and also French, enterprises from capturing markets that the Germans had temporarily lost in many industries. But during the interwar years when British enterprises did develop and maintain such capabilities, as they did in oil, containers, and chemicals, their industries did become competitive in international trade.

In these same interwar years organizational capabilities that were developed through the exploitation of scale permitted American enterprises to grow by expanding their activities abroad. They did so in oil; rubber; glass; abrasives; branded, packaged foods; and consumer chemicals, as well as in a wide variety of machinery, including automobiles. Capabilities based on the economies of scope stimulated growth by diversification. They made it possible for American and German (but fewer British) companies to expand into new product markets related to their original ones.

After World War II, such organizational capabilities became even more central to the competitiveness of enterprises, industries, and economies, as expansion into new geographical and product markets became the primary routes to growth for the modern industrial enterprise, and as such multinational and inter-industry expansion intensified competition in many markets. By the 1960s this intensified competition, the result of continued growth and of the competitive power of the managerial industrial enterprises based on their organizational capabilities—the central dynamic of modern industrial capitalism—was bringing underlying changes in the strategy, organization, and financing of such enterprises. Indeed, the competition of the 1960s may be seen as a turning point in the evolution of the managerial enterprise. The significance of this turning point can be better understood through a brief review of two interrelated issues: the concept of first movers and that of challengers; and how and why challengers arise in the industrial world.

FIRST MOVERS AND CHALLENGERS

The creators of the modern industrial enterprise (as defined in Chapter 2) were, of course, entrepreneurs, not managers. And the creation of this new type of enterprise called for entrepreneurial skills of the highest order. Joseph Schumpeter defined the entrepreneur as the creator of new combinations in production, marketing, sources of supply, and organization.[1] The first movers—those entrepreneurs that established the first modern industrial enterprises in the new industries of the Second Industrial Revolution—had to innovate in all these activities. They had to be aware of the potential of new technologies and then get the funds and make investments large enough to exploit fully the economies of scale and scope existing in the new technologies. They had to obtain the facilities and personnel essential to distribute and market new or improved products on a national scale and to obtain extensive sources of supply. Finally, they had to recruit and organize the managerial teams essential to maintain and integrate the investment made in the processes of production and distribution.

In Britain and the United States before the end of the 1890s, the first movers in the new industries rarely looked to established capital markets for funds. The initial capital that was not provided by an entrepreneur and his partners came from local investors, with some assistance from local financial institutions. In the United States the first large-scale funding of industrial enterprises by investment-banking houses and other financial institutions came only with the turn-of-the-century merger movement. And this funding was used to rationalize production and distribution facilities and management organizations after the merger. Only in industries where such rationalization permitted enterprises to exploit fully the economies of scale did the American financial institutions play a role in establishing modern industrial enterprises. In Germany, on the other hand, banks did play a significant role in providing capital for new ventures to entrepreneurs making the investments necessary to exploit the potential economies of scale and scope. In both Germany and the United States the funds provided by the financiers brought them into the decision-making process as outside directors. Once the new consolidated enterprises in the United States and the managerial enterprises in Germany were firmly established, the financiers had less and less influence on decisions concerning current operations and the allocation of resources for future growth. Bankers preferred to remain bankers and to let industrialists run the enterprises. Moreover, retained earnings provided industrial managers with most of the funding needed to finance continuing growth.

Once modern industrial enterprises were established, the managers began to take charge. As soon as the interrelated investments in production and distribution were made and a managerial staff was recruited, organized, and trained, the critical skills needed for continued growth and successful performance of both the enterprises and the industries in which they operated became more managerial than entrepreneurial or financial.

Of the three levels of management in these new enterprises—lower, middle, and top (see Figure 1)—the tasks of both the middle and the top managers were brand-new. In production the new middle managers—both line and staff—had to learn intimately the technology of the products made and the processes used in the different factories under their control. So, too, in marketing and distribution middle managers had to come to know the similarities, differences, vagaries, and opportunities of different regional markets. In both production and distribution the line managers had to recruit, train, and motivate their own staffs as well as the lower-level managers under their command—the managers of plants, branch sales and purchasing offices, and laboratories. And even more than these lower-level executives, the middle managers had to learn to administer; that is, they had to learn to coordinate, to evaluate and act on such evaluations, in addition to recruiting, training, and motivating subordinates. For top managers such administrative duties were paramount. They not only had to learn to coordinate and monitor the activities of the functional departments but also to plan, allocate resources for, and implement long-term programs to maintain the enterprise's facilities and skills, if they were to retain their share of existing markets and to move into new ones. Equally important, they had to select and reward the functional executives—the middle managers responsible for the different functional activities within the enterprise.

These functional and administrative skills were highly product-specific. For this reason, once the new organizations were in place, the middle and top managers were normally recruited from within. Nearly all those who came from the outside had had experience in the same industry. The managerial capabilities of individual enterprises varied, of course, from enterprise to enterprise. They reflected the training, experience, and innate abilities of the members of the organization and, above all, of its leadership—the full-time executives at the corporate office. Obviously, too, such managerial abilities changed within a firm as time passed and as younger sets of managers replaced the founding entrepreneurs and the managers they had recruited.

As has been repeatedly emphasized in the collective histories of the individual industries told in the preceding chapters, the first movers' initial, interrelated, three-pronged investments in manufacturing, marketing, and management created powerful barriers to entry. Challengers had to make comparable investments at a greater risk, precisely because the first movers had already learned the ways of the new processes of production, were already dominating the markets for the new or greatly improved products, and were already reaping returns from their initial investments. As the first movers' functional and administrative skills were honed, the barriers to entry by newcomers became even more formidable. In the sale of consumer products, particularly branded, packaged goods, these barriers were reinforced by advertising, tying contracts, and exclusive franchises. In the more technologically advanced, producer-goods industries the barriers were reinforced by patents. In Europe, first movers strengthened their position still further by arranging interfirm agreements as to price, output, and marketing territories.

Nevertheless, challengers appeared. Even where a single first mover came to dominate a national industry, as occurred in Britain and Germany, it competed with foreign firms in distant markets and often in its own home market. Challengers were rarely new entrants, new entrepreneurial enterprises. Some were mergers of established firms, or established firms that exploited specialized marketing or technological opportunities. Most, however, were first movers from other nations or from related industries that used their organizational capabilities to enter new markets. Other challengers were smaller firms that had established themselves in specialized products or particular geographical markets.

Challengers succeeded for various reasons. Occasionally, although this was rare, a first mover simply dissipated its advantages. Henry Ford's automobile company and Judge Elbert Gary's United States Steel are two well-known examples. Ford, after his brilliant achievements in production and distribution had made him the world's lowest-cost producer of automobiles, destroyed his company's competitive capabilities in the years immediately following World War I. He did so by driving out nearly all his experienced and highly competent senior managers. William S. Knudsen, the top production executive, and Norval A. Hawkins, the company's sales chief, moved to General Motors, where after 1920 a new management transformed that enterprise into its modern form. The executive most responsible for that transformation, Alfred Sloan, often said that Henry Ford should be given as much credit as Sloan himself for the success of General Motors in the 1920s and 1930s.[2] In Britain at the same time, Ford, by removing Percival Perry and other managers, opened the way for Austin Motor Company and Morris Motors to obtain their initial stronghold in the British market for low-priced cars. Judge Gary, by continually overruling the senior managers trained by Andrew Carnegie (they finally resigned in frustration), permitted Bethlehem Steel, Republic Steel, and other challengers to make the investments and develop the organizational capabilities needed to capture a substantial market share from the United States Steel Corporation.

Government action was another means of creating successful challengers. Before World War II direct government funding was rare. Indeed, in the years before World War I, the one example in the three countries was the funding of Anglo-Persian Oil by the British government in order to have an assured supply of fuel oil for the Navy. This funding assisted that company to rise into the global oil oligopoly. So, too, during World War I the German government financed the building of a new giant aluminum enterprise. But without the coming of World War I, it is unlikely that either enterprise would have become a successful challenger. Wartime demand and government subsidy also permitted British Aluminium to remain at least a secondary player in the global oligopoly. During the depression many companies received government support, but in nearly every case the motive was to keep the enterprise alive rather than to convert it into an aggressive competitor. Only after World War II did governments support a nation's "champion" in international markets.

Other government aids, such as tariffs, patents, and government regulations, and in Germany the purchasing of equipment by government-owned railroads and telegraph systems, usually benefited first movers as much as challengers. Occasionally, however, such government action helped to deter foreign challengers and assist local ones. Thus the decision of the state-owned railways in Germany to purchase air brakes from the German firm Knorr-Bremse helped that firm to challenge the Westinghouse Air Brake Company, the first mover in that industry, in Germany.

In the United States, and only in the United States, did antitrust action play a role in encouraging challengers. The federal courts, by ordering the dissolution of Standard Oil, American Tobacco, and Du Pont in 1911 and 1912, created several new firms out of a single dominant one—more than ten out of Standard Oil, four out of American Tobacco, and two out of Du Pont. At the end of World War II the federal government, by turning over government-financed aluminum plants built by Alcoa to Reynolds Metals and Kaiser Aluminum, provided them with production facilities on the scale essential to compete with the first mover. Two of these actions (those pertaining to Alcoa and American Tobacco) converted near monopolies into oligopolies, and the other two increased the number of players in the two existing oligopolies. These antitrust cases, however, did not bring new investment in facilities, except for those by Reynolds and Kaiser in marketing and research. The production and distribution facilities of the new companies were taken from the original enterprises. So were most of their managerial personnel.

More significant opportunities for challengers were provided by major shifts in sources of supply and in basic markets. None were more dramatic than those that occurred in the oil industry during the first decade of the twentieth century. The opening of the vast new fields in Texas, California, Rumania, and Russia about the same time that gasoline was beginning to replace kerosene as the industry's major product permitted Gulf Oil, Texas Company, Sun Oil, Union Oil of California, and two new major oil companies in Germany to make the investments essential to become effective challengers. Although in no other industry were changes in supplies and markets that dramatic, slower shifts in both of those areas provided opportunities for the rise of new competitors. In meatpacking, for example, the competitive advantages of the first movers in the United States, which had established themselves in the 1880s, were being dissipated in the years immediately after World War II as the coming of the supermarket and the replacement of refrigerated railway cars by refrigerated trucks permitted other packers and the retailers to bypass the Continental distribution networks that the first movers had created.

Another historic development was as important as shifts in supply and demand. This was the continuing growth of markets for the products of the challengers' industries. It was this growth that permitted smaller firms operating in niches, that is, specialized markets, to build plants of optimal size. Such firms could establish themselves in niches because the first movers concentrated on high-volume, standardized production, where the cost advantages of scale were the greatest, and thus were less able to meet the less-standardized, more-specialized requirements of certain industrial customers or of specific regional markets. These smaller challengers might enjoy as much as 5%, but rarely more than 10%, of a major market dominated by first movers. Nevertheless, that market niche often gave them a secure base for further growth as the industry expanded. For example, the rapid expansion of the tire industry made it possible for General Tire and Fisk Rubber to become significant secondary players in their domestic oligopoly by meeting the demand for replacements. So, too, Minnesota Mining & Manufacturing moved into a niche by supplying abrasives and then tapes needed in grinding and polishing the finishes used in the burgeoning automobile industry. Again, Heinrich Lanz and G. M. Pfaff and Dürkoppwerke in Germany were able to cut into the market share of International Harvester and Singer Sewing Machine, respectively, by expanding their footholds gained in providing products for specialized local needs.

General growth of *national* markets also provided opportunities for challengers, although these opportunities arose more often before World War I and after World War II than in the years between 1914 and 1945—years when war, postwar recession, prosperity, depression, and again war brought sharp fluctuations in demand. Even so, in the 1930s in Britain, where the worldwide Great Depression had much less impact than it did in Germany and the United States (indeed, for Britain the 1930s were more dynamic years than the 1920s), the demand for automobiles and appliances soared. Although subsidiaries of American firms benefited from this increase in demand, it assured the continuing growth of the British challengers to the Americans in the British automobile and electrical-machinery industries.

CHALLENGERS FROM ABROAD AND FROM OTHER INDUSTRIES
Nevertheless, the major challengers in the capital-intensive industries of the twentieth century were not smaller firms that took advantage of changes in technologies and markets. To repeat, far more often the successful challengers

were long-established companies, usually first movers, from other countries or from other industries in the same country. These established firms had the facilities and skills—the organizational capabilities—that simply were not available to new entrepreneurial entrants into an industry and that were difficult for smaller specialized firms to acquire. The capabilities of the firms from abroad were normally based on managerial experience developed from exploiting economies of scale, and the capabilities of those moving from related industries were based more on skills developed in exploiting those of scope.

A number of first movers in one country also became first movers in others, as did the European rayon, chemical, and pharmaceutical companies in the United States and the American light-machinery companies in Europe. But more first movers went abroad as challengers. American tire, food, and consumer-chemical companies moved into Europe to challenge first movers there, and Nestlé, Stollwerck, and Lever Brothers became challengers in the United States. As Shell established itself in the United States, so did the Texas Company, Standard Oil of New York (Socony), and Standard Oil of California in Europe and Asia.

Even more competitors came from related industries. In some cases the products developed for new markets were, indeed, entirely new. Here the established enterprise became Schumpeter's entrepreneur. The products were invented by the company's research department and then were scaled up to obtain the maximum advantages of scale or scope. The necessary market organization was created and the necessary managers recruited. Such interrelated, tripartite investments made the diversifying enterprise a first mover in new product markets, as Du Pont was in nylon, Dacron, and neoprene, and ICI was in polyethylene.

In most cases, however, a challenger's product was not brand-new. Cumulative innovation within the production, distribution, and research and development (R&D) departments permitted an enterprise to develop a product that was competitive in existing related industries. Thus Libbey-Owens—a first mover in bottle making—used its technological abilities to challenge Pittsburgh Plate Glass in plate glass. In Europe the German chemical firm Henkel moved into the production of soap powder to become Lever Brothers' strongest competitor. In more far-ranging ways, as early as the 1890s dye companies in Germany became major challengers in pharmaceuticals and film. Chemical companies in the United States after World War I, and in Britain with the formation of ICI, became challengers in paints, varnishes, and finishes, and also in plastics and other synthetic materials. After the European first movers in rayon established themselves in the United States, their only significant challengers were Du Pont and Tennessee Eastman. Both were successful because they had the organizational capabilities to exploit the economies of scope in cellulose chemistry. Other chemical companies, such as Dow Chemical and Griesheim-

Elektron, became major producers of magnesium and alloys. At the same time the leading makers of paint, pharmaceuticals, rubber, and even food began to produce and distribute a variety of chemical products. Soap producers, notably Procter & Gamble, and much more hesitantly Lever Brothers, moved into foodstuffs.

In machinery before the First World War, International Harvester began to manufacture plows, harrows, and other agricultural equipment, while Deere and other plow makers moved into harvesters. In the 1930s, as the depression in farming contracted the agricultural-equipment market, International Harvester began to produce construction equipment, trucks, and other commercial vehicles. Allis-Chalmers, a producer of machinery for the milling and lumber industries, began to make electrical equipment before World War I and agricultural machinery immediately after the war. In both the United States and Germany the first movers in electrical equipment—generators, transformers, motors, streetcars, meters, circuit breakers, and lamps—diversified very widely. In addition to closely related products such as appliances, instruments, and radios, they produced plastics and alloys, which they had developed in the process of improving wire and insulation.

Such increasing diversification gave birth to a new phenomenon—a single enterprise competing, not only with companies within its own industry, but also with those in several other industries, and competing with different firms in each of those oligopolistic product markets. Thus in the 1920s Du Pont's Paint and Finishes Department competed functionally and strategically with Hercules Powder, Sherwin-Williams, Glidden, and National Lead; and its Dyestuffs Department (later the Organic Chemical Department) competed in the same manner with Allied Chemical, American Home Products, and I.G. Farben's General Aniline & Film. For the other Du Pont departments the pattern was the same. In Germany the chemical giant I.G. Farben competed with Vereinigte Glanzstoff-Fabriken (VGF) in rayon, with Zeiss Ikon in cameras, with both German and Swiss firms in pharmaceuticals, with Deutsche Solvay-Werke in synthetic alkalies, with Vereinigte Stahlwerke (VSt) and Metallgesellschaft in alloys, and even in dyes with Kali-Chemie; and these companies, in turn, competed with other firms in other product markets. In Britain, on the other hand, before World War II only ICI developed the capabilities necessary to diversify competitively into related industries. But Unilever, Burroughs Wellcome, and Beechams were already beginning to develop the facilities and skills that permitted them to pursue a comparable strategy of diversification after the war.

Organizational capabilities in research and development, besides permitting established first movers to move into related industries, also played a critical role in improving products, processes, and productivity in the core industries in which they had started. Thus it was the established firms, not the new ones, that carried out the revolution in pharmaceuticals which began with the introduction of sulfa drugs and penicillin. They did so in Germany and Britain as well as in the United States. Between the world wars major improvements in products and processes were brought to completion by established enterprises—in oil, rubber, glass and other materials, chemicals, most metals, a variety of food processing, and light and heavy machinery, including automobiles and electrical equipment.

Such capabilities, it should be stressed once again, were primarily those of development and not of invention. For the function of management in the modern industrial corporation was to determine first, through pilot plants and market studies, whether the new products and processes could be produced with the quality and at the price that permitted them to be sold on a global scale, and then to make—and to maintain a constant watch over—the investments essential to achieve this goal. Invention was largely left to individuals or groups outside of the enterprise and often working in universities and institutes, and many times even the initial commercialization of the product and process was left to small entrepreneurial firms.

Before the Second World War very few major industrial enterprises made extensive investments in fundamental research. Such investments by European leaders—ICI, I.G. Farben, and the German electrical companies—remained small. The tiny number investing in fundamental research in the United States, notably Du Pont, GE, and AT&T, did achieve important results: Du Pont with nylon and neoprene in the late 1930s; and GE, even earlier, in developing tungsten filament that was ductile rather than brittle, as well as vacuum tubes and then radio and other electronic equipment. Such successes encouraged other enterprises in technologically advanced industries, particularly in the United States, to begin to make comparable investments after 1945.

The capabilities in product development that permitted established firms to move into related product markets and those that provided competitive advantages in foreign markets allowed the modern industrial enterprise to be entrepreneurial and innovative in the Schumpeterian sense. They permitted these enterprises to produce and improve products for markets other than those for which their enterprise had been originally established. They could obtain and maintain profit share in these other markets because they had development, production, marketing, and financial skills and resources not available to individual entrepreneurs attempting to break into the same markets. But existing enterprises could only remain entrepreneurial in this manner if their middle managers maintained functional facilities and skills and if their top managers effectively monitored internal operations and adjusted strategies to constantly changing technological and market opportunities.

Finally, I want to emphasize yet again that the organizational capabilities—the facilities and skills—that provided the core dynamic for the continuing evolution of the modern industrial enterprise and of the industries which it dominated were created primarily in those capital-intensive industries where the interrelated investment in manufacturing, marketing, and management provided powerful competitive advantages. In other industries where the technologies of production remained relatively simple and where markets required little in the way of product-specific distribution and services, there was less need, and less incentive, to develop such capabilities. In textiles, apparel, leather, lumber, furniture, publishing and printing, and specialized machinery, modern industrial enterprises had fewer competitive advantages and so appeared in much smaller numbers. When they did appear, they rarely acquired a dominant position. In such industries the management of production and distribution remained much more personal. In such industries more small, single-unit firms continued to buy and sell through commercial intermediaries. In such industries size could be more of a disadvantage than an advantage. There organizational capabilities resulted more from exploiting the firm's flexibility for action than from utilizing economies of scale and scope.

Even so, in lines where the minimum efficient scale of production was low and where a retailing enterprise could take all the output of a factory of optimal size, manufacturers often established their own retail outlets and retailers often invested in manufacturing plants. This was true of apparel (particularly shoes) and furniture, where marketing organizations could easily absorb the output of works operating at minimum efficient scale. In textiles, lumber, and specialized machinery, where more opportunities for economies of scale or scope existed, the industry's leaders were those that integrated production and distribution by investing in facilities and personnel for wholesaling or direct selling to industrial customers. In these industries, however, such integration did not permit them to dominate at home or abroad in the manner of first movers in the more capital-intensive sectors of the economy. Such firms only occasionally went abroad. Moreover, because the technologies of production remained relatively simple, there was little incentive to invest in research and development. In addition, their investment in wholesaling remained small in comparison with that of the leaders in capital-intensive industries. Therefore, these enterprises had little opportunity to develop capabilities based on the exploitation of scope. They rarely diversified. They and the industries in which they operated played a much smaller role in economic growth and transformation after the 1880s than did the enterprises in the capital-intensive industries that enjoyed the cost advantages of scale and scope and thus provided an underlying dynamic for the growth of modern industrial capitalism.

Post–World War II Developments

The historic trends described in this book culminated in the years after World War II. Before that, in the decades following 1914, the drive for long-term profits through growth by expansion into new markets had been held back by the traumatic events of world history. The devastating First World War, followed by continuing crises into the 1920s, the Great Depression of the 1930s, the even more gigantic, global war of 1939 to 1945, and the massive reconstruction that had to follow—all these delayed the increased international and inter-industry competition that such growth made almost inevitable.

Once the long-established European industrial enterprises had revived their organizational capabilities, and the newer Japanese firms had developed theirs, and both European and Japanese companies had begun to move into foreign markets, international competition intensified. So did inter-industry competition as leading firms in the United States and Europe expanded their investment in research and development. This heightened competition may mark that turning point in the evolution of the modern industrial enterprise to which I have already referred. As increased competition threatened to lower profits and reduce opportunities to reinvest earnings in industries where firms' organizational capabilities gave them competitive advantages, their managers began to seek new ways of growth and to devise new ways of management. Because the events of the late 1960s and the 1970s appear to have marked the end of one era in the history of managerial capitalism and the start of another, a summary of postwar developments in the 1950s and 1960s provides a fitting afterword to this history of the modern industrial enterprise from its beginnings in the 1880s until the 1940s.

This afterword, which relates postwar developments to those described in the previous chapters, is not based on detailed data, as those chapters were. Instead, it is an impressionistic analysis designed to show the kinship between postwar developments and the earlier history. For example, after World War II the environment was just as turbulent, though in new ways; the basic institutional arrangements to carry out production and distribution remained much the same, at least until the late 1960s; and the growth of the modern industrial enterprise continued, but because of intensified competition it began to move into new paths.

American industrial enterprises came out of the war with enhanced competitive positions, but nevertheless, the devastated European and Japanese economies and the major enterprises in their core industries recovered with impressive speed. The same large multinational enterprises continued to dominate the same industries as they had before the war and for much the same reasons. Even the German chemical and machinery firms, whose facilities had been destroyed, whose personnel had been scattered, and whose homeland was divided, returned to positions in national and global markets as strong as those that they had held before the advent of the Hitler regime.

THE TRANSFORMATION OF THE GLOBAL ECONOMY

Politically the world changed fast in the postwar years. Although during this period of American hegemony the United States and the countries of Western Europe long continued to dominate world trade (with Japan as the one new challenger before the 1970s), a host of new nations appeared, many of them former colonies or dependencies of the dismembered empires. Nearly all hoped to industrialize and to achieve economic growth by adopting the existing technologies of production and methods of distribution. Moreover, the world was quickly divided between the East and the West—the Communist and noncommunist—with very little trade between the two. As significant as political change, however, was the transformation of technologies and markets.

The pace of technological innovation, stimulated by the demands of war, gathered speed. The impact of the new technologies was almost as profound as the impact of those which had led to the creation of modern industrial enterprise in the last decades of the nineteenth century. Of particular importance were the innovations in compiling, collating, and communicating information, which required the application of the science of electronics.

Indeed, the electronic revolution not only brought into existence a number of new industries but also transformed the processes of production and distribution, as the coming of electricity had before the turn of the century. In the 1960s and 1970s a wide variety of industries shifted from electromechanical to electronically controlled processes of production that began to transform the work place and alter the materials used in production. They realigned the economies of scale and scope, often reducing minimum efficient scale and at the same time expanding the opportunities for exploiting the economies of scope.

In transportation and communications new technologies had a more immediate impact. In transportation the substitution of oil for coal as an energy source did not significantly change the speed or regularity of the movement of goods across land and sea, even though techniques of containerization did increase the volume carried by individual ships. But the jet plane, the new telecommunication technology, and the computer achieved, in Raymond Vernon's words, "the spectacular shrinkage of space."[3] In the 1950s the introduction of the jet plane for civilian travel greatly expanded the possibility of face-to-face communication. Between 1960 and 1974 passenger volume on international commercial flights rose from 26 billion passenger-miles to 152 billion. The coming of the teleprinter made cable communication more effective. In 1956 the first transatlantic telephone cable went into operation, greatly improving the speed and reliability of overseas telephone communication, which since 1927 had depended on radio transmission. In 1965 global communication was further improved when the first commercial communications satellite went into operation.

Even more significant has been the integration of the electronic computer into the new international communications networks. In the late 1950s the computer was being rapidly adapted for a multitude of business purposes. Then in 1963 Honeywell demonstrated the computer's potential for international coordination by placing a terminal in Britain to control a computer at a plant in

Massachusetts, with control signals being sent by the standard Telex line.[4] At first the new trans-border computer networks were used largely by service companies for hotel and airline reservations, stock-market quotations, and banking and insurance transactions. By the early 1970s, multinational industrial enterprises, according to one authority, were increasingly relying on such computer data, usually through leased lines, "to coordinate production and marketing; to coordinate financial management; to share data-processing resources; to reduce costs of telephone circuits; to share scientific and technical research; to improve accuracy and security of information transfer (e.g., by using standard message formats and data encryption techniques)."[5] By the mid-1970s such international computer communication was becoming an integral part of the control and information systems of American, European, and Japanese multinational enterprises.

The globalization of communication encouraged the internationalization of markets, while individual domestic markets boomed. Indeed, the two decades after the close of World War II probably witnessed the greatest growth of demand in history. Not only did population increase, but, more important, so did per capita output and income.[6] At the same time the continuing migration from country to city rapidly enlarged the numbers of customers for processed and manufactured products.

During these same two decades of United States hegemony, tariffs and other barriers that divided markets melted away. Where trade restrictions lingered, they were often the result of legislation to encourage the growth and health of the economies of newer nations. In the 1950s and 1960s the national policies of economic self-sufficiency of the interwar years all but disappeared. The formation of the European Community by the Treaty of Rome in 1957 began to create a domestic market for European manufacturers large enough and fast-growing enough to permit scale economies in production comparable to those that had long existed in the United States.

The decline of trade barriers was accompanied by the breakdown of prewar cartels and other interfirm contractual agreements. Free trade and competition, basic tenets of the United States economic creed, were exported abroad. The victorious American authorities dismantled the cartels in Germany and dissolved I.G. Farben and VSt into their major constituent parts. Then in 1956 the British Parliament passed the Restrictive Practices Act, the first British legislation to challenge the legal and economic validity of maintaining market power through contractual cooperation. Soon the European Community began to develop a body of legislation that did much the same for the broad new Continental market.

CONTINUING ROLE OF THE MODERN INDUSTRIAL ENTERPRISE

Despite these profound changes in the environment, the modern industrial enterprise continued to dominate capital-intensive industries, whether established or new. In the United States and Germany most of the same individual enterprises—those that had acquired organizational capabilities before the war—continued to be the industrial leaders. There was little turnover among the top two hundred. In Britain, where a smaller number had developed such capabilities before the war, the turnover was greater. British firms began to make investments in new and improved facilities and to recruit and expand their managerial hierarchies, pushing aside other firms that failed to do so. As before, turnover at the top in all three countries resulted either from major technological innovations—innovations that created new industries and transformed old ones—or from mergers and acquisitions which caused some firms to disappear and others to grow in size.

In the United States the firms that moved onto the list of the top two hundred between 1948 and 1973 for reasons other than mergers and acquisitions were those in the information-related industries and other technologically new industries, particularly those based on innovations in electronics.[7] These firms included new entrepreneurial enterprises—Xerox, Control Data, Texas Instruments, Raytheon, Emerson Electric, and Dana. They also included established firms—General Telephone & Electric (GTE), Motorola, Carrier (a first mover in air-conditioning equipment during the 1930s), Clark Equipment, and Honeywell. The newly created enterprises became first movers by making the three-pronged investment in manufacturing, marketing, and management. The established firms increased their assets by making the similarly large investments that were necessary to volume-produce new products, much as the established drug firms had done in exploiting the pharmaceutical revolution.

In Germany, on the contrary, the majority of the relatively small number of firms, established or new, to move into the top rank were in consumer goods—in branded, packaged products, including consumer chemicals, consumer electronics and appliances, and publishing and printing.[8] The rapid growth of these consumer-goods producers reflected a higher per-capita income and a larger aggregate consumer demand in Germany, and in Europe as a whole, than before World War II.

In Britain the firms that had made the three-pronged investment before the Second World War continued to dominate their industries. In the early 1970s these included established chemical and pharmaceutical firms that had begun after the war to make the necessary investment in production, distribution, and management. They benefited from developing the technologies of antibiotics, polymer chemicals, and other new products. Still other firms that joined the top group were older federations that had begun, though not until the 1960s, to create central offices and rationalize their facilities. Those established between 1948 and 1973—and there were many more in Britain than in the United States and Germany—came primarily in chemicals; in stone, clay, and glass; and in electrical and nonelectrical (though not transportation) machinery. In addition to those absorbed by merger, the firms that were no longer among the top two hundred in 1973 were those that had failed to make the necessary investments. In Britain, with some notable exceptions, the managerial hierarchies within firms remained smaller than those in the United States and Germany.[9]

In all three countries the successful exploiters of the new technologies, whether they were long-established firms or new entrepreneurial enterprises, made investments in physical facilities and managerial personnel on a scale similar to those made by first movers in the new industries of the 1880s and 1890s (if differences in relative size of industries and national economies are taken into account). Indeed, what is striking is how similar the evolution of the new industries in the 1950s and 1960s was to the evolution of those of the 1880s and 1890s, even though the rapidity of technological change in the later period was much greater than it had been before World War II, so that one set of new products was often quickly replaced by an improved "second generation," and then by a third. But what really differentiated the first movers in the new industries of the post–World War II era from those of earlier times was that in the later years the first movers in new industries included long-established firms.

Among the best-known American postwar companies, Xerox, in the copier industry, provides an example of an entrepreneurial firm which became dominant through its impressive investment in production, distribution, and management. And International Business Machines (IBM) is an example of a long-established firm, for decades a member of the top two hundred, that was not a pioneer in mainframe computers but became a first mover in that industry by making a massive investment in new, product-specific production facilities to exploit fully the economies of scale, and also by expanding its experienced marketing network and recruiting a multitude of new executives.

The history of the computer industry—one central to the postwar information revolution—parallels that of the American machinery industries a half-century earlier. This is true even though the technologies of production were far more complex than those of the earlier electrical industry, and the markets served were more numerous and more varied than those of the earlier industries. Here the one fundamental difference—the role of the established firm—is particularly striking. In 1965, a little more than a decade after the mainframe computer had first been commercialized, IBM had completed its System 360, which made it the first mover in the production and distribution of general-purpose mainframes for a wide variety of users. At almost precisely the same time Digital Equipment Corporation (DEC) completed comparable though smaller investments in its PDP-8, which made it the first mover in low-price minicomputers—machines that employed a different technology for more specialized users.

IBM's resulting competitive advantage was as powerful as that of any first mover described in this history. Except for Control Data, IBM's mainframe rivals were all, like IBM itself, established enterprises. (Except for Honeywell Heat Regulator, their earlier histories are all reviewed in Chapter 6.) Of these, GE, RCA, and Philco, finding IBM's advantages too powerful, dropped out. Sperry Rand—the industry's most successful pioneer—was able to maintain a stable position well behind IBM, and eventually (in 1986) it merged with Burroughs to form UNISYS. In that same year Honeywell, which had purchased the computer operations of another pioneer, Raytheon, and then those of GE, abandoned the manufacturing of computers. Meanwhile National Cash Register integrated its computers into its existing end products and concentrated on two specialized markets—banking and retailing. Control Data (a merger of many small firms), once it had rationalized its product lines and facilities, was the only company formed after 1950 to become a major competitor in the mainframe industry.

In minicomputers DEC maintained its strength. Its first strong competitor was Data General, established in 1968 by a former DEC executive who had played a critical part in the development of the PDP-8. Nevertheless, by 1980 DEC and Data General were ranked second and fourth in revenues generated in minicomputers. IBM was first, Burroughs third, and Hewlett-Packard, a producer for thirty years of measuring and testing instruments, was fifth. The sixth was Wang Laboratories, a first mover in word processing and office systems. And these six accounted for 75% of the revenues generated in that branch of the industry.[10]

The pattern was much the same in personal (micro-) computers—machines that employed a still different architecture for a still different market, the individual user. The first entrepreneurial firms to make extensive interrelated investments—Apple Computer, Tandy (Radio Shack), and Commodore—accounted in 1980 for 68% of dollar sales in the United States (Table 24). By then the three pioneers who together had accounted for 50% of sales in 1976, but who had failed to make such an investment, had already dropped by the wayside. Two years later (1982), however, three established firms—IBM, the Nippon Electric Company (NEC) of Tokyo, and Hewlett-Packard—accounted for 35%, driving the market share of the three first movers down to 48%.[11]

Like American machinery firms of earlier years these computer companies quickly moved abroad. IBM almost immediately became the leading producer of mainframe computers in Europe. DEC also led in minicomputers but was seriously challenged by Nixdorf, a German company. By the mid-1980s Apple and IBM, along with NEC, accounted for half of the world's production of personal computers.

Abroad, established firms developed and continued to dominate all lines. Nixdorf, the minicomputer producer, was the only new entrepreneurial firm in Europe to become a major player. In Germany the other leaders included Siemens, Mannesmann, and BASF (Siemens in mainframes and the other two

Table 24. Share of the U.S. market in the personal computer industry, 1976–1982.

Company	1976	1978	1980	1982
MITS	25%	—	—	—
IMSAI	17	—	—	—
Processor Technology	8	—	—	—
Radio Shack	—	50%	21%	10%
Commodore International	—	12	20	12
Apple	—	10	27	26
IBM	—	—	—	17
NEC	—	—	5	11
Hewlett-Packard	—	—	9	7
Others	50	28	18	17
Total	100%	100%	100%	100%
Total units	15,000	200,000	500,000	1,500,000

Sources: Gary N. Farner, "A Competitive Analysis of the Personal Computer Industry" (Master's thesis, Alfred P. Sloan School of Management, MIT, 1982), p. 18, and Deborah F. Schreiber, "The Strategic Evolution of the Personal Computer Industry" (Master's thesis, Alfred P. Sloan School of Management, MIT, 1983), p. 7, cited in John Friar and Mel Horwitch, "The Emergence of Technology Strategy: A New Dimension of Strategic Management," *Technology in Society* 7:152 (1985).

in specialized market niches). In Japan all the major computer makers were enterprises that had originally been established by the 1920s. As in technologically advanced industries of earlier years, the British lagged behind. By 1974 only 25% to 30% of all installations in Britain came from British producers.[12]

Thus in the 1960s and 1970s, as in the 1880s and 1890s, new capital-intensive industries quickly came to be dominated by the few firms which made large enough investments in manufacturing, marketing, and management to develop the capabilities to exploit fully the economies of scale and scope. In computers, the most dynamic of the postwar industries, established companies accounted for a much greater proportion of the revenues produced than did the new entrepreneurial firms.

CONTINUING GROWTH

After World War II growth based on the defensive strategies of horizontal combination and vertical integration became even less common. At the same time, as the experience of the computer industry indicates, growth based on the underlying dynamic of managerial enterprise—the exploitation of organizational capabilities by expansion abroad and into related product lines—became even more usual. Legal barriers to horizontal combinations of industrial giants became almost as formidable in Europe as they had been for decades in the

United States. In established industries the need for assured supplies and outlets through vertical integration lessened. As economies expanded and as markets were internationalized, alternative stable sources of supply and greater
numbers of outlets became available. Therefore companies had less need to
reduce transaction costs by owning their suppliers and outlets. Indeed, many
companies performed vertical *dis*integration by spinning off earlier investments
made in suppliers and, to a lesser extent, in outlets. In fact, such vertical
disintegration had already begun during the interwar years. On the other hand,
expansion abroad and into related product lines—often both at the same time—
became the strategy of growth for an increasing number of leading industrial
enterprises, both European and American; and in general that strategy was
carried out more aggressively than before the war.

Growth by expansion abroad. In the early postwar years American firms
continued to lead the way in overseas expansion. The number of subsidiaries
established abroad by American companies after 1948 increased substantially.
Whereas the number of new manufacturing subsidiaries of American industrial
firms in Britain rose from 22 to 93 between 1917 and 1948 for an increase of 71,
the number had grown to 544 by 1971 for a further increase of 451; whereas
in Germany the number of such subsidiaries moved from 14 in 1913 to 33 in
1953 for an increase of 19, the number reached 330 by 1971 for a further
increase of 297 (see Tables 14 and 15). The firms setting up these subsidiaries
continued to be concentrated in the same industries as before the war, that is,
in food, chemicals, and machinery, where both markets and the technologies of
production offered the greatest potential for exploiting the economies of scale
and scope. (In the years between 1948 and 1971 the U.S. subsidiaries in these
three sets of industries accounted for 66.2% of all U.S. subsidiaries established
in Britain, and in the period 1954–1971 for 65.1% of those in Germany. The
figure for France was 71.7%.) The major changes between the two periods
were a decrease in the percentage of U.S. food subsidiaries in Britain and an
increase in the percentage of U.S. chemical subsidiaries in Germany. One other
difference was that before the Second World War, American firms had entered
through building new facilities. After 1945 they did so through acquisition,
followed by increased direct investment in the acquired subsidiary in order to
benefit more fully from the economies of scale and scope.

By the 1960s most of the major American corporations with sizable investments abroad had adopted the multidivisional structure to administer their foreign holdings (Table 25). As they expanded their foreign direct investment,
they put aside their international departments, which had long coordinated and
monitored foreign activities, replacing them either by area divisions or by worldwide product divisions. Where the enterprise continued to concentrate on a
small number of products, its managers usually divided foreign operations into
geographical (area) divisions. The more the enterprises diversified, the more

Table 25. Multinational enterprises, classified by structure and by diversity of products made abroad for 162 American industrial enterprises, 1966.

Structure	Total number of firms	Number of firms classified by foreign product diversity[a]		
		None	Low	High
International departments				
Centralized, functional structure	8	7	1	0
Multidivisional structure	82	39	39	4
Area divisions	17	11	4	2
Worldwide product divisions	30	0	11	19
Mixed	22	0	13	9
Grid	3	0	0	3
Total	162	57	68	37

Sources: John M. Stopford and Louis T. Wells, Jr., *Managing the Multinational Enterprise: Organization of the Firm and Ownership of the Subsidiaries* (New York, 1972), p. 41. Table based on *News Front,* November 1965, January 1966, and February 1966, and annual reports of the firms.

a. "None" indicates that all the products made by a firm were in a single two-digit SIC industry. "Low" indicates that a firm has products in more than one industry but that one product line is of dominating importance. "High" indicates that a firm has products in many industries and no dominant product line.

their managers turned to using worldwide product divisions.[13] By the late 1960s a substantial number used mixed area and product structures—usually area divisions for regions with smaller markets, and product divisions where the demand was more concentrated.[14]

As European industries recovered from the war of the 1940s and as their domestic markets again became large enough to take the output of plants built at optimal size, their leaders once again looked to foreign markets. Not surprisingly, those enterprises which had had strong organizational capabilities before the war, primarily German firms, soon regained their prewar position at home and then abroad, just as they had done in the 1920s. Others, particularly those in Britain, began to develop such capabilities as they transformed themselves from federations or alliances into legally and administratively consolidated enterprises, and as family firms began to make more extensive investments in production and distribution and to recruit larger managerial staffs. In this transformation many firms acquired organizational structures and control-and-accounting systems of the sort developed earlier in the United States.

Because during the interwar years American managers had competed more aggressively (both functionally and strategically) than the Europeans, they had paid close attention to such essential management techniques. It was these American-perfected administrative procedures, and the skills that came from using them, that J. J. Servan-Schreiber had had in mind when he wrote *The American Challenge*. The opening passage of that book, published in 1968, reads: "Fifteen years from now it is quite possible that the world's third greatest industrial power, just after the United States and Russia, will not be Europe, but American industry in Europe. Already, in the ninth year of the Common Market, this European market is basically American in organization."[15] For Servan-Schreiber, the United States challenge was not one of financial power, nor was the problem the European "technological gap." "On the contrary, it is something quite new and considerably more serious—the extension to Europe of an *organization* that is still a mystery to us."[16]

It did not remain a mystery for long. When Servan-Schreiber wrote, the transfer of techniques was already well under way. By 1970, for example, more than half of the largest one hundred industrials in Britain had used the services of a single United States consultant, McKinsey & Company, to reorganize their management structures. Even in Germany, where more attention had been paid to internal administration, American consultants, including McKinsey, played an important role.[17] Nevertheless, these techniques were only aids in enhancing organizational capabilities.

Far more important in the development of competitive strength were the extensive recruitment of managers (particularly by British but also by French and Italian enterprises), the increasing knowledge of production processes and markets, and the molding of the management teams and the units they administered into integrated, coordinated organizations. These capabilities, sharpened by increasing functional and strategic competition at home and then in the European Common Market, provided the competitive edge needed to move into the United States, the world's largest market for both industrial and consumer products.

Among the Europeans the British moved first to expand abroad in the immediate postwar years. They were most successful in food, chemicals, glass, and other materials—lines in which they had developed organizational capabilities before the war. They were less successful in automobiles, electrical equipment, and light, volume-produced machinery, where they had been slower in developing such capabilities.

In automobiles, for example, Britain remained Europe's largest producer only until 1956; and within Britain the strong American presence continued. In 1960, 96% of the passenger cars produced in Great Britain came from the "Big Five": the British Motor Corporation, the subsidiaries of Ford and General Motors, Standard Motor Company, and Rootes Motors. After Chrysler purchased Rootes in 1966, just over half the production of passenger cars in Britain came from subsidiaries of the American "Big Three." (The British Motor Corporation, formed in 1952, long remained a typical British alliance between Austin and Morris, in which each firm continued to operate almost independently.) By 1956 Germany's "Big Four" consisted of Volkswagen, Daimler-Benz, and two American companies, Ford and GM's Opel. These four, which accounted for 87% of the passenger cars sold in Germany, outproduced and outexported the British. France's four leading firms, with 98% of the output in the domestic market, were less aggressive abroad. Fiat in Italy and a little later Volvo and Saab in Sweden became respected members of the global oligopoly.[18]

By the 1960s industrialists on the Continent, particularly Germans, were rapidly taking market share from the British in international trade, not only in automobiles but in appliances, electrical equipment, and heavy machinery. German enterprises also quickly regained their prewar chemical and pharmaceutical markets. German and Italian firms, including the Italian typewriter company Olivetti, were effectively challenging American producers of light machinery in Continental markets.

In many industries these were the first successful challengers to the American first movers that had established themselves in Europe early in the century. By the mid-1960s these European makers of mass-produced automobiles and light machinery had developed the organizational capabilities—the facilities and skills in production, marketing, and management—that made them effective challengers to the long-established American first movers not only outside the United States but even in the American market. They were able to compete successfully with American first movers in the American market because they had a strong base in their own domestic markets. As those domestic markets expanded, the firms were able to build plants of optimal size, using improved, best-practice facilities. Such domestic markets gave the European challengers a base that was not available to potential domestic challengers within the United States. This is why in automobiles, light machinery, and many other industries, challengers to first movers in industrial nations have come from abroad and not from the homeland.

In these same years a new industrial power was rising in the Far East. For the Japanese the creation of organizational capabilities required much more than just recovery from wartime devastation. Before the war Japan had relied on the Western companies for its mass-produced light machinery, automobiles, much of its basic industrial machinery, its chemicals (except fertilizer and other agricultural chemicals), and its oil. In its prewar capital-intensive industries Japan's organizational capabilities had been strongest in electrical equipment, where the leading firms had long had close ties with the four Western first movers—General Electric, Westinghouse, Siemens, and AEG. As a result, postwar recovery and continued industrial and economic growth called for a massive transfer of technology from the West to Japan comparable to that which had been required for the transformation of their premodern economy into an industrial economy in the 1880s and 1890s. As Hirschmeier and Yui noted in their *Development of Japanese Business, 1600–1973:*

> Between 1950 and 1967 Japanese industry set records of technological transfers. A total of 4,135 licenses were purchased by Japanese industry, mainly from the USA, over half in the field of machinery construction and about 20 per cent in the field of chemical industries. During the same time exports of licenses amounted to only about 1 per cent of the money spent on imports of patents and licenses.[19]

In addition, American engineers and consultants went to Japan to impart the know-how that was essential for the successful transfer of production processes.

This unprecedented transfer of technology, along with the rapid growth of the Japanese domestic market, permitted that nation to adopt new, capital-intensive processes of production on a scale reminiscent of that which had occurred in the United States and Europe at the end of the nineteenth century. The Japanese firms, particularly those in mass-produced automobiles and appliances and later those that had moved into computers, made large-scale investments in production and distribution. Their enterprises became even more management-intensive than those of the West. As an example of growth, the Japanese market, which had absorbed fewer than 500,000 new cars in 1964, took 1.13 million in 1967, 2.38 million in 1970, 2.93 million in 1973, and 3.10 million in 1979.[20] Once the home market provided a large enough base to exploit the economies of scale, the automobile makers and also the appliance producers moved abroad. The growth of these metal-using consumer-goods industries and the increasing urbanization of Japan permitted steel and other metal-making firms to employ new technologies in giant works that produced far greater throughput and enjoyed much lower unit costs than the largest American and European works.[21] By the 1970s the Japanese in these established industries and also those in the new electronically based telecommunication industries were becoming powerful challengers in both American and European markets.

Growth by diversification into related industries. At the same time the growth of European and Japanese industrial enterprises were enlarging the number of firms in many global oligopolies, the number of competitors within countries was being further increased as established domestic firms moved into related industries. Studies by Richard Rumelt for the United States, Derek Channon for Britain, and Heinz Thanheiser for Germany document the rapid adoption of diversification as a strategy for growth in all three countries.[22] In the United States the number of "single business" firms among the Fortune 500 (that is, firms that derived 95% or more of their sales from a single, main product line) dropped from 28% of the total in 1949 to only 7% in 1969. The number of "dominant-product" firms (firms that derived from 70% to 95% of their sales from a single business or a vertically integrated chain of businesses) dropped slightly from 38.7% to 35.8% during the same twenty years. By contrast, those which had diversified into related business, and in which no single, main product line accounted for more than 70% of sales, rose from 29.2% to 44.5% of the total. Firms operating in businesses unrelated through technology or markets grew from 2.9% to 12.4%. (These were the conglomerates—firms that grew by acquisition in unrelated industries.) By 1969, then, diversification into new product lines had become an accepted, indeed a preferred, route to growth for the large American industrial enterprise.

In Britain and Germany the broad pattern of diversification was much the same, although its extent quite naturally varied. Of the one hundred largest manufacturers in Britain, fourteen of which were foreign subsidiaries, an even greater proportion moved into related industries between 1950 and 1970, the percentage going from 23% to 54%. Before the mid-1970s, American-style conglomerates remained rare. As Derek Channon noted in his *Strategy and Structure of British Enterprise,* by 1969 "there was no real emergence of the acquisitive conglomerate in Britain." Of the six companies in unrelated businesses in the top one hundred, "only two bore a real resemblance to the American conglomerates."[23]

Of the one hundred largest German manufacturing companies in 1970, twenty-two were still single-line producers, twenty-two were dominant-product firms, forty-six were in related products, and ten operated in unrelated industries.[24] Prewar firms such as Bosch, Krupp, Enka-Glanzstoff (VGF), Henkel, Linde, and Felten-Guilleaume, and two new entrants to the top one hundred, Melitta and Bertelsmann (both producers of consumer products), diversified by exploiting the economies of scope and did so more extensively than did the leading prewar German diversifiers in chemicals and machinery.[25]

Also in Germany, firms operating in unrelated industries differed from the American conglomerates. Such firms were either family holding companies (Konzerne) or government holding companies. The three government-sponsored enterprises—VEBA, Preussag, and Saarberg—were primarily used to take over weak firms in a variety of industries. The four private, family Konzerne were those of Flick, Quandt, Werhahn Bereich, and Roechling. They were less diversified than the American conglomerates in terms of the industries in which they operated and in the numbers of divisions administered. Moreover, the family holding companies appear to have carried on the tradition of the earlier family Konzerne. The central office remained small, and it concentrated on managing and maintaining the long-term health and growth of subsidiaries or divisions.

The studies by Rumelt, Channon, and Thanheiser also emphasize that structure followed strategy. The multidivisional structure was normally adopted to assist in administering the increasingly diversified firms and to facilitate their expansion. It was this type of organization that McKinsey & Company advised the British companies, particularly the existing federations, to adopt. In Germany such structures also replaced the looser Konzerne that used the holding-company form of control. German firms that were employing centralized, functionally departmentalized structures made the change as they moved into new product lines, much as Schering and Rütgerswerke had begun to do before World War II.[26]

In the postwar years the leading industrial enterprises in all three countries diversified by using capabilities based on the economies of scope. But these were economies of scope in *production* and *R&D* more than in distribution. These firms commercialized products whose innovation had come from their own research laboratories. After World War II American industrial enterprises invested much more extensively in fundamental research than they had before 1941 (see Chapter 6). But they also continued to rely on research carried out in universities and institutes, or by small, usually entrepreneurial, firms. The large, established enterprises then made the heavy investment in time and money essential to transform the innovation into an internationally marketable and profitable product or process.

As a result, overall R&D investment in technologically advanced industries was much greater than it had been before World War II. In the United States, funding for R&D rose from $6,605 million in 1956 to $17,858 million in 1970. Research continued to be concentrated, as it had been before the war, in chemicals and the three machinery groups. Expenditures by firms in these groups accounted for roughly 70% of the total. Of the total funding, 50% came from federal sources in 1956 and 44% in 1970. The great part of such federal funding went to electrical and electronic equipment, instruments, and aircraft and missiles. As had been true before the war, research personnel continued to be concentrated in companies with ten thousand or more employees.[27]

Intensified R&D investment and the organizational capabilities based on economies of scope led many more companies into making many more products than had been the case before the war. The extent of such diversification in the United States is suggested by the increase, between 1948 and 1973, in the number of different SIC categories in which the largest firms operated. Whereas in 1948 relatively few of those firms operated in as many as five three-digit industries, by 1973 a sizable number were operating in ten such industries, and many in even more.[28] These moves into new product lines intensified competition in these and other American industries. At the same time, the greatly increased investment in R&D made the development of new or improved products more costly and also more risky. By the 1960s there was a much greater chance than in prewar years that a firm would spend five to eight years developing a product, only to have a competitor reach much the same market with much the same product a few months earlier.

In these ways, by the mid-1960s challengers from across national boundaries and from related industries intensified the competition in capital-intensive industries. This was particularly true in the United States, but it was also true in Europe. In those American industries where competitive advantages had rested on the economies of scale—such as automobiles and farm, office, and sewing machinery—the major new competitors came from other countries. In those where the competitive advantages lay in exploiting the economies of scope—such as food, chemicals, and electrical equipment—they tended to come from related industries. In both cases these competitors were established firms with well-developed organizational capabilities.

Challengers in established industries were hardly ever new entrepreneurial firms. This continued to be as true after World War II as it had been before the war, even though the institutionalization of research in universities, institutes, and consulting firms had greatly increased the opportunities for innovation, and even though the institutionalization of the supply of venture capital made funding for such innovations more available. Such institutionalization, however, did assist the new entrepreneurial firms to move into specialized market niches or occasionally to become first movers in industries based on new technologies.

During the 1960s the modern industrial enterprise and the system of industrial capitalism that it engendered were in full flower. By then the managerial enterprise dominated the capital-intensive industries—old and new—even more completely than it had before World War II. In Great Britain these enterprises were replacing prewar, personally managed companies. In Japan, rapidly growing industrial firms were becoming even more management-intensive than those in the West. Moreover, managerial enterprises were becoming more numerous in the more fragmented, labor-intensive industries as new technologies of production altered capital-labor ratios and as managerial enterprises diversified into these industries. And in those dynamic, global industries whose technologies of production and distribution permitted the exploitation of the cost advantages of scale and scope, decisions as to current operations and allocation of resources for future production and distribution were made by salaried managers.

Yet the very success of the modern, managerial industrial enterprise created unprecedented challenges for its managers. The continuous growth of the enterprise through expansion abroad and into related industries led to competition as intense as those managers had ever known. In the established industries, intensified competition and reduced market share increased excess capacity and so raised unit costs. Moreover, the sharpened competition came just at the moment when those managers were facing the full impact of the new technologies, particularly those affected by the electronics revolution. The need to shift from electromechanical to electronic processes of production required heavy investment in new facilities and the development of new skills by both working and managerial personnel. The accelerated rate of technological change thus increased the costs and risks of reinvesting earnings within the enterprise's existing industries.

A New Era of Managerial Capitalism?

It was in these ways, then, that the powerful dynamic of industrial capitalism—the drive for new geographical and product markets based on the organizational capabilities of the modern industrial enterprise—led to what may prove to be the important turning point in the evolution of that institution. During the 1960s, intensified inter-nation and inter-industry competition began to reshape the strategies of growth, the internal organization of managerial enterprises, and the relationships between individual firms and between owners and managers. The causes for these changes and the ways in which they have begun to trans-form the modern industrial enterprise must be the subject of another study. Because these transformations are still under way and because they reflect rapidly changing markets, technologies, and public policies, the historian is not yet in a position to analyze or evaluate them.

Nevertheless, the historian who has studied the past experience of the institution is in a better position than most analysts to identify which developments are truly new. And such identifications can provide a point of departure for any careful investigation of the history of the managerial industrial enterprise in what may prove to be a new era of industrial capitalism. They also provide a fitting conclusion to this history of the modern industrial enterprise during the period of growth from its beginning in the Second Industrial Revolution through World War II.

Of the many recent changes in the growth, management, and financing of the modern industrial enterprise, six have no historical precedents. These include: the adaptation of a new strategy of growth—that of moving into new markets where the organizational capabilities of the enterprise do not provide competitive advantages; the separation of top management in the corporate office from middle management in the operating divisions; the extensive and continuing divestiture of operating units; the buying and selling of corporations as a distinct business in its own right; the role played by portfolio managers in the capital markets; and the evolution of those capital markets to facilitate the coming of what has been termed "a market for corporate control." All of these changes are interrelated.

Because large, managerial industrial enterprises were more numerous in the United States than in the rest of the world and because in the early 1960s they dominated the international economy, these six new phenomena have become most obvious in the United States. More than half of the four hundred largest industrial firms in the noncommunist world in 1973 were still American-owned and -operated (Table 5). It was these American firms that first felt the brunt of the new competition as European enterprises revived and Japanese firms began to create their own organizational capabilities.

An initial response to intensified competition—a response that came first in the United States, then in Britain, and still later in continental Europe—was the decision of top managers to have their industrial enterprises grow by acquiring companies in markets that were only distantly related or even unrelated to the core facilities and skills of their enterprise, that is, to move into markets where they had little or no competitive advantage. Not all managers responded in this way. Those in many of the large American industrial enterprises reacted to the new competition, as they had done earlier to less intensive competition, by making state-of-the-art investments in production, distribution, and R&D, and by adjusting the roles and responsibilities of their management teams in order to maintain their competitive strength by developing strategies that continued to exploit fully their organizational capabilities. But in many other cases, managers failed to respond in this way. Many senior executives believed that the opportunities for profit from investment in their own or closely related industries had become limited. Instead, they searched for industries with greater growth potentials. For the first time in history, American managers began to invest extensively and systematically in facilities and enterprises in businesses in which they had had little or no experience. The only appropriate historical analogy is the Konzern building in Germany following World War I. But there such diversification occurred only during a totally unprecedented period of superinflation and military occupation. Once the Dawes Plan had restored relatively stable economic and business conditions by the end of 1924, such Konzern building all but stopped.

Precisely because the American firms had little or no competitive advantage in the markets which they entered, they could not carry out such expansion, as they had in closely related industries, through direct investment in new facilities and skills; instead, they had to expand through merger and more often acquisition. Tax, accounting, and other financial considerations entered into the decisions to move into new, distantly related, or unrelated markets in which the initiating company had little distinct competitive advantage. Nevertheless, the primary motive for such acquisitions—both at home and abroad—appears to have been the desire of managers to assure the continuing expansion of their enterprises by entering industries that promised more growth and less competition than those on which their organizational capabilities rested.

By the late 1960s the drive for growth through acquisition and merger had almost become a mania. The number of mergers and acquisitions rose from just over 2,000 in 1965 to more than 6,000 in 1969, dropping back to 2,861 in 1974. The purpose of the largest number of these acquisitions was not to combine horizontally or vertically but to diversify. During the period 1963–1972, close to three-fourths of the assets acquired were for product diversification. One-half of these were in unrelated products. And after the merger wave receded, the trend still continued. In the following period, 1973–1977, one-half of all assets acquired through merger and acquisition came from acquisitions of enterprises in unrelated industries.[29]

Such unprecedented diversification created another new phenomenon in the evolution of the managerial industrial enterprise: it often led to a separation, that is, a breakdown of communications, between top management at the corporate office—the executives responsible for coordinating, managing, and planning and allocating resources for the enterprise as a whole—and the middle managers who were responsible for maintaining the competitive capabilities of the operating divisions in the battle for market share and profits (Figure 2). Massive diversification led to such a separation for two reasons. First, the top managers often had little specific knowledge of and experience with the technological processes and markets of many of the divisions or subsidiaries they had acquired. Second, the large number of different businesses that were being acquired created a decision-making overload in the corporate office. Whereas before World War II the corporate office of large, diversified international enterprises had rarely managed more than ten divisions and only the largest as many as twenty-five, by 1969 companies were operating from forty to seventy divisions, and a few even more. Moreover, because these divisions were responsible for production, marketing, purchasing, and research facilities on a worldwide basis, they were often larger in terms of assets and employees than many of the enterprises that have been described in this study.

The increase in the number of divisions administered and the wide variety of businesses in which they operated combined to create an overload for the decision-makers in top management that was even more daunting than that at Du Pont and other enterprises which had pioneered in developing the strategy of diversification after World War I. While the earlier overload had resulted in the innovation of the multidivisional structure, that of the 1960s led only to an increase in the number of executives in the corporate office. Divisions were grouped together, administered by group vice-presidents who often had their own subordinate line and staff executives. These top managers in the corporate office no longer had, unlike their predecessors, the time to make and maintain personal contacts with the heads of the operating divisions. Nor did the senior executives have the product-specific experience needed to evaluate the proposals and to monitor the performance of their operating managers. Instead, in carrying out those critical tasks they had to rely on impersonal statistical data that had become far less relevant than the information systems devised and used in the 1920s and 1930s by corporate officers of diversified firms to carry out comparable functions.[30] The overload resulted, not from any lack of information, but from its lack of quality and from the senior decision-makers' lack of ability to evaluate it. Top managers were beginning to lose the capabilities needed to maintain a unified enterprise whose whole was more than the sum of its parts.

The managerial weaknesses resulting from the separation of top from operating executives quickly led to still another new phenomenon—the selling off of divisions and other operating units in unprecedented numbers. The costs of unbridled diversification were soon learned. Before the mid-1960s such divestitures had been rare. To be sure, facilities had been sold off and personnel let go in the post-merger rationalizations early in the century. Outdated facilities had also been spun off as firms in the 1920s and 1930s improved their product and processes or as they moved into dynamic related industries that more effectively used their organizational capabilities. So, too, integrated divisions and subsidiaries had been divested in the process of vertical disintegration that came when managers felt they no longer needed to have assured sources of supplies or outlets.

What was unprecedented in the early 1970s was the number and continuing flow of divestitures that followed the merger and acquisition wave of the late 1960s. What had been until then an occasional transaction became an accepted business activity. In 1965 the ratio of divestitures to acquisitions and mergers was less than 1 to 11 (195 divestitures to 2,125 acquisitions and mergers). By 1969, when the number of acquisitions and mergers had soared to 6,107, those of divestitures rose to 801, or a ratio of 1 divestiture to every 8 mergers and acquisitions. Then as mergers and acquisitions dropped, divestitures rose sharply. In 1971 the ratio was 1 to 2.3 (1,960 to 4,608). From 1974 to 1977 there was one divestiture to every two mergers and acquisitions. And, of course, many of the divestitures became the acquisitions or parts of mergers of other enterprises.[31]

This unprecedented number of mergers and acquisitions, followed so shortly by an unprecedented number of divestitures, helped to bring into being another new phenomenon—the buying and selling of corporations as an established business, and a most lucrative one at that. Although industrialists pioneered in this business, the financial community prospered most from it. Before the 1960s it was rare for financial institutions, including investment banks, to have specialized merger and acquisitions departments. The primary function of investment bankers in the United States and abroad was to provide their clients with long-established services. The most important of these was the underwriting of securities used to supplement retained earnings in funding long-term growth. The new and highly profitable business that began with the financing of acquisitions in the late 1960s and the continuing flow of divestitures in the 1970s warranted the creation of the specialized departments. Soon, too, specialists in "deconglomeration" appeared.

This brand-new business of buying and selling corporations was further stimulated by an unprecedented change in the nature of the "ownership" of American industrial companies, that is, of the holders, buyers, and sellers of their shares. Before World War II the majority of such securities were held by relatively wealthy individuals and families. The major institutional investors were insurance companies and the trust departments of banks. Such institutional investors, like wealthy individuals, normally invested for the long term—for growth in assets rather than for current dividends. The turnover of the shares of individual companies was small (that is, the number of shares sold was only a small percentage of the shares outstanding).

After World War II, increasingly large amounts of the voting shares of industrial enterprises were held in the portfolios of pension and mutual funds. These funds had their beginnings in the 1920s, but they achieved little growth in the depressed years of the 1930s. By the 1960s, however, they had come into their own. The managers of these funds properly considered their primary function to be that of increasing the short-term return (dividends plus appreciation) on their overall portfolio. They did so by constantly buying and selling securities. Their goal was to have the return on the securities they held be greater than the average return of stocks listed, as indicated by Standard and Poor's index of the five hundred leading corporations. Such portfolio managers had neither the time, the information, nor the need to be concerned about the long-term health and growth of the individual firms whose securities they daily bought and sold. Such shareholders had little incentive to become outside directors on boards of companies in which they were so temporarily involved. The criterion for the securities they constantly traded was short-term profit, rarely long-term gain. And as time passed, these portfolio managers—the new "owners" of American industry—increasingly traded securities in large blocks of stock of ten thousand shares or more.

As the number of such funds and the volume of the securities they individually traded increased, the turnover of the securities of industrial enterprises also rose. The ratio of the volume of shares traded annually on the New York Stock Exchange to its total shares listed grew from between 12% and 16% in the early 1960s to well over 20% during the acquisition wave. Then that percentage began to soar, reaching over 50% by the mid-1980s. The growth in block trading in the same period was just as striking. In 1965 block trading accounted for only 3.1% of total sales on the New York Stock Exchange. By 1978 it accounted for 22.9%, and by 1985 for 51%. Finally, in those same years the volume of total transactions rose dramatically. On the New York Stock Exchange the volume of shares went from close to half a billion shares annually in the early 1950s to 1.5 billion in 1965, to 3 billion in the late 1960s, to more than 5 billion in 1976, and to 27.5 billion in 1985.[32]

The great increase in the total volume of transactions, the rise in the rate of turnover, and the growth of block sales made possible the last new phenomenon—the coming of an institutionalized market for corporate control. For the first time, individuals, groups, or companies could obtain control of well-established companies in industries with which the buyers had no previous connection, simply by purchasing the companies' shares on the stock exchange. Large blocks of stock were being traded regularly; and such buyers had little difficulty in raising funds for these purchases from financial institutions.

Thus the diversifications of the 1960s, the divestitures of the 1970s, the business of buying and selling corporations (stimulated by the shift in ownership), and finally the coming of the market for corporate control greatly facilitated the ease with which the modern industrial enterprise could be restructured. Such firms could be bought, sold, split up, and recombined in ways that would have been impossible before the acquisition wave of the 1960s.

In Britain the response of large industrial enterprises to the intensifying competition was closest to that in the United States. There, where the London money market was second in size only to that of New York, the story appears to have been a rather pale reflection of the American experience. Mergers and acquisitions did increase in 1968 and 1969 and again in 1972, but on a much smaller scale than in the United States. A number of conglomerates were formed and unrelated acquisitions were made, but again on a smaller scale. In addition, there were more horizontal mergers than in the United States, often carried out at government instigation. Divestitures, as new a phenomenon in Britain as they were in the United States, followed in the 1970s. But the buying and selling of companies did not become as lucrative a business, and a market for corporate control was slower in coming.[33]

Developments in Germany and on the rest of the Continent have been different. Although mergers and acquisitions occurred in the late 1960s and the 1970s, there was no significant acquisition wave. In Europe, therefore, there were much less expansion through acquisition, less overloading of the corporate office, and fewer resulting divestitures; the buying and selling of companies did not become a profitable business, nor did an active market for corporate control appear. One reason for these differences may have been the smaller size of the European capital markets, in terms of volume and turnover of transactions, and the continuing strength of the banks (particularly in Germany) and of the financial holding companies. As competition increased, however, Europe's large industrial enterprises also began to move into distantly related and unrelated markets, and overdiversification into other industries and overexpansion into foreign markets certainly occurred. But because European firms continued to rely on long-established relationships with banks and other financial institutions, they were able to pull back when such expansion did not prove profitable, and they appear to have done so in a more orderly fashion than their American counterparts.[34]

Japan had little in the way of a merger movement. There were almost no expansions into unrelated areas, no large-scale divestitures, no business of buying and selling companies, and no market for corporate control. Once the first movers had firmly established themselves in the domestic market, they grew in the German manner, cooperating as well as competing at home and competing vigorously abroad on the basis of their organizational capabilities.

The unprecedented developments resulting from the intensified competition of the 1960s have brought a basic reshaping of the structure of the modern industrial enterprise, particularly of the relationships between the corporate office and the operating divisions. Many firms in the United States and Europe have reduced the overload at the top by spinning off divisions whose activities were not closely related to the core capabilities of the enterprise. Others have reduced the size and altered the planning, control, and resource-allocation functions of the corporate office, and at the same time have given the operating units still greater autonomy. Few, however, have followed the example of the Japanese kieretsu or "enterprise groupings" by letting the operating organizations have full financial autonomy—that is, control over the use of their profits, the raising of capital, and even the making of strategic plans. Still others rely, as they move into new geographical or product markets, on joint ventures and other interfirm cooperative arrangements.

The goal of this restructuring of enterprises in the capital-intensive industries must be to maintain, renew, or expand the organizational capabilities of the enterprise. The continuing productivity, competitiveness, and profitability of these enterprises and of the industries and nations in which they operate depend on constant reinvestment in order to maintain and improve product-specific facilities and to maintain and develop product-specific technical and managerial skills. A crucial theme of this history of the modern industrial enterprise is that creating and maintaining such capabilities is a continuing, long-term process— a process that requires sound, long-term perspectives from the decision-makers responsible for the health and growth of their enterprise.

In cases where the unprecedented developments of recent years have contributed to these long-term perspectives by motivating managers and financiers to define and implement long-term plans for restoring, maintaining, and improving organizational capabilities, they have helped to make enterprises, industries, and nations more competitive and profitable. But where these developments have encouraged short-term gains—where decisions and actions have been motivated by the desire to obtain high current dividends or profits based solely on the transactions involved in the buying and selling of companies—at the expense of maintaining long-term capabilities and profits, they appear to have reduced and even destroyed the capabilities essential to compete profitably in national and international markets. The rapidity with which a number of capital-intensive industries in the United States—those that have driven industrial growth—have lost market share at home and abroad since the merger and acquisition wave of the 1960s suggests that, in those American industries at least, long-term investment may have been sacrificed for short-term gain.

*

This brief review of the post–World War II history of the modern industrial enterprise and the system of managerial capitalism it has brought forth has shown how the institution and the system reached their fullest strength and how that very success ushered in a new era—one characterized by more competition than growth. The purpose of these final words was, as stated earlier, to bring the implications of the historical story closer to current developments.

The institution's postwar history has only begun to be studied. Its history after the intensified competition of the 1960s and 1970s is even more vaguely understood. The events are too close; the interrelationships between the institution and its environment are too complex; and the data needed for description and analysis have still to be collected and collated. Valid description and analysis on which generalizations can be made must await an in-depth, industry-by-industry, country-by-country historical study comparable to the one presented here on the evolution of the institution in the United States, Great Britain, and Germany from the 1880s to the 1940s.

Indeed, this book has only begun to map the history of the institution before World War II. Much more work needs to be done at every level on each industry in each country. New information, more detailed evidence, will certainly modify the patterns of institutional change that have been outlined and so will alter and enrich the explanatory theory derived from the patterns of dynamic change recorded here.

Appendix Tables · Notes · Credits · Index

Appendix Tables

The following tables rank the 200 largest industrial enterprises in the United States, Great Britain, and Germany by industry for three different sets of years: a year around World War I, a year at the end of the prosperity of the 1920s, and a year at the beginning of the post-World War II era. Slightly different years were selected for each country because the sources used sometimes had inconsistent coverage of companies for certain years, and, in the case of Germany, an attempt was made to avoid the direct influence of war and defeat.

A fourth table for each country (A.4, B.4, and C.4) shows the turnover in the list of the leading firms in the most dynamic industries—food, chemicals, and machinery. The companies in these turnover tables are listed under their main product line within each of the major industries, and their ranking for each of the three years follows the company name. If a company is not among the 200 largest for one or two of the three years, it is listed in brackets, with its assets for those years, when available. If a firm was merged with or fully acquired by another, the name of the acquiring or merged enterprise and the year of acquisition or merger is given in parentheses. If a company is foreign owned, its parent's name and nationality are added. The aim of these tables is to show at a glance the turnover and stability of the leading firms in these industries.

The primary source in ranking the U.S. industrial enterprises was the balance sheets for the years 1917, 1930, and 1948 in *Moody's Manual*. German ranking came from the data in the 1913/14, 1930, and 1953/54 volumes of the *Handbuch der deutschen Aktiengesellschaften*. Total assets in consolidated balance sheets, if available, were used. Such balance sheet data are usually not included in the British *Stock Exchange Yearbook*, therefore the British rankings are based on the market value of shares for the years 1919, 1930, and 1948 in the *Stock Exchange Daily Official List*.

Included are industrial enterprises which operated domestic production facilities. British-American Tobacco Co., for example, was excluded because the company did not have manufacturing facilities within Great Britain until well after World War II. Occasionally a nonmanufacturing company had a manufacturing firm large enough to reach the top 200. For instance, Western Electric, the telephone manufacturer, is included with electric and electronic equipment because its parent company, American Telephone & Telegraph, a utility company, is not listed here.

Not included are most privately held companies and many subsidiaries of foreign firms, because directories rarely list companies whose securities are not traded, and the information necessary to rank them is therefore not available. Privately owned companies large enough to compete in their industries do appear in the text, however, as competitors of the companies that are ranked here.

Information on the industries in which individual firms had their products comes from the same directories used for ranking purposes and from the sources on these companies cited in the text. Information on specialized lines and by-products is particularly difficult to obtain, so these product lines may not always be complete. The first of the three tables for each country lists only the major product line because of the paucity of information in the early twentieth century. If total output of a process is used internally, such as pulp produced by a paper company that is wholly used in the processing of newsprint or paper, it is not listed in the company's product lines.

The industrial categories in which the firms are classified are those used by the U.S. government, in particular the Bureau of the Census in its Standard Industrial Classifications. Firms are grouped by their SIC two-digit group and listed with their major product line (the three- or four-digit SIC code). Some categories have been modified or combined. For example, some kinds of light machinery such as sewing machines, typewriters, office machinery, and some appliances, which the SIC lists as electrical equipment because they are run by electric motors, are listed here with nonelectrical machinery because these machines relied on human power until well into the twentieth century. The Standard Industrial Classification list below is from U.S. Office of Management and Budget, *Standard Industrial Classification Manual, 1972* (Washington, D.C., 1972).

Industry groups according to U.S. Standard Industrial Classification

Group	Industry title
20	FOOD AND KINDRED PRODUCTS
201	Meat products
202	Dairy products
203	Preserved fruits and vegetables
204	Grain mill products
205	Bakery products
206	Sugar and confectionery products
	2062 Cane sugar refining
	2063 Beet sugar
	2065 Confectionery and cocoa products
207	Fats and oils
208	Beverages
	2082 Malt beverages
	2085 Distilled liquor
	2086 Bottled and canned soft drinks

209 Miscellaneous foods and kindred products
    2091 Canned and packaged fish
    2097 Manufactured ice
    2099 Food preparations

21 TOBACCO MANUFACTURES
211 Cigarettes
212 Cigars
213 Chewing and smoking tobacco
214 Tobacco stemming and redrying

22 TEXTILE MILL PRODUCTS
221 Weaving mills, cotton
222 Weaving mills, synthetics
223 Weaving and finishing mills, wool
224 Narrow fabric mills
225 Knitting mills
226 Textile finishing, except wool
227 Floor covering mills
228 Yarn and thread mills
    2285 Synthetic yarn
229 Miscellaneous textile goods
    2296 Tire code and fabric

23 APPAREL AND OTHER TEXTILE PRODUCTS
231 Men's and boys' suits and coats
232 Men's and boys' furnishings
233 Women's and misses' outerwear
234 Women's and children's undergarments
235 Hats, caps, and millinery
236 Children's outerwear
237 Fur goods
238 Miscellaneous apparel and accessories
239 Miscellaneous fabricated textile products

24 LUMBER AND WOOD PRODUCTS
241 Logging camps and logging contractors
242 Sawmills and planning mills
243 Millwork, plywood and structural members
244 Wood containers
245 Wood buildings and mobile homes
249 Miscellaneous wood products

25 FURNITURE AND FIXTURES
251 Household furniture
252 Office furniture
253 Public building and related furniture
254 Partitions and fixtures
259 Miscellaneous furniture and fixtures

26	PAPER AND ALLIED PRODUCTS
261	Pulp mills
262	Paper mills, except building paper
263	Paperboard mills
264	Miscellaneous converted paper products
265	Paperboard containers and boxes
266	Building paper and board mills

27	PRINTING AND PUBLISHING
271	Newspapers
272	Periodicals
273	Books
274	Miscellaneous publishing
275	Commercial printing
276	Manifold business forms
277	Greeting card publishing
278	Blankbooks and book binding
279	Printing trade services

28	CHEMICALS AND ALLIED PRODUCTS
281	Industrial inorganic chemicals
282	Plastics materials and synthetics
283	Drugs
284	Soap, cleaners, and toilet goods
285	Paints and allied products
286	Industrial organic chemicals
287	Agricultural chemicals
289	Miscellaneous chemical products
2892	Explosives
2895	Carbon black

29	PETROLEUM AND COAL PRODUCTS
291	Petroleum refining
295	Paving and roofing materials
299	Miscellaneous petroleum and coal products

30	RUBBER AND MISCELLANEOUS PLASTICS PRODUCTS
301	Tires and inner tubes
302	Rubber and plastics footwear
303	Reclaimed rubber
304	Rubber and plastics hose and belting
306	Fabricated rubber products
307	Miscellaneous plastics products

31	LEATHER AND LEATHER PRODUCTS
311	Leather tanning and finishing
313	Boot and shoe cut stock and findings
314	Footwear, except rubber
315	Leather gloves and mittens
316	Luggage

The 200 largest industrial enterprises in the United States, ranked by assets, 1917.

Rank	Firm	Assets ($ millions)	Major product line (SIC code)
Group 20: Food and kindred products			
4	Armour & Co.	314.1	201
5	Swift & Co.	306.3	201
28	American Sugar Refining Co.	137.3	2062
40	Corn Products Refining Co.	112.0	204
44	Wilson & Co.	102.0	201
49	Morris & Co.	91.1	201
63	National Biscuit Co.	73.5	205
66	Cudahy Packing Co.	64.7	201
76	Distillers Securities Corp.	55.7	2085
78	Great Western Sugar Co.	54.0	2063
82	Cuban American Sugar Co.	51.4	2062
86	Borden's Condensed Milk Co.	47.5	202
104	American Cotton Oil Co.	42.4	207
108	E. Anheuser Brewing Association	41.5	2082
111	Quaker Oats Co.	40.0	204
129	American Ice Co.	35.2	2097
136	Fleischmann Co.	34.5	2099
139	California Packing Corp.	33.7	203
153	American Beet Sugar Co.	30.5	2063
159	Royal Baking Powder Co.	30.0	2099
161	Standard Milling Co.	29.3	204
170	Booth Fisheries	27.5	2091
174	Coca-Cola Co.	27.0	2086
177	Utah-Idaho Sugar Co.	26.7	2063
183	Libby, McNeill & Libby	26.0	201
186	Southern Cotton Oil Co.	25.9	207
188	H. J. Heinz Co.	25.0	203
190	Jos. Schlitz Beverage Co.	25.0	2082
197	Ward Baking Co. of New York	24.6	205

Rank	Firm	Assets ($ millions)	Major product line (SIC code)
Group 21: Tobacco manufactures			
18	American Tobacco Co.	164.2	211
41	Liggett & Myers Tobacco Co.	111.2	211
68	P. Lorillard Co.	63.4	211
93	American Cigar Co.	45.0	212
123	R. J. Reynolds Tobacco Co.	37.4	211
127	General Cigar Co.	35.7	212
Group 22: Textile mill products			
34	American Woolen Co.	123.0	223
106	Pacific Mills	42.4	221
160	American Thread Co.	29.8	228
176	Botany Worsted Mills	27.7	223
198	Arlington Mills	24.4	223
199	Plymouth Cordage Co.	24.4	229
Group 23: Apparel and other textile products			
134	Cluett, Peabody & Co.	34.9	232
175	Hart, Schaffner & Marx	26.9	231
196	National Cloak & Suit Co.	24.7	231
Group 24: Lumber and wood products			
21	Weyerhaeuser Timber Co.	153.2	242
184	Red River Lumber Co.	26.0	242
194	Long-Bell Lumber Co.	24.8	242
Group 26: Paper and allied products			
57	International Paper Co.	77.6	262
109	American Writing Paper Co.	41.3	264
116	Bemis Brothers Bag Co.	39.2	264
158	Great Northern Paper Co.	30.0	262
165	West Virginia Pulp & Paper Co.	28.7	262
Group 27: Printing and publishing			
131	Hearst Publications	35.0	271
137	Curtis Publishing Co.	34.2	272
Group 28: Chemicals and allied products			
8	E.I. du Pont de Nemours & Co.	263.3	286
20	Union Carbide & Carbon Corp.	155.9	281
47	Virginia-Carolina Chemical Co.	94.4	287
55	American Agricultural Chemical Co.	82.1	287
70	Procter & Gamble Co.	62.8	284
72	National Lead Co.	58.7	285
74	General Chemical Co.	56.9	281
87	United Drug Co.	47.4	283
95	Barrett Co.	44.9	281
97	National Aniline & Chemical Co.	44.2	286
101	United States Industrial Alcohol Co.	43.5	286
113	H. Koppers Co.	40.0	286

Rank	Firm	Assets ($ millions)	Major product line (SIC code)
115	American Linseed Co.	39.4	285
126	International Agricultural Corp.	36.4	287
128	Semet-Solvay Co.	35.6	281
144	Hercules Powder Co.	32.5	286
147	United Dyewood Corp.	31.9	286
157	Grasselli Chemical Co.	30.0	281
162	Aetna Explosives Co.	29.0	2892
180	Atlas Powder Co.	26.1	2892
Group 29: Petroleum and coal products			
2	Standard Oil Co. of New Jersey	574.1	291
14	Standard Oil Co. of New York	204.3	291
24	Texas Co.	144.5	291
26	Gulf Oil Co.	142.9	291
32	Standard Oil Co. of Indiana	126.9	291
33	Standard Oil Co. of California	126.9	291
35	Magnolia Oil Co.	122.8	291
42	Pure Oil Co.	110.0	291
48	Sinclair Oil & Refining Corp.	93.8	291
53	Pan American Petroleum & Transport Co.	83.0	291
56	Associated Oil Co.	80.6	291
58	Union Oil Co. of California	77.5	291
59	Vacuum Oil Co.	76.1	291
71	Atlantic Refining Co.	60.7	291
80	Midwest Refining Co.	52.4	291
88	Pierce Oil Corp.	46.7	291
92	Cosden & Co.	45.5	291
103	Tide Water Oil Co.	42.7	291
110	General Asphalt Co.	40.9	295
132	Shell Co. of California	35.0	291
145	General Petroleum Corp.	32.2	291
191	Sun Co.	25.0	291
Group 30: Rubber and miscellaneous plastics products			
9	United States Rubber Co.	257.5	301
22	B. F. Goodrich Co.	146.1	301
54	Goodyear Tire & Rubber Co.	82.5	301
81	Firestone Tire & Rubber Co.	51.6	301
107	Fisk Rubber Co.	41.9	301
Group 31: Leather and leather products			
23	Central Leather Co.	145.3	311
94	Endicott Johnson & Co.	45.0	314
99	American Hide & Leather Co.	43.9	311
125	International Shoe Co.	36.6	314

Rank	Firm	Assets ($ millions)	Major product line (SIC code)
Group 32: Stone, clay, and glass products			
105	Harbison-Walker Refractories Co.	42.4	325
119	Pittsburgh Plate Glass Co.	38.7	321
155	Atlas Portland Cement Co.	30.0	324
171	Lehigh Portland Cement Co.	27.5	324
192	Owens Bottle Machine Corp.	24.9	322
Group 33: Primary metal industries			
1	United States Steel Corp.	2,449.5	331
3	Bethlehem Steel Corp.	381.5	331
6	Midvale Steel & Ordnance Co.	270.0	331
10	Phelps Dodge Corp.	232.3	333
12	Anaconda Copper Corp.	225.8	333
13	American Smelting & Refining Co.	221.8	333
19	Jones & Laughlin Steel Co.	159.6	331
27	Kennecott Copper Corp.	142.4	333
37	Republic Iron & Steel Co.	122.3	331
38	Lackawanna Steel Co.	117.3	331
43	Aluminum Co. of America	104.0	333
45	Youngstown Sheet & Tube Co.	97.0	331
46	Colorado Fuel & Iron Co.	95.3	331
50	Crucible Steel Co. of America	90.3	331
51	United States Smelting, Refining & Mining Co.	88.7	333
60	New Jersey Zinc Co.	75.0	333
69	International Nickel Co.	63.1	333
73	Inland Steel Co.	57.4	331
89	La Belle Iron Works	46.5	331
91	Brier Hill Steel Co.	45.9	331
112	M. A. Hanna & Co.	40.0	331
114	Trumbull Steel Co.	40.0	331
118	American Steel Foundries	38.9	331
135	Pittsburgh Steel Co.	34.7	331
146	Woodward Iron Co.	32.0	331
151	United States Cast Iron Pipe & Foundry	31.3	331
154	American Rolling Mill	30.3	331
164	American Metal Co.	28.9	333
168	United Alloy Steel Corp.	28.0	331
169	Sloss-Sheffield Steel & Iron Co.	27.8	331
173	St. Joseph Lead Co.	27.1	333
Group 34: Fabricated metal products			
30	American Can Co.	133.1	341
79	Crane Co.	53.8	343
85	Weirton Steel Co.	50.0	344
90	American Brass Co.	46.1	343

Rank	Firm	Assets ($ millions)	Major product line (SIC code)
120	National Enameling & Stamping Co.	38.6	346
121	Winchester Repeating Arms Co.	37.8	348
141	Scovill Manufacturing Co.	33.5	342
150	National Acme Co.	31.3	345
166	American Radiator Co.	28.1	343
185	Continental Can Co.	25.9	341
189	Remington Arms-Union Metallic Cartridge Co.	25.0	348
Group 35: Machinery, except electrical			
7	International Harvester Co.	264.7	352
15	Singer Manufacturing Co.	192.9	3636
61	United Shoe Machinery Corp.	74.1	3636
64	Deere & Co.	69.9	352
77	Allis-Chalmers Manufacturing Co.	54.8	3531
117	J. I. Case Threshing Machine Co.	39.2	352
124	Niles-Bement-Pond Co.	37.3	354
130	Babcock & Wilcox, Ltd.	35.1	351
138	Ingersoll-Rand Co.	34.2	3532
142	Advance-Rumely Co.	33.2	352
148	Worthington Pump & Machinery Corp.	31.9	3561
149	Remington Typewriter Co.	31.6	3572
156	Burroughs Adding Machine Co.	30.0	3573
163	Moline Plow Co.	28.9	352
167	Otis Elevator Co.	28.0	3534
172	Emerson-Brantingham Co.	27.4	352
200	E. W. Bliss Co.	24.4	354
Group 36: Electric and electronic equipment			
11	General Electric Co.	231.6	361
17	Westinghouse Electric & Manufacturing Co.	164.7	361
36	Western Electric Co.	122.6	366
143	Victor Talking Machine Co.	33.2	3652
195	Electric Storage Battery Co.	24.7	3691
Group 37: Transportation equipment			
16	Ford Motor Co.	165.9	3711
25	Pullman Co.	143.3	374
29	General Motors Corp.	133.7	3711
31	American Car & Foundry Co.	127.2	374
39	Willys-Overland Co.	113.2	3711
52	American Locomotive Works	84.1	374
62	Baldwin Locomotive Works	73.8	374
65	Studebaker Corp.	69.6	3711
75	United Motors Corp.	56.3	3711
83	Maxwell Motor Co.	50.8	3711

Rank	Firm	Assets ($ millions)	Major product line (SIC code)
84	Dodge Brothers	50.0	3711
96	Pressed Steel Car Co.	44.7	374
98	Westinghouse Air Brake Co.	44.0	374
100	Packard Motor Car Co.	43.6	3711
102	Railway Steel Spring Co.	43.0	374
122	New York Shipbuilding Corp.	37.7	373
133	Standard Steel Car Co.	35.0	374
140	American Ship Building Co.	33.6	373
152	Newport News Shipbuilding & Dry Dock Co.	31.1	373
178	Curtiss Aeroplane & Motor Co.	26.3	372
179	Todd Shipyards Corp.	26.3	373
181	Standard Parts Co.	26.1	3714
182	Pierce Arrow Motor Car Co.	26.0	3711
187	White Motor Co.	25.5	3711
Group 38: Instruments and related products			
67	Eastman Kodak Co.	63.9	386
Group 39: Miscellaneous manufacturing industries			
193	Aeolian-Weber Piano & Pianola Co.	24.8	393

The 200 largest industrial enterprises in the United States, ranked by assets, 1930.

Rank	Firm	Assets ($ millions)	Major	Others
Group 20: Food and kindred products				
16	Armour and Co. (Illinois)	421.3	201	204, 207, 283, 284, 287, 311, 329
24	Swift and Co.	321.7	201	204, 207, 284, 287, 311, 329
36	National Dairy Products Co.	233.1	202	206, 2086
46	Borden Co.	188.0	202	203
59	American Sugar Refining Co.	148.4	2062	
63	National Biscuit Co.	138.6	205	2065
65	Corn Products Refining Co.	127.3	204	206, 207
87	Wilson and Co., Inc.	92.2	201	
90	Great Western Sugar Co.	88.5	2063	
100	Cuban Dominican Sugar Corp.	80.1	2062	
107	California Packing Corp.	76.5	203	2091
110	Standard Brands Inc.	73.7	2099	2095, 2081
111	Cudahy Packing Co.	72.6	201	202, 2077
114	General Foods Corp.	69.8	204	206, 2095, 2099
116	City Ice and Fuel Co.	69.5	2097	358
121	Cuban-American Sugar Co.	67.1	2062	
126	Continental Baking Co.	65.0	205	
127	Libby, McNeill & Libby	64.6	201	203, 2091
128	Quaker Oats Co.	64.2	204	
129	Wm. Wrigley Jr. Co.	63.0	2065	
131	Coca-Cola Co.	61.5	2086	
140	General Mills, Inc.	56.8	204	
141	Cuban Cane Products Co., Inc.	56.7	2062	
163	American Ice Co.	47.9	2097	

Rank	Firm	Assets ($ millions)	Major	Others
167	General Baking Co.	45.1	205	
172	Wesson Oil and Snowdrift Co., Inc.	43.4	207	2097, 285, 287
174	South Porto Rico Sugar Co.	42.9	2062	
179	American Beet Sugar Co.	42.3	2063	
180	Ward Baking Corp.	42.0	205	202
181	Purity Bakeries Corp.	41.5	205	202
186	Gold Dust Corp.	40.6	207	204, 284
Group 21: Tobacco manufactures				
28	American Tobacco Co.	277.2	211	212, 213
50	Liggett & Myers Tobacco Co.	174.7	211	212, 213
53	R. J. Reynolds Tobacco Co.	168.3	211	213
73	P. Lorillard Co.	111.3	211	212, 213
195	United States Tobacco Co.	36.8	211	213
Group 22: Textile mill products				
77	American Woolen Co.	106.2	223	
123	Pacific Mills	65.9	221	222, 223, 226, 229
190	Celanese Corp. of America	39.3	2285	
196	Riverside & Dan River Cotton Mills, Inc.	36.7	221	226
Group 24: Lumber and wood products				
75	Long-Bell Lumber Corp.	108.8	242	243, 286
169	Red River Lumber Co.	44.1	242	243
184	Hammond Lumber Co.	40.7	242	243
198	Pickering Lumber Co.	36.5	242	243
Group 25: Furniture and fixtures				
106	Simmons Co.	76.6	251	
Group 26: Paper and allied products				
4	International Paper & Power Co.	820.6	262	263
72	Crown Zellerbach Corp.	118.1	262	263, 264, 265, 266
83	Minnesota & Ontario Paper Co.	98.2	262	263, 266, 242, 243, 244, forestry
89	St. Regis Paper Co.	89.7	262	263, 264, 266, 242
92	Brown Co.	85.8	262	242, 243, 281
136	West Virginia Pulp & Paper Co.	57.6	262	261, 263, 264, 242
159	Great Northern Paper Co.	49.4	262	263
160	Kimberly-Clark Corp.	49.2	262	264, 281, forestry
Group 27: Printing and publishing				
66	Hearst Consolidated Publications, Inc.	124.9	271	272

Rank	Firm	Assets ($ millions)	Product lines (SIC codes)	
			Major	Others
105	Curtis Publishing Co.	77.8	272	
Group 28: Chemicals and allied products				
12	E.I. du Pont de Nemours & Co.	617.6	286	281, 282, 285, 287, 2892, 386
18	Allied Chemical & Dye Corp.	402.2	286	281, 331
22	Union Carbide & Carbon Corp.	358.2	281	286, 2895, 363, 3714
30	Koppers Co. of Delaware	250.0	286	285, 331, 353, 356
51	Drug Inc.	171.1	284	207
58	Procter & Gamble Co.	155.8	284	207
78	National Lead Co.	105.8	285	207, 333
91	American Cyanamid Co.	87.3	287	281
97	McKesson & Robbins, Inc.	82.0	283	284
109	American Agricultural Chemical Co.	74.3	287	
117	Colgate-Palmolive-Peet Co.	68.5	284	
125	American I. G. Chemical Corp.	65.8	286	
161	Sherwin Williams Co.	48.3	285	284, 286, 287
168	Columbian Carbon Co.	45.1	2895	281
170	Hercules Power Co.	43.7	286	282, 284, 2892
177	Davison Chemical Co.	42.5	287	281, 2074
188	Parke, Davis and Co.	40.4	283	
192	Virginia-Carolina Chemical Corp.	38.0	287	
197	United States Industrial Alcohol Co.	36.6	286	
200	International Agricultural Corp.	36.1	287	
Group 29: Petroleum and coal products				
2	Standard Oil Co. (New Jersey)	1,770.9	291	295, 299
5	Standard Oil Co. (Indiana)	801.1	291	295, 299
7	Gulf Oil Corp. of Pennsylvania	761.5	291	295, 299
9	Standard Oil Co. of New York	720.3	291	
11	Shell Union Oil Corp.	676.9	291	299
13	Standard Oil Co. of California	610.2	291	295, 299
14	Texas Corp. (Texaco)	581.8	291	295, 296
17	Sinclair Consolidated Oil Corp.	404.8	291	
19	Union Oil Co. of California	394.3	291	295, 296

Rank	Firm	Assets ($ millions)	Major	Others
31	Tide Water Associated Oil Co.	248.3	291	299
34	Vacuum Oil Co.	240.5	291	
39	Pure Oil Co.	216.5	291	299
40	Ohio Oil Co.	215.0	291	
42	Philips Petroleum Co.	214.4	291	299
45	Prairie Oil and Gas Co.	195.9	291	
49	Continental Oil Co.	179.4	291	299
55	Atlantic Refining Co.	160.1	291	
84	Sun Oil Co.	94.1	291	295, 299
93	Richfield Oil Co. of California	85.1	291	
94	Columbia Oil & Gasoline Corp.	83.0	291	
98	Mid-Continent Petroleum Corp.	81.9	291	
119	Standard Oil Co. of Ohio	68.0	291	295, 299
120	Barnsdall Corp.	67.3	291	286
150	Rio Grande Oil Co. (Delaware)	53.1	291	
151	Deep Rock Oil Corp.	52.9	291	
165	General Asphalt Co.	46.0	295	291

Group 30: Rubber and miscellaneous plastics products

Rank	Firm	Assets ($ millions)	Major	Others
37	Goodyear Tire and Rubber Co.	227.7	301	304, 306, 2296
43	United States Rubber Co.	211.7	301	302, 303, 304, 306, 2296
56	B.F. Goodrich Co.	159.0	301	302, 304, 306, 2296
61	Firestone Tire & Rubber Co.	147.3	301	302, 303, 307, 2296, 3714
137	Fisk Rubber Co.	57.2	301	2296

Group 31: Leather and leather products

Rank	Firm	Assets ($ millions)	Major	Others
74	International Shoe Co.	110.2	314	
166	Endicott Johnson Corp.	45.2	314	

Group 32: Stone, clay, and glass products

Rank	Firm	Assets ($ millions)	Major	Others
82	Pittsburgh Plate Glass Co.	99.6	321	323, 325, 327, 281, 285, 287, mining
115	United States Gypsum Co.	69.8	327	285
135	International Cement Corp.	57.6	327	
148	Lehigh Portland Cement Co.	53.8	327	
153	Harbison-Walker Refractories Co.	52.2	325	
164	Owens-Illinois Glass Co.	46.3	322	329, 244, 264, 265, 307, 346

Rank	Firm	Assets ($ millions)	Product lines (SIC codes)	
			Major	Others
173	Johns-Manville Corp.	43.4	329	
178	Libbey-Owens-Ford Glass Co.	42.5	321	
Group 33: Primary metal industries				
1	United States Steel Corp.	2,394.5	331	332, 327, 344, 345, 349
8	Anaconda Copper Mining Co.	739.1	333	335
10	Bethlehem Steel Corp.	719.7	331	332, 344, 345, 373
25	Kennecott Copper Corp.	308.5	333	335
26	Republic Steel Corp.	308.5	331	344
27	Phelps Dodge Corp.	285.4	333	281
29	Youngstown Sheet and Tube Co.	258.2	331	
33	Aluminum Co. of America	242.9	333	334, 335, 336, 344, 345
35	American Smelting & Refining Co.	237.1	333	334
38	Jones & Laughlin Steel Corp.	219.5	331	343, 344
57	National Steel Corp.	157.4	331	
60	American Rolling Mill Co.	148.3	331	
67	Wheeling Steel Corp.	124.8	331	
68	Crucible Steel Co. of America	122.6	331	
79	Inland Steel Co.	103.0	331	
86	American Metal Co., Ltd.	92.6	333	
101	Pittsburgh Steel Co.	79.5	331	
102	United States Smelting Refining and Mining Co.	79.4	333	
103	Interlake Iron Corp.	78.1	331	
104	Colorado Fuel & Iron Co.	78.0	331	
154	General Cable Corp.	52.1	331	
185	St. Joseph Lead Co.	40.7	333	
189	Otis Steel Co.	39.7	331	
Group 34: Fabricated metal products				
41	American Radiator & Standard Sanitary Corp.	215.0	343	344, 349, 358
44	American Can Co.	198.4	341	
69	Crane Co.	119.9	343	344, 349, 326, 358
96	Continental Can Co.	82.2	341	346, 354
132	Gillette Safety Razor Co.	61.1	342	284
138	American Steel Foundries	57.1	344	

Rank	Firm	Assets ($ millions)	Product lines (SIC codes) Major	Others
152	General Steel Castings Corp.	52.6	346	
162	Scovill Manufacturing Co.	48.2	342	343, 349
183	United States Pipe & Foundry Co.	41.3	346	
194	A. O. Smith	37.8	349	
Group 35: Machinery, except electrical				
20	International Harvester Co.	383.8	352	371
48	Singer Manufacturing Co.	183.2	3636	
71	Deere and Co.	118.7	352	
85	United Shoe Machinery Corp.	93.4	3636	
99	National Supply Co. of Delaware	81.1	3533	
108	Allis-Chalmers Manufacturing Co.	75.7	353	351, 352, 355, 356, 361
118	Remington Rand Corp.	68.4	357	252
134	J. I. Case Co.	58.9	352	
143	Otis Elevator Co.	55.3	3534	
144	Oliver Farm Equipment Co.	54.5	352	
146	Caterpillar Tractor Co.	54.3	352	353
149	International Combustion Engineering Corp.	53.4	3559	343
155	National Cash Register Co.	52.1	357	
156	Timken Roller Bearing Co.	50.9	3562	
157	Ingersoll-Rand Co.	50.0	3532	351, 3561, 3567
171	International Business Machines Corp.	43.6	357	
175	Burroughs Adding Machine Co.	42.9	357	
191	Underwood Elliott Fisher Co.	38.3	357	
193	Fairbanks, Morse and Co.	37.9	351	3561, 361, 374
Group 36: Electric and electronic equipment				
15	General Electric Co.	493.9	361	363, 364, 369, 374
21	Western Electric Co., Ltd.	379.3	366	3861
32	Westinghouse Electric & Manufacturing Co.	246.1	361	363, 364, 369, 3534, 354, 374
52	Radio Corp. of America	168.5	3651	367, service
187	Electric Storage Battery Co.	40.6	3691	
Group 37: Transportation equipment				
3	General Motors Corp.	1,315.8	3711	3714, 363
6	Ford Motor Co.	781.9	3711	3714
23	Pullman Inc.	532.2	374	

Rank	Firm	Assets ($ millions)	Product lines (SIC codes)	
			Major	Others
47	Chrysler Corp.	184.1	3711	3714, 3732
70	Studebaker Corp.	119.9	3711	3714
76	American Car & Foundry Co.	106.9	374	3711
80	American Locomotive Co.	102.4	374	3533, 358
81	Baldwin Locomotive Works	100.1	374	
88	General American Tank Car Corp.	90.0	374	
95	Newport News Shipbuilding & Dry Dock Corp.	82.8	373	351
112	Packard Motor Car Co.	71.6	3711	3714, 351
113	Westinghouse Air Brake Co.	70.0	374	3662
122	Curtiss-Wright Corp.	67.1	372	
124	Bendix Aviation Corp.	65.8	372	374
130	Mack Trucks, Inc.	62.0	3713	374
139	Willys-Overland Co.	57.1	3711	3714
142	Hudson Motor Car Co.	56.4	3711	3714
145	Nash Motor Co.	54.4	3711	3714
147	Pressed Steel Car Co.	54.2	374	3711
158	White Motor Co.	49.6	3713	3711, 3714
176	United Aircraft and Transport Corp.	42.8	372	transportation
182	Briggs Manufacturing Co.	41.4	3711	3714
199	Borg-Warner Corp.	36.1	3714	354, 356, 357
Group 38: Instruments and Related Products				
54	Eastman Kodak Co.	167.1	386	
64	General Theatres Equipment, Inc.	129.0	386	service
Group 39: Miscellaneous manufacturing industries				
62	International Match Corp.	145.5	399	
133	Armstrong Cork Co.	59.5	399	249, 266

The 200 largest industrial enterprises in the United States, ranked by assets, 1948.

| Rank | Firm | Assets ($ millions) | Product lines (SIC codes) | |
			Major	Others
Group 20: Food and kindred products				
26	Swift & Co.	522.5	201	204, 207, 281, 284, 287, 311, 329
29	Armour & Co. (Illinois)	477.7	201	204, 207, 284, 287, 311, 329
37	Schenley Industries, Inc.	341.9	2085	283, 204
41	National Dairy Products Corp.	317.6	202	206, 207, 208
45	Joseph E. Seagram & Sons, Inc.	301.0	2085	
50	Anderson, Clayton	284.3	207	355, distribution
62	Borden Co.	242.2	202	204, 207, 209, 283
67	General Foods Corp.	222.4	204	203, 206, 208, 209
69	National Distillers Products	214.5	2085	204
73	Coca-Cola Co.	204.9	2086	
85	National Biscuit Co.	161.8	205	
90	Wilson & Co., Inc.	154.0	201	206, 284, 394
100	Corn Products Refining Co.	139.0	204	206, 207
104	American Sugar Refining Co.	133.5	2062	
113	General Mills	124.8	204	207, 363
116	Standard Brands Inc.	122.5	2099	203, 207, 208, 209
122	H.J. Heinz Co.	114.9	203	204, 2099
134	California Packing Co.	102.7	201	2095
139	Cudahy Packing Co.	98.9	201	202, 204, 207, 287
150	Quaker Oats Co.	87.7	204	205
151	Archer-Daniels-Midland Co.	87.5	207	
153	Anheuser-Busch	87.2	2082	204, 283
154	Wesson Oil & Snowdrift Co., Inc.	86.2	207	285, 287
159	Carnation Co.	82.7	202	204

Rank	Firm	Assets ($ millions)	Product lines (SIC codes) Major	Others
162	Libby, McNeill & Libby	82.0	201	203, 2091
189	Wm. Wrigley, Jr., Co.	69.1	2065	
198	Great Western Sugar Co.	67.2	2063	
Group 21: Tobacco manufacturing				
18	American Tobacco Co.	686.6	211	212, 213
25	R. J. Reynolds Tobacco Co.	530.6	211	213
30	Liggett & Myers Tobacco Co.	425.0	211	212, 213
124	Philip Morris & Co., Ltd., Inc.	113.7	211	
141	P. Lorillard Co.	96.4	211	212, 213
Group 22: Textile mill products				
59	Celanese Corp. of America	256.6	2285	307
66	American Viscose Corp.	226.8	2285	
79	Burlington Mills Corp.	176.8	221	222, 223, 224, 225, 228
84	J.P. Stevens & Co., Inc.	164.4	221	222, 223
106	United Merchants & Manufacturers, Inc.	128.2	221	222, 223, 225, 226
117	American Woolen Co.	122.4	223	228
119	Cannon Mills Co.	120.1	221	228
181	Pacific Mills	72.8	221	222, 223, 226
Group 24: Lumber and wood products				
71	Weyerhaeuser Timber Co.	210.1	242	243, 261
164	Crown Cork & Seal Co., Inc.	80.5	249	341, 3559
Group 25: Furniture and Fixtures				
190	Simmons Co.	68.9	251	
Group 26: Paper and allied products				
40	International Paper Co.	323.2	263	262, 264, 265, 266
87	St. Regis Paper Co.	157.6	262	264
88	Crown Zellerbach Corp.	155.7	262	263, 364
111	Kimberly-Clark Corp.	125.4	262	263, 266
170	Champion Paper & Fibre Co.	76.8	262	263, 264, 265, 286
174	West Virginia Pulp & Paper	75.8	262	263, 264
Group 27: Printing and publishing				
86	Hearst Consolidated Publications, Inc.	161.7	271	272
185	Time, Inc.	71.5	272	
Group 28: Chemicals and allied products				
8	E.I. du Pont de Nemours & Co.	1,189.3	286	281, 282, 285, 287, 2892, 222, 386

Rank	Firm	Assets ($ millions)	Product lines (SIC codes)	
			Major	Others
15	Union Carbide and Carbon Corp.	722.6	281	282, 286, 289, 369
38	Allied Chemical and Dye Corp.	338.6	281	282, 284, 286, 287, 331
42	Procter & Gamble Co.	316.3	284	207
54	Dow Chemical Co.	271.4	281	282, 283, 286, 287
70	American Cyanamid Co.	212.0	287	281, 282, 283, 286
76	National Lead Co.	183.4	285	281, 336, 343
78	Monsanto Chemical Co.	176.9	286	281, 282, 283, 284, 285, 287
103	Publicker Industries, Inc.	134.6	286	283, 2082, 204
109	Koppers Co., Inc.	126.1	286	282, 283, 284, 285, 249, 331, 344, 353, 371, 396
127	General Aniline & Film Corp.	110.5	286	386
130	Sterling Drug, Inc.	107.6	283	284
131	McKesson & Robbins, Inc.	107.5	283	wholesaling
135	Colgate-Palmolive-Peet Co.	102.6	284	
138	Sherwin-Williams Co.	101.0	285	284, 286, 287
144	Air Reduction Co., Inc.	94.4	281	354
152	Johnson & Johnson	87.3	283	284, 384
155	Rexall Drug Inc.	86.0	283	306, 384, 208, 221, 206, distribution
157	Hercules Powder Co.	85.3	286	282, 286, 2892
158	American Home Products Corp.	84.5	283	284, 204, 209
175	Glidden Co.	75.6	285	
195	Parke, Davis & Co.	68.1	283	384
200	Abbott Laboratories	66.1	283	
Group 29: Petroleum and coal products				
1	Standard Oil Co. (New Jersey)	3,526.0	291	295, 299, 286, 287
4	Standard Oil Co. (Indiana)	1,500.0	291	295, 299, 286
5	Socony-Vacuum Oil Co., Inc.	1,443.0	291	
6	Texas Co. (Texaco)	1,277.0	291	295, 299, 286, 2895
7	Gulf Oil Corp.	1,191.0	291	295, 299, 286
11	Standard Oil Co. of California	1,074.5	291	295, 299, 286, 287
13	Cities Service Co.	991.8	291	utility
16	Sinclair Oil Corp.	710.1	291	
21	Shell Union Oil Corp.	640.5	291	299, 286
22	Philips Petroleum Corp.	579.2	291	299, 289

Rank	Firm	Assets ($ millions)	Product lines (SIC codes)	
			Major	Others
33	Atlantic Refining Co.	382.5	291	
46	Union Oil of California	298.4	291	295, 299
49	Tide Water Associated Oil Co.	287.7	291	299
51	Sun Oil Co.	278.5	291	295, 299, 373
55	Pure Oil Co.	270.9	291	299
56	Continental Oil Co.	261.9	291	299
64	Standard Oil Co. (Ohio)	237.3	291	295, 299
74	Ohio Oil Co.	203.3	291	
83	Skelly Oil Co.	169.0	291	
97	Richfield Oil Corp.	146.9	291	
101	Mid-Continent Petroleum Corp.	137.1	291	299, 286
102	Sunray Oil Corp.	136.0	291	
Group 30: Rubber and miscellaneous plastics products				
31	Goodyear Tire & Rubber Co.	424.9	301	304, 306, 2296, 396, 399
35	United States Rubber Co.	348.5	301	302, 303, 306, 2296, 282, 396
36	Firestone Tire & Rubber Co.	344.3	301	303, 304, 306, 307, 2296, 396
57	B.F. Goodrich Co.	261.7	301	302, 303, 304, 306, 307, 2296, 282, 396
188	General Tire & Rubber Co.	69.8	301	304, 306, 309, 2296
Group 31: Leather and leather products				
120	International Shoe Co.	117.8	314	
160	Endicott Johnson Corp.	82.5	314	
Group 32: Stone, clay, and glass products				
65	Pittsburgh Plate Glass Co.	227.3	321	322, 281, 285, 289
77	Owens-Illinois Glass Co.	180.2	322	329, 382
93	United States Gypsum Co.	150.7	327	329, 295, 285
108	Johns-Manville Corp.	127.9	329	
148	Minnesota Mining & Manufacturing Co.	88.9	329	289, 307, 384
161	Libbey-Owens-Ford Glass Co.	82.2	321	322
Group 33: Primary metal industries				
3	United States Steel Corp.	2,534.9	331	332, 327, 344, 345, 346, 347, 349, 373, 374
12	Bethlehem Steel Corp.	1,029.0	331	322, 344, 345, 373, 374

Rank	Firm	Assets ($ millions)	Product lines (SIC codes) Major	Others
20	Anaconda Copper Mining Co.	660.3	333	335, 342, 343
23	Kennecott Copper Corp.	575.4	333	335, 242, 287, 342, 343, 346
27	Aluminum Co. of America	503.6	333	334, 335, 336, 344, 345, 349, 356
28	Republic Steel Corp.	489.1	331	344, 345
34	Jones & Laughlin Steel Corp.	379.1	331	343, 344
39	National Steel Corp.	329.8	331	
43	Armco Steel Corp.	316.2	331	344
44	Youngstown Sheet & Tube Co.	311.6	331	291
47	Inland Steel Co.	292.8	331	341, 344
48	American Smelting & Refining Co.	290.4	333	334
53	Phelps Dodge Corp.	274.3	333	281
81	Wheeling Steel Corp.	172.2	331	344, 346
123	Reynolds Metal Co.	114.1	333	344
125	American Metal Co., Ltd.	112.7	333	
126	Crucible Steel Co. of America	112.0	331	
156	Colorado Fuel & Iron Corp.	85.6	331	349, 353
167	U.S. Smelting, Refining & Mining Co.	78.8	333	
171	American Brake Shoe Co.	76.6	332	346, 356, 374
186	Pittsburgh Steel Co.	70.5	331	
193	Allegheny Ludlum Steel Corp.	68.4	331	
196	Sharon Steel Corp.	67.9	331	

Group 34: Fabricated metal products

Rank	Firm	Assets ($ millions)	Major	Others
52	American Can Co.	275.8	341	
68	Continental Can Co.	221.7	341	346, 265, 307, 354
82	American Radiator & Sanitary Corp.	171.3	343	344, 349, 358
99	Crane Co.	142.0	343	344, 349, 326, 358
168	Gillette Safety Razor Co.	78.3	342	284
183	Scovill Manufacturing Co.	72.1	346	344, 345, 349, 361, 363

Group 35: Machinery, except electrical

Rank	Firm	Assets ($ millions)	Major	Others
19	International Harvester Co.	671.8	352	353, 3711
58	Deere & Co.	257.5	352	
60	Allis-Chalmers Manufacturing Co.	253.8	353	3523, 3551, 361

Rank	Firm	Assets ($ millions)	Product lines (SIC codes) Major	Others
63	International Business Machines Corp.	341.9	357	387
72	Singer Manufacturing Co.	209.1	3636	362, 361
95	Caterpillar Tractor Co.	147.3	352	3531
98	National Cash Register	143.9	357	
107	Remington Rand Inc.	127.9	357	264, 363, 386
133	United Shoe Machinery Corp.	104.6	3636	
137	National Supply Co.	101.6	353	351
142	Ingersoll-Rand Co.	96.1	353	351, 356
146	Food Machinery & Chemical Corp.	90.3	3551	355, 353, 356, 281, 286, 287
165	Babcock & Wilcox Co.	79.3	351	355, 249, 341
166	Timken Roller Bearing Co.	78.8	3562	331
169	Fairbanks, Morse & Co.	77.4	351	362, 374
172	J. I. Case Co.	76.6	352	
177	Sperry Corp.	74.2	356	352, 354, 355, 362, 381
178	Otis Elevator Co.	73.6	3534	
180	Oliver Corp.	73.2	352	
184	Worthington Pump & Machinery Corp.	72.1	3561	351, 353, 358, 361, 382
187	Dresser Industries, Inc.	69.9	3533	356
191	Burroughs Adding Machine Co.	68.5	357	264
192	Combustion Engineering-Superheater Inc.	68.4	356	

Group 36: Electric and electronic equipment

Rank	Firm	Assets ($ millions)	Major	Others
9	General Electric Co.	1,177.3	361	363, 364, 365, 366, 367, 282
14	Western Electric Co.	785.9	366	367
17	Westinghouse Electric Corp.	693.6	361	363, 364, 365, 366, 367, 3534
61	Radio Corporation of America	248.2	3651	367
140	Philco Corp.	96.6	365	363, 369
147	Avco Manufacturing Co.	89.8	365	363, 3724, 352, 358
194	Sylvania Electric Products Inc.	68.3	365	364, 366, 367, 386

Group 37: Transportation equipment

Rank	Firm	Assets ($ millions)	Major	Others
2	General Motors Corp.	2,957.7	371	336, 374
10	Ford Motor Co.	1,149.2	371	352
24	Chrysler Corp.	541.4	371	351, 356

Rank	Firm	Assets ($ millions)	Product lines (SIC codes) Major	Others
75	Pullman Inc.	194.7	374	3559
80	American Car & Foundry Co.	174.8	374	3714, 332, 343, 344
89	Curtiss-Wright Corp.	155.6	372	
91	Nash-Kelvinator	153.5	371	356, 363
92	Borg-Warner Corp.	151.3	371	331, 346, 352, 355, 356
94	General American Transportation Corp.	148.1	374	307, 344, 355, 358
96	United Aircraft Corp.	147.0	372	
105	Studebaker Corp.	129.2	371	
110	Boeing Airplane Co.	125.5	372	
112	Kaiser-Frazer Corp.	124.9	371	
114	Bendix Aviation Corp.	123.6	372	3714, 366
115	Electric Auto-Lite Co.	122.8	3714	364, 3692
118	North American Aviation, Inc.	121.0	372	
121	Budd Co.	116.5	371	374, 352
129	Hudson Motor Car Co.	108.3	371	
132	Packard Motor Car Co.	107.2	371	351
136	Douglas Aircraft Co., Inc.	102.4	372	
143	Baldwin Locomotive Works	94.7	374	332, 336, 344, 351
145	American Locomotive Co.	93.1	374	351, 358
149	Westinghouse Air Brake Co.	88.3	374	
163	Willys-Overland Motors, Inc.	80.7	371	
173	Fruehauf Trailer Co.	76.3	3715	379
176	Briggs Manufacturing Co.	74.7	3714	343, 344
179	Lockheed Aircraft Corp.	73.3	372	
182	Mack Trucks	72.7	371	
197	Dana Corp.	67.9	371	
Group 38: Instruments and related products				
32	Eastman Kodak Co.	411.6	386	282, 286, 287
Group 39: Miscellaneous manufacturing industries				
128	Armstrong Cork Co.	109.1	399	249
199	Diamond Match Co.	67.0	399	

Turnover in the list of those of the 200 largest industrial enterprises in the United States that are in the food, chemical, and machinery industries, 1917, 1930, 1948. Rank number follows the company name.

1917 (Assets over $24.4 million)	1930 (Assets over $36.1 million)	1948 (Assets over $66.1 million)
Group 20: Food and kindred products		
201: Meat products		
Armour 4	Armour 16	Armour 29
Swift 5	Swift 24	Swift 26
Wilson 44	Wilson 87	Wilson 90
Morris 49	(Armour 1923)[a]	
Cudahy Packing 66	Cudahy Packing 111	Cudahy Packing 139
Libby, McNeill & Libby 183	Libby, McNeill & Libby 127	Libby, McNeill & Libby 162
202: Dairy products		
Borden 86	Borden 46	Borden 62
	National Dairy Products 36	National Dairy Products 41
[Carnation $17.2][b]	[Carnation $26.7]	Carnation 159
203: Canned fruits and vegetables		
California Packing 139	California Packing 107	California Packing 134
H. J. Heinz 188	[H. J. Heinz pvt.]	H. J. Heinz 122
204: Grain mill products		
Corn Products Refining 40	Corn Products Refining 65	Corn Products Refining 100
Quaker Oats 111	Quaker Oats 128	Quaker Oats 150
Standard Milling 161	(Gold Dust 1928)	
	General Foods 114	General Foods 67
[Washburn Crosby $20.0]	General Mills 140	General Mills 113
205: Bakery products		
National Biscuit 63	National Biscuit 63	National Biscuit 85
Ward Baking 197	Ward Baking 180	[Ward Baking $25.9]
	Continental Baking 126	[Continental Baking $59.2]

a. If a firm was merged with or fully acquired by another, the name of the acquiring or merged enterprise and the year of acquisition or merger is given in parenthesis.

b. Brackets indicate that a company's assets were not sufficient for it to be included in the 200 largest industrial enterprises for the year in which it is listed (in which case total assets are given), or that the company was privately held (pvt.) and total assets are not available.

1917 (Assets over $24.4 million)	1930 (Assets over $36.1 million)	1948 (Assets over $66.1 million)
[General Baking $16.0]	General Baking 167	[General Baking $37.0]
	Purity Bakeries 181	[Purity Bakeries $29.4]

206: Sugar and confectionery products

2062: Cane sugar refining

American Sugar Refining 28	American Sugar Refining 59	American Sugar Refining 104
Cuban-American Sugar 82	Cuban-American Sugar 121	[Cuban-American Sugar $47.1]
	Cuban Dominican Sugar 100	[West Indies Sugar $61.6]
[Cuban Cane Sugar $8.3 agri. only]	Cuban Cane Products 141	[Cuban Cane Products $54.1]
[South Porto Rico Sugar $15.5]	South Porto Rico Sugar 174	[South Porto Rico Sugar $43.3]

2063: Beet sugar

Great Western Sugar 78	Great Western Sugar 90	Great Western Sugar 198
American Beet Sugar 153	American Beet Sugar 179	[American Beet Sugar $37.5]
Utah-Idaho Sugar 177	[Utah-Idaho Sugar $29.9]	[Utah-Idaho Sugar $32.2]

2065: Confectionery and cocoa products

[Wm. Wrigley Jr. $23.0]	Wm. Wrigley Jr. 129	Wm. Wrigley Jr. 189

207: Fats and oils

American Cotton Oil 104	Gold Dust 186	[Best Foods $44.1]
Southern Cotton Oil 186	Wesson Oil and Snowdrift 172	Wesson Oil and Snowdrift 154
	[Anderson, Clayton pvt.]	Anderson, Clayton 50
	[Archer-Daniels-Midland $23.6]	Archer-Daniels-Midland 151

208: Beverages

2082: Malt beverages

E. Anheuser Brewing Assn. 108	[Anheuser-Busch pvt.]	Anheuser-Busch 153
J. Schlitz Beverage 190	[J. Schlitz Brewing pvt.]	[J. Schlitz Brewing pvt.]

2085: Distilled liquor

Distillers Securities 76	[National Distillers Products $26.8]	National Distillers Products 69
	[Schenley Products pvt.]	Schenley Industries 37
		Joseph E. Seagram & Sons 45

2086: Soft drinks

Coca-Cola 174	Coca-Cola 131	Coca-Cola 73

209: Miscellaneous foods and kindred products

2091: Canned and packaged fish

Booth Fisheries 170	[Booth Fisheries $20.6]	[Booth Fisheries $7.7]

1917 (Assets over $24.4 million)	1930 (Assets over $36.1 million)	1948 (Assets over $66.1 million)
2097: Manufactured ice		
American Ice 131	American Ice 163	[American Ice $12.4]
[City Ice & Fuel pvt.]	City Ice & Fuel 116	[City Products $57.5]
2099: Food preparations		
Fleischmann 136	(Standard Brands 1929)	
Royal Baking Powder 159	Standard Brands 110	Standard Brands 116
Group 28: Chemicals and allied products		
281: Industrial inorganic chemicals		
Union Carbide & Carbon 20	Union Carbide & Carbon 22	Union Carbide & Carbon 15
General Chemical 74	(Allied Chemical & Dye 1920)	
Barrett 95	(Allied Chemical & Dye 1920)	
Semet Solvay 128	(Allied Chemical & Dye 1920)	
Grassalli Chemical 157	(Du Pont 1928)	
[Solvay pvt.]	Allied Chemical & Dye 18	Allied Chemical & Dye 38
[Dow Chemical pvt.]	[Dow Chemical $21.5]	Dow Chemical 54
[Air Reduction pvt.]	[Air Reduction $35.8]	Air Reduction 144
283: Drugs (consumer chemicals)		
United Drug 87	Drug Inc. 51	Rexall Drug 155
	McKesson & Robbins 97	McKesson & Robbins 131
[Parke, Davis $18.1]	Parke, Davis 188	Parke, Davis 195
[Sterling Drug pvt.]	[Sterling Drug pvt.]	Sterling Drug 130
[Johnson & Johnson pvt.]	[Johnson & Johnson pvt.]	Johnson & Johnson 152
	[American Home Products $21.9]	American Home Products 158
[Abbott Laboratories pvt.]	[Abbott Laboratories $3.6]	Abbott Laboratories 200
284: Soap, cleaners, and toilet goods (consumer chemicals)		
Procter & Gamble 70	Procter & Gamble 58	Procter & Gamble 42
	Colgate-Palmolive-Peet 117	Colgate-Palmolive-Peet 135
285: Paints and allied products (consumer chemicals)		
National Lead 72	National Lead 78	National Lead 76
American Linseed 115	(Gold Dust 1928)	
[Sherwin Williams $20.4]	Sherwin Williams 161	Sherwin Williams 138
	[Glidden $35.0]	Glidden 175
286: Industrial organic chemicals		
E.I. du Pont de Nemours 8	E.I. du Pont de Nemours 12	E.I. du Pont de Nemours 8

1917 (Assets over $24.4 million)	1930 (Assets over $36.1 million)	1948 (Assets over $66.1 million)
National Aniline & Chemical 97	(Allied Chemical & Dye 1920)	
U.S. Industrial Alcohol 101	U.S. Industrial Alcohol 197	[U.S. Industrial Chemical $46.7]
H. Koppers 113	Koppers 30	Koppers 109
Hercules Powder 144	Hercules Powder 170	Hercules Powder 157
United Dyewood 147	[United Dyewood $25.6]	[United Dyewood $3.8]
	American I.G. Chemical 125 controlled by I. G. Farben, Germany	General Aniline & Film 127
[Monsanto Chemical pvt.]	[Monsanto Chemical pvt.]	Monsanto Chemical 78
[Publiker-Ward Distilling pvt.]	[Publiker Commercial Alcohol pvt.]	Publiker Industries 103
287: Agricultural chemicals		
Virginia-Carolina Chemical 47	Virginia-Carolina Chemical 192	[Virginia-Carolina Chemical $44.3]
American Agricultural Chemical 55	American Agricultural Chemical 109	[American Agricultural Chemical $37.7]
International Agricultural 126	International Agricultural 200	[International Minerals & Chemical $56.5]
[American Cyanamid $15.8]	American Cyanamid 91	American Cyanamid 70
[Davison Chemical $11.4]	Davison Chemical 177	[Davison Chemical $25.1]
289: Miscellaneous chemical products		
2892: Explosives		
Aetna Explosives 162	(Hercules Powder 1921)	
Atlas Powder 180	[Atlas Powder $33.8]	[Atlas Powder $32.9]
2895: Carbon black		
[Columbian Carbin pvt.]	Columbian Carbon 168	[Columbian Carbon $48.8]
Group 35: Machinery, except electrical		
351: Engines and turbines		
Babcock & Wilcox 130	[Babcock & Wilcox $20.6]	Babcock & Wilcox 165
[Fairbanks, Morse $19.6]	Fairbanks, Morse 193	Fairbanks, Morse 169
352: Farm and garden machinery		
International Harvester 7	International Harvester 20	International Harvester 19
Deere 64	Deere 71	Deere 58
J. I. Case 117	J. I. Case 134	J. I. Case 172
Advance-Rumely 142	[Advance-Rumely $30.7]	(Allis Chalmers 1931)

1917 (Assets over $24.4 million)	1930 (Assets over $36.1 million)	1948 (Assets over $66.1 million)
Moline Plow 163	[Minneapolis-Moline Power Implement $23.6]	[Minneapolis-Moline $43.2]
Emerson-Brantingham 172	(J. I. Case 1928)	
[Oliver Chilled Steel Plow pvt.]	Oliver Farm Equipment 144	Oliver 180
	Caterpillar Tractor 146	Caterpillar Tractor 95

353: Construction and related machinery

3531: Construction machinery

Allis-Chalmers Mfg. 77	Allis-Chalmers Mfg. 108	Allis-Chalmers Mfg. 60

3532: Mining machinery

Ingersoll-Rand 138	Ingersoll-Rand 157	Ingersoll-Rand 142

3533: Oil field machinery

[National Supply pvt.]	National Supply 99	National Supply 137
[Dresser Industries pvt.]	[Dresser Industries $3.3]	Dresser Industries 188

3534: Elevators and moving stairways

Otis Elevator 167	Otis Elevator 143	Otis Elevator 178

354: Metal working machinery

Niles-Bement-Pond 124	[Niles-Bement-Pond $13.6]	[Niles-Bement-Pond $18.0]
E. W. Bliss 200	[E. W. Bliss $24.8]	[E. W. Bliss $18.7]

355: Special industry machinery

3551: Food products machinery

	[Food Machinery $7.9]	Food Machinery & Chemical 146

3559: Special industry machinery, nec.

	International Combustion Engineering 159	(Super Heater 1933)

356: General industrial machinery

3561: Pumps and pumping equipment

Worthington Pump & Machinery 148	[Worthington Pump $29.5]	Worthington Pump & Machinery 183

3562: Ball and roller bearings

[Timken Roller Bearing $15.0]	Timken Roller Bearing 156	Timken Roller Bearing 166

357: Office and computing machines

3572: Typewriters

Remington Typewriter 149	Remington Rand 118	Remington Rand 107
[Underwood Typewriter $21.8]	Underwood Elliott Fisher 191	[Underwood $41.6]

1917 (Assets over $24.4 million)	1930 (Assets over $36.1 million)	1948 (Assets over $66.1 million)

3573: Electronic computing equipment
3574: Calculating and accounting machines

Burroughs Adding Machine 156	Burroughs Adding Machine 175	Burroughs Adding Machine 191
[National Cash Register $19.6]	National Cash Register 155	National Cash Register 98
[Computing-Tabulating-Recording $22.2]	International Business Machines 171	International Business Machines 63
		Sperry 177

358: Refrigeration and service machinery

[Locomotive Superheater pvt.]	[Superheater $22.5]	Combustion Engineering-Superheater 192

3636: Sewing machines (from Group 36)

Singer Mfg. 15	Singer Mfg. 48	Singer Mfg. 72
United Shoe Machinery 61	United Shoe Machinery 85	United Shoe Machinery 133

Group 36: Electric and electronic equipment
361: Electric distribution and industrial equipment

General Electric 11	General Electric 15	General Electric 9
Westinghouse Electric & Mfg. 17	Westinghouse Electric & Mfg. 32	Westinghouse Electric 17

365: Radio and TV receiving equipment
3651: Radio and TV receiving sets

	Radio Corp. of America 52	Radio Corp. of America 61
[Philadelphia Storage Battery pvt.]	[Philadelphia Storage Battery pvt.]	Philco 141
	[Aviation $25.2]	Avco Manufacturing 147
	[Hygrade Lamp $3.9]	Sylvania Electric 194

3652: Phonograph records

Victor Talking Machine 143	(RCA 1929)	

366: Communication equipment

Western Electric 36	Western Electric 21	Western Electric 14

369: Miscellaneous electrical equipment and supplies
3691: Storage batteries

Electric Storage Battery 195	Electric Storage Battery 187	[Electric Storage Battery $65.8]

Group 37: Transportation equipment
371: Motor vehicles and equipment
3711: Motor vehicles and car bodies

Ford Motor 16	Ford Motor 6	Ford Motor 10
General Motors 29	General Motors 3	General Motors 2
Willys-Overland 39	Willys-Overland 139	Willys-Overland 163

1917 (Assets over $24.4 million)	1930 (Assets over $36.1 million)	1948 (Assets over $66.1 million)
Chevrolet Motor 46	(General Motors 1918)	
Studebaker 65	Studebaker 70	Studebaker 105
United Motors 75	(General Motors 1918)	
Maxwell Motor 83	Chrysler 47	Chrysler 24
Dodge Brothers 84	(Chrysler 1928)	
Packard Motor Car 100	Packard Motor Car 112	Packard Motor Car 132
Pierce Arrow Motor Car 182	(Studebaker 1928)	
White Motor 187	White Motor 158	[White Motor $58.8]
[International Motor Truck pvt.]	Mack Trucks 130	Mack Truck 182
[Hudson Motor Car $10.9]	Hudson Motor Car 142	Hudson Motor Car 129
[Nash Motor Car pvt.]	Nash Motor 145	Nash Kelvinator 91 Kaiser-Frazer 113

3714: Motor vehicle parts and accessories

Standard Parts 181	liquidated 1923	
[Briggs Mfg. $20.0 in Group 35]	Briggs Mfg. 182 in Group 35	Briggs Mfg. 176
	Borg-Warner 199	Borg-Warner 92
	[Electric Auto-Lite $24.8]	Electric Auto-Lite 115
[Spicer Mfg. $15.0]	[Spicer Mfg. $13.9]	Dana 197

3715: Truck trailers

	[Fruehauf Trailer $1.9]	Fruehauf Trailer 173

372: Aircraft and parts

Curtiss Aeroplane & Motor 178	Curtiss-Wright 122	Curtiss-Wright 89
	Bendix Aviation 124, 24% controlled by General Motors	Bendix Aviation 114
	United Aircraft and Transport 176	United Aircraft 96
	[North American Aviation $30.1, no manufacturing, controlled by General Motors]	North American Aviation 118
	[Douglas Aircraft $3.6] from United Aircraft	Douglas Aircraft 136 Boeing Airplane 110 Lockheed Aircraft 179

1917 (Assets over $24.4 million)	1930 (Assets over $36.1 million)	1948 (Assets over $66.1 million)
373: Ship and boat building and repairing		
New York Shipbuilding 122	[New York Shipbuilding pvt., controlled by American Brown Boveri Electric]	[New York Shipbuilding $21.2, controlled by Avco Mfg.]
American Shipbuilding 140	[American Shipbuilding $13.3]	[American Shipbuilding $11.9]
Newport News Shipbuilding & Dry Dock 152	Newport News Shipbuilding & Dry Dock 95	[Newport News Shipbuilding $43.5]
Todd Shipyard 179	[Todd Shipyard $22.7]	[Todd Shipyard $53.1]
374: Railroad equipment		
Pullman 25	Pullman 23	Pullman 75
American Car & Foundry 31	American Car & Foundry 76	American Car & Foundry 80
American Locomotive Works 52	American Locomotive 80	American Locomotive 145
Baldwin Locomotive Works 62	Baldwin Locomotive Works 81	Baldwin Locomotive Works 143
Pressed Steel Car 96	Pressed Steel Car 147	[Pressed Steel Car $25.2]
Westinghouse Air Brake 98	Westinghouse Air Brake 113	Westinghouse Air Brake 149
Railway Steel Spring 102	(American Locomotive 1926)	
Standard Steel Car 133	(Pullman 1934)	
Union Tank Line 170	[Union Tank Car $48.3 no manufacturing]	[Union Tank Car $47.2]
[General American Tank Car $12.8]	General American Tank Car 88	General American Transportation 94
[E. G. Budd Mfg. pvt.]	[E. G. Budd Mfg. $30.9]	Budd 121

The 200 largest industrial enterprises in Great Britain, ranked by market value of shares, 1919.

Rank	Firm	Market value of shares (£ millions)	Major product line (SIC code)
Group 20: Food and kindred products			
7	Arthur Guinness, Son & Co., Ltd.	19.0	2082
22	Watney, Combe, Reid & Co., Ltd.	6.9	2082
28	Maypole Dairy Co., Ltd.	6.2	202
34	Bass, Ratcliffe & Gretton, Ltd.	5.3	2082
36	Scotch Whisky Brands, Ltd.	5.2	2085
45	Distillers' Co., Ltd.	4.3	2085
46	J. Lyons & Co., Ltd.	4.3	205
47	Liebig's Extract of Meat Co., Ltd.	4.3	201
57	John Walker & Sons, Ltd.	3.6	2085
60	British Oil & Cake Mills, Ltd.	3.5	207
61	Mitchells & Butlers, Ltd.	3.5	2082
63	Bovril, Ltd.	3.4	201
64	Union Cold Storage Co., Ltd.	3.4	201
72	Joseph Rank, Ltd.	3.0	204
73	Lipton, Ltd.	3.0	2099
75	Huntley & Palmers, Ltd.	2.9	205
76	Walker & Homfrays, Ltd.	2.9	2082
78	British Cocoa & Chocolate Co., Ltd. (Cadbury)	2.7	2065
81	Abram Lyle & Sons, Ltd.	2.6	2062
82	British & Argentina Meat, Co., Ltd..	2.6	201
85	Mann, Crossman & Paulin, Ltd.	2.5	2082
88	Threlfall's Brewery Co., Ltd.	2.3	2082
89	Whitbread & Co., Ltd.	2.3	2082

Rank	Firm	Market value of shares (£ millions)	Major product line (SIC code)
93	Van den Berghs, Ltd.	2.3	207
99	Samuel Allsopp & Sons, Ltd.	2.2	2082
102	Charrington & Co., Ltd.	2.1	2082
107	Peter Walker & Son, Warrington & Burton, Ltd.	2.0	2082
108	W. & A. Gilbey, Ltd.	2.0	2085
110	Jurgens, Ltd.	2.0	207
114	Cannon Brewery Co., Ltd.	1.9	2082
122	Crosse & Blackwell (Manufacturing Co.), Ltd.	1.8	203
123	Courage & Co., Ltd.	1.8	2082
125	Barklay, Perkins & Co., Ltd.	1.8	2082
126	John Smith's Tadcaster Brewery Co., Ltd.	1.8	2082
127	Rowntree & Co., Ltd.	1.8	2065
128	James Keiller & Son, Ltd.	1.8	203
130	Spillers & Bakers, Ltd.	1.7	204
133	Truman, Hanbury, Buxton & Co., Ltd.	1.7	2082
137	Henry Tate & Sons, Ltd.	1.6	2062
138	Home & Colonial Stores, Ltd.	1.6	2099
144	United Dairies, Ltd.	1.5	202
149	J. S. Fry & Sons, Ltd.	1.5	2065
153	Ind, Coope & Co. (1912), Ltd.	1.4	2082
154	William Younger & Co., Ltd.	1.4	2082
156	Northampton Brewery Co., Ltd.	1.4	2082
160	Holt Brewery Co., Ltd.	1.3	2082
164	Robert Cain & Sons, Ltd.	1.3	2082
167	C. & E. Morton, Ltd.	1.3	2082
170	Bristol Brewery, Georges & Co., Ltd.	1.3	2082
171	Worthington & Co., Ltd.	1.3	2082
173	E. Lazenby & Son, Ltd.	1.3	203
174	Groves & Whitnall, Ltd.	1.2	2082
175	P. Phipps & Co. (Northampton & Towcester Breweries), Ltd.	1.2	2082
176	City of London Brewery Co., Ltd.	1.2	2082
179	Eastmans, Ltd.	1.2	201
182	Meux's Brewery Co., Ltd.	1.2	2082
189	Style & Winch, Ltd.	1.1	2082

Rank	Firm	Market value of shares (£ millions)	Major product line (SIC code)
192	Wilson's Brewery, Ltd.	1.1	2082
194	Olympia Oil & Cake Co., Ltd.	1.1	207
197	Peek, Frean & Co., Ltd.	1.1	205
199	Mackie & Co. Distillers, Ltd.	1.0	2085
Group 21: Tobacco manufactures			
5	Imperial Tobacco Co. (of Great Britain & Ireland), Ltd.	22.8	211
148	Ardath Tobacco Co., Ltd.	1.5	211
172	Gallaher, Ltd.	1.3	211
Group 22: Textile mill products			
2	J. & P. Coats, Ltd.	45.0	228
11	Courtaulds, Ltd.	16.0	2285
15	Fine Cotton Spinners & Doublers' Association, Ltd.	9.9	228
23	Bleachers' Association, Ltd.	6.7	226
27	Calico Printers' Association, Ltd.	6.4	226
31	Bradford Dyers' Association, Ltd.	6.1	226
37	English Sewing Cotton Co., Ltd.	5.0	221
42	Horrockses, Crewdson & Co., Ltd.	4.5	221
44	Linen Thread Co., Ltd.	4.4	229
58	Rylands & Sons, Ltd.	3.6	229
71	British Cellulose & Chemical Manufacturing (Parent) Co., Ltd.	3.1	2285
96	John Haslam & Co., Ltd.	2.2	228
100	Lister & Co., Ltd.	2.1	228
115	Tootal Broadhurst Lee Co., Ltd,	1.9	228
118	Tunnicliffe & Hampson, Ltd.	1.9	228
152	A. & S. Henry & Co., Ltd.	1.4	228
159	Cox Brothers, Ltd.	1.3	229
162	Winterbottom Book Cloth Co., Ltd.	1.3	221
163	F. Steiner & Co., Ltd.	1.3	228
165	Crosses & Winkworth, Ltd.	1.3	228
178	John Bright & Brothers, Ltd.	1.2	228
180	Patons & Baldwins, Ltd.	1.2	228
185	Joshua Hoyle & Sons, Ltd.	1.2	221
187	Barlow & Jones, Ltd.	1.1	228

Rank	Firm	Market value of shares (£ millions)	Major product line (SIC code)
191	Sir Titus Salt Baft, Sons & Co., Ltd.	1.1	228
193	United Turkey Red Co., Ltd.	1.1	228
Group 26: Paper and allied products			
59	Wall Paper Manufacturers, Ltd.	3.6	264
129	John Dickinson & Co., Ltd.	1.7	264
150	Edward Lloyd, Ltd.	1.4	262
Group 27: Printing and publishing			
32	E. Hulton & Co., Ltd.	6.0	271
48	Associated Newspapers, Ltd.	4.2	271
49	Amalgamated Press, Ltd.	4.2	272
117	Pictorial Newspaper Co. (1910), Ltd.	1.9	271
155	Waterlow & Sons, Ltd.	1.4	276
Groups 28: Chemicals and allied products			
4	Lever Brothers, Ltd.	24.3	284
8	Brunner, Mond & Co., Ltd.	18.7	281
10	Nobel Explosives Co., Ltd.	16.3	2892
18	Reckitt & Sons, Ltd.	8.8	284
20	Levinstein, Ltd.	8.0	286
30	United Alkali Co., Ltd.	6.1	281
38	Boots Pure Drug Co., Ltd.	5.0	283
43	Borax Consolidated, Ltd.	4.4	281
68	J. & J. Colman, Ltd.	3.3	284
77	Salt Union, Ltd.	2.8	2899
132	British Dyes, Ltd.	1.7	286
146	Cassell Cyanide Co., Ltd.	1.5	281
166	Beecham Estates & Pills, Ltd.	1.3	283
168	John Knight, Ltd.	1.3	284
Group 29: Petroleum and coal products			
1	Burmah Oil Co., Ltd.	62.8	291
3	Anglo-Persian Oil Co., Ltd.	29.1	291
9	Shell Transport and Trading Co., Ltd.	18.2	291
Group 30: Rubber and miscellaneous plastics products			
17	Dunlop Rubber Co., Ltd.	8.9	301
140	Charles Macintosh & Co., Ltd.	1.5	302
151	India Rubber, Gutta Percha & Telegraph Works Co., Ltd.	1.4	307
Group 31: Leather and leather products			
145	Barrow Hepburn & Gale, Ltd.	1.5	314

Rank	Firm	Market value of shares (£ millions)	Major product line (SIC code)
Group 32: Stone, clay, and glass products			
16	Associated Portland Cement Manufacturers, Ltd.	9.1	324
83	Pilkington Brothers, Ltd.	2.6	321
Group 33: Primary metal industries			
13	United Steel Companies, Ltd.	23.2	331
24	Consett Iron Co., Ltd.	6.6	331
26	Dorman, Long & Co., Ltd.	6.5	331
29	Richard Thomas & Co., Ltd.	6.2	331
33	Mond Nickel Co., Ltd.	5.6	333
35	Hadfields, Ltd.	5.3	331
39	Stewarts & Lloyds, Ltd.	5.0	331
51	Ebbw Vale Steel, Iron and Coal Co., Ltd.	4.0	331
53	John Lysaght, Ltd.	3.9	331
55	Bolckow, Vaughan & Co., Ltd.	3.7	331
62	Stanton Ironworks Co., Ltd.	3.5	331
65	Staveley Coal & Iron Co., Ltd.	3.4	331
67	British Insulated & Helsby Cables, Ltd.	3.4	335
69	Baldwins, Ltd.	3.3	331
70	Pease & Partners, Ltd.	3.1	331
79	British Aluminium Co., Ltd.	2.7	333
95	P. Davies	2.3	331
97	South Durham and Cargo Fleet	2.2	331
98	Sheepbridge Coal & Iron Co., Ltd.	2.2	331
103	Wigan Coal & Iron Co., Ltd.	2.1	331
104	Consolidated Cambrian, Ltd.	2.1	331
113	Telegraph Construction & Maintenance Co., Ltd.	1.9	335
116	John Summers & Sons, Ltd.	1.9	331
120	Tredegar Iron & Coal Co., Ltd.	1.9	331
121	Butterley Co., Ltd.	1.9	331
124	Park Gate Iron & Steel Co., Ltd.	1.8	331
131	David Colville & Sons, Ltd.	1.7	331
136	Thomas Bolton & Sons, Ltd.	1.7	331
143	Vulcan Foundry, Ltd.	1.5	332
147	British Mannesmann Tube Co., Ltd.	1.5	331
157	Alfred Hickman, Ltd.	1.4	331

Rank	Firm	Market value of shares (£ millions)	Major product line (SIC code)
158	Darlington Forge, Ltd.	1.4	331
161	Callender's Cable & Construction Co., Ltd.	1.3	335
169	Coltness Iron Co., Ltd.	1.3	331
177	Barrow Haemetite Steel Co., Ltd.	1.2	331
183	Thomas W. Ward, Ltd.	1.2	331
184	W. T. Henley's Telegraph Works Co., Ltd.	1.2	335
190	Glasgow Iron & Steel Co., Ltd.	1.1	331
195	William Jessop & Sons, Ltd.	1.1	331
198	Herbert Morris, Ltd.	1.1	331
Group 34: Fabricated metal products			
19	Guest, Keen & Nettlefolds, Ltd.	8.2	345
Groups 35: Machinery, except electrical			
25	Babcock & Wilcox, Ltd.	6.5	351
52	Platt Brothers & Co., Ltd.	4.0	3552
80	Howard & Bullough, Ltd.	2.7	3552
91	Linotype & Machinery, Ltd.	2.3	3559
105	Ruston & Hornsby, Ltd.	2.1	352
112	Mather & Platt, Ltd.	2.0	3552
135	British United Shoe Machinery Co., Ltd.	1.7	3636
Group 36: Electric and electronic equipment			
50	Metropolitan-Vickers Electrical Co., Ltd.	4.0	361
54	English Electric Co., Ltd.	3.8	361
94	Siemens Brothers & Co., Ltd.	2.3	361
119	General Electric Co., Ltd.	1.9	361
181	British Thompson-Houston Co., Ltd.	1.2	361
200	Gramophone Co., Ltd.	1.0	3652
Group 37: Transportation equipment			
6	Vickers, Ltd.	19.5	373
12	Metropolitan Carriage, Wagon, & Finance Co., Ltd.	14.4	374
14	Sir W. G. Armstrong, Whitworth & Co., Ltd.	12.2	373
21	John Brown & Co., Ltd.	7.7	373
40	Cammell, Laird & Co., Ltd.	4.8	373
41	Birmingham Small Arms Co., Ltd.	4.6	375

Rank	Firm	Market value of shares (£ millions)	Major product line (SIC code)
56	Swan, Hunter & Wigham-Richardson, Ltd.	3.6	373
66	Austin Motor Co., Ltd.	3.4	3711
74	William Doxford & Sons, Ltd.	3.0	373
84	Pearson & Knowles Coal & Iron Co., Ltd.	2.5	373
86	North British Locomotive Co., Ltd.	2.4	374
90	Harland & Wolff, Ltd.	2.3	373
92	Leyland Motors, Ltd.	2.3	3711
101	William Beardmore & Co., Ltd.	2.1	373
106	Workman, Clark & Co., Ltd.	2.1	373
109	Ford Motor Co. (England), Ltd.	2.0	3711
134	Birmingham Railway Carriage & Wagon Co., Ltd.	1.7	374
139	R. & W. Hawthorn, Lesley & Co., Ltd.	1.5	373
141	William Gray & Co. (1918), Ltd.	1.5	373
142	Rolls-Royce, Ltd.	1.5	3711
186	H. & C. Grayson, Ltd.	1.2	373
188	Dennis Brothers, Ltd.	1.2	3711
196	Aircraft Manufacturing Co., Ltd.	1.1	372
Group 39: Miscellaneous manufacturing industries			
87	Bryant & May, Ltd.	2.4	399
111	Michael Nairn & Co., Ltd.	2.0	399

The 200 largest industrial enterprises in Great Britain, ranked by market value of shares, 1930.

Rank	Firm	Market value of shares (£ millions)	Product lines (SIC codes) Major	Others
Group 20: Food and kindred products				
8	Distillers' Co., Ltd.	45.5	2085	2099, 281
9	Arthur Guinness, Son & Co., Ltd.	43.0	2082	
16	Watney, Combe, Reid & Co., Ltd.	18.5	2082	
19	Union Cold Storage Co., Ltd.	14.1	201	
22	Bass, Ratcliff & Gretton, Ltd.	13.3	2082	
25	J. Lyons & Co., Ltd.	12.1	205	202, 2065
27	Bovril, Ltd.	10.8	201	
28	British Cocoa and Chocolate Co., Ltd. (Cadbury-Fry)	10.3	2065	
31	P. Walker (Warrington) & Robert Cain & Sons, Ltd.	10.0	2082	
32	Mitchells & Butlers, Ltd.	9.9	2082	
36	Tate & Lyle, Ltd.	9.3	2062	
43	Hoare & Co., Ltd.	7.6	2082	
45	Taylor, Walker & Co., Ltd.	7.5	2082	
47	United Dairies, Ltd.	7.3	202	
48	Barclay, Parkins & Co., Ltd.	7.1	2082	
50	Liebig's Extract of Meat Co., Ltd.	6.9	201	
54	Samuel Allsopp & Sons, Ltd.	6.4	2082	
57	Lipton, Ltd.	6.3	2099	201, 202
59	Courage & Co., Ltd.	6.0	2082	
64	Threlfall's Brewery Co., Ltd.	5.5	2082	
65	Ind, Coope & Co., Ltd.	5.3	2082	
72	Charrington & Co., Ltd.	5.0	2082	
74	City of London Brewery Co., Ltd.	4.8	2082	

Rank	Firm	Market value of shares (£ millions)	Product lines (SIC codes)	
			Major	Others
75	Mann, Crossman & Paulin, Ltd.	4.7	2082	
77	Truman, Hanbury, Buxton & Co., Ltd.	4.6	2082	
81	Whitbread & Co., Ltd.	4.4	2082	
82	Joseph Rank, Ltd.	4.4	204	
86	John Smith's Tadcater Brewery Co., Ltd.	4.1	2082	
89	Spillers, Ltd.	4.0	204	
91	Manbré & Garton, Ltd.	3.8	2082	
92	Rowntree & Co., Ltd.	3.7	2065	
93	Ansells Brewery, Ltd.	3.7	2082	
94	Crosse & Blackwell (Manufacturing Co.), Ltd.	3.7	203	
107	Cerebos, Ltd.	3.3	2099	
112	Meux's Brewery Co., Ltd.	3.2	2082	
113	Barratt & Co., Ltd.	3.1	2065	
115	Associated Biscuit Manufacturers, Ltd.	3.1	205	
125	Groves & Whitnall, Ltd.	2.8	2082	
127	Matthew Brown & Co., Ltd.	2.7	2082	
129	Benskin's Watford Brewery, Ltd.	2.5	2082	
132	Wolverhampton & Dudley Breweries, Ltd.	2.4	2082	
137	H. & G. Simonds, Ltd.	2.3	2082	
139	H. P. Sauce, Ltd.	2.3	2099	203
143	W. & A. Gilbey, Ltd.	2.3	2085	
146	Holt Brewery Co., Ltd.	2.1	2082	
149	Schweppes, Ltd.	2.1	2086	
151	Aerated Bread Co., Ltd.	2.1	205	203, 2099
153	Tamplin & Son's Brewery, Brighton, Ltd.	2.0	2082	
157	Bristol Brewery, Georges & Co., Ltd.	2.0	2082	
158	Marston, Thompson & Evershed, Ltd.	2.0	2082	
159	P. Phipps & Co. (Northampton & Towcester Breweries), Ltd.	2.0	2082	
164	James Shipstone & Sons, Ltd.	1.8	2082	
167	Walker & Homfrays, Ltd.	1.7	2082	
170	Usher's Wiltshire Brewery, Ltd.	1.7	2082	

Rank	Firm	Market value of shares (£ millions)	Product lines (SIC codes)	
			Major	Others
177	Aplin & Barrett & the Western Countries Creameries, Ltd.	1.6	202	
181	Parker's Burslem Brewery, Ltd.	1.6	2082	
185	Brooke, Bond & Co., Ltd.	1.5	2099	
189	Associated Breweries, Ltd.	1.4	2082	
190	William Younger & Co., Ltd.	1.4	2082	
193	Wenlock Brewery Co., Ltd.	1.4	2082	
194	Friary Holroyd & Healy's Breweries, Ltd.	1.4	2082	
195	Associated British Maltsters, Ltd.	1.4	2082	
199	W. Butler & Co., Ltd.	1.4	2082	
Group 21: Tobacco manufactures				
2	Imperial Tobacco Co. (of Great Britain & Ireland), Ltd.	130.5	211	213
30	Carreras, Ltd.	10.0	211	213
141	Godfrey Phillips, Ltd.	2.3	211	213
144	Gallaher, Ltd.	2.3	211	213
Group 22: Textile mill products				
6	Courtaulds, Ltd.	51.9	2285	
7	J. & P. Coats, Ltd.	47.4	228	
35	Fine Cotton Spinners' & Doublers' Association, Ltd.	9.8	228	
51	Bleachers' Association, Ltd.	6.9	226	
52	British Celanese, Ltd.	6.9	2285	285
56	Combined Egyptian Mills, Ltd.	6.3	228	
61	Winterbottom Book Cloth Co., Ltd.	5.8	221	226
66	Bradford Dyers' Association, Ltd.	5.4	226	
70	Lancashire Cotton Corp., Ltd.	4.9	228	
73	English Sewing Cotton Co., Ltd.	4.9	221	
76	Linen Thread Co., Ltd.	4.6	229	
78	Calico Printers' Association, Ltd.	4.5	226	
96	Rylands & Sons, Ltd.	3.6	229	
108	Patons & Baldwins, Ltd.	3.2	228	
154	Fleming, Reid & Co., Ltd.	2.0	228	225
172	Woolcombers, Ltd.	1.6	229	
183	Joshua Hoyle & Sons, Ltd.	1.5	221	
188	Whitworth & Mitchell, Ltd.	1.5	221	

Rank	Firm	Market value of shares (£ millions)	Product lines (SIC codes) Major	Others
197	Porritts & Spencer, Ltd.	1.4	229	
198	Lister & Co., Ltd.	1.4	228	
200	Cook, Son & Co. (St. Paul's), Ltd.	1.3	228	
Group 23: Apparel and other textile products				
174	Wolsey, Ltd.	1.6	232	252
Group 26: Paper and allied products				
41	Wall Paper Manufacturers, Ltd.	7.9	264	
62	Inveresk Paper Co., Ltd.	5.7	262	
90	Wiggins, Teape & Co. (1919), Ltd.	3.8	264	
120	E. S. & A. Robinson, Ltd.	2.9	264	265, 275
124	John Dickinson & Co., Ltd.	2.8	264	262
Group 27: Printing and publishing				
12	Allied Newspapers, Ltd.	27.6	271	
17	Daily Mail Trust, Ltd.	15.6	271	
37	Daily Mirror Newspapers, Ltd.	8.8	271	
100	Odhams Press, Ltd.	3.4	272	271, 273, 275
114	George Outram & Co., Ltd.	3.1	271	
123	Liverpool Daily Post & Echo, Ltd.	2.8	271	
142	London Express Newspaper, Ltd.	2.3	271	
156	George Newnes, Ltd.	2.0	272	
178	Waterlow & Sons, Ltd.	1.6	276	
186	Times Publishing Co., Ltd.	1.5	271	
Group 28: Chemicals and allied products				
1	Unilever, Ltd.	132.0	284	203, 204, 2091
4	Imperial Chemical Industries, Ltd.	77.3	281	285, 286, 287, 204, 327, 333, 335, 348, 352, 364, 375
21	Reckitt & Sons, Ltd.	13.4	284	281, 203, 204
23	Boots Pure Drug Co., Ltd.	12.8	283	
55	Pinchin, Johnson & Co., Ltd.	6.3	285	
105	Goodlass, Wall & Co., Ltd.	3.3	285	
109	Borax Consolidated, Ltd.	3.2	281	
116	Salt Union, Ltd.	3.1	2899	2099
136	Cooper, McDougall & Robertson, Ltd.	2.4	287	
138	Beechams Pills, Ltd.	2.3	283	
160	British Briquettes, Ltd.	1.9	286	

Rank	Firm	Market value of shares (£ millions)	Product lines (SIC codes) Major	Others
Group 29: Petroleum and coal products				
3	"Shell" Transport & Trading Co., Ltd.	104.6	291	
5	Anglo-Persian Oil Co., Ltd.	59.8	291	
10	Burmah Oil Co., Ltd.	33.4	291	
40	Candles, Ltd.	8.0	299	
Group 30: Rubber and miscellaneous plastics products				
11	Dunlop Rubber Co., Ltd.	28.2	301	2296, 375, 394
162	India Tyre & Rubber Co. (Great Britain), Ltd.	1.8	301	
180	Goodyear Tyre & Rubber Co. (Great Britain), Ltd.	1.6	301	
Group 31: Leather and leather products				
38	J. Sears & Co. (True-form Boot Co.), Ltd.	8.5	314	
Group 32: Stone, clay, and glass products				
20	Associated Portland Cement Manufacturers, Ltd.	13.9	324	
24	Turner & Newall, Ltd.	12.6	329	249, 283
103	London Brick Co. & Forders, Ltd.	3.4	325	
106	Morgan Crucible Co., Ltd.	3.3	325	
117	Pilkington Brothers, Ltd.	3.0	321	
165	United Glass Bottle Manufacturers, Ltd.	1.8	322	
176	Allied Cement Manufacturers, Ltd.	1.6	324	
Group 33: Primary metal industries				
29	Mond Nickel Co., Ltd.	10.3	333	
33	Dorman, Long & Co., Ltd.	9.8	331	
46	British Insulate Cables, Ltd.	7.5	335	
49	Stewarts & Lloyds, Ltd.	7.1	331	332
53	United Steel Companies, Ltd.	6.7	331	
63	British Aluminium Co., Ltd.	5.5	333	
69	Callender's Cable & Construction Co., Ltd.	5.1	335	
71	John Summers & Sons, Ltd.	5.0	331	
83	Amalgamated Metal Corp., Ltd.	4.3	333	
87	W. T. Henley's Telegraph Works Co., Ltd.	4.1	335	
88	Baldwins, Ltd.	4.0	331	
102	Stavely Coal & Iron Co., Ltd.	3.4	331	

Rank	Firm	Market value of shares (£ millions)	Product lines (SIC codes) Major	Others
104	Consett Iron Co., Ltd.	3.3	331	
110	Hadfields, Ltd.	3.2	331	3532
111	Stanton Ironworks Co., Ltd.	3.2	331	
122	Richard Thomas & Co., Ltd.	2.9	331	
133	Consolidated Tin Smelters, Ltd.	2.4	333	
147	Ebbw Vale Steel, Iron & Coal Co., Ltd.	2.1	331	
155	Enfield Cable Works, Ltd.	2.0	335	
161	South Durham and Cargo Fleet	1.8	331	
171	Allied Ironfounders, Ltd.	1.6	332	
179	British Ropes, Ltd.	1.6	331	229
182	Coltness Iron Co., Ltd.	1.5	331	
192	Thos. W. Ward, Ltd.	1.4	331	324, 325, 353
Group 34: Fabricated metal products				
14	Guest, Keen & Nettlefolds, Ltd.	20.3	345	344, 346, 349
68	Radiation, Ltd.	5.1	343	358
98	J. Stone & Co., Ltd.	3.5	344	
99	Tube Investments, Ltd.	3.5	344	
126	Crittall Manufacturing Co., Ltd.	2.8	344	336
140	J. G. Graves, Ltd.	2.3	344	
163	Metal Box, Ltd.	1.8	341	342, 344, 346
168	Parkinson & Cowan, Ltd.	1.7	344	
Group 35: Machinery, except electrical				
26	Babcock & Wilcox, Ltd.	11.0	351	344
42	British United Shoe Machinery Co., Ltd.	7.7	3636	
119	Mather & Platt, Ltd.	3.0	3551	356, 361
131	Linotype & Machinery, Ltd.	2.4	3555	
148	W. & T. Avery, Ltd.	2.1	3576	
166	Platt Brothers & Co., Ltd.	1.7	3552	
Group 36: Electric and electronic equipment				
18	General Electric Co., Ltd.	14.5	361	364, 354
34	Associated Electrical Industries, Ltd.	9.8	361	363, 364, 365
58	Gramophone Co., Ltd.	6.2	3652	
67	Columbia Graphophone Co., Ltd.	5.3	3652	
95	Siemens Brothers & Co., Ltd.	3.7	361	366
118	Chloride Electrical Storage Co., Ltd.	3.0	3691	

Rank	Firm	Market value of shares (£ millions)	Product lines (SIC codes)	
			Major	Others
130	English Electric Co., Ltd.	2.4	361	363
145	Ever Ready Co. (Great Britain), Ltd.	2.2	3691	
173	A. Reyrolle & Co., Ltd.	1.6	361	
187	International Automatic Telephone Co., Ltd.	1.5	366	
Group 37: Transportation equipment				
13	Ford Motor Co., Ltd.	21.2	3711	352
15	Vickers, Ltd.	19.6	373	331
44	Morris Motors, Ltd.	7.6	3711	
60	Armstrong Whitworth Securities Co., Ltd.	6.0	373	331
84	John Brown & Son, Ltd.	4.3	373	331
85	Austin Motor Co., Ltd.	4.3	3711	
97	Joseph Lucas, Ltd.	3.6	3714	
101	Birmingham Small Arms Co., Ltd.	3.4	375	348
121	Swan, Hunter & Wigham-Richardson, Ltd.	2.9	373	
134	Harland & Wolff, Ltd.	2.4	373	
135	Leyland Motors, Ltd.	2.4	3711	
152	Dennis Brothers, Ltd.	2.1	3711	
169	Cammell, Laird & Co., Ltd.	1.7	373	
175	Rolls-Royce, Ltd.	1.6	3711	
184	Birmingham Railway Carriage & Wagon Co., Ltd.	1.5	374	
191	D. Napier & Son, Ltd.	1.4	372	
196	S. T. D. Motors, Ltd.	1.4	3711	
Group 38: Instruments and related products				
128	Amalgamated Dental Co., Ltd.	2.7	3843	
150	Ilford, Ltd.	2.1	386	
Group 39: Miscellaneous manufacturing industries				
39	British Match Corp., Ltd.	8.1	399	
79	Barry & Staines Linoleum, Ltd.	4.4	399	
80	Michael Nairn & Co., Ltd.	4.4	399	

The 200 largest industrial enterprises in Great Britain, ranked by market value of shares, 1948.

Rank	Firm	Market value of shares (£ millions)	Major	Others
Group 20: Food and kindred products				
6	Distillers' Co., Ltd.	127.6	2085	207, 2099, 281, 283, 286
7	Arthur Guinness Son & Co., Ltd.	67.0	2082	
17	Tate & Lyle, Ltd.	29.8	2062	
19	J. Lyons & Co., Ltd.	28.0	205	202, 2086, 2099, hotels
23	Bass, Ratcliffe & Gretton, Ltd.	27.3	2082	
28	Watney, Combe, Reid & Co., Ltd.	24.3	2082	
38	Union Cold Storage Co., Ltd.	19.2	201	shipping
40	Ranks, Ltd.	18.3	204	
42	Walker Cain, Ltd.	17.3	2082	2085
43	Mitchells & Butlers, Ltd.	17.3	2082	2085
44	United Dairies, Ltd.	16.9	202	3551, 342
47	Charrington & Co., Ltd.	15.7	2082	
52	Spillers, Ltd.	14.7	204	
59	Ind, Coope & Allsopp, Ltd.	13.5	2082	
60	Ansell's Brewery, Ltd.	13.1	2082	
64	Allied Bakeries, Ltd.	12.6	205	
70	Taylor, Walker & Co., Ltd.	11.3	2082	
73	British Cocoa & Chocolate Co., Ltd. (Cadbury-Fry)	10.9	2065	
76	Courage & Co., Ltd.	10.7	2082	
78	Cerebos, Ltd.	10.3	2099	
86	Barclay, Perkins & Co., Ltd.	9.5	2082	
87	Manbré & Garton, Ltd.	9.3	2082	
90	H. & G. Simonds, Ltd.	8.9	2082	
92	Truman, Hanbury, Buxton & Co., Ltd.	8.8	2082	

Rank	Firm	Market value of shares (£ millions)	Product lines (SIC codes)	
			Major	Others
102	Threlfall's Brewery Co., Ltd.	8.0	2082	2086
108	Liebig's Extract of Meat Co., Ltd.	7.5	201	shipping
111	Bristol Brewery, Georges & Co., Ltd.	7.4	2082	
112	Bovril, Ltd.	7.3	201	
117	John Smith's Tadcaster Brewery Co., Ltd.	7.0	2082	
118	Whitbread & Co., Ltd.	7.0	2082	
120	John Mackintosh & Sons, Ltd.	6.9	2065	
127	Associated Biscuit Manufacturers, Ltd.	6.7	205	2065
128	H. P. Sauce, Ltd.	6.6	2099	203
131	Scottish Brewers, Ltd.	6.6	2082	
137	Mann, Crossman & Paulin, Ltd.	6.1	2082	
142	W. & A. Gilbey, Ltd.	6.0	2085	
151	British Sugar Corp., Ltd.	5.6	2063	
153	Brooke, Bond & Co., Ltd.	5.5	2099	
154	City of London Brewery Investment Trust, Ltd.	5.5	2082	
160	Rowntree & Co., Ltd.	5.2	2065	
163	Cow & Gate, Ltd.	5.2	202	
164	United Biscuits, Ltd.	5.1	205	
165	Joshua Tetley & Son, Ltd.	5.1	2082	
167	Hammonds United Breweries, Ltd.	5.1	2082	
175	Benskin's Watford Brewery, Ltd.	4.9	2082	
182	Matthew Brown & Co., Ltd.	4.8	2082	
185	Wolverhampton & Dudley Breweries, Ltd.	4.7	2082	
186	W. Butler & Co., Ltd.	4.7	2082	
187	P. Phipps & Co., Ltd.	4.7	2082	
189	Vaux & Associated Breweries, Ltd.	4.6	2082	hotels
190	McDougalls Trust, Ltd.	4.6	2041	
193	Brickwood & Co., Ltd.	4.5	2082	
195	Strong & Co. of Romsey, Ltd.	4.5	2062	
Group 21: Tobacco manufactures				
1	Imperial Tobacco Co. (of Great Britain & Ireland), Ltd.	257.8	211	212, 213
25	Carreras, Ltd.	25.6	211	213, 3559

Rank	Firm	Market value of shares (£ millions)	Product lines (SIC codes) Major	Others
45	Gallaher, Ltd.	16.4	211	212, 213
99	Charles Phillips & Co., Ltd.	8.3	211	
173	Arthur Lewis & Co. (Westminster), Ltd.	4.9	211	212, 213
184	Amalgamated Tobacco Corp., Ltd.	4.8	211	

Group 22: Textile mill products

Rank	Firm	Market value of shares (£ millions)	Major	Others
8	Courtaulds, Ltd.	57.1	2285	
11	J. & P. Coats, Ltd.	53.9	226	
32	British Celanese, Ltd.	23.3	2285	
56	Fine Spinners & Doublers, Ltd.	13.8	226	
68	Patons & Baldwins, Ltd.	12.0	226	
88	Calico Printers' Association, Ltd.	9.2	226	221, 226
89	Lancashire Cotton Corp., Ltd.	9.1	228	221
95	Winterbottom Book Cloth Co., Ltd.	8.5	221	226
114	Bradford Dyers' Association, Ltd.	7.2	226	
116	Linen Thread Co., Ltd.	7.2	229	
121	Bleachers' Association, Ltd.	6.9	226	
138	Combined Egyptian Mills, Ltd.	6.0	228	
139	English Sewing Cotton Co., Ltd.	6.0	221	
168	James Templeton & Co., Ltd.	5.0	227	228
178	Allied Industrial Services, Ltd.	4.8	221	228
183	James Nelson, Ltd.	4.8	222	228
198	Joshua Hoyle & Sons, Ltd.	4.5	221	222, 226, 228

Group 23: Apparel and other textile products

Rank	Firm	Market value of shares (£ millions)	Major	Others
49	Montague Burton, Ltd.	15.0	231	
133	Price's Trust Co., Ltd. (Price Tailors)	6.2	231	

Group 26: Paper and allied products

Rank	Firm	Market value of shares (£ millions)	Major	Others
26	Bowater Paper Corp., Ltd.	24.9	262	
65	Wall Paper Manufacturers, Ltd.	12.4	264	
69	Wiggins Teape & Co. (1919), Ltd.	11.9	264	262
85	John Dickinson & Co., Ltd.	9.5	264	262, 277, 278, 307, 395
110	E. S. & A. Robinson, Ltd.	7.4	264	265, 275
124	Inveresk Paper Co., Ltd.	6.8	262	

Rank	Firm	Market value of shares (£ millions)	Product lines (SIC codes) Major	Others
Group 27: Printing and publishing				
16	Kemsley Newspapers, Ltd.	31.8	271	
50	Daily Mail & General Trust, Ltd.	14.8	271	
66	Amalgamated Press, Ltd.	12.3	272	
77	Daily Mirror Newspapers, Ltd.	10.6	271	
113	Odhams Press, Ltd.	7.3	272	271, 275
126	London Express Newspaper, Ltd.	6.8	271	
194	"News of the World," Ltd.	4.5	272	
Group 28: Chemicals and allied products				
3	Imperial Chemical Industries, Ltd.	197.5	281	282, 283, 285, 286, 2892, 333, 335
4	Unilever, Ltd.	183.6	284	203, 204, 2091
14	Reckitt & Sons, Ltd.	33.6	284	281, 283, 203, 2099
29	Boots Pure Drug Co., Ltd.	23.7	283	
34	Beecham Group, Ltd.	22.4	283	284, 286, 287, 203, 205, 2065
36	British Oxygen Co., Ltd.	21.2	281	
61	Pinchin, Johnson & Associates, Ltd.	13.0	285	
72	Monsanto Chemicals, Ltd.	10.9	286	
75	Fisons, Ltd.	10.7	287	
97	Borax Consolidated, Ltd.	8.3	284	mining
104	Goodlass Wall & Lead Industries, Ltd.	7.9	285	333
132	Albright & Wilson, Ltd.	6.3	281	
169	Lewis Berger & Sons, Ltd.	5.0	285	
174	Sangers, Ltd.	4.9	283	
177	International Paint & Compositions Co., Ltd.	4.8	285	
188	Yardley & Co., Ltd.	4.7	284	
192	Glaxo Laboratories, Ltd.	4.5	283	
Group 29: Petroleum and coal products				
2	Anglo-Iranian Oil Co., Ltd.	204.4	291	299
5	"Shell" Transport & Trading Co., Ltd.	173.1	291	299
9	Burmah Oil Co., Ltd.	56.4	291	299, 284, 399
Group 30: Rubber and miscellaneous plastics products				
10	Dunlop Rubber Co., Ltd.	55.9	301	302, 306, 2295, 239, 375, 394
158	British Tyre & Rubber Co., Ltd.	5.3	301	

Rank	Firm	Market value of shares (£ millions)	Product lines (SIC codes) Major	Others
Group 31: Leather and leather products				
74	J. Sears & Co. (True-form Boot Co.), Ltd.	10.9	314	313
Group 32: Stone, clay, and glass products				
21	Associated Portland Cement Manufacturers, Ltd.	28.0	324	
24	Turner & Newall, Ltd.	25.9	329	
80	British Plaster Board, Ltd.	10.1	327	264, 266
81	Morgan Crucible Co., Ltd.	9.8	325	329
84	Pilkington Brothers, Ltd.	9.6	321	
123	London Brick Co., Ltd.	6.9	325	
125	United Glass Bottle Manufacturers, Ltd.	6.8	322	
199	Tunnel Portland Cement Co., Ltd.	4.4	324	
Group 33: Primary metal industries				
15	Stewart & Lloyds, Ltd.	31.9	331	332
22	Richard Thomas & Baldwins, Ltd.	27.7	331	335
33	Steel Co. of Wales, Ltd.	22.5	331	
35	British Insulated Callender's Cables, Ltd.	21.2	335	
37	United Steel Companies, Ltd.	21.0	331	
48	Staveley Coal & Iron Co., Ltd.	15.1	331	332
51	British Aluminium Co., Ltd.	14.7	333	
53	John Summers & Sons, Ltd.	14.5	331	
54	Dorman, Long & Co., Ltd.	14.5	331	construction
58	Mond Nickel Co., Ltd.	13.5	333	
62	Lancashire Steel Corp. Ltd.	13.0	331	
71	Colvilles, Ltd.	11.0	331	
96	Wm. Baird & Co., Ltd.	8.5	331	mining
98	Consett Iron Co., Ltd.	8.3	331	325, 299
106	British Ropes, Ltd.	7.8	331	229
107	Allied Ironfounders, Ltd.	7.7	332	
135	Thos. W. Ward, Ltd.	6.2	331	324, 325, 353
140	Amalgamated Metal Corp., Ltd.	6.0	333	
147	Imperial Smelting Corp., Ltd.	5.8	333	281
155	Pease and Partners, Ltd.	5.5	331	332, 285, 299
156	Murex, Ltd.	5.4	333	
166	Sheepbridge Coal & Iron Co., Ltd.	5.1	331	353, mining
170	Butterley Co., Ltd.	5.0	331	344, mining, construction

Rank	Firm	Market value of shares (£ millions)	Product lines (SIC codes)	
			Major	Others
180	Whitehead Iron & Steel Co., Ltd.	4.8	331	
200	Renold & Coventry Chain Co., Ltd.	4.4	331	349
Group 34: Fabricated metal products				
13	Guest, Keen & Nettlefolds, Ltd.	35.3	345	344, 346, 349, 325
30	Tube Investments, Ltd.	23.4	344	347, 251, 252, 285, 331, 335, 375
63	Metal Box Co., Ltd.	12.8	341	342, 344, 346, 264, 265, 275, 386
109	Radiation, Ltd.	7.5	343	358
171	Superheater Co., Ltd.	5.0	343	344
172	Crittal Manufacturing Co., Ltd.	4.9	344	
179	J. Brockhouse & Co., Ltd.	4.8	346	344, 349, 331, 354, 356, 3714
Group 35: Machinery, except electrical				
41	British United Shoe Machinery Co., Ltd.	17.5	3636	
46	Babcock & Wilcox, Ltd.	16.3	351	344
129	Platt Brothers & Co. (Holdings), Ltd.	6.6	3552	
130	Ruston & Hornsby, Ltd.	6.6	351	344
136	R. A. Lister & Co., Ltd.	6.1	351	352, 364, 371
148	G. & J. Weir, Ltd.	5.7	356	
150	Skefco Ball Bearing Co., Ltd.	5.6	3562	
157	Alfred Herbert, Ltd.	5.4	354	
162	W. & T. Avery, Ltd.	5.2	3576	332
196	Herbert Morris, Ltd.	4.5	353	344
Group 36: Electric and electronic equipment				
18	Associated Electrical Industries, Ltd.	28.9	361	363, 364, 365, 366
20	General Electric Co., Ltd.	28.0	361	364, 321, 326, 354
57	English Electric Co., Ltd.	13.8	361	363, 372
79	Crompton Parkinson, Ltd.	10.2	361	3691, 335
91	Electric & Musical Industries, Ltd.	8.9	3652	3561
103	Ever Ready Co. (Great Britain), Ltd.	8.0	3692	364
105	Hoover, Ltd.	7.9	363	
152	Chloride Electrical Storage Co., Ltd.	5.5	3691	
176	Siemens Brothers & Co., Ltd.	4.9	361	364, 366, 3692, 335

Rank	Firm	Market value of shares (£ millions)	Product lines (SIC codes)	
			Major	Others
191	Plessey Co., Ltd.	4.6	361	364
197	Automatic Telephone & Electric Co., Ltd.	4.5	366	361
Group 37: Transportation equipment				
12	Vickers, Ltd.	39.3	373	307, 348, 3551, 358, 382
27	Morris Motors, Ltd.	24.8	3711	354, 359
31	Ford Motor Co., Ltd.	23.3	3711	372, 352
55	Austin Motor Co., Ltd.	14.1	3711	
67	John S. Brown & Sons, Ltd.	12.1	373	353
82	Joseph Lucas, Ltd.	9.8	3714	372, 375, 364
83	Hawker Siddeley Group, Ltd.	9.6	372	3714
93	Associated Commercial Vehicles, Ltd.	8.7	3711	
100	Standard Motor Co., Ltd.	8.0	3711	
101	Harland & Wolff, Ltd.	8.0	373	
115	Raleigh Industries, Ltd.	7.2	375	
119	Cammell, Laird & Co., Ltd.	6.9	373	
122	Leyland Motors, Ltd.	6.9	3711	
134	Bristol Aeroplane Co., Ltd.	6.2	372	3714, 344
141	Rootes Securities, Ltd.	6.0	3711	
143	Vauxhall Motors, Ltd.	6.0	3711	
144	Swan, Hunter, & Wigham-Richardson, Ltd.	5.9	373	
145	Pressed Steel Co., Ltd.	5.9	3711	372, 358
146	Birmingham Small Arms Co., Ltd.	5.8	375	3714, 348, 354
149	Rolls-Royce, Ltd.	5.6	3711	372
181	Briggs Motor Bodies, Ltd.	4.8	3711	346
Group 38: Instruments and related products				
161	Ilford, Ltd.	5.2	386	
Group 39: Miscellaneous manufacturing industries				
39	British Match Corp., Ltd.	18.6	399	
94	Michael Nairn & Greenwich, Ltd.	8.6	399	
159	Barry & Staines Linoleum, Ltd.	5.3	399	

Turnover in the list of those of the 200 largest industrial enterprises in Great Britain that are in the food, chemical, and machinery industries, 1919, 1930, 1948. Rank number follows the company name.

1919 (Market value of shares over £1.0 million)	1930 (Market value of shares over £1.3 million)	1948 (Market value of shares over £4.4 million)
Group 20: Food and kindred products		
201: Meat products		
Union Cold Storage 64	Union Cold Storage 19	Union Cold Storage 38
British & Argentina Meat 82	(Union Cold Storage 1923)[a]	
Liebig's Extract of Meat 47	Liebig's Extract of Meat 50	Liebig's Extract of Meat 108
Bovril 63	Bovril 27	Bovril 112
202: Dairy products		
Maypole Dairy 28	(Home & Colonial Stores 1924)	
United Dairies 144	United Dairies 47	United Dairies 44
[Aplin & Barrett pvt.][b]	Aplin & Barrett 177	[Aplin & Barrett £1.1]
[West Surrey Central Dairy pvt.]	[Cow & Gate £0.7]	Cow & Gate 163
203: Canned fruits and vegetables		
Crosse & Blackwell 122	Crosse & Blackwell 94	[Crosse & Blackwell (Holdings) £2.5]
J. Keiller 128	(Crosse & Blackwell 1919)	
E. Lazenby 173	(Crosse & Blackwell 1919)	
204: Grain mill products		
J. Rank 72	J. Rank 82	Ranks 40
Spillers & Bakers 130	Spillers 89	Spillers 52
[McDougalls pvt.]	[McDougalls pvt.]	McDougalls Trust 190
205: Bakery products		
J. Lyons 46	J. Lyons 25	J. Lyons 19

a. If a firm was merged with or fully acquired by another, the name of the acquiring or merged enterprise and the year of acquisition or merger is given in parenthesis.

b. Brackets indicate that a company's assets were not sufficient for it to be included in the 200 largest industrial enterprises for the year in which it is listed (in which case total assets are given), or that the company was privately held (pvt.) and total assets are not available.

1919 (Market value of shares over £1.0 million)	1930 (Market value of shares over £1.3 million)	1948 (Market value of shares over £4.4 million)
Huntley & Palmers 75	Associated Biscuit Manufacturers 115	Associated Biscuit Manufacturers 127
Peak, Frean 197	(Associated Biscuit Manufacturers 1921)	
[Aerated Bread £0.8]	Aerated Bread 151	[Aerated Bread £4.1] Allied Bakeries 64 United Biscuits 164

206: Sugar and confectionery products
2062: Cane sugar refining

Abram Lyle 81	Tate & Lyle 36	Tate & Lyle 17
Henry Tate 137	(Tate & Lyle 1921)	

2063: Beet sugar

British Sugar 151

2065: Confectionery and cocoa products

British Cocoa and Chocolate (Cadbury) 78	British Cocoa and Chocolate (Cadbury-Fry) 28	British Cocoa and Chocolate (Cadbury-Fry) 73
Rountree 127	Rountree 91	Rountree 160
J. S. Fry 149	(British Cocoa & Chocolate 1920)	
[Barratt £0.5]	Barratt 113	[Barratt £2.3]
[John Mackintosh pvt.]	[John Mackintosh & Sons £0.8]	John Mackintosh 120

207: Fats and oils

British Oil & Cake Mills 60	(Lever Brothers 1925)	
Van den Berghs 93	Unilever 1 in Group 28	Unilever 4 in Group 28
Jurgens 110	Unilever 1 in Group 28	Unilever 4 in Group 28
Olympia Oil & Cake 194	(Jurgens 1920)	

208: Beverages
2082: Malt beverages

Guiness 7	Guiness 9	Guiness 7
Watney, Combe, Reid 22	Watney, Combe, Reid 16	Watney, Combe, Reid 28
Bass, Ratcliffe & Gretton 34	Bass, Ratcliffe & Gretton 22	Bass, Ratcliffe & Gretton 23
Mitchells & Butlers 61	Mitchells & Butlers 32	Mitchells & Butlers 43
Walker & Homfrays 76	Walker & Homfrays 167	[Walker & Homfrays £1.8]
Mann, Crossman & Paulin 85	Mann, Crossman & Paulin 75	Mann, Crossman & Paulin 137
Threlfall's Brewery 88	Threlfall's Brewery 64	Threlfall's Brewery 102
Whitbread 89	Whitbread 81	Whitbread 118

1919 (Market value of shares over £1.0 million)	1930 (Market value of shares over £1.3 million)	1948 (Market value of shares over £4.4 million)
Samuel Allsopp 94	Samuel Allsopp 54	(Ind Coope & Allsopp 1934)
Charrington 102	Charrington 72	Charrington 47
P. Walker & Son Warrington & Burton 107	P. Walker & Robert Cain & Sons 31	Walker Cain 42
Cannon Brewery 114	(Taylor, Walker 1930)	
Courage 123	Courage 59	Courage 76
Barclay, Perkins 125	Barclay, Perkins 48	Barclay, Perkins 86
John Smith's Tedcaster Brewery 126	John Smith's Tedcaster Brewery 86	John Smith's Tedcaster Brewery 117
Truman, Hanbury, Buxton 133	Truman, Hanbury, Buxton 77	Truman, Hanbury, Buxton 92
Ind, Coope 153	Ind, Coope 65	Ind, Coope & Allsopp 59
William Younger 154	William Younger 190	(Scottish Brewers 1931)
Northampton Brewery 156	[Northampton Brewery £0.7]	[Northampton Brewery £1.7]
Holt Brewery 160	Holt Brewery 146	(Ansells Brewery 1934)
Robert Cain 164	(P. Walker & R. Cain 1921)	
C. & E. Morton 167	[C. & E. Morton £1.1]	(Beecham Food Products 1948)
Bristol Brewery, Georges 170	Bristol Brewery, Georges 157	Bristol Brewery, Georges 111
Worthington 171	(Bass, Ratcliffe & Gretton 1926)	
Groves & Whitnall 174	Groves & Whitnall 125	[Groves & Whitnall £2.6]
P. Phipps 175	P. Phipps 159	P. Phipps 187
City of London Brewery 176	City of London Brewery 74	City of London Brewery & Investment 154
Meux's Brewery 182	Meux's Brewery 112	[Meux's Brewery £3.5]
Style & Winch 189	(Barclay Parkins 1928)	
Wilson's Brewery 192	[Wilson's Brewery £1.9]	[Wilson's Brewery £2.9]
[Hoare £0.9]	Hoare 43	(Charrington 1933)
[Ansells Brewery £1.0]	Ansells Brewery 93	Ansells Brewery 60
[Wolverhampton & Dudley Brewery £1.0]	Wolverhampton & Dudley Breweries 132	Wolverhampton & Dudley Breweries 185
[Taylor, Walker pvt. small]	Taylor, Walker 45	Taylor, Walker 70
[Manbré Sugar & Malt £0.5]	Manbré & Garton 91	Manbré & Garton 87
[Matthew Brown £0.5]	Matthew Brown 127	Matthew Brown 182

1919 (Market value of shares over £1.0 million)	1930 (Market value of shares over £1.3 million)	1948 (Market value of shares over £4.4 million)
[Benskin's Watford Brewery £0.5]	Benskin's Watford Brewery 129	Benskin's Watford Brewery 175
[H. & G. Simonds £0.5]	H. & G. Simonds 137	H. & G. Simonds 90
[Tamplin & Son's Brewery, Brighton £0.5]	Tamplin & Son's Brewery, Brighton 153	[Tamplin & Son's Brewery, Brighton £1.9]
[Marston, Thompson & Evershed £0.5]	Marston, Thompson & Evershed 158	[Marston, Thompson & Evershed £3.2]
[James Shipstone & Sons £0.6]	James Shipstone & Sons 164	[James Shipstone & Sons £1.4]
[Usher's Wiltshire Brewery £0.6]	Usher's Wiltshire Brewery 170	[Usher's Wiltshire Brewery £1.8]
[Parker's Burslem Brewery £0.7]	Parker's Burslem Brewery 181	[Parker's Burslem Brewery £2.8]
[North Eastern Breweries £0.7]	Associated Breweries 189	Vaux & Associated Breweries 190
[Wenlock Brewery £0.8]	Wenlock Brewery 193	[Wenlock Brewery £1.5]
[Friary Holroyd & Healy's Breweries pvt.]	Friary Holroyd & Healy's Breweries 194	[Friary Holroyd & Healy's Breweries pvt.]
[Gilstrap, Earp pvt.]	Associated British Maltsters 195	[Associated British Maltsters £2.5]
[W. Butler £0.6]	W. Butler 199	W. Butler 187
[Dutton's Blackburn Brewery £0.5]	[Dutton's Blackburn Brewery £1.3]	[Dutton's Blackburn Brewery £1.6]
[Brickwood £0.6]	[Brickwood £1.3]	[Brickwood £1.6]
		Scottish Brewers 131
[Joshua Tetley & Son pvt.]	[Joshua Tetley & Son pvt.]	Joshua Tetley & Son 165
[Hammonds Bradford Brewery pvt.]	[Hammonds Bradford Brewery £0.6]	Hammonds United Brewery 167
[Strong pvt.]	[Strong pvt.]	Strong 195

2085: Distilled liquor

Scotch Whisky Brands 36	(Distillers 1920)	
Distillers 45	Distillers 8	Distillers 6
John Walker & Sons 57	(Distillers 1925)	
W. & A. Gilbey 108	W. & A. Gilbey 143	W. & A. Gilbey 142
Mackie & Co. Distillers 199	(Distillers 1924)	

2086: Soft drinks

[Schweppes £1.0]	Schweppes 149	[Schweppes £3.3]

1919 (Market value of shares over £1.0 million)	1930 (Market value of shares over £1.3 million)	1948 (Market value of shares over £4.4 million)

209: Miscellaneous foods and kindred products
2099: Food preparations

Lipton 73	Lipton 57	(Home & Colonial Stores 1931)
Home & Colonial Stores 138	[Home & Colonial Stores no mfg.]	[Home & Colonial Stores no mfg.]
[Cerebos £0.3]	Cerebos 107	Cerebos 78
[Midland Vinegar pvt.]	H. P. Sauce 139	H. P. Sauce 128
[Brooke, Bond £0.3]	Brooke, Bond 185	Brooke, Bond 153

Group 28: Chemicals and allied products
281: Industrial inorganic chemicals

Brunner, Mond 8	Imperial Chemical Industries 4	Imperial Chemical Industries 3
United Alkali 30	(Imperial Chemical Industries 1926)	
Borax Consolidated 43	Borax Consolidated 109	Borax Consolidated 97
Cassell Cyanide 146	(Imperial Chemical Industries 1927)	
[Albright & Wilson pvt.]	[Albright & Wilson pvt.]	Albright & Wilson 132

283: Drugs (consumer chemicals)

Boots Pure Drug 38	Boots Pure Drug 23, controlled by Drug, Inc., U.S.	Boots Pure Drug 29
Beecham Estates & Pills 166	Beechams Pills 138	Beecham Group 34
	Cooper, McDougall & Robertson 136	[Cooper, McDougall & Robertson £3.0
	[Sangers £0.7]	Sangers 174
		Glaxco Laboratories 192

284: Soap, cleaners, and toilet goods (consumer chemicals)

Lever Brothers 4	Unilever 1	Unilever 4
Reckitt & Sons 18	Reckitt & Sons 21	Reckitt & Sons 14
J. & J. Colman 68	[J. & J. Colman pvt.]	[J. & J. Colman pvt.]
John Knight 168	(Lever Brothers 1920)	
[Yardley pvt.]	[Yardley pvt.]	Yardley 188

285: Paints and allied products (consumer chemicals)

[Pinchin, Johnson pvt.]	Pinchin, Johnson 55	Pinchin, Johnson 61
[Goodlass, Wall & Lead pvt.]	Goodlass, Wall 105	Goodlass, Wall & Lead Industries 104
[Lewis Berger pvt.]	[Lewis Berger 208]	Lewis Berger 169
[International Paint & Compositions £0.5]	[International Paint & Compositions £1.1]	International Paint & Compositions 178

1919 (Market value of shares over £1.0 million)	1930 (Market value of shares over £1.3 million)	1948 (Market value of shares over £4.4 million)
286: Industrial organic chemicals		
Levinstein 20	(Imperial Chemical Industries 1926)	
British Dyes 132	(Imperial Chemical Industries 1926)	
	British Briquettes 160	(Powell Duffryn Associated Collieres 1939)
287: Agricultural chemicals		
[James Fison pvt.]	[Fison, Packard & Prentice pvt.]	Fisons 75
289: Miscellaneous chemical products		
2892: Explosives		
Nobel Explosives 10	(Imperial Chemical Industries 1926)	
2899: Chemicals and chemical preparations (salt)		
Salt Union 77	Salt Union 116	(Imperial Chemical Industries 1937)
Group 35: Machinery, except electrical		
351: Engines and turbines		
Babcock & Wilcox 25	Babcock & Wilcox 26	Babcock & Wilcox 46
[R. A. Lister pvt.]	[R. A. Lister pvt.]	R. A. Lister 136
352: Farm and garden machinery		
Ruston & Hornsby 105	[Ruston & Hornsby £0.6]	Ruston & Hornsby 130
353: Construction and related machinery		
[Herbert Morris £0.6]	[Herbert Morris £0.9]	Herbert Morris 196
354: Metalworking machinery		
[Alfred Herbert pvt.]	[Alfred Herbert pvt.]	Alfred Herbert 157
355: Special industry machinery		
3552: Textile machinery		
Platt Brothers 52	Platt Brothers 166	Platt Brothers 129
Howard & Bullough 80	(Platt Brothers 1932)	(Platt Brothers 1932)
Mather & Platt 112	Mather & Platt 119	[Mather & Platt £4.1]
3555: Printing trades machinery		
Linotype & Machinery 91, subsidiary of Mergenthaler Linotype, U.S.	Linotype & Machinery 131, subsidiary of Mergenthaler Linotype, U.S.	[Linotype & Machinery £3.3, subsidiary of Mergenthaler Linotype, U.S.]
356: General industrial machinery		
[G. & J. Weir pvt.]	[G. & J. Weir pvt.]	G. & J. Weir 148

1919 (Market value of shares over £1.0 million)	1930 (Market value of shares over £1.3 million)	1948 (Market value of shares over £4.4 million)
[Skefco Ball Bearing pvt., subsidiary of SKF, Sweden]	[Skefco Ball Bearing pvt., subsidiary of SKF, Sweden]	Skefco Ball Bearing 150, subsidiary of SKF, Sweden

357: Office and computing machines

[W. & T. Avery £0.7]	W. & T. Avery 148	W. & T. Avery 162

3636: Sewing machines (from Group 36)

British United Shoe Machinery 135, subsidiary of United Shoe Machinery, U.S.	British United Shoe Machinery 42, subsidiary of United Shoe Machinery, U.S.	British United Shoe Machinery 41, subsidiary of United Shoe Machinery, U.S.

Group 36: Electric and electronic equipment

361: Electric distribution and industrial equipment

Metropolitan-Vickers Electrical 50, controlled by Vickers and Metropolitan Carriance, Wagon, & Finance	Associated Electrical Industries 34, controlled by General Electric, U.S.	Associated Electrical Industries, 18
English Electric 54	English Electric 130	English Electric 57
Siemens Brothers 94	Siemens Brothers 95	Siemens Brothers 176
General Electric Co. 119	General Electric Co. 18	General Electric Co. 20
British Thompson Houston 181, subsidiary of General Electric, U.S.	(Associated Electrical Industries 1928)	
[A. Reyrolle pvt.]	A. Reyrolle 173	[A. Reyrolle £4.2]
[Crompton £0.6]	[Crompton Parkinson £1.2]	Crompton Parkinson 79
[Plessey pvt.]	[Plessey pvt.]	Plessey 191

363: Household Appliances

[Hoover pvt.]	[Hoover Holdings pvt.]	Hoover 105, subsidiary of Hoover, U.S.

365: Radio and TV receiving sets

3652: Phonographic records

Gramophone 200, controlled by Victor Talking Machine, U.S.	Gramophone 58	Electric & Musical Industries 91
	Columbia Graphophone 67	(Electric & Musical Industries 1931, then Radio Corp. of America, 1932)

366: Communication equipment

	International Automatic Telephone 187	Automatic Telephone & Electric 197

1919 (Market value of shares over £1.0 million)	1930 (Market value of shares over £1.3 million)	1948 (Market value of shares over £4.4 million)

369: Miscellaneous electrical equipment and supplies
3691: Batteries

[Chloride Electrical Storage pvt., subsidiary of Electrical Storage Battery, U.S.]	Chloride Electrical Storage 118, subsidiary of Electrical Storage Battery, U.S.	Chloride Electrical Storage 152
[British Ever Ready £0.3, subsidiary of Union Carbide & Carbon, U.S.]	Ever Ready (Great Britain) 145	Ever Ready (Great Britain) 103

Group 37: Transportation equipment
371: Motor vehicles and equipment
3711: Motor vehicles and car bodies

Austin Motor 66	Austin Motor 85	Austin Motor 55
Leyland Motors 92	Leyland Motors 135	Leyland Motors 122
Ford Motor 109, subsidiary of Ford Motor, U.S.	Ford Motor 13, subsidiary of Ford Motor, U.S.	Ford Motor 31, subsidiary of Ford Motor, U.S.
Rolls-Royce 142	Rolls-Royce 175	Rolls-Royce 149
Dennis Brothers 188	Dennis Brothers 152	[Dennis Brothers £2.2]
[Morris Motors pvt.]	Morris Motors 44	Morris Motors 27
[A. Darraq £1.0]	STD Motors 196	Standard Motors 100
[Associated Equipment pvt.]	[Associated Equipment pvt.]	Associated Commercial Vehicles 93
[Rootes pvt.]	[Rootes Motors pvt.]	Rootes Securities 141
[Vauxall Motors £0.8]	[Vauxall Motors pvt., subsidiary of General Motors, U.S.]	Vauxall Motors 143, subsidiary of General Motors, U.S.

3714: Motor vehicle parts and accessories

[Joseph Lucas £0.7]	Joseph Lucas 97	Joseph Lucas 82
		Briggs Motor Bodies 181, subsidiary of Briggs Mfg., U.S.
	[Pressed Steel Co. of Great Britain, subsidiary of Pressed Steel Car, U.S.]	Pressed Steel 145, subsidiary of Pressed Steel Car, U.S.

372: Aircraft and parts

Aircraft Manufacturing 196	liquidated 1921	
[D. Napier & Son £1.0]	D. Napier & Sons 191	(English Electric 1942) Hawker Siddeley 83
[Bristol Aeroplane pvt.]	[Bristol Aeroplane pvt.]	Bristol Aeroplane 134

1919 (Market value of shares over £1.0 million)	1930 (Market value of shares over £1.3 million)	1948 (Market value of shares over £4.4 million)

373: Ship and boat building and repairing

Vickers 6	Vickers 15	Vickers 12
Armstrong, Whitworth 14	Armstrong Whitworth Securities 60	liquidated 1943
John Brown 21	John Brown 84	John Brown 67
Cammell, Laird 40	Cammell, Laird 169	Cammell, Laird 119
Swan, Hunter & Wigham-Richardson 56	Swan, Hunter & Wigham-Richardson 121	Swan, Hunter & Wigham-Richardson 144
William Doxford 74	(Shipbuilders' Investment 1926)	
Pearson & Knowles Coal & Iron 84	(Armstrong, Whitworth 1920)	
Harland & Wolff 90	Harland & Wolff 134	Harland & Wolff 101
William Beardmore 101	[William Beardmore £0.8]	[William Beardmore £3.0]
Workman, Clark 106	(John Brown 1928)	
Hawthorn, Lesley 139	[Hawthorn, Lesley £0.5]	[Hawthorn, Lesley £2.0]
William Gray 141	[William Gray pvt.]	[William Gray £3.0]
H. & C. Grayson 186	[Grayson, Rollo & Clover Dock pvt.]	[Grayson, Rollo & Clover Docks £0.3]

374: Railroad equipment

Metropolitan Carriage, Wagon, & Finance 12	(Vickers 1929)	
North British Locomotives 86	[North British Locomotives £1.0]	[North British Locomotives £3.4]
Birmingham Railway Carriage & Wagon 134	Birmingham Railway Carriage & Wagon 184	[Birmingham Railway Carriage & Wagon £2.0]

375: Motorcycles, bicycles, and parts

Birmingham Small Arms 41	Birmingham Small Arms 101	Birmingham Small Arms 146
		Raleigh Industries 116

The 200 largest industrial enterprises in Germany, ranked by assets, 1913.

Rank	Firm	Assets (M millions)	Major product line (SIC code)
Group 20: Food and kindred products			
45	Schultheiss' Brauerei AG	46.9	2082
53	Aktienbrauerei zum Löwenbräu	39.9	2082
66	Verein deutscher Oelfabriken	32.7	207
80	Gebrüder Stollwerck AG	28.3	2065
84	Aktien-Brauerei-Gesellschaft Friedrichshöhe vorm. Patzenhofer	27.5	2082
85	Zuckerfabrik Frankenthal	26.5	2063
90	Gesellschaft für Brauerei, Spiritus- u. Presshefe-Fabrikation vorm. G. Sinner	26.0	2082
99	Bremer-Besigheimer Oelfabriken AG	24.1	207
106	Zuckerraffinerie Tangermünde Fr. Meyers Sohn AG	22.2	2063
115	Unionbrauerei Schülein & Co. AG	20.6	2082
124	Hartwig & Vogel AG	18.8	2065
129	Zuckerfabrik Klein-Wanzleben vorm. Rabbethge & Gieseeke	17.1	2063
130	AG Hackerbräu	16.9	2082
135	Breslauer Spiritfabrik AG	16.8	2085
140	H. Schlinck & Cie. AG	16.1	207
143	Brauhaus Nürnberg	16.1	2082
144	Leipziger Bierbrauerei zu Reudnitz Riebeck & Co.	16.0	2082
146	F. Thörl's Vereinigte Harburger Ölfabriken AG	15.6	207
148	Oelfabrik Gross-Gerau-Bremen	15.5	207

Rank	Firm	Assets (M millions)	Major product line (SIC code)
153	Zuckerraffinerie Halle	15.1	2063
154	Bürgerliches Brauhaus München	15.0	2082
170	"Sarotti" Chokladen & Cacao-Industrie AG	14.0	2065
196	Württembergische-Hohenzollern'sche Brauereigesellschaft	12.8	2082
198	Pommersche Provinzial-Zuckersiederei	12.7	2063
199	Rheinischer Aktien-Verein für Zuckerfabrikation	12.7	2063
200	AG Schlossbrauerei Schöneberg	12.6	2082
Group 21: Tobacco manufactures			
98	Georg. A. Jasmatzi AG	24.2	211
Group 22: Textile mill products			
26	Norddeutsche Wollkämmerei u. Kammgarnspinnerei	74.1	228
50	Dollfus-Mieg & Co. AG	41.1	228
68	Kammgarnspinnerei Stöhr & Co. AG	32.6	228
81	Mech. Baumwoll-Spinnerei u. Weberei in Augsburg	28.3	221
100	Bremer Woll-Kämmerei	23.5	223
120	Kullman & Cie AG	19.1	221
137	Zwirnerei u. Nahfadenfabrik Gögginen	16.7	228
152	Manufakturen Hartmann & fils	15.2	221
159	Kammgarnspinnerei vorm. Schwartz & Co. AG	14.7	228
164	Vereingte Glanzstoff-Fabriken AG (VGF)	14.6	2285
168	Neue Braumwoll-Spinnerei u. Weberei Hof	14.1	221
174	Etablissments Herzog AG	13.7	221
177	Schoellersche u. Eitorfer Kommgarn Spinnerei AG	13.5	228
180	Wöll-Wäscherei u. Kammerei u. Döhren	13.2	223
183	Vögtländische Baumwollspinnerei	13.2	228
Group 23: Apparel and related products			
181	Conrad Tack & Cie. AG	13.2	236
Group 24: Lumber and wood products			
157	Berliner Holz-Comptoir	14.8	242

Rank	Firm	Assets (M millions)	Major product line (SIC code)
Group 26: Paper and allied products			
19	Zellstofffabrik Waldhof	97.9	262
56	AG für Maschinenpapier-Zellstoff-Fabrikation	36.8	262
116	Feldmühle, Papier- u. Zellstoffwerke AG	19.9	262
176	Varziner Papier-Fabrik zu Hammermühle-Varzin	13.6	262
Group 28: Chemicals			
8	Badische Anilin- u. & Soda-Fabrik (BASF)	128.2	286
9	Farbenfabriken vorm. Friedr. Bayer & Co.	121.3	286
15	Farbwerke vorm. Meister Lucius & Brüning in Höchst a.M.	111.2	286
16	Deutsche Solvay	110.3	281
34	Deutsche Gold- u. Silber-scheide-Anstalt vorm. Roessler (DEGUSSA)	58.3	281
40	Chemische Fabrik Griesheim-Elektron	51.1	286
42	Dynamit AG vorm. Alfred Nobel & Co.	48.4	2892
44	Vereinigte Köln-Rottweiler Pulverfabriken	47.3	2892
48	AG für Anilin-Fabrikation in Berlin-Trepton (AGFA)	42.9	286
60	Rütgerswerke AG	35.4	286
64	Sloman & Co.	33.6	281
65	AG für chemische Produkte vorm. H. Scheidemandel	33.1	289
77	Holzverkohlungs-Industrie AG	30.7	281
83	Consolidirte Alkaliwerke Westeregeln	27.6	281
91	Anglo-Continentale (vorm. Ohlendorff'sche) Guano-Werke	25.9	287
92	Chemische Werke vorm. H. & F. Albert	25.5	287
95	Alkaliwerke Ronnenberg	24.6	281
113	Gerb- u. Farbstoffwerke H. Renner & Co. AG	20.9	286
126	Elektrochemische Werke GmbH	18.6	281
128	"Union" Fabrik chemischer Produkte	17.1	287

Rank	Firm	Assets (M millions)	Major product line (SIC code)
142	Chemische Fabrik von Heyden AG	16.1	283
150	Chemische Fabriken vorm. Weiler-ter Meer	15.4	286
151	Chemische Fabrik auf Actien vorm. E. Schering	15.2	283
162	Reinisch-Westfälische Sprengstoff AG	14.6	2892
163	Vereinigte Chemischefabriken Leopoldshall	14.6	281
171	Chemische Fabrik AG vormals Moritz Milch & Co.	14.0	287
173	Chemische Fabrik Hönningen u. vormals Messingwerk Reinickendorf R. Seidel AG	13.9	281
184	"Silesia" Verein chemischer Fabriken, Ida- u. Marienhütte	13.1	281
185	Verein chemischer Fabriken in Mannheim	13.1	281
197	Chemische Fabrik Buchau	12.7	281
Group 29: Petroleum refining and coal products			
39	Deutsche Erdöl AG	51.6	291
103	Deutsche Petroleum AG	22.9	291
123	Deutsche Mineralöl-Industrie AG	19.0	291
133	Deutsche Vacuum Oil Company	16.8	291
136	Gesellschaft für Teerverwertung m.b.H.	16.8	295
Group 30: Rubber products			
37	Continental-Caoutschouc- u. Gutta-Percha-Co.	52.5	301
109	Vereinigte Gummiwaren-Fabriken Hamburg-Wien	21.5	301
175	Mitteldeutsche Gummiwarenfabrik Louis Peter AG	13.6	301
195	Hannoversche Gummiwerke Excelsior AG	12.8	301
Group 31: Leather and its products			
76	Adler u. Oppenheimer Lederfabrik AG	30.8	311
131	Lederfabrik Hirschberg vorm. Heinrich Knoch & Co.	16.9	311
Group 32: Stone, clay, and glass products			
96	Portland-Cementwerke Heidelberg u. Mannheim AG	24.4	324

Rank	Firm	Assets (M millions)	Major product line (SIC code)
102	AG für Glasindustrie vorm. Friedr. Siemens	23.2	322
105	Rheinisch-Westfälische- Kalkwerke	22.5	327
110	Alsen'sche Portland-Cement- Fabriken	21.1	324
138	Portland-Cementfabrik Germania AG	16.7	324
139	AG der Gerresheimer Glashüttenwerke vorm. Ferd. Heyl	16.4	322
193	Porzellanfabrik Kahla	12.8	326
Group 33: Primary metal industries			
1	Friedrich Krupp AG	599.5	331
4	Deutsch-Luxemburgische Bergwerks-Hütten AG	278.2	331
5	Phoenix AG für Bergbau u. Hüttenbetrieb	223.9	331
7	Gutehoffnungshütte Aktienverein u. Hüttenbetrieb (Oberhausen)	130.4	331
12	Mannesmannröhren-Werke	115.1	331
13	Felten & Guilleaume Carlswerk AG	114.2	331
14	Rombacher Hüttenwerke	112.8	331
20	Vereinigte Königs-und Laurahütte	92.4	331
21	Oberschlesische Eisenbahn- Bedarfs AG	85.2	331
22	Metallgesellschaft	84.4	331
23	Rheinische Stahlwerke	84.3	331
25	Bochumer Verein für Bergbau u. Gusstahlfabrikation	78.1	331
27	Kattowitzer AG für Bergbau u. Eisenhüttenbetrieb	72.6	331
29	Dillinger Hüttenwerke AG	63.9	331
30	Ilseder Hütte	63.7	331
31	Eisen- und Stahlwerk "Hoesch" AG	62.8	331
32	Oberschlesische Eisen-Industrie AG	58.7	331
35	Röchling'sche Eisen- und Stahlwerke GmbH	56.3	331
41	Georgs-Marien-Bergwerks- u. Hütten Verein	50.3	331

Rank	Firm	Assets (M millions)	Major product line (SIC code)
47	Schlesische AG für Bergbau u. Zinkhüttenbetrieb	45.7	333
49	Bismarckhütte	41.9	331
51	Buderus'sche Eisenwerke AG	40.7	331
55	AG für Bergbau, Blei- und Zinkfabrikation	38.1	333
57	Eisenwerk-Gesellschaft Maximilianhütte	36.4	331
59	Rheinische Metallwaren- und Maschinenfabrik	35.6	331
62	Vereinigte Stahlwerk van der Zypen u. Wissener Eisenhütten AG	34.7	331
63	Eisenwerk Kraft	34.2	331
69	Façoneisen-Walzwerk L. Mannstaedt AG	32.4	331
74	AG für Hüttenbetrieb in Duisberg-Meiderich	31.5	331
78	Th. Goldschmidt AG	28.5	333
79	Gebr. Böhler & Co. AG	28.1	331
82	Hasper Eisen und Stahlwerk	27.7	331
94	Donnermarckhütte Oberschles. Eisen- und Kohlenwerke AG	24.8	331
97	AG Lauchhammer	24.3	331
107	Heddernheimer Kupferwerk u. Süddentsche Kabelwerke AG	22.1	333
108	Westfalische Stahlwerke AG	21.7	331
118	Eisenhüttenwerk Thale AG	19.5	331
119	Norddeutsche Affinerie	19.3	333
125	Westfälische Drahtindustrie	18.8	331
127	Stahlwerk Becker AG	17.4	331
132	Westfälische Eisen- u. Drahtwerke AG	16.9	331
134	Eisenhütte Silesia AG	16.8	331
145	Hirsch, Kupfer u. Messingwerke AG	15.8	333
155	Norddeutsche Hütte AG	14.9	331
156	Hochofenwerk Lübeck AG	14.9	331
161	Geisweider Eisenwerke AG	14.7	331
167	Vereinigte Deutsche Nickel-Werke AG	14.4	333
172	Krefelder Stahlwerk AG	13.9	331
190	Blechwalzwerk Schulz Knaudt AG	12.9	331

Rank	Firm	Assets (M millions)	Major product line (SIC code)
Group 34: Fabricated metal products			
36	Deutsche Waffen- und Munitions-fabriken	52.7	348
104	Württembergische Metallwarenfabrik Geislingen-st.	22.7	349
112	Maschinen-u. Daupfkessel-Armaturen-Fabrik Schäffer & Budenberg GmbH	21.0	344
122	C. Hackmann AG	19.0	343
187	Balche, Tellering & Cie. AG	13.1	344
Group 35: Machinery, except electrical			
11	Maschinenfabrik Augsburg-Nürnberg AG (MAN)	117.5	351
28	Singer & Co. Nähmaschinen AG	68.2	3636
38	Maschinenfabrik-Anstalt Humboldt	52.2	351
43	Deutsche Maschinenfabrik AG (DEMAG)	47.5	351
46	Gasmotoren-Fabrik Deutz	46.0	351
54	Gebr. Körting AG	39.3	358
61	Julius Pintsch	34.8	356
71	Stettiner Chamottefabrik AG vorm. Didier	32.1	3567
72	Ludw. Loewe & Co. AG	31.8	354
73	Berlin-Anhaltische Maschinenbau AG (BAMAG)	31.8	351
75	Maschinenfabrik Esslingen	31.3	351
86	Sächsische Maschinenfabrik vorm. Rich. Hartmann	26.5	3552
87	Hannoversche Maschinenbau AG (HANOMAG)	26.4	352
89	Berliner Maschinenbau AG vormals L. Schwartzkopff	26.0	351
117	Gesellschaft für Linde's Eismaschinen AG	19.6	358
121	Vogtländische Maschinenfabrik vormals J. C. & H. Dietrich AG	19.1	3552
141	Vereinigte Fabriken Landwirt-schaftlichen Maschinen vorm. Epple u. Buxbaum	16.1	352
149	Maschinenfabrik Thyssen & Co. AG	15.4	351

Rank	Firm	Assets (M millions)	Major product line (SIC code)
165	Mühlenbauanstalt u. Maschinen-fabrik vormals Gebrüder Sack	14.6	355
178	Maschinenfabrik Gritzner AG	13.5	3636
179	Schubert & Salzer Maschinenfabrik AG	13.4	3552
189	AG-für Görlitzer Maschinenbau-Anstalt u. Eisengiesserei	13.0	351
191	Amme, Giesecke & Konegen AG	12.9	355
192	Maschinenfabrik Buckau AG (R. Wolf)	12.9	351
194	Dürkoppwerke AG	12.8	3636
Group 36: Electric and electronic equipment			
2	Allgemeine Elektricitäts-Gesellschaft (AEG)	463.0	361
3	Siemens-Schuckert Werke GmbH	323.5	361
6	Siemens & Halske AG	189.6	361
17	Bergmann-Elektricitäts-Werke AG	104.2	361
67	Accumulatoren-Fabrik AG	32.7	3691
93	Brown Boveri & Cie. AG	25.0	361
147	AG Mix & Genest Telephon- u. Telegrapheu-Werke	15.5	366
Group 37: Transportation equipment			
10	Vulkan Werke Hamburg u. Stettin AG	118.6	373
18	Orenstein & Koppel-Arthur Koppel AG	100.1	374
24	Blohm & Voss KG	83.2	373
33	Benz & Cie. Rheinische Automobil-u. Motoren-Fabrik AG	58.6	3711
52	AG "Weser"	40.2	373
58	Linke-Hofmann-Werke Breslauer AG	36.2	374
70	Howaldtswerke Kiel	32.4	373
88	Bremer Vulkan Schiffbau u. Maschinenbau	26.2	373
101	Daimler-Motoren-Gesellschaft	23.2	3711
111	Neue Automobil-Gesellschaft AG	21.1	3711
114	Adlerwerke vorm. Heinrich Kleyer AG	20.7	3711
158	Flensburger Schiffbau-Gesellschaft	14.8	373

Rank	Firm	Assets (M millions)	Major product line (SIC code)
160	Reiherstieg Schiffwerfte u. Maschinenfabrik	14.7	373
169	Joh. C. Tecklenborg AG Schiffbau u. Maschnenfabrik	14.0	373
186	Eisenbahnsignal-Bauanstalt Maxjüdel & Co. AG	13.1	374
188	Deutsche Waggon Leinhanstalt AG	13.0	374
Group 38: Instruments and related products			
166	Gebrüder Junghans AG	14.5	384
182	Optische Anstalt C. P. Goerz AG	13.2	385

The 200 largest industrial enterprises in Germany, ranked by assets, 1929.

Rank	Firm	Assets (RM millions)	Product lines (SIC codes) Major	Others
Group 20: Food and kindred products				
23	Schultheiss-Patzenhofer Brauerei-AG	121.6	2082	204, 2097
41	Ostwerke AG	78.2	2085	2099, 322, 324
44	Deutsche Jurgens-Werke AG	73.2	207	
49	Van den Bergh's Margarine AG	66.9	207	
54	Süddeutsche Zucker-AG	59.7	2063	
74	Engelhardt-Brauerei AG	45.0	2082	204
81	Getreide-Industrie & Commission AG	43.4	204	distribution
86	Leipziger Bierbrauerei	42.0	2082	
93	Pfeifer & Langen AG	39.6	2063	
103	Dortmunder Actien-Brauerei	35.5	2082	
106	Zuckerfabrik Klein-Wanzleben	35.4	2063	agriculture
109	F. Thörl's Vereinigte Harburger Ölfabriken AG	34.4	207	
118	Aktienbrauerei zum Löwenbräu in München	32.9	2082	
132	"Nordsee," Deutsche Hochseefischerei Bremen-Cuxhafen	29.1	2091	207
134	Zuckerraffinerie Tangermünde Fr. Meyers Sohn AG	28.1	2063	
137	Dortmunder Union-Brauerei AG	27.7	2082	
142	Gebrüder Stollwerck AG	26.4	2065	203, 2052, 358

Rank	Firm	Assets (RM millions)	Product lines (SIC codes) Major	Others
149	Actiengesellschaft Paulaner-bräu Salvatorbrauerei und Thomasbräu	24.3	2082	204, 2097
155	"Sarotti" AG	21.6	2065	2082, 205
157	von Rath, Schoeller & Skene AG	21.3	2063	
158	Haake-Beck Brauerei AG	21.3	2082	
160	Löwenbrauerei-Böhmisches Brauhaus AG	21.1	2082	
162	Bavaria- u. St.-Pauli-Brauerei	21.0	2082	
164	Sinner AG	20.9	2082	204, 2099
170	Holsten-Brauerei	19.9	2082	
173	Berliner Kindl Brauerei AG	19.3	2082	
193	Brauerei zum Felsenkeller	17.0	2082	2099
197	Gabriel u. Jos. Sedlmayr Spaten-Franziskaner-Leistbräu AG	16.6	2082	204, 2097
Group 21: Tobacco manufactures				
131	Martin Brinkmann AG	29.3	211	212, 213
Group 22: Textile mill products				
10	Norddeutsche Wollkämmerei & Kammgarnspinnerei	239.8	228	223, 225
13	Vereinigte Glanzstoff-Fabriken AG	231.2	2285	222, 287
46	J. P. Bemberg AG	70.9	2285	222, 225, 232, 3552
51	Christian Dierig AG	64.6	221	228, 229
67	Vereinigte Seidenwebereien AG	47.8	222	
68	Kammgarnspinnerei Stöhr & Co. AG	47.4	228	
73	Mechanische Weberei zu Linden	45.8	221	
84	F. H. Hammersen AG	42.5	221	226, 228
85	Vereinigte Jute-Spinnereien und Webereien	42.2	229	
98	Toga Vereinigte Webereien AG	38.2	223	
113	Baumwollindustrie Erlangen-Bamberg AG	33.9	221	228
121	Fr. Küttner AG	32.1	2285	3552
125	"Sapt" AG für Textilprodukte	31.2	221	
159	Bremer Woll-Kämmerei	21.2	223	
167	Gruschwitz Textilwerke AG	20.6	228	

Rank	Firm	Assets (RM millions)	Product lines (SIC codes) Major	Others
172	Hanfwerke Füssen-Immenstadt AG	19.4	229	
182	Deutsche Acetat-Kunstseiden AG "Rhodiaseta"	18.1	2285	
187	Mez AG	17.8	228	
188	Schlesische Textilwerke Methner u. Frahne AG	17.6	229	
189	Kulmbacher Spinnerei in Kulmbach	17.5	228	
192	Alrowa Deutsche Strickerei-AG	17.1	225	
198	Johs. Girmes & Co. AG	16.5	223	3552
199	Meyer Kauffmann Textilwerke AG	16.4	221	
200	Deutshe Wollenwaren-Manufaktur AG	16.0	223	
Group 23: Apparel and other textile products				
138	Allgemeine Textil-Fabrikations-und Handels-AG & A. Breminhmeyer	27.4	231	232, 233, 221
Group 26: Paper and allied products				
22	Zellstoffabrik Waldhof	121.6	262	261, 263
58	A.G.-für Zellstoff- & Papierfabrikation	54.6	262	261, 282, 286
63	Feldmühle, Papier-u. Zellstoffwerke AG	49.2	262	261, 263
75	Königsberger Zellstoff-Fabriken u. Chemische Werke Koholyt AG	45.0	262	264, 2285, 281, 282, 286, 329
184	Natronzellstoff-u. Papierfabriken AG	18.0	262	261
Group 27: Printing and publishing				
78	Ullstein AG	44.3	271	272, 273
Group 28: Chemicals and allied products				
2	I. G. Farbenindustrie AG	2,090.2	286	281, 282, 283, 287, 289, 291, 386
6	Kali-Industrie AG (Wintershall)	413.1	281	287
11	Burbach-Kaliwerke AG	235.3	281	
18	Obersschlesische Kokswerke & Chemische Fabriken AG	135.6	286	287, 295, mining
19	Deutsche Solvay-Werke AG	134.0	281	mining
31	Rütgerswerke-AG	101.0	286	281, 287, 295, 299

Rank	Firm	Assets (RM millions)	Major	Others
			Product lines (SIC codes)	
47	Deutsche Gold- und Silber-Scheideanstalt vormals Roessler (DEGUSSA)	68.1	281	281, 287, 333, 384, banking
50	Schering-Kahlbaum AG	65.6	283	386
53	Ruhrchemie AG	61.5	286	287, mining
55	Kali-Chemie AG	58.0	281	287, mining
64	Kaliwerke Salzdetfurth AG	49.1	281	287, mining
65	Dynamit-AG. vorm. Alfred Nobel & Co.	48.8	2892	282
69	Kaliwerke Aschersleben	47.2	281	mining
72	Rheinisch-Westfälische Sprengstoff-AG	46.4	2892	282
91	Consolidirte Alkaliwerke Westeregeln	40.9	281	287, 289, mining
147	Mitteldeutsche Stickstoffwerke AG	24.4	287	
148	Siemens-Planiawerke AG	24.3	286	329
153	Chemische Fabrik von Heyden	21.6	283	281, 284, 286
165	Westfälisch-Anhaltische Sprengstoff AG	20.8	2892	282
166	Saccharin-Fabrik AG vorm. Fahlberg, List & Co.	20.7	283	281, 286, 287
169	J.D. Riedel-E. de Haën AG	19.9	283	281, 286, mining, distribution
180	AG für Chemische Produkte vorm. H. Scheidemandel	18.2	289	283, 287
195	AG Georg Egestorffs Salzwerke u. Chemische Fabriken	16.8	289	286
196	Chemische Werke vorm. H. & E. Albert	16.6	287	283
Group 29: Petroleum and coal products				
8	Rhenania-Ossag Mineralölwerke AG	259.3	291	299
17	Deutsche Erdöl-AG	142.0	291	299
27	Deutsch-Amerikanische Petroleum-Gesellschaft	103.3	291	285, 299
77	Deutsche Petroleum-AG	44.9	291	299
119	Deutsche Vacuum Oel AG	32.7	291	299
139	Deutsche Gasolin AG	27.1	291	299
186	Ebano Asphalt-Werke AG	17.9	295	

Rank	Firm	Assets (RM millions)	Product lines (SIC codes) Major	Others
Group 30: Rubber and miscellaneous plastic products				
30	Continental Gummi-Werke AG	102.0	301	306, 2296, 384, 394
179	Harburger Gummiwaren-Fabrik "Phoenix" AG	18.5	301	302, 306, 384, 394
Group 31: Leather and leather products				
71	Adler u. Oppenheimer AG	46.7	311	
82	Cornelius Heyl AG	42.7	311	
133	J. Sigle & Cie. Schuhfabriken AG (Salamander)	28.8	314	
156	Lederfabrik Hirschberg vorm. Heinrich Knoch & Co.	21.4	311	
181	J. Mayer & Sohn, Lederfabrik AG	18.2	311	
Group 32: Stone, clay, and glass products				
60	Wickingsche Portland-Cement-u. Wasserkalkwerke	53.5	324	
96	Schlesische Portland-Cement-Industrie AG	38.4	324	
115	Portland-Cementwerke Heidelberg-Mannheim-Stuttgart	33.7	324	325
152	Porzellanfabrik Kahla	21.7	326	325, 261
171	Villeroy & Boch	19.8	326	325
177	AG für Glasindustrie vorm. Friedrich Siemens	18.9	322	321, 325
178	Vereinigte Portland-Zement-und Kalkwerke Schimischow, Silesia und Frauendorf AG	18.7	324	325
Group 33: Primary metal products				
1	Vereinigte Stahlwerke AG	2,145.7	331	332, 325, 344, 345, 349, 373, 374, mining
4	Fried. Krupp AG	472.7	331	352, 353, 371, 374
9	Mannesmannröhren-Werke	251.0	331	325, 344, 351, 356, mining, construction
12	Klöckner-Werke AG	233.7	331	287, 327, 345, 347, 348, 373, mining
14	Metallgesellschaft AG	211.1	331	333, 281, mining
15	Eisen-und Stahlwerk Hoesch AG	188.2	331	281, 354, 374, mining

Rank	Firm	Assets (RM millions)	Product lines (SIC codes) Major	Others
16	Gutehoffnungshütte Oberhausen AG	159.8	331	327, 333
20	Ilseder Hütte	128.7	331	281
21	Felten & Guilleaume Carlswerk AG	124.5	335	333, 349
26	Gutehoffnungshütte, Nürnberg	104.0	331	373
28	Mansfeld AG für Bergbau u. Hüttenbetrieb	103.2	333	335, 281, 286, 289, 322, 325, 342, 367, mining
32	Mitteldeutsche Stahlwerke AG	100.9	331	346, 373, 374, 384, mining
37	Vereinigte Oberschlesische Hüttenwerke AG	95.1	331	374
42	Deutsche Edelstahlwerke AG	77.9	331	346, 371, 374
56	Berg-Heckmann-Selve AG	58.0	333	335, 342, 348, 349, 356, 371, 374
57	Vereinigte Aluminium-Werke AG zu Lautawerk	55.4	333	281, 286
66	Eisenwerk-Gesellschaft Maximiliansütte	48.7	331	287, 374
76	Buderus'sche Eisenwerke	45.0	331	325, 327, 346
80	*"Rheinmetall"* Rhein. Metallwaren-und Maschinenfabrik	43.4	331	346, 348, 357, 3714, 372, 374
83	Hirsch, Kupfer u. Messingwerke AG	42.6	333	335, 374
89	Eisen-und Hüttenwerke AG Bochum	41.2	331	
92	Deutsche Industrie-Werke AG	40.4	331	333, 229, 344, 352, 374
97	Th. Goldschmidt AG	38.3	333	2899
102	Oberschlesische Eisenbahn-Bedarfs-AG	35.8	331	335, 386, 344, 346, 356, 374
111	Norddeutsche Affinerie	34.2	333	281
117	Hochofenwerk Lübeck AG	33.0	331	333, 286, 327
124	Stahlwerk Becker AG	31.3	331	352
141	Schlesische Bergwerks-u. Hütten AG	26.6	333	
146	Sachtleben AG für Bergbau u. Chemische Industrie	24.5	333	
154	Deutsche Kabelwerke AG	21.6	335	333, 366
183	C. J. Vogel Draht-u. Kabelwerke AG	18.0	335	

Rank	Firm	Assets (RM millions)	Product lines (SIC codes) Major	Others
190	Vereinigte Deutsche Nickel-Werke AG	17.3	333	335, 342
191	"Kronprint" AG für Metallindustrie	17.2	331	346
Group 34: Fabricated metal				
94	Württembergische Metallwarenfabrik	39.2	342	346, 322, 364, 395
95	Berlin-Karlsruher Industrie-Werke AG	38.9	348	342, 346, 354, 355, 357, 382
176	Bing Werke vorm. Gebrüder Bing AG	19.1	342	341, 346, 251, 357, 363
Group 35: Machinery, except electrical				
29	M.A.N.—Maschinenfabrik Augsburg-Nürnberg AG	102.8	351	353, 355, 358, 344, 371, 374, construction
38	Singer Nähmaschinen AG	94.1	3636	361
48	Demag AG	67.7	351	353, 355, 356, construction
59	Vereinigte Kugellager-Fabriken AG	54.5	3562	
88	"Miag" Mühlenbau u. Industrie AG	41.5	353	351, 352, 355, 373, construction
90	Gesellschaft für Linde's Eismaschinen AG	41.1	358	351, 355, 356, 281, 374
100	Schubert & Salzer Maschinenfabrik AG	37.3	3552	357, 375
101	"Hanomag" Hannoversche Maschinenbau-AG	36.0	352	351, 344, 374
104	Maschinenbau-Anstalt Humboldt	35.5	351	353, 355, 344, 3711, 374, construction
107	Motorenfabrik Deutz AG	35.4	351	
108	Stettiner Chamottfabrik AG vorm. Didler	34.4	3567	325
114	Berliner Maschinenbau-AG vormals L. Schwartzkopff	33.8	351	355, 356, 332, 374
120	Wanderer-Werke vorm. Winkelhofer & Jaenicke AG	32.6	357	371, 375
123	Heinrich Lanz AG	31.3	352	
128	Bamag-Meguin AG	30.0	351	353, 355, 356, 358, 343, 344, 373, 374
151	Maschinenfabrik Buckau R. Wolf AG	22.6	351	352, 353, 355, 356, 358, 344, 374

Rank	Firm	Assets (RM millions)	Product lines (SIC codes) Major	Others
161	Sächsische Maschinen-fabrik vorm. Rich. Hartmann	21.0	3552	351, 353, 355, 356, 358, 344, 3714, 374
175	Gebr. Körting AG	19.1	358	351, 356
194	Dürkoppwerke AG	17.0	3636	346, 3714, 375
Group 36: Electric and electronic equipment				
3	Allgemeine Elektricitäts-Gesellschaft (AEG)	579.4	361	363, 364, 365, 366, 281, 287, 326, 335, 371, 374, 382
5	Siemens-Schuckertwerke AG	420.7	361	363, 333, 335, 351
7	Siemens & Halske AG	406.4	361	364, 366, 356, 358, 372, 374, 382
34	Bergmann-Elektricitäts-Werke AG	96.7	361	363, 364, 335, 351, 356, 358, 374, 382
52	Brown, Boveri & Cie AG	63.5	361	321, 327, 353, 356, 358, 374, mining
62	Accumulatoren-Fabrik AG	50.5	3691	
110	Polyphonwerke AG	34.3	3652	
122	Julius Pintsch AG	31.7	364	361, 351, 356
130	Mix & Genest AG	29.7	366	
135	C. Lorenz AG	27.9	366	
163	Voigt & Haeffner AG	21.0	361	
Group 37: Transportation equipment				
24	Daimler-Benz AG	116.5	3711	372, 351, 352, 354
25	Henschel & Sohn AG	108.1	374	3714, 353, mining
33	Adam Opel AG	99.4	3711	
35	Blohm & Voss	96.5	373	374
39	Knorr-Bremse AG	85.2	374	
40	Robert Bosch AG	83.0	3714	364, 369, 382
43	Deutsche Schiff-und Maschinenbau AG Bremen	76.5	373	371, 344, 355
45	Linke-Hofmann-Busch-Werke AG	71.0	374	371, 344, 351, 353, 355, 356, forestry, mining
61	Orenstein & Koppel AG	53.4	374	344, 353, 354
70	Deutsche Werke Kiel AG	46.8	373	374, 344, 351, 354, 361
78	Adlerwerke vorm. Heinrich Kleyer AG	44.8	3711	375, 357
87	Nationale Automobil-Gesellschaft AG	41.7	3711	372, 374
99	Deutsche Werft AG	37.8	373	

Rank	Firm	Assets (RM millions)	Product lines (SIC codes) Major	Others
106	Bayerische Motoren-Werke AG (BMW)	35.5	3711	
112	Borsigwerk AG	33.9	374	331, 351, 353
116	Bremer Vulkan, Schiffbau u. Maschinenfabrik	33.0	373	3714
127	Zschopauer Motorenwerke J.S. Rasmussen AG	30.5	3711	351, 375
129	Vereinigte Westdeutsche Waggonfabriken AG	29.7	374	
140	Fichtel & Sachs AG	26.8	3714	3562
144	Eisenbahn-Verkehrsmittel-AG	25.0	374	3714
145	Horchwerke AG	24.9	3711	
150	NSU Vereinigte Fahrzeugwerke AG	23.3	375	3711
168	Ford Motor Company AG	20.5	3711	352
185	Waggon-u. Maschinenbau AG Görlitz	17.9	374	371, 344, 351
Group 38: Instruments and related products				
126	Gebrüder Junghans AG	31.2	387	
136	Kodak AG	27.8	386	382, 354
143	Zeiss Ikon AG	26.1	386	382, 383, 349, 357, 364, 3714
Group 39: Miscellaneous manufacturing industries				
36	Deutsche Linoleum-Werke AG	96.3	399	
174	Deutsche Zündholzfabriken AG	19.2	399	

The 200 largest industrial enterprises in West Germany, ranked by assets, 1953.

Rank	Firm	Assets (DM millions)	Product lines (SIC codes) Major	Product lines (SIC codes) Others
Group 20: Food and kindred products				
20	Margarine-Union AG	349.6	207	202
53	Süddeutsche Zucker-AG	152.2	2063	204, 2086, agriculture
110	"Nordsee" Deutsche Hochseefischerei AG	52.6	2091	2097
118	Dortmunder Union-Brauerei AG	47.6	2082	2097
119	"Löwenbräu" München	46.9	2082	2097
126	Deutsche AG für Nestle Erzeugnisse AG	41.3	202	204, 2065, 209
137	Heinr. Auer Mühlenwerke	37.1	204	
139	Schultheiss-Brauerei AG	36.5	2082	
141	F. Thörl's Vereinigte Harburger Oelfabriken AG	36.1	207	
150	Fritz Homann AG	33.5	207	243
160	C. H. Knorr AG	31.7	203	204, 209
170	Dortmunder Actien-Brauerei	29.0	2082	2097
174	Zuckerfabrik Jülich AG	28.0	2063	
179	Paulaner-Salvator-Thomasbräu AG	25.3	2082	2097
183	"Sarotti" AG	23.8	2065	203, 204, 205, 2086
185	Wicküler-Küpper-Brauerei AG	23.0	2082	2086, 2097
187	Holsten-Brauerei AG	22.9	2082	2097
188	Gebrüder Stollwerck AG	22.7	2065	203, 204, 205, 358
193	Bavaria- und St. Pauli-Brauerei	19.8	2082	2086
195	Binding-Brauerei AG	19.5	2082	2097

Rank	Firm	Assets (DM millions)	Product lines (SIC codes) Major	Others
196	Berliner Kindl Brauerei AG	18.9	2082	2086, 2097
199	Haake-Beck Brauerei AG	17.0	2082	
Group 22: Textile mill products				
23	Chemische Werke Hüls AG	307.6	2285	281, 282, 284, 286
34	Vereinigte Glanzstoff-Fabriken AG (VGF)	218.7	2285	222, 3552
71	Christian Dierig AG	98.0	228	221, 222
87	Vereinigte Seidenwebereien AG	70.3	222	221, 223
90	Baumwollindustrie Erlangen-Bamberg AG	67.8	221	222, 228
91	Chemie Faser	66.6	2285	282
120	Mech. Baumwoll-Spinnerei und Weberei Augsburg	45.9	221	222, 223
127	J.F. Adolff AG	40.5	228	226
128	Bremer Woll-Kämmerei	39.1	223	281, 287, 299
131	Val. Mehler AG	38.0	229	239
134	Kulmbacher Spinnerei	37.5	228	229
135	Deutsche Rhodiaceta AG	37.4	2285	
136	Mez AG	37.3	228	
138	Norddeutsche Wollkämmerei und Kammgarn-spinnerei AG	36.6	228	
143	Württembergische Cattunmanufactur	35.8	221	222, 223
144	Süddeutsche Zellwolle AG	35.7	228	
148	Augsburger Kammgarn-Spinnerei	34.0	228	229, 239
151	J. P. Bemberg	33.2	2285	
167	Hanfwerke Füssen-Immenstadt AG	30.1	229	
171	Neue Augsburger Kattunfabrik	28.7	221	222, 228
178	Vereinigte Jute-Spinnereien und Webereien AG	26.3	229	239
181	Wollgarnfabrik Tittel & Krüger und Sternwoll-Spinnerei AG	24.3	228	
191	Zwirnerei Ackermann AG	21.2	228	
192	Kammgarnspinnerei Stöhr & Co. AG	20.6	228	221, 229
197	Zwirnerei und Nähfadenfabrik Göggingen	18.8	228	229

Rank	Firm	Assets (DM millions)	Product lines (SIC codes) Major	Others
198	Woll-Wäscherei und Kämmerei in Döhren	18.8	223	

Group 23: Apparel and other textile products

Rank	Firm	Assets (DM millions)	Major	Others
180	Gebhard & Co.	24.6	233	222

Group 26: Paper and allied products

Rank	Firm	Assets (DM millions)	Major	Others
45	Zellstofffabrik Waldhof	169.9	262	263, 265
61	Aschaffenburger Zellstoff-werke AG	134.0	262	263
70	Feldmühle Papier- und Zellstoffwerke	99.5	262	263, 265, 286 329

Group 28: Chemicals and allied products

Rank	Firm	Assets (DM millions)	Major	Others
2	Farbenfabriken vorm. Friedr. Bayer & Co.	1,086.0	286	281, 283, 284, 285, 287, 289, 299, 333, 386
4	Badische Anilin & Sodafabrik AG (BASF)	835.0	286	281, 282, 284, 287, 289, 386
7	Farbwerke Hoechst AG vorm. Meister Lucius & Brüning	700.6	286	281, 282, 283, 284, 287, 289, 354, 386
25	Wintershall AG	297.0	281	287, 291, 299
31	Rheinpreussen AG für Bergbau u. Chemie	247.5	286	mining, utility
39	Deutsche Gold- und Silber-Scheideanstalt vormals Roessler (DEGUSSA)	203.7	281	283, 285, 286, 287, 333, 384
41	Dynamit AG vorm. Alfr. Nobel & Co.	187.3	2892	281, 282, 354, 357
49	Schloven-Chemie AG	159.7	286	291
57	Kali-Chemie AG	145.8	281	286, 287, 2086, 283, mining
62	Ruhrchemie AG	129.6	286	
63	Vereinigte Kaliwerke Salzdetfurth AG	119.2	281	287
73	Burbach-Kaliwerke AG	94.6	281	287, 289
78	Schering AG	87.7	283	284, 287, 383, 386
82	Cassella Farbwerke Mainkur AG	81.6	286	282, 283, 287, 2285
86	Süddeutsche Kalkstickstoff-Werke AG	73.2	281	282, 2285
97	Rütgerswerke AG	62.6	286	284, 285, 287, 295, 299
105	E. Merck AG	54.5	283	287
122	"Sachtleben" AG für Bergbau und Chemische Industrie	45.1	286	281, 282, mining

Rank	Firm	Assets (DM millions)	Product lines (SIC codes) Major	Others
125	P. Beiersdorf & Co. AG	41.6	284	283, 384
129	Chemische Werke Albert	39.0	287	281, 282, 283, 285
146	Wasag-Chemie AG	34.7	281	286
182	Chemische Werke Bergkamen AG	24.1	286	281, 291
184	Sunlicht Gesellschaft AG	23.6	284	281, 283
189	Riedel-de Haën AG	22.4	283	281, 286, 287, 289
Group 29: Petroleum and coal products				
13	ESSO AG	448.3	291	
15	Deutsche Shell AG	428.5	291	299
18	Gelsenberg Benzin AG	377.3	291	351
26	Deutsche Erdöl-AG	286.6	291	299, 284, 399
40	Deutsche Vacuum Oel AG	203.2	291	299
92	Deutsche Gasolin AG	66.3	291	299
Group 30: Rubber and miscellaneous plastics products				
33	Continental Gummi-Werke AG	227.8	301	306, 2296, 384, 394
81	Deutsche Dunlop Gummi Compagnie AG	82.6	301	306, 394
85	Phoenix Gummiwerke AG	73.7	301	302, 204, 306, 384
116	Metzeler Gummiwerke AG	48.3	301	304, 306, 384, 394
173	Gummi-Werke Fulda	28.3	301	
Group 31: Leather and leather products				
79	Salamander AG	84.7	314	319, 284
185	Cornelius Heyl AG	23.4	311	
Group 32: Stone, clay, and glass products				
72	Dyckerhoff Portland-Zementwerke AG	95.5	324	
74	Portland-Zementwerke Heidelberg AG	92.5	324	
93	Rheinisch-Westfälische Kalkwerke AG	66.2	327	
124	AG der Gerresheimer Glashüttenwerke	41.9	322	329, 381
142	Deutsche Libby-Owens-Gesellschaft für maschinelle Glasherstellung AG	36.0	322	321
162	Deutsche Tafelglas AG	31.4	321	
Group 33: Primary metal products				
1	Mannesmann AG	1,091.1	331	325, 356
3	Hoesch Werke AG	969.9	331	353, 354, 3714, 374

Rank	Firm	Assets (DM millions)	Product lines (SIC codes) Major	Others
5	Dortmund-Hörder Hüttenunion AG	753.7	331	325
8	Hüttenwerke Phönix AG	694.6	331	
10	Nordwestdeutscher Hütten- und Bergwerksverein AG (Klöckner-Werke)	652.0	331	345, 374
11	Rheinische Röhrenwerke AG	469.4	331	
12	Hüttenwerk Rheinhausen AG	452.2	331	327, 374
14	Gusstahlwerk Bochumer Verein AG	434.8	331	374
16	Hüttenwerk Oberhausen AG	409.8	331	327
17	Rheinische Stahlwerke AG	398.0	331	353
19	Metallgesellschaft AG	350.6	331	333, 281, 282, 283, 284, 286, 299, 306, 355, 356, transportation
29	Ruhrstahl AG	257.9	331	344, 346, 352, 354, 356
30	Ilseder Hütte	248.6	331	281, 286, 351
35	August-Thyssen-Hütte AG	217.4	331	
36	Eisenwerk-Gesellschaft Maximilianshütte AG	214.7	331	
37	Vereinigte Aluminium-Werke AG	212.8	333	281, 325
38	Deutsche Edelstahlwerke AG	205.9	331	
42	Hüttenwerke Siegerland AG	185.0	331	
46	Felten & Guilleaume Carlswerk AG	169.4	335	333, 361, 364, 366
50	Niederrheinische Hütte AG	155.6	331	325
52	Stahl- und Walzwerke Rasselstein/Andernach AG	154.8	331	
54	Duisburger Kupferhütte	152.0	333	331, 281, 287
58	Stahlwerke Südwestfalen AG	145.7	331	
59	Norddeutsche Affinerie	144.4	333	281, 287
60	Buderus'sche Eisenwerke	135.3	331	327, 344, 356, 358
64	Stahlwerke Bochum AG	119.1	331	
66	Hütten-und Bergwerke Rheinhausen AG	111.8	331	
67	Gusstahlwerk Witten	104.3	331	
84	Hüttenwerk Salzgitter AG	74.8	331	281, 351, 353, 354, 356, 361
89	Stolberger Zink AG für Bergbau und Hüttenbetrieb	69.4	333	281
101	Metallhüttenwerke Lübeck	58.4	333	281

Rank	Firm	Assets (DM millions)	Product lines (SIC codes) Major	Others
106	Th. Goldschmidt AG	54.3	333	281, 283, 286, 287, 289, 366
117	Capito & Klein AG	48.1	331	
123	Stahlwerke Röchling-Buderus AG	43.0	331	
130	Wieland-Werke AG	38.5	335	
133	Luitpoldhütte AG	37.8	331	327
159	Kabelwerk Rheydt AG	31.7	335	
165	Westfälische Drahtindustrie	30.5	335	331, 349
169	Mansfeld AG für Bergbau u. Hüttenbetrieb	29.6	333	332, 281, 286, 295, mining
190	Vereinigte Deutsche Nickel-Werke AG	21.4	333	331, 342, 343
Group 34: Fabricated metal products				
94	Busch-Jaeger Dürener Metallwerke AG	65.6	346	361, 381
108	Zahnradfabrik Friedrichshafen AG	53.3	346	3714
140	J.A. Schmalbach Blechwarenwerke AG	36.3	341	
157	Württembergische Metall-warenfabrik	32.1	342	346, 322, 328, 364, 395
163	W. Krefft AG	31.3	343	342, 346, 333, 355, 358, 363, 367
Group 35: Machinery, except electrical				
24	DEMAG AG	307.1	351	353, 354, 331, 361, 374
28	Klöckner-Humboldt-Deutz AG	262.2	351	352, 331, 344, 3714, 374
55	Deutsche Babcock & Wilcox-Dampfkessel-Werke AG	151.3	356	351, 354, 355, 358
56	Gesellschaft für Linde's Eismaschinen AG	148.7	358	351, 352, 354, 355, 356, 281, 286, 363
75	Maschinenfabrik Buckau R. Wolf AG	91.4	351	353, 355, 358, 348
80	Heinrich Lanz AG	83.4	352	
88	Industrie-Werke Karlsruhe AG	69.5	354	355, 358, 331, 382
96	Vereinigte Kesselwerke AG	63.1	351	356, 343, 344
98	Didier-Werke AG	60.8	3567	325
100	Schiess AG	58.6	354	353, 3552
103	Westfalia Dinnendahl Gröppel AG	56.8	353	354, 356

Rank	Firm	Assets (DM millions)	Product lines (SIC codes) Major	Others
104	Maschinenfabrik Fahr AG	55.8	352	
112	Rheinmetall-Borsig AG	52.3	355	354
114	Dürrwerke AG	49.9	358	353, 344
115	G.M. Pfaff AG	48.5	3636	
132	Motoren-Werke Mannheim	38.0	351	3561, 374
145	Atlas-Werke AG	34.8	351	353, 355, 356, 366, 373, 381, 384
147	Anker-Werke AG	34.5	357	375, 384
152	Schubert & Salzer Maschinenfabrik AG	33.2	3552	354, 3636, 343
153	Ernst Heinkel AG	32.9	351	
156	Dürkoppwerke AG	32.3	3636	3562, 3714
158	Singer Nähmaschinen AG	32.1	3636	361, 228
161	Klein, Schanzlin & Becker AG	31.5	356	358
166	Kamphagel AG (vorm. Nagel & Kaemp)	30.4	353	352, 3551, 373, 382
172	Bergedorfer Eisenwerke AG Astra-Werk	28.7	3551	3552, 352, 358
175	Maschinen-AG Balcke	26.6	358	356, 344
194	L. Schuler AG	19.5	354	3636
200	Eisenwerk Wülfel	16.7	356	353, 354
Group 36: Electric and electronic equipment				
6	Siemens & Halske AG	739.8	361	363, 364, 365, 366, 367, 333, 335, 351, 352, 353, 354, 355, 356, 358, 371, 374, 381, 382, 384, 387
9	Allgemeine Elektricitäts-Gesellschaft (AEG)	658.0	361	363, 364, 365, 366, 367, 351, 354, 355, 356, 371, 374, 381, 382, 384, 387
27	Brown, Boveri & Cie. AG	278.1	361	335, 351, 355, 374
51	Accumulatoren-Fabrik AG	154.9	3692	
107	Pintsch BAMAG AG	53.5	361	351, 356
113	Voigt & Haeffner AG	51.2	361	363, 356
121	C. Lorenz AG	45.7	366	
154	Schorch-Werke AG	32.8	361	
Group 37: Transportation equipment				
21	Daimler-Benz AG	340.2	3711	351, 354
22	Adam Opel AG	335.3	3711	358

Rank	Firm	Assets (DM millions)	Product lines (SIC codes) Major	Others
32	Robert Bosch GmbH		3714	351, 356, 361, 364, 369, 382
43	Kieler Howaldtswerke AG	175.5	373	344, 351
44	AG "Weser"	175.0	373	344, 351, 353
47	Deutsche Werft AG	165.7	373	
48	Howaldtswerke Hamburg AG	161.4	373	344
65	Orenstein-Koppel u. Lübecket Maschinenbau AG	114.0	374	373, 352, 353, 356
68	Bremer Vulkan Schiffbau u. Maschinenfabrik	102.8	373	344, 351
69	Ford-Werke AG	102.5	3711	
76	Lübecker Flender-Werke AG	90.3	374	
77	BMW	87.8	3711	375
83	NSU Werke AG	80.4	375	3711, 351
99	Adlerwerke	59.5	3711	375, 356, 357
102	Fichtel & Sachs AG	58.1	3714	375, 351, 3562
109	Krauss-Maffei AG	52.9	374	371, 344, 346, 353, 354, 355, 356
149	Flensburger Schiffsbau-Gesellschaft	33.5	373	344
155	Waggonfabrik Uerdingen AG	32.5	374	3711
Group 38: Instruments and related products				
111	Zeiss Ikon AG	52.4	386	
164	Kodak AG	30.6	386	
168	Gebrüder Junghans AG	29.9	387	
Group 39: Miscellaneous manufacturing industries				
95	Deutsche Linoleum-Werke AG	64.6	399	307, 384
176	Matth. Hohner AG	26.6	393	274
177	Deutsche Zündholz Fabriken	26.5	399	

Turnover in the list of those of the 200 largest industrial enterprises in Germany that are in the food, chemical, and machinery industries, 1913, 1929, 1953. Rank number follows the company name.

1913 (Assets over M 12.6 million)	1929 (Assets over RM 16.0 million)	1953 (Assets over DM 16.7 million)
Group 20: Food and kindred products		
202: Dairy products		
[Deutsche Nestle pvt. subsidiary of Nestlé, Switzerland][a]	[Deutsche Nestle RM11.4, subsidiary of Nestlé, Switzerland]	Deutsche Nestle 126 subsidiary of Nestlé, Switzerland
203: Canned and preserved fruit and vegetables		
[C. H. Knorr M9.1]	[C. H. Knorr RM9.6]	C. H. Knorr 160
204: Grain mill products		
	Getreide-Industrie & Commission 81	[Getreidehandel DM19.0 distribution only]
	[Heinr. Auer Mühlenwerke RM11.6]	Heinr. Auer Mühlenwerke 137
206: Sugar and confectionery products		
2063: Beet sugar		
Zuckerfabrik Frankenthal 85	Süddeutsche Zucker 54	Süddeutsche Zucker 53
Zuckerraffinerie Tangermünde Fr. Meyers Sohn 106	Zuckerraffinerie Tangermünde Fr. Meyers Sohn 134	[Zuckerraffinerie Tangermünde Fr. Meyers Sohn DM3.1]
Zuckerfabrik Klein-Wanzleben 129	Zuckerfabrik Klein-Wanzleben 106	[Klein-Wanzlebener Saatzucht agriculture only]
Zuckerraffinerie Halle 153	[Zuckerraffinerie Halle RM7.6]	East Germany
Pommersche Provinzial-Zuckersiederei 198	[Pommersche Provinzial-Zuckersiederei RM8.0]	[Pommersche Provinzial-Zuckersiederei DM0.8]
Rheinischer Aktien-Verein zur Zuckerfabrikation 199	(Pfeiffer & Langen 1928)[b]	

a. Brackets indicate that a company's assets were not sufficient for it to be included in the 200 largest industrial enterprises for the year in which it is listed (in which case total assets are given), or that the company was privately held (pvt.) and total assets are not available.

b. If a firm was merged with or fully acquired by another, the name of the acquiring or merged enterprise and the year of acquisition or merger is given in parenthesis.

1913 (Assets over M 12.6 million)	1929 (Assets over RM 16.0 million)	1953 (Assets over DM 16.7 million)
	Pfeifer & Langen 93	liquidated 1932
	von Rath, Schoeller & Skene 157	Poland
[Zuckerfabrik Jülich Alex. Schoeller pvt.]	[Zuckerfabrik Jülich Alex. Schoeller RM2.1]	Zuckerfabrik Jülich 174

2065: Confectionery and cocoa products

1913	1929	1953
Gebrüder Stollwerck 80	Gebrüder Stollwerck 142	Gebrüder Stollwerck 188
Hartwig & Vogel 124	[Hartwig & Vogel RM15.2]	
Sarotti 170	Sarotti 155	Sarotti 183

207: Fats and oils

1913	1929	1953
Verein deutscher Oelfabriken 66	(Deutsche Jurgens 1920)	
Bremer-Besigheimer Oelfabriken 99	(Deutsche Jurgens 1920)	
H. Schlinck & Cie. 140	[H. Schlinck & Cie. RM11.3]	(Deutsche Jurgens 1938)
F. Thörl's Oelfabrik Gross-Grerau-Bremen 148	F. Thörl's 109 (Deutsche Jurgens 1920)	F. Thörl's 141
	Deutsche Jurgens Werke 44 subsidiary of Jurgens, Netherlands	Margarine-Union 20 subsidiary of Unilever, Netherland-Great Britain
	Van-den Bergh's Margarine 49	(Deutsche Jurgens 1930)
	[Fritz Homann pvt.]	Firtz Homann 150

208: Beverages
2082: Malt beverages

1913	1929	1953
Schultheiss' Brauerei 45	Schultheiss-Patzenhofer 23	Schultheiss-Brauerei 139
Aktienbrauerei zum Löwenbräu 53	Aktienbrauerei zum Löwenbräu 118	Löwenbräu München 119
Brauerei Patzenhofer 84	(Schultheiss' Brauerei 1920)	
G. Sinner 90	Sinner 164	[Sinner DM10.3]
Unionbrauerei Schülein 115	liquidated 1914	
Hackerbräu 130	[Hackerbräu RM11.5]	[Hackerbräu DM11.0]
Brauhaus Nürnberg 143	[Brauhaus Nürnberg RM12.4]	[Brauhaus Nürnberg DM11.2]

1913 (Assets over M 12.6 million)	1929 (Assets over RM 16.0 million)	1953 (Assets over DM 16.7 million)
Reudnitz Riebeck 144	Reudnitz Riebeck 86	East Germany
Bürgerliches Brauhaus München 154	(Aktienbrauerei zum Löwenbräu 1921)	
Württembergische Hohenzollern'sche Brauerei 196	[Württembergische Hohenzollern'sche Brauerei RM13.8]	
Schlossbrauerei Schöneberg 200	[Schlossbrauerei Berlin- Schöneberg RM8.6]	[Berliner Schlossbrauerei DM9.5]
[Brauerei Ernst Engelhardt M5.9]	Engelhardt-Brauerei 74	[Engelhardt-Brauerei DM4.1]
[Dortmunder Actien- Brauerei M9.8]	Dortmunder Actien- Brauerei 103	Dortmunder Actien- Brauerei 170
[Dortmunder Union- Brauerei M6.3]	Dortmunder Union- Brauerei 137	Dortmunder Union- Brauerei 118
[Paulanerbräu Salvatorbrauerei M11.0]	Paulanerbräu Salvatorbrauerei u. Thomasbräu 149	[Paulaner-Salvator- Thomasbräu 179
[Kaiserbrauerei Beck M11.1]	Haake-Beck Brauerei 158	Haake-Beck Brauerei 199
[Böhmisches Brauhaus M8.6]	Löwenbrauerei- Böhmisches Brauhaus 160	[Löwenbrauerei- Böhmisches Brauhaus DM3.2]
[Bavarra Brauerei M8.4]	Bavaria- u. St. Pauli- Brauerei 162	Bavaria- u. St. Pauli Brauerei 193
[Holstein Brauerei M6.9]	Holstein Brauerei 170	Holstein Brauerei 187
[Berliner Kindl Brauerei M8.5]	Berliner Kindl Brauerei 173	Berliner Kindl Brauerei 195
[Brauerei zum Felsenkeller M6.9]	Brauerei zum Felsenkeller 193	(Aktienbrauerei zum Löwenbräu 1933)
	Gabriel u. Jos. Sedlmayr 197	East Germany
[Wicküler-Küpper- Brauerei M11.7]	[Wicküler-Küpper- Brauerei RM11.8]	Wicküler-Küpper- Brauerei 185
[Brauerei Binding M12.4]	[Schöfferhof-Binding- Bürgerbräu RM13.3]	Binding-Brauerei 195
2085: Distilled liquor Breslauer Spiritfabrik 135	Ostwerke 41	(Schultheiss-Patzenhofer Brauerei 1930)
2091: Fish products [Deutsche Dampffischrei Nordsee in Bremen RM6.9]	Nordsee Deutsch Hochseefischerei 83	Nordsee Deutsch Hochseefischerei 110

1913 (Assets over M 12.6 million)	1929 (Assets over RM 16.0 million)	1953 (Assets over DM 16.7 million)

Group 28: Chemicals and allied products
281: Industrial inorganic chemicals

Deutsche Solvay 16 subsidiary of Solvay, Belgium	Deutsche Solvay 19 subsidiary of Solvay, Belgium	[Deutsche Solvay pvt.]
DEGUSSA 34	DEGUSSA 47	DEGUSSA 39
Sloman 64	[Sloman RM2.5 distribution only]	
Holzverkohlungs-Industrie 77	(DEGUSSA 1929)	
Consolidirte Alkaliwerke Westeregeln 83	Consolidirte Alkaliwerke Westeregeln 91	(Vereingte Kaliwerke Salzdetfurth 1937)
Alkaliwerke Rohnenberg 95	(Kali-Industrie 1927)	
Elektrochemische Werke 126	liquidated 1925	
Vereinigte Chemische-fabriken Leopoldshall 163	(Kaliwerke Aschers-Iden 1922)	
Chemische Fabrik Hönningen 173	[Chemische Fabrik Hönningen pvt.]	
Silesia Verein 184	(Rütgerswerke 1920)	
Verein chemischer Fabriken in Mannheim 185	liquidated 1920	
Chemische Fabrik Bachau 197	(Th. Goldschmidt 1927)	
	Kali-Industrie 6	Wintershall 25
[Kaliwerke Kruegershall M13.2]	Burbach-Kaliwerke 11	Burbach-Kaliwerke 73
[Kaliwerke Friedrichshall M11.3]	Kali-Chemie 55	Kali-Chemie 57
	Kaliwerke Salzdetfurth 64	Vereingte Kaliwerke Salzdetfurth 63
	Kaliwerke Aschersleben 69	(Vereingte Kaliwerke Salzdetfurth 1937)
		Wasag Chemie 146 controlled by German government

283: Drugs (consumer chemicals)

Chemische Fabrik von Heyden 142	Chemische Fabrik von Heyden 153	[Chemische Fabrik von Heyden DM8.5]

1913 (Assets over M 12.6 million)	1929 (Assets over RM 16.0 million)	1953 (Assets over DM 16.7 million)
Chemische Fabrik auf Actien vorm E. Schering 151	Schering-Kahlbaum 50	Schering 78
[Saccharin-Fabrik Fahlberg, List M6.1]	Saccharin-Fabrik Fahlberg, List 166	[Fahlberg-list Chemische Fabriken DM0.8]
[J. D. Riedel M11.3]	J. D. Riedel-E. de Haën 169	Riedel-de Haën 189
[E. Merck pvt.]	[E. Merck pvt.]	E. Merck 105

284: Soap, cleaners, and toilet goods (consumer chemicals)

	[P. Beiersdorf pvt.]	P. Beiersdorf 125
[Sunlicht Gesellschaft pvt.]	[Sunlicht Gesellschaft pvt.]	Sunlicht Gesellschaft 184

286: Industrial organic chemicals

BASF 8	I. G. Farben 2	BASF 4
Bayer 9	I. G. Farben 2	Bayer 2
Hoechst 15	I. G. Farben 2	Hoechst 7
Griesheim-Elektron 40	I. G. Farben 2	
AGFA 48	I. G. Farben 2	
Rütgerswerke 60	Rütgerswerke 31	Rütgerswerke 97
H. Renner & Co. 113	liquidated 1920	
Chemische Fabriken Weiler-ter Meer 150	I. G. Farben 2	
[Oberschlesische Kokswerke & Chemische Fabriken mining only]	Oberschlesische Kokswerke & Chemische Fabriken 18	(Schering 1937)
	Ruhrchemie 53	Ruhrchemie 62
	Siemens-Planiawerke 148 controlled by Siemens & Halske and Rütgereswerke	[Siemens-Planiawerke pvt. subsidiary of Siemens & Halske]
[Gewerkschaft Rheinpreussen pvt. mining]	[Gewerkschaft Rheinpreussen pvt. mining]	Rheinpreussen AG für Bergbau u. Chemie 31
		Schloven-Chemie 49 controlled by Bergwerks- gesellschaft Hibernia
[Leopold Cassella pvt.]	I. G. Farben 2	Cassella Farbwerke Mainkur 82
		Sachtleben 122
		Chemische Werke Bergkamen 182

1913 (Assets over M 12.6 million)	1929 (Assets over RM 16.0 million)	1953 (Assets over DM 16.7 million)

287: Agricultural chemicals

1913	1929	1953
Anglo-Continentale Guano Werke 91	[Guano-Werke RM13.0]	[Guano-Werke DM20.5 subsidiary of Wasag Chemie]
Chemische Werke H. & E. Albert 92	Chemische Werke H. & E. Albert 196	Chemische Werke Albert 129
Union Fabrik Chemischer Produkte 128	[Union Fabrik Chemischer Produkte RM10.2]	
Moritz Milch & Co. 171	(AG Pommerensdorf 1927)	
	Mitteldeutsche Stickstoffwerke 147 controlled by Vereinigte Industries Unternehmungen AG	(Bayerischen Stickstoffwerke 1933)
[Bayerische Stickstoffwerke pvt.]	[Bayerische Stickstoffwerke pvt.]	Süddeutsche Kalkstickstoffwerke 86 controlled by Vereinigte Industrie Unternehmungen

289: Miscellaneous chemical products
2892: Explosives

1913	1929	1953
Dynamit AG Nobel 42	Dynamit AG Nobel 65	Dynamit AG Nobel 41
Vereinigte Köln-Rottweiler Pulverfabriken 44	(I. G. Farben 1926)	
Rheinische Westfälische Sprengstoff 162	Rheinische Westfälische Sprengstoff 72	(Dynamit 1931)
	Westfälisch-Anhaltische Sprengstoff 165	(I.G. Farben 1945)

2899: Chemicals, not elsewhere classified

1913	1929	1953
H. Scheidemandel 65	H. Scheidemandel 180	[H. Scheidemandel-Motard DM15.6]
	Georg Egestorffs Salzwerke 195	(Kali Chemie 1932)

Group 35: Machinery, except electrical
351: Engines and turbines

1913	1929	1953
MAN 11	MAN 29 controlled by Gutehoffnungshütte	[MAN DM414.7 subsidiary of Gutehoffnungshütte]
Maschinenfabrik-Anstalt Humboldt 38	Maschinenbau-Anstalt Humboldt 104	Klöckner-Humboldt-Deutz 28

1913 (Assets over M 12.6 million)	1929 (Assets over RM 16.0 million)	1953 (Assets over DM 16.7 million)
DEMAG 43	DEMAG 48	DEMAG 24
Gasmotoren-Fabrik Deutz 46	Motorenfabrik Deutz 107	Klöckner-Humboldt-Deutz 28
BAMAG 73	Bamag-Meguin 128	Pintsch BAMAG 107 in Group 36
Maschinenfabrik Esslingen 75	(Gutehoffnungshütte 1927)	
Berliner Maschinenbau L. Schwartzkopff 89	Berliner Maschinenbau L. Schwartzkopff 114	[Berliner Maschinenbau L. Schwartzkopff pvt.]
Maschinenfabrik Thyssen 149	(Vereinigte Stahl Werke 1926)	
Görlitzer Maschinenbau 189	liquidated 1921	
Maschinenfabrik Buchau R. Wolf 192	Maschinenfabrik Buchau R. Wolf 151	Maschinenfabrik Buchau R. Wolf 75
	[Vereinigte Kesselwerke RM6.7]	Vereinigte Kesselwerke 96
	[Motoren-Werke Mannheim RM9.1]	Motoren-Werke Mannheim 132
	[Atlas-Werke RM9.7]	Atlas-Werke 145
		Ernst Heinkel 153

352: Farm and garden machinery

HANOMAG 87	HANOMAG 101	(Rheinstahl-Union 1952) liquidated 1933
Landwirtschaftlichen Maschinen Epple u. Buxbaum 141	[Vereinigte Fabriken Landwirtschaftlichen Maschinen Epple & Buxbaum RM8.8]	
	Heinrich Lanz 123	Heinrich Lanz 80
[Maschinenfabrik Fahr M3.0]	[Maschinenfabrik Fahr RM6.5]	Maschinenfabrik Fahr 104

353: Construction and related machinery

	Miag 88	East Germany
		Westfalia Dinnendahl Gröppel 103
		Kamphagel 166

354: Metalworking machinery

Ludw. Loewe 72	(Ges. für Elektrische Unternehmungen 1929)	
Deutsche Waffen- u. Munitions-fabriken 36 in Group 34	Berliner-Karlsruher Industrie-Werke 95 in Group 34	Industrie-Werke Karlsruhe 88

1913 (Assets over M 12.6 million)	1929 (Assets over RM 16.0 million)	1953 (Assets over DM 16.7 million)
[Ernst Schiess Werkzeugmaschinenfabrik pvt.]	[Schiess-Defries RM13.9]	Schiess 100

355: Special industry machinery

Gebr. Sack 165	(Miag 1925)	
Amme, Giesecke & Konegen 191	(Miag 1925)	
Rheinmetall 59	Rheinmetall 80 [Astra-Werke RM2.3]	Rheinmetall-Borsig 112 Astra-Werke 172

3552: Textile machinery

Vogtländische Maschinenfabrik J. C. & H. Dietrich 121	[Vogtländische Maschinenfabrik J. C. & H. Dietrich pvt.]	liquidated 1934
Schubert & Salzer 179	Schubert & Salzer 100	Schubert & Salzer 152
Sächsische Maschinenfabrik Rich. Hartmann 86	Sächsische Maschinenfabrik Rich. Hartmann 161	East Germany

356: General industrial machinery

Julius Pintsch 61	Julius Pintsch 122 in Group 36	Pintsch BAMAG 107 in Group 36
Didier 71	Didier 108	Didier 98
	Vereinigte Kugellager- Fabriken 59	[Vereinigte Kugellager- Fabriken pvt.]
[Deutsche Babcock & Wilcox M7.0]	[Deutsche Babcock & Wilcox RM12.5]	Deutsche Babcock & Wilcox 55
		Klein, Schanzlin & Becker 161
[Eisenwerk Wülfel M5.7]	[Eisenwerk Wülfel RM4.4]	Eisenwerk Wülfel 200

357: Office and computing machines

[Wanderer-Werke M9.3]	Wanderer-Werke 120	[Wanderer-Werke DM11.5] Anker-Werke 147

358: Refrigeration and service machinery

Linde's Eismaschinen 117	Linde's Eismaschinen 90	Linde's Eismaschinen 56
Gebr. Körting 54	Gebr. Körting 175	[Gebr. Körting pvt.]
		Dürrwerke 114
		Maschinen AG Balcke 175

3636: Sewing machines (from Group 36)

Singer 28	Singer 38	Singer 158
Maschinenfabrik Gritzner 178	[Maschinenfabrik Gritzner RM11.3]	[Gritzner-Kayser DM16.0]
Dürkoppwerke 194	Dürkoppwerke 194 [G. M. Pfaff RM16.0]	Dürkoppwerke 156 G. M. Pfaff 115

1913 (Assets over M 12.6 million)	1929 (Assets over RM 16.0 million)	1953 (Assets over DM 16.7 million)

Group 36: Electric and electronic equipment
361: Electric distributing and industrial equipment

AEG 2	AEG 3	AEG 9
Siemens-Schuckert Werke 3 controlled by Siemens & Halske and Schuckert	Siemens-Schuckert Werke 5 controlled by Siemens & Halske and Schuckert	[Siemens-Schuckert Werke DM817.5 subsidiary of Siemens & Halske]
Siemens & Halske 6	Siemens & Halske 7	Siemens & Halske 6
Bergmann-Elektricitäts-Werke 17	Bergmann-Elektricitäts-Werke 34	[Bergmann-Elektricitäts-Werke DM1.7]
Brown, Boveri & Cie 93 subsidiary of Brown, Boveri, Switzerland	Brown, Boveri & Cie 52 subsidiary of Brown, Boveri, Switzerland	Brown, Boveri & Cie 27 subsidiary of Brown, Boveri, Switzerland
[Voigt & Haeffner M12.4]	Voigt & Haeffner 163	Voigt & Haeffner 113
		Schorch-Werke 154

364: Electric lighting and wiring equipment

Julius Pintsch 61 in Group 35	Julius Pintsch 122	Pintsch BAMAG 107

365: Radio and TV receiving equipment

[Polyphon Musikwerke M2.8]	Polyphonewerke 110	[Deutsche Grammophon pvt. controlled by Siemens & Halske]

366: Communication equipment

Mix & Genest 147	Mix & Genest 130 controlled by ITT, United States	Mix & Genest pvt. controlled by ITT, United States
[C. Lorenz AG, Telephon u. Telegraphen Werke M2.9]	C. Lorenz 135 controlled by ITT, United States	C. Lorenz 121 controlled by ITT, United States

369: Miscellaneous electrical equipment and supplies
3691: Storage and other batteries

Accumulatoren Fabrik 67	Accumulatoren Fabrik 62	Accumulatoren Fabriken 51

Group 37: Transportation equipment
371: Motor vehicles and equipment
3711: Motor vehicles and car bodies

Benz & Cie. 33	Daimler-Benz 24	Daimler-Benz 21
Daimler-Motoren-Ges. 101	Daimler-Benz 24	Daimler-Benz 21
Neue Automobil 111 controlled by AEG	Nationale Automobil Ges. 87	[Nationale Automobil Ges. DM10.0]
Adlerwerke 114	Adlerwerke 78	Adlerwerke 99
	Adam Opel 33 controlled by General Motors, U.S.	Adam Opel 22 subsidiary of General Motors, U.S.

1913 (Assets over M 12.6 million)	1929 (Assets over RM 16.0 million)	1953 (Assets over DM 16.7 million)
	BMW 105	BMW 77
	Zschopauer Motorenwerke 127	[Auto Union DM5.0]
	Horchwerke 145	(Zschopauer Motorenwerke 1932)
	Ford Motor Co. 168 subsidiary of Ford Motor, U.S.	Ford-Wierke 69 subsidiary of Ford Motor, U.S.

3714: Motor vehicle parts and accessories

1913	1929	1953
	Robert Bosch 40	Robert Bosch 32
	Fichtel & Sachs 140	Fichtel & Sachs 102

373: Ship and boat building and repairing

1913	1929	1953
Vulkan Werke 10	(Deutsche Schiff u. Machinenbau 1926)	
Blohm & Voss 24	Blohm & Voss 35	[Blohm & Voss DM8.5]
AG Weser 52	Deutsche Schiff- u. Maschinenbau Bremer 43	AG Weser 44 controlled by F. Krupp
Howaldtswerke Kiel	[Howaldtswerke Kiel RM7.8]	Kieler Howaldtswerke 43
Bremer Vulkan Schiffbau 88	Bremer Vulkan Schiffbau 116	Bremer Vulkan Schiffbau 68
Flensburger Schiffbau-Ges. 158	[Flensburger Schiffbau-Ges. RM5.3]	Flensburger Schiffbau-Ges. 149
Reiherstreg Schiffwerfte u. Maschinenfabrik 160	[Reiherstieg Schiffwerke u. Maschinenfabrik RM0.1]	
Joh. C. Tecklenborg 169	(Aktiengesellschaft Weser 1926)	
	Deutsche Werke Kiel 70	[Deutsche Werke Kiel pvt.]
	Deutsche Werft 99	Deutsche Werft 47 controlled by Gutchoffnungshütte and AEG
		Howaldtswerke Hamburg 48

374: Railroad equipment

1913	1929	1953
Orenstein & Koppel 18	Orenstein & Koppel 61	Orenstein & Koppel 65
Linke-Hofmann-Werke 58	Linke-Hofmann-Busch-Werke 45	East Germany

1913 (Assets over M 12.6 million)	1929 (Assets over RM 16.0 million)	1953 (Assets over DM 16.7 million)
Eisenbahnsignal-Bauanstalt Max Jüdel 186	[Eisenbahnsignal-Bauanstalt Max Jüdel RM12.5]	liquidated 1931
Deutsche Waggon Leinhanstalt 188	Eisenbahn-Verkehrsmittel 144	[Eisenbahn-Verkehrsmittel pvt.]
	Henschel & Sohn 25	[Henschel & Sohn pvt.]
	Knorr-Bremse 39	[Knorr Bremse DM10.9]
	Borsigwerk 112	(Rheinmetall 1932)
	Vereinigte Westdeutsche Waggonfabriken 129	(Klöckner-Humboldt-Deutz 1948)
	Waggon- u. Maschinenbau Görlitz 185	East Germany
	[Lübecker Flander-Werke RM3.6]	Lübecker Flander-Werke 76
		Krauss-Maffei 109
[Waggonfabrik Uerdingen M5.0]	[Waggonfabrik Uerdingen RM7.6]	Waggonfabrik Uerdingen 155
375: Motor cycles, bicycles, and parts		
[Neckausulmer Fahrradwerke M7.5]	NSU Vereinigte Fahrzeugwerke 150	NSU Werke 83

Notes

1. The Modern Industrial Enterprise

1. Simon Kuznets, *Economic Growth of Nations: Total Output and Production Structure* (Cambridge, Mass., 1971), pp. 144–151, 160–161, 316–317.
2. In recent years a large literature has appeared on the core-peripheral approach to analyzing modern economies. Before that, Robert Averitt, *The Dual Economy: The Dynamics of American Industry* (New York, 1968), was the pioneering study. Joseph Bowering, *Competition in a Dual Economy* (Princeton, 1986), provides a newer overview of this literature. Bowering concludes that for the years 1969–1973 "core firms tend to dominate industries which grow significantly more rapidly than other industries. Core firms' growth rates also tend to be closer to their industry growth rate than do periphery firm growth rates" (p. 179). The approach and findings of sociologists writing on core-peripheral firms, particularly in relation to labor and labor organization, are reviewed in Charles Tolbert, Patrick H. Horan, and E. M. Beck, "The Structure of Economic Segmentation: A Dual Economy Approach," *American Journal of Sociology* 85:1095–1116 (March 1980), and Randy Hudson and Robert L. Kaufman, "Economic Dualism: A Critical Review," *American Sociological Review* 47:727–739 (1982).
3. The evolution and implications of the separation of ownership from management have, of course, been a concern of economists and economic historians since the publication of the classic study by Adolf A. Berle, Jr., and Gardiner C. Means, *The Modern Corporation and Private Property* (New York, 1932).

2. Scale, Scope, and Organizational Capabilities

1. Most succinctly defined by Oliver Williamson in his "Modern Corporation: Origins, Evolution, Attributes," *Journal of Economic Literature* 19:1539–44 (Dec. 1981); also in his "Organizational Innovation: The Transaction Cost Approach," in Joshua Ronen, ed., *Entrepreneurship* (Lexington, Mass., 1983), ch. 5.
2. David Teece, "Economies of Scope and the Scope of the Enterprise," *Journal of Economic Behavior and Organization* 1:223–247 (Sept. 1980); John C. Panzar and

Robert D. Willig, "Economics of Scope," *American Economic Review* 71:268–272 (May 1981). See also Elizabeth E. Bailey and Ann F. Friedlaender, "Market Structure and Multiproduct Industries," *Journal of Economic Literature* 20:1084–1148 (Sept. 1982). The emphasis of this literature is on economies of scope in production, not in distribution.

3. Again the most succinct definition comes from Williamson, "The Modern Corporation," pp. 1547–49, which builds on Ronald Coase's classic article, "The Nature of the Firm," *Economica* 4:386–405 (Nov. 1937). In his piece Williamson states that "the criterion for organizing commercial transactions is assumed to be the strictly instrumental one of cost economizing. Essentially this takes two parts: economizing on production expenses and economizing on transaction costs. In fact, these are not independent and need to be addressed simultaneously." Williamson, however, does not differentiate between *distribution* expenses and transaction costs—costs that are largely defined in contractual terms. As Herman Daems has suggested, three types of transaction costs can be identified: contractual arrangements with customers, those with suppliers, and those with banks or other financial institutions or individuals.

4. A compilation by Herman Daems indicates that these firms generated an impressive share of the noncommunist world's employment in industry. Of the broad industrial categories in which the large firm clustered—food, chemicals, petroleum, metals, and the three machinery SIC groups—those firms employing more than 30,000 accounted in all the categories except food and nonelectrical machinery for from 39.5% to 72% of the total world's labor force in their industry. Herman Daems, "Power versus Efficiency: A Cross-Section Study of Chandler's *Visible Hand*," in François Caron, ed., *Entreprises et Entrepreneurs* (Paris, 1983).

5. I use the term "minimum efficient scale" as defined by such industrial organization economists as F. M. Scherer and William G. Shepherd, whose work, in turn, rests on that of George Stigler and Joe S. Bain, done in the 1950s and 1960s, on the relationship of "minimum optimal scale" to market share. This literature is effectively summarized by F. M. Scherer, "Economies of Scale and Industrial Concentration," in Harvey J. Goldschmid et al., eds., *Industrial Concentration: The New Learning* (Boston, 1974), esp. pp. 51–55; and by William G. Shepherd, *The Economics of Industrial Organization*, 2d ed. (Englewood Cliffs, N.J., 1985), chs. 9–10. My definition differs in emphasizing that minimum efficient scale depends on both capacity and throughput and thus can only be achieved by managerial coordination. An early and particularly useful application of these concepts to long-term development is Leonard W. Weiss, "The Survival Technique and the Extent of Suboptimal Capacity," *Journal of Political Economy* 72: 246–261 (June 1965). The term "scale" as used in this chapter and the following ones refers primarily to continuous flow processes, but it can pertain to batch processes, as suggested in Armen Alchian, "Costs and Outputs," in Moses Abramovitz et al., *The Allocation of Economic Resources: Essays in Honor of Bernard Francis Haley* (Stanford, 1959), pp. 23–40.

6. Ralph W. Hidy and Muriel E. Hidy, in their *Pioneering in Big Business, 1882–1911* (New York, 1955), pp. 14–23, 44–46, describe the financial arrangements that unified the Standard Oil alliance.

7. Hidy and Hidy, *Pioneering in Big Business*, p. 107, gives costs and profits for 1884 and 1885; also Harold F. Williamson and Arnold R. Daum, *The American Petroleum Industry: The Age of Illumination, 1859–1899* (Evanston, Ill., 1959), pp. 482–484.

8. L. F. Haber, *The Chemical Industry during the Nineteenth Century: A Study of the Economic Aspect of Applied Chemistry in Europe and North America* (Oxford, 1958), pp. 128–136; and John J. Beer, *The Emergence of the German Dye Industry* (Urbana, 1959), p. 119; Sachio Kaku, "The Development and Structure of the German Coal-Tar Dyestuffs Firms," in Akio Okochi and Hoshimi Uchida, eds., *Development and Diffusion of Technology* (Tokyo, 1979), p. 78.

9. Alfred D. Chandler, Jr., *The Visible Hand: The Managerial Revolution in American Business* (Cambridge, Mass., 1977), p. 379.

10. Scott J. Moss, *An Economic Theory of Business Strategy: An Essay in Dynamics without Equilibrium* (Oxford, 1981), pp. 110–111. The application of the concept of minimum efficient scale to the understanding of the evolution of the enterprise is one of several major contributions of Moss's study. Particularly valuable are the concepts spelled out in his chapters 6 and 7 on vertical integration.

11. A detailed example of recruiting and organizing such a hierarchy is given in Alfred D. Chandler, Jr., and Stephen Salsbury, *Pierre S. du Pont and the Making of the Modern Corporation* (New York, 1971), pp. 132–148.

12. In the United States, General Electric, Westinghouse, Eastman Kodak, and Du Pont all provide good examples of this relationship during their pioneering years. See Harold C. Passer, *The Electrical Manufacturers, 1875–1900: A Study in Competition, Entrepreneurship, Technical Change, and Economic Growth* (Cambridge, Mass., 1960), pp. 263–264; Reese V. Jenkins, *Images and Enterprise: Technology and the American Photographic Industry, 1839–1925* (Baltimore, 1975), pp. 116, 120, 183–187 (esp. 184); Chandler and Salsbury, *Pierre S. du Pont*, pp. 140, 142–143; David A. Hounshell and John Kenly Smith, Jr., *Science and Corporate Strategy: Du Pont R&D, 1902–1980* (Cambridge, Eng., 1988), esp. chs. 1, 2, and 8. For German examples see Chapters 12 and 14 of this study.

13. David C. Mowery, "The Emergence and Growth of Industrial Research in American Manufacturing, 1899–1945" (Ph.D. diss., Stanford University, 1981), ch. 5, and Mowery, "The Relationship between Intrafirm and Contractual Forms of Industrial Research, 1900–1941" (Paper, Harvard Business School, July 1982).

14. The term "pioneers" as used here is close to "innovators" as used by Joseph Schumpeter, that is, entrepreneurs who put new processes of production and new products into use. Because the words "innovator" and "innovation" have been so widely used in so many contexts since Schumpeter's day, I prefer the more neutral descriptive term "pioneers."

15. The literature on functional and strategic competition is voluminous. Because such competition has been central in the administration of industrial companies, this literature has been used for decades in courses in production, marketing, purchasing, control, and policy taught in American business schools. Michael Porter, *Competitive Strategy: Techniques for Analyzing Industries and Competitors* (New York, 1980), cogently describes the current thinking about such competition.

16. Stephen H. Hymer was the first to point out that the modern industrial enterprise moved abroad to exploit the competitive advantages based on the organizational capabilities of a managerial hierarchy. See particularly his "Multinational Corporation and the Law of Uneven Development," in J. W. Bhagwati, ed., *Economics and World Order* (New York, 1971), pp. 113–140, and his "Efficiency (Contradictions) of Multinational Corporations," *American Economic Review* 60:441–448 (May 1970). See also Charles P. Kindleberger, *American Business Abroad: Six Lectures on Direct Investment* (New Haven, 1969); and Richard E. Caves, "Inter-

national Corporations: The Industrial Economics of Foreign Investment," *Economica* 38: 1–27 (Feb. 1971).

17. For example, S. J. Nicholas reports from a sample of 119 British firms: "In all cases for which information was available, 99% of all British multinationals had agency agreements and 70% had overseas travelers before the initial foreign investments." S. J. Nicholas, "British Multinational Investment before 1939," *Journal of Economic History* 11:620–621 (Winter 1982). This was true of both North American and German multinationals. Also, as John H. Dunning has noted concerning manufacturing subsidiaries established abroad by multinationals before 1914, 87.7% of those that were U.S.-based were in developed economies, as were 73.7% of those that were U.K.-based and 81.0% of those that were European-based. John H. Dunning, "Changes in Level and Structure of International Production: The Last One Hundred Years," in Mark Casson, ed., *The Growth of International Business* (London, 1983), p. 90.

18. Those stimuli to growth by diversification were first emphasized by Edith Penrose, *A Theory of the Growth of the Firm* (Oxford, 1959), esp. chs. 5 and 7; they were more fully developed by Scott J. Moss in his *Economic Theory of Business Strategy*, esp. pp. 51–64 (where he considers carefully the effect of the external environment). David Teece's excellent "Towards an Economic Theory of the Multiproduct Firm," *Journal of Economic Behavior and Organization*, 3:39–63 (March 1982), considers the economics of scope inherent in the modern industrial enterprise. Teece says (p. 47), "A specialized firm's generation of excess resources, both managerial and technical, and their fungible character is critical to the theory of diversification advanced here."

19. Alfred D. Chandler, Jr., *Strategy and Structure: Chapters in the History of the American Industrial Enterprise* (Cambridge, Mass., 1962), esp. chs. 2, 3, and 7.

20. Ibid., ch. 4.

21. This generalization refers, of course, to enterprises that moved into related products by direct investment and not, as did the conglomerates of the 1960s and 1970s, into unrelated products through acquisition. See the concluding chapter of this book.

3. The Foundations of Managerial Capitalism in American Industry

1. B. R. Mitchell and Phyllis Deane, *Abstract of British Historical Statistics* (Cambridge, Eng., 1962), pp. 19, 24–27; and, for the United States, U.S. Bureau of the Census, *Historical Statistics of the United States, Colonial Times to 1970* (Washington, D.C., 1975), I, 8, 13.

2. Kuznets noted: "The much higher rate of growth of population in the United States, combined with the same or roughly the same rate of growth of per capita product, means that there was a correspondingly higher rate of growth in aggregate product here than in the European countries." Simon Kuznets, "Notes on the Pattern of U.S. Economic Growth," in Edgar O. Edwards, ed., *The Nation's Economic Objectives* (Chicago, 1964), p. 17.

3. The United States mileage figures are given in U.S. Bureau of the Census, *Historical Statistics*, II, 728–729; those for Great Britain in Peter Mathias, *The First Industrial Nation: An Economic History of Britain, 1700–1914* (New York, 1969), p. 488; and those for Germany in Brian R. Mitchell, *European Historical Statistics, 1790–1970* (New York, 1975), p. 315. Mileage for France was 14,500 in 1880 and

25,200 in 1910. Telegraph mileage and messages for the United States are in U.S. Bureau of the Census, *Historical Statistics*, II, 788. There is no readily available information on telegraph mileage in Britain and Germany.

4. Alfred D. Chandler, Jr., *The Visible Hand: The Managerial Revolution in American Business* (Cambridge, Mass., 1977), chs. 3 and 4, reviews these developments in railroad organization and management in much more detail.

5. Chandler, *The Visible Hand*, p. 125, taken from the *10th Annual Report of the Pennsylvania Rail Road* (Philadelphia, 1857), pp. 74–75.

6. Chandler, *The Visible Hand*, ch. 5.

7. Alfred D. Chandler, Jr., ed., *The Railroads: The Nation's First Big Business* (New York, 1965), pts. II, IV–VI.

8. Chandler, *The Visible Hand*, ch. 7.

9. Ibid., pp. 223, 229.

10. Ralph M. Hower, *History of Macy's of New York, 1858–1919: Chapters in the Evolution of the Department Store* (Cambridge, Mass., 1943), pp. 105–106. The major part of the business continued to be in dry goods and apparel.

11. Boris Emmet and John E. Jeuck, *Catalogues and Counters: A History of Sears, Roebuck & Company* (Chicago, 1950), pp. 132–133.

12. Ibid., pp. 118–119, 241–243. The data are not clear on whether the operating units were owned or whether Sears "controlled the output."

13. As Emmet and Jeuck point out, the number of Sears-controlled factories increased in times of prosperity, when it was difficult to obtain goods, and decreased in depressed periods, when supply exceeded demand. Thus at Sears in 1935 the total output of the company-owned or partially controlled factories was 7% of total sales, whereas in 1947 it was 16%. Emmet and Jeuck, *Catalogues and Counters*, pp. 412–413.

14. Nathan Rosenberg, "Technological Interdependence in the American Economy," *Technology and Culture* 20:28 (Sept. 1979).

15. Chandler, *The Visible Hand*, ch. 9 and pp. 388–389.

16. For the transformation in grain processing, ibid., pp. 250–253; for the transformation of the canning process by the "automatic-line" canning factory, ibid., p. 253.

17. William Haynes, *American Chemical Industry*, vol. VI, *The Chemical Companies* (New York, 1949), pp. 320–324 (for Parke, Davis) and 385–390 (for Sherwin-Williams).

18. Richard B. Tennant, *The American Cigarette Industry* (New Haven, 1950), p. 250.

19. By 1907 Armour was slaughtering 7.3 million animals a year and Swift 8.0 million. Chandler, *The Visible Hand*, p. 392. See pp. 393–401 for a description of the very large managerial organization at Armour in 1900, and pp. 299–302 for an account of the initial growth of the mass producers of perishable products. For breweries see Chandler, *The Visible Hand*, p. 301; Thomas C. Cochran, *The Pabst Brewing Company* (New York, 1948), pp. 171–173; and, for a sketch of Adolphus Busch by Irving Dillard, Supplement I of *Dictionary of American Biography* (New York, 1944), pp. 141–143. The Fleischmann story is indicated in Secretary, The Fleischmann Yeast Company, to W. E. Hallon and Company, December 3, 1920, in Corporate Records Division, Baker Library, Harvard Business School. See *Dictionary of American Biography* (New York, 1946), VI, 458, for a sketch of Charles Lewis Fleischmann by George H. Genzmer.

20. David A. Hounshell, *From American System to Mass Production, 1800–1932: The*

Development of Manufacturing Technology in the United States (Baltimore, 1984), chs. 2, 4; also Chandler, *The Visible Hand,* pp. 302–309.

21. William T. Hutchison, *Cyrus Hall McCormick: Harvest* (New York, 1935), pp. 711–712.

22. Chandler, *The Visible Hand,* pp. 297, 302–309.

23. Glenn Porter and Harold C. Livesay, *Merchants and Manufacturers: Studies in the Changing Structure of Nineteenth Century Marketing* (Baltimore, 1971), p. 193. Remington Typewriter soon had branches in 16 American cities. Porter and Livesay also indicate that National Cash Register had a similar sales force. For Eastman, see Chandler, *The Visible Hand,* pp. 296–297; and Reese V. Jenkins, *Images and Enterprise: Technology and the American Photographic Industry* (Baltimore, 1975), chs. 8–10.

24. Chandler, *The Visible Hand,* pp. 310–312.

25. Ibid., p. 368.

26. Harold Passer, *The Electrical Manufacturers, 1875–1900: A Study in Competition, Entrepreneurship, Technical Change, and Economic Growth* (Cambridge, Mass., 1960), ch. 20; and Mira Wilkins, *The Emergence of Multinational Enterprise: American Business Abroad from the Colonial Era to 1914* (Cambridge, Mass., 1970), pp. 52–59, 93–96.

27. Wilkins, *The Emergence of Multinational Enterprise,* pp. 51, 200, 213.

28. See Chapter 10 for Electric Storage Battery and AFA, and Chapters 6 and 9 for the phonograph and record companies.

29. The histories of these chemical companies are told in more detail in Chapter 5.

30. For histories of these metal-makers, see Chapter 4.

31. Harold Sharlin, "The First Niagara Falls Power Project," *Business History Review* 35:59–74 (Spring 1961), and Chapters 6 and 9 of this book.

32. Useful statistical tests of the broad impact of the economies of scale in the late nineteenth century are presented in John A. James, "Structural Change in Manufacturing, 1850–1890," *Journal of Economic History* 43:433–459 (June 1983).

33. Chandler, *The Visible Hand,* ch. 10, esp. p. 318 on trade associations in hardware.

34. The Standard Oil story, described more fully in Chapter 4, is told in more detail in Alfred D. Chandler, Jr., "The Standard Oil Company: Combination, Consolidation, and Integration," in Alfred D. Chandler and Richard Tedlow, *The Coming of Managerial Capitalism: A Casebook on the History of American Economic Institutions* (Homewood, Ill., 1986), case 14, pp. 359–364.

35. In the 1880s the new company, instead of exchanging shares with the companies joining the combination, often used its stock to purchase their assets. The most important of such companies was the Diamond Match Company formed in 1881 before Standard Oil had devised the trust. James C. Bonbright and Gardner C. Means, *The Holding Company: Its Public Significance and Its Regulation* (New York, 1932), pp. 67–72. Even after New Jersey had passed its general holding company corporation laws in 1889 and 1890, consolidators often preferred this method until the Supreme Court in the E. C. Knight case of 1895, concerning the American Sugar Refining Company, ruled that holding companies financed through exchange of shares of stock were legal.

36. George Bittlingmayer, "Did Antitrust Policy Cause the Great Merger Wave?" *Journal of Law and Economics* 28:77–118 (April 1985), indicates that antitrust policy did make a critical difference. The author documents the importance of state

action, court decisions, and difficulties of cartel enforcement in the timing and methods of the turn-of-the-century merger movement. See also Lester G. Telser, *A Theory of Efficient Cooperation and Competition* (Cambridge, Eng., 1987), ch. 2, "Perceptions and Reality: The Genesis of the Sherman Act," which is particularly useful in relating the author's "core theory" of oligopoly to the coming of antitrust regulation; and Hans B. Thorelli, *The Federal Antitrust Policy: Origination of an American Tradition* (Baltimore, 1955), pp. 258–259.

37. Alfred D. Chandler, Jr., and Stephen Salsbury, *Pierre S. du Pont and the Making of the Modern Corporation* (New York, 1971), pp. 83–85, 93–95.

38. A. J. Moxham to T. C. du Pont, June 18, 1903, Du Pont Archives, Hagley Library, Greenville, Delaware: Accession 1075–23. The four well-established companies not coming into the merger were Giant, Lent, King, and Olin (a forerunner of Olin-Mathieson). Chandler and Salsbury, *Pierre S. du Pont*, p. 104; and see pp. 137–148, "Department Building," on the creation of the integrative managerial hierarchy.

39. Malcolm B. Burns, "Economies of Scale in the Manufactured Tobacco Industry, 1897," *Journal of Economic History* 43:461–474 (June 1983), describes the way in which Duke's American Tobacco Company carried out the same strategy. As a result of rationalizing production and consolidating processing in plants of optimal scale, the number of factories producing smoking tobacco was reduced by 82%, those in chewing and fine cut tobacco by 88.2%, and those in snuff by 90.0%.

40. Chandler, *The Visible Hand*, pp. 334–336.

41. Shaw Livermore, "The Success of Industrial Mergers," *Quarterly Journal of Economics* 50:68–95 (Nov. 1935); and Chandler, *The Visible Hand*, pp. 337–344.

42. Thomas K. McCraw, *Prophets of Regulation: Charles Francis Adams, Louis D. Brandeis, James M. Landis, Alfred E. Kahn* (Cambridge, Mass., 1984), pp. 144–147.

43. C. Hax McCullough, *One Hundred Years of Banking: The History of Mellon National Bank and Trust Company* (Pittsburgh, 1969), p. 29. The Mellons incorporated their long-established private bank in 1902.

44. Thomas R. Navin and Marion V. Sears, "The Rise of a Market for Industrial Securities, 1887–1902," *Business History Review* 24:105–138 (June 1953). The authors report that the first money raised in Wall Street for new capital facilities was that found in 1901 by J. P. Morgan for the Federal Steel Company (which was then becoming part of United States Steel).

45. Vincent D. Carosso, *The Morgans: Private International Bankers, 1854–1913* (Cambridge, Mass., 1967), pp. 438–453, 458–460; for German banks, see Chapter 10 of this book.

46. David Bunting and Mark S. Mizruchi, "The Transfer of Control in Large Corporations, 1905–1919," *Journal of Economic Issues* 16:985–1003 (Dec. 1982). The quotation is from p. 1001. The obvious reasons for the default are not explained.

47. Chandler, *The Visible Hand*, p. 282; Monte A. Calvert, *The Mechanical Engineer in America* (Baltimore, 1967), chs. 3–5.

48. David Noble, *America by Design: Science, Technology, and the Rise of Corporate Capitalism* (New York, 1979), esp. ch. 6.

49. Chandler, *The Visible Hand*, pp. 466–468.

50. Melvin Copeland, *And Mark an Era: The Story of the Harvard Business School* (Boston, 1958), p. 43.

51. Of all the companies with plants overseas in 1914 listed by Wilkins, *The Emergence of Multinational Enterprise,* pp. 211–214, 43 were in the top 200 in 1917, and another 17 of the top 200 had plants in Canada.

52. David C. Mowery, "The Emergence and Growth of Industrial Research in American Manufacturing, 1899–1905" (Ph.D. diss., Stanford University, 1981), p. 66.

53. David M. Kotz, *Bank Control of Large Corporations in the United States* (Berkeley, 1978), makes a distinction between managing and control: "In contrast to managing, which is an activity, control is a power" (p. 17). But the exercise of power in a large modern bureaucracy requires information about complex existing situations and the realities of alternative courses of action as well as the ability to carry out decisions and to review and revise them. Power without the instruments of control is only potential power. It is rarely brought into use unless the organization gets into financial difficulties or other enterprises or financial groups try to obtain control of its assets. The holders of such power have helped create, maintain, or destroy existing capabilities, but they cannot maintain a healthy, competitive enterprise without the support of a managerial hierarchy with product-specific administrative and functional skills. Kotz, like Bunting and Mizruchi, believes that the influence of bankers, even as he defines influence, lessened during the interwar years.

4. Creating Organizational Capabilities

1. This stability is indicated by the turnover tables for the food, chemical, and machinery industries listed in Appendix A.2. For the other industries a comparison of leaders in each, listed in Appendix A.1 for 1917, 1930, and 1948, makes the same point. These data are reinforced by the findings of more general studies of the top 100, including Richard C. Edwards, "Stages of Corporate Stability and Corporate Growth," *Journal of Economic History* 35: 428–457 (July 1975).

2. Harold F. Williamson and Arnold Daum, *The American Petroleum Industry: The Age of Illumination, 1859–1899* (Evanston, Ill., 1959), pp. 489, 493.

3. Allan Nevins, *Study in Power: John D. Rockefeller, Industrialist and Philanthropist* (New York, 1953), I, 59.

4. Williamson and Daum, *The American Petroleum Industry, 1859–1899,* p. 273; on pp. 274–286 the authors review the processes and costs of refining at this scale, while on pp. 228–230, 283–285, and 482–483 they indicate the relationship between increased throughput and unit costs. A more detailed review of the rise of the Standard Oil alliance can be found in Alfred D. Chandler, Jr., and Richard Tedlow, *The Coming of Managerial Capitalism: A Case Book in the History of American Economic Institutions* (Homewood, Ill., 1985), pp. 348–356.

5. Nevins, *Study in Power,* I, 87, quotes a letter written by Rockefeller to his wife on April 19, 1868, when his enlarged refinery establishment was coming into full operation. It indicates the eagerness with which both Vanderbilt, the nation's best-known entrepreneur, and Stone, Cleveland's leading businessman, sought Rockefeller's business. "We were sent for by Mr. Vanderbilt yesterday at 12:00, but did not go. He is anxious to get our business & said he thought he could meet us on terms. We sent our card by messenger, that Van might know where to find our offices, & later in the day, at the St. Nicholas, saw the card in the hand of Amasa

Stone, Jr., who was figuring with Van for the business. I made a proposition to draw 100,000 barrels & Mr. Stone desired [us] to meet Van last eve at the Manhattan Club Room & Will [John's brother] engaged to meet them at 9:00. We talked business to Amasa & guess he thinks we are rather prompt young men."

6. Williamson and Daum, *The American Petroleum Industry, 1859–1899,* pp. 443–444, 465.

7. The story of legal consolidation, administrative centralization, and vertical integration can be followed in more detail in Chandler and Tedlow, *The Coming of Managerial Capitalism,* pp. 356–368.

8. Williamson and Daum, *The American Petroleum Industry, 1859–1899,* pp. 581–588 (on both Crescent and Tide Water); also John Moody, ed., *Moody's Manual of Industrial and Miscellaneous Securities for 1900* (New York, 1900), p. 1011. Partially because of Pennsylvania legislation passed in June 1883 prohibiting the combination of pipelines, Tide Water remained legally and administratively "an ally" rather than a constituent company. It operated as "a quasi-independent enterprise." Ralph W. Hidy and Muriel E. Hidy, *Pioneering in Big Business, 1882–1910* (New York, 1955), pp. 86, 326, 379, 417, 455, and 686.

9. For the impact of the opening of the Ohio-Indiana fields, see Williamson and Daum, *The American Petroleum Industry, 1859–1899,* ch. 22; and Harold F. Williamson et al., *The American Petroleum Industry: The Age of Energy, 1899–1959* (Evanston, Ill., 1963), p. 87. For Sun Oil's investment in the new fields, see August W. Giebelhaus, *Business and Government in the Oil Industry: A Case Study of Sun Oil, 1876–1945* (Greenwich, Conn., 1980), pp. 208–231.

10. Chandler and Tedlow, *The Coming of Managerial Capitalism,* pp. 364–366.

11. Williamson et al., *The American Petroleum Industry, 1899–1959,* pp. 28, 27–89, 116; and Giebelhaus, *Business and Government in the Oil Industry,* pp. 40–50. Security, Standard's subsidiary, did not move into crude-oil production. When Standard was taken to court in 1907 by the state of Texas for antitrust violations in that state, Security was sold to Magnolia Petroleum. By 1907, before this antitrust action by the state had taken place, Gulf, Texas, and Sun were already major integrated companies competing successfully with Standard Oil.

12. Williamson et al., *The American Petroleum Industry, 1899–1959,* p. 13.

13. Alfred D. Chandler, Jr., *The Visible Hand: The Managerial Revolution in American Business* (Cambridge, Mass., 1977), pp. 350–353.

14. Williamson et al., *The American Petroleum Industry, 1899–1959,* pp. 65 and 563, gives percentages of crude-oil stocks controlled by the 20 largest oil companies.

15. The nature and importance of this investment is carefully detailed in Williamson et al., *The American Petroleum Industry, 1899–1959,* pp. 216–230 and ch. 13.

16. U.S. Bureau of the Census, *Distribution of Manufacturers' Sales, 1939* (Washington, D.C., 1942), p. 105, summarizes data for 1929, 1935, and 1939. Williamson et al., *The American Petroleum Industry, 1899–1959,* pp. 477–481, breaks down the figures for distribution by wholesalers of gasoline.

17. Williamson et al., *The American Petroleum Industry, 1899–1959,* p. 482.

18. Vacuum Oil Company, a Rochester, New York, maker of lubricants and a part of the Standard Oil Trust, had set up its European marketing organization in 1885 in Liverpool and had established small works in 1896 and 1901. That firm became the base for the Socony-Mobil European operations, after Socony and Mobil

merged in 1931. J. C. Gridley, "Expansion and Organization of Mobil Oil Company Limited," in Ronald S. Edwards and Harry Townsend, eds., *Studies in Business Organization* (London, 1961), pp. 35–38.

19. Henrietta M. Larson, Evelyn H. Knowlton, and Charles S. Popple, *New Horizons, 1927–1950* (New York, 1971), p. 200.

20. Mira Wilkins, *The Maturing of Multinational Enterprise: American Business Abroad from 1914 to 1970* (Cambridge, Mass., 1975); see pp. 84–88 for investments in refineries in Canada and Europe.

21. U.S. Bureau of Foreign and Domestic Commerce, *American Branch Factories Abroad,* 73d Cong., 2d sess., S. Doc. 120 (Washington, D.C., 1934), table 3.

22. Wilkins, *The Maturing of Multinational Enterprise,* pp. 238–241. As Wilkins points out, these three, plus Standard of California, Atlantic Refining, Cities Service, Sinclair, Sun, and Tide Water, represented "well over 90% of American investment abroad." All retained small, usually specialized marketing organizations abroad. Of these, Sinclair and Tide Water kept small refinery facilities. Jean Francois G. Landeau, *Strategies of U.S. Independent Oil Companies Abroad* (Ann Arbor, Mich., 1977), p. 66.

23. Alfred D. Chandler, Jr., *Strategy and Structure: Chapters in the History of Industrial Enterprise* (Cambridge, Mass., 1962), pp. 189–193, describes the organizational innovations at Jersey Standard to coordinate such flows and indicates the complexity of that task.

24. Wilkins, *The Maturing of Multinational Enterprise,* ch. 9, for expansion and contraction of investment in crude oil abroad; also Landeau, *Strategies of U.S. Independent Oil Companies Abroad,* pp. 66–67, 133–134, 137, 138, 141.

25. Williamson et al., *The American Petroleum Industry, 1899–1959,* pp. 235–241, 498–505, and 709–715, succinctly reviews this evolution of price leadership.

26. Quoted from the Federal Trade Commission Report of 1920, "High Cost of Gasoline," p. 375; Williamson et al., *The American Petroleum Industry, 1899–1959,* pp. 235–236. Until 1930 Jersey Standard based its price structure on costs of refined products at Gulf Coast refineries plus rail charges to principal distribution points. After 1930 the pricing formula was based on delivery costs of gasoline and kerosene at major East Coast terminals or at local refineries plus handling and delivery charges to distribution centers within its territory. Williamson et al., *The American Petroleum Industry, 1899–1959,* pp. 710–715.

27. Williamson et al., *The American Petroleum Industry, 1899–1959,* p. 238.

28. Quoted ibid., pp. 235–236, from the FTC Report, 1920, p. 53.

29. Williamson et al., *The American Petroleum Industry, 1899–1959,* chs. 4, 11, and 17. These chapters, which tell the complex story of technological innovation in refining, emphasize the constant reduction of costs and the increase in refinery output during the interwar years and the contribution of research and development to this improvement.

30. Ibid., pp. 439–440 and also 374–375.

31. Ibid., pp. 679–680.

32. Ibid., ch. 6, esp. pp. 231–234; ch. 11, esp. pp. 493–499; and ch. 19.

33. Ibid., chs. 5, 13, and 18 for changes in demand for petroleum products.

34. Ibid., pp. 502–503, 712, drawn from tables based on FTC data.

35. David C. Mowery, "The Emergence and Growth of Industrial Research" (Ph.D. diss., Stanford University, 1981), pp. 66–74. These individuals amounted to 3.7%

of total staff personnel and 4.4% of scientific personnel employed in American industry in that year. Because of the capital-intensive nature of the industry, research intensity (as measured by the ratio of scientific personnel in research laboratories per 1000 workers) was the third largest, 1.83, after chemicals and rubber. By 1946 the research intensity was 26.28, just under chemicals with their ratio of 27.81. Mowery's tables on employment and research intensity for 1921, 1933, and 1946 are printed in Alfred D. Chandler, Jr., "From Industrial Laboratories to Departments of Research and Development," in Kim B. Clark, Robert H. Hayes, and Christopher Lorenz, eds., *The Uneasy Alliance: Managing the Productivity-Technology Dilemma* (Boston, 1985), pp. 55, 57–58.

36. Quoted in George S. Gibb and Evelyn H. Knowlton, *The Resurgent Years, 1911–1927* (New York, 1956), p. 524.

37. Howard R. Bartlett, "The Development of Industrial Research in the United States," in National Research Planning Board, *Research in National Resources* (Washington, D.C., 1940), pp. 45–49.

38. Williams Haynes, *American Chemical Industry*, vol. V, *Decade of New Products* (New York, 1954), p. 211.

39. Williams Haynes, *American Chemical Industry*, vol. VI, *The Chemical Companies* (New York, 1949), pp. 399–403; and Alfred D. Chandler, Jr., "Development, Diversification, and Decentralization," in Ralph E. Freeman, ed., *Post-War Economic Trends in the United States* (Cambridge, Mass., 1960), pp. 268–269.

40. William Haynes, *American Chemical Industry*, V, 210–211, 220; ibid., VI, 436; Williamson et al., *The American Petroleum Industry, 1899–1959*, pp. 422–430.

41. Williamson et al., *The American Petroleum Industry, 1899–1959*, pp. 79–83; John N. Ingham, *Biographical Dictionary of American Business Leaders* (Westport, Conn., 1983), II, 924. In 1902 Mellon enlarged the capacity of Gulf's refinery from 125 barrels to 10,000 barrels a day.

42. U.S. Temporary Natural Economic Committee, *Investigation of Concentration of Economic Power*, Monograph 29, *The Distribution of Ownership in the Two Hundred Largest Nonfinancial Corporations* (Washington, D.C., 1940), p. 511, shows that at the Texas Corporation in 1939 no officer or director held as much as 1% of the voting stock outstanding. Indeed, the company's 19 officers and directors held a total of 1.18% of the stock. At Tide Water (p. 512) none of the 15 senior executives held as much as .05%, and, except for one nonexecutive (outside) director, no director held as much as 1%. That one director had only 2.2%. At Pure Oil (p. 496), no director held as much as 1%. The total held by 12 directors and executives was 0.52%. At Shell Union Oil (p. 503), a foreign subsidiary, the story was much the same. Nor did the total stock held by the directors of the former Standard companies reach as much as 1% (pp. 339, 405, 509, and 510). This was also true of Richfield (p. 500), where Harry F. Sinclair, chairman of the board, the largest stockholder, held 0.7% of the stock. At Union (p. 513) a total of 21 officers and directors held a total 1.72% of the stock outstanding.

43. The value of shipments for petroleum refining in 1947 was $6.6 billion. For tires it was $1.5 billion, and for rubber footwear $0.2 billion. U.S. Bureau of the Census, *Concentration Ratios in Manufacturing Industries, 1958* (Washington, D.C., 1962), pp. 26–27.

44. This story can be followed in Glenn D. Babcock, *History of the United States Rubber Company* (Bloomington, Ind., 1966), pp. 12–49, and in Nancy P. Norton, "Indus-

trial Pioneer: The Goodyear Metallic Rubber Shoe Company" (Ph.D. diss., Radcliffe College, 1950), esp. pp. 126–131 and 193–194. As time passed, tennis and golf balls and other recreational items became another profitable product line.

45. Chandler, *The Visible Hand,* pp. 433–434; for Goodrich, see Haynes, *American Chemical Industry,* VI, 190–192.

46. Besides rationalizing and expanding the sales organization, Colt formed the General Rubber Company in 1904 to buy crude rubber. This organization soon had offices in Liverpool and London and in the rubber-growing areas of Brazil and the Dutch East Indies. In 1909 the company obtained its first rubber plantations in Sumatra. As early as 1904 the board decided to produce its own sulphuric acid for its rubber reclaiming processes and to have its own fleet of tank cars. Then at the end of 1905, to house the enlarged company headquarters, Colt moved into a large building at 42 Broadway. Babcock, *History of the United States Rubber Company,* pp. 53–64.

47. Daniel Nelson, "Mass Production in the U.S. Tire Industry," *Journal of Economic History* 47:329–339 (Sept. 1987). U.S. Rubber made the investment in production in 1906, when Colt moved the tire-production facilities of Rubber Goods Manufacturing from Chicago to Detroit. "Including the equipment the new plant was valued at $15 million, had a floor area of 900,000 sq. ft. and was able to produce 300 tires a day." Babcock, *History of the United States Rubber Company,* pp. 114–115. As Goodyear's plant moved into full production, daily output rose from 50 tires in 1905 to 900 in 1909. Maurice O'Reilly, *The Goodyear Story* (Elmsford, N.Y., 1983), pp. 16–22. Before beginning to produce the "quick detachable" auto tire in 1905, Goodyear had become a leading producer of carriage and bicycle tires (pp. 13–15). B. F. Goodrich established itself in tires by merging in 1912 with Diamond Tire, which had built its tire plant and established its marketing organization a few years earlier.

48. "General Tire on the Loose," *Fortune* 34: 115–116 (July 1946).

49. U.S. Bureau of the Census, *Concentration Ratios, 1958,* p. 27. U.S. Bureau of the Census, *Distribution of Manufacturers' Sales, 1939,* pp. 112–113, includes data on establishments for 1929 and 1935. Michael J. French, "Structural Change and Competition in the U.S. Tire Industry, 1920–1937," *Business History Review* 60:32–39, 42–45 (Spring 1986), reviews the collapse of the smaller firms, which began even before the depression.

50. See U.S. Bureau of the Census, *Concentration Ratios, 1958,* pp. 112–113, for concentration and distribution of rubber footwear; and U.S. Bureau of the Census, *Distribution of Manufacturers' Sales, 1939,* pp. 117–119, for figures on establishments in leather footwear. Total sales were, of course, smaller for rubber footwear—$52.4 million as compared with $716.9 million for leather shoes—but the average sales per rubber establishment were $4.79 million, compared with $0.72 million for shoes.

51. See Babcock, *History of the United States Rubber Company,* pp. 110–111, 304–313, for the development of the original equipment and replacement tire markets. In the 1930s the tire makers, some of whom had attempted rather unsuccessfully to set up retail outlets during World War I, expanded these outlets so that in 1939 15.4% of production was sold through manufacturers' retail establishments as compared with 2.2% in 1929. This move was partly in response to the success of

mass retailers, particularly Sears, Roebuck and Montgomery Ward, in selling tires under a special brand name—tires that were often produced by the smaller independents. French, "Structural Change and Competition," pp. 39–40.

52. From annual reports, B. F. Goodrich Company, for 1917 and 1921. *Moody's Manual, 1928*, p. 1567, states that Goodrich had an investment of 11% in Continental Gummiwerke. (I have found little information on the output of the French works.) Goodrich may have acquired some technical know-how from Continental. It did use Continental as a brand name. (See Chapter 10 of this study.)

53. Michael J. French, "The Emergence of a Multinational Enterprise: The Goodyear Tire and Rubber Company, 1910–1939," *Economic History Review* 40:75–79 (1987); Wilkins, *The Maturing of Multinational Enterprise*, pp. 75, 144. Goodrich had a joint venture with Mitsubishi in Japan to produce rubber insulating materials, and it built a tire plant in Australia. Babcock, *History of the United States Rubber Company*, pp. 208–210, describes the expansion of that company's overseas branch sales offices.

54. Bartlett, "Industrial Research," pp. 55–56; Haynes, *American Chemical Industry*, VI, 190–197, 452–455; and John D. Gaffey, *The Productivity of Labor in the Rubber Tire Industry* (New York, 1940), pp. 80–81.

55. Mowery, "Industrial Research," p. 70, tables printed in Chandler, "From Industrial Laboratories to Departments of Research and Development," p. 55.

56. The quotation is from French, "Structural Change and Competition," original draft, p. 21. For U.S. Rubber's changing market share, see Babcock, *History of the United States Rubber Company*, pp. 212, 310. Babcock's figures differ only slightly from a table on sales of replacements for the four leaders in 1926–1933, given in Securities & Exchange Commission Report of 1942, "Investment Trusts and Investment Companies," p. 245. That report gives U.S. Rubber's share for 1928 as 9.5% and 14.6% for 1933. Between 1926 and 1933 Goodyear's share rose from 15.3% in 1926 to 29.3% in 1929 and went back to 19.8% in 1933. In 1930 General Motors offered a new purchasing plan for original tires to reduce costs and prices, which was turned down first by Goodyear and then by Goodrich before it was accepted by U.S. Rubber; as a result U.S. Rubber had 50% of General Motor's original equipment orders (pp. 306–307). See also French, "Structural Change and Competition," p. 32.

57. French, "The Emergence of a Multinational Enterprise," pp. 40, 65–69. Wilkins, *The Maturing of Multinational Enterprise*, pp. 89–90, 98–103; and Haynes, *American Chemical Industry*, VI, 164. Firestone also set up a large plant in Singapore for the initial processing of crude rubber. U.S. Rubber did not expand its early prewar investment in Sumatra. As French points out (p. 67), "Plantation investments were defensive responses to supply constraints."

58. Babcock, *History of the United States Rubber Company*, pp. 230–244, 326, 333; and Haynes, *American Chemical Industry*, VI, 164, 192–197, 452–455. Goodrich Sales Training Department, *Growth of an Idea* (Akron, 1918), pp. 33–37; its "Advertising Department" is described on p. 32.

59. Chandler, *Strategy and Structure*, pp. 350–351. Goodrich, under pressure from contracting markets during the depression, returned temporarily to a functional structure.

60. U.S. Bureau of Foreign and Domestic Commerce, *American Branch Factories*

Abroad, p. 18. Of the $232.5 million invested abroad by paper companies, $224.2 was in Canada. Wilkins, *The Maturing of Multinational Enterprise,* pp. 9–10, 93–102, 176, 194, reviews this investment.

61. Naomi Lamoreaux, *The Great Merger Movement in American Business, 1895–1904* (Cambridge, Eng., 1985), pp. 44. The second quotation is from Avi J. Cohen, "Technological Change as Historical Process: The Case of the U.S. Pulp and Paper Industry, 1915–1940," *Journal of Economic History* 44:779 (Sept. 1984). Cohen points out (p. 791) that by 1934, 81.5% of U.S. pulp makers were integrated with paper mills. Victor S. Clark makes the same point in his *History of Manufacturers in the United States* (New York, 1929), II, 487, and III, 246. The adoption of the new wood pulp papermaking machinery and ancillary mechanical and chemical developments that accompanied it is very well told in Judith A. McGaw, *Most Wonderful Machine: Mechanization and Social Change in Berkshire Paper Making, 1801–1885* (Princeton, 1987), ch. 7, esp. pp. 199–206, 224–233. See also Lamoreaux, *The Great Merger Movement,* pp. 140–141.

62. Lamoreaux, *The Great Merger Movement,* pp. 106, 127, 139, 140–141; *International Paper Company, 1898–1948* (n.p., 1948); and *Fortune* 1:65 (May 1930) and 16:13ff (Dec. 1937). Lamoreaux, *The Great Merger Movement,* pp. 126–134, 139–141, gives an excellent review of the way in which International Paper came to define its role as a price leader. International Paper's drop in market share is shown in an unpublished Appendix I to Richard E. Caves, Michael Fortunato, and Pankaj Ghemawat, "The Decline of Dominant Firms, 1905–1929," *Quarterly Journal of Economics* 99:523–527 (Aug. 1984). (I am indebted to the authors for the appendix.) For investment in research, see Mowery, "Industrial Research," p. 74.

63. Warren C. Scoville, *Revolution in Glassmaking: Entrepreneurship and Technological Change in the American Industry, 1880–1920* (Cambridge, Mass., 1948), pp. 176–178.

64. See *The Pittsburgh Plate Glass Company: Organization* (Pittsburgh, 1942), p. 4, for the plant at Creighton. Other useful information on the beginning and early growth of the company is in "Life Goes On," *Fortune* 9: 42–46, 86–88 (Jan. 1934).

65. Scoville, *Revolution in Glassmaking,* p. 236; Lamoreaux, *The Great Merger Movement,* pp. 122–123. For National Wall Paper, see Chandler, *The Visible Hand,* p. 336.

66. Pearce Davis, *The Development of the American Glass Industry* (Cambridge, Mass., 1949), pp. 175–191. According to Henry Pelling, *American Labor* (Chicago, 1960), pp. 66–67, the Window Glass Workers' Union "was in virtually complete control of the entire window glass working force in the United States" by the turn of the century.

67. Scoville, *Revolution in Glassmaking,* pp. 124–130, 191–194. Emile Fourcault, a Belgian inventor, developed a comparable process that was adopted after World War I.

68. T. C. Barker, *The Glassmakers Pilkington: The Rise of an International Company, 1826–1976* (London, 1977), pp. 284–285, 287.

69. George W. Stocking and Myron W. Watkins, *Monopoly and Free Enterprise* (New York, 1951), pp. 124–126. By 1926, 2% of output at American Window Glass was still produced by hand; by 1929 none was. The appendix to Caves, Fortunato, and

Ghemawat, "Decline of Dominant Firms," shows Pittsburgh Plate Glass's market share declining from 78% to 50% but does not define the product market.

70. Scoville, *Revolution in Glassmaking,* chs. 4–6, tells the story in detail. Both "Billions of Bottles," *Fortune* 10: 70–73 (April 1932), and "Owens Again and Why," *Fortune* 13: 113–120 (May 1936) take up the story after the 1929 merger.

71. Wilkins, *The Maturing of Multinational Enterprise,* pp. 41, 498; Barker, *The Glassmakers,* p. 288. In 1917 Libbey and the Sumitomo group had set up the American-Japanese Glass Company, of which Libbey-Owens owned 35%. Wilkins, *The Maturing of Multinational Enterprise,* pp. 29, 291.

72. Scoville, *Revolution in Glassmaking,* pp. 118–124. The cartel was the Europaischer Verband des Flaschenfabriken Gesellschaft.

73. Barker, *The Glassmakers,* pp. 311–316, 357–362. To avoid American antitrust action the two American firms and the Franklin Glass Corporation, a subsidiary of a Belgian enterprise, formed a "Webb-Pomerene company," the Plate Glass Export Corporation (p. 361). (The Webb-Pomerene Act, passed in February 1918, permitted competing firms to form joint ventures in the export trade without becoming liable for violation of antitrust laws.) See also Chapter 6.

74. "The Haughtons of Corning," *Fortune* 32: 129–132, 253–260 (July 1945). The *Fortune* articles on Pittsburgh Plate Glass and Owens-Illinois already cited also provide information on research. Barker, *The Glassmakers,* pp. 372–373, 376–378, 415, refers to Corning and Owens-Illinois and to the development work at Libbey-Owens and Pittsburgh Plate Glass.

75. For information on Carborundum, see Haynes, *American Chemical Industry,* VI, 66–68; and William H. Wendell, *The Scratch Heard 'Round the World'* (Princeton, 1965), pp. 5–15.

76. Charles W. Cheape, *Family Firm to Modern Multinational: Norton Company, A New England Enterprise* (Cambridge, Mass., 1985), ch. 2. As this product had an aluminum base, Norton integrated backward into bauxite mining but sold its holdings to Alcoa in 1909, when that company signed a 40-year contract guaranteeing Norton the supplies it needed at $5.50 a ton (pp. 85–90).

77. Cheape, *Family Firm to Modern Multinational,* p. 95. From 1938 to 1942 Norton had 34% to 39% of the market (p. 226); for a good description of price leadership in the industry, see pp. 96–99, 243–246.

78. Ibid., ch. 5, esp. pp. 191–198.

79. Information on Minnesota Mining and Manufacturing is from Haynes, *American Chemical Industry,* VI, 279–282; and Virginia Huck, *Brand of the Tartan: The 3M Story* (New York, 1955), esp. ch. 8, where pp. 185–186 describe briefly the product lines of the divisions in the late 1930s. The complex story of Durex, a joint venture, formed under the provisions of the Webb-Pomerene Act, can be followed in Cheape, *Family Firm to Modern Multinational,* pp. 172–173, 219–222, 248.

80. Huck, *Brand of the Tartan,* p. 177; ch. 20 is entitled "The Great Depression: A Golden Era."

81. Dean Richmond, *Design for Growth* (Buffalo, 1960), chs. 1 and 2. After 1935 National Gypsum grew more through acquisition than direct investment. John P. Hayes, *National Gypsum Company: The Power of Balance* (Princeton, 1985), pp. 9–13.

82. The appendix to Caves, Fortunato, and Ghemawat, "Decline of Dominant Firms," gives United States Gypsum's market share. Haynes, *American Chemical Industry*, VI, 236–237, and Bartlett, "Industrial Research," p. 68, indicate how Johns-Manville's extensive investment in research, beginning in 1915, helped to develop and improve its full line of products. Information on both firms is taken from *Moody's Manual*.

83. Thomas R. Navin, *Copper Mining and Management* (Tucson, 1978), pp. 225–227. According to the appendix to Caves, Fortunato, and Ghemawat, "Decline of Dominant Firms," American Brass's share dropped from 40% in 1901 to 25% in 1929, but whether its share refers to basic shapes or manufactured products, or both, is not indicated.

84. Chandler, *The Visible Hand*, pp. 253, 296.

85. Charles H. Hession, "The Tin Can Industry," in Walter Adams, ed., *The Structure of American Industry* (New York, 1954), pp. 404–409. Market-share figures are on p. 407. Between 1927 and 1929 Continental also grew by acquisition. Another useful study is James W. McKie, *Tin Cans and Tin Plate: A Study of Competition in Two Related Markets* (Cambridge, Mass., 1959), pp. 103–107.

86. Hession, "Tin Can Industry," p. 406.

87. U.S. Bureau of the Census, *Distribution of Manufacturers' Sales, 1939*, pp. 85, 125–126, 136–138.

88. George Smith, *From Monopoly to Competition: The Transformations of Alcoa, 1886–1986* (Cambridge, Eng., 1988), pp. 84–93. Also useful is Martin R. Perry, "Forward Integration by Alcoa," *Journal of Economics* 29:37–51 (Sept. 1980).

89. The account of Alcoa's beginning and growth is based primarily on Smith, *From Monopoly to Competition*, chs. 2 and 3. The cost figures are from his table 1.1.

90. Smith, *From Monopoly to Competition*, pp. 98–100.

91. George W. Stocking and Myron W. Watkins, *Cartels in Action: Case Studies in International Business Diplomacy* (New York, 1946), ch. 6, reviews the international interfirm agreements. The initial cartel fell apart in the fall of 1908, but Alcoa and AIAG negotiated an agreement that protected the American market for another year.

92. These developments and postwar cartel arrangements are covered in Smith, *From Monopoly to Competition*, chs. 2 and 3; and in Stocking and Watkins, *Cartels in Action*, pp. 242–254. Stocking and Watkins and also Perry, "Forward Integration," rely heavily on Donald H. Wallace, *Market Control in the Aluminum Industry* (Cambridge, Mass., 1937).

93. Navin, *Copper Mining and Management*, p. 54. Martha Moore Trescott, *The Rise of the American Electrochemicals Industry: Studies in the American Technological Environment* (Westport, Conn.), pp. 96–98. These refineries handled other non-ferrous metals besides copper.

94. Navin, *Copper Mining and Management*, pp. 63–69, for location of these refineries and for increase in demand; U.S. Bureau of Census, *Historical Statistics*, pt. 1, p. 602, for increase in output. In 1890, 129,882 tons of recoverable copper were mined in the United States and in 1910, 554,119 tons. By 1910, 711,020 tons were being refined from both domestic and foreign ores, compared with 539,526 tons for 1906. See also U.S. Federal Trade Commission, *Report on the Copper Industry*, pt. I, *The Copper Industry of the United States and International Copper Cartels* (Washington, D.C., 1947), ch. 3.

95. The histories of these enterprises are succinctly told in Navin, *Copper Mining and Management*, chs. 19–23. See also U.S. FTC, *Report on the Copper Industry*, pt. I, ch. 4.

96. Navin, *Copper Mining and Management*, p. 86.

97. U.S. Bureau of the Census, *Concentration Ratios, 1958*, p. 141.

98. U.S. FTC, *Report on the Copper Industry*, pt. I, pp. 187–231; the quotation is from p. 191. For legal reasons the foreign members were called "associates" (p. 209). George W. Stocking and Myron W. Watkins, *Cartels or Competition: The Economics of International Controls by Business and Government* (New York, 1948), pp. 124–131; Navin, *Copper Mining and Management*, ch. 10. Because of the failure of Copper Exporters the American firms played only a peripheral role in the international cartel that existed from 1935 to 1939. For the Webb-Pomerene Act, see note 73.

99. Navin, *Copper Mining and Management*, pp. 67, 312–313.

100. *Fortune* 10: 64, 102 (Aug. 1934); John F. Thompson and Norman Beasley, *For the Years to Come: A Story of International Nickel* (New York, 1960), pp. 85–90. The new process brought a drop in prices from 60¢ to less than 25¢ a pound; see also Trescott, *American Electrochemicals Industry*, p. 96. For Mond Nickel, see Chapter 7 of the present volume. John P. McKay, "House of Rothschild (Paris) as a Multinational Enterprise, 1875–1914," in Alice Teichova, Maurice Lévy-Leboyer, and Helga Nussbaum, eds., *Multinational Enterprise in Historical Perspective* (Cambridge, Eng., 1986), pp. 79, 83–84, tells the story of the French nickel enterprise.

101. For the role of the families, see the chapters in Navin, *Copper Mining and Management*, on these companies; for their organizational structure, see Chandler, *Strategy and Structure*, pp. 327–330.

102. These differences are suggested by figures on output per establishment in U.S. Bureau of the Census, *Census of Manufactures, 1929*, vol. II, *Reports by Industries* (Washington, D.C., 1933), pp. 906, 1085.

103. Chandler, *The Visible Hand*, pp. 259–269; Joseph F. Wall, *Andrew Carnegie* (New York, 1970), ch. 11 and pp. 500–506; and Peter Temin, *Iron and Steel in Nineteenth-Century America: An Economic Inquiry* (Cambridge, Mass., 1964), pp. 181–182.

104. Victor Clark, *History of Manufacturers in the United States* (New York, 1929), III, 269, 655; Temin, *Iron and Steel in Nineteenth-Century America*, p. 185.

105. The equipment, products, and annual capacity of American steel works are listed in the annual edition of the American Iron and Steel Association's *Directory of the Iron and Steel Works of the United States*, published in Philadelphia. In the 1894 edition those of Carnegie Steel Company are given on pp. 115–116, of Illinois Steel on pp. 169–170, and of Jones & Laughlin on p. 114. The Carnegie output was probably larger than it appears, for the *Directory* lists only ingot output for Homestead and not finished rails and structures. For the rest, the capacity of "ingots" and rails has been combined in the figures presented here. For Jones & Laughlin the capacity was 350,000 gross tons of "steel billets and blooms," 50,000 of "muck bars," and 450,000 of "finished materials."

106. Harold C. Livesay, *Andrew Carnegie and the Rise of Big Business* (Boston, 1975), p. 199; Wall, *Andrew Carnegie*, pp. 585–586; Chandler, *The Visible Hand*, p. 314.

107. Temin, *Iron and Steel in Nineteenth-Century America*, pp. 164–165.

108. Ibid., pp. 284–285. David Brody, *Steelworkers in America: The Nonunion Era* (Cambridge, Mass., 1960), pp. 3–6. Jack Blicksilver, "United States Steel Corporation: Exercising Industrial Leadership, 1901–1941" (Harvard Business School, Case BH 123R-1963). Livesay, *Andrew Carnegie and the Rise of Big Business,* pp. 128, 155–156, 166, summarizes cost reductions and profits.

109. By this agreement Carnegie Steel leased the ore properties for 50 years, agreeing, in addition to paying the royalty of 25¢ a ton, to ship a minimum tonnage over the railroad and steamship lines that Rockefeller had built to transport the Mesabi ore. Livesay, *Andrew Carnegie and the Rise of Big Business,* pp. 153–154.

110. Vincent P. Carosso, *The Morgans: Private International Bankers, 1854–1913* (Cambridge, Mass., 1987), pp. 391–392. Federal Steel's holdings are listed in *Moody's Manual, 1900.* Wall, *Andrew Carnegie,* pp. 726, 767, gives market shares. In 1900 Federal's output was 1.23 million tons to Carnegie's 2.97 million. Blicksilver, "United States Steel Corporation," p. 2.

111. D. E. Dunbar, *The Tin-Plate Industry: A Comparative Study of Its Growth in the United States and in Wales* (Boston, 1915), pp. 47–49, 77–82. Naomi Lamoreaux, in her "Competitive Behaviour of Small versus Large Firms: The American Steel Industry in the Late-Nineteenth Century," *Business and Economic History,* 2d ser., 9:32 (1980), is apparently aware of these innovations. She writes, "Giant tin-plate mills that produced the common grades of materials pioneered in automating their finishing processes and integrating both the primary and finishing processes in a single works." Yet in her *Great Merger Movement,* p. 39, she states that in tin plate "there were no economies of scale over a wide range of production." For the impact of these innovations and the resulting scale economies on international competition, see Chapter 7 of the present volume. For wire, see William Z. Ripley, ed., *Trusts, Pools, and Corporations* (New York, 1905), ch. 3 and pp. 305–309; also Joseph M. McFadden, "Monopoly in Barbed Wire: The Formation of American Steel and Wire," *Business History Review* 52: 469–489 (Winter 1978). McFadden gives excellent information on the failure of wire firms to control prices or output through either licensing or pooling.

112. Wall, *Andrew Carnegie,* pp. 330–338, 347–348; Livesay, *Andrew Carnegie and the Rise of Big Business,* pp. 205–206. William E. Belcher, "Industrial Pooling Agreements," in Ripley, *Trusts, Pools, and Corporations,* pp. 80–82.

113. Dunbar, *Tin-Plate Industry,* p. 83 (quotation); Blicksilver, "United States Steel Corporation," p. 4; Abraham Berglund, *The United States Steel Corporation* (New York, 1907), pp. 64–66; Wall, *Andrew Carnegie,* pp. 767–776.

114. The often told story of the Morgan-Carnegie deal is best covered in Wall, *Andrew Carnegie,* pp. 783–793, and Carosso, *The Morgans,* pp. 466–474. Blicksilver, "United States Steel Corporation," pp. 3–4, effectively summarizes the story of the merger after Carnegie's agreement. It is given in more detail in Berglund, *United States Steel Corporation,* p. 67–72.

115. McFadden, "Formation of American Steel and Wire," pp. 476–489; Carosso, *The Morgans,* p. 392. The normally lengthy process of such mergers is described in Alfred D. Chandler, Jr., and Stephen Salsbury, *Pierre S. du Pont and the Making of the Modern Corporation* (New York, 1971), pp. 54–130.

116. Robert Hessen, *Steel Titan: The Life of Charles M. Schwab* (New York, 1975), pp. 128–129. Berglund, *United States Steel Corporation,* pp. 75–88, esp. pp. 75–76, 85–87, for the redefinition of boundaries; and Carosso, *The Morgans,* pp. 488–

490. For some reason, the United States Steel Products Export Company (formed in 1904), with general offices in New York, was placed under the "direct control" of Federal Steel. The activities of the steel corporation's export subsidiary are well described by Ken Ballen, "American Firms and the Foreign Market, 1900–1914" (Paper, Fletcher School of Law and Diplomacy, Tufts University, Jan. 1975), pp. 4–9, which is based on testimony from the 1909 Congressional hearings investigating U.S. Steel and on the Corporation's Annual Reports.

117. Dunbar, *Tin-Plate Industry,* pp. 95, 101–102; also p. 19.

118. Hessen, *Steel Titan,* pp. 124–129; John A. Garraty, *Right-Hand Man: The Life of George W. Perkins* (New York, 1957), pp. 96–100, 119.

119. Lamoreaux, *The Great Merger Movement,* pp. 135–137.

120. Hessen, *Steel Titan,* p. 186.

121. Letter of August 10, 1904, quoted in Hessen, *Steel Titan,* pp. 186–187.

122. Both quotations are from Hessen, *Steel Titan,* p. 187. The second is taken from a letter from Dickson to Corey, Feb. 16, 1909.

123. From Ida Tarbell's biography of Gary, quoted in Blicksilver, "United States Steel Corporation," p. 12. Although the immediate cause of Corey's departure was a controversy over the removal of a junior executive (see Garraty, *Right-Hand Man,* pp. 120–125), the long-standing basis of conflict was certainly pricing policy.

124. The story of the rapid growth of the independents, summarized in Figure 5, is reviewed in Gertrude Schroeder, *The Growth of Major Steel Companies, 1900–1950* (Baltimore, 1953), esp. chs. 2 and 3.

125. Devices for carrying out price leadership, such as Pittsburgh-plus pricing, uniform list of extras, and the use of the American Iron and Steel Institute as a clearing house for information, are described in Walter Adams, "The Steel Industry," in Adams, ed., *The Structure of American Industry,* pp. 167–170; and William T. Hogan, *Economic History of the Iron and Steel Industry in the United States* (Lexington, Mass., 1971) vol. III, pts. IV and V, pp. 1101–15.

126. In 1952 the 12 largest steel companies produced 83.1% of finished hot rolled steel. Adams, "The Steel Industry," p. 155. For a summary of acquisitions in the steel industry, see Chandler, *The Visible Hand,* p. 360, and the historical sketches of the different companies in Schroeder, *The Growth of Major Steel Companies.* The only companies on the list of the top 200 between 1917 and 1948 that are not covered in Schroeder are Columbia Coal and Iron, Allegheny Ludlum, and Otis Steel; Jones & Laughlin acquired Otis in 1942 (p. 59).

127. See, for example, Schroeder, *The Growth of Major Steel Companies,* pp. 47, 55, 62, 71, 76; and Chandler, *The Visible Hand,* p. 360.

128. Adams, "The Steel Industry," pp. 154–158, reviews U.S. Steel's decline in market share. These markets are described in Hogan, *Economic History of the Iron and Steel Industry,* chs. 29 and 37. Lamoreaux, *The Great Merger Movement,* p. 153, asserts: "Under the guidance of Judge Gary, the Steel Corporation adopted a successful policy of forestalling entry by limiting access to vital raw materials. In this manner it managed both to protect its market share and to earn handsome profits." In fact, Table 11 tells a very different story. Between 1901 and 1927 the U.S. Steel Corporation produced between 41% and 46% of the iron ore mined in the United States. Not only was more than half of the ore in the United States mined by other U.S. companies, but steel mills in the East relied on both Canadian and Cuban ore. Nor, as Table 11 indicates, was the U.S. Steel Corporation able

to protect its market share from its competitors. Schroeder's chart (Figure 6.5) emphasizes the rapid growth of U.S. Steel's challengers that came as they took market share from the corporation.

129. Chandler, *Strategy and Structure,* pp. 332–333.

130. U.S. Bureau of the Census, *Distribution of Manufacturers' Sales, 1939,* p. 142. The census reports a sharp drop in products sold through intermediaries between 1929 (when it was 39.4%) and 1935.

131. Wilkins, *The Maturing of Multinational Enterprise,* pp. 151–152; and Ballen, "American Firms and the Foreign Market." In 1914 U.S. Steel had 40 warehouses around the world, besides a plant in Canada. By 1928 it had only 24 warehouses and two Canadian plants.

132. Mowery, "Industrial Research," pp. 66, 70; Adams, "The Steel Industry," p. 157; and Bartlett, "Industrial Research," pp. 58–59.

133. Schroeder, *The Growth of Major Steel Companies,* p. 52. Eaton immediately recruited Tom Girdler, an experienced steel executive, to administer Republic, and Girdler continued to be chief executive officer for many years after Eaton had left the scene. Marcus Gliesser, *The World of Cyrus Eaton* (New York, 1965), pp. 45–49, 58–59.

134. Ralph W. Hidy, Frank Ernest Hill, and Allan Nevins, *Timber and Men: The Weyerhaeuser Story* (New York, 1963), pp. 317–323, 361–368, and ch. 25. *Moody's Manuals* provide information on Simmons and Armstrong Cork.

135. It was also true of Dan River, which appeared on the 1930 list. Jesse W. Markham, "Integration in the Textile Industry," *Harvard Business Review* 28: 74–88 (Jan. 1950); see pp. 76, 83–84 for the leading enterprises, p. 82 for integration, and pp. 85–86 for competition and pricing in this nonconcentrated industry. Additional information comes from *Moody's Manual.*

136. Arthur H. Cole, *The American Wool Manufacturers* (New York, 1926), pp. 234–250. In 1917 American Woolen established the American Wool Products Company for selling abroad. It had set up branch offices and sales agencies in 14 foreign countries before it was liquidated in 1921 (p. 242). Sam Bass Warner, *Province of Reason* (Cambridge, Mass., 1984), pp. 127–132, describes Wood's plans. See also Chandler, *The Visible Hand,* pp. 337–338, 340.

137. Mowery, "Industrial Research," pp. 66, 70.

138. See notes 46 and 53 to Chapter 3 of this study.

5. Expanding Organizational Capabilities: Food and Chemicals

1. This information is from U.S. Federal Trade Commission, *Report on Distribution Methods and Costs,* pt. V, *Advertising as a Factor in Distribution* (Washington, D.C., 1944), esp. pp. xii–xiii and 5–16.

2. Daniel Pope, *The Making of Modern Advertising* (New York, 1983), pp. 41–42 and ch. 4.

3. Alfred D. Chandler, Jr., *The Visible Hand: The Managerial Revolution in American Business* (Cambridge, Mass., 1977), pp. 256–258, 289–299.

4. Ibid., pp. 326–329.

5. Ibid., pp. 334–336; also Arthur S. Dewing, *Corporate Promotions and Reorganizations* (Cambridge, Mass., 1914), chs. 3 and 4. For Distillers Securities see Alfred

D. Chandler, Jr., "The Beginnings of Big Business in American Industry," *Business History Review,* 33:10–11 (Spring 1959).

6. Chandler, *The Visible Hand,* pp. 295–296 (p. 291 for American Tobacco); see *Dictionary of American Biography* (New York, 1973), supp. 3, p. 358, for Hershey.

7. Chandler, *The Visible Hand,* p. 296; Williams Haynes, *American Chemical Industry,* vol. VI, *The Chemical Companies* (New York, 1949), pp. 320–324 (for Parke, Davis), pp. 385–390 (for Sherwin-Williams), pp. 341–345 (for Procter & Gamble); and Alfred Lief, *It Floats: The Story of Procter & Gamble* (New York, 1958). The two drug companies larger than Parke, Davis on the 1917 and 1930 lists—United Drug (and its successor, Drug, Inc.) and McKesson & Robbins— were primarily distributing companies whose manufacturing facilities produced technologically simple toilet articles and pills mainly for their own outlets. Their cost advantages derived almost wholly from their investment in distribution.

8. Perhaps, however, the Great Western Sugar Company, a 1905 merger, should be considered as having come after the turn-of-the-century merger movement.

9. Alfred S. Eichner, *The Emergence of Oligopoly: Sugar Refining as a Case Study* (Baltimore, 1969), p. 327. As Eichner points out, after World War I American Sugar Refining, which was "approximately three times the size of its largest competitor . . . remained the undisputed price leader" (p. 329).

10. These developments can be followed in *Moody's Manual* and in the annual reports of American Linseed (Best Foods) and American Cotton Oil (Gold Dust) from 1921 to 1929. Gold Dust acquired several firms in the 1920s, including Standard Milling. The parent company's name was changed to Hecker Products in 1936 and then to Best Foods, Inc. The other two bulk producers of vegetable oil and comparable commodities to be listed in the top 200—Anderson, Clayton, and Archer-Daniels-Midland—appeared there briefly because of the great increase in commodity processing carried on by these companies (they were primarily commodity traders) during the Second World War; their size in 1948 represented only a temporary condition. Information on Southern Cotton Oil is in Chandler, *The Visible Hand,* pp. 327, 567, and in *Moody's Manual*; for Wesson Oil see *Moody's Manual.*

11. See Chandler, *The Visible Hand,* pp. 326–327, 334–336, for American Cotton Oil, National Biscuit, and Corn Products Refining. See Haynes, *American Chemical Industry,* VI, 323, for Parke, Davis, and 390 for Sherwin-Williams. For more on Sherwin-Williams see *The Story of Sherwin-Williams* (Cleveland, n.d.); Arthur W. Steudel, *George A. Martin, 1864–1944: Beloved Industrialist* (Princeton, 1949); and particularly the company's *Representatives' Handbook* in Baker Library, Harvard Business School. The *Handbook,* published about 1912, includes an organizational chart and discusses distribution and marketing procedures. For Fleischmann, see Secretary, The Fleischmann Company, to W. E. Dutton & Company and Harris, Forbes & Company, December 3, 1920; and report of statistical department, Otis & Company, September 11, 1928, in Baker Library, Corporate Archive Division. See also *Dictionary of American Biography* (New York, 1946), VI, 458–459.

12. Haynes, *American Chemical Industry,* VI, 323.

13. Oscar Schisgall, *Eyes on Tomorrow: The Evolution of Procter & Gamble* (New York, 1981), pp. 88–89.

14. Ibid., ch. 8.

15. This decline in market share is documented in the unpublished appendix to Richard

E. Caves, Michael Fortunato, and Pankaj Ghemawat, "The Decline of Dominant Firms, 1905–1929," *Quarterly Journal of Economics* 99: 523–546 (Aug. 1984).

16. Jean Herr, *World Events, 1866–1966: The First Hundred Years of Nestlé* (Rivas, Switzerland, 1966), pp. 117–118; *Report of Federal Trade Commission on Milk and Milk Products, 1914–1918* (Washington, 1921), pp. 34–39, 56–60. The report explains in detail the complex arrangements that led Nestlé to move into the production of milk in the United States and to purchase two United States companies during the war. For the other two challengers, see Martin L. Bell, *A Portrait of Progress: A Business History of Pet Milk Company from 1885 to 1960* (St. Louis, 1962), esp. ch. 2; John D. Weaver, *Carnation: The First Seventy-Five Years, 1899–1974* (Los Angeles, 1974), esp. chs. 2 and 3.

17. U.S. Bureau of Foreign and Domestic Commerce, *American Branch Factories Abroad,* 73d Cong., 2d sess., S. Doc. 120 (Washington, D.C., 1934). As Mira Wilkins points out, many of the consumer-drug and chemical plants overseas were small mixing and packaging establishments; this was especially true in Latin America. Mira Wilkins, *The Maturing of Multinational Enterprise: American Business Abroad from 1914 and 1970* (Cambridge, Mass., 1974), p. 84. The paper industry's large investment in Canada was a special case, because paper companies built their plants there to be close to timber supplies; their investment in the rest of the world was negligible.

18. For firms with subsidiaries abroad before 1914, see Mira Wilkins, *The Emergence of Multinational Enterprise: American Business Abroad from the Colonial Era to 1914* (Cambridge, Mass., 1970), pp. 212–213. For direct investment after the war, Wilkins, *The Maturing of Multinational Enterprise,* pp. 63–64, 81–84, 143–145, 495. Pet Milk and Carnation Milk, which formed a joint Webb-Pomerene venture in 1919 to market canned milk in Europe, soon had a plant operating in France. Wilkins, *The Maturing of Multinational Enterprise,* p. 63; Weaver, *Carnation,* pp. 42–43, 63–64.

19. Wilkins, *The Maturing of Multinational Enterprise,* p. 83.

20. For Procter & Gamble in Britain, see Chapter 9.

21. W. T. Brady, *Corn Products Refining: A Half Century of Progress and Leadership, 1906–1959* (Princeton, N.J., 1958), pp. 13–15; "Corn Products," *Fortune* 18: 57–58, 102, 103 (Sept. 1938). Abroad, Corn Products concentrated on producing more branded bulk products than packaged ones. Brady, *Corn Products Refining,* pp. 14–15.

22. The annual report of the American Cotton Oil Company, dated November 1893, lists the Central Laboratory as one of its "executive departments"; see *Who Was Who* (Chicago, 1942), I, 1323, for David Wesson; also Charles Wilson, *The History of Unilever: A Study in Economic Growth and Social Change* (London, 1954), II, 36–37.

23. Haynes, *American Chemical Industry,* VI, 332 (for Parke, Davis), and 385–386 (for Sherwin-Williams); and Schisgall, *Eyes on Tomorrow,* p. 136 (for Procter & Gamble). For Duisberg's praise, see Chapter 12 of this study.

24. These product lines of the first two vegetable-oil companies are reported in *Moody's Manual*; the third appears in "Corn Products," *Fortune* 18: 51; Brady, *Corn Products Refining,* pp. 19–21.

25. Alfred D. Chandler, Jr., *Strategy and Structure: Chapters in the History of the Industrial Enterprise* (Cambridge, Mass., 1962), p. 348; Haynes, *American Chemical Industry,* VI, 69–70.

26. These emergent product lines are reported in *Moody's Manual.*

27. Haynes, *American Chemical Industry,* VI, 348–350.

28. Ibid., pp. 334–385; an article in *Fortune* 4:92 (Dec. 1931), and another in *Fortune* 19:77ff (April 1939); Lief, *It Floats,* p. 118; and Schisgall, *Eyes on Tomorrow,* pp. 136–140.

29. Haynes, *American Chemical Industry,* VI, 387–390, for Sherwin-Williams; ibid., 189–190, for Glidden; and also *A Report on Diversification: The Glidden Company* (n.p., 1956). By 1937 Glidden had 26 research and control laboratories.

30. Haynes, *American Chemical Industry,* makes no reference to research activities at McKesson & Robbins or at United Drug; nor does Samuel Merwin, *Rise and Fight Again* (New York, 1935), the biography of United Drug's founder, Lewis K. Liggett.

31. Peter Temin, *Taking Your Medicine: Drug Regulation in the United States* (Cambridge, Mass., 1980), pp. 75–80.

32. Haynes, *American Chemical Industry;* VI, 1–3 (Abbott), 26–30 (American Home Products), 271–275 (Merck), 321–323 (Parke, Davis), 333–335 (Pfizer), 395–398 (Squibb), 407–408 (Sterling).

33. Summaries of these mergers, as well as other information, come from Chandler, *Strategy and Structure,* pp. 346–349 (quotation from p. 347). Information on Standard Brands and Best Foods is from *Moody's Manual* and annual reports. In 1931 Gold Dust acquired the Richard Hellmann division of General Foods. Gold Dust (Best Foods) was acquired by Corn Products in 1958. For Fleishmann's yeast, see note 11 above. For the one horizontal merger see David R. Foster, *The Story of Colgate-Palmolive: One Hundred and Sixty-Nine Years of Progress* (Princeton, N.J., 1975), pp. 16–17; after the merger, production was consolidated and the enlarged sales forces integrated.

34. Haynes, *American Chemical Industry,* VI, 26–30 (quotation on 28).

35. Chandler, *The Visible Hand,* pp. 300–301 (brewers), 391–402 (meatpackers). For the importance of American technical innovations in brewing, see Chapter 11, note 9.

36. For the impact of the motor vehicle on the meatpacking oligopoly see Richard J. Arnould, "Changing Patterns of Concentration in American Meat Packing, 1880–1963," *Business History Review* 45:18–34 (Spring 1971).

37. U.S. Bureau of the Census, *Distribution of Manufacturers' Sales, 1939,* pp. 22–23.

38. Chandler, *Strategy and Structure,* p. 348; *Fortune* 46:144 (Dec. 1952).

39. Chandler, *The Visible Hand,* pp. 393–399; U.S. Federal Trade Commission, *Report on the Fertilizer Industry* (Washington, D.C., 1916), p. 172 and ch. 4.

40. Again United Drug/Rexall, because of the nature of its business, was an exception. Its diversified line, listed in Appendix A.1, resulted primarily from a policy of vertical integration rather than from one based on exploiting the economies of scope. It produced small, packaged, surgical and cloth products, candy, and soft drinks in small, relatively labor-intensive plants for its retail chain of drug stores. Rexall remained much more a distributor than a manufacturer.

41. Glidden's divisions included Paints and Varnish, Chemicals and Pigments, Metal Refining, Naval Stores, Vegetable Oil, Food Products, and Feed Mill. Hayes, *American Chemical Industry,* VI, 189.

42. Chandler, *Strategy and Structure,* pp. 347–348.

43. Alfred D. Chandler, Jr., "From Industrial Laboratory to Department of Research

and Development," in Kim B. Clark, Robert H. Hayes, and Christopher Lorenz, eds., *The Uneasy Alliance: Managing the Productivity-Technology Dilemma* (Boston, Mass., 1985), pp. 55, 58, based on David C. Mowery, "The Emergence and Growth of Industrial Research in American Manufacturing, 1899–1945" (Ph.D. diss., Stanford University, 1981), pp. 66–74.

44. Of the 23 chemical firms among the top 200 in 1948 (Appendix A.3), none were founded after 1915 and only 3 of those after 1910—Publiker Industries in 1913, Air Reduction in 1915, and Koppers (in its modern form) in 1914. Of the 2 companies—Hercules and Atlas—that were spun off from Du Pont as a result of the antitrust action of 1912, Hercules was on both the 1930 and the 1948 list. Nearly all the constituent companies of American Home Products, as well as those of Union Carbide & Carbon and Allied Chemical, were established before 1910.

45. David A. Hounshell and John Kenly Smith, Jr., *Science and Corporate Strategy: Du Pont R&D, 1902–1980* (Cambridge, Eng., 1988), pp. 275–285; Jean-Claude Guédon, "Conceptual and Institutional Obstacles to the Emergence of Unit Operations in Europe," in William F. Furter, ed., *History of Chemical Engineering,* Advances in Chemistry Series, vol. 190 (Washington 1980), pp. 45–75.

46. U.S. Bureau of the Census, *Distribution of Manufacturers' Sales, 1939,* p. 99, lists distribution channels for chemicals in 1929, 1935, and 1939. For example: in 1935, 83.7% of explosives were sold through the manufacturing company's wholesale organization, 12.6% went directly to customers, and only 3.7% were sold through independent commercial intermediaries. For the overall category of coal-tar products, 39.8% went through the manufacturer's own wholesale organization, 42.2% to industrial users, and 17.3% to commercial intermediaries. The census does not provide a detailed breakdown of industrial chemical products as it does for foods, consumer chemicals, and other industries. Presumably because of the complexity of product and process, it makes no attempt to indicate either sales volumes or outlets for a wide variety of industrial chemicals. Even for major subcategories of coal-tar products, the amounts of goods sold through company-owned wholesalers and those sold through independent intermediaries are lumped together in order "to avoid detection," that is, to maintain the confidentiality of data acquired. Of the industries listed, only in the case of ammunition, cleaning and finishing preparations, fireworks, and lubricating oils not made in petroleum refineries did wholesalers handle, on average, more than a quarter of the sales in the decade 1929–1939. The concentration in these four subindustries was the lowest of any in Group 28. U.S. Bureau of the Census, *Concentration Ratios, 1958,* like its *Distribution of Manufacturers' Sales, 1939,* failed to break down the larger industries by the different intermediate and end-products produced.

47. Chandler, *Strategy and Structure,* pp. 57–63; and in much more detail, Alfred D. Chandler, Jr., and Stephen Salsbury, *Pierre S. du Pont and the Making of the Modern Corporation* (New York, 1971), chs. 3 and 4. Jeffrey L. Sturchio, "DuPont, Dynamite and Diversification: A Study of Chemical Research in Industry" (Paper presented at History of Science Society meeting, Dec. 1981), pp. 4–16, reviews the evolutionary nature of the technology used in the production of dynamite before the merger.

48. Martha Moore Trescott, *The Rise of the American Electrochemicals Industry, 1880–1910: Studies in the American Technological Environment* (Westport, Conn., 1981), pp. 157–158. General Chemicals came to have a centralized structure similar to Du Pont's. L. F. Haber, *The Chemical Industry, 1900–1930: Interna-*

tional Growth and Technological Change (Oxford, 1971), p. 338; also L. F. Haber, *The Chemical Industry during the Nineteenth Century: A Study of the Economic Aspects of Applied Chemistry in Europe and North America* (Oxford, 1958), p. 179. See Haynes, *American Chemical Industry,* VI, 179–181, for General Chemical and 45–47 for Barrett.

49. Trescott, *American Electrochemicals Industry,* pp. 64, 67–68; Haber, *Chemical Industry, 1900–1930,* p. 179; and the unpaged report of the U.S. Office of Alien Property Custodian, *Bureau of Sales: Alien Property Custodian* (n.p., 1920). Roessler & Hasslacher, which became the only large American producer of cyanide, revolutionized the gold-recovery process.

50. Haynes, *American Chemical Industry,* VI, 429–435; Trescott, *American Electrochemicals Industry,* pp. 73–75.

51. Trescott, *American Electrochemicals Industry,* pp. 94–95; Haynes, *American Chemical Industry,* VI, 113–114; also Don Whitehead, *The Dow Story: History of the Dow Chemical Company* (New York, 1968), pt. I. Penn Salt established a comparable electric alkali chlorine plant at Wyandotte, Michigan, in 1898 and became a large producer after 1908.

52. Trescott, *American Electrochemicals Industry,* pp. 83–84.

53. W. J. Reader, *Imperial Chemical Industries: A History,* vol. I, *The Forerunners, 1870–1926* (Oxford, 1970), pp. 98–100, 292–293; Haynes, *American Chemical Industry,* VI, 391–393.

54. Haynes, *American Chemical Industry,* VI, 367–368; Reader, *Imperial Chemical Industries,* I, 95, 292–293.

55. Haynes, *American Chemical Industry,* VI, 367.

56. See Chapter 12 of the present volume; also U.S. Office of Alien Property Custodian, *Bureau of Sales,* provides a detailed description of Bayer's direct investment in the United States.

57. Haynes, *American Chemical Industry,* VI, 183. For Merck and von Heyden, see Chapter 12 of the present volume.

58. Haynes, *American Chemical Industry,* VI, 282–284.

59. For Du Pont see Wilkins, *The Maturing of Multinational Enterprise,* pp. 78–80, 184–185; also Reader, *Imperial Chemical Industries,* I, 417–418; and Graham D. Taylor and Patricia S. Sudnik, *DuPont and the International Chemical Industry* (Boston, 1984), pp. 137–141. For Union Carbide see Trescott, *American Electrochemicals Industry,* p. 210; and for Monsanto, Haynes, *American Chemical Industry,* VI, 429–438.

60. U.S. Bureau of Foreign and Domestic Commerce, *American Branch Factories Abroad,* p. 13. As Table 14, which was compiled by Peter Williamson from the Harvard Business School data base on multinationals, indicates, American *industrial* chemical companies organized only 4 subsidiaries in Great Britain before 1930 and 12 between 1930 and 1948, as compared with American consumer-chemical companies, which set up 7 and 19 in the same periods, and food companies, which established 6 and 24 in the same time spans. In Germany, no American chemical companies (either consumer or industrial) established subsidiaries before 1914. Three industrial producers did so between 1914 and 1930 and three more immediately after the war (Table 15). In France only one such industrial chemical company did so before 1931, while seven did so between 1931 and 1953, most of those appearing after the war.

61. This story is told in detail in Chandler, *Strategy and Structure,* pp. 78–90.

62. The quotation from the Executive Committee is given in Chandler, *Strategy and Structure*, p. 88; see also Arthur P. Van Gelder and Hugo Schlatter, *History of the Explosives Industry in America* (New York, 1927), pp. 301, 430, 537, 541–544.

63. *Annual Report of the E. I. du Pont de Nemours & Co. for 1924*, p. 6.

64. Hounshell and Smith, *Science and Corporate Strategy*, pp. 155, 211, 608–610. Metallic sodium was also used in the production of indigo.

65. *Annual Report of the E. I. du Pont de Nemours & Co. for 1947*, pp. 18–20; Haynes, *American Chemical Industry*, VI, 133; William S. Dutton, *Du Pont: One Hundred and Forty Years* (New York, 1949), p. 377. Forty percent of total sales volume in 1939 came, Dutton writes, from "new products, developed largely since 1928," giving "direct employment to 18,000 men and women on the Du Pont wage and salary rolls" (p. 377).

66. Hounshell and Smith, *Science and Corporate Strategy*, pt. II and ch. 13.

67. Haynes, *American Chemical Industry*, VI, 203–207, for Hercules, and 39–44 for Atlas; also Edith T. Penrose, "The Growth of the Firm—A Case Study: The Hercules Powder Company," *Business History Review* 34:1–23 (Spring 1960).

68. Haynes, *American Chemical Industry*, VI, 21–23; *Fortune* 22:102–104 (Sept. 1940).

69. Haynes, *American Chemical Industry*, VI, 113–125, for Dow, and 282–287 for Monsanto. Also Whitehead, *The Dow Story*, pp. 120–122.

70. Haynes, *American Chemical Industry*, VI, 242–244; also Fred C. Foye, *Ovens, Chemicals, and Men!: Koppers Company, Inc.* (New York, 1958), esp. pp. 11–15, 22. To assure a massive and constant supply of the coal that it processed, Koppers also owned and operated several coal mines.

71. The quotation is from Haynes, *American Chemical Industry*, VI, 9–10. For the histories of the Allied Chemical divisions (the subsidiaries became divisions in the 1930s), ibid., VI, 45–49, 292–296, 367–370, 391–395; and Haber, *Chemical Industry, 1900–1930*, p. 187. Useful information on Allied Chemical is also available in *Fortune* 1:81ff (June 1930); 16:83ff (Dec. 1937); 20:44ff (Oct. 1939); and 50:119ff (Oct. 1954). Haber, *Chemical Industry, 1900–1930*, pp. 349–350, documents Allied Chemical's poor performance.

72. Information on Union Carbide comes from Haynes, *American Chemical Industry*, VI, 429–433; from *Fortune* 23:61ff (June 1941), 24:33 and 57ff (July 1941), and 55:123ff (Feb. 1957); and from Haber, *Chemical Industry, 1900–1930*, p. 373. By 1934 Union Carbide's corporate office consisted of the offices of the general managers for each of the four major operating groups—gases, electric furnaces, chemical products, and carbon products—and a corporate staff which by 1929 included a central research laboratory. *Annual Report for 1929*, p. 12. In 1939 Union Carbide acquired Bakelite, which had begun in 1909 as part of the German firm Roessler & Hasslacher. After being acquired by Americans, it joined with two other producers of resin in 1922. Bakelite became Union Carbide's plastics division. Because National Carbon with its Ever Ready products was the only division producing consumer goods, it sold Prestone antifreeze and the occasional consumer product developed by other divisions in the corporation.

73. For information on these three, see Haynes, *American Chemical Industry*, VI, 94–96, 346, 440–448. Publiker Industries came on the list largely because of World War II demands, particularly for alcohol used in a synthetic rubber program.

U.S. Industrial Alcohol (it became U.S. Industrial Chemicals in 1943) built a national sales organization, replacing former sales agents, after merger, with two other companies in 1915, and then invested in research. The fact that Air Reduction had an equity interest in U.S. Industrial Alcohol may have slowed its diversification. Only after World War II did it begin to diversify substantially.

74. Haynes, *American Chemical Industry,* VI, 5–9.

75. Chandler, *Strategy and Structure,* pp. 91–113, for Du Pont, and pp. 375–377 for the others, excepting Atlas. *Moody's Manual* describes the structure of Atlas.

76. Hounshell and Smith, *Science and Corporate Strategy,* ch. 5. This section on Du Pont diversification is based almost wholly on Hounshell and Smith's impressive study.

77. A. P. Tanberg to J. A. Burckel, Sept. 20, 1938, as quoted in Hounshell and Smith, *Science and Corporate Strategy,* p. 309.

78. Ibid., ch. 3, for the dye story; also Haynes, *American Chemical Industry,* VI, 134.

79. Hounshell and Smith, *Science and Corporate Strategy,* pp. 157–158. These market figures come from a company memorandum entitled "Approximate Percent of United States Market Enjoyed by Du Pont Products, March 1928," General Motors Suit, PD, p. 3879, and also from D. W. Jayne to Fin Sparre, Sept. 20, 1930, Accession 1813, Box 5, both at Hagley Museum and Library, Greenville, Del. Sterling Products had taken over the Bayer Company's facilities following World War I, keeping its pharmaceutical business but selling the dye business to Grasselli, which in 1928 sold it with its own dye works to the recently formed German giant, I. G. Farben (see Chapter 14).

80. Hounshell and Smith, *Science and Corporate Strategy,* p. 150.

81. See Hounshell and Smith, *Science and Corporate Strategy,* pp. 126–132, for tetraethyllead; and Joseph C. Robert, *Ethyl: A History of the Corporation and the People Who Made It* (Charlottesville, Va., 1983), ch. 4.

82. For Freon and Teflon see Hounshell and Smith, *Science and Corporate Strategy,* pp. 155–157.

83. Ibid., pp. 233–236, 251–257.

84. For the work of the Ammonia Department, ibid., ch. 9 and pp. 476–480. Haynes, *American Chemical Industry,* VI, 394. The original joint venture with Claude included a third party, the National Ammonia Company—a Wilmington-based producer which was initially slated to sell the product that Du Pont made. Hounshell and Smith, *Science and Corporate Strategy,* pp. 185–186.

85. Haynes, *American Chemical Industry,* VI, 59, 133. Also U.S. Federal Trade Commission, *Report on Fertilizer Industry, January 9, 1950* (Washington, 1950), p. 25; in 1939 these two plants produced 71.1% of all the nitrogen (natural as well as synthetic) used in fertilizers in the United States (pp. 23–26).

86. Hounshell and Smith, *Science and Corporate Strategy,* pp. 161–169; Jesse W. Markham, *Competition in the Rayon Industry* (Cambridge, Mass., 1952), pp. 14–24.

87. Markham, *Competition in the Rayon Industry,* p. 47. For profits see Hounshell and Smith, *Science and Corporate Strategy,* pp. 167–169; Donald C. Coleman, *Courtaulds: An Economic and Social History,* vol. II, *Rayon* (Oxford, 1969), p. 389.

88. Hounshell and Smith, *Science and Corporate Strategy,* pp. 170–171.

89. For example, Du Pont engineers laid out entire finishing areas for bakeries. One office at departmental headquarters worked full-time on packaging-design services. Ibid., pp. 172–180.

90. Ibid., ch. 8, and for Sylvania's share, p. 177.

91. Ibid. ch. 6. Market shares are given in the company memorandum "Approximate Percent of U.S. Market Enjoyed by Du Pont Products," and also in Jayne to Sparre, Sept. 20, 1930 (see note 79 above).

92. The histories of all these departments as well as the neoprene and nylon stories are reviewed in detail in the Hounshell and Smith study.

93. U.S. Temporary National Economic Committee, *The Distribution of Ownership in the Two Hundred Largest Non-financial Corporations* (Washington, D.C., 1940), app. VII. For stockholdings in 1965, see Philip H. Burch, Jr., *The Managerial Revolution Reassessed: Family Control in America's Large Corporations* (Lexington, Mass., 1972), pp. 36–67.

6. Expanding Organizational Capabilities: Machinery

1. Mira Wilkins, *The Emergence of Multinational Enterprise: American Business Abroad from the Colonial Era to 1914* (Cambridge, Mass., 1970), pp. 215–217. Fritz Blaich, *Amerikanische Firmen in Deutschland, 1890–1914* (Wiesbaden, 1984), esp. pp. 1–7.

2. In Group 36, Electric Storage Battery ranked 203d in 1948. In Group 35 a second machine-tool maker, E. W. Bliss, ranked 200th in 1917. Like Niles-Bement-Pond, it failed to grow. General American Transportation, the one new company on the list, was a transportation firm that also made railroad cars for specialized uses. In the 1920s it began to build cars, including refrigerated and oil cars, which the meatpacking and oil companies had earlier built for themselves.

3. David A. Hounshell, *From the American System to Mass Production, 1800–1932: The Development of Manufacturing Technology in the United States* (Baltimore, 1984), ch. 2, esp. pp. 98–119. Alfred D. Chandler, Jr., *The Visible Hand: The Managerial Revolution in American Business* (Cambridge, Mass., 1977), pp. 302–305, 402–406.

4. See Chandler, *The Visible Hand*, p. 308, for typewriters; also Blaich, *Amerikanische Firmen*, pp. 48–54. The quotation is from the sketch of John Thomas Underwood, *Dictionary of American Biography* (New York, 1973), supp. 2, pp. 673–674. Richard Current, *The Typewriter and the Men Who Made It* (New York, 1954), provides the best review of the industry's history. For cash registers, mimeograph machines, and adding machines, see Chandler, *The Visible Hand*, pp. 308, 313, 564–565.

5. Hounshell, *From American System to Mass Production*, pp. 178–182; Chandler, *The Visible Hand*, pp. 406–410.

6. For the merger, see Fred V. Carstensen, "... a dishonest man is at least prudent': George W. Perkins and the International Harvester Steel Properties," *Business and Economic History*, 2d series, 9:87–102 (1980); John A. Garrity, *Right-Hand Man: The Life of George W. Perkins* (New York, 1957), pp. 89–97; also, Chandler, *The Visible Hand*, p. 409.

7. Wayne G. Broehl, Jr., *John Deere's Company: A History of Deere & Company and Its Times* (New York, 1984), pp. 230–235, 239–259, 279–287. Developments at

Moline Plow and J. I. Case can be followed in this excellent history of Deere. For the ineffectiveness and failure of associations and combinations before 1901, see pp. 150–151, 166, 172, 187–189; for competition from International Harvester, pp. 324–328, 340–350.

8. For these companies see Chandler, *The Visible Hand*, p. 310. Fairbanks, Morse & Company acquired the pioneering American scale manufacturer E. & T. Fairbanks in 1916.

9. Although listed in Group 34 by the U.S. Bureau of the Census, American Radiator had both the production and the distribution characteristics of a large firm in Group 35. Its story is well told in Mira Wilkins, "American Enterprise Abroad: American Radiator in Europe, 1895–1914," *Business History Review* 43: 326–346 (Autumn 1969).

10. U.S. Bureau of the Census, *Distribution of Manufacturers' Sales, 1939* (Washington, D.C., 1940), p. 177. Of the remaining agricultural machinery, 20.1% was sold through "other" wholesalers and 4.9% through retailers, including chain stores. By 1939 sales through firm-owned wholesalers had dropped to 51.9%, while sales through other wholesalers had risen 38.6%. This rapid change needs to be studied.

11. The census data emphasize that during the depression both sewing-machine and office-machinery producers sold off many of their retail stores. In 1929, 16.6% of sewing-machine sales were made through independent wholesalers, 65.1% through firm-owned retail stores, and 18.3% directly to customers.

12. These are listed in Chandler, *The Visible Hand*, p. 368, and described in more detail in Mira Wilkins, *The Emergence of Multinational Enterprise*, pp. 212–213 in a table that shows location as well as number of foreign plants.

13. Blaich, *Amerikanische Firmen*, pp. 48–58.

14. Fred W. Carstensen, *American Enterprise in Foreign Markets: Studies of Singer and International Harvester in Imperial Russia* (Chapel Hill, 1984), pp. 68–71 and 75 for Singer.

15. Ibid., p. 230, and also pp. 193–195, 208.

16. Information on Remington Rand, Underwood, and IBM comes from Robert Sobel, *I.B.M.: Colossus in Transition* (New York, 1981), chs. 3–4, supplemented by data from *Moody's Manual*. For Food Machinery Corporation, see Colleen A. Dunlevy, "Food Machinery & Chemical Corporation's Central Research Department: A Case Study in Research and Development, 1942–1954" (Senior Honors Thesis, University of California, Berkeley, 1981), pp. 77–88. Information on International Combustion Engineering is from *Moody's Manual*.

17. Walter F. Peterson and C. Edward Weber, *An Industrial Heritage: Allis-Chalmers Corporation* (Milwaukee, 1976), p. 129; see chs. 5–8 for details of the history summarized here. E. D. Adams, a partner of Winslow & Lanier, was the Deutsche Bank's American representative. The figures on income for the Tractor and Farm Equipment Division are on p. 273. Also see Alfred D. Chandler, Jr., *Strategy and Structure: Chapters in the History of the Industrial Enterprise* (Cambridge, Mass., 1962), p. 370.

18. The story of Harvester's successful competition with Ford is well told in Jane S. Weaver, "Ford and International Harvester: Competition and Development in the U.S. Tractor Industry, 1918–1928" (Undergraduate Honors Thesis, Harvard College, 1981). Market-share figures are on p. 3; the quotation from the 1907 Annual

Report is from p. 5. For John Deere's comparable move into tractors, see Broehl, *John Deere's Company,* pp. 351–360, 412, 478–485.

19. Chandler, *Strategy and Structure,* p. 371.

20. Information on structure can be found in *Moody's Manual,* which lists the autonomous, integrated divisions of these companies. See also Chandler, *Strategy and Structure,* pp. 370–372; Peterson and Weber, *An Industrial Heritage,* p. 355; and Dunlevy, "Food Machinery Corporation," p. 83.

21. Information on product lines at these two companies can be found in *Moody's Manual.* In 1928 Elmer Sperry sold his company to North American Aviation. It became independent again in 1933 when North American Aviation was reorganized. For information on North American Aviation see Thomas P. Hughes, *Elmer Sperry: Inventor and Engineer* (Baltimore, 1971), pp. 321–322, and the citations in note 38.

22. Census figures are reproduced in Alfred D. Chandler, Jr., *Giant Enterprise: Ford, General Motors, and the Automobile Industry* (New York, 1964), p. 5. See Jean-Pierre Bardou et al., *The Automobile Revolution: The Impact of an Industry* (Chapel Hill, 1982), p. 120, for U.S. share of world output.

23. Bardou et al., *The Automobile Revolution,* pp. 54–62, gives an excellent overview of Ford's accomplishments. Allan Nevins, *Ford: The Times, the Man, and the Company* (New York, 1954) ch. 18, provides a dramatic description of the introduction of the moving assembly line at the Highland Park plant. Chandler, *Giant Enterprise,* p. 108, lists prices.

24. Market-share figures, from U.S. Federal Trade Commission, *Report on the Motor Vehicle Industry* (Washington, D.C., 1939), p. 29, are given in Chandler, *Giant Enterprise,* p. 3. For the importance of the innovation of the closed car, see Alfred P. Sloan, Jr., *My Years with General Motors* (Garden City, N.Y., 1963), pp. 158–159.

25. The General Motors story is summarized in Chandler, *Strategy and Structure,* ch. 3; it is given in more detail in Alfred D. Chandler, Jr., and Stephen Salsbury, *Pierre S. du Pont and the Making of the Modern Corporation* (New York, 1971), chs. 16–22.

26. Allan Nevins and Frank E. Hill, *Ford: Expansion and Challenge, 1915–1933* (New York, 1957), ch. 6; Sloan, *My Years with General Motors,* p. 62.

27. Sloan, *My Years with General Motors,* pp. 176–182.

28. Between 1929 and 1933 the total share enjoyed by Hudson, Nash, Packard, and Studebaker fell from 12.3% to 6.6% and the cars produced fell from 563,000 to 104,000. By 1937 the four companies' total share had risen to 9.2% and the total number of cars produced was 358,200. Chandler, *Giant Enterprise,* p. 3. For Chrysler's success in following the General Motors strategy, see Bardou et al., *The Automobile Revolution,* pp. 94, 98.

29. The market-share and profit-and-loss figures for Ford and General Motors from the 1939 FTC report are given in Chandler, *Giant Enterprise,* pp. 5–7; see also Chandler, *Strategy and Structure,* p. 160. The views of Sloan and du Pont on backward integration are described in Chandler and Salsbury, *Pierre S. du Pont,* pp. 257–263.

30. Chandler, *Giant Enterprise,* p. 26.

31. For the direct investments of American automobile manufacturers see Mira Wilkins, *The Maturing of Multinational Enterprise: American Business Abroad*

from 1914 to 1970 (Cambridge, Mass., 1974), pp. 72–75; also Bardou et al., *The Automobile Revolution,* ch. 6; James Foreman-Peck, "The American Challenge of the 1930s: Multinationals and the European Motor Industry," *Journal of Economic History* 42:868 (December 1982); and Sloan, *My Years with General Motors,* pp. 315–328 (sales figures on p. 328). See also *New York Times,* Nov. 9, 1930, pp. 11, 12.

32. Foreman-Peck, "American Challenge," pp. 868–871. Masaru Udagawa, "The Prewar Japanese Automobile Industry and the American Manufacturers," in Keiichiro Nakagawa and Hidemasa Morikawa, eds., *Japanese Yearbook on Business History: 1985* (Tokyo, 1985), p. 82.

33. David C. Mowery, "The Emergence and Growth of Industrial Research in American Manufacturing, 1899–1945" (Ph.D. diss., Stanford University, 1981), p. 71. (See Chapter 4, note 35, above.)

34. Nevins and Hill, *Ford: Expansion and Challenge,* pp. 238–246, for the venture into airplane making; and Weaver, "Ford and International Harvester," for tractors.

35. Information on the product lines of Borg-Warner and Bendix comes from *Moody's Manual* and from *Standard & Poor's Corporation Records* for 1939 and 1948. A. P. Fontaine, *Where Ideas Unlock the Future: The Story of the Bendix Corporation* (Princeton, 1967), briefly reviews the Bendix story. Sloan, *My Years with General Motors,* pp. 363–364, 367–369, provides important additional information. As Sloan stresses, the great growth of Bendix came with the unprecedented wartime demand for aviation parts and systems. By 1942, 82% of sales went to aircraft "during this peak of war production"; with the return of peace the company shifted to automotive products. Even so, 1948 aviation still accounted for 48% of the corporation's sales and automotive for 28%. *Moody's Manual, 1948,* p. 1391.

36. See, for example, Sloan, *My Years with General Motors,* p. 251.

37. Ibid., pp. 105–111, 249–258, 358–359. Stuart W. Leslie, *Boss Kettering* (New York, 1983), chs. 5–7.

38. Leslie, *Kettering,* ch. 10. See Sloan, *My Years with General Motors,* pp. 346–353 for the diesel story, and pp. 362–367 for aircraft and engines; the quotations from Sloan and from the General Motors Executive Committee are on pp. 363 and 373. Sloan suggests that the company's production skills were particularly important in the volume production of North American's AT-6. General Motors' commercialization of the diesel locomotive appears to have been homegrown; at least, the available sources make no reference to comparable developments in Germany.

39. Wilkins, *The Emergence of Multinational Enterprise,* pp. 212–213.

40. See the description in Thomas P. Hughes, *Networks of Power: Electrification in Western Society* (Baltimore, 1983), ch. 1. The formative years of the industry and its leaders is analyzed in Harold C. Passer, *The Electrical Manufacturers, 1875–1900: A Study in Competition, Entrepreneurship, Technical Change, and Economic Growth* (Cambridge, Mass., 1953), esp. chs. 2, 7–11, 16, 17, and 21; and in Hughes, *Networks of Power,* chs. 2–6.

41. Passer, *Electrical Manufacturers,* ch. 20; also D. G. Buss, *Henry Villard: A Study of Transatlantic Investments and Interest, 1870–1895* (New York, 1978), pp. 218–220.

42. By the agreement signed in March 1896, "General Electric patents were considered to represent 62½ percent of the value of the patents and Westinghouse 37½ percent." Passer, *Electrical Manufacturers,* p. 331 (quotation), and pp. 263–270,

331–333. Hughes, *Networks of Power*, chs. 5–6, places the story in its international context.

43. Henry F. Prout, *A Life of George Westinghouse* (New York, 1922), pp. 279–281. Cyrus Adler, *Jacob H. Schiff: His Life and Letters* (New York, 1929), pp. 158–161, gives a good example of the role of investment bankers who provided regular but short-term financing before and after receivership. Schiff, a senior partner at Kuhn Loeb, was primarily concerned with the recruitment of top managers who could keep the company profitable. In refinancing Westinghouse, Kuhn, Loeb worked with the Chase National Bank so that Schiff came to be the chairman of the Board's Proxy Committee and Albert H. Wiggin of Chase a member of its Executive Committee. *Moody's Manual, 1916*, p. 3823.

44. These Board members included the Boston capitalists Gordon Abbot, George Gardner, T. Jefferson Coolidge, Oliver Ames, Henry Lee Higginson, and Robert Treat Paine. The Morgan representatives were J. P. Morgan, Charles Steele, and G. F. Peabody, according to *Moody's Manual, 1900*, p. 316. At the time of the merger the Boston and Morgan representatives were evenly divided. Passer, *Electrical Manufacturers*, p. 323. On Morgan's role see Vincent P. Carosso, *The Morgans: Private International Bankers, 1854–1913* (Cambridge, Mass., 1987), pp. 390–391, 604.

45. Wilkins, *The Emergence of Multinational Enterprise*, pp. 52–59, 93–96.

46. Ibid., pp. 43, 69; Prout, *A Life of Westinghouse*, pp. 263–266.

47. Mowery's tables show the electrical-machinery group as second in the employment of scientific personnel in 1921 with 7.2% of the total, as compared with 30.4% in the chemical industries. In terms of research intensity, however, the much greater employment in processes of electrical-machinery production put it behind both rubber and petroleum. In 1946 the figures for the percentage of scientific personnel employed were 15.2% of the total of such personnel in American manufacturing for electrical equipment and 30.6% for chemicals. Electrical equipment was still behind petroleum in research intensity. Mowery, "Industrial Research," pp. 66, 70. (See my Chapter 4, note 35.)

48. Kendall Birr, *Pioneering in Industrial Research: The History of the General Electric Research Laboratory* (Washington, D.C., 1957), provides a useful overview of the history of research and development at GE; also Leonard S. Reich, *The Making of American Industrial Research: Science and Business, 1876–1926* (Cambridge, Eng., 1985), esp. pp. 82–96; William Haynes, *American Chemical Industry*, vol. VI, *The Chemical Companies* (New York, 1949), pp. 156–159; George Wise, *The Corporation's Chemist: A Biography of Willis R. Whitney* (New York, 1985). On Westinghouse's research, see Ronald Kline, "The Origins of Industrial Research at the Westinghouse Company, 1886–1922" (Paper delivered at the annual meeting of the Society for the History of Technology, Pittsburgh, Pa., October 1986).

49. Hugh G. J. Aitken, *The Continuous Wave: Technology and American Radio, 1900–1932* (Princeton, 1985), pp. 13, 25, 231–232, 248 on GE, and pp. 67, 434–435, 457, 465 on comparable developments at Westinghouse and Western Electric.

50. This route to diversification and the initial organizational responses are summarized in Chandler, *Strategy and Structure*, pp. 363–365.

51. Aitken, *Continuous Wave*, ch. 10, esp. pp. 502–509. Josephine Y. Case and Everett Needham Case, *Owen D. Young and American Enterprise: A Biography* (Boston, 1982), chs. 11 and 13, and pp. 349–352, 417–418.

52. *Moody's Manual, 1943*, pp. 1261–63, 1267–68.

53. Chandler, *Strategy and Structure*, pp. 365–370.

54. Harold C. Passer, "Development of Large-Scale Organization: Electrical Manufacturing around 1900," *Journal of Economic History* 12:386 (Fall 1952); for GE's product lines, see *Professional Management at General Electric: Book One—General Electric's Growth* (n.p., 1951), p. 19.

55. Chandler and Salsbury, *Pierre S. du Pont*, pp. 572–587. At General Motors, where Pierre du Pont stayed on as chairman of the Board after leaving the presidency in 1929, he took issue with Sloan only once. After learning that John J. Raskob had become chairman of the National Committee, Sloan insisted that Raskob resign from the chairmanship of the General Motors Finance Committee. Du Pont then threatened that he too would resign if Raskob was forced to. Raskob did resign, as did Pierre, and Sloan continued as the corporation's chief executive officer.

56. U.S. Temporary National Economic Committee, *The Distribution of Ownership in the Two Hundred Largest Non-financial Corporations* (Washington, D.C., 1940), app. VII; and Philip J. Burch, *The Managerial Revolution Reassessed: Family Control in America's Large Corporations* (Lexington, Mass., 1972), pp. 36–37.

57. Of the firms among the top 200 listed in Appendix A, only those in SIC Group 38 (instruments and related products) and Group 39 (miscellaneous) have not been specifically reviewed in these last three chapters. The very few firms listed in the top 200 in these two categories evolved according to the patterns already described. International Match, the American subsidiary of Swedish Match, was an exception. The two firms that were in the top 200 in all three sets of years—Diamond Match and Eastman Kodak—are impressive examples of first movers in their industries. Both came into being in the 1880s and quickly became the leaders in their global oligopolies. Their activities are briefly reviewed in Chandler, *The Visible Hand*, pp. 292–293, 297–298, and 374–375. More details on Diamond Match can be found in Hakan Lindgren, *Corporate Growth: The Swedish Match Industry in Its Global Setting* (Stockholm, 1979), pp. 49, 51–58, 69–70, 102–103, 112, 115, 157, 196–197, 286–289, and esp. 294–309. These pages tell a fascinating tale of oligopolistic competition and cooperation on a global scale in the branded, packaged product industry. For International Match, see the Lindgren study, pp. 108, 110, and 113. For more details on Eastman Kodak, see Reece Jenkins, *Images and Enterprise: Technology and the American Photographic Industry* (Baltimore, 1975), chs. 4–11, which provide a picture of global dominance by the American first mover in a technologically advanced industry where Germans were the only challengers. Also see Chapter 14 of the present volume.

58. Simon Kuznets, *Economic Growth of Nations: Total Output and Production Structure* (Cambridge, Mass., 1971), p. 319. On pp. 315 and 318 Kuznets describes his long table in this manner: "Using two simple and seemingly mechanical criteria—the size of the share in 1880, and the rate of growth (or multiplication) from 1880 to 1914—I formed four broad groups of these branches. Group A includes branches whose product accounted for 0.6 percent or less of total value product in 1880, and whose output grew by a factor of at least 6 between 1880 and 1914. Group B includes branches whose product accounted for more than 0.6 percent of total product in 1880, and whose product grew by a factor of at least 6 from 1880 to 1914. Group C includes the branches whose output grew during 1880–1914 by a factor of less than 6 but more than 3, regardless of the size of their product (in

relation to the total) in 1880. Group D comprises all other branches, that is, those whose output grew by a factor of 3 or less from 1880 to 1914. It should be noted that the growth factor for the total output of the thirty-eight branches over the 1880–1914 period was 4.33." Kuznets emphasizes the problems of classification faced in developing this table: "It is frustrating that available sectoral classifications fail to separate new industries from old, and distinguish those affected by technological innovations" (p. 315).

59. A useful summary of the traditional view of the foundation and exercise of market power is given in Joe S. Bain and David Qualls, *Industrial Organization: A Treatise* (Greenwich, Conn., 1987), ch. 9. See also Edward S. Herman, *Corporate Control, Corporate Power* (Cambridge, Mass., 1981), ch. 7.

60. The story of Henry Ford and the Selden patent is revealing: Nevins, *Ford, The Times, the Man, and the Company,* ch. 13.

61. Richard H. Schallenberg, *Bottled Energy: Electrical Engineering and the Evolution of Chemical Energy Storage* (Philadelphia, 1982), pp. 210–211.

62. Jenkins, *Images and Enterprise,* p. 184.

63. Richard Tennant, *The American Cigarette Industry* (New Haven, 1950), p. 31; see also Chandler, *The Visible Hand,* pp. 389–390.

64. This point was strongly argued in *The Visible Hand,* as shown in the summary on pp. 334–339.

7. The Continuing Commitment to Personal Capitalism in British Industry

1. Leslie Hannah, *The Rise of the Corporate Economy: The British Experience* (Baltimore, 1976), p. 6 and app. 2; Leslie Hannah, "Introduction," in Leslie Hannah, ed., *Management Strategy and Business Development: An Historical and Comparative Study* (London, 1976), p. 6; and S. J. Prais, *The Evolution of Giant Firms in Britain: A Study of the Growth of Concentration in the Manufacturing Industry in Britain, 1909–1970* (Cambridge, Eng., 1976), p. 47.

2. For a rough estimate of assets for 1948, see Alfred D. Chandler, Jr., "The Development of Modern Management Structures in the U.S. and U.K.," in Hannah, *Management Strategy and Business Development,* pp. 41–43, taken from National Institute of Economic and Social Research, *Company Income and Finance, 1949–1953* (London, 1956), app. C.

3. As there is no study for Britain comparable to the TNEC reports on concentration of economic power (see note 13 below), it is difficult to get data on the amount of stock held by senior executives in the companies they managed. But Philip Sargent Florence, *Ownership, Control, and Success of Large Companies: An Analysis of British Industrial Structure and Policy, 1936–1951* (London, 1961), indicates that more family members were full-time managers and held larger blocks of stock in their companies than was the case for comparable industry leaders in the United States.

4. [Cadbury Brothers, Ltd.], *Industrial Record, 1919–1939: A Review of the Inter-War Years* (Bournville, Eng., 1944), pp. 6–7 (quotation). In addition to this study the following provided more detailed information: Iolo A. Williams, *The Firm of Cadbury, 1831–1931* (New York, 1931); T. B. Rogers, *A Century of Progress, 1831–1931* (Bournville, Eng., 1931); Robert J. Finch, *A Worldwide Business*

(London, 1948). An excellent recent review and analysis of the Cadbury experience is Charles Dellheim, "The Creation of a Company Culture: Cadbury's, 1861–1931," *American Historical Review* 92:13–44 (Feb. 1987); particularly relevant are pp. 17–23. Cadbury's ranking in terms of its work force comes from the "List of Largest Employers in 1935" provided by Professor Leslie Hannah. The firm was 29 on the list, which included four railways and government-owned and -operated ordnance factories.

5. For specific developments in overseas distribution, purchasing, and production, see Rogers, *A Century of Progress,* pp. 150–152; and Geoffrey Jones, "Multinational Chocolate: Cadbury Overseas, 1918–1939," *Business History* 29:59–76 (March 1984). Jones points out that by 1897 Cadbury had agents in Australia, Canada, India, South Africa, France, and Turkey. By 1900 exports represented 10% of the value of its domestic sales of cocoa and 22% of the value of its domestic chocolate sales (p. 60). See also Jones, "The Chocolate Multinationals: Cadbury, Fry, and Rowntree," in Geoffrey Jones, ed., *British Multinationals: Origins, Management, and Performance* (Aldershot, Eng., 1986), ch. 5.

6. [Cadbury Brothers], *Industrial Record,* pp. 6–7.

7. *Stock Exchange Year-Book, 1919.*

8. The formation of Imperial Tobacco and an evaluation of its governance structure is given in Bernard W. E. Alford, "Strategy and Structure of the U.K. Tobacco Industry," in Hannah, *Management Strategy and Business Development,* ch. 3, which can be supplemented by Alford's *W. D. and H. O. Wills and the Development of the U.K. Tobacco Industry, 1786–1965* (London, 1973), esp. pp. 309–314 and 330–333. For British American Tobacco see also Mira Wilkins, *The Emergence of Multinational Enterprise: American Business Abroad from the Colonial Era to 1914* (Cambridge, Mass., 1970), pp. 92–93; Mira Wilkins, *The Maturing of Multinational Enterprise: American Business Abroad from 1914 to 1970* (Cambridge, Mass., 1974), p. 152; and Sherman Cochran, *Big Business in China* (Cambridge, Mass., 1980), pp. 12–24.

9. Ronald S. Edwards and Harry Townsend, *Business Enterprise: Its Growth and Organization* (London, 1958), pp. 65–66.

10. Alford, "Strategy and Structure," p. 75.

11. Alfred D. Chandler, Jr., *The Visible Hand: The Managerial Revolution in American Business* (Cambridge, Mass., 1977), pp. 382–398.

12. *Dictionary of American Biography* (New York, 1974), supp. 4, pp. 370–371.

13. U.S. Temporary National Economic Committee, *The Distribution of Ownership in the Two Hundred Largest Non-financial Corporations* (Washington, D.C., 1940), pp. 391–392.

14. See the beginning of Chapter 3.

15. Angus Maddison, *Phases of Capitalist Development* (New York, 1982), pp. 8, 44. Graeme M. Holmes, *Britain and America* (London, 1976), p. 25, provides very similar estimates.

16. Holmes, *Britain and America,* p. 89.

17. Peter Mathias, *The First Industrial Nation: An Economic History of Britain, 1700–1914* (London, 1969), p. 468; and B. R. Mitchell and Phyllis Deane, *Abstract of British Historical Statistics* (Cambridge, Eng., 1962), pp. 302–306; and for the United States, U.S. Bureau of the Census, *Historical Statistics of the United States, Colonial Times to 1970* (Washington, D.C., 1975), II, 898–899.

18. For Britain: Phyllis Deane and W. A. Cole, *British Economic Growth, 1688–1959: Trends and Structure* (Cambridge, Eng., 1962), p. 142. For the United States: U.S. Bureau of the Census, *Historical Statistics*, I, 138. For British urban population: Mathias, *First Industrial Nation*, pp. 243–248, 451.

19. For U.S. railroad mileage statistics, see U.S. Bureau of the Census, *Historical Statistics*, p. 731. For Great Britain: Mathias, *First Industrial Nation*, pp. 280, 287, 488. The story of the building, financing, and operations of the American railroad network is reviewed in Chandler, *The Visible Hand*, chs. 5–6; and that of the British network is well summarized in T. R. Gourvish, *Railways and the British Economy, 1830–1914* (London, 1980).

20. Gourvish, *Railways*, pp. 10–11; and T. R. Gourvish, *Mark Huish and the London North Western Railway* (Leicester, 1972), pp. 265–267.

21. Robert J. Irving, *The Northeastern Railway Company, 1870–1914: An Economic History* (Leicester, 1976). Pages 218 and 254–256 refer to visits of that road's senior managers to the United States to learn management and organizational techniques; p. 157 describes the organization of the road in 1887; and pp. 213–218 indicate later organizational changes.

22. Gourvish, *Railways*, pp. 16–19; Gourvish, *Mark Huish*, pp. 167–171, 259–260. The total capital raised for the British rail network was, of course, less than that needed for the American. By 1900 the amount raised for the British railways was $5,762 million (close to half of which had been raised by 1870), while $10,263 million was the amount for the U.S. railways (a quarter of which had been raised by 1870). Gourvish, *Railways*, p. 42; U.S. Bureau of the Census, *Historical Statistics*, II, 734. (The figures used here represent book value.)

23. See Gourvish, *Railways*, pp. 27–29 and ch. 7. Although 70% of the system was completed by 1875, the first encroachment on rate-making freedom of the individual roads did not come until the 1899 decision of the Railway and Canal Commission, which had been established in 1888—a decision that brought improved performance. R. J. Irving, "The Profitability and Performance of British Railways, 1870–1914," *Economic History Review*, 2d ser., 31:54–55, 63–65 (Feb. 1978).

24. Gourvish, *Railways*, p. 31.

25. Ibid., pp. 30–31.

26. James B. Jefferys, *Retail Trading in Britain, 1850–1950: A Study of Trends in Retailing with Special Reference to the Development of Cooperative, Multiple Shop, and Department Store Methods of Trading* (Cambridge, Eng., 1954), p. 6.

27. Peter Mathias, *Retailing Revolution: A History of Multiple Retailing in the Food Trades Based upon the Allied Suppliers Group of Companies* (London, 1967), pp. 38–41; and W. Hamish Fraser, *The Coming of the Mass Market, 1859–1914* (London, 1981), pp. 110–111.

28. For department stores see Jefferys, *Retail Trading in Britain*, pp. 18–21, 325–331; and Fraser, *The Coming of the Mass Market*, pp. 128–133 (quotations are from pp. 131–132 and 132, respectively).

29. For multiple shops see Jefferys, *Retail Trading in Britain*, pp. 128–133; and Fraser, *The Coming of the Mass Market*, pp. 111–121. Jefferys, p. 23, and Fraser, pp. 116–117, give details on many multiple-shop firms with the number of branches operated.

30. Mathias, *Retailing Revolution*, has a good description on pp. 44–46; see also Fraser, *The Coming of the Mass Market*, pp. 112–113.

31. For cooperatives see Jefferys, *Retail Trading in Britain,* pp. 16–18 (quotation on p. 16); Fraser, *The Coming of the Mass Market,* pp. 16–18; and the two histories of the C.W.S. by Percey Redfern: *The Story of the C.W.S.: The Jubilee History of the Cooperative Wholesale Society, Limited, 1863–1913* (Manchester, 1913), and *The New History of the C.W.S.* (London, 1938).

32. G. D. H. Cole, *A Century of Cooperation* (Manchester, 1945), pp. 163–167 and ch. 11. Fraser, *The Coming of the Mass Market,* p. 125, notes that 83% of sales came from food but does not give the date for that statistic.

33. Jefferys, *Retail Trading in Britain,* pp. 29–30, 74.

34. Fraser, *The Coming of the Mass Market,* pp. 101–113.

35. Mathias, *Retailing Revolution,* pp. 46 (quotation), 97.

36. Victor Clark, *History of Manufactures in the United States, 1860–1893* (New York, 1929), p. 477. On the 1930 list used to construct Appendix B.2, Saxon Shoe ranked 202d.

37. The statistics for Sears are from Boris Emmet and John E. Jeuck, *Catalogues and Counters* (Chicago, 1950), pp. 290, 294–295, 301. (The 9.6% is for profits as a percentage of sales before income tax.) Redfern, *The New History of the C.W.S.,* pp. 33–36. Christine Shaw, "The Large Manufacturing Employer," *Business History* 25:52 (March 1983), ranks the C.W.S. as the eleventh largest manufacturing employer in Britain in 1907, employing 13,203 workers in 36 manufacturing plants. In 1912 the number was 13,307. Redfern, *The Story of the C.W.S.,* p. 313.

38. Redfern, *The Story of the C.W.S.,* pp. 320–325; and Redfern, *The New History of the C.W.S.,* pp. 550–561.

39. These generalizations are based on company histories, memoirs, and articles cited for these industries in Chapter 9 and supplemented by the essays on the bread, cereal, chocolate, and grocery industries in D. J. Oddy and D. S. Miller, eds., *The Making of the Modern British Diet* (London, 1976).

40. S. J. Nicholas, "British Multinational Investment before 1939," *Journal of Economic History* 11:618–621; also Charles Wilson, *The History of Unilever: A Study in Economic and Social Change* (Cambridge, Eng., 1954), II, 42–43, 50–52. An example of a distribution and delivery system similar to that set up by Cadbury, which Fry then joined, is that set up by Peek Frean, which Huntley & Palmers then joined; T. A. B. Corley, *Quaker Enterprise in Biscuits: Huntley and Palmers of Reading, 1822–1972* (London, 1972), p. 213.

41. Terry Nevett, "London's Early Advertising Agents," *Journal of Advertising History* 1:15–17 (Dec. 1977).

42. J. Othick, "The Cocoa and Chocolate Industry in the Nineteenth Century," in Oddy and Miller, *The Making of the Modern British Diet,* p. 79. Othick notes (p. 89) that, according to one estimate, by the turn of the century the "Big Three" accounted for two-thirds of retail imports of raw cocoa into Great Britain.

43. Fraser, *The Coming of the Mass Market,* p. 167 (quotation). Also, T. A. B. Corley, "Nutrition, Technology, and the Growth of the British Biscuit Industry, 1820–1900," in Oddy and Miller, *The Making of the Modern British Diet,* pp. 20–22. Huntley & Palmers' major investment in production came between 1867 and 1873, when its work force grew from 910 to 2,500. By 1898 it had reached 5,057. Corley, *Quaker Enterprise in Biscuits,* p. 96. Corley tells on pp. 88 and 135 about the collaboration with Peek Frean. He notes that "again and again, Peek Frean recognized Huntley and Palmers as a price leader."

44. Fraser, *The Coming of the Mass Market,* p. 168. Crosse & Blackwell also had a venture in tinned salmon (p. 160) and tomato "catsup" (p. 142).

45. Wilson, *The History of Unilever,* I, 246–248, 313; and H. R. Edwards, *Competition and Monopoly in the British Soap Industry* (Oxford, 1962), pp. 183–186.

46. David Daiches, *Scotch Whiskey: Its Past and Present* (Glasgow, 1976), pp. 66 (quotation), 72, and chs. 4–6 (esp. pp. 110–113, 122–123); and company reports.

47. Alford, *Wills and the Development of the U.K. Tobacco Industry,* chs. 10 and 11. By 1901 Wills accounted for 63.7% of total sales of cigarettes and 55.2% of total tobacco sales in Great Britain (p. 223).

48. John M. Stopford, "The Origins of British-Based Multinational Manufacturing Enterprises," *Business History Review* 48:316–317, 321–322 (Autumn 1974); and data from histories of companies cited in Chapter 9. In addition, information on the match industry comes from Hakan Lidgren, *Corporate Growth: The Swedish Match Industry in Its Global Setting* (Stockholm, 1979), pp. 57–58. Bryant & May purchased the American Diamond Match Company's factory in Liverpool in 1901, its plant in Germany in 1903, and then ten years later its facilities in Brazil. In addition to the companies listed, Schweppes & Mackintosh had "outposts," small factories supplying selling agencies. Stopford, "The Origins," pp. 323–324. Mackintosh, makers of toffee, set up a plant in the United States in 1903, but it failed. One reason was that the product was not packaged but sold in bulk, and while it sold and traveled well in winter, it melted in the summer. Peter J. Buckley and Brian R. Roberts, *European Direct Investment in the U.S.A. before World War I* (New York, 1982), p. 38. In 1922 Mackintosh set up an American factory that individually wrapped and branded the product. For Cadbury, see Rogers, *A Century of Progress,* p. 85. For Burroughs Wellcome, see William S. Haynes, *American Chemical Industry,* vol. VI, *The Chemical Companies* (New York, 1949), pp. 60–62; and *Burroughs Wellcome Company, 1880–1980: Pioneer in Pharmaceutical Research* (Princeton, 1980), pp. 10–12. For Keiller's German plant, built in 1908, see *The Times* (London), Jan. 23, 1919, p. 3—a report on a merger of this company with Crosse & Blackwell.

49. Buckley and Roberts, *European Investment in the U.S.A.,* p. 91; Wilson, *The History of Unilever,* vol. I, chs. 7, 12 (the quotation is from p. 190). Lever Brothers established factories in Switzerland, Germany, Holland, Australia, and Canada between 1898 and 1901; in Belgium in 1904; in France, Sweden, and Norway in 1910; and in Japan in 1913.

50. A memorandum entitled "Duties of Directors, 1917" is in file L.C. 6391 in the Unilever archives, Unilever House, Blackfriars, London.

51. John Vaizey, *The Brewing Industry, 1886–1951* (London, 1960), chs. 1, 6. Only the largest brewers had established laboratories before World War I, including Guinness, Whitbread, Allsopp, and Ind Coope, but these were quality-control, not research, laboratories.

52. Kristof Glamann, "Founders and Successors: Managerial Change during the Rise of the Modern Brewing Industry" (Paper presented at the E.B.C. Conference, Copenhagen, 1981), p. 2. *Trumans, the Brewers: The Story of Truman Hanbury Buxton and Co., Ltd., London & Burton* (London, 1966), provides a good example of the operation of a continuing, family-managed brewing enterprise.

53. Vaizey, *The Brewing Industry,* pp. 8–9, 31–32, 143–148; Walter P. Serocold, *The Story of Watney's* (London, 1949), pp. 27, 40. Also, Patrick Lynch and John Vaizey,

Guinness's Brewery in the Irish Economy, 1759–1876 (Cambridge, Eng., 1960), ch. 12.

54. William D. Rubinstein, "The Victorian Middle Classes: Wealth, Occupation, and Geography," *Economic History Review,* 2d ser., 30:605 (Nov. 1977), shows that in the period 1880–1899, 14 out of 59 millionaires were located in the food, drink, and tobacco category. (These included 23.7% of the millionaires whose wealth was not based on land.) In manufacturing, textiles came next with 5. Moreover, 2 of the 3 millionaires in chemicals produced branded, packaged products. Finance included 13 and agricultural 10. For 1900–1914, out of 73 millionaires, 14 were in food, drink, and tobacco; 8 in textiles; 14 in agriculture; and 22 in finance. Rubinstein's data are further documented in his *Men of Property: The Very Wealthy in Britain since the Industrial Revolution* (London, 1981), ch. 3.

55. Glenn D. Babcock, *History of the United States Rubber Company: A Case Study in Corporation Management* (Bloomington, Ind., 1966), pp. 90–91; B. F. Goodrich Company, *The Growth of an Ideal* (Akron, 1918), p. 52.

56. Jean-Pierre Bardou et al., *The Automobile Revolution: The Impact of an Industry* (Chapel Hill, 1982), pp. 12, 25–26; and Geoffrey Jones, "The Growth and Performance of British Multinational Firms before 1939: The Case of Dunlop," *Economic History Review,* 2d ser., 37:35–44 (Feb. 1984). Dunlop did set up factories in the 1890s in France, Germany, and the United States for the production of bicycle tires. None of these was particularly successful, in part because the production of such tires did not have the cost advantages of scale that the making of auto tires had.

57. Theodore C. Barker, *The Glassmakers: Pilkington—The Rise of an International Company, 1826–1976* (London, 1977), chs. 8–14 (pp. 133–141 for adoption of Siemens process; ch. 9, p. 163, for quotation on warehouses; pp. 193–198 for negotiation with Continental cartels; pp. 130–131, 171–172, 234–236 for middle and top management; and pp. 170–171 for financing growth through retained earnings). As Barker writes, continuing expansion was "self-financed." During the 1880s and early 1890s "profits were high enough to permit a massive ploughing back in order to renew obsolescent buildings and equipment . . . and to allow for innovation and expansion" (p. 170). At the same time the four partners received income far above their original expectations. See also T. C. Barker, "The Glass Industry," in Derek H. Aldcroft, ed., *The Development of British Industry and Foreign Competition, 1875–1914: Studies in Industrial Enterprise* (London, 1968), which provides an excellent summary of the industry's development. Barker's article and book both provide information on Chance Brothers.

58. William J. Reader, *Imperial Chemical Industries: A History* vol. I, *The Forerunners, 1870–1926* (London, 1970), chs. 2, 4, 5, and 7. These chapters describe in great detail the rise of the Nobel enterprise and the coming of the complex network of international arrangements among members of the new global oligopoly in the 1880s. Two "International Conventions" in 1885 and 1886 defined the markets in Europe; and then in 1888, on the basis of the "American Convention," the Europeans agreed to withdraw from the United States and the Americans agreed to keep out of Europe, while Latin America and Southeast Asia became "neutral territories" (pp. 159–161).

59. Ibid., p. 106.

60. Again, the story is told in Reader, *Imperial Chemical Industries,* vol. I, chs. 3, 4,

6, and 10. Also important is Ludwig F. Haber, *The Chemical Industry during the Nineteenth Century: A Study of the Economic Aspect of Applied Chemistry in Europe and North America* (Oxford, 1958), pp. 87–90, 92–102, 157–159.

61. Reader, *Imperial Chemical Industries,* I, chs. 6 and 10. Pages 218–221 in ch. 10 provide a good description of one of the best-managed entrepreneurial firms in Britain in the early twentieth century. Sales were carried out by branch offices at home in London and abroad in China, and also by exclusive agents (pp. 221–226, 230; p. 96 in ch. 6 gives the division of markets for the Solvay group).

62. See Donald C. Coleman, *Courtaulds: An Economic and Social History,* vol. II, *Rayon* (Oxford, 1969), pp. 55–56 and 58 for figures on the British enterprise, and pp. 113 and 125 for those on its American subsidiary; p. 122 lists shares held in 1912.

63. Ibid., chs. 3–6.

64. See Chapter 8 and Chapter 11.

65. Wilson, *The History of Unilever,* I, 204, 228, 245, 278; II, 101–103.

66. Shaw, "The Large Manufacturing Employer," p. 53. Wilkins, *The Emergence of Multinational Enterprise,* pp. 212–213, lists the American firms operating factories in Britain before 1914.

67. For these companies, see Wilkins, *The Emergence of Multinational Enterprise,* pp. 212–213, and my Chapter 6.

68. Ian C. R. Byatt, *The British Electrical Industry, 1875–1914: The Economic Returns to a New Technology* (Oxford, 1979), pp. 47–48, 187.

69. Ibid., pp. 138, 150 for market share and value of output; pp. 139–151, 166–170 for historical development; and pp. 184–188 for British electrical engineers. Moreover, Dick Kerr, a maker of traction equipment, was from the start managed by an American engineer. S. B. Saul, "The American Impact upon British Industry," *Business History* 3:32–33 (Dec. 1960). T. C. Barker and Michael Robbins, *A History of London Transport: Passenger Travel and the Development of the Metropolis,* vol. II, *The Twentieth Century* (London, 1974), p. 43.

70. S. B. Saul, "The Engineering Industry," in Aldcroft, ed., *British Industry and Foreign Competition,* p. 192, also makes this point.

71. For agricultural machinery see Saul, "Engineering Industry," p. 211. Saul notes that "in 1900 the total British output of harvesting machinery was not 1/10th that of McCormick alone in America," and that "during the 1870s improved American models made at home and shipped over the Atlantic began to drive out the British product in Europe and made huge inroads in markets further afield." Also see S. B. Saul, "The Market and the Development of the National Engineering Industries in Britain, 1860–1914," in S. B. Saul, ed., *Technological Change: The United States and Britain in the Nineteenth Century* (London, 1970), pp. 152–153.

72. Saul, "National Engineering Industries," pp. 194–195. The importance of Platt's textile engineering to the development of the Japanese textile industry is emphasized in Gary Saxonhouse, "A Tale of Japanese Technological Diffusion in the Meiji Period," *Journal of Economic History* 34:162–163 (March 1974).

73. Saul, "American Impact upon British Industry," pp. 24–25.

74. D. A. Farnie, "Samuel Radcliffe Platt (1845–1902)," in David J. Jeremy, ed., *Dictionary of Business Biography* (London, 1985), IV, 729–731, mentions that the second-generation Platt worked with six senior managers. Little information is available in secondary sources on Mather & Platt or Howard & Bullough.

75. For overseas marketing see Stephen J. Nicholas, "Overseas Marketing: Performance of British Industry, 1870–1914," *Economic History Review*, 2d ser., 37: 489–506 (Nov. 1984).

76. Saul, "Engineering Industry" pp. 194–195. The tariff barrier was the main reason for building the Howard & Bullock plant in the United States. Mira Wilkins, in her *History of Foreign Investment in the United States to 1914* (Cambridge, Mass., 1989), lists this factory as the only one established by the British textile-machinery makers in the United States before 1914.

77. Haber, *The Chemical Industry during the Nineteenth Century*, pp. 81–84; and L. F. Haber, *The Chemical Industry, 1900–1930: International Growth and Technological Change* (Oxford, 1971), pp. 13–14. John J. Beer, *The Emergence of the German Dye Industry* (Urbana, Ill., 1959), ch. 5.

78. Haber, *The Chemical Industry, 1900–1930*, pp. 121, 145, 179.

79. Haber, *The Chemical Industry during the Nineteenth Century*, pp. 92–98 and ch. 9; Haber, *The Chemical Industry, 1900–1930*, pp. 77–80, 151. Also, D. W. F. Hardie and J. Davidson Pratt, *A History of the Modern British Chemical Industry* (Oxford, 1966), pp. 86–95. Besides the Niagara Falls plant of Albright and Wilson and that of Castner-Electrolytic, United Alkali built a potassium chlorate plant at Bay City, Michigan, in 1889, to be near an ample supply of chlorine. Reader, *Imperial Chemical Industries*, I, 117–121; Haber, *The Chemical Industry during the Nineteenth Century*, pp. 160–161; Martha Moore Trescott, *The Rise of the American Electrochemicals Industry, 1880–1910: Studies in the American Technological Environment* (Westport, Conn., 1981), pp. 67–68; and Haynes, *American Chemical Industry*, VI, 264–265.

80. Haber, *The Chemical Industry during the Nineteenth Century*, pp. 93–95, 160–161; Donald H. Wallace, *Market Control in the Aluminum Industry* (Cambridge, Mass., 1937), pp. 6, 36–68; and George W. Stocking and Myron W. Watkins, *Cartels in Action: Case Studies in International Business Diplomacy* (New York, 1946), pp. 220–233.

81. Charles E. Harvey, *The Rio Tinto Company: An Economic History of a Leading International Mining Concern, 1873–1954* (Penzance, Eng., 1981), p. 66.

82. John Morton, *Thomas Bolton & Sons, Limited, 1783–1983* (Worcester, Eng., 1983), pp. 75–95. The development of continuous-wire drawing, an important innovation for increasing throughput, is described on pp. 80–86, and the alliance with Callender's Cable on p. 91; also, Robert R. Toomey, *Vivian and Sons, 1809–1924: A Study of the Firm in the Copper and Related Industries* (New York, 1985), pp. 19, 292–302. Franz W. Franke, "Abriss der neusten Wirtschaftsgeschichte des Kupfers" (Ph.D. diss., Hessenischent, Ludwig's University, Giessen, 1920), p. 94, lists the refineries operating in Britain as well as on the Continent in 1903. Byatt, *British Electrical Industry, 1875–1914*, pp. 152–157, lists and describes the development of the cable companies.

83. Toomey, *Vivian and Sons*, pp. 21–24, 340–341. As Toomey reports (p. 301), in 1902 the daily throughput of the smelting furnaces at the Vivian works was 16 tons a day, whereas in the United States 150 tons a day was "standard" capacity. Little information is available on Elliott's Metal Company with its Pembrey Copper Works at Burry Port near Swansea, which was the size of Bolton's Froghall works and larger than Vivian's.

84. Charles E. Harvey, "Business History and the Problem of Entrepreneurship: The

Case of the Rio Tinto Company, 1873–1939," *Business History* 21:15 (Jan. 1979); also Harvey, *Rio Tinto Company*, pp. 148–159.

85. See Chapter 12 for Metallgesellschaft; Toomey, *Vivian and Sons*, pp. 339–340; and D. J. Rowe, *Lead Manufacturing in Britain: A History* (London, 1983), pp. 170, 281. Rowe outlines (chs. 6, 8) the rise of many small family firms in the industry and the not-too-successful attempt of the "Lead Convention" to control prices and production; see pp. 182–188 for the history of the cartel.

86. John F. Thompson and Norman Beasley, *For the Years to Come: A Story of International Nickel of Canada* (New York, 1960), ch. 7; and *Stock Exchange Official Year-Book*; also John M. Cohen, *The Life of Ludwig Mond* (London, 1956), ch. 7.

87. Prices and imports are given in Peter Temin, *Iron and Steel in Nineteenth-Century America: An Economic Inquiry* (Cambridge, Mass., 1964), pp. 282, 284.

88. Frank W. Taussig, *Some Aspects of the Tariff Question* (Cambridge, Mass., 1929), p. 159. In Germany, Steven B. Webb notes: "Tariffs were redundant in many cases, however, because Germans produced steel cheaply enough to export." He adds that "even with free trade, Germans would have regularly imported only tin plate and special types of pig and bar iron." Steven B. Webb, "Tariffs, Cartels, Technology, and the Growth of the German Steel Industry, 1879–1914," *Journal of Economic History* 40:310 and 312 (June 1980).

89. Peter Temin, "The Relative Decline of the British Steel Industry, 1880–1913," in Henry Rosovsky, ed., *Industrialization in Two Systems* (New York, 1966), p. 148.

90. Donald M. McCloskey, *Economic Maturity and Entrepreneurial Decline: British Iron and Steel, 1870–1913* (Cambridge, Mass., 1973), p. 84.

91. Duncan L. Burn, *The Economic History of Steelmaking, 1867–1939: A Study in Competition* (Cambridge, Eng., 1940), p. 203. Pages 218–233 emphasize the growing differences in scale of operations and the extent of integration after 1900 between the United States and Great Britain. McCloskey, in his attack on Burn in *Economic Maturity and Entrepreneurial Decline,* does not consider in detail the differences in minimum efficient scale, but he rightly stresses that the growth of demand was much slower in Britain and required a different array of products than elsewhere. Particularly useful in reviewing these issues and the development of the steel industry in general is Bernard Elbaum, "The Steel Industry before World War I," in Bernard Elbaum and William Lazonick, eds., *The Decline of the British Economy* (Oxford, 1986), pp. 51–81. Elbaum points out (p. 61): "With some backward extrapolation, we can infer from the available data that in 1910 roughly 50 percent of British output was made with hand-charged, cold metal practice, and 25% with hot metal practice. By contrast, in the United States only a handful of old plants employed hand charging, and vertically integrated practice dominated heavy steel-making."

92. Elbaum, "Steel Industry," pp. 61–62. W. E. Minchinton, *The British Tin Plate Industry* (Oxford, 1957), pp. 67–68, shows that U.S. imports declined from 223.1 tons in 1895 to 63.5 tons in 1899.

93. Elbaum, "Steel Industry," p. 51. By contrast, in 1870 Britain's share of world tonnage output had been 50% for pig iron, 37% for wrought iron, and 43% for steel. Temin, "Relative Decline," p. 148.

94. Peter L. Payne, "Iron and Steel Manufacturers," in Aldcroft, ed., *British Industry and Foreign Competition*, p. 88. Payne's article, like Elbaum's more detailed analysis, provides a balanced view of the lengthy debate on whether the high cost of

production, resulting in loss of markets, was or was not an example of entrepreneurial failure in Victorian Britain.

95. On July 10, 1889, British Westinghouse's board approved the sale in Britain of £500,000 shares to the public and another £500,000 to the parent company, U.S. Westinghouse, and "by July 20 applications had been received for £632,280 shares—the issue was a success." Robert Jones and Oliver Marriott, *Anatomy of a Merger: A History of G.E.C., A.E.I., and English Electric* (London, 1970), p. 100. R. C. Mitchie, "Options, Concessions, Syndicates, and Other Provisions of Venture Capital, 1880–1913," *Business History* 23:147–164 (July 1981), reviews the debate over financial constraints to investment in new industries in Britain in this period. Mitchie concludes that "the risk capital was available for new domestic industries. It was other limitations that restricted their establishment and growth" (p. 154), and that "investors appeared to have been keen to exploit all these opportunities, neglecting none" (p. 160). The problem was not, Mitchie emphasizes, that investors were unwilling to invest. It was rather that manufacturers were reluctant to go to capital markets for funds (and so to dilute further their control over their enterprise).

96. Leslie Hannah, "Mergers in British Manufacturing Industry, 1880–1918," *Oxford Economic Papers*, n.s., 26:10 (March 1974).

97. Mathias, *First Industrial Nation*, pp. 388–389.

98. Morton Keller, "Regulation of Large Enterprise: The United States in Comparative Perspective," in Alfred D. Chandler, Jr., and Herman Daems, eds., *Managerial Hierarchies: Comparative Perspectives on the Rise of the Modern Industrial Enterprise* (Cambridge, Mass., 1980), pp. 164–165.

99. [Balfour] Committee of Industry and Trade, *Factors in Industrial and Commercial Efficiency* (London, 1927), p. 10.

100. As Hannah points out, there were far fewer vertical than horizontal mergers. By his count of mergers between 1880 and 1918, 64 were horizontal, 9 vertical, and 1 "diversifying." Hannah, "Mergers in British Manufacturing Industry," p. 11.

101. Peter L. Payne, "The Emergence of the Large-Scale Company in Great Britain, 1870–1914," *Economic History Review,* 2d ser., 20:534 (Dec. 1967).

102. Ibid., pp. 528–529; and M. A. Utton, "Some Features of the Early Merger Movement in the British Manufacturing Industry," *Business History* 14:53 (Jan. 1972). Utton expands the number of directors of Calico Printers given by Payne to 128.

103. Henry W. Macrosty, *The Trust Movement in British Industry* (London, 1907), p. 157.

104. Ibid., pp. 124–132 for J. & P. Coats (p. 128 for Coats's statement). Also Payne, "Emergence of the Large-Scale Company," pp. 528–530. For Coats abroad, see Peter J. Buckley and Bryan R. Roberts, *Direct European Investment in the U.S.A. before World War I* (New York, 1982), pp. 48–49. Simon H. Whitney, *Antitrust Policy: An American Experience in Twenty Industries* (New York, 1958), I, 528.

105. A. C. Howe, "Sir Alfred Herbert Dixon, Bart (1857–1920)," in David Jeremy, ed., *Directory of British Business Leaders* (London, 1984), II, 107–110.

106. Yuichi Kudo, "Strategy and Structure of United Alkali Co., Ltd.," *Academia: Nanzan Journal of Economic and Business Administration* 66:148 (March 1980).

107. Reader, *Imperial Chemical Industries,* I, 104–123, 227–231; Kudo, "Strategy and Structure of United Alkali," pp. 74–149; also Haber, *The Chemical Industry during the Nineteenth Century,* pp. 180–185.

108. Reader, *Imperial Chemical Industries,* vol. I, chs. 5 and 7, esp. pp. 126–137. The quotation is from p. 127.
109. R. P. T. Davenport-Hines, *Dudley Docker: The Life and Times of a Trade Warrior* (Cambridge, Eng., 1984), pp. 24–43.
110. Macrosty, *The Trust Movement,* p. 16. This same argument for merger was used in 1916 by a leading lead producer who had been secretary of the industry's trade association. David J. Rowe, *Lead Manufacturing in Britain: A History* (London, 1983), pp. 183–184, 285. Merger did not come until the mid-1920s, however.
111. Macrosty, *The Trust Movement,* p. 17.
112. Donald C. Coleman, "Gentlemen and Players," *Economic History Review,* 2d ser., 26:92–116 (Feb. 1973).
113. Reader, *Imperial Chemical Industries,* I, 230–231. Reader describes the nature of the criss-cross web of agreements in the heavy-chemical industry.
114. For this review of the connection between educational institutions and the needs of the new industrial enterprises, I rely on Robert Locke's article, "The Relationship between Higher Educational and Managerial Cultures in Britain and West Germany: A Comparative Analysis of Higher Education from an Historical Perspective," in Pat Joynt and Malcolm Warner, eds., *Managing in Different Cultures* (Oslo, 1985), pp. 96–102.
115. Eric Ashby, *Technology and the Academics* (London, 1948), quoted by Locke in "Higher Educational and Managerial Culture," p. 99.
116. Locke, "Higher Educational and Managerial Cultures," p. 96.

8. Creating Organizational Capabilities: The Stable Industries

1. Alexander Gerschenkron referred to Germany as a "late industrializer" catching up to Britain. For example, Alexander Gerschenkron, *Economic Backwardness in Historical Perspective: A Book of Essays* (Cambridge, Mass., 1962), p. 16.
2. The impact of the war on British industry is summarized in Sidney Pollard, *The Development of the British Economy, 1914–1967,* 2d ed. (London, 1969), pp. 42–63. Also valuable are L. F. Haber, *The Chemical Industry, 1900–1930: International Growth and Technological Change* (Oxford, 1971), pp. 188–193 for chemicals; R. W. Ferrier, *The History of the British Petroleum Company,* vol. I, *The Developing Years, 1902–1932* (Cambridge, Eng., 1982), pp. 270–294 for oil; Jean-Pierre Bardou et al., *The Automobile Revolution: The Impact of an Industry* (Chapel Hill, N.C., 1982), pp. 79–82 for automobiles; R. P. T. Davenport-Hines, *Dudley Docker: The Life and Times of a Trade Warrior* (Cambridge, Eng., 1984), ch. 5 for machinery, electrical equipment, and attitudes of industrialists; and Howard L. Gray, *War Time Control of Industry: The Experience of England* (New York, 1918), pp. 39–48 for iron and steel.
3. Davenport-Hines, *Dudley Docker,* pp. 84–86. The quotation, on p. 84, is from a speech by Docker printed in the *Economist,* June 3, 1916.
4. Bardou et al., *The Automobile Revolution,* pp. 81–82, shows that Ford produced 50,000 vehicles during the four war years in Britain; Leyland was next with 6,000, primarily trucks; while Morris produced only 1,344. Associated Equipment Company supplied 40% of the military trucks, producing annually 4,000. It installed an assembly line in 1915.

5. Pollard, *The British Economy,* p. 57.

6. Ibid., pp. 53 (quotation on government control), and 62 (quotation from Parliamentary Committee on Trusts).

7. Ferrier, *History of the British Petroleum Company,* I, 487, refers to Anglo-American Oil as "not legally, but almost in practice, a Standard Oil subsidiary." The Court decreed that the existing Standard Oil stockholders would become stockholders in the independent company on a share-to-share basis. For the continuing relationship, see Ralph W. Hidy and Muriel E. Hidy, *Pioneering in Big Business* (New York, 1955), p. 711; George Sweet Gibb and Evelyn H. Knowlton, *The Resurgent Years* (New York, 1956), pp. 499, 502. For Royal Dutch–Shell and EPU see Chapter 11.

8. Ferrier, *History of the British Petroleum Company,* vol. I, ch. 3. At its formation 97% of its stock was held by Burmah Oil (ibid., I, 12). Also T. A. B. Corley, *History of the Burmah Oil Company, 1886–1924* (London, 1983), ch. 9. Even after the sale of 51% of the Anglo-Persian Oil Company's stock to the British government in 1914, Burmah Oil remained the one large private stockholder. Because of this the value of its shares was even greater than that of Anglo-Persian's (see Appendix B.1).

9. Ferrier, *History of the British Petroleum Company,* vol. I, ch. 5.

10. For Greenway, who joined Shaw, Wallace in 1898, see R. W. Ferrier, "Charles Greenway (1857–1934)," in David J. Jeremy, ed., *Dictionary of Business Biography* (London, 1984), I, 639–641. For Greenway's change in strategy in 1912, see Ferrier, *History of the British Petroleum Company,* I, 149–153. (C. A. Walpole of Strick, Scott took over the refining and commercial departments at Abadan; Ferrier, *History,* pp. 161–162.) For the activities of the managing agents, see Ferrier, *History,* pp. 264–269.

11. Greenway's words are from a speech he gave in 1925; as with all direct quotations from Anglo-Persian managers, the speech is taken from the archives of the British Petroleum Company. Ferrier, *History of the British Petroleum Company,* I, 160 (quotation); see also pp. 13, 294, 461.

12. Ibid., I, 274–277, 316–319.

13. For investment in tankers, ibid., I, 292–294, 525–537; for refinery investment at Swansea, pp. 214–217, 429–452, 483–484; and for investment in marketing, pp. 217–219, 243–247, 291–294. The Greenway quotation is from page 291. For his appointment as both chairman and managing director, pp. 296–297.

14. For investment in research, ibid., I, 277–279, 452–460. The quotation is from p. 453. In addition to research on product and process, Anglo-Persian pioneered in oil-field geology and oil-field use, for unlike American companies it had complete control over one of the world's largest oil fields. Ferrier describes this accomplishment (ibid., I, 412, 422). In this work the company's petroleum engineers continued to have close contact with oil and mining engineers who were on the faculty of the University of Birmingham.

15. Ibid., vol. I, ch. 11, for postwar expansion in marketing and distribution; and pp. 487–490 for pumps as well as garage- and service-station activities.

16. Ibid., I, 373. Ferrier documents the reinvestment of retained earnings (ibid., I, 341–348).

17. Ibid., I, 248.

18. Ibid., I, 336–341. The quotations are from p. 337 and p. 338.

19. Much has been written about the "As is" agreement. Mira Wilkins, *The Maturing of Multinational Enterprise: American Business Abroad from 1914 to 1970* (Cambridge, Mass., 1974), pp. 89, 233–234, provides a brief review. Ronald Ferrier, in chapter 3, "Downstream Activities, 1928–1939," in the forthcoming volume of his history of British Petroleum, gives a detailed and complete analysis. R. W. Ferrier, *The History of British Petroleum Company: The Years of Growth and Crises, 1928–1954* (Cambridge, Eng., forthcoming). The quotation is from Ferrier's manuscript. See also Chapter 13 of this study.

20. For facts on the formation of Shell-Mex & BP and the market share it held, see Ferrier's forthcoming volume.

21. The data on Dunlop come from Geoffrey Jones, "The Growth and Performance of British Multinational Firms before 1939: The Case of Dunlop," *Economic History Review* 37: 35–53 (Feb. 1984); Geoffrey Jones, "The Performance of British Multinational Enterprise, 1890–1945," in Peter Hertner and Geoffrey Jones, eds., *Multinationals: Theory and History* (Aldershot, Eng., 1986), pp. 97, 99–108; Sir Ronald Storrs, *Dunlop in Peace and War* (London, 1946), pp. 6–16; and P. Jennings, *Dunlopera* (London, 1961). Sir Eric Geddes's career is reviewed by R. J. Irving and R. P. T. Davenport-Hines in their sketch of Geddes in Jeremy, *Dictionary of Business Biography*, II, 507–514. For de Paula see Leslie Hannah, *The Rise of the Corporate Economy: The British Experience* (Baltimore, 1976), p. 90. F. R. M. de Paula, *Development in Accounting* (London, 1948) was one of the first British treatises on modern corporate finance and budgetary controls. The India Rubber Gutta Percha and Telegraph Works (Appendix B.1) moved into tires in the 1920s and in 1933 was purchased by British Goodrich Rubber. In 1934 British Goodrich changed its name to British Tyre & Rubber (BTR) (see Appendix B.3) and in 1936 sold out to British interests. India Tyre & Rubber Company, Ltd. (Appendix B.2) was originally a subsidiary of a small American company based in Akron. The British company became independent of American control in 1929 and was acquired by Dunlop in 1933.

22. Jones, "The Growth and Performance," p. 44 (quotation). Besides the tire division these divisions included General Rubber Goods, Footwear, Garment, and Sport. Ronald S. Edwards and Harry Townsend, *British Enterprise: Its Growth and Organization* (London, 1958), pp. 218–220; and Leslie Hannah, "Strategy and Structure in the Manufacturing Sector," in Leslie Hannah, ed., *Managerial Strategy and Business Development* (London, 1976), p. 190.

23. Jones, "The Growth and Performance," pp. 44–52; Jones, "Performance of British Multinational Enterprise," pp. 100–104; and Michael French, "Structural Change and Competition in the U.S. Tire Industry, 1920–1927," *Business History Review* 60:41–42 (Spring 1986).

24. Quoted in Jones, "The Growth and Performance," p. 47, from Report to Board, April 26, 1924, in Dunlop archives. For investments in the 1930s in India, Australia, and Ireland, ibid., pp. 50–51.

25. Wilkins, *The Maturing of Multinational Enterprise*, pp. 98–102.

26. D. C. Coleman, *Courtaulds: An Economic and Social History*, vol. II, *Rayon* (Oxford, Eng., 1969), pp. 180–184 for the beginnings of British Celanese, and pp. 183, 266 for British Enka and Bemberg. For number of plants see pp. 325, 400, and also 189–191.

27. *Fortune* 16:39–43, 106–112 (July 1937).

28. Jesse W. Markham, *Competition in the Rayon Industry* (Cambridge, Mass., 1952), pp. 16–20, for foreign investment in the United States after Courtaulds. Tubize merged in 1930 with American Chatillon, a subsidiary of a second Italian enterprise, the Chatillon Group, and then combined in 1946 with Celanese. Coleman, *Courtaulds,* II, 190–191; Markham, *Competition in the Rayon Industry,* p. 87.

29. For German rayon developments, Chapters 12, 14 of this study; also Markham, *Competition in the Rayon Industry,* pp. 17–18.

30. Coleman, *Courtaulds,* II, 293 for tariff, 389–400 for Salvadge as lobbyist, 18 and 178–179 for A. D. Little's innovation.

31. Markham, *Competition in the Rayon Industry,* pp. 52–53.

32. For Du Pont, Chapter 5 of this study; for Tennessee Eastman, Markham, *Competition in the Rayon Industry,* p. 20.

33. Markham, *Competition in the Rayon Industry,* p. 47. In 1938 the figure for total output produced by the seven firms was 93%; for AVC's share see Coleman, *Courtaulds,* II, 384–409 (esp. p. 389), and 411–420.

34. See, for example, Coleman, *Courtaulds,* II, 392–393. Courtaulds even suggested the formation of a single marketing and sales syndicate in the German manner. For the role of the German companies in developing rayon staples, ibid., p. 190.

35. Ibid., pp. 189–198, 241–242, 281–284, 286–287, 294–300. The quotation is from p. 242.

36. Ibid., pp. 375–377.

37. Ibid., pp. 232–233 for these three quotations, two of which are from the Courtaulds archives.

38. Ibid., p. 495 (quotation); for cellophane, pp. 372–374.

39. Ibid., pp. 227–231. The quotation is from p. 229.

40. Ibid., pp. 256–257, and also 316. The quotation is from p. 256.

41. *Fortune* 60:124ff (Dec. 1959); and the many references on British Celanese in Coleman, *Courtaulds.*

42. As pointed out earlier, the Webb-Pomerene Act modified the Sherman Antitrust Act so that American firms might combine to sell their products abroad. The complete story of Durex is told in Charles W. Cheape, *Family Firm to Multinational: Norton Company, a New England Enterprise* (Cambridge, Mass., 1985), pp. 173, 218–223. See also Virginia Huck, *Brand of the Tartan: The 3M Story* (New York, 1955), pp. 125–133.

43. Hannah, *The Rise of the Corporate Economy,* p. 23; Derek F. Channon, *The Strategy and Structure of British Enterprise* (Boston, Mass., 1973), p. 122.

44. Hannah, "Strategy and Structure in Manufacturing," pp. 189–190; Channon, *The Strategy and Structure of British Enterprise,* pp. 185–186. While Hannah points to rationalization within the enterprise and reorganization of divisions, Channon writes that until the 1960s "the organization of Turner & Newall remained that of a holding company." In 1934 the Turner & Newall organization was described in the following manner: It "is built around the principle of a grouping by consent of allied interests and activities, based on self-operating units (i.e., branch or control companies, each with its own board of directors, composed of men actually engaged and experienced in the business) linked up for purposes of co-operation and co-ordination through executives of the branch and the control company directors with a board of your [i.e., the parent] company which confines its attention to general matters such as finance and policy." Quoted in Alfred Plummer, *Inter-*

national Combines in Modern Industry (London, 1934), p. 279. The excerpt also states that Turner & Newall were part of a cartel which included asbestos manufacturers in at least ten European countries.

Somewhat similar is the story of the British Plaster Board group. The largest member of that holding company began expansion after a new process to produce plaster board was developed in the early 1930s. From 1935 to 1939 the company gained control of ten competitors and then of two more during the war. But until after the end of the war British Plaster Board made less effort to centralize controls and rationalize production and distribution than did Turner & Newall. John Routley and Harold Mattingly, *A Saga of British Industry: The Story of the British Plaster Board Group* (London, 1959). There is little published information on United Glass Bottle, but the *Stock Exchange Year-Book* shows that it too was a federation.

45. T. C. Barker, *The Glassmakers: Pilkington, the Rise of an International Company, 1826–1976* (London, 1977), ch. 19, "Reorganization in the 1930s," reviews these administrative developments. Quotations are from p. 325. For Couzens-Hardy see pp. 235–236.

46. Ibid., p. 335 for accounting and finance control, pp. 340–343 for investment in research.

47. Ibid., ch. 20, pp. 390–391 for dividends and profits; 373–375 for purchase of control of Chance Brothers; 372, 376–378, 415 for moving into glass fibers and glass brick; 378–390 for overseas expansion; and 357–362 for international agreements. Pilkington had rejoined the cartel, the Convention Internationale des Glaceries, in 1929 (pp. 305–314).

48. The 1935 census showed that 96% of the output of wallpaper was produced by the category "the three largest firms." H. Leak and A. Maizel, "Structure of British Industry," *Journal of the Royal Statistical Society*, series A, vol. 108 (1945), p. 163. As there is little evidence of any substantial competition to Wallpaper Manufacturers, that firm must have accounted for nearly all of that output.

49. Alfred D. Chandler, Jr., *The Visible Hand: The Managerial Revolution in American Business* (Cambridge, Mass., 1977), p. 336.

50. This and other references to the percentage of output accounted for by the three largest companies in an industry come from Leak and Maizel, "Structure of British Industry," tables 12 and 13, pp. 161, 163. Table 14 on pp. 164–165 lists the commodities whose output is concentrated in one or two firms.

51. W. J. Reader, *Bowater: A History* (Cambridge, Eng., 1981), pp. 27, 30. For the Bowater-Lloyd combination, ibid., pp. 116–118; and Channon, *The Strategy and Structure of British Enterprise*, pp. 180–182.

52. Reader, *Bowater*, p. 189.

53. Channon, *The Strategy and Structure of British Enterprise*, pp. 180–182; Reader, *Bowater*, pp. 29, 54, 183–196. In Reader, chs. 11 and 12 describe expansion into the United States; ch. 13, difficulties met in carrying out expansion abroad and into packaging materials; chs. 14 and 15, financial difficulties and later takeover. These managerial weaknesses encouraged the rise of a successful challenger, Reed Papers.

54. Channon, *The Strategy and Structure of British Enterprise*, pp. 179–180. See also *Stock Exchange Year-Book* for the members of the board.

55. For example, in 1948 Pilkington's paid-in capital was £3,192,000 (approximately $12,864,000), as compared with $89,802,000 for Pittsburgh Plate Glass and

$15,958,000 for Libbey-Owens-Ford. Bowater's assets were £27 million (approximately $108 million), as compared with International Paper Company's $323 million. Courtaulds' assets were of course much smaller than Du Pont's. Only Johns-Manville and Turner & Newall were of comparable size—$128 million as compared with £31 million (approximately $124 million).

56. Hannah, *The Rise of the Corporate Economy,* p. 97 (quotation); Channon, *The Strategy and Structure of British Enterprise,* p. 153. The directors are listed in the annual *Stock Exchange Year-Book.*

57. For Radiation, *Stock Exchange Gazette,* Mar. 14, 1930, p. 556.

58. William J. Reader, *Metal Box: A History* (London, 1976), chs. 4, 5.

59. Ibid., p. 47, for both quotations.

60. Ibid., pp. 22, 152.

61. Ibid., p. 54. In the exchange of stock Continental Can received £50,000 Metal Box shares, and Metal Box received £100,000 worth of Continental shares.

62. Ibid., chs. 6, 7. The program, quoted by Reader on page 85, is from a memorandum of Robert Barlow to F. N. Hepworth, Nov. 21, 1934. Channon indicates that centralized coordination of production was not fully achieved until 1944; see *The Strategy and Structure of British Enterprise,* p. 184.

63. Reader, *Metal Box,* ch. 8.

64. Channon, *The Strategy and Structure of British Enterprise,* p. 184.

65. For Mond Nickel see *Fortune* 10:102 (Aug. 1934). For developments in the lead industry see D. J. Rowe, *Lead Manufacturers in Britain: A History* (London, 1983), chs. 9, 10; for organization of Associated Lead, p. 341; for Great Britain and international conventions, pp. 324–330. In 1931 Associated Lead acquired Goodlass Wall, a leading maker of paints and varnishes, "not only a defensive base against possible entrance by paint companies into the manufacture of lead pigments but also a major outlet for its own product" (p. 307).

66. Charles E. Harvey, *The Rio Tinto Company: An Economic History of a Leading Mining Concern, 1873–1954* (Penzance, Eng., 1981), ch. 8. By 1932 "acute financial problems" of British Mining Corporation and Amalgamated Metal had rendered "their shares almost worthless" (p. 221).

67. George W. Stocking and Myron W. Watkins, *Cartels in Action: Case Studies in International Business Diplomacy* (New York, 1946), pp. 227 (quotation), 238, 244–254; Donald H. Wallace, *Market Control in the Aluminum Industry* (Cambridge, Mass., 1937), pp. 88–89.

68. "Black Decade" is the title of chapter 15 in D. L. Burn, *The Economic History of Steelmaking, 1867–1939: A Study in Competition* (Cambridge, Eng., 1940), which provides an excellent review of the difficult decade 1921–1931. As Burns points out, imports rose from 1.1 million tons in 1920 to 3.7 million in 1926 (p. 394). The story can also be followed in detail in J. C. Carr and W. Taplin, *History of the British Steel Industry* (Cambridge, Mass., 1962), chs. 33, 34, 37, 38. The return of Britain to the gold standard in 1925 probably further depressed the foreign markets for British steel by increasing the value of the pound. Probably this was also true for the production of textiles from natural fibers.

69. This review of the interwar steel industry and the largest steelmakers in Britain relies heavily on Steven Tolliday, *Business, Banking, and Politics: The Case of British Steel, 1918–1939* (Cambridge, Mass., 1987). Tolliday's arguments are summarized in his "Steel and Rationalization Policies, 1918–1950," in Bernard

Elbaum and William Lazonick, eds., *The Decline of the British Economy* (Oxford, 1986). Also useful was K. Warren, "Iron and Steel," in Neil K. Buxton and Derek H. Aldcroft, eds., *British Industry between the Wars: Instability and Industrial Development, 1919–1939* (London, 1979), pp. 103–128.

70. Tolliday, *Business, Banking, and Politics*, pp. 221–235; and Jonathan Boswell, *Business Policies in the Making: Three Steel Companies Compared* (London, 1983). Boswell describes and analyzes the prewar history of Stewarts & Lloyds on pp. 49–51, and the history of the interwar years on pp. 63–70, 90–95, 121–130, 154–159. The quotations are from pp. 64–65 and 66. The reference to the "centralized coordinating authority" (p. 65) is from the Board minutes of Nov. 11, 1918, in the Stewarts & Lloyds archives in the British Steel Corporation East Midlands Regional Records Centre, Irthlingborough, Northants, England.

71. Boswell, *Business Policies*, p. 94, quoting a report from MacDiarmid at the Board meeting of July 15, 1926.

72. For Brassert's plan, see Tolliday, *Business, Banking, and Politics*, pp. 221–231, and also Boswell, *Business Policies*, pp. 125–126.

73. Tollliday, *Business, Banking, and Politics*, pp. 227–231. The quotation is from p. 228.

74. As part of the arrangement Colvilles, the largest Scottish steelmaker, took over Stewarts & Lloyds' plate business in Scotland and in world markets and agreed to supply Stewarts & Lloyds with the plates needed in its tube trade. Peter L. Payne, *Colvilles and the Scottish Steel Industry* (Oxford, 1979), pp. 206–208.

75. Boswell, *Business Policies*, pp. 122–124. For Tube Investments, see *Stock Exchange Gazette*, April 18, 1930, p. 865, and Oct. 17, 1930, p. 2532.

76. Tolliday, *Business, Banking, and Politics*, pp. 125–126. For the history of Richard Thomas, ibid., ch. 5.

77. Thomas was described by an associate "as an impossible man to work with because of his 'arrogant and overbearing disposition.'" Ibid., p. 133.

78. For Brassert's plan at Richard Thomas, ibid., pp. 130–146; for quotation on first-mover advantages, p. 142; for alternatives to building a mill at optimal size, pp. 198–206.

79. Ibid., pp. 153 (quotation), 250–258; Tolliday, "Steel and Rationalization Policies," pp. 91–92, 99–100; and Warren, "Iron and Steel," pp. 118–120. The story is summarized in P. W. S. Andrews and Elizabeth Brunner, *Capital Development in Steel: A Study of the United Steel Companies, Ltd.* (New York, 1951), pp. 542–548; also Carr and Taplin, *History of the British Steel Industry*, pp. 447–448.

80. Tolliday, *Business, Banking, and Politics*, ch. 4 for the story of Colville and the Scottish steel industry (the quotation is from p. 95). For more detail see Payne, *Colvilles*, chs. 6–9. Because it was owned by Harland & Wolff, Colvilles' shares were not traded on the London Stock Exchange until the 1936 merger. Therefore Colvilles is not listed in Appendix B.1 or B.2.

81. Tolliday, *Business, Banking, and Politics*, p. 95.

82. Payne, *Colvilles*, pp. 151–170 and, for Brassert's report, pp. 170–180. Tolliday, *Business, Banking and Politics*, pp. 140–146, also reviews the report. With the acquisition of Dunlop, David Colville & Sons became Colvilles, Ltd.

83. Payne, *Colvilles*, p. 174.

84. Tolliday, *Business, Banking, and Politics*, p. 122.

85. For the story of Dorman Long and northeast coast steel, ibid., ch. 3; and Boswell,

Business Policies, pp. 35–42, 77–83, 103–110, 115–121, 156–159. Tolliday, *Business, Banking, and Politics*, p. 48.

86. Tolliday, *Business, Banking, and Politics*, p. 71 (quotation); for the position of the two banks, pp. 76–78.

87. Ibid., p. 79.

88. Boswell, *Business Policies*, pp. 42–49, 70–77.

89. The managerial reorganization of the United Steel Companies is described in detail in Andrews and Brunner, *Capital Development*, ch. 5. It is summarized in Boswell, *Business Policies*, pp. 141–154 (quotation from p. 144); see also pp. 95–102.

90. Tolliday, *Business, Banking, and Politics*, pp. 157–158, 214–221, 259–268.

91. Ibid., p. 161.

92. Carr and Taplin, *History of the British Steel Industry*, chs. 43, 44, and 47, reviews interfirm cooperation, especially the role of the British Iron and Steel Federation (BISF) in controlling competition at home, working with international cartels abroad, and obtaining the tariff in 1932; see p. 425 for Stewarts & Lloyds' role in the European cartel. The role of government and the BISF are major themes of the Tolliday study.

93. Gertrude Schroeder, *The Growth of Major Steel Companies, 1900–1950* (Baltimore, 1953), p. 43.

94. Another, smaller, specialized cloth processor was United Turkey Red, a merger of four Scottish firms completed in 1898.

95. C. H. Lee, "The Cotton Textile Industry," and E. M. Sigsworthy, "The Woolens Industry," in Roy Church, ed., *The Dynamics of Victorian Business* (London, 1980), pp. 173, 182. William Lazonick, "The Cotton Industry," in Elbaum and Lazonick, *The Decline of the British Economy*, pp. 18–20. My review of the cotton-textile industry rests largely on Lazonick's essay. Also see Robert Robson, *The Cotton Textile Industry in Britain* (London, 1954), pp. 103–117.

96. Lazonick, "The Cotton Industry," p. 34. In 1930 at least two of the largest integrated firms remained family-dominated, with J. C. Hoyle as chairman of one and William Whitworth as chairman of the other. Horrockes, Crewdson became part of Amalgamated Cotton Mill Trust, Ltd., a speculative holding company, and in 1932 became an independent enterprise. Robson, *The Cotton Textile Industry*, pp. 157, 166; and *Stock Exchange Year-Book*. In this reorganization only a small amount of stock was issued. Therefore Horrockes, Crewdson is not on either the 1930 or the 1948 list.

97. Lazonick, "The Cotton Industry," pp. 18–20.

98. Ibid., p. 19; also William Lazonick, "Factor Costs and the Diffusion of Ring Spinning Economy prior to World War I," *Quarterly Journal of Economics* 96: 89–109 (Feb. 1981). The primary restraint was that shipping ring yarn required a bobbin which was expensive and was not always returned. As Lazonick points out: "In 1913 almost all British automatic looms were in firms that combined spinning and weaving." Lazonick stresses that strong labor unions in spinning and weaving held back the adoption of the improved machines. See also Jesse W. Markham, "Integration in the Textile Industry," *Harvard Business Review* 27:74–88 (Jan. 1950).

99. Lazonick, "The Cotton Industry," p. 19. R. E. Tyson, "The Cotton Industry," in Derek H. Aldcroft, ed., *The Development of British Industry and Foreign Competition, 1875–1914: Studies in Industrial Enterprise* (London, 1968), p. 121, shows that in 1913, when Great Britain had 18.7% of its spindles in rings, the U.S. had

86.0% and Japan 95.7%. In 1909 there were nearly 200,000 Northrup looms in the United States (they had first been marketed there in 1894), and in the same year there were only 8,000 in Britain.

100. Quoted in Lazonick, "The Cotton Industry," p. 32, from D. Moggridge, ed., *Collected Works of John Maynard Keynes* (Cambridge, Eng., 1981), XIX, 631.

101. The quotation is from a letter from Geddes to E. R. Peacock, Dec. 7, 1931 (Bank of England archives), quoted in Hannah, *The Rise of the Corporate Economy,* p. 85; see also pp. 73–75, 137. See Robson, *The Cotton Textile Industry,* pp. 157–168.

102. Warren, "Iron and Steel," p. 125.

103. Geoffrey Jones, ed., *British Multinationals: Origins, Management, and Performance* (Aldershot, Eng., 1986), p. 13.

9. Creating Organizational Capabilities: The Dynamic Industries

1. By 1930 Babcock & Wilcox had three works in Britain and ran several partially owned subsidiaries with plants in France, Germany, Holland, Italy, Spain, and Japan; it also operated a worldwide network of sales branches. In short, it had become a larger multinational, managerial enterprise than its American parent. *Federation of British Industries Register for 1930,* p. 320. In addition, see references to Babcock & Wilcox in Geoffrey Jones, "The Gramophone Company: An Anglo-American Multinational, 1898–1931," *Business History Review* 59: 78 (Spring 1985); also *Moody's Manual.*

2. Mira Wilkins, *The Emergence of Multinational Enterprise: American Business Abroad from the Colonial Era to 1914* (Cambridge, Mass., 1970), pp. 212–213. American Radiator and Eastman Kodak, while not listed in Group 35 (the former is in Group 34 and the latter in Group 38), had much the same production and distribution characteristics as the companies listed here. The branch and sales offices of most of the subsidiaries of American companies, as well as those of Babcock & Wilcox, are listed for the interwar years in *Federation of British Industries Register.*

3. Compare the pumps and equipment produced by Weir, given in William J. Reader, *The Weir Group: A Centenary History* (London, 1971), ch. 5, with those listed for Worthington in *Moody's Manual* during the same years.

4. *Federation of British Industries Register,* 1930, p. 404. The same *Register* lists branch offices and sales agencies overseas for Platt Brothers.

5. The information on Platt Brothers (and the 1931 merger, Textile Machinery Makers, Ltd.) comes largely from *Stock Exchange Year-Book.* Platt's laboratory is included by David Mowery in a list of those firms among the 200 largest enterprises in Britain which had made investments in separate research and development establishments.

6. The Lister and Herbert Morris directors are listed in the *Stock Exchange Year-Book,* as is Alfred Herbert's title. Lister appears to have had its beginnings as a producer of sheep-shearing and other agricultural equipment in Australia. Roy Church, *Herbert Austin: The British Motor Car Industry to 1941* (London 1979), p. 164. For Weir, see Reader, *The Weir Group,* chs. 5–7.

7. Reader, *The Weir Group,* p. 94; J. R. Parkinson, "Shipbuilding," in Neil K. Buxton and Derek H. Aldcroft, eds., *British Industry between the Wars: Instability and Industrial Development, 1919–1939* (London, 1979), pp. 95–98.

8. Quoted in J. D. Scott, *Vickers: A History* (London, 1962), p. 83. The Vickers story has been well told by Scott and even more authoritatively (for the period preceding World War I) by Clive Trebilcock, *The Vickers Brothers: Armaments and Enterprise, 1864–1914* (London, 1977).

9. Trebilcock describes the management of both Armstrong Whitworth and Vickers in *The Vickers Brothers,* pp. 143–148.

10. Scott, *Vickers,* p. 140.

11. Quoted in R. P. T. Davenport-Hines, *Dudley Docker: The Life and Times of a Trade Warrior* (Cambridge, Eng., 1984), p. 175. The comparable story at Du Pont is mentioned in Chapter 4 of this study and is told in detail in Alfred D. Chandler, Jr., *Strategy and Structure: Chapters in the History of the Industrial Enterprise* (Cambridge, Mass., 1962), ch. 3. For the Westinghouse purchase, Davenport-Hines, *Dudley Docker,* pp. 159–175, and Robert Jones and Oliver Marriott, *Anatomy of a Merger: A History of G.E.C., A.E.I., and English Electric* (London, 1970), pp. 58–61; for Armstrong Whitworth's Newfoundland venture, W. J. Reader, *Bowater: A History* (Cambridge, Eng., 1981), pp. 32–59; for Beardmore, Peter L. Payne, *Colvilles and the Scottish Steel Industry* (Oxford, 1979), pp. 145–146; for Hadfields, Geoffrey Tweedale, "Business and Investment Strategies in the Inter-War British Steel Industry: A Case Study of Hadfields, Ltd., and Bean Cars," *Business History* 29:47–68 (June 1987); and for the failure of Hadfields' joint venture with an American firm to make manganese steel and castings in the United States, see Geoffrey Tweedale, "Transatlantic Specialty Steels: Sheffield High-Grade Steel Firms and the USA, 1860–1940," in Geoffrey Jones, ed., *British Multinationals: Origins, Management, and Performance* (Aldershot, Eng., 1986), pp. 88–89.

12. Steven Tolliday, *Business, Banking, and Politics: The Case of British Steel, 1918–1939* (Cambridge, Mass., 1987), pp. 192–197; Davenport-Hines, *Dudley Docker,* pp. 175–186; Scott, *Vickers,* ch. 15 (quotation from p. 162); and J. C. Carr and W. Taplin, *History of the British Steel Industry* (Cambridge, Mass., 1962), pp. 441–447.

13. Payne, *Colvilles,* pp. 168–169, 183, 259; Scott, *Vickers,* p. 167; Tolliday, *Business, Banking, and Politics,* pp. 236–247; Tweedale, "Business and Investment Strategies," pp. 63–66.

14. Steven Tolliday, "Steel and Rationalization Policies, 1918–1950," in Bernard Elbaum and William Lazonick, eds., *The Decline of the British Economy* (Oxford, 1986), pp. 97–98. In addition to its role in reorganizing Vickers and Armstrong Whitworth and in forming English Steel and Lancashire Steel, the Bank of England supported the formation in 1930 of National Shipbuilding Security, Ltd., a firm created to purchase and dismantle redundant shipyards. Parkinson, "Shipbuilding," pp. 96–97.

15. Davenport-Hines, *Dudley Docker,* pp. 48–52 and ch. 11; also Barry Ryerson, *The Giants of Small Heath: The History of BSA* (Yeovil, Eng., 1980), chs. 2–5.

16. Even so, BSA was unsuccessful in making automobiles. Davenport-Hines writes that "the real cause of this uneven performance [during much of the interwar period] was that the financial and managerial ills of BSA's motor division were contaminating the whole group" (*Dudley Docker,* p. 222). Between 1927 and 1932 the group had four chairmen. Docker retired as deputy chairman in 1912 but continued to watch over the company in the years following World War I. He finally

turned the chairmanship over to his son, who led the firm to near disaster in the years following World War II.

17. Church, *Herbert Austin*, p. 185; Roy Church and Michael Miller, "The Big Three: Competition, Management, and Marketing in the British Motor Industry, 1922–1939," in Barry Supple, ed., *Essays in British Business History* (Oxford, 1977), ch. 9, also provides an excellent detailed review of the industry's interwar years. Jean-Pierre Bardou et al., *The Automobile Revolution: The Impact of an Industry* (Chapel Hill, N.C., 1982), pp. 104–106, places these developments in their international setting.

18. Allan Nevins and Frank Ernest Hill, *Ford: Expansion and Challenge, 1915–1933* (New York, 1957), pp. 361–366; Mira Wilkins and Frank Ernest Hill, *American Business Abroad: Ford on Six Continents* (Detroit, 1964), pp. 82–87, 106–107, 110–111, 140–145; Roy Church, "The Marketing of Automobiles in Britain and the United States before 1939," in Akio Okochi and Koichi Shimokawa, eds., *Development of Mass Marketing: The Automobile and Retailing Industries* (Tokyo, 1981), pp. 70–71. The dealers' demoralization resulted more from fixed and unrealistic quotas than from the demand for exclusive franchises; both Morris and Austin used the same type of exclusive franchise.

19. Bardou et al., *Automobile Revolution*, p. 105. Ford's failure to adjust its product meant also that the company was hit hard by the tax on horsepower passed by Parliament in 1920.

20. Ibid., p. 143 (quotation); this page also gives production figures. See in addition James Forman-Peck, "The American Challenge of the Twenties: Multinationals and the European Motor Industry," *Journal of Economic History* 42:112 (March 1982).

21. Nevins and Hill, *Ford: Expansion and Challenge*, pp. 542–549, 564–565; Wilkins and Hill, *American Business Abroad*, pp. 190–191, 204–206, and ch. 14; Church and Miller, "The Big Three," pp. 170–173.

22. Church and Miller, "The Big Three," pp. 164, 173. Ford's share dropped to 19% in 1938 and 15% in 1939 as Austin and Morris responded quickly to Ford's new growth.

23. Alfred P. Sloan, Jr., *My Years with General Motors* (New York, 1963), pp. 318–322, 327–328, reviews General Motors' move into Britain through the use of internal company documents.

24. Church and Miller, "The Big Three," p. 180; Forman-Peck, "The American Challenge," p. 112.

25. Bardou et al., *Automobile Revolution*, p. 144; Graham Turner, *The Leyland Papers* (London, 1971), ch. 1. Roy Church points out that Singer's fall from the Big Three was not so much the result of marketing policy as of the costly purchase of the Daimler Works, which was "too large and too uneconomic for success at that time." Church, *Herbert Austin*, pp. 200–201. The listing in Appendix B.2, where Ford is still first in terms of market value of its shares among the automobile producers in 1930, suggests that securities buyers remained unaware of Ford's miserable performance, and that they continued to believe in Ford's ability to pay dividends.

26. Roy Church, "Innovations, Monopoly, and the Supply of Vehicle Components in Britain, 1880–1930: The Growth of Joseph Lucas, Ltd.," *Business History Review* 52: 226–249 (Spring 1978). For a much more detailed history, see Harold Nock-

olds, *Lucas: The First Hundred Years,* vol. 1, *The King of the Road* (London, 1976). Mira Wilkins, *The Maturing of Multinational Enterprise: American Business Abroad from 1914 to 1970* (Cambridge, Mass., 1974), p. 293; and *Stock Exchange Year-Book.* In the 1920s Lucas and Smith had market-allocating agreements with America's Electric Auto-Lite and Germany's Bosch (Church, "Innovations, Monopoly, and the Supply of Vehicle Components," pp. 244–245).

27. See Derek Channon, *The Strategy and Structure of British Enterprise* (Boston, 1973), pp. 156–158; and Sir Roy Dobson, "Development and Organization of the Hawker Siddeley Group, Ltd.," in Ronald S. Edwards and Harry Townsend, eds., *Business Growth* (London, 1966), ch. 15.

28. Forman-Peck, "The American Challenge," p. 112.

29. Roy Church, "The Transition from Family Firm to Managerial Enterprise in the Motor Industry: An International Comparison," in Leslie Hannah, ed., *From Family Firm to Professional Management: Structure and Performance of Business Enterprise* (Budapest, 1982), pp. 28–38.

30. Wayne Lewchuk, "The Motor Vehicle Industry," in Elbaum and Lazonick, *The Decline of the British Economy,* pp. 141, 147–148 for the policy of high dividends, and pp. 144–146 for turning managerial functions over to labor.

31. Ibid., p. 153. "This strategy [that of giving the worker some degree of control over the pace of work] was successful in the short run, but eventually the under-development of the managerial function, the rise of strong labor institutions, and the post-1945 changes in technology produced a situation in which British firms were unable to compete."

32. This information is from Sir William McFadzean, "Development and Organization of British Insulated Callender's Cables, Ltd.," in Edwards and Townsend, *Business Growth,* pp. 287–292; *Stock Exchange Year-Book*; I. C. R. Byatt, *The British Electrical Industry, 1884–1914* (Oxford, 1979), pp. 152–154, 157, 167, 174–175; also R. E. Catterall, "Electrical Engineering," in Buxton and Aldcroft, *British Industry between the Wars,* pp. 248–249. Henley was a pioneer in the making of telegraphic wire and cable. Callender's Cable and British Insulated Wire exploited a new type of conductor—both better and cheaper—in the 1890s. Because of the intensive use of rubber for insulation, Henley easily turned to the manufacturing of tires and golf balls when the other two competitors took over its market share in electrical equipment. (For the later experience of another traditional telegraph-wire producer, India Rubber Gutta Percha, see Chapter 8, note 21.) The extent of the sales-office network of the first of these three companies (Henley) is indicated in the *Federation of British Industries Register for 1930,* pp. 333–334, 341–342, 381. It is uncertain if family management still predominated at Henley's, but there was little turnover on the board. The electric-cable companies are discussed here, even though the U.S. Census (and, therefore, Appendixes B.1–B.3) lists them in Group 33, because they were such an important part of the electrical-equipment industry in Britain. In the United States and Germany electric cables were produced by the major electrical-equipment companies.

33. Dane Sinclair's firm, Automatic Telephone & Electric Company, had produced 200 of his switchboards by 1889. When Sinclair joined British Insulated Wire, his switchboard company became part of that firm. It was spun off in 1911 but remained under the control of its founder.

34. Jones and Marriott, *Anatomy of a Merger,* pp. 80–81, 129–130 (quotation from

p. 130). As part of the agreement between Siemens and Dick, Kerr, the two formed a joint venture in light bulbs. (English Electric, Dick, Kerr's successor, sold its half-share back to Siemens in 1927.) At the same time Siemens and Dick, Kerr agreed not to encroach on each other's businesses. Before the war GEC had a broader product line than its competitors, which included dynamos, motors, and switching and other smaller units, but not streetcars or other traction equipment. Dick, Kerr, meanwhile, concentrated mostly on traction equipment but did produce some power-generating machinery. Adam P. Whyte, *Forty Years of Electrical Progress: The Story of the G.E.C.* (London, n.d.), ch. 7.

35. Davenport-Hines, *Dudley Docker,* pp. 156–159; Jones and Marriott, *Anatomy of a Merger,* pp. 58–61; John Dumelow, *Metropolitan-Vickers Electrical Company, Ltd., 1899–1949* (Manchester, 1949), pp. 73–74 (published by the company). Jones and Marriott note that Docker had worked with the German giant, AEG, to obtain contracts for the electrification of British railways.

36. Whyte, *Forty Years of Electrical Progress,* pp. 70–76. The quotation is from p. 74.

37. Ibid., pp. 96–99; Jones and Marriott, *Anatomy of a Merger,* pp. 83–84.

38. Quoted in Davenport-Hines, *Dudley Docker,* p. 178, from the British Electrical and Allied Manufacturers' Association, *The BEAMA Book: Combines and Trusts* (London, 1927), pp. 96–97.

39. Owen D. Young to Montague Norman, April 4, 1927, and to Sir Robert M. Kindersley, July 27, 1926, from the Owen D. Young Papers at the Owen D. Young Library, St. Lawrence University, Canton, New York. I am deeply indebted to Josephine and Everett Case for providing copies of Young's papers concerning his plans for merger in Britain. These plans are briefly reviewed in their work, *Owen D. Young and American Enterprise: A Biography* (Boston, 1982), pp. 418, 426, 444, 461, 519, 852, 853, 856, 861. In July 1927, Young had written Kindersley that the general strike and the resulting "economic uncertainty have discouraged further efforts since my visit on my part to forward a program of unification of the electrical manufacturers." Young Papers, St. Lawrence University, Canton, New York. Jones and Marriott, *Anatomy of a Merger,* pp. 93–94, indicates that Swope, the president of International General Electric, was considering the merger of IGE's Thomson-Houston subsidiary with GEC in 1921.

40. Owen D. Young to Lord Weir, August 15, 1928; also Young to Josiah Stamp, Aug. 28, 1928. Young Papers.

41. Jones and Marriott, *Anatomy of a Merger,* ch. 6, "The Easter Plot (1929)," tells the story of a fairly straightforward negotiation.

42. Young's letter to Pole, from the Owen D. Young Papers, had on it a hand-written note: "not sent."

43. Ibid. Information regarding the 60% ownership by General Electric is from an article, "The World's Electrical Industry: The Predominance of the American General Electric Company," *European Finance,* Aug. 2, 1929, pp. 100, 102, 107; this article is also in the Young Papers.

44. Young's letter to Pole, Nov. 29, 1929, from the Young Papers.

45. *New York Times,* Aug. 2, 1929, and "The World's Electrical Industry," both from the Young Papers. Wilkins, *The Maturing of Multinational Enterprise,* pp. 67–68, 469, uses the FTC report of 1948 on the international electric-equipment cartel to analyze this move in much the same terms as those indicated by documents in the Young Papers.

46. In "Remarks of Young at Camp General, Association Island, July 30, 1930," made shortly after Swope's return, Young noted that the company now held "a substantial interest in every principal [electrical] manufacturing company in the world," and he added, "not of course that it had pushed itself into those corners against the will of either the stockholders or the managers, but on the invitation of the management [sic] themselves." Young Papers, St. Lawrence University, Canton, New York.

47. Wilkins, *The Maturing of Multinational Enterprise,* pp. 68–69, reviews the formation of the Electrical Apparatus Export Association. She points out that by the agreement "each company was required to 'notify' an international secretary of customers in certain specified territories; bids were discussed, and the successful tenderer of the bid had to 'compensate' the international secretary as well as the other members who had been 'notified.'" For GE's withdrawal from international markets in this industry, ibid., pp. 294–296.

48. Jones and Marriott, *Anatomy of a Merger,* ch. 8; and for the size of GE's holdings in AEI, see p. 160.

49. Jones and Marriott, *Anatomy of a Merger,* pp. 131–140 (and see pp. 142 and 172 on Crompton Parkinson); Leslie Hannah, *Electricity before Nationalization: A Study of the Development of the Electricity-Supply Industry in Britain to 1948* (London, 1980), pp. 227–232.

50. Jones and Marriott, *Anatomy of a Merger,* chs. 7, 10, 11. For Parkinson, see Philip Sargent Florence, *Ownership, Control, and Success of Large Companies: An Analysis of English Industrial Structure and Policy, 1936–1951* (London, 1961), p. 223.

51. Jones and Marriott, *Anatomy of a Merger,* p. 142–143.

52. This summary comes primarily from Jones, "Gramophone Company," pp. 76–100. See also Ronald Gelatt, *The Fabulous Phonograph, 1877–1977* (London, 1977), esp. pp. 107, 177, 197, 209–210, 225–226, 255, 258, and 274; as well as "Columbia Graphophone Company, Ltd.: Analysis by Willington & Co., New York, Dec. 11, 1928," in Baker Library, Harvard Business School, Boston, Mass. See, in addition, the company's annual reports.

53. Jones, "Gramophone Company," p. 100. EMI's diversification is described on the same page.

54. Ibid., p. 98; *Stock Exchange Gazette,* Mar. 17, 1930, p. 556, and May 2, 1930, p. 972. By 1935 the American shares had been sold off to British interests. Columbia disposed of its American factory a few years after the merger.

55. Richard E. Threlfall, *The Story of One Hundred Years of Phosphorus Making, 1851–1951* (Oldbury, Eng., 1951), esp. pp. 152–154, 186–217; L. F. Haber, *The Chemical Industry, 1900–1930: International Growth and Technological Change* (Oxford, 1971), pp. 115, 143–144, 152, 272. Griesheim Elektron had become the major force in the industry following its development of a high-volume electrolytic process for producing phosphorus. Martha Ward Trescott, *The Rise of the American Electrochemical Industry, 1880–1910: Studies in American Technological Development* (Westport, Conn., 1980), p. 80.

56. Threlfall, *One Hundred Years of Phosphorus Making,* p. 158. The date of this incident is uncertain, but the text indicates that it was probably just before World War I. That 40% of the company's voting stock was controlled by Albrights, Threlfalls, and Wilsons is indicated in Florence, *Ownership, Control, and Success of Large Companies,* pp. 223–224.

57. For Fisons, see D. W. Hardie and J. Davidson Pratt, *A History of the Modern British Chemical Industry* (London, 1966), p. 292; and W. J. Reader, *Imperial Chemical Industries: A History,* vol. II, *The First Quarter Century, 1926–1952* (London, 1975), pp. 106–109. For Salt Union, see W. J. Reader, *Imperial Chemical Industries: A History,* vol. I, *The Forerunners, 1870–1926* (London, 1970), pp. 103–104; for its acquisition by Imperial Chemical Industries, Reader, *Imperial Chemical Industries,* II, 269. For British Briquettes, see *Stock Exchange Year-Book.* For Borax, see Hardie and Pratt, *A History of the Modern British Chemical Industry,* p. 268; and Norman J. Travis and Carl G. Randolph, *United States Borax & Chemical Corporation* (Princeton, 1973). Although Borax had chemical-processing plants in Britain and abroad, it was much more a mining than a manufacturing enterprise. British Oxygen began its modern existence in 1900 after obtaining the Carl von Linde patents, for which the inventor received 25% of the company's voting shares. Haber, *The Chemical Industry, 1900–1930,* pp. 144; J. S. Hutchinson, "Development and Organization of British Oxygen Company, Ltd.," in Edwards and Townsend, *Business Growth,* pp. 301–312 (quotation from p. 307).

58. Reader, *Imperial Chemical Industries,* vol. I, ch. 17, for the postwar history of Nobel's Explosives.

59. "Report of the Committee on Organization—to the Chairman and Board of Directors of Explosives Trades Limited," signed by B. E. Todhunter and dated April 2, 1919, from the archives, ICI Record Center, Imperial Chemical House, Millbank, London. Unless otherwise indicated, all other ICI documents cited are from these archives. Reader puts this report in its historical setting in *Imperial Chemical Industries,* I, 390–391. The report began by pointing out: "The movement towards large combinations originated in the United States, and in that country has been continuously in the direction of closer organization and centralized control, and the policy of large American amalgamations after passing through a phase of some form of loose agreement: a pool, a holding, is now crystallizing into the complete Merger, in which the separate management and personnel of the individual units disappear, even if the units themselves retain their nominal existence, and a single executive and operating staff is created in which the entire control is centralized." The report further stated: "The keynote of the American system appears to be (1) complete centralization of control, (2) reliance on individuals and not on committees, (3) full authority and responsibility for each individual within his own sphere, (4) the employment of young persons in positions of importance." The initial Du Pont reorganization, which went into effect in April 1919, quickly proved incapable of administering Du Pont's recent diversification into related industries. After a series of organizational experiments, the company created one of the earliest multidivisional forms, which went into effect in September 1921. Chandler, *Strategy and Structure,* pp. 67–78, 91–112. The British visitors took back copies of the studies and reports that are cited in *Strategy and Structure,* pp. 67–78.

60. Reader, *Imperial Chemical Industries,* I, 393. Chamberlain made this point strongly at a meeting of the Organization Committee, Aug. 28, 1919. The minutes indicate the issues raised.

61. Reader, *Imperial Chemical Industries,* I, 390–393.

62. Ibid., pp. 381, 382.

63. Ibid., chs. 13, 16.

64. Ibid., pp. 357 (quotation), and 331–370.

65. Ibid., chs. 12, 19 (reference to a British I.G. is from p. 459); and Haber, *The Chemical Industry, 1900–1930*, pp. 207–208, 292–293.

66. Reader, *Imperial Chemical Industries*, vol. I, ch. 19.

67. Until Mond's death in 1930, nearly all the documents in the ICI records that I could find dealing with organizational matters had been drafted and signed by Mond, with little evidence to suggest that they had grown out of special studies and reports.

68. From "Notes on the proposed amalgamation of Brunner, Mond & Company, Ltd., and Nobel Industries, Ltd.," by D. Marsh (New York, Oct. 5, 1926); and from the minutes of the meeting in Sir Harry McGowan's room, Oct. 14, 1926. Both documents are in ICI's amalgamation files for 1918 and 1925–26. Besides sales, the Commercial Department included purchasing, transport ("traffic" was the American term), and insurance offices. Central Administration included labor, welfare, accounting, statistics, and patents. Reader, *Imperial Chemical Industries*, II, 22–30. Mond provided a good description of the working out of this new structure in two memoranda: "Organization: Imperial Chemical Industries," Mar. 15, 1927; and "Organization: Imperial Chemical Industries," Apr. 6, 1927.

69. Reader, *Imperial Chemical Industries*, II, 22–23. The accounting and control systems are described in Mond's "Functions of the Financial Controller," Oct. 25, 1926; also, "Imperial Chemical Industries: Report of the Financial and Technical Subcommittees of the Costs Committee, March 17, 1927"; and H. J. Mitchell to Chairman and President, undated, but referring to Mitchell's Memorandum of Oct. 28, 1927.

70. Reader, *Imperial Chemical Industries*, II, 140–143 and 70–94; and three memoranda written for J. H. Wadsworth on the proposed group structure, forwarded to the Executive Directors by Mitchell (as Chairman of the Executive Committee), Dec. 31, 1928; also J. H. Wadsworth, "To The Board," June 6, 1929; and Imperial Chemical Industries, Executive Committee minutes, Jan. 8, June 6 and 25, Aug. 18, Sept. 10, and Nov. 5, 1929, in ICI archives material file #14. The offices in the Central Administration Department were listed simply as the Central Services Departments.

71. See Reader, *Imperial Chemical Industries*, II, 234–239, for McGowan, "the dictator supreme."

72. Ibid., pp. 46–54; and David A. Hounshell and John Kenly Smith, Jr., *Science and Corporate Strategy: Du Pont R & D, 1902–1980* (Cambridge, Eng., 1988), ch. 10.

73. Reader, *Imperial Chemical Industries*, vol. II, ch. 10.

74. Ibid., pp. 145–155.

75. Ibid., ch. 11. The first quotation is from p. 194 and the second from p. 187. Reader took the second quotation from *USA* v. *ICI et al.;* "Preliminary Draft of Dr. Cronshaw's Testimony," box 173, file 173, Library Department Historical Collection, ICI Organics Division, Blackley, Eng.

76. Reader, *Imperial Chemical Industries*, II, 93. Both quotations are from this page. The first is taken from R. E. Slade, "The Dupont Research Organization," Jan. 6, 1938, ICI General Purposes Committee Minutes.

77. Reader, *Imperial Chemical Industries*, II, 331–336, 351–354.

78. Hounshell and Smith, *Science and Corporate Strategy*, p. 204; see also P. J. Wingate, *The Colorful Du Pont Company* (Wilmington, Del., 1982), p. 103.

79. Hounshell and Smith, *Science and Corporate Strategy,* pp. 191–205 (quotation from p. 203).

80. Reader, *Imperial Chemical Industries,* II, ch. 13, entitled "Dictatorship in the Thirties: The Baron's Revolt."

81. Ibid., p. 245. The quotation is from Harold J. Mitchell's draft letter, Jan. 13, 1938, ICI Secretary's Confidential Paper.

82. Reader, *Imperial Chemical Industries,* II, 92.

83. B. J. T. Cronshaw, "Memorandum on Organization—A Note in Reply to Mr. Lutyens," undated, received by W. F. Lutyens, Jan. 4, 1941. "ICI Ltd. Organization," a memo dated June 30, 1943, notes: "The war . . . particularly the dispersal of the Staff to the provinces, has necessitated variations from the [prewar] organization which tend to accelerate weaker points and to raise costs without at the same time achieving the advantage of de-centralized responsibility."

84. Reader, *Imperial Chemical Industries,* II, 305–306.

85. Channon, *The Strategy and Structure of British Enterprise,* pp. 144–145; and *Annual Report of Imperial Chemical Industries, Ltd., for 1963,* p. 15.

86. For Liebig and Brooke Bond, see Channon, *The Strategy and Structure of British Enterprise,* pp. 168–169. For Bovril, Richard Bennett, *The Story of Bovril* (London, 1953); and John Armstrong, "Hooley and the Bovril Company," *Business History* 19:22 (1978). For Mackintosh and Schweppes, *Stock Exchange Year-Book.* For Mackintosh only, see also David J. Jeremy, "John Mackintosh" and "Harold Vincent Mackintosh," in David J. Jeremy, ed., *Dictionary of Business Biography,* IV (London, 1986), 41–57. In 1948 the directors of Mackintosh included Lord Mackintosh (as chairman), J. D. V. Mackintosh, E. D. Mackintosh, and J. H. Guy.

87. For Lewis Berger see *Stock Exchange Year-Book;* and William Haynes, *American Chemical Industry,* vol. VI, *The Chemical Companies* (New York, 1949), p. 98.

88. Information on Sangers is from *Stock Exchange Year-Book;* on Beechams, from Anne Francis, *A Guinea a Box: A Biography* (London, 1968).

89. The Boots' experience is given in Stanley Chapman, *Jesse Boot of Boots the Chemist* (London, 1974), esp. ch. 7. Contemporary documents available in the Boots archives in Nottingham provide a useful case study of the transfer of organizational techniques to a British company under American tutelage. Due to limitations of space, that story cannot be told here. Although Boots, like the C.W.S., manufactured a number of the products it sold, only a little over a quarter of its assets and sales were related to manufacturing.

90. Information on Burroughs Wellcome is from Channon, *The Strategy and Structure of British Enterprise,* pp. 146–147; from Haynes, *American Chemical Industry,* VI, 60–63; and from *In Pursuit of Excellence: One Hundred Years of Burroughs Wellcome, 1880–1980* (London, 1980), p. 23–30.

91. Rowntree, the third member of the Big Three in chocolate, failed to join British Cocoa & Chocolate only because of the opposition of its 80-year-old founder. Geoffrey Jones, "The Chocolate Multinationals," in Jones, *British Multinationals,* pp. 97–99. For Huntley & Palmers and Peek Frean, see T. A. B. Corley, *Quaker Enterprise in Biscuits: Huntley & Palmers of Reading, 1822–1972* (London, 1972), pp. 204–207, 212–213. For Tate & Lyle, Phillipe Chalmin, *Tate & Lyle: Géant du Sucre* (Paris, 1983), pp. 109–111.

92. For the Crosse and Blackwell merger, *Stock Exchange Year-Book* for 1918, p. 1893. Information on constituent companies in the merger is given in London *Times,* Jan. 23, 1919, pp. 3, 13 (quotation).

93. For H. P. Sauce and Cerebos, see *Stock Exchange Year-Book*; for Cerebos, Richard Everly and I. M. D. Little, *Concentration in British Industry: An Empirical Study of the Structure of Industrial Production, 1935–1951* (Cambridge, Eng., 1960), p. 117.

94. For McDowell, Robertson, see *Stock Exchange Year-Book*. For Reckitt and Colman, see Basil N. Reckitt, *The History of Reckitt and Sons, Limited* (London, 1952), esp. chs. 8–13 (pp. 87–88 provide a brief summary of the cooperation with J. & J. Colman that led to the merger in 1938).

95. D. J. Rowe, *Lead Manufacturing in Britain: A History* (London, 1983), pp. 306–308. Another merger listed in Appendixes B.3 and B.4 is the British Sugar Corporation—a combination of 18 sugar companies carried out by political fiat through the Sugar Industry (Reorganization) Act of 1936. Everly and Little, *Concentration in British Industry*, pp. 244–247. It is not indicated whether rationalization occurred or what kind of management structure resulted. For Pinchin Johnson, *Stock Exchange Year-Book*.

96. Huford Jones, *The Master Millers: The Story of the House of Rank* (London, 1954), pp. 64–68 (the quotation is divided by a series of pictures).

97. Information on Spillers comes from *Stock Exchange Year-Book*. Spillers' reorganization is reviewed in the London *Times*, Jan. 25, Feb. 5, and particularly May 9, 1927; also Everly and Little, *Concentration in British Industry*, p. 187.

98. H. G. Lazell, *From Pills to Penicillin: The Beecham Story* (London, 1975), pp. 30–35.

99. Ibid., p. 30.

100. Lazell, *Beecham Story*, pp. 21, 86–87, 133.

101. Information on this expansion comes from annual reports. Particularly useful is that of 1956. See also David Daiches, *Scotch Whiskey: Its Past and Present* (Glasgow, 1976), ch. 4 and pp. 113, 122–123. The developments leading to the 1925 merger are outlined in Brian Spiller, *The Chameleon's Eye: James Buchanan & Company Limited, 1884–1984* (London, 1984), pp. 58–62.

102. Reader, *Imperial Chemical Industries*, II, 322–327, 340, reviews the place of Distillers' Company, Ltd., in the chemical industry; also Daiches, *Scotch Whiskey*, p. 113.

103. Daiches, *Scotch Whiskey*, pp. 85–86, 111–113; and annual reports. Ross was succeeded by his son, Henry J. Ross, who had long been one of the two assistant managing directors.

104. Jones, "Chocolate Multinationals," pp. 99–114.

105. Tobacco makers, however, continued to concentrate primarily on the British market. After the creation of Imperial Tobacco and British American Tobacco, Imperial operated (exclusively) in the domestic market and British American (which after the war became British-financed and -managed) produced and marketed overseas—including the United States, where it operated a subsidiary, Brown & Williamson. Channon, *The Strategy and Structure of British Industry*, p. 101; and Wilkins, *The Maturing of Multinational Enterprise*, p. 152.

106. *Stock Exchange Year-Book*; London *Times*, Apr. 30, 1936; and post-World War II annual reports. Crosse & Blackwell owned a South African company, the Sweet Cake Flour Company, suggesting backward integration in that area, but the *Stock Exchange Year-Book* fails to mention a plant there.

107. Reckitt, *Reckitt and Sons*, pp. 64–65, 77–79, 87. The quotation is from page 79.

108. See *Stock Exchange Year-Book* for both paint companies.

109. R. P. T. Davenport-Hines, "Glaxo as a Multinational before 1963," in Jones, *British Multinationals,* pp. 139–151; Haynes, *American Chemical Industry,* VI, 60–63; Channon, *The Strategy and Structure of British Enterprise,* pp. 146–147. Beecham had built a small factory in Brooklyn, N.Y., in the 1890s, but made little effort to expand its American operations after World War I.

110. Jones, "Chocolate Multinationals," p. 103.

111. Geoffrey Jones, "Origins, Management, and Performance," in Jones, *British Multinationals,* p. 15 (Rowntree did not establish a comparable committee until the 1950s); and Reckitt, *Reckitt and Sons,* p. 79.

112. Jones, "Origins, Management, and Performance," p. 14.

113. Charles Wilson, *The History of Unilever: A Study in Economic Growth and Social Change* (New York, 1968), I, 227–233; Reckitt, *Reckitt and Sons,* pp. 72–75, 83–86.

114. Jonathan Liebenau, "Industrial R & D in Pharmaceutical Firms in the Early Twentieth Century," *Business History* 26: 337, 342–343 (1984); Davenport-Hines, "Glaxo," pp. 142–143.

115. For example, Chapman, *Jesse Boot,* pp. 97–98; and for an earlier period, A. E. Musson, *Enterprise in Soap and Chemicals: Joseph Crosfield & Sons, Limited, 1815–1965* (Manchester, Eng., 1965), p. 147.

116. Channon, *The Strategy and Structure of British Enterprise,* p. 117; Ronald Ferrier, "H. M. Stanley Award, 15th November 1978," in British Petroleum archives, Britannic House, Moor Lane, London.

117. Besides what is available in *Stock Exchange Year-Book,* information on United Dairies comes from Jefferys, *Retail Trading in Britain* (Cambridge, Eng., 1954), pp. 228–229, 232–234.

118. Information on J. Lyons and Aerated Bread is from Jefferys, *Retail Trading in Britain,* pp. 211, 213–214; J. Salmons, "The Development and Organization of J. Lyons and Company, Ltd.," in Edwards and Townsend, *Business Growth,* pp. 163–177; also John Hendry, "The Teashop Computer Manufacturer: J. Lyons, LEO, and the Potential and Limits of High-Tech Diversification," *Business History* 29:73–75 (Jan. 1987).

119. Information on Allied Bakeries and Cow and Gate is from *Stock Exchange Year-Book* and Channon, *The Strategy and Structure of British Enterprise,* pp. 166, 168.

120. One firm in this category on which almost no information is available, Alpin and Barrett of Yeovil, cheese producers, may have been formed by wholesalers.

121. John Vaizey, *The Brewing Industry, 1886–1951* (London, 1960), pp. 143–148; for Guinness, see Viscount Boyd of Merton, "Guinness—Ten Years On," in Edwards and Townsend, *Business Growth,* pp. 193–202; Channon, *The Strategy and Structure of British Enterprise,* pp. 96–97; also M. W. Cumming, "The History of Guinness" (Paper, Trinity College, Dublin, 1978), p. 82.

122. In 1877 James Bell, the Scottish shipper, became an agent for T. C. and Joseph Eastman, an American firm that began to ship meat in crude cooling devices. Bell merged with Eastman to form Eastman's, Ltd., in 1889. For the Bell and Eastman enterprises, see James T. Critchell and Joseph Raymond, *A History of the Frozen-Meat Trade: An Account of the Development and Present-Day Methods of Preparation, Transport, and Marketing of Frozen and Chilled Meats* (London, 1912), pp. 24–26, 209, 253; and Jefferys, *Retail Trading in Britain,* p. 187. For Eastman, see also Mary Yeager, *Competition and Regulation: The Development of Oligopoly*

in the Meat-Packing Industry (Greenwich, Conn., 1981), pp. 55–58. The Nelson experience is described in Critchell and Raymond, *History of the Frozen-Meat Trade,* pp. 63–64, 80–81, 143–144, 168–170, 221, 309, 348, 378–379. The cost of shipping a live steer from New York to London was £8/10s as opposed to 10s dressed.

123. For the River Plate Fresh Meat Company, Critchell and Raymond, *History of the Frozen-Meat Trade,* pp. 76–79, 140–141, 209; and also Jefferys, *Retail Trading in Britain,* p. 187; for W. and R. Fletcher, Critchell and Raymond, *History of the Frozen-Meat Trade,* pp. 265, 281, 365.

124. U.S. Federal Trade Commission, *Food Investigation: Report on the Meat-Packing Industry, 1919* (Washington, D.C., 1919), pt. I, pp. 164–177.

125. The joint operations of Armour and Swift were carried out through the short-lived National Packing Company. In 1901, 40,000 cwts. (hundredweights) of beef were imported into Britain from Argentina and 3,180,291 from the United States. By 1910, 2,710,747 came from Argentina and 469,444 from the United States. Critchell and Raymond, *History of the Frozen-Meat Trade,* p. 249. A useful summary of the American move into Argentina, Uruguay, and Brazil is Frederick M. Halsey, *Investments in Latin America and the British West Indies,* Special Agent Series No. 169, Department of Commerce, Bureau of Foreign and Domestic Commerce (Washington, D.C., 1918), pp. 94–96, 202, and 208.

126. U.S. Federal Trade Commission, *Food Investigation,* pt. I, pp. 167, 174.

127. A "quarter" is one-quarter of a hundredweight.

128. London *Times,* June 17, 1917. American firms remained profitable, the statement read, "even when prices of cattle in Argentina had greatly increased, while meat prices in Great Britain have suffered some decline, and at the same time when heavy losses are being incurred by the British and Argentine companies."

129. London *Times,* Mar. 30, 1914.

130. U.S. Federal Trade Commission, *Food Investigation,* pt. I, p. 174.

131. Critchell and Raymond, *History of the Frozen-Meat Trade,* pp. 170–172; U.S. Federal Trade Commission, *Food Investigation,* pt. I, pp. 172–173, 189–190; and Richard Perren, "William Vesty and Sir Edmund Hoyle Vesty," in Jeremy, *Dictionary of Business Biography,* V (1986), 618–621; also Jefferys, *Retail Trading in Britain,* pp. 190–193.

132. "Britain: The Vestey Empire Tells Some Secrets," *Business Week,* Aug. 26, 1972.

133. Lewis Johnman, "The Largest Manufacturing Companies of 1935," *Business History* 28:239 (April 1986), for employment figures; my Appendix B.2 for the market value of its shares.

134. Lever's American subsidiary, under the exceptional guidance of Francis Countway, built a large plant in Cambridge, Mass., in 1914 but used its own marketing organization to make sales in New England only. It relied until after World War I on Lamont, Corliss to distribute its products in the rest of the United States. It continued to do its own advertising and brand development as well as manufacturing for the national markets. Charles Wilson, *The History of Unilever: A Study in Economic Growth and Social Change* (New York, 1968), I, 205–206. Only after World War I did Lever become a significant factor in the national American market.

135. See Wilson, *The History of Unilever,* vol. I, ch. 11, and pp. 51–52 for its purchasing organization. For its transportation facilities, see W. J. Reader, *Hard Roads and Highways: S.P.D., Ltd., 1918–1968* (London, 1969), pp. 14, 17–18.

136. Wilson, *The History of Unilever,* vol. I, ch. 6; Musson, *Enterprise in Soap and Chemicals,* pp. 225–227. The quotation from Lever is given in Musson, pp. 225–226. (Neither Musson nor Wilson cites the Lever archives directly.)

137. Wilson, *The History of Unilever,* I, 246–247.

138. Musson, *Enterprise in Soap and Chemicals,* pp. 144–149. Musson points out that Crosfield registered a variety of brand names between 1886 and 1899 and that the new works were built in 1894 (pp. 80–85, 97–104). By World War I Crosfield had a hierarchy totaling 33 managers with three executives assisting the Crosfield partners at the top. Because of its involvement in chemicals production, it employed "a number of university graduates, some with doctorates, especially those engaged in research and development" (p. 147).

139. Wilson, *The History of Unilever,* vol. I, ch. 18. D. K. Fieldhouse, *Unilever Overseas: The Anatomy of a Multinational, 1895–1965* (London, 1978), pp. 31–32, gives a summary of these acquisitions.

140. The managerial growth is well summarized in Fieldhouse, *Unilever Overseas,* pp. 27–32. This information has been supplemented by material gleaned from the Unilever archives, in Unilever House, Blackfriars, London. Especially useful was the 1917 memorandum on the duties of the directors, in file LC6391.

141. The quotations are from Fieldhouse, *Unilever Overseas,* pp. 31, 34.

142. For a useful summary, ibid., pp. 32–36 (quotation from p. 32). The details are in Wilson, *The History of Unilever,* vol. I, ch. 19.

143. Fieldhouse, *Unilever Overseas,* p. 32.

144. Ibid., pp. 36–37; and Wilson, *The History of Unilever,* vol. I, ch. 20.

145. For purchasing, Musson, *Enterprise in Soap and Chemicals,* p. 290; for transportation, Reader, *Hard Roads and Highways,* p. 302.

146. Everly and Little, *Concentration in British Industry,* p. 261, for Lever's market share. For Palmolive, see Wilson, *The History of Unilever,* I, 302; for British Oil & Cake, Wilson, I, 278–280; for the margarine business, Wilson, vol. I, ch. 14; for passing the dividends, Wilson, I, 298.

147. Wilson, *The History of Unilever,* II, 345.

148. Ibid., I, 302.

149. Quotations are from Musson, *Enterprise in Soap and Chemicals,* p. 292, and Wilson, *The History of Unilever,* I, 303.

150. Wilson, *The History of Unilever,* vol. II, ch. 16, for the merger. The merger's formal name was Margarine Unie/Union. For the entry of the Dutch margarine makers into the British market by way of the grocery and drug chains, see Peter Mathias, *Retailing Revolution: A History of Multiple Retailing in the Food Trades Based upon the Allied Suppliers Group of Companies* (London, 1967), pp. 195–258.

151. Of the grocery chains in Britain with 400 or more stores, only the International Tea Company and the Star Tea Company were not controlled by the two Dutch margarine makers. Jefferys, *Retail Trading in Britain,* pp. 139–141.

152. Wilson, *The History of Unilever,* II, 301–302 (quotation), and 301–306 for negotiations and the merger.

153. Ibid., pp. 306–308 for legal arrangements. In order to avoid double taxation the consolidators set up two holding companies—one British and one Dutch—with identical boards, a solution already used at Margarine Union/Unie.

154. Mathias, *Retailing Revolution,* pp. 262, 265–275, 285–292. Allied Suppliers remained almost wholly a purchasing intermediary. Manufacturing accounted for only 10% of its income.

155. The story of the folding of Margarine Unie's operations into the Lever structure is summarized in Fieldhouse, *Unilever Overseas,* pp. 39–46 (quotation on 41). The subjects of ending committee management and of new personnel for the Continental Committee were discussed at the July 27, 1933, meeting of the Special Committee. In these years the Special Committee met at least three times a week and often daily.

156. Wilson, *The History of Unilever,* II, 292–296, for rationalization of the margarine industry; 342–343, 347–348, for rationalization of the Continental soap trade; and 343–347 for rationalization of the British companies. For the last see also Musson, *Enterprise in Soap and Chemicals,* pp. 320–328.

157. Musson, *Enterprise in Soap and Chemicals,* pp. 328–329, 349–350, 364.

158. Everly and Little, *Concentration in British Industry,* p. 261. The Continent counted "for the biggest part of the increase" of 100,000 tons for 1933–34, and for a total of close to 550,000 tons by the second half of the 1930s. Wilson, *The History of Unilever,* II, 349.

159. Fieldhouse, *Unilever Overseas.* This study does not deal specifically with Lever's activities in the United States or on the European Continent, but only examines the firm's activities in the rest of the world; it mentions Colgate-Palmolive-Peet and Procter & Gamble as Unilever's only significant competitors, and then only in a few areas.

160. Chandler, *Strategy and Structure,* ch. 4.

161. From 1901 to 1906 the pay-out ratio (dividends to net profits) for Brunner, Mond is estimated to have ranged from 74% to 92%; for Vickers, from 1903 to 1905, to have averaged 80%; for Armstrong Whitworth from 1902 to 1906, 91.7%; for J. & P. Coats from 1897 to 1906, 68%; for Bleachers' Association from 1901 to 1906, 80%; and for Bradford Dyes from 1900 to 1905, close to 90%. Eugene A. Miao, "The Unused Resources: The Role of the London Stock Exchange in Industrial Development, 1880–1910" (Research paper, Harvard Business School, Boston, Mass., 1986–87).

10. The Foundations of Managerial Capitalism in German Industry

1. The information on Stollwerck comes from Bruno Kuske, *100 Jahre Stollwerck Geschichte, 1839–1939* (Cologne, 1939).

2. Ibid., p. 136.

3. Ibid., p. 80 ("Der Vertrieb wurde der Schrittmacher für Fabrikation und deren Technik"); pp. 64–80 review marketing developments.

4. Ibid., p. 130.

5. For overseas expansion of the chocolate business, ibid., pp. 100–112. See also U.S. Office of Alien Property Custodian, *Bureau of Sales: Alien Property Custodian,* 3 vols. (Washington, D.C., 1920), an unpaged report of properties held in 1920.

6. Kuske, *100 Jahre Stollwerck Geschichte,* pp. 87–95, 104–107, reviews the development of the vending-machine business.

7. Charles Wilson, *The History of Unilever: A Study in Economic Growth and Social Change* (London, 1954), I, 101, 103, 108, for Lever Brothers; *Handbuch der deutschen Aktiengesellschaften* (Berlin, 1913), for Jasmatzi. Kuske mentions the alliance with Diamond Match.

8. *Moody's Manual, 1916,* p. 3946. The connection with Edison is mentioned in

Thomas R. Kabisch, *Deutsches Kapital in den USA: Von der Reichsgründung bis zur Sequestrierung (1917) und Freigabe* (Stuttgart, 1982), p. 253.

9. Kuske, *100 Jahre Stollwerck Geschichte,* p. 127.

10. Ibid., pp. 131–132, for the size, growth, and role of the central headquarters.

11. For financing growth before and after World War I, ibid., pp. 119–129.

12. Richard H. Schallenberg, *Bottled Energy: Electrical Engineering and the Evolution of Chemical Energy Storage* (Philadelphia, 1982), describes the evolution of the technologies and use of the electrical storage battery.

13. Ibid., pp. 210–211.

14. Ibid., pp. 92–95. See also Burkhard Nadolny and Wilhelm Treue, *Varta: Ein Unternehmen der Quandt-Gruppe, 1888–1963* (Munich, 1963), pp. 39–50; Albert Müller, *25 Jahre der Accumulatoren-Fabrik Aktiengesellschaft, 1888–1913* (n.p., 1913); Oskar Clemens, *50 Jahre Accumulatoren-Fabrik Aktiengesellschaft, 1888–1938* (n.p., 1938); Peter Czada, *Die Berliner Elektroindustrie in der Weimarer Zeit* (Berlin, 1969), pp. 257–262. All of these works provide information on the beginnings of AFA.

15. The only area of electrical technology in which the United States lagged was that of storage batteries. In 1892 the Edison Electric Illuminating Company of Boston and other electrical utility firms had placed orders with AFA. The following year Müller visited the United States to evaluate the American market. It was then that he met with Gibbs. Richard H. Schallenberg, "The Automatic Storage Battery: An American Lag in Electrical Engineering," *Technology and Culture* 22:725 (Oct. 1981).

16. Schallenberg, *Bottled Energy,* pp. 202–213. S. Wyman Rolf, *"Exide," the Development of an Engineering Idea: A Brief History of the Electric Storage Battery Company* (Princeton, 1951), pp. 8–17. *Moody's Manual, 1900,* p. 312–313, lists the company's board of directors. For the maintenance contract, see Schallenberg, *Bottled Energy,* p. 220.

17. Schallenberg, *Bottled Energy,* p. 212. The French company was the Société Anonyme pour le Travail des Metaux (TEM). Nadolny and Treue, *Varta,* p. 49. As the latter study points out, the high cost of sending a heavy lead product across the Atlantic, the high tariffs, and the building by ESB of a plant of optimal size all provided strong disincentives for AFA to attempt to compete in the United States.

18. Schallenberg, *Bottled Energy,* pp. 213–214. Also I. C. R. Byatt, *The British Electrical Industry* (Oxford, 1979), pp. 47–49, 142–143. National Carbon and Presto-O-Lite, which became part of Union Carbide & Carbon in 1917, only began to produce batteries (primarily for telephone systems and automobiles) after 1910. Schallenberg, *Bottled Energy,* p. 289; William Haynes, *American Chemical Industry,* vol. VI, *The Chemical Companies* (New York, 1949), pp. 429, 435.

19. Schallenberg, *Bottled Energy,* p. 221.

20. Clemens, *50 Jahre AFA,* p. 76.

21. Nadolny and Treue, *Varta,* pp. 51–52. Because of its economic power in production and distribution, AFA only participated in a cartel with smaller competitors from 1900 to 1902 (p. 50). See also Clemens, *50 Jahre AFA,* pp. 75–78.

22. The organization chart is accompanied by a description of each of the offices on it. Müller, *25 Jahre der AFA,* pp. 169–270.

23. They only say, for example, that in the 1920s the Vorstand included a manager of the former Russian subsidiary and a manager of a branch whose activities had been

consolidated into a larger works. Clemens, *50 Jahre AFA*; also Nadolny and Treue, *Varta*, p. 48.

24. Nadolny and Treue, *Varta*, pp. 48, 85–86; Clemens, *50 Jahre AFA*, pp. 247–250.
25. Müller, *25 Jahre der AFA*, organization chart and pp. 171–173.
26. On AFA's nine-member Supervisory Board were Emil Rathenau (AEG), Wilhelm von Siemens (Siemens & Halske), and five bankers, including Georg Siemens of the Deutsche Bank. *Saling's Börsen-Jahrbuch, 1895–1896*, p. 691.
27. B. R. Mitchell, *European Historical Statistics, 1750–1970* (New York, 1978), pp. 4–6 (the British figures are for 1871 and 1911). J. H. Clapham, *The Economic Development of France and Germany, 1815–1914*, 4th ed. (Cambridge, Eng., 1955), p. 278, for rural-urban percentages in Germany; also Robert Gellately, *The Politics of Economic Despair: Shopkeepers and German Politics, 1810–1914* (London, 1974), p. 14. See U.S. Bureau of the Census, *Historical Statistics of the United States: Colonial Times to 1970* (Washington, D.C., 1975), I, 8, for population, and p. 428 for area. The area is for the coterminous United States.
28. Mitchell, *European Historical Statistics*, pp. 12–14; U.S. Bureau of the Census, *Historical Statistics*, I, 11. In addition to its six largest cities, Britain had three more with populations of over 100,000. See Angus Maddison, *Phases of Capitalist Development* (Oxford, 1982), p. 8, for estimates of per-capita income.
29. Mitchell, *European Historical Statistics*, pp. 300, 302, 304, 307; Peter Mathias, *The First Industrial Nation: An Economic History of Britain, 1700–1914* (London, 1969), p. 468; Christoph Buchheim, "Deutschland auf dem Weltmarkt am Ende des 19. Jahrhunderts," *Vierteljahrschrift für Sozial-und Wirtschaftsgeschichte* 71:201, 211, 214 (1984). The export of textiles and consumer goods was important to German economic growth because it provided foreign exchange.
30. See Robert A. Brady, *The Rationalization Movement in German Industry: A Study in the Evolution of Economic Planning* (Berkeley, 1933), p. 250 for chemicals, and p. 170 for electrical equipment. Also Ludwig F. Haber, *The Chemical Industry, 1900–1930: International Growth and Technological Change* (Oxford, 1971), pp. 108–109; Czada, *Berliner Elektroindustrie*, p. 143.
31. Clapham, *The Economic Development of France and Germany*, p. 280.
32. Rainer Fremdling, "Railroads and German Economic Growth: A Leading Sector Analysis with a Comparison of the United States and Great Britain," *Journal of Economic History* 37:601 (Sept. 1977).
33. Mitchell, *European Historical Statistics*, pp. 315–317. Mileage in Germany doubled from 3,281 miles operating in 1846 to 6,605 in 1852 and to 10,593 in 1859. The German railway boom was stimulated by the French war indemnity of five billion francs. As Werner Sombart wrote, "You might say that by way of war indemnity France finished off our main railway network for us." Quoted in Clapham, *The Economic Development of France and Germany*, p. 346. I am indebted to Colleen Dunlavy for much of the information presented here, which she first explored in "A Comparative Study of Railroads: The United States, France, and Germany," (Seminar paper, Harvard Business School, July 1981), and more fully developed in "Politics and Industrialization: Early Railroad Development in the United States and Prussia" (Ph.D. diss., Massachusetts Institute of Technology, 1988).
34. W. Robinson et al., *Modern Railway Practice: A Treatise on the Modern Methods of the Construction and Working of German Railways. Approved by the Prussian Minister of Public Works, the Bavarian Minister of Communications, and the*

Railway Authorities of German States and [written] by Engineers and Managers of the German Administrative Boards and Professors of the Technical Colleges, English ed., rev. (London, New York, Berlin, 1914), pp. 18–24.

35. The Austrian roads retained their membership during the Prussian-Austrian War of 1866, indicating where the priorities of the engineers and railroad managers lay.

36. Robinson et al., *Modern Railway Practice,* pp. 23–24.

37. Hira M. Jagtiani, *The Role of the State in the Provision of Railways* (London, 1924), pp. 66–71, 84–86; Robinson et al., *Modern Railway Practice,* pp. 24–27; also Fritz R. Stern, *Gold and Iron: Bismarck, Bleichröder, and the Building of the German Empire* (New York, 1977), pp. 208–219. In 1879 the Prussian Minister of Railways became President of the Imperial Railway Office. Robinson et al., *Modern Railway Practice,* p. 24; also *Statistisches Jahrbuch für das Deutsche Reich* (Berlin, 1882), III, 115.

38. Robinson et al., *Modern Railway Practice,* pp. 27–29. These developments are summarized in B. H. Meyer, "The Administration of Prussian Railways," *Annals of the American Academy of Political and Social Sciences* 10:403–412 (1897).

39. Robinson et al., *Modern Railway Practice,* p. 29. Meyer writes in his "Administration of Prussian Railroads," pp. 410–411: "The treaty governs all shipments of goods from or through one of the states to another. It provides for uniform through-bills of lading, prescribes routes for international traffic, fixes liability in cases of delay and loss, prohibits special contracts, rebates, and reductions, except when publicly announced and available to all, and prescribes certain custom-house regulations." To oversee and enforce these codes a "central bureau" was established in Berne, Switzerland.

40. Detlev F. Vagts, "Railroads, Private Enterprise, and Public Policy: Germany and the United States, 1870–1920," in Norbert Horn and Jürgen Kocka, eds., *Law and the Formation of the Big Enterprises in the Nineteenth and Early Twentieth Centuries* (Göttingen, 1979), p. 613.

41. This is described in William J. Cunningham, "The Administration of the State Railways of Prussia-Hesse," *Official Proceedings of the New York Railroad Club* (New York, 1913), pp. 3127–3130.

42. Quoted in Clapham, *The Economic Development of France and Germany,* p. 349.

43. Richard Tilly, "Germany, 1815–1870," in Rondo E. Cameron, ed., *Banking in the Early Stages of Industrialization: A Study in Comparative Economic History* (New York, 1967), pp. 174–175. Also useful here is Richad Tilly, "Financing Industrial Enterprise in Great Britain and Germany in the Nineteenth Century: Testing Grounds for Marxist and Schumpeterian Theories?" in H.-J. Wagner and J. W. Drukker, eds., *The Economic Law of Motion of Modern Society: A Marx-Keynes-Schumpeter Centennial* (Cambridge, Eng., 1986), ch. 9, esp. pp. 127–130.

44. Jacob Riesser, *The German Great Banks and Their Concentration in Connection with the Economic Development of Germany* (Washington, D.C., 1911), p. 48. (The third edition of Riesser's classic study, published in 1909, was translated by the [U.S.] National Monetary Commission in 1911.)

45. Riesser, *German Great Banks,* ch. 2, esp. pp. 49–56.

46. Norbert Horn, "Aktienrechtliche Unternehmensorganisation in der Hochindustrialisierung, 1860–1920: Deutschland, England, Frankreich, und die USA im Vergleich," in Horn and Kocka, *Law and the Formation of the Big Enterprises,* pp. 138–139.

47. These differing relationships between banks and industrial enterprises may be seen by comparing the story told in Fritz Seidenzahl, *100 Jahre Deutsche Bank, 1870–1970* (Frankfurt am Main, 1970), with that in Harold van B. Cleveland and Thomas F. Huertas, *Citibank, 1812–1970* (Cambridge, Mass., 1985).

48. Quoted in Harold F. Williamson and Arnold R. Daum, *The American Petroleum Industry: The Age of Illumination, 1859–1899* (Evanston, Ill., 1959), p. 502.

49. Brady, *Rationalization Movement*, p. 283, and also references to these companies.

50. *German American Trade News* 13:4–6 (Nov. 1959).

51. Erwin Hasselman, *Consumers' Cooperation in Germany* (Hamburg, 1953), pp. 8–18; Brady, *Rationalization Movement*, pp. 284–286; [Cooperative Wholesale Society], *The People's Year Book, 1931*, pp. 138–139.

52. Hasselman, *Consumers' Cooperation*, p. 18.

53. Percy Redfern, *The New History of the C.W.S.* (London, 1938), pp. 533, 536.

54. Gellately, *Politics of Economic Despair*, p. 45.

55. Karl H. Lampert, *Strukturwandlungen des deutschen Einzelhandels* (Ph.D. diss., University of Nüremberg, 1956), table 19. The multiple-shop percentages included three categories: variety and small department stores, 5.0%; manufacturers' outlets, 2.8%; and others, 0.4%. The British figures are given in James B. Jefferys, *Retail Trading in Britain, 1850–1950: A Study of Trends in Retailing with Special Reference to the Development of Cooperative, Multiple Shop, and Department Store Methods of Trading* (Cambridge, Eng., 1954), p. 73. Eduard Gartmayer and Heinz-Dieter Meindorf, *Nicht für Gewinn allein: Die Geschichte des deutschen Einzelhandels* (Frankfurt am Main, 1970), concentrates on the post-World War II period but includes some useful background tables and materials, especially in ch. 1.

56. Morton Keller, "Regulation of the Large Enterprise: The United States Experience in Comparative Perspective," in Alfred D. Chandler, Jr., and Herman Daems, eds., *Managerial Hierarchies: Comparative Perspectives on the Rise of the Modern Industrial Enterprise* (Cambridge, Mass., 1980), p. 164; Ulrich Wengenroth, "Die Entwicklung der Kartellbewegung bis 1914," in Hans Pohl, ed., *Kartelle und Kartellgesetzgebung in Praxis und Rechtsprechung vom 19. Jahrhundert bis zur Gegenwart* (Stuttgart, 1985), pp. 15–27. Erich Maschke, "Outline of the History of German Cartels from 1873 to 1914," in F. Crouzet, W. H. Challnor, and N. M. Stern, eds., *Essays in European Economic History, 1798–1914* (New York, 1969), pp. 226–258.

57. Jürgen Kocka, "Entrepreneurs and Managers in German Industrialization," in Peter Mathias and M. M. Postan, eds., *The Cambridge Economic History of Europe*, vol. VII, *The Industrial Economies: Capital, Labour, and Enterprise* (Cambridge, Eng., 1978), pt. 1, p. 563.

58. Fritz Blaich, "Ausschliesslichkeitsbindungen als Wege zur industriellen Konzentration in der deutschen Wirtschaft bis 1914," in Horn and Kocka, *Law and the Formation of the Big Enterprises*, pp. 317–341; Gerald D. Feldman, *Iron and Steel in the German Inflation, 1916–1923* (Princeton, 1977), pp. 29–30; Brady, *Rationalization Movement*, pp. 132–134; L. F. Haber, *The Chemical Industry during the Nineteenth Century: A Study of the Economic Aspect of Applied Chemistry in Europe and North America* (Oxford, 1958), p. 125.

59. Horn, "Unternehmensorganisation," p. 183.

60. Haber, *The Chemical Industry, 1900–1930*, p. 44; see pp. 42–50 for a summary of the place of these engineering schools, universities, and research institutes in

chemistry and the chemical industry. The most detailed study of the relationships between higher education and industry is Robert R. Locke, *The End of the Practical Man: Entrepreneurship and Higher Education in Germany, France, and Great Britain, 1880–1940* (Greenwich, Conn., 1984), ch. 2, esp. pp. 37–42, 58–66. His data and findings are summarized in his "Relationship between Higher Educational and Managerial Cultures in Britain and West Germany: A Comparative Analysis of Higher Education from an Historical Perspective," in Pat Joynt and Malcolm Warner, eds., *Managing in Different Cultures* (Oslo, 1985), esp. pp. 184–186.

61. In addition, there were three schools devoted to mining engineering, in Berlin, Freiberg, and Clausthal.

62. Locke, "Higher Educational and Managerial Cultures," p. 185.

63. Georg Siemens, *History of the House of Siemens*, vol. I, *The Era of Free Enterprise* (Munich, 1957), p. 112; Haber, *The Chemical Industry, 1900–1930*, p. 49.

64. Two other such schools were set up: at Königsberg in 1915 and at Nuremberg in 1929.

65. Locke, "Higher Educational and Managerial Cultures," p. 186.

11. Creating Organizational Capabilities: The Lesser Industries

1. J. H. Clapham, *The Economic Development of France and Germany, 1815–1914*, 4th ed. (Cambridge, Eng., 1955), p. 217. Other information is from *Handbuch der deutschen Aktiengesellschaften*, various years. The minimal information that is available gives no evidence that the sugar companies invested in extensive sales networks.

2. Charles Wilson, *The History of Unilever: A Study in Economic Growth and Social Change* (London, 1954), II, 45–46, 73–75, 101–107, 134–135, 198–202. See also *75 Jahre Thörl's Vereinigte Harburger Oelfabriken AF* (Hamburg, 1958), pp. 7–10.

3. Gerhard Genest, *Sechzig Jahre Sarotti, 1868–1928* (Berlin, 1928), pp. 51–62; Jean Heer, *World Events, 1866–1966: The First Hundred Years of Nestlé* (Lausanne, 1966), p. 143.

4. Wilson, *The History of Unilever*, II, 216 (quotation); pp. 214–224 tell the Schicht story before 1914.

5. The Henkel story is told in detail in *Henkel & Cie GmbH, 100 Jahre Henkel: 1876–1976* (Düsseldorf, 1976), esp. pp. 30–77, 189–191. For Lever's response, see Wilson, *The History of Unilever*, I, 121, 189–191, 216; II, 214–222. For the Crosfield deal, A. E. Musson, *Enterprise in Soap and Chemicals: Joseph Crosfield & Sons, Limited, 1815–1965* (Manchester, 1965), pp. 199–201. The arrangements in France are not clear. After World War I Lever obtained control of the French rights to Persil as well as those in Great Britain and the British Empire. The British rights were acquired after Crosfield became part of Lever Brothers in 1919.

6. The information on Georg Jasmatzi comes from the *Handbuch der deutschen Aktiengesellschaften*, as does that on Knorr and "Nordsee" Deutsche Dampffischerei.

7. Werner Link, *Die amerikanische Stabilisierungspolitik in Deutschland, 1921–32* (Düsseldorf, 1970), p. 72. For Quaker Oats and Corn Products, see Chapter 5.

8. From the Statistische Reichsamt, in *Dortmunder Actien-Brauerei* (Dortmund, 1927), p. 4.

9. Kristof Glamann, "The Scientific Brewer: Founders and Successors during the Rise

of the Modern Brewing Industry," in D. C. Coleman and Peter Mathias, eds., *Enterprise and History: Essays in Honour of Charles Wilson* (Cambridge, Eng., 1984), pp. 187–188; for the new "method for pure cultivation of yeast" that was developed in the 1880s, see pp. 187, 193–194. Glamann emphasizes the importance of the American experience to German brewers (p. 191).

10. William Mayer, "Bavaria's 'Fifth Element'" (Seminar paper, Harvard University, 1981), pp. 10–13; and Glamann, "Scientific Brewer," pp. 192, 197.

11. Hans Ehlers, *1871–1921, Schultheiss-Patzenhofer: Ein Rückblick* (Berlin, 1921), pp. 13–14; and also see, for regional divisions, Erich Borkenhagen, *125 Jahre Schultheiss-Brauerei: Die Geschichte des Schultheiss-Bieres von 1842 bis 1967* (Berlin, 1967), pp. 33–100. See also *Handbuch der deutschen Aktiengesellschaften, 1939.*

12. The Nobel story up to the mid-1880s is summarized in John P. McKay, "Entrepreneurship and the Emergence of the Russian Petroleum Industry, 1813–1883," *Research in Economic History* 8:47–91 (1983). It is told in more detail in Robert W. Tolf, *The Russian Rockefellers: The Saga of the Nobel Family and the Russian Oil Industry* (Stanford, 1976), chs. 3–6.

13. Tolf, *Russian Rockefellers*, p. 67 (quotation); McKay, "Entrepreneurship," p. 75. As Tolf points out, this refinery "had the first multistill continuous system ever adopted for commercial use." McKay describes the coordinating organizations on pp. 70–71.

14. Tolf, *Russian Rockefellers*, chs. 7–8; John P. McKay, "Baku Oil and Transcaucasian Pipelines, 1883–1891: A Study in Tsarist Economic Policy," *Slavic Review* 43: 613, 617 (Winter 1984). At the beginning of 1886, 1,250 tank cars were operating; by September 1889 there were 4,195, with 2,290 controlled by the Rothschilds. As early as 1882 the Rothschilds had built a refinery in Fiume. Frederick C. Gerretson, *History of the Royal Dutch* (Leiden, 1953–1957), III, 70.

15. McKay, "Entrepreneurship," p. 86. By 1893 Nobel's share of the kerosene refined in Russia had dropped to 21% from more than 60% in 1883; also Tolf, *Russian Rockefellers*, ch. 9. McKay, "Baku Oil and Transcaucasian Pipelines," emphasizes that the inability of the Russian producers, refiners, and the Tsarist government to agree delayed the pipeline from the Caspian to the Black Sea from coming into full operation until after 1903, thus putting Russian oil refiners at a disadvantage in competing with Standard Oil.

16. Tolf, *Russian Rockefellers*, pp. 116–117.

17. Gerretson, *History of the Royal Dutch*, esp. vol. III; Tolf, *Russian Rockefellers*, chs. 10, 14; Ralph W. Hidy and Muriel E. Hidy, *Pioneering in Big Business, 1882–1911* (New York, 1955), pp. 526, 554–558, 563, 565; Fren Förster, *Geschichte der Deutschen BP* (Hamburg, 1979), ch. 3.

18. Gerretson, *History of the Royal Dutch*, III, 72–106; and Förster, *Geschichte der Deutschen BP*, ch. 5, for the activities of the Deutsche Bank and the formation of DPAG, DPVG, and EPU. Of EPU's authorized capital of M 37 million, the Deutsche Bank held 28.2%, Nobel 36.19%, and Rothschild 29.61%. Tolf, *Russian Rockefellers*, p. 185.

19. Gerretson, *History of the Royal Dutch*, III, 95.

20. Ibid., pp. 81–82, and also 66–69; Förster, *Geschichte der Deutschen BP*, ch. 4; Hidy and Hidy, *Pioneering in Big Business*, pp. 513–515.

21. Gerretson, *History of the Royal Dutch*, III, 119.

22. Hidy and Hidy, *Pioneering in Big Business*, pp. 503–521, 555–566.

23. Tolf, *Russian Rockefellers*, p. 185; Förster, *Geschichte der Deutschen BP*, p. 89; Hidy and Hidy, *Pioneering in Big Business*, pp. 564–566; George Gibb and Evelyn Knowlton, *The Resurgent Years, 1911–1927* (New York, 1956), pp. 204–205; Gerretson, *History of the Royal Dutch*, III, 101–102.

24. Hidy and Hidy, *Pioneering in Big Business*, pp. 564–565, 571; Gibb and Knowlton, *Resurgent Years*, pp. 210–211; Förster, *Geschichte der Deutschen BP*, pp. 89–91.

25. Gerretson, *History of the Royal Dutch*, III, 96; Förster, *Geschichte der Deutschen BP*, p. 88. Stauss remained as much a banker as an oil executive. Ronald Ferrier identifies him as the Deutsche Bank oil adviser in negotiations held in 1914: *History of the British Petroleum Company*, vol. I, *The Developing Years, 1901–1932* (Cambridge, Eng., 1982), p. 197.

26. Hidy and Hidy, *Pioneering in Big Business*, p. 569.

27. Gibb and Knowlton, *Resurgent Years*, pp. 214–220; Förster, *Geschichte der Deutschen BP*, ch. 6; Gerretson, *History of the Royal Dutch*, IV, 179–180, and 178 for EPU's continuing investment in transportation and seagoing tankers.

28. Tolf, *Russian Rockefellers*, pp. 189–190; Gerretson, *History of the Royal Dutch*, IV, 136–138.

29. Karl Weigand, *1871–1921: Gedenkbuch zum 50jährigen Bestehen der Continental-Caoutchouc-und Gutta-Percha-Compagnie* (Hannover, 1921), esp. pp. 47–49; H. Th. Schmidt, *Continental: Ein Jahrhundert Fortschritt und Leistung* (Hannover, 1971), chs. 2–4, esp. pp. 15–32.

30. Otto A. Friedrich, *The Phoenix Story on the 100th Anniversary of Phoenix Gummiwerke A.G., 1856–1956* (Hamburg-Harburg, 1956), esp. pp. 15, 18–20.

31. Weigand, *1871–1921*, pp. 76–79. Also Schmidt, *Continental*, pp. 30–32. Before 1914 sales companies were established in Britain (1905), Sweden (1906), Austria (1906), Denmark (1909), Hungary (1911), Italy (1912), and Norway (1913). Schmidt does not explicitly refer to Goodrich as a partner in the production of the Continental tire, but, when telling of postwar arrangements with Goodrich, he says that they were based on "the foundation of old friendly relationships" (p. 47).

32. D. C. Coleman, *Courtaulds: An Economic and Social History* (Oxford, 1969), II, 21–22, 50, 89–92. See also *Vereinigte Glanzstoff-Fabriken A.G. Elberfeld* (Elberfeld, [1924?]), pp. 46–88.

33. The Bemberg story is briefly outlined in Hugo Kaulen, *Die internationalen Beziehungen der deutschen Kunstseidenindustrie* (Cologne, 1929), pp. 27–29; it is also mentioned in Coleman, *Courtaulds*, II, 190. The one other pioneer rayon producer in Germany, Vereinigte Kunstseide-Fabriken AG (VKF), was formed in 1900 to use the oldest, that is, the nitrocellulose, Chardonnet process. Unable to exploit the economies of scale, it never became a major competitor. In 1911 when the VGF plant at Elberfeld and its Austrian works at St. Pölten produced annually 1,273,000 kg, the output of all other German factories was 180,000 kg. Coleman, *Courtaulds*, II, 94.

34. Coleman, *Courtaulds*, II, 89–102.

35. Ibid., p. 92.

36. W. J. Reader, *Imperial Chemical Industries: A History*, vol. I, *The Forerunners, 1876–1926* (Oxford, 1970), pp. 61, 95, 107; as Reader stresses, the company went into the production of lignite and potash as well as heavy chemicals. See also J. Bolle, *L'Invention, L'Homme, L'Enterprise Industrielle* (Brussels, 1963), p. 132.

37. Reader, *Imperial Chemical Industries*, I, 115–116.
38. Ibid., chs. 2, 5, 7.
39. Ibid., pp. 76, 81–87.
40. Ibid., pp. 131–136, 149–153.
41. T. C. Barker, *The Glassmakers: Pilkington, the Rise of an International Company, 1826–1976* (London, 1977), pp. 145, 162. Pilkington invested in the French plant in the early 1890s and had full control by 1907.
42. Barker, *The Glassmakers*, pp. 196–198, 267–268.
43. Charles W. Cheape, *Family Firm to Modern Multinational: Norton Company, a New England Enterprise* (Cambridge, Mass., 1985), pp. 193–198. Carborundum built its plant in Düsseldorf in 1907 and Norton built one in Cologne in 1909. The latter did so at the urging of Schuchardt and Schütte, which took a 30% stock interest and continued to handle sales.
44. Fritz Blaich, *Amerikanische Firmen in Deutschland, 1890–1918* (Wiesbaden, 1984), pp. 15–16; Fritz Wegeleben, *Die Rationalisierung im deutschen Werkzeugmaschinenbau: Dargestellt an der Entwicklung der Ludwig Loewe & Co., A.G., Berlin* (Berlin, 1924), pp. 26–41, and also *Ludwig Loewe & Co. A.G., Berlin, 1869–1929* (n.p., 1930), esp. pp. 67–85. The book *50 Jahre deutsche Waffen-und Munitionsfabriken Aktiengesellschaft* (Berlin, 1939), reviews in detail the history of that arms maker; see esp. pp. 53–59. See also Reader, *Imperial Chemical Industries*, I, 148–153.
45. Blaich, *Amerikanische Firmen*, pp. 77–78.
46. For an excellent review of the story of Singer and its competitors in Germany, ibid., pp. 24–40. Some firms stayed alive by developing machines for highly specialized needs. Pfaff, in order to assure itself of high-quality parts, convinced the Griest Manufacturing Company of New Haven to establish a branch plant in Germany in 1911. Singer was the only American company whose subsidiary was listed in *Handbuch der deutschen Aktiengesellschaften* and so appears in Group 35 in Appendixes C.1–C.4.
47. Blaich, *Amerikanische Firmen*, pp. 41–46; *Schubert & Salzer, Maschinenfabrik Aktiengesellschaft Ingolstadt* (Ingolstadt, 1958), esp. pp. 21–44.
48. Blaich, *Amerikanische Firmen*, pp. 54–58 for adding and calculating machines, and pp. 48–54 for typewriters. For Wanderer Werke, see Conrad Matschoss, *Vom Werden der Wanderer Werke* (Berlin, 1935), pp. 167–174. This is supplemented by Rudolph Schneider, "Die Entwicklung der Wanderer-Werke" (Ph.D. diss., University of Tübingen, 1922).
49. Blaich, *Amerikanische Firmen*, pp. 69–75; Wayne G. Broehl, *John Deere's Company: A History of Deere and Company and Its Times* (New York, 1984), pp. 629–632; M. Hofer, *Die Landmaschinenbau Heinrich Lanz AG, Mannheim* (Berlin, 1929), pp. 28–29, 78–83; also Klaus H. Gachring, *Ein Lebenswerk für die Landwirtschaft* (Frankfurt am Main, n.d.), pp. 3–4, 6.
50. Blaich, *Amerikanische Firmen*, p. 85 for Otis, pp. 60–66 for United Shoe, p. 7 for Westinghouse Air Brake, p. 88 for Chicago Pneumatic Tool Company, pp. 83–85 for International Steam Pump, and p. 6 for American Radiator; also Mira Wilkins, "American Business Abroad: American Radiator in Europe, 1895–1914," *Business History Review* 43: 326–346 (Autumn 1962), and Mira Wilkins, *The Emergence of Multinational Enterprise: American Business Abroad from the Colonial Era to 1914* (Cambridge, Mass., 1970), pp. 100, 212–213. For Knorr-Bremse's success in

getting the Association of German Railway Administrations to use a domestic supplier, see Franz Ludwig Neher, *Fünfzig Jahre Knorr-Bremse, 1905–1955* (Berlin, 1955), p. 48.

51. Gustav Goldbeck, *Kraft für die Welt: 1864–1964, Klöckner-Humboldt-Deutz AG* (Düsseldorf, 1964), pp. 227–233; Lynwood Bryant, "The Beginnings of the Internal Combustion Engine," in Melvin Kransberg and Carroll W. Pursell, Jr., eds., *Technology and Western Civilisation*, I (Oxford, 1967), 648–661.

52. Theodor Heuss, *Robert Bosch: Leben und Leistung* (Munich, 1975), pp. 73–88, 150, 288, 487–488; Bryant, "Internal Combustion Engine," p. 661; Peter Hertner, "German Multinational Enterprise before 1914: Some Case Studies," in Peter Hertner and Geoffrey Jones, eds., *Multinationals: Theory and History* (Aldershot, Eng., 1986), pp. 119–121. The facilities and activities of Bosch's American subsidiary are detailed in the unpaged report, U.S. Office of Alien Property Custodian, *Bureau of Sales: Alien Property Custodian*, 3 vols. (Washington, D.C., 1920). See also statement on Ernst Eisenmann & Co., in same report. In the United States, Bosch purchased before World War I the subsidiaries of the smaller German firm, Eisenmann & Booton Rubber Company.

53. *50 Jahre Kältetechnik 1879–1929: Geschichte der Gesellschaft für Linde's Eismaschinen AG Wiesbaden* (Wiesbaden, 1929), tells the Linde story in detail. It is summarized in E. W. von Rosenberg, *Das ist Linde* (Frankfurt am Main, 1964); Glamann, "Scientific Brewer," p. 187.

54. The details of this complex story of what was essentially a failure to develop the new machine in overseas markets through patents is told in *Geschichte für Linde's*, pp. 30–32.

55. Ibid., pp. 178–180. The Linde enterprise held 25% of the shares of British Oxygen; Ludwig F. Haber, *The Chemical Industry, 1900–1930* (Oxford, 1971), p. 144. Gunnar Nerhlim, *Growth through Welding: Perspectives on the History of a Norwegian Welding Firm, Norgas AS, 1908–1983* (Oslo, 1983), esp. pp. 28–72, describes the operation of the Scandinavian daughter companies.

56. Blaich, *Amerikanische Firmen*, pp. 37–38 for Opel, pp. 49–50 for Adlerwerke; Schubert & Salzer, *Maschinenfabrik Aktiengesellschaft Ingolstadt* (Ingolstadt, 1958), for that firm.

57. Blaich, *Amerikanische Firmen*, pp. 20–21; *Maschinen für die Welt: Schiess A.G., 1866–1966* (Düsseldorf, 1966), pp. 8–12.

58. Gerhard Egbers, "Innovation, Know-How, Rationalization, and Investment in the German Textile Industry during the Period 1871–1935," in Hans Pohl, ed., *Innovation, Know-How, Rationalization, and Investment in the German and Japanese Economies, 1868/1871–1930/1980* (Wiesbaden, 1982), p. 235. This article reviews the technological developments in the industry.

59. Ferdinand Bachmann, *Organisationsbestrebungen in der deutschen Tuch-und Wollwarenindustrie* (Karlsruhe, 1915), p. 20. The largest growth occurred in the enterprises employing 201–1000 workers in spinning and in those employing 51–200 workers in weaving (p. 21).

60. Jürgen Kocka, "Entrepreneurs and Managers in German Industrialization," in Peter Mathias and M. M. Postan, eds., *The Cambridge Economic History of Europe*, vol. VII, *The Industrial Economies: Capital, Labour, and Enterprise* (Cambridge, Eng., 1978), pt. 1, p. 564. The industry with the largest number of such agreements was iron and steel (with 62), followed by chemicals and textiles.

61. Bachmann, *Organisationsbestrebungen*, p. 22.
62. *Alien Property Custodian Report*, Senate Document No. 435, 65th Congress, 3rd Session (Washington, D.C., 1919), pp. 128–133; and report on Botany Worsted Mills in *Bureau of Sales*, the unpaged report of property held by the Custodian.
63. Bachmann, *Organisationsbestrebungen*, ch. 3, refers to interfirm agreements but says almost nothing about banks financing the industry.

12. Creating Organizational Capabilities: The Great Industries

1. The three light-machinery firms described in the previous chapter—Deutz, Bosch, and Linde's Eismaschinen—were subtracted from the total number of firms in these industries given in Table 8.
2. *Führer durch die Maschinenbau-Anstalt Humboldt: 60 Jahre technischer Entwicklung, 1856–1916* (n.p., 1919), pp. 17–33.
3. Ibid., pp. 20–25, 136–147. Division VII is described in the text but not indicated on the Lageplan.
4. Ibid., p. 25 and unpaged listing of sales offices including 48 in Germany, 55 in Europe, 6 in Africa, 17 in America, 14 in Asia, and 2 in Australia.
5. Ibid., p. 26.
6. *Deutscher Maschinenbau, 1837–1937: Im Spiegel des Werkes Borsig* (Berlin, 1937), pp. 34–48; *75 Jahre Borsigwerk* (Glogau, 1929), p. 13; and Kurt Pierson, *Borsig: Ein Name geht um die Welt* (Berlin, 1973), pp. 176, 185–189. Krupp built the other open-hearth works. (I am indebted to Wilfried Feldenkirchen for this information.)
7. Walther Däbritz and Erich Metzeltin, *Hundert Jahre Hanomag* (Düsseldorf, 1935), esp. pp. 96–121.
8. For BEMAG see Friedrich Kleinhaus, *100 Jahre Wirken und Werden* (Berlin, 1952), pp. 9–44; *75 Jahre Schwartzkopff* (Berlin, 1927), pp. 5–42; Fritz Blaich, *Amerikanische Firmen in Deutschland, 1890–1918: US-Direktinvestionen im deutschen Maschinenbau* (Wiesbaden, 1984), p. 78. The information on Gebrüder Korting AG is from the *Handbuch der deutschen Aktiengesellschaften*.
9. Otto Bitterauf, *Die Maschinenfabrik Augsberg-Nürnberg AG* (Nuremberg, 1924), fills in the story in detail to 1924. *Werden und Wirken der MAN* (n.p., 1931), pp. 4–13, summarizes the output and product lines of the three works. See also Fritz Büchner, *Hundert Jahre Geschichte der Maschinenfabrik Augsburg-Nürnberg* (Frankfurt am Main, 1940).
10. Gerald D. Feldman, *Iron and Steel in the German Inflation, 1916–1923* (Princeton, 1977), pp. 18–19, 35; and Bitterauf, *Die Maschinenfabrik Augsburg-Nürnberg AG*, pp. 206–207.
11. *DEMAG: Deutsche Maschinenfabrik AG* (Duisburg, [1965?]), pp. 12–14.
12. *Stettiner Chamottefabrik AG vormals Didier: 50 Jahre Aktiengesellschaft, 1872–1922* (Berlin, n.d.), pp. 21–34.
13. *100 Jahre BAMAG, Köln-Bayenthal* (Darmstadt, [1965?]), pp. 12–14; also *Zur Halbjahrhundertfeier der BAMAG, 1872–1922* (Berlin, 1922).
14. Conrad Matschoss, *Die Maschinenfabrik R. Wolf Magdeburg-Buckau, 1862–1912* (Magdeburg, 1912), pp. 120–149. *Die Geschichte unseres Hauses von 1838 bis 1938: Maschinenfabrik Buckau R. Wolf* (Magdeburg, [1938?]), pp. 203–232,

reviews the product line. Wolf appears to have been one of the few German companies to build complete factories (that is, turnkey projects) for industrialists in less-developed nations.

15. *100 Jahre Hartmann Textilmaschinenbau im Jahre 1937* (Berlin, 1937), pp. 41–48. A plan of the company's works in Chemnitz in 1900 (p. 43) shows the physical layout of five divisions—one for locomotives, a second for spinning machinery, a third for weaving machinery, a fourth for machine tools, and a fifth for steam engines, hydraulic motors, and machinery for grain and other mills.

16. For Linke-Hofmann, see Feldman *Iron and Steel,* pp. 274–276. This firm in eastern Germany did not participate in the locomotive cartels—either the early, weak cartel of 1890 or the more successful of 1909. There is little information on Henschel, a privately held locomotive firm, which had the largest share of the 1909 cartel, with 26.8% of the output. Hanomag and Schwartzkopff were second, each with 15.5%. Däbritz and Metzeltin, *Hundert Jahre Hanomag,* p. 97.

17. *Denkschrift anlässlich der Fertigstellung der 5000: Lokomotive mit einem Rückblick auf die Entwicklung der Orenstein & Koppel-Arthur Koppel AG* (Berlin, 1913), pp. 11–23, 45ff. The company had a large plant producing dump cars and other light railway cars that had its own distributing organization in the United States. At the time of World War I, it was taken over by the Press Steel Car Company for $1.3 million. *Alien Property Custodian Report,* Senate Document No. 435, 65th Congress, 3rd Session (Washington, D.C., 1919), pp. 120, 218–219; and an unpaged, three-volume report by the U.S. Office of Alien Property Custodian entitled *Bureau of Sales: Alien Property Custodian* (Washington, D.C., 1920).

18. Wilhelm Treue, "Innovation, Know-How, Rationalization, and Investments in the German Shipbuilding Industry, 1860–1930," in Hans Pohl, ed., *Innovation, Know-How, Rationalization, and Investment in the German and Japanese Economies, 1868/1871–1930/1980* (Wiesbaden, 1982), pp. 107–115. One large shipbuilder, Schichau (a private firm), appears to have been as diversified as the others.

19. Bitterauf, *Die Maschinenfabrik Augsburg-Nürnberg AG,* table 8 (in 1907 and 1908 MAN had 11,380 and 11,232 employees, respectively); Matschoss, *Die Maschinenfabrik R. Wolf,* p. 151 (in 1907 there were 2,200 workers and 200 Beamte); *100 Jahre Hartmann,* p. 48. British data are from Christine Shaw, "The Large Manufacturing Employers of 1907," *Business History* 25:51 (March 1983). (In Group 36 the three firms in Britain, employing over 5,000 were the subsidiaries of General Electric, Westinghouse, and Siemens.)

20. *Deutscher Maschinenbau,* pp. 34–36, 47; *Führer durch die Maschinenbau-Anstalt Humboldt,* introduction and p. 48.

21. These firms are mentioned in Georg Siemens, *History of the House of Siemens* (Freiburg, 1957), I, 133–134 (Mix & Genest); 291, 293–294 (Bergmann); I, 295, and II, 64 (Voigt & Haeffner); and I, 69, 316, 331–332 (Felten & Guilleaume). For information on Deutsche Grammophon, see Chapter 8 of this study. Information on Bergmann can also be found in its annual reports for 1912–1914; in *Das Band: Werkzeitschrift der Betriebsgemeinschaft Bergmann-Elektricitäts-Werke AG,* vol. 6, no. 25 (May 1941), pp. 4–11; and in Siemens, *History of the House of Siemens,* I, 293–294.

22. This story is told in Siemens, *History of the House of Siemens,* vol. I, and is summarized in Sigfrid von Weiher and Herbert Goetzeler, *The Siemens Company: Its Historical Role in the Progress of Electrical Engineering, 1847–1980* (Berlin,

1977), chs. 1–3. See also Peter Hertner, "German Multinational Enterprise before 1914: Some Case Studies," in Peter Hertner and Geoffrey Jones, eds., *Multinationals: Theory and History* (Aldershot, Eng., 1986), pp. 125–127. Jürgen Kocka, *Unternehmensverwaltung und Angestelltenschaft am Beispiel Siemens, 1847–1914* (Stuttgart, 1969), is the most careful study on Siemens. For the development of its organizational structure, see Jürgen Kocka, "Family and Bureaucracy in German Industrial Management, 1850–1914: Siemens in Comparative Perspective," *Business History Review* 45: 133–156 (Summer 1971). For the life of Werner von Siemens, see his book *Inventor and Entrepreneur: Recollections of Werner von Siemens* (London, 1966).

23. The role and functions of these agents are defined in detail in "General directions for representatives of the firm Siemens & Halske" (Allgemeine Vorschriften für die Herren Vertreter der Firma Siemens & Halske in Berlin für den Vertrieb von Maschinen, Apparaten, und Materialien für elektrische Beleuchtung), March 1886, Werner von Siemens Institut zur Geschichte des Hauses Siemens, Munich (Siemens Archives), SAA 68/Li 80.

24. For these agreements and their modifications see *50 Jahre Berliner Elektricitäts-Werke, 1884–1934* (Berlin, 1934), pp. 10, 16. See also *50 Jahre A.E.G.* (Berlin, 1956), pp. 46–115; and Thomas P. Hughes, *Networks of Power: Electrification in Western Society* (Baltimore, 1983), pp. 68–78; von Weiher and Goetzeler, *The Siemens Company*, pp. 41, 42; Siemens, *History of the House of Siemens*, I, 91–100; Hugh Neuburger, "The Industrial Politics of *Kreditbanken*, 1880–1914," *Business History Review* 51: 193–195 (Summer 1977).

25. Peter Hertner, "Financial Strategies and Adaptation to Foreign Markets: The German Electro-technical Industry and Its Multinational Activities, 1890s to 1939," in Alice Teichova, Maurice Lévy-Leboyer, and Helga Nussbaum, eds., *Multinational Enterprise in Historical Perspective* (Cambridge, Eng., 1986), p. 149.

26. Siemens, *History of the House of Siemens*, I, 304–305 (quotation from 305).

27. *50 Jahre A.E.G.*, pp. 116–149; Siemens, *History of the House of Siemens*, I, 153; Hertner, "Financial Strategies," p. 150.

28. Hertner, "Financial Strategies," p. 149; Siemens, *History of the House of Siemens*, I, 151; *50 Jahre A.E.G.*, p. 149.

29. Siemens, *History of the House of Siemens*, I, 151; Hertner, "Financial Strategies," pp. 149–150; Jacob Riesser, *The German Great Banks and Their Concentration in Connection with the Economic Development of Germany* (Washington, D.C., 1911), p. 713; and also, for Lahmeyer, *50 Jahre A.E.G.*, pp. 166, 177–180; and for Brown, Boveri, Siemens, *History of the House of Siemens*, I, 226–229, 247–249.

30. See Chapter 6.

31. Siemens, *History of the House of Siemens*, I, 206–207, 210–211.

32. L. F. Haber, *The Chemical Industry, 1900–1930: International Growth and Technological Change* (Oxford, 1971), pp. 78–79.

33. Siemens, *History of the House of Siemens*, I, 184–185, 290. Siemens reluctantly entered into this venture under strong pressure from the government.

34. Hertner, "Financial Strategies," pp. 151–152. For these negotiations with Schuckert see Siemens, *History of the House of Siemens*, I, 194–197; *50 Jahre A.E.G.*, pp. 149–169. There are also many letters in the Siemens Archives on the negotiations and completion of the agreement.

35. *50 Jahre A.E.G.*, pp. 167–169 (quotation on 169). Harm Schröter, "A Typical Factor of German International Market Strategy: Agreements between the U.S. and German Electrochemical Industries up to 1939," in Teichova, Lévy-Leboyer, and Nussbaum, *Multinational Enterprise*, pp. 161, 164.

36. In 1904 the two other Siemens representatives on the SSW Supervisory Board were Emil Budde, a veteran manager, and Carl Lueg, a lawyer.

37. Von Weiher and Goetzeler, *The Siemens Company*, pp. 59–60; Siemens, *History of the House of Siemens*, I, 196–275. These terms can be followed in correspondence in the Siemens files, particularly the memo to the bureau head clerks, Jan. 17, 1903; and the following circular letters: No. 20323, Feb. 19, 1903; No. 34821 II, March 20, 1903; No. 44539 II, April 20, 1903; No. 54607 I, June 11, 1903; No. 110857, Aug. 8, 1903; and the letter from Werner Siemens to Kommerzienrat Weinand und Siegen, Feb. 6, 1903. Siemens Archives, SAA 68/Li 180 and SAA 68/Li 278.

38. Von Weiher and Goetzeler, *The Siemens Company*, pp. 36, 57–58; Siemens, *History of the House of Siemens*, I, 167–172, 268–275, 297, 323–325. Also see table of organization for Siemens-Schuckert, 1908 ("Interne Organisation der Siemens-Schuckert Werke," Berlin, May 1908) Siemens Archives, SAA 68/Li 180.

39. Siemens, *History of the House of Siemens*, I, 269.

40. Ibid., p. 321.

41. Sources include a four-volume typescript, the history of ZW of SSW compiled in the 1960s, "ZW-Chronik," Siemens Archives, SAA 68/Li 83, esp. pp. 8–36; Siemens, *History of the House of Siemens*, I, 159, 320–321; and most important of all, "Organisation des Stammhauses und Verkehr der Geschäftsstellen mit dem Stammhause," with enclosed "Arbeitsplan der bilanzierenden Abteilungen," July 31, 1913, Siemens Archives, SAA 68/Li 278/1; and the detailed manual of organization for Siemens & Halske and Siemens-Schuckert Werke in "Siemens-Rhein-elbe-Schuckert-Union Auskunftsbuch, 1921," in the same file.

42. Siemens, *History of the House of Siemens*, II, 28. See *Handbuch der deutschen Aktiengesellschaften* for 1913 for overlapping boards; also Kocka, "Siemens," pp. 152–154. For the secretariat, Wilfried Feldenkirchen, "Big Business in Interwar Germany: Organizational Innovation at Vereinigte Stahlwerke, I.G. Farben, and Siemens," *Business History Review* 61: 443 (Autumn 1987).

43. *50 Jahre A.E.G.*, pp. 147–169 (quotation from p. 160). Tilmann Buddensieg et al., *Industriekultur: Peter Behrens and the AEG, 1907–1914*, trans. Iain B. Whyte (Cambridge, Mass., 1984), pp. 270–357, provides photographs of the massive amount of new construction after 1905, while the map on p. 336 indicates that AEG's industrial complex was comparable to but somewhat smaller than Siemensstadt.

After I had sent the manuscript of this book to press, Clemens Verenkotte of the University of Freiburg notified me that he had come across a major souce of information on AEG in the Owen D. Young Papers at the Owen D. Young Library, St. Lawrence University, Canton, N.Y. This included letters, memoranda, and other documents exchanged between managers of the General Electric Company of the United States and AEG, and reports of GE's managers on AEG's products, markets, organizations, finances, and on the relationship between the two companies and also between them and Siemens. The documents Mr. Verenkotte uncovered support the statements made here. He plans to write an article based

on these documents that will, for the first time, illuminate the story of AEG—
its organizational development, its weak top management, and its changing relationship with the other members of the global oligopoly.

Documents at the Young Library that are of particular value for AEG's organizational structure include Gerard Swope, "Memorandum of a Conversation with
Direktor [sic] Deutsch of A.E.G., June 23rd, 1910, in Berlin"; and Anson W.
Burchard to E. W. Rice, Jr., July 13, 1912, and to C. A. Coffin, August 1, 1912,
both relating to "A. E. G. Organization—Mr. Patterson's Report." These documents, which provide a detailed description of AEG's organization, indicate the
size of its managerial hierarchy, particularly its international marketing and distribution network, and the decentralized nature of its operations.

44. See Appendixes A.1–A.3 and C.1–C.3.

45. Peter Czada, *Die Berliner Elektroindustrie in der Weimarer Zeit* (Berlin, 1969),
    p. 118, quoted in Hertner, "Financial Strategies," p. 145; see also Hertner,
    p. 150.

46. Hughes, *Networks of Power,* p. 179.

47. Peter Hertner, "Financial Strategies," p. 152; Peter Hertner, "Case Studies on
    German Multinational Enterprises before the First World War," in Norbert Horn
    and Jürgen Kocka, eds., *Law and the Formation of the Big Enterprises in the
    Nineteenth and Early Twentieth Centuries* (Göttingen, 1979), pp. 409–413, 443;
    Siemens, *History of the House of Siemens,* I, 316; von Weiher and Goetzeler, *The
    Siemens Company,* p. 62. AEG also had "joint ventures with GE in Italy and with
    Brown, Boveri for producing turbines," *50 Jahre A.E.G.,* pp. 156 (quotation),
    159, 160, 169.

48. The role played by the Deutsche Bank and Georg von Siemens (who was ennobled
    in the late 1890s and died in 1901) in the early financing of both AEG and Siemens
    can be followed in *50 Jahre A.E.G.,* pp. 73–121; Siemens, *History of the House
    of Siemens,* I, 154–158; von Weiher and Goetzeler, *The Siemens Company,* p.
    44; Neuburger, "The Industrial Politics," pp. 193–207.

49. Siemens, *History of the House of Siemens,* I, 322 (quotation). For AEG's purchase
    of Lahmeyer, see *50 Jahre A.E.G.,* pp. 179–180; and on the bank's role in
    Siemens' obtaining control of Bergmann, see Wilfried Feldenkirchen, "Competi-
    tion and Cartelization" (Paper presented at the Business History Seminar, Har-
    vard Business School, March 1986), p. 24.

50. Neuburger, "The Industrial Politics," p. 200. Neuburger stresses the important
    role the Deutsche Bank played in mediating conflict between Siemens and AEG.

51. The history of these seven companies is outlined in John J. Beer, *The Emergence
    of the German Dye Industry* (Urbana, Ill., 1959), chs. 8 and 9 (the drop in dye
    prices is listed on p. 119); and it is summarized in L. F. Haber, *The Chemical
    Industry during the Nineteenth Century: A Study of the Economic Aspect of Applied
    Chemistry in Europe and North America* (Oxford, 1958), pp. 83–88, 128–136,
    169–180, and in Haber, *The Chemical Industry, 1900–1930,* pp. 120–134. A more
    detailed introduction is Ernst Bäumler, *A Century of Chemistry* (Düsseldorf,
    1968), which is a history of Hoechst; see esp. pp. 1–69.

52. Sachio Kaku, "The Development and Structure of the German Coal-Tar Dyestuff
    Firms," in Akio Okochi and Hoshimi Uchida, eds., *Development and Diffusion of
    Technology: Electrical and Chemical Industries* (Tokyo, 1980), p. 84, notes that
    of 2,750 patents granted to dyestuffs firms from 1877 to 1900 Bayer received

647, Hoechst 533, and BASF 367. See also W. J. Reader, *Imperial Chemical Industries: A History*, vol. I, *The Forerunners, 1870–1926* (London, 1970), pp. 262–267. Of the five dye companies in Britain in 1914 only two did not have a Continental connection. One of these concentrated on a single line, alizarin, and the other on the lowest-quality dyes.

53. Beer, *The German Dye Industry*, pp. 94–96; Haber, *The Chemical Industry during the Nineteenth Century*, pp. 174–175. The role of branch offices is indicated in W. R. Murling to Carl Duisberg, Feb. 3, 1896; Carl Duisberg to H. T. Boettinger and Carl Huelsenbusch, April 8, 1903, and May 14, 1903, in Werksarchiv der Bayer AG, Leverkusen (Bayer Archives). The investment in research at Bayer after 1878 is described in George Meyer-Thurow, "The Industrialization of Invention: A Case Study from the German Chemical Industry" *Isis* 93: 365–375 (Sept. 1982).

54. Haber, *The Chemical Industry during the Nineteenth Century*, pp. 135–136.

55. The quotation is from a printed copy of Duisberg's "Memorandum," p. 3, in the Bayer Archives. The works layout is described on pp. 3–6. See also Hans Joachim Flechtner, *Carl Duisberg: Vom Chemiker zum Wirtschaftsführer* (Düsseldorf, 1961), pp. 141–152. Haber, *The Chemical Industry during the Nineteenth Century*, p. 136, citing Hermann Pinnow, *Werksgeschichte* (Munich, 1938), sets the figure of total employment at Bayer at 10,000, including 7,900 at Leverkusen; the rest were presumably at Elberfeld, the original works. But the *Handbuch der deutschen Aktiengesellschaften* lists employment at 33,168 for the same period. This figure probably included the worldwide sales force, the finishing and packing plants abroad, and the larger plant in New York State.

56. Duisberg Memorandum, pp. 7–8, Bayer Archives.

57. These duties are described in Duisberg's 10-page memorandum, dated Elberfeld, June 1899, entitled "Die Direktion der Farbenfabriken vorm. Fried. Bayer & Co., Elberfeld, im Juni 1899." It is a copy of the memorandum sent to a lawyer, Rechtsanwalt Justizrat Krüll, on Feb. 18, 1908, for legal review. Bayer Archives.

58. *Handbuch für die Abteilungsvorstände der Farbenfabriken vorm. Fried. Bayer & Co.* (Leverkusen, 1912), in Bayer Archives. The foreword indicates the change in the top directorate.

59. Haber, *The Chemical Industry during the Nineteenth Century*, pp. 133–136; Beer, *The German Dye Industry*, pp. 97–102. For Hoechst see also Bäumler, *A Century of Chemistry*, pp. 14–42.

60. Beer, *The German Dye Industry*, p. 100.

61. Haber, *The Chemical Industry, 1900–1930*, pp. 145, 148, 158–159, 173; Hertner, "German Multinational Enterprise before 1914," pp. 123–135. For the Bayer plant in the United States, see U.S. Office of Alien Property Custodian, *Bureau of Sales*, unpaged report; and for Hoechst in Great Britain, Reader, *Imperial Chemical Industries*, I, 265–266. From 1890 to 1895 AGFA and Bayer together held two-thirds of the shares of Levenstein, Ltd., the largest British firm, but in 1897 they withdrew completely from that company. Haber, *The Chemical Industry, 1900–1930*, p. 148.

62. Haber, *The Chemical Industry during the Nineteenth Century*, pp. 175–176. The most significant cartel in the early 1880s, which controlled the price of alizarin dyes, lasted only three years, collapsing in 1885. Beer, *The German Dye Industry*, p. 199.

63. Beer, *The German Dye Industry*, pp. 124–125. Flechtner, *Carl Duisberg*, pp. 183–187. Duisberg's grand tour began with a visit to the major textile mills in the South. He then traveled to the nation's heartland, calling at St. Louis (Anheuser Busch), Milwaukee (Pabst and Allis-Chalmers), Cleveland (Grasselli Chemical and Frank Rockefeller), Pittsburgh (Westinghouse, Carnegie Steel, Jones & Laughlin, Pittsburgh Plate Glass, and American Locomotive), the Niagara Falls complex (Alcoa, Norton, Carborundum, International Paper, and others), the Boston area (Harvard University and various textile manufacturers), the New York area (Singer, Wheeler & Wilson, Corn Products, American Smelting & Refining), and Hartford (Pope Bicycle and Colt). Correspondence about the trip and the route taken is in the Bayer Archives.

64. These negotiations, including those involved in the Hoechst-Cassella combination, are reviewed in detail in Beer, *The German Dye Industry*, pp. 125–134, and summarized in Haber, *The Chemical Industry, 1900–1930*, pp. 124–126.

65. Haber, *The Chemical Industry, 1900–1930*, p. 126.

66. Duisberg's statement is from a piece written by him in 1910 that appears in an unpublished history of Bayer in the Bayer Archives.

67. Haber, *The Chemical Industry, 1900–1930*, pp. 121, 145.

68. Haber, *The Chemical Industry during the Nineteenth Century*, pp. 171–174; Haber, *The Chemical Industry, 1900–1930*, p. 123.

69. Haber, *The Chemical Industry, 1900–1930*, pp. 133–134. The development of this group of firms can be followed in more detail in Hans Holländer, *Geschichte der Schering Aktiengesellschaft* (Berlin, 1955), and in *150 Jahre Riedel de Häen: Die Geschichte eines deutschen Unternehmens* (Seelze-Hannover, 1964). According to the U.S. Office of Alien Property Custodian, *Bureau of Sales*, unpaged report, Riedel's advertising was "directed exclusively to the attention of the medical profession." See also O. Schlenk, *Chemische Fabrik von Heyden, 1874–1934* (Radebeul, Germany, 1934), pp. 17–52.

70. Duisberg in a letter to two other members of Bayer's Directorium, May 14, 1903, in the Bayer Archives, reported that the equipment in Parke, Davis's Detroit laboratory was the finest he had ever seen.

71. The production and distribution activities of Merck and von Heyden and the sales organization of Riedel within the United States are reviewed in detail in U.S. Office of Alien Property Custodian, *Bureau of Sales*, unpaged report. Holländer, *Geschichte der Schering*, pp. 36–37, lists foreign plants. Hertner, "German Multinational Enterprise before 1914," pp. 115–119, reviews Merck's multinational activities before 1914.

72. Haber, *The Chemical Industry, 1900–1930*, p. 134. Although the representative of the Darmstädter Bank joined the members of the Heyden family on the Heyden Supervisory Board, there is little evidence that banks were influential in the pharmaceutical industry.

73. *Rütgers: Zur Geschichte der Rütgerswerke* (n.p., 1975), pp. 5–18; Theodor Lingens, *Aufbau und Entwicklung der deutschen Teerderivate-Industrie* (Jena, 1926), pp. 49–74, and esp. p. 61 for the company's purchase of shares in C. Weyl in 1905; also Siemens, *History of the House of Siemens*, II, 76–78; William Haynes, *American Chemical Industry*, vol. VI, *The Chemical Companies* (New York, 1949), 437–438.

74. Haber, *The Chemical Industry during the Nineteenth Century*, p. 123; Haber, *The*

Chemical Industry, 1900–1930, p. 114; Hermann Pinnow, *Werden und Wesen der Deutschen Gold-und Silber-Scheideanstalt* (n.p., 1948), pp. 43–74. HIAG was long associated with DEGUSSA, although the connecting links are not made clear by either Haber or Pinnow.

75. Haber, *The Chemical Industry during the Nineteenth Century*, p. 125; Haber, *The Chemical Industry, 1900–1930*, pp. 78–80, 113–115. For more detail see G. Pistor, *Hundert Jahre Griesheim, 1856–1956* (n.p., 1958); *Messer Griesheim Heute: Bericht über das 75. Geschäftsjahr* (n.p., 1972); and Pinnow, *Werden and Wesen, DEGUSSA.*

76. Haber, *The Chemical Industry during the Nineteenth Century*, pp. 124, 151, 158; Haber, *The Chemical Industry, 1900–1930*, pp. 77–78, 113–114, 179; and Pinnow, *Werden und Wesen, DEGUSSA*, pp. 18–59. After Aluminium, Ltd., was liquidated in 1900, its assets were taken over by the Castner-Kellner Alkali Company.

77. See U.S. Office of Alien Property Custodian, *Bureau of Sales*; and *Moody's Manual, 1916*, pp. 379–380. One of R&H's subsidiaries was the General Bakelite Co., which became a part of Union Carbide in 1939.

78. Haber, *The Chemical Industry during the Nineteenth Century*, pp. 126–127; and Haber, *The Chemical Industry, 1900–1930*, pp. 113–114, 120.

79. Haber, *The Chemical Industry, 1900–1930*, pp. 117–120, 199–204, and also pp. 89 and 268; and F. Rüsberg, *Fünfzig Jahre Kali-Chemie Aktiengesellschaft* (n.p., 1948).

80. Haber, *The Chemical Industry, 1900–1930*, pp. 116–117, 201. During the war the German government supported the first of the two superphosphate companies; consequently, the third, the 1912 joint venture, had to shut down its plants.

81. For example, DEGUSSA came to manage the selling syndicate that distributed cyanamids.

82. *50 Jahre A.E.G.*, pp. 88–90; Siemens, *History of the House of Siemens*, I, 214; Haber, *The Chemical Industry during the Nineteenth Century*, p. 92.

83. Walther Däbritz, *Th. Goldschmidt A.G., Essen: Neun Jahrzehnte Geschichte einer deutschen chemischen Fabrik, 1847–1937* (Essen, 1937), pp. 3–14, 24–32, 54–63. Carl Duisberg, "The Latest Achievements and Problems of the Chemical Industry" (Paper delivered at Eighth International Congress of Applied Chemistry, College of the City of New York, New York, Sept. 9, 1912), printed in pamphlet form (New York, 1912), pp. 1–31; reprinted in *Smithsonian Institution, Annual Report, 1912* (Washington, D.C., 1913), pp. 231–256. Martha Moore Trescott, *The Rise of the American Electrochemicals Industry, 1800–1910: Studies in the American Technological Environment* (Westport, Conn., 1981), pp. 95–96.

84. Thomas R. Navin, *Copper Mining and Management* (Tucson, Ariz., 1978), pp. 273–274, 340–346, and also 65–69; Walther Däbritz, *Fünfzig Jahre Metallgesellschaft* (Frankfurt am Main, 1931), chs. 2–5; Haber, *The Chemical Industry during the Nineteenth Century*, p. 125. Information on Metallgesellschaft, including production figures, is in *Alien Property Custodian Report*, pp. 68–93, and also in the supplemental U.S. Office of Alien Property Custodian, *Bureau of Sales*, unpaged report. Only in zinc did Germany have enough ore to meet its requirements. Gertrud Milkereit, "Innovation, Know-How, Rationalization, and Investment in the German Mining and Metal-Processing Industries, including the Iron and Steelmaking Industries," in Pohl, *Innovation, Know-How, Rationalization, and Investment in the German and Japanese Economies*, pp. 161–163, reviews inno-

vation in the German nonferrous metals industries. Franz W. Franke, *Abriss der neuesten Wirtschaftsgeschichte des Kupfers* (Giessen, 1920), pp. 83, 94, lists 1903 output of copper refineries worldwide.

85. Däbritz, *Metallgesellschaft,* pp. 151–165.

86. Two other German trading companies played a major role in the international metals trade, Aron Hirsch & Sohn and Beer, Sondheimer & Co., but they remained traders and did only a small amount of processing. Aron Hirsch's American representative, L. Vogelstein & Co., helped to finance the refinery of the United States Smelting, Refining & Mining Company in Chrome, N.J., becoming the refiner's selling agent, but production and other activities of the larger company remained in American hands. *Alien Property Custodian Report,* p. 85. For the zinc and lead syndicates, ibid., pp. 65–68; and D. J. Rowe, *Lead Manufacturing in Britain: A History* (London, 1983), pp. 281, 308–309.

87. Navin, *Copper Mining and Management,* p. 273.

88. A most impressive study of the early German steel industry is Ulrich Wengenroth, *Unternehmensstrategien und technischer Fortschritt: Die deutsche und die britische Stahlindustrie, 1865–1895* (Göttingen, 1986); examples of parallel development are not only the timing of railroad demand for steel (pp. 44–59), but also the influence in Germany of the work of Alexander Lyman Holley, the builder of the major American Bessemer works (pp. 79–84), and the expansion of output resulting from the new technologies for new markets (ch. 5). Useful references in English are Wilfried Feldenkirchen, "The Banks and the Steel Industry in the Ruhr: Developments in Relations from 1873 to 1914," in Wolfram Engels and Hans Pohl, eds., *German Yearbook on Business History, 1981* (Berlin, 1982), pp. 28–34. Founding dates for leading German steel firms are given in Jürgen Kocka and Hannes Siegrist, "The Hundred Largest German Industrial Corporations, Late Nineteenth and Early Twentieth Centuries: Expansion, Diversification, and Integration in Comparative Perspective," in Horn and Kocka, *Big Enterprises,* pp. 100–102. See also Milkereit, "Innovation in German Mining and Metal-Processing Industries," pp. 156–159; David S. Landes, *The Unbound Prometheus: Technological Change and Industrial Development from 1872 to the Present* (Cambridge, Eng., 1969), pp. 254–269, and esp. 258–259 for the Thomas Gilchrist process; Feldman, *Iron and Steel,* pp. 13–16.

89. For example, two important steelmakers entered the industry at the turn of the century by investing in existing enterprises. One was Peter Klöckner, who obtained in 1903 a controlling interest in Lothringer Hütten- und Bergwerks-Verein, and later an interest in two machinery firms, Hanomag and Humboldt. The other was Hugo Stinnes, who put together the Deutsch-Luxemburg group.

90. Feldenkirchen, "Banks and Steel," pp. 28–34; Riesser, *The German Great Banks,* pp. 725–749.

91. Feldman, *Iron and Steel,* pp. 21 (quotation), 24–25; Feldenkirchen, "Banks and Steel," pp. 36–37; and Wilfried Feldenkirchen, "Middle Management: The Role and Function of Middle Management," in Keiichiro Nakagawa and Tsunehiko Yui, eds., *Organization and Management, 1900–1930* (Tokyo, 1980), esp. p. 123. By 1896 Krupp employed 187 middle managers; by 1914 the number was 522. GHH, Phoenix, Rheinstahl, and Hoesch had comparable numbers of middle managers. Reusch's activities are reviewed in detail in Erich Maschke, *Es entsteht ein Konzern: Paul Reusch und die GHH* (Tübingen, 1969).

92. Feldman, *Iron and Steel,* p. 21. Wilhelm Treue, *Die Feuer verlöschen nie: August*

Thyssen-Hütte 1890–1926 (Düsseldorf, 1966), p. 157; and Organization Manual for Gelsenkirchener Bergwerks-AG, Siemens Archives, SAA 54/Lc 563 (this manual was drawn up shortly after World War I when the enterprise was rebuilding its prewar network). H. A. Brassert & Company of Chicago, the steel-industry consultant that played an important role in the attempted rationalization of British steel companies (see Chapter 8) on p. 68 of its "Report to Dillon, Reed & Co. on the properties of Gelsenkirchener Bergwerks, Deutsch-Luxemburg, and Bochumer Verein," dated Dec. 15, 1925, noted that these firms, "the Big Three, as well as their competitors, had built up an extensive sales organization through sales agencies owned outright or controlled through stock ownership." This report is in the Baker Library, Harvard Business School.

93. Feldman, *Iron and Steel,* p. 18 (quotation); National Conference Board, *Rationalization of German Industry* (New York, 1931), pp. 89–91.

94. Feldman, *Iron and Steel,* p. 17 for the percentages of the Ruhr mills in the Steel Works Association in 1904, and pp. 34–35 for percentage of allocation of primary products in 1912–1913 by the association. For Carnegie and Federal's share of the market see Chapter 4.

95. Feldman, *Iron and Steel,* p. 30.

96. Ibid., p. 37 (quotation); pp. 30–38 cover the formation of the 1895 Coal Syndicate, the Pig Iron Syndicate, and the Steel Works Association. See also Treue, *August Thyssen-Hütte,* p. 140. For the larger setting, Erich Maschke, "Outline of the History of German Cartels from 1873 to 1914," in F. Crouzet, W. H. Challnor, and N. M. Stern, eds., *Essays in European Economic History, 1798–1914* (New York, 1969), pp. 226–258.

97. Feldman, *Iron and Steel,* p. 33 (quotation). Treue, *August Thyssen-Hütte,* p. 33. For the effectiveness of the association's cartel, Steven B. Webb, "Tariffs, Cartels, Technology, and Growth in the German Steel Industry, 1879–1914," *Journal of Economic History* 40: 332 (June 1980).

98. Feldman, *Iron and Steel,* p. 23; Feldenkirchen, "Banks and Steel," pp. 38–39; Riesser, *The German Great Banks,* pp. 706–708; Hermann Brinchmeyer, *Hugo Stinnes* (New York, 1921), pp. 40–45. Stinnes had also acquired a major coal mine in 1906.

99. Webb, "Tariffs, Cartels, Technology, and Growth in the German Steel Industry," pp. 318–319; Jürgen Kocka, "Rise of Modern Industrial Enterprise in Germany," in Alfred D. Chandler, Jr., and Herman Daems, eds., *Managerial Hierarchies* (Cambridge, Mass., 1980), pp. 87–88; Feldman, *Iron and Steel,* pp. 18, 32–33. By 1912 GBAG with its allocation of 4.4% had become the ninth largest producer of primary steel in Germany.

100. Feldenkirchen, "Banks and Steel," pp. 38–39 (quotation from p. 39); Feldman, *Iron and Steel,* pp. 19–20. Wilfried Feldenkirchen, "Competition and Cartelization," pp. 22–23. For Mannesmann and the Deutsche Bank, see Alice Teichova, "The Mannesmann Concern in East Central Europe in the Interwar Years," in Alice Teichova and P. L. Cottrell, eds., *International Business and Central Europe, 1918–1939* (New York, 1983), pp. 103–106; and Peter Hertner "German Multinational Enterprise before 1914," pp. 121–123.

101. Feldman, *Iron and Steel,* p. 21, where Feldman notes: "The general directors or prominent directors could and did play an increasingly important independent role in the development of general policy and, in their turn, became dependent on the industrial bureaucracy below them for day-to-day operations."

102. Webb, "Tariffs, Cartels, Technology, and Growth in the German Steel Industry," pp. 310, 312.

103. Haber, *The Chemical Industry during the Nineteenth Century*, p. 203 (quotation), and for an excellent review of the impact of both patents and tariffs on the chemical industry, pp. 198–204, 210–224.

104. Jürgen Kocka, "The Entrepreneur, the Family, and Family Capitalism: Some Examples from the Early Base of Industrialism in Germany," *German Yearbook on Business History, 1981* (Berlin, 1981), pp. 68–75, suggests the importance of family in business at the beginning of the Second Industrial Revolution; and for an awareness of the conflict between the claims of family and those of business efficiency, see pp. 75–82.

105. Fritz Blaich, *Kartell-und Monopolpolitik im kaiserlichen Deutschland* (Düsseldorf, 1973), p. 153, cited in Feldman, *Iron and Steel*, p. 38.

106. Richard Tilly, "Mergers, External Growth, and Finance in the Development of Large-Scale Enterprise in Germany, 1880–1913," *Journal of Economic History* 42: 633–639 (Sept. 1982). Tilly's sample of mergers also included ten transportation and utility firms. By another, more restrictive measure (external growth) merger and acquisition accounted for one-sixth of total growth.

13. War and Crises: The Lesser Industries

1. The impact of the war on different industries can be followed in Gerald D. Feldman, *Iron and Steel in the German Inflation* (Princeton, 1977), pp. 51–82 for iron and steel; in L. F. Haber, *The Chemical Industry, 1900–1930: International Growth and Technological Change* (Oxford, 1971), pp. 227–230 for chemicals; and in Georg Siemens, *History of the House of Siemens: The Era of the World Wars* (Munich, 1957), vol. I, ch. 20 for electrical equipment.

2. As Feldman points out, the government made use of cartels to control output and price, "One of the great transformations brought by the war was that the state was now directly and openly concerned with the preservation and operations of cartels and syndicates." Feldman, *Iron and Steel*, p. 65. See Charles S. Maier, *Recasting Bourgeois Europe: Stabilization in France, Germany, and Italy in the Decade after World War I* (Princeton, 1975), pp. 57–58 for the role of industrialists in mobilization.

3. Ibid., pp. 51–53; B. R. Mitchell, *European Historical Statistics, 1750–1970* (New York, 1975), pp. 187, 190, 217, 219, 224.

4. James W. Angell, *The Recovery of Germany* (New Haven, 1929), pp. 15, 58. Angell still provides a useful, brief contemporary account in English of the postwar crises and the recovery that followed. The best scholarly review and analysis is Maier, *Recasting Bourgeois Europe*, pt. 3. A good brief summary of the course of inflation and the literature about it is Steven B. Webb, "Four Ends of the Big Inflation in Germany" (Paper given at Economic History Workshop, Harvard University, November 1985). Stephen A. Schuker, *The End of French Predominance in Europe: The Financial Crises of 1924 and the Adoption of the Dawes Plan* (Chapel Hill, N.C., 1976), provides a detailed account of the events and the negotiations that brought stabilization; particularly useful are chs. 6 and 8.

5. Duisberg's memorandum, "Die Vereinigung der deutschen Farbenfabriken," is published with annotation in Wilhelm Treue, "Carl Duisbergs Denkschrift von 1915 zur Gründung der 'Kleinen IG,'" *Tradition* 8:193–227 (1963). Haber, *The Chemical*

Industry, 1900–1930, pp. 279–282, briefly describes the formation of the I.G. As Haber records in a footnote, three very small specialized companies also joined the I.G. at that time. See also J. J. Beer, *The Emergence of the German Dye Industry* (Urbana, Ill., 1959), pp. 137–140.

6. Feldman, *Iron and Steel,* pp. 71, 116–119 (quotation from 118).
7. Ibid., pp. 260–263; Angell, *Recovery of Germany,* p. 48. Angell estimates that, as of 1929, 20% to 25% of existing industrial equipment had been built or purchased during the inflation period.
8. This account follows Feldman, *Iron and Steel,* pp. 213–244.
9. The quotation from Jastrow, dated April 7, 1920, is from Feldman, *Iron and Steel,* p. 222; the quotation on the GHH/MAN negotiations is from pp. 233–234. Both were taken from internal documents.
10. For control of Bochumer and the Austrian steel mill, ibid., pp. 235, 271.
11. Ibid., pp. 272–273, 277–279.
12. Otto Bitterauf, *Die Maschinenfabrik Augsburg-Nürnberg AG (MAN)* (Nuremberg, 1924), p. 206. Feldman, *Iron and Steel,* pp. 229–230, 266–271, 384–385. The member companies of the GHH Konzern are listed in *Saling's Börsen-Jahrbuch für 1925–1926: Ein Handbuch für Bankiers und Kapitalisten* (Berlin and Leipzig, 1925), "Deutsche Konzerne," pp. 14–16. Arnold Tross, *Der Aufbau der Eisen-und eisenverarbeitenden Industrie-Konzerne Deutschlands: Ursachen, Formen und Wirkungen des Zusammenschlusses unter besonderer Berücksichtigung der Maschinen-Industrie* (Berlin, 1923), pp. 50–57, lists dates of acquisitions and product lines of firms coming into GHH before 1923. In 1923 the GHH Konzern was divided legally into two major enterprises, GHH Nuremberg and GHH Oberhausen.
13. *Liste der Gesellschaften die als Teil der Eisen- und Stahlindustrie angesehen werden und gemäss Allgemeiner Verfügung Nr. 7 bzw. Nr. 3 (Krupp) zum Gesetz Nr. 52 unter Kontrolle stehen, zusammengestellt von der Treuhandverwaltung im Auftrage der North German Iron and Steel Control* (n.p., n.d.).
14. Feldman, *Iron and Steel,* p. 269.
15. Ibid., pp. 245–251. For detailed listings of the members of the Krupp Konzern see the Konzern section of *Saling's Börsen-Jahrbuch, 1925–1926;* and Tross, *Eisen- und eisenverarbeitenden Industrie-Konzerne Deutschlands.* For Klöckner, see Gustav Goldbeck, *Kraft für die Welt: 1864–1964, Klöckner-Humboldt-Deutz AG* (Düsseldorf and Vienna, 1964), pp. 168–169. For acquisition of shipyards by these Konzern builders see listing in *Saling's Börsen-Jahrbuch, 1925–1926.*
16. For locomotive makers, Feldman, *Iron and Steel,* pp. 274–276, 283–284. Linke-Hofmann, which was actually the majority holder of the Hanomag shares, also worked closely with AEG to coordinate turbine and generator production.
17. Angell, *Recovery of Germany,* p. 24.
18. Quoted in Feldman, *Iron and Steel,* p. 256.
19. I am indebted to Wilfried Feldenkirchen for this observation. For Schultheiss-Patzenhofer see Hans Ehlers, *1871–1921, Schultheiss-Patzenhofer: Ein Rückblick* (Berlin, 1921), pp. 3, 16–19.
20. "Mit der Fusion von fünf Zuckerfabriken fing es an: 50 Jahre Südzucker," *Frankfurter Allgemeine Zeitung,* no. 102, May 6, 1976. For agreements between sugar-producing countries see Philippe Chalmin, *Tate and Lyle: Géant du sucre* (London, 1983), pp. 153–160.
21. Charles Wilson, *The History of Unilever: A Study in Economic Growth and Social Change* (New York, 1968), II, 199–202.

22. Gerard Genest, *Sechzig Jahre Sarotti, 1868–1928* (Berlin, 1928), pp. 51–86; Jean Heer, *World of Events, 1866–1966: The First Hundred Years of Nestlé* (Rivaz, Switzerland, 1966), p. 143.

23. Bruno Kuske, *100 Jahre Stollwerck Geschichte, 1839–1939* (Cologne, 1939), pp. 107–114, 110–134.

24. The information on these two companies is from the *Handbuch der deutschen Aktiengesellschaften, 1929.* I have been unable to locate precise data on the nature and extent of Corn Products' financial control.

25. Wilson, *The History of Unilever,* I, 288 (quotation), and II, 348; *100 Jahre Henkel, 1876–1976* (Düsseldorf, 1976), pp. 83–115, 191–195.

26. Wilson, *The History of Unilever,* II, 348 (quotations). In 1917 Ernst von Seiglin, one of the founders of Dr. Thompson's Seifenpulver, had gained full control of that company. *100 Jahre Henkel,* pp. 192–193.

27. Information on the cigarette producers is from the *Handbuch der deutschen Aktiengesellschaften, 1929.*

28. Robert A. Brady, *The Rationalization Movement in German Industry: A Study in the Evolution of Economic Planning* (Berkeley, 1933), pp. 268–269.

29. Information on these five companies is from *Saling's Börsen-Jahrbuch, 1929–1930,* pp. 17–19, 35–37, 70–72, 93–94; and in the same source for 1932–1933, p. 1811.

30. See Chapter 8. Fren Förster, *Geschichte der Deutschen BP, 1904–1979* (Hamburg, 1979), ch. 8 and pp. 140, 173, outlines this complex story. In 1940 Deutsche Erdöl absorbed Deutsche Petroleum.

31. George S. Gibb and Evelyn H. Knowlton, *The Resurgent Years, 1911–1927* (New York, 1956), p. 518.

32. Ronald Ferrier, *History of British Petroleum, 1928–1954,* vol. II, *Years of Growth and Crisis* (London, forthcoming), ch. 4, "Downstream Activities, 1928–1939."

33. Henrietta Larson, Evelyn H. Knowlton, and Charles S. Popple, *New Horizons, 1927–1950* (New York, 1971), table 9.

34. Ferrier, *History of British Petroleum,* II, ch. 4 (ms. draft, p. 121).

35. Useful for the development of crude oil and also synthetic gasoline in Germany is Raymond G. Stokes, "The Oil Industry in Nazi Germany," *Business History Review* 59: 254–277 (Summer 1985); also for crude oil see Dietrich Hoffmann, *Die Erdölgewinnung in Norddeutschland* (Hamburg, 1970), pp. 111, 130; and Ferrier, *History of British Petroleum,* vol. II, ch. 4 (in draft of ch. 4, pp. 120–121).

36. The information on Continental comes almost wholly from H. Th. Schmidt, *Continental: Ein Jahrhundert Fortschritt und Leistung* (Hannover, 1971), pp. 47–90; this study relies on and cites internal company records.

37. For the financing from Goodrich see Werner Link, *Die Amerikanische Stabilisierungspolitik in Deutschland, 1921–1932* (Düsseldorf, 1970), p. 72.

38. Schmidt, *Continental,* pp. 71–72. Schmidt stresses that the coming of the depression sharply reduced demand. For product development in synthetic rubber and fiber in the 1930s, ibid., pp. 53–85.

39. Donald C. Coleman, *Courtaulds: An Economic and Social History,* vol. II, *Rayon* (Oxford, 1969), pp. 190–191, 241, 278–284, 376–387. Paul H. Boeddinghaus, *Die Konzentration in der Kunstseidenindustrie* (Cologne, 1931), pp. 38, 45–65; p. 49 lists the members of the two boards.

40. Eva Flügge, *Kunstseidenindustrie: Der internationale Aufbau der Kunstseidenindustrie und seine Folgen* (Leipzig, 1936), pp. 64–66. Also see Chapters 5 and 8 of the present volume.

41. Haber, *The Chemical Industry, 1900–1930*, pp. 288, 290, 291.

42. The information on the dynamite companies comes largely from W. J. Reader, *Imperial Chemical Industries: A History*, vol. I, *The Forerunners, 1870–1926* (London, 1975), pp. 406–413.

43. Reader, *Imperial Chemical Industries*, II, 411; and Alfred D. Chandler, Jr., and Stephen Salsbury, *Pierre S. du Pont and the Making of the Modern Corporation* (New York, 1971), pp. 571, 703–704. The purchase of Köln-Rottweiler by I. G. Farben gave Du Pont a tiny share, less than 1%, of the Farben stock.

44. In Hermann Gross, *Further Facts and Figures Relating to the Deconcentration of the IG Farbenindustrie* (Kiel, 1950), list 7 (opposite p. 57) gives the I.G. holdings in the two dynamite companies. Rhenish-Westfälische, one of the smaller units of the prewar Dynamite Trust had been part of the Stinnes Konzern in the early 1920s.

45. See M. Hofer, *Die Landmaschinenbau Heinrich Lanz AG Mannheim* (Berlin, 1929), pp. 81–86 for foreign sales and service organization, pp. 78–81 for domestic sales force, and also pp. 28–29, 58–61.

46. Feldman, *Iron and Steel*, p. 245.

47. *Schubert und Salzer, Maschinenfabrik Aktiengesellschaft Ingolstadt* (Ingolstadt, 1958), pp. 32, 42–53 (quotation on 52).

48. Conrad Matschoss, *Vom Werden der Wanderer Werke* (Berlin, 1935), pp. 178–179.

49. For Deutz see Goldbeck, *Kraft für die Welt*, pp. 166–170. The pattern of recovery was much the same for Bergedorfer Eisenwerk, the German subsidiary of the Swedish makers of dairy machinery, Alfa-Laval.

50. Theodor Heuss, *Robert Bosch: Leben und Leistung* (Munich, 1975), pp. 283, 327–330, 498–499; also *Was ist Bosch?* (Stuttgart, 1950), pp. 28–29. For the joint venture and Bosch's technological superiority, see Harold Nockolds, *Lucas: The First Hundred Years*, vol. I, *The King of the Road* (London, 1976), pp. 252–258.

51. See *50 Jahre Kältetechnik, 1879–1929: Geschichte der Gesellschaft für Linde's Eismaschinen AG Wiesbaden* (Wiesbaden, 1929), pp. 32–33, 163–164 for refrigeration machinery, and pp. 121–123 for liquid oxygen.

52. Oscar Clemens, *50 Jahre Accumulatoren-Fabrik Aktiengesellschaft, 1888–1938* (Berlin, 1938), pp. 90–102, esp. pp. 94–96, 250–251. In order to become acquainted with the new technology used in the new products, Günther Quandt, who had obtained control of AFA during the inflation, made an extensive visit to the United States in 1925 (see p. 95).

53. Information on Knorr-Bremse is from *50 Jahre Knorr-Bremse*, pp. 60–61; that on Orenstein & Koppel is from the *Handbuch der deutschen Aktiengesellschaften*.

54. Jean-Pierre Bardou et al., *The Automobile Revolution: Impact of an Industry* (Chapel Hill, N.C., 1982), pp. 71–72, 74, 83. For early postwar plans concerning the auto industry, see Feldman, *Iron and Steel*, pp. 273–274; and Förster, *Deutsche BP*, p. 129.

55. From a report on the German automobile industry written for the General Motors Executive Committee, March 8, 1929, quoted in Alfred P. Sloan, Jr., *My Years with General Motors* (New York, 1964), p. 325.

56. Bardou et al., *The Automobile Revolution*, pp. 106–107, 144–145; and Mira Wilkins and Frank Ernest Hill, *American Business Abroad: Ford on Six Continents* (Detroit, 1964), pp. 74, 138–140; and also *75 Jahre Motorisierung des Verkehrs, 1886–1961: Jubiläumsbericht der Daimler-Benz AG* (n.p., 1961), pp. 136–137, 163–165.

57. One other automobile company listed among the top 200 in 1929 (Appendix C.2), which is not mentioned in the text, is Nationale Automobil-Gesellschaft (originally called Neue Automobil-Gesellschaft), the automobile-producing subsidiary of the electrical-equipment giant, AEG, which, like its competitor, Siemens, had begun before the war to make electric automobiles and had then turned to making large, gasoline-driven vehicles. Neither proved to be successful. Nationale Automobil-Gesellschaft is not listed among the top five producers in Bardou et al., *Automobile Revolution*, or in Wilkins and Hill, *American Business Abroad*. For BMW and DKW see Bardou et al., *Automobile Revolution*, p. 107; and *Weltrekorde-Sporterfolge: 50 Jahre BMW* (Munich, 1966).

58. The information on financing comes from *Saling's Börsen-Jahrbuch* for the years mentioned.

59. Sloan, *My Years with General Motors,* pp. 197, 322–327. Also "Memorandum . . . on Walter Carpenter's visit to England, Germany, and France in 1937," pp. 10–12, in Du Pont Archives, Hagley Museum and Library, Greenville, Del. For British production see Roy Church and Michael Mitter, "The Big Three: Competition, Management, and Marketing in the British Motor Industry, 1922–1939," in Barry Supple, ed., *Essays on British Business History* (Oxford, 1977), p. 164.

60. Wilkins and Hill, *American Business Abroad,* pp. 204, 207, 232–235, 278–283.

61. Ibid., p. 283. In 1938 Opel sold 114,200 passenger vehicles; DKW (Auto Union), 50,340; Daimler, 25,330; and Ford, 23,969.

62. Wilkins and Hill, *American Business Abroad,* p. 206.

63. Sloan, *My Years with General Motors,* pp. 256, 327.

14. Recovery in the Great Industries

1. For BAMAG's acquisition of Meguin, see *100 Jahre BAMAG Köln-Bayenthal* (Darmstadt, [1965?]), p. 17. Information on BAMAG is from *Handbuch der deutschen Aktiengesellschaften,* various years. One firm, Deutsche Waffen-und Munitionsfabriken, was forced by the Treaty of Versailles to develop a whole new set of product lines. It attempted to move into sewing machines, spinning machinery, packaging machinery, ball bearings, and tubing, but with little success. It only began to prosper again after 1933 when Germany began to rearm and it could return to its original product lines. *50 Jahre Deutsche Waffen-und Munitionsfabriken AG* (Berlin, 1939), esp. pp. 140–141.

2. *Deutscher Maschinenbau, 1837–1937: Im Spiegel des Werkes Borsig* (Berlin, 1937), esp. pp. 47–48.

3. *100 Jahre Hartmann Textil-Maschinenbau im Jahre 1937* (Berlin, 1937), pp. 54–56, 163–164. Less is known about another merger, "Miag"—Mühlenbau und Industrie AG—an American-financed merger in 1925 of five makers of grain and milling machinery.

4. Erich Maschke, *Es entsteht ein Konzern: Paul Reusch und die GHH* (Tübingen, 1969), pp. 196–197; *50 Jahre Kältetechnik, 1879–1929: Geschichte der Gesellschaft für Linde's Eismaschinen AG Wiesbaden* (Wiesbaden, 1929), pp. 32–36; *MAN: Bilder, Daten, Objekte zur Geschichte* (n.p., 1977), pp. 6–7, suggests the pioneering work done by MAN in diesel and printing machinery.

5. Gustav Goldbeck, *Kraft für die Welt: 1864–1964, Klöckner-Humboldt-Deutz AG* (Düsseldorf and Vienna), 1964), pp. 168–170, 187–189, 198–199, 210.

6. For Bergmann, see Chapter 12, including note 21; and the chart of the joint

holdings of AEG, Siemens Archives SAA 54/Li 258 (I am indebted to Professor Wilfried Feldenkirchen for this chart). For Voigt and Haeffner, *50 Jahre Voigt & Haeffner* (Frankfurt, 1941); for J. Pintsch, see Paul Lindenberg, *Julius Pintsch* (Berlin, 1924), and Georg Siemens, *History of the House of Siemens* (Munich, 1957), I, 291. For Polyphonwerke and Deutsche Grammophon, see Geoffrey Jones, "The Gramophone Company: An Anglo-American Multinational, 1898–1931," *Business History Review* 59:90–93 (Spring 1985). *65 Jahre Deutsche Grammophon Gesellschaft, 1898–1963* (n.p., n.d.), provides a detailed history of Deutsche Grammophon.

7. Robert A. Brady, *The Rationalization Movement in German Industry: A Study in the Evolution of Economic Planning* (Berkeley, 1933), p. 177.

8. Peter Hertner, "L'Industrie electrotechnique allemande entre les deux guerres: A la recherche d'une position internationale perdue," *Relations Internationales* 43:304 (Autumn 1985). Hermann Levy, *Industrial Germany: A Study of Monopoly Organization and the Control of the State* (Cambridge, Eng., 1935), p. 75, says that the Dresdner Bank estimated that Germany had 50% of the world's trade in these products in 1913, 25% in 1925, and 29% in 1928.

9. Peter Hertner, "Financial Strategies and Adaptation to Foreign Markets: The German Electro-technical Industry and Its Multinational Activities, 1890s to 1939," in Alice Teichova, Maurice Lévy-Leboyer, and Helga Nussbaum, eds., *Multinational Enterprise in Historical Perspective* (Cambridge, Eng., 1986), p. 153; also Siemens, *History of the House of Siemens,* II, 147–148.

10. Levy, *Industrial Germany,* p. 78; Robert Jones and Oliver Marriott, *Anatomy of a Merger: A History of G.E.C., A.E.I., and English Electric* (London, 1970), pp. 36–41.

11. Harm Schröter, "A Typical Factor of German International Market Strategy: Agreements between the U.S. and German Electrotechnical Industries up to 1939," in Teichova, Lévy-Leboyer, and Nussbaum, *Multinational Enterprise,* pp. 164–165. Also Wilfried Feldenkirchen, "Big Business in Interwar Germany: Organizational Innovation at Vereinigte Stahlwerke, IG Farben, and Siemens," *Business History Review* 61:445 (Autumn 1987).

12. Heidrun Homburg, "Die Neuordnung des Marktes nach der Inflation: Probleme und Widerstände am Beispiel der Zusammenschlussprojekte von AEG und Siemens 1924–1933, oder 'Wer hat den längeren Atem?'" in Gerald D. Feldman, ed., *Die Nachwirkungen der Inflation auf die deutsche Geschichte, 1924–1933* (Munich, 1985), pp. 117–156 (review of these negotiations) and pp. 153–154 (changing market share). Two letters, Felix Deutsch to Anson W. Burchard, Aug. 7, 1925, and Burchard to C. A. Coffin, O. D. Young, Gerard Swope, and C. H. Minor, Aug. 6, 1925, in Owen D. Young Papers (6–16), Owen D. Young Library, St. Lawrence University, Canton, N.Y., contain detailed information on AEG's preparation for the merger.

13. Gerald D. Feldman, *Iron and Steel and the German Inflation, 1916–1923* (Princeton, 1977), pp. 454–456 and ch. 13.

14. Sigfrid von Weiher and Herbert Goetzeler, *The Siemens Company: Its Historical Role in the Process of Electrical Engineering, 1847–1980* (Berlin, 1984), pp. 90–91; Feldenkirchen, "Big Business," p. 448; Brady, *Rationalization Movement,* pp. 175–176.

15. Feldenkirchen, "Big Business," p. 445; and Brady, *Rationalization Movement*, p. 177.

16. Harm Schröter, "Siemens and Central and Southeast Europe between the Two World Wars," in Alice Teichova and P. L. Cottrell, eds., *International Business and Central Europe, 1918–1939* (New York, 1983), pp. 173–196.

17. Hertner, "L'Industrie electrotechnique allemande," pp. 257–258.

18. C. F. v. Siemens to Linsley Fiske of Dillon, Read, Jan. 26, 1925; L. Fiske to M. Haller, March 10, 1925; M. Haller to L. Fiske, March 16–25, 1925 (references to "the Krupp and Thyssen loan and the financial relationship between General Electric and AEG"), from Siemens Archives, SAA 11/L5 946 (I am indebted to Clemens Verenkotte for the sources listed in this and the next two notes). Hertner, "Financial Strategies," pp. 154–155; Schröter, "Siemens and Central and Southeast Europe," pp. 182–184. Clemens Verenkotte, "Amerikanisches Investment und die Rationalisierung der deutschen Industrie, 1925–1933" (M.A. thesis, University of Freiburg, 1987), pp. 113–116, puts the total that Siemens received at $48 million. Siemens, *History of the House of Siemens*, II, 202–206; von Weiher and Goetzeler, *The Siemens Company*, p. 96. For American loans to both Siemens and AEG, Robert R. Kuczynski, *Bankers' Profits from German Loans* (Washington, 1932), pp. 155–156. Also for AEG, *Wall Street Journal*, Jan. 22 and April 18, 1925; and Verenkotte, "Amerikanisches Investment," p. 110. Finally, chapter 6 of Robert Sobel's forthcoming history of Dillon, Read provides valuable information on the role played by that investment house in raising funds for Siemens in the United States.

19. Von Weiher and Goetzeler, *The Siemens Company*, p. 96; Verenkotte, "Amerikanisches Investment," pp. 163–166, 170–171. The nominal capital of Osram was RM 1,740,000, and International General Electric paid an unusually high price of RM 600,000 for its 16.66% share. Early in 1929 Kuhn, Loeb began negotiating with Siemens to carry out a "Consolidation of various European Electrical Manufacturers." Otto H. Kahn to C. F. von Siemens, Jan. 26, 1929; memorandum of Aug. 20, 1929, on subjects to be discussed by Mr. Schiff and C. F. v. Siemens on "Organization of 'Siemens public utility financing corp.,' a Holding, Financing, and Operating Company organized in the United States." Siemens Archives, SAA 4/Lp 157.

20. G. Swope to C. F. von Siemens, Jan. 29, 1930, and C. F. v. Siemens to Swope, also Jan. 29, 1930, Siemens Archives. I am indebted to Clemens Verenkotte for this citation.

21. Particularly valuable is an 11-page letter from C. F. v. Siemens to G. Swope, June 18, 1932, Siemens Archives. For later agreements see Mira Wilkins, *The Maturing of Multinational Enterprise: American Business Abroad from 1914 to 1970* (Cambridge, Mass., 1974), pp. 67–68, 496; and Chapter 9 of the present study.

22. Feldenkirchen, "Big Business," p. 445. I am indebted to Professor Feldenkirchen for a chart from the Siemens Archives that indicates the joint holdings: SAA 54/Li 258. For ITT, AEG, and Felten & Guilleaume, the joint venture which ITT soon controlled, see Verenkotte, "Amerikanisches Investment," pp. 173–174.

23. "Organisation des Stammhauses und Verkehr der Geschäftsstellen mit dem Stammhause" with enclosed "Arbeitsplan der bilanzierenden Abteilungen," Siemens Archives, SAA 68/Li 278/1. An earlier, detailed organization chart, dated Oct. 1922, of both S&H and SSW, from SAA Siemens-Rheinelbe-Schuckert-Union

Auskunftsbuch 1921 (pp. 157–184 for S&H and pp. 185–271 for SSW) provides an excellent picture of the company's organizational structure shortly after World War I. As it is similar to Figures 13 and 14, this chart has not been reproduced here. See also von Weiher and Goetzeler, *The Siemens Company*, p. 88.

24. Besides the 1927 organization chart for SSW (Figure 14), there is a useful chart dated August 1926 in ZW Chronik, pt. IV, typescript, Siemens Archives, SAA 68/Li 83 and 1927 Elmo 7152.

25. One line, electrical cooking and heating equipment, was obtained in 1920 with the purchase of a small Dresden company. Because of the unsettled economic conditions, instead of moving its manufacturing facilities to Siemensstadt as had been planned, Siemens enlarged the Dresden plant. Siemens, *History of the House of Siemens*, II, 66–67.

26. See the chart on joint holdings of AEG and Siemens in Siemens Archives, SAA 54/Li 258; also Schwennicke, "Organisation des Hauses Siemens" (Kaufmännisches Ausbildungswesen der Siemensfirmen), October 1940, pp. 51–53, Siemens Archives, SAA 33/Lp 866; von Weiher and Goetzeler, *The Siemens Company*, pp. 91–93; Brady, *Rationalization Movement*, p. 175; Siemens, *History of the House of Siemens*, II, 78.

27. Both quotations are from Brady, *Rationalization Movement*, p. 178.

28. Schröter, "Siemens and Central and Southeast Europe," pp. 176, 182. For the two internal I.G.'s, see Feldenkirchen, "Big Business," pp. 445, 447; also my Figure 13.

29. See Feldenkirchen, "Big Business," p. 447, for the subsidiary to handle military orders; and von Weiher and Goetzeler, *The Siemens Company*, p. 95, for the reshaping of the joint ventures.

30. The force at Western Electric numbered 64,253. When added to that of GE and Westinghouse the work forces of the major producers in these industries in the two countries were about the same: 179,600 for the American (1930) and 186,000 for the German (1929).

31. Brady, *Rationalization Movement*, pp. 103–104. Accurate comparisons of total assets are almost impossible to calculate because of the different accounting systems used (for example, those employed for the determination of depreciation) and because assets of subsidiaries may or may not have been included.

32. Ibid., p. 127. Brady notes that the capacity for European crude steel increased by 8.3 million tons between 1913 and 1929 and that 5 million tons of this were exported from the country of origin.

33. The best reviews in English of the formation of VSt are Feldman, *Iron and Steel*, pp. 454–461; Feldenkirchen, "Big Business," pp. 420–423; Brady, *Rationalization Movement*, pp. 107–108; and Hans Pohl, "On the History of Organization and Management in Large German Enterprises since the Nineteenth Century," *German Yearbook on Business History, 1982* (Berlin, 1982), pp. 113–115.

34. Horst Mönnich, *Aufbruch ins Revier: Aufbruch nach Europa—Hoesch, 1871–1971* (Munich, 1971), pp. 65–67; Feldman, *Iron and Steel*, pp. 460–461; Feldenkirchen, "Big Business," p. 421.

35. Jefferson Caffery, Counselor of the American Embassy, Berlin, to Secretary of State Frank B. Kellogg, Oct. 5, 1925, U.S. National Archives, Washington, D.C., RG59, 862.51/2059. I am indebted to Clemens Verenkotte for this citation. Verenkotte's review of the correspondence in the State Department Archives further substantiates the story told here of the formation of VSt.

36. Feldman, *Iron and Steel,* p. 457.
37. For the new structure, Feldenkirchen, "Big Business," pp. 424–425; Pohl, "Organization and Management," pp. 114–115.
38. Quoted in Brady, *Rationalization Movement,* p. 119.
39. Ibid., pp. 109–112. Feldenkirchen, "Big Business," pp. 424–425. For the Dillon, Read underwriting see Kuczynski, *Bankers' Profits,* pp. 150–155; and Verenkotte, "Amerikanisches Investment," p. 104; and most important of all, Robert Sobel's forthcoming history of Dillon, Read, ch. 6.
40. The first quotation is from Brady, *Rationalization Movement,* pp. 110–111, and the second from p. 111. Feldenkirchen, "Big Business," p. 425.
41. For the 1933 reorganization see Feldenkirchen, "Big Business," pp. 426–428; and Wilhelm Treue and Helmut Uebbing, *Die Feuer verlöschen nie: August-Thyssen-Hütte,* vol. II, *1926–1966* (Düsseldorf, 1969), pp. 59–72.
42. Alfred D. Chandler, Jr., *Strategy and Structure: Chapters in the History of the Industrial Enterprise* (Cambridge, Mass., 1962), p. 334.
43. This information is given in *Moody's Manual* and the *Handbuch der deutschen Aktiengesellschaften* beginning in 1927.
44. The best brief survey of the enterprises controlled by these Konzerne is in *Saling's Börsen-Jahrbuch, 1925–1926.* For Krupp and GHH financing, see Kuczynski, *Bankers' Profits,* p. 150; and Verenkotte, "Amerikanisches Investment," pp. 55–57, 59, 106–109.
45. Alice Teichova, "The Mannesmann Concern in East Central Europe in the Interwar Period," in Teichova and Cottrell, *International Business and Central Europe,* ch. 5, esp. pp. 106–126. After Mannesmann regained its holdings in the Saar, following the 1935 plebiscite, and integrated them into its operating structure, it dropped out of the cartel. In 1937, under pressure from Stewarts & Lloyds, it rejoined.
46. *Liste der Gesellschaften die als Teil der Eisen- und Stahlindustrie angesehen werden und gemäss Allgemeiner Verfügung Nr. 7 bzw. Nr. 3 (Krupp) zum Gesetz Nr. 52 unter Kontrolle stehen: Zusammengestellt von der Treuhandverwaltung im Auftrage der North German Iron and Steel Control, Abt. Vermögenswerte/Beteiligungen* (n.p., n.d.).
47. Brady, *Rationalization Movement,* p. 133.
48. The Germans remained the strongest participants in the so-called first international Steel Cartel formed on Sept. 30, 1926, which included only Germany, France, Belgium, Luxemburg, and the Saar. The Germans were quickly able to increase their assigned share, which was originally set at 40.45%, with France at 31.89% and Belgium at 12.57%. By 1930 the cartel was in complete disarray and in 1931 it collapsed. A second international steel cartel began in June 1937, which was later enlarged to include Britain, Czechoslovakia, Poland, and the Steel Exporters Association (the last was an American Webb-Pomerene Company). In this cartel the Germans may have had the power to provide the discipline necessary to stabilize prices. But the Nazi mobilization and the response of other European nations to it were far more effective than the cartel in raising prices. The most detailed review of the international steel cartels is George W. Stocking and Myron W. Watkins, *Cartels in Action: Case Studies in International Business Diplomacy* (New York, 1946), ch. 5.
49. These moves can be followed in Günther Ogger, *Friedrich Flick der Grosse* (Bern, 1971), esp. pp. 85–95.

50. Maschke, *Es entsteht ein Konzern,* pp. 219–220.
51. Walther Däbritz, *Fünfzig Jahre Metallgesellschaft, 1881–1931* (Frankfurt am Main, 1931), pp. 224–226.
52. Ibid., p. 261. Th. Goldschmidt AG lost its properties in Britain, Australia, France, and the United States during the war. In the 1920s it regained world markets, expanded its product lines into alloys, electrochemicals, and other chemicals, and reshaped its management along functional lines. Walther Däbritz, *Th. Goldschmidt A.G., Essen: Neun Jahrzehntegeschichte einer Deutschen chemischen Fabrik, 1847–1937* (Essen, 1937), pp. 75ff.
53. Hans Radandt, *Kriegsverbrecher-Konzern Mansfeld* (East Berlin, 1958), pp. 25–66, traces this complex interrelationship. In the 1930s when Mansfeld had financial problems, AEG and Metallgesellschaft pulled out and Mansfeld had to be supported by a large government subsidy.
54. Däbritz, *Metallgesellschaft,* pp. 233–235. Thomas R. Navin, *Copper Mining and Management* (Tucson, Ariz., 1978), pp. 121–122, 341–342.
55. Däbritz, *Metallgesellschaft,* pp. 234–235; Navin, *Copper Mining and Management,* p. 283.
56. Däbritz, *Metallgesellschaft,* pp. 253–255.
57. Ibid., pp. 258–259.
58. L. F. Haber, *The Chemical Industry, 1900–1930: International Growth and Technological Change* (Oxford, 1971), pp. 248–249.
59. Brady, *Rationalization Movement,* p. 250.
60. Haber, *The Chemical Industry, 1900–1930,* pp. 283–284, is the best brief review in English of the formation of I.G. Farben. A longer account is Wolfram Fischer, "Dezentralisation oder Zentralisation: Kollegiale oder autoritäre Führung? Die Auseinandersetzung um die Leitungsstruktur bei der Entstehung des IG Farben-Konzerns," in Norbert Horn and Jürgen Kocka, eds., *Law and the Formation of the Big Enterprises in the Nineteenth and Early Twentieth Centuries* (Göttingen, 1979), pp. 480–484.
61. Haeuser (of Hoechst) to senior members of the General Council, Dec. 13, 1924, in Werksarchiv der Bayer AG, Leverkusen (Bayer Archives).
62. Final version of memorandum presented by Carl Duisberg to the General Council, Nov. 8, 1924, Bayer Archives.
63. Quotations are from the memorandum by Duisberg cited in note 62.
64. Carl Bosch outlined his views in a short memorandum to senior members of the General Council, Dec. 11, 1924, Bayer Archives. The quotations are from this memorandum.
65. Memorandum of Carl Bosch, Feb. 24, 1925, Bayer Archives; also Fischer, "Dezentralisation oder Zentralisation," p. 484.
66. The text of the merger agreement, Oct. 2, 1925, is in the Bayer Archives. The quotation is from that agreement.
67. Ibid. The merger agreement also called for the Governing Board to appoint "four gentlemen [*Herren*], two from the Operating Communities and two from the Sales Communities, to assist the [Working] Committee in secret and personnel affairs."
68. The list of the existing I.G. committees appears in *Tabellarische Übersichten über die Organisation der Farbenfabriken vorm. Fried. Bayer & Co., 1924,* pp. 20–23, Bayer Archives. The memorandum "Organisation der Zentralbuchhaltung Frank-

furt," Dec. 18, 1925, Bayer Archives, concerns the opening of the Frankfurt office. See also Feldenkirchen, "Big Business," pp. 433–437.

69. Haber, *The Chemical Industry, 1900–1930,* pp. 285–287.
70. An excellent source on the organization of the I.G. Farben research establishment is the report of E. K. Bolton, Director of the Chemical Department (Du Pont's Central Research Department) to Jasper Crane, Vice-President, June 11, 1936, about a four-day visit to the major research laboratories at I.G. Farben, in Du Pont Company files at Hagley Museum and Library, Greenville, Del. The quotation is from p. 24. Earlier in the memorandum (p. 7) Bolton noted: "There is no standardization of practice in the operations of these different laboratories as it is felt very desirable to maintain as far as possible the old traditions and independence of functioning of each laboratory. Many of these laboratories have had administrative practices in operation for many years and no attempt has been made to standardize a particular procedure."
71. Ibid., p. 15.
72. For reorganization of sales, see Fritz ter Meer, *Die I.G. Farbenindustrie Aktiengesellschaft: Ihre Entstehung, Entwicklung, und Bedeutung* (Düsseldorf, 1953), pp. 45ff. And from the Bayer Archives: report of P. Haefliger, Aug. 31, 1931, esp. pp. 5–13; P. Haefliger to Carl Duisberg, Nov. 9, 1931; and Sales Department Dye and Dyestuffs and Products, "Rules of the Dye Committee 1929." Important also are the entries for I.G. Farbenindustrie in the *Handbuch der deutschen Aktiengesellschaften,* which outlines the changes in the organization of the several Sales Communities and lists I.G. Farben's holdings in Deutsche Gasolin. For the holdings of Standard Oil in that enterprise, see Henrietta M. Larsen, Evelyn H. Knowlton, and Charles S. Popple, *New Horizons, 1927–1950* (New York, 1971), p. 334; and for those of Shell, W. J. Reader, *Imperial Chemical Industries: A History,* vol. II, *The First Quarter Century, 1926–1952* (London, 1974), p. 170.
73. For General Dyestuffs and GAF see William Haynes, *American Chemical Industry,* vol. VI, *The Chemical Companies* (New York, 1949), pp. 174–177, 183–184; also the chart "IG Farben in the Americas, New York, 1942," in Bayer Archives. For 1939 market share, see Stocking and Watkins, *Cartels in Action,* p. 508; for 1929 market share, Chapter 5 of this study. For pharmaceuticals, Haynes, *American Chemical Industry,* VI, 407; and Werner Link, *Die amerikanische Stabilisierungspolitik in Deutschland, 1921–1932* (Düsseldorf, 1970), p. 369.
74. Reese Jenkins, *Images and Enterprise: Technology and the American Photographic Industry, 1839–1925* (Baltimore, 1975), pp. 330–337 (quotation on p. 330).
75. Feldenkirchen, "Big Business," p. 439. The American I.G. included, besides those three enterprises, a producer of photographic printing machines. Walter Carpenter of Du Pont was amused and totally skeptical when at a meeting in Germany two senior I.G. Farben executives, ter Meer and von Schnitzler, "advised repeatedly and unreservedly that the German IG did not own directly or indirectly the General Aniline Works or American IG." Walter S. Carpenter to Jasper Crane, Oct. 23, 1935, p. 5, Carpenter Papers, Hagley Museum and Library. I.G. Farben executives continued to maintain this position in public and in private.
76. Reader, *Imperial Chemical Industries,* II, 185 (quotation), and chs. 9 and 11. Verena Schröter, "The I.G. Farbenindustrie AG in Central and Southeastern Europe, 1926–1938," in Teichova and Cottrell, *International Business and Central Europe,* pp. 139–172.

77. Memorandum from H. Kühne to Carl Bosch, Feb. 12, 1927, Bayer Archives. All the quotations are from this memorandum.

78. Ter Meer, *I.G. Farben,* pp. 45ff. The basic organization in 1929 is described in an undated memorandum in Bayer Archives and also in the directive cited in note 80.

79. In a letter written about three years later Bosch stated emphatically: "The Central Committee was created on my own wish and for my own assistance, because the Working Committee had not worked well [because of its large membership]." Bosch to P. Haefliger, March 10, 1933, Bayer Archives. For the ending of Duisberg's policy of internal competition see ter Meer, *I.G. Farben,* p. 35.

80. This quotation is from a directive on the functions of committees, "Kommissionen der IG," Sept. 1931, Bayer Archives.

81. The quotation, referring specifically to the Technical Committee, is in a memorandum, "Besprechung über Zusammenarbeit zwischen Zentralfinanzverwaltung, Zentralbuchhaltung, Tea-Büro und Z. A. -Büro," Nov. 5, 1931, Bayer Archives.

82. Ibid., pt. 5, p. 4.

83. E. Weber-Andreae to Carl Duisberg, Sept. 8, 1931, enclosing a review of a report by the office on organization concerning the structure of marketing activities. Peter Hayes points out in his *Industry and Ideology: I.G. Farben in the Nazi Era* (Cambridge, Eng., 1987), p. 21, that the Chemical Committee, the Dyes Committee, and the Pharmaceutical Committee all came to operate quite independently of the senior manager of Sparte II, Fritz ter Meer.

84. The "Organisationsplan der I.G. Berlin, NW7," Sept. 19, 1937, Bayer Archives, outlines in detail the functions of each of the Zentralstellen offices in Berlin. Hayes, *Industry and Ideology,* pp. 30–31 and 392 (chart), gives an excellent brief review of the development and work of these Berlin staff offices that collectively became known as Berlin NW7—particularly the economics and statistical office (Vovi) and the office entitled Wirtschaftspolitische Abteilung (Wipo), which assisted the Central Committee in matters of foreign trade, economic negotiations with foreign states, and dealings with government agencies.

85. Hayes, *Industry and Ideology,* pp. 23–26; ter Meer, *I.G. Farben,* p. 56.

86. Hayes, *Industry and Ideology,* pp. 198–205; Joseph Borkin, *The Crime and Punishment of I.G. Farben* (New York, 1978), pp. 72–73.

87. Hayes, *Industry and Ideology,* pp. 182–185.

88. Reader, *Imperial Chemical Industries,* II, 44–45, 191–192; and documents cited in David A. Hounshell and John Kenly Smith, Jr., *Science and Corporate Strategy: Du Pont R&D, 1902–1980* (Cambridge, Eng., 1988), ch. 9, p. 653, n. 101.

89. For discussion of organization at Du Pont and General Motors in the United States, see Chandler, *Strategy and Structure,* chs. 2 and 3, esp. pp. 67–72.

90. Hayes, *Industry and Ideology,* pp. 24 (first quotation) and 19 (second quotation).

91. These products were all sold through the product divisions of the Sales Communities in Sparte II; in Figure 19 they would be included with dyes and pharmaceuticals. In 1937 dyestuffs and dyestuff auxiliaries accounted for 92,360 metric tons and pharmaceuticals for 2,676; while "waxes," plastics, and insecticides and fungicides totaled 2,975, 3,161, and 5,050, respectively (there were no figures for cellophane). These figures are from Richard Sasuly, *I.G. Farben* (New York, 1947), pp. 298–299. So the tonnage in the new lines accounted for just under 5% of the output of Sparte II, which, as Figure 19 indicates, constituted 20% of total I.G. Farben sales in 1937. Although volume is certainly not equivalent to income

received from these products, their importance to I.G. Farben, as compared with Du Pont, is clear.

92. In Bayer Archives a copy of an article by P. Maguenne, "The I.G. Farbenindustrie and the Best Business Organization" (Die I.G. Farbenindustrie und die beste Geschäftsorganisation), *Chimie und Industrie* 22:1205–16 (1929), marked up by Carl Duisberg, tells of the difficulties in rayon. The *Handbuch der deutschen Aktiengesellschaften* for 1930 shows the VGF withdrawal in that year.

93. Those plans were reported in a memorandum covering a visit of Walter Carpenter to England, Germany, and France in 1937. The visit extended from April 18 to May 7. In 1935 I.G. Farben undertook self-funded expansion of rayon staple to 11,000 or 12,000 tons and did not expand cellulose filament capacity. Walter S. Carpenter to members of the Executive Committee (Du Pont Company) Oct. 23, 1935: a memorandum on "the meeting with the German last night," p. 5, Hagley Museum and Library (File DuP-68-30). Hayes, *Industry and Ideology,* pp. 144–147, describes the expansion of rayon production under Wilhelm Keppler, Hitler's economic advisor. In 1937 the output of rayon staple reached 100,000 tons, up from 5,400 tons in 1933. Much of the output was produced by new plants. The only other major producer in Germany during the late 1930s was Deutsche Rhodiaseta, the subsidiary of the French acetate producer. See Arthur Missbach, *Die Deutschen Spinnstoffe* (Berlin, 1943), pp. 102–103, 108–115. Chemische Werke Hüls, founded in 1938, carried out massive wartime production in rayon and synthetic rubber.

94. See E. Weber-Andreae's enclosed report to Carl Duisberg, Sept. 8, 1931, Bayer Archives. Weber-Andreae wrote that two managers of one of his product departments spent 65 days traveling during the first half of 1931 "in safeguarding the conventions and talks with major customers."

95. Chapter 12 of this study; Haber, *The Chemical Industry, 1900–1930,* p. 288 (also p. 213); *Aller Anfang ist schwer: Bilder zur hundertjährigen Geschichte der Degussa* (n.p., 1973), pp. 57–64; Hermann Pinnow, *Werden und Wesen der Deutschen Gold- und Silber-Scheideanstalt* (n.p., 1948), pp. 43–44, 72–95.

96. Haber, *The Chemical Industry, 1900–1930,* p. 288.

97. For rayon, *Handbuch der deutschen Aktiengesellschaften* for 1927; for Norsk Hydro, Haber, *The Chemical Industry, 1900–1930,* p. 327.

98. The formation of these cartels is described in Hayes, *Industry and Ideology,* pp. 33–35; and in Reader, *Imperial Chemical Industries,* vol. II, chs. 9–11. Hayes summarizes the dye and nitrogen cartels on pp. 32–36 and the relationship of I.G. Farben, Standard Oil (N.J.), Shell, and ICI in the development of synthetic gasoline on pp. 36–38, 115, 119, 140. Because that development became a major political issue after the outbreak of World War II, much has been written about this connection. Borkin's account, *The Crime and Punishment of I.G. Farben,* which is based primarily on the testimony given in the Nuremberg War Trials and Senate Hearings in 1942, should be collated with Reader, ch. 10, and with Larsen, Knowlton, and Popple, *New Horizons,* pp. 153–157, 167–195, 431–443 (based on company records as well as on legal testimony in Congressional hearings). Borkin, for example, makes no mention of the role of ICI or Shell in these developments.

99. Garath P. Dyas and Heinz T. Thanheiser, *The Emerging European Enterprise: Strategy and Structure of French and German Industry* (Boulder, Colo., 1976), pp. 92–93, 125, 144.

100. *Handbuch der deutschen Aktiengesellschaften* for 1930. In his letter to Duisberg of Sept. 8, 1931, E. Weber-Andreae listed as I.G. Farben's leading competitors all the firms described in this section on the independents. Only Bayerische Stickstoffwerke was not included.

101. Haber, *The Chemical Industry, 1900–1930*, pp. 288, 290–291; also F. Rüsberg, *50 Jahre Kali-Chemie* (n.p., 1949), esp. pp. 14, 56–74; and "75 Jahre Kali-Chemie AG, 1899–1974," in the company's monthly house journal *KC Nachrichten: Werkzeitschrift für die Mitarbeiter der Kali-Chemie AG,* Sept. 1974.

102. Haber, *The Chemical Industry, 1900–1930*, pp. 268–269.

103. Ibid., p. 326.

104. *Rütgers: Zur Geschichte der Rütgerswerke* (n.p., [1975?]), pp. 18–21.

105. For von Heyden, see O. Schlenk, *Chemische Fabrik von Heyden, 1874–1934* (Radebeul, 1934), pp. 78–85. For Merck, *E. Merck AG: Chemische Fabrik Darmstadt* (Berlin, 1927), pp. 37–47. Merck's arrangement with its former American subsidiary is summarized in Milton Miskosvitz, Michael Katz, and Richard Levering, eds., *Everybody's Business: An Almanac* (New York, 1980), p. 230. For von Heyden's arrangement with its American branch, see Haynes, *American Chemical Industry,* VI, 207.

106. Haynes, *American Chemical Industry,* VI, 279; *150 Jahre Riedel–de Haën: Die Geschichte eines deutschen Unternehmens* (Berlin, 1964), pp. 74–86; and the *Handbuch der deutschen Aktiengesellschaften.*

107. This was definitely the case for Schering and undoubtedly so for the others.

108. Haber, *The Chemical Industry, 1900–1930*, p. 289. Hans Holländer, *Geschichte der Schering AG* (n.p., n.d.), pp. 45–95; during the interwar period Schering's exports accounted for more than 60% of production (p. 69), and it built several finishing plants abroad (p. 46).

109. I.G. Farben's production in 1937 as compared with total German production by products is from Exhibit No. 13, ch. 1, Kilgore Committee Report, U.S. Senate, Feb. 1946, printed in Sasuly, *I.G. Farben,* pp. 298–299.

110. Haber, *The Chemical Industry, 1900–1930*, pp. 154, 194–195, 303–306. In chemicals St. Gobain remained primarily a producer of superphosphates and fertilizers.

111. George W. Edwards, *American Dollars Abroad: A Discussion of Our International Financial Policy* (New York, 1928), p. 32. In order to finance their domestic activities both the Deutsche Bank and the Disconto had raised funds in New York, including a $25 million issue for the Deutsche Bank in 1927 underwritten by Dillon, Read. See Robert Sobel's forthcoming history of Dillon, Read, ch. 6.

112. T. C. Barker, "Business Implications of Technical Developments in the Glass Industry, 1945–1965: A Case-Study," in Barry Supple, ed., *Essays in British Business History* (Oxford, 1977), p. 191.

Conclusion: The Dynamics of Industrial Capitalism

1. For Schumpeter the principal role of the entrepreneur was innovation; and such entrepreneurial innovation was central to economic development. Schumpeter writes, in speaking of innovation: "To produce other things, or the same things by a different method, means to combine these materials and forces differently . . . Development in our sense is then defined by the carrying out of new combinations.

"This concept covers the following five cases: (1) The introduction of a new good—that is one with which consumers are not yet familiar—or of a new quality of a good. (2) The introduction of a new method of production, that is one not yet tested by experience in the branch of manufacture concerned, which need by no means be founded upon a discovery scientifically new, and can also exist in a new way of handling a commodity commercially. (3) The opening of a new market, that is a market into which the particular branch of manufacture of the country in question has not previously entered, whether or not this market has existed before. (4) The conquest of a new source of supply of raw materials or half-manufactured goods, again irrespective of whether this source already exists or whether it has first to be created. (5) The carrying out of the new organization of any industry, like the creation of a monopoly position (for example through trustification) or the breaking up of a monopoly position." This statement is from Schumpeter's *Theory of Economic Development,* trans. Redvers Opie (Cambridge, Mass., 1934), pp. 65–66. The work was first published in German in 1911.

2. Sloan said this to me more than once when I was assisting him in the writing of *My Years with General Motors.* The story of Henry Ford's destruction of the capabilities of his management team is summarized in Keith Sward, *The Legend of Henry Ford* (New York, 1948), ch. 14, "Ford Alumni Association."

3. Raymond Vernon, *Storm over the Multinationals: The Real Issues* (Cambridge, Mass., 1977), p. 3.

4. Christiano Antonelli, *Cambiamento tecnologico e impresa multinazionale: Il ruolo delle reti telematiche nelle strategie globali* (Milan, 1984), esp. chs. 2 and 3. Much of the information given in these two chapters was presented in "The Diffusion of a New Information Technology as a Process Innovation: International Data Telecommunications and Multinational Industrial Companies" (Paper completed at the Center for Policy Alternatives, MIT).

5. Richard H. Veith, *Multinational Computer Nets: The Case of International Banking* (Lexington, Mass., 1981), pp. 15–19 (quotation from pp. 17–18).

6. Simon Kuznets, *Economic Growth of Nations: Total Output and Production Structure* (Cambridge, Mass., 1971), ch. 1, esp. table 4.

7. The list of the top 200 industrial enterprises in the United States in 1973 was prepared at the same time as the lists that appear as Appendixes A.1–A.3. GTE was the last large survivor among AT&T's early competitors. After the war it moved aggressively into manufacturing by acquiring Sylvania and other industrial enterprises.

8. This can be observed by referring to Gareth P. Dyas and Heinz T. Thanheiser, *The Emerging European Enterprise: Strategy and Structure in French and German Industries* (Boulder, Colo., 1976), and comparing their appendix 1, "The Top 100 Industrial Enterprises in Germany" (1970), with the list of the largest 200 in 1953 given in Appendix C.3 of this study. Eleven of the top 100 in 1969 which were not on the 1953 or earlier lists were in these consumer-goods industries. See also Frank Vogel, *German Business after the Economic Miracle* (New York, 1973); Volker R. Benghahn, *The Americanisation of West German Industry, 1945–1973* (Cambridge, Eng., 1986); Peter A. Lawrence, *Managers and Management in West Germany* (New York, 1980).

9. These generalizations are based on comparing Appendix B.3 with a list of the 200 largest industrials in Britain compiled for 1973 and prepared with Appendixes B.1–

B.3. For a review of British business after World War II, see Graham Turner, *Business in Britain*, rev. ed. (Harmondsworth, Eng., 1971); and Derek F. Channon, *The Strategy and Structure of British Enterprise* (Boston, 1973).

10. The best summary of the developing structure of the computer industry is Kenneth Flamm, *Creating the Computer: Government, Industry, and High Technology* (Washington, D. C., 1986), ch. 4, "IBM and Its Competitors," ch. 5, "Competition in Europe," and ch. 6, "Computers in Japan," supplemented by Flamm, *Targeting the Computer: Government Support and International Competition* (Washington, D.C., 1987). Summaries of the histories of individual firms are given in alphabetical order in James W. Cortada, *Historical Dictionary of Data Processing* (New York, 1987). Also useful is Nancy S. Dorfman, *Innovation and Market Structure: Lessons from the Computer and Semiconductor Industries* (Cambridge, Mass., 1987), particularly chs. 4 and 5. IBM's massive investment in System 360 is described in detail in Robert Sobel, *IBM: Colossus in Transition* (New York, 1981), ch. 10. Glenn Rifkin and George Harrar, *The Ultimate Entrepreneur: The Story of Ken Olsen and Digital Equipment Corporation* (Chicago, 1988), provides details on that entrepreneur and his enterprise. The journal *Datamation* provides, from 1975 on, excellent information on annual revenues produced by individual companies. Those for the minicomputer in 1982 come from its June 1983 issue, p. 92.

11. Chapter 6 of Mel Horwitch, *Postmodern Management*, forthcoming, supplements Flamm's information on personal computers. See also Charles H. Ferguson, "From the People Who Brought You Voodoo Economics," *Harvard Business Review* 66:59 (May–June 1988), for share of world market by IBM, NEC, and Apple. Tandy purchased Radio Shack in 1962. Both firms had been established in the 1920s.

12. Flamm, *Creating the Computer,* p. 150, says, "For all intents and purposes, the wave of important technological innovation that marked the British entries into the computer marketplace in the 1950s had entirely receded by the middle of the 1960s." Flamm, p. 168, gives market share in Europe of the leading European companies, including the Bull Group in France, a joint venture of Bull with GE (Honeywell had purchased GE shares in 1970), and a small, government-sponsored company, Compagnie International pour Information, which was, in turn, a merger of the computer operations of three long-established enterprises; International Computers, Ltd. (ICL), in Britain, the firm that merged the computer activities of the (British) General Electric Company, EMI, Ferranti, and Plessey; Olivetti (Italy); Philips (Netherlands); and L. M. Ericcson (Sweden). Flamm, p. 201, gives the market shares of the leaders in Japan—Fujitsu, NEC, Hitachi, Toshiba, Matsushita, Nippon Telegraph and Telephone, and Mitsubishi—which accounted for more than 75% of the Japanese market; while IBM and the subsidiaries of Sperry-Rand and NCR accounted for more than 20% of that market.

13. John M. Stopford and Louis T. Wells, Jr., *Managing the Multinational Enterprise: Organization of the Firm and Ownership of the Subsidiaries* (New York, 1972), pp. 39–46.

14. The one other structure listed in Table 25—the grid structure, in which a local executive reported to two or more corporate executives for different functions and activities—has rarely provided effective administration. Stopford and Wells, *Managing the Multinational Enterprise,* pp. 86–91.

15. J. J. Servan-Schreiber, *The American Challenge* (New York, 1968), p. 3.

16. Ibid., pp. 10–11.

17. This influence can best be documented by reviewing the references to McKinsey & Company in the index to Channon, *The Strategy and Structure of British Enterprise*, p. 254. Dyas and Thanheiser, *Emerging European Enterprise*, pp. 112–123, has information on the transfer of American methods to Germany.

18. Jean-Pierre Bardou et al., *The Automobile Revolution: The Impact of an Industry* (Chapel Hill, N.C., 1982), pp. 172–175.

19. Johannes Hirschmeier and Tsunehiko Yui, *The Development of Japanese Business, 1600–1973* (Cambridge, Mass., 1975), p. 258.

20. Bardou et al., *The Automobile Revolution*, p. 199, and also pp. 182–183.

21. Thomas K. McGraw and Patricia A. O'Brien, "Production and Distribution: Competition Policy and Industry Structure," in Thomas K. McCraw, ed., *America versus Japan: A Comparative Analysis* (Boston, 1986), ch. 3.

22. Richard P. Rumelt, *Strategy, Structure, and Economic Performance* (Boston, 1974); Channon, *The Strategy and Structure of British Enterprise*, pp. 52–68; and Dyas and Thanheiser, *Emerging European Enterprise*, p. 72 (Thanheiser did the work on Germany and Dyas on France). The pattern in France is quite similar to that of Germany. A preliminary summary of the findings in these studies is Bruce R. Scott, "The Industrial State: Old Myths and New Realities," *Harvard Business Review* 51:133–145 (March–April 1973).

23. Channon, *The Strategy and Structure of British Enterprise*, p. 188. An acquisitive conglomerate is one that carries out a strategy of growth through aggressive acquisitions of companies rather than by concentrating on managing the firms it has acquired.

24. Dyas and Thanheiser, *Emerging European Enterprise*, pp. 72, 144–151, and ch. 7. Twenty-one of the 100 largest German enterprises were foreign subsidiaries.

25. Thanheiser lists eight of these firms in the unrelated category, but he points out (p. 151) that five could be classified as related diversifiers, as they had grown by gradual evolution and had only a small portion of their business in unrelated fields. Three others—Enka-Glanzstoff and the two new entrants, Melitta and Bertelsmann—also grew primarily by exploiting the economies of scope.

26. Rumelt, *Strategy, Structure, and Economic Performance*, pp. 63–77 (esp. pp. 66–67, 70–72); Channon, *The Strategy and Structure of British Enterprise*, pp. 68–75; and Dyas and Thanheiser, *Emerging European Enterprise*, p. 72.

27. National Science Foundation, *Research and Development in Industry, 1970: Funds, 1970, Scientists and Engineers, January 1971*, NSF72-309 (Washington, D.C., 1971), pp. 32–35. Postwar developments in industrial research in the United States are summarized in Margaret B. W. Graham, "Corporate Research and Development: The Latest Transformation," *Technology in Society* 7:179–195 (1985); and in her "Industrial Research in the Age of Big Science," in Richard S. Rosenbloom, ed., *Research on Technological Innovation, Management, and Policy* (Greenwich, Conn., 1985), pp. 47–79.

28. The extent of diversification is indicated in a list of the top 200 industrial enterprises in the United States compiled for 1973 and prepared with Appendixes A.1–A.3. An extract taken from that list, which gives the product lines of those companies in food, chemicals, and the three machinery groups, has been published in Alfred D. Chandler, Jr., and Richard S. Tedlow, *The Coming of Managerial Capitalism:*

A Casebook on the History of American Economic Institutions (Homewood, Ill., 1985), case 28, "The Conglomerates and the Merger Movement of the 1960s," pp. 765–775.

29. David J. Ravenscraft and F. M. Scherer, *Mergers, Sell-offs, and Economic Efficiency* (Washington, D.C., 1987), ch. 6.

30. See Chapter 5. For a detailed explanation of overloading, see my *Strategy and Structure*, ch. 2. H. Thomas Johnson and Robert S. Kaplan, *Relevance Lost: The Rise and Fall of Management Accounting* (Boston, 1987), p. 205, points out that "contemporary cost accounting and management control systems . . . are no longer providing accurate signals about the efficiency and profitability of internally managed transactions . . . Without the receipt of appropriate cost and profitability information, the ability of the 'visible hand' to effectively manage the myriad of transactions that occur in a complex hierarchy has been severely compromised." Particularly useful are ch. 6, "From Cost Management to Cost Accounting: Relevance Lost," and ch. 7, "Cost Accounting and Decision Making: Academics Strive for Relevance."

31. W. T. Grimm & Company, *Mergerstat Review, 1987* (Chicago, 1988), pp. 103–104.

32. New York Stock Exchange, *New York Stock Exchange Fact Book, 1987* (New York, 1987), p. 71.

33. Leslie Hannah, *The Rise of the Corporate Economy*, 2d ed. (London, 1983), pp. 150–155, 177.

34. Herman Daems, "Determinants of Changes of Industrial Diversification: The Experience of European Industrial Groups" (Seminar paper, Harvard Business School, April 18, 1988). This paper summarized findings from Professor Daems's study of the diversification patterns of leading European industrial enterprises between 1973 and 1985.

Credits

Permission has been granted from the following authors, publishers, and corporations to use material from the works cited. References to specific page numbers can be found where these works are used throughout the text.

Barker, T. C., "Business Implications of Technical Developments in the Glass Industry, 1945–1965: A Case-Study," in Barry Supple, ed., *Essays in British Business History* (Oxford: Oxford University Press, 1977); reprinted with permission of Oxford University Press. Cadbury Brothers, Ltd., *Industrial Record, 1919–1939* (Bournville: Cadbury Brothers, 1944); reprinted with permission of Cadbury Ltd. Chandler, Alfred D., and Stephen Salsbury, *Pierre S. du Pont and the Making of the Modern Corporation* (New York: Harper & Row, 1971); reprinted with permission of Harper & Row Publishers, Inc. Deane, Phyllis, and W. A. Cole, *British Economic Growth, 1688–1959* (New York: Cambridge University Press, 1962, 1967); reprinted with permission of Cambridge University Press. Dummelow, John, *Associated Electrical Industries Limited, 1899–1949* (Manchester: Metropolitan-Vickers Electrical Co., 1949); reprinted with permission of General Electric Co. PLC. Feldenkirchen, Wilfried, "Big Business in Interwar Germany," *Business History Review* 61 (Autumn 1987); reprinted with permission of Harvard Business School. Friar, John, and Mel Horwitch, "The Emergence of Technology Strategy," *Technology and Society* 7 (1985); Copyright 1986 Pergamon Press Ltd., reprinted with permission of Pergamon Press, Inc. Hayes, Peter, *Industry and Ideology: IG Farben in the Nazi Era* (New York: Cambridge University Press, 1987); reprinted with permission of Cambridge University Press. Hessen, Robert, *Steel Titan: The Life of Charles M. Schwab* (New York: Oxford University Press, 1975); reprinted with permission of the Oxford University Press. Jefferys, James B., *Retail Trading in Britain, 1850–1950* (New York: Cambridge University Press, 1954); reprinted with permission of the Cambridge University Press. Kuznets, Simon, *Economic Growth of Nations*, pp. 315–319 (Copyright 1971 by Simon Kuznets, Cambridge, Mass.: Belknap Press of Harvard University Press); reprinted by permission. Maschinenbauanstalt Humboldt, "Lageplan der Maschinenbau-Anstalt Humboldt, 1916"; reprinted with permission of Klöckner-Humboldt-Deutz AG. Müller, Albert, *25 Jahre der Accumulatoren-Fabrik Aktiengesellschaft, 1888–1913* (n.p., 1913); reprinted with permission of VARTA. Reader, W. J., *Imperial Chemical Industries: A History*, vol. II: *The First Quarter-Century, 1926–1952* (Oxford: Oxford University Press, 1975); reprinted with the permission of Oxford University Press, England. Rostow, W. W., *The World Economy: History & Prospect* (Austin: University of Texas Press, 1978); reprinted with permission of the University of Texas Press. Schroeder, Gertrude G., *The Growth of Major Steel Companies, 1900–1950* (Baltimore: Johns Hopkins Press,

Index